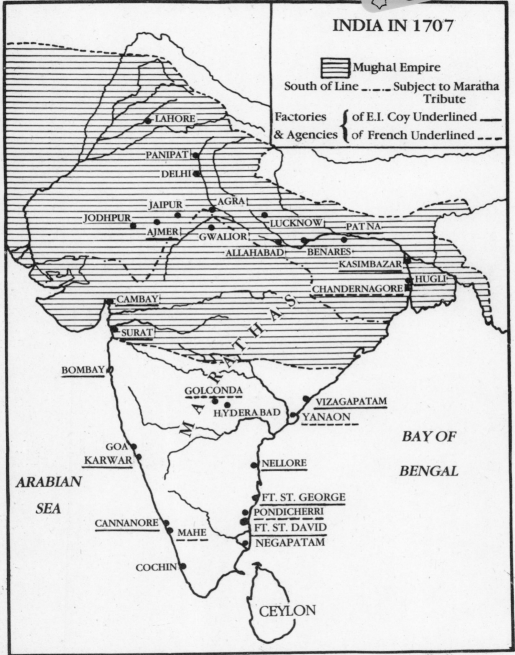

INDIA IN 1707

- Mughal Empire
- South of Line ⋅–⋅– Subject to Maratha Tribute
- Factories { of E.I. Coy Underlined ___
- & Agencies { of French Underlined ⋅–⋅–

ARABIAN SEA

BAY OF BENGAL

LAHORE
PANIPAT
DELHI
JAIPUR
JODHPUR
AJMER
AGRA
GWALIOR
LUCKNOW
PAT NA
ALLAHABAD
BENARES
KASIMBAZAR
CHANDERNAGORE
HUGLI
CAMBAY
SURAT
BOMBAY
GOLCONDA
HYDERABAD
VIZAGAPATAM
YANAON
GOA
KARWAR
NELLORE
FT. ST. GEORGE
PONDICHERRI
CANNANORE
MAHE
FT. ST. DAVID
NEGAPATAM
COCHIN

MARATHAS

CEYLON

The map represents the *actual* rather than the formally correct distribution of political authority in 1707 for even though the imperial troops were in occupation of important strongholds in the Deccan, the balance of power had tilted in favour of the Marathas who had virtually wrested the imperial provinces (of the Deccan).

A DICTIONARY OF
MODERN INDIAN HISTORY, 1707–1947

For
Arjun and Anuradha

A DICTIONARY OF
MODERN INDIAN HISTORY
1707–1947

PARSHOTAM MEHRA

DELHI
OXFORD UNIVERSITY PRESS
BOMBAY CALCUTTA MADRAS

Oxford University Press, Walton Street, Oxford, OX2 6DP
New York   Toronto
Delhi   Bombay   Calcutta   Madras   Karachi
Petaling Jaya   Singapore   Hong Kong   Tokyo
Nairobi   Dar es Salaam
Melbourne   Auckland
and associates in
Beirut   Berlin   Ibadan   Nicosia

© Oxford University Press 1985

Reprinted with corrections 1987

SBN 19 561552 2

Printed by Rekha Printers Pvt. Ltd., New Delhi 110020
and published by S. K. Mookerjee, Oxford University Press
YMCA Library Building, Jai Singh Road, New Delhi 110001

Contents

List of Maps

Acknowledgements

The preparation of this work has entailed a number of obligations, both personal as well as institutional, and it is pleasant to record them here. At the outset it was my students who, for over a quarter century, pushed and provoked me, year in year out, in delving deeper into what I taught. To endeavour to keep abreast of new works and research in an area as vast and varied as the history of modern India is by no means an easy task. But the seemingly invisible yet remorselessly relentless pressures that were mounted by my young friends kept me glued as it were to the grindstone. They alone are the true forebears of this venture: my indebtedness to their often annoying yet well-meaning probes and pin-pricks remains abiding.

A singular development impelled me to give shape and form to this nebulous, inchoate idea to help them and myself. In 1971 or thereabouts, the University Grants Commission awarded me a project under its scheme for 'Writing of University-Level Textbooks', Initially, I thought a 'dictionary' was far too ambitious for the kind of studies envisaged by the Commission, but for once, and uncharacteristically, enthusiasm got the better of me. The award gave me a small budget to travel to and work at libraries and research centres outside Chandigarh. Additionally, I was given modest secretarial assistance and, for a couple of years, the services of a research scholar. A student who initially read with me for her M.A., Indarjit Khurana, matured into a good, dependable researcher and she it was who prepared in her own hand the first draft of the *Dictionary*, then barely one-tenth of its present size. This volume owes her a debt that is not easy to spell out: she helped to knock into some sort of shape my own then far from clear ideas as to what I was about.

It is pleasant to record that the Commission, for its part, has been extremely understanding and kept me relatively free from embarrassing inquiries. I should perhaps confess that it was soon clear to me that in terms of the parameters mapped out by the scheme, there was far too much on my plate than could be managed with any assurance. Two results ensued. For one, it took longer and longer to finalize the end-product: there was always good reason for including an individual, an institution, a movement, and this meant ever more time and effort. Deadlines became meaningless and irrelevant. There was the corollary of many an omission— some glaring—even at the stage when things seemed to get finalized. I plead guilty, in advance, to many a valid criticism about names and titles that do not find a mention and sometimes of those that do. There must also have crept in despite a rigorous scrutiny, some errors of fact or judgement. Here too I would crave the readers' indulgence and hope to make amends as and when an opportunity offers itself.

A large part of the work on the preliminary drafts was undertaken at the Panjab University Library. Close proximity, familiarity with the holdings and the general friendliness of the staff were a great help. Some were cordial and generous both with their time and understanding.

Over the years I became a regular if an unabashedly frequent commuter to Delhi, and most of my work was done there at the Nehru Memorial Museum and Library. Before long, it was difficult not to be convinced that for any worthwhile work on modern India no scholar could do without resort to this graciously conceived, well-run, neat complex. In its rich holdings—of books, private papers, microfilms, learned journals—and congenial surroundings, one finds oneself so much at ease and at home. The staff, it is pleasant to say, were both courteous as well as patient. For the final shape that the *Dictionary* took, both in terms of its volume and contents, the NMML's contribution must remain singular, and unrivalled.

Besides Teenmurti House, I had the benefit of working at the libraries of the Indian Council of World Affairs, India International Centre, the Archaeological Survey of India and the National Archives of India. Their staff were generous with their time and attention and proved to be of great help.

I have deliberately eschewed all mention of individual names. For one, they are far too numerous; more, not a few would prefer anonymity. And yet some stick out in my mind. At Chandigarh, the young and resourceful G. S. Thakur helped me to rummage through shelves for little-known books and references. At Teenmurti House, S. K. Sharma, Naveen Mahajan and Indu Sharma were not only of great help but also untiring. Among those who helped locate books and journals—I have been unusually stubborn in my determination not to master the cataloguing—two names stand out, Benedict Minjh and Dhirendra Singh. As always, my good friend Dr S. R. Bakshi, no mean scholar of modern Indian history in his own right, and A. K. Awasthi, who mans the reprographic cell, gave invaluable help and advice.

Discussions with a host of friends and colleagues helped. Here too a few stand out. Professor Ravinder Kumar, who is both a friend and philosopher; Dr D. N. Panigrahi, at once gracious and well-informed. Professor Sri Ram Mehrotra read a part of the manuscript; Professor B. B. Misra has always remained a source of inspiration for his insights, singular devotion, tireless application. For running successive drafts of a considerably large manuscript, two young men did a wonderful job of work. Ved Prakash straightened out the initial drafts; the more definitive work fell to the lot of Atam Prakash. In between, Vishwa Mohini Dogra lent a helping hand. They were all competent in their professional skills, besides being generous in understanding. This was the more marked, considering my chronic penchant for adding and subtracting, criss-crossing, pushing in, pulling out. Even the most patient of them may have felt annoyed, if not exasperated. Mercifully, they all bore with me over the years without any major mishap.

Through the various incarnations that the draft saw, Kesar Singh helped to organize the bulk of an unmanageable, ever-bulging mass. He managed to put all manner of bits and pieces together; he bound, unbound and rebound an infinite number of volumes into viable shapes and forms.

For the publishers I have a special word. In the initial stages they kept me at my job with a deft mixture of encouragement and incentive. Later, some minor irritants notwithstanding, we were yoked in a common endeavour to help improve the finished product. No effort was spared, no suggestions brushed aside. I made a number of good friends but the contribution of my editor at the O.U.P. and his colleagues in the production department have been invaluable.

The *Dictionary* has been a long time in the making. During these many years my wife showed a brave resolve to put up with me and my new venture. And this despite all the stresses and strains to which my not infrequent travels and long absences from home, added to a relative lack of interest in managing its affairs, exposed her. Owing to their extra-marital interests, and loyalties, university dons do not, by definition, make for ideal married companions! That we have lasted so long is a tribute at once to her devotion and resilience. This book owes a lot to her. My two grandchildren, Arjun and Anuradha, arrived on the scene only after the bulk of the manuscript had gone to the publishers. Over the years that I have supplemented it and pored over the numerous galleys and page proofs, sketch maps and prelims, they have been a source of such unalloyed fun and frolic, play as well as pleasure. In gratitude, this book is dedicated to them.

Introduction

The *Dictionary* was born largely out of a sorely-felt need that, as a teacher, I was so acutely conscious of: a handy compendium that may, at short notice, furnish the essential details about men and affairs in the modern period of Indian history. And yet outside the small, somewhat exclusive world of academe, there are any number of people—journalists, littérateurs, civil servants, technocrats, laymen—who, one way or another, would need some authoritative information on such diverse subjects as Sati and Thuggee, the Khilafat Movement, Jallianwala Bagh, the Nehru Report, the Government of India Act, 1935, the Moplahs, etc. For these and a lot more the *Dictionary* offers a succinct guide designed to cater to their individual specialist as well as generalist requirements.

The modern period for the limited purview of the *Dictionary* may be deemed to commence with the reign of Bahadur Shah I (r. 1707–12), the last of the Great Mughals. It spans roughly the succeeding two and a half centuries and brings the story, through the eventful days of the Peshwas, Ranjit Singh, the John Company, and the Crown that succeeded it, down to 1947, marking the transfer of political power from Whitehall to an independent India. There are some exceptions to this broad schema: both Jawaharlal Nehru (d.1964) and Jayaprakash Narayan (d.1979) spill across the watershed but have entries to themselves; Mountbatten (d. 1978) does not. Within the parameters of this time-frame, the subject-matter is encompassed in nearly 400 entries, arranged in an alphabetical order so structured as to cater to the needs of the layman as well as the scholar. For the more curious, whether amateur or professional, who would fain pursue his quarry further there is, for almost every entry, a bibliographic note that cites all that is relevant: books, papers, research articles.

Each entry is intended to be self-contained, complete in itself. And yet, where it is desirable for a fuller understanding of an individual, a subject or an interpretation to consult other entries, cross references to these are clearly indicated by *q.v./qq.v.* There is also a general index at the end of the volume through which the reader should be able to trace all references to a specific person or subject that may not have claimed separate treatment as an independent, individual entry.

In compiling this work the aim has been to synthesize the results of modern research so as to present to the reader an up-to-date, coherent and cogent introduction to the fascinating saga of men and matters that comprehends modern India. The objective has been to offer a new treatment or interpretation based upon an integrative approach wherein scholarly research has been meshed into a narrative that has the colour and pace of the generalist. For the beginner or the lay reader or even the scholar who is rushed, the task of obtaining updated as well as relevant and adequate data for an understanding of modern Indian history may seem well-nigh impossible. Simply put, this volume is dedicated to making this exercise less difficult.

Most of the references cited in the bibliographic notes are spelt out in full. However, to avoid repetition, some abbreviations have been used. These have also been employed for honours bestowed on the John Company and, later, the Crown's personnel who saw service in India. A list of such abbreviations and what they stand for has been appended.

A conscious effort has been made to explain in the body of the text itself such words or phrases as are special to the subject matter. It was none the less felt that a few might have escaped this net. A small glossary has therefore been compiled to help the reader for a fuller, more comprehensive understanding. A few sketch maps have been inserted to illustrate place-names or scenes of hostilities in battles fought, wars won or lost. These have also been provided to indicate the growth of the Indian railways as well as the jig-saw puzzle of Indian States on the eve of Independence. Maps on the end papers broadly comprehend the political configuration in 1707, marking the advent of Bahadur Shah's accession and 1961, in the aftermath of the fall-out from the States Reorganization Commission.

A word on the historian and his craft. Like all academic disciplines, history too is essentially an exercise of thought and entails the constant restoring of the given elements in a new, ever-evolving generalizing pattern. More, it implies the imposition of organizing concepts on the historical process so as to open up fresh vistas of understanding. History has the unique distinction of encompassing the totality of relations between the various structures of society and to view the totality in terms of its (societal) development. Ideally, the historical quest should yield not only a deeper understanding of the present but also a more appropriate orientation to its varied facets. Recollecting, and in the process restructuring, the past is a social act of the present undertaken by men of the present and affecting the social system of the present. The grave disadvantage of those not knowing the past is that they do not know the present. History is not unlike a hill or a high point of vantage from which alone one may see the town in which one lives or the age of which one is an integral part.

Two other aspects may be briefly touched on. Contrary to popular belief, history is not a mere rattling of dead men's bones: as a matter of fact, it treats of full-blooded *homo sapiens* in the totality of their surroundings and not without their emotional stresses and strains. It is not a bare catalogue but a complete version of events. Our views of history come from the impact of experience upon reading and of reading upon experience. Objectivity has its place in historical study but it is a subordinate place: 'the heart of the subject is not in the method, but in the motor; not in the technique but in the historian'. And finally, it is not the proper function of the historian to pass moral judgements. And yet, writing that does not one way or another reveal the principles, predilections and prejudices of its author lacks in colour and taste and may be almost worthless.

Abbreviations

A. C. Banerjee   *Constitutional History of India*, 3 vols, New Delhi, 1977–78

Indian Constitutional Documents, 3 vols, 3rd edition, Calcutta, 1961

Advanced History of India   R. C. Majumdar, H. C. Raychaudhuri, Kalikinkar Datta, *An Advanced History of India*, 3rd ed., London, 1967

Aitchison   C. U. Aitchison (compiler): *A Collection of Treaties, Engagements and Sanads relating to India and Neighbouring Countries*, 14 vols, 5th ed., Calcutta, 1929–31

AICC   All-India Congress Committee

Balfour, The
Cyclopaedia of India   Edward Balfour, *The Cyclopaedia of India and of Eastern and Southern Asia*, 3 vols, Graz (Austria), 3rd ed., 1967

Beale   Thomas William Beale, *An Oriental Biographical Dictionary* (rev. ed., Henry George Keene), Indian reprint, Ludhiana, 1972

British Paramountcy
and Indian Renaissance   R. C. Majumdar (ed.), *British Paramountcy and Indian Renaissance*, Parts i–ii, Bombay, 1963–65

Buckland   C. E. Buckland, *Dictionary of Indian Biography*, reprint, Varanasi, 1971

CHI   *Cambridge History of India*, 6 vols, 2nd Indian reprint, Delhi, 1962–3

CHI, V–VI   H. H. Dodwell (ed.), *British India, 1497–1858*, 2nd Indian reprint, Delhi, 1963

H. H. Dodwell (ed.), *The Indian Empire, 1858–1918*, 2nd Indian reprint, Delhi, 1963

C.I.E.   Companion of the Order of the Indian Empire

C.S.I.   Companion of the Order of the Star of India

DNB   Leslie Stephen and Sidney Lee (eds.), *The Dictionary of National Biography*, 22 vols, reprint, Oxford, 1964–5

DNB 1901–1911   Sidney Lee (ed.), *The Dictionary of National Biography: Twentieth Century*, reprint, Oxford, 1966

DNB 1912–1921   H. W. C. Davis and J. R. H. Weaver (eds.), *The Dictionary of National Biography, 1912–1921*, reprint, Oxford, 1961

DNB 1922–1930   J. R. H. Weaver (ed.), *The Dictionary of National Biography, 1922–1930*, reprint, Oxford, 1961

DNB 1931–1940	L. G. Wickham Legg (ed.), *The Dictionary of National Biography, 1931–1940*, reprint, Oxford, 1961
DNB 1941–1950	L. G. Wickham Legg and E. T. Williams (eds.), *The Dictionary of National Biography, 1941–1950*, Oxford, 1959
DNB 1951–1960	E. T. Williams and Helen M. Palmer (eds.), *The Dictionary of National Biography, 1951–1960*, Oxford, 1971
DNB 1961–1970	E. T. Williams and C. S. Nicholls (eds.), *The Dictionary of National Biography, 1961–1970*, Oxford, 1981
G.C.B	Knight Grand Cross of the Bath
G.C.I.E.	Grand Commander of the Indian Empire
G.C.M.G.	Knight (or Dame) Grand Cross of St Michael and St George
G.C.S.I.	Grand Commander of the Star of India
G.C.V.O.	Knight (or Dame) Grand Cross of Royal Victorian Order
Gribble	J. D. B Gribble, *History of the Deccan*, 2 vols, London, 1896
Gwyer and Appadorai	M. Gwyer and A. Appadorai (eds.), *Speeches and Documents on the Indian Constitution 1921–1947*, 2 vols, Oxford, 1957
HMG	His (Her) Majesty's Government
Hobson-Jobson	Henry Yule and A. C. Burnell, *Hobson-Jobson: A glossary of colloquial Anglo-Indian words and phrases, and of kindred terms, etymological, historical, geographical and discursive*, 2nd ed., Delhi, 1968
Imperial Gazetteer	*The Imperial Gazetteer of India*, 26 vols, new ed., Oxford, 1908–9
JAS	*Journal of Asian Studies*, Ann Arbor (Michigan)
JIH	*Journal of Indian History*, Trivandrum
JMAS	*Journal of Modern Asian Studies*, Cambridge (UK)
K.C.B.	Knight Commander of the Bath
K.C.I.E.	Knight Commander of the Indian Empire
K.C.S.I.	Knight Commander of the Star of India
K.G.	Knight of the Garter
Majumdar: History and Culture of the Indian People	R. C. Majumdar (ed.): *The History and Culture of the Indian People*, 11 vols., Bombay, 1955–77
Maratha Supremacy	R. C. Majumdar (ed.) *The Maratha Supremacy (1707–1818 AD)*, Bombay, 1977
Mitra, Quarterly Register	N. N. Mitra, *The Indian Quarterly Register*, Calcutta, 1919–1929
Mitra, Annual Register	N. N. Mitra, *The Indian Annual Register*, Calcutta, 1930–46
NMML	Nehru Memorial Museum and Library (Teenmurti House, New Delhi)
NWP	North-Western Provinces (later United Provinces)

NWFP	North-West Frontier Province (est. 1901)
Roberts	P. E. Roberts, *History of British India under Company and the Crown,* 3rd ed., Oxford, 1952
Sardesai	G. S. Sardesai, *A New History of the Marathas*, 3 vols, Bombay, 1958
Sen, 1857	Surendra Nath Sen, *Eighteen Fiftyseven,* New Delhi, 1957
Sen: DNB	S. P. Sen (ed.), *Dictionary of National Biography,* 4 vols, Calcutta, 1972–4
Struggle for Freedom	R. C. Majumdar (ed.), *Struggle for Freedom,* 2nd ed., Bombay, 1978
Tara Chand	Tara Chand, *History of the Freedom Movement in India,* 4 vols, New Delhi, 1961–72
UP	United Provinces of Agra and Oudh (later Uttar Pradesh)

Ahmad Shah Abdali (c. 1722-73)

Ahmad Khan, popularly known as Ahmad Shah Durrani and Baba-i-Afghan (literally, 'father of the Afghan [nation]'), was the son of Malik Muhammad Zaman Khan, who lived in the vicinity of the city of Herat. He was among the prisoners taken by Nadir Shah (q.v.), the Persian ruler (notorious for his 1739 sack of Delhi), when the latter captured Kandahar a year earlier. Starting as a mace-bearer Ahmad Khan was, by degrees, promoted to a considerable command in the army and was later part of the *corps d'elite* of Afghan mercenaries which constituted the Persian ruler's most trusted bodyguard.

The preference shown by the Persian ruler for his Afghan hirelings led to a great deal of jealousy among his own Turkmen, the Qizilbash (literally, 'red heads'), and was to be the principal cause of his assassination (1747) by Muhammad Khan Qajar, founder of the new dynasty in Persia that succeeded him.

Earlier, the close affinity between Malik Saddo and Persia's Safavi dynasty over the struggle for Kandahar had laid the foundation for the employment of the Abdalis as the spearhead of Nadir Shah's army. And when the latter died, Ahmad Khan Abdali, Malik Saddo's lineal descendant, was able to build, for the first time, an Afghan kingdom with a Persian bias. It rose on the ruins of his master's conquests.

On the morrow of Nadir Shah's assassination, Ahmad Khan made an unsuccessful attack on the Persian troops, waylaid a large convoy of their treasure and returned by forced marches to his patrimony. He was chosen ruler by Sabir Shah, a holy man, at the shrine of Sher Surkh, near Kandahar. Later he took for himself the title of 'Durr-i-Durrani' (literally, 'pearl of pearls') whence his tribe, the Abdalis, came also to be known as Durranis.

The Afghan chief not only subdued Kandahar and Kabul but also took Peshawar and Lahore and, emboldened by the weakness of the later Mughals, resolved upon the conquest of Delhi.

In his reign of 26 years (1746-73) Ahmad Shah swept eight times across the Indus; his first two expeditions (1748-9) were designed to obtain in his own name the Mughal emperor's confirmation of the cession of Peshawar and such other trans-Indus districts as had been made over to Nadir.

His expedition in 1752 led to the annexation of Lahore and Multan, thereby incorporating nearly the whole of West Panjab into his empire and fixing a boundary at Sirhind beyond the eastern limits of what is now Pakistan. Later in the year the Durranis overran Kashmir which they conquered, and held, largely with the aid of the Yusufzais and other tribesmen around Peshawar.

In 1756 Ahmad Shah marched up to Delhi and would have proceeded against Oudh (q.v.) and Bengal but for an outbreak of cholera in his own camp that compelled him to beat a hasty retreat. Each time he came, the

1

returning Afghan hordes were harassed by the Sikhs, their acerbity and fierceness growing every successive year.

While Sikh power was gradually gaining in importance and political strength, by 1758 the Marathas had extended their influence right up to Peshawar, largely in the wake of the Afghan invasions. As a result, the fury of the Durrani and his erstwhile Indian allies (who also included, apart from Muslim rulers, some Hindu and Jat chiefs) was now directed principally against the Marathas; in 1761 the latter were badly routed at the Third Battle of Panipat (q.v.).

In a larger perspective, the Afghan ruler's campaigns led not so much to the downfall of the Marathas as the completion of the process of disintegration of the Mughal empire begun by Nadir Shah. Additionally, the Afghans threw the Panjab into a state of anarchy which, as noticed before, made possible the emergence of a new power, the Sikhs. The Abdali also gave to Lahore and Multan, and to Peshawar and Derajat 'that contradiction in terms, a new orientation towards the west'.

The last three invasions of the Afghan ruler were directed against the Sikhs. He declared jihad against what he regarded as an unruly, irresponsible foe, yet failed to extirpate them, mainly because of the Sikh refusal to face him in pitched battles. Additionally, his own not always successful efforts to unite Afghanistan and suppress its internal dissensions prevented him from consolidating his hold over the Panjab. He did not return to India after 1769 and died four years later at Mirgha in the Achakzai Toba hills, where he had gone to escape the summer heat. His tomb at Kandahar is still respected as a sanctuary.

Sir Olaf Caroe, a well-known authority on the Pathans, rates Sher Shah as 'the most illustrious Afghan in history' who was 'greater even' than Ahmad Shah. All the same, he contends that although the former left a record more memorable in the sphere of effective governance and power, he 'failed to display those human and endearing qualities' for which the first of the Saddozai monarchs is 'so well-known'.

J. D. Cunningham, historian of the Sikhs, has compared Ahmad Shah to the Roman emperor Galba—'fitted for conquest, yet incapable of empire'. He has called him the very ideal of the Afghan genius—hardy, enterprising and successful in founding an Afghan monarchy that endured. With a bold and commanding turn of natural genius, he was an adept in the difficult art of management of men and tribes. Never losing the common touch, he kept up the same equal and popular demeanour with his Durrani and Ghalji counsellors. Himself a divine, he wrote poetry not only in Persian but also in Pushtu.

Ganda Singh, a percipient biographer, maintains that the Shah's genius found its fullest expression in his remarkable military exploits and in having knit together a large number of heterogeneous warring tribes into a homogeneous Afghan nation.

In the political map of northern India, Ahmad Shah's invasions were responsible for many momentous changes—the sharp decline of Mughal authority, the extension of Maratha influence to the north, the rise of the Sikhs as a political power in the Panjab and, indirectly, the emergence and consolidation of the East India Company (q.v.) in and around Bengal.

Ganda Singh, *Ahmad Shah Durrani*, Bombay, 1959; Olaf Caroe, *The Pathans: 500* B.C.-A.D. *1957*, London, 1958.

Abdur Rahman, Amir of Afghanistan (1844–1901)

Abdur Rahman was the son of Mohammad Afzal Khan and a grandson of Amir Dost Mohammad (q.v.). When he was barely 13 years old his father, then governor or Mizar-i-Sharif, the northern province of Afghanistan, put him in charge of Tashkurgan. Later he was removed from this post for failure to collect taxes. After a couple of years, his father relented and gave him command of the army. In 1863, following the death of Dost Moham-mad, he fought alongside his father in the civil war that ensued and openly challenged Sher Ali's right to the Afghan throne. A bitter, five-year struggle ensued ending, in 1868, in his father's death and his own discomfiture. Worsted in battle, he was forced to flee to Russian Turkestan. He was given asylum in Samarkand, and residing there for nearly a decade (1870-80), studied closely the Russian system of administration while keeping in touch with events in his own country. He calculated that Sher Ali's death (1880) in the course of the Second Anglo-Afghan War (q.v.), offered a favourable opportunity to stage a come-back. By now nearly 40, he is said to have looked a 'personification of watchful strength moved by an inflexible will' and was endowed with his grandfather's vigour, judgement and ferocity.

In 1880 Ayub Khan's defeat of a British force at Kandahar conspired to bring about his return. With Afghanistan visibly falling apart, the British were at their wits' end and understandably looked upon Abdur Rahman as the proverbial ram in the thicket. He was welcome to his people too who, no doubt, considered him a suitable successor to the throne of Kabul. A formal declaration of his accession was made on 22 July 1880 after he signed a treaty with the British agreeing not to establish relations with any other European power. In 1881, the ruler of Kandahar abdicated in his favour and six years later he occupied Herat.

Known as 'the Iron Amir', he succeeded to a difficult legacy. In his own words, 'Every priest, mullah and chief of every tribe and village considered himself an independent king, and for about 200 years past . . . the Mirs of Turkestan, the Mirs of Hazara, the chiefs of Ghilzai were all stronger than their Amirs.'

The Amir extended his territorial domain further by taking Roshan and Shignan in 1882, though these were to remain disputed territory for another decade. Maimana was occupied in 1885, Hazurajat in 1893 (after defeating the rebellious Hazuras), and Kafiristan two years later. He also successfully contended with two major rebellions—of the Ghilzais (also Ghaljis) in 1886 and of his cousin Ishak Khan. The latter held a quasi-independent position as governor of Afghan Turkestan and, in 1888, proclaimed himself Amir. The revolt was crushed, ham-handed justice meted out to the rebels and a semblance of law and order restored.

A great step forward was the demarcation of well-defined and viable physical boundaries for Afghanistan. The Amir agreed to delineation of the Russo-Afghan boundary by a mixed Anglo-Russian commission, helped by Afghan experts. Begun in 1884 but seriously interrupted by the Panjdeh affair, the work was completed in 1888 when the boundary—all the way from the Hari Rud to Khojah Saleh (more correctly, Khwajah Salar)—was at last formally laid down. Six years of comparative peace followed, until the revival of disputes regarding the Pamirs. Here, too, after a great deal of bargaining, an agreement was reached (March 1895) with Russia whereby Afghanistan was to surrender territory north of Panjdeh while Russia gave up part of Darwaz, lying to the south of the river Oxus.

In 1893 the Amir agreed to receive a diplomatic mission from India with the principal objective of working out a more exact definition of the Indo-Afghan frontier. The agreement arrived at resulted in the delimitation (1894-6) of the boundary known as the Durand Line (q.v.).

Earlier, the British acquisition of the Kurram valley in 1892 followed and in some cases preceded punitive expeditions against the Shiranis of Takht-i-Sulaiman, the Orakzais in the neighbourhood of the Samana range, the Isazais of the Black Mountains and the chiefs of Hunza and Nagar: to the Amir, these were manifestations of an active, 'forward' policy. The result was that between 1890 and 1898, Anglo-Afghan relations were 'so strained, that on several occasions war seemed imminent'. The British charged the Amir with receiving deputations from the (British) tribal zone, failure to prevent his regular troops and subjects from joining tribal levies, and granting asylum to their enemies. They also alleged that the Amir had addressed assemblies of mullahs and exhorted them to wage jihad, that he had assumed the title of 'Zia-ul-Millat wa-ud-Din' and published a book entitled *Taqwim-ud-Din* which affected British interests. All this, the British argued, did not encourage peaceful, much less friendly, relations between neighbours.

Among his own people, political fission was the order of the day and the Amir spent most of his time and energy trying to penetrate and pacify zones of relative inaccessibility; it was a policy of what has been called 'internal imperialism'. Thus, in the late 1880s and early 1890s, Abdur Rahman shifted thousands of Ghilzai Pushtun, his principal enemies, and others from southern and south-central Afghanistan to north of the Hindu Kush. In this he accomplished two immediate objectives: he removed dissidents from areas which they might again infect with the germs of revolt and he created a force loyal to himself. For even though the Ghilzai (Pushtun) might be anti-Durrani (Pushtun) while living in their own territorial-tribal zones, they were pro-Pushtun in the northern non-Pushtun (Tajik/Uzbeck/Hazara/Turkoman) areas.

Abdur Rahman created Boards of Treasury and Trade, Bureaus of Justice and Police, Offices of Records, Public Works, Posts and Communications, Directorates of Education and Medicine. All these were equated to modern Cabinet Departments or Ministries. He created a Supreme Council, similar to the modern Cabinet, albeit with a purely advisory role. He also appointed a General Assembly (*Loya Jirga*) which included three groups of Afghan citizens. The practice of selling public offices was discontinued and a civil administration established. The country was divided into four major administrative provinces—Turkestan, Herat, Kandahar and Kabul—and into seven administrative districts.

The Amir made important reforms in the legal field which owed their effectiveness to his own firm grip and control over the kingdom in general and its religious establishments in particular. All laws were divided into three categories: Islamic laws (*Sharia*), administrative or civil laws (*kanun*), and tribal laws. It followed that there were three types of courts: religious courts that dealt with religious and civil affairs; criminal courts which were administered by the chiefs of police or kotwals; and judges. There was also a board of commerce made up of merchants, Afghan as well as non-Afghan, Hindu as well as Muslim, which settled business disputes.

Essentially a military autocracy, his government relied on a standing and centralized Afghan army. The Amir had created it from a tribal and feudal force that was weak in administration, discipline, logistics and armaments and lacked a trained officer corps.

Abdur Rahman encouraged the development of trade and internal communications and hired European advisors in an attempt to introduce some western technology. A single monetary unit, the (Kabuli) rupee, was instituted and a mint opened in Kabul. He imported mining machinery and established a number of state-owned workshops in Kabul: saw mills, steam hammers and lathes. In all this special emphasis was placed on the requirements of the armed forces. He also improved the condition and security of roads and postal services. His government made noteworthy though modest gains in the sphere of public health. In this, as in other fields of endeavour, his chief obstacles were financial and political constraints.

The Amir did not intend to disturb the basic socio-economic structure of his kingdom. His dependence on his Durrani kinsmen and other Afghan tribes made any such undertaking highly dangerous, if not impossible. His reliance on Islamic fundamentalism as a spiritual weapon against Britain and Russia, even though serving Afghan interests by rallying disparate ethnic groups, promoted xenophobia and traditionalism. Thus, despite his benevolent despotism, he was not unsuccessful in formulating a definite programme of modernization. The real difficulty was that he was unable to find the means to bring such a programme into operation.

In the field of foreign policy, the Amir resented the demarcation of the boundaries of his kingdom to which reference has been made in preceding paragraphs, for he viewed it as 'demarcation without representation'. He vigorously condemned railway building close to the borders of Afghanistan and the Indian government's avowed intention to push the line into his domain. This was, he wrote, tantamount to 'pushing a knife into my vitals'.

Abdur Rahman once likened his kingdom to a swan in the middle of a lake: 'When the swan approached too near to one bank, the tigress [Britain] clawed out some of his feathers, and when the opposite bank, the wolves [Russia] tried to tear him to pieces.' On another occasion, he compared Afghanistan to a goat on which a lion and a bear had fixed their eyes. In any case, he had no intention of allowing his country to become a battleground for the two contenders.

The Amir was succeeded by Habibullah Khan (q.v.), his eldest son and close confidant. He had shrewdly kept his sons in Kabul, refusing to make them provincial governors. It would seem few, if indeed any, of them apart from Habibullah, harboured any political ambitions. The new provincial governments had succeeded, as well as Abdur Rahman's ruthless policy of killing or exiling all his enemies, real or potential. So also the forced migration of dissidents inside the country. In the bargain, Afghans were denied the rights of free travel without the express consent of their government.

Mir Sultan Muhammad Khan Munshi (ed.), *The Life of Amir Abdur Rahman: Amir of Afghanistan*, 2 vols, London, 1920; Vartan Gregorian, *The Emergence of Modern Afghanistan: Politics of Reform and Modernisation, 1880-1946*, Stanford, 1969, pp. 129-62; Ludwig W. Adamec, *Afghanistan, 1900-1923: A Diplomatic History*, Berkeley, 1967, pp. 1–27; Louis Dupree, *Afghanistan*, Princeton, 1973.

First (Anglo-) Afghan War (1838–42)

British India's relations with Afghanistan may be traced to the western powers' sustained attempts at imperialist expansion in the heart of Asia. Simply put, the John Company (q.v.) feeling its way towards Sind (q.v.) and the Panjab, came into collision with Tsarist Russia's expansion southward. While the British viewed Russia's Asian involvement and growing interest in Afghanistan and lands on its periphery as a threat to their Indian empire, Russia was deeply concerned that the British were cutting it off from Central Asia's markets. Russia took advantage of initial British indifference and ineptitude and established its predominance in Persia with the treaty of Turkomanchai (1828). Jolted by imminent danger, the British then began strengthening diplomatic relations with the Amirs of Sind (q.v.) and the Sikhs in the Panjab. However, their efforts to conclude a treaty with Dost Mohammad (q.v.), the Barakzai ruler of Afghanistan, proved abortive.

Initially, Dost Mohammad had reacted favourably to the mission of Alexander Burnes (q.v.) and British overtures, thanks to his fear of Persia or, more accurately, a strong Russia working through a weak Persian regime. Calcutta however was very cool to their envoy's fervid plea for a categorical assurance to the Afghan ruler. Unfortunately for him, Burnes hedged his bets, pointing out that Shah Shuja had only to appear in Peshawar with 'an [British] agent and two of its [British] regiments, as an honorary escort, and an avowal to the Afghans that we have taken up his cause to insure his being fixed for ever on the throne'. In the result, the question of Peshawar, then held by the Sikhs and coveted by the Amir, assumed dangerous proportions with Lord Auckland (q.v.) insisting that his government could not interfere in the affairs of an independent state—viz., Ranjit Singh's (q.v.) Panjab.

In 1837 the Russians encouraged Persia to lay siege to Herat. Moreover, Teheran's new Qajar ruler, Mohammad Shah (r. 1834–48), staked his claim to the sovereignty of Afghanistan. Meanwhile, Burnes's objective of bringing about a rapprochement between Ranjit Singh and Dost Mohammad and working out a mutual security agreement with the Amir seemed destined to prove abortive. Burnes, increasingly suspect in Calcutta, had no authority to make any firm promises of substantial assistance to the Afghan ruler who, by March 1838, felt equally convinced that the British would 'do nothing to upset' their alliance with the Sikh chief. No wonder he next turned a ready ear to the Russian adventurer, Captain Ivan Vitkevich who, in sharp contrast to the British envoy, was profuse in his promises. As a prerequisite to any formal treaty with the Amir, the British demanded the dismissal of the Russian agent and Kabul's clear disavowal of any claims to provinces occupied by the Sikhs.

At this stage the British matured their plans for a friendly Afghan state under a puppet ruler. Shah Shuja, the deposed Saddozai Afghan chief who

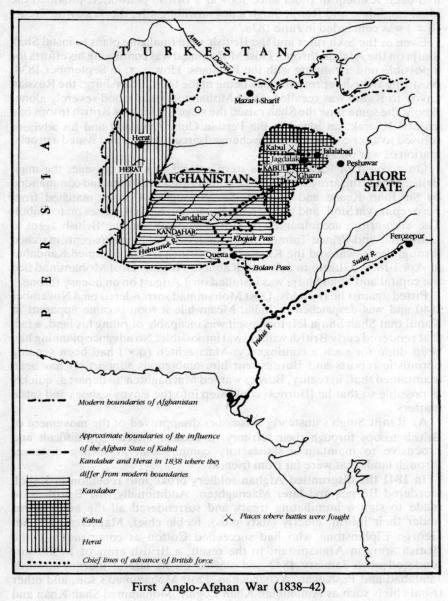

First Anglo-Afghan War (1838–42)

had been resident in India since 1809 as a British pensioner, provided the ideal candidate and Ranjit Singh a not unwilling ally; the Tripartite Treaty (q.v.) was concluded in June 1838.

Even as the Sikh ruler and the British were finalizing plans to instal Shah Shuja on the Afghan throne, Dost Mohammad was continuing his efforts for a possible understanding with the Russians. However, in September 1838, on strong British representations being made to St. Petersburg, the Russian envoy to Kabul was recalled. Dost Mohammad thus stood severely alone. About the same time the Shah raised the siege of Herat as British troops had reached Kharak, an island in the Persian Gulf. Auckland and his advisers refused to alter course under the changed circumstances and issued a proclamation of war on 1 October.

On account of Ranjit Singh's stern refusal to allow passage, the main British force, the army of the Indus, numbering 21,000 men and commanded by Sir John Keane and Lt.-Gen. Sir Willoughby Cotton, marched from Ferozepur, via Sind, and through the Bolan and Khojak passes on to Kabul. The Sikh army, accompanied by Col. Claude Wade, the British agent at Ludhiana, and Prince Taimur Shah, Shah Shuja's heir apparent, marched through Peshawar and the Khyber pass. British troops occupied Kandahar in April 1839, Ghazni in July and Kabul in August. Dost Mohammad fled the capital and Shah Shuja was installed on 7 August on an uneasy throne.

Pitted against heavy odds, Dost Mohammad surrendered on 4 November 1840 and was despatched to India. Meanwhile it soon became apparent in Kabul that Shah Shuja left to himself was incapable of ruling his land, a fact that rendered early British withdrawal impossible. No advance planning had been done for such a contingency: Macnaghten (q.v.) had been sending optimistic reports and Burnes lent him ambiguous support. It has been maintained that, in reality, Burnes wanted Macnaghten 'to depart as quickly as possible so that he [Burnes] could step into the Envoy's shoes and settle matters'.

As Ranjit Singh's unsteady successors disapproved of the movement of British troops through their territory, it became increasingly difficult and expensive to maintain a satisfactory commissariat at such a distance, through lands that were far from friendly.

In 1841 the disgruntled Afghan soldiery broke into rebellion in Kabul, murdered Burnes and later Macnaghten. Additionally, the British were made to sign a humiliating treaty and surrendered all the army stores under their infirm, elderly (sixty plus), feeble chief, Maj.-Gen. William George Elphinstone who had succeeded Cotton as commander of the British army in Afghanistan. In the result, a British army of 16,500 surrendered on 6 January 1842 and started on its fateful journey towards Jalalabad and Peshawar. Akbar Khan, Dost Mohammad's son, and other tribal chiefs such as Amanullah Khan Logari, Mohammad Shah Khan and Shamsuuddin Abdullah Khan Achakzai, continued harassing the retreating rabble, of which 120 were taken hostage and all but one of the rest perished; the solitary survivor (Dr William Brydon) reached Jalalabad half-dead, on a famished donkey's broken back.

Ellenborough (q.v.) who replaced Auckland, though initially in favour of vindicating British honour, changed his mind and ordered a withdrawal of all the British forces. It is said he replaced the policy of folly with one of pomp. None the less, he was determined on the 're-establishment of our military reputation by the infliction of some signal and decisive blow'. In the result, Maj.-Gen. George Pollock commanding 'the army of retribution', marched from Peshawar to Jalalabad and defeated the Afghans en route at Mamu Kheyl, Jagdalak and Tezir, reaching Kabul on 15 September 1842. Two days later he was joined by Maj.-Gen. William Knott who had earlier destroyed the fortifications of Ghazni. On 12 October, after all British prisoners has been freed, the armies marched back and were accorded a rousing welcome. Dost Mohammad was released and reoccupied his throne.

Clearly the war severely damaged British prestige and resulted in draining the exchequer of 15 million pound sterling, apart from claiming a toll of 20,000 lives. Blame for it has been traditionally saddled on to Auckland, his own and his advisors' 'misunderstandings and miscalculations'. Kaye's time-worn account has over the years held Auckland and his advisers squarely responsible for the fiasco, refusing to notice any redeeming features or extenuating circumstances in the situation. Sir Kerr Fraser-Tytler has however pointed out that they were by no means the only rulers of India who blundered over Afghan policy. Another careful scholar of the First Afghan War has brought out the fact that Auckland 'served as a pawn in the meaningful (though often misguided) Whig policies' of Palmerston 'to contain Russian advances in Central Asia'. To quote Norris, it was the British government's determination to 'avoid [a] European war at all costs that disguised the truth and doctored the record of events in Persia and Afghanistan in 1838. The disguise has hampered historians ever since.'

Michael Yapp, a keen student of British Indian 'strategies', has held Auckland and Macnaghten 'squarely' responsible for the 'disaster' insofar as they pursued a policy of 'greater intervention in which they did not believe and without the resources to make it work, created a situation in which decisive superiority in Afghanistan was lost.'

Louis Dupree, a percipient observer of Afghanistan and its people, calls the campaign 'an abortive experiment in imperialism'. More, the 'realistic results of the First Anglo-Afghan war can be stated simply: after four years of disaster, both in honor, material and personnel, the British left Afghanistan as they found it, in tribal chaos and with Dost Mohammad Khan returned to the throne of Kabul.'

J. A. Norris, *First Anglo-Afghan War 1838-1842*, Cambridge, 1967; W. K. Fraser-Tytler, *Afghanistan: A Study of Developments in Central and Southern Asia*, 2nd ed., Oxford, 1953; Louis Dupree, *Afghanistan*, Princeton, 1973; M. E. Yapp, *Strategies of British India: Britain, Iran & Afghanistan, 1798-1850*, Oxford, 1980.

Second (Anglo-) Afghan War (1878–80)

With Dost Mohammad (q.v.) re-installed in Kabul and the British following a policy of scrupulous non-interference coupled with a rapprochement between England and Russia in 1844, Anglo-Afghan relations showed considerable improvement in the decade following the First Afghan War (q.v.). This, however, did not last, for by the late fifties Russian pressure towards the Caspian had been renewed following its amazing recovery from the humiliating military debacle in the Crimean war (1854-6). Steadily but surely Tsarist Russia inched its way towards the rickety, ill-administered Central Asian khanates of Bukhara (1866), Tashkent (1867), Samarqand (1868) and Khiva (1873) and her 'progress' created powerful repercussions, both far and near.

In Afghanistan, Dost Mohammad's death (1863) was followed by a bloody civil war in which Sher Ali eventually emerged victorious (1866). The new Amir had viewed Russia's movement towards his northern frontiers with apprehension and, to forestall it, sought an offensive and defensive alliance with British India. Here John Lawrence (q.v.) and his so-called policy of 'masterly inactivity' held sway, albeit his two immediate successors, Mayo (q.v.) and Northbrook (q.v.), were neither its uncritical nor yet over-enthusiastic supporters. This was especially the case as their political masters at home appeared complacent—being supremely satisfied with the Tsar's repeated assurances that Afghanistan was outside his sphere of influence. Presently, the Amir, sore with the British for their refusal to

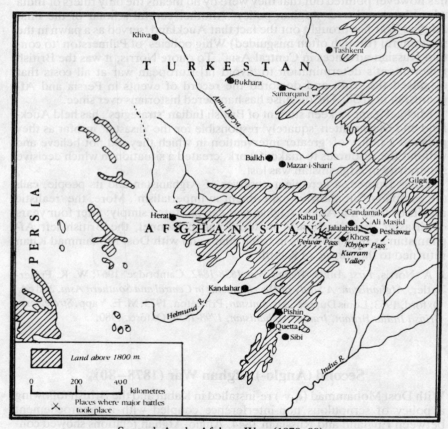

Second Anglo-Afghan War (1878–80)

accept Abdulla Jan, his favourite younger son, as his heir-apparent, turned towards Russia to ensure the safety of his kingdom.

Disraeli's (1804–81) return to power (1874) in England spelt a radical change in the home government's policy in foreign affairs in general and towards Afghanistan in particular. Northbook, unable to implement 'Whitehall's new instructions of forcing a British envoy on an unwilling Sher Ali, was replaced by Lytton (q.v.). With detailed guidelines drawn up by Salisbury, the new Secretary of State for India, the stage appeared set for a second massive British intervention in Afghan affairs. The new Governor-General soon communicated to the Amir his intention of sending a British envoy to Kabul and refused to be discouraged by the latter's protestations. As the Viceroy viewed it, a British envoy would become an adviser, not simply a resident representative.

On 10 October 1876 Lytton reasserted his intention of making the Afghan ruler accept a British resident at Kabul and agents at Herat and elsewhere, apart from guaranteeing free entry for all Englishmen to his country. In addition, Sher Ali was to sever communications with Russia. Should the Amir prove recalcitrant, he was warned that he would face the prospect of total extinction.

Failing an exclusive alliance with Kabul, Lytton was determined to extend India's borders beyond Peshawar. The Governor-General's bellicose attitude received an unexpected boost thanks to the explosive situation between England and Russia over Turkey (1877-8). Outraged by an impending revision of the Treaty of San Stefano (March 1878) at the Congress of Berlin (June-July 1878), the Russians retaliated by the dispatch of a mission to Kabul under General Stolietoff, an envoy of Russian Turkestan's new chief, General von Kaufmann. This was accomplished in July 1878 in the teeth of Sher Ali's violent protests. No sooner was the news received than Lytton demanded corresponding representation for India.

Neville Chamberlain, who headed the British mission, proceeded to the Afghan frontier despite Sher Ali's urgent requests for delay. Eventually, as the mission was denied entry at the frontier post of Ali Masjid, Lytton served the Amir with an ultimatum (2 November). He had already strengthened his position by concluding a treaty with the Khan of Kalat and, in turn, occupied Quetta. At the same time, by an agreement with the ruler of Kashmir he had established an agency at Gilgit. These two important observation posts had enabled him to organize an effective espionage system throughout Afghanistan. Meanwhile, British protests in St Petersburg led to Stolietoff's departure from Kabul. But in the absence of a satisfactory communication from that end, Lytton declared war on 20 November.

Having earlier signed a defensive alliance with Russia, Sher Ali appealed for aid when the British invaded Afghanistan. Russia and Britain had already come to terms at Berlin, and General Kaufmann refused, tactfully emphasizing the impossibility of transporting troops and material across the Hindu Kush in winter. Refusing to take no for an answer, the Amir journeyed to Mizar-i-Sharif to plead his case in person before the Tsar. Across the Amu Darya, however, the Russian constabulary blocked his attempts to reach St Petersburg arguing that he should make his peace with the British. Broken in spirit, Sher Ali was taken ill and died near Balkh on 21 February 1879.

The principal attack was launched by three British armies converging on Kabul: General Samuel Browne, through the Khyber pass; General Fredrick Sleigh (later Lord) Roberts, through the Kurram valley and General John Biddulph, through the Bolan. A fourth army, under General Donald Stewart, proceeded towards Kandahar. No effective opposition from the Afghan host was encountered by any British commander, and before long British troops were in occupation of Jalalabad, the Peiwar pass and Kandahar itself. Out-generalled as well as outmanoeuvred, the Amir had fled towards Russian Turkestan to solicit help, but this was denied him, for Russia and Britain had already come to terms at Berlin.

In February 1879, while Sher Ali was in exile and before his death, the British concluded the Treaty of Gandamak (q.v.) with his son and successor, Yakub Khan. The treaty is still considered 'the most disgraceful agreement' ever signed by an Afghan Amir. In all fairness, however, it should be pointed out that little unity existed among the tribal leaders. Unorganized and sporadic resistance against the British continued. The result was an uneasy truce.

On 3 September 1879 there was an uprising in Kabul. The Afghans revolted against the occupying forces and murdered the British envoy, Sir Louis Cavagnari. It was soon evident that the British would not be able to hold out for long. In the result, Lytton contemplated handing over Kandahar to Wali Sher Ali, negotiating the future of Herat with Persia and accepting Abdur Rahman (q.v.), as the new ruler at Kabul. However, before any of these moves could take shape and form, he was recalled. His policy had claimed a heavy toll in men and money as well as the friendship of the Afghans, and was admittedly a dismal failure.

The military disaster of the first war did not repeat itself in the second, however. Two factors helped—the leadership of General Roberts and the quality of his subordinates. The General reoccupied Kabul (October 1879) with Yakub Khan, the Afghan Amir in tow, a virtual British prisoner. His brother Ayub proclaimed himself the new ruler and succeeded in defeating a British army at Maiwund, near Kandahar (July 1880). But the British commander marched from Kabul and lent substantial assistance to Abdur Rahman who soon worsted Ayub in battle.

Ripon (q.v.), the new Viceroy, made haste to confirm Abdur Rahman. The latter, in return for a subsidy, agreed to refrain from maintaining relations with any other country without the prior approval of the Indian government, and to let the latter hold the districts of Pishin and Sibi. In return, the British committed themselves to bail him out in the event of unprovoked opposition. Ayub Khan who had earlier worsted a British force was pushed back into Herat. Later, considerable assistance was given to the Amir to reoccupy the town. Similarly Wali Sher Ali was persuaded to abdicate in his favour thereby enabling the Amir to consolidate his position anew.

It appears Lytton was convinced that the real solution to the Afghan question lay in securing Kandahar and the Peshawar-Kurram valley. This was what Salisbury had instructed him to aim at. But the Governor-General had fixed his eyes on Kabul, the master key to India. The 'mountain wall', the passes and the glacis, were still to be effectively held. Unfortunately, the Kabul campaign had failed to secure an ally commanding a reasonable mandate over the Afghans. Thus the grandiose dream of a triumphant march of the British army into the heart of Central Asia backed by its Afghan feudatories and supported by the anti-Russian forces of the Muslim world, remained unrealized.

There is no doubt that Lytton's initiative had forced the hands of the home government and the Cabinet found it expedient to support him in practice. But the Viceroy was soon to discover that his action was not worth it. His policies were censured officially, his objectives scrutinized diligently and his initiative circumscribed seriously. To cap it all, Salisbury was determined not to forgive his disobedient representative.

It is interesting to recall that in March 1880, Lytton's government, in sore straits, had sent Lepel Griffin to Kabul to undertake diplomatic and administrative superintendence of affairs and negotiations—in other words, to find someone to whom charge of Kabul and the surrounding country could be entrusted. In his instructions, the Viceroy mentioned, but rejected, the alternatives of annexation, or military occupation, or temporary occupation until the establishment of a friendly ruler had been secured. None of these would be in accordance with previous British declarations nor yet likely to produce a safe and comparatively speedy settlement of affairs. In fact, their adoption would greatly irritate the people of the country, entail enormous additional cost to the finances of India and place a heavy strain on the army.

Of all the Viceroys in India and Ministers at home, only Mayo appears to have realized the true nature of Afghan loyalties. In his attempts to revive the Durrani hegemony or to divide Afghanistan, Lytton backed the wrong horse. Sher Ali died—tired of war. But it was Abdur Rahman, another Barakzai, who was to step into his shoes.

D. P. Singhal, *India and Afghanistan 1876-1907*, St Lucia (Australia), 1963; Suhash Chakravarty, *From Khyber to Oxus, A Study in Imperial Expansion*, New Delhi, 1976.

Third (Anglo-) Afghan War (1919)

A variety of reasons have been put forth to explain the Third Afghan War. According to some, its genesis lay in Kabul's anxiety to take advantage of a weakened British government on the morrow of World War I. Others maintain that British preoccupations with the nationalist agitation in India provided the Afghans an ideal opportunity to regain the Panjab. Still another explanation suggests that the war was a 'diversionary tactic' to unite the divergent factions in Afghanistan so as to reduce internal tensions. Indirectly, the war may be traced to Amir Habibullah's (q.v.) failure to secure independence, followed by his son King Amanullah's (q.v.) unilateral declaration to that effect at the time of his coronation. British disavowal of the latter action made it evident that they would not relinquish such control as they exercised without a struggle.

Preparations were made on both sides. By 1 May 1919 Afghan troop movements towards the border began to increase tension in the neighbouring tribal areas. The British declared war on 6 May and hostilities began with the first battle of Bagh three days later. In the Khyber area a British contingent under Major General Fowler faced a large force commanded by Saleh

Mohammad Khan, Commander-in-Chief of the Afghan army. With the
timely arrival of their equipment, the British won both at Bagh as well as
Dakka, beyond the Khyber. Kandahar saw no action under Abdul Quddus
Khan, except for the British capture of Spin Baldak, opposite Chaman. At
Khost, Afghan troops under Mohammad Nadir Khan forged ahead and
occupied Spinwan and Shewa on 23 May; four days later they invested Thal.
British :einforcements were rushed under Brig.-Gen. R. F. H. Dyer
(q.v.) but before he could attack, news of the armistice was received and
Afghan troops retreated swiftly. Operations in Chitral and Baluchistan were
brief, British forces for the most part dispersing multitudes of ill-equipped
Afghan soldiery.

Both sides were keen to end hostilities. In essence, the poorly equipped
Afghan forces were no match for the British, aided by modern weaponry:
bombs, aeroplanes, wireless communications. At the same time, Whitehall
felt, continued hostilities were undesirable, especially in view of a disturbed
tribal frontier and mounting political disaffection in India. Besides,
Delhi was understandably keen to maintain Afghanistan as a buffer state
and pacify Indian Muslims who constituted a powerful and vocal minority.

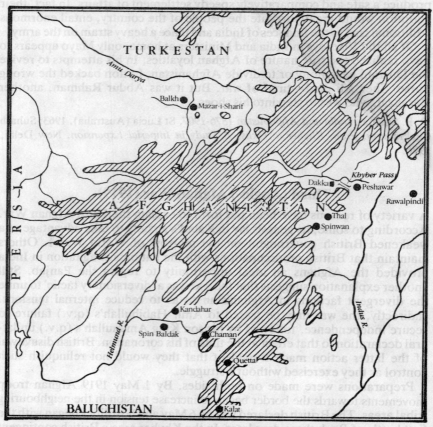

Third Anglo-Afghan War (1919)

To negotiate a settlement, an Afghan delegation led by Ali Ahmad Khan was met by its British counterpart under Sir Hamilton Grant, then Foreign Secretary in Delhi. The Treaty of Rawalpindi, initialled on 8 August 1919 (supplemented by further agreements of 23 November 1921), recognized Afghanistan as an independent sovereign state, while the latter agreed, albeit somewhat reluctantly, to recognize the Durand Line (q.v.) as its frontier with India. British subsidies were discontinued while Afghanistan's right to direct relations with other powers was accepted without qualification.

Afghan, British and Russian historians disagree on the origin, course and outcome of the war. The Afghans claim that the war was forced on them by the British, but are ambiguous on the question of who started actual hostilities. All Afghan historical literature claims a total Afghan military and political victory. The British maintain that the genesis of the war lay in the wild hopes and plots of the Afghans. According to this view the Afghans wanted to make use of the Indian nationalist movement and Pathan strength and support to regain the Panjab. Brigadier Sykes appears to suggest that international political considerations forced the hand of King Amanullah; that the latter was strongly suspected of complicity in the murder of his father and that he attacked India as a 'suitable and popular diversion.'

Russian accounts squarely blame the British imperialists, maintaining that the latter launched an aggressive war forcing the Afghans to 'take up arms for the defence of their motherland and their freedom'. More, it was the Red army's 'liberation' of Merv (May 1919) and the Soviets' diplomatic recognition of Afghanistan that thwarted British plans to renew the war with an attack from Persia or Bukhara.

The major reason for the war appears to be the development of 'Afghan nationalism and the rising social and political expectations in the country'. Amanullah had promised to lead his people to 'total liberation' in his first royal proclamation and this did much to rally Afghan public opinion to his support. More, Afghan leaders urged their people 'who were true Muslims and patriots' to prepare themselves for the struggle against Great Britain, 'the traditional foe of Afghan independence'.

Lt.-Gen. G. N. Molesworth, *Afghanistan: 1919*, Bombay, 1962; Ludwig W. Adamec, *Afghanistan 1900-1923: A Diplomatic History*, Berkeley, 1967, pp. 108–68.

Afzal-ud-Daula, Nizam (1827–69)

Born in October 1827, Atzal-ud-Daula succeeded his father, Nasir-ud-Daula (q.v.), to the gaddi in May 1851. His minister, Mir Turab Ali Khan, popularly known as Salar Jang (q.v.), was a protege of the British. During the Rebellion of 1857 (q.v.) the Nizam remained loyal to the John Company (q.v.) although his people were incited by 'rebel' sympathizers from time to time and several cases of insurrection were reported. These were ruthlessly put down.

During what were some of the most critical days for the Company, the Hyderabad contingent served with a British force in central India for thirteen months. The Nizam was persuaded by the Government of India to remove the Mughal emperor's name from his coinage, but an attempt to proclaim him independent was viewed as a breach of friendship. After the suppression of the 1857 Rebellion Canning (q.v.), on behalf of the British sovereign, thanked the Nizam for his loyalty and bestowed many presents on him.

By a treaty concluded in 1860 all territories assigned to the British, other than Berar, were restored to the Nizam; Sholapur was ceded to the Nizam and Rs 50 lakhs of his debt cancelled. A nominal head now, he was created KCSI in August 1861. He died on 26 February 1869.

Thomas William Beale, *An Oriental Biographical Dictionary*, rev. ed., reprint, Ludhiana, 1972, p.36; J. D. B. Gribble, *A History of the Deccan*, London, 1924, 2 vols, II.

The Aga Khan (1877–1957)

Sir Sultan Muhammad Shah, Aga Khan III, was the hereditary spiritual leader or Imam of the Khoja Ismaili community in India, Burma, Malaya, Persia, Syria, Central Asia and South Africa.

Way back in the 19th century, the Aga Khan's grandfather who was governor of the province of Mahallats and Qum in Iran under its Qajar rulers was involved in dynastic quarrels and obliged to migrate to Sind (q.v.). He later helped the British in the First Anglo-Afghan War (q.v.) and in the campaign against the Amirs of Sind (q.v.). The tradition of fidelity to the British was thus well ingrained in the family.

A politician, diplomat and religious head, the Aga Khan preferred to be called an internationalist. He also earned fame for his extensive stables which bred race-horses that won the English Derby five times. His principal source of income came from the contributions of his followers which he invested wisely.

The Aga Khan played an active and indeed crucial role in early Muslim politics in India, and this despite his many European preoccupations. Besides taking a keen interest in Muslim political and educational activities he was also involved in the economic and social welfare of his followers who prospered under his able direction. He infused them with his own broadmindedness, exhorting them to adapt themselves to the customs and style of life of the country of their adoption without sacrificing their religion.

Though acquainted with Sir Syed Ahmed (q.v.), it was mainly through Mohsin-ul-Mulk (q.v.) that he became actively associated with the Aligarh movement (q.v.). Besides making generous contributions in men and money to help the movement tide over its financial difficulties, he was also a co-founder of the All-India Muslim League (q.v.) and its President for the first seven years (1906-13).

There was, he wrote, no hope 'of a fair deal for us [Muslims] within the fold of the Congress party or in alliance with it...we asked [1906] that the Muslims of India should not be regarded as a mere minority, but as a nation within a nation whose rights and obligations should be guaranteed by statute.'

The Aga Khan's role in the establishment of the Muslim League needs no emphasis. Years later he was to admit in his *Memoirs* that Minto's (q.v.) acceptance 'of our demands was the foundation of all future constitutional proposals made for India by successive British governments, and its final, inevitable consequences was the partition of India and the emergence of Pakistan.' Concerning 1906: 'Our achievement...seemed important enough, and it was obvious to those of us most closely associated with it—especially Nawab Muhsin-ul-Mulk and myself—that since we had obtained separate electoral recognition we should make that separate representation effective.'

As for his importance, the British were more than fully cognisant of it. Minto's private secretary, Dunlop Smith noted that 'Men like the Aga Khan plainly feel that in pressing for large separate treatment for Mohammedans they are fighting our battle much more than their own. We have far more to lose than the Muslims by an entente between Islam and Hinduism.'

For his part, the Aga Khan confided in Minto's private secretary: 'I have asked all the members of the Muslim League Deputation...to form a permanent committee, and I have given to my old friend Muhsin-ul-Mulk...certain instructions regarding the methods by which he is to proceed.'

In the wake of a quarrel between the trustees of the MAO College and its English principal (1909), the Aga Khan, at the behest of the provincial Lt. Governor, Sir John Prescott Hewett (1854-1941), as well as the Viceroy (Minto), was responsible for shifting the headquarters of the Muslim League from Dacca to Lucknow thereby placing it 'under the direct, watchful eye of the authorities'.

In 1913 the Aga Khan, who had hitherto been permanent president of the League, resigned and for well-nigh a decade chose to remain in the political wilderness. He was convinced that by adopting a resolution in favour of a system of self-government suitable to India the League had drawn considerably closer to the Indian National Congress (q.v.). This, he argued, was premature and even 'unfortunate,' more so as he had led the famous deputation demanding separate electorates for his community.

An additional reason for his ouster was that he was the only Muslim leader of importance who had viewed the annulment of the Partition of Bengal (q.v.) as 'a boon' to the community. His action was severely criticized by his compatriots and, finding his position 'inconvenient', he quit.

In sum, his disapproval of the League's new stance, its involvement in the Khilafat Movement (q.v.) and earlier (1916) rapprochement with the Congress were responsible for his temporary retirement from active politics.

During World War I, the Aga Khan was criticized by Muslims for being a henchman of the British who, they alleged, were working against the interests of his community. In two diplomatic missions on behalf of the Allies, he tried to dissuade the Sultan of Turkey from joining the Central Powers. Later, he worked assiduously to cultivate the loyalty of the Khedive of Egypt to the British cause. To appease his followers and quieten Muslim agitators over Turkey's losses in the war, he urged sympathetic handling of its case at the Paris Peace Conference (1919).

At the end of the war, the anti-British Khilafat leaders chose the Aga Khan and Syed Ameer Ali (q.v.) to present their case to the new Turkish regime and demand restoration of the last Caliph, Abdul Majid. Both Kemal Ataturk and Ismet Inonu, leaders of a resurgent nation, chose however to spurn the advice of these 'pillars of British rule' in India.

The Aga Khan re-entered active political life with the Congress boycott of the Simon Commission (q.v.). Earlier, in September 1928, as 'leader of the blue-blooded loyalists since 1906', he had poured ridicule on the Nehru Report (q.v.), and dubbed its proposals as 'degrading'. In particular he took exception to its emphasis on a strong centre, declaring that 'each Indian province should have the freedom to proclaim independence'.

As president of the Muslim All-Parties Conference which was convened in Delhi on 1 January 1929, the Aga Khan declared *inter alia* that India could not be a prosperous and self-governing country if "such a large and important section of the people as the Muslims remain in doubt as to whether their cultural entity is safe or not . . . There is a lot of talk about the term **"communal"**. I **may again remark in passing that Muslims of India are not a community, but a nation composed of many communities.'**

Muslims, he averred, must be armed with the right to elect their own representatives through separate electorates. Earlier, he had advocated the same line of reasoning in his book, *India in Transition* (1918).

In 1931-2, the Aga Khan attended the Round Table Conference (q.v.) not only as a Muslim League representative, but as head of the entire Indian delegation. Here he successfully fought for recognition of the minority status of Muslims. Separate representation for Muslims was later accepted in the British government's Communal Award (q.v.).

On 13 November 1931, the Aga Khan presented the Round Table Conference with what came to be known later as the 'minorities pact' on behalf of the Muslims, the depressed classes, the Anglo-Indians, the Europeans and a section of Indian Christians. In an 11-point charter of safeguards, the demand for statutory representation was given up in favour of representation of the different minorities by convention.

Later (April 1933), he was one of the five Muslim co-optees who helped the joint committee of both Houses of Parliament to consider the British government's White Paper on India's constitutional reforms.

The Aga Khan swore by Hindu-Muslim unity and amity, but was of the firm view that this could be achieved only if the majority community recognized the genuine political claims of the minority.

Deeply interested in education which he considered to be 'key to a rewarding life', the Aga Khan advocated both a dispersion of modern scientific knowledge and technology as well as a study of Islamic history and religion. He encouraged Ismaili women to abandon purdah and educate themselves. He urged the setting up of an autonomous Muslim University patterned after Oxford to make all these programmes viable, and collected a sum of Rs 80 lakhs for its establishment. He also supported a scheme for compulsory elementary education. After the Partition (1947), he exhorted his followers in Pakistan to modernize their educational system, and gave generous donations to encourage research and scholarship among the Muslims.

Early in life the Aga Khan was much impressed by Gandhi's (q.v.) movement in South Africa and gave it all possible support. Later, however, he denounced the Mahatma's Civil Disobedience Movement (q.v.), declaring that through it Hindus aimed at subjugating the Muslim masses.

A moderate loyalist who favoured continuance of the British connection, he responded to Gandhi's appeal for relief for the Jallianwala Bagh (q.v.) victims, but declined to contribute towards a memorial which, he argued, would encourage bitterness between the communities. In 1942, in the wake of the Quit India Movement (q.v.), he offered the government his house in Poona for the Mahatma's detention.

Earlier, the British had appointed him India's representative to the Disarmament Conference in Geneva (1932) and to the Assembly of the League of Nations (1932, 1934-7); in 1937 he was voted President of the Assembly. Thereafter, he virtually retired from active political life, spending most of his time in Europe where he died in 1957.

Sir Sultan Muhammad Shah, *The Memoirs of Aga Khan: World Enough and Time*, London, 1954; Stanley Jackson, *The Aga Khan: Prince, Prophet and Sportsman*, London, 1952; Harry J. Greenwall, *His Highness the Aga Khan, Imam of the Ismailis*, London, 1952; G. A. Natesan (ed.), *Eminent Musalmans*, Madras, n.d.

C. U. Aitchison (1832–96)

Charles Umpherston Aitchison was placed fifth in the first competitive examination for the Indian Civil Service held in 1855, and is said to have been 'the most distinguished among the competition-wallahs'.

He studied law and Hindustani for a year in London, prior to which he had obtained an M. A. degree from Edinburgh. He started service in the Panjab as assistant to the judicial commissioner. From then on till 1878 he alternated between that province and the Government of India. He was an adviser (1859-65) to Canning (q.v.) and continued in the central government as under-secretary in the foreign department (1859-65) when Sir John Lawrence (q.v.) posted him to the Panjab as Deputy Commissioner.

Aitchison was strongly influenced by Lawrence's policy of non-interference in the Central Asian and Afghan questions, a policy which he had sought to implement as Foreign Secretary (1868-78). Apprehensive of Lytton's (q.v.) 'forward' stance, Aitchison was away on furlough in England when Indo-Afghan relations hit a sharp trough, resulting in the second Anglo-Afghan War (q.v.)

As Chief Commissioner of British Burma (1878-81), Aitchison tried, albeit unsuccessfully, to stop the sale of opium and improve standards of morality among English officers. He was next appointed Lieutenant-Governor of the Panjab (1882-7). To his persistent efforts goes the credit for establishing the Panjab University. In 1886, as President of the Public Service Commission (q.v.), he proposed to retain a European *corps d'elite* while extending employment opportunities to Indians. Briefly (1887-8) a member of Dufferin's (q.v.) Council, he retired on grounds of ill-health, repaired home (1889) and settled down in London and, later, Oxford. A great supporter of missionary work, he was actively engaged in it until his death in 1896.

A serious-minded officer, Aitchison compiled *A Manual of the Criminal Law of the Panjab* in 1860. Between 1862-92 he put together *A Collection of Treaties, Engagements and Sunnuds Relating to India and the neighbouring countries*, of which the first volume appeared in Calcutta in 1862; 11 volumes had been issued by 1892. This was a monumental undertaking, but, in addition, 'So valued had his office minutes been found, that he may be said to have written most of the dispatches relating to the great questions of foreign and feudatory policy from Lord Canning to Lord Northbrook.'

In 1875 Aitchison published a treatise on *The Native States of India* with some leading cases illustrating the principles which governed their relations with the British. He also wrote the *Life of Sir John Lawrence* in Sir William Hunter's 'Rulers of India' series.

George Smith, *Twelve Indian Statesmen*, London, 1897, pp. 287-307; *Dictionary of National Biography*, Vol. XXII, Supplement, London, 1964-5, pp. 25-6 (Arthur Jacob Ashton).

Ajit Singh (d. 1947)

Born at Khatkar Kalan, a village in Jullundur district (Panjab), Ajit Singh came of a Jat Sikh family and was an uncle of Bhagat Singh, the well-known revolutionary. He received his education at the Sain Dass Anglo-Sanskrit High School in Jullundur and, later, at D. A. V. College, Lahore. Subsequently, ill-health prevented his completing a law course at Bareilly.

Panjab's decision to raise the rates of revenue assessment and irrigation and the adoption of the Canal Colonies Act depriving land grantees of some of the rights they had initially enjoyed brought Ajit Singh into active politics. He joined hands with Lala Lajpat Rai and other leaders mainly from the urban areas, in a popular agitation against these laws.

Bal Gangadhar Tilak's (q.v.) famous declaration, 'Swaraj is my birthright and I shall have it', appears to have had a profound impact on Ajit Singh. He is also said to have come in contact with the extremists of Calcutta while some revolutionaries in Bengal are said to have visited him. His subsequent political education was rounded off by association with such well-known Panjab revolutionaries as Lala Pindi Das, Lal Chand Falak and Sufi Amba Prasad.

At a public meeting at Rawalpindi on 21 April 1907 Ajit Singh launched a violent attack on the enhanced land assessment referred to above, and exhorted cultivators to stop tilling until the rate was reduced. So powerful was his appeal that the angry mob began setting fire to government property, and, as a result, he along with Lajpat Rai was arrested and deported to Mandalay in Burma.

After his return, Ajit Singh started a paper, the *Peshwa*, in collaboration with Sufi Amba Prasad and later, after it was banned, published it under different names—*Bharat Mata* and *Sahsik*. Among the booklets he published mention may be made of *Baghi Museah*, *Mahabban-i-Watan*, *Bandar Bant*, *Ungli-Pakarte Punja Pakara* and *Ghadar 1857*. He also founded the revolutionary Bharat Mata Society and, in association with Syed Hyder Riza, the Indian Patriots' Association. His speeches and writings in 1908 persuaded the government to order his arrest but before this could occur, Ajit Singh escaped to Persia where he started a paper (in Persian) to advocate the cause of Indian independence.

Ajit Singh travelled on to Rome and, for a short spell, was lecturer in a college there. Later he went to Geneva and thence to Paris. During World War I he moved to Rio de Janeiro but kept in touch with the Ghadr Party (q.v.) in San Francisco. Understandably he rejected the policy of political mendicancy then advocated by the Indian National Congress (q.v.) and favoured a militant revolutionary movement to achieve independence.

Ajit Singh met Subhas Chandra Bose (q.v.) on his return to Europe in the course of World War II. On 15 August 1947, soon after his return home, he died.

S. P. Sen (ed.), *Dictionary of Nationalist Biography*, 4 Vols., Calcutta, 1972-4, I, pp. 32-3 (Fauja Singh); Fauja Singh, *Eminent Freedom Fighters of Panjab*, Patiala, 1972, pp. 61-4; *Who's Who: Panjab Freedom Fighters*, Patiala, 1972, pp. lv-lvi, introduction.

Akbar Shah II (d. 1837)

Akbar Shah II succeeded his father, Shah Alam II (q.v.), in 1806. He was young, energetic and ambitious, anxious to restore some of the old glory and authority of the Mughal empire. The East India Company (q.v.) was by then firmly entrenched and had given shape and form to its vast dominion. The emperor tried to live up to his imperial pretensions by appointing Mirza Jahangir, a favourite son of his, as heir-apparent. The British resident who supported the cause of his eldest son Alam Zafar successfully out-manoeuvred him, forcing the emperor to announce officially in January 1810 the appointment of the British nominee.

Mughal authority was by then considered a mere fiction. Thus Lord Hastings (q.v.), while touring the north refused to call on the emperor or present the traditional *nazr;* instead, he sent him a gaudy present through Metcalfe (q.v.). It was the emperor, however, who had sought an interview with the Governor-General which the latter declined—unless all ceremonial implying Mughal supremacy over the Company's dominions was waived.

During the tenures of Bentinck (q.v.) and Auckland (q.v.) the fiction was finally extinguished; in 1835, the coinage which had since 1778 been issued in the regnal year of the emperor, was replaced by the Company's rupee bearing the English monarch's image and superscription.

The question of the imperial stipend remained a perennial source of dispute. Any augmentation promised (as in 1809) was countermanded before it could be effected, and the emperor's helplessness in forcing issues was now more apparent than ever before. Akbar Shah finally decided to approach the British sovereign direct, entrusting Raja Rammohun Roy (q.v.), then proceeding to England for the renewal of the Charter Act of 1833 (q.v.), to represent his case. The Raja forcefully pleaded that the emperor deserved better than the sum agreed to by the Court of Directors, and demanded an increase of Rs 3 lakhs, to bring the total to Rs 15 lakhs. The Raja's own death in 1833, however, left matters unsettled, the enhanced payment was deferred and, in fact, never made, for Akbar Shah died four years later (June 1837), a poor and disillusioned man.

The emperor is said to have been a competent poet and was succeeded by his son Bahadur Shah II (q.v.), the last Mughal ruler of Delhi, also remembered as a poet of distinction.

Beale, pp. 46-7; *The Cambridge History of India*, reprint, New Delhi, n.d., 6 vols, H. H. Dodwell (ed.), V, pp. 605-6; T. G. P. Spear, *Twilight of the Mughals*, Cambridge, 1951, pp. 39–42, 45–9.

Alamgir II (1699–1759)

Aziz-ud-din, son of Jahandar Shah, was crowned Mughal emperor on 2 June 1754 and took the title Alamgir II. This followed the deposition and imprisonment of Ahmad Shah, son of emperor Muhammad Shah by the Wazir, Imad-ul-mulk Ghazi-ud-din Khan in collaboration with the Marathas.

A quiet, religious and scholarly man, with no taste for, nor experience of, administrative work, Alamgir was a mere figurehead. **Real power was** wielded by his wazir, the wily, selfish and unscrupulous Imad-ul-mulk. His brief (1754-9) yet eventful reign witnessed the near disappearance of the Mughal emperor's authority. The Marathas, encouraged by court intrigue and a ruthless struggle for power, spread their control northwards and captured Lahore (1758). Meanwhile Ahmad Shah Abdali (q.v.) led two devastating invasions that wreaked havoc on Delhi in 1757 and 1759. The Emperor, who is widely believed to have invited the invader, was treacherously assassinated by his wazir on 29 November 1759. While the Afghans thus eliminated the immediate Maratha threat, Alamgir's son, Ali Gauhar, later Shah Alam II (q.v.), who was then in Bengal, made important concessions to the British in the grant of the Diwani Rights (q.v.).

According to Spear, Alamgir affected the culture and austerity of the great Mughal emperor Aurangzeb (1658-1707) without possessing either his vigour or shrewdness.

Beale, p. 49; T. G. P. Spear, *Twilight of the Mughals*, Cambridge, 1951, pp. 14, 16.

Aligarh Movement

The genesis of the Aligarh movement may be traced to the combined efforts of Sir Syed Ahmad Khan (q.v.) and his junior partners, and the foundation of the Muslim Anglo-Oriental College in Aligarh.

Essentially, it was a 'cultural movement' with the objective of 'regeneration of liberal values in literature, social life, education and religion'. Aiming at the modernization of the Muslim community, then allegedly trapped in the vice of medieval obscurantism, it appealed mainly to the well-to-do classes through whom, it was hoped, it would filter down to the masses. Its main objectives were the popularization of education and rationalization of religious tenets.

In pursuance of its educational programme, Indian Scientific Society was formed in 1863, the MAO College established in 1875 and the All-India Muhammadan Educational Conference in 1886. Stress was laid on the learning of western science and literature, besides the traditional study of Islam. The Urdu language received encouragement.

Some members who adhered to the movement questioned Islam's age-old dogma and refused to conform to orthodox custom. This brought upon them the wrath of the Ulama and less educated masses. The movement however soon gathered momentum and gained adherents as more and more Muslims were educated.

The movement eschewed active politics to ensure continued British support for its programmes. It assiduously supported all government legislation with a view to stamping out the stigma of disloyalty with which the entire

Muslim community had been branded since the Rebellion of 1857 (q.v.). Additionally, the aim was to obtain for the Muslims an equal share of representation in the future administration of the country: Muslims were to avoid all participation in agitations sponsored by the Indian National Congress (q.v.).

The objective was not merely to bring about the modernization of Indian Muslims but also to make them play a dominant role in the religious, political, economic and cultural life of the country. With this end, it was deemed essential to introduce them to the western system of education and civilization, besides imparting to them some knowledge of Islamic theology, history and culture. In sum, western education and British patronage were the principal means for the attainment of these objectives.

Broadly, the movement aimed at Muslim regeneration. Sir Syed's advocacy of Hindu-Muslim unity, it has been suggested, was 'a myth continued for generations by interested parties'; his was a 'separatist' movement that led, in course of time, to the demand for partition and the creation of Pakistan. It claimed for the Muslims of India a separate status—viz., separate from the Hindus. It emphasized the historical superiority of the Muslims in India and resolved on a different line of action for them. Muslims were not to be equated with Hindus, much less dominated by them; special safeguards were advocated for the protection of their rights and interests. Even as the All-India Muslim League (q.v.) was the outcome of the Aligarh movement, so were many leaders of the League and of the community. They employed every conceivable device—separate electorates, special weightage and reservation of seats—to safeguard Muslim interests.

Nor did the movement influence Muslim activities in northern India alone; it established its sway over Hyderabad too. Thus both Mohsin-ul-Mulk (q.v.) as well as Viqar-ul-Mulk (q.v.), who passed the best part of their lives in Hyderabad, succeeded in establishing Urdu as the medium of instruction in the state as well as founding the Hyderabad College. It is true that the latter did not attract many students from northern India, but Aligarh's pre-eminent role and leadership came to be accepted and a certain liaison established between Aligarh, Hyderabad, Lahore, Karachi and Dacca.

A Muslim historian has maintained that the Aligarh movement was aimed at the uplift of the Muslims on the religious, moral and educational planes and that at the inauguration of the Muhammadan Educational Conference, in December 1886, Sir Syed strongly deprecated political discussion for the Muslims of the day. Politics, it has been suggested, was no part of the movement nor would Sir Syed allow Hindu-Muslim rancour to enter the four walls of the institution he had nurtured. His *Atharu's-Sanadid* (first ed. 1887) lent a strong leverage to true historical research and a probe into the activities of the past. With the death of Sir Syed in March 1898 and the appointment of Nawab Mohsin-ul-Mulk as Secretary of the MAO College, the movement entered what has been called 'the penumbra stage', while the Nawab's death (1907) brought about 'the umbra stage of its eclipse'. Its other end may be said to be the final resignation of Nawab Viqar-ul-Mulk as Secretary of the MAO College in July 1912. Between these two stalwarts, the lamp of the movement had been kept burning for 15 years, the one nurturing it by his great qualities of head and heart, the other by his strong, unbending character. With their passing away the last flicker of the movement seems to have died out. This, in turn, gave birth to new movements which bore only a distant resemblance to the original one.

In terms of its ideal of a self-governing all-India institution, it is suggested that the movement had come to a close in 1920 with the assent of the Governor-General to the Aligarh Muslim University Bill.

A recent compiler of 'basic documents' relating to the movement has characterized it 'as a reform movement resembling in some respects and with its own limited means, the Reformation in Europe having as its prelude the echoes of a new culture, new learning and new approach to life. Sir Syed impressed upon the Muslims that in the struggle for existence only the fittest could survive. This movement was intended to make them the fittest.'

A perceptive critic has suggested that the success of the Congress aroused among leaders of the Aligarh movement a desire to form a purely Muslim political body to represent their point of view to the government. This was encouraged by the principals of the MAO College, especially Colone Theodore Beck, who may be said to have originated the so-called two-nation theory. The move was welcome to a beleaguered government as a counter-poise to nationalist agitation. To give it shape and form, a Muhammadan Anglo-Oriental Defence Organization of Upper India was set up, to be followed a few years later by the foundation of the Muslim League.

Apart from education, in literature the Aligarh movement stood for 'simplicity of diction, purity of ideas and imitation of nature'; in social life, for 'honesty in daily intercourse, communal sympathy and the cultivation of unaffected habits'; in religion, for 'a shift towards reason' and 'anti-fanaticism'.

Among the stalwarts of the movement, mention may be made of Altaf Hussain Hali, the poet; Shibli Nomani, the theologian and Nazir Ahmad, the politician. Syed Ameer Ali (q.v.), though 'not of the movement', shared its ideals and, in his own way, 'furthered them'. In retrospect, knowledge-able Muslim authorities view it as a social movement that preached the gospel of the 'good life' in the Aristotelian sense. Its role in the cultural regeneration of Muslim India would be hard to exaggerate; for a strong cultural base was to serve as a necessary prerequisite for an enduring political fabric. It produced public men who played important roles in politics and, in education, inculcated some discipline in the mass of men.

A great deal of credit for the regeneration of the Muslim community goes to the movement. But in so far as it cared for and promoted only Muslim interests it was no doubt responsible for inducting the aims of communal separation in the body-politic.

M. S. Jain, *The Aligarh Movement, its origin and development, 1858-1906*, Agra, 1965; H. K. Sherwani, *The Aligarh Movement, Sir Syed Memorial Lectures 1969*, Aligarh, 1969; K. K. Aziz, *The Making of Pakistan*, London, 1967, pp. 18-22, 124-5; Shan Muhammad (ed.), *The Aligarh Movement: Basic Documents 1869-1898*, 3 vols, Meerut, 1978; David Lelyveld, *Aligarh's First Generation*, Princeton, 1977.

Treaty of Alinagar (1757)

Calcutta (q.v.) was re-named Alinagar after its capture by Siraj-ud-Daula (q.v.) on 1 June 1756. On 5 February 1757 the Nawab's men encamped just outside the town where they are said to have been worsted by a small English force in a night attack mounted by Robert Clive (q.v.). This impelled the Nawab to come to an understanding and establish peace with the English four days later. Dodwell refers to it as the 'Treaty of February 1757'.

Called a 'Treaty and Agreement' with the Nawab, it comprised (i) a 7-article 'list of demands' made by the John Company (q.v.) which bears no date; (ii) an 'agreement' signed by the Governor and Committee on 9 February 1757, affirming, on 'solemn attestation', to return to the *status quo ante;* (iii) a number of 'Perwannahs and dustucks' issued by the Nawab bearing the dates 9 and 31 March (1757) giving effect to the terms agreed to; and (iv) an 'agreement of Colonel Clive with the Nawab' that 'as long, as he [the Nawab] shall observe his agreement, the English will always look upon his enemies as their enemies' and grant him all assistance in their power. The last was dated 12 February (1757).

In sum, all the trade privileges held earlier by the Company stood confirmed, and these could not be called into question. English trade was to be exempt from all taxes or imposts. Additionally, the Company was authorized to fortify Calcutta against possible French attack and to strike its own coins. While the Nawab agreed to make good all losses the Company had incurred and abide by other articles of the treaty, the English promised him their friendship and goodwill.

C. U. Aitchison (comp.), *A Collection of Treaties,Engagements and Sunnuds Relating to India and the Neighbouring Countries*, 5th ed., Calcutta, 1929–31, 14 vols, II, pp. 197–200; Dodwell, *CHI*, V, p. 245; S. C. Hill, *Three Frenchmen in Bengal*, London 1903, pp. 27–8.

Treaty of Allahabad (1765)

In 1764 Mir Kasim (q.v.), who had been deposed in favour of Mir Jafar (q.v.), made a last desperate bid to oust the British from Bengal. The Mughal emperor Shah Alam II (q.v.) and Nawab Shuja-ud-Daula (q.v.) of Oudh (q.v.) espoused his cause. The confederate forces were however decisively defeated at Buxar (q.v.) and, while retreating, were pursued vigorously until they surrendered.

Subsequently, an 11-clause tripartite treaty was concluded at Allahabad on 16 August 1765 by Robert Clive (q.v.) on behalf of the John Company (q.v.), Najm-ud-Daula, Mir Jafar's son and successor (and the then titular ruler of Bengal) and Shuja-ud-Daula. According to its terms, Oudh was to be restored to the Nawab with the exception of the two districts of Allahabad and Karra, which were given to Shah Alam . The restoration of the state was to be effected by English forces 'being withdrawn from the dominions of His Highness' as soon as 'this treaty is executed' (Art. 10). A pledge of mutual assistance between the parties in the event of an attack by another power was made, it being stipulated that, if the Company's troops were employed 'in His Highness's service', he was to defray their expense. The Nawab agreed to a payment of Rs 50 lakhs as war indemnity, partly in cash and jewels immediately, the rest in monthly instalments spread over a period of 13 months (Art. 6). Raja Balwant Singh was to continue to hold Banaras, Ghazipur and other districts. Shuja was to maintain, at his expense, an English garrison; it was to be stationed in his territory so as to defend his frontier and protect his interests. He was also to grant trading privileges to the Company throughout his dominion and pledge that no other Europeans would henceforth be employed by him.

Four days before the conclusion of the treaty, the Mughal Emperor Shah Alam had conferred upon the Company the Diwani Rights (q.v.) of the provinces of Bengal, Bihar and Orissa. In return, he was to receive from the revenues of Bengal an annual grant of Rs 26 lakhs but revert his royal jagir to the Company.

The treaty and the settlement that preceded it have been assailed as a breach of faith by the Company with the emperor in so far as it took away what had been promised to him (the province of Oudh). Additionally, it has been suggested, it bestowed territory (Allahabad and Karra) on one who was not able to hold it on his own. In extenuation, it may however be pointed out that the aim here was to make some provision for a helpless ruler who had none. Again, the restoration of Oudh to Shuja meant placating an ally who was at the time too grateful to attack and later too severely handicapped to think of doing so.

Clive's apologists contend that the settlement was a middle course, which afforded more advantages and posed fewer dangers than any other course of action. On the basis of the grant of Karra and Allahabad to the emperor the English were able to demand from him the Diwani of Bengal, Bihar and Orissa alluded to above.

With the conclusion of this treaty, Oudh became a friendly buffer state that would protect English possessions in Bengal from any threat that a Maratha advance towards the north might pose.

Dodwell, *CHI*, V, pp. 176, 273–4; *Aitchison*, I, pp. 60–5; II, pp. 76–9.

Jean Francois Allard (1785–1839)

Born in 1785 at St Tropez on the Mediterranean littoral in France, Allard served in the French cavalry until 1814. Thereafter he travelled to Persia and came to Lahore (1822) where he found service under Ranjit Singh (q.v.). Initially placed in charge of training two cavalry regiments, he was promoted after his men acquitted themselves creditably in the battle of Naushera (1824). In 1826 he saw action at Peshawar, and was actively associated with the Lahore Darbar's later expeditions to the frontier.

His cavalry enjoyed a cycle of favour, for the new cuirasses so pleased the Maharaja that he ordered that the two regiments be equipped with them. These were made at Wazirabad and were of creditable workmanship.

Unlike Ranjit Singh's other commanders, Allard had a literary flair. On leave in Europe for a year and a half, he returned in 1834 as envoy of King Louis Philippe to the court of Lahore. The British protested violently and Allard was forced to disavow the intention.

Allard was a favourite of Ranjit Singh's and is said to have had considerable hold on the Maharaja. He lost a great deal of money when the notorious William Palmer & Co (q.v.) was declared bankrupt. Allard died in Peshawar in January 1839 and was buried at Lahore.

Amanullah, King of Afghanistan (1890–1939)

Amanullah's accession is credited to his 'personal popularity, the rallying of the Barakzais and the support of the Army'. Maintaining that his legitimacy and mandate to rule emanated from the 'Afghan nation', he addressed his first proclamation to his people and the army, deliberately omitting any mention of the religious establishment. He was crowned ruler on 1 March 1919. In charge of the state treasury and the garrison stationed in Kabul at the time of his father Amir Habibullah's (q.v.) death, Amanullah was in a strong position to assert his claim. With a view to winning popular support, he had emphasized the independence of his country and his intent of introducing reform and modernization.

To buttress his strength, he declared war on the British and so timed his action as to synchronize with an expected mutinous outbreak in India. His intelligence however turned out to be faulty, with the result that the attempted invasion, leading to the Third Anglo-Afghan War (q.v.) proved a military fiasco. None the less, by the Treaty of Rawalpindi signed in August 1919 (and later elaborated in an agreement of November 1921), Amanullah was able to free Afghanistan completely from any extraneous constraints on the conduct of its foreign policy.

Fortified by the prestige accruing to him as a liberator, he lost no time in entering into diplomatic relations with other countries. A flurry of missions followed, resulting (1921-2) in treaties of friendship with Russia, France, Germany and Italy. The king, as he now styled himself, lent active countenance to pan-Islamism in Turkey and Iran as well as the Khilafat Movement (q.v.) in India. It was only after the Afghan-aided Amir of Bukhara was badly worsted by Soviet troops that Amanullah finally gave his assent to the sharply debated agreement with the British briefly alluded to above.

In foreign policy, Amanullah followed three distinct paths—establishing diplomatic relations with Soviet Russia, gradually normalizing relations with Britain, striving for solidarity within the Muslim world. In this way, he was able to re-establish the balance of power that had been destroyed by the provisions of the Anglo-Russian convention of 1907. More important, his new freedom of action allowed him to check the ambitions of Soviet Russia and the British by playing off one against the other.

The treaty with Russia, signed on 13 September 1920 at Kabul, placed Afghanistan in a much stronger bargaining position vis-a-vis Great Britain. Amanullah's establishment of diplomatic relations with Turkey and Russia which followed were particularly important in this context. His support to the pan-Islamic cause was equally pronounced. Later, he took credit for securing Russia's commitment to the independence of Bukhara and Khiva, and lent support to the Khilafat cause.

Amanullah's pan-Islamic stance was to be drastically modified after 1922. Economic and political constraints at home demanded that he seek normalization of relations with Great Britain and abandon the policy of active intervention in Soviet Central Asia. It was obvious that his limited financial resources and the country's land-locked position precluded such expensive indulgences.

The British viewed him as a Soviet 'Trojan horse'. In the result, they insisted that all Russian arms sent to Afghanistan for eventual use in a

national liberation movement in India be transported out and Indian revolutionaries entering Afghanistan disarmed.

Once his treaty with Britain had been concluded—an important feature
being Afghanistan's agreement to keep Soviet consulates out of eastern
Afghanistan—Amanullah concentrated on domestic reform, even though
he continued to lend moral support to various pan-Islamic activities. Anti-
British revolutionaries like Raja Mahendra Pratap, Obaid-ullah Sindhi and
Mohammad Barkatullah—President, Prime Minister and Foreign Minister
respectively of the 'Provisional Government of India'—no longer found
refuge in Afghanistan.

Amanullah's reign heralded a period of modernization at a rapid pace, a
contingency for which his people were singularly unprepared. His ultimate
goal was the transformation of Afghanistan into a modern state. In particular, he attached great importance to reform in education, which was made
free. At the same time he encouraged the import of printing machinery and
assisted in the establishment of an Afghan press.

Existing roads were repaired and plans made for new highways to link the
capital with Afghan Turkestan, Peshawar and Kandahar. He expanded the
telephone system and introduced the telegraph. Hotels too were set up on
the European model, but remained largely in a primitive state of maintenance and service. Airplanes were bought, pilots trained and the army
equipped with sophisticated weapons drilled on Turkish and German lines.

Important military, economic, administrative and legal reforms were
introduced, mostly of a progressive nature, even though many Afghans
found them to be obnoxious. This was particularly true of the orthodox
Mullahs who pronounced them incompatible with Quranic injunctions.
Especially galling to them were measures concerning the position of women.
Amanullah's methods were 'often exceedingly tactless', and were also
ill-considered and hasty. Moreover, only a small élitist group spearheaded
by Mahmud Beg Tarzi, a close confidant, was committed to the ideal of a
modern Afghanistan and to the ruler's ambitious, if nebulous, programme
for realizing that ideal.

Amanullah inducted a constitutional monarchy of sorts while upholding
the principles of hereditary rule. The first Afghan constitution was promulgated in 1923. Two consultative bodies were established—with only a few
members being popularly elected. Cabinet members were to be chosen by
the King and were responsible only to him. A penal code was also promulgated between 1924-5. Having thus established what he believed to be firm
foundations for his rule, the king embarked on a foreign tour (1927-8)
touching, among other areas, India, Europe, Turkey and Iran. Impressed by
the progress he witnessed in these lands, he announced on his return a
further acceleration of the programme of domestic reform.

The King's penchant for modernization and the rapidity with which he went
ahead with it was soon matched by the ferocity of reaction that set in. 1924-5
was to witness a widespread rebellion by the Mullahs and the Mangal
Pushtun tribesmen of Khost against the liberalization of laws relating to
women. Anti-government demonstrations in Kabul (1928) had hardly been
subdued when the Shinwari tribe broke out in open rebellion and was soon
joined by others. Habibullah, an illiterate Tajik from Kohistan and a notorious highwayman known to posterity as 'Bacha-i-Saqao' (literally, 'son of a

water-carrier'), took advantage of these insurrections to threaten Kabul from the north. With the second attack on the capital, Amanullah sought safety and escaped to Kandahar. The Bacha now took over the administration and was to rule the country for nine brutal months. In the meanwhile, the deposed Amanullah made a feeble and unsuccessful attempt to regain Kabul. Later, he fled to Italy. Reluctantly given asylum by King Victor Emmanuel III, he died (1939) in exile.

Amanullah's real contribution lay in asserting the independence of his country, establishing diplomatic relations with many European nations and opening the doors of his kingdom to outsiders. He established schools on modern lines, encouraged the study of foreign languages and sent many Afghans abroad for advanced study, brought about improvement in communications and even initiated archaeological explorations.

Leon B. Poullada, *Reform and Rebellion in Afghanistan, 1919-29: King Amanullah's Failure to Modernise a Tribal Society*, Cornell, 1973; Vartan Gregorian, *The Emergence of Modern Afghanistan*, Stanford, 1969, pp. 227-74; Ludwig W. Adamec, *Afghanistan's Foreign Affairs to the Mid-twentieth Century*, Tucson, Arizona, 1974, pp. 42-8; Hasan Kakar. 'Trends in Modern Afghan History' , in Louis Dupree and Linette Edward (ed.), *Afghanistan in the 1970s*, New York, 1974.

Bhimarao Ramji Ambedkar (1891–1956)

Bhimarao Ramji was born on 14 April 1891 of Mahar, Hindu untouchable, parents at Mhow in Madhya Pradesh. His father was a subedar in the army and a Kabirpanthi hailing from a village, Ambad, in Ratnagiri district of the then Bombay presidency. It was a large family, Bhimarao being the fourteenth child. Educated at Satara and later Bombay, he took his surname 'Ambavadekar' from his native village; a Brahmin teacher at the high school in Satara who was fond of his young pupil changed the name to Ambedkar in the school records—and it stuck.

In 1913, awarded a Baroda state scholarship, Ambedkar proceeded to the United States and joined Columbia University in New York, where two years later he took his M.A. in Economics with a dissertation on 'Ancient Indian Commerce'. In 1926, he obtained a doctorate from the same university. While at Columbia, John Dewey, the philosopher, was among his teachers and helped reinforce the young man's commitment to social reform.

In 1916, Ambedkar moved to the London School of Economics and prepared for the Bar. A year later, however, he had to discontinue his studies owing to financial exigencies. He briefly taught at Bombay's Sydenham College of Commerce as Lecturer in Political Economy, but in 1921 resumed his studies in London and obtained an M.Sc. (1921) and D.Sc. (1923). His D.Sc. thesis, later published, was entitled 'The Problem of the Rupee'.

All through the years, the indignities, humiliations and hardships to which he was subjected because of his low-caste origins had stirred in his proud, intelligent and sensitive mind a bitter resentment against the rigidities of the social system. They lingered with him to the very end.

On returning home in June 1924 Ambedkar started legal practice at the Bombay High Court. This was the beginning of an active public career as social worker, politician, writer, educationist. The same year he founded the Depressed Classes Institute ('Bahishkrit Hitkarnini Sabha') in Bombay for the moral and material progress of untouchables. Three years later, he started a Marathi fortnightly, *Bahishkrit Bharat*, and in November 1930, a weekly, the *Janata*.

Another organization that Ambedkar established in 1927 was the Samaj Samata Sangh, its objective being to propagate the gospel of social equality among untouchables and caste Hindus. Inter-caste marriages and inter-caste meals were an integral part of the programme. The Sangh's organ, the *Samata*, was started in March 1929.

In December 1927 Ambedkar led a satyagraha to establish the right of untouchables to draw water from a public tank at Malad, in Kolaba district; three years later he led another satyagraha to establish his community's right to enter the famous temple of Kalaram at Nasik. This satyagraha was not withdrawn until March 1930.

Soon, Ambedkar's eminence as a jurist began to be widely recognized. In 1928 he was appointed Professor at Government Law College, Bombay; seven years later, he was offered the coveted Perry professorship of Jurisprudence. In the meantime he was emerging as a leader of the Depressed Classes, in which capacity he continued to be a nominated member (1926-34) of the Bombay Legislative Council. This vantage position enabled him to sponsor several bills for the welfare of his community, of which he now emerged as the principal spokesman. He was an official nominee to the Round Table Conference (q.v.) and continued to serve on some of its committees down to 1934. His appointment, it has been said, 'marked a milestone' in the socio-political struggle of his community which had never hitherto been consulted in the governance of the country.

While his powerful solicitude for his people was shared by many, Ambedkar's more militant stance, that they be organized politically and treated as distinct from the Hindus, had fewer supporters. This led to a long drawn-out conflict with Gandhi (q.v.), punctuated by threats of fast unto death on the one hand and uneasy compromises on the other.

The British government's 'Communal Award' (q.v.) had conceded separate electorates to a number of communities, including the untouchables. Understandably, Gandhi's reaction was one of bitter opposition; he proceeded on a fast unto death in the Yarvada jail (20 September 1932). Four days later, leaders of the untouchables, including Ambedkar, agreed *inter alia* to an accord called the Poona Pact which provided for reservation of seats for the community in the general (Hindu) constituencies.

The compromise was something to which Ambedkar had agreed with great mental reservations; he was bitter and voiced his strong personal resentment against it. From then on, it would seem, his attitude to the Indian National Congress (q.v.) in general and caste Hindus in particular 'grew increasingly bitter and demanding.' With an uncanny political acumen, he set up an Independent Labour Party in October 1936 which captured all the Scheduled Caste seats in Bombay presidency in the 1936-7 general elections. Later, in April 1942, he organized the All-India Scheduled Castes Federation as a political party. To promote the interests of his community he established the Peoples Education Society in July 1945; it was instrumental in starting a number of colleges for scheduled caste students in Bombay presidency.

On the declaration of World War II, Ambedkar stoutly repudiated the claim made by the Congress of representing the Depressed Classes and, politically, drew closer to Jinnah (q.v.) and his All-India Muslim League (q.v.), in decrying what he called caste Hindu chauvinism. His *Thoughts on Pakistan,* published in 1940, although critical of some aspects of Jinnah's leadership, was not overly hostile to the concept *per se.*

From July 1942 to March 1946 Ambedkar served on the Governor-General's Executive Council as Member for Labour. Later, the Congress nominated him to the Constituent Assembly (q.v.) in whose deliberations he was to play a prominent role. His thorough knowledge and understanding of constitutional law marked him out as one of the chief architects of independent India's republican constitution.

While Law Minister in Jawaharlal Nehru's Cabinet, Ambedkar was also chairman of the Constituent Assembly's drafting committee and presented before it the draft constitution on 4 November 1948. Later, he was to pilot it successfully through the cut and thrust of debate in the House. He also made a signal contribution towards the drafting of the Hindu Code Bill, which made him known as 'a modern Manu' (after the celebrated Hindu law giver). Ambedkar resigned from the Cabinet in September, 1951. Later, in 1952 and 1953, he lost two successive elections to Parliament.

In October 1935 Ambedkar announced for the first time that his followers would leave the Hindu faith altogether for, within it, they would never win social equality. During 1938-40 he briefly turned to Sikhism, but his efforts to gain a special place for his community within the Sikh fold proved unsuccessful. On 14 October 1956 Ambedkar embraced Buddhism and at a well-attended ceremony at Nagpur advised his followers to accept the new faith; himself giving *Deeksha* to hundreds of thousands. In retrospect, however, the exercise was to prove futile, for it did not alter existing realities; furthermore, before long, many reverted to their earlier, older faith. In November 1956, he attended the fourth conference of the World Fellowship of Buddhists at Kathmandu. This was his last public appearance.

A prolific writer, some of Ambedkar's works are: *Castes in India: their mechanism, genesis and development,* 1916; *Pakistan or Partition of India,* 1946 (originally, *Thoughts on Pakistan,* 1940) and *Thoughts on Linguistic States,* 1955.

Dhananjay Keer, *Dr Ambedkar: Life and Mission,* 3rd ed., Bombay, 1971; Chandra Bharill, *Social & Political Ideas of B. R. Ambedkar,* Jaipur, 1977; D. R. Jatava, *The Political Philosophy of B. R. Ambedkar,* Agra, 1965; Sen, *DNB,* I, pp. 46-99 (C.B. Khairmoday); *DNB 1950-60,* pp. 15-16 (Frank Moraes).

Syed Ameer Ali (1849–1928)

The son of Syed Saadut Ali of Mohan in the Unnao district of Oudh (q.v.), Ameer Ali was born at Cuttack in Orissa. His family claimed descent from the Prophet through the eighth Imam, Ali Raza; they were Shias who came to India with Nadir Shah (q.v.). His forbears were prominent in the service of the Nawab of Oudh till shortly before that state's annexation.

Ameer Ali was educated at Hooghly College, Chinsura, and later graduated in arts and law from Calcutta University. He is said to have been the first Muslim in India to take the M.A. degree. Later he won a government scholarship to England, where he was one of the first Indians to be called to the bar in 1873. On returning home, he set up practice in Calcutta (q.v.). In 1876 he founded the Central National Mohammedan Association of which he was secretary for a quarter century; for about the same time he was the president of the Hooghly Imambara Committee.

Professionally Ameer Ali rose high. In 1878 he was Presidency magistrate; a year later, Chief Presidency magistrate. In 1897, he was a member of the commission set up to inquire into the affairs of the ex-king of Oudh. He was a member of the Bengal Legislative Council during 1878-83; in 1883 one of the three additional Indian legislative members of the Governor-General's Council. During 1890-1904 he was a judge of the Calcutta High Court; in the latter year, he retired to England, but continued to remain active in Indian affairs.

At each stage in the formulation of constitutional reforms between 1907 and 1909, Ameer Ali and his London branch of the All-India Muslim League (q.v.) played an important part. They fought hard, and successfully, to ensure that the price paid for their support for the proposals was high.

As a pamphleteer, a speaker and an organizer, Ameer Ali was continually before the public in defence of his co-religionists. For modern developments of nationalism, whether in Turkey or India, he had little sympathy: Islam and the British empire, both transcending merely racial or geographical barriers, were the objects of his loyalty. Although a Shia, he protested against the abolition of the Khilafat (q.v.) and, along with the Aga Khan (q.v.), wrote (1923) to the Turkish National Assembly against its suppression. That year the two had led a deputation to Turkey too in its support. They were coldly received by the leaders of the Turkish revolution—Ismet Inonu and Kemal Ataturk—who pointed out that a Shia and a Khoja had no *locus standi* to advise Sunni Turkish Muslims. More, not only were they heretics but also 'pillars of British rule in India'.

Glorification of the Islamic past by Ameer Ali, and Shibli Nomani (1857-1914), strengthened separatist ideas among the educated Muslims. Proud of his Persian descent, Ameer Ali told the Hunter Committee on Education (q.v.) that Urdu should be to the Muslims of Bengal what Bengali was to the Hindus. He regarded Indian nationalism as a mere cloak for Hindu domination. As a corollary, he was a staunch advocate of community representation and separate treatment for Indian Muslims.

The regeneration of Muslims was the cry of the day and in January 1910, at the third annual session of the AIML, it formed the main theme of Ameer Ali's presidential address. He warned an unprecedented number of 300 delegates—and 4,000 visitors—in Delhi that 'a steady process of disintegration and demoralization, partly induced by circumstances and forces beyond our control, has been going on in our midst'. He urged the community to consider 'how best to prevent the impoverishment of Mussalmans and the passing of Mussalman estates in other hands'. In presenting his programme of economic regeneration, Ameer Ali asked them 'to foster industries, encourage trade and commerce and make more practical use of academic learning'.

He wrote extensively not only on law but also on Muslim history and institutions and was the author of a number of books on historical, religious and legal subjects of which the following bear mention: *Mohammedan Law* (2 vols), which has been published in several editions; *Critical Examination of the Life and Teachings of Mohammad*; *Spirit of Islam*; *Ethics of Islam*; *A Short History of the Saracens*.

Among Ameer Ali's other interests were the reform of Muslim family law in India and the foundation of a mosque in London. In the latter capacity, he was Chairman of the Woking Mosque Committee. In 1908, he founded the London branch of the All-India Muslim League, of which he remained president for many years.

Francis Robinson, *Separatism among Indian Muslims*, Delhi, 1975; V. V. Nagarkar, *Genesis of Pakistan*, Bombay, 1975; *Islamic Culture*, vols IV & V, 1931, 1932; *DNB 1922-30*, pp. 18-19 (S. V. FitzGerald).

Amherst (1773–1857)

Before his arrival in India, William Pitt (later Earl Amherst) had served in a diplomatic capacity in Naples (1809–11) and later (1816–17) as head of an abortive commercial mission to China. On his return from the latter assignment, he was appointed Governor-General of India in the hope that his would be a period of peace and consolidation following the expansionist policy pursued earlier by the Marquess of Hastings (q.v.). But Amherst proved as uncompromising an imperialist as his predecessor and was responsible for bringing a foreign land, Burma, under British sovereignty in India. He also put into practice the unwritten right of the paramount power to interfere, whenever necessary, in the affairs of India States (q.v.).

The First Anglo-Burmese War (q.v.) occupied most of his time. The Burmese 'threat' to the Indian empire had begun to loom large after their occupation of Arakan, Manipur and Assam. Amherst's predecessors, preoccupied with other problems, had largely ignored this one; efforts to settle the dispute through diplomatic channels had borne no fruit either. While the Burmese took Calcutta's inaction to imply that it was weak, Amherst was guided by a Council that was not always well-informed. Disputes arose about the possession of the island of Shahpuri near Chittagong (now in Bangladesh) and Cachar (Assam). It has been held that the immediate cause of the war was the declaration that Assam was a British protectorate.

The John Company (q.v.) soon realized the true extent of the Burmese 'threat' and their 'preparations' to attack Bengal simultaneously from the Brahmaputra valley, Cachar and Arakan. More important, it was not unmindful either of the commercial advantages which would accrue, should it control the Burmese coastal regions. When the Company declared war in February 1824, Amherst hoped to secure the Bengal frontier and establish control over Burma's coastal areas. Accordingly, operations were launched both in Assam as well as Lower Burma. Though the plan was excellent on paper, unfamiliarity with the terrain and local climate led to a prolongation of hostilities. Dogged by a faulty system of supplies and an outbreak of tropical diseases, the campaign proved to be well-nigh disastrous. By 1826, however, the Burmese were defeated and a peace treaty signed at Yandaboo (q.v.). Initially, the home government had to resist the Court of Directors' plea to recall Amherst for having allegedly mismanaged the campaign; in the end, he was rewarded with an earldom!

Two problems flowed from the war. It had been an expensive campaign, both in terms of men and money. The financial difficulties however were tided over to some extent by large loans from the Nawab of Oudh (q.v.) and the Raja of Gwalior. On a more serious plane, there was the mutiny at Barrackpore (near Calcutta) in 1824. Disaffection amongst the sepoys over loss of life due to disease, besides glaring differentials in pay and a strong taboo against crossing of the seas, flared into an open revolt which was put down with a heavy hand.

Amherst continued with the earlier policy of non-interference in the internal affairs of Indian states. Accordingly, he refused to take sides in the disputed succession in Bharatpur and peremptorily ordered the suspension of military preparations made by Ochterlony (q.v.) and recalled him. However Charles Metcalfe (q.v.), who took Ochterlony's place, lost no time in convincing the Governor-General of the need to intervene. The fort of Bharatpur was stormed and occupied by General Combermere (December 1825) and the Raja reinstalled, with British help.

Towards the close of 1826 the Governor-General made a tour through the North-West Provinces and in the following summer inaugurated Simla as a viceregal sanatorium. In February 1828 Amherst's tenure drew to a close. It has been held that while he was a capable official in a subordinate capacity, he was hardly qualified to be the head of a government and that he was a man of 'very mediocre' abilities who had no 'real grasp' of the problems with which India was then beset.

On returning to England, Amherst served as Lord of the Bed Chamber both to George IV and William IV. In 1835 he was designated Governor-General of Canada, but surrendered the appointment because of a change in the ministry. Thereafter he gradually faded out from active public life and spent his time in retired comfort until his death in 1857.

Hiralal Gupta, 'India under Lord Amherst', unpublished D. Phil thesis, University of Allahabad, 1946; A. T. Ritchie and R. Evans, *Earl Amherst*, Rulers of India, Oxford, 1909.

Treaty of Amritsar (1809)

Between 1805-7, Maharaja Ranjit Singh (q.v.) had established his sway over almost all the cis-Sutlej states without so much as a whimper of protest from John Company (q.v.). It thus remained for the latter to give him formal recognition. In 1805, the Sikh ruler had suggested to the British, through General Gerard Lake, that the Sutlej serve as a boundary between their respective dominions. Earlier, distraught and panic-stricken by Ranjit Singh's continued aggression against them, the Malwa chiefs had appealed to the British for help but, for a time, were completely ignored.

In 1807 when the danger of a Franco-Russian advance on India loomed large in the wake of Napolean's alliance with Tsar Alexander I at Tilsit, the Company resolved to extend its territorial boundary from the Jamuna to the Sutlej by using Malwa (whose chiefs had meanwhile made another appeal) as a 'power in the game'. Metcalfe (q.v.) was sent to negotiate a treaty with Ranjit Singh directed against a possible French advance into India. The parleys were protracted as both parties devised ways and means to further their own selfish ends.

Presently, British policy underwent a major metamorphosis as news of the Spanish insurrection against Napoleon sharply reduced such chances as there might have been of the grandiose French designs on India. British interest, understandably, now shifted to checking the ambitions of the Sikh ruler by persuasion if possible, or by force if necessary. Colonel Ochterlony's (q.v.) march to Ludhiana and Ranjit Singh's ignorance of developments in Europe under-scored the latter's weakness. On the other hand, the British advance coupled with the adroitness of the young Metcalfe who assured the Sikh chief that he could make conquests in other directions without British interference, made Ranjit Singh pause. On 9 February 1809, Ochterlony issued a warning to the effect that any further encroachments by the Lahore darbar south of the Sutlej would be resisted. British armed presence coupled with the fear that some more Panjab chiefs might flock to the British banner and seek their protection brought the Sikh ruler to his knees.

The 4-article treaty, signed formally at Amritsar on 25 April 1809, provided for (a) perpetual friendship and 'most-favoured power' treatment for the 'Lahore Rajah'; (b) recognition of Ranjit Singh's sovereignty over 'territories and subjects' north of the Sutlej; (c) permission to keep troops on the left bank of the river only to the extent that these were deemed necessary for the internal duties of that territory'.

The transaction was completed by a British proclamation on 3 May 1809 which dealt primarily with arrangements regarding the country occupied by the rulers of Malwa and Sirhind, while Ranjit Singh gave up all territorial acquisitions made by him after the arrival of Metcalfe. Disregard of any clause by either party was to render the treaty 'null and void'.

The treaty has been rated 'a grievous blow' to Ranjit Singh's dreams of a united Panjab, and he was no longer free to pursue his territorial expansion west of the Indus. He was to lay no claims to allegiance from the cis-Sutlej chiefs and gave up Faridkot and Ambala; henceforth, he was to direct his energies elsewhere other than southwards. At the same time, the effective British frontier had moved from the Jamuna to the Sutlej.

Aitchison, II, pp. 237-38; Khushwant Singh, *Ranjit Singh, Maharaja of the Punjab 1780-1839*, London, 1962; Dodwell, *CHI*, V, pp. 540-1.

Mukhtar Ahmad Ansari (1880–1936)

Mukhtar Ahmad Ansari was born in 1880 at Yusufpur, in Ghazipur district of U.P. He was educated at Allahabad and Hyderabad. He was a medical student at Madras and later in London, where he earned his M.D. and M.S. degrees. Ansari spent about ten years (1900-10) in England where he became acquainted with Pandit Motilal Nehru (q.v.) and his son Jawaharlal as well as Hakim Ajmal Khan. On returning home in 1910, he established a medical practice and settled down in Delhi.

He was initially active both in the Indian National Congress (q.v.) as well as the All-India Muslim League (q.v.) and played an important role in bringing about the 1916 Lucknow Pact (q.v.). Two years later he presided over the annual session of the Muslim League. In his presidential address he called upon his co-religionists to take a bold and fearless stand on the

Khilafat (q.v.) question which had been agitating their minds. He also pleaded for the community's unconditional support for complete independence for the country. So forthright and unorthodox was his stance that all the copies of his address were proscribed by the government.

In 1920 Ansari was elected President of the Nagpur session of the Muslim League where the All-India Khilafat Conference meeting under Maulana Abul Kalam Azad (q.v.) and the Congress under Dr Vijayaraghavachari had also convened. The three met in joint session. In January 1920, Ansari was leader of the Khilafat delegation that waited upon the Viceroy and impressed upon the latter the 'necessity for preservation of the Turkish empire and of the sovereignty of the Sultan as Khalif.'

In his address to the Madras session (1927) of the Congress over which he presided, Ansari devoted the bulk of his speech to the question of communal amity and goodwill. He summarized Congress policy as one of co-operation for 35 years (1885-1920); Non-cooperation (q.v.) for a year and a half (1921-22); followed by obstruction within the Council and constitutional deadlock for four years (1923-27). 'Non-cooperation did not fail us', he remarked, 'we failed non-cooperation'.

In 1928 the All-Parties conference under Ansari's chairmanship appointed a committee to draft the principles of India's future constitution. Headed by Motilal Nehru it was this committee that wrote the Nehru Report (q.v.).

Despite Lord Irwin's (q.v.) 'distinct promise' to nominate Ansari to the Round Table Conference (q.v.), Willingdon (who succeeded Irwin) scored out his name, pleading that Muslim delegates were opposed to his inclusion. It was clear that the new Governor-General was keen to demonstrate that Muslim India was opposed to Swaraj; additionally, he would beat the Congress by cutting out its Muslim limb.

When the Congress launched Civil Disobedience (q.v.) in January 1932, Vallabhbhai Patel (q.v.), then the party's president, drew up a list of names to succeed him one after another in the event of mass arrests. Ansari's name was second on the list, after Rajendra Prasad (q.v.).

Ansari occupied a position of eminence in the Congress. For a number of years he was a member of the party's Working Committee, was the party Joint Secretary for six years and its President in 1927. He lent strong support to higher education and, in particular, to the establishment of Jamia Millia Islamia in Delhi and the Kashi Vidya Peeth at Banaras. After the retirement of Hakim Ajmal Khan he acted as Chancellor of Jamia (1928-36).

His palatial Delhi home, 'Darus-salam', was for all practical purposes the headquarters of Congress activity; Gandhi (q.v.) used to stay there, whenever he was in the city.

A percipient observer of trends among Indian Muslims rates Dr Ansari higher than Maulana Azad in 'clarity of outlook, broader vision and preciseness' and calls him 'one of the noted spokesmen of radical nationalist school in India and a fine product of the progressive movement in Muslim society. He even excels Maulana Azad in his deep accent on secularism'.

Despite his political preoccupations, Ansari found time for his professional work. He was the author of *Regeneration of Man* (1935), a work in which he recorded his experiments of surgical cases regarding rejuvenation. In 1912 he led what came to be known as the Ansari Medical Mission to

Turkey to provide medical and surgical aid to its forces then fighting in the Balkan wars (1912-13) against its hostile neighbours. A surgeon of the highest eminence, his outlook on life was said to be 'essentially scientific'.

B. Pattabhi Sitaramayya, *History of the Indian National Congress*, 2 vols, Reprint, New Delhi, 1969, I; Moin Shakir, *Khilafat to Partition: A survey of major political trends among Indian Muslims during 1919-1947*, New Delhi, 1970; Mushirul Hasan, *Muslims & the Congress: Correspondence of Dr. M. A. Ansari*, New Delhi, 1979; Sen, *DNB*, I, pp. 65-7 (Mushirul Haq).

Arbitral Tribunal (1947)

The Arbitral Tribunal was set up about the same time as the Partition Council (q.v.) with a view to resolving questions on which the two new dominion governments of India and Pakistan were unable to reach agreement. The Tribunal was composed of one representative each of India and Pakistan.

By 15 August (1947) the Partition Council was able to sort out most of the problems referred to it through its expert and steering committees. This left only a few matters for settlement by the Tribunal. For fear that the latter may not be able to arrive at any agreed conclusions, Lord Louis Mountbatten (1900–79), the then Viceroy, was keen that few if any matters come before it. At his suggestion, the Pakistani representatives, Ghulam Mohammed and Sir Archibald Rowlands, met their counterparts, Vallabhbhai Patel (q.v.), Rajendra Prasad (q.v.) and C. Rajagopalachari (q.v.), in a final effort to resolve outstanding issues at the level of the Partition Council. After a brief discussion they remitted the issues to the two steering committee members, Chaudhari Mahommed Ali and H. M. Patel. The latter were able to evolve compromise formulae which were accepted by their respective principals. This meant that all references to the (Arbitral) Tribunal stood withdrawn.

V. P. Menon, *The Transfer of Power in India*, New Delhi, 1957, pp. 397–8.

Army Reorganization (1947)

With the acceptance of June 3rd Plan (q.v.), the two dominions of India and Pakistan on whom power was to devolve insisted on having their own armed forces under their respective control before the date of transfer of power, viz., 15 August 1947. Both M. A. Jinnah (q.v.) and Acharya J. B. Kripalani (1888–1982), presidents respectively of the All-India Muslim League (q.v.), and the Indian National Congress (q.v.) agreed that division should be on a territorial (citizenship) basis, subject to the stipulation that an opportunity be afforded to those who happened to be resident in that part of India in which their community was in a minority to transfer their homes and citizenship to the other part. Subsequently, the Partition Council (q.v.) decided that as from 15 August the Indian Union and Pakistan would each have within its territory armed forces under its own operational control and composed predominantly of non-Muslims and Muslims respectively.

The decision involved the splitting up the three wings of the armed forces and the establishment of separate headquarters in India and Pakistan with a view to each taking over its respective command as on 15 August. While, in due course, the existing armed forces were to be sorted out, it was ruled that in the transitional period they should remain under a single administrative control. The task was entrusted to Field-Marshal Sir Claude Auchinleck who, as from 15 August, was redesignated Supreme Commander. He was to work under the direction of a Joint Defence Council consisting of four members including himself, the other three being Lord Louis Mountbatten (1900–79) the then Viceroy who was to be Chairman, and the Defence Ministers of India and Pakistan. The original idea that the Council include the Governors-General of the two new Dominions was later dropped.

The Joint Defence Council continued to function until 1 April 1948, but the Supreme Commander ceased to be a member as from 1 December 1947, when his post was abolished. To be fair, Auchinleck had himself proposed that the command end on 31 December 1947, but Vallabhbhai Patel (q.v.), then India's Home Minister, had begun questioning his impartiality and insisted that his command be wound up at once. In the absence of 'necessary goodwill and co-operation', Auchinleck found it difficult to function, and the British government also agreed that the Supreme Command be wound up as from 30 November.

It may be noted that initially Auchinleck had been very reluctant to split up the Army and other defence forces. He was deeply distressed at the prospect of tearing apart an organization that had been reared with such care, apart from the fact that he thought the division of the forces an impossibly complicated operation. There was the difficulty that, despite the appointment and promotion of Indians during World War II, 'the main cadre of officers—and certainly all the General Staff were British'. When Lord Ismay, Mountbatten's Chief of Staff, asked him to prepare a plan, Auchinleck is reported to have replied that the Army 'cannot be broken up' and argued that it would be ruined if split. It appears that ultimately Auchinleck 'had to be ordered to it, and [he] was very resentful'.

The withdrawal of British troops from India started as from 17 August 1947 and was completed on 28 February 1948. The last to withdraw were the Somerset Light Infantry.

V. P. Menon, *The Transfer of Power*, pp. 398–400; *Tara Chand*, IV, pp. 532–3.

Arya Samaj

Rated as one of the most powerful revivalist movements in modern India, the Arya Samaj was founded by Swami Dayanand Saraswati (q.v.) at Rajkot (Saurashtra) in 1875; another body answering to that name was set up at Ahmedabad and Bombay later that year. The principal objective of the organization was to counteract the proselytizing activities of Muslims and Christians, and to launch a programme of social reform.

The Samaj does not believe in caste based on birth, but in one resting on function or work; nor in inequality of man and man or between the sexes. Arya Samajists regard the Vedas as infallible, eternal and divine. The Samaj maintains that the Vedic religion alone was true and universal. Aryans were the chosen people, the Vedas their gospel and India their homeland. It followed that all other religions were a shade less than perfect. One way or another, Dayanand's call was: 'Back to the Vedas'.

Members of the Samaj undergo training in the manner prescribed in the Vedas and are required to contribute 1% of their earnings to the organization. Later, members also swore by the ten principles (*niyams*) laid down by Dayanand. A procedure for worship at the weekly meetings is prescribed.

Elaborately organized at the village level on a democratic basis, the Samaj graduates through a hierarchy to the general assembly which is the top policy-making body. Some of the workers who preach its tenets are paid; others work in an honorary capacity. Apart from the main body, its front organizations include the Arya Kumar Sabha, the Stri Samaj and a tract society responsible for publications.

The Samaj's message resulted in changed attitudes towards prevalent practices and the Depressed Classes. Idolatory was condemned, as was untouchability and child marriage. The subjection of women was decried, inter-caste marriages encouraged as well as the remarriage of widows. Members involved themselves actively in such social work as famine relief, and running orphanages and widow homes.

From the purely defensive, the Samaj soon veered round to the offensive. Dayanand's *Satyartha Prakash* (1879), in so far as it underlined the weaknesses in Islam and Christianity, became highly polemical. So also did such movements as protection of the cow and 'Shuddhi', reconversion to the faith of those who willingly, or under duress, had renounced it earlier.

The Samaj aimed at achieving 'social, religious and political unity', created great interest in the initial stages but later provoked rabid controversies. While it succeeded in a 'national awakening' restricted to a narrow Hindu base, it also encouraged retaliatory measures by other religious groups (viz., 'Tabligh' among the Muslims). Similarly, the protection of the cow, for most part unexceptional, became a subject of controversy for some Muslim theologians and their followers among the poor and uneducated sections of the community. All this led to an upsurge of communal tension inspired by religious jealousies which continued, especially in the Panjab, until the partition of the country in 1947.

The Samaj's greatest contribution lay in the field of education, although the choice of the system to be followed became a matter of some controversy and debate. The *Gurukula* school was a hark-back to Vedic times; the rival *College* group recognized the value of English education and spread a network of Dayanand Anglo-Vedic schools and colleges throughout the country. The premier Dayanand Anglo-Vedic College, established in 1886 at Lahore with the veteran Lala Hans Raj as its Principal, served as a model for similar institutions all over northern India. The curriculum attempted to achieve a synthesis between modern and traditional learning.

Because of its unrelenting opposition to alien rule, the British accused the Samaj of being a political body. Assuredly some leading Arya Samajists like Lala Lajpat Rai and Bhai Parmananda were political activists, but the Samaj *per se* had no political affiliations. None the less the contrary impression somehow persisted during the extremist agitation (1907-17) and some known Samajists were dismissed from government service.

Gandhi's (q.v.) principle of satyagraha, though supported by Swami Shradhananda, was vigorously opposed by Lala Hans Raj. The Samajists also decried Indian National Congress (q.v.) support of the Khilafat movement (q.v.), as also the two-nation theory and the demand for a separate Muslim homeland. During the Hindu-Muslim disturbances on the eve of Partition (1947), the Samaj organized a Veer Dal (youth volunteers) to protect Hindu property and rights. The Congress later accused it of inciting communal tendencies and disharmony and the Samaj was temporarily forced out of the national scene, even though its social and educational activities continued unabated.

The Arya Samaj is not merely a society which from the time of its inception has initiated drastic reform in Hindu society, customs and practices; it also stands for a cosmopolitan religion and a precise, and profound philosophy derived from the Vedas and its founder. Its religion and philosophy are, in a true sense, the religion and philosophy of the Vedas. God, Soul and Matter are the dominant factors in the metaphysics of the Arya Samaj, while its theory of knowledge is based on the knowledge of the two—the knower and the knowable.

Swami Dayanand's programme was practical; he insisted on the superiority of practice over belief and devotion. The field of service of the Arya Samaj included all—women and untouchables among the Hindus, indeed all afflicted people without distinction of caste or creed. Dayanand's followers rejected idol worship, scoffed at contemporary belief in astrology and refused to concede that heavenly bodies were either interested in human affairs or could be propitiated.

Dayanand's presentation of India's past made the Arya Samaj a revivalist body. The golden age that he pictured was certainly a thing of the past but he believed—and inspired millions to believe—that it could be recaptured.

Unlike the Brahmo Samaj (q.v.), the Prarthana Samaj and several other 19th century reformist movements, the Arya Samaj never cut itself aloof from the mainstream of Hindu thought. Even as Dayanand had done, its members rather claimed to be true Hindus, basing themselves as they did on the Vedas which every Hindu equally respected.

In bringing about a national awakening in the country, the Samaj played a dual role: at once progressive and retrogressive. Thus in attacking religious superstition, propagating mass education, inculcating equality of man to man as well as between man and woman, it acted as a catalyst for progressive reform. Yet in proclaiming the Vedas to be infallible, it denied the individual the exercise of his own independent judgement and substituted one tyranny, that of the Brahmins, by another. In its formative phase the Samaj made a signal contribution to the nationalist upsurge, yet after the twenties it contributed, however unwittingly, to the growth of what has been called a 'belligerent religio-communal atmosphere'.

Founded in Bombay, the Samaj threw deep roots in the Panjab alone, even though its branches spread all over the north. After Swami Dayanand's death (1883), his work was continued by a band of zealous followers, with the result that, to this day, the Samaj has remained a live organization.

Vaidyanath Shastri, *The Arya Samaj, its cult and creed*, 2nd ed., New Delhi, 1967; Lajpat Rai (revised, expanded and edited by Sri Ram Sharma), *A History of the Arya Samaj*, New Delhi, 1967; Kenneth Jones. *Arya Dharm: Hindu Consciousness in 19th-century Punjab*, New Delhi, 1976; J. F. Jordens, *Dayanand Saraswati*, Delhi, 1978.

Asaf-ud-Daula (c. 1749–97)

Mirza Amani, the eldest son of Shuja-ud-Daula (q.v.), was enrolled (1761) a mansabdar in the Mughal court and given the title of 'Asaf-ud-Daula'. Declared heir apparent in his father's lifetime, he succeeded as Nawab of Oudh (q.v.) in 1775 and was appointed (1776) Nawab Wazir by the emperor. On his accession, he signed the treaty of Faizabad (q.v.) and on the intervention of Nathaniel Middleton, then British resident, was able to secure Rs 50 lakhs from his father's Begums to clear his arrears with the Calcutta Council on the understanding that no more would be demanded. The Resident appears to have 'incurred the displeasure' of Warren Hastings (q.v.) by his slowness in pressing Asaf-ud-Daula for the treasure of the Begums. The Nawab later moved his capital from Faizabad to Lucknow.

During his reign conditions in Oudh worsened precipitately. Indifferent to civil and criminal administration, he left affairs of state entirely in the hands of subordinates who, while enriching themselves, fleeced the populace indiscriminately. He paid heavily for the British subsidiary force over which he had little control and was asked to disband his own troops so as to relieve the state's financial distress, all efforts to modernize their equipment being summarily rejected. This, coupled with his craze for new buildings, curios, etc. increased his indebtedness to the John Company (q.v.). It was to meet these growing obligations that he seized the property of the Begums briefly alluded to above. This was done with the approval of Warren Hastings whose role in this sordid business was later the subject of acute controversy.

Since the Company had taken over the defence of Oudh, the Nawab's control over his state's foreign relations passed into its hands; it took all important decisions, viz., in his dealings with the Marathas and the Rohillas. Before long, the Resident began interfering in the internal administration of the state—in the appointment and dismissal of ministers—while, at the same time, complaining about the Nawab's lax administration. John Shore (q.v.) noted in 1795 that 'disaffection and anarchy' prevailed in Oudh and nothing but the presence of British troops 'prevented open insurrection'. Asaf-ud-Daula did not recover, it is believed, from the shock administered by the Company's removal of his favourite minister Ghao Lal. The Nawab died on 21 September 1797.

P. Basu, *Oudh and the East India Company, 1785-1801*, Lucknow, 1943; *Beale*, p. 81; Dodwell, *CHI*, V, pp. 299-301, 349-51.

Asiatic Society

The Asiatic Society was founded on 15 January 1784 by Sir William Jones (q.v.) and thirty other members who had responded to his call for pursuing various branches of Asiatic studies. It was modelled on the Royal Society of England with elaborate rules and regulations to guide its functioning. Membership was voluntary but, until 1829, no Indians were admitted. The Society attracted a large foreign clientele after its activities became better known. Initially its meetings were held every week and later every month.

The first of its publications, *Asiatic Researches*, was brought out in

1789 and included articles written by eminent British scholars. Credit for widespread interest in the field of indological studies in England and the west is deservedly given to the work of the Society.

Lord Auckland (1784–1849)

George Eden, later Earl of Auckland, was Governor-General of India, 1835-42. Educated at Eton and Christ Church, Oxford, he sat in the House of Commons as a Whig in 1810 and the Lords four years later. He served as President of the Board of Trade (1830-2) and, two years later, was appointed First Lord of the Admiralty. In 1835 he was chosen by Lord Palmerston, then Britain's Foreign Secretary, to succeed Bentinck (q.v.) as Governor-General and a year later took over from Charles Metcalfe (q.v.). A vivid account of his tenure of office and experiences is given in *Up the Country* by his sister Emily (Eden): it describes a tour by the Governor-General of the John Company's (q.v.) domain in and around the Doab that lasted nearly 2½ years, October 1837-March 1840.

The widespread famine then prevalent in the North-Western Provinces deeply distressed the Governor-General and an official famine policy to provide relief dates back to his efforts to allay human suffering and undertake preventive measures. A sum of Rs 40 lakhs was spent on famine relief in 1839.

A prey to indecision and hesitancy, Auckland followed a policy of expediency towards the 'native' Indian States (q.v.). On the death of Nasiruddin Haidar of Oudh (q.v.), he forcibly enthroned his old uncle Nasir-ud-Daula who, in gratitude, agreed to sign any treaty proposed by the Governor-General. Oddly, the latter failed to communicate to the Nawab the fact that the Court of Directors did not approve of the treaty actually signed, a piece of carelessness not easy to explain away.

While acknowledging the right of the ruler of Orcha to adopt an heir, the Governor-General, as if in anticipation, followed Dalhousie's (q.v.) policy of abandoning no fit opportunity for annexation and applied it on the slightest of pretexts. The Raja of Satara was deposed on allegedly trumped-up charges of conspiracy and the ruler of Karnal for attempting to wage a war against the Company.

It was at Simla, the summer headquarters of the Government of India, that Auckland launched the First Anglo-Afghan War (q.v.). A Russophobe to the backbone, any activity by that country in Persia and Afghanistan persuaded him of the dire need to dispatch a diplomatic mission to Kabul, a course of action supported by the home authorities. But the mission sent was foredoomed to failure in so far as the choice of Alexander Burnes (q.v.) appears to have been an unhappy one.

In essence, the Governor-General had refused to forsake Ranjit Singh's (q.v.) friendship by failing to hand back Peshawar to the Afghan ruler. In the result, Dost Mohammad's (q.v.) negotiations with the Russians were viewed as hostile intrigue that looked larger than life in the light of the Russian-inspired Persian siege of Herat. This gave added support to Auckland's plans to replace Dost Mohammad by a dependable ally such as Shah Shuja and led to the conclusion of the Tripartite Treaty (q.v.).

Apologists contend that this course of action was forced upon Auckland by his advisers, but it would be hard to acquit him of blame for listening to them and thereby allowing the outbreak of a foolish and, eventually, disastrous war. If he were to receive credit for the successful issue of the Afghan campaign of 1839, he must in equal measure bear responsibility for the disaster of 1841.

Unscrupulously, Auckland made Sind (q.v.) a base for operations as well as a scapegoat to finance his Afghan campaign. Not honest enough to annex the province straightaway, he disguised his aggressive designs under the garb of friendship. The manifesto issued in October 1838, justifying his policy towards the Afghan ruler, blatantly misrepresented and distorted facts regarding negotiations with Dost Mohammad.

Although the siege of Herat had been raised in September 1838, Auckland plunged into the war in the hope of winning military glory. Initial successes to British arms, in particular the capture of Kabul, earned him an Earldom. Later, however, through lack of far-sightedness and ill-chosen measures of economy he reduced the strength of the Kabul garrison and appointed the weak and incompetent General Elphinstone its commander. Defeat, humiliation and tragedy struck the British at Kabul when the slender peace that had subsisted for two years was rudely shattered by the discontented Afghan host which rose as one man.

Unwilling to accept the harsh truth, Auckland proclaimed in January 1842 that the British discomfiture was only a 'partial reverse'. On returning to England, he was once more sworn in as First Lord of the Admiralty. Failing health however soon put an end to his career and he died on 1 January 1849.

A biographer has charged Auckland with financial mismanagement, underlining that 'an exhausted treasury and an increasing debt' were the 'chief legacies' of his tenure of office. Thus 'whereas the first year of his rule had opened with a surplus revenue of a million and a half, he left behind a deficit of two millions and an addition of 12 to the public debt'. It has also been contended that another failing was 'his engrossing pursuit of a foreign policy in which he had never heartily concurred'.

L. J. Trotter, *The Earl of Auckland*, Rulers of India, Oxford, 1905; *DNB*, VI, pp. 357–8 (Henry Morse Stephens); Edward Thompson (ed.), Emily Eden, *Up the Country: Letters written to her sister from the Upper Provinces of India*, reprint, London, 1978.

August (1917) Declaration

On 20 August 1917, Edwin Samuel Montagu (1879-1924), then Secretary of State for India, made a momentous declaration in the House of Commons on the policy of HMG towards future political reform in India. Under considerable pressure from Indian militant nationalists and the advocates of Home Rule (q.v.), and in recognition of Indian loyalty and ungrudging support in the war-effort, the British government considered it imperative that some political concessions be made. Delay, it was argued, might alienate moderate opinion in the country. Mature deliberation on the question had led British policy-makers to the conclusion that India be granted self-government as soon as it was fully prepared. This, it was felt, would bring about a change in a hitherto autocratic system.

Montagu's declaration read in part: 'The policy of His Majesty's Government, with which the Government of India are in complete accord, is that of the increasing association of Indians in every branch of the administration and the gradual development of self-governing institutions, with a view to the progressive realisation of *responsible government* in India as an integral part of the British empire.'

To prevent its commitment to a rigid schedule, HMG went on to clarify 'that progress in this policy can only be achieved by successive stages. The British Government and the Government of India on whom the responsibility lies for the welfare and advancement of the Indian people must be the judges of the time and measure of each advance and they must be guided by the cooperation received from those upon whom new opportunities of service will thus be conferred and by the extent to which it is found that confidence can be reposed in their sense of responsibility.'

Earlier, Montagu's memorandum circulated to the Cabinet on 30 July 1917 drew its pointed attention to the deteriorating situation in India and the increasing insistence by the Viceroy and heads of provincial governments for an immediate enunciation of policy. But he could not get the Cabinet to find any time to discuss the question. 'The number of times that I have sat trembling for a Cabinet summons', he confided to Austen Chamberlain on 15 August 1917, 'the number of times that I have hoped to see the Prime Minister; all this would make a story that would bring tears to your eyes.'

The 30 July memorandum referred to noted *inter alia*: 'HMG and the Government of India have in view the gradual development of free institutions in India with a view to ultimate self-government within the Empire.' The Cabinet's approval of the Curzon (q.v.) draft was given on 14 August; Montagu used it six days later in the House of Commons.

The skilful phraseology of the declaration, beginning with the substitution of the words 'responsible government' for 'self-government'; of progress to be made by 'successive stages', leaving the determination of those stages in the hands of India's rulers who would lay down the 'time and measure of each advance'—was the painstaking work of Curzon. He had assumed the role of a *rapporteur* during the War Cabinet's deliberations on Indian problems and appeared determined to introduce an element of delay until such time as Indian opinion became more representative. Understandably, he had not reckoned with the imminent transformation of the Indian National Congress (q.v.) into a mass movement under Gandhi (q.v.), a fact that would compel HMG to quicken the pace of reform. Nor had he visualized that responsible government would be interpreted in terms of Indian ministers being held accountable to an electorate envisaged in the scheme of dyarchy.

The genesis of the August Declaration needs a word by way of explanation. It all began with Austen Chamberlain, who, in 1915, succeeded Lord Crewe at the India Office. He asked Charles Hardinge (q.v.), then Governor-General, for a memorandum on the political reforms that may be necessary *after* the war. On its receipt, in October 1915, he asked the British Cabinet to meet the 'powerful and increasing demand for a greater share by Indians in the administration of the country'. Chelmsford (q.v.), who succeeded Hardinge, wrote a despatch on 24 November 1916 suggesting that the British objective should be thus defined: 'To associate them [Indians] with ourselves in a continuously increasing degree in the administration of the country'. Earlier, he had suggested that British India should form 'an integral part of the Empire with self-government', but the rate of its progress in that direction was to be determined by a number of imponderables.

The Viceroy's proposals were scrutinized by an India Office committee which submitted its report on 18 March 1916. Earlier that year a Round Table group had issued 'suggestions for constitutional progress', while Indian members of the Imperial War Conference as well as the Imperial War Cabinet had pleaded the country's cause without demur.

In July 1917 Chamberlain resigned on the issue of the military disaster that Indian troops had met in Mesopotamia and was succeeded by Montagu. The latter's immediate task was to take a decision on an issue that had been debated by Hardinge, Chelmsford and officials in India as well as Britain. After a great deal of political manoeuvring—Asquith had left the government and Lloyd George was far from well-disposed—the Cabinet's approval was forthcoming on 14 August. Because of Curzon's strong disapproval, the expression 'responsible government' was substituted for 'self-government'.

The declaration of 20 August signified the passing away of the second British Empire and the beginning of what A. E. Zimmern has called 'the third British Empire'; the transformation, in principle, of the Empire into a commonwealth of nations. Perhaps the most important feature of the Montagu declaration was that it represented a break from the policy of the Minto-Morley reforms (q.v.), of associating Indians in government *by* the British, towards a policy of giving Indians responsibility for governing *themselves*.

The announcement, it has been pointed out, was intended to deal with ends, *not* means. The end of policy could have been Indian self-government, but the step towards it was one of increasing association.

The announcement of 20 August has been viewed as a powerful and revolutionary document, both in itself and the effect it had on the course of constitutional reforms. The stunning fact however is that the phrase that was most important was inserted by the reforms' greatest critic, Curzon. He was later to reject the logical conclusion drawn from his words. Called to comment on dyarchy during a House of Lords debate on 31 July 1924, he said, '...I profoundly detest it...'

The August declaration made a tremendous impact on the Indian political scene: it inaugurated a more liberal era of reform. In its recognition of India emerging as a self-governing dominion lay the foundation of the later multi-racial Commonwealth in which member countries of the former British Empire would work together on a basis of complete equality.

S. R. Mehrotra, 'The politics behind the Montagu declaration of 1917', in C. H. Philips (ed.), *Politics and Society in India*, London, 1963, pp. 71-96; and *India and the Commonwealth, 1885–1949*, London, 1965; Richard Danzig, 'The Announcement of August 20th 1917', *Journal of Asian Studies*, Ann Arbor, XXVIII, I, November 1968, pp. 19-37.

August 8, 1940 Offer

With the outbreak of World War II in September 1939 and India's automatic involvement in it without consultation by Whitehall, the Indian National Congress (q.v.) demanded a clear-cut definition of the British government's war and peace aims as applicable to India. Shortly afterwards, there was a change of government in England with Winston Churchill (1874-1965) taking over as Prime Minister from Neville Chamberlain. Churchill's mental outlook about India, it was well known, had not progressed beyond his early twentieth-century imperialist mould and many in his own country viewed him as 'the crustiest of the Tories'.

In India, in the early years of what came to be called the 'phoney' war, public opinion had crystallized but, owing to divided loyalties, remained remarkably ambivalent. While on the one hand there was understandable resentment at the casual fashion in which India had been treated by its British masters, many people were making their full contribution to the swelling quota of recruits for the war machine and raising public funds. The initial Congress reaction of asking the provincial governments to resign was not universally acclaimed; there was sizeable dissent in the party's own ranks too. In the meanwhile, in 1940 L. S. Amery replaced Lord Zetland as Secretary of State for India. Lord Linlithgow's (q.v.) correspondence with Whitehall reveals that both in New Delhi and London there was growing emphasis on the intractability of the Hindu-Muslim problem which, nationalist opinion charged, was trotted forth as an excuse to postpone any transfer of authority to Indian hands.

On 21 June 1940 the Congress Working Committee adopted a resolution stating emphatically that its creed of non-violence was relevant only in terms of its struggle for independence and was by no means suited to facing a national challenge or resisting an external enemy. The resolution signified a clear break between Gandhi (q.v.) and the Congress; the former now ceased to be even an ordinary, or symbolic 4-anna, member of the organization or to accept the party's policies or programmes.

In the first week of July, the Congress executive formally asked HMG to affirm its adherence to the goal of independence for India and to induct immediately into office, at the centre, a national government. The Governor-General's response was to hold consultations with a wide range of political leaders. On 8 August 1940, he issued from Simla a statement that was intended to break the constitutional deadlock. It made three points: (i) an immediate expansion of the Viceroy's Executive Council by inducting into that body a number of representative Indians; (ii) the establishment of a War Advisory Council comprising representatives of British India and the Indian States (q.v.), the Council to meet at regular intervals; (iii) the promotion of practical steps to arrive at an agreement among Indians on the form which the post-War representative body would take, the method by which it should arrive at its conclusions and a definition of the principles and outlines of the constitution itself.

As if to qualify what had been said in New Delhi, the Secretary of State declared on 14 August that if 'Dominion Status for India can be finalized after the war, there is nothing to prevent a preliminary discussion and negotiations during the war.'

Nationalist reaction to what came to be known as the 'August offer' was hostile. It was clear that all it amounted to was the addition of a few more Indians to the Governor-General's Executive Council without transferring responsibility from the British Parliament to the Indian legislature. The only party that was happy about this was the All-India Muslim League (q.v.). On

22 April 1941, Amery declared that the 'Constitution itself and also the body which is to frame it, must be the outcome of agreement between the principal elements in Indian national life. That is an essential pre-requisite to the success of the future constitution.'

Not long after Adolf Hitler (1889-1945) had launched his massive invasion of Russia (June 1941), Whitehall finally made up its mind to give effect to the 'August (1940) offer'. In pursuance thereof, in July 1941 the Viceroy's Executive Council was enlarged from 7 to 12 members, of whom 4 were British and 8 Indians as against 3 (Indians) earlier. No member of the Congress or the League joined the new Council except Sultan Ahmed, a prominent Leaguer of Patna. Later, Jinnah (q.v.) took the Viceroy severely to task for inducting a member of his party without his (Jinnah's) permission.

In the new Council, some existing charges were separated and redistributed while new portfolios of 'information' and 'civil defence' were added. Additionally, a National Defence Council of 30 members, including the Premiers of Panjab, Bengal and Assam, was constituted. The Council was designed to serve as a safety-valve and a forum to improve liaison between the central government on the one hand and the provinces and states on the other, but it had no executive authority.

The members of the new Executive Council were: Sir Edward Benthall, Sir Jeremy Raisman, Sir Reginald Maxwell, Sir Sultan Ahmed, Sir Ramaswami Mudaliar, Sir Firoz Khan Noon, Sir Mohammed Usman, Sir Ashok Roy, Sir Azizul Huque (Haque), Sir J. P. Srivastava, Dr B. R. Ambedkar (q.v.), Sir Jogendra Singh and Dr N. B. Khare.

Tara Chand, III, p. 308; V. P. Menon, *The Transfer of Power*, pp. 86–114.

Aurobindo Ghosh (Sri Aurobindo) (1872–1950)

Aurobindo Ghosh, a leading Bengal revolutionary later turned yogi, belonged to an educated and completely anglicized middle-class family. His father, Dr Krishnadhone Ghosh, had sent Aurobindo, then barely 7 years old, along with his two elder brothers to England to study there so as to remain unaffected, and literally untouched, by influences at home. Considered somewhat of a prodigy, Aurobindo mastered Greek and Latin at school and won a scholarship to King's College, Cambridge where later he took the classical tripos.

With its tangible material rewards and the prestige of belonging to the ruling élite, the I.C.S. was, then as for many years later, the El Dorado of brilliant and ambitious young men. At 18, Aurobindo effortlessly passed its entrance examination, but the charm of a bureaucratic career appears to have worn off even while he was undergoing his probation. He knew how much store his family set by his success; if he resigned, it would break his father's heart. He none the less failed to appear in the riding test and was disqualified.

Broadly, Aurobindo's career may be divided into three parts. To start with, there is his early youth and education (1879-92) in England: this is followed by his work and service under the Gaekwad in Baroda (1892-1906), followed by his meteoric, barely four-year (1906-10) political career in

Calcutta (q.v.) which gathered intensity during the great agitation caused by the Partition of Bengal (q.v.); and finally, the remaining forty years (1910-50) in philosophical and religious work in Pondicherry where he developed into a seer whose thought continues to inspire men and women throughout the world.

Aurobindo lived in England for nearly 13 years: Manchester, 1879-1884; London, 1884-90; and finally Cambridge. All through he showed a great aptitude for classical studies—in language as well as literature. Briefly, the fruits of his education were a thorough knowledge of several western European languages, an elegant English prose style and an extreme hostility to India's British rulers.

Aurobindo returned home in 1893, a member of the Baroda civil service, and served in varied capacities in different departments of the state's administration. Presently he found more suitable employment as a lecturer in English in Baroda College, and rose to be Professor and later Vice-Principal. He also handled the Gaekwad's foreign correspondence. With his immense aptitude for and interest in the learning of languages, he soon picked up a good working knowledge of Bengali, Gujarati, Marathi, Hindi and Sanskrit. A great deal of his time was taken up in writing poetry, plays and essays in English.

While abroad, Aurobindo had been fascinated by the revolutionary movement and its leaders. He came into close contact with Indian students and joined the Indian Majlis, delivering impassioned speeches from its platform. In the result, he returned to India more a dedicated patriot and less an anglicized babu.

Aurobindo was in the political field for less than ten years, 1901-10; in the first half a silent, behind-the-scenes spectator; in the latter, an activist. Initially, the Indian National Congress (q.v.) programme appealed to him, but closer contact and a sterner look at its aims and objectives convinced him that it was neither representative of nor yet designed to serve the interests of the masses. He referred to it as an élitist body; to call it the 'National Congress', he argued, was entirely inappropriate and misleading. *Inter alia*, he criticized the party policy of 'prayer, petition and protest', and assailed its timid repetition of loyalty to the Raj. He put forward his views forcefully in a series of articles, 'New Lamps for Old', published (1893-94) anonymously in *Indu Prakash*, a paper edited by K. G. Deshpande, an acquaintance from his Cambridge days.

On the lookout for more effective ways of attracting mass support against British rule, his young mind was powerfully influenced by the ideology of the revolutionary group. Consequently, during his twelve years at Baroda, besides establishing contacts with such groups in Maharashtra where they constituted a wing of the extremist or nationalist party, he also tried to channelize kindred developments in Bengal into a regular movement. His Baroda years may thus be viewed as a period of 'Indianization'. He now read extensively Sanskrit literature and philosophy and, in due course, adopted ancient Indian thought and values—as he interpreted them—for his own.

As it evolved over the years, appears to have put trust in two strategies: the line of mass movement and the path of secretly plotted violent revolution. In this framework, it would appear that during his years at

Baroda he was inching towards a viable alternative to what the moderates in the congress preached.

In 1902, under his direction a revolutionary organisation was started in Calcutta. Margaret Elizabeth Noble, better known as Sister Nivedita (1867-1911) was associated with it from its inception and contributed revolutionary literature for its library. As if preordained to lead the anti-partition agitation, he accepted the post of principal of the newly-established Bengal National College (later Jadavpur University) and, by 1906, moved to Calcutta. He began to be closely associated with the Bengali daily *Jugantar* and, assisted by B. C. Pal (q.v.), revived the *Bande Mataram*, a daily published in English.

Aurobindo's plan of action included a boycott of British trade, the substitution of national schools for government institutions, the establishment of arbitration courts in place of the existing courts of law and the creation of a volunteer force that was to serve as a nucleus for an army of open revolt. He coined the catch phrase 'No control, no co-operation' and defined the latter as 'refusal of co-operation in the industrial exploitation of our country, in education, in government, in judicial administration, in the details of official intercourse'. He expressed the view that political freedom was 'the life and breath of a nation' and that without it no people could 'fully realise its destiny'. He listed three kinds of resistance: armed revolt; aggressive resistance short of armed revolt; defensive resistance, whether passive or active. In justifying violence, he cited the *Bhagvada Gita*, comparative historical experience of many peoples as well as the 'general conscience' of humanity. It was during this period that he expounded his political philosophy and popularized theories of nationalism and passive resistance. The two newspapers with which he was associated lasted less than two years but had a powerful impact; the Government dubbed them 'seditious' and labelled Aurobindo a 'dangerous character'.

Aurobindo emphasized that nationalism does not necessarily imply complete national unity from within—it should, on the other hand, be a spiritual nationalism, involving a feeling of dedication to the motherland, as of the son to a mother. He put forth the concept of land as mother and pleaded for its emancipation from the shackles of foreign rule. In a pamphlet entitled *Bhawani Mandir*, published secretly and circulated while he was at Baroda, he advocated the establishment of a workshop of Bhawani and the institution of an order of *karamayogis* devoted to the service of the goddess. The fulfilment of the latter's destiny would help the achievement of universal spiritual unity. Through the use of religious symbols he explained nationalism and appealed to the emotions of the masses so as to bring them into the vortex of the freedom movement. The terms and concepts used in the pamphlet are taken from the *Markendya Purana*, while Bankim Chandra's *Anandmath* appears to have exercised considerable influence too. The religious and political categories are however fused.

Aurobindo dubbed colonial self-government as a 'political monstrosity'. The ideal for India, he argued, must be 'unqualified swaraj' without which it was impossible to progress. It was foolish to accept reforms from the British Government; indeed the worse the government, the better it would be for Indian nationalism: disaffection could only hasten the day of liberation.

'It is out of no hostility to the English people, no hatred, that we seek absolute autonomy', he insisted; it was the first condition for developing India's national self and realizing her destiny. The means of achieving it lay through passive resistance, elaborated into two main theories—Boycott (q.v.) and Swadeshi (q.v.). To Aurobindo revolution was not incompatible with passive resistance, for there was inherent in the latter the right to resist actively any injustice or violent coercion.

Aurobindo's prose was like heady wine to the young radicals of Bengal. He organized the Extremists, or Nationalists as they called themselves in the Bengal Congress, and promoted an alliance between them and their counterparts in Maharashtra, led by Balgangadhar Tilak (q.v.). He set out to radicalize the policies and programmes of the Congress and advocated a boycott not only of British goods but also of government-aided schools and, indeed, of the whole alien administration. He was confident that the Congress would eventually adopt an all-India boycott resolution.

Nor was Aurobindo's approach entirely negative. On the contrary, along with his theory of economic boycott, he postulated the necessity of Swadeshi; along with an educational boycott, he put forward his views on national education; along with the judicial boycott, he stressed the necessity of national arbitration courts; along with the executive boycott, he underlined the importance of national organization and, as a sanction behind the whole boycott theory, he placed the concept of a social boycott.

From July 1906, when he left Baroda for good, Aurobindo concentrated on widening the base of the revolutionary movement by encouraging the alliance between Tilak's group and the Bengal revolutionaries. His was a three-fold programme of action: first, he would help to educate the public through his writings; next, he would work with other Extremists to capture the Congress organization from the Moderates and, finally, he would secretly help people prepare for a violent insurrection.

All this added up to an attempt at transforming the Congress into a radical stronghold. The party's annual sessions in 1906 and 1907 witnessed noisy scenes as the Nationalists (or Extremists) tried to capture power in the organization. At the Surat session (1907) Aurobindo and Tilak finally provoked a split in the party. The Bengal Government's assessment of him makes interesting reading: 'He is regarded and spoken of by all as the disciples regard a great Master. He has been in the forefront of all . . .But he has kept himself, like a careful and valued general, out of sight of the enemy. We cannot get evidence against him such as would secure his conviction in a Court.'

Thereafter dubbed by the government as undesirable, his activities were closely watched. Minto (q.v.), then Viceroy, tried to persuade Whitehall to deport Aurobindo, but no fool-proof case could be brought against him. As to his writings, he had, in the opinion of his detractors, developed the 'art of safe slander' to perfection. On 25 May 1910, Minto confided in Morley, the Secretary of State, that Aurobindo was 'the most dangerous man we now have to reckon with'.

Earlier, the government had involved Aurobindo in the Maniktala bomb conspiracy case (1908-9). Imprisoned for a year, he was brilliantly defended by C. R. Das (q.v.) and, eventually, acquitted. Das prophesied that Aurobindo would emerge as 'the poet of patriotism, as the prophet of nationalism and the lover of humanity', that long after he was dead his words 'would be echoed and re-echoed, not only in India but across distant seas and lands'.

Contrary to popular belief, Aurobindo was not an anarchist; he sought to replace British rule not by anarchy but by national rule. As for his links with terrorism, 'there is now little doubt that he was not closely in touch with secret revolutionary groups throughout the country, but, in Bengal was for a considerable time their secret leader and inspirer.' Much of his time in jail was devoted to yoga, meditation and study. Soon after his release, he brought out two publications, *Karamyogi* and *Dharma*, to take up his programme, attended the Bengal provincial conference at Hooghly and privately met Surendranath Banerjea (q.v.) to work out a *rapprochement* with the Moderates. Unity however proved elusive.

In the meantime, there was a marked change in Aurobindo's political ideals. He began to advocate 'spiritual and moral regeneration' as a prelude to political advancement and warned that the government was intensifying its efforts to round up revolutionaries. He later claimed to have received divine instruction to leave Chandernagore (q.v.) in February (1910) and a month later left for Pondicherry. With his departure ends that brief yet tumultous phase of his deep and powerful influence on contemporary Indian politics.

At Pondicherry, where he was soon joined by his wife and a number of friends, Aurobindo concentrated on *Sadhana*, study and writing. Most of what he wrote was published in *Arya*, a monthly that a French couple, Paul and Mira Richard, helped start and which Aurobindo edited for seven years (1914-21). He now spoke of a world society and of the unity of mankind. Though he continued to speak and write on problems of the day, he failed to make any impact and firmly refused all attempts to stage a comeback to political life. Mira Richard, later known as the Mother, helped establish and run the proliferating ashram, while Aurobindo devoted himself to yoga, writing and the training of his disciples. He felt that he had tremendous power, could shape the working of the world by soul force and carried out what has been called the 'ritual interiorization' of the cosmic process.

Education, Aurobindo argued, must cater to Indian needs and culture. The medium of instruction should be the mother tongue and the curriculum so designed as to enable the child to develop according to its abilities. Yoga must form a part of the curriculum. He never denied that modern, scientific knowledge was essential to progress, but social reform, he declared, could be instituted only in an emancipated society. Understandably, he deprecated the obsession of the Congress with social uplift.

In 1926 Aurobindo entered into seclusion which was mantained till his death in 1950.

Aurobindo believed that man is destined to evolve a principle of force and harmony. Even for social reform he would not support any legislation or imposition from without, for, to be truly effective, reform must come from within. To transform life, body and mind, a Supreme Power, above the mind, was essential. This was the super mind. Essentially, the emphasis in his teaching was on the spiritualization of the phenomenal world and of all human activity through the emergence of a disciplined religious élite, extending widely to embrace all mankind.

His ashram which grew into a large centre after 1926 became an international community drawn from all parts of the world. Among its multi-faceted activities were the Sri Aurobindo Society, the work union and the Sri Aurobindo International Centre of Education.

Aurobindo died on 5 December 1950. A keen student of his writings has summed up his contribution to modern Indian political thought: (i) His concept of spiritual nationalism and the divinity of the motherland which imparted an esoteric significance to the movement of Indian liberation; (ii) His exposition of the ideal of complete freedom from foreign rule and his role in invigorating, inspiring and radicalising the national movement; (iii) His contribution to the theory of boycott and passive resistance as also to the use of force, if necessary, to achieve freedom; (iv) His vision of the broader role that India was destined to play in world affairs and his enlightened ideal of human unity that must ultimately transcend mere national development.

His work is all the more significant in that Aurobindo compressed it in the short period of hardly five years. His overall contribution is a strange medley, at once progressive as well as retrogressive in character. On the one hand, he bequeathed a legacy of religious sectarianism by appealing to the religious sentiments of Hindus and decrying the *Mlecchas*, which term would include the Muslims. Unwittingly perhaps, he succeeded in alienating them from the national mainstream. On the other hand, he provided a coherent revolutionary ideology and a well thought-out mass programme based on passive resistance which Gandhi (q.v.) was later to employ so successfully.

V. C. Joshi (ed.), *Sri Aurobindo: an interpretation*, Delhi, 1973; A. B. Purani, *The Life of Sri Aurobindo, A Source-book*, 3rd ed., Pondicherry, 1964; Karan Singh, *Prophet of Indian Nationalism: A study of the political thought of Sri Aurobindo Ghosh, 1893-1910*, London, 1963; Leonard A. Gordon, *The Religious Roots of Indian Nationalism: Aurobindo's Early Political Thought*, Calcutta, 1974; David L. Johnson, 'Aurobindo Ghosh and Indian Nationalism: a religious analysis', University of Iowa thesis, 1972, microfilm, *NMML*; Purushotman M. Krishna. 'Political Philosophy of Sri Aurobindo: an exposition and assessment of the integral system of a leading Indian thinker', New School for Social Research, New York, thesis, 1963, microfilm, *NMML*; Amales Tripathi, 'Sri Aurobindo, a study in messianic Nationalism', *Calcutta Historical Journal*, 4,1, July-December 1979, pp. 62–79.

Avitabile (1791–1850)

Born at Agerola, in southern Italy, Paolo di Bartolomew Avitabile served in the Neapolitan army (1807-9) and later in the imperial French army under Joseph Bonaparte. During 1820-6 he saw service in Persia but later returned to Italy. Finding no gainful employment there, he sought work with Ventura (q.v.) in India. In December 1826 he reached Lahore via Kabul with Court (q.v.) as a travelling companion, and was employed by Ranjit Singh (q.v.).

A successful but ruthless administrator, Avitabile ruled by fear and torture. Appointed Governor of Wazirabad in December 1829, thenceforth he always added a civil governorship to the command of a military brigade.

Five years later (1834) Avitabile became Governor of Peshawar. The methods he had used earlier against the Kurds while in Persia were now employed on the 'border ruffians', as he called them, of Peshawar and the

Khyber. He did indeed look upon them as no more than human vermin whose most useful purpose was to exterminate one another. One Kalandar Khan is said to have held his jagir from the Governor of Peshawar for a yearly tribute of 50 Afridi heads!

Avitabile's presence at Peshawar both before and after the First Anglo-Afghan War (q.v.) proved to be indispensable to the British, for the force furnished by the Darbar under the conditions of the Tripartite Treaty (q.v.) 'were more inclined to fight against than for' the British. In 1842, in the wake of their retreat from Kabul, he rendered the East India Company (q.v.) troops all possible assistance.

He continued serving under Ranjit Singh's successors, but, conscious that the Sikh state would not last, sought permission to leave. This was granted him in 1843. Behind the scenes he is said to have been in treasonable correspondence with Henry Lawrence (q.v.), giving the British useful information about the deployment of Sikh forces. He left for Naples in September 1843, where he was honoured; similar honours were conferred on him by King Louis Philippe of France and the John Company. He died at Agerola on 28 March 1850.

H. L. O. Garrett (ed.) C. Grey, *European Adventurers of Northern India, 1785 to 1894*, reprint, Patiala, 1970.

Abul Kalam Azad (1888–1958)

The son of Shaikh Mohammad Khairuddin Sahib, Azad was born in Mecca in 1888. His father was a mystic and a scholar of eminence. He was the second son and named Feroz Bakht—'of exalted destiny'—but was commonly called Muhiyuddin Ahmed. His father was famous as a 'Pir' or a 'Murshid' while his Arab mother, daughter of the Mufti of Medina, knew little Urdu and he therefore conversed at home in Arabic. Azad married Zulaikha Begum (d. 1944) and a son, Hussain, was born; the boy died when only 4.

He was educated mostly at home and *not* at the Al-Azhar University in Cairo as is widely believed. Later, he was admitted to the Dars-i-Nizami course in Calcutta (q.v.) to study Islamic theology and divinity. Soon after completing his studies at the young age of 16, he adopted the pen name of Abul Kalam Azad which stuck. In view of his learning and scholarship, he was acclaimed a 'Maulana' (i.e., teacher).

Azad's education was on the traditional pattern: knowledge of Persian and Arabic followed by geometry, arithemetic, algebra and Islamic theology. Convinced that literature and philosophy could flourish only in a free society, he was attracted towards the revolutionary movement in Bengal after the Partition (q.v.) of that province in 1905 and joined the activist group.

At 16, Azad undertook a tour of Egypt, Syria, Palestine and Iraq. At Cairo, he imbibed the reformist movement of Jamaluddin Afghani and Shaikh Muhammad Abduh. It was during this period that he spent some time at Al Azhar. As he recorded, his contacts with the nationalist, revolutionary groups in these countries 'confirmed my political beliefs. They expressed their surprise that Indian Mussalmans were either indifferent to

or against nationalist demands. They were of the view that Indian Mussalmans should have led the national struggle for freedom and could not
understand why [they] were camp followers of the British.'

Azad did not follow his father (d. 1909) to become a religious leader, and
took to journalism instead. Soon he was editor of *Nairang-i-Alam* and later
of his own paper *Lisan-us-Sido* (literally, 'Tongue of the Truth'). He was
soon acclaimed by well-known Urdu poets of the time, Altaf Hussain Hali
and Maulana Shibli as well as Nawab Mohsin-ul-Mulk (q.v.) as 'an old head
on young shoulders'. It is said that when Hali and Shibli met Azad who was
then 16 years old, they took him to be the son of the famous man! In 1905 he
edited *Al-Nadwah* and later (1907), the *Vakil*.

In his writings, Azad challenged the basic principles of the Aligarh Movement (q.v.), repudiated the policy of co-operation with the British and of
separation of Muslims from Hindus. In June 1912, he founded his own
weekly paper *Al-Hilal*, then rated 'a rare amalgam of rhetoric, wit, poetry,
biting sarcasm and lofty idealism'. Though deeply soaked in Islamic tradition, his outlook was that of an Indian nationalist who wanted to interpret
Islamic scriptures from a rational point of view.

The demand for *Al-Hilal* was so great that within the first three months
all the old issues had to be reprinted, 'as every new subscriber wanted the
entire set'. Within two years it reached a circulation of 26,000 copies per
week, a figure then unheard of in Urdu journalism.

Azad felt that the Aligarh tradition, though modern in its acceptance of
western education, was otherwise conservative 'and to a certain extent even
feudal'.

He espoused the cause of the Turks in the Balkan wars (1912-13). His
paper, which was radical in tone and content, attracted notice and soon its
security of Rs 2,000 was declared forfeit and a fresh bond of Rs 10,000
demanded. Finding it too harsh a blow to sustain, 'after 5 months I started a
new press called *Al-Balagh* and brought out a journal under the same name'.
Presently (1916) he was externed from Bengal and interned at Ranchi where
he was to remain until 1920.

During his internment at Ranchi (1916-20) Azad wrote *Tazkira*, an account of his ancestors, and prepared the first draft of his famous translation,
with a commentary, of the Quran, *Tarjuman-ul-Quran*. Through police
negligence, the manuscript was misplaced and work on it had to be redone.
Originally plannned in three volumes, only two were later plublished. Many
scholars have viewed it as the most important commentary on the Quran
during the last 300 years; it has since been translated into English.

Azad refused to accompany the Khilafat (q.v.) delegation that waited on
the Viceroy (March 1920), for he made no secret of the fact that he hated
begging, petitioning, waiting in deputations. In December 1921, he was
arrested by the government, prosecuted and sentenced to a year's rigorous
imprisonment. In 1923-4 he was President of a Hindu-Muslim unity conference, to help solve the communal problem. In 1929 a Nationalist Muslim
Party (q.v.) was formed within the Congress and Azad was chosen its
President at the first session held at Allahabad. He condemned Muslim
separatism, viewed partition as a sin and stoutly disputed the All-India
Muslim League (q.v.) claim to represent the Muslims. Jinnah (q.v.), in
return, was to call him 'a Congress show-boy'.

Perhaps Azad's most conspicuous talent was his ability to effect a viable compromise between conflicting and contradictory views. It was because of this gift that he was elected president of the Indian National Congress (q.v.) when only 35, the youngest to hold that office. In 1940 he was elected a second time and continued to hold that position unil June 1946.

As Congress chief, he conducted negotiations with Cripps (q.v.) in 1942; with Wavell (q.v.) at the Simla Conference (q.v.). In January 1947 he became Member in-charge of Education in the Viceroy's Executive Council and retained the portfolio after the country became independent. After independence and until his death on 22 February 1958 Azad was Education Minister in Nehru's Cabinet. In this capacity, he was responsible for the appointment of the University Education Commission in 1948, the Secondary Education Commission in 1952 and the establishment of a large number of national laboratories for scientific research. He was also associated with the setting up of the Kharagpur Institute of Higher Technology, the University Grants Commission, the three National *Akademis* and the Indian Council for Cultural Relations. Under his fostering care, the Departments of Archaeology, Anthropology and Archives were further developed and strengthened. He opposed those who wanted to oust the English language.

In politics, as in other walks of life, Azad's was essentially a voice of reason, moderation and sanity. He was shy of the crowd and not of it. A percipient student of Muslim politics has coined the phrase 'romantic' for that period of Azad's life spanning the publication of *Al-Hilal* to the end of the Khilafat movement. He is rated one of the few non-Wahabi religious scholars who remained absolutely uninfluenced by Muslim *tasawuf* or mysticism; he only approved of them when they challenged the government or public opinion.

It has been suggested that Azad, 'did not possess all the qualities of a leader in the situation which faced him'. But then no one did. His critics maintain that a mass movement among Muslims 'is a very recent phenomenon and in the whole history of Muslim India no one thinker or scholar has been more intensely hated by his co-religionists' than the Maulana during the ten years preceding the country's partition. Jinnah took every opportunity of insulting him; the Muslim press kept on cursing him; he was abused from every communal platform.

Jinnah, a lay person by descent, training and temperament, chose to espouse the cause of religious communalism and, despite the contradictions between his personality and career, was audacious enough to proclaim his ideal, loud and clear. On the other hand, Azad, who was a religious person by education and social classification, decided upon secularism as his goal but was not courageous enough to call a spade a spade.

It has been held by Azad's detractors that while the Maulana may have distinguished himself as the chancellor of an institution for theological research on Islamic studies, like Al-Azhar, as Minister for Education, he was completely out of his depth. More, he perpetuated a system that had no relevance to national needs.

Azad has noted in one of his books that at the outset of his political career, the revolutionaries in Bengal saw the Muslims play the British game and viewed them as 'an obstacle to the attainment of freedom'. Later, he openly avowed that, to him, non-violence was a matter of policy, not of creed. In this he had strong differences with Gandhi (q.v.) and, as a result, after 1930 he did not waver when many others did.

In his writings (e.g., *India Wins Freedom*) there is not even a passing reference to 'the invective, the abuse and the gross insults heaped upon him by his Muslim opponents'. Mujeeb maintains that 'Particularly in the years after independence he stood out as one who could be relied upon for absolute impartiality of judgement and for an unimpeachable integrity. He was too aloof to concern himself with persons, too intellectual to relish political small talk, too proud to think in terms of alliance, affiliation or opposition. He was a statesman who would not accept the normal functions of a politician, and he was engrossed in principles that he could not become an efficient administrator. He had to be taken for what he was, with no credentials other than his personality.'

Azad's political ideas were the expression of his innermost belief. The Maulana's writings, except for *India Wins Freedom* and two collections of letters, had a deeply religious colour and tone. Indeed, he seemed always to be talking of the Quran. He considered it the real basis of a faith, and it inspired all his thinking.

During his internment in the Ahmadnagar fort (1942-5) Azad wrote *Ghubar-i-Khatir*, rated as a compendium of the 'most exquisite personal eassays' in Urdu or any other language. As Minister for Education in independent India he was mainly responsible for sponsoring a *History of Philosophy: Eastern and Western*, later published (1952-3) in two volumes.

Azad the rebel abhorred the adoration of shrines. The greatest deterrent to man's mental progress, he declared, were his traditional beliefs. He himself was unconventional and firmly believed in carving out his own course, whether in politics or in social customs and practices.

Mujeeb has maintained that Azad was as detached and uninvolved as a fakir. He dressed well, ate good food, knew how to live with taste, but he never bothered to run after wealth. Although not rich, Azad had richness of life; he loved his friends and relatives, helped and appreciated artists and men of letters and was a person of true refinement.

Abul Kalam Azad, *India Wins Freedom: an autobiographical narrative*, New Delhi, 1959; Arsh Malsiani, *Abul Kalam Azad*, Builders of Modern India, New Delhi, 1976; Mahadev Desai, *Maulana Abul Kalam Azad*, London, 1941; M. Mujeeb, *The Indian Muslims*, London, 1967; Mushirul Haq, *Muslim Politics in Modern India, 1857-1947*, Meerut, 1970; Moin Shakir, *Khilafat to Partition: A survey of major political trends among Indian Muslims during 1919-1947*, New Delhi, 1970; *DNB 1951-60*, pp. 48-9 (Humayun Kabir); Sen, *DNB*, I, pp. 92-5 (Mushirul Haq).

Azad Hind Fauj (1944–5)

The Azad Hind Fauj, also called the Indian National Army or INA for short, aimed to liberate India from British rule. Its principal battles were fought in Burma and the north-east frontier in Assam during 1944-5. Subhas Chandra Bose (q.v.) was its *Neta* or leader.

Bose had left Germany early in 1943 and, after a perilous three-four month voyage in a submarine, arrived in Singapore on 2 July 1943. Two days later he took over from Rashbehari Bose as leader of the Indian independence movement in East Asia, reorganized the Fauj and on 25 August became its first Supreme Commander. On 21 October 1943 he proclaimed the 'Provisional Government of Azad Hind'.

The Andaman and Nicobar islands were occupied by the Japanese in November 1943 and renamed Shaheed and Swaraj islands respectively. The headquarters of the INA were shifted to Rangoon in January 1944. Later, marching across Burma with the war cry '*Chalo Dilli*', they stood on Indian soil on 13 March 1944. In May (1944), Kohima and Imphal were taken with deafening cries of 'Jai Hind' and 'Netaji Zindabad'.

Soon however, the INA experienced severe reverses largely because the Japanese forces were under unrelenting strain in Burma and elsewhere in South-East Asia. The Fauj meanwhile was badly depleted by casualties through war, disease, desertions and lack of assistance from the Japanese command. They surrendered—demoralized, starving and in rags.

Bose's efforts to infuse his troops with new vigour—he visited Tokyo in October 1944 and toured South-East Asian countries to raise funds—proved singularly unavailing. There were large-scale desertions in the face of the sweeping British victories in Burma; by May 1945 the INA had been completely shattered and Bose himself was reportedly killed in an air crash over Taipeh on 18 August 1945.

Before the Azad Hind Fauj took shape, a conference of 16 representatives of Indian organizations in territories occupied by the Japanese in South-East Asia was held in Tokyo, 28-30 March 1942. The conference resolved that the time was opportune to start a liberation movement among Indians in East Asia. To attain the 'Independence of India complete and free from domination', it was decided that military action under Indian command should be taken against the British. The conference ruled that 'after the liberation of India', representatives of the Indian people would frame the 'future' constitution for their country.

At the Tokyo conference, Raja Mahendra Pratap (d. 1979), the legendary hero of India's war for freedom, and Rashbehari Bose held numerous consultations with the Japanese and thereafter resolved to convene a meeting of Indian representatives from all parts of Asia, in Bangkok, on 15 June. A total of 120 delegates, half from the army and half civilians, were to attend. Among them were Indian representatives from Japan, Manchukuo, Hong Kong, Shanghai, the Philippines, Java, Thailand, Malaya and Burma. Indian prisoners of war who had volunteered to fight for the freedom of India were represented by 60 delegates headed by Captain Mohan Singh. Others present included Major-General A. C. Chatterjee, Cols. N. S. Gill, Habib-ul-Rahman, Ghulam Qadir Gilani, Burhanuddin and Prakash Ram Sarup. Rashbehari Bose was unanimously elected president.

The Bangkok conference was in session on 16-22 June. 35 resolutions adopted by it are said to have been forwarded to the Japanese authorities for confirmation on its final day. No formal communication was received but a letter dated 10 July addressed to Rashbehari Bose asked him to keep the resolutions of the conference secret as well as the Japanese reply.

Among the decisions of the conference the following deserves notice, 'Resolved that the Indian Independence League shall immediately proceed to raise an Army called the Indian National Army from among the Indian soldiers (combatants and non-combatants) and such civilians as may hereafter be recruited for military service in the cause of Indian Independence.'

The headquarters of the organisation were established on Wireless Road, Bangkok and five members of its Council of Action named. The INA was born in September 1942; by December, its strength had risen to 17,000.

A word on the prisoners of war joining the INA.

In Malaya, out of 85,000 taken prisoner, 60,000 were Indians. The Japanese who hardly ever surrendered—they fought to the last man—despised prisoners of war and treated them badly. Determined to make use of the Indians, they separated them from their British officers, kept information from them and offered them every inducement to co-operate. The men were told that the war was over and the British were defeated; they were harangued by their educated fellow countrymen about the new Asia that was growing up under Japanese leadership; they were offered the choice of joining a new Indian army with Japanese backing or of harsh and degrading treatment, to which there seemed no prospect of any end. Some of the Indian officers were starved, tortured and beaten; Captain P. K. Dhargalkar of the 3rd Cavalry is an instance in point. For 88 days he was confined in a cage less than 5'-6" long and about the same in width, in which there were, sometimes, as many as four people!

The captain did not surrender—he later tendered evidence against the INA—and after 1947 rose to the rank of Lt. General.

But Dhargalkar and his ilk were an exception. Lesser mortals surrendered in their thousands to swell the ranks of the Azad Hind Fauj.

Presently (November 1942–January 1943) the Independence League was up against a critical situation as the result of a clash between the Burmese Territorial Committee of the League and the Japanese military authorities. Mohan Singh suspected the latter of harbouring ulterior motives. This precipitated a crisis as the League's Council of Action quit in a body. Some members were arrested but Rashbehari Bose continued to be at the top. The crisis dealt a severe blow to the cause of the League.

A conference of the League and its territorial committees was held in April 1943 at Singapore; another on 4 July 1943. Bose who had arrived two days earlier was invited to assume presidentship of the League. On 5 July he took the salute at an impressive parade of the INA at the maidan opposite the Municipal office at Shohan, in Singapore. Later that day, he was sworn in as the new head of the organisation.

Bose's 'special order of the day on the occasion of taking over direct command of the Army' was dated 25 August 1943 wherein he signed as 'Supreme Commander'. He said *inter alia*: 'Our work has already begun. With the slogan 'Onward to Delhi' on our lips, let us continue to labour and fight till our National Flag flies over the Viceroy's House in New Delhi and the Azad Hind Fauj holds its victory parade inside the ancient Red Fortress of India's metropolis.'

The INA, albeit a complete military disaster, served to inspire the Indian national movement with its saga of bravery and fortitude. Bose's 'Provisional Government' which was accorded recognition by the Axis Powers and their allies served as the harbinger of a new liberated India.

Mohan Singh, *Soldier's Contribution to Indian Independence*, New Delhi, 1974;

Durlab Singh (ed.), *Formation and Growth of the Indian National Army*, Lahore, 1946; P. B. Roy. *The Glory that is INA*, Calcutta, 1946; Hugh Toye, *Subhash Chandra Bose: The Springing Tiger: A study of a revolutionary*, London, 1959; Tara Chand, *History of the Freedom Movement in India*, New Delhi, 1961–72, 4 vols, IV, pp. 414–23.

Bahadur Shah I (r. 1707–12)

Surnamed Qutb-ud-din Shah Alam, and formerly Prince Muazzam, Bahadur Shah was the second son of the last great Mughal emperor, Aurangzeb (r. 1658–1707). On hearing of his father's death, he left Kabul post haste, crowned himself at Pul-i-Shah Daullah and assumed the title of Shah Alam Bahadur Shah. He then headed towards Delhi to wrest authority from his younger brother, Prince Azam. His second son, Azim-ush-Shan, had, in the meantime, seized Agra for his father's cause. At the hotly-contested battle of Jajau, near Samugarh, in June 1707, Azam lost his life along with his two grown-up sons; in the aftermath, Muazzam assumed regal authority.

The new emperor's two major problems in the north were the Rajputs and the Sikhs under Guru Gobind Singh, their tenth and last Guru. In so far as the emperor was up against a major revolt from his younger brother Kam Bakhash in the Deccan, the Rajput rulers banded themselves together into a confederacy, marched towards Agra and bore down on Sambhar, the garrison town of the Mughals. Asad Khan and the Mughal commanders retaliated in full force, Rajput ranks were broken and the Kachhwaha chief, Jai Singh of Amber, opened negotiations for peace. In victory, the emperor was large-hearted and restored Jai Singh and his ally Ajit Singh their capitals as well as homelands.

Guru Gobind Singh was received by the emperor at Agra with great honour and successfully persuaded to accompany the imperial army to the Deccan. At Nander, on the Godavari, the Guru parted company with the emperor; it was here, in November 1708, that he was murdered. The Guru's political heir, Banda Bahadur (q.v.), had been charged with the task of repairing to the Panjab and, in consultation with his five councillors, 'punish' the enemies of the Khalsa. Fired with a new zeal, he soon established himself at Sadaura; his followers seized Sirhind and dared advance as far as the suburbs of Lahore.

Imperial retaliation was sharp and swift. Banda and his men were driven out of Thanesar, ousted from Sirhind, expelled from Lahore and closely besieged at their new stronghold, Lohgarh. The emperor's sudden death at this juncture, however, was a god-send and, for a time, the Sikhs succeeded in harassing the Mughal hosts and recovering a part of their lost domain.

Despite his woefully short reign, Bahadur Shah initiated measures to conciliate the Marathas. It was, however, much too much for him to accept their principal claim for *Chauth* and *Sardeshmukhi* for the six subhas of the Deccan. In the result, the stalemate persisted as did Maratha plundering raids on imperial domain.

After a brief reign of less than five years, Bahadur Shah died in February 1712 at Lahore, while engaged in the task of improving and making alterations to the Shalimar gardens, outside the city. He was later buried at Delhi. He left behind four sons, three of whom were killed in the bloody war of succession that followed; the sole survivor, Jahandar Shah, ascended the throne.

Bahadur Shah's reign witnessed a sharp deterioration in the financial situation' and a further accentuation of the crisis of the jagirdari system. For this a primary responsibility rested with the emperor who had granted jagirs recklessly and given promotions to all and sundry. In the result, the imperial treasury was well-nigh empty, with the salaries of some army units falling into sizeable—in some cases 6 years'—arrears. Attempts made by his wazir, Munim Khan, to check the rot were not particularly successful, and chroniclers cited with approval the gibe of the 'witty, sarcastic people [who] found the rule of his [emperor's] accession in the words Shah-i-bi-Khabr'.

In the domain of general policy, a 'cautious if hesitating' departure from Aurangzeb is evident in the sphere of religious policy and in the emperor's dealings with his Hindu subjects. Thus, while discrimination against their employment as news-reporters in the provinces and the use of palkis and Arabi and Iraqi horses continued, the hated poll-tax or *jizyah* 'while not formally abolished, seems to have fallen gradually into disuse'. More, Aurangzeb's 'rigid approach' to the Rajput and Maratha problems was gradually modified'. In sum, the emperor 'was feeling his way towards a more liberal and acceptable policy . . . [none the less] he failed to reap any definite political advantages from his policy of cautious compromise, and bequeathed to his successors a more difficult situation than the one he had inherited.'

With Bahadur Shah's death disappeared the last semblance of Mughal pomp and pageantry. All in all, he was 'a mild and generous man and although possessed of great dignity of behaviour . . . proved to be a weak ruler. His policy was to allow matters to drift and to postpone decision. He was fond of compromise even in important political and administrative matters.'

Satish Chandra, *Parties and Politics at the Mughal Court, 1707–1740,* Aligarh, 1959, pp. 22–60; A. L. Srivastava, *The Mughul Empire (1526–1803 A.D.),* 3rd ed., Delhi, 1959, pp. 439–42; Richard Burn (ed.), *CHI,* IV. pp. 319–25; *Beale,* p. 95.

Bahadur Shah II (1775–1862)

Abu Zafar, the last Mughal emperor, was the eldest son of Akbar Shah II (q.v.) and his Rajput wife Lal Bai, and ascended the throne in 1837, having assumed the title of Abul Muzaffar Sirajuddin Muhammad Bahadur Shah. Earlier, he had survived, through British support, two attempts on his life, besides a sustained effort to replace him as heir apparent by his father's favourite son Jahangir.

Educated in the traditional style, he was well-versed in Urdu and Arabic, besides being a reputed Persian scholar and a fine calligraphist. He was deeply learned in Sufi philosophy. Among his tutors were the famous poets Ibrahim Zauq and Asad Ullah Khan Ghalib, under whose tutelage his poetic talent blossomed. Much of his verse is of indifferent quality but his ghazals, composed mainly during his exile (1858–62), have earned him literary fame. He wrote under the pen-name of 'Zafar'.

Not unlike his predecessors, Bahadur Shah could not easily reconcile himself to the thought that his was only a titular sovereignty. He tried to assert his authority in seemingly vain attempts to have his monthly stipend of Rs 100,000 enhanced, and later to have Jawan Bakht, a younger son by his favourite queen Zeenat Mahal, recognized as heir apparent.

Bahadur Shah was living in shabby despondency when the Rebellion of 1857 (q.v.) broke out at Meerut. On 11 May the soldiers reached Delhi and with great enthusiasm proclaimed Bahadur Shah Emperor. No wonder, that at 82, frail of body, senile and virtually penniless, the 1857 revolt found him 'bewildered'. He was however candid enough to tell the 'rebels': 'I have neither troops, magazines nor treasury. I am not in a condition to join any one.' Reviving old Mughal glory was a distant daydream, but there were other compulsions of the situation: 'For distraught by his position and offended by the familiarity of the soldiers, he had neither means of resistance nor possibility of escape ... He had not very much to lose and possibly something very great to gain. He bowed to destiny and the force of circumstances.'

The initial outburst of patriotic zeal, however, soon spent itself and presently well-nigh chaotic conditions prevailed in the city as no effective leadership or plan of action emerged. Prince Mirza Moghul was appointed Commander-in-Chief of the forces and Jawan Bakht as Wazir. The Emperor personally undertook to organize the defences of the city, but was without any resources. Money was extorted from bankers and businessmen alike. Reports of soldiers ravaging the countryside and disrupting normal life in the city poured in continually, while the civilian population were terrorized into submission. Unfortunately, shortage of supplies was as chronic as lack of funds.

In the meantime, the British relief forces were converging on the imperial capital, while Mughal levies, such as they were, failed to hold them back. Though fighting valiantly, in the absence of any concerted plan of action they were defeated at Hindon, Badli-ki-sarai and finally on the ridge outside Delhi.

Unfortunately for him, Bahadur Shah was not fit to serve even as a symbol. He was so weak that he could not control either the soldiers or the nobility. In spite of his personal failings, no one thought of an alternative to him; to the very end, the soldiers and the people looked to him as the head of state. There was, in fact, unanimous agreement that he alone had the right to become the Emperor of India. Thus Nana Saheb's (q.v.) coins were struck in the name of the Emperor and for that matter, all the coins were issued in Bahadur Shah's name.

As the Mughal forces continued to fare badly and conditions in the city worsened, Bahadur Shah, his wife Zeenat Mahal and advisers Ahsanullah Khan and Mahbub Ali tried to establish some rapport with the British. Their overtures, however, were spurned. The Emperor's pronouncedly weak condition failed to cope with the exertions of leading a revolt and, in the final count, he was prepared to relinquish all that he had. This was of no avail either.

The siege of Delhi lasted from June through September 1857. As its fall seemed imminent, Bahadur Shah was urged by Subahdar Bakht Khan, who had been the chief commander of the Indian forces, to accompany his army to Oudh (q.v.). The Mughal ruler rejected this offer, repairing instead to Humayun's tomb, just outside the city's gates. There on 21 September, he surrendered to Lt W.S.R. Hodson, of 'Hodson's Horse', who had earlier defeated the 'rebels' at Rohtak. The Emperor's sons Mirza Moghul and Mirza Khawaja Sultan and a grandson, Mirza Abu Bakr, who were known to have taken a prominent part in the rebellion, were captured the following day and shot.

Until his trial began on 27 January 1858, Bahadur Shah was huddled into a tiny, dimly-lit room of the palace, within the city's Red Fort. Tried by a military commission instructed by John Lawrence (q.v.), he was accused of aiding and abetting the rebellion of Bakht Khan and Mirza Moghul and of declaring himself sovereign of India while still a pensioned subject of the British government. Additionally, he was saddled with the responsibility for the death, on 16 May 1857, of 49 Europeans. The Emperor's defence was weakly conducted and failed to put forth the juristic argument that he was heir to subsisting imperial (Mughal) rights; that, in fact, the boot was on the other leg—it was the John Company (q.v.) that had rebelled against him!

To be fair, Bahadur Shah was a victim of *force majeure* and acted through-out under duress. The evidence for conspiracy prior to the outbreak of the rebellion is slender; his collusion in the murders of 16 May is open to question; his distrust and distaste for the rebel army was well-known, indeed pronounced, and therefore the question of his waging a war against the British as a free agent does not bear serious scrutiny.

In the trial that lasted till 9 March 1858 Bahadur Shah was found guilty on all counts and sentenced to life imprisonment. It has been said that this was more a court of inquiry than a judicial tribunal, that it was a 'travesty of justice' and in the nature of a reprisal. Exiled to Rangoon with his wife Zeenat Mahal, he died four years later (7 November 1862).

Bahadur Shah's role in the uprising has been grossly exaggerated. Competent observers believe that he was 'too weak, too ignorant, too inexperienced in the art of warfare and too resourceless' to have played any active part; that 'neither a hero, nor a villain', he was a simple soul catapulated into the limelight by events over which he had little if any control.

T. G. P. Spear, *Twilight of the Mughals*, Cambridge, 1951; G.D. Khosla, *The Last Mughal*, Delhi, 1969; *Beale*, p. 95.

Balaji Baji Rao (1720–61)

Also known as Nana Sahib or Bala Rao Pandit Pradhan, Balaji succeeded his father, Baji Rao I, to the Peshwaship in June 1740. Nine years later, after the death of Shivaji's grandson, Shahu (q.v.), he skilfully outmanoeuvred the rival factions, put Raja Ram in confinement and officially assumed control of the Maratha state. He was not a soldier by profession or inclination, but was fortunate in having capable generals who successfully executed his military policies.

After subjugating Bundelkhand and being formally invested as Deputy Governor of Malwa by the Mughal Emperor, Balaji concentrated his attention on exacting tribute from the Hindu and Muslim states of the south—

Mysore, Bedmur, Shira, Savanur, etc. About the same time, Raghuji Bhonsle revived Maratha claims for *chauth* in Bihar and Bengal, while Jayappa Sindhia and Malhar Rao Holkar, confining themselves to the north, claimed *chauth* and interfered actively in the internal affairs of various Rajput states.

Safdar Jang, wazir at the Mughal court in Delhi, had called for Maratha help twice, in 1750 against the Pathans and two years later against Ahmed Shah Abdali (q.v.). In return, he had promised Rs 50 lakhs and the governorship of Agra and Ajmer to the Peshwa. Though the promise was not fulfilled, it whetted the Maratha appetite and ambition to extend their empire northwards. The Peshwa took advantage of Imad-ul-Mulk's support (the Marathas had helped him to power in 1754) to send an army under his brother Raghunath Rao (q.v.) a second time to gain their objective. The latter, after subjugating the Doab, proceeded to the Panjab where he defeated its Afghan Governor and established control at Lahore (1757). A year later, Dattaji Sindhia extended Maratha sway right up to Attock, replacing the Muslim governor of the province by Sahaji Sindhia and Tukoji Holkar.

Notwithstanding these impressive, albeit superficial, military successes, Baji Rao was not a far-sighted statesman; in the result, he ignored many important developments which were later to prove fatal to the Maratha cause. Thus, his critics point out, he lost sight of the ideal of *Hindu-pad-padshahi* and, instead of consolidating his power over the conquered territories through a sound system of administration, let organized plunder continue, a fact that helped in alienating both Hindu and Muslim rulers. Additionally, Maratha preoccupations with the south came in the way of his taking a deeper interest in the activities of his generals who quarrelled among themselves, alienated the Rajputs and the Jats by their high-handed behaviour and severely antagonised the Afghan and other Muslim chiefs by their continuous interference in the affairs of the Mughal court. He let his brother Raghunath Rao, an incompetent lad, command expeditions to the north which, besides incurring heavy expenditure, failed to consolidate the gains which the Peshwa had achieved earlier. Having incurred the wrath of the Abdali, he left an insufficient and unprepared Maratha force to contend with the hardy Afghans.

In 1759 Ahmed Shah Abdali recaptured the Panjab and marched to Delhi. Balaji dispatched a large force under Sadashiv Rao Bhau, who had just returned triumphant after defeating the Nizam's levies at Udgir. At the Third Battle of Panipat (q.v.) in January 1761 the Marathas suffered severe reverses, losing the cream of their soldiery on the battlefield. Unable to withstand the shock, the Peshwa died six months later (June 1761) at Poona.

After Shahu's death, the Peshwa had moved Maratha administration from Satara to Poona, thereby incurring the charge of usurpation against his master, the Chhatrapati. In the affairs of his own people, he could not reconcile the differences between Holkar and Sindhia and allowed them a free hand against the Rajputs who thereby became estranged. Nor was he able to rectify the mismanagement of Raghunath Rao. To crush Tulaji Angria, the naval sardar, he called in the help of the British who, in retrospect, were to prove too strong for him and the Maratha state. Towards the end, he lost control of affairs and died in a demented state, deeply mourning the deaths of Vishwas Rao, his son, and Bhausaheb, his brother, both worsted by the Abdali at Panipat.

A man of refined taste, Balaji was fond of leading a luxurious life and enjoyed splendour and the fine arts. In the bargain, the Maratha camp lost its original vitality and simplicity and fashioned itself after the enervating splendour of the imperial Mughal court. The public debt multiplied; at his death, it amounted to Rs 50 lakhs.

The Peshwa was nevertheless an expert in accounts and penmanship and attempted to exercise strict control over receipts and expenditure. Public servants were trained in a special institution of the secretariat called the *Phad*, where Nana Phadnis (q.v.) too received his training.

A contemporary, Sir Richard Temple, noted of the Peshwa: 'He allowed Maratha rule to continue to what it had been from the first, more an organization of plunder than a system of administration. Personally he was unscrupulous in this respect, morally inferior to his father and grandfather.'

Grant Duff is of the view that Balaji was a man of considerable political sagacity, polished manners and great address.

Denis Kincaid noted that the Peshwa spent vast sums in attracting to Poona learned scholars, devout Brahmins and famous poets. He encouraged trade, built fountains, improved roads and created fresh *peths* or quarters in the town.

G. S. Sardesai, A *New History of the Marathas*, 2nd impression, Bombay, 1958, 3 vols, II.

Baji Rao II (1775–1851)

Baji Rao II, the last Peshwa to occupy the *masnad* at Poona, was the eldest son of Raghunath Rao (q.v.). Born at Dhar on 10 January 1775, he was brought up and privately tutored at Kopargaon and later Anandwalli, near Nasik. On moving to Shivner he developed a close intimacy with his cousin, the Peshwa Sawai Madhav Rao; it is believed that the attempt by Nana Phadnis (q.v.) to obstruct this intimacy led the Peshwa to suicide (27 October 1795). As he left no issue and Baji Rao was the next of kin, he hoped to become the Peshwa. This outcome was, however, prevented by Nana Phadnis, with the result that his younger brother, Chimnaji Appa, was placed on the *masnad*.

Aided by Daulat Rao Sindhia (q.v.), who was promised over Rs 100,000 in reward, Baji Rao's authority was successfully established by December 1796. After a brief interval, Nana Phadnis was restored to the Prime Ministership but, to start with, it was Daulat Rao Sindhia, with a powerful military machine to back him, who was the real power behind the new Peshwa's throne.

Baji Rao's reign was marked by growing internal dissensions and mutual bickerings among the Maratha chiefs. *Inter alia*, they carried on depredations in each other's territories thereby laying waste the countryside. While the Peshwa busied himself in putting down dissident chieftains and the Rajas of Kolhapur and Satara, in foreign policy he vacillated between friendship with the English and the Nizam on the one hand and with Tipu Sultan (q.v.) on the other.

Poona had made an alliance with the John Company (q.v.) and the Nizam in 1790, but at the same time entertained vakils from the Mysore ruler. Baji Rao's principal adviser, Daulat Rao Sindhia, alienated Yaswant Rao Holkar (q.v.) by murdering Madhav Rao and kidnapping his son Khande Rao after Tukoji's death. Later the Peshwa mercilessly killed Yaswant Rao's brother Vithoji Holkar, a development that precipitated a major crisis. Yaswant Rao marched towards Poona at the head of a formidable force, simultaneously sending messages that he meant only to chastise Daulat Rao and had nothing against the Peshwa as such. Baji Rao's frantic appeals to his chiefs in the north brought some help but his forces were defeated at Hadaspur (25 October 1805).

In the wake of this debacle the Peshwa fled to Bassein to solicit British aid. The latter, long awaiting an opportunity to control affairs in the Maratha state, made Baji Rao sign the subsidiary Treaty of Bassein (q.v.). As a result, the Peshwa was restored to the gaddi by British arms. The Maratha chiefs who had opposed this overt interference and disapproved of the subsidiary alliance, were now brought to book in what came to be known as the Second Anglo-Maratha War (q.v.). Ostensibly on the side of the John Company whose cause he espoused, Baji Rao secretly encouraged his chieftains to resist its onslaughts but, after their defeat, resigned himself to British tutelage.

The last Peshwa was neither a good administrator nor an accomplished warrior. Constant British interference in the management of his affairs with the chiefs and in the administration annoyed him and friction increased as the years rolled by. By 1810, he began to make plans to rally his feudatory chiefs in a combined effort to oust the Company.

In 1816, Ganga Dhar Shastri, an emissary from Baroda's Gaekwad to the Peshwa at Poona, was murdered. It was a foul, dastardly crime for which Trimbakji Danglia, the Peshwa's favourite minister, was widely believed to be responsible. Baji Rao was forced to deliver him to the British who imprisoned him. Later Trimbakji managed to escape, while the Peshwa declined all knowledge of his whereabouts.

Baji Rao now augmented his armed forces. The British, suspicious of his true intent and in order to avert a military confrontation, forced him to sign the Treaty of Poona (q.v.). Mountstuart Elphinstone (q.v.), stationed at the Peshwa's court, also made preparations as he found Maratha troops gathering near the capital. On 5 November 1817 his Residency was burnt down by Baji Rao's irate soldiers, a development that heralded the start of the Third Anglo-Maratha War (q.v.). After his defeat at Kirkee later the same day, the Peshwa fled from pillar to post while trying to rally Sindhia, Holkar and Bhonsle to his forlorn cause. The latter two responded but, in the absence of a joint plan, were each singly defeated.

Sardesai maintains that with the fall of Poona the result of the war became 'a foregone conclusion', that all that remained was 'to pursue the fugitive Peshwa and run him to ground', that 'even in flight (November 1817–May 1818) he did not fail to exhibit his inborn indecision and cowardice'.

Subsequently, the Peshwa's forces were worsted at Kopargaon and Asti and, by May 1818, Baji Rao, deserted by a large number of troops, was ready to surrender. Malcolm (q.v.) dictated terms by which the Peshwa gave up in perpetuity for himself and his successors all 'right, title and claim' to sovereign authority over the Maratha confederacy. He was escorted to

Bithur, near Kanpur, which was to be his permanent place of residence, on a pension of Rs 8 lakhs annually. Although he had a large retinue of wives, no son survived Baji Rao. In 1827, he adopted Dhondo Panth, alias Nana Saheb (q.v.) and, subsequently, three more children—Dada Sahib, Bala Sahib and a daughter, Matiabai. The British, however, were circumspect and kept a close watch on his activities through their Commissioner stationed at Bithur. A spate of rumours were always linked with his person, of intrigues and plots to restore him to the *masnad*. A private firm even cheated him of a sizeable sum of money on the promise of helping him in his lost cause.

Contemporary Maratha accounts describe Baji Rao as handsome of person, a good speaker and intensely religious. Not without accomplishments in private life, his character was marked by an utter want of morality. In public life, even if his many faults are borne in mind, one cannot but feel that he was singularly unfortunate. In his early years he was ill-served by those around him; later, he was surrounded by a politically vicious atmosphere.

It would be unfair to hold Baji Rao solely responsible for the ruin of the great Maratha empire. Its decline had set in before his time and it did not lie in him to arrest the decay. To be sure, after the treaty of Bassein, Baji Rao was like moving in a blind alley from which there seemed to be no escape. In the aftermath of this suicidal compact, British power and prestige took deep roots in the country and flourished; by 1818, when he sought to recover his authority, he confronted a superior enemy in a battle that had already been lost.

At Bithur, Sardesai has suggested, Baji Rao spent his life 'in religious pursuits without apparent regret or compunction' at the loss of his power and position, or of the independence of the Maratha state. Gupta has expressed the view that even as a conspirator Baji Rao lacked initiative. In his 'younger days he had hardly proved to be a leader of men and his life in confinement was not likely to bring about any change in his character. The last 35 years he passed in a backwater, cut off from the political issues of his time.'

It may be noted that when Baji Rao first began his life in exile the John Company had become the *dominant power* in India, and when he died it was *the only power* that had survived.

Pratul Chandra Gupta, *Baji Rao II and the East India Company, 1796-1818*, 2nd ed., New Delhi, 1964; and *The Last Peshwa and the English Commissioners, 1818-1851*, Calcutta, 1944; G. S. Sardesai, *New History of the Marathas*, III.

Balaji Vishwanath (d. 1720)

A Brahmin *kulkarni*, and hereditary *deshmukh* of Shriwaradhan in the Konkan, Balaji Vishwanath's original name was Bhairo Pant Pingle. From the outset he had been a steadfast supporter of Raja Shahu (q.v.); the latter after gaining authority, appointed him his Peshwa (Prime Minister) in November 1713. Earlier, the family had left the Konkan and migrated to Maratha country, allegedly because of troubles with the Sidi rulers of Janjira. Bhairo Pant's native cleverness, his experience as a revenue officer and pleasant manners brought him immediate employment and secured his advancement. He had been *subahdar* of Poona division since 1696 and of Daulatabad division from 1704 onwards, both tension-ridden areas with parallel Mughal-Maratha governance. In as much as he had worked success- fully as *subahdar*, administrator and revenue collector in Poona and Au- rangabad districts in Raja Ram's difficult times, he doubtless was *au fait* with the currents and cross-currents of Mughal-Maratha politics as well as leading personalities in both camps.

Since Shahu's return to the Deccan, Balaji had faithfully followed his fortunes and in furthering them shown great organizing capacity and skill as a mediator. It was his advocacy that had brought to Shahu's cause the veteran leader Dhanaji Jadhav in 1707 and secured the Maratha chief his ancestral throne. By his alacrity, watchfulness and tact, four years later he had foiled Chandrasen's conspiracy and thereby helped defeat Shahu's rivals. By worsting Krishna Rao Khatavkar in battle, he had taught a stern lesson to the rebels. No wonder, Shahu was convinced that Balaji was the one man who could safeguard his interests and bring order out of chaos. Later, the Peshwa was able to conciliate Kanhoji Angria, the great naval commander who had initially inclined towards Tara Bai (q.v.), the widow of Raja Ram.

In his handling of the Nizam-ul-Mulk (q.v.), the Peshwa was equally successful. A number of indecisive actions were fought (1712–14) as a result of which the Nizam must have come to the conclusion that a settlement with the Marathas subserved his own interests. In the end, he withdrew his troops from Poona district and repaired to Hyderabad.

The high water-mark of Balaji's achievement was his treaty with Husain Ali, one of the Sayyid brothers (q.v.), who had, in 1715, been transferred to the Deccan in place of Nizam-ul-Mulk. A pragmatist, Husain Ali soon concluded that a *modus vivendi* had to be worked out with Raja Shahu and his Peshwa. With great patience he wrought a settlement granting the Maratha ruler the rights of *chauth* and *sardeshmukhi* in the 6 provinces of Aurangabad, Berar, Khandesh, Bidar, Golconda and Bijapur. In return, the Marathas were to maintain 15,000 troops with the Mughal *subahdar* to aid the emperor, pay him 10% of the annual income from *sardeshmukhi*, swear loyalty to the imperial cause and, in lieu of the *swaraj* for old territory, pay an annual tribute of Rs 10 lakhs.

Convinced that the agreement was tantamount to a complete abdication of his authority, the Mughal emperor, Farrukh Siyar (q.v.), refused to ratify it. Apart from the emperor's recalcitrance in this particular instance, the Sayyid brothers who were far from happy with his unending intrigues against their authority struck, had him deposed and killed. A puppet ruler, Rafi-ud- darjat, was installed in his place. The latter ratified the treaty with Raja Shahu by two or perhaps three imperial *firmans*, variously dated between 3 and 24 March (1719). No sooner were these ready to hand, than the Peshwa, who had accompanied Husain Ali to the capital, returned home in great triumph. Additionally, the mother and wife of the Maratha ruler were released and allowed to accompany the Peshwa. Raja Shahu's authority, it was evident, was now accepted by the Mughal emperor, a face that gave Shahu a 'distinct advantage' over his political rivals.

There was no dearth of critics who pointed out that the Peshwa's treaty was a retrograde step, that while the great Shivaji (1627–80) had fought for an independent Maratha state, his grandson (acting on the advice of his

Peshwa) 'threw away the jewel of liberty' and accepted, in exchange, 'the badge of Mughal slavery'. Apologists however maintain that, as realists, the Maratha state had grabbed true political authority, leaving 'ostentatious display' to Aurangzeb's effete successors.

With the death of the last great Mughal emperor (1707) and the withdrawal of the Mughal armies from the Deccan, a sea-change had come over the political landscape. *Inter alia*, the stark divergence between the interests of the Maratha sardars and the Maratha peasantry was there for all to see. Intent on personal gain and plunder, the sardars refused to subordinate their selfish, individual gains to the larger national good, thereby making the re-establishment of a centralized administrative system impossible. Balaji Vishwanath who, in 1719, effected a complex revenue division between Shahu and his sardars institutionalized the new arrangements. Broadly, what he sought to do was to place on the Maratha sardars the entire responsibility for the collection of *chauth* and *sardeshmukhi* with a fixed share (*sardeshmukhi* plus 34% of the *chauth*) for the Raja. In the result, the latter was to become largely dependent upon his sardars for his finances.

Nor was that all. Inside Maharashtra, care was taken to divide the responsibility for the collection of *chauth* and *sardeshmukhi* in such a manner that no individual Maratha sardar could easily dominate a large, compact area. At the same time, in Maharashtra itself, the semblance of a centralized system of administration under the care and supervision of the Peshwa was kept up.

An important line of criticism against Balaji holds that he undermined the monarchical order, buttressed the authority of local chieftains such as the Bhonsles of Nagpur and the Angrias in the Konkan, so that, in due course, the latter paid scant attention to the dictates of central authority. Here, it has been suggested, was the beginning of the jagir system or feudalization of the Maratha state which, even though responsible for the speedy expansion of its power base, at the same time led to its rapid dissolution. This was a clear departure from the great Shivaji. Putting the gears in reverse, Balaji had now substituted for the autocracy of the sovereign the authority of the Maratha confederacy.

The Peshwa's apologists point out that as a practitioner of *realpolitik*, Balaji realized that Shahu lacked both 'commanding talents and energy', that to plug the void he had perforce to conjure the support of the common people, of the peasants as well as the *shiledars*, as against the warlords. With a view to harnessing their energies to a great purpose, he had, in the bargain, compromised royal authority. In the result, he was able to build a solid base for a Maratha confederacy.

It is said that Balaji could ride a horse with difficulty and was not gifted with soldierly talent. He was one of the few characters in the India of that era who reached a high position *without* being a soldier. A reputable British historian maintains that Balaji Vishwanath 'had a calm, comprehensive and commanding intellect, an imaginative and aspiring disposition and an aptitude for ruling rude natures by moral force, a genius for diplomatic combinations, and a mastery of finance.'

Truly called 'the second founder' of the Maratha state, Balaji brought 'order out of chaos, helped national interests and preserved the unity of the state'. His greatness has been dimmed by the brilliant victories of his son and successor. All the same, his brief tenure would appear to mark the transition from the royal period to the age of the Peshwas and ushers in a new era in Maratha history. From then on, the feeble successors of Shivaji fade into insignificance, while the reins of government pass into the hands of their able Prime Ministers who were to direct the course of Maratha polity for nearly a hundred years.

R. C. Majumdar (ed.), *The Maratha Supremacy*, Bombay, 1977, Vol. VIII, in 'History and Culture of the Indian People', Vols I-XI; Yusuf Husain, *The First Nizam: the life and times of Nizam-ul-Mulk Asaf Jah I*, 2nd ed., Bombay, 1963.

Treaty of Banaras (1773)

Warren Hastings (q.v.) had long anticipated a clash with the Marathas. Lately they had held the Mughal emperor, Shah Alam II (q.v.), under their protection and tutelage demanding from him the districts of Karra and Allahabad, besides threatening Rohilkhand. To counter their designs, the British were keen on maintaining Oudh (q.v.) as a strong and friendly power that would, at the same time, act as a powerful buffer. A meeting between the Nawab Wazir and Warren Hastings was arranged at Banaras on 18 August 1773; on 7 September, a 2-article treaty was concluded.

Article 1 dealt with the sale of Karra and Allahabad to the Wazir. Since the emperor, to whom these districts had been initially ceded in return for his conferment of the rights of Diwani (q.v.) on the East India Company (q.v.) in 1765, had transferred his allegiance to the Marathas and to that extent forfeited his claim to British gratitude and these territories, they were now sold to the Nawab. In lieu, the latter was required to pay Rs 50,00,000 to the Company, in prescribed instalments. Article 2 stipulated that the Nawab defray the expenses of the troops maintained by the Company for his help and assistance at Rs 2,10,000 per month for a brigade whenever needed.

A secret agreement was also entered into by the two sides at the same time. Under its terms, the British were to furnish a brigade of troops to help the Nawab punish the Rohillas for their alleged evasion of treaty engagements and to conquer the country for him. The Nawab was to bear all the expenses of the campaign. For allowing him to retain the Rohilla country, he was to pay the Company Rs 40 lakhs; if, however, the latter did not assist him, he was absolved from paying the stipulated sum. Warren Hastings did however give an undertaking that this help would be rendered whenever it was required.

It may be noted that the strength of a brigade was defined as comprising two battalions of Europeans, six battalions of sepoys and one company of artillery. The expenses for the troops were to be defrayed by the Nawab 'from the time they shall have passed the borders of his dominions till they return within the borders of the province' of Bihar.

It is obvious that the treaty made the Nawab more dependent on the English in so far as he would, by joining them, earn the undoubted enmity of the Marathas. It would at the same time free the latter from the possession of two remote districts. Finally, British frontiers would be protected by a force maintained at someone else's expense.

Hastings' action in depriving the emperor of the two districts and stopping the payment of tribute to him was later severely criticized as a 'shocking, horrible and outrageous breach of faith' with Shah Alam. Apologists however contend that 'it is difficult to see' what other course was possible for the Governor-General in the existing circumstances.

Aitchison, II, pp. 84-6; Dodwell, *CHI*, pp. 215-16, 218.

Banda Bahadur (1670–1716)

Guru Gobind Singh, the tenth and last Sikh Guru who had accompanied the Mughal emperor Bahadur Shah I (q.v.) to the Deccan, had briefly so-journed at Nander, on the banks of the Godavari. There he came in touch with a *bairagi* sadhu named Lachhman Dev; the son of a Rajput ploughman, he originally came from Poonch in West Kashmir. As a sorcerer under the name of Madhodas, he had won great fame and commanded a large following. To Lachhman Dev, who had by then spent 15 years in his hermitage, the Guru gave a new name which the former had himself chosen—*banda* or, literally, the (Guru's) slave. According to Ganda Singh, in so far as Banda had been formally baptised and initiated into the Khalsa fold, his correct name should be Banda Singh, *not* simply Banda.

Prior to his own ghastly murder, the Guru had commissioned Banda to repair to the Panjab and, in consultation with 5 of his councillors (appointed by the Guru), to punish the enemies of the Khalsa. He gave Banda 5 arrows from his quiver and his own standard and battle drum, apart from issuing *hukamnamas* to the Sikhs, urging them to volunteer for service. The Guru's specific target was Wazir Khan, the governor of Sirhind, who had killed the Guru's two youngest sons, been responsible for taking the lives of his two elder ones as well as his mother and thousands of Sikhs and Hindus.

The Guru's choice of Banda in preference to some of his own companions has never been adequately explained. It has been suggested that Banda was only one of a number of Sikhs sent by the Guru to foment rebellion in the Panjab. In so far as he was the most successful, Banda was able to gain preponderance over the others and was thus pitchforked into the leadership of the entire community.

Strictly warned against assuming or aspiring to spiritual leadership, Banda arrived in the Panjab, collected a large following and, making his way into the less accessible hilly areas, established himself at Sadhaura in Nahan district, now in Himachal Pradesh. Presently Banda and his men spread to the entire country between the Sutlej and the Jamuna, succeeded in capturing Sirhind and moved towards Thanesar. Before long they had occupied half of the sarkar of Saharanpur, seized Sultanpur and extended their depredations to the vicinity of Lahore itself.

Banda fought against Wazir Khan near Ropar (May 1710); the Mughal commander was killed and his army routed. Two days later he stormed Sirhind when the town is said to have been destroyed 'in detail'. In the old town of Mukhlisgarh (also Mukhilspur), a small fortress situated in the lower Shivalik hills in the safety of the Himalaya, Banda established his headquarters, renamed it Lohgarh and proclaimed himself padshah. He introduced a new calendar dating from his capture of Sirhind and had coins struck marking his reign. His seal had inscribed on it not only the names of the Gurus but also Guru Gobind's *degh* (cauldron) and *tegh* (sword).

In the second half of 1710, the emperor Bahadur Shah himself moved against Banda. In the result, he and his men were driven out of Thanesar, removed from Sirhind, expelled from Lahore, closely invested at Lohgarh. In sum, they were made to suffer crushing defeats at numerous places. Fortunately for him, owing to rivalries between two imperial generals, Muhammad Amir Khan and Rustam Dil Khan, Banda was able to effect his escape; more, the sudden death of the emperor in February 1712 gave him some respite. Before long, he regained his authority, now sustained by powerful peasant armies. In 1711 he took Bahrampur, Raipur and Batala, recovered Sadhaura and Lohgarh and put up a huge fort at Gurdaspur. The viceroy of Lahore marched against Banda but was worsted in a pitched battle. Later, the governor of Sirhind fared no better.

The final round was joined (1715) in the reign of Farrukh Siyar (q.v.). Banda's adversary was Adbus Samad Khan, a Turani noble, then governor of Kashmir. The battle was fought at Gurdas Nangal, not far from Gurdaspur, where Banda finally laid down his arms on 17 December (1715) after a grim siege lasting a little over 8 months (April-December). With his hands manacled, his feet bound in fetters and an iron collar mounted around his neck, Banda and his guards were locked inside an iron cage and, flanked by 700 Sikh prisoners, marched to the imperial capital.

On the arrival of this veritable cavalcade in Delhi, Banda and his 26 officials were separated from his men. The latter were divided into 7 groups of 100 each, to be beheaded all the 7 days of the week. The execution itself began on 5 March 1716. Deeply struck, a 3-man embassy of the East India Company (q.v.), then in the imperial capital, reported on 10 March to their superiors, 'It is not a little remarkable with what patience they undergo their fate, and to the last it has not been found that one apostatized from their new formed religion.'

That, however, was not the end. Banda and his officials were tortured for another 3½ months to disclose the whereabouts of their hidden treasure! When all attempts to extort any confessions failed, it was decided to execute Banda on 9 June 1716, and his officials the following day. According to Ganda Singh, the execution took place near the dargah of Qutb-ud-Din Bakhtiyar Kaki and *not* at the *chabutra* of the *kotwali* in Chandni Chowk.

Before his execution, Banda was offered pardon if he renounced his faith and accepted Islam. He refused to oblige and was brutally tortured to death.

Critics aver that although the last Guru had specifically restricted Banda's role to that of military commander of a punitive expedition, he widened it to embrace a spiritual ministry as well. He preached sermons and gave benedictions. His proclamation affording protection to all those 'threatened by thieves, dacoits, highway robbers, troubled by Mohammadan bigots', it has been argued, opened the floodgates to a sea of pent-up hatred. The best he could do under the circumstances was to ride the crest of the resultant wave of violence that he had let loose, 'a wave whose course he neither perhaps could nor yet tried to direct'.

Nor was that all. Banda's religious innovations which 'transgressed and disregarded' the Guru's commandments, were resented by the orthodox in the community who disapproved of his becoming 'a petty king, living in regal pomp, with courtiers and a couple of wives'. Ganda Singh refutes 'the allegation' that Banda 'had contravened' any injunction of Guru Gobind Singh, suggesting it has no historical basis.

On the other hand, Banda has been hailed as the harbinger of revolutionary change, for 'in seven stormy years Banda changed the class structure of land holdings in the southern half of the state by liquidating many of the big Muslim zamindar families of Malwa in the Jullundur Doab . . .[at the same time] the movement to infuse the sentiment of Panjabi nationalism in the masses received a setback with Banda.' In other words, even though guilty of mass killings, the followers of Banda led what was 'clearly an agrarian revolt and not an anti-Islamic crusade'. In the process, large estates were first broken up into smaller holdings, albeit then in the hands of Sikh or Hindu peasants. Later, with the rise of Sikh political power, these holdings were grouped together to form large estates, but in the hands of Sikh chieftains.

The above notwithstanding, the charge of gruesome massacre is hard to wash. Banda, it is suggested, destroyed about 50,000 Muslims, a brutality that 'cannot be approved in any age by any people'. More, 'his savagery hardened the hearts of the Muslim peasants and made them as anti-Sikh as their government. The Muslims looked upon him as a barbarian, whom nature had formed for a butcher . . . an infernal monster.'

On the other hand, by dealing 'a severe blow to the intolerant' Mughal rule in the Panjab, Banda was 'to break the first sod' in the conquest of that province by the Sikhs. In other words, in 1710, he had 'laid the foundation' of the Sikh empire.

In a wider perspective, Banda's achievement has been compared with Shivaji's (1627–80). Between the two, it has been suggested, their success 'encouraged' the Rohillas, Rajputs and Jats and, further afield, the satraps in Bengal, Uttar Pradesh and the Deccan 'to elevate their status from one of viceroyalty to kingship'.

Hari Ram Gupta, *History of the Sikhs*, 3rd ed., New Delhi 1978, 8 vols, 2, pp. 1–38; Gurdev Singh Deol, *Banda Bahadur*, Jullundur, 1972; Ganda Singh, *A Life of Banda Singh Bahadur*, Amritsar, 1935; and 'Banda Singh Bahadur, his achievements and his place of execution', *Panjab Past & Present*, vol. 9, part 2 (1975), pp. 441–80.

Gooroodass Banerjee (1844–1918)

Gooroodass Banerjee who rose to be a celebrated lawyer and judge as also a renowned educationist, was born in a lower middle class family in the Calcutta (q.v.) suburb of Narkeldanga. He lost his father while still a child and was brought up by his mother. Austere and orthodox to the core, she so moulded him as to imbibe the true Brahmanical virtues of integrity, simplicity and humility.

A student of the David Hare School and later of Presidency College, Banerjee was always first in his class. He obtained an M.A. in Mathematics (1865), a B.L. in Law (1866) and was appointed Professor of Mathematics at Berhampur, which enabled him to practice law alongside. He soon established a lucrative practice and became the retained pleader of the Nawab of Murshidabad as well as of other well-known zamindars. In 1872, he left Berhampur to practice at the Calcutta High Court. Within the next six years he obtained a Doctorate in Law and was appointed (1879) Honorary Presidency Magistrate. He reached the acme of his legal career in 1888 when he replaced Justice Cunningham as an Additional Judge of the Calcutta High Court. On attaining the age of 60, he resigned voluntarily (1904) and was knighted the same year.

Deeply interested in education, Banerjee had all along been active in Calcutta University affairs as a Fellow of the Senate and a member of its Syndicate. In addition, he was president of studies in Mathematics and Bengali (later Sanskrit too), examiner in arts and law and president of the central textbook committee. In recognition of his services in this field, Lord Lansdowne (q.v.), then Governor-General and Chancellor, appointed him Vice-Chancellor of Calcutta University (1890-92), the first Indian to be so honoured. He was reappointed in 1902 but resigned a year later. He heavily underscored flaws in the then system of education and, as a corrective, helped to start a 'Society for the Higher Education of Young Men' and later, **in collaboration with Dr M. L. Sirkar, an 'Indian Association for the** Cultivation of Science'.

As a member of Curzon's (q.v.) Universities Commission (1902) Banerjee appended a strong note of dissent to the majority report. The latter would, in his view, tend to check the spread of education and introduce bureaucratic control. After the partition of Bengal (q.v.) he took an active interest in the programme of national education, as a member of the 'Banga Jatiya Vidya Parishad'. The scope of education, as he envisaged it, was tri-dimensional— literary, scientific and technical. He encouraged the use of Bengali, Hindi and Urdu as the media of instruction; in fact, he was emphatic that instruction be imparted through the medium of the mother tongue. He foresaw the necessity for technical and agricultural education and pleaded strongly for the constitution of the faculties of technology and agriculture in universities. His basic objective, however, was to 'supplement and *not* supplant' governmental efforts in this field.

Banerjee's somewhat inflexible and orthodox religious and social ideas limited his perspective. He approved of the 'zenana' (segregation of of ladies) and early marriage though aware of their ruinous effect on women's education. Acknowledging that social regeneration depended on educated women he proposed a system of instruction that would equip the fair sex to perform their household duties efficiently. He rigorously followed the rituals and ceremonies in the caste system enjoined by the shastras, laying the utmost emphasis on religious instruction in schools.

Though not actively engaged in politics on account of the limitations placed by his station in life, Banerjee was not altogether immune from their impact. Thus he attended a public meeting called for 16 October 1905 to protest against the partition of Bengal and proposed Ananda Mohan Bose (q.v.) to the chair. He attended the national conference in 1885, and was a member of the Calcutta municipality which he represented in the Bengal legislative council in 1887.

In 1906 he became a member of the national council of education which proved to be the nucleus for the later establishment of Jadavpur university. He was also a member of the Sahitya Parishad and of the Bharat Dharma Mahamandal.

In 19th century Bengal, Gooroodass Banerjee occupies a unique position. An unswerving adherence to certain basic principles and the old-world charm of his manner distinguished him from many. Curzon described him, not inaptly, as 'a quite remarkable blend of the best that Asia can give or Europe teach'. Among his books special mention may be made of *Hindu Law of Marriage and Stridhan* and *The Education Problem in India.*

Anath Nath Basu (ed.), *Sir Gooroodass Banerjee Centenary Commemoration Volume*, Calcutta University, 1948; U. N. Banerjee (comp), *Reminiscences, Speeches and Writings of Sir Gooroodass Banerjee*, Calcutta, 1927.

Surendranath Banerjea (1848–1925)

Surendranath Banerjea who rose to be a well-known nationalist leader was at the same time a popular journalist and a dedicated educationist. He came of a reputable *kulin* Brahmin family, long settled in Calcutta. Educated in Anglo-Indian institutions, both in school and college, he competed successfully for the Indian Civil Service examination held in London (1869) and was placed second. Owing to a technical lacuna, he was initially disqualified; a court judgement in his favour however resulted in his induction into the service and posting as Assistant Magistrate at Sylhet. This was soon followed by his dismissal on a flimsy technicality for an apparently inadvertent procedural error. His appeal against this arbitrary action was as abortive as his subsequent efforts to be called to the bar in Bengal. Indomitable and undaunted, qualities for which he was known as 'Surrender Not', he plunged into the role of a 'public agitator', fighting to redress the grievances of all those who had suffered.

Banerjea was convinced that his caste, status, education and personal talents entitled him to assume leadership. While his grandfather was a traditionalist, his father was what may be called a 'modern man' and rudely shocked by his son's dismissal from the service. Banerjea convinced himself that he had suffered because he came of a subject race 'that lay disorganized, had no public opinion and no voice in the counsels of their government'. He further argued that the personal wrong done to him was illustrative 'of the helpless impotency of our people'.

Banerjea was soon Professor of English at the Metropolitan Institution, later Vidyasagar College, and subsequently at Ripon College, which he founded in 1882. It is now known, after him, as Surendranath College. He involved himself actively with students' associations, enthusing their members with the new political consciousness and the ideal of a united India. In July 1876 he became a founder-member of the Indian Association (q.v.) whose principal objective was to organize public agitations to seek redressal of grievances. A powerful and fiery orator, Banerjea collected a substantial following through his speeches and writings. Two years later, he bought over the proprietary rights of the *Bengalee* which was gradually converted into a popular daily and a formidable exponent of nationalism. Soon a municipal councillor (1875-99), Banerjea later represented the Calcutta Corporation in the Imperial Legislative Council (1893-1901).

In an effort to organize an all-India movement inspired by the 1877 Imperial Darbar (q.v.), Banerjea set out on a lecture tour of northern India and later Bombay and Madras, arousing support for such causes as opposition to the lowering of examination age for entry into the Indian Civil Service (from 21 to 19 years), approval of the Ilbert Bill (q.v.) and a denunciation of Lytton's (q.v.) Vernacular Press Act (q.v.).

His tour constitutes a major landmark in the history of India's political regeneration. Soon Banerjea emerged a popular hero—from his prosecution for contempt of court resulting from vehement criticism of a Calcutta High Court judge who insisted on the production, in his court, of an idol of Saligram for identification! His conviction and imprisonment provoked an outburst of indignation followed by a *hartal*.

Banerjea mooted the idea of holding a 'National Conference' of representatives from political associations all over the country. Two such conferences were actually held, in 1883 and 1885; the latter, convened in Calcutta, explains his absence from the inaugural session of the Indian National Congress (q.v.). From 1886, however, he attended nearly all its annual sessions, except that at Karachi, and was twice (1895 and 1902) elected party President. Owing to the important role he and his colleagues played in its deliberations, the Congress came to be looked upon as the handiwork of Bengalis.

Banerjea was also a member of the party delegation to England (1890) which demanded greater participation of Indians in the administration which, they pleaded, should be based on the elective principle.

A political moderate, Banerjea believed in the beneficence of British rule and advocated constitutional agitation as a means for achieving a representative form of government. To keep the British public informed, he advocated the institution of a 'National Fund' to maintain a permanent delegation in London so as to project and propagate the Indian viewpoint. He stressed the need for Hindu-Muslim unity as a prerequisite to the attainment of Swaraj and tried to convince the Muslims that it was to their advantage to join hands with the Congress. He discouraged his party men from dissociating themselves completely from government when the younger group exhibited signs of frustration at the failure of the 'Moderates' to make any substantial gains in the post-1890 period. Though participating actively in the Partition of Bengal (q.v.) and Swadeshi (q.v.) movements, he repeatedly stressed that their aim was not to alienate the English rulers. On the contrary, he viewed it as an appeal to their conscience; it was the latter's representatives in India who, he argued, had perpetrated these enormities.

Rated as the 'most distinguished of Bengal's National Congressmen' apart from being secretary of the main political organization of the province, the Indian Association, Banerjea was the leader of the first phase in the anti-Partition agitation. Earlier, he had dramatized opposition to Curzon's (q.v.) reconstruction of municipal government by leading 28 Indian members out of the Calcutta Corporation with a pledge never to return until non-official control was restored. His weapons—press articles, public meetings of protest, petitions and deputations—were of a constitutional character but proved, in the short run, to be of no avail.

At the Surat Congress split (q.v.) in 1907, Banerjea and other Moderates succeeded in preventing the Extremists from capturing power. Later he joined the Moderates at Allahabad, supporting reform rather than revolution. Nevertheless, his estrangement from the militants was to mark the beginning of the end of his political leadership.

The annulment of the Partition (December 1911) was claimed to be a victory for the Moderates. Their Extremist rivals, whom they had succeeded in ousting from the Congress, had been arrested, deported and virtually hounded out from active politics. In 1912 Banerjea and his group who had boycotted the Bengal legislative council elections three years earlier, decided to contest. The result was a great disappointment, they won only 4 of the 23 elective seats. Their small numbers notwithstanding, Banerjea and another of his group were chosen by the non-official members of the provincial council as their representatives on the Imperial Legislative Council. His work in the latter body drew attention to injustices and inequalities perpetrated by moving resolutions and calling for divisions on legislative amendments.

In July 1915 Banerjea submitted a scheme for constitutional reform which contains 'the essence of important later proposals', viz., the memorial presented to the Viceroy in October 1916 by 19 members of the Imperial Legislative Council and the Congress-League scheme of December 1916.

His differences with the Congress grew with the emergence of Gandhi (q.v.) on the political stage. Banerjea differed with the latter's views and opposed his advocacy of the Khilafat (q.v.) and the Non-cooperation (q.v.) Movements. In 1918 he finally broke away from the Congress, which had decided to boycott the Montagu-Chelmsford reforms (q.v.) and formed the All-India Liberal Federation (q.v.). The Moderates' influence began to decline and when they walked out of the Congress (1918), Surendranath too practically walked out of the history of India's struggle for freedom.

Self-government meant to Banerjea 'colonial self-government', *not* independence. He attempted therefore to make the scheme of reforms a success and contested elections thereunder. In January 1921 the Bengal Governor, Lord Ronaldshay, nominated him—'my old critic'—as his first 'chief minister', investing him with the portfolios of Local Self-Government and Health. He thus became the first Indian to hold that position.

His support of dyarchy was unqualified: 'The Government thus formed on the whole a happy family, despite differences of opinion inseparable from the discussion of public affairs. Of heated conflict or collision we had little or none; and in our discussions we had not much of the taste of the alleged evils of dyarchy.'

As Minister, the Act to amend Curzon's earlier (1904) Calcutta municipal law 'was to be his magnum opus'; he refers to it as the 'most important measure of municipal legislation' during his tenure. The proposed legislation, however, provoked considerable controversy, particularly on the question of Muslim representation. Despite his known opposition, he accepted communal electorates and, in the result, was 'reviled as a traitor to his own principles'.

Banerjea adduced cogent reasons, for accepting office. He noted 'that it would have been unwise, unpatriotic, almost treacherous to do so [not to accept office]. Therefore in all sincerity and singleness of heart, which even the voice of slander will not be able to cloud, did I join the government in a ministerial position. The familiar trick is to urge that we have changed. It is not *we* who have changed, but the Government.'

Banerjea's acceptance of office provoked strong protest. The nationalists now bade him 'a sad farewell', labelling 'Surrender Not Banerjea' of Partition fame as 'Sir Surrender' and referring to him as 'the Lost Leader'. As a result, in the 1923 elections to the Bengal Council, Banerjea suffered a decisive defeat. Thereafter he retired from active public life and, until his death two years later, occupied himself with writing his autobiography, *A Nation in Making*. He died at Barrackpore in August 1925.

Banerjea held liberal social and religious views, advocated widow remarriage and raising the age of marriage of girls. Essentially he viewed himself as a competitor, usually winning, infrequently losing, but never daunted. He likened himself to Mazzini who raised a fallen and degraded Italy. His varied activities, including membership of the Calcutta Corporation, the Senate of the University, and Legislative Councils in the province and the Centre, were integrated with the roles of an instructor, teacher, and spokesman. His most critical function was the transmission of ideas, rather than creative thought. He was also an able organizer and indefatigable collector of funds.

Surendranath Banerjea, *A Nation in Making: Being the Reminiscences of Fifty years of Public Life*, reprint, Calcutta, 1963; S. K. Bose, *Surendranath Banerjea*, Builders of Modern India, New Delhi, 1968; Daniel Argov, *Moderates and Extremists in the Indian National Movement 1883-1920, with special reference to Surendranath Banerjea and Lajpat Rai*, Bombay, 1967; Jyoti Prasad Suda, *Main Currents of Social and Political Thought in Modern India*, Vol. I, The Liberal and National Traditions, Meerut, 1963, pp. 151-74.

Woomesh Chandra Bonnerjee (1844–1906)

Woomesh Chandra Bonnerjee, born Bandhopadyaya, besides being a successful lawyer was the first President of the Indian National Congress (q.v.) and the first Indian to contest an election to the British House of Commons. In school, he was more interested in developing his histrionic talents than in academic pursuits. Soon he left it and was articled to an attorney (1861). As a clerk (1862-4) to W. P. Gillanders, a reputed Calcutta law firm, he secured the Rustomji Jamsetji Jeejeebhoi scholarship for law studies abroad. Called to the Bar from Middle Temple he returned home to practise at the (Calcutta) High Court. His outstanding performance in court resulted in his appointment as standing counsel to the government, the first 'native' to occupy that position and one in which he was to officiate four times. His famous defence of Surendranath Banerjea (q.v.) in the contempt of court and the Burdwan libel cases brought him fame.

Bonnerjee's undoubted affluence accounted for his stylish and thoroughly anglicized way of living and annual trips to England, where he bought a house. Twice he was offered a judgeship of the Calcutta High Court, 'but he refused the honour on account of his poverty.' His monthly income was not less than Rs 20,000 whereas the salary of a judge was only Rs 4,000!

Himself a Hindu, he allowed his wife to embrace Christianity. In 1880 he had been appointed Fellow of Calcutta University and six years later became president of its law faculty. He also represented the University in the Bengal Legislative Council. While studying in England, he made his first speech advocating representative government for India and forcefully asserted that his people were intelligent enough to be trusted with the right of franchise and greater responsibility in administration. The Secretary of State and his Council, generally ignorant of Indian affairs, could scarce be sympathetic administrators. The solution, he averred, lay in a representative assembly and a senate in India, with the power of veto vesting in the Governor-General who should, however, be restrained like the American President.

Bonnerjee believed Indian nationalism to be a product of English education. A founder member of the Indian National Congress, he was twice
(1885 and 1892) chosen its President. The aims and objectives of the
Congress as enunciated by him at its first session bear repetition: '(i) The
promotion of personal intimacy and friendship among all the more earnest
workers in our country's cause in the various parts of the Empire; (ii) The
eradication by direct friendly personal intercourse of all possible race, creed
or provincial prejudices...and consolidation of those sentiments of national
unity that had their origin in our beloved Lord Ripon's ever memorable
reign.'

He had also proposed the establishment of 'standing committees' in all
provinces so that there could be 'correspondence' between different parts of
the country.

A moderate in politics, Bonnerjee placed great faith in the British sense of
justice, imploring Congress to resort to constitutional agitation only and
supporting it with a party movement in England. He accompanied a Congress delegation to London in 1890 to press for political reform and advised
the party to lay down an official policy for the year ahead, constitute
provincial committees and establish a close rapport between its workers and
the people. He also urged it to set aside all personal, religious and provincial
differences and concentrate on discussing wider, national problems. He
believed the party should confine its activities to political matters only and
leave questions of social reform to other parties or groups.

A 'large portion' of Bonnerjee's income, computed at Rs 20,000 to Rs
30,000 a month, was spent for the Congress. It has been said that he 'stood
by the cradle of the National Congress which he nurtured with parental
solicitude and affection'. An ardent advocate of the British connection, he
believed that changes in the system of administration could be made in a
constitutional manner through a process of gradual evolution.

Bonnerjee believed that social problems should be dealt with at the
provincial level and strongly deprecated the British policy of restricting
Indian activity to social rather than political problems. In his presidential
address to the Congress session at Allahabad (1892) be pleaded; 'What we
want is that there should be a responsible government for India. I have
always felt that the one great evil of the Indian administration is that our
rulers are responsible to no one outside of their own conscience.'

As a typical representative of his age, he had little faith in the common
people of India. Essentially, he was an aristocrat not only in his way of life
but also in his way of thinking. It should follow that his appeal was not to the
masses but to the intelligentsia. According to Surendranath Banerjea, WCB
lent to the Congress a dignity and an air of respectability in official eyes,
which otherwise it would not perhaps have possessed .

Legal reform was his forte. He advocated trial by jury as well as separation
of the executive from legislative functions. He was at the same time a great
champion of the freedom of the Press—viz., his defence of Surendranath
Banerjea in the *Bengalee* case. Although opposed to early marriage, he was
clearly of the view that the Age of Consent Bill which raised the age of
marriage had disregarded the feelings of the people.

From 1902 onwards Bonnerjee lived in London where he practiced before
the judicial committee of the Privy Council. He remained in touch with the

national movement to the very end of his life in 1906. Besides establishing the (London) Indian Society, for many years he financed the Parliamentary Standing Committee and a journal called *India*.

Gokhale said of him that he was 'pre-eminent as a lawyer' in addition to being 'an ardent patriot, a wise and far-sighted leader, an incessant worker', one whose 'nobility of mind and greatness of soul' were unrivalled. But the collective Congress tribute to him was meagre and measly, for its resolution (1906) lumped him with other leaders in an omnibus obituary.

Many have grieved that 'this grand patriarch of national renaissance' has remained 'a forgotten patriot'. Srinivasa Sastri has expressed the view that the country 'will never know the exact amount of her pecuniary indebtedness to him'.

Sadhona Bonnerjee, *Life of W.C. Bonnerjee: First President of the Indian National Congress*, Calcutta, 1944; P. Thankappan Nair, 'W. C. Bonnerjee and the National Renaissance,' *Radical Humanist*, July 1971, pp. 17–22, 31; Kalyan Kumar Sen, 'W. C. Bonnerjee and the Growth of National Consciousness, *Modern Review*, CIX, i, January 1961, pp. 70-2.

Robert Barker (1729–89)

Robert (later Sir Robert) Barker came to India in 1749 as an officer in the employment of the East India Company (q.v.). He served as a captain of artillery under Robert Clive's (q.v.) command in Bengal, first at Chandernagore (q.v.) and later Plassey (q.v.), which won him the former's friendship and esteem. After three years (1726–5), Barker returned as a colonel in the infantry and was posted at Allahabad. Later he rose to be commander-in-chief of the British forces in Bengal, in which capacity he was deputed by Warren Hastings (q.v.) to witness the signing of a treaty of alliance (June 1772) between the Rohillas and the Nawab Wazir of Oudh. Subsequently, in 1773, he accompanied the Nawab's men to Rohilkhand when the Marathas invaded that territory and helped in successfully repulsing them.

Barker resigned in 1774 because he disapproved of reforms in the army introduced by Warren Hastings, and sailed for England just before the Rohilla War (q.v.). In September 1786, he tendered evidence before the Select Committee of the House of Commons on the impeachment of Warren Hastings. He died three years later at Bushbridge.

Dodwell, *CHI*, V, pp. 216–18; Charles Edward Buckland, *Dictionary of Indian Biography*, London, 1905, p. 27.

George Hilaro Barlow (1762–1846)

George (later Sir George) Hilaro Barlow came out to India in 1778 as a member of the Bengal Civil Service, served in Gaya and later Calcutta in the revenue department where he implemented Cornwallis's (q.v.) Permanent Settlement (q.v.). Designated Chief Secretary in 1796 by Sir John Shore (q.v.) he became five years later a member and thereafter Vice-President of the Supreme Council under Wellesley (q.v.). In October 1805, after Cornwallis's death, he took over as provisional Governor-General and functioned as such until Minto's (q.v.) arrival in July 1807.

A man of mediocre abilities and crude, even uncivilized, manners, he carried out to the letter the wishes of the Court of Directors. Earlier, a zealous subordinate to Wellesley, he now assiduously reversed the latter's policies which, *inter alia,* had completely depleted the treasury. In concrete terms, he made concessions to the Maratha chiefs, Sindhia and Holkar, and annulled the East India Company's (q.v.) earlier protective treaties with the chiefs of Rajasthan. His elevation to the top position did not receive the approval of the Whig ministry then in office, with the result that he was replaced. Thereafter he was nominated to the governorship of Madras, taking over from William Bentinck (q.v.) who had resigned. The economy drive he pursued in terms of scaling down the salaries and allowances of men and officers brought about a clash between the Indian regiments and the king's troops at Seringapatam.

Barlow suppressed the Vellore mutiny (1806) vigorously, relying on the king's officers and the sepoys themselves against the Company's men. The dispute gravely affected his reputation; in tackling it, he had shown singular want of tact though plenty of courage. Hostile propaganda and pamphlets by the cashiered officers on their return home poisoned the atmosphere and brought about his recall in 1812. He lived in retirement in England till his death, in December 1846.

An able man and a faithful lieutenant, Barlow failed utterly when placed in supreme command at times of crises. It was widely held that his supersession (1807) was justified.

Buckland, p. 27; *DNB*, I, pp. 1140–41 (Henry Morse Stephens).

Treaty of Bassein (1802)

In the opening years of the 19th century, the Maratha confederacy had shown signs of drifting apart, what with the weakness of the central authority and personal wrangles and growing selfish ambitions of its warring chiefs. Thus Daulat Rao Sindhia (q.v.) and Yashwant Rao Holkar (q.v.) fought for supremacy at the Peshwa's court; the latter had Malhar Rao Holkar murdered and took his son Kande Rao prisoner; a little later Peshwa Baji Rao II (q.v.) had Vithoji Holkar cruelly done to death. Enraged beyond measure, Yashwant Rao marched to Poona to settle scores. Sindhia, even though preoccupied in the north, sent troops to the Peshwa's rescue but their combined forces were worsted by Holkar's at Hadaspur (25 October 1802). Baji Rao, fleeing from pillar to post, finally reached Bassein and solicited an alliance with the John Company (q.v.) to re-establish his authority. In the result, on 31 December 1802, a subsidiary treaty of 19 articles was signed whereby the Peshwa bartered away, in goodly measure, his own independence as well as that of his people.

The treaty of Bassein stipulated that the Peshwa (in return for a defensive alliance which was reciprocal) (i) was to maintain a subsidiary force of 6,000 regular native infantry with the usual proportion of field pieces and European artillerymen attached. It was to be stationed in his dominion. in perpetuity. While the annual expense on the force was estimated at Rs 25 lakhs, districts yielding Rs 26 lakhs as revenue were assigned as payment (Art IV) with all articles required for the upkeep of the troops being exempt from duty; (ii) agreed not to entertain any foreign national hostile to the British in his service. In addition, he accepted British intercession to settle his differences with the Nizam and the Gaekwad and undertook not to negotiate with any other state his differences with the two of them; (iii) pledged not to negotiate with any other state without the Company Bahadur's prior permission; (iv) relinquished 'for ever' all his rights and claims to the city of Surat.

A schedule attached to the treaty listed all the territories 'ceded in perpetuity' by the Peshwa (in pursuance of Article IV).

A year later, on 16 December, 1803, a supplementary treaty of 8 articles was concluded at Poona. It stipulated *inter alia* the addition of a regiment of native cavalry to the British subsidiary force. Again, in place of 10,000 cavalry and 6,000 infantry, to be furnished by the Peshwa in the event of war, it would now be 5,000 cavalry and 3,000 infantry. While territories yielding a revenue of Rs 19,16,000 were restored to the Peshwa out of what he had ceded earlier (1802), he was now to surrender to the Company territory in Bundelkhand yielding a revenue of Rs 36,16,000. The latter was to be taken from those quarters of the province that were 'most contiguous to the British possessions and in every respect most convenient'.

The treaty gave the British a legitimate claim to interfere in the Peshwa's domestic squabbles and turn to advantage the endless distractions of his dominion. Its rejection by the other Maratha chiefs led to the Second Anglo-Maratha War (q.v.) and the subsequent break-up of the confederacy. According to Sardesai, the news of the treaty 'greatly dismayed' Holkar and Sindhia. Their confabulations led them to conclude that Bassein 'has destroyed the Maratha state', enabling the British 'to deal the same blow to it that they did to Tipu Sultan' (q.v.).

The import of the treaty cannot be over-emphasized. Later historians rated it as 'one of the most important landmarks' of British dominion in India; contemporary observers noted that it marked a distinct change in 'the footing on which' the Company stood in western India. Having brought itself into definite relations with the formal head of the Maratha confederacy, it 'had either to control' the latter or 'was committed to hostilities' with it.

Unfortunately, the Peshwa was a broken reed to lean upon and, as Arthur Wellesley put it, it was 'a treaty with a cipher [viz., the Peshwa]'. It involved the British in that endless maze of intrigue with which a once-great empire, now on its political death-bed, was riddled.

A word on Bassein. Situated on the Malabar coast, it was originally known as 'Wasai' or 'Wasi'; the Portuguese later called it 'Basain' and the English 'Bessi'. With an area of 1,926 acres, it appears to have been initially an island but, over the aeons, the creek that separated it from the mainland had silted up. In 1534, Bassein was ceded to the Portuguese by Bahadur Shah, king of Gujarat, and two years later a fort was built there. It gained in prosperity and many beautiful buildings came up. In the 18th century when Portuguese power was no more, Chimnaji Appa, a Maratha general, captured (1739) the fort and utterly destroyed it. A possession of the Peshwa, it was held by British forces under Brig. Gen. Thomas Goddard in 1780 but was restored to the Marathas two years later by the Treaty of Salbai (q.v.). In 1818 when Maratha power was decisively worsted, Bassein was passed over to the British.

Aitchison, III, pp, 63–75; G. S. Sardesai, *A New History of the Marathas*, III, pp. 384–5; Henry Yule & A. C. Burnell, *Hobson-Jobson*, reprint, Delhi, 1968, pp. 70–1.

Paul Benfield (d. 1810)

Paul Benfield came to India as a civil servant of the John Company (q.v.) in 1764. Like its other employees, he too amassed a fortune through private trade. He earned notoriety in a caricature, 'Court Rupee', wherein he is depicted with a black face riding in Hyde Park on a stout cob. It stemmed largely from his involvement in the Nawab of Carnatic's debts and the subsequent charges levelled on this count against him by the well-known British parliamentarian, Edmund Burke (1729–97).

Briefly, Benfield had lent large sums of money to the Nawab to settle Dutch claims to Tranquebar, a part of the Tanjore ruler's territory. The transaction was questioned by the Court of Directors who ordered him to return to England in 1779. Back home, he sought to prove that his loans had been no secret, that by his efforts he had actually averted a war and promoted 'the most essential interests' of his employers. He was honourably acquitted, restored to service and returned to Madras. He was to stay there till 1793, when he repaired home and made an unsuccessful bid to set up a business. He died in Paris, in 1810, in indigent circumstances.

DNB, II, pp. 220-1 (Alexander John Arbuthnot); *Buckland*, p. 35.

Bengal Famine (1943)

The Bengal famine, at its worst from July to December 1943, claimed a heavy toll of human life variously estimated between 1.5 and 3.5 millions. It has been held to have been more 'man-made' than God-made, although nature as well as World War II (1939–45) made no small contribution to this ghastly human tragedy.

The ineptitude and inefficiency in New Delhi in handling the overall food problem had been apparent over the years. Thus, whereas in 1896-1905 the total output of foodgrains was priced at Rs 28.7 billion, the figure had declined to Rs 27.2 billion for the period 1939-45. This was the more pronounced in so far as the increase in population during the same period was 24%. Statistics suggest that the per capita output came down from 100 to 91%—more specifically, from 560 lbs in 1936-7 to 399 in 1945-6. It is also worth noting that whereas prior to 1919 India had been a net exporter of foodgrains, it subsequently become a major importer.

In 1942, with Linlithgow (q.v.) as Viceroy, the food situation in Bengal assumed alarming proportions. Essentially a rice producing area, at a low level of consumption, Bengal was then just about able to meet its requirements. In 1941 the *aman* (winter) crop had failed and production was less by nearly 2 million tons. This deficiency could not be met by imports because of the earlier (1942) fall of Burma to the Japanese. In 1943 both the autumn as well as the spring crops failed. 1942 had been, food-wise, a slightly better year albeit not good enough to meet the deficits which had accumulated over the years.

Natural calamity apart, there was a number of other factors that made the situation grim. One was the suspension of imports and the dislocation of trade in the countryside because of bureaucratic controls consequent upon threats of war on the frontier. Again, there was a considerable tightening of provincial and district barriers against the movement of foodgrains, an abnormal increase in army demands, an influx of refugees from Burma and Malaya and last, though by no means the least, an overall rise in commodity prices.

The up-swing in prices was largely due to the prevailing psychosis of shortages created partly by the failure of the *aman* crop of 1942 and partly by the events of war. The provincial government not only failed to dispel these fears but, by its policies, actually aggravated the situation and contributed to a rise in prices.

Essentially, the government's direct contribution to the tragedy lay in its failure to foresee, at the beginning of World War II, or even as late as April 1942 when Burma fell, the gravity of the food situation as it developed and the need for timely action to meet it.

Among other causes the following may be listed: the provincial government's lack of experience and utter unpreparedness to meet the situation; private domination and control of the grain trade; indecision and fatal delays in enforcing orders; the conduct and integrity of officials of the Food Department and private procurement agencies set up by the government, which left a lot to be desired; political wrangles in Bengal and the unfortunate lack of co-operation between the provincial Governor and his Ministers on the one hand and between the central and Bengal governments on the other.

The fact was that New Delhi had minimized the acuteness of the problem although portents of the impending tragedy were all too apparent. An index was Calcutta, where the price of coarse rice alone went up from Rs 5.10 per maund in January 1942 to Rs 8 in July.

A bad situation was made worse by the incompetent Muslim League (q.v.) ministry headed by the well-meaning, if incapable, Khwaja Nazimuddin with H. S. Suhrawardy as his Food Minister. The provincial government had started by taking over control of supplies, and then employing corrupt officials and inexperienced, greedy trade agents to purchase and distribute grain. J. P. Srivastava, Food Member of the Governor-General's Executive Council, did no better for he continued to deny in the Central Legislative Assembly the existence of any scarcity conditions, a misrepresentation dutifully echoed by the Secretary of State in Whitehall. Thus all the three limbs—the provincial ministry in Calcutta, the Governor-General's Executive Council at New Delhi and the Secretary of State in London—exhibited gross lack of knowledge of the situation and a singular degree of incompetence and inefficiency to grapple with it.

From July to December 1943, when the famine was at its worst, the number of deaths in Bengal, according to estimates of the Famine Enquiry Commission, was 1.5 million. However, K. P. Chattopadhayaya, who has computed figures on the basis of sample surveys of mortality, puts these at 3.5 million. Harrowing as these statistics are, it was the manner of dying by slow starvation—in October (1943) it was estimated that 700 persons were dying every day in Calcutta's streets—that represented perhaps the most shameful part of this great human tragedy.

It was under Lord Wavell's (q.v.) stewardship that the tide began to turn. The new Viceroy wanted to dismiss the provincial ministry. On 6 January (1944) he noted in his *Journal*: 'Discussed with Jenkins and Abell [his principal aides] result of latter's visit to Calcutta and approved draft of telegram to S. of S. [Secretary of State for India, L. S. Amery] recommending Section 93 administration for Bengal. It is against my principles to take over from an Indian Government . . . . But this Government has been given a long run, and too much is at stake.'

Four days later, 'I saw Nazimuddin, the Bengal Premier, and told him I was dissatisfied with the state of Bengal. He said things would be alright if his Ministry was given a chance and supported against his political enemies. I rather like him and think he is straight but incapable. I have little opinion of his Food Minister [H. S.] Suhrawardy.'

On 13 January 1944 Wavell learnt that the War Cabinet had turned down his proposal for taking over the provincial government in Bengal. He did however succeed in appointing the Australian politician R. G. Casey (later Lord Casey, Australia's Governor-General) as the new Governor and handed over the work of distribution of relief to the army. A system of food rationing too was introduced in all the large towns in the country. Gradually the situation was brought under control and, by June 1944, it was well on its way to normalcy.

B. M. Bhatia, *Famines in India—A study in some aspects of the Economic History of India (1860–1945)*. Bombay, 1963, pp. 321–4; *Tara Chand*, IV, pp. 410–12; Penderel Moon (ed.), *Wavell: The Viceroy's Journal*, Oxford, 1973, pp. 46–7; A. K. Sen, 'Famine Mortality: A study of the Bengal Famine of 1943' in E. G. Hobsbawm *et al* (ed.), *Peasants in History: Essays in Honour of Daniel Thorner*, New Delhi, 1980, pp. 194–220.

Partition of Bengal (1905)

The province of Bengal had, over the years, become large and unwieldy. Every territorial addition to the John Company's (q.v.) dominion extending from Assam (1826) in the east to Delhi and beyond in the west had been added on to it. Even after the creation of the North-West Provinces (1836), the attachment of Arakan to British Burma (1862), and the constitution of Assam into a chief commissionership (1874), the province still embraced Bengal, Bihar, Orissa, Chhota Nagpur and its hilly tracts and certain other tributary states. By the end of the century, it extended over an area of 189,000 square miles with a population of 78½ million, creating in its wake vast administrative problems.

In 1843, a provincial secretariat was established. 11 years later the Governor-General was relieved of the direct administration of territories comprising the presidencies of Bengal and a separate post of Lieutenant-Governor was created. A civilian, he governed alone—viz, without an Executive Council—and was responsible, in the first instance, to the Governor-General.

Since 1854 Bengal had been reduced in area by nearly a quarter; despite this, its population had risen from 40 or 50 to almost 80 million—well over that of a quarter of the entire subcontinent. This had entailed a corresponding increase in governmental activity.

A proposal from the Government of India to give the Lieutenant-Governor of the province an Executive Council was rejected by Whitehall because it involved delegation of power and authority. So was another suggestion to divide the province on ethnic and linguistic grounds, this time in deference to the wishes of its Bengali-speaking civil servants whose promotions would thereby be adversely affected. The more popular interpretation however is that partition was the most effective way of checking the rapid growth of nationalism by breaking the unity of the Hindus, widening the gulf between them and the Muslims and weakening the already emboldened public press. The political motive behind the partition was not new as it had been mooted as far back as 1896 by one W. B. Oldham. Having decided that partition was an ideal solution out of the dilemma, administrative and otherwise, that the government faced, an official announcement to give it shape and form was made in Calcutta on 4 July 1905.

Another way of looking at it would be to view it as a problem in Lord Curzon's (q.v.) viceroyalty. Towards the close of his tenure, it had become abundantly clear that the Lower Provinces in general and the eastern half of Bengal in particular were administratively starved. The latter's communications were bad; its government buildings, mean and inadequate; its police stations, few and far between. Several districts were too large for administration by a single magistrate or collector. Its agricultural population was becoming richer and more litigous; its law courts and district establishments over-burdened with work; its scattered schools and colleges multiplying and producing a large crop of educated unemployed. Disappointment bred discontent, which was aggravated by political agitators and newspaper headlines that foreign rule was the source of all mischief.

In the last decade of the 19th century, there was an enormous increase in litigation with the result that the energies of district and sub-divisional officers were confined more and more to the business of trying cases. District officers were also burdened by mounting correspondence with various provincial departments, which prevented them from moving about their districts freely and thus becoming sufficiently acquainted with local conditions. Partition or a re-arrangement of charges appeared to be the only effective remedy, but it implied some disturbance of vested interests and, however desirable, a signal for loud newspaper protest.

Curzon, in 1902, had written: 'Bengal is ungovernably too large a charge for any single man'. His words had by then become a cliché dishonoured by 70 years of official inaction. What followed was truly remarkable: within ten years, Bengal was partitioned twice; its government was provided with an Executive Council; its Lieutenant-Governor replaced by a Governor; the capital moved from Calcutta to Delhi.

There were two alternatives: division of the province or expansion of its government. The second was overruled. The ideas of giving the Lieutenant-Governor a Council was thrown out on the plea that 'personal methods of government are better suited to the circumstances of India, and produce superior results'.

The unwillingness to delegate authority is faithfully reflected in the relations between the Government of India and Bengal. It was typical of Curzon—and indeed of normal relations between the governments—that it was he who made a tour of East Bengal in February 1904 to enlist support for partition and *not* the Lieutenant-Governor. One vainly asks why the latter was not asked to handle this essentially local question.

It may also be recalled that until well into the present century, the tendency was to govern, for the sake of the government, *not* the governed. Too often in the discussions on Bengal, both in 1867-8 and 1902-3, it was the concurrence of the administration which was deemed of primary importance. The violent Bengali hatred of partition was born out of the fact that the measure was pushed through in the name of administrative convenience, which was considered 'all sufficient', while the opposition was characterized as ignorant or, more often, 'selfish and subversive'. Bengali, and particularly Calcutta, interests were severely affected by the partition—but it was for the Europeans, official and non-official, that adjustments were made.

The question of moving the Government of India out of Calcutta so as to give Bengal a Governor and an Executive Council was raised as early as 1868—it was ruled out in Calcutta, although both Bombay and Madras supported it for they believed that the Government of India was 'inordinately' influenced by Calcutta opinion. Apart from the 'secretariat wallahs'—for whom Calcutta was a stronghold in the 19th century—there was the European business community. Through the Bengal Chamber of Commerce and private influence, they could, and did, exert strong pressure on the government. And, if thwarted, their displeasure found expression in the columns of *The Englishman, Capital* and *Commerce*.

The ascendancy of Calcutta was important in finding a solution to the Bengal problem. Any attempt to partition the province was seen as a threat to Calcutta as a metropolis; any suggestion to shift the imperial capital was viewed as a threat to non-official European influence! Both the Governments of India and of Bengal were thus bound hand and foot by Calcutta until freed by the growth of counter-forces in the late 19th century.

By 1905, there was the legacy of 70 years of procrastination and delay. Bengal's administrative malaise was by then so acute that to have postponed a cure any longer would have been fatal. The disclosures of the Indian Police Commission in 1903 on the neglect of East Bengal had left no doubt on the point. There was also the personality of Curzon who had set his heart on solving the Bengal problem and it was unfortunate that he chose partition as the way out. It was left to his 'liberal' successor to repair the damage.

Curzon's announcement of the partition, even though rated administratively 'expedient', came at a 'peculiarly unfortunate' time. Revolution was being preached in Bengal—even Vivekananda (q.v.) had combined 'nationalism with religious tendencies'. There was, in addition, the cumulative impact of Japan's 'resounding victories' over Russia and a firm belief among the educated classes that the Governor-General's reforms were designed to cramp their growing influence in the community. The anti-partition agitation, with its vehement invective, its appeals to Hindu sentiment, its clarion call that Bengal as the motherland had been torn into two, its bold plan for enforcing a punitive boycott (q.v.) of foreign goods (and supplementing them entirely by 'Swadeshi' (q.v.), its enlistment of youths, students and schoolboys in picketing operations, gave ample scope to the British to dub it as sedulous preaching of revolutionary doctrines. In East Bengal, there were growing disturbances; in both Bengals it was widely proclaimed that the government was setting Muslims against Hindus. Under cover of a storm of passions, the revolutionaries organized secret societies, collected arms and manufactured bombs.

As a backdrop it may be recalled that in 1896–7 a proposal was mooted to the effect that some parts of Bengal be incorporated into Assam—the former was too large, the latter too small. Curzon's view was that Bengal apart, the boundaries of Assam, the Central Provinces and Madras were 'antiquated, illogical and productive of inefficiency'. More, he endorsed the views of Denzil Charles Ibbetson, then a member of his Council, that the influence of Eastern Bengal in the politics of the province was out of all proportion to its real political importance, that it was a 'hotbed of the purely Bengali movement, unfriendly if not seditious in character'. It followed that for him it was imperative to destroy the influence of the intelligentsia over Bengal and of the latter over the whole of India.

Curzon was impervious to criticism of his proposed scheme and agreed with H. H. Risley, then Home Secretary, that 'Bengal united is a power, Bengal divided will pull several…different ways'. To many among the ruling élite that appeared to be the great merit of the Viceroy's scheme.

The argument that partition was demanded by the Muslims or was designed to improve the condition of their backward brethren in Bengal's eastern districts does not, in the face of evidence to the contrary, carry conviction. Tara Chand has expressed the view that neither Hindus nor Muslims had expressly demanded partition. To be sure, the real reason was not 'because the administrative problem could not be solved otherwise, but because the British rulers were alarmed at the growth of national solidarity in India and were anxious to thwart it.'

Curzon's proposals were sent to Whitehall on 2 February 1905, the latter's approval accorded on 9 June. Royal assent was given on 1 September and re-organization effected on 16 October, the same year.

The English as well as the 'native' Indian press had been critical of the proposed measure from the very outset. It has been suggested that between December 1903 and October 1905 'over 2,000 public meetings attended by 500 to 50,000 people were held in the two parts of Bengal at which Hindus and Mohammedans with equal zeal and earnestness joined in the protest.'

The partition, as has been noticed, came into effect on 16 October 1905. Under its terms, the districts of Dacca, Mymensingh, Faridpur, Bakargunj, Tippera, Noakhali, Chittagong and its hill tract of Rangpur, Pabna, Malda and Bogra were to form part of the new province of East Bengal and Assam with a predominantly Muslim population. The western half of Bengal, Bihar and Orissa were placed under another Lieutenant-Governor. The district of Sambalpur with the exception of a few zamindaris was transferred from the Central Provinces to the Bengal division of the presidency of Fort William. In 1910, the latter was given an Executive Council of two British civil servants and one non-official Indian.

Bengal's reaction to the partition was unprecedented—16 October was observed as a day of mourning, protest meetings were held and the foundaton of a 'Federal Hall' laid. The latter was to serve as a venue for similar gatherings in the future. A resolution was passed to launch the Swadeshi movement (q.v.) and adopt the slogan of '*Bande Mataram*'.

Among the prominent leaders of the anti-partition agitation mention may be made of Gooroodass Banerjee (q.v.), Surendranath Banerjea (q.v.),

Rabindranath Tagore (q.v.), Satish Chandra Mukherji, Motilal Ghose, Ananda Mohan Bose (q.v.), Romesh Chandra Dutt (q.v.), Bipin Chandra Pal (q.v.), Ashvini Kumar Dutt, Ambika Charan Mazumdar and K. K. Mitra. The principal organizations that took part were the Dawn Society, the Bande Mataram Sampradaya, the Anti-Circular Society and the Swadeshi Samaj.

The government came down heavily on the protestors. Public meetings were banned as was the cry of 'Bande Mataram'. All this however was to no apparent avail, for the earlier political mendicancy of the nationalist movement had now given place to organized 'revolutionary pressure'.

The importance of the movement lies in the fact that it aided in 'crystallising' national sentiment. It has been said that from Bengal's partition 'can be dated the end of British rule in India'.

Both the Swadeshi movement and the boycott propaganda that followed in its wake made a deep impact; their most enthusiastic supporters being the youth of Bengal. To be sure, the partition had acted as a catalytic agent that precipitated the slow developing process of anti-British sentiment. The Russo-Japanese war (1904–5), the worsening economic conditions in India and the 'haughty apathy' of the British acted as additional predisposing causes.

To start with, the government played down the agitation. As it spread and became more virulent, policy changed. Between 1906-8, a spate of repressive measures on the one hand and a resolute effort to wean away the Muslims on the other were vigorously launched. In the result, while propaganda activity through public meetings and the press continued unabated, the Swadeshi and boycott movements buttressed it further. The latter led to an outburst of revolutionary activity in the two Bengals and, to suppress it, the government resorted to a vast array of more repressive measures.

In 1911, as has been noticed, partition was set aside. As a result, the two divided provinces emerged as three political entities: united Bengal became the charge of a governor in council; Bihar and Orissa were placed under a lieutenant-governor in council; Assam was entrusted to a chief commissioner.

The most celebrated casualty of Bengal's partition was the unity of the Indian National Congress (q.v.). The disagreement over agitational methods in Bengal led to the division of the Congress into two factions—the Moderates and the Extremists; to a clash between the two at Surat (q.v.) in December 1907 and to the latter's exclusion from the Congress for a decade thereafter.

S.Z.H. Zaidi, 'The Partition of Bengal and its annulment—a survey of territorial redistribution of Bengal (1902–1911)', unpublished Ph. D. thesis, 1964, University of London; J. M. Broomfield, 'The Partition of Bengal: A problem in British Administration, 1830–1912', in *Indian History Congress*, Proceedings, Aligarh, 1960, Calcutta, 1961, 2 parts, II, pp. 13-24; P. C. Chakravarty, 'Genesis of the Partition of Bengal (1905)', in *Indian History Congress*, Proceedings, Trivandrum, 1958, Bombay, 1959, pp. 549-53; Pardaman Singh, 'The Annulment of the Partition of Bengal', *Bengal Past and Present*, XCII, 1973, pp. 77-83.

Bengal Tenancy Act (1885)

The oppressed peasantry in Bengal, as elsewhere, posed a serious problem to British authorities in India. Legislative measures—the Permanent Settlement (q.v.) of 1793 and the Rent Act of 1859, seeking to effect a better landlord-tenant relationship—had failed to offer a worthwhile solution, for the ryot was continuously harassed by eviction, rent increases and undue exactions as before. The result was large-scale anti-zamindari riots in the years 1872-6. Need was thus felt for legislation to provide some sort of relief and security to the tenant farmers without at the same time antagonizing the zamindars. In Bihar a Rent Law Commission was set up in 1879 to inquire into the problem and on the basis of its report, submitted a year later, a Bill was introduced (1883). It provided the ryot with liberalized occupancy rights, security against enhancement of rent and compensation for loss during disturbances. The proposed legislation, however, caused an uproar among the zamindars. To placate them, a select committee was appointed to review the Bill; it was adopted in its amended form in March 1885.

A comparison between the original Bill and the law as finally enacted makes instructive reading. Briefly according to the Bill, (i) the right of occupancy was to be conferred on all settled ryots who held land in the same village or estate; the Act limited this to land held in the same village; (ii) the Bill had made the right of occupancy heritable and freely transferable; the Act left the right to transfer to be regulated by local custom; (iii) in regard to enhancement, the Bill had provided that the rent paid by an occupancy ryot should not exceed 1/5th of the gross produce and that no enhancement could at once double the rent or take place except at an interval of ten years. The rent of a non-occupancy ryot was not to exceed 5/16th of the gross produce. The Act removed all such restrictions on enhancement of rent; (iv) the Bill laid down that in case of ejectment, the non-occupancy ryot was to receive compensation; the Act deleted this provision.

It should follow that the Act of 1885 was very much an emasculated version of the original Bill. Among other things, it failed to give any protection to the under-tenant of the occupancy ryot.

Under the new law, the ryot was given occupancy rights if he had held land in the same village for 12 years; the practice of shifting was stopped and no eviction was possible except for misuse of land or breach of contract. Though occupancy rights were hereditary, they were not transferable. A sub-lease by a ryot was also deemed invalid unless it had the landlord's consent. Limits on enhancement of rent were set aside, and the rent itself could now be increased by 2 annas in a rupee by a contract out of court. Any further increase was ruled out for fifteen years, except through a law suit.

Compensation for improvement in cases of eviction was provided. A landlord could, however, by applying to a civil court, claim land for a reasonable purpose requiring his tenant to sell the whole or part of his holding. By providing a simple and summary procedure for rent suits, the zamindar's powers remained virtually unaffected, for the latter was still able to intimidate his tenants and even, at times, break down their privileged status by the threat of legal proceedings.

The complexities of the Act afforded ample opportunity for resort to law and it was the zamindar, *not* the tenant, who was an adept at going to the law court. A mere threat to do so was enough to persuade a recalcitrant tenant to agree to an increase.

To say all this is not to deny the gains made by the tenant. In many respects, the new law resembled the Irish Land Act of 1881. The tenant had now secured his 3 F's: fair rent, fixity of tenure and free sale of occupancy rights. Tenant-farmers received protection in a small measure, and the importance of the new law lay essentially in its recognition of their rights, and in setting a precedent for future legislation. The Act empowered the central government to order a survey and the preparation of a record of rights in any area. Additionally, the provincial government could direct similar operations in any estate on their own or on request. The work was to be undertaken by a staff presided over by a director of land records, with operational expenses to be shared between the state, the landlord and the tenant.

In adopting the new law, it has been said, a first step had been taken towards introducing a modicum of 'system, justice and clarity' in the jungle of revenue administration in Bengal.

T. R. Metcalf, *The Aftermath of Revolt*, Princeton, 1965; Bipin Chandra, *The Rise and Growth of Economic Nationalism in India*, New Delhi, 1966; *Selections from Papers Relating to the Bengal Tenancy Act, 1885*, Calcutta, 1885.

Young Bengal

The followers of Henry Louis Derozio (q.v.) were collectively known as the Young or New Bengal, the term being also used for the movement they initiated. Their activities embrace roughly the first half of the nineteenth century, and its prominent members were Krishna Mohan Bandyopadhyaya, Rasik Krishna Malik, Radhanath Shikdar, Dakshina Ranjan Mukhopadhyaya, Pearay Chand Mitra and Ramtanu Lahiri.

A majority in Derozio's group consisted of students of Hindu College. Deeply influenced by western literature, philosophy and revolutionary ideas, theirs was an appeal to reason and a revolt against the superstitions and malpractices then prevalent in Hindu society. Holding radical views, they openly spurned and ridiculed orthodox beliefs and adopted western ways of living. Of liberal persuation in politics, they advocated benevolent government and free trade. Young Bengal, it has been said, 'read Tom Paine, admired revolutionary France, hated the British Tories, wrote poems about the fallen state of the motherland and dreamt of a free and self-governing India in the future'.

The movement's primary aim was to expose the corrupt priesthood and evil social customs, diffuse education especially among women, use freedom of the press to bring about radical social change, encourage patriotism and improve conditions in the country. They publicized their views through several journals such as the *Bengal Spectator*, *Parthenon* (or the *Athenium*), *Hesperus*, *Inquirer*, *Quill*, *Gyaneveshwar*, *Hindu Pioneer*, etc. A number of its members were also actively associated with the (Bengal) British India Society, founded by George Thompson in 1843.

Variously criticized as anglicists and atheists, these young men were, in reality, idealists in search of a utopia. Understandably, they failed to develop a popular base, or an ideology that would work. The result was that the movement had petered out by the mid-nineteenth century.

The assault which Young Bengal made on orthodoxy in the community led the latter to re-examine their beliefs and practices. Additionally, by their integrity, dignified conduct, conscientiousness and intellectual honesty these 'youthful zealots' enhanced the country's self-respect and elevated the moral stature of society. They were men in whom the nationalist movement first manifested itself; their major contribution lay in the impetus they gave to free and rational thinking and a spirit of inquiry that was the hallmark of the age of reason.

K. S. Bhattacharya, 'Social and Political Thinking of Young Bengal', *JIH*, LVII, I, April, 1979, pp. 29–61; T. Banerji, 'The Young Bengal: A General Estimate, in *Renascent Bengal (1817–1857)*, The Asiatic Society, Calcutta, 1972; N. S. Bose *Indian Awakening and Bengal*, Calcutta, 1960; *Tara Chand*, II, pp. 244–7.

William Bentinck (1774–1839)

William Henry Cavendish Bentinck first came to India as Governor of the then Madras presidency. Earlier, he had served in some military expeditions as well as civil missions in Europe and was, intermittently, a member of the British parliament. In 1808, he was blamed for an alleged failure to control the sepoy mutiny at Vellore and recalled home. Later he served in several diplomatic assignments in Europe on behalf of his country.

Bentinck actively sought and successfully secured his appointment in 1827 as Governor-General to demonstrate that he had been wronged for his earlier removal with its stigma of inefficiency and incapacity. He assumed office in July 1827.

In his new assignment he had specific and, in fact, explicit instructions to enforce reform in the civil as well as military services and to slash expenditure. He instituted two committees of inquiry and later based his measures on their reports. In the result, the salaries of civil servants were reduced and **batta** (daily allowance) to army personnel halved. The latter measure, opposed by members of his Executive Council, including Metcalfe (q.v.) and W. B. Bayley, led to the resignation of Lord Combermere, then Commander-in-Chief of the armed forces. Additionally, it aroused a great deal of general discontent among the European community. It would only be fair however to mention that in all this Bentinck was merely carrying out the express wishes of his political bosses, even though he himself considered some of their directives both 'impolitic and unnecessary'.

On the judicial side, he abolished the provincial Courts of Appeal and Circuit and instituted in their place a Civil and Sessions Judge in every district. Some junior administrative posts had been anticipated by his predecessors but it fell to him to implement their recommendations.

Bentinck also undertook some measures of social reform such as the abolition of sati (q.v.) and female infanticide, grounds for which had already been prepared. Under his instructions Colonel William Sleeman (q.v.) successfully suppressed the Thugs (q.v.). The Governor-General also announced rules relating to succession as affected by change of religion; this freed the new converts to Christianity from some anxiety and secured them a measure of inheritance. Bentinck is also given credit for introducing western education based on Macaulay's (q.v.) minute of 1835. That decision was taken in the face of a long and bitter controversy between the 'Anglicists' and the 'Orientalists'. Macaulay's one-sided view, couched in vigorous prose, held out extravagant hopes that the measure would result in a complete transformation of the social milieu. Strictly, the decision was that funds earmarked by the government for education should henceforth be devoted *not* to the fostering of oriental learning but to instruction in English and western science.

Despite his policy of non-intervention in relation to Indian States (q.v.) for which his period of administration is known, Bentinck assumed the government of Mysore and Coorg on grounds of mismanagement, and annexed Cachar in Assam on the death of its ruler. It would thus seem that his policy regarding the states was both inconsistent and vacillating; the 'native' rulers complained that they were neither permitted to manage their affairs nor yet furnished with assistance necessary to bring about reform. All that they received were threats of annexation if the internal administration did not improve, as was the case in Oudh (q.v.), Berar, Gwalior; in Rajput states he did not interfere even when asked to, on the plea that he believed in non-intervention. In all cases, he let things get out of control before stepping in.

In what has been rated a valuable minute (1835), Bentinck was the first to underscore that threat of a Russian advance towards India. To counter it, he sent Alexander Burnes (q.v.) to Persia to conclude an agreement with the Shah who, *inter alia*, gave a solemn pledge neither to join the Tsar nor allow Russian armies to march to India. He also concluded a treaty of friendly alliance with Ranjit Singh (q.v.) and a treaty of commerce with the Amirs of Sind (q.v.) to secure Britain's Indian frontiers. In terms of the Charter Act of 1833 (q.v.), Bentinck assumed the title of Governor-General of India. In March 1835 he resigned on grounds of ill-health, and four years later died in Paris.

Contemporary historians of British India have rated his performance favourably. Thus James Mill thought his Indian achievement remarkable 'in a most important and difficult situation'; H. H. Wilson who continued Mill's *History* assigned him 'an honourable place' among British statesmen who ruled India. Marshman has called his tenure 'the most memorable between Cornwallis (q.v.) and Dalhousie (q.v.)'. More recently, Bentinck has been compared to Ripon (q.v.) in his enthusiasm for progressive causes and in innovation and reform that laid the foundations of India's progress along western lines.

Rosselli has expressed the view that while Macaulay's panegyrics—'He infused into oriental despotism the spirit of British freedom'—may be exaggerated, there is no doubt that Bentinck was among the first British statesmen who acted on the maxim of governing India in the interests of her people. His partisans invest him with two great qualities—personal indifference to popular applause and high moral courage; his detractors underline the fact that he was an exponent of the views of others either pressed upon him from home or by those he trusted—and never dared assert his own.

John Rosselli, *Lord William Bentinck: The making of a Liberal Imperialist 1774–1839,* Delhi, 1974; C. H. Philips (ed.), *The Correspondence of Lord William*

Cavendish Bentinck, *Governor-General of India, 1828–35*, Oxford, 1977, 2 vols; *DNB*, II, pp. 292–7 (John A. Alexander).

Annie Besant (1847–1933)

A renowned theosophist, Mrs Annie Besant (*née* Wood), figures prominently in the history of the freedom movement as the initiator of the Home Rule League (q.v.). This was during the years of World War 1 (1914–18) when moderate opinion hesitated, in view of England's preoccupations, to voice their demands for political reform long deemed overdue.

Of predominantly Irish lineage, Mrs Besant's bold and independent thinking had resulted in separation from her husband, vicar Frank Besant, in 1873. Initiated soon afterwards into Charles Bradlaugh's (1833–91) Secular Society, she became its Vice-President, actively engaged in preaching and publishing articles on atheism and the political and social rights of women.

As a member of the Fabian Society from 1885 onwards, Annie Besant pursued equally actively the socialist principles it had espoused. She contributed articles on socialism to the *Fabian Essays*, organized successful strikes of factory working girls and fought for every reform then under discussion. In 1889 she enrolled as a member of the Theosophical Society (q.v.) whose ideology furnished the answers she had long sought. Devoted and diligent, she was chosen President of the Society after the death of Col. Olcott in 1907. In turn, she chose J. Krishnamurti to succeed her, and just when he was all but declared world messiah, he broke away from the movement (1929). Some rate this as one of the primary causes of her rapidly failing health after 1930 and her death soon afterwards (1933).

Initially, Annie Besant's interest in Theosophy, Hinduism and the land of its origin had brought her out to India in 1893. In the course of that year and the one following, she lectured on Hindu religion and culture in several towns of southern and northern India. She expostulated against the loss of faith by the Hindus in their great, and ancient, religion, glorifying it as the fount of all other religions and the 'cradle of civilization'. From 1895 to 1907 she made Banaras her home, where her untiring efforts resulted in the establishment of the Central Hindu College. With the help of Dr Bhagvan Das, she translated the Bhagavad Gita into English, to revive an interest in its study among educated Indians. Later she was to supervise the compilation of a textbook on Hindu religion and morals.

Annie Besant's interest in politics during these years remained peripheral, although she was acutely conscious of the emergence of Indians in the political field as well as their demand for political reform. She felt that India should not adopt western institutions and methods, but alter these to suit her peculiar conditions and way of life. In brief, she opposed all attempts to abandon the old traditions.

Annie Besant emerged on the political stage in 1913 when she publicly recommended that the House of Commons set up a Standing Committee for Indian affairs. On a visit to England the following year, she pleaded that India be recognized as a nation, allowed to govern itself as one of the other self-governing nations composing the Empire, and that a programme to achieve this inevitable end be charted out. On her return, she started two papers, the weekly *Commonwealth* (January 1914) and the daily *New India*

(July 1914) to propagate her political ideas and scheme of work. She also attended the annual session of the Indian National Congress (q.v.). In 1915, at a meeting in Bombay, she enunciated her plan to organize a Home Rule League. This was established in September 1916, after she had failed in her efforts to persuade Balgangadhar Tilak (q.v.) to combine the League he had established with her own.

Her slogan 'England's difficulty is India's opportunity' became a catchphrase in the nationalist armoury. The educated middle-class all over the country was impressed by her powerful oratory and bold demand for Dominion Status (q.v.) on the basis of equality, and rallied to the League. Another important achievement to her credit was the reconciliation she brought about between Tilak and the Congress. She played no small role in the cause of Hindu-Muslim unity and the Lucknow Pact (q.v.) which consummated it.

In May 1916, Annie Besant forfeited her deposit on the *New India* under the Press Act regulations. She paid the additional security of Rs 10,000 and continued the legal battle, moving from the Madras High Court to the Privy Council. Meanwhile, Lord Pentland, Governor of Madras, attempted to persuade her to abandon the Home Rule campaign and agree to be deported to England for the period of the War. On her declining to do so, she and her assistants, B. P. Wadia and J. S. Arundale, were interned without trial. This not only resulted in her emergence as the country's foremost freedom fighter, but in widespread agitation for her release, leading finally to a withdrawal of the order of her internment. She came forth triumphant and was honoured by being nominated President of the Congress session at Calcutta the same year.

The Montagu-Chelmsford Reforms (q.v.), for which her Home Rule campaign was responsible in large measure, were not up to her expectations, but she urged that they be given a trial. Her leadership was eclipsed by the emergence of Gandhi (q.v.) on the national scene, with his yet novel method of non-violent non-cooperation, of which she soon became an 'avowed opponent'. In the result, her influence soon began to wane.

A word on Annie Besant's politics. She could not compromise her constitutional methods of resistance with what seemed to her to be Gandhi's anarchical approach. Satyagraha as a means to achieve political ends held no appeal for her. In government action taken at Amritsar following the Rowlatt Act (q.v.) satyagraha, she supported official policy, maintaining that no government could look on while mobs indulged in orgies of large-scale destruction and violence. She exhorted everyone to stop criticizing the government and to make a stand against revolution. This alienated not only the extremist nationalists, but some Home rulers as well. She eschewed active politics after that. Convinced however that India must frame her own constitution, she staged a brief comeback in 1925 with the Commonwealth of India Bill, which several eminent Indian friends had helped her draft. It was introduced in the House of Commons by the well-known Labour leader, George Lansbury, and had the support of the (Labour) Party. Foredoomed to failure, it barely managed to receive a first reading. Years later however she did stand vindicated, with independent India voluntarily choosing to remain in the Commonwealth.

The range of her interests was wide and varied. To her credit goes the establishment of the Boy Scouts Association of which, for years, she was Honorary Commissioner. It brought her the Distinguished Order of the

Silver Wolf. She was also responsible for starting the Indian Women's Association so as to involve educated Indian women in their own welfare. A great educationist, she spared no effort in her determination to help establish new schools and colleges. Rabindra Nath Tagore (q.v.) was designated chancellor of the National University she established at Adyar, near Madras in 1918; the Central Hindu College she had helped to found later grew into Banaras Hindu University.

She gave the Congress its first flag which was green and red—a white portion with the spinning wheel was added later.

In sum, she worked in three different fields of India's national life: the British connection; the influence of the west; and the reaction of the new forces on the minds of the orthodox.

Annie Besant's appeal was more to the English-educated middle classes while Gandhi's was to the vast masses of the country. Hers was to the head; his to the heart.

She was known for efficiency in action and strength of will, her meticulous care of little as of great things. With her high regard for everyone, small as well as big, and appreciation of values and of men, she verily served as an ideal and an inspiration.

Annie Besant, *Autobiography*, reprint, London, 1915; Arthur Hobart Nethercot, *The First Five Lives of Annie Besant*, Chicago, 1960; and *The Last Four Lives of Annie Besant*, Chicago, 1963; Anne Fremantle, *This Little Band of Prophets: the Story of the Gentle Fabians*, London, 1960; Warren S. Smith, *The London Heretics, 1870-1914*, London, 1967; C.P. Ramaswami Aiyar, *Annie Besant,* Builders of Modern India Series, Delhi, 1963; Sri Prakasa, *Annie Besant: As Woman and Leader*, 3rd ed., Bombay, 1962; Esther Bright, *Old Memories and Letters of Annie Besant*, London, 1939; Raj Kumar, *Annie Besant's Rise to power in Indian politics 1914–1917*, New Delhi, 1981.

Bhutan

Bhutan, an independent kingdom and since 1971 a member of the United Nations, is situated on the southern slopes of the Himalaya. With an area of 18,000 square miles and a population of over a million, it is bounded on the north by Tibet and the east by Arunachal Pradesh; to its south lies Assam; to its north-east Bengal; on its west are Sikkim and the Chumbi valley. The country falls broadly into three physical divisions: the southernmost, contiguous to India and called the 'duars' (literally 'doorways' or 'passes') is mountainous and has a heavy rainfall; the central, which abounds in valleys with a moderate rainfall, is the most populous and produces nearly all the food; the northern, coterminous with Tibet, is full of mountains. It has five passes leading into Tibet, a strong factor influencing settlement and trade. The principal rivers are the Manas, the Torsa and the Sankosh.

The term 'Bhutan' comes from the Sanskrit word *Bhutanta*, literally 'end of Tibet'; the Bhutanese call their country *Drukyul* or 'land of the thunderbolt'. Apart from the Bhutias who are the dominant community, there are also the Lepchas, Tibetans and Nepalese. Lamaism is the state religion. The country is broadly run on a feudal basis, all power vesting in the hands of its landed chiefs called *penlops* who govern in the provinces and districts they hold, called *dzongs*. The natural wealth of the land is meagre and a major source of income is the Indian subsidy available in varied fields of human endeavour.

Broadly, Bhutan's history may be divided into three periods: the first, from the birth of the country till the advent of Tibet's influence; the second, from about the 10th century till the consolidation of Bhutan as a national entity in the 18th. The period is marked by the disappearance of the original inhabitants, the advent of Tibetan influence, consolidation of Buddhism under the Drukpa hegemony and emergence of Bhutan as a national entity. The third is the period of Indo-Bhutanese relationship both under the British and the government of free India, and covers developments from the early 19th century to date. There is hardly any reliable historical material for the first period; in the second, it is sketchy; in the third, it is both considerable and reliable.

Bhutan figures in modern Indian history from the time of Warren Hastings (q.v.), principally as a land providing a trade and transit route to Tibet. It came into conflict with the British because of the latter's occupation of the duars which the Bhotias had wrested from the Ahom rulers of Assam in the 18th century and which had provided them their principal source of income. With the annexation of Assam (1826) after the first Anglo-Burmese war (q.v.), the British inherited what was virtually a never-ending conflict, resulting from the duars territory located between the Teesta and Dhansiri rivers. The area had been taken from the Muslim rulers of Assam by the Bhutanese who, though by no means in absolute possession of the country,

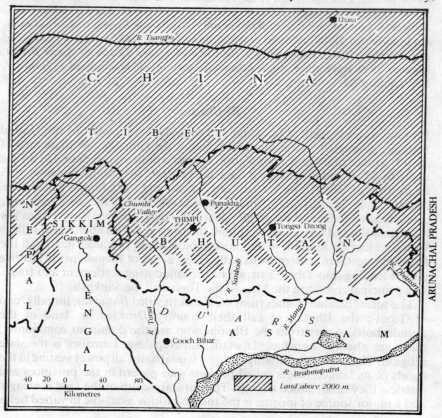

Bhutan

yet succeeded in extracting an annual tribute by pledging to refrain from launching raids or committing other outrages.

Trade relations with Bhutan initiated by Warren Hastings were broken off following the Anglo-Nepalese War (q.v.). Captain Robert Pemberton's mission (1837) failed to persuade the ruler to surrender the duars in Darrang district which he had occupied. In the result, the British took the Assam duars (1841) in return for an annual subsidy of Rs 1,000. All this notwithstanding, Bhutanese incursions into British-held territory, which had increased during the Rebellion of 1857 (q.v.), persisted and the failure of British missions to settle pending disputes convinced the government of the dire need for a 'forward' policy. Accordingly, it took over the Ambari Talakota district in 1860. Three years later, Ashley Eden (q.v.) led an unsuccessful mission in which, having forced his way in, he was treated somewhat harshly and compelled to sign a treaty that was clearly humiliating to the British.

War was declared on 22 November 1864 and all the Bengal as well as Assam duars annexed. By October 1865, the Bhutanese were ready to negotiate and signed the treaty of Sinchula, accepting, for the first time, a subordinate position and a subsidy.

With China, Bhutan has age-old ties. The right of granting a seal of office to the ruler was revived by the C'hing emperor, Chien Lung in 1736. The British envoy Pemberton reported that China's power, exercised through the Amban in Lhasa, was recognized with marked deference. Annual imperial mandates arrived through the Lhasa ambans while presents in kind were sent in return. In 1877 Chinese and Tibetan officials were despatched to sustain the Deb Raja in his refusal to let a British agent build a road. In 1890, the Chinese emperor sanctioned titles for the *penlops*.

The Tashi Lama, next in importance to the Dalai Lama (q.v.), in his correspondence with Warren Hastings in 1774 claimed that Bhutan was a dependency of the Dalai Lama. Subsequently, Bhutan maintained an agent at Lhasa.

In the 1880s, Bhutan began to figure prominently in British Indian politics. This was due partly to trade as also to Britain's increasing interest in counteracting Chinese influence in Tibet. Calcutta none the less scrupulously refrained from interfering in the civil strife then raging in the country, resulting from the intense rivalry and irreconcilable differences between its Dharam and Deb Rajas. In 1885, Ugyen Wangchuk, then *penlop of* Tongsa, emerged as the country's most powerful leader and sought to strengthen his position further by developing cordial relations with the British. In 1903 he lent his full support to Colonel Younghusband's Expedition (q.v.) and, as a mediator at Lhasa, was responsible for the convention signed there by the British commissioner. A year later, the British awarded him the KCSI and invited him to meet the Prince of Wales, then (1906) on a visit to India.

Indian authorities welcomed the emergence of Ugyen Wangchuk as the King of Bhutan in 1907, a development that signified the birth of hereditary monarchy in the family of the Tongsa *penlop* in west Bhutan.

In 1910 negotiations were initiated with British India so as to rule out the possibility of any interference by the Chinese in the country's internal affairs. The resultant treaty of Punakha, while it increased the subsidy to Rs 1 lakh, gave Britain added control over the country's external affairs, bringing it more or less on par with other princely Indian States (q.v.). Anglo-Bhutanese relations continued to be amicable and after the Chinese threat faded out, the British began treating the land virtually as a protectorate. In 1924, Whitehall defined Bhutan's political status thus: 'under the suzerainty of His Majesty, but not an Indian state, though its transition to that status could easily be affected by the concurrence of both parties.'

The Government of India Act 1935 (q.v.) excluded Bhutan from British Indian domain. In 1946 the country affirmed its separate identity before the (British-sponsored) Cabinet Mission (q.v.). To define its post-1947 status, a 10-article Indo-Bhutanese treaty was signed on 8 August 1949. The compact, as the preamble underlined, was between two 'peoples'. Free trade and commerce were provided for, India agreeing to grant every facility for the carriage, by land or water, of Bhutan's produce. Additionally, Bhutan was free to import 'whatever arms, ammunition, machinery, warlike materials or stores' it required. India also ceded 32 square miles of territory in the area known as Dewangiri. New Delhi was to 'exercise no interference' in the internal administration but Bhutan was 'to be guided by the advice of the Government of India in regard to its external affairs' and was to receive an annual subsidy of Rs 5 lakhs.

In 1952 King Jigme Dorji Wangchuk succeeded to the throne. Six years later, at his invitation, Prime Minister Nehru visited the country, travelling via Tibet. In the late 1960s, Bhutan became a member of the Colombo Plan Consultative Committee and of the Universal Postal Union; in 1971, of the United Nations—in all three cases her membership being sponsored by India. In July 1972, on the death of the king, his only son, Jigme Singye Wangchuk became the new Druk Gyalpo.

Nari Rustomji, *Enchanted Frontiers: Sikkim, Bhutan and India's North-eastern Borderlands,* Delhi, 1971; also, *Imperilled Frontiers: India's North Eastern Borderlands,* Delhi, 1983; Pradyumna P. Karan and William M. Jenkins, *The Himalayan Kingdoms: Bhutan, Sikkim and Nepal,* Princeton, 1963; Nirmala Das, *The Dragon Country: the general history of Bhutan,* Bombay, 1974; P. L. Mehra, 'Sikkim and Bhutan: an historical conspectus', *JIH,* XLVI, 1, April 1968, pp. 89-124; Michael Aris, *Bhutan: the early history of a Himalayan kingdom,* London, 1979; Burke Inlow, 'Report from Bhutan', *Asian Affairs* (Journal of Royal Central Asian Society, London) IX, 3, Oct. 1978, pp. 295–308.

Treaty of Bhyrowal (1846)

A series of '11 articles of agreement' concluded at Lahore on 16 December 1846 and ratified by the Governor-General at Bhyrowal (on the left bank of the Beas) ten days later, further modified the earlier Treaty of Lahore (q.v.) between the British government and the Sikh state. The new compact was necessitated by the fact that the Darbar and its 'principal chiefs and Sardars' had expressed their 'anxious desire' to solicit British 'aid and assistance' in maintaining the administration of the Lahore state during the minority of Maharaja Dalip Singh (q.v.).

A sequel to the treaty of Lahore, the new 'agreement' helped further to tighten the John Company's (q.v.) control over the Panjab. Understandably, the British took advantage of the discordant elements in the state to make themselves powerful and indispensable. Lal Singh, a one-time paramour of Maharani Jind Kaur (q.v.), was found guilty of an anti-British conspiracy, tried and exiled on 13 December 1846, to the delight of other envious Sardars. A two-way diplomatic manoeuvre followed, for while the Darbar was cajoled into signing another treaty, a decision was taken to remove the minor Maharaja Dalip Singh's widowed mother, the Maharani.

The 'articles of agreement' stipulated *inter alia* that:

i) a British officer, 'with an efficient establishment of assistants' was to have 'full authority' to direct and control all matters in all departments of the state;

ii) a Council of Regency of eight Sardars who were signatories to the new compact would conduct the administration of the country 'in consultation with' the British Resident;

iii) a British force 'of such strength and numbers and in such positions' as deemed fit was to be stationed at Lahore and was free to occupy 'any fort or military fort' as it may deem necessary;

iv) the Darbar was to pay Rs 22 lakhs in two instalments for the maintenance of the British force;

v) the 'preceding arrangements' were to be operative 'only during the minority of the Maharaja' and were to terminate on his attaining 'the full age of 16 years' (4 September 1854).

Aitchison, II, pp. 267-70; Khushwant Singh, *History of the Sikhs*, II, pp. 59-60.

Syed Husain Bilgrami (1842–1926)

Syed Husain Bilgrami was an eminent Muslim educationist and one of the first two Indians (the other being Sir K. S. Gupta) to be a member of the India Council of the Secretary of State in London. Hailing from the village of Bilgram in Bihar (from which he took his name), he was born in 1842, and received his early education in the traditional Muslim fashion. Later, he studied at Patna, Bhagalpur and Calcutta. As Professor of Arabic at Canning College, Lucknow, where he was also put in charge of the *Lucknow Times*, a bi-weekly organ of the talukdars of Oudh, he attracted the attention of the visiting Sir Salar Jang (q.v.), who persuaded him to move to Hyderabad. From 1873 onwards he was to serve there for nearly fifty years in various capacities—as private secretary to the state's prime minister, as education secretary and, later, Director of Public Instruction. He was tutor and secretary to Nizam Mir Mehboob Ali Khan (q.v.) as well as the last of the line, Mir Osman Ali Khan (q.v.), and later (1912-13), after retirement, adviser to the third Salar Jang, the young grandson of his benefactor.

The programme for educational reform implemented in the erstwhile state of Hyderabad was largely structured by Bilgrami and almost all educational institutions in the state, barring perhaps Osmania University and New Girls' School, owe their origin to his efforts. Besides encouraging female, industrial and vocational education, he took great interest in the preservation and publication of old and valuable books. To encourage oriental learning and scholarship, the Dar-ul-Ulam or Oriental College was founded as well as the State Library, originally a repository for rare and priceless Arabic works. A member of the Imperial Legislative Council, he was one of the two Indians, the other being Gooroodass Banerjee (q.v.), to be a member of Lord Curzon's (q.v.) Universities Commission of 1902. Though by no means a political activist, his interest in and devotion to the cause of Muslim regeneration and association with Syed Ahmad Khan (q.v.) drew him unwittingly into the vortex of (Muslim) politics in the country. Bilgrami was among the leading ashrafs (aristocrats) who joined the Syed in his anti-Indian National Congress (q.v.) chorus.

Characteristically, Bilgrami exhorted his co-religionists to steer clear of the Congress and to concentrate on the educational progress of the community. As President of the Muhammadan Anglo-Oriental Educational Conference in 1896 and 1901, he appealed to Muslims to throw off the shackles of traditionalism and adopt the new ideas and learning of the west. In the larger interests of the community, he opposed competition as a means of recruitment to the civil service which, he argued, must guarantee a modicum of Muslim representation. He opposed it not only because it would deprive the Muslims of all share in the government but because 'competition' did not test anything 'but the power of assimilating knowledge'. 'Capacity for physical endurance, power of muscle and sinew, moral capability, fearlessness of character'—these 'are not measured by a literary test'.

While lending his support to the Statutory Civil Service (q.v.), instituted in 1879, he was emphatic on excluding 'men of low caste', for he would, 'as a rule', look with suspicion 'on men who had risen from low positions'.

Bilgrami's address to the Muhammadan Anglo-Oriental Educational Conference at Meerut in December 1896 offered 'more a literary treat' than a practical discourse. Five years later, addressing the 14th annual session of the same conference at Rampur (January 1901), he tried to give a new orientation to education by his emphasis on acquiring western skills. 'Rarely before', it has been noted, 'was such an uncompromising stand taken by a responsible leader before a representative Muslim gathering.'

In 1906 Nawab Mohsin-ul-Mulk (q.v.) requested Bilgrami to draft an address to the Viceroy which the proposed Muslim deputation was to present. To be sure, W. A. J. Archbold, then Principal of MAO College, had communicated with him and Nawab Ali Chowdhry of Dacca concerning the address and the composition of the delegation. A 'formal request' was drawn up for which numerous signatures were collected. An address too was knocked into shape whose contents were discussed between Mohsin-ul-Mulk, Bilgrami and Archbold. Thus it was that he became the author of what has been regarded as the classic document of Muslim separatist demands.

In doing so, Bilgrami, who had cultivated good relations with Charles Stuart Bayley, then British Resident at Hyderabad, was voicing with added emphasis the apprehensions of the Muslim community to a Secretary of State (viz., Morley) who, he maintained, 'knows more about Voltaire and eighteenth-century literature than the condition of contemporary India'. He warned that men who knew 'nothing of the conditions' yet wished 'to carry out their theories' could only 'bring about ruin of the country'.

In 1907 Bilgrami was a member of the 3-man delegation comprising, apart from himself, the Aga Khan (q.v.) and Syed Ameer Ali (q.v.) that waited on the Secretary of State and demanded separate electorates and weightage at all stages for the Muslim community as also 50% representation in the Viceroy's Executive Council. A year later Morley asked him to join the India Council. In 1909 he returned home on grounds of ill-health. During

World War I he appealed to his community to remain loyal to Britain even though Turkey was the enemy.

Bilgrami was the recipient of many honours from the Nizam and was officially referred to as 'Nawab Ali Yar Khan Bahadur, Motman Jung, Imad-ud-Daulah, Imad-ul-Mulk, CSI'. The grand old man of Hyderabad, as he was frequently called, died in 1926.

G. A. Natesan (ed.), *Eminent Musalmans*, Madras, n.d., pp. 353-63; Rafiq Zakaria, *Rise of Muslims in Indian Politics: an Analysis of Developments from 1885 to 1906*, Bombay, 1970.

Benoit de Boigne (1751–1830)

Initially Benoit Leborgne, but known to posterity as Benoit de Boigne, he was born at Chembery (Savoy) in Italy on 8 March 1751. With no regular schooling, he yet acquired a good knowledge of books and a tolerable proficiency in Latin. There is more than one version of his making the overland journey to India. Here he raised disciplined armies from the virile people of the north and trained them to fight and conquer. His famous battalions formed, as it were, a connecting link between the era of the Mughal empire and that of British dominion in the east.

De Boigne arrived in Madras in 1778 and joined the 6th Native Infantry as a lieutenant. It was during this period that he acquired a good working knowledge of British army organization, training and tactics. Superseded owing to a social misdemeanour, he resigned his command and proceeded north in search of a fortune. Around 1784 he was commissioned by Madhava Rao Sindhia (q.v.) to raise two battalions of disciplined infantry with a suitable complement of artillery. Consisting of 850 men each, they were patterned as nearly as possible on the lines of those in the John Company's (q.v.) service with similar accoutrements, arms and discipline.

The Battle of Agra (June 1788), in which the Mughals and their allies were severely repulsed, extinguished for all time any hope of independence for the successors of Akbar and Aurangzeb and completely established Maratha ascendancy. It assured an easy reconquest of the Doab and made Sindhia the undisputed master of Hindustan. For de Boigne, Agra had been a partial reverse; later, at Lalsot, Sindhia retreated against his commander's better judgement. Both meant his temporary retirement (1789-90). Subsequently, as a result of the victories of Patna and Mesta, a second (1791) and a third (1793) brigade were formed. In organizing them, de Boigne somewhat remodelled their earlier constitution. The Battle of Lakhairi (September, 1793) between Sindhia and Holkar resulted in a decisive victory for the former and settled for a time the hitherto ding-dong Sindhia-Holkar struggle in favour of the former.

At the height of his power, de Boigne employed a fine set of subordinate officers, ran his own arsenals and paid his troops well and in time. His battalions, known as the 'Cheria Fauj', successfully reduced the Rajput rulers of Jodhpur and Ajmer and defeated Tukoji Holkar. Madhava Rao appointed him governor of Hindustan. After the Maratha ruler's death, de Boigne resigned his command and repaired home with a large fortune, worth more than a quarter million pounds sterling, securely invested.

A contemporary described his appearance thus: frame and stature, herculean; aspect, mild and unassuming; habit and demeanour, unostentatious. Rated to be a born leader of men, he was an adventurer of a rare type, a self-made soldier of fortune.

Even though an Italian, de Boigne had pronouncedly Anglophile sympathies. He rated the English 'the first in the world' and was convinced that 'there are not many men like them'.

De Boigne died in June 1830.

Desmond Young, *Fountain of the Elephants*, London, 1959; Shelford Bidwell, *Swords for Hire: European Mercenaries in Eighteenth-century India*, London, 1971; Herbert Compton, *A Particular Account of the European Military Adventurers of Hindustan from 1784 to 1803*, reprint, Oxford, 1976.

Ananda Mohan Bose (1847–1906)

A pioneering educationist, social reformer and nationalist, Ananda Mohan Bose was born on 23 September 1847 at a village in Mymensingh district, now in Bangladesh. After a brilliant school career, he won distinctions in Calcutta University and finished his mathematical tripos at Cambridge, thereby becoming India's first wrangler. Simultaneously he had kept his terms at the Inns of Court and was duly called to the bar in April 1874.

His work as an advocate in the Calcutta High Court and later in the mofussil was designed principally to earn a living; his heart lay in the uplift of the masses through religious, social and political reform. An active member of the Brahmo Samaj (q.v.), he was co-founder with Sivanath Sastri of the Sadharan Brahmo Samaj (1878), after the parting of ways with Keshab Chandra Sen had become irrevocable.

Bose strove to popularize the spread of education with a view to ameliorating the condition of women. To him credit is due for the City College of Calcutta (1879) and the Banga Mahila Vidyalaya. For his services in the field of education, he was nominated a Fellow of Calcutta University and a member, in 1877, of its faculties of Arts and Law. A year later he became a member of its syndicate and was nominated a member of the Education (Hunter) Commission of 1882 (q.v.). The scheme he drew up for the popularization of primary education was accepted by the government.

Bose's interest in politics may be traced to his student days in England. There he had started the (London) Indian Society 'to foster the spirit of nationalism among Indian residents' and advocated the gradual establishment of representative government in the country. To activise student interest in politics, he started the Calcutta Students Association, it being the earliest known attempt to organize students for political work. Later he left most of its work to Surendranath Banerjea (q.v.) whom he had befriended and come to admire.

Aware of the lack of a purely political association, he founded along with Banerjea the Indian Association (q.v.) in 1876. Its establishment was sought to be justified on the ground that none of the existing associations represented the 'oppressed cooly or the oppressed ryot' or was capable of 'keeping up and stimulating public opinion'. As its secretary, Bose called in December 1883 a 'National Conference' in Calcutta to discuss 'the burning questions' of the day. Among the resolutions adopted at this meeting, one related to the raising of a national fund, another to the desirability of establishing 'representative assemblies' in the country. At the same time, a vigorous constitutional agitation was launched to protest against such legislation as the Vernacular Press Act (q.v.) and the Ilbert Bill (q.v.).

To recoup his failing health, Bose left for Germany in 1879. During a brief stop-over in England, on his way home, he lectured extensively, pleading the cause of his country and its people. He had, as noticed above, mooted the idea of a 'National Conference' and years later was nominated president of the Madras annual session (1898) of the Indian National Congress (q.v.); his presidential address was hailed for its 'passionate patriotism and spiritual fervour' coming 'from the inmost depths of a noble heart, throbbing with passion, sincerity and conviction'. In later years, even though incapacitated by poor health, his spirit remained undaunted and he made his last protest speech from a stretcher, in October 1905, against the Partition of Bengal (q.v.). He died on 20 August 1906.

Bose's biographer has maintained that 'with a kind heart, he joined an ever-ready hand'. His sympathy was of a practical nature; for to every good cause he gave liberal help. Besides the service he personally rendered to a number of movements, religious, political and educational, he contributed an immense amount of money to them. His religion was an important feature of his life. Although the outside world knew him as a worker, a patriot, an educationist and a reformer, in his inmost nature 'he was a saint and a rishi'.

Hem Chandra Sarkar, *A Life of Ananda Mohan Bose*, Calcutta, 1929; Sen, *DNB*, I, pp. 207-9 (Kshitis Roy).

Subhas Chandra Bose (1897–1945)

Subhas Chandra Bose was born on 23 January 1897 at Cuttack, the ninth child in a family of fourteen and the son of a lawyer of the kayasth caste. He studied at Ravenshaw Collegiate school in Cuttack; later, at college in Calcutta, he developed a strong religious streak, spending considerable time in meditation, and was particularly impressed by the teachings of Ramakrishna, Vivekananda (q.v.) and even Aurobindo (q.v.). He graduated in 1919 with a First Class in Philosophy and repaired to England for further studies. Two years earlier, he had had a taste of military discipline as a member of the University Training Corps.

In 1920 he appeared in the I.C.S. examination in England and, allegedly to his own surprise, came out 4th in order of merit. He had also secured a Cambridge Tripos in Moral Sciences. Much against the wishes of his parents, he resigned from the I.C.S. and returned home in July 1921.

Bose met Gandhi (q.v.) in Bombay and was advised to serve under C.R.Das (q.v.) whom he took to be his political guru. When Das became Mayor of Calcutta, Bose assumed office as the Corporation's Chief Executive Officer. Presently, he was arrested in a round-up of terrorists and sent to prison in Mandalay. There he was detained without trial for three years under the notorious Regulation III of 1818 and was released in 1927 on grounds of ill health—in jail he had contracted tuberculosis and was taken seriously ill.

At the Calcutta session of the Indian National Congress (q.v.), Bose commanded the Seva Dal, the party's volunteer corps. He also collaborated with Jawaharlal Nehru and S. Srinivasa Iyengar, members of the Independence League, and helped queer the pitch for Gandhi and the 'old guard' on the question of complete independence versus Dominion Status (q.v.) as the Congress goal.

Bose joined the Civil Disobedience Movement (q.v.) and when released after the Gandhi-Irwin Pact (q.v.), bitterly opposed the Mahatma's tantrums. He was detained again but constant jail-going had shattered his health. While in Europe recouping, he is said to have tried, unsuccessfully, to establish liaison with the Nazi leader Adolph Hitler. He avowed he had 'no ideological inhibitions', in his search for collaborators so as to achieve the principal objective of overthrowing British imperialism.

Bose's differences with Gandhi were of a fundamental nature. Non-violence, which was an article of faith with the Mahatma, was only a weapon for Bose—'to be used or discarded', according to the exigencies of the moment. This ideological stance helped him all through the 30s and until the eve of World War II to find points of contact with the left wing of the Congress. More, it helped him bitterly oppose the latter's acceptance of office on any conditions under the Government of India Act, 1935 (q.v.).

Bose had been elected Congress President at the Haripur (1938) session, where he made a bold stand for unqualified Swaraj and the use of force against the British, 'if necessary'. At Tripuri, the following year, he was elected by a narrow margin in the teeth of Gandhi's opposition. It proved to be a pyrrhic victory—within months, Bose 'was hounded out of the party'.

Interestingly, at Tripuri, where he was a sick man moving about on a stretcher, Bose forecast an imperialist war in Europe within months and urged the Congress to serve a 6-month ultimatum to the British. In the event of its rejection, Bose urged a countrywide struggle for complete independence. He quit in April 1939. For the 'democratization, radicalization and reorientation' of the party which, in his view, should serve as a sharp instrument of the people's will, he founded the Forward Bloc. To start with, it functioned within the Congress fold.

It was time for Gandhi and his men to hit back. Bose was removed from the presidentship of the Bengal Provincial Congress Committee (August) and debarred from holding an elective office for 3 years. In March 1940 Bose convened an Anti-Compromise Conference at Ramgarh in Bihar under the joint auspices of the Forward Bloc and the Kisan Sabha. At the Nagpur session of his Bloc in June, he demanded the immediate establishment of a Provisional National Government in India.

Arrested in July 1940, Bose threatened a fast in jail and was let out in December under strict surveillance. On 26 January 1941 the world learnt of his disappearance from 'house arrest'. He surfaced in Berlin in November (1941) and, in his broadcasts, affirmed that he had escaped so as 'to supplement from outside the struggle going on at home'. The burden of his song was that Britain's difficulty was India's opportunity, that 'our enemy's enemy is our friend'.

Bose met Hitler only once, on 27 May 1942, when the latter is said to have approved of his plans to go to S.E. Asia. The long delay in his departure—he was not to leave Germany until February 1943—has been attributed to technical problems and the bad liaison between Berlin and Tokyo. His return to the east and organization of the Azad Hind Fauj (q.v.) is now history. On assuming the command of the army, Bose, now Netaji, declared: 'I am conscious of the magnitude of the task that I have undertaken and I feel weighed down with a sense of responsibility . . . It is only on the basis of undiluted nationalism and perfect justice and impartiality that India's army of liberation can be built up. We must weld ourselves into an army that will have only one goal, namely, the freedom of India, and only one will, namely to do or die in the cause of India's freedom. When we stand, the Azad Hind Fauj has to be like a wall of granite; when we march, the A.H.F. has to be like a steam roller.'

The Fauj's victories, great morale-boosters as they were, proved short-lived. The tide soon turned (end 1944). Retreat became inevitable under circumstances of increasing difficulty—shortage of supplies, harassment by aerial strafing. The Fauj fell back on Mandalay, then on Rangoon, and finally made for Bangkok. It was a sad story of disillusionment and of hope turning to dust and ashes just as it was near fulfilment. Presently, desertions from its ranks became the order of day and Bose felt compelled to issue a *diktat* imposing summary trial and death. To his Japanese allies, he had now become a liability, for they themselves were reeling under heavy blows.

Tall, well above average in height and predisposed to obesity, Bose had a chubby face with a cherubic smile.

It has been suggested that Bose's creation of the A.H.F. was a mixture of military necessity, political idealism as well as rank opportunism. Actually, an interesting sidelight on the raising of the Azad Hind Fauj, more popularly called the Indian National Army or I.N.A., was provided by the 'I.N.A. trials' in Delhi's Red Fort (1946) which attracted much public attention. Three Indian army officers who played important roles in the A.H.F. under Bose were charged with desertion. It was urged on behalf of their defence that the Fauj became a necessity in so far as Japan was threatening to send a large number of Indian prisoners of war to starvation and death in the south-west Pacific unless they organized themselves to fight on their behalf; that, on some occasions, the Japanese had actually carried out their threats.

Bose's detractors charge that he had always exhibited 'strong authoritarian ambitions', that he loved wearing uniforms, that he had all the makings of a benevolent dictator—dedicated, fearless and a strict disciplinarian. A biographer has maintained that Bose did nothing for those I.N.A. cadres who were arrested by the Japanese before he arrived to take over command, that he totally forgot the fate of thousands of Indians slaving in Thailand on the infamous 'Death railway'. Essentially, he concludes, Bose was an extremist who evoked extreme reactions—'people were either for him to the point of idolatry or they were totally opposed'.

Hugh Toye, *Subhash Chandra Bose: The Springing Tiger: A study of a revolutionary*, London, 1959; Subbier Appadurai Ayer, *Unto him a Witness: the story of Netaji Subhas Chandra Bose in East Asia*, Bombay, 1951; Dilip Kumar Roy, *Netaji, the man: Reminiscences*, rev. ed., Calcutta, 1966; Gerald H. Corr, *The war of the Springing Tigers*, London, 1975; Khosla, *Last Days of Netaji*, New Delhi, 1974.

Boundary Commission (1947)

After the acceptance of the June 3rd Plan (q.v.), it was deemed necessary to have a body to settle the boundaries of the new dominions of India and Pakistan. Two commissions were accordingly constituted, the first to deal with the partition of Bengal, as also the separation of the district of Sylhet from Assam; the second, with the partition of the Panjab. Each was to consist of a Chairman and four members—two nominated by the Indian National Congress (q.v.) and two by the All-India Muslim League (q.v.). It was understood that all the members would have the status of High Court Judges. They were for Bengal, Justices C. C. Biswas, B. K. Mukherji, Abu Salah Mahmud Akram and S. A. Rahman; for the Panjab, Justices Mehr Chand Mahajan, Teja Singh, Din Mahommed and Muhammad Munir. Sir Cyril (later Lord) Radcliffe was to be the common chairman of the two bodies.

The terms of reference laid down that the commissions were to demarcate the boundaries of the two parts of the respective provinces of Bengal and the Panjab on the basis of ascertaining the contiguous majority areas of Muslims and non-Muslims. The Bengal commission, in addition, was required to demarcate the Muslim majority areas of Sylhet district and the contiguous non-Muslim majority areas of the adjoining districts of Assam.

In Bengal there were the indisputably non-Muslim majority districts of Midnapore, Bankura, Hooghly, Howrah and Burdwan and the Muslim majority areas of Chittagong, Noakhali, Tippera, Dacca, Mymensingh, Pabna and Bogra. Except for them, all other areas, including Calcutta, were subject to contention and rival claims. Similarly in the Panjab, there was a great deal of controversy over the three divisions of Lahore, Multan and Jullundur and a part of the Ambala division. There were differences not only among those tendering evidence but also among the members themselves. Neither as regards the Panjab nor Bengal, were the members able to reach satisfactory agreement among themselves. It was therefore resolved that the chairman would give his own conclusions in both cases.

The final award itself was ready on 13 August and Lord Mountbatten's original plan was to hand it over to the two parties immediately. It was none the less clear that he had to go to Karachi that day (13 August) to inaugurate the new dominion of Pakistan. Thus, the earliest that party leaders could be summoned together was 17 August. No one, not even Mountbatten, it has been suggested, had seen the text of the award before then.

The Congress had claimed for West Bengal about 59% of the area and 46% of the population; under the Radcliffe Award it got only 36% of the area and 35% of the population. Of the total Muslim population of Bengal 16% was in West Bengal; there were 42% non-Muslims in East Bengal. In the Panjab, the Sikhs had claimed territory on the basis of religion and culture, a rational distribution of canal colonies, river waters and irrigation systems. Thus they claimed for East Panjab all portions of the river Chenab. The Radcliffe Award gave to East Panjab only 13 districts comprising the whole of Jullundur and Ambala divisions, the Amritsar district of the Lahore division and certain tehsils of Lahore and Gurdaspur districts.

Additionally, East Panjab obtained control over three of the rivers of the united Panjab—the Beas, Sutlej and the upper waters of the Ravi. Roughly

38% of the area and 45% of the population were assigned to East Panjab; West Panjab obtained 62% of the area and 55% of the population, together with a major percentage of the income of the old province.

The Radcliffe Award satisfied no one. The Indian press characterized it as self-contradictory, anomalous, arbitrary and palpably unjust to the Hindus of Bengal and the Panjab. The Pakistani press declared that the country had been cheated, that the award was a biased decision and an act of shameful partiality.

V. P. Menon, *The Transfer of Power*, pp. 401–3.

De La Bourdonnais (1699–1753)

Bertrand Francois Mahe de La Bourdonnais, a French adventurer, came to India several times after the age of ten and stayed back in Pondicherry after one such trip to study civil engineering. On his return to Europe he was appointed governor of Mauritius and Bourbon for five years (1735-40) but continued to hold that office until 1748. An excellent sailor and navigator, he equipped a squadron to challenge England's might in the Indian Ocean. In September 1746, after some indecisive engagements with a British naval force, La Bourdonnais sailed to the Coromandel coast and successfully brought about the capitulation of Madras.

Dupleix (q.v.) repudiated the treaty his compatriot had concluded with the English to restore the town for a ransom of £440,000. While the battle continued, a storm destroyed the French naval squadron; La Bourdonnais is said to have been bribed by the British to ransom Madras and later sailed away to Mauritius. Subsequently, he was recalled to France and imprisoned in the Bastille for 3 years on various charges of dereliction of duty preferred against him by Dupleix. Tried, he was acquitted by the Privy Council but died on 9 September (1753), broken both in body and spirit.

Buckland, p. 240; Dodwell, *CHI*, V, pp. 118-22.

Boycott (c. 1905)

The term 'boycott' came to be coined in Ireland. Here agricultural labour served with eviction notices by one Captain Charles Cunningham Boycott (1832-97) refused the demand without at the same time resorting to violence. Their leader was Charles Stewart Parnell (1846-91), the great Irish nationalist and anti-British rebel. In his capacity as agent for a large landowner in county Mayo (Ireland), Captain Boycott found himself completely ostracized by the Irish agrarian insurgents of 1880.

In India calls for boycott were made intermittently between 1876-84 as a protest against British commercial policy. The latter allegedly aimed at ruining Indian industry as well as against the seemingly contemptuous British disregard for Indian feelings. Later, in February-March 1905, boycott of British goods was openly preached in Bengal, then seething with resentment over the Partition (q.v.) of the province, by a north Indian Arya Samajist, Tahal Ram Ganga Ram. His speeches, coupled with the successful boycott of American goods by the Chinese, made a powerful impact when the cry was taken up by Krishna Kumar Mitra in *Sanjibani* followed by the *Amrita Bazar Patrika* in July of the same year. On 7 August 1905, a pledge of boycott was taken at a mass meeting at the Town Hall in Calcutta.

The bulk of the moderates, however, accepted the boycott only after considerable hesitation. It was on 12 August that Surendranath Banerjea's (q.v.) *Bengalee* echoed *Sanjibani*'s call of the previous month. Narendranath Sen's speech moving the boycott resolution (7 August 1905) at the Town Hall meeting bordered on the apologetic: 'I sincerely wish that the occasion had not arisen at all to formally move such a resolution…I do not know whether and to what extent it will be effective…our object is not retaliation but vindication of our rights, our motto is 'Defence, not Defiance'.'

To start with at any rate, the boycott was viewed as a last desperate effort to draw attention to the plight of Bengal through pulling at the purse-strings of British manufacturers and workers. Its purpose was not primarily the encouragement of the spirit of self-reliance or the development of a movement of full-scale passive resistance as others were interpreting it.

Economic boycott, the nationalists stressed, ought to be vigorously preached and practised. It was a necessary handmaid to a constructive Swadeshi movement (q.v.) and actively contributed to its growth. Capital was of course required to complete the work; scientific and technical knowledge was equally necessary. But boycott was the pioneer.

In a certain sense, boycott may be viewed as a practical if also dynamic aspect of the doctrine of passive resistance preached by Aurobindo Ghosh (q.v.). It was expected, eventually, to extend to educational, judicial and administrative spheres, besides the economic. To most people it was a weapon aimed at combating British commercial exploitation of India by eschewing use of British goods and encouraging the purchase of indigenous products instead, even if it meant sacrificing money and quality. *Inter alia*, it was designed to encourage the growth of an indigenous industry. The movement began as a graduated boycott of certain British goods like cotton, sugar, cigarettes, enamelled ware etc. Swadeshi industry, it was recognized, could prosper only if the boycott agitation was successful.

Apart from the economic, many considered it to be a political weapon. It was argued that a general boycott of British goods and government activity with resultant efforts to contain the movement would involve mass arrests and repressive legislation. This would increase the British public's awareness of the Indian national cause and mount pressure on the governing élite to adopt measures beneficial to the country. As a necessary corollary, boycott envisaged a dislocation of administrative services, for no government could function without the support of the people.

While the Indian National Congress (q.v.) approved of the Swadeshi movement it gave only lukewarm support to boycott, its logical corollary. To the moderates who dominated its counsels, the movement was too defiantly anit-British and rested on a feeling of hatred which, they argued, engendered violence. To the extremists, on the other hand, it was an act of self-preservation, their major weapon of defence against imperialist exploitation. The moderates however prevented the passing of a boycott resolution in 1905; the following year they accepted it as a temporary expedient necessitated by the partition of Bengal. In 1908, following the Surat Split (q.v.), the moderates revoked their earlier resolution on the subject.

A wholesale boycott of English goods was obviously never practical politics; the development of Swadeshi industries, in fact, stimulated the import of machinery and even of certain varieties of cotton yarn. The *Bande Matram* favoured no more than a 'graduated boycott', with Manchester piecegoods, Liverpool salt and foreign sugar as the principal targets. The boycott of sugar however was to prove a total flop while the impact on most other imports was little more than marginal if the period as a whole be taken into account. And not only in Bengal but also 'on the overall trade figures in British India, the boycott left hardly a dent'.

Sumit Sarkar, *The Swadeshi Movement in Bengal*, New Delhi, 1973, pp. 137-48; Ambalal Sakarlal Desai, 'Economic Swadeshism—an analysis', *Modern Review*, I, 2, February, 1907, pp. 123-8; *Tara Chand*, III, pp. 339-41.

Brahmo Samaj (founded 1828)

Initially called the Brahma Sabha and later the Brahmo Samaj, the movement was started by Raja Ram Mohan Roy (q.v.) in Calcutta on 20 August 1828. At its weekly meetings, open to all, passages were read from the Upanishads and explained in Bengali, followed by sermons and devotional songs. Yet, to start with, there were more sympathisers than members. Premises were acquired in 1830 to serve as a permanent place of worship, although after Ram Mohan Roy's death in 1833 the Samaj languished for a while.

Thirteen years later, Debendra Nath Tagore (1817-1905) assumed charge as Acharya and infused new life into the movement. He introduced initiation, norms for membership and a form of prayer and worship called 'Brahmopasna'. Though he and his young followers questioned the infallibility of the Vedas, he took relevant excerpts from the Upanishads and compiled them into a text called *Brahmo Dharma*, which served as a guide for prayer and devotion. Earlier on, he had established a 'Tattva Bodhini Sabha' to propagate the Brahmo faith and the *Tattvabodhini Patrika* to carry its message far and wide.

The Samaj became much more live and dynamic after Keshab Chandra Sen (1838–84) joined it in 1857. Religious and social problems were discussed in the Sangat Sabha which he formed three years later. Soon, the Brahmo Samajists gave up idolatry and caste symbols, devoting more time and effort to social service and educational activities. Preachers were sent out and as a result of Sen's own tours throughout the country (1864 and 1868) organized groups such as the Veda Samaj in Madras and the Prarthana Samaj in Bombay came into being.

Debendra Nath could not reconcile himself to Keshab Chandra's radically reformist ideas; in 1865 there was a split when Sen and his followers broke away. They established what was called the 'Brahmo Samaj of India'; Debendra Nath's more orthodox group now came to be known as the 'Adi Brahmo Samaj'.

The Sen group, while enthusiastic supporters of the emancipation of women, the education of girls and remarriage of widows, was dead set against polygamy and child marriage. Through its efforts, the government legalized Brahmo marriages by the Native Marriage Act II of 1872 which laid down fourteen (14) as the minimum (marriageable) age for girls.

Schools for girls and vocational institutions for boys were opened too. The daily *Indian Mirror* and the weekly *Sulabh Samachar* were started to disseminate knowledge. Thus, under Keshab Chandra, social reform assumed a wider, all-India character. Doctrinal changes too brought about a 'very rich and comprehensive synthesis of religions' which he called Nava Vidhan.

Greatly influenced by Vaishnav and Christian teachings, Keshab Chandra had introduced devotional singing to the accompaniment of music at the Samaj's prayer meetings. Gradually, however, his claims to be the 'divinely commissioned' leader of the movement and his doctrine of 'Adesh' or 'Divine command' alienated all those who preferred a more democratic set-up. Differences arose over the content of social reform, especially with regard to women. Sen, then under the influence of Ramakrishna Parmahansa, advocated meditation and renunciation, with less time spent on philanthropic activities. The schism came to a head in 1878 when he performed the marriage of his 13-year old daughter to the Prince of Cooch-Behar in accordance with Hindu rites. Both the bride as well as the bridegroom were under age and the marriage was in clear violation of the 1872 enactment which Sen himself had so zealously advocated. In the result, a powerful and influential section under Sivanath Sastri and Ananda Mohan Bose (q.v.) seceded from the main body to form the Sadharan Brahmo Samaj, organized on more democratic lines. Sen, still the undisputed leader of his group, however, continued to be active until his death, in 1884.

Sen's 'contributions' to the Samaj were significant and may be briefly listed: his enunciation, and accentuation, of the doctrine of 'Adesh' or 'Divine command'; bringing man's social life within the domain of his religious duty; infusion of the spirit of 'repentance' and 'prayer'; inculcation of a spirit of self-surrender for the propagation of the cause; infusion of bhakti or devotional fervour into the movement. In addition, he emphasized the sense of universality of theism, re-emphasized that in the service of man was the service of god, underlined his faith in the divine mission of the Brahmo Samaj and enforced the habit of daily devotion on the part of his friends and followers.

Most of his impact was, however, lost with the Cooch-Behar marriage; it lowered his as well as the Samaj's credibility. It has been maintained that the Samaj 'rose with K. C. Sen; with him perhaps it has gone down in public regard'.

Even while Sen was active, the Sadharan Brahmo Samaj made steady progress, sending out missionaries from time to time. Its work was directed by a general committee of 100 members elected from Calcutta and the provincial units; it published two newspapers, the *Indian Messenger* and *Tattva Kaumudi*. The Samaj had, over the years, moved away from its Hindu moorings and was based on 'abstract principles like reason, truth and morality'. Bereft of any popular appeal, its following soon dwindled. In 1911, there are said to have been 183 Brahmo Samajs all over the country with a total membership of 5,504. Of the three branches of the Brahmo Samaj, the 'Adhi Samaj' soon became indistinguishable from Hinduism and gradually faded away. So did Keshab Chandra's 'Nav Vidhan'. The Sadharan Samaj however showed a certain vitality and made some headway.

The role of the Brahmo Samaj as the 'first intellectual movement which spread the ideas of rationalism and enlightenment in modern India' cannot be over-emphasized. Its liberal approach to social and religious questions won the approbation of Europeans and Indians alike. Its educational and social reform activities instilled a new confidence which, in turn, contributed to the growth of nationalism; a number of Brahmo Samajists were later prominent in the struggle for independence.

Sivanath Sastri, *History of the Brahmo Samaj*, 2 vols, 2nd ed., Calcutta, 1919; David Kopf, *The Brahmo Samaj and the Shaping of the Modern Indian mind*, Princeton, 1979.

British Indian Association (1851)

Some Indians who had been active in the Landholders' Society and the Bengal British India Society (defunct, 1846) met in Calcutta on 29 October 1851 and resolved to form 'for a period of not less than three years', a British Indian Association. The object was 'to promote the improvement and efficiency of the British Indian Government by every legitimate means in its power' and thereby advance 'the common interests of Great Britain and India and ameliorate the condition of the native inhabitants of the subject territory'. Branches of the Association were soon formed in Bombay and Madras—and later in Poona, the North-West Provinces and Oudh. Drawn principally from the élitist groups, mostly zamindars, in the large towns, it was pledged to constitutional means of agitation, more specifically with legislation concerning India pending in the British parliament or in the Governor-General's Council. Understandably, the Association maintained an Agent in London to safeguard its interests and propagate its cause.

Even though it professed to be an organization open to all, its sponsors as well as those that came later kept the membership fee at a high enough figure to keep out a large number of people from its rolls. The agitation over the 'Black Acts' (viz, the Ilbert Bill (q.v.) and the Vernacular Press Act (q.v.)) appears to have alienated the European community with the result that not a single Englishman ever joined the Association.

Of the three political associations organized in the three presidencies, the British Indian Association in Calcutta enjoyed the longest lease of life. The zamindars of Bengal were its most stable members; the two other presidencies had lacked such a body of rich, educated and comparatively leisured class of citizens. Besides, the government invariably chose from among its members its own nominees to the Legislative Council, conferring on them honorary titles of 'Raja' and 'Rai Bahadur'. Of a total of 49 members nominated to the Bengal Council between 1862 and 1882, 35 were members of the Calcutta branch of the (British Indian) Association.

Beginning with reform and suggestions for improvement in the Charter Act of 1853 (q.v.), the Association continued throughout the 19th century to press its demand for a greater participation of Indians in the administration and their induction into the civil, judicial and legislative services without discrimination. Yet all this was dominated by its loyalty to the British government.

On matters of religious and social reform, the Association followed a policy of cautious moderation advocating change from within rather than through legislation. With the rise of national consciousness among the middle class, the influence of the Association began to wane. It encouraged the establishment of the Indian National Congress (q.v.) but refused to merge with it. Thereafter, it remained in the background, its activity restricted to Bengal even though it voiced opinion on national problems too. Thus, it opposed the Congress policy of Non-cooperation (q.v.) and Civil Disobedience (q.v.), official pampering of Muslims, the Communal Award (q.v.), and the Land Tenancy Acts (q.v.). It welcomed the Simon Commission (q.v.) which was boycotted by almost all other political groups in the country.

It has been suggested that the real importance of the Association lay in its attempt to initiate Indians into public life.

P.N.Singh Roy (ed.), *Chronicle of the British Indian Association*, Calcutta, 1967; Sujata Ghosh, 'The British Indian Association (1851–1900)', *Bengal Past and Present*, 77 (144), 2, July-December, 1958, pp. 99-119; Bimanbehari Majumdar, *Indian Political Associations and Reform of Legislature, 1818–1917*, Calcutta, 1965.

First (Anglo-) Burmese War (1824–6)

The first Anglo-Burmese war may be viewed as an inevitable clash of interests between two advancing empires. The Burmese had extended their sway over Arakan, Manipur and Assam and were poised menacingly, as the British viewed it, on the borders of a rapidly-growing Indian empire. The British, on their part, (*c.* 1820) free from their preoccupation with the Marathas, were keen to secure their eastern frontier against foreign incursions. They had been singularly unsuccessful in their attempts to establish diplomatic relations with the Burmese so as to straighten out their disputes and eliminate French designs on that country. The Burmese resented the British refusal to accept their bidding and to surrender the refugees from Assam who had taken shelter in Bengal. As if that were not enough, the governor of Arakan claimed Bengal for his kingdom.

The security of British India's eastern frontier may not have been the sole reason that animated the British; the establishment of a firm base in south Burma, which possessed good harbours and provided facilities for rich trade, may well have been the real objective. Disputed claims over the island of Shahpur in the Gulf of Bengal, off the Arakan coast, resulted in alternate attempts by both sides to occupy it. To forestall a potential Burmese threat to Sylhet, the British re-installed the ruler of Cachar and put him under their protection. The Burmese, who claimed sovereignty, resented this overt interference, yet the force they sent to meet this challenge was defeated. The siezure of the commander of a British schooner (January 1824) brought matters to a head and Lord Amherst (q.v.) declared war on 24 February 1824.

A two-pronged campaign was launched: one force operated in Assam while the other made lower Burma its objective. The Burmese, expecting to fight in Bengal, were unprepared for this change in strategy. The British force in Assam met no serious reverses except at Ramu (17 May). By January 1825 Rangpur, then capital of Assam, and by June, Cachar and Manipur, had been occupied.

In Burma, ignorance of topography, poor communications, an impossible climate and lack of provisions made British movement slow, at best. The Burmese showed remarkable mobility and built strong stockades but, in

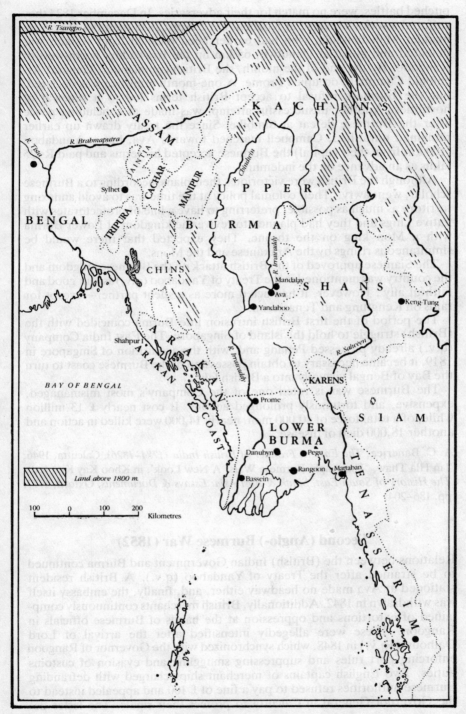

Anglo-Burmese Wars

pitched battles, were no match for their adversaries. In December 1824 they suffered a serious reverse at Kokeen. On 2 April 1825 their doughty commander Mahabandula, who had earlier been recalled from Assam, was defeated and killed at Danubyn, 65 km up the Irrawaddy, north-west of Rangoon. By the end of the month, the British commander, General Archibald Campbell, occupied Prome. A one-month armistice was declared, but the Burmese refusal to accept British terms led to a renewal of hostilities. Another unsuccessful attempt was made at concluding peace after the Burmese defeat at Simbike. Since the treaty drawn up earlier remained unratified, Campbell marched towards Ava, but at Yandaboo (100 km from their capital) the Burmese accepted his terms and paid Rs 25 lakhs as an advance on the indemnity.

Although the British were victorious, their plans, according to a Burmese scholar, went awry: 'Their colonial policy at the time was to avoid annexing territory as much as possible, preferring to have a line of protectorates with native kings and they had planned to revive the kingdom of Lower Burma with a Mon king on the throne. They expected that there would be simultaneous risings by the Arakanese and the Mons.'

The Siamese approved of the British attack on the Burmese kingdom and the country was mentioned in the Treaty of Yandaboo (q.v.) as 'our good and faithful ally'. However, it had acted more as a silent partner—except for raids on Kengtung and Tenasserim.

The period of the first British intrusion into Burma coincided with the (British) struggle to hold the island of Singapore. The East India Company (q.v.) already possessed Penang and, with the acquisition of Singapore in 1819, it became necessary to obtain possession of the Burmese coast to turn the Bay of Bengal virtually into a British lake.

The Burmese war is rated one of the Company's most mismanaged, expensive, and tortuously prolonged actions. It cost nearly £ 13 million while, of a total force of 40,000 men, nearly 14,000 were killed in action and another 18,000 died of disease.

A. C. Banerjee, *The Eastern Frontier of British India (1784–1826)*, Calcutta, 1946; Tin Hla Thaw, 'The Anglo-Burmese Wars: A New Look', in Khoo Kay Kim (ed), *The History of South East, South & East Asia: Essays & Documents*, Oxford, 1977, pp. 186–204.

Second (Anglo-) Burmese War (1852)

Relations between the (British) Indian Government and Burma continued to be strained after the Treaty of Yandaboo (q.v.). A British resident stationed at Ava made no headway either, and, finally, the embassy itself was withdrawn in 1842. Additionally, British merchants continuously complained of extortions and oppression at the hands of Burmese officials in Rangoon. These were allegedly intensified after the arrival of Lord Dalhousie (q.v.) in 1848, which synchronized with the Governor of Rangoon enforcing port rules and suppressing smuggling and evasion of customs duties. Two English captains of merchant ships charged with defrauding Burmese authorities refused to pay a fine of £ 100 and appealed instead to the Governor-General in Calcutta to protect their rights. The latter despatched Commodore Lambert with 'the ships under his command and any other available vessels of war' to obtain reparations in a claim amounting to less than Rs 1,000!

On Lambert's complaint that the Rangoon chief had refused to see him, King Paganwin, in a bid to avoid hostilities, transferred the chief. Bent upon provocation, the British officer despatched a deputation of junior members of his staff who were denied an audience by the Burmese ruler. The Commodore thereupon seized the king's ship, attacked other Burmese vessels, and declared the waterways of Rangoon to be in a state of blockade.

Dalhousie outwardly disavowed his Commodore's inflammatory actions, but never the less started vigorous preparations for an eventual confrontation. The advantages, he must have reckoned, were immense—a continued coastline up to Malacca and Singapore, an inland trade route to China along the Irrawaddy and possession of the rich deltaic region of Pegu boasting three Burmese ports.

Convinced of the justice of his cause, the Governor-General changed his earlier stance, issued an insolent ultimatum asking the Burmese king and his ministers to apologize, demanded the payment of Rs 10 lakhs as indemnity and the cession of Rangoon and Martaban until the amount had been paid. When the Burmese refused to comply, Dalhousie, who had already made up his mind that on a question of prestige England would not submit to Ava, declared war on 1 April 1852.

General Henry Godwin was given command of the land forces and Admiral Charles Austen of the navy. The total strength of the force was 8,429 men with 159 guns and 19 ships. The war was short and swift. On 5 April 1854 Martaban was captured; Rangoon was occupied nine days later; Bassein fell on 19 May. Additionally, Burmese land forces were defeated at Prome and Pegu. Lying low and waiting for the monsoon to fight their battles, the king and his ministers failed to make any overtures for peace. The British took Prome (October), while Pegu was reoccupied (21 November). Dalhousie, in the absence of any feelers for peace, decided to annex Pegu and issued a proclamation to that effect (19 December).

The annexation had great advantages for the British. To start with, it united the (British) provinces of Arakan and Tenasserim, the whole forming a consolidated unit giving the British command over the entire coast and sea-trade. The fact that upper Burma depended upon the trade and produce of Pegu gave them a decisive edge. The province had an excellent climate, fertile soil and rich resources, particularly in teak. Naturally the Burmese did not like the annexation, but they 'did not retaliate'. In 1853 their ruler Mindon Min made an unsuccessful bid, through a deputation to the Indian Governor-General, to retrieve Pegu. Two years later Sir Arthur Phayre tried, equally unsuccessfully, to persuade the king to sign a treaty. Cordial relations were, however, restored as British prisoners were released and the Irrawaddy opened to trade from upper Burma.

It would be useful to look at the other side of the coin. Without any access to the sea except through British occupied territory, Burma and the Burmese people lay at British mercy. Dalhousie resolved also that there should not be another treaty of Yandaboo for the Burmese to debate and dispute. He boldly proclaimed that Pegu was now the third province of British Burma. In doing so, the Governor-General underlined that, should

the Burmese misbehave 'it must of necessity lead to the total subversion of
the Burman state and to the ruin and exile of the king and his race.'

Such a method of acquisition of territory by brute force alone—without
negotiation, without a treaty, and without a declaration of peace—was
unprecedented. A Burmese scholar maintains that it was 'not in keeping'
with the expression of liberalism repeatedly made by European political
thinkers. It should follow that the second Anglo-Burmese war was a war of
'naked imperialism' in the true sense of the term.

But perhaps to Commodore Lambert and Lord Dalhousie it seemed only
fitting that the tragedy of Burmese Pegu should begin with an act of piracy by
one and close with an act of piracy by the other. Richard Cobden, the British
radical leader, had this to say: 'Lord Dalhousie begins with a claim on the
Burmese for less than a thousand pounds, which is followed by an additional
demand of an apology from the Governor of Rangoon for the insult offered
to our officers; next, his terms are raised to one hundred thousand pounds
and an apology from the king's ministers; then follows the invasion of
Burmese territory; when, suddenly, all demands for pecuniary compensation and apology cease and his lordship is willing to accept the cession of
Pegu as a compensation and a reparation.'

This war, it has been aptly said, marked the 'beginning of the end' of
Burmese independence.

Maung Htin Aung, *A History of Burma,* New York, 1967; Dorothy Woodman, *The
Making of Burma,* London, 1962; Tin Hla Thaw, 'The Anglo-Burmese Wars: A New
Look' in Khoo Kay Kim (ed.), *The History of South East, South & East Asia:
Essays & Documents,* Oxford, 1977, pp. 186–204.

Third (Anglo-) Burmese War (1885)

In the aftermath of the second war (1852), Anglo-Burmese relations,
diplomatic as well as commercial, took a favourable turn in the post-1860
period. The Burmese ruler, Mindon Min, not only accepted an agent at his
court, but also allowed British boats to navigate the river Irrawaddy for
purposes of trade with China, right up to Bhamo; the British, in turn,
allowed Burmese traders reciprocal rights in lower Burma, which they now
controlled. This phase, however, was short-lived, for in the 1870s the two
countries began drifting apart. The Burmese ruler allegedly refused an
audience to a British envoy on the plea that he was wearing shoes!
Whitehall expressed its horror at the barbarous murder of royal relatives
which, added to its other outstanding grievances, led it to withdraw its
embassy (1879).

Meanwhile, from their recently established base in Indo-China, French
interests were securing a foothold in upper Burma, a development that the
British viewed as a challenge to their trade in Yunnan. French technical and
scientific experts soon appeared and in 1883 Thibaw (also Thebaw), the new
Burmese ruler, sent an ostensibly commercial mission to Paris seeking aid
for his country's industrial and scientific undertakings. The real aim, the
British feared, was to negotiate and finalize the unratified treaty of 1873,
providing for French arms and ammunition. Their worst fears were
confirmed when, two years later, the French pointed to the need of a treaty

between the neighbouring countries of Burma and French Indo-China, and despatched an envoy to Mandalay. Plans for establishing a bank as well as the construction of railways were drawn up. Despite this, Paris clearly disavowed any intention of supplanting the British politically.

Coupled with the French menace was the much-advertised disability of British merchants to operate in upper Burma where the king claimed monopoly rights, both on exports as well as imports. The merchants had complained of chaotic conditions and a corresponding decline in trade. The alleged arrogance of the Burmese, growing French influence and the unduly exaggerated fears of the traders brought Anglo-Burmese relations to a point of near-rupture. Even as the French envoy was withdrawn as a result of Whitehall's protests, the Bombay-Burma Trading Company added fresh fuel to the smouldering fires.

Initially, operating under a contract with the Burmese government, the Company was illegally conducting extensive deforestation of the southern provinces of upper Burma for which it had failed to pay the required customs duty. It was also discovered that it had defrauded the state to the tune of Rs 10 lakhs by removing, without authorization, nearly 57,000 logs. A fine of Rs 24 lakhs was thereupon imposed on the Company which it was required to pay in four annual instalments.

Completely at bay, the Company now pulled wires at the highest level, in Whitehall. Since Burma did not relent, the British Chief Commissioner demanded (22 October 1885) *inter alia* that: (i) an envoy from the Governor-General of India be received in Mandalay and authorized to adjudicate the dispute; (ii) the envoy reside in the Burmese capital in future; (iii) Burma regulate its relations with foreign powers in accordance with British advice; and (iv) Burma afford unfettered facilities for British trade with China.

In reply, the Burmese ruler accepted all the demands barring (iii). Herein too he showed himself willing to refer the propriety of the demand to a decision by other friendly powers, viz., France, Germany and Italy, with whom both Burma and Britain maintained diplomatic relations.

Among the various reasons for Burma's annexation there was the ineptness of King Thibaw and the treachery of those who surrounded him; the stolidity of the highest authorities in Britain who were clearly averse to an adventurist policy; the unwillingness of Dufferin (q.v.) to force issues, and the crucial behind-the-scene activities of British commercial interests. There was the additional fact that the race for the exploitation of Burma's unbounded natural wealth between British and French commercial interests, in which British officials played a nefarious role, led to large-scale ruination of the land which, in turn, set off a veritable chain reaction. Thus, in the years immediately preceding annexation (1883-5), there was severe drought followed by an almost complete breakdown of law and order that led, in its wake, to a sharp decline in the sale of British goods in upper Burma. Thibaw's alleged 'mismanagement' was at best a secondary factor.

Diplomatic negotiations notwithstanding, the military authorities had already worked out plans for operations in upper Burma and troops had been assembled, ready for the battle line. Dufferin ordered General Harry Prendergast into action with an expeditionary force of 10,000 men and 67 guns, supported by artillery and a naval brigade. Two forts were taken without much resistance and Mandalay itself occupied on 28 November—

the war lasting a bare ten days! King Thibaw surrendered and, along with Queen Supayalat, was given exactly forty-five minutes to start on his journey into exile on the western coast of India.

The sight of the tiny, dignified figure, helpless, humiliated and pale, riding on a common cart surrounded by hundreds of red-coated and bearded giants, won for Thibaw the hearts of his people, whom he had never known before.

Through a royal proclamation issued on 1 January 1886, upper Burma was to become 'part of HM's Dominions...[to] be adminisered by such officers as the Viceroy and Governor-General of India may from time to time appoint'. The country was made into a province of British India. To obtain Chinese concurrence to this arrangement, the British modified some articles of the Chefoo convention (1876) relating to a mission from India which was to have proceeded to China, via Tibet.

While, on the face of it, the conquest was easy, it took a long time to establish any semblance of law and order. An army of 32,000 men and 8,500 military police, both continuously mobile, fighting most of the time and carrying out summary executions took five years to pacify the country, especially its northern regions. For many years thereafter, British troops were engaged in campaigns against the peripheral peoples—the Shans, Kachins, Karens and Chins. The traders' ambition of a cultural revolution combined with political stability proved to be illusory. The Irrawaddy Flotilla Company continued to operate what was a virtual monopoly of rail traffic until it was nationalized in 1948. The development of Burma's large mineral resources did not really begin until after 1914. The deposition of Thibaw dislocated the delicate inter-dependence of the monarchy and Theravada Buddhism, and by declining to interfere in religious matters, the British undermined and destroyed the Buddhist hierarchy. The demoralization of the Sangha, the Buddhist monastic order, was amply demostrated by the number of *pongyis* who became active rebels between 1886 and 1890.

The annexation itself was by no means untypical of an expanding imperialism's tactical moves. For whatever the truth of King Thibaw's alleged cruelties and high-handedness, British motives are amply borne out in a contemporary's apt observation: 'The arrogance and barbarity of a native court, the oppression of British subjects, the hindrance to British commerce, the intrigues of foreign nations, are for ever terminated in upper Burma.'

Thibaw died in December 1916, an exile at Ratnagiri on the Konkan coast.

A. C. Banerjee, *Annexation of Burma*, Calcutta, 1944; Charles Lee Keeton, *King Thebaw and the Ecological Rape of Burma: the Political and Commercial Struggle between British India and French Indo-China in Burma, 1878-86*, New Delhi, 1974; A. T. O. Stewart, *The Pagoda War: Lord Dufferin and the Fall of the Kingdom of Ava, 1885-6*, London, 1972; Tin Hla Thaw 'The Anglo-Burmese Wars: A New Look' in Khoo Kay Kim (ed.), *The History of South East, South & East Asia: Essays & Documents*, Oxford, 1977, pp. 186–204.

Alexander Burnes (1805–41)

Alexander Burnes was born at Montrose in Scotland, and enrolled as an ensign in the Bengal army in 1821. Good at languages, he rapidly picked up Hindustani, Persian and Arabic. As assistant resident in Cutch (1823-9), he exhibited great talent as a cartographer, producing a map of a hitherto unknown tract and exploring the Indus. In 1830, he was chosen to travel through the countries of the lower Indus on the pretext of a complimentary mission to Maharaja Ranjit Singh (q.v.).

Fearing a Russian advance into Asia, Burnes volunteered to find an overland route from Attock to Astrakhan, exploring the countries bordering on the Oxus and the Caspian. An interesting account of his travels which included the Panjab, Afghanistan, Bukhara, the Turkoman country, the Caspian and Persia was published in 1834. In London, the Royal Geographical Society awarded him a gold medal; in Paris, he earned a silver medal; he was elected member of many learned and exclusive societies and was lionized as a traveller.

In 1836, Burnes was assigned an ostensibly commercial, albeit actually political, mission to Afghanistan. Credulous, and to a degree easily swayed, his critics have argued that he was totally unequipped for such a venture. In Kabul, he advocated the conclusion of a treaty with Amir Dost Mohammad (q.v.) which was designed to put an end to Russian influence at the cost of Ranjit Singh's friendship, a course of action which Auckland (q.v.) summarily rejected. It was then that he made the sensible suggestion supporting Dost Mohammad, but the British chose to support the unpopular Shah Shuja.

Burnes was next sent to Sind (q.v.) and Baluchistan to smooth the way with the Amirs (q.v.). The Khan of Kalat was to be asked for passage through his territories of a British army which was to go to Afghanistan to aid the restoration of Shah Shuja. Later, Burnes accompanied the army to Kabul as the second political officer, Macnaghten (q.v.) being the first. He was knighted and received the brevet-rank of lieutenant-colonel. At Kabul (1839-41) he had little to do, with virtually no power or responsibility, offering advice which was seldom acted upon and thereby becoming thoroughly dissatisfied with the prevalent state of affairs. His 'lack of dignity and diplomatic caution'—he is said to have acquired, *inter alia*, a large harem—alienated the respect of Afghan chiefs. Unwilling to accept Shah Shuja as their ruler, they rose in rebellion. Burnes was almost the first victim of their unrestrained fury; he was attacked and assassinated in his house by an unruly mob (2 November 1841).

A man of unbounded energy and talent, Burnes' judgement with reference to Central Asian affairs has often been called into question. It may be that he exaggerated the Russian threat, but there is little doubt that the advice he gave in favour of an alliance with Dost Mohammad was far sounder than that upon which Auckland eventually acted. But even though his views were rejected, he zealously exerted himself to give effect to the policy adopted by his superiors. The Afghans probably distrusted him as the 'treacherous cause' of their country's invasion, but it is not easy to sustain that charge.

DNB, III, 389–91 (Alexander John Arbuthnot); *Buckland*, pp. 62–3.

Marquis de Bussy (1718–85)

Charles Joseph Pattisiar, better known as Marquis de Bussy-Castelnau, was
in consonance with Dupleix's (q.v.) ambitious plans, chiefly responsible for
the establishment of French influence in the Deccan. This was in the second
half of the 18th century when the English and the French were vying with
each other for greater control over 'native' Indian rulers in the peninsula.

Having joined the French East India Company in 1737, Bussy
participated in the capture of Madras under la Bourdonnais (q.v.) in 1746.
Able and courageous, he was appointed commander of the French troops
charged with supporting their proteges Chanda Sahib and Nasir Jang in the
struggle for succession to the masnads of Carnatic and Hyderabad respectively. With great presence of mind he appointed Salabat Jang as Nizam in
1751, when Muzaffar Jang (Nasir Jang's successor) was killed; he defeated
the Nawab of Kurnool and brought about the retreat of Peshwa Balaji Baji
Rao's (q.v.) Maratha forces. With Salabat Jang's recognition as Nizam by
the Mughal emperor, French hegemony over the Deccan appeared to be
well-nigh complete.

The ultimate objective of the French was to have the whole country up to
the Krishna leased to them as well as to obtain concessions for duty-free
trade. A clever diplomat, Bussy had the Northern Circars, yielding an
annual revenue of Rs 40 lakhs, turned over to him in 1753 ostensibly for the
efficient maintenance of his troops. He undertook several expeditions for
the Nizam, securing Daulatabad and putting down refractory rajas and
zamindars. At the same time, he captured several English settlements,
including Vizagapatam along the eastern sea-board. His growing influence
in the Nizam's court created many enemies and, in 1756, he was summarily
dismissed and assaulted while leaving. His military superiority, however,
soon compelled the Nizam to reinstate him.

Unwilling to endanger French interests in the Deccan, Bussy refused
Shuja-ud-Daulah's (q.v.) request for help against the English. At the zenith
of his power and influence, he was however recalled by Count de Lally
(q.v.), the new French commander, when hostilities with the English broke
out afresh in 1758. Taken prisoner after the battle of Wandiwash in January
1760, he was sent to Europe where he fought a long-drawn law suit against
the Count.

With the renewal of Anglo-French hostilities in 1781, Bussy was appointed commander of the troops sent out to India. He was detailed by
Admiral Sufferin to reinforce Cuddalore, then besieged by the English. He
withdrew his support to Tipu (q.v.) shortly after peace had been concluded
between the English and the French in Europe. Dupleix is said to have
thought highly of his abilities. He died at Pondicherry in January 1785.

A. Martineau (trans. A. Carmmiade), *Bussy in Deccan*, Pondicherry, 1941.

Butler Committee Report (1929)

The question of Berar had been a matter of considerable controversy between
the Government of (British) India and the Nizams of Hyderabad. In a communication dated 20 September 1925 to the Viceroy, Lord Reading (1860-1935),

the Nizam Mir Osman Ali Khan (q.v.), raised some important issues concerning his status and position vis-a-vis the paramount power. The Viceroy's reply dated 27 March 1926 was quite categorical: 'The sovereignty of the British Crown is supreme in India, and therefore no Ruler of an Indian State can justifiably claim to negotiate with the British Government on a footing of equality. Its supremacy is not based upon treaties and engagements, but exists independently of them and, quite apart from its prerogative in matters relating to foreign powers and policies, it is the right and duty of the British government, while scrupulously respecting all treaties and engagements with the Indian States (q.v.), to preserve peace and good order throughout India . . . It is the right and privilege of the Paramount Power to decide all disputes that may arise between States, or between one of the States and itself . . . the title "Faithful Ally" which your Exalted Highness enjoys has not the effect of putting your Government in a category separate from that of other States under Paramountcy of the British Crown.'

When the exchanges were published, the rulers of Indian States were understandably restive and anxious. At a conference with the Viceroy at Simla in May 1927 they expressed their 'deep concern' over 'certain phrases employed and doctrines enunciated' in this correspondence. In sum, they demanded an impartial inquiry into the whole gamut of relationship between themselves and the Paramount Power.

The appointment of the Simon Commission (q.v.) was deemed to offer a good opportunity to accept this demand and Whitehall announced on 16 December 1927 the constitution of a 3-member committee consisting of Sir Harcourt Butler (1869-1938), Professor W. S. Holdsworth and the Hon'ble S. C. Peel. It was to inquire into the relationship between the Indian states and the Paramount Power and to suggest ways and means for the more satisfactory adjustment of the existing economic relations between them and British India.

Officially called the Indian States Committee, its three members came to India and visited 16 States. Although it refused to receive representatives of the States' subjects, the committee did acknowledge a written statement from the All-India States' Peoples' Conference, whose declared objective was 'attainment of responsible government for the people in the Indian States through representative institutions under the aegis of their rulers'.

The Princes spared neither time nor money to represent their viewpoint forcefully. Briefly, they argued that the 'paramount power is the British Crown and no one else; it is to it that the States have entrusted their foreign relations and external and internal security'; that the obligations and duties which the States and the paramount power had undertaken required faith and trust. It followed, they insisted, that the States could not be compelled to transfer to a third party their loyalty to the British Crown.

The Committee's report was submitted on 14 February 1929. Among the points made, the following may bear mention: 'The relationship of the Paramount Power with the States is not merely a contractual relationship, resting on treaties made more than a century ago. It is a living, growing relationship shaped by circumstances and policy, resting...on a mixture of history, theory and modern fact...It is not in accordance with historical fact that when the Indian States came into contact with the British power they were independent, each possessed of full sovereignty...Nearly all of them were subordinate or tributary to the Moghul empire, the Mahratta confederacy or the Sikh kingdom, and dependent on them...'

As for paramountcy, it defied definition: 'Conditions alter rapidly in a changing world. Imperial necessity and new conditions may at any time raise unexpected situations. Paramountcy must remain paramount; it must fulfil its obligations defining or adapting itself according to the shifting necessities of the time and progressive development of the States....'

Nor could the Princes be handed over to another government in British India, 'If any government in the nature of a Dominion Government should be constituted in British India, such a government would clearly be a new Government resting on a new and written constitution. The contingency has not arisen; we are not directly concerned with it; the relations of the States to such a Government would raise questions of law and policy which we cannot now and here foreshadow in detail. We feel bound, however, to draw attention to the really grave apprehensions of the Princes on this score, and to record our strong opinion that, in view of the historical nature of the relationship between the Paramount Power and the Princes, the latter should not be transferred without their own agreement to a relationship with a new Government in British India responsible to an Indian Legislature.'

In the wake of the Butler Committee report, Sir John Simon sought and obtained the British Prime Minister Ramsay MacDonald's (q.v.) approval of his proposal that his commission should have an 'extended interpretation' to its terms of reference by 'not excluding' the relationship between British India and the Indian States from its 'purview'.

Later in its report, the Simon Commission endorsed the Butler Committee's findings in substantial measure and agreed that the Viceroy, and *not* the Governor-General in Council, should be the 'agent of the Paramount Power' in its relations with the Princes. The framers of the Government of India Act 1935 (q.v.) went to the logical extreme by stipulating that the two offices of the Governor-General and the Crown Representative were indeed separate and distinct in their functions.

M. Gwyer and A. Appadorai, *Speeches & Documents on the Indian Constitution 1921-47*, 2 vols, London, 1957, II, pp. 715–23; A. C. Banerjee, *Constitutional History of India*, 3 vols, Delhi, 1977–78, III, pp. 92–4.

Battle of Buxar (1764)

The town of Buxar lies some 120 kilometers to the west of Patna and gives its name to a district which is a subdivision of Shahabad (in Bihar) on the southern banks of the Ganges.

A battle was fought here on 22 October 1764 between British troops under Major Hector Munro (q.v.) and the combined forces of Mir Kasim (q.v.), Shuja-ud-Daula (q.v.) and Shah Alam II (q.v.). It lasted from around 9 a.m. to mid-day.

British troops engaged in the fighting numbered 7,072, comprising 857 Europeans. 5,297 sepoys and 918 Indian cavalry. Estimates of the 'native' forces vary from 40,000 to 60,000. Lack of co-ordination among the three disparate allies, each with a different axe to grind, was responsible for their decisive debacle. The defeated troops were pursued until they surrendered.

British losses are said to have been 847 killed and wounded, while the three Indian allies accounted for 2,000 dead; many more were wounded. 133 pieces of artillery were captured while the cash that fell to the victors amounted to Rs 12 lakhs.

At Buxar, as earlier at Plassey (q.v.), British commanders used their fire power to maximum advantage and it was this more than anything else that brought them victory. The Indian forces on the other hand, poorly led and hopelessly out-manoeuvred, attempted to overwhelm their adversaries by sheer numbers thereby providing convenient targets for the latter's artillery. This would largely explain their heavy casualties and ultimate flight. Interestingly enough, Mir Kasim who fought the British, was not a general and even lacked the physical courage to lead his men. More, he depended heavily upon his European mercenaries—the brigades of Marker and Sumroo—who, when it came to fighting fellow Europeans, invariably were half-hearted.

The battle established the claims of the John Company (q.v.) as real conquerors of Bengal, much more than Plassey did. It has been said that whereas Plassey 'transferred power', Buxar 'created rights'. No less significant was the defeat of the titular head of the Mughal empire, Shah Alam II, who was henceforth to be no better than a hapless pensioner. Equally important was the debacle of Shuja-ud-Daula, now at the mercy of the Company which dictated to him the Treaty of Allahabad (q.v.). The Company Bahadur, with the Diwani Rights (q.v.) bestowed on it soon afterwards (1765), were now the *de facto* rulers of Bengal.

With Buxar, British rule entered a new phase: the era of legitimate economic trade came to an end while that of trade under the aegis of political power and with the help of state revenue was inaugurated. For Buxar not

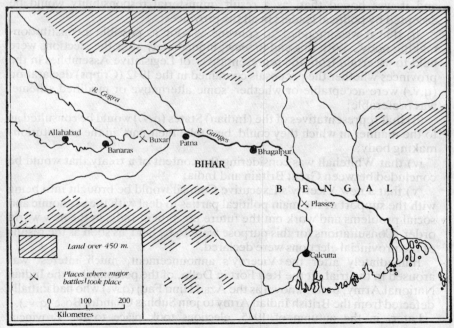

Battle of Buxar (1764)

only made the British into the lawful government of Bengal, it bound the Nawab of Oudh in an alliance which secured Bengal's western frontier. With the Mughal emperor now a (British) pensioner, it ruled out forever the recovery of his patrimony.

Dodwell, *CHI*, V, pp. 173–4; D. C. Verma, *Plassey to Buxar: A military study*, New Delhi, 1976.

Cabinet Mission Plan (16 May 1946)

A word on the background to the despatch of the British Cabinet Mission to India may be useful. A general election in England was held in July 1945, while the war against Japan was still in progress; the Conservatives under Winston Churchill (1874–1965) were badly mauled in the returns. The Labour party leader, C. R. Attlee (1883–1967) took over as Prime Minister of the new government with Lord Pethick-Lawrence as Secretary of State for India. On 6 and 9 August, the Americans dropped atom bombs on Hiroshima and Nagasaki respectively; nine days later, Japan surrendered unconditionally.

On 24 August, Lord Wavell (q.v.), then Governor-General, was summoned to London for consultations. It is understood that the Labour Prime Minister made it clear to him that Britain had made up its mind to quit India. On 19 September, after his return, Wavell made a broadcast in which he spelt out the main points of a statement he had been authorized to make on behalf of HMG. *Inter alia*, he affirmed:

　　i) that elections to the Central and Provincial legislatures so long postponed, thanks to the war, were to be held during the following cold weather and it was hoped that, as a result, ministerial responsibility would be accepted by political leaders in all the provinces;

　　ii) that it was intended 'to convene as soon as possible a constitution-making body'. With this end in view, immediately after the elections were held to ascertain from the representatives of Legislative Assemblies in the provinces whether the proposals contained in the 1942 (Cripps) declaration (q.v.) were acceptable or whether 'some alternative or modified scheme' was preferable;

　　iii) that representatives of the (Indian) States (q.v.) would be consulted as to the manner in which they could 'best take their part' in the constitution-making body;

　　iv) that Whitehall was considering the content of a treaty that would be concluded between Great Britain and India;

　　v) that a new Viceroy's Executive Council would be brought into being with the support of the main political parties to deal with the economic and social problems and work out the future position of India in the new world order. Consultations for this purpose were to be held 'as soon as the results of the provincial elections were declared.'

Immediately after the Viceroy's announcement, much interest was aroused in the trial, at the Red Fort in Delhi, of the personnel of the Indian National Army, better known as the Azad Hind Fauj (q.v.) who had initially defected from the British Indian Army to join Subhas Chandra Bose (q.v.).

Later, in the autumn of 1945, elections took place to the Provincial

Assemblies and the Legislative at the Centre. Shortly afterwards, a ten-member British Parliamentary delegation under the auspices of the Empire Parliamentary Association visited India. The delegation, led by Professor Robert Richards, a Labour party member who had been at one time (1924) Under Secretary of State for India, was in the country for about a month (January-February 1946). It met almost all the important Indian political leaders but, despite its fund of goodwill, appears to have made no deep impact on the political situation in the country.

In the general elections, the Indian National Congress (q.v.) won 57 seats as against the 44 it held in the Central Legislative Assembly elected in 1934; the All-India Muslim League (q.v.) annexed all the 30 seats reserved for Muslims.

In the provinces, while in 1937 the Congress was able to win 714 out of a total of 846 general seats, now (in 1946) it won 923, including seats in the special constituencies. The Muslim League did even better: in 1937, its representatives numbered a bare 109, less than 25% of the Muslim quota of 492; in 1946, it won 425 seats, its percentage going up to 86.

It was now clear that the League leader M. A. Jinnah (q.v.) stood fully vindicated as the pre-eminent spokesman of the party which had staked its claim to be the sole representative of the Muslim community.

On 19 February 1946 Lord Pethick-Lawrence announced in Parliament that the following steps were contemplated in conjunction with leaders of Indian opinion:

    i) to hold 'preparatory discussions with elected representatives of British India and with Indian States in order to secure the widest measure of agreement, as to the method of framing a constitution';

    ii) to set up a 'constitution-making body';

    iii) to bring into being 'an Executive Council having the support of the main (political) parties.'

He also announced that a three-man special mission of Cabinet ministers consisting of himself, Sir Stafford Cripps (q.v.), President of the Board of Trade, and A. V. Alexander, First Lord of Admiralty, would proceed to India 'to act in association with the Viceroy in this matter'.

On 15 March 1946, Attlee further clarified that 'His [three] colleagues were going to India with the intention of using their utmost endeavour to help her to attain freedom as speedily and as fully as possible.'

Eight days later (24 March), the Cabinet Mission arrived in New Delhi, Lord Pethick-Lawrence declaring that their primary objective was to set up 'an acceptable machinery' whereby India could realize her 'full independent status' as determined by herself and also, to make 'interim arrangements' for this purpose.

The mission spent nearly five weeks in discussions with the Premiers of the provinces, members of the provincial governments and of the Viceroy's Executive Council, party leaders, representatives of minorities and special interests, prominent leaders as also representatives of the Indian States.

On 5 May, a conference of leaders of the Congress and Muslim League was begun at Simla to consider (a) the grouping of provinces; (b) the character of the federal union; (c) the setting up of a constitution-making machinery.

The Congress and the League reactions were sharply different to the Cabinet

Mission's paper circulated earlier to their leaders. The differences were found to be irreconcilable, with the result that on 12 May the conference was declared officially closed. Four days later, the mission published a statement putting forward their recommendations whereby Indians might decide for themselves their future constitution and, in the meantime, set up an interim government to carry on the country's day-to-day administration. The framework thus spelt out came to be known as the Cabinet Mission Plan.

Its chief proposals were:

i) There should be a Union of India embracing both British India and the States which should deal with three subjects: Foreign Affairs, Defence and Communications and have the powers necessary to raise the finances, etc., required for these subjects;

ii) The Union should have an executive and a legislature of representatives chosen from British India and the States; any question concerning a major communal issue in the legislature should require for its decision a majority of the representatives present and voting of each of the two major communities as well as a majority of all the members present and voting;

iii) All subjects other than the Union subjects and all residuary powers should vest in the provinces;

iv) The States will retain all subjects other than those ceded to the Union;

v) Provinces should be free to form groups (sub-federal) with executives and legislatures and each group could determine the provincial subjects to be taken in common;

iv) The constitution of the Union and the groups should contain a provision whereby any province could by a majority vote of its legislative assembly call for a reconsideration of the terms of the constitution after an initial period of ten years, and at ten-yearly intervals thereafter.

With regard to the constitution-making body, the Mission proposed:

i) the formation of an Assembly on the basis of the recently-elected provincial legislatures by alloting to each province a total number of seats proportional to its population roughly in the ratio of one to a million; elections were to be held by a method of proportional representation with single transferable vote;

ii) the division of the provincial allocation of seats between the main communities in each province in proportion to their respective populations;

iii) the provision of election of representatives of the community by its members in the provincial legislature.

This proposal contemplated a Constituent Assembly of 292 members from British India and 93 from the Indian States. The British India members would be divided into 210 General (viz., all those who were not Muslims or Sikhs), 78 Muslim and 4 Sikh seats. It was stipulated that:

iv) in the preliminary meeting, the Assembly would decide its order of business, elect a Chairman and other office bearers, and an advisory committee to determine the rights of citizens, safeguards for minorities, and administration of tribal and excluded areas. The Assembly would then divide itself into three sections consisting of groups of Provinces 'A', 'B', 'C'. (Provinces placed in group 'A' were Madras, Bombay, the United Provinces, Bihar, the Central Provinces and Orissa; Group 'B' comprised Panjab, the North-West Frontier Province and Sind; Group 'C', Bengal and Assam.) These sections would settle (provincial) constitutions of provinces included in the Sections and also decide whether any group constitution should be set up and, if so, with what provincial subjects it should deal.

As soon as the new constitutional arrangements came into operation it would be open to any province to elect to come out of any group in which it had been placed. Such a decision would be taken by the legislature of the province after the first general election under the new constitution;

v) After (iv), the sections would meet together and along with the States' representatives proceed to prepare the Union constitution. The Advisory Committee (*infra* vii) recommendations would also be considered by the Union Constituent Assembly;

vi) In the Union Constituent Assembly, any resolutions varying the recommendation made by the Cabinet mission as to the basic form of the constitution, or the raising of any major communal issue, would require a majority of the representatives present and voting of each of the two major constitutions;

vii) The Advisory Committee on the rights of citizens, minorities and Tribal and Excluded areas will contain due representation of the interests affected and their function will be to report to the Union Constituent Assembly upon the list of fundamental rights, clauses for protecting minorities and a scheme for the administration of Tribal and Excluded Areas, and to advise whether these rights should be incorporated in the Provincial/Group/Union constitutions;

viii) The Viceroy was to request the Provincial Legislatures 'forthwith' to proceed with the election of their representatives and the States to set up a negotiating committee;

ix) The Assembly would negotiate the treaty contemplated between the Union Assembly and the United Kingdom 'to provide for certain matters arising out of the transfer of power';

x) To carry on the country's day-to-day administration while the constitution-making was proceeding the Mission recommended the setting up of an interim government having the support of the major political parties. This was a task to which it attached 'the greatest importance'.

Both the Congress and the League seemed to be in two minds with regard to the Cabinet Mission proposals; they were reluctant to reject them outright and yet equally unwilling to accept them as they stood. The Sikhs were against the division of India, of the grouping of provinces and a weak centre. The Scheduled Castes were divided into two factions: the B. R. Ambedkar (q.v.) group opposed the framing of the constitution by a sovereign assembly; a rival faction led by Jagjivan Ram accepted the Congress point of view.

On 31 May, Wavell noted in his *Journal*:
'So end two months of negotiation without any decision. Perhaps we shall get one in June, and very much good work has been done by the Delegation, but I shall not alter my view that a more firm and definite line, and less pandering to the Congress, would have produced quicker and better results . . . . Indian politics and Indian politicians are disheartening to deal with, and we British seem to have lost faith in ourselves and the courage to govern at present.'

In the correspondence that now ensued between the Viceroy on the one hand and the Congress and League leaders on the other for filling posts in the proposed interim government there was little or no agreement. Finally, on 16 June the Viceroy proposed an Executive Council of 14: 6 belonging to the Congress, including a Scheduled Caste representative; 5 to the Muslim League; 1 Sikh; 1 Indian Christian and 1 Parsi. He announced the names of the persons chosen.

On 19 June, the Viceroy wrote to Jinnah. Six days later, the Congress Working Committee stated that it would not give up its right to nominate a Nationalist Muslim to the Executive Council or accept the principle of parity with the Muslim League. Because of these considerations, and the Viceroy's letter to Jinnah referred to above, the Committee rejected Wavell's proposal of 16 June. At the same time with regard to the statement of 16 May relating to the formation and functioning of the Constitution-making body, while adhering to its reservations and interpretations, the League indicated its acceptance of the Cabinet mission proposals. In reply, the Viceroy informed Jinnah that he would not proceed with his statement of 16 June and would instead take steps to form a government on his own.

The Cabinet Mission felt completely frustrated in its efforts to find a meeting ground between the two major political parties. According to Hodson: 'In his [Cripps'] view the Mission must at all costs come to an accommodation with the Congress; they could manage without the League if they had the Congress with them, but not with the League alone without the Congress. Lord Wavell and with less certainty, Mr Alexander ranged themselves on the opposite side. While Sir Stafford felt he must resign if they broke with the Congress before making reasonable concessions, the Viceroy was not prepared to carry on if they gave way to Congress demands.'

In the event, members of the Mission fell between two stools; they could neither satisfy the Congress nor the League and left for England on 29 June.

In his statement to the House of Commons on 16 July 1946 Cripps noted that when the Mission arrived in India 'the atmosphere for an agreement between the parties was not propitious'. He summed up the mission's work as falling into four periods: 'i) from the time of our arrival to the end of April; ii) from the end of April to 16 May when the Plan was spelt out; iii) from 16 May to 16 June when a second main statement was issued and iv) from 16-29 June, when the mission left.'

In summing up the achievements of the Mission it has been noted that while the Congress and the League 'had indeed accepted the long-term plan, (but) their acceptances had been conditioned by their own interpretations of almost all the controversial issues.'

There were, however, two 'positive' gains: 'First, the problem of the future of India had been brought down from the clouds of nebulous theories to the plane of hard realities; secondly, there had been the welcome realisation that the Labour party in England meant to keep their pledge to withdraw from India as soon as possible. Hereafter it was not to be so much a struggle to wrest power form the British, as a dispute as to how that power, once inherited, should be shared by the parties concerned.'

Tara Chand, IV, pp. 466-73, 473-5; H. V. Hodson, *The Great Divide*, London, 1969, pp. 151, 156; Wavell: *The Viceroy's Journal*, Oxford, 1978, p. 282; *Gwyer and Appadorai*, II, pp. 571–640; V. P. Menon, *The Transfer of Power*, pp. 236–79.

Calcutta

Situated on the left bank of the Hooghly, Calcutta lies some 140 kilometres from the Bay of Bengal. It grew out of three straggling villages of Sutanuti, Govindapur and Kalikata, which were part of the larger barony of Kalikshetra where the British had initially settled.

The first mention of the town is in a poem of 1495; later, Portuguese ships used to anchor at what is now Garden Reach. Job Charnock (1630-92) of the English East India Company (q.v.) arrived here in 1686 after some skirmishes with the Mughals on the Hooghly. After an initial expulsion, he returned four years later.

The Hooghly tapped the rich trade of the Gangetic valley and Calcutta was situated at the highest point at which the river was navigable for sea-going vessels. Besides, the town was protected against attack by the river on the west and by morasses on the east, and it could be defended by guns mounted on ships.

The three villages listed above were formally bought from the Roy Choudhuries in November 1698 for a sum of Rs 1,300. The middle territory of Kalikat was the area where construction of buildings and fortifications initially began, and gave its name to the entire settlement which, in its anglicized form, came to be known as Calcutta.

In 1707, the Company declared it a separate presidency accountable only to its Directors in London. The new settlement was perpetually harassed by the Mughal governors of Bengal and, in 1717, the Calcutta Council sent an embassy to Delhi to procure the recognition of their rights in the country and permission to purchase property. The growth of the town was phenomenal; by 1756 its trade was worth a million pounds sterling annually while 50 vessels visited the port every year from abroad. Broadly, the town was divided into two sections: the English and the well-do-do 'native' merchants lived in the north, while the poorer Indians were housed in the south.

The town was captured by Siraj-ud-Daula (q.v.) on 1 June 1756 and re-captured by Robert Clive (q.v.) on 1 January 1757. After Plassey (q.v.), Mir Jaffar (q.v.) gave the English the zamindari of the 24-Parganas as well as a free gift of the town and some adjacent villages. Permission was also granted to establish a mint. From then on Calcutta was to enjoy uninterrupted prosperity.

Initially the headquarters of the Bengal presidency, it became British India's capital in 1833, for the Governor-General and the offices of the supreme government were located here. It continued to enjoy that status until the central government moved to Delhi in 1912.

An important industrial and commercial centre, Calcutta soon became a hub of political activity too, being the venue of meetings of the Indian National Congress (q.v.) from time to time.

Tapan Mohan Chatterjee, *Road to Plassey*, New Delhi, 1960, pp. 1–113; *The Imperial Gazetteer of India*, new edition, reprint, New Delhi, n.d., IX; Desmond Doig, *Calcutta: an artist's impression*, Calcutta, 1968.

Calcutta Municipal Act (1899)

Local or municipal government in India in the 19th century stemmed largely from the need of her British rulers to enlist popular support for the collection of taxes. With a growing awareness of their rights, Indians had also begun to demand a greater participation in local affairs. There was, however, a noticeable governmental retreat from its earlier policy operative roughly until 1863.

As the issue of reform of municipal administration came up before Lord Curzon's (q.v.) administration, it was decided *inter alia* to strengthen executive authority and give representation to European commercial interests. This tended to diminish the influence of the mass of rate payers who reacted by organizing themselves as an opposition in all municipal deliberations.

The Act of 1899, III of 1899 (Bengal Council), also known as the Mackenzie Act (after Sir Alexander Mackenzie who had been Lieutenant-Governor of Bengal, 1895-8) became law as of 27 September 1899. It provided for a strong municipal executive and furnished it with a law adequate enough to meet the sanitary requirements of the city and to modernize standards of municipal administration. The Council's powers were seriously curtailed—it had to devote its attention to the completion and extension of the drainage works throughout Calcutta and to the permanent and progressive improvement of the areas newly added to the metropolis by the Calcutta Act of 1888.

Additionally, the functions of the Corporation were divided among three corporate bodies. The corporation, a deliberative body, was to consist of 25 elected members: 15 nominated by the government, 4 each elected by the Calcutta Traders Association and the Bengal Chamber of Commerce and 2 by the Port Commissioners. A general committee of 12 members composed of 4 representatives of European commercial interests, 4 elected by the Ward Commissioners and 4 nominated by government with the Chairman of the Municipality as its President was to serve as a link between the deliberative body and the supreme executive authority. The latter consisted of a Chairman, a Vice-Chairman and a Deputy Chairman.

The Chairman was to be a member of the I.C.S. endowed with the right to exercise power independently or with the advice of the Corporation. His emoluments and perquisites were to be fixed by the provincial government which in fact vested him with enormous independent powers. Other provisions of the law made for direct governmental interference in municipal activities. In the result, the Corporation tended to become self-governing only in name with the elective element in a minority and real power vested in an executive supported by the general committee. What was more, the powers of the Corporation were confined to fixing rates of assessment and laying down general policy.

Curzon's justification for introducing the new measure was not far to fathom. The Corporation, he argued, talked more and worked less. Besides, the town's sanitary conditions were scandalous and no effective action would be possible unless there was a strong executive free from the control of the Corporation or its committees. The latter being large bodies were unsuited, it was pointed out, to deal with details of administration and had made effective governance impossible.

Under the new dispensation, the Corporation directed its efforts to the punctual collection of rates, completion of the drainage system and improvement of its water supply. Great strides were made in the health and sanitary improvement of the town. But even its most fervent appologists conceded that this was far from being 'popular government'. Public opinion opposed it as a 'reactionary and retrograde' measure, its induction heralded by a series of resignations by the elected members. In the Bengal Legislative Council repeated protests were voiced, especially by those belonging to the Indian National Congress (q.v.).

As the measure had been adopted in the teeth of their protests, 28 Indian members of the corporation led by Surendranath Banerjea (q.v.) resigned their seats when it came to be implemented. This is said to have been the earliest known instance of collective non-cooperation in British India.

The Act, its critics averred, was 'entirely subversive of the principles of local self-government in the municipal administration of Calcutta' and likely to establish a machinery instituting 'local self-effacement' in place of local self-government.

Far better, said Surendranath Banerjea, 'to do away with semblance of a show—this mockery of local self-government—and convert the Calcutta municipality into a government bureau, controlled and directed by government'.

Twenty-four years later, Banerjea, as Minister for Local Self-Government in Bengal, was responsible for repealing the old law. A new measure—providing for abolition of the office of official Chairman, an entirely elected body of Councillors, a Mayor chosen by the latter, and an Executive Officer appointed by and responsible to the corporation—was enacted in its place and remained operative until 1951.

Keshab Choudhuri, *Calcutta: Story of its Government*, Bombay, 1973.

Lord Canning (1812–62)

Charles John (later Earl) Canning, was the first Governor-General and Viceroy to be appointed under the Indian Councils Act (q.v.) of 1858. A member of Parliament (1836), he was elevated to the House of Lords a year later and served in various capacities in government, including that of Under-Secretary for Foreign Affairs and Post Master General, before his appointment in India (August 1855). Fervently hoping for a peaceful tenure, he was not altogether unaware of a gathering storm in the wake of an aggressively expansionist policy pursued by his predecessor, Lord Dalhousie (q.v.).

To counter the refusal of Indian troops to serve overseas, occasioned partly by the difficulty of providing British Burma with a sufficient force of 'native' troops, he broad-based their terms of enlistment to include countries beyond the seas and territories held by the John Company (q.v.). In deciding upon this military reform, later described as a potent cause of the Rebellion of 1857 (q.v.), the Governor-General had the support of the army top brass.

No sooner had he met the Persian threat to Afghanistan, than he was confronted by a far more formidable foe: the sepoys rebelled at

Barrackpore, near Calcutta, in March (1857). The contagion soon caught on. On 10 May there was a mutiny at Meerut and the sepoys proceeded towards Delhi where they proclaimed Bahadur Shah II (q.v.) emperor. Soon the civilian population broke out in revolt too, actively supporting the mutineers. The disgruntled princes and zamindars followed suit.

Canning's personal superintendence of the effort to suppress the revolt delayed action if partly because of his inability to take quick decisions while his headquarters were in distant Calcutta. He was compelled, however, to restrict himself to general policies—arranging for and dispatching troops, vesting authority and control in the hands of his army commanders and provincial administrators.

Among the steps taken to check the rebellion was the Press Act, which covered all newspapers, Indian as well as English, that published inflammatory or slanderous articles. The General Arms Act, which he next put into force, restricted the possession of arms without a licence, irrespective of race. Besides arousing the hostility of 'natives', these measures antagonized Europeans too for no distinction was sought to be made between the ruling 'whites' and the native 'blacks'. Additionally, they took strong exception to any efforts to moderate the fierceness of retribution involving, in some cases, the sacrifice of innocent lives for the outrages committed by the mutineers. They described his policy as an amalgam of 'too late' and 'too little'. To add to his discomfiture, Ellenborough (q.v.), then President of the Board of Control, censured Canning for his proclamation regarding the zamindars of Oudh (q.v.), the nerve-centre of opposition and resistance to the state. In this Canning firmly stood his ground, thereby forcing Ellenborough's resignation. This apart, many other attempts to remove him were defeated by the Queen, said to be the 'strongest of Canningites'.

Even as the smouldering embers of the mutiny were dying down, one of the Governor-General's primary concerns was to ensure that just treatment was meted out to those who had taken no part in it. Not only did he seek to distinguish between those who had mutineed and those who had not (i.e. Act XIV), he also wanted the rebels to know of his promise of pardon, so as to restore confidence in his government's just policies. Unshaken in his resolve not to 'govern in anger', his detractors derisively called him 'clemency Canning'. It should be noted however that he made it explicit that sentences already passed would be enforced and that charges of murder against Europeans would not be withdrawn. In Oudh, he insisted, that justice be administered with a heavy hand, authorizing *inter alia* the award of capital punishment, so that, in reality, he was not as clement as his detractors asserted.

Soon after the proclamation of a general pardon, Canning set out on a grand tour of India marked by the worst of what has been called 'Anglo-Mughal' pageantry. He made it a point to visit the areas affected by the revolt and the princely states so as to impress on all the 'reality' of Queen Victoria's 'power and authority'! His proclamation was rendered into regional languages and read all over India on 1 November 1858.

Canning disliked the prevalent practice of discussing all policy matters in the Governor-General's Executive Council which he termed a 'gigantic essay club'. In its place he suggested that departmental secretaries should dispose of routine business while special subjects could be discussed and finalized with the (departmental) chiefs. Unable to implement this scheme, he initiated the 'portfolio system', doing away with joint deliberations with all the councillors on every subject.

A number of laws, the end-result of initiatives taken much earlier, were finalized during Canning's tenure. The law codes (viz., the Indian Penal Code and the Criminal Procedure Code) drawn up by Macaulay (q.v.) were introduced in 1860-1 and the Indian States (q.v.) asked to adhere to them as far as possible. In 1862, the old Supreme Court and the Company's 'Adalats' were replaced by chartered High Courts at Calcutta, Madras and Bombay. Additionally, a police force was organized and Charles Wood's Education Dispatch of 1854 (q.v.) implemented by the University Act (1857), leading to the establishment of universities in Calcutta, Bombay and Madras. The Indian Councils Act (q.v.) of 1861 was adopted and enforced. Even though the Viceroy had not been directly consulted, many of his recommendations were included in its provisions, viz., the introduction of non-official Indians in the Legislative Council at the centre and greater (legislative) powers for the Governor-General.

While Canning did not actively pursue Dalhousie's policy to dispose of, as he chose fit, all cases of misgovernment in a princely state, he did not abandon it either. At the same time, he was conscious that the safety and strength of government lay in the support it received from the princes and the zamindars. In rewarding loyal princes and ensuring the continuity of their titles and possessions, encouraging zamindars to consolidate their holdings, introducing a land revenue system favourable to their interests and conferring judicial powers on them, he succeeded in wooing this influential class to the side of the government.

To placate European opinion, he proposed the sale of waste lands and the redemption of land tax, but neither of these measures were implemented during his tenure. Similarly, while aware of the injustices and abuses prevalent among the indigo plantations in Bihar and Bengal and inclined to act impartially by eradicating the evil of 'coercive cultivation', he none the less bowed to local English criticism and withdrew a bill favouring the ryots. This had followed the outbreak of the widespread Indigo Riots (q.v.). Later, he appointed a commission to inquire into the grievances of tenants against the European indigo planters.

Indian finances, then in bad shape with a deficit of £ 14 million, were reorganized by John Wilson and later Samuel Laing. A budget, paper currency and direct taxation were introduced for the first time. Duties on opium and salt were enhanced as well as an import durty of 5% on many unenumerated articles and 20% on wines, spirits, coffee, etc.

Canning was responsible for the reorganization of the Indian army and the re-establishment of India's financial solvency strained by the enormous expenditure involved in suppressing the 1857 revolt. Additionally, he deprecated the abolition of the system of raising British regiments for employment exclusively in India.

A policy of non-interference in Afghanistan, which was to be brought fully into play during John Lawrence's (q.v.) tenure had, in fact, originated with Canning. To him, Russia's threatened advance towards India was only an act intended to worry the British, and should create no alarm. While opposed to acquiring new territory, as advised in the case of Sikkim, he did not favour the cession of territory already under British control, as in the case of Peshawar.

Strictly just and conscientious, Canning possessed the rare virtue of magnanimity. His defects were a cold and reserved manner and an over-anxious temperament that frequently occasioned delay in the dispatch of public business.

Canning was awarded the much-coveted G.C.B. in March 1859, followed by an Earldom two months later. He survived only by three months his retirement and departure from India in March 1862.

M. Maclagan, *Clemency Canning*, London, 1962; Bhupen Qanungo, 'Lord Canning's administration and the modernization of India, 1856–62', Indiana University thesis, 1962, microfilm, *NMML*; H. S. Canning, *Earl Canning*, Rulers of India, Oxford, 1891.

John Cartier (d. 1802)

John Cartier arrived in India as a 'writer' in the employ of the East India Company (q.v.). He served in Dacca till 1756 and was among the fugitives who sought shelter at Fulta. Subsequently, while serving under Robert Clive (q.v.) in the Bengal campaigns, he was given due recognition. His work won appreciaton from the Court of Directors who appointed him chief of their Dacca factory in 1761; six years later he was promoted to the second place in the Council and made a member of the Select Committee at Calcutta. On 26 December 1769 he succeeded Harry Verelst (q.v.) as Governor of Bengal.

The Diwani Rights (q.v.) and its aftermath, and the Dual government (q.v.) introduced by Clive, had created governmental and fiscal chaos, and Cartier's administration inherited two major problems—a depleted treasury and an impending famine. Known as 'Virtuous Cartier', he was eulogized by Edmund Burke for his government of Bengal. He was, however, a poor administrator, lacking in self-confidence and assertiveness, with the result that most decisions were taken by the Select Committee and forced on him. The famine (1769-70) in Bengal and Bihar was a major upheaval, resulting *inter alia* in a complete breakdown of the administrative machinery. Relief measures were inadequate while corruption was rampant and the Company's servants enriched themselves by monopolizing the purchase of food-grains. Cartier suggested moving troops out of Bengal to afford relief to the people, but his proposal was rejected by the Directors.

In external affairs, the home authorities insisted on a policy of peace, a fact that persuaded the Marathas to make a fresh bid for power in northern India (1771). Albeit assured they would not touch the Company's posses-sions, Cartier was apprehensive for his new-gained ally, Shah Shuja (q.v.) and his principality of Oudh (q.v.). He also failed to prevent the Marathas from chaperoning the Mughal emperor Shah Alam II (q.v.) to Delhi. Unable to carry on the administration, Cartier resigned in 1772 and returned to England where he lived in retirement until his death in June 1802.

Buckland, p. 75; Mani Gopal Chander, *Cartier, Governor of Bengal 1769-72*, Calcutta, 1970.

Chait Singh (d. 1810)

Chait Singh (also rendered Chet Singh) who succeeded his father Raja Balwant Singh as zamindar of Banaras, Jaunpur and Chunarghar in 1770, belonged to the Dhunihar caste and was the grandson of Mansa Ram, the founder of the dynasty. In 1775, by the Treaty of Faizabad (q.v.), these districts were ceded in perpetuity to the East India Company (q.v.).

With the assumption of the Company's suzerainty, a new era began in the life of Banaras: 'It was drawn within the Company's orbit, at first retaining some autonomy which it had lost by the end of the century.' More specifically, by an agreement reached with Chait Singh and the *sanad* and *putta* granted to him on 15 April, 1776, the Raja was left free in the internal management of his kingdom 'under the acknowledged sovereignty of the Company'. Besides the right to collect the revenues, he was entrusted with the administration of civil and criminal justice and of the mint. In return, he was to pay a sum of Rs 23,40,249 as annual revenue to the Company. It was recommended—though not obligatory—that he maintain 2,000 horse and assured that as long as he adhered to these engagements no further demand or 'any augmentation' of the annual tribute would be made. The spirit of the agreement was designed to obtain 'revenue without territory'

Meanwhile wars with the Marathas and Haidar Ali (q.v.) had drawn heavily on the Company's purse. To meet this enormous expenditure, Warren Hastings (q.v.) demanded (1778) from the Raja an additional payment of Rs 5 lakhs for a year only. Similar demands were however repeated, and complied with, in 1779. In the following year, additional demands for 2,000 cavalry and Rs 50 lakhs as fine for the Raja's alleged failure to make the earlier payments were made. Unable to comply with these seemingly endless extortions, Chait Singh offered Rs 2 lakhs to Hastings, which he accepted and yet continued to march towards Banaras to force payment of the rest of the amount. Chait Singh was arrested while his people revolted against British high-handedness; in the melee that followed, he managed to escape while Warren Hastings retreated to Chunar. Chait Singh now rallied help from some neighbouring principalities but was defeated by a relief force under Major (later Lt. Gen.) William Popham (1740-1821). He fled to Gwalior where he sought refuge with its Maratha chief; he was to stay there until his death in 1810.

In Banaras, Chait Singh was replaced by his nephew Mohip Narain, a minor; the tribute was raised to Rs 40 lakhs, while civil and criminal administraton was taken over by the Company.

It is widely held that Warren Hastings' arbitrary and overbearing treatment of the Banaras ruler was largely the result of a personal grudge he bore Chait Singh for intriguing with Lt. Gen. Sir John Clavering (1722-77), a hostile member of the Bengal Council under the Regulating Act (q.v.). This would also explain why he was singled out from among many rich zamindars to make such enormous payments. Credence is lent to this belief by the fact that Elijah Impey (q.v.) collected testimonials and affidavits to demonstrate that there had been an insurrection in Banaras so as to justify the Governor-General's precipitate and injudicious conduct.

Aitchison, I, pp. 59-62; *Beale*, p. 113; Dodwell, *CHI*, V, pp. 295-9; Kamala Prasad Mishra, *Banaras in Transition (1738-1795): A Socio-Economic Study*, New Delhi, 1975.

Chandernagore

Chandernagore or Chandannagar, literally 'city of sandalwood', is situated on the right bank of the Hooghly. Shaista Khan, governor of Bengal under the Mughal emperor Aurangzeb (r. 1658–1707), granted the site to the French East India Company in 1674 to build a factory.

The settlement founded by Bourreau Desplandes in 1690 was later (1731-41) enlarged and turned into an important commercial centre by Dupleix (q.v.). Dependent on it were the factories of Kasimbazar, Patna, Dacca, Javgdia and Balasore. Maritime trade flourished in commodities such as salt, saltpetre and opium. By 1757, the town had an annual revenue of 60,000 French livres.

During the Seven Years' War (1756-63) the town was captured (1757) by the John Company (q.v.), but later (1763) restored to the French. None the less, while their trade privileges were renewed, the French were not allowed to maintain any military presence, and even their monopoly of trade was gradually taken away. In the result, by 1768 only three or four ships visited Chandernagore annually. Recaptured by the English in 1778, after the outbreak of the American War of Independence (1776-84), it was restored to the French by the Treaty of Paris (1785). The town however now wore a deserted look, for its trade had dried up, the French trading agency itself moving to Calcutta (q.v.) in 1791. Wrested again by the British in 1793, on the outbreak of the revolutionary wars in Europe, it was finally restored to the French in 1815 and remained part of their overseas Empire until its transfer to the Indian republic on 2 February 1951.

Imperial Gazetteer of India, vol. III; S. P. Sen, *The French in India*, Calcutta, 1958.

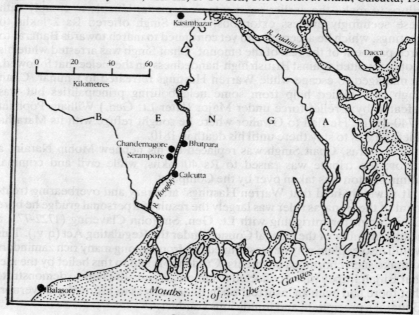

Chandernagore

Charter Acts (1793–1853)

On 31 December 1600, Elizabeth I, Queen of England (r. 1558-1603) granted a royal charter to a group of enterprising merchants registered under the name of 'the Governor and Company of merchants of London trading into the East Indies'. The charter contained the name of the first Governor along with 24 'committees' and gave the Company the right of exclusive trade with India for fifteen years.

A purely commercial enterprise to start with, the East India Company (q.v.) gradually developed a territorial character and as a result began exercising political power. This fact was recognized by the successive Charter Acts which extended the Company's monopoly of trade in India and China and outlined its administrative, legislative and judicial functions in the presidency towns where its first factories and trade emporia (in India) were established. Through the Regulating Act of 1773 (q.v.). Parliament had evinced keen interest in controlling the administration and activities of this 'joint stock company' whose ability to exercise effective political power it severely doubted. The periodic renewal of the Company's charter provided Parliament with opportunities to probe into its affairs and slowly but steadily extend control over its administration.

1781. The Act prolonged the Company's privileges for ten years and extended the control of the state in two specific directions: (1) three-quarters of the surplus, after paying a dividend of 8%, was to go to the Treasury; (2) the Directors were to communicate to the ministers of the Crown all dispatches sent to or received from India.

1793. The Act confirmed the Company's territorial possessions and monopoly of trade for twenty years. Essentially a consolidating measure, it reinforced the provisions of the previous (Pitt's India) Act of 1784 (q.v.). A few modifications however were introduced, viz., membership of the Governor-General's council was reduced from four to three and the latter was empowered 'to superintend, direct and control' the presidencies of Bombay and Madras.

1813. The provisions of this measure were based on the report of a Parliamentary secret committee submitted in 1812, which was powerfully influenced by the then widely accepted theory of laissez-faire, the aggressive war policy pursued by Whitehall with its consequent depletion of the Company's resources and its growing indebtedness. While affirming the Company's right to the territorial possessions and revenues of India, the Act proclaimed the sovereignty of the Crown over them. The Indian administration was asked to maintain separate accounts for its commercial and political activities. Trade was thrown open to all British subjects, the Company retaining only its monopoly over tea and the China trade. The Directors kept their rights of patronage but all important appointments were henceforth to be subject to the approval of the Crown. It was however the Board of Control that looked after Haileybury College (q.v.) at Addiscombe and the Calcutta and Madras Colleges.

The Act marks the beginning of an ecclesiastical establishment in India, for missionaries were now permitted to settle in the country. An educational policy was also initiated by the grant of Rs 1 lakh out of the Company's Indian revenues for the encouragement of education, literature and science.

1833. The Act was the combined result of a detailed inquiry and heated debates in Parliament and outside, and proved to be the most comprehensive piece of legislation between Pitt's India Act of 1784 and the transfer of power to the crown in 1858. The charter was renewed for twenty years but government was to be held 'in trust for His Majesty, his heirs and successors'. The trade monopoly of the Company was abolished and it was now asked to discontinue all its commercial transactions. The restriction on licenced immigration of Europeans into India was removed, which necessitated an extension of legislative powers. The Governor-General of India—in supersession of the earlier (since 1773) non-descript Governor-General of the presidency of Fort William in Bengal—and his council were empowered to make laws affecting all persons and for all courts. Such laws did not require the Calcutta Supreme Court's approval to become operative, but were subject to alteration or rejection by Parliament. A law commission headed by a jurist was appointed to codify existing laws. The most vital improvements were made in legislative procedures which were clearly differentiated from administration. A fourth, extraordinary member, called the Law Member, was added to the council; he was entitled to sit and vote only at such meetings where legislative business was transacted. A new, fourth, Presidency of Agra was created (it did not last, being wound up in 1835). The presidencies were deprived of their power of independent legislation and were, without qualification, definitely made subordinate to the Governor-General and his council in all financial matters.

An important impact of the liberal ideas then widely held was the recognition that all people, irrespective of their caste, creed or colour were eligible to seek employment under the Company—a pious platitude which long remained a dead letter. A directive was also issued to the Governor-General to propose measures for the abolition of slavery.

1853. The significance of this Act lies in the enhanced parliamentary control which came in its wake. The number of Directors was reduced from twenty-four to eighteen, six to be appointed by the Crown. The quorum for the Board's meetings was fixed at ten. The patronage of the Directors was withdrawn—appointment to all civil services being thrown open to competition.

The distinction between the governor-general's council as an executive and a legislative organ was now clearly drawn; for legislative purposes the council was enlarged to include, besides the Governor-General and the Commander-in-Chief, a representative from each presidency (with at least ten years' standing as a civilian) and two non-official European and Indian members (the last provision was never implemented). A Lieutenant-Governor was also appointed for Bengal.

In a sense the five Charter Acts mark the varied stages through which Parliament paved the way for a final take-over of the Company in 1858.

A. C. Banerjee, *Constitutional History of India*, 3 vols, Delhi, 1977-78, I; M. V. Pylee; *A Short Constitutional History of India*, Bombay, 1967; Sri Ram Sharma, *A Constitutional History of India 1765–1954*, 2nd ed., Bombay, 1954.

Lord Chelmsford (1868–1933)

Frederic John Napier Thesiger, later Viscount Chelmsford, could boast of no special qualifications for his appointment as India's Governor-General. This was especially so in view of the troubled times in which it was made: England was deeply involved in World War I while the fiasco suffered by the Indian army in Mesopotamia (1916) had lowered its prestige and lowered Delhi's reputation. Meanwhile, the Indian nationalist movement was becoming more activist.

Educated at Winchester and Oxford, Thesiger was called to the Bar in 1893. His first political appointment as Governor of Queensland (1905-9) was followed by a term in New South Wales (1909-13). Back in England, he had only recently joined his regiment and gone with it to India, when his appointment was announced. He took over in April 1916.

As Governor-General, Chelmsford propounded the view that he would pacify nationalist opinion by announcing 'Dominion Home Rule' as the goal for India's constitutional progress. This was designed to maintain a certain continuity in policy introduced by his predecessor, while at the same time conceding the substance of S. P. Sinha's (q.v.) demand at the 1915 session of the Indian National Congress (q.v.). In doing so, the Governor-General set himself a difficult task, for it was clear that conditions in India were undergoing a rapid change and the impact of the war was tending to reduce the influence of the Moderates in the Congress. He realized too that an unequivocal declaration of the British attitude towards Indian constitutional advance was an urgent necessity. A dispatch containing proposals to this effect was sent to the Secretary of State, Austen Chamberlain, in November 1916.

The dispatch is typical of Chelmsford's somewhat excessive caution and his near-surrender to the opinion of his notoriously conservative Council, who were unwilling to make any major political concessions. The antithesis of Curzon (q.v.), he did not dominate his Executive Council and his minute merely suggested expanding the legislative councils, developing local self-government and ensuring greater employment of Indians in the administration. Whitehall, convinced that all this would be far from satisfactory to public opinion in India, set out to devise something more meaningful.

While HMG was deliberating on the political concessions to be announced, the Viceroy and his Council maintained an ominous silence. With nationalist fervour increasing and inspired further by the Red revolution in Russia (1917), Indians were getting increasingly impatient. Earlier (1916) a group of Indian legislators presented the government with proposals that came to be called the 'Memorandum of the nineteen'. It revealed, *inter alia*, that even the so-called loyalists among the Muslims had been alienated by British policy towards Turkey. In an unprecedented move, the All-India Muslim League (q.v.) and the Congress joined hands leading to the Lucknow Pact (q.v.) and together pressed hard for far-reaching political reform.

The Viceroy's dilemma worsened as moderate supporters of government policy gradually melted away while a Cabinet reshuffle in Britain installed E. S. Montagu as the new Secretary of State. An unsparing critic of the Indian bureaucracy and the India Office, as well as a well-known liberal, Montagu's appointment raised new hopes and, to an extent, helped ease the political situation. In his historic declaration of 20 August 1917 (q.v.), he removed the ban on Indians for regular commissions in the army and released Mrs Annie Besant (q.v.) and her colleagues from detention. This was followed by his visit to India to confer with the Viceroy and Indian leaders, a course he had himself suggested to his predecessor (Austen Chamberlain). The joint report (1918) formed the basis for the Montagu-Chelmsford Reforms (q.v.) of 1919. Reactions to it were mixed, with the moderates willing to try the Act, the extremists convinced they had been cheated, and the British bureaucrats feeling visibily insecure under the new constitutional dispensation.

To curb nationalist fervour, Chelmsford's government used far-reaching provisions of the law which operated during the war to intern and deport for life many national leaders who allegedly posed a threat to public peace. He also refused to repeal the Indian Press Act of 1910 (q.v.), viewing it as a means for checking anti-government propaganda. With the end of the war approaching and the draconian law becoming obsolete, the Governor-General clearly hoped that an equally strong measure would replace it. With this end in view, Justice Sydney A. T. Rowlatt was appointed chairman of a committee to study the situation. Its report later became the basis for the introduction of two laws, one of which, the Rowlatt Act (q.v.), acquired great notoriety. Chelmsford was not fully prepared for the storm of protest that broke out in its wake.

Gandhi (q.v.) appealed to Indians to observe an all-India *hartal* on 6 April 1919 in protest against the 'black law'; his success was overwhelming. There was rioting at some places, even the burning of government buildings by excited mobs. The Governor-General accepted the Panjab Governor, Michael O'Dwyer's (q.v.) request for the army to take over civil administration at Amritsar. In the result, on 13 April Brigadier Dyer (q.v.) fired on a peaceful gathering at Jallianwala Bagh (q.v.). Though the Governor-General did not approve of Dyer's action, he clearly delayed the institution of an inquiry into his conduct for nearly six months.

Martial law regulations imposed on the Panjab after 13 April were even harsher. So widespread and intense was Indian indignation that riots broke out in several parts of the country. Eventually the Viceroy bowed to mounting public pressure and set up the Hunter Committee (q.v.) whose seemingly lenient attitude towards British officers deemed guilty of excesses infuriated Indian public opinion. The Muslims too were disgruntled with the terms of the treaty of peace with Turkey. One result was the Khilafat Movement (q.v.), another a nationwide response to Gandhi's appeal to start the Non-cooperation Movement (q.v.), the formal pledge to launch it being taken in August 1920. In its wake, the Congress boycotted the first elections held under the 1919 reforms as well as the visit to India of King George V's brother, the Duke of Connaught.

A strange duality now marked the course of events: as the 1919 constitutional reforms were being launched, the Rowlatt Acts, followed by the Non-cooperation Movement and the Khilafat campaigns were being mounted. Not long after, the National Liberal Federation (q.v.) and the Swaraj Party (q.v.) found themselves acting in close liaison in the legislative councils.

Chelmsford carried to its logical conclusion the policy initiated by his predecessors to organize a body of loyal princes. The Chamber of Princes, a consultative body, was brought into being by a Royal proclamation of 8 February 1921. The Viceroy was entitled to consult its Standing Committee on matters relating to the Indian States (q.v.) and such others as they shared in common with British India. He also pleaded for the inclusion of Indian representatives in the Imperial Conference.

In foreign affairs, King Amanullah (q.v.), the new ruler of Afghanistan, under pressure at home, launched hostilities leading to the Third (Anglo-) Afghan War (q.v.), and the Treaty of Rawalpindi.

Chelmsford left India in April 1921 after a stormy tenure. Back in England, he resumed his interest in education, serving on several committees and commissions. He also acted (1924) briefly as first Lord of the Admiralty. Five years later he was elected Fellow of All Souls College, Oxford and, in 1932, its Warden. He died a year later.

Speeches by Lord Chelmsford, Viceroy & Governor-General of India, Simla, 2 vols, 1919, 1921; *DNB 1931–40*, pp. 854–5 (R. Coupland); V. B. Kulkarni, *British Statesmen in India*, Bombay, 1961, pp. 280–315.

Civil Disobedience Movements (1930-41)

Civil disobedience, the defying of civil authority or the refusal to obey it, was the principal weapon Gandhi (q.v.) wrought in his fight against British rule in India. Under his stewardship, it became an integral part of the various campaigns launched from time to time by the Indian National Congress (q.v.); its story, for the most part, is inextricably linked with those campaigns.

To begin with, in the early twenties the Non-cooperation (q.v.) and the Khilafat Movements (q.v.) marked the first phase of Gandhi's emergence as a national leader. Civil disobedience was an important part of these struggles which culminated in the Moplah Rebellion (q.v.) in Kerala on the one hand and the Chauri Chaura holocaust in U.P. on the other. The end-result was an abandonment of the movement and a temporary retracing of steps.

Towards the end of the third decade, the appointment of the all-white Simon Commission (q.v.) fuelled the fires of political agitation. The inept handling of the situation by Whitehall precipitated events leading to the refusal of the Congress to attend the first session of the Round Table Conference (q.v.). This was followed by Gandhi's Dandi March (q.v.) to launch the salt satyagraha and all that came in its wake. Briefly, in so far as the British wished to bring the Congress into the discussions in London, the Viceroy, Lord Irwin (q.v.) was ready for a compromise which was effected through what came to be known as the Gandhi-Irwin Pact (q.v.). Broadly, Civil Disobedience was countermanded, prisoners released and the Mahatma participated in the second session of the Round Table Conference.

The peace purchased through the Pact proved to be a temporary truce. Gandhi returned (end-December 1931) from London, a thoroughly frustrated man, convinced that he and the movement he represented had been cheated.

To recapitulate: even though on the surface, the Government had been very sanguine about combating the salt satyagraha, at the highest levels of

administration, it was getting increasingly worried. This is borne out from
some of the reports the Viceroy made to his political masters.

On March 13 (1930)

Most of my thought at the moment is concentrated upon Gandhi. I wish I felt
sure what the right way to deal with him is.

April 24 (1930)

Their [Congress'] main object was to prepare the country for widespread
defiance of law and from a given date to proclaim by widespread demonstrations their contempt for lawful authority. In this object they have attained a
considerable measure of success.

Both these reports were made before Gandhi's arrest (5 May). Not that
the situation improved as a result. Thus on 22 May, the Viceroy was writing,
'There is no doubt that Gandhi has evoked a much wider nationalist movement than any observer, British or Indian, so far as I know, anticipated. Nor
has the policy of cutting off the tall poppies been so successful as we hoped in
defeating it.' On 2 June he noted: 'It [civil disobedience] has caught their
(peoples') imagination and swept them off their feet and obviously has
dangerous potentialities. I am satisfied that we shall not solve the real
problem merely by repressive measures, and it is therefore necessary to
examine possibilities of constructive action in the light of various possible
developments in future.'

Two diversionary tactics were the publication of the Simon Commission
report in May-June and the first session of the Round Table Conference in November (1930). Neither succeeded. The report proved to be a
non-starter and the Conference an exercise in futility. The *Times* correspondent expressed a widely-shared view that 'no Indian delegation without
Gandhi, the two Nehrus, Malaviya or Patel could possibly be looked on as
representative.'

Nor had the movement slackened. In January 1931, H. N. Brailsford, the
Manchester Guardian correspondent in India, wrote in his paper, 'To face the
lathi charges became a point of honour and in a spirit of martyrdom volunteers went out in hundreds to be beaten. They gave a display of disciplined
passive courage . . . . The great mass of the people is not in a normal state of
mind. It has been roused to a high pitch of sustained exaltation . . . to anger,
it doubts our sincerity and above all it is passionately devoted to its imprisoned leaders . . . . So long Gandhi is in prison, I doubt whether the main
body of the movement will abandon or even slacken, its resistance.'

Gandhi was let out and, as has been noticed earlier, his Pact with the
Viceroy followed. Subsequently, he attended the Round Table Conference
but returned a disappointed man 'oppressed with premonitions of another
struggle'.

The Congress alleged that the letter and spirit of the Pact had been
shamelessly violated. The rule of 'lawless laws', the ordinances, had continued, as had repression on the poor peasantry in Uttar Pradesh and the
Khudai Khidmatgars under Khan Abdul Ghaffar Khan (q.v.) in NWFP; in
Bengal, a virtual reign of terror had been unleashed. Gandhi's request to the
new Viceroy, Willingdon (who had replaced Irwin), for parleys was turned
down unceremoniously.

On 1 June (1932) the Congress resolved that 'in the event of a satisfactory response not forthcoming [from the Viceroy] the Working Committee calls upon the nation to resume Civil Disobedience, including non-payment of taxes.'

Less than twenty-four hours later the Government, in a pre-emptive strike, promulgated five ordinances assuming to itself extraordinary powers. Every Congress organization and its allied or branch organizations were banned. Mass arrests followed involving, it has been estimated, 100,000 people. Whitehall had made it unmistakably clear that it was 'determined to take every action' in its power to suppress this challenge to authority. Meanwhile, even as the movement continued, the Communal Award (q.v.) was announced. Gandhi's fast in jail against its provisions, in so far as these related to the Scheduled Castes or Harijans, resulted in the Poona Pact. Opposition to the latter by orthodox Hindus and Dr B. R. Ambedkar (q.v.) persuaded the Mahatma on 8 May (1933) to announce another 21-day fast. The same evening he was released from prison.

No sooner was he free than Gandhi advised the Congress to suspend the civil disobedience movement and asked the government to release its prisoners. Neither was willing to oblige: top Congress leaders were indignant at Gandhi's sudden *volte face*; Willingdon refused unless the movement was unconditionally withdrawn and turned down the Mahatma's request for a meeting.

The Congress leadership decided to launch individual civil disobedience and from August 1933 to March 1934 thousands of Congress workers, at the centre, in the provinces as well as districts courted arrest. Gandhi himself was arrested on 1 August and sentenced to a year's imprisonment. He was however released three weeks later owing to a deterioration in his health.

Government machinery was ruthless in its oppression. Civil disobedience was crushed and Gandhi obliged to face the fact. Yet two aspects need to be heavily underlined. One, the growth of terrorist activity and increasing restlessness in the labour movement resulting in a rash of strikes. Two, economic distress leading to disillusionment among the intelligentsia. The potentialities of this discontent were grim portents for the future.

A healthy aspect was that the movement helped inculcate among the people qualities of fearlessness, self-reliance, sacrifice. The age-long dependence on the British and their promises was shattered. Another revealing facet was the coming into its own of Indian womanhood.

The years 1934-40 were witness to a series of rapid developments. To start with, there was the introduction of the Government of India Act, 1935 (q.v.) which created acute controversy and division in nationalist ranks. While condemning the Act, the Congress decided to contest the elections under it and, with convincing electoral majorities in 6 out of the 11 Governor's provinces, to accept responsibility for government. In office, it gave a good account of itself on the whole, although its rule was dogged by unseemly controversies with the All India Muslim League (q.v.).

At the outbreak of World War II, and against the better judgement of some of its leaders, the party decided to quit office in the 8 provinces it then ruled (September 1939) on the issue of the British government's far from explicit war aims and their application to India. New Delhi and Whitehall's dithering led to the hopelessly inadequate, if vague, 8 August (1940) offer (q.v.). The Congress responded and, to vindicate its self-respect, launched individual civil disobedience under Gandhi's leadership. The first satyagrahi, Vinoba Bhave, was arrested on 21 October.

From its inception in October (1940) through December (1941) the movement passed through four phases. In the first (Oct.-Nov. 1940) only select persons were asked—Bhave and Jawaharlal Nehru; in the second (Nov. 1940-Jan. 1941), satyagrahis were chosen to represent the Congress Working Committee, the All-India Congress Committee and the central and provincial legislatures. Altogether nearly 600 people courted arrest. In the third phase (Jan.-Apr. 1941) a wider choice was exercised and as many as 2,207 people were jailed. In the fourth phase (Apr.-Dec. 1941) the net was wider still—as many as 22,000 courted imprisonment.

The Congress campaign continued till Japanese armies began to approach India and constituted a direct threat to the country's territorial integrity. In its wake, the Congress abjured its faith in absolute non-violence, whereupon on 15 December 1941 Gandhi quit its official leadership. The Government helped; it released all political prisoners it had taken. Civil disobedience was at an end.

Judith M. Brown, *Gandhi and Civil Disobedience: the Mahatama in Indian Politics. 1928-34,* Cambridge, 1977; *Tara Chand,* IV, pp. 129–32, 157–9, 197–8; 304–12.

Robert Clive (1725–74)

Popularly regarded as the founder of British dominion in India, Robert Clive's family came from Shropshire in the English Midlands. Averse to study, he was appointed a writer in the East India Company (q.v.) and landed in Madras, a boy of 19, in 1744. Clive was essentially a recluse, but Anglo-French rivalry and later wars in all parts of the globe, including India, pitchforked him into action and importance. The capture of Madras by the French deprived Clive of his civil employment, forcing him to take to the profession of arms. He took part in the capture of Fort St David, an establishment on the south coast of Madras, and was employed in Edward Boscawen's siege, both by sea and land, of the French settlement at Pondicherry. On the conclusion of peace, he returned to his desk job, but presently hostilities were resumed and he opted for military service.

In 1751, Thomas Saunders, president of Fort St George in Madras, bestowed on the intrepid British commander the rank of Captain. In July that year Clive was ordered to join the British force in Tiruchchirapalli (misspelt, Trichinopoly). At the instance of Muhammad Ali, its then Nawab, Arcot which lay defenceless en route was captured by the Company's troops. This was followed by Clive's first success in an open field encounter, at Arni. The young Captain also distinguished himself in subsequent armed bouts with the French forces, till the latter finally surrendered to Major Stringer Lawrence (1697–1775) at Trichinopoly in 1752. His military successes were due in no small measure to Major Lawrence's expert stewardship. By no means a strategist, Clive did however possess initiative, courage and determination and his victory at Arcot gave him the abounding self-confidence he was to exhibit in his subsequent career.

Returning to England in 1753, Clive made an unsuccessful attempt to enter Parliament. Later he secured permission to return to India and reached Bombay in 1755. Before long, he was commissioned as a Lieutenant Colonel in the East Indies only', and appointed Governor and Commander of Fort St David. On his way to Madras from Bombay, Clive and Admiral Charles Watson worsted the Maratha admiral Angria's stronghold at Gheria. Soon news came of an upheaval in Bengal resulting in the notorious, if half-fictitious, tragedy of the Black Hole; Clive was ordered to march to Calcutta (q.v.) with the help of Watson's fleet. He reached Bengal towards the end of December 1756. By simultaneous use of bribes to the Nawab's men as well as threats of armed action, he endeavoured to weaken the enemy's resolve. In January 1757, Hooghly was captured, even though there had been some initial reverses. Calcutta was taken too, thanks to the seemingly misplaced orgies of a drunken soldier. Soon afterwards, through the machinations of some treacherous nobles in the Nawab's court, riddled with intrigue and fear of an impending Afghan onslaught from the north, Siraj-ud-daula (q.v.) signed the peace Treaty of Alinagar (q.v.). Some chroniclers attribute this to Clive's successful assault on the Nawab's camp, but this is no longer widely accepted.

Apprehending that the Nawab and the French might join forces, the politician in Clive came to the fore. Emulating the example of Dupleix (q.v.), he began his intrigues with the disgruntled nobles to replace Siraj-ud-daulah by the more pliant Mir Jafar (q.v.). To this effect a regular treaty was drawn up and signed. Clive also resorted to forgery to deprive Seth Omi Chand (q.v.), a fellow conspirator, of the latter's share of the anticipated loot. The British commander marched to Plassey (q.v.) where he was confronted by the Nawab's large if ill-organized and poorly equipped army. The battle that followed was little more than an 'armed demonstration', since the Nawab found himself deserted by Mir Jafar, Rai Durlabh (q.v.) and their combined forces, thus giving the British an easy victory. The suggestion for an immediate battle came from Eyre Coote (q.v.), the initiative was taken by Major John Kilpatrick (d. 1787) but the honours for the success that crowned it went to Clive. The British commander swiftly followed Mir Jafar to Murshidabad to reap the fruits of his victory. In retrospect, he confessed to being 'astonished at his moderation' in accepting only £ 234,000 as reward for his services; later, he was to persuade Mir Jafar to grant him a jagir too. Suspecting the newly-proclaimed Nawab of conspiring with the Dutch against the English, Clive took the initiative and defeated the Dutch at Biderra in 1759.

In 1760, he returned to England and was raised to the (Irish) peerage, as Lord Clive, baron of Plassey. He won a seat in the House of Commons but did not figure prominently in politics. Defeating opposition from the Court of Directors that was led by Laurence Sullivan, Clive was appointed Governor of Bengal.

By the time he arrived in Bengal (1765), the decisive Battle of Buxar (q.v.) had been fought and won leaving the British in a highly advantageous position on which Clive was now determined to improve. He concluded a treaty with Shuja-ud-daula (q.v.), making Oudh (q.v.) a friendly buffer state and preventing further protracted warfare. Next, he obliged the Mughal emperor Shah Alam II (q.v.) by granting the latter the districts of Karra and Allahabad, in return for which he secured for the Company the Diwani Rights (q.v.) over Bengal, Bihar and Orissa.

Since he had specific instructions from the Court of Directors to effect reforms in the civil service, Clive set about putting things in order. Aware of the rampant corruption, he asked the Company's functionaries not to accept bribes or presents and further sought to check the abuse of private trade. He made an effort to increase the salaries of officers and introduced a system of rewards. His critics however doubted whether one who had amassed a huge fortune by dubious means—in 1766, he had inherited a jagir worth Rs 5 lakhs annually from Mir Jafar—could afford to censure others. His reform, aimed at drastically reducing 'batta', a special daily allowance admissible to army officers, provoked a near mutiny which Clive boldly, and resolutely, put down.

Later, Clive was to introduce the system of Dual Government (q.v.), so as to put the Diwani rights won from the Mughal emperor into operation. Though much criticized, it formed the basis of administration he bequeathed to his successors. In January 1767 Clive returned to England where he was subsequently charged with corruption and nepotism; after a prolonged and agonising trial he was acquitted in 1773. But his long and eventful career soon drew to a tragic end for, broken in body and in spirit, he committed suicide in 1774.

In military matters Clive's real contribution is said to have been in raising the morale of the Company's troops, rather than in any particular action in which he was engaged. Plassey, it has been maintained, was 'not really a title to fame' though fame came to him on its account. None the less, he could legitimately claim to be the founder of the Indo-British army in Bengal.

Two images of Clive persist: one, that of the daring, forward-looking leader, ruthless towards his foes and magnanimous towards the defeated; the other, a venal, corrupt politician who at the same time professed devotion to duty.

In 1757-60 Clive viewed his critics as envious and weak-kneed creatures who grudged a great man his well-deserved success and its rewards. In 1765, on the other hand, he saw many of his former colleagues as squalid and venomous destroyers of society and the Company. As Spear points out, in 1757, 'the taking of presents from Mir Jafar was right, very right; in the years 1760-5, the taking of presents by others from Mir Jafar, Mir Kasim and Najm-ud-Daulah was wrong, very wrong.'

Clive went to Bengal with the idea of the sponsored state in his mind, resting on Bussy's (q.v.) successful management of Hyderabad and his 'home-grown' experience of the Carnatic itself. There was however a vital distinction: the Deccan experiments were mainly political in character designed to preserve control of strategic areas; in Bengal, considerations were primarily commercial, to give the Company's merchants a free hand. The failure in the latter case was due to the fact that the hand was taken too freely. Clive's contribution lay in evolving the theory of a controlled state—*through* Indian agency.

Clive's claim to greatness, his biographers maintain, would be advanced 'independently' of any faults or shortcomings. What he wanted was money for the Company's dividends and ultimately his own influence in England, 'not lands to administer or subjects to nourish'. His work was not the laying of foundations, for the later edifice had a different base: 'It was rather a foretaste of things to come, an anticipation of something which posterity realised. Clive was not a founder but a harbinger of the future. He was not a planner of empire but an experimenter who revealed something of the possibilities. Clive was the forerunner of the British Indian empire.'

T. G. P. Spear, *Master of Bengal: Clive and his India*, London, 1975; H. H. Dodwell, *Dupleix and Clive*, London, 1938; A. Mervyn Davies, *Clive of Plassey: A Biography*, London, 1939; Norman Partington, *Master of Bengal*, London, 1974; Mark Bence-Jones, *Clive of India*, London, 1974; Nirad Chaudhuri, *Clive of India*, London, 1975.

The Communal Award (1932)

On 16 August 1932, Prime Minister Ramsay MacDonald (q.v.) announced in the British Parliament HMG's decision with regard to what he called 'representation of the British Indian communities in the Provincial Legislatures' envisaged in the proposed scheme of constitutional reform in India which was to emerge, later, as the Government of India Act, 1935 (q.v.). In so far as 'the size and composition' of the Central legislature had still to be decided, including questions relating to the representation of the Indian States (q.v.), a decision on representation in that body was deferred. An 'annexed table' to the Prime Minister's statement showed a detailed distribution of seats in the Legislative Councils in the Governors' Provinces, or in the Lower Houses, 'if there is an Upper Chamber'.

The announcement came to be popularly known as HMG's 'Communal Award'. It provided, *inter alia*, for separate electorates for Muslims, Sikhs, Christians, Anglo-Indians and Europeans. Voters not belonging to any of these communities would vote in a 'general' constituency. The Depressed Classes were assured separate special constituencies with a right to vote in the remaining general constituencies also. Special constituencies with separate communal electorates were to be constituted for women in all provinces except the NWFP. Seven seats were to be reserved for the Marathas in certain selected plural-member constituencies in the Bombay Presidency. Labour seats were to be filled from non-communal constituencies. The Award retained weightage given to Muslims in the minority provinces. In the Panjab, Muslims were given 86 out of 175 seats in the reformed Council and further assured of three more seats from the landholders' constituencies.

In Bengal, Muslims were given 48.4% seats. Hindus in the Panjab were given 27% and Sikhs 18.8% seats; in Bengal, Hindus obtained 39.2% seats.

The announcement made it clear that while HMG 'themselves can be no parties to any negotiations which may be initiated with a view to the revision of their decision...they are most anxious to close no door to any agreed settlement should such happily be forthcoming. If therefore...they are satisfied that the communities who are concerned are mutually agreed upon a practicable alternative scheme...they will be prepared to recommend to Parliament that alternative should be substituted for the provision now outlined.'

Again, the Constitution itself was 'to empower a revision of this electoral arrangement...after 10 years with the assent of the communities affected, for the ascertainment of which suitable means will be devised.'

It may be noted that the provision regarding Depressed classes became the subject of an acute controversy. Gandhi (q.v.) who was then in jail for his participation in the Civil Disobedience Movement (q.v.) was determined to have it changed. His decision (September 1932) to go on a fast unto death brought about negotiations culminating in the Poona Pact. which secured a major modificaton of the original Whitehall proposals. The report of Parliament's Joint Select Committee noted that the Pact 'in the view of HMG was within the terms of the announcement made by them (HMG) and therefore properly to be included as an integral part of the Communal Award.'

What may be termed as a supplement to the Award was appended at the third session of the Round Table Conference (q.v.) where, on the last day of its meeting, Sir Samuel Hoare, then Secretary of State for India. averred that 'the (British) Government consider that the Moslem community should have a representation of 33–1/3 per cent of British India seats in Federal Chambers. So far as India is concerned, that must be a matter for arrangement between the communities affected and the India of the Princes.'

In July 1934, New Delhi announced what has been called 'the third instalment' of the Communal Award pertaining to communal representation in the services. Twenty-five per cent of the posts under the Government of India and the Railway Services, it was affirmed, were to be reserved for Muslims and 8–3/4% for other minorities. In case suitable candidates for posts reserved for other minorities were not available, the vacancies allotted to these minorities were to be filled in by suitable Muslim candidates.

The Joint Select Committee in its report of 31 October 1934 noted that while 'We may deplore the mutual distrust of which the insistence on this demand (for communal electorates) by the Minorities (viz., Mahomedans, Sikhs, Indian Christians, Anglo-Indian and European communities) is so ominous a symptom, but it is unhappily a factor in the situation which cannot be left out of account.'

Political parties in India gave the Award a mixed reception. In a resolution on 25-26 November 1933, the All-India Muslim League (q.v.) noted that while it 'falls short of the Muslim demands, the Muslims have accepted it in the best interests of the country reserving to themselves the right to press for the acceptance of all their demands.'

The Indian National Congress (q.v.) Working Committee resolution of 13–15 June 1934 however was somewhat ambivalent: 'Since however the different communities in the country are sharply divided on the question of the Communal Award…and the Congress claims to represent equally all the communities composing the Indian nation…(it) can neither accept nor reject the Communal Award as long as the division of opinion lasts.'

A little over three years later, in October 1937, the Congress shifted its stance materially. Thus, the AICC at its meeting in Calcutta noted that the party was 'opposed to this decision (i.e. Communal Award) as it is anti-national, anti-democratic and is a barrier to Indian freedom and the development of Indian unity.' At the same time 'a change in or supersession of the communal decision should only be brought about by the mutual agreement of the parties concerned. The Congress has always welcomed . . .such a change by mutual agreement.'

Gwyer & Appadorai, I, pp. 261-70: Pattabhi Sitaramayya, II, pp. 67-8.

Indian National Congress

The Indian National Congress, founded in 1885 by Allan Octavian Hume (q.v.), a retired member of the Indian Civil Service, held its first session in Bombay at Christmas that year. As then defined, the party's principal objectives were:

a) fusion into one national whole of all the different and discordant elements that constituted the population of India;

b) gradual regeneration along all lines, mental, moral, social and political, of the nation thus evolved; and

c) consolidation of the union between England and India by securing the modification of such conditions as may be unjust or injurious to the latter country.

Hume's motives were an amalgam of liberalism and imperialism, and he found in the proposed plan an efficacious 'safety-valve' for the escape of great dangers that faced the British empire. He established the loyal Indian National *Congress* to thwart the Indian National *Conference* of 'Bengali baboos' of 'advanced' views.

Lord Dufferin's (q.v.) attitude, it may be recalled, was one of 'indifference' towards the movement. The prevalent Russophobia, however, worked more in the nature of a catalytic agent.

The first phase in the history of the Congress, often described as a period of political mendicancy, lasted until 1907. Despite its then largely loyalist, armchair politics, the party did succeed in inducting a spirit of national unity among India's diverse peoples; in focussing attention on their major political grievances and providing a training ground for Indian politicians.

Its outer facade notwithstanding, at the Surat (q.v.) session in 1907, the 'extremists' who hailed principally from the Deccan and the Central Provinces and had chafed under the leadership of the older generation, wrecked the party's unity and brought about a split. The older, more senior members who continued to hold together reiterated their belief that the Congress' objective was the attainment by the Indian people 'of a system of government similar to that enjoyed by the self-governing members of the British Empire'. Additionally, there was to be participation, 'on equal terms', in the rights and responsibilities of the Empire. These objectives were to be achieved by bringing about a reform in the existing system of administration and by promoting national unity, fostering public spirit and developing and organizing the intellectual, moral, economic and industrial resources of the country.

For some time efforts at unity continued to be made, but to no avail. At the Lucknow session in 1916, under the presidentship of Babu Ambika Charan Mazumdar of Faridpur (in Bengal) a superficial union between the two wings was effected for the differences were of a fundamental character and hard to bridge. After the special Calcutta session (September 1920), the party leadership was virtually taken over by Mahatma Gandhi (q.v.) and his lieutenants.

In the early twenties came the Non-cooperation (q.v.) and Khilafat Movements (q.v.) which confirmed the Mahatama's growing hold over the Congress machine. To the superficial eye they were a dismal failure, yet there is little doubt that the two brought about a great measure of politicization of the masses. In 1927, the party adopted 'purana Swaraj' as the country's political goal yet, according to its extremist detractors, the following years witnessed a climb-down. Thus at its 1928 session the party, while reiterating its earlier stance, affirmed its willingness to accept Dominion Status (q.v.) 'if granted before the end of 1929'.

The climate for a political compromise was propitious in the latter half of 1929. Yet the opportunity was lost, for the party insisted on the immediate grant of Dominion Status coupled with an assurance that it form the basis for parleys at the Round Table Conference (q.v.). All through 1930 it launched a Civil Disobedience Movement (q.v.), convinced it would lead the country to its political goal. The following March there were parleys leading to the Gandhi-Irwin Pact (q.v.); civil disobedience was temporarily suspended and the Mahatma was to attend the second session of the Round Table Conference.

While the Mahatma was away, the government set its energies to crushing the movement as well as the party that had launched it. On his return, and the resumption of the movement, the government came down with a heavy hand. To all outward appearances, the Congress was completely annihilated while all forms of political activity throughout the country were rigorously suppressed. In the middle of 1934, the movement was countermanded and the ban on Congress withdrawn. Gandhi, released in the autumn, announced his complete dissociation from the party of which he ceased to be 'even a 4-anna member'. In the years that followed, until the outbreak of World War II, the Congress functioned as a constitutional organization and successfully contested the general elections to the provincial and central legislatures held in 1936-7 under the Government of India Act, 1935 (q.v.). The results were extremely gratifying for its morale as it formed governments in 8 of the 11 British-ruled Governor's provinces.

There was an abrupt change after World War II was declared. Congress demanded that Whitehall categorically declare how far its professed war aims of protection of democratic rights were applicable to India. With HMG singularly reluctant to make any commitment, the result was that the Congress withdrew its ministries from the provinces where it held control. It decided upon organizing a mass campaign to galvanize the country politically. At Ramgarh (April 1940) it reiterated its demand for complete independence and the convening of a Constituent Assembly (q.v.) 'where the rights of all recognized minorities will be fully protected by agreement as far as possible between the elected representatives of various majority and minority groups, or by arbitration if agreement is not reached on any point'.

After the fall of the Low countries and France in the middle of 1940, the Congress resolved upon abandoning the Mahatma's creed of non-violence as a vehicle of state policy. It affirmed its belief that should a genuinely representative national government be constituted at the Centre, it would cooperate fully in the war effort. Apart from an ideological breach with the Mahatma, the Poona resolution, as it came to be called, constituted a revolutionary departure, from non-participation in the war effort, the party now pledged itself to active help in its prosecution.

New Delhi's response to the Poona resolution was the measly August 8, 1940 offer (q.v.) whereby it agreed to invite a certain number of representative Indians to join an enlarged Executive Council of the Viceroy.

Additionally, a War Advisory Council was to be constituted comprising representatives of British India as well as those of Indian States (q.v.). The Congress reacted by rejecting the August offer as being opposed not only to the principle of democracy but to the best interests of the country as well.

In September 1940, the AICC ruled its rejection of the August offer, at the same time requesting the Mahatama to resume the leadership of the party. Individual civil disobedience, restricted to a limited number of satyagrahis, was the answer; the first in the line being Acharya Vinoba Bhave. There were large scale arrests all over the country which included the members of the party working committee, ex-Premiers and Ministers of provincial governments, a host of members of central as well as provincial legislatures and prominent Congressmen. By the end of 1941, New Delhi had set at liberty all the arrested leaders with a view to breaking the political impasse. The annual party session held at Bardoli in Assam formally suspended the civil disobedience movement, leaving the door open for negotiations with the British government for a political settlement. Japan's entry into the war (December 1941) coupled with her rapid military successes led her slowly but surely towards India's doorstep. It was against this background that the Cripps mission (q.v.) was sent which, as has been noticed elsewhere, was a political disaster.

On the eve of the AICC meeting at Allahabad (April 1942), the Madras Congress legislative party under the leadership of C. Rajagopalachari (q.v.) adopted a resolution recommending that the party 'acknowledge the All India Muslim League's (q.v.) claim for separation should the same be persisted in when the time comes for framing the future constitution of India'. Additionally, the League was to be invited for consultations 'for the purpose of arriving at an agreement and securing the installation of a national government to meet the present emergency'. Furthermore, the resolution stressed the need for a popular government in which the Muslim League 'should be invited to participate'.

C.R.'s lead met with widespread criticism, as a result of which, he resigned his membership of the party high command as well as the leadership of the Madras (Congress) legislative party. At the same time, he launched a vigorous campaign in favour of a national government in which the Muslim League should participate. All the while the Mahatma was busy with his call for a 'final struggle' with the British and of 'open rebellion'.

The Congress call for 'Quit India' (q.v.) was the subject of lively controversy, many front rank Congress leaders questioning the wisdom of launching a political movement when the enemy was at the door-step. Eventually, however, near-unanimity was reached and the resolution adopted by an overwhelming majority. Out of 253 AICC members who attended, the tally was 240 for and 13 against.

Mass arrests followed. New Delhi charged that the party had no desire to negotiate; that, with peace on its lips, it was in fact secretly planning a widespread subversive movement. The government had therefore, it argued, no alternative but to act firmly and quickly.

The Muslims by and large kept out of the movement as did Dr. Ambedkar's (q.v.) followers among the scheduled castes. Authority held that except for the cessation of work by the textile industrial workers in Ahmedabad, the wheels of industry did not stop moving. The public services—the police, the post and telegraphs, the railways, the urban utility services—continued to function. Enthusiasm among the student community did not last either. Later, Gandhi's 21-day fast in February 1943 led to a widespread demand for his release, echoed among others by an All-Parties Conference. New Delhi however refused to budge. There was, it argued, no change in the situation to warrant a re-consideration of the ,question; and yet three members of the Governor-General's Executive Council—Sir Homi Mody, M. S. Aney and N. R. Sarkar resigned their posts.

Gandhi was eventually released in May 1944. This was followed by the publication of the C. R. (q.v.) and Desai-Liaqat formulae (q.v.) to break the political impasse. Followed the Simla Conference (q.v.) which, it may be recalled, proved infructuous. Shortly afterwards, the government revoked its ban on the Congress which now resumed its activity in full swing.

In September 1945, the party decided to contest elections to the central and provincial legislatures then being held all over the country. The Hindu Mahasabha (q.v.) and the independents were badly routed; in the Panjab, the Congress bagged nearly one-third of the Sikh seats. As for the Muslim seats, the Congress was convincingly defeated in all the Hindu majority provinces except for U.P. and, to a limited extent, in Assam. In the NWFP, however, it emerged triumphant.

In May 1946 the British Cabinet Mission (q.v.) presented its plan. Both the Congress and the League accepted it, albeit with reservations. Later, however the League, charging that the Congress had gone back on its promise, resiled from its earlier stance.

With Congress participation, the interim government (q.v.) was formed on 2 September, 1946; the League, after an initial refusal, trooped in, towards the end of October (1946). The conflict within the government led to the British Prime Minister Attlee's statement of February 1947 fixing a deadline (June 1948) for British withdrawal and the appointment of Lord Louis Mountbatten as Governor-General for the specific purpose of arranging the transfer of power. His June 3rd Plan (q.v.) spelt out the basis on which the two independent dominions of India and Pakistan emerged in August 1947.

Anil Seal, *The Emergence of Indian Nationalism*, London, 1974; S.R. Mehrotra, 'The organisation of the Indian National Congress 1885–1920' and 'The Objectives and Methods of the Indian National Congress, 1885–1920' in *Towards India's Freedom and Partition*, New Delhi, 1979, pp. 67–90 and 91–114 also *The Emergence of Indian National Congress*, Delhi, 1974; B. Pattabhi Sitaramayya, *History of Indian National Congress* 2 vols., reprint, New Delhi, 1969; Bimanbehari Majumdar and Bhakat Prasad Mazumdar, *Congress and Congressmen in the pre-Gandhian Era, 1885-1917*, Calcutta, 1967; P.D. Kaushik, *The Congress Ideology and Programme, 1920–47*, New Delhi, 1964; B.R. Tomlinson, *The Indian National Congress and the Raj, 1929–42*, London, 1976.

The Constituent Assembly (1946–50)

By the end of June 1946 elections to the Constituent Assembly which was an integral part of the Cabinet Mission plan (q.v.), were over. Out of a total of 296 seats allotted to British India, 4 remained vacant because the Sikhs refused to join the Assembly. The remaining 290 were divided into three sections: 'A', 'B' & 'C'. In Section 'A', were the provinces of Madras, Bombay, Orissa, U.P., C.P. and Bihar, where the Indian National Congress (q.v.) won 162 general and two Muslim seats, the All India Muslim League (q.v.) 19 and the Independents 1. In group 'B' comprising Panjab, the NWFP, Sind and Baluchistan, the Congress won 7 general and 2 Muslim seats; the Muslim League 19, the Unionist Party 3, Independents 1. In Group 'C', embracing Bengal and Assam, the Congress won 32, the Muslim League 35, the Communists 1, the Scheduled Castes 2 and the Krishak Praja Party 1.

The total number of seats taken by the Congress was 201; by the Muslim League 73; there were 8 independents and 6 members from other parties. The Congress won all the general seats, except 9; the League all the Muslim seats, except 5.

On 20 November, Lord Wavell (q.v.) issued invitations for the meeting of the Constituent Assembly scheduled for 9 December. The very next day M.A. Jinnah (q.v.) expressed regret at the Viceroy's decision and declared that no representative of the Muslim League would attend. Jawaharlal Nehru reacted by making it clear that the Constituent Assembly would meet whether the Muslim League came in or not. Wavell told Liaqat Ali Khan (q.v.) that he would not agree to the representatives of the League remaining in the government unless his party accepted the long-term plan of the Cabinet Mission. Liaqat Ali countered with the remark that his party would not accept the long-term plan except on its own terms and was ready to resign from the government, if need be.

To break this unseemly deadlock, the Congress, the League and Sikh leaders were invited to London along with the Governor-General. In the result Jinnah, Nehru, Liaqat Ali Khan and Baldev Singh visited the British capital between 3–6 December; the deadlock, however, persisted. To get around it, on 6 December, HMG affirmed that as the Cabinet mission statement of 16 May had made it clear, the formation of the sections was a precondition to the convening of the Constituent Assembly for the purpose of preparing provincial and group constitutions and that the disputed matters in the sections would be decided by a simple majority of votes of representatives in the sections. Part of the statement read: 'Should a Constitution come to be framed by a Constituent Assembly in which a large section of the Indian population had not been represented, HMG could not, of course, contemplate, as the Congress have stated that they would not contemplate, forcing such a constitution upon any unwilling parts of the country.'

Critics pointed out that HMG's decision to observe a code of Gandhian non-violence and abstention from forcing issues so as to effect a communal settlement was an amazingly gratuitous encouragement to intransigence. The British attitude appeared to be starkly self-contradictory. It would seem that the use of force was legitimate enough when the Congress was making what, in the British view, were unreasonable demands viz., the Non-Cooperation (q.v.) and Khilafat (q.v.) movements of 1920–2, the Dandi March (q.v.) and salt satyagraha of 1930–2 and the Quit India movement (q.v.) of 1942. Yet, however unreasonable the Muslim demands appeared, the use of force could not be envisaged.

As scheduled, the Constituent Assembly convened on 9 December, in the

Library of the Council Chamber. 205 members attended and were seated in separate blocks, province-wise. The Muslim League representatives abstained, as did those from the Indian States (q.v.).

The preliminary business of the Assembly was to appoint a Rules Committee and elect a Chairman. A Committee of 15 was elected to frame the rules of procedure of the Assembly, of the Sections and its Committees. Dr Rajendra Prasad (q.v.) was elected Chairman.

On 5 February and again on the 13th, the resignation of Muslim League members in the Interim government (q.v.) was demanded by the Congress party while Sardar Vallabhbhai Patel (q.v.) insisted that if the League did not resign, they would. HMG however ruled that the resignation of the interim government would spell political disaster.

The most important and politically significant resolution known as the 'objectives resolution' was moved by Jawaharlal Nehru on 21 December 1946. After 6 days' discussion, consideration was deferred to 31 December in the hope the Muslim League would join the Assembly before long. As the League refused to oblige, the Assembly discussed the resolution on 20-22 January (1947) at its second session. Nehru replied to the debate after which all amendments were withdrawn and the Assembly adopted the resolution on 22 January in a solemn manner with all members standing.

Inter alia, the resolution read:

'This Constituent Assembly declares its firm and solemn resolve to proclaim India as an Independent Sovereign Republic and to draw up for her future governance a constitution;

wherein all power and authority . . . its constituent parts, organs of government, are derived from the *people*;

wherein shall be guaranteed and secured to all the people of India justice, social, economic and political;

wherein adequate safeguards shall be provided for minorities, backward and tribal areas, and depressed and other backward classes;

whereby...this ancient land attains its rightful and honoured place in the world and makes its full and willing contribution to the promotion of world peace and the welfare of mankind.'

On 20 February 1947 the British Prime Minister Attlee made a statement in the House of Commons that Britain would quit India by June 1948 and that Wavell would be replaced by Lord Mountbatten as Viceroy.

The objectives resolution was later to be incorporated substantially into the Preamble of the Indian Constitution, both in its 'spirit and, as far as possible, the language'.

The first draft of the constitution was ready by October 1948. Meanwhile the rulers of Indian States having acceded to the Union, accepted the premise that sovereignty resided in their people—*not* in themselves.

After nearly three years of strenuous work, the constitution was finally adopted by the Assembly on 26 November 1949 and came into force as from 26 January 1950 when India emerged as a 'sovereign, independent, democratic' Republic.

Tara Chand, IV pp. 490–5; V. P. Menon, *The Transfer of Power*, pp. 318–29, 330–1, 412–13.

Eyre Coote (1726–83)

Eyre (later Sir Eyre) Coote joined the army early in life and, in 1754, was sent to India with the 39th Regiment, the first to see service overseas. From Madras he was soon (1756) posted to Bengal where he served with distinction under Robert Clive (q.v.)—in recapturing Calcutta (q.v.), Chandernagore (q.v.), as well as taking part in the battle of Plassey (q.v.). In recognition of his services, he was promoted Lieutenant Colonel and took over the 84th Regiment at Madras in 1759.

As soon as the Anglo-French conflict began, Coote successfully commanded British troops at the battles of Wandiwash (q.v.) and Pondicherry After nearly six years (1762–68) in England, he returned to India as Commander-in-Chief, at Madras; unfortunately, he was not able to get along with the local governor and soon (1770) left for home. He returned nine years later, this time as Commander-in-Chief (India) and member of the Supreme Council in Calcutta. In 1780 he was deputed to Mysore to meet the new challenge posed by Haidar Ali (q.v.) who was up in arms against the John Company (q.v.). After some initial reverses, Coote defeated the Mysore ruler at Portonovo. It has been held that the latter victory as surely saved Madras from Haidar Ali as Wandiwash had saved it from the French commander, de Lally (q.v.). Failing health forced Coote to return to Bengal in 1782 and he died a year later (26 April, 1783).

Coote's military capacity has been rated very high, as also his patience, equable temper, activity and energy. 'Daring valour and cool reflection' are said to have been his other great qualities which contemporaries noted, and admired.

Buckland, p. 93; Dodwell, *CHI*, V, pp. 163-5, 284-7; *DNB*, IV, pp. 1083-6 (Henry Morse Stephens.)

Cornwallis (1738–1805)

Of Irish descent, Charles (later first Marquis and second Earl) Cornwallis was born in the eastern county of Suffolk in England and educated at Eton. At 18, he joined the army and four years later entered Parliament as member for Eyer. From 1776–1783 he served as British commander in the rebellious American colonies, where he was singularly unsuccessful, his disastrous campaigns culminating in the surrender of British forces at Yorktown. During 1784–85, twice over, he declined to accept the office of Governor-General and Commancer-in-Chief of the John Company's (q.v.) dominion in India; a year later, however, he accepted the offer, landing in Calcutta (q.v.) on 12 September 1786.

Desirous of establishing British authority in India on a firm foundation, he found an excuse in the confused state of affairs in Oudh (q.v.) to impose on its ruler, Asaf-ud-Daula (q.v.), the maintenance of an enlarged British force, securing at the same time a reduction of the Nawab's own troops.

Finding Tipu (q.v.) a formidable foe in the Carnatic, Cornwallis forged an alliance with the Nizam and the Marathas in 1790. On the plea that the Mysore ruler was contemplating an invasion of Tanjore, the British launched an attack ending in the Third Anglo-Mysore War (q.v.) which culminated in the rout of Tipu's forces and the Treaty of Seringapatam (q.v.). It is held that in this manner, Cornwallis vindicated his failure at Yorktown and made Britain's first acquisition of territory in India by right of conquest.

His place in the history of British India rests primarily on the Permanent Settlement (q.v.) of land revenue and the Cornwallis Code (q.v.), a manual that settled several long standing administrative, and judicial, matters. He was also responsible for creating an efficient civil service but one from which Indians were to be scrupulously excluded. In the law courts too English judges replaced Indians for, it was argued, all regulations would be 'useless and nugatory' as long as their execution depended on the 'natives'. For much the same reason, English law was substituted for Muhammadan law as the latter was deemed barbarous. In all his reforms a basic assumption appeared to be that a system suited to one society could work equally well in another. It was during his tenure of office that the first English envoy, Lord George Macartney, was sent to Peking and Colonel Fitzpatrick to Nepal. The objective in both cases was to conclude a commercial treaty.

Cornwallis returned to England in 1793 and after seeing service on the continent and in Ireland was re-appointed Governor-General of India (July 1805), charged with inaugurating a pacific regime in place of the policy of large-scale territorial expansion under Wellesley (q.v.). His second term, however, was tragically brief, lasting a bare three months; he died, at Ghazipur, on 5 October 1805.

Though by no means brilliant, Cornwallis inspired confidence in others by his devotion to duty, modesty, perseverance, moderation, the art of conciliation, and a willingness to accept the advice of those who possessed more expert knowledge of a subject than himself. He was fortunate in having the confidence of the Court of Directors and the friendship of the Prime Minister and the President of the Board of Control.

In some respects, Cornwallis completed the work of Warren Hastings (q.v.). It was the latter who, in 1772, had decided to implant the sovereignty of the Company in place of the Nawab's—exactly as Robert Clive (q.v.) had envisaged. The judicial and police reforms introduced by Cornwallis completed the constitutional change. In much the same manner, in bringing the administration of criminal justice under English control in 1790, he was only continuing the policy of Hastings.

Cornwallis had the best of intentions—a deep and genuine anxiety to improve the condition of the people. Yet his knowledge of the means by which this was to be attained was singularly inadequate. It has been said that he was anxious 'to make everything as English as possible in a country which resembles England in nothing'. Besides, it implied stigmatizing a whole people as unworthy of trust, incapable of honourable conduct and fit to be employed only in menial situations. Notwithstanding the advantages conferred by his reforms, the 'natives' had no share in making the laws under which they lived and very little in administering them.

A. Aspinall, *Cornwallis in Bengal*, Manchester, 1931; W. S. Seton-Karr, *The Marquus Cornwallis*, Rulers of India, Oxford, 1914.

Cornwallis Code (1793)

The Code was a compendium of forty-eight regulations promulgated on 1 May 1793 by Cornwallis (q.v.). Its aim was to regulate the system of John Company's (q.v.) internal government in so far as it related to its Indian possessions. It defined *inter alia* the revenue, judicial and police systems, created procedures and guarded against miscarriage of justice by setting limits to executive authority.

Among the most important features of the Code were the Permanent Settlement (q.v.) of land revenue, separation of revenue administration and the administration of justice in the hands of Collectors. There was also the creation of a civil service from which Indians were to be scrupulously excluded.

The earlier distinction between revenue and civil cases was abolished and the trial of suits formerly cognizable by the revenue courts was transferred to the Diwani courts which were continued, one in each district.

Four Provincial Courts of Civil Appeal were set up at Patna, Dacca, Murshidabad and Calcutta; each court consisting of three English judges. Another regulation provided for the appointment of a number of licensed Hindu and Muhammadan vakils or pleaders as the legal representatives of suitors who preferred not to conduct their own cases.

The reforms comprising the Code were designed as the basis of a great legal code. The judges were authorized to propose new regulations.

Despite the additional expenditure these entailed, Cornwallis was certain the reforms were 'essential for the national honour and the future prosperity' of the Company's Indian dominions.

In many respects the new regulations were of importance merely as defining the existing system but while re-stating it they contemplated further change. Thus special procedures were laid down for fresh proposals by officials charged with working the prevalent system.

In the reforms carried out in the early years of his first tenure, Cornwallis's aim was economy, purification and simplification. For this purpose Englishmen, adequately remunerated, and *not* foisted by influence, were appointed and vested with exceptional powers. In the second period of reform, of which the Code was the culmination, the principal objective was to safeguard the 'natives' trom oppression. The 'Code' barely helped to create an administrative machinery; upon the spirit that informed it, depended its success. It was to remain operative, virtually unaltered, until about 1813.

Dodwell, *CHI*, V, pp. 437-55; A. Aspinall, *Cornwallis in Bengal*, Manchester, 1931.

Claude Auguste Court (1793–1861)

Born at Grasse in France, Claude Auguste Court was educated at the Ecole Polytechnique in Paris (1812-13). He served in the French army from 1813 to 1818 and later in Persia for a couple of years; in 1827, he along with Avitabile (q.v.) joined Ranjit Singh's (q.v.) service, there he helped in improving greatly the Maharaja's artillery arm.

Court spoke Persian fluently, and was a shrewd and keen observer of men and things. Essentially, a scholar and gentleman, his recorded observations provide a valuable source of information. He paid much attention to archaeology and numismatics. Educated, dignified and respectable, he was however a very unpopular officer, being unable to manage his own soldiers. Initially saved by Ventura (q.v.) whenever his regiments rebelled, he later (1841 and 1843) sought British help in controlling them. Pandit Jalla, a prominent courtier, proclaimed him a deserter and the Lahore Darbar declared forfeit his right to the jagirs he had acquired. This made Court retire from the army and leave for his native Grasse where he lived until his death in 1861.

Court is said to have been the best of the four principal Frenchmen in Sikh employ and was especially useful to Ranjit Singh as an ordnance officer. The guns he forged were put to excellent use by the Khalsa artillery in the Second Anglo-Sikh War (q.v.) and wreaked havoc on the British army.

In 1833 the whole of the Khalsa army was re-organized, on the model of 'Francese Campo', into brigades composed of 3 or 4 infantry battalions, a regiment or so of cavalry and a battery or two of artillery. These brigades were cantoned or quartered in a circle around Lahore—those of Allard (q.v.) and Ventura at Anarkali, those of Avitabile at Naulakha and of Court at Begampura (later Moghalpura).

More of a 'departmental administrator' than an active soldier, Court barely capable of controlling the disorderly soldiers of the Khalsa army under Ranjit Singh 'was quite unable to manage them' in the exceptional times after the death of the Maharaja.

A person of high literary attainments, cautious and retiring disposition, Court was the most respectable of all the French officers in Ranjit Singh's service.

H. L. O. Garret (ed.), *European Adventurers of Northern India 1785 to 1849*, reprint, Patiala, 1970; *Buckland*, pp. 77–8.

Richard Stafford Cripps (1889–1952)

Richard Stafford Cripps' mother had willed that her children be 'trained to be undogmatic and unsectarian Christians, charitable to all churches and sects; studying the precepts and actions of Christ as their example; taking their religious inspiration directly from the spirit of the New Testament'.

From his father's side came the hoary tradition of public service for its own sake, strongly reinforced by powerful but simple religious beliefs. Parental influences thus managed to produce in Cripps the highest possible ideals in personal as well as public life.

Viewed in their proper perspective, his nature cures, teetotalism, vegetarianism, often put down to crankiness, were, in reality, the products of trial and error in an attempt to ease his chronic physical disabilities. His successes did not come from his unflagging energy and long hours alone; he had one of the most acute minds of his generation.

In 1927 Cripps became the youngest of King's Counsels and soon emerged as a distinguished lawyer. In 1930 he became Solicitor-General and was knighted; in January 1931 he was elected Labouor member for East Bristol.

Always irritated by delays, Cripps' logical mind had concluded that if socialism were the right answer to social and economic problems, it had better be brought in 'at once, lock, stock and barrel, with barely a transitional period.' He was a leading member of the Socialist League, a militant group within the Labour party. In the public mind he was confirmed as an out-and-out revolutionary while to Labour party militants of the left wing, he was a hero.

In 1936 Cripps was a prime mover in creating a 'United Front' designed to bring together the Labour party, the Communists as well as the Independent Labour Party (ILP), all into one political organization. A new journal, the *Tribune*, was launched in 1937 to help further the cause. In 1938 he advocated an even broader-based grouping so as to remove the Tory leader Neville Chamberlain's government from office. This was the 'popular front' he now sought and it was to include, apart from the groups listed, a section of the Conservatives as well. When he refused to withdraw this programme of action, despite a directive from the party's national executive, Labour expelled him from its membership in January 1939. He was not to be re-admitted until 1945.

Cripps' public image of the French revolutionary hero Robespierre was belied by private charm and great kindliness. His work for the miners in successfully fighting their legal battles without remuneration won him many friends. In June 1940 Winston Churchill then Prime Minister sent him to Moscow as Britain's Ambassador to the Soviet Union. He remained there for nearly 2 years but could not claim to have advanced the cause of friendship with Joseph Stalin until the German invasion of Russia in June 1941. No sooner did this happen than he negotiated, in July (1941), the Mutual Assistance Pact with the Soviet Union.

In January 1942, on his return from Moscow, Cripps was made Lord Privy Seal, Leader of the House of Commons and a member of the British War Cabinet.

Of the Cripps Mission (q.v.) to India that he headed in March-April (1942), L.S. Amery, then Secretary of States, is reported to have said later that it was thought better that Cripps fail (than that he, Amery, should). As it was, Cripps very nearly succeeded. In retrospect, he felt fully convinced that it was Gandhi (q.v.) who sabotaged the hopes of success after taking no part in the official parleys. As a result, he was to put the utmost emphasis on the Mahatma being involved in any future constitutional confabulations.

In November 1942, Cripps quit the leadership of the House of Commons and his seat in the War Cabinet to become Minister for Aircraft Production, a post in which he is said to have been extremely successful. In 1945, C. R. Attlee, then Prime Minister, made him President of the Board of Control in the first post-war Labour government.

In the three-man Cabinet Mission (q.v.) that came to India (March-June 1946), Cripps was the principal moving force. The Mission's plan of 16 May in all its complex details is said to have been drafted by him one morning before breakfast! It was to become the basis of all subsequent political discussions with the Indian leaders.

In October 1947 Cripps was appointed Minister for Economic Affairs and a few weeks later, after Dr. Hugh Dalton's resignation, Chancellor of the Exchequer. Through sheer persuasion he was able to enforce a voluntary wage freeze on labour and later made industry accept a dividend limitation: an arrangement that worked well for nearly two years. In September 1949, he was obliged to announce a devaluation of the pound sterling.

Owing to failing health, Cripps resigned in October, 1950. His wife Isabel who shared with her husband his simple Christian faith was always by his side and helped in creating a happy home. They had three daughters and a son.

Cripps, who was Fellow of University College, London (1930), Rector of Aberdeen University (1942-45) and Fellow, Royal Society (1948), was appointed Companion of Honour (CH) in 1951. A year later he was dead.

DNB 1950–60, pp. 270–4 (Woodrow Wyatt); Eric Estorick, *Stafford Cripps: A Biography*, London, 1949.

Cripps Mission (1942)

Through the mission of Sir Stafford Cripps (q.v.), then Lord Privy Seal and a member of the British War Cabinet, Whitehall made a big effort to break the political impasse in India which had been heightened by the Indian National Congress (q.v.) decision to quit office in the provinces (September 1939), the abortive August 8, (1940) Offer (q.v.) followed by the somewhat erratic Civil Disobedience Movement (q.v.) under Gandhi (q.v.). The outbreak of World War II, the initial victories of the Axis powers, and mounting US and Chinese pressures on their British allies to make political concessions in India had further complicated a difficult situation.

As a backdrop to the Cripps mission it may be noted that all through 1941-42 there had been a series of resounding German victories in Europe matched by growing Japanese pressure in Asia. The latter had invaded the Philippines, Malaya and Burma. Singapore had fallen on 15 February 1941 when two British warships, the aircraft carriers 'Prince of Wales' and the 'Repulse', were sunk.

On 30 December 1941 the Congress Working Committee had convened: it resolved, *inter alia*, to offer full cooperation to the British war effort *if* conditions were created in which Indians could fight with honour and dignity for the cause of freedom and democracy. In London, Prime Minister Winston Churchill (1874-1965) was averse to any concessions being made to Indian political demands albeit the Labour leader C. R. Attlee (1883–1967), who was also Deputy Prime Minister, was getting increasingly restive with the then Viceroy Linlithgow's (q.v.) unhelpful attitude. He considered the latter to be a defeatist and thought it worthwhile if a high level effort was mounted to bring the Indian political leaders together.

Chiang Kai-shek (1887-1975), Kuomintang leader and Nationalist China's head of state and government, visited India from 8 to 25 February 1942. On his return home he warned HMG that 'if the Indian political problem is not immediately and urgently solved, the danger will be daily increasing . . . If the Japanese should know of the real situation and attack India they would be virtually unopposed.' To the American President, Franklin Delano Roosevelt (1882-1945), he had expressed the view that British policy was tantamount to 'presenting India to the enemy and inviting them to quickly occupy India'. He confessed to being 'both worried and alarmed'.

In the United States, the American Under Secretary of State. Summer Welles, had noted in Feburary 1942 that there had been 'a serious undercurrent of anti-British feelings'. The need for Indian cooperation in the war had been underlined, among others, by General Eisenhower who expressed the view that, unless held, a 'junction between the Japanese and German forces would be accomplished through the Persian Gulf'.

It was against the above background that the British government took the decision to despatch Cripps. As noted earlier, there was mounting pressure from Chungking as well as the White House. The latter was particularly unhappy with Churchill's pronouncement that the Atlantic Charter (14 August 1941) between the President and the Prime Minister (which *inter alia* respected the right of nations to choose their form of government and pledged the restoration of sovereign rights and self-government to those forcibly deprived of these) did *not* apply to India. Washington left Whitehall in no doubt that, in its view, the political problem of India needed urgent attention.

It should be evident that Cripps was to negotiate on the basis of a 'statement of policy' authorized by the War Cabinet. He was to offer Indian political leaders, if he considered it 'wise or necessary', positions in the (Viceroy's) Executive Council 'provided this does not embarrass the defence and good government of the country during the present critical time'. He would consult the Viceroy (who evidently had no foreknowledge) and Commander-in-Chief and 'bear in mind the supreme importance' of the military situation.

This point is doubly underlined by Cripps' biographer who maintains that he (Cripps) did not go 'as a plenipotentiary to negotiate the terms of an agreement' but 'to explain and clarify the terms of a statement of policy that could not be altered'.

The Cripps scheme was in two parts. The *first* prescribed the procedure for framing the Dominion constitution. The preliminary move here was the holding of fresh elections to all the provincial legislatues. Together with the representatives of the Indian States (q.v.) they were to constitute an electoral college whose business it was to elect the constitution-making body. The latter's strength was to be 1/10 of the total membership of the electoral college which was to be chosen according to a system of proportional representation. As for the constitution-making body, it was laid down that if at the final stage 'a province expressed its unwillingness, through a vote of its legislature, to accept the constitution, it was free to refuse accession to the Indian Union'. It would then proceed to formulate its own constitution which would have the same status, powers and functions as that of the Union of India.

It was made clear that the Indian Dominion would have the right to secede from the Empire. The conclusion of a treaty between HMG and the constitution-making body was envisaged.

It may be noted that both Linlithgow and Wavell (q.v.), (then Commander-in-Chief), had argued against the inclusion of the right of a province not to accede to the Union of India but Churchill and the War Cabinet had been obdurate.

The *second* part of the Cripps scheme related to immediate and interim arrangements during the war. It contemplated no change in the Government of India Act 1935 (q.v.) nor in the responsibility of HMG for the governance of india nor yet in its control and direction over the defence of the country. It was recognized that organizing the military, moral and material resources of the country was New Delhi's responsibility which it was to discharge with the co-operation of the people.

As for the *first* part, the Congress objected to the provision for the local (viz., provincial) option referred to, which, it felt, implied acceptance of the principle of Pakistan. Nor was the mode of selection of representatives of the princely states by their rulers to the constitution-making body to its liking.

In regard to the *second* part, the question of the status of the Executive Council and especially its Defence Minister, was a subject of acute controversy. Congress was prepared to accept the position that Indian independence would be recognized *after* the war but argued that unless *de facto* power and responsibility were conceded *now*, the change contemplated would not be of any significance. Congress had proffered satisfactory assurances on the question of the proposed 'National government' which along with the question of the Defence portfolio ultimately proved to be the principal bone of contention.

Unfortunately for him, in two specific instances—the composition and authority of the Executive Council as well as the provision about the Defence portfolio—Cripps is said to have exceeded his instructions. It is also suggested that he worked at cross purposes with the Viceroy and the government of India. It was clear that he wanted Indian leaders to join in preparing the constitution of a free India, while New Delhi completely lacked such a faith or objective and heaved a sigh of relief when Cripps did eventually fail. eventually fail.

Maulana Azad (q.v.) has maintained that Cripps changed his position between his first and second interviews. Possible explanations are: *One*, that he had hoped 'to persuade the Congress to accept the proposals even though there was no change in the basic situation by his persuasive powers and manners.' *Two*, that during the interval referred to, the inner circle of the government of India had started to influence him, that he was constantly surrounded by the Viceroy and his entourage. *Three*, messages between London and New Delhi had been exchanged; the former, it would appear, had sent 'fresh instructions which made him (Cripps) feel that if he went too far he might be repudiated'.

Glendevon (Linlithgow's son, biographer and apologist) has charged that the Viceroy would have forgiven Sir Stafford anything except 'stealing his (L's) cheese to bait his own (C's) trap'; in other words, 'offering control of the Executive Council as an inducement to accept the declaration'.

For Cripps' offer of 29 March—'You cannot change the constitution. All you can do is to change the conventions of the constitution. You can turn the Executive Council into a Cabinet'—was, to Linlithgow, a sell-out. To start with, the Viceroy maintained, Cripps had no instructions to say anything of the kind; for another, it appeared to be a rash and irresponsible suggestion. The Viceroy's anxiety was already beginning to prove justified and Cripps was naive enough to show him a suggested list of members of the new Executive Council. Linlithgow is said to have reacted: 'That's my affair'.

All through the negotiations, the Viceroy continued to complain that

Cripps did not consult him and had even offered a wholly Indian Executive Council, barring the Defence portfolio. Linlithgow had told H.V. Hodson, 'I think he (Cripps) will fail with HMG's policy' and that the entire exercise was 'like hawking rotten fish'. The fact is that difficulties between Cripps and Linlithgow reflected differences between Churchill and Amery on the one hand and Attlee and Churchill on the other; that Attlee completely distrusted Linlithgow's judgement and his handling of the Indian situation.

Thus in a letter to Amery on 24 January 1942, the Labour leader had noted: 'I must confess that the general effect of the despatch (from New Delhi) does not increase my confidence in the Viceroy's judgement. . . .Linlithgow seems to be defeatist. . . .It is worth considering whether some one should not be charged with a mission to try to bring the political leaders together. There is a lot of opinion here which we cannot ignore which is not satisfied that there is nothing to be done, but to sit tight on the declaraton of August (8) 1940.'

Eventually, Cripps *was* repudiated by the British Cabinet both on the question of a 'National' government as well as on Defence. Whitehall accepted Linlithgow's contention that there could be no surrender of the authority conferred on the Viceroy by the Act of 1935.

A word on the Cripps-Johnson (Col. Louis A. Johnson (1891-1966), President Roosevelt's Personal Representative stationed in New Delhi) formula on Defence. It stipulated that an Indian may be appointed Defence Member in the Governor-General's Executive Council but that he would delegate his powers to the Commander-in-Chief as the War Member who, in turn, would control the war operations and the armed forces and be responsible to General Headquarters as well as Naval and Air Headquarters.

Cripps later complained to Amery that on the Johnson formula, Linlithgow had gone beyond his (C's) back. Considering the treatment to which he (Cripps) had subjected the Viceroy, argues Glendevon, 'it would be an understatement to call this an odd reaction'. For whichever way it was, he maintains, Cripps went well beyond his brief and was 'manifestly baiting the trap with the Viceroy's cheese'.

In the final count, the hopes which Cripps had initially raised of establishing a National government could not immediately be realized, nor was the Cripps-Johnson formula substantially different from an earlier version which the Congress had rejected. The War Cabinet decided in favour of Linlithgow and against Cripps, taking note of the fact that 'there can be no question of any convention limiting in any way your (Viceroy's) powers in the existing situation and no departure from it could be contemplated during the war'.

Cripps offered his resignation but was persuaded not to press it. On 10 April, the Congress rejected his proposals and accused Cripps of going back on his word; the next day Cripps charged that what the Congress aimed at was the establishment of 'an oligarchic, irresponsible and irreplaceable government.' A brute majority would, he argued, be thus in a position to dominate the minorities; he was satisfied that the minorities would never accept such a situation. The day following (12 April) he left India, his mission a complete failure.

In retrospect, it would appear that in sending him Whitehall's principal objective had been to win over public opinion for it should be plain that it had no intention to transfer power to Indian hands. Linlithgow, Glendevon affirms, had given both Churchill and the Cabinet ample warning but they felt impelled to take the risks in response to heavy pressures from their war-time allies.

Neither Cripps nor Linlithgow, it has been said, believed that the mission would succeed. The Cabinet had noted that the 'present declaration is intended not to supercede, but to clothe those general declarations [i.e., declaration of August 1940] with precision and to convince people of India of the Cabinet's sincere resolve'.

Maulana Azad noted that Cripps 'was essentially an advocate and as such he was inclined to paint things in a rosier colour than was warranted by the facts.' Cripps believed, a knowledgeable Indian journalist has suggested, that 'his personal relation with Nehru' would help him win over the Congress Working Committee. He was reinforced in this faith by the powerful support given to his proposals by C. Rajagopalachari (q.v.). Gandhi however viewed his scheme as worse than that of the Act of 1935 in so far as the principle of partition was to be decided by people chosen on a very limited franchise. No wonder he is reported to have told Cripps that his proposals were tantamount to 'an undated cheque on a crashing bank.'

Hodson has held that the 'fault clearly lay with Sir Stafford in negotiating on such an issue (the Defence portfolio) to a point of vital commitment without the clearest understanding with the Viceroy. The busy body Colonel Johnson made matters worse. But the blame did not rest with him alone for the War Cabinet and especially its India Committee made a fundamental mistake, strange in a body so experienced, when they sent an emissary to promote a policy in India which had not been fully argued with the Viceroy, though he would have to carry it out.'

A biographer of Cripps has put forth the view that it was 'as clear as daylight from the details of the negotiations what was obvious from the document the moment it was handed to the Indian leaders and published to the world—the British government were not prepared to yield one inch of power to the Indians *now* and wanted their willing co-operation as complete subordinates on the strength of 'a post-dated cheque' of questionable character. Neither the earnest advocacy of Stafford nor his drive nor his eloquence could persuade the Indian leaders that there was more than this in the proposals he had brought.'

In a letter to Linlithgow on 11 April Amery confided: 'It now seems to me that the longer he stayed out there the more his keenness on a settlement drew him away from the original plan, on which we had agreed, and in the direction of something to which we were all opposed...What puzzles me a little is that Cripps should have been prepared to go that far with Congress without realizing that this was the very thing against which Jinnah (q.v.) said the Muslims would rise in revolt.'

Glendevon has charged that Linlithgow trusted Cripps and was shabbily treated in return.

R. J. Moore has argued that if the Cripps mission had been fully supported, India's eventual partition might have been averted.

Despite Cripps' failure, British gains, on the whole, were impressive. The American urgency regarding Indian autonomy was now sharply subdued and Japan's credibility put under a shadow. Chinese apprehensions and fears were reduced to verbal protests by Chiang to Roosevelt; the radical section of the Labour party and Labour members of the British Cabinet became reconciled to HMG's policy towards India and were annoyed with the Congress attitude.

Speaking in the British Parliament on 28 April (1942) Cripps declared that his failure was due to the

i) involvement of government in the war;

ii) propaganda of the Axis powers producing a defeatist atmosphere;

iii) growth of communal antagonism and the conflicting demands of the (Indian political) parties and the communities;

iv) objection of the Congress primarily to the first part of the Declaration and secondly about the form and character of the Executive Council and the position of the Defence member in it.

The British parliamentary debate that followed was a brave effort in projecting the curious paradox that while Great Britain was anxious to lay down the burden of empire and entrust India with independence, Congress leaders, especially Gandhi, were so blind as to fail to recognize what was in their own interest and so crazy as to reject a generous British offer! All told, because of the cussedness of the Congress, Whitehall convinced itself, an opportunity for a settlement was lost. Both Amery and Churchill gave repeated if fatuous assurances that despite failure to break the deadlock, the proposals remained in force in all their scope and integrity.

It may be noted that only the Muslim League (q.v.) accepted the Cripps proposals while most of the other political parties—the Akalis, the Hindu Mahasabha (q.v.), the National Liberal Federation (q.v.) and the Indian Christians—were opposed to them.

Nicholas Mansergh and E. W. R. Lumby (eds.), *The Transfer of Power, 1942-47*, Vol. I, *The Cripps Mission, January-April 1942*, HMSO, London, 1970; H. V. Hodson, *The Great Divide: Britain, India & Pakistan*, London, 1969; Maulana Abul Kalam Azad, *India Wins Freedom: An Autobiographical Narrative*, Bombay, 1959; John Glendevon, *The Viceroy at Bay: Lord Linlighgow in India 1936–43*, London, 1971; Durga Das, *Indian from Curzon to Nehru and After*, rev. enl. ed., Calcutta 1973; R. J. Moore, *Churchill, Cripps & India 1939–1945*, Oxford, 1979.

Lionel George Curtis (1872–1955)

Born in March 1872, Lionel George Curtis was educated at Wella House, Haileybury and New College, Oxford.

In 1900 he acted as secretary to Sir Alfred (later Viscount) Milner. After the latter's departure in 1905 and the arrival of Lord Selborne, 'Milner's kindergarten', a group of bright young civilians headed by Curtis, set themselves to prepare a formal memorandum showing the imperative need for uniting the four (Cape Province, Natal, Orange Free State, Transvaal) South African colonies. In 1909, when the Union (of South Africa) constitution was completed, he returned to England and founded the *Round Table*, a quarterly review of which Phillip Kerr, later the Marquess of Lothian, became the first editor. The journal advocated a federation of self-governing countries of the 'British Commonwealth', thereby introducing that connotation for the first time. Later, as Beit Professor of Colonial History at Oxford, Curtis devoted himself to the cause of a closer union of the British Commonwealth, forming Round Table groups.

In 1916-17 Curtis took a prominent part in discussions relating to the progress of India towards self-government. His activities and the Montagu-Chelmsford report led him to publish a book entitled *Dyarchy* (1920) which also contained his 'Letters to the People of India'. In 1920-21, it was through his efforts that the Royal Institute of International Affairs (Chatham House) was founded and endowed. He assisted the British government in framing the Irish treaty (1921) and the Irish constitution and remained, until 1924, 'Advisor to the Colonial Office on Irish Affairs'.

During 1924-34 Curtis was engaged in writing his book *Civites Dei*, published in 3 volumes over the years 1934-37. Herein he set forth his gospel of the Commonwealth, and indeed world unity under free and democratic institutions.

Curtis was a man of action and an enthusiast who exercised a compelling influence on others. Although in later life he held no important position and was not well-known in public, his influence was great: in the creation of the Union of South Africa, in the progress of India towards self-government and in the Irish treaty.

DNB 1951-60, pp. 279-80 (Robert Henry Brand); Lionel Curtis, *Dyarchy: Papers Relating to the Application of the Principle of Dyarchy to the Government of India*, Oxford, 1920.

Curzon (1859–1925)

George Nathaniel Curzon, later Marquess Curzon of Kedleston, had an eventful tenure as Viceroy (1899-1905); it was to mark the end of an epoch in British rule in India. He had long aspired and indeed prepared himself thoroughly for this appointment which he had assiduously sought after a brilliant and, in some respects, outstanding academic career at Eton and later Balliol College (Oxford). A Balliol composition summed up his early upbringing:

> My name is George Nathaniel Curzon,
> I am a most superior person
> My cheek is pink, my hair is sleek,
> I dine at Blenheim once a week.

Thus was cast the image of the 'Superior Person' and for a time Curzon, it would appear, was not unhappy with it. Years later when he wished desperately to shed it, it stuck. 'Never has more harm been done to one single individual than that accursed doggerel has done to me', he confided in his second wife, Grace.

A faithful representative of his age, Curzon was, both by upbringing and training, a great believer in Tory democracy seasoned by a strong flavour of individual than that accursed doggerel has done to me', he confided to his Lytton's (q.v.) 'forward policy', including the war against Afghanistan.

Some aspects of Curzon's thinking come out clearly in his early works—*Russia in Central Asia in 1889* (1889), *Persia and the Persian Question* (1892) and *Problems of the Far East* (1894). More especially his pronounced, and indeed uncompromising, Russophobia and his belief in Great Britain's divine mission to counter it are heavily underlined.

Curzon entered Parliament in 1885 and served as Under-Secretary for India

(1891-2) and later (1895-8) for foreign affairs. A thorough study and understanding of Asia and the Near East, he was convinced, were essential prerequisites to good statesmanship. Beginning in 1887 he had travelled extensively in Central Asia, Persia, Afghanistan, India, the Pamirs, Siam, Indo-China and Korea not to mention Canada, the United States and China, with visits to St. Petersburg and Moscow. The result was the three voluminous tomes, referred to in the preceding paragraph, the end-products of extensive study and wide-ranging travels.

His thinking did not take long to crystallise. *Inter alia*, Curzon was convinced of England's civilizing mission, of the seemingly self-evident truth that 'India was the strength and greatness of England'. It followed that 'without India the Empire would not exist' and that in the then global struggle for new markets and colonies England was the best equipped, and should, for that reason, never recede before the claims of other colonial powers. Some of these conclusions which before long took the form of firm convictions were to become the guidelines for policies that he later adopted during his viceroyalty.

Curzon found his fervent, almost religious, faith in the imperial destiny of England confirmed for him both on the Yangtze and in the defiles of the Khyber Pass; his great journeys rendering him at once a xenophobe and a nationalist. He came to view the British empire as 'a majestic responsibility' rather than as 'an irksome burden' and affirmed that it be 'strong in small things as in big'.

Curzon's Indian viceroyalty (January 1899–November 1905) falls broadly into two uneven halves with the Delhi Darbar (January 1903) serving as a convenient dividing line. During the first four years, despite the 'mingled bewilderment and pain' of the bureaucrats, he was admired in India and supported at home; in the last two, while his popularity in India, began to wane, his differences with those 'who rule and overrule from Whitehall' 'became increasingly bitter.

A thoroughbred imperialist, Curzon felt the urgent necessity of establishing British influence in the landward periphery surrounding India, and of preventing rival powers from encroaching on it and thereby posing a threat to the British empire. To achieve this objective, he did not sometimes hesitate to defy the home government or use *force majeure*, should the situation so warrant. A confirmed Russophobe, he felt that the Tsarist advance towards the empire's Indian frontiers, whether by land or sea, must be kept under a stern check.

His stubborn resistance to such an advance in Persia, elaborated in a masterly despatch to Whitehall, underlined the insecurity to which India would be exposed and, if unchecked, the additional defence and maritime expenditure that it would have to incur. He browbeat, on his own initiative, the petty sultanates in the Gulf and such foreign agents as he thought were allies of Russia, from securing bases on their soil. He strengthened and further increased the number of British consulates in Persia and prevented the Tsar's government from advancing southwards and gaining control over the Persian Gulf. Initially, he felt hurt by the home government's declaration that his actions were short-sighted; it was only in 1903 that Lansdowne (q.v.) officially supported his policy. Elated by this recognition Curzon, escorted by a naval flotilla, paid a much-publicized and highly dramatised visit to the Gulf.

In Afghanistan, the Viceroy had hoped to strengthen the British position by reviewing the old treaty relations which he deemed unsatisfactory. Yet no suitable opportunity came his way as Amir Abdur Rahman (q.v.) while sedulously keeping his pledges refused to kowtow to the Viceroy. Even though feeling outraged, Curzon was prevented by the home government from sending an ultimatum and thereby precipitating a crisis. With Habibullah (q.v.) he was particularly tactless—threatening to withhold the subsidy and the arms consignment until the earlier treaty had been negotiated *de novo*. Curzon maintained that the compact had been personal to the new Amir's father and was convinced that Habibullah's recalcitrance had been instigated by Russia. Anyway, the Amir refused to be over-awed while Whitehall, fearing the worst, ordered Lord Ampthill (who was acting for the Viceroy while Curzon was away home on leave) to despatch a mission under Louis Dane, then foreign secretary to government. Much to Curzon's chagrin, an agreement entirely favourable to Habibullah was concluded which, *inter alia*, denied the Indian government 'all means of putting pressure on the Amir'.

The Viceroy's Tibetan policy too revealed an ambitious design. Lacking a formal link, the only source of information for the Indian government for all that happened in Tibet was Nepal's envoy stationed at Lhasa. Curzon was desirous of establishing a direct link ostensibly to facilitate commerce but in reality to preclude any possibility of Russian influence and intrigue. Reports of Tsarist agents operating had been sporadically received from different sources while the declining influence of a moribund (Manchu) China encouraged the Viceroy to despatch his own emissaries to the 13th Dalai Lama (q.v.). His letters however elicited no response, being returned, unopened. Curzon took this to be a personal affront both to himself as well as the government he represented. This looked particularly offensive when it was revealed that the Lama had despatched one Aguan Dorjieff, a Buryat Mongol of Russian nationality, as his 'diplomatic' envoy to St. Petersburg. Consequently, the Viceroy strongly urged Whitehall to order an armed expedition.

Overruled, Curzon none the less persuaded a reluctant HMG to sanction a commercial mission with an armed escort to confer with the Chinese and Tibetan officials *inside* Tibetan territory and chose Francis Younghusband (q.v.) to be its leader. The objective, as was only too apparent, was to reach Lhasa and there dictate terms to the lama hierarchy. China disavowed any control over the country (Tibet) and categorically repudiated the widely accepted rumour of its treaty with Russia in regard to the Dalai Lama's domain. Curzon meticulously catalogued the 'warlike preparations' of the Tibetans and persuaded an increasingly recalcitrant Cabinet at home to sanction a move up to Gyantse and later, in the face of 'Tibetan resistance', to Lhasa itself. There Younghusband was to defy Whitehall's specific instructions in regard to the Lhasa Convention (q.v.) partly because of the support, both overt as well as covert, which he had received from the Viceroy himself.

Curzon's approach towards the problem of the north-west frontier which he tackled at the very outset of his reign may be rated among his most successful. He ordered the withdrawal of large numbers of troops stationed close to the border and substituted them by tribal levies who, he argued, would succeed in maintaining peace better. The regular troops, in order to be easily available for emergencies, were to be stationed at nearby well-entrenched, well-defended cantonments. Although his policy broke down completely by the time of World War I, and sporadic risings had occurred even earlier, it certainly brought a measure of peace and drastically reduced the cost of military operations (from an estimated Rs 4,584,000 between 1894-8 to Rs 248,000 during 1899-1905).

Closely tied to his tribal policy was the long-contemplated separation of the frontier province from the Panjab, though, in the process, the provincial governor, badly ruffled by Curzon's inept handling, resigned. The Viceroy's ostensible aim was to improve the administration of the area, extend communications right up to the border with Afghanistan and thereby strengthen the imperial hold. The new North-West Frontier Province, placed under a chief commissioner responsible directly to the government in Calcutta, was differentiated from the old North-West Provinces by designating the latter as the 'United Provinces of Agra and Oudh.'

The Viceroy, determined to make his administration memorable, spared neither himself nor his subordinates in his great zeal to ensure the permanence of the British impact. Aware of the strong dislike of the 'natives' of foreign rule, he hoped to win them over by an efficient and just administration and launched a programme of administrative reform covering twelve major fields. At the same time he wished to set aright the mistakes of his predecessors.

Commissions were constituted to deal with irrigation, railways, agricultural banks and police. His financial reforms soon began to bear fruit while the currency reform was widely applauded. His work for Indian historical monuments including restorations at Delhi and Agra was a source of great satisfaction. Curzon struck his reforming axe at the superfluous minuting in government offices, reducing the verbiage of printed reports from some 18,000 pages to 8,000 and statistics from about 35,000 to 20,000. These measures, he hoped, would leave bureaucrats more time for constructive thinking.

Most of the Viceroy's well-intentioned endeavours, however, bore a stigma in that there was not even the slightest involvement of the people for whom he laboured so hard. His failure may be explained partly by his conceited retort to all such criticism: 'I know best'; by his adamant refusal to recognize the upsurge of nationalism and his incurable habit of underestimating the capabilities of his adversaries. To which may be added a stern refusal to delegate to others either work or responsibility.

Opposed to decentralization, Curzon's first attempt to establish official control over local government was the Calcutta Municipal Act (q.v.). In essence, it tended to officialise municipal administration and diminish the control exercised over it by the abhorred 'Bengali babu'. The measure proved to be extremely controversial and Curzon lived to see it undone, in 1923.

The widespread famine of 1897-8 brought to the fore the stark inadequacy of official methods with the result that Curzon now ordered the earlier Famine Code to be revised. Flaws in revenue assessement, as had been pointed by Romesh Chunder Dutt (q.v.) among others, were a major cause of India's poverty. Curzon worked diligently to set things right and in his Land Resolution of 1902, declared the vagaries of the monsoon, *not* revenue assessment, to be the controlling factor in the situation. He assured his critics that government aimed at reducing taxation demands and making revenue assessments more elastic. Thus the Panjab Land Alienation Act (1901) sought to protect cultivators from eviction. To help boost agricultural production, he established an Agricultural Research Institute at Pusa in Delhi. He also instituted a rapid land survey (under Sir Colin Scott Moncrieff) which identified widespread irrigation as an ideal remedy for all agricultural ills. Sir Colin recommended the irrigation of 6,500,000 additional acres at a cost of Rs 30 crores—a scheme that would, he computed, provide employment to 300,000 labourers.

A new Department of Commerce and Industry was set up to encourage, among other things, railway construction. Sir J. N. Tata (1839-1904) was given permission to set up an iron and steel plant.

Curzon rated education to be the 'most clamant necessity of all'. The products of (Thomas Babington) Macaulay's (q.v.) time-worn system were, he argued, the empire's foremost critics. He therefore departed from the hitherto pursued policy of state non-interference in education by declaring it to be a state responsibility. In this manner, he hoped to change the direction of education policy to serve the interests of the empire: emphasizing primary rather than college education and shifting control from the hands of non-official Indians to that of government officials. To effect these changes, a meeting of educationists was called at Simla where Indian representatives or invitees were conspicuous by their absence. All the 150 resolutions debated at the conference were drafted by Curzon himself!

A committee was set up to look into the functioning of universities and its recommendations implemented by the University Act VIII of 1904. A strong, hostile, almost unprecedented, public reaction to this measure has been called a 'dress rehearsal' for the events that were to follow.

Elaborate plans were spelt out for primary education while stringent rules were laid down for recognizing secondary schools. At the same time the Viceroy encouraged the teaching of European children, helped re-open hill schools and sanctioned a recurring grant of Rs 2.46 lakhs beginning in 1906. Though merely skirting the surface of the problem, he deserves credit for recognizing Hindi as the language of a majority of the people and initiated measures to have official documents translated into that language.

Curzon's lively interest in the preservation of Indian historical monuments referred to in a preceding paragraph led to the appointment of John (later Sir) Marshall as the first Director General of Archaeology.

Curzon's own principal architectural contribution was the Victoria Memorial at Calcutta assailed by his critics as a 'bizarre creation in marble'.

To restore the people's faith in the police a commission under Sir Andrew Fraser (q.v.) began a detailed enquiry into all facets of the problem. In the light of its report, a new covenanted Police Service was constituted and a criminal intelligence department established. Long before Kitchener (1850-1916) appeared on the scene as Commander-in-Chief, Curzon realizing the indispensability of artillery, well-organized transport, and improved communications for an efficient defence force had been able to achieve a measure of self-sufficiency both in ammunition and armaments.

An ostentatious coronation Darbar at Delhi (1903) to mark the accession of King Edward VII (r. 1902-12) was a result of the Governor-General's misconceived notion that Indians would respond heartily to regal pomp and pageantry and to the equal status of citizenship that the empire represented. So prominently did the Viceroy himself figure in the entire proceedings that critics nicknamed it as the 'Curzonation Darbar'.

A firm believer in the pre-eminence of the paramount power, Curzon tried unsuccessfully, albeit valiantly, to prevent Queen Victoria as well as Edward VII from attaching too much importance to the 'native' princes. In his efforts to dissuade the latter from making too frequent trips abroad, he waxed eloquent on the duties of the rulers to their own people. Coercion and intimidation were the weapons the Viceroy used whenever necessary in his dealings with the Indian States (q.v.). The Nizam was bullied into leasing the Berar territory in perpetuity.

Despite warnings to the contrary, Curzon went ahead with the Partition of Bengal (q.v.), ostensibly for administrative convenience, but in reality, critics suggest, for curbing a growing restiveness among the nationalists. He had convinced himself that opposition to the measure would be purely temporary. Unfortunately for him the passive resistance in the form of the Swadeshi Movement (q.v.) and the resultant Boycott (q.v.) of foreign goods were responsible for widespread discontent all over India. Not long afterwards (1911), it was countermanded.

By 1905 the new form of nationalism which from the lofty heights of abstract idealism had come down to draw a powerful response from the masses was further stimulated by the challenge of Curzon's imperialism. It had now captured the imagination of a large segment of the educated classes. Curzon's challenge to it was 'the challenge of benevolent British imperialism as an alternative to developing Indian nationalism. But in so doing, he had carelessly overstepped the bounds of political prudence, and by pursuing such measures as educational reform and the partition of Bengal in the face of widespread popular opposition, he presented the extremists with ready-forged weapons with which to attack his whole concept of paternal despotism. Guided as he was by the maxim that administrative efficiency is synonymous with the contentment of the governed, Curzon sought to stifle nationalism with bureaucracy. In fact in his singlemindedness he aided rather than deterred the forces undermining the British position in India. His regime therefore marks if not the beginning of the end, at any rate the end of the beginning.'

Towards the close of his viceroyalty Curzon faced more grievous danger in a head-on clash with Lord Kitchener whose appointment as India's Commander-in-Chief had been made at his own behest. Agreeable initially, the Army chief soon came to the conclusion that his power was flagrantly curtailed by a junior military member in the Viceroy's council. On the face of it, it was an administrative anomaly which could have been corrected but fearing that it would diminish the power of civil authority, Curzon would have none of it. While the Governor-General remained complacent about the soundness of his position, Kitchener intrigued behind his back and built up strong support for himself in London. As the two failed to effect a compromise, the matter was referred to the home government. Backed by the powerful support both of the Prime Minister and the Secretary of State Kitchener managed to have the military member's position downgraded. Curzon accepted the new compromise, but with ill-grace. Later his appointment of Sir Edmund Barrow as the new military supply member brought the crisis to a second deadlock for Kitchener strongly disapproved of the new incumbent. Confident of his own indispensability, Curzon submitted his resignation—not for the first time. It was, to his utter and everlasting disbelief, accepted!

The sad fact was that his continuous defiance of the home government had gradually undermined his standing while the events of the last few years (1903-5) had been none too happy from his point of view. By 1905 his relations with Henry St. John Brodrick (later Earl of Midleton), Secretary of State for India, as well as (Arthur James) Balfour, then Prime Minister, were unfriendly, even bitterly hostile. There was some truth in his later charge that the two had treated him with 'tortuous malignity'.

After his return home, though temporarily in eclipse, Curzon held successive important posts, both in and outside government. For a time he was Warden of the Cinque ports and later Chancellor of the University of Oxford. He abandoned the idea of seeking an election to the House of Commons and was instead elevated to the House of Lords. Prior to World War I, he was Lansdowne's right-hand man. Lord Privy Seal in Asquith's Cabinet, he was president of the Air Board (1916). Later, under Lloyd George he was a member of the War Cabinet, subsequently (1919) taking over the Foreign Office which he retained until 1924.

Curzon's service in the War Cabinet and as Foreign Secretary was the second peak in his career. But his role in the Foreign Office was not as successful as it might well have been in an earlier era.

The ex-Viceroy proved to be a bitter opponent of the Montagu-Chelmsford Reforms (q.v.), convinced that these would lead to parliamentary government in the Indian empire and thus shatter the very basis of British rule. This was seemingly inconsistent, for he was the author of the August (1917) Declaration (q.v.) with its promise of 'progressive realization of responsible government'. He was heart-broken when, in 1924, his lifelong dream of becoming Prime Minister was shattered and Stanley Baldwin, Tory leader in the House of Commons, was selected to head the government as well as the party. Later, he was passed over even for Foreign Office. Unable to bear the great mental and physical strain, his health broke down suddenly. He died in London in March 1925.

Curzon's life span may, for convenience, be divided into three, unequal, parts: 1859–98, youth and early promise; 1899–1905, Indian viceroyalty, at once a triumph and a disaster; 1905–25, sure yet steady decline. Winston Churchill has remarked that the morning of his career was golden, the noontide bronze and the evening lead. India, it has been said, was 'the watershed and a microcosm of the whole: brilliant promise, precociousness tempered by responsibility; fierce personal clashes and, in the end, bitter disappointment.' The harsh truth is that the manner of his resignation from the Viceroyalty did lasting damage to his chances of becoming Prime Minister for it 'alienated him from his former friends and gave him a reputation for unreliability. In his relations with his superiors he was thought to be quick to take offence, with his subordinates unbalanced; in the details of administration his industry was at the expense of the practical; in negotiations he was thought to be obdurate; in policy, unsound.' His abandonment of Asquith (1916) and later of Lloyd George (1922) was not easily forgotten, or even forgiven. A. J. P. Taylor put it with characteristic terseness when he described the ex-Viceroy as 'one of nature's rats'.

Curzon has been rated a study in sublime failure. Viceroy at 39, when he quit seven years later he was in the political wilderness for over a decade. Foreign Secretary after a convincing victory over Kitchener, his adversary, he was yet not able to fortify his country's triumph in a great war. Worse, the supreme prize of his ambition was denied him at the very last minute. A biographer has summed up his personal tragedy thus: 'He acquired great possessions and resounding titles; he left his mark upon the art and literature of his country; and yet he achieved successes rather than success. Had his will been as forceful as his intellect, his determination as constant as his industry...But the tense self-preoccupation of the chronic invalid robbed him of all elasticity and he failed to adapt himself to the needs of a transitional age which did not like him and which he did not like.'

David Dilks, *Curzon in India*, 2 vols, London, 1969-70; Kenneth Rose, *Superior Person: A Portrait of Curzon and his circle in late Victorian England*, London, 1969; Earl of Ronaldshay, *The Life of Lord Curzon: Being the Authorised Biography of George Nathaniel, Marquess Curzon of Kedleston*, 3 vols, London, 1928; Harold Nicolson, *Curzon, the Last Phase, 1919-25*, New York, 1934; Leonard Mosley, *Curzon: the End of an Epoch*, London, 1960; V. C. Bhutani, *Apotheosis of Imperialism: Indian Land Economy under Curzon*, New Delhi, 1976; D. R. Thorpe, 'George Nathaniel Curzon' in *The Uncrowned Prime Ministers*, London, 1981, pp. 92-163; Peter Harnetty, 'Nationalism and Imperialism in India: the Viceroyalty of Lord Curzon, 1899-1905', *JIH*, 41 (2), August 1963, pp. 391–403.

The Thirteenth Dalai Lama (1876–1933)

The Dalai Lama is, traditionally, the spiritual and temporal ruler of Tibet. The title 'Dalai', which means ocean and corresponds to the Tibetan *Gyatsho*, is Mongolian in origin. It was conferred on the 5th Dalai Lama, spiritual successor of the Gelug-pa or the yellow hat sect of lamaism, by the Mongol chief Altan Khan. In Tibet itself he is known by such other epithets as *Kyam Rim-po-che* (The Precious Protector), *Gye-Wa-Rim-po-che* (The Precious Sovereign), *Kyam-gon Buh* (The Inner Protector), *Lama Pon-po* (The Priest Officer), *Kundun*, etc.

The 13th Dalai Lama, Thupten Gya-tsho, who came of ordinary peasant stock in the province of Dak-po, not far from Lhasa, was born in June 1876. Discovered as the unmistakable and unchallenged reincarnation of Chenre-si (or Lord of Mercy), the Tibetan god, he was brought to Lhasa in 1878. However, the Amban, the Chinese emperor's official viceroy stationed in Lhasa, had not been consulted, with the result that the Lama's enthronement was delayed by a whole year. Later the Dalai Lama went through traditional training in meditation and learning religious text under the guidance of senior monks. During his minority, as was customary, he was guided by a Regent and his Cabinet.

Unlike some of his immediate predecessors, the 13th Dalai Lama attained majority; the then Regent and the Prime Minister who were conspiring to get rid of him were apprehended in time and later executed. To start with, the intricacies of government eluded him, slowing down the pace of improvement and efficiency that he aspired to inject into the mediaeval mode and manner of administration in his country.

Aware of Chinese hostility to his exercising full temporal and ecclesiastical control, as well as the growing weakness of Manchu authority in the mainland itself, the Dalai Lama attempted to break free. Having scotched an attempt by the Amban to appoint his own protege in the Cabinet, the Dalai Lama proceeded to obtain Russian help as a counterpoise to the Chinese. His principal instrument in this exercise was Aguan Dorjieff, a Buryat Mongol who even though a subject of the Tsar had studied in Lhasa and was very close to the person of the Lama

Unfortunately for him, the Dalai Lama's policy aroused the British government's ire. Deeply suspicious of Russian motives, the latter was further irked by the fact that the Lama had refused to reply to communications sent to him by the Indian Viceroy, Lord Curzon (q.v.). To forestall possible Russian hegemony over Tibet, the Younghusband Expedition (q.v.) was mounted. Initially charged with negotiating a settlement on the frontier itself, it eventually marched into Lhasa. As a result of this relentless and, to the Tibetans, unashamed onslaught, the Dalai Lama fled—initially to Outer Mongolia but, later, to China. The Lhasa Convention (q.v.) was signed in his absence; earlier, he had been denounced and deposed by his political masters in Peking. He returned home in December 1909, after a five-year exile. A few months later a large Chinese invading force sent from the eastern marches appeared in the Tibetan capital. Compelled again to flee, he sought and received asylum in India, where he pleaded with the British for support to drive the Chinese out and later supplicated that Tibet be declared a (British) protectorate. Unfortunately for him, all this was to no avail. The British refused to be tempted and earlier, in the Anglo-Russian convention (1907), had pledged to Russia a 'hands-off' policy in Tibet.

With the overthrow of Manchu rule in February 1912 and the subsequent ousting of Chinese troops from Tibet itself, the Dalai Lama staged a triumphant come-back. He spurned attempts made by the newly installed Chinese Republic under its first President, later briefly turned Emperor, Yuan Shih-kai, to accord him recognition. The Dalai Lama's objective was to assert temporal as well as ecclesiastical independence from China.

In Tibet, the Dalai Lama who, in conjunction with his Cabinet, the National Assembly and the Ecclesiastical Council constituted the country's supreme government, slowly but surely assumed all power to himself. He appointed his men to the Cabinet, seldom called the Assembly and succeeded in reducing the influence of the monks in his administration by replacing them with lay officials. The strength of the army was increased and it was now better trained and equipped—some of the arms being imported from India, as were the drill-sergeants. In 1921, a threatened civil war between the army and the monks was narrowly averted. The Dalai Lama was equally autocratic in matters relating to the monasteries, insisting that they concentrate only on religious study and spiritual pursuits.

A breach occurred between the 13th Dalai and the 9th Panchen Lamas in 1925 when the latter fled to China. Attempts at reconciliation failed, for while the Dalai Lama took an increasingly independent stance, the Panchen Lama came more and more under the influence of Kuomintang China. Though critized by a section of the people and the principal monasteries for becoming 'earthly' and concentrating on secular matters, the Dalai Lama's regime was notably less oppressive than earlier ones and was welcomed by a majority of his countrymen. Outside observers noted its relative efficiency, the maintenance of law and order, a proper administration of justice and a lessening of corruption.

The Dalai Lama tried to strengthen Tibet's relations vis-a-vis her neighbours in Asia. He was particularly impressed by Japan's progress. In 1913 he sent a Tibetan representative to the tripartite Simla Conference (1913-14) agreeing to the boundary between India and Tibet known in the eastern sector as the McMahon Line after the British Plenipotentiary, Sir Arthur Henry McMahon (q.v.). The abortive treaty also conceded Peking's control over Eastern Tibet, subject to an unqualified acceptance by China of Tibet's autonomy. A year later the Dalai Lama offered 1,000 men to fight on the British side in World War I. He was averse to joining the League of Nations, strongly questioning the ability of other countries to help Tibet in the event of a Chinese invasion. Before his death in December 1933 he lent countenance to two Kuomintang attempts, in 1927 and again in 1931, to normalize relations with Tibet.

Charles Alfred Bell, *Portrait of the Dalai Lama*, London, 1946; Tokan Tada, *The Thirteenth Dalai Lama*, the Toyo Bunko, Tokyo, 1965; Parshotam Mehra, *Tibetan Polity, 1904–37*, Wiesbaden, 1976.

Dalhousie (1812–60)

James Andrew Broun Ramsay, tenth Earl, later Marquess of Dalhousie and Governor-General of India (1848-56), came of Scottish lineage and was educated at Harrow and Christ Church, Oxford. He had served a successful decade in Parliament in varied capacities, as Vice-President and later President of the Board of Trade in Sir Robert Peel's administration.

Dalhousie was the youngest in age to assume the responsibilities of governing the Indian empire. Ambitious, and possessed of indefatigable energy, he came out determined to complete and consolidate Britain's Indian empire. Conditions in the country favoured his policies and added to his own ability to create opportunities where none had existed.

To 'rationalize the map of India', foster internal security and figure out continuous borders for the Company's domain, he undertook to incorporate through conquest, annexation and abolition of titles, a large number of hitherto independent territories and bring them under British rule.

Within three months of his arrival, Diwan Mulraj (q.v.), governor of Multan in the then tension-ridden Panjab, broke into open revolt. Dalhousie's deliberate effort for a time to underplay this challenge would appear to have been part of a master plan to let the disaffection catch on and spread, thereby making later British interference on a large scale imperative. In Sher Singh's revolt the Governor-General found the *casus belli* to justify the entry of British troops into the Panjab (November 1848). Although his clear-cut aim was to crush the Sikh army and annex the state, he refrained from openly declaring his intent so as to prevent the community from rallying to a common cause and offering united resistance. As it was, the Second Anglo-Sikh war (q.v.) took a heavy toll on both sides.

Lacking faith in his Commander-in-Chief, General Hugh (later Field Marshal, first Viscount) Gough (1779-1869), the Governor-General asked for a replacement. However, before Charles Napier (q.v.), could arrive to take over as the new chief, the war had been won with the British victory at Gujrat. Dalhousie annexed the Panjab, rejecting the advice of such moderates as Henry Lawrence (q.v.) and Sleeman (q.v.) and, in the bargain, gave the British empire a much-sought-for northern frontier.

For the administration of the state, a 3-member board, consisting of among others Henry and John Lawrence (q.v.) was constituted. Later during his tenure, the Governor-General was involved in a controversy with Napier regarding certain directives he had given on the issue of allowances paid to Indian troops without the government's prior approval. Dalhousie demanded and obtained Napier's resignation, in which action he was backed by his political superiors in London.

Despite the Afghan Amir Dost Mohammad's (q.v.) participation in hostilities against the British, Dalhousie wanted to maintain peace on the frontier so as to be able to continue his work in the interior. A treaty was concluded with Afghanistan in 1855; a year earlier, a subsidiary treaty had been negotiated with the Khan of Kalat.

A brief war in Sikkim was precipitated by the superintendent of Darjeeling, Dr John Campbell, and his companion Sir Joseph Dalton Hooker (1817-1911), the botanist, who allegedly attempted to cross over into Chinese territory. They were released after strong British protests while, in the process, the Raja was mulcted of some 1,670 square miles of territory for his reported insult to British subjects.

The Governor-General's activist policy emboldened British merchants in Rangoon who intensified their complaints of Burmese maltreatment. Dalhousie, at once impatient and intolerant, could brook no slight to British prestige and was determined to have the alleged wrongs redressed. An expeditionary force commanded by Commodore Lambert was despatched to Rangoon to demand reparations. Careful plans had been made for the invasion and occupation of Lower Burma while outwardly a pretence had been kept up to disapprove of Lambert's actions. The Governor-General was also not oblivious of the fact that the implementation of his plan would mean not only additional territory but protection to the far-flung outposts of the empire in the east, and increased trade as well as free markets for British goods. Over a minor dispute, an ultimatum which the Burmese were bound to reject was delivered and war declared. The Governor-General made sure that the mistakes of the First Burmese War (q.v.) were not repeated during the Second Burmese War (q.v.) at the speedy conclusion of which the province of Pegu, comprising Lower Burma, was unilaterally declared annexed.

More by accident than design, Dalhousie embarked on what looked like a systematic campaign to extinguish all princely Indian States (q.v.) and titles. Any pretext which served the purpose appears to have been adopted and justified. The maximum number of annexations were made through the application of the Doctrine of Lapse (q.v.). Among others, the states of Satara, Nagpur, Jhansi, Udaipur, Balghat, Sambhalpur, Jaitpur, Carnatic and Tanjore were thus incorporated. Some titular sovereignties were discontinued as in the case of Nana Saheb (q.v.). Oudh (q.v.) was annexed at the behest of the Directors on the plea of misgovernment, although its case was by no means worse than that of the so-called 'independent' states. Earlier, the Governor-General had instituted an inquiry under James Outram (q.v.) to legalize his anticipated action. Wajid Ali, the last Nawab of Oudh, preferred to surrender his crown to being disgracefully removed. By and large, only such princely states were spared as were conveniently surrrounded by a ring-fence of British territories. The Nizam paid heavily for his 'independence' by ceding the rich province of Berar.

In sum, most of Dalhousie's annexations were accomplished under the cover of lapse or misgovernment, as in the case of Oudh, or even the abolition of titular sovereignties (Carnatic) that he viewed as obsolete.

Dalhousie's activity was not confined to territorial expansion and consolidation; he aimed at creating a modern state with a streamlined system of government and economy. A step in this direction was the creation in 1854 of the office of Lieutenant-Governor of Bengal, thereby freeing the Governor-General of the minutiae of local government. A uniform system of centrally controlled administration was spelt out. He insisted on 'unity of authority' and an administrative structure run by civilians with an over-riding authority over military officials. In the newly-acquired territories, a non-regulation system was adopted.

Additionally, British-ruled territories were to be inter-linked with a network of communications. Drawing on his experience of railroad building and administration as President of the Board of Trade in England, Dalhousie sketched out a plan for railway construction. His railway minute of 20 April (1853) has been regarded as 'one of the most remarkable and comprehensive' of his many important state papers. It details convincingly the political and military as well as commercial reasons which underlined the need for speedy introduction of a vast network of Indian Railways (q.v.) throughout the country. These were designed to consolidate newly-acquired areas, enhance the mobility and striking power of the troops, facilitate trade and encourage the investment of British capital in India.

With equal vigour, Dalhousie took up the construction of telegraph lines in 1853 and the institution of a modern postal system. While the railways had been the subject of correspondence with the home government before his assumption of office, the introduction of the electric telegraph was his own idea carried out entirely on his recommendation.

A uniform half-anna (thrҽe naya paise) postage rate all over India was introduced. The loss of Rs 9 lakhs in revenue, the Governor-General was convinced, would be made up by an increase in the mail handled. A Public Works Department too was set up to encourage road and canal construction. The Grand Trunk Road was laid and the Ganges Canal finalized in 1854.

Army reform did not escape the Governor-General's vigilant eye either and he outlined his proposals on the subject in nine masterly minutes. He suggested among other things the strengthening of the Company's troops and a corresponding reduction in the 'native' force, promotion based on merit rather than seniority, adequate medical services, etc. It was the home government which, sensing no urgency, postponed taking any action. On his own initiative, he created an irregular force to strike a balance between the John Company's (q.v.) and the 'native' troops. A disagreement between him and Charles Napier, his commander-in-chief, over the question of *batta* or daily allowance had led, as has been noticed earlier, to the latter's resignation.

Dalhousie welcomed revision of the government's educational policy embodied in the Education Despatch of 1854 (q.v.) by Sir Charles Wood. He also established an Engineering College at Roorkee and a Medical College in Calcutta.

In his enthusiasm for consolidating the John Company's possessions, establishing its supremacy and modernizing the administrative structure, Dalhousie undertook all manner of reform. He possibly overlooked the impact of his actions on the dispossessed zamindars, the deposed princes as well as the populace in general. Both Charles Napier and William Sleeman in regard to conditions in the army and the political repercussions of the annexation of Oudh had warned him of an impending mutiny. Conditions presaging civil strife were not absent either and the Santal Rebellion (q.v.) proved to be a forerunner of more widespread revolts culminating in the Rebellion of 1857 (q.v.).

The strain of seven years of vigorous and unremitting activity took a heavy toll on a delicate physique; for Dalhousie lived for a bare four years after his departure from India in March 1856. His policy and administration came in for severe criticism when fourteen months later the Great Rebellion broke out. Yet he felt no need to justify his actions. His papers (sealed for fifty years after his death), he was sure, would vindicate his honour.

The key to Dalhousie's success was his dauntless character. He was seldom prepared to act as an obedient servant of his masters at home, seldom prepared to accept their orders without protest. Few Governors-General moved as widely and as frequently as he did over the length and breadth of India, when there were no railways, and the roads were far from modern. Few too could work as hard as he did. The truth is he came in not too good health and, through over-work, ruined himself completely. A biographer has noted: 'and of many great names which adorn the annals of our Indian empire, not one stands out more brightly than that of Dalhousie.'

The total effect of the changes brought about during 1848-56 contributed to the development, besides other things, of a changed economy, a new social outlook, and finally a concept of Indian unity.

The military and political grievances were themselves enough for the outbreak of the Rebellion. The social grievances have 'rather been exaggerated or their significance over-emphasized.' The rapid expansion of the railways and the telegraphs immediately after the Mutiny and their immense popularity everywhere would appear to falsify the theory of Indian antipathy towards them.

In bringing about change, Dalhousie was guided by the utilitarian philosophy of Jeremy Bentham and John Stuart Mill. By transforming oriental India into a westernized India, he thought he was 'strengthening the hold' of Britain. He did not visualize the future. He is remembered today 'more as a catalyst in the growth of Indian nationalism, albeit an inadvertent one', than as a torch-bearer of British imperialism and as a man at the root of the Rebellion of 1857.

Dalhousie ranks among the ablest, if at the same time the most controversial, of Governors-General of British India. To him the country owes its railways and telegraphs, the reform of its postal system and the development of irrigation and road-making. He removed imposts which shackled internal trade and promoted popular education. He had great capacity for work. His relations with his Council were good. He was tenacious—at times perhaps over-tenacious—in maintaining his own authority. He has been compared with Wellesley (q.v.) but had an edge in that he 'spent more energy in organizing than in acquiring.' He has also been compared with Bentinck (q.v.) but, unlike the latter who established a few signposts in his vision of a westernized India, Dalhousie laid down the 'roads of progress.' Curzon (q.v.) was a great systematizer, but Dalhousie 'created' what Curzon sought to perfect. His weakness, it has been said, 'was that of going too far too fast. He was a sick man in a hurry. He was the apostle of a westernized India with all an apostle's zeal and faith.'

M. N. Das, *Studies in the Economic and Social Development of Modern India, 1848-56*, Calcutta, 1959 and 'The Marquis of Dalhousie, a sketch of his character and personality', in *IHC*, proceedings of the twentieth session, 1957, Bombay, 1958, pp. 266-74; Suresh Chandra Ghosh, *Dalhousie in India, 1848-56: A study of his social policy as Governor-General*, New Delhi, 1975; William Lee-Warner, *The Life of the Marquis of Dalhousie*, 2 vols, reprint, Irish University Press, 1972.

Maharaja Dalip Singh (1838–93)

Dalip Singh, youngest son of Maharaja Ranjit Singh (q.v.) was born on 4 September 1838 and ascended the throne on 18 September 1843 after the gruesome murder of his brother Sher Singh. With his accession, his mother, Maharani Jind Kaur (q.v.), became Regent. Shortly after the conclusion of the first Anglo-Sikh War (q.v.), the Maharani was exiled, ostensibly on grounds of hatching a conspiracy, but in reality to curb her growing anti-British influence on the young prince. By the Treaty of Lahore (q.v.), following the Second Anglo-Sikh War (q.v.), Dalip Singh was placed under British protection, compelled to give up his several estates and pensioned off for Rs 4 lakhs annually. His personal property was sold and the proceeds distributed among the troops.

From 1850 to 1854 Dalip Singh stayed as Dr John Login's ward at Fatehgarh, during which period he was converted to Christianity. Later he was given an estate at Elveden in Suffolk (England) and became a great favourite of Queen Victoria who treated him affectionately, as though he were her own godson. On 1 July 1854, Dalip Singh was received at the Palce. The 35-year old Queen was taken in by the 15-year old ex-Maharaja: 'He has been carefully brought up . . . is a Christian. He is extremely handsome and speaks English perfectly, and has a pretty, graceful and dignified manner . . . I always feel so much for these poor deposed Indian Princes.'

A recent study has revealed that it was at the Queen's instance and *against* the advice of her Government that the former Maharaja was given an allowance of £15,000 a year and the rank of a European Prince with the title of His Serene Highness.

Dalip Singh was permitted to visit his mother in India in 1861, when the latter accompanied him back to England where she died two years later (1863). It was at her behest that he studied the Blue Book on the Panjab and

staked his claims to his father's estates; but all to no avail. In a letter to the
Times (8 September 1888), Dalip Singh maintained that he was 'a ward of
the British nation' and that it was unjust on the part of the guardian to
deprive him of his kindgom in consequence of a failure in the guardianship.
Peeved by his change of stance, the British instituted an inquiry into his
debts.

It were largely his financial difficulties, for which he may have been partly
responsible himself, that finally drove him to claim compensation for his
private estates in the cis-Sutlej territory. The British offer of a measly few
thousand pounds frustrated him. Consequently, he turned his thoughts
towards the possibility of becoming the ruler of the Panjab with support
from his collaterals.

In 1883, Dalip Singh's attempt to return to India was foiled by the British
arresting him at Aden. The simmering discontent led to a great deal of strain
in his relations with Whitehall in the years that followed. A London
newspaper commented: 'For upwards of 30 years has he been at issue with
them at various points, small questions no doubt at first...but which, as time
went on, become more and more of vital importance to the Maharaja and, in
corresponding ratio, less and less interesting to the officials who had to deal
with the case....Is he, therefore, entirely to blame for his present attitude
towards the British nation?'

With the British refusal to allow him to return home he endeavoured to
formulate a seemingly visionary scheme for obtaining Russian support. His
letter dated 10 May 1887 to the Tsar is eloquent testimony to this day-
dreaming: 'I guarantee an easy conquest of India. For besides the promised
assistance of the Princes of India with their armies, it is in my power to raise
the entire Panjab in revolt and cause the inhabitants to attack in their rear
the British forces sent to oppose the Imperial Army.....

At this moment the whole of India is with me and as soon as the People of
Hindustan are assured of my arrival in Russia their joy will know no bound
at their coming deliverance.....

I would venture to state that, should the invasion of India be entertained
in the Imperial councils, an army of not less than 200,000 men and 2,000
cannons be provided for that purpose.....

I have been deputed simply to make an appeal on behalf of 250,000,000 of
my countrymen for deliverance from the cruel yoke of British rule and
having done so my duty is ended.....'

The Maharaja, who is said to have entered Russia surreptitiously around
April 1887, remained at Kiev until sometime in October 1888. From
Geneva, in June 1889, he issued a proclamation to his 'beloved fellow-
countrymen' in India asking them to rally to his cause. He warned them of
England's 'perfidious designs' and of the impending 'conflict' in which 'the
great Emperor of Russia' would be arrayed on the side of 'our friends' and
render 'material support.' He described himself as 'Sovereign of the Sikh
Nation' and an 'implacable foe of the British Government.'Additionally, he
announced his reconversion to the Sikh faith and entered into correspondence with several Indian princes and Sikh chieftains.

The poor response his frantic appeals evoked was bitter disappointment.
He therefore beat a hasty retreat. In July 1890, the Maharaja wrote to the
Queen expressing 'deep regret' for his past conduct and 'humbly' asking for

her 'pardon' and 'clemency', promising at the same time 'obedience to her wishes for the future.' As a result, his debts were paid off and he was accorded the Queen's pardon 'you have sought.' The Queen was deeply touched by her last meeting with 'the poor misguided maharajah' which took place (March 1891) in France: 'He is quite bald and vy. (very) grey ... I asked him to sit down—and almost directly he burst out into a most terrible and violent fit of crying almost screaming ... and I stroked and held his hand and he became calm and said, 'Pray excuse me and forgive my faults' and I answered 'They are forgotten and forgiven' ... but it was vy (very) sad—; still I am so glad that we met again and I cld. (could) say I forgave him.'

Dalip Singh died in Paris on 22 October 1893 of paralysis and was buried a week later at Elveden.

Khushwant Singh has bemoaned the fact that 'for some strange reason', Sikh historians have made him into a hero: 'Dalip Singh was as much of a non-hero as any produced by the Sikhs.'

In June 1863 Dalip Singh married Bamba Muller, the daughter of a German merchant and an Abyssinian mother. A Christian, she was a student and later teacher at the American Presbyterian Mission School in Cairo. She died sometime in September 1887, leaving six children, three sons and three daughters. Two years later, in May 1889, the Maharaja married Ada Douglas Wetherill in Paris. She outlived him and died much later, in August 1930.

Lena Login, *Sir John (Spencer) Login and Duleep Singh*, London, 1899, reprinted, Patiala, 1970; Ganda Singh (ed.), *History of the Freedom Movement in the Punjab, Vol. III, Maharaja Duleep Singh's Correspondence*, Panjabi University, Patiala, 1972; 'Maharaja Duleep Singh's letter to the Emperor of Russia, May 10, 1887', *Panjab, Past and Present*, 1, 2, April 1967. pp.352–5; Michael Alexander and Sushila Anand, *Queen Victoria's Maharajah: Duleep Singh 1838–93*, London, 1980; Khushwant Singh, 'Maharajah Dalip Singh', *Hindustan Times*, New Delhi, 18 May 1980.

Dandi March and Salt Satyagraha (1930–1)

The five years that elapsed after Chauri Chaura and the collapse of the Non-cooperation Movement (q.v.) were for the nationalist cause a period of great discouragement and still greater disillusionment. This lean phase came to an end with the appointment of the Simon Commission (q.v.) towards the close of 1929. The 'all-white' commission was widely viewed by nationalist opinion as an inquisition by foreigners into India's fitness for self-government. Presently, the 'Simon seven' and their 'blood-red' progress through the country became symbolic of a new national resurgence.

Both overtly and covertly the Commission posed a challenge to Indian politicians to produce on their own an agreed solution to the constitutional tangle. The result was the Nehru Report (q.v.) which, later, a vocal section of the Muslim community refused to accept. The Calcutta session of the Indian National Congress (q.v.) in 1928 had split over the issue of Dominion Status (q.v.) versus complete independence. An irreparable breach was narrowly averted by Gandhi's (q.v.) compromise formula to the effect that, if by

31 December 1929 the goal of Dominion Status was not accepted by the British, the Congress would opt for complete independence.

1927 however was marked by a rash of large-scale disturbances. In April that year a bomb was thrown into the visitors' gallery of the Central Legislative Assembly. Shortly afterwards a number of trade union leaders were arrested in the notorious Meerut Conspiracy case. Two years later, Lord Irwin's (q.v.) visit to England for consultations with Whitehall, followed by his announcement of 31 October (1929) that Dominion Status was India's political goal created a stir. However, the goodwill thus generated was presently dissipated by debates in Parliament which revealed the existence of a powerful lobby against the grant of any political concessions to the nationalist cause in India. Understandably, the Indian reaction was a strong revulsion against any political compromise.

With 'the year of grace' over, at the Lahore session of the Congress (December 1929), the flag of *purna swaraj* (complete independence) was unfurled. On 26 January 1930 'independence day' was observed throughout the country with a clarion call to the people that 'it was a crime against God and man' to submit to the 'satanic British rule' (Gandhi's words). It was at this stage that the Mahatma announced his decision to open his campaign by breaking what he called the pugnacious Salt Laws.

On the morning of 12 March, Gandhi with a band of 78 or 79 volunteers started on his 385-kilometre trek from Sabarmati Ashram at Ahmedabad to Dandi on the west coast. The march turned out to be a great popular upsurge although the Government had hoped it would be an utter disaster.

A word on salt and the tax. In the late twenties, nearly 35% of India's needs were met by salt produced by, or sold to the Government; 30% was imported, another 35% manufactured by licence subject to payment of excise. Gross revenue from salt duty, for fiscal 1923-4, was Rs 10.12 crores and for 1924-5, Rs 7.86 crores. The salt monopoly had been defended so far on the plea that the same amount of revenue could not be raised so cheaply and with so little inconvenience to the country in any other manner.

To revert to the Satyagraha, Dandi is situated in Jalalpur district in Gujarat. Of the total number of Satyagrahis accompanying the Mahatma, 2 were Muslims, 1 Christian and the rest Hindus—two of them representing the untouchables. They were drawn from all parts of India and were aged between 16 and 61, the oldest being the Mahatma himself. They were selected as people who had been obedient to the Ashram discipline.

The march began at 6.00 a.m. on 12 March 1930. That day meetings were held and processions taken out all over the country; it had been declared to be Civil Disobedience (q.v.) Day. The Dandi marchers covered approximately 16 kilometres a day. Meantime, on 23 March 1930, the A.I.C.C. meeting held at the Sabarmati Ashram endorsed its Working Committee's resolution authorizing the Mahatma to launch civil disobedience on a mass scale. It was decided to break the salt laws in so far as salt was an item of daily use and its price affected large masses of people.

Not everyone was persuaded; but all were mystified. Salt, Jawaharlal Nehru (q.v.) recorded later, 'suddenly became a mysterious word, a word of power. The salt tax was to be attacked, the salt laws were to be broken. We were bewildered and could not fit in a national struggle with common salt.'

Gandhi reached Surat on 1 April 1930. Out of the 25 days which the journey took, the party had walked every day barring three when the Mahatma observed *Maun Vrat* (fast of silence). Four days after Surat, on the morning of 5 April, Gandhi and his party reached Dandi. His prayers early next morning were unusually solemn. Immediately afterwards, accompanied by 84 volunteers from the Gujarat Vidyapith and Seth Punjabhai of Ahmedabad, the Mahatma proceeded, exactly at 6 in the morning, for a bath in the sea. Gandhi and his volunteers picked up salt lying on the sea-shore. At this, Sarojini Naidu who was present, hailed him as a 'law breaker.'

With Gandhi's satyagraha, salt became the symbol of India's will to freedom. The Salt Satyagraha which had begun with the carefully staged drama of Gandhi's month-long march lasted another two months after his inaugural gesture on the Dandi shore, petering out as soon as the monsoon arrived. This phase of civil disobedience was 'peculiarly Gandhi's own.' It was a point of conflict he had carefully chosen to create the maximum unity so pivotal to his plans, and for most of the time he led the Satyagraha in person.

Dennis Dalton has suggested that mindful of the hot mid-afternoons, Gandhi confined the marching schedule to the mornings and evenings and 'provided ample advance publicity' to ensure a good press coverage, both Indian and foreign. More, 'Gandhi's influence and impact as a mass leader derived in large part from his performers' sense of his advice; he staged and executed his events with an uncanny sensitivity to the mood and temper of those around him.'

The march was not strictly part of civil disobedience, but its dramatic prelude. It was peaceful but impressive. Gandhi's stark figure, staff in hand, outstriding his companions; fearless, with a messianic zeal for his cause, quietly confident in combat with the Raj, compelled respect and awe as he made his symbolic journey to the sea.

Congress leaders were arrested on 5 May 1930 at the village of Karadi where later that day Gandhi was also taken into custody. Mass-scale arrests were made throughout the country. There was police firing in Delhi, Peshawar and other places.

Earlier, the Mahatma's non-arrest after he had broken the law made him shift his stance. He now moved to a temperance and anti-foreign cloth campaign which would bring women into the movement and appeal to international opinion as righteous issues.

Gandhi had planned raiding and taking possession of the Dharsana Salt Works located in Surat district and had written to the Viceroy to that effect. But before he could do so, he was stopped in the early hours of 5 May. Later, on 21 May, 2,500 volunteers from all parts of Gujarat led by Imam Abdul Qadir Bawazir, an old colleague of Gandhi in South Africa, took part in the 'raid'. Abbas Tyabji, Sarojini Naidu, Pyarelal and Manilal Gandhi who were with the volunteers, were arrested and the latter mercilessly beaten up. The toll was 2 dead, 320 injured.

The scope of the civil disobedience movement was now extended to include, apart from salt, breach of forest laws, non-payment of taxes, boycott of foreign cloth, banks, as well as shipping and insurance companies. The Government retaliated by issuing a series of ordinances which brought within the ambit of the law a number of new offences and conferred extraordinary powers on the executive. For all practical purposes, a virtual reign of terror was unleashed. 'Salt making, salt-pedalling, courting arrest, suffering brutal police attacks . . . forcible breaking of meetings, shootings, confiscation of property' became the order of the day. About 100,000 persons are said to have filled the jails.

On 23 April 1930 there was a big demonstration at Peshawar following the arrest of Khan Abdul Ghaffar Khan (q.v.). It claimed a heavy toll, 30 dead and 33 wounded. In May, martial law was proclaimed at Sholapur. This was an eye-opener. To start with, as has been noticed, the Government had viewed the movement as 'a mad gesture on the part of a crazy visionary', fondly hoping it would 'fall completely flat' and that either Gandhi would have to recall it or it would die of ennui. In the Viceroy's own words, 'the march, inauspiciously begun, would peter out in failure and ridicule, and I had no desire to martyrise Gandhi prematurely.'

In July 1930 the London-based *Daily Herald* journalist, George Slocombe interviewed Motilal Nehru (q.v.). Subsequently, T. B. Sapru (q.v.) and M. R. Jayakar met Motilal as well as Jawaharlal Nehru in Naini Jail and Mahatma Gandhi and others in Poona. On 31 January 1931, after a conciliatory speech by Prime Minister Ramsay MacDonald (q.v.) at the Round Table Conference (q.v.), the Government released unconditionally all members of the Congress Working Committee.

This was the first link in the chain of events that culminated in the Gandhi-Irwin Pact (q.v.). The withdrawal of the satyagraha campaign and of the ordinances that had been issued in its wake as well as the release of civil disobedience prisoners led to Gandhi's visit to England (September-December 1931) to attend the second session of the Round Table Conference.

Outside Bombay, the only provinces where the Salt Satyagraha proved more than a token gesture were Bengal, Madras and U.P. It created 'rather less interest' than had been expected. This is not to suggest that it did not create a deep impression; in fact, it did.

Neither in India as a whole, nor in any province was the Government's salt monopoly ever threatened by the Salt Satyagrahis. Nor had Gandhi, much less the Congress Working Committee, either expected or intended this. Nor yet did it succeed in Gandhi's objective of uniting the Hindus and the Muslims in a common struggle. But it performed an important preparatory function in the civil disobedience campaigns by generating widespread demonstrations of contempt for laws considered oppressive and for British authority. It had also given local Congress committees occasion to try out their publicity mechanisms and organizational links.

Years later, recalling his many memories of Gandhi, Jawaharlal noted that the dominant picture in his mind was of the Mahatma marching to Dandi: 'He was the pilgrim in quest of truth; quiet, peaceful, determined and fearless who would continue that quiet pilgrimage regardless of consequences.'

S. R. Bakshi, *Gandhi and Salt Satyagraha*, Malayalttor (Kerala), 1981 and 'The Dandi March of Gandhi', *Modern Review*, CXXXIV. 4, April 1974, pp. 249-58; Dennis Dalton, 'The Dandi Drama' in Peter Robb and David Taylor (eds.), *Rule, Protest and Identity: aspects of modern South Asia*, London, 1978, pp. 133-44; Judith M. Brown,

Gandhi and Civil Disobedience: the Mahatma in Indian Politics 1928-34, Cambridge, 1977, pp. 100-16; Penderel Moon, *Gandhi and Modern India*, London, 1968; D. G. Tendulkar, *Mahatma: Life of Mohandas Karamchand Gandhi*, new edition, July 1961, 8 vols, III, pp. 20-38; *Dandi March: Freedom Struggle of India, 1928-31: an Exhibition of Photographs and Documents*, NMML, 1969, pp. 1-3.

Imperial Darbar (1877)

The idea of an imperial darbar was mooted by the British Tory leader and Prime Minister Benjamin Disraeli (1804-81) and later ably and enthusiastically executed by Lytton (q.v.). The occasion was the assumption to the title of 'Empress of India' by Queen Victoria in accordance with the Royal Titles Act (q.v.). Harold Laski's later comment that the Act was due to the personal initiative of the Queen does not bear scrutiny. In actual fact, it was Disraeli's brainchild in furtherance of a larger imperial design.

The ostensible objective of the British in indulging in this impressive display of 'Anglo-Mughal pageantry' was to forge unity with the influential class of princes and chiefs by bringing them closer to the monarchical system of government to which they had been long accustomed. An illusion of power was sought to be conveyed by making them lieutenants of a sovereign power now vested in the Queen. The establishment of an Indian privy council comprising, to start with, the leading princes to consult with and advise the Governor-General on matters of common interest was an idea originating with the Governor-General himself. He would fain make an announcement of its institution at the darbar!

Opposition to this proposal in the Secretary of State's India Council, however, was far too strong; as a result, the Governor-General backtracked and the empty title 'Councillors of the Empress' was bestowed on some of the leading princes.

In a notification of 18 August 1876, the Indian government announced its intent to hold the 'imperial assemblage' on 1 January 1977. The invitees included the governors of different provinces, heads of administration, nobles, princes and chiefs. Instructions were at the same time issued to local governments to stage 'public rejoicings' by appropriate demonstrations of loyalty to mark the 'historical importance of the occasion.'

Invitations to the Darbar, held on 1 January 1877 at Delhi, went out *inter alia* to zamindars and 'loyal' citizens of consequence. Elaborate arrangements for their stay, rehearsals of the princes paying court to the Queen—now represented by the Viceroy—colourful flags, bunting and gun salutes marked the pageantry and the parade. Conspicuous by his absence was the common man or any genuine representatives of the country's vast teeming millions.

Lytton pardonably exaggerated when he described the spectacle as an 'unqualified success' coming as it did at a time when half the country was in the throes of a harsh, cruel famine. The unsurpassed magnificence of the Darbar involving heavy expenditure was vigorously criticized by the very class the Viceroy had hoped to placate and silence into submission through closer bonds with the landed aristocracy. Be that as it may, apologists of the Darbar averred that it had produced, among those attending it, a 'feeling of unity and a vision of one India.'

1876 had witnessed grave tragedies. There was the immense loss of human life in the cyclone of 1876 in Bengal, apart from one of the worst famines ever to visit the land. One may add that in the face of these calamities, the financial health of the country was none too sound. The total cost of the Darbar is reckoned at Rs 19,54,000 including ceremonies held throughout the country on 1 January 1877.

The Darbar re-affirmed the hereditary rights of the 'native' princes who were acknowledged as the cornerstone in the facade of the empire of which the Queen was the apex and the crown.

V. C. P. Chaudhry, *Imperial Policy of the British in India*, Calcutta, 1968.

Chittaranjan Das (Deshbandhu) (1870–1925)

Chittaranjan Das was born in 1870 in an upper middle class Baidya family of Talirbagh, Vikrampur in Dacca district, now part of Bangladesh. He was educated at Presidency College, Calcutta. Later, failing to get into the I.C.S. despite two attempts, he was called to the bar (Inner Temple) in 1894.

Socially, Das was everything a Bhadralok should be. His family were Brahmos (originally Baidyas) from Dacca district. His father and uncle were Calcutta High Court lawyers. He had been educated at Presidency College where he had been an active member of the Students Association in the exciting days following Surendranath Banerjea's (q.v.) dismissal from the I.C.S.

Das was powerfully influenced by Bankim Chandra and Brahmabandhar Upadhyaya and in the decade 1907-17 attracted a lot of attention. As a lawyer, his defence of Aurobindo Ghosh (q.v.) in the Alipore bomb case (1908) in which the young revolutionary was acquitted brought him a great deal of fame. Later he was defence counsel in the Dacca conspiracy case of 1910, the Delhi conspiracy case of 1914, the Alipore trunk murder case of 1918 and the Kutubdia detenue case. He was one of the lawyers in the Dumraon case involving a complex inheritance suit.

In the agitation against the Partition of Bengal (q.v.), Das was a co-worker of Surendranath Banerjea, Bipin Chandra Pal (q.v.) and Sri Aurobindo. He was also associated with *New India* and *Bande Matram*, both leading nationalist organs at the time.

His period of active political association may be said to begin in 1917. Early that year Das presided over the Bengal provincial conference at Bhowanipore where his address was rated a landmark; in retrospect, it was to herald his political debut. Herein he touched, *inter alia*, on the uniqueness of the Bengalis—'a distinct type, a distinct character and a distinct law of his own.' He showed concern for the development of the Bengali language, and called for a national movement tied to the regional culture and language to bring the high-cast westernized Bengali in line with the lower-caste Hindus and Muslims. Additionally, he underlined the need for rural uplift and of our 'oppressed and downtrodden fellow brethren.' Another theme he underscored in his whirlwind campaign during 1917-18 had a strong regional bias. He maintained that government repression alone had caused the revolutionary movement to develop and only extensive concessions leading to self-government could end it.

In 1918 Das was president both of the special session of the Indian National Congress (q.v.) at Bombay and the annual session of the party in Delhi. He opposed the Montagu-Chelmsford Reforms (q.v.) as being at once inadequate and disappointing. That year he was a member of the unofficial Jallianwala Bagh (q.v.) inquiry committee. In 1920 he joined Gandhi's Non-cooperation Movement (q.v.) and renounced his own lucrative practice at the bar. The following year, apart from non-cooperation, the large-scale exodus of coolies from the Assam tea gardens and the strike of the Assam-Bengal railway employees engaged his active attention.

By 1918, Das and his friends had captured a majority in the Bengal Provincial Congress Committee, having ousted the moderates. Once in power, they drastically slashed the Indian Association's (q.v.) representation in the body. At the annual Congress session at Nagpur, towards the end of December 1920, Gandhi scored a complete victory. Das himself moved the resolution on non-cooperation and was seconded by Lajpat Rai. This was paradoxical, for the Bengal delegates had come determined to oppose Gandhi and non-cooperation—but lived to support it! In doing so, Das assumed the active leadership of the Bengal contingent of delegates.

From the Nagpur session onwards, Gandhi became what Jawaharlal Nehru (q.v.) later called the 'permanent super president of the Congress', and the young Nehru described the Mahatma as 'consciously humble' but at the same time 'imperious.' Until his arrest (late 1921), Das worked hard to make non-cooperation a success, his speeches strongly reminiscent of Aurobindo Ghosh and B. C. Pal in their Swadeshi Movement (q.v.) hey-day.

As has been noticed earlier, in January 1921, to symbolize his conversion to non-cooperation, Das renounced his legal practice, gifted away his property and possessions to the nation and donned *khadi*. His followers gave him the title of *Deshbandhu* (Friend of the Nation) and the Bengali vernacular press hailed him as worthy of the honour.

Das's great work lay in taking the national movement down to the level of the mofussil. The novelty of a virile Congress organization at the district level captured public imagination and gave the rural Bhadralok in particular a stake they had not known before. Hand in hand went an increasing association of the Muslims with the movement.

By the end of 1921 Gandhi's adamant attitude in negotiations with the government was apparent. Swaraj was nowhere in sight. Das was angry with Gandhi, but was himself in jail. There was violence in Bombay in the latter half of 1921 and a year later at Chauri Chaura. To the apparent discomfiture of not a few, the Mahatma reversed political gears. In retrospect, Gandhi's call for the triple boycott of council, courts, and schools was impressive; once Das had overcome his doubts about the first, he had no hesitation in accepting the other two. He was an advocate of council entry with a view to, as he put it, 'non-cooperation from within.' In 1922 at the Gaya session of the Congress, his views were bitterly opposed; consequently, he lost and resigned. Later, along with Motilal Nehru (q.v.), Maulana Mohamed Ali (q.v.), Shaukat Ali (q.v.) and Ajmal Khan, he organized the Congress-Swarajya-Khilafat party, better known as the Swaraj Party (q.v.). At its special session at Delhi in 1923 the Congress approved entry into the councils.

Earlier, at the A.I.C.C. meeting in Calcutta in November 1922, Das supported Motilal Nehru on a resolution in favour of council entry but their political opponents had its consideration postponed to the annual session at Gaya in December. Das presided at the session and appealed for support for entry into the councils; the principal opposition came from C. Rajagopalachari (q.v.). The result, as has been noticed, was that Das and his supporters decided to form the Swaraj party; its programme as spelt out in the preceding paragraph was endorsed by the special Delhi session of the Congress. At the end of the year (1923), in elections to the Bengal Provincial Congress Committee, the Swarajists gained an outright majority; Das resumed the leadership with the youthful Subhas Chandra Bose (q.v) as the Committee's Secretary.

The Swaraj party was founded on 31 December 1922 although its manifesto was not signed till a few weeks later. From then on the Swarajists were called 'pro-changers', the Gandhians being labelled 'no changers' or 'whole-hoggers.' These terms defined factional attitudes towards the Gandhian programme.

In the Bengal council elections, the Swarajists triumphed. Thus on 1 December 1923, the Calcutta *Statesman*,noted, 'Bengal has declared itself Swarajist. In every kind of Bengali constituency the Swarajists have triumphed. Even the Muhammadan electorate which was considered to be a safe asset for government has been rent asunder.' Non-official opinion apart, a Bengal government report averred, 'By 1923 the Swarajist party had arisen with improved organization, a definite political programme, substantial party funds and a declared policy of contesting on behalf of the party as many seats in the Council as possible. The party discipline was also good.'

The Swarajists in some cases had supported independent candidates. One such was Dr B. C. Roy who defeated Surendranath Banerjea in the 24-Pargana municipal north constituency.

The All India Hindu Mahasabha (q.v.) in Bengal faced stiff opposition from Das. This flowed from his firm conviction that political and social security could be assured only if the Bhadralok were willing to admit the lower orders, Muslims as well as Hindus, to some form of partnership.

By 1923, the terrorist movement in Bengal had revived, apart from the activization of the revolutionary *samitis* of the earlier (viz., Partition) period. Das personally disapproved of their activities but it would appear that some of his followers in the party, including Bose, favoured violence. The latter, it was surmised, served as Das's liaison with the terrorists. In the long run this linkage strained his relations with the government with whom, at times, it appears, he wanted to co-operate. Whatever its long term impact, in the short run, however, it was a considerable electoral asset as it secured Hindu Bhadralok sympathy.

In the 1923-4 elections to the legislative council, the Swarajists, as noted earlier, swamped Bengal and later helped to defeat the provincial government on its budget demands. As a result of this, not only was dyarchy killed in Bengal, but the all-powerful bureaucracy in the country was rudely shaken. In 1924, the Swarajists swept the Calcutta corporation with Das being elected Mayor, a performance he repeated the following year. He now doubly underlined the fact that his concept of Swaraj was 'for the masses, *not* for the classes'; that he stood for 'government by the people and for the people'.

In 1924-5, Das again dominated the B.P.C.C. with his new-found recruit, 24-year old Subhas Chandra Bose who had recently achieved fame by having resigned from the ICS and returning from Cambridge to join Gandhi's non-cooperation.

Meanwhile there was a vigorous intra-communal debate in eastern Bengal where Das was willing to make a deal with the Muslims if they would lend support to his party. Details were left to be worked out after the elections but in the meantime many Muslim candidates accepted the Swarajist label and the party acquired a measure of general goodwill from the community.

In the wake of his electoral triumph in the provincial council, Das was invited to accept office by Lord Lytton, the then provincial governor. The latter was, in a manner of speaking, 'holding open a door that the Deshbandhu dared not enter,' no matter how tempted he might have felt. Council entry yes, but ministerial office would surely have split the party and alienated its Bhadralok support.

Early in December (1923), in discussions with a number of leading Muslims, the terms of a Hindu-Muslim pact were settled and later endorsed at a meeting of the Swaraj party in the provincial council. Amongst other provisions, representation in the latter body was to be directly proportional to population and through a separate electorate. In local bodies, the majority community in each district was to have 60% of the seats, the minority, 40%. 55% of all government jobs were to be reserved for Muslims and until such time as that percentage was reached, the community was to supply up to 80% of all new entrants. No resolution affecting the religious beliefs or practices of any community was to be passed by the legislative council without the consent of three-fourths of the elected representatives of that community. There was to be no music in processions before mosques and cow-slaughter was not to be interfered with.

Das, his critics averred, had paid a high price for the 21-odd Muslims who followed him into the Council. It is important to remember, however, that in the B.P.C.C. in 1924-5, Muslims constituted only 13% of the membership while in the Bengal legislative council, 50% of the Swarajists were Muslims. It should be evident that Das had gained considerable Muslim support for his party at the ballot box and in the Council and many believed in his strong determination to create better communal relations in Bengal.

To underline this, it may be recalled that Chaudhri Muhammad Ali, a Muslim leader and later (1955) Prime Minister of Pakistan, put forth the view that 'C.R.Das's death in the summer of 1925 removed the one Hindu leader who inspired unreserved confidence among Muslims; never again was Hindu leadership to rise to his height.'

It may be recalled that when Das entered the new Council with its total of 139 members he had the support of 46 Swarajists and 19 independent nationalists. The Swarajists and their allies defeated the popular ministers who resigned (26 August 1924) and Lytton temporarily suspended the constitution. It was finally suspended in March 1925.

Gandhi's determination to bring the masses into the nationalist movement was matched by the British decision to extend the electoral base. Das was badly enmeshed between the two: his experience in the Council (Dec. 23–Aug. 24) had failed to strengthen his hold on either section of the electorate: the Bhadralok or the non-Bhadralok.

One feature of the non-cooperation period which did continue into later years was the development of small ashrams, or communities, where education, spinning and other elements, of what soon came to be called the Gandhian constructive programme, were centred. One such was the Abhay Ashram in east Bengal.

Another characteristic of the post-war years in general and of the non-cooperation period in particular was the growth of Trade Union Movement (q.v.) and the rash of strikes that accompanied its birth. Das presided over the first session of the All-India Trade Union Congress where he gave a call for 'Swaraj for the 98 per cent' and tried to identify the Congress with the best interests of the masses.

In June 1924 when the A.I.C.C. convened at Ahmedabad, Maharashtra and Bengal lined up in refusing to accept non-violence under any circumstances. In *Young India* Gandhi wrote his piece under the caption, 'Defeated and Humbled.' By the year-end, he had concluded with Das the so-called Calcutta Pact which would allow both the Gandhians and the Swarajists to work from the Congress platform, albeit in their own separate ways.

In the wake of the failure of Dyarchy and its abandonment in Bengal, there was increasing terrorist activity and, in March 1925, Das made a bold bid for a clear-cut renunciation of violence. This, he vainly hoped, would produce an adequate British response. His Faridpore speech eschewing violence—both on religious grounds as well as its intrinsic impracticability—was unreservedly in line with his earlier thinking. Neither he nor Gandhi felt he was taking a new line. At the time of his departure for Darjeeling in May 1925, in failing health, his own large house had been placed in trust and he had divested himself of many of his worldly goods. While in Darjeeling, Gandhi visited him; with the latter he had maintained a warm relationship 'even through political strife.' Das died on 16 June 1925.

Lytton, the provincial governor, and Broomfield, the historian, have pictured Das as a weak man, an opportunist, one led rather than leading. Das's biographers on the other hand have shown him marching from triumph to triumph and have underplayed the conflicts and hostilities on the Bengal as well as the Indian political scene in the early 1920s. M. R. Jayakar, a fellow Swarajist, recalls Das as the boss of a political machine with autocratic tendencies and at the same time an emotional man. As a mature person, he was a fascinating combination of the emotional and the practical; the Vaishnava and the worldly lawyer; the Swarajists' passionate ideologue and successful fund-raiser. In retrospect, however, it would appear that his pacts and alliances (1921-5) were 'fragile creations' based more on his personal tact and ability than on party strength or impersonal forces. Within three years of his passing away, the Swaraj party, the B.P.C.C. and communal relationships in Bengal were to be torn by sharp divisions.

In their heyday, however, the Swarajists showed 'an eagerness to learn and to improve the quality of life in Calcutta during the early years of their participation in the corporation.' At the same time, their successful prevention of the working of Dyarchy may have been good short-term tactics: there was no logical way of slowly escalating tactics within the councils, for work therein to be meaningful had to be co-ordinated with mass pressures from outside.

Apart from politics, Das was a man of letters. His first book of verse was published in 1895; later he brought out four volumes of lyrics. In 1914 he was responsible for a literary quarterly, the *Narayana*; in 1914 and, again in

1922, an evening daily, the *Banglar Katha*; in 1923, the Swaraj party organ, *Forward* and the following year the Calcutta corporation's official organ, the *Municipal Gazette.*

Under Brahmo influence, Das was at first a Vedantist but later turned to the Sakta (Mother) cult and Vaishnavism. In 1924, as has been noticed, he formulated his 'Communal Pact' to promote what he deemed to be permanent peace between Hindus and Muslims. On a wider plane, he envisioned a pan-Asiatic federation of the oppressed nations and advocated India's participation in it.

Prithwis Chandra Ray, *Life and Times of C. R. Das: the story of Bengal's Self-expression*, Oxford, 1927; Hemendranath Das Gupta, *Deshbandhu Chittaranjan Das*, Delhi, 1960; Sukumar Ranjan Das, *Chitta Ranjan*, Calcutta, 1921; Dilip Kumar Chatterjee, *C. R. Das and Indian National Movement: a study in his political ideals*, Calcutta, 1965; P. C. Roy Chaudhury, *C. R. Das and his Times*, Mysore, 1979; Leonard Gordon, *Bengal: The Natonalist Movement 1876-1940*, London, 1974; J. H. Broomfield, *Elite Conflict in a Plural Society*, Berkeley, 1968.

Dayanand Saraswati (1824–83)

Mul Shankar, later known as Dayanand Saraswati, was born into a Brahmin family in Tankara, Kathiawar, Gujarat. An orthodox Samavedi Brahmin to start with, a change in his religious outlook took place on a Sivaratri evening when he was barely fourteen years old. Subsequently, he studied religious literature seriously to solve his doubts and at 21 escaped from home, and an impending marriage, to continue his 'academic pursuits.' For 15 years he wandered all over India as an ascetic visiting temples, discoursing with learned Brahmins and studying religious texts and yoga. His quest remained unsatisfied until, in 1860, he met Swami Virjananda, a blind sanyasi, at Mathura. A 2½-year stay and study under the latter cleared most of his doubts and he launched a movement against the distortions of the true Hindu faith and the pretensions of the Brahmins.

Through those years Dayanand acquired a mastery of the Sanskrit language and its grammar. He was also well-versed in Hindu philosophy and religious literature. Virjananda interpreted the Vedas for him and charged him with the mission of purging Hinduism of its ugliness and impurities.

From 1863 onwards, Dayanand devoted himself to preaching his new gospel as embodied in the teachings of the Arya Samaj (q.v.) he had founded. His active missionary life began in 1865 when he travelled up and down the country—Calcutta (1872-3), Poona and Bombay (1875) though most of his time was taken up in Uttar Pradesh, Rajasthan and the Panjab.

Keshab Chandra Sen, the Brahmo Samaj (q.v.) leader counselled the Swami to speak in the language of the people, in Hindi, rather than in Sanskrit and to dress more generously than in a bare loin-cloth. The Swami was the first to publish religious commentaries on the Vedas in Hindi. Before he died, nearly a hundred Samajs had been established in the Panjab, U.P., Rajasthan and Bombay—apart from some Sanskrit *pathshalas,* an orphanage, a public trust for publication of his works and an 'Indian academy'.

A man of great intellectual honesty, a learned scholar of Sanskrit, a forceful speaker and a doughty debator, Dayanand soon made a powerful impact, particularly at a celebrated disputation at Banaras in 1869. It has been said that 'his choice of the dogmas and doctrines concerning the unity of God, the rejection of the plurality of the Hindu gods and the doctrines of metempsychosis and law of action (Karma), the relations of man, nature and god, were the result of a process of his own analysis and ratiocination, in which he was not guided by tradition or history.'

In 1875 he founded branches of the Arya Samaj in Rajkot, Ahmedabad and Bombay. There members would worship according to Vedic *sanskaras*, and subscribe to a set of prescribed rules. These were elaborated two years later when, after attending the Imperial Darbar (q.v.), the Swami was invited to Lahore, a town that was soon to emerge as the headquarters of his movement. In 1879, an unsuccessful attempt was made to merge the Samaj with the Theosophical Society (q.v.).

Dayanand's aim was to reclaim and reconvert those who had been lost to the Hindu fold, as well as to revive pride in India's cultural heritage, its glorious past and its Vedic religion. He spent the rest of his life, till his death in 1883, touring India, opening new branches of the Samaj and propagating the tenets of his faith. The *Satyartha Prakash*, published in 1877 from Banaras, offers the sum and substance of his teaching.

The Swami taught that there is one God, that the Vedas are his utterance, that there is no incarnation, all divine names being the epithets of the one and only God. His doctrine of the infallibility of the Vedas was a challenge to the supernatural revelations of Christianity and Islam. He maintained that social customs had no religious sanction and denounced *shraddha*, pilgrimages and child marriage while favouring widow-remarriage. The study of the Hindu scriptures was to be open to all, irrespective of caste, class or creed. He however accepted the doctrine of Karma, the transmigration of souls. and the sanctity of the cow. Though he decried the caste system, he believed in the four varnas resting on merit and occupation, *not* birth. He laid stress on the uplift of the depressed classes to prevent, *inter alia*, their conversion to other faiths.

The Satyartha Prakash has been called the Arya Samajists' Bible. Its purport is to offer an exhaustive treatise on Hinduism, defining its attitude to all questions—be they religious, social or political. It discusses the most abstruse religious and philosophical issues, an exercise hitherto available only in Sanskrit. A whole chapter in the book is devoted to a discussion on the best form of government. The Swami believed that 'good government is no substitute for self-government.' To him government was the agent of a community in promoting the good of society, besides defending the latter against external dangers. He therefore held compulsory education and social reform to be a state responsibility.

Dayanand disliked alien control and was convinced of the impermanence of British rule. None the less he was sensible enough to realize that the country was as yet disunited and unprepared to challenge their mastery. He therefore contented himself with spreading the message of liberalism and nationalism among the masses. What was essential, he maintained, was a common religion and language. His propagation of *Shuddhi* and the sanctity of the cow, however laudable and to many even unexceptional, later created a degree of communal tension which, to the Swami's mind, may have been altogether unintentional.

Dayanand was a prolific writer; an edition of his collected writings, it has been said, 'would run to some 10,000 pages.' A great Vedic scholar, he always went to the original text for all that he wrote or interpreted.

His attitude to the world was quite revolutionary, for he placed the goal of active social service as the duty of the individual. In matters of social reform, his impact has been the most profound in the Panjab, Uttar Pradesh, Hyderabad and Rajasthan; his followers were leading reformists—be the milieu social, religious or even political.

A recent biographer has summed up the Swami aptly as 'an individualist consumed by a passion for action, principled yet pragmatic; a man with great inner depth yet totally involved in the present and always working for a better future; a mind receptive to the rapidly changing world around him but never passively submitting to its pressure; a man consumed by the dream of a better life for all, a happiness not only religious but also social and economic.' More, his limitations such as they were may be viewed as the 'contrasting shadows that accentuate the basic greatness of a man who made himself into one of the giant figures of nineteenth-century India.'

J. T. F. Jordens, *Dayananda Saraswati: His Life and Ideas*, Delhi, 1978; Suraj Bhan, *Dayanand: his life and work,* Jullunder, 1956; B. B. Majumdar, *History of Indian Social and Political Ideas from Ram Mohan to Dayanand*, Calcutta, 1967.

Treaty of Deogaon (1803)

Concluded on 17 December 1803 between Raghuji Bhonsle and the John Company (q.v.), the 12-clause treaty of Deogaon brought hostilities between the two to a close in the course of the protracted Second Anglo-Maratha War (q.v.). Facing successive reverses in battle and threatened by Major-General Arthur Wellesley (later, Duke of Wellington) with an attack on his capital at Nagpur, Raghuji agreed to accept the terms proffered. He also undertook to cede the province of Cuttack, including Balasore, which gave the Company control over a continuous stretch of the eastern seaboard and linked the presidencies of Bengal and Madras. The steadfastly 'loyal' Nizam now received the whole of western Berar, i.e., the territory lying to the west of the river Wardha over which Bhonsle waived all claims. The latter also agreed to (i) expel all foreigners from his service; (ii) accept British arbitration in all his disputes with the Nizam or the Peshwa; (iii) respect treaties concluded by the British with his feudatories; (iv) dissociate himself and his successors from the confederacy 'and other Maratha chiefs' and agree not to assist them any more.

Bhonsle agreed to accept a British envoy at his court and Mountstuart Elphinstone (q.v.) was appointed in that capacity. The Maratha ruler further undertook that 'no European or American or a nation at war with the English, or any British subject was to be entertained' by him without the Company's prior consent.

The treaty was to mark the first step towards ending the second Maratha war. Completely isolated now, Sindhia too hastened to make his peace with the English.

Aitchison, III, 97–9; R. C. Majumdar, H. C. Raychaudhuri, Kalikinkar Datta, *An Advanced History of India*, 3rd ed., London, 1967, pp. 696-7.

Henry Louis Vivian Derozio (1809–31)

A talented Eurasian and one of the pioneers of the renaissance in Bengal, Henry Louis Vivian Derozio left a deep impress as a poet, teacher, reformer and journalist. Of mixed parentage, his father was a Portuguese, his mother an Indian. Even as a young boy he was rated somewhat of a prodigy. Besides doing well in studies, he imbibed a taste for literature, philosophy and free thinking from David Drummond, then Principal of the Dharamtala School. Later Derozio considered these qualities to be necessary prerequisites for any 'dissemination of European learning and science' among the Indian people.

After a short spell in his father's business and owing to ill-health, Derozio moved to an uncle's indigo plantation at Tarapur in Bhagalpur, now in Bihar. Inspired by the estate's pastoral surroundings he began composing verse that was intensely patriotic and some of which was published later in Calcutta's *India Gazette.*

Derozio's literary fame—at 18 he had published a volume of poems—brought him (1827) the job of assistant master in the senior department of Hindu College in Calcutta. After a year, he was promoted Lecturer in English Literature and History. Before long he had established a rapport with his students, inculcating in them a spirit of inquiry in the pursuit of truth and giving them opportunities for free discussion at his home. In 1828 he started the Academic Association where, at weekly meetings, his students debated such challenging questions as patriotism, idolatry, priestcraft and more philosophical issues like free will, fate, virtue and vice, the existence of God, etc. These meetings were sometimes attended by such men of eminence as David Hare, Edwin Ryan of the Supreme Court and Dr Mill, Principal of Bishop's College. Derozio also gave weekly lectures on morals and literature at David Hare's school and impressed his listeners as one whose attachment to knowledge, love of truth and hatred of evil was unique. Under his tutelage some of his students also started the short-lived *Parthenon* in the columns of which they advocated suppression of social evils, encouragement of women's education, provision of cheap justice, etc. Deeply involved in active literary pursuits he served on the editorial staff of *The Hesperus, The Calcutta Literary Gazettee* and *The India Gazette* while contributing to *The Calcutta Magazine, The Indian Magazine, The Bengal Annual* and *Kaleidoscope.*

Derozio and his followers, popularly known as 'Derozians' or 'Young Bengal' (q.v.), were the early harbingers of radical thought and practice, which seriously alarmed the orthodox sections of the community. Rumours maligning him went around and it was alleged that his misconduct was responsible for parents withdrawing their wards from the college where he taught. Thus, despite a spirited defence of his conduct and stout repudiation of the charge of propagating atheism and encouraging disobedience, he was asked to leave (April 1831). Subsequently, he started an evening daily, *The East Indian* but died of cholera a few months later.

Derozio published two books of poems, the second containing the famous 'Fakeer of Jhungheera.' His critical approach had the effect of liberating the minds of his young pupils; it opened up their intellectual horizons and gave them the capacity to value truth above all.

Amongst his youthful pupils were such names as Ram Gopal Ghosh,

Dakshinaranjan Mukherjee, Rashik Krishna Malik, the Rev. K. M. Baner-jee, Radhanath Sikdar, Ramtanu Lahiry and Peary Chand Mitra. By their integrity, dignified conduct, conscientiousness, and intellectual honesty they enhanced the self-respect and elevated the moral stature of society. They were men in whom the nationalist sentiment first manifested itself.

Eliot Walter Madge (Subir Ray Choudhuri, ed.), *Henry Derozio: the Eurasian Poet and Reformer*, new ed., Calcutta, 1967; Thomas Edwards, *Derozio: the Eurasian Poet, Teacher and Journalist*, Calcutta, 1884; *Buckland*, pp. 117-18.

Desai–Liaqat Pact (1945)

Talks between Bhulabhai Jivanji Desai (1877-1946) and Liaqat Ali Khan (q.v.), leaders respectively of the Indian National Congress (q.v.) and the All India Muslim League (q.v.) parties in the Central Legislative Assembly, were aimed at finding a way out of the 1942-5 political impasse. Desai revealed the fact of an understanding having been reached at the Provincial Political Conference at Peshawar on 22 April 1945. Subsequently, Liaqat Ali published the gist of the agreement prefaced by a statement to the press. The text read:

'The Congress and the League agree they will join in forming the interim Government at the Centre.

The composition of such a government will be on the following lines:

(a) equal number of persons nominated by the Congress and the League in the Central Executive. Persons nominated need not be members of the Central Legislature;

(b) representatives of the minorities, in particular of the Scheduled Castes and the Sikhs;

(c) the Commander-in-Chief.

The government so formed would function within the framework of the existing constitution (viz. Government of India Act 1935 (q.v.)). It was under-stood however that if the Cabinet could get a particular measure passed by the Legislative Assembly, it will not enforce it by resort to any of the reserve powers of the Governor-General. This will make it function reasonably independent of the Governor-General.

The next step would be the withdrawal of Section 93 in the provinces and the installation, as soon as possible, of provincial governments on the lines of a coalition at the Centre.'

Known as the Desai-Liaqat pact, the agreement was never formally endorsed either by the Congress or the League. On the contrary, M. A. Jinnah (q.v.) denied all knowledge and, in fact, frowned upon it; Liaqat Ali therefore had to repudiate it later. The principal Congress leaders were in detention when the 'pact' was made public, but on reading about it in the press they were furious. It has been suggested that Desai's political career came to a virtual dead-end as a consequence.

The two-party formula evolved in the 'pact' was welcome to Lord Wavell (q.v.) and was later to form the basis of his recommendations about the reconstruction of his Executive Council.

Pattabhi Sitaramayya, II, p. 652; *Tara Chand*, IV, pp. 434-5.

Direct Action Day: 16 August 1946

On 27 July 1946 M. A. Jinnah (q.v.), addressing the All-India Muslim
League (q.v.) Council, attacked the Cabinet Mission Plan (q.v.) in general
and Lord Wavell (q.v.) in particular. He charged them with playing into the
hands of the Indian National Congress (q.v.), treating the latter's conditional acceptance of the Mission's (16 May) plan as genuine and postponing
the formation of the Interim Government (q.v.) in accordance with its
statement of 16 June. He maintained that the Congress had unequivocally
repudiated the essential provisions of the scheme of 16 May regarding
grouping and rejected outright the proposals of 16 June. Yet 'a fantastic and
dishonest construction was put on the clause (viz. 8 of June 16) by that
ingenious juggler of words (Sir Stafford) Cripps (q.v.) to evade the formation of the interim government.'

In the light of these observations, the Council of the Muslim League
resolved that any participation by Muslims in the proposed constitution-
making machinery was fraught with danger and withdrew its earlier acceptance of the Mission's plan. Jinnah explained that while the British had
machine-guns to enforce their will, and Congress the weapon of civil resistance, the Muslims alone remained defenceless, with their hands and feet
tied. It followed, he argued, that they too must bid good-bye to constitutional methods and prepare for self-defence and self-preservation by resort
to direct action.

The Working Committee of the Muslim League met on 30 July and fixed
16 August for observing 'Direct Action day' throughout the country.

In a statement two days earlier (viz. on 14 August) the League leader
explained that the object and purpose behind his call was to make the
Muslims understand fully the situation that was facing them so that they
could prepare themselves for any eventuality that they may have to face.

In the tense situation thus building up the Viceroy's decision to invite the
Congress to form the interim government at the Centre proved the proverbial last straw. Jinnah declined Jawaharlal Nehru's (q.v.) invitation to participate in it while the theologian Shabbir Ahmad Usmani, then President of the
All-India Jamiatul Ulma-i-Islam, declared that 'no power on earth can crush
the Muslims. Living he is a *Gazi*, and killed in action he is a martyr.'

In Calcutta (q.v.), 16 August began with public demonstrations, hartals and
hoisting of Muslim League flags. Soon resistance led to clashes and rioting
spread all over the city. Utter confusion and widespread disturbances gripped the common people while the hooligans had a field day indulging in
stabbing, killing, arson and criminal assaults on women. The mob fury continued for four consecutive days after which life in the city gradually limped
back to normal. During this mass killing and orgy of destruction,
the forces of law and order proved utterly ineffective to meet the emergency.
The police proved to be supine and indifferent and, many believed, partial.

The Bengal government led by the League leader H. S. Suhrawardy had
declared 16 August a public holiday which made it possible for students, office
staff and others to join the crowds that roamed about the streets. Nor was the
army called out until the situation had got completely out of hand.

According to H. V. Hodson, then Constitutional Adviser to the
Governor-General, the tragedy claimed 5,000 killed and 15,000 seriously

wounded in Calcutta alone. How many Hindus and Muslims were killed in the mofussil is anybody's guess nor is there any official count of the number of houses destroyed or the value of property looted.

The Congress blamed the Bengal government for inaction. Suhrawardy on the other hand reversed the blame. He put the onus squarely on Congress for attempting to thwart the League's proposed demonstration designed to pressurize government into modifying the offer it had made to Nehru to form an interim government. He held his political adversaries principally responsible for creating the panic that had led to the catastrophe.

While Jinnah accused Congress of deliberately provoking the riots, Liaqat Ali Khan (q.v.) charged that the party had plunged Calcutta into anarchy with the twin objectives of discrediting the Muslim League government and demonstrating that India had already passed under Hindu rule as a result of Wavell's offer to Nehru.

On 18 August Wavell recorded in his *Journal:* 'Calcutta is as bad as ever and the death-toll mounts steadily. Sarat Chandra Bose rang up in the afternoon with a message of protest to me that the police were favouring the Muslims against the Hindus, whereas the Governor tells me the casualties are higher among the Muslims. Anyway it is a thoroughly bad business.'

A day later, 19 August, he noted: 'I had an hour in the afternoon with (Maulana Abul Kalam) Azad (q.v.) about the Calcutta riots and the Interim Government. He criticized the Bengal Ministry severely and said that although they had apprehended trouble they had not taken sufficient precautions; also they have been too late in enforcing total curfew and the troops had not been called out soon enough.'

And, on 26 August (after he had visited Calcutta the previous day): The city had been pretty well cleared up by the time and except for some burnt out shops and houses there was not a great deal of evidence of recent occurrences. . . . The chief points to my mind were Suhrwardy's continual presence in the control room on the first day with many M. League friends and his obvious communal bias; that the victims were almost entirely goondas and people of the poorest class; that there were no attacks on the Police; and that any hesitation of the Police to open fire and take firm action was partly due to the political criticism directed against them after the riots of last February and November.'

Tara Chand, IV, pp. 447-84; Penderel Moon, *Wavell, the Viceroy's Journal,* pp. 334-5, 338-9.

Diwani Rights (1765)

The defeat and debacle of the combined forces of Mir Kasim (q.v.), Shuja-ud-Daula (q.v.) and Shah Alam II (q.v.) at Buxar (q.v.) brought in its wake a very significant development. The prime mover was Robert Clive (q.v.) who, in 1765, had been appointed governor of Bengal for the second time. On arrival in Madras, he had come to the conclusion that the time was ripe for John Company (q.v.) to become 'nabobs in fact, if not in name, perhaps totally so without disguise.' In pursuance of this new policy, he decided at first to placate the principal victim of the battle of Buxar, Shuja-ud-Daula, to whom, in lieu of a war indemnity of 50 lakhs, he magnanimously returned all his possessions, except for the districts of Karra and Allahabad. The latter were gifted to the homeless, and now resourceless, Shah Alam, in return for which the emperor issued three separate '*firmaunds*' conferring on the John Company the rights of 'Dewanny (or civil and revenue administration) of Bengal, Behar and Orissa.' At the same time, the accession of the pro-British Najm-ud-Daula as the new Nawab of Bengal, was confirmed.

The grant of Diwani secured for the British full control over Bengal's affairs without at the same time incurring the responsibility, or inconvenience, of a territorial dominion. The principal disadvantage was that it divorced power from responsibility. It must be recognized though that the Company was at the time far from ready to accept on its own the administration of large tracts of the country.

As against the disadvantage listed, the immediate gains were sizeable. The Diwani secured a measure of control over the Nawab which was regarded as the most pressing need of the time; additionally, it promised some protection against the complaints of foreign powers and the demands of the home government. It may also be conceded that something short of the assumption of full dominion would be less likely to excite legal difficulties in England or provoke the interference of Parliament. In sum, a complete control over Bengal's affairs was secured without the inconvenience of formal and avowed dominion.

The Company was henceforth to administer the province as the Diwan of the Mughal emperor. In return, it agreed to pay the Emperor Rs 20 lakhs as revenue and an additional Rs 53 lakhs to the Nawab (Najm-ud-Daula) for his expenses, retaining whatever was surplus for itself.

It would appear that the Company now virtually came to occupy the position of a 'Nawab-maker', although it had no *locus standi* yet in the political life of Bengal from the constitutional viewpoint.

The expenses of the Nizamat were settled by an agreement between the Nawab and the Company on 30 September 1765. Under this arrangement, the Nawab agreed to accept a sum of Rs 53, 86,181 as 'adequate allowance' for the support of the Nizamat: Rs 17,788,54 towards meeting all his household expenses and Rs 36,07,277 towards the upkeep of horses, sepoys, peons, *burcandazes* as were deemed necessary 'for the support of his dignity only.' In sum, the Nawab thus not only parted with his authority as Dewan but also became a stipend-holder of the Company. The management of his household affairs and the administration of criminal justice were, no doubt, retained by him. But here also the Nawab was made to accept a nominee of the Company as 'Naib Subah and guardian of his household during his minority.'

Nor was that all. The military defence of the Company was now no longer within the Nawab's purview. It followed that he was not in a position to harm the interests of the Company even if he wanted to do so.

In regard to his functions as Nazim, the Nawab received the 'usual marks of civility and respect' from the Company, albeit there was no concealing the fact that he was 'in a position of complete dependence' upon the latter. More, the Company 'not only prevailed upon him to part with a substantial portion of the powers of the Nizamat.. but (exercised) considerable influence over him and his government in exercising the remaining powers, though for the sake of form it was ordinarily done under a veil, the ostensible grounds being that he was a minor in age and quite inexperienced and was thus incapable of exercising his authority judicially and likely to play into the hands of the self-seeking individuals.'

It has been estimated that the Company had thus gained, besides an empire, a revenue of something like Rs 4,000,000. The Nawab would have, in theory at any rate, retained military power and the exercise of judicial functions while the Company became masters of revenue. Thereby they controlled the purse-strings, even though retaining in service 'native' (Indian) collectors. This was the Dual System (q.v.) with all its attendant evils.

As a trading corporation, the Company was, understandably, interested in making a profit. Despite the rights it acquired, it did not take the responsibility of collecting the land revenue, not to speak of administering the country—in both cases 'native' agents were employed. Later, when it was to turn its attention to the task of administration, its commercial character stood in the way of evolving 'an adequate and honest machinery.'

Niranjan Dhar, *The Administrative System of the East India Company in Bengal, 1714-86*, Calcutta, 1964; *Aitchison*, II, pp. 241-3; Dodwell, *CHI*, V, pp. 176-7; Ram Gopal, *How the British Occupied Bengal*, Bombay, 1963. ·

Dominion Status

A demand for the grant of Dominion Status was made by the Indian National Congress (q.v.) as early as 1908. Nearly a decade later, E. S. Montagu's pronouncement of August 1917 (q.v.) had spoken *inter alia* of 'the gradual development of self-governing institutions with a view to the progressive realization of responsible government.' Albeit far-reaching in scope, its impact was short-lived for Sir Malcolm (later Baron) Hailey, then Home Member in the Viceroy's Executive Council, had declared on 8 February 1924 that the 'objective' of the Montagu-Chelmsford Reforms (q.v.) was 'responsible government', *not* Dominion Status. The latter, he averred, was 'not indeed the same thing' as the former.

Not long afterwards, the Nehru Report (q.v.) had categorically affirmed: 'There certainly are those among the parties represented in the (All-Parties) Conference who put their case on the higher plane of complete independence but we are not aware of any who would be satisfied with anything lower than full Dominion Status.'

Earlier, at the Imperial Conference (q.v.) of 1926, the status of a 'Dominion' had been defined as one of 'autonomous communities within the British Empire, equal in status, in no way subordinate one to another in any aspect of their domestic or external affairs, though united by a common allegiance to the Crown, and freely associated as members of the British Commonwealth of Nations.'

At the Commonwealth Labour Conference in London (1921), Ramsay MacDonald (q.v.), on the eve of taking over as Britain's first Labour Prime Minister, had declared: 'I hope that within a period of months rather than years, there will be a new Dominion added to the Commonwealth of our nations, a Dominion that will find self-respect as an equal within this Commonwealth. I refer to India.'

The first official pronouncement on the subject, however, had to wait another 8 years and was made in a statement by Lord Irwin (q.v.) on 31 October 1929 on his return after prolonged consultations with the British government in London. While announcing HMG's decision to convene a Round Table Conference (q.v.), the Viceroy said: 'But in view of the doubts which have been expressed both in Great Britain and India regarding the interpretation to be placed on the intentions of the British government in enacting the Statute of 1919, I am authorized on behalf of His Majesty's Government to state clearly that in their judgement it is implicit in the declaration of 1917 that the natural issue of India's constitutional progress as therein contemplated is the attainment of Dominion Status.'

The goodwill generated by this declaration was soon dissipated by the tone and temper of official pronouncements in the British Parliament. Thus it was explained that the aim of the Viceroy's declaration had been two-fold: (a) to allay doubts that had arisen regarding British intentions; and (b) to make 'a good atmosphere' for the Simon Commission's (q.v.) impending report. The nationalist demand that the projected Round Table Conference convene for the specific purpose of drafting India's constitution on the basis of Dominion Status was summarily rejected. The Viceroy's declaration, therefore, soon became a matter of mere academic interest and, with the passage of time, an historical curiosity.

It may be recalled that the Lahore session of the Congress, held in December 1929, had declared 'that the word Swarajya in Art. I of the Congress constitution shall mean complete independence...' Earlier. Gandhi (q.v.) had made it clear that, to him, Dominion Status meant 'complete independence plus a voluntary partnership with Britain...'

It may also be relevant to mention that the Government of India Act, 1935 (q.v.) fell far short of Dominion Status in several important respects. Thus a scheme of Dyarchy was sought to be introduced at the centre in so far as several safeguards vesting autocratic powers in the Governor-General were provided. It was also stipulated that all laws passed in India were subject to approval by the Crown.

It should be evident that this definition of Dominion Status was far removed from that laid down in the Statute of Westminster (1931). To be sure, the latter had implied the right of secession and full autonomy as well as observation of complete neutrality in case of war.

The constitutional 'offer' made by Sir Stafford Cripps (q.v.) in March 1942 regarding the treatment of India as a Dominion of the Crown was far from enthusiastically received at the time and was, in fact, later rejected by nearly all political parties in India.

In August 1947, with the transfer of power, the then British-ruled India was split into two independent Dominions of India and Pakistan. Three years later, India, now a sovereign democratic republic, decided on its own to continue to be a member of the Commonwealth of Nations.

Gwyer and Appadorai, I, pp. 220–5; B. Shiva Rao, *The Framing of India's Constitution: A Study*, New Delhi, 1968, p. 15.

Dost Mohammad, Amir of Afghanistan (1826–63)

Dost Mohammad, the founder of the Barakzai or Mohammedzai dynasty, was the youngest son of Payenda Khan, the chief of the clan. He was appointed governor of Ghazni after Shah Shuja, the grandson of Ahmad Shah Abdali (q.v.) had fled to India in 1809. Thirteen years later, the Barakzais rose in revolt against Mahmud Shah (Shah Shuja's brother who had succeeded him at Kabul) so as to avenge the execution of one of their chiefs, Fateh Khan. Dost Mohammad helped defeat Mahmud and eventually drove him out of the country. In the subsequent parcelling out (1826) of the kingdom he received Ghazni, Jalalabad, Charikar and later (after his brother's death) Kabul. From then on he occupied himself in consolidating his authority, subjugating the weaker Durrani sub-tribes in and around his territories, and improving and modernizing the armed forces so as to meet the aggressive designs of his country's European neighbours. He also reformed the judicial system, took measures to encourage trade and to establish law and order.

In 1836 Dost Mohammad made a strong bid to recover Peshawar from Ranjit Singh (q.v.) but failed to follow up his victory at Jamrud. A year later he virtually invited British interference in his affairs by making the restoration of Peshawar a pre-condition to a binding commitment. The abortive mission of Alexander Burnes (q.v.) was largely inspired by a desire to ensure the Amir's co-operation with the British against the spectre of Russian aggression through their instigation of the Persian siege of Herat.

Burnes had orders to investigate the prospects for commercial relations between India and Central Asia, 'to work out the policy of opening the river Indus to commerce.' In reality, the economic situation served as a front for his real mission: to bring about a rapprochement between Ranjit Singh and Dost Mohammad and to conclude a mutual security agreement with the Amir based on the Shah Shuja-Mountstuart Elphinstone (q.v.) treaty of 1809.

The Amir's letter to Lord Auckland (q.v.) asking for assistance in settling Anglo-Sikh differences elicited the curt reply that the British government followed a consistent policy of non-interference in the affairs of independent nations. 'Subsequent history', an astute observer of the Afghan scene has noted, 'made this declaration one of the more laughable events in a series of unlaughable blunders.'

Since the British were reluctant to offer anything substantial, much less pressurize Ranjit Singh, Dost Mohammad turned a ready ear to the promises made by the Russian envoy, Captain Vikovitch. Auckland took the opportunity to take the fatal plunge to instal Shah Shuja, the exiled Amir, at Kabul. The First Anglo-Afghan War (q.v.) that followed resulted in an Afghan defeat and debacle. Dost Mohammad, forced to flee his capital, surrendered on 2 November 1840 and was bundled out to India along with his family.

As a British guest-cum-detainee, the Amir covertly, if not overtly, continued encouraging his son Akbar Khan to oust the unwanted British. In November 1841, Burnes and W. H. Macnaghten (q.v.) were murdered by an infuriated Afghan mob frustrated in its attempts to free their land from alien yoke. Subsequently, almost the entire British army with its large retinue of women and children and camp followers was done to death during its retreat (December-January 1841-2) from Kabul to Jalalabad. A few months later Shah Shuja too fell prey to an assassin's bullet.

In 1843 Dost Mohammad, released from detention, was permitted to return to Kabul. He now concentrated on extending his authority to all parts of the country and uniting them into one. Gradually he regained control over Kandahar, Mazar-i-Sharif, Qataghan, and Kunduz; he conquered Balkh in 1850 and Khulm, Kunduz and Badakshan five years later; by 1863, he had acquired Herat.

In 1848, during the Second Anglo-Sikh War (q.v.), Dost Mohammad was induced to aid the erstwhile rulers of the Panjab. But the adventure was ill-conceived for in the battle of Gujrat (February 1849) his cavalry was ignominiously routed and pursued as far as the hills, while Peshawar was annexed to British India.

For nearly a decade after his restoration, British relations with the Amir remained 'undefined but sullen'. They were later modified under the pressure of Persia's eagerness to expand eastwards and reconquer Herat and Kandahar. The former town, seized by Persia in 1852, was relinquished only under threat of vigorous British action. In 1854 the Amir held Herat briefly but it was attacked again. Dost Mohammad secured the treaty of Peshawar (30 March 1855), signed by John Lawrence (q.v.), then Chief Commissioner of the Panjab and Ghulam Haider Khan, heir-apparent to the Afghan throne. India pledged non-interference in the Amir's affairs while he, in turn, agreed to be 'the friend of the friends and the enemy of the enemies' of the British. This favoured the 'British version of the status quo.'

In October 1856, Herat was seized afresh by the Persians, a development that led to a 3-month war with Britain. A force was despatched from Bombay and the Amir assisted with money as well as munitions. In 1857, the Amir met John Lawrence at Peshawar. A supplementary treaty was signed (26 January 1857) whereby he was promised a subsidy of Rs 1 lakh per month for as long as hostilities with Persia lasted. He was to maintain an army capable of resisting aggression from the west and the north as well as a sizeable quantity of ammunition. Troops under James Outram (q.v.) landed at Kandahar, and the Persian siege was promptly raised. Later, a British mission under Major H. B. Lumsden was admitted with 'much misgiving.' Its aim was 'to co-ordinate activities' in the fight against the Persian aggressor.

Deeply indebted to the British, the Amir refrained from taking advantage of their apparent discomfiture during the Rebellion of 1857 (q.v.) to occupy Peshawar. This was contrary to what many of his advisers, particularly the religious leaders, suggested, they wanted him to swoop down if only to 'liberate' the Indian Muslims. Afghan historians have taken Dost Mohammad severely to task for not being more aggressive during the Indian revolt.

In 1862 the Amir attacked Herat and, even though to all appearances he was not the aggressor, the British signified disapproval by recalling their vakil, a Muslim agent who had been maintained at Kabul since 1857. Dost Mohammad died on 9 June 1863 after occupying the town in May (1863)— his dream of a united Afghanistan fulfilled at last!

To modernize his army in the hope that it would help consolidate his position and check the encroachments of his neighbours, the Amir was willing to hire Burnes or an Englishman of comparable rank. Among some western adventurers at his court, mention may be made of Josiah Harlan, Lt. Campbell and Colonel Leslie (alias Rattray).

The Amir's efforts to ensure his dynasty's continued rule through an uncontested law of succession were frustrated first by the death of his eldest son, Mohammad Akbar Khan, followed by the one whom he named his successor, Ghulam Haider Khan.

In the aftermath of the Afghan war, when he regained his throne, Dost Mohammad was in a stronger position than ever before to work for the political unity of Afghanistan. His major achievement in fact lay in the political unification of his country, apart from the establishment of relative internal stability and maintenance of a standing army.

A fitting epitaph to Dost Mohammad is to be found in the Afghan saying, 'Is Dost Mohammad dead that there is now no justice in the land?'

Vartan Gregorian, *The Emergence of Modern Afghanistan 1880-1946*, Stanford, 1969, pp. 73-85; Mohan Lal, *Life of the Ameer Dost Muhammad Khan of Kabul*, 2 vols, London, 1846.

Dual Government (1765–74)

The Dual system of government was instituted by Robert Clive (q.v.) as a result of the Mughal Emperor Shah Alam II's (q.v.) grant to the East India Company (q.v.) in 1765 of the Diwani Rights (q.v.) for the provinces of Bengal, Bihar and Orissa. This was the aftermath of the Mughal ruler's earlier defeat and discomfiture at the Battle of Buxar (q.v.). The Diwani conferred on the Company the right of collection and appropriation, of land revenue. This gave it virtual control over the purse-strings, making it the *de facto* ruler, while the Nawab with his vaunted boast of territorial jurisdiction became a mere figurehead, a pensioner of state, forced to act under or in conjunction with the Company's officials. He was 'treated with outward respect but only as a pageant.'

Clive continued the then prevalent practice of revenue administration, including the employment of 'native' collectors, Mohammed Reza Khan for Bihar and Shaitab Rai for Bengal, under European supervisors. The appointment of the Company's servants as collectors, he felt, would expose it for what it was—the real Subehdar. Other European powers engaged in trade or alternative avocations might then, he further argued, refuse to make to the English payments for privileges they enjoyed and quit rents for districts they had acquired. Besides, the Company's English officials, he reasoned, lacked adequate knowledge of Indian conditions and might therefore be tempted to take undue advantage of their newly-won position.

The system was far from fool-proof. By and large, the collectors and the supervisors oppressed, exploited and fleeced the ryots or the actual tillers. The Nawab dared not use his judicial authority to punish offenders, because of his own heavy indebtedness to the English. The raising of large sums of money led to the ruin of agriculture and was responsible for the disastrous famines in these provinces in 1770 and later years.

The experiment spelt disaster from the beginning. The emperor was a ruler in name only; his Diwan, 'Kampani Sahib Bahadur,' was represented by a victorious, and masterful, foreign soldier. The Company's men were assisted by people who were avowed traders, whose interests were principally involved in maintaining its dividends and who lacked completely the professional training essential to efficient administration. The result was that confusion reigned both in the administration of justice as well as collection of land revenue. At the end of seven years, it was still difficult to ascertain the difference between the sum received as land revenue by the government and the sum actually paid by the ryot to the zamindars.

Dodwell, *CHI*, V, pp. 176-7, 409-13; D. N. Banerjee, *The Administrative System of the East India Company in Bengal, 1765-74*, 2 vols, London, 1943, I, pp. 83–6.

Dufferin (1826–1902)

Frederick Temple Hamilton-Temple Blackwood, first Marquis of Dufferin and Ava, was appointed Governor-General in 1884, a fitting climax to a successful public career. Having entered the House of Lords in 1850, he was twice (1849-52 and 1854-8) Lord-in-Waiting to Queen Victoria. Subsequently, he embarked on a long and distinguished diplomatic career which took him as Assistant to the British Ambassador to Turkey (1860), and Governor-General of Canada (1872-8) from where he was again transferred to the Porte. In 1882 he proceeded to Egypt to reorganize and reform the Khedive's administration. In between, he had served at home as Under Secretary for India (1864-6) and, in a similar capacity, at the war office. In 1868 he became chancellor for the duchy of Lancaster. For services rendered to the state he was honoured by the award of a K.C.B. (1861), the Riband of St. Patrick (1863), an Earldom (1871), a G.C.M.G. (1876) and G.C.B. (1883).

In December 1884 Dufferin succeeded Ripon (q.v.) as Governor-General. His friend and mentor Kimberley was then Secretary of State for India. The new Viceroy was determined to make an all-out effort to restore the balance between Indian and imperial interests. Priority was to go to the latter, so as to divert attention from domestic issues that agitated the British public. An experienced diplomat, he followed a policy laid down by Whitehall, arguing that that was one way of ensuring a smooth administration.

Soon after his arrival, the Afghan question came to the fore. In 1884, Merv had fallen into Russian hands, a development that renewed British fears of a possible advance into India through Herat. A joint boundary commisson had been constituted at Russia's request, but disputed territories had prevented any settlement being effected. While Amir Abdur Rahman (q.v.) was visiting the Governor-General at Rawalpindi, the Russians forcibly ousted the Afghans from Panjdeh, then widely believed to be part of Afghan territory. A virtual war hysteria gripped both countries as troops began to be massed on their respective borders. Frenzied diplomatic activity and Abdur Rahman's cool common sense in waiving Afghan claims prevented the incident from blowing up into a full-fledged conflict, in which the Amir rightly envisaged his recently-united and badly-mauled country to be a major battleground between the two super-powers.

Subsequently, boundary negotiations were revived and after much deliberation the physical contours delineated in 1887. With his long diplomatic experience, Dufferin sorted out the difficulties, quietly withdrawing his proposal to strengthen the fortifications in Herat, a course of action to which the Amir had raised strong objections. Relations with Afghanistan were now happily established so that the Amir's confidence in British bona fides was not shaken even during the crisis occasioned by his cousin Ishak Khan's rebellion (1888).

Dufferin improved railway communications with Quetta and the Afghan border; he increased the strength of the army (by 10,600 British and 20,000 Indian soldiers); introduced the concept of linked battalions and reserves into the 'native' army and constituted a new force, the Burma Military Police. In 1888, Tibetans were expelled from Lingtu in Sikkim and expeditions mounted on the North-West Frontier (q.v.) in the area of the Black Mountains.

In the mean time, the spectre of French expansion into upper Burma was posing a serious threat. British commercial interests in China felt threatened by French intrusions coupled with the Burmese ruler, Thibaw's unfriendly policies. English merchants urged annexation; British industry, in the throes of an economic depression at home and a Whig regime face to face with a critical electorate, advocated much the same course of action. The only opposition came from those who questioned the benefits of this policy to India. Though initially in favour of establishing a protectorate as against an outright annexation, Dufferin switched over to the latter view as both France and China were preoccupied with hostilities elsewhere. The Third Anglo-Burmese War (q.v.) precipitated by issues which were easily negotiable, lasted a bare 10 days. Burma was annexed and became one of the provinces of the Indian empire. For the Governor-General, it was a personal triumph 'worthy of immortalization' and was responsible for the addition of the Burmese town of Ava as part of his title. Another small town in Burma was also named after him.

On the domestic front, the Governor-General was not even half as popular, or successful, as in matters of foreign policy. Early on, he had realized how important the educated middle class were, especially through their monopoly of the press, itself a powerful factor in informing public opinion. Yet an instinctive dislike of this class came in the way of his taking a balanced or even rational attitude towards it. While applauding the patriotism of English volunteers for active service against Russia, a corresponding reaction from Indian personnel put him in a quandary—he was not prepared to arm them! His alternative plan to recruit some Indian officers was rejected by Whitehall, a development that further confirmed the Viceroy's standing as a 'reactionary' among vocal nationalist leaders.

As a foil to hostile criticism from the educated class, the Viceroy is said to have placated the well-to-do élitist group of Indian princes. The Bengal Tenancy Act (q.v.), originally initiated by Ripon's government, was further watered down to favour the zamindars. In Oudh, Rent Act XXII of 1886 enabled tenants-at-will to secure compensation for improvements, while they were further guaranteed possession for seven years. At the same time the landlords' rights were fully safeguarded. By the Panjab Act XVI of 1887, the rights of occupancy and profits from agriculture were judicially divided without undue opposition from any quarter. To win over the princes, the Gwalior fort was restored to Sindhia, a university established at Allahabad and a legislative council instituted in the North-Western Provinces. Dufferin also advocated an enlargement of the legislative councils elsewhere vesting them with powers of interpellation and the right of discussing the annual provincial budget.

The idea of establishing an 'officious' if not official organ of the Government for expressing its viewpoint and to counteract the 'lies' propagated by the 'native' press was contemplated by the Viceroy, but did not materialize. He was all for the imposition of some sort of restrictions on the press and other forms of propaganda, and had, on a number of occasions, ventilated his grievances against its extreme sections charging them with spreading deliberate misrepresentation. Nor was his government, it would appear, 'very enthusiastic about launching on prosecutions'—more a matter of policy than otherwise.

Initially persuaded by A. O. Hume (q.v.) to support the formation of an 'Indian National Union, where educated Indians could ventilate their grievances and keep the government' informed of public reaction to its policies, Dufferin withdrew his support when informed that it was planned as a memorial to Ripon's progressive policies. He refused any official representation at its meetings, thereby converting what was intended to be an association for a mutual exchange of ideas into a body engaged in criticizing the government and its policies. He however seized upon the opportunity provided by the rejection, in 1886, of the Indian National Congress (q.v.) by the Mohammadan National Association and the (Mohammadan) Literary Society to encourage Muslim separatism. In the bargain, Dufferin appointed a large number of educated Muslims to jobs in the public services so as to encourage political rivalry with the majority community.

By 1887, the Congress had become a somewhat important political force, especially as the princes and the zamindars were aiding it financially. To cut it to size Dufferin proposed that an announcement of the long-awaited constitutional reforms of the legislative councils and the civil service be made. This, he argued, would serve the dual purpose of subverting Congress popularity and blunting criticism of official policy in the press. Before his departure, he assailed it (the Congress) as Hume's brain-child, an 'unrepresentative, misguided and disloyal body' which, in as much as it represented 'a microscopic minority' of the Indian people, could not be trusted to control the destiny of multitudes in the country.

Dufferin adjudged the nationalist leadership as representative of 'only an infinitesimal section' of the people, indifferent and even hostile to the true interests of the masses. He charged that the so-called 'Babu agitator' and 'important Native Association' had offered 'strenuous resistance to our recent land legislation.' Further, that while the government was 'always working in the interests of the great body of people', the educated classes instinctively promoted 'their own interests at the expense of those of the bulk of our subjects.'

His financial policy was guided by considerations in which the paramountcy of imperial interests appeared uppermost. Heavy expenditure incurred in preparing for an Afghan war, then deemed imminent; the annexation and pacification of Burma; imposition of the administrative expenses of the war on the Somali coast of Africa on the Indian exchequer—all these had meant an empty treasury and an over-burdened tax-payer. To meet these expenses, a direct tax on income was imposed, followed by an increase in salt duties and petroleum. The Governor-General was later criticized for not imposing simultaneously an import duty on English cotton goods.

Dufferin retired of his own accord in 1888. Despite sustained efforts to win popular support, he did not receive the rousing send-off given to his predecessor. None the less, he was amply rewarded by the Home government with a marquisate. Later he was to serve in two diplomatic assignments—at Rome (1889-91) and in Paris (1891-6), promoting better relations between these lands and his own. The failure of the London and Globe Corporation, of which he had become Chairman in 1897, caused great financial loss and mental anguish. Dufferin called it 'an indescribable calamity which will cast a cloud over the remainder of my life.' His biographer has called it 'one ruinous mistake'—in dealing with a class of business of which he had no experience.

Lyall concludes his long account with the words, 'if the two final years be struck out of his account, Lord Dufferin's life may be reckoned to have been singularly happy and fortunate.' He died, a sad, broken man, in 1902.

Alfred Lyall, *Life of the Marquis of Dufferin and Ava*, 2 vols, London, 1905; Kalpanna Bishui, 'Lord Dufferin and the Indian Press', *IHC*, proceedings of the Ranchi session, 1964, Aligarh, 1967, 2 Parts, II, pp. 199-208; Bipin Chandra, 'Lord Dufferin and the character of the Indian Nationalist leadership', *loc cit*, pp. 208–14; *DNB 1901-11*, pp. 171-6 (William Lee-Warner).

Frederick William Duke (1863–1924)

Frederick (later Sir) William Duke came of an old Scottish family; an ancestor had fought in the rebellion of 1745. He passed the I.C.S. examination in 1882; his two-year probation being spent at University College, London. Duke was assigned to Bengal and had no secretariat experience until, after 24 years in the districts, he took over as Chief Secretary in 1909.

Over the years Duke had acquired a thorough knowledge of district administration and of the people of Bengal. Yet his modesty and lack of ambition meant that his good and unobtrusive work came to little notice. Quiet and reserved in utterance, of cautious temperament, he was at the same time a shrewd though kindly judge of men.

Duke's tenure, 1897-1902, of the magistracy of Howrah which carried with it the chairmanship of its municipality restored its disorganized finances for a time especially when he acted as Chairman of the Calcutta Corporation. In 1905 he was promoted as Commissioner of Orissa. His appointment as officiating Chief Secretary in 1908 came as somewhat of a surprise. When an Executive Council under the Lieutenant-Governor was established in 1910, Duke was one of the senior members and, in July (1911), took over as acting Lieutenant-Governor. He was the last of the Lieutenant-Governors for, in 1912, with the Partition of Bengal (q.v.) annulled, it became a full-fledged presidency.

In April 1912, Duke became a senior member of Bengal's Executive Council under Sir Thomas David Gibson-Carmichael (later Lord Carmichael)

(1859-1926) who had been transferred from Madras . In November 1914 Duke retired and was appointed member (1914-20) of the Secretary of State's Council of India.

In London he came into contact with a group of students associated with the *Round Table* quarterly review and with them as a nucleus as well as some officials of the India Office engaged in discussions leading to the formulation of a scheme of Dyarchy. In a 'Memorandum' dated 1 May 1916, they sketched out how an Indian province could be governed under a scheme of 'partial' responsibility. This unofficial document acquired importance and when Edwin Montagu visited India (November 1917-March 1918), he took Duke along and relied heavily upon his advice. The Montagu-Chelmsford Reforms (q.v.) of 1919 drew on the scheme though by no means fully.

Duke died suddenly on 11 June 1924. Apart from rich administrative experience, he possessed considerable knowledge of the fauna and flora of Bengal largely because he was an indefatigable foot-slogger and was known as 'the sahib who does all his daks on foot.' Generally interested in Indian archaeology, he was able to do useful work at Gaya for the conservation of Buddhist remains.

DNB 1922-1930, pp. 275-7 (M. C. C. Seton).

Henry Dundas (1742–1811)

Henry Dundas, first Viscount Melville, dominated the Indian scene as a member of the East India Company's (q.v.) Board of Control for well-nigh two decades, 1784–1801. A Tory, his interest in Indian affairs was initially aroused with his appointment in April 1781 as Chairman of Parliament's Secret Committee to report on the causes of the war in the Carnatic and the state of the Company's Indian possessions. While presenting six reports on the subject a year later, he strongly condemned mismanagement of affairs in the three presidencies. More specifically, he demanded that both Warren Hastings (q.v.) and William Hornby, then president of the council in Bombay, having acted in a manner 'repugnant to the honour and policy of England', be removed from their respective offices. In April 1783 he brought forward a bill for the regulation of the government of India proposing *inter alia* an enhancement of the powers of the Governor-General, subordinating the Presidencies of Bombay and Madras to Bengal and suggesting that Cornwallis (q.v.) be the next Governor-General. The bill failed but Charles James Fox (1749–1806), and later William Pitt the Younger (1759–1806), borrowed from it appreciably to introduce measures bearing their respective names. The latter as Prime Minister was responsible for what came to be known as Pitt's India Act (q.v.) and appointed Dundas as member of the Board of Control envisaged in the new law.

Although he did not formally become President of the Board until 1793, the management of affairs was left practically in the hands of Dundas from the very outset. By 1796 he had emerged as the supreme authority on Indian affairs advising and controlling the Governor-General's foreign policy, in the appointment of personnel, introduction of judicial and administrative reform as well as presenting and pushing through the Company's budget. He was also the sole means of communication between the King and the

Governor-General. He defended Warren Hastings against Edmund Burke's (1729-97) charge of criminal conduct in the Rohilla War (q.v.) although on the question of Chait Singh (q.v.) he voted with Pitt, against Hastings. At the same time, he strongly recommended the impeachment of Sir Elijah Impey (q.v.).

Deeply interested in his new charge, Dundas gathered vast and varied information about the country's customs, its rulers, and land revenue system; he was in intimate correspondence with the distinguished orientalist, Sir William Jones (q.v.). He was also responsible for the appointment of John Bruce (1745-1826), the Company's first historiographer.

The self-imposed task of seeing through the renewal of the Company's charter, initially due in 1793, prevented him from taking over from Cornwallis as Governor-General either that year or, again, in 1796. His powerful advocacy of the renewal of the charter was noticed by Pitt who complimented him on his comprehensive grasp of the history of India and of the various sources of British commerce. For years Dundas continued to influence Britain's Indian policy and it was his apprehension of French and Russian danger through Afghanistan that persuaded Lord Wellesley (q.v.) to send John Malcolm (q.v.) to Persia in 1800. Later, he persuaded the Company's Directors to open a British Residency in Baghdad.

With a change of government in England in 1801, Dundas lost his post to Lord Lewisham and reluctantly accepted a pension of £2,000 offered by the Company. A year later he was elevated to the peerage as Viscount Melville and in 1804, with Pitt's return to power, was, briefly, First Lord of the Admiralty. Impeachment proceedings were started against him in 1806 on charges relating to naval matters, but he was soon acquitted on all counts. Though restored to the Privy Council (1807) and still actively interested in politics, he refused ministerial office that was now offered to him. He died on 28 May 1811.

An intimate and trusted lieutenant of Pitt, Dundas, though lacking in refinement and literary taste, was possessed of great political acumen and indefatigable industry. Apart from Indian affairs, he was deeply involved in Scottish politics and, as an active agent for the ruling party, controlled elections of the Scottish representative peers as well as members of the House of Commons from Scotland. As treasurer of the navy for a number of years he introduced various improvements in admiralty departments and for the welfare of seamen and their families.

As a virtual head of the Board of Control, Dundas managed Indian affairs for 16 years. His friends rated his reports on the most complicated questions of Asian policy as major repositories of information that were unrivalled both for their clarity as well as comprehensiveness. James Mill (1773-1836), on the other hand, charged him with being both 'active and meddling' and maintained that 'any advice which he ever gave' was either 'very obvious, or wrong.' A popular doggerel was none too complimentary: For true to public virtue's patriot plan, He loves the minister and not the man; Alike the Advocate of North and Wit, The friend of Shelburne and the guide of Pitt.

Holden Furber, *Henry Dundas*, Oxford 1931; Cyril Matheson, *Henry Dundas*, London, 1933.

Joseph Francois Dupleix (1697–1764)

Joseph Francois Dupleix, second son of a former general who was also one of the directors of the French Indies, was born in January 1697. After a few years at sea he was appointed, through his father's influence, as First Counsellor and Military Commissioner of the Superior Council at Pondicherry in 1720. Successful as a merchant, he made a quick fortune. In 1730 he was promoted and sent as Intendant of the factory at Chanderna-gore (q.v.) which under his expert supervision soon became a prosperous trading centre.

In 1742 Dupleix rose to be Governor of Pondicherry and Director-General of the French factories in India. Ambitious, resourceful and strong-willed, he was also a keen observer of local politics which, he realized, could be exploited with a view to establishing French predominance.

A shrewd diplomat, Dupleix occupied himself in building up French prestige in Indian eyes. He seized the opportunity offered by the Anglo-French war in Europe (1744) to extend hostilities to India and hoped to put an end to British power and commercial rivalry in the south of the peninsula. Madras was captured (1746) but an unfortunate dispute between him and La Bourdonnais (q.v.), the French chief, helped the rival English East India Company (q.v.) whose reinforcements soon arrived and Pondicherry itself was besieged (1748). When hostilities in Europe drew to a close by the treaty of Aix-la-Chapelle, Madras was restored to the British.

Taking advantage of the confused state of political conditions in the south, Dupleix began dabbling in local squabbles, taking an active interest in the disputed successions in the Carnatic and Deccan. In the latter, he supported Muzaffar Jang, the Nizam's grandson, against Nasir Jang who had suc-ceeded his father (1748); in the former, Chanda Sahib against Anwar-ud-din Khan and his son, Mohammad Ali. Convinced that French trade could be extended faster by political processes he was keen to buttress the claims of his proteges. By 1751 he had reached the apogee of his power having successfully set up his candidates in the most strategic centres and having acquired from the Nizam, through Bussy (q.v.), a grant of the Northern Circars and a vague title as ruler of India south of the river Krishna. A year later, in recognition of his great success, King Louis XV made him a Marquis while, after Chanda Sahib's murder (1752), he was designated Nawab of the Carnatic.

Earlier, Mohammad Ali, besieged at Tiruchhirappalli (Trichinopoly), sought British help which put the latter back in the political arena by the middle of 1751. More fortunate in their local commanders, the British won successive victories at Arcot (September 1751) and Arni against Chanda Sahib and his French allies.

An excellent diplomat, albeit a poor general, Dupleix never commanded his troops in the battlefield and at this critical juncture failed to recall Bussy, his only able commander, from Hyderabad. As if that were not bad enough, he lost La Touche and his detachment at sea. Consequently, his forces lacked effective military leadership and suffered severe reverses. Never despairing in the face of heaviest of odds and always confident of ultimate success, he appointed commanders from among those available, recruited crews of merchant vessels and Indians as soldiers, plotted hard to detach

English allies and, since French finances were low, drew on his personal fortune to pay for his campaigns.

The Directors of the French Company, which was a state enterprise, had little knowledge of Dupleix's plans, being far more interested in trade and profit, both of which had, during his tenure, suffered badly. Understandably, they asked him to discontinue his adventurous policies and negotiate for peace after the French defeat at Tiruchhirappalli referred to earlier. The belligerents met at Sadras, a Dutch settlement between Madras and Pondicherry, in January 1754, but Dupleix would not abandon his gains while the British refused to compromise on the terms laid down by him. Hostilities were therefore resumed.

Dupleix's plan of campaign could not have been conducted without arousing British opposition while his own principals at home were loath to risk another war. Before the French commander could make good his reverses, Dupleix was recalled to France and replaced by Charles Robert Godeheu who reached Pondicherry in August 1754.

In Paris, Dupleix was disgraced in every conceivable way: accused of corruption, his accounts were overhauled, his personal loans ignored. He had to wage a relentless battle for his very survival, but all to no avail and, in November 1764, died in dire poverty.

Dodwell repudiates the suggestion that Dupleix's failure was due to lack of military support from his political masters in France. He argues that in four years (1750-53) Dupleix received nearly 400 recruits more than did the English; that at a time when the latter started with a garrison of 800, he had as many as 1,200 European recruits: 'the conclusion must be that he was appreciably better supplied with soldiers than the English were.' Dodwell maintains that Dupleix 'was not the victim of neglect, that Godeheu was not the betrayer of French interests in India but rather that both countries were exhausted by the struggle in which they had been engaged and both urgently felt the need of a breathing space in which to recover themselves. It is noteworthy that when the war in the Carnatic was renewed, it was renewed with all the advantage to the English of superior sea power.' On this occasion the John Company's unaided struggle attracted notice 'in part because its objectives had become evidently of national importance.'

Dupleix's main failure, Dodwell concludes, lay in finance 'giving colour to the reports of mismanagement or roguery. It has been strenuously argued that Dupleix made his wars pay for themselves; but never was such a delusion (more untrue)....We have ample evidence to show that his policy involved a heavy expenditure out of the funds provided for other purposes by the French Company...that a considerable proportion of the French Company's funds were absorbed by Dupleix, that he succeeded no better than did the English then or later in making war in the Carnatic pay for itself. Like the Deccan it was too poor. It was ruinous to dispute it against another European power. Dupleix's schemes and policy demanded a wealthier province than either the Carnatic or the Deccan for their realization.'

The English success in the Carnatic against Dupleix must be ascribed to Major Stringer Lawrence and Thomas Saunders as well as to Robert Clive (q.v.). Lawrence was an eminently capable soldier, Saunders a remarkably successful politician. Without them there could have been no defence of Arcot or surrender of Seringapatam. Nor could Clive observe without learning from the ambitious schemes of his adversary.

The essence of Dupleix's policy lay in using his diplomatic skill and military advantage to secure a local Indian power amenable to his grand design. In this fashion, he may well have argued, he would satisfy the French company by ruining British trade. What was more, by making Indian authorities dependant on himself he would become the *de facto* ruler of south India. He no doubt suffered from misfortune and, except for Bussy, was generally ill-served by his military lieutenants; on the other hand, he had to contend with talent in the person of Lawrence and genius in that of Clive. More, he treated his political masters, the French Company, in a cavalier fashion, informing them of his victories but concealing his defeats.

His faults were of an over-sanguine temperament, an autocratic disposition that made it difficult to work with equals and provided a fruitful source of quarrels. He dazzled but also divided his intelligence relying too much on artifice in dealing with opponents. His departure created a void that no one could fill; his impact being that of the flood which destroys, not of the rain that enriches.

Dupleix's political conceptions were bold, daring and imaginative, ingenious as well as far-reaching. His is a striking and scintillating figure in the history of 18th century India.

S. P. Sen, *The French in India: First Establishment and Struggle*, Calcutta, 1946; Henry Dodwell, *Dupleix and Clive: The Beginning of Empire*, Indian reprint, Gorakhpur, 1962; G. B. Malleson, *Dupleix*, Rulers of India, Oxford, 1892; C. S. Srinivasachari (ed.), *Ananda Ranga Pillai: the Pepys of French India*, Madras, 1940.

Henry Mortimer Durand (1850–1924)

Son of General Sir Henry Marion Durand and born in Bhopal, Henry Mortimer Durand joined the I.C.S. in 1870 and came out to India three years later. Earlier, he had been called to the bar. Except for a tenure of eighteen months in Bengal, and later in Rajputana, he remained part and parcel of what was then called the Foreign and Political Department of the government of India and rose to be its head.

Durand's most conspicuous contribution lies in the settlement of Afghanistan's frontiers. His first contact with that country was in the years of the Second Afghan War (q.v.) when he served under Sir Frederick Sleigh (later Field Marshal Earl) Roberts as his political secretary; later he was awarded the Afghanistan medal for gallantry. For a decade (1884-94) he was Foreign Secretary. Tactful and sincere, apart from being well-versed in Persian, he was accepted (1893) by Amir Abdur Rahman (q.v.) in preference to General Roberts as Lansdowne's (q.v.) envoy to settle the question of the Indo-Afghan boundary. The agreement and the line delineating the limits of their respective territories are known, after him, as the Durand Agreement and the Durand Line (q.v.). While the processs of demarcation was still in progress, he was posted out to Persia.

An internal reform in which he was keenly interested was the institution of the Imperial Service troops, sometimes referred to as 'Durand's fad.' Comprising the best trained forces of the princely Indian States (q.v.), they augmented by nearly 26,000 men the British fighting forces both in and outside India.

The Durand football matches which continue to be played as of date were started by him in Simla in 1886. He had organized association football with a view to fostering good relations among all classes and communities. Two years later, he presented a silver football to be competed for annually. The game became exceedingly popular.

His tenure of six years (1894-1900) in Persia was not a great success, but at Madrid where he subsequently (1900-4) served as Ambassador he helped promote better relations. His stiff manner and rigid views spelt the end of his term (1904-5) as British envoy in the U.S.A. His feelings hurt, Durand declined appointment as Governor of Bombay. After an unsuccessful attempt to be elected to Parliament in 1910, he retired from active public life and devoted himself principally to literary pursuits until his death in 1924.

Durand as noticed earlier was mainly responsible for the boundary between the two empires—and largely because of his profound knowledge of Central Asian problems and the statesmanlike views he expressed, it has stood the test of more than a generation. Further, by removing sources of grave misunderstanding and constant irritation, he paved the way for the Anglo-Russian agreement of 1907. 'Of secondary, yet of first-rate importance' was the settlement of a statutory boundary on the North-West Frontier (q.v.) with Afghanistan, a boundary that, to date, bears his name.

Owing to these two achievements, Durand stands out in his generation as the great boundary-maker and, consequently, as the great peace-maker.

In 1879 Durand edited his father's *History of the First Afghan War* and wrote a biography called *The Life of Major-General Sir H. M. Durand* (1883). His *Life of Sir Alfred Lyall* (1913) has been rated as his best book. He served as Director of the Royal Asiatic Society (1911-19) and President of the Royal Central Asian Society (1914-17).

A man of fine appearance and physique, he rode, shot and played games well. Outwardly, however, he appeared to be somewhat formal and forbidding.

Percy Sykes, *The Right Honourable Sir Mortimer Durand: A biography*, London, 1926; *DNB 1922-30*, pp. 277-9 (H. V. Lovett).

Durand Line

The Durand Line, named after Sir Mortimer Durand (q.v.), lays down the Indo-Afghan (now the Pakistan-Afghan) boundary. The agreement to demarcate it was part of the settlement of 12 November 1893 between the Government of India and the Afghan Amir, Abdur Rahman (q.v.). The demarcation itself took place between 1894-6 with the help of four Anglo-Afghan commissions working simultaneously; they helped to divide the respective spheres of influence between the two countries.

By 1895, the frontier between Nawa Kotal on the outskirts of the Mohmand country and the Bashgal valley on the borders of Kafiristan had been demarcated—an agreement was concluded on 9 April 1895. A similar agreement regarding the Kurram frontier was made on 21 November 1894. The Afghan-Baluch boundary from Domandj to the Persian frontier was not finally demarcated until 1896. A small portion of the Line in the Khyber remained undemarcated until the conclusion of the Third Anglo-Afghan War (q.v.).

As laid down on the ground, the line extends over 1,400 miles from Gilgit in Kashmir to Koh-i-Malik Siah—over deserts, barren hills and mountain ranges. It contains a number of important passes (the Khyber, Bolan, Tochi and Gomal) and was considered to be of vital importance in frontier defence, though of little strategic value. The work of the commissions that put it on the ground proved far from easy or smooth. Before it was completed, Durand had been transferred to Persia; additionally, the Afghan commissioners often worked at cross purposes with their counterparts, for they were given maps different from those which Calcutta had supplied Kabul!

Durand's main purpose, as he saw it, was 'to delineate once and for all, British and Afghan responsibilities in the Pushtun area.' While, to all appearances, the Amir agreed, his autobiography and other papers indicate his opposition to the Durand Line as a *permanent* boundary. He later insisted that the boundary delineated zones of responsibility and did *not* draw an international boundary. It has been suggested that the Amir did *not* actually write the crucial 'I renounce my claims' sentence. Moreover, even Durand, it has been remarked, 'did not propose to move forward the administrative border of India, but merely pushed for' political control.

Sir Olaf Caroe has put forth the view that the 'agreement did not describe

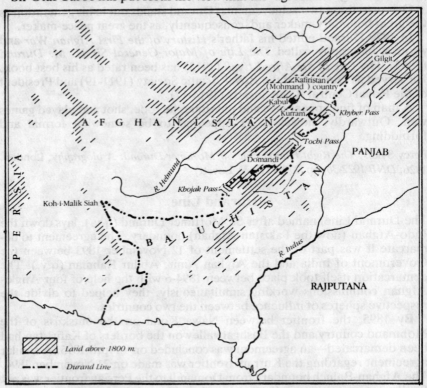

Durand Line

the line as a boundary of India but as the frontier of the Amir's dominions and the lines beyond which neither side would exercise interference. This was because the British government did *not* intend to absorb the tribes into their administrative system, only to extend their own, and exclude the Amir's authority in the territory east and south of the line. In the international aspect this was of no account, for the Amir had renounced sovereignty beyond this line.' An India Office document underlines that the Durand Agreement 'was an agreement to define the spheres of influence of the British government and the Amir.'

The importance of the Line has been somewhat over-rated. While it was designed no doubt to put an end to the existing uncertainty on the border and facilitate frontier administration, in actual fact it failed to do either. As it turned out, it saddled India with increased responsibilities for keeping the peace in an area it did not directly administer, thereby adding to the chance of collision with the tribes as well as the Amir.

The Line was not based on sound topographical data, for places marked on the map were not always located on the ground. Nor, it appears, were the tribes ever consulted. It would seem, in retrospect, that the political issues were rated far more important and over-rode ethnological considerations. The Amir's opposition may have been compromised by the increase in his subsidy (from Rs 12 to 18 lakhs) and the recognition of his right to import munitions of war.

An observer of the Afghan scene has noted that the tribes between British India's administrative border and the Durand Line were 'a buffer to a buffer and the line had none of the rigidity of other international frontiers. It was the usual British compromise but there was no other acceptable solution and considering the complexities of the problem, it worked very well.'

Actually, between the British-administered areas and the Durand Line stretched an extensive tribal belt and many an ethnic absurdity was perpetrated by splitting the tribes on either side of the boundary now laid down. The handing over to the Amir of the Birmal tract of Waziristan and cutting the Mohmand tribal area into two parts are cited as cases in point.

The Durand Line, designed to bring stability to the frontier regions, failed in its objective. In reality it little resembled the line agreed to by Durand and the Amir. Again, politically, geographically and strategically, the Line proved untenable. British and Indian troops fought many bloody engagements with the fiercely independent border mountaineers. Much of the fighting was the direct result of British attempts to demarcate the hated Line—or, to control the tribes near it.

Nor did the Line see the end of the tribal problem, for the Amir maintained his contacts with the tribes on the other side and could, and in fact did, call them into action whenever the need arose. The result was that the tribal question, in terms of a disturbed frontier, became for all practical purposes a British problem. The latter could neither abandon the frontier nor occupy the tribal areas and thus found themselves, for most part, engaged in an interminable war with the tribes. Afghanistan, however, got a measure of respite, for its ruler found it easy to maintain contact and exercise influence with the tribes in the British sphere, across the Durand Line.

Afghan historians contend that the Durand Line was 'imposed on Afghanistan under the threat of war and economic blockade', that it deprived the country of a quarter million Afghan nationals of military age. British historians on the other hand maintain that the Line was a negotiated settlement and refer to the positive references made to it in Abdur Rahman's 'Life'—the Afghans question the very authenticity of this portion of the Amir's autobiography. Frazer-Tytler, the British diplomat so knowledgeable on the country and its people, has suggested that Abdur Rahman, unfamiliar with reading maps, did not understand all the implications when the Line was drawn on a map before him, but was too conceited to say so.

According to Singhal, there were considerable differences between the map the Amir supplied his representatives and the one on which the Durand Line was sketched out at Kabul: 'For the Amir it can properly be argued that the map prepared in 1853 had been prepared in a hurry and was not without inaccuracies.'

According to Forrest, a biographer of Lord Roberts, 'the Amir signed the treaty but he did not sign the official maps indicating the boundary. He disliked the boundary because he considered it damaged his authority and prestige and he determined by all the indirect means in his power to prevent its demarcation.' In view of the military potential of the borderland and the close inter-tribal and family ties between the Afghan and Pathan tribes, the Durand Agreement resulted in strengthening the political position of the tribes of Afghanistan. Thus, in its wake, the policies of the Afghan rulers became more sensitive to the wishes of the major border tribes on whom they were dependent for the defence of their country.

The Durand Agreement gave the British control of the border passes and thus the power to prevent Afghan nomads from entering India or reentering Afghanistan. With this diplomatic and economic weapon, the authorities in India believed they could 'induce the Afghans to compose any differences they might have with the British government.' The tribal territory was put within the British sphere of influence—much against the wishes of the Amir. British insistence on this was dictated by increasing Tsarist influence round and about Afghanistan in the first instance. Secondly, there was the responsibility of guarding Britain's Indian empire.

The Amir had to consolidate his position and centralize his authority in the face of many rivals. For such a task he wanted peace—at least on his most turbulent frontier—on the Yagistan side. By delegating to Britain authority to deal with the Yagistani tribes, he solved his major difficulty. He also badly needed the financial assistance that was given him under the Agreement.

In July 1949, after the British had quit India and Pakistan came into being, Afghanistan declined to acknowledge the Durand Line as an international boundary and gave its full support to the cause of an independent Pakhtunistan.

C. Colin Davies, *The Problem of the North West Frontier, 1890-1908*, with a Survey of Policy since 1849, 2nd ed., London, 1975; S. R. Tikekar, 'The Durand Line—A Survey', *India Quarterly*, VI, 4, 1950, pp. 326-31; R. I. Malhotra, *Afghan Search for Identity: Frontier Settlements 1872-1893*, New Delhi, 1982; Leon B Poullada, 'Some International Legal Aspects of Pushtunistan Dispute', *Afghanistan* (Kabul), XXI, 4, Winter 1969, pp. 32–49.

Romesh Chunder Dutt (1848–1909)

Born in August 1848, Romesh Chunder Dutt belonged to a highly educated and cultured Bengali family of Calcutta (q.v.). His father was one of the first Indians to become a deputy collector in Bengal; his great-uncle was the first to be secretary to the Sanskrit College (Calcutta) and a judge of the court of small causes. His two female cousins, Aru and Toru Dutt, accomplished scholars of French and English, showed great poetic promise at the time of their early deaths.

A typical product of Macaulay's (q.v.) system of education, Dutt's early schooling was in indigenous institutions. Prior to his acquiring the B.A. degree from Presidency College, he left for England (1868) with Surendranath Banerjea (q.v.) and Behari Lal Gupta to take the Indian Civil Service examination. There, in 1871, he ranked third in order of merit, out of 320 candidates. He utilized the interim period, before his selection, by undertaking legal studies, reading English history and literature and travelling extensively in Europe. He developed faith in the democratic institutions as operating in the west and in the traditional sense of justice and fair-play of the British nation. He returned to India, after being called to the bar, in June 1871.

Beginning his 26 years of distinguished civil service work as Assistant Magistrate of Alipore, Dutt rose, by dint of sincere hard work, to be officiating Commissioner of Burdwan (1894). Prospects for higher promotion were somewhat bleak because of the ingrained European prejudice to being ruled by a 'native', a sentiment powerfully reflected in the Anglo-Indian press. In the result, in October 1897, he sought premature retirement so as to be able to devote more time to literary pursuits, and take part freely in Indian politics.

Dutt's literary and other output was impressive. His first book, *Three Years in Europe* (1872), ran into four editions. A few years later appeared his *Peasantry in Bengal*, wherein he expressed the view that the Permanent Settlement (q.v.) of Cornwallis (q.v.) was unwise and ill-conceived, unfairly benefitting the zamindars at the cost both of the cultivator as well as the state. At once biographical as well as critical, his *History of Bengali Literature* (1877) was published under a pseudonym. By 1879 appeared half a dozen of his historical and social romances in Bengali, three of these being later published in English.

Dutt's translation of the Rig Veda in Bengali appeared in 1885. Based on Sanskrit sources, his *History of Civilisation in Ancient India* appeared in three volumes (1888-90).

After his superannuation, Dutt settled in London and published *England and India: a Record of Progress during 100 Years* (1899) wherein he pleaded for a larger popular share of Indians both in legislation as well as administration. In 1900 appeared his *Famines in India*, a series of open letters addressed to Lord Curzon (q.v.), then Governor-General, setting forth his views on agrarian policy and attributing the incidence of famine to high land assessments. Curzon's rejoinder wherein Dutt was accused of inaccuracy was contained in his government's Land Resolution of 1902. Dutt's counter-reply was given in two substantial volumes, *Economic History of British India, 1757-1837* (1902) and *India in the Victorian Age* (1904). Here he analysed the impact of colonialism which had made India a producer and exporter of raw materials and a market for the metropolitan power's finished products. In the result, Dutt argued, his country's indigenous industry and agriculture had been crippled and its people impoverished.

While in London, Dutt published in English verse large extracts of the two great epics, the *Mahabharata* and the *Ramayana*. These were published in book-form in 1899-1900 and their value acknowledged by as great an authority as Max Muller, the famous German indologist.

In 1899 Dutt presided over the fifteenth annual session of the Indian National Congress (q.v.) at Lucknow, and affirmed his faith in the party ideal of a widely representative body informing the government of prevalent public opinion, and gradually seeking, through constitutional means, a greater participation of Indians in the country's administration. He deplored the adoption of retrograde measures, like the Calcutta Corporation Act (q.v.) and the sedition laws then on the statute book. Famines and increasing poverty however were issues which caused him the greatest anxiety. For these he laid the blame squarely on the faulty land-assessment policy of the government and the enormous drain of Indian wealth to England. He co-operated with Dadabhai Naoroji (q.v.) and W. C. Bonnerjee (q.v.) in keeping the English public informed on Indian questions.

In 1904 Dutt returned to India, having accepted the post of Revenue Minister in Baroda. Here he attempted to put his ideas on reform into practice. He also presided over the first Indian Industrial Conference, held alongside the Congress session, at Banaras in December 1905. He supported the Swadeshi Movement (q.v.) and its objective but did not approve of the violent agitation launched by the Extremists. He was appointed (1908) a member of the Decentralization Commission which attempted to seek ways of involving a large number of Indians at all levels in the administrative hierarchy. He signed the Commission's report with a strong note of dissent on many details. Later, he was consulted by John Morley, then Secretary of State for India, on the impending (1909) scheme of constitutional reforms.

Moderate and restrained, Dutt abhorred all revolutionary activity; western ideas, he felt, should be carefully adapted to suit Indian conditions. He considered the Minto-Morley Reforms (q.v.) to be a great step forward, 'calculated to give the people of India a substantial share in the control and direction of their affairs.'

His ideas on social change, especially regarding the position of women, are explicit in his writings. He never placed Hinduism above other religions and was appalled by the inequities that (Hindu) society accepted. He pleaded none the less that certain customs were necessary and good and should be retained.

In an overall eventful career, the last twelve years of his life are of great significance in so far as he made a signal contribution in the field of economic administration as well as politics. His work in the economic field would probably stand out as his most outstanding contribution—his *Economic History* and *Famines* deeply influenced the future course of the nationalist movement. In the colonial situation that prevailed, he argued, the highest priority was to analyse the economics of colonialism, to challenge the complacent theories of economic prosperity, create the right perspective and the correct consciousness among the people. He demonstrated how the economic interests of India had been subordinated to those of a colonial power and the country reduced to a mere appendage to subserve Britain's economic needs.

From his own analysis, Dutt however failed to draw the logical conclusion that to rectify the prevalent situation, colonial control should end and believed that the aberrations of the system could be set aright through the working of the democratic processes in Britain. He was concerned therefore with building up a strong public opinion in India and projecting it to the British public.

A biographer has referred to Dutt's career as 'an unanswerable demonstration' of the capacity of India to produce citizens of the highest calibre borne out by 'his passionate love of his country, his unbiased championship of the cause of India as a whole' and his willingness to subordinate all other considerations 'to the service of his motherland.'

It has been suggested that his long experience in administration had convinced him that British rule in India could be more efficient and more popular by admitting the people to a share in the control and direction of governmental processes. And he felt an irresistible impulse to take part in the national upsurge to secure this share for his countrymen. Dutt combined in his person the triple role of an administrator, a patriot and an author. In addition there was his 'astonishing power of work', an unerring mental grasp combined with a strong will and the 'habit of industry.'

R. C. Dutt, *Romesh Chunder Dutt,* New Delhi, 1968; J. N. Gupta, *Life and work of Romesh Chunder Dutt,* London, 1911; R. C. Majumdar, 'Romesh Chunder Dutt', *JIH,* XLVIII, 1, April 1970, pp. 1–5; G. A. Natesan (ed.), *Indian Statesmen: Dewans and Prime Ministers of Native States,* Madras, n.d., pp. 241-72.

Michael Francis O'Dwyer (1864–1940)

Son of an Irish landowner, Michael (later Sir Michael) O'Dwyer competed successfully for the I.C.S. which he joined in 1882. Intelligent and persevering, he utilized his two years training to complete successfully a degree in jurisprudence. He began service at Shahpur in the Panjab and rose to be the Director of Land Records and Agriculture in the province. Except for a brief stint in some Indian States (q.v.)—at Bharatpur and Alwar 1897-1900, Resident in Hyderabad (1909), and Agent to the Governor-General in Central India (1910-12)—he remained in the north.

A practical administrator, O'Dwyer was hand-picked by Lord Curzon (q.v.) to be Revenue Commissioner of the newly-organized North-West Frontier Province (q.v.) and served in that capacity during 1901-8. In December 1912, he was appointed Lieutenant-Governor of the Panjab, from which post he retired in 1919. As head of the administration, he was determined to hold aloft the banner of imperial prestige and to crush ruthlessly all those who dared agitate. This policy culminated in the large-scale massacre of Jallianwala Bagh (q.v.), followed by measures of barbaric cruelty and humiliation which revived unhappy memories of James George Neill's (1810-57) blood-thirstiness in the Rebellion of 1857 (q.v.).

O'Dwyer is rated one of the 'worst specimens of Morley's Tohinovniks.' The Rowlatt Act (q.v.) had, as it were, sprinkled salt over the Panjab's wounds. It brooked 'no vakil, no appeal, no dalil' and threatened every political worker with dire consequences at the bidding of executive authority.

As the strains and stresses in the Panjab were considerable, the agitation there was more widespread and even more intense than in any other province. There was great fervour, strident emotion, large agitated crowds all of which tended to alarm authority and led to frequent clashes. Worse, the Panjab acquired an invidious distinction for turbulence since the agrarian troubles of 1907; conditions on land had since greatly deteriorated.

O'Dwyer belonged to that coterie of hard-headed, unimaginative administrators who considered British rule to be the best thing that could have happened to India and thus saw no logical reason for unrest, much less demands for freedom. It was inevitable that he grew to dislike the Indian National Congress (q.v.) and the educated classes who were in the vanguard of the political agitation. He was convinced that the well-fed peasant, whose revenue assessments were fair and low, had no cause for complaint and concluded that political agitation was restricted only to the urban areas and needed to be put down by force. He lamented Montagu's August 1917 Declaration (q.v.) as a capitulation to the extremists and refused to believe that administration could, at any stage, be handed over to Indians.

Forewarned on his appointment as Lieutenant-Governor about the existence of 'inflammable material' in the Panjab, O'Dwyer effectively manoeuvred and manipulated the administrative machinery to outwit the members of the Ghadr Party, (q.v.) and other extremists pouring into the province. Their influx had been a cause of grave apprehension during the war years. At the same time, he successfully organized and secured a steady flow of military recruits and monetary remittances to the government in Delhi. In recognition of his services during these years, he was awarded the KCSI (1913) and GCIE (1917).

Scheduled to retire in March 1919, O'Dwyer would have escaped, but for a two-month extension, the ignominy he later earned on account of the disorders in the Panjab culminating in the Jallianwala Bagh holocaust. He approved of Brigadier Dyer's (q.v.) action, viewing it as inevitable and even necessary, to quell the opposition. He opposed the composition of the Hunter Inquiry Committee (q.v.) since it included C. H. Setalvad who had earlier been disallowed entry into the province. Later, he tried hard to prevent Dyer's resignation. While the majority of the Hunter Committee absolved him of all blame, the minority held him guilty on a number of counts.

The Congress Inquiry Committee, which comprised Motilal Nehru (q.v.), Fazlul Haq (q.v.), M. R. Jayakar, C. R. Das (q.v.), Abbas Tyabji and Gandhi (q.v.) with K. Santanam as Secretary went even further and ruled that O'Dwyer 'invited violence from the people, so that he could crush them. The evidence shows that he subjected the Panjab to the greatest provocation under which they momentarily lost self control.'

In England, he challenged Sir Sankaran Nair for publishing (1922) libellious information against him in his book *Gandhi and Anarchy* and won the suit. Though secure in his pension and honour, O'Dwyer could not escape retribution and fell victim to Udham Singh's bullets at a meeting of the Royal Central Asian Society in London, on 13 March 1940.

His *India As I knew It, 1885-1925* (1925) is a vivid, frank and a highly provocative account.

Sir Michael O'Dwyer, *India as I Knew It, 1885-1925*, London, 1925; Arthur Swinson, *Six Minutes to Sunset*, London, 1964, pp. 54-62, 159-177; Sir C. Sankaran Nair, *Autobiography*, Madras, 1966; *Report of the Commissioners Appointed by the Punjab sub-Committee of the Indian National Congress*, Reprint, New Delhi, 1976.

R. E. H. Dyer (1864–1927)

Reginald Edward Harry Dyer was born at the hill-station of Murree, now in Pakistan. He was educated at Bishop Cotton School, Simla and Middleton College in county Cork (Ireland). Later he graduated from the Royal Military College, Sandhurst and received a commission (1885) in the Queen's royal regiment. In 1888 he was transferred to the Indian army where the rest of his military career was spent.

Dyer saw active service in the Burma campaign of 1886-7, the Hazara expedition (1888), the relief of Chitral (1893), the Waziristan blockade (1901-2) and the Zakka Khel operations (1908). In 1916 he took part in military action in south-east Persia where by his energy, courage, and bluff he achieved a notable success and received a well-earned Companion of the Order of Bath.

Posted to the command of a training brigade at Jullundur in the spring of 1917 Dyer met with a serious accident that incapacitated him for a whole year. Always a full-blooded man and liable to attacks of gout, he suffered for the rest of his life from frequent severe headaches while the internal injuries sustained may account for a gradual loss of power over his lower limbs.

Dyer earned notoriety on account of the Jallianwala Bagh Massacre (q.v.) which he ordered and, later, justified. The salient facts may be briefly stated. Posted at Jullundur as commander of a training brigade as noticed above, he was asked by Michael O'Dwyer (q.v.), then Lieutenant-Governor of the province, to take over control of the deteriorating law and order situation at Amritsar, following the earlier hartal and riots in the town. After a brief survey of the situation Dyer came to the conclusion that he was far from adequately equipped to face frenzied mobs even though the necessity to punish the rabble-rousers existed. Having issued an order banning all public meetings, he is said to have waited for an infringement 'to wreak his vengeance and punish the offenders.'

On the afternoon of 13 April 1919, apprised of a gathering at Jallianwala Bagh, Dyer marched there with his officers and men and ordered them to open fire, without prior warning. Subsequently, he ordered a curfew and made sure that his victims went unaided. He then imposed martial law and, confident of support from civil authority, carried out his sadistic, if notorious, 'crawling order.' Later, he directed the flogging of six men allegedly responsible for assaulting a lady missionary.

Three of his actions were the subject of a bitter controversy: (a) on 13 April when a dense crowd of several thousand persons had assembled Dyer marched a small force of 50 rifles to the spot and opened fire without warning. The panic-stricken mob endeavoured to disperse, the exits were inadequate and Dyer, apparently thinking that the mob was massing to attack him, did not give the order to cease fire until 1,650 rounds had been expended; (b) on 19 April he issued an order that no Indian should be permitted to pass; except in a crawling posture, along the street in which the English missionary had been assaulted; (c) on the spot where the assault had taken place, he caused to be whipped, after conviction on an entirely different charge, six persons whom he believed to have been guilty of committing the assault.

After Amritsar, Dyer commanded a brigade (May 1919) on active service in the Third Afghan War (q.v.) and distinguished himself in the relief of the small fort of Thal which was threatened by the Afghan commander, General (afterwards King) Nadir Shah, with a force greatly exceeding his own.

In his evidence before the Hunter Inquiry Commitee (q.v.), Dyer conceded that he could have dispersed the crowd at the Bagh without use of force. He attempted to justify the severity he had shown by reference to eventualities that had not arisen, but might have and to the impression he hoped to produce in other parts of India. Much of what he said appeared to be tinged with racial arrogance. The committee concluded, *inter alia*, that the crawling order was indefensible, the firing a great tragedy and their effect on alienating responsible opinion disastrous.

Earlier, in his report to the Army Council, Dyer had concluded, 'if any dominant motive can be extracted, it was the determination to avert from the European women and children and those of the law-abiding Indian community that fate which I was convinced would be theirs, if I did not meet the challenge and produce the required effect to restore order and I am conscious that it was this motive which gave me the strength of will to carry out my duty.' Datta, a careful student of the Amritsar tragedy, has concluded that, in view of the elaborate arrangements made by one Hans Raj of the CID to assemble a crowd into the Bagh and manoeuvre to keep it there, it would be obvious that Dyer was primarily motivated by the desire for revenge.

General Sir Charles (later Lord) Carmichael Monroe, then Defence Member in the Governor-General's Executive Council, changed his mind regarding Dyer after the latter's appearance before the Hunter Committee. There was, the Defence Member noted, unqualified acknowledgement of the fact that Dyer had decided to fire even before he reached the Bagh, that his aim was to strike terror or make a wide impression, that if he had been able to get the armoured cars into the Bagh, he would have used machine-guns and caused even greater slaughter. Monroe concluded that Dyer had shown want of wisdom, a foolhardiness, a lack of sensitivity that were inexcusable. It may be conceded that he stood condemned *not* for what he did but for what he said, *not* for his action but for his motives.

A word on Dyer's mental disorder. A biographer, Rupert Furneaux, has put forth the view that medical factors were affecting the brigadier's actions. Arteriosclerosis has a retrograde effect and it may have been creeping upon Dyer in 1919. Briefly, Furneaux argues, that *after* Dyer opened fire, his mind became confused and he went on firing.

Dyer's case history suggests a plausibility in Furneaux's theory. Thus, in November 1921, almost 2½ years after Amritsar, he suffered a stroke that brought on partial paralysis. Earlier, on 2 June 1919, and at another moment of stress, he collapsed when giving orders for the final attack on Thal. It is reasonable to argue that if he was as ill as this from June 1919 onwards, he could not have been in first-class mental condition the preceding April.

Furneaux has not gone unchallenged. According to Arthur Swinson, Dyer's bodyguard. W. J. Anderson, has revealed that when Captain F. C. Briggs plucked at Dyer's sleeve it wasn't (as Anderson seems to have imagined) to get him to cease firing; he wanted to draw his attention to sections of the crowd deploying to left and right. Dyer mistakenly imagined that they were planning to outflank him and directed the fire on to them. In fact, they were trying to reach the exits. Anderson's evidence, it has been suggested, clearly destroys the theory developed by Furneaux that Dyer was subject to a mental disorder at this time. It confirms, in fact, the evidence of R. Plomer, Deputy Superintendent of Police, and others that he was calm and in control of himself. Rightly or wrongly, it would appear, he knew just what he wanted to do and did it.

The debate in the House of Commons on the issue was heavily weighted against the General but the House of Lords vindicated him. The latter concluded, *inter alia*, that the Hunter Committee had unfairly censured him for performing his duty in the maintenance of law and order and had thereby set a bad precedent. Understandably, at home, Dyer received a great deal of sympathy and understanding. A collection of £ 26,000 was made by an English daily and gratefully accepted. While some held his actions to be solely responsible for alienating moderate public opinion, others expressed the view that the Indian authorities, under fire from the home government, had made him a convenient scapegoat. Typical of his apologists, the following two bear mention. Sir Michael O'Dwyer: 'General Dyer's action that day in the Jallianwala Bagh was the decisive factor in crushing the rebellion of the Panjab.' And R. Craddock: 'what happened in Amritsar had started to happen in other places and would have gone on happening anywhere if General Dyer's stern action had not quelled it.'

A trenchant critic was B. G. Horniman: 'The Jallianwala Bagh has created for Dyer a special niche in the gallery of frightfulness.'

Afflicted by a paralytic attack in November 1921, after his retirement, Dyer died, in 1927, of cerebral haemorrhage.

Ian Colvin, *The Life of General Dyer*, London, 1929; Arthur Swinson, *Six Minutes to Sunset, the story of General Dyer and the Amritsar affair*, London 1964; V. N. Datta, *Jallianwala Bagh*, Ludhiana, 1969; Raja Ram, *The Jallianwalah Bagh Massacre*, Chandigarh, 1969; *DNB 1922-30,* pp. 280-2 (S. V. FitzGerald); Rupert Furneaux, *Massacre at Amritsar*, London, 1963.

The East India Company

The English East India Company, popularly nicknamed John Company (after John Bull), was founded at the end of the 16th century. It was incorporated by Royal Charter on 31 December 1600, under the title: 'The Governor and Company of Merchants of London, trading into the East Indies.' Its main objective was to compete with the Dutch merchants who had obtained an almost unchallenged monopoly of trade with the Spice Islands and raised the price of pepper from 3 to 8 shillings per pound!

The Charter conferred upon the Company the sole right of trade with the East Indies (viz., all the countries beyond the Cape of Good Hope or the Straits of Magellan) for a term of 15 years. Unauthorized interlopers were liable to forfeiture of ships and cargo. There were 217 subscribers and 125 shareholders in the original (London) Company, which had a capital of £72,000, its first Governor being Sir Thomas Smythe. Its 24 'committees' (i.e., committee-men) nominated in the Charter were afterwards to be annually elected.

The early voyages of the London Company, 1601-12, reached as far as Japan and are designated separate voyages' as the subscribers individually bore the cost of each and reaped the entire profits. After 1612, however, the voyages were conducted on a joint-stock basis, for the benefit of the Company as a whole. The first English factories in India were established at Masulipatam and Petapoli, in the Bay of Bengal.

Mounting friction between the English and the Dutch companies led to a rash of conflicts, culminating in the massacre of English merchants at Amboyna (in the Moluccas of Indonesia) in 1623. 'A bloody and brutal piece of work', the slaughter resulted in the English company admitting tacitly the Dutch claim to a monopoly of the spice trade. Henceforth it turned its back on Indonesia and concentrated its interests, and efforts, on India.

As its trade grew, the Company built (1609) its own dockyard at Deptford, heralding the inception of 'great ships in England.' From now on to the mid-19th century the 'East Indiamen' held unquestioned sway among the merchant vessels of the world. This was particularly so in the 17th century, when they had to be prepared at any moment to fight not merely Malay pirates but the armed vessels of their Dutch, French and Portuguese rivals.

For the first 100 years of its life the Company's monopoly of trade was far from unfettered. In 1657 Oliver Cromwell (1599-1658), the great Lord Protector, had renewed the Charter of 1609 (it re-endorsed the Company's trade in perpetuity, unless it should prove unprofitable) on condition that the Indian trade shoud be in the hands of a single joint-stock company. Thus, as W. W. Hunter noted years later, the Company 'passed from its mediaeval to its modern basis.'

The reign of Charles II (1660-85) marks a period of boom in the Company's fortunes. He granted it five Charters and helped its growth from a single trading company into a great chartered company, with the right to acquire territory, coin money, command fortresses and troops, form alliances, make war and peace and exercise both civil and criminal jurisdiction.

The Company's prosperity, however, was by no means an unmixed blessing; it attracted a large number of 'interlopers' who wanted to make profits from its trade. Parliament's affirmation (1694) that 'all the subjects of England' had equal rights to trade, unless otherwise prohibited, helped their cause. The result was the establishment, in 1698, of a rival East India Company—in consideration of a loan of £ 2 million to the state. The resultant unseemly rivalry between the old and the new continued until they were finally amalgamated as a result of the tripartite indenture between the companies and Queen Anne (1702), ratified under the Godolphin award (1708). The latter gave it a new name—'the United Company of the Merchants of England Trading to the East Indies.' From now on, this body received at intervals new charters prolonging the period of its monopoly.

It may be useful at this stage to review the Company's working in relation to its dominion in the East. Even though strongly opposed to each other, the English and the Dutch Companies fought long and bitterly against the Portuguese. In 1612 an English fleet led by Captain Thomas Best repulsed Portuguese attacks and began trading at Surat; a year later, a Mughal imperial *firman* secured its trading rights there. In 1622 the English Company's capture of Ormuz in the Persian Gulf helped it further against any opposition from the Portuguese.

Earlier, Sir Thomas Roe, as the Ambassador (1615-19) of King James I to the court of the Mughal emperor Jahangir, had secured some privileges. Roe, who intensely disliked the military and commercial policies of the Dutch and the Portuguese, exhorted his own countrymen to forswear them: 'Let this be received as a rule that if you will profit, seek it at sea, and in quiet trade; for without controversy, it is an error to affect garrisons and land wars in India.'

In 1640 the Company acquired the site of modern Madras, where it quickly built Fort St George. In 1668 King Charles II transferred to it the site of Bombay which he had received as part of his dowry when marrying the Portuguese princess, Catherine of Braganza. This he did for £ 10 annually as rent. Between 1669 and 1677, the Company's Governor, Gerald Aungier, laid the foundations of the modern city of Bombay, to which the western headquarters of the Company were transferred in 1687. Three years later, Job Charnok, a faithful servant of the Company, at the invitation of Nawab Ibrahim Khan of Bengal laid the foundations of Calcutta (q.v.). The site was a swampy land on the Bhagirath comprising the village of Sutanati to which, in 1698, were added the adjoining villages of Kalikata and Govindapur. From now on, with the three Presidencies of Madras, Bombay and Bengal established, the Company's history merges, for all practical purposes, with that of British India's.

In 1691 the Nawab of Bengal exempted the Company from payment of customs duty in return for an annual payment of Rs 3,000 only. This right was later (1715) confirmed by the Mughal emperor, Farrukh Siyar (q.v.).

The acquisition of sovereignty over India was neither a swift nor sudden process. For one thing, it entailed wars with the Company's European rivals—the Portuguese, the Dutch and, most formidable of them all, the French—as well as the 'native' powers in India. By the Battle of Wandiwash (q.v.). the French threat was eliminated, while the Battle of Plassey (q.v.), 3 years earlier, gave it a foothold over Bengal, Bihar and Orissa.

As long as the Company's chief business was trade, it was left to manage its own affairs. As already noted, the original (December 1600) charter had placed it in the hands of a Governor and a committee of 24, who exercised unlimited control over their factors in India. But after Plassey, when the Company acquired territory and became a ruling power, Lord North's Regulating Act, (q.v.) was deemed necessary. In 1784 Pitt's India Act (q.v.), created a Board of Commissioners as a department of the English government to exercise control, at once political, military and financial, over British possessions in India. The Act for the first time used the historic phrase 'Governor-General in Council', an entity that was soon to emerge as politically all-powerful.

The latter half of the 18th century found the Company at war with the rulers of Mysore and the Marathas. The Nizam was never a serious contender but both Haidar Ali (q.v.) and his son Tipu (q.v.) proved formidable foes, as did Nana Phadnavis (q.v.), the Maratha leader. Yet slowly but surely the Company worsted its rivals in the field and sapped where it could not storm. The long and short of it was that by 1799 Tipu had not only been routed in bloody combat but killed; within less than two decades thereafter, the mighty power of the Maratha confederacy had been reduced to dust and ashes. In the meantime, the Mughal emperor in Delhi had shrunk to a mere shadow of his former self; presently, he was to become a helpless pensioner of the Company and its virtual prisoner. More, by 1818 the proud Rajputs, driven by petty jealousies, had become feudatories of the Company.

All that now remained was the conquest of Sind (q.v.) and of the Panjab. The former fell in the aftermath of the disastrous First Anglo-Afghan War (q.v.) being both 'morally and politically' its sequel; the latter, a victim to the anarchy created by the successors of Maharaja Ranjit Singh (q.v.). By this time, thanks to the exertions of Amherst (q.v.) and Dalhousie (q.v.), Burma's coastal provinces and lower half had fallen securely into the British lap.

All this while, under the general direction of Pitt's India Act, the Company continued to administer British India and its Directors at home wielded considerable influence in Parliament. To some extent the growth of government control over the Company was matched by the growth of the latter's influence over the former. The Charter Act of 1813 [Charter Acts (q.v.)] gave the Board of Control authority over the Company's commercial transactions and abolished its monopoly of the Indian trade. The Act of 1833 [Charter Acts (q.v.)] took away the valuable China trade—chiefly in tea. The Company's property was now secured on its Indian possessions and its annual dividend of 10 guineas per £ 100 stock made a charge upon the Indian revenues. From now on it ceased to be a trading concern and exercised only administrative powers.

During the period that elapsed between Pitt's India Act (1784) and the Charter Act of 1833, the Company was gradually relieved of its long-held trading privileges in the East; simultaneously, it grew to be the paramount power in India responsible for the government of a very large population spread over an immense area. In all these developments and in the administration of its dominion, the Company's government in London which maintained a close scrutiny and control over its Indian possessions, played an important, even essential, role. As a result of Pitt's India Act, the Court of Proprietors could be by-passed if a decision of the Court of Directors was approved by the Board of Commissioners, more popularly, the Board of Control. While it greatly weakened their power, the Directors still continued to perform a useful, indeed valuable, function of giving expression to public opinion on the Company's government in India and England.

The most important function of the Proprietors was to elect the 24 Directors who formed the executive body of the Company in England. The necessary and formal qualification for admission to the Direction was the possession of £2,000 of India stock. The Court had long shown a tendency to becoming co-optive and, by 1784, it was customary for the Directors in office to unite to ensure the return of the 6 Directors 'out by rotation.' In practice, therefore, the Directors consisted of 30 members who were virtually elected for life.

Throughout the half century 1784-1834 there existed in the Company a strong and well-organized City and shipping interest, as also a large, well-organized Indian interest; after 1813, when the Indian monopoly vanished, the Indian interest gave place to the City, shipping and private trade interest.

The most important committee of the Directors, in so far as the Government of India was concerned, was the Secret Committee, its origins going as far back as 1683. In 1784, however, a permanent statutory committee consisting of not more than three Directors had been constituted. It was not merely the channel through which secret despatches passed; in practice, it often originated secret despatches particularly on commercial subjects.

With a view to keeping the Crown from 'corrupt influence', Pitt had left the patronage of India in the hands of the Directors. Accordingly, the Act had vested in the Court nominations to the superior posts in India—namely the Governor-General, Governors of Presidencies, and the chief army commands—subject to the approbation of the Crown. In practice, however, these nominations were made by the Ministry and the Directors' legal right (of nomination) became, in effect, a power of veto. In the main, therefore, the Directors' patronage consisted of appointments of writers, civil servants for the administration of the Company's territories, of cadets and assistant surgeons for the Company's armies. Between 1793-1813, the yearly average for these posts came to: 40 writers, 240 cadets and 30 assistant surgeons.

The strength, influence and independence of the Court of Directors, as against the Board of Control and the Cabinet, varied in proportion to the strength of East India interests in Parliament. Beginning with a representation of 60 members in July 1784, the East India membership increased by August 1802 to 95 and, in October 1806, to 103. Coincidentally, between 1802 and 1806, the Directors' powers grew to their maximum—the Court scored its greatest triumphs at home and forced its external policy on the Indian government. From 1806, however, the number of East India members in Parliament gradually decreased and in the general elections between 1830 and 1834 it fell from 62 to 45.

Even though it was hardly possible to govern India from England, the influence of the home government on British Indian policy was profound between 1784-1834. The strong support of at least one party, as in the case of Minto (q.v.) and Amherst (q.v.), was essential for a successful Governor-Generalship. Only two Governors-General—Wellesley (q.v.) and the Marquess of Hastings (q.v.)—were bold or rash enough to ignore the principles of Indian policy laid down in London. Paradoxically, it was they who most extended the Company's territories in India. Hastings' policy was partly thrust on him by the march of events; even so, it was severely conditioned by directives from home.

Keen students of the Company's affairs maintain that the part played by the Directors in moulding the home government's Indian policy has, in general, been either misrepresented or ignored. By acting as a brake on the speed of the Company's expansion they unwittingly benefited British power in India, which was thereby afforded periodic intervals of peace in which to consolidate and organize its resources.

The Company's Directors have been criticized, even lampooned—having been described variously as 'those worthy cheesemongers', 'those mean-spirited men', 'those paltry shabroons.' The fact, however, is that whenever their conduct failed to satisfy the government, the latter usually turned round and called the Board either 'factious' or 'parsimonious.' Wellesley and the Grenville Whigs 'fostered the legends' which some historians later dutifully accepted and repeated. Thus it has been maintained that the Directors' India policy was determined by their anxiety to keep the Company's dividends at a high level, and by their desire to increase their patronage; that it was uniformly marked by financial and commercial mis-management. The truth, as Philips has suggested, is 'less one-sided than this.'

By 1833 there was the incessant propaganda, widely broadcast, that the Directors were constantly borrowing from the Indian territorial revenues to bolster up the Company's declining, ill-managed, commerce. Nothing, it has been pointed out, could be 'more untrue.' Throughout the 1784-1834 period the Company's territorial branch was indebted to its commercial branch and *not* the other way round. It is said that the Directors' 'Financial Letters' to India were 'models of sound advice' and by their own unremitting attention to the Company's financial interests, they facilitated the task of the Governor-General.

With increasing demands made on it, the machinery the home government devised in 1784 to supervise the Indian government proved to be inadequate and yet it lasted, with minor changes, down to 1858. It has been suggested that it was not the Board of Commissioners, but the Court of Directors which provided the necessary knowledge and stability in the home government. Differences of opinion between the two authorities arose frequently over appointments to high office and over the conduct of commercial, financial and external policy. Serious differences however were few and the machine worked with 'relative noiselessness', so long as the Court maintained its independence and constituted a check on an otherwise uncontrolled President of the Board of Control. This 'noiselessness', Philips suggests, 'was a sign of the machinery's efficiency.' But towards the mid-thirties the Directors began to lose their independence and the resultant noiselessness 'was now indicative of the Court's subservience' to the Board.

With Dalhousie's stewardship India's political contours, so far as British domain was concerned, had been firmly sketched. What remained of the princely Indian States (q.v.) would have been mopped up but for the trauma of the Rebellion of 1857 (q.v.). That rude shock shook the empire to its very foundations and sounded the Company's death knell. It now ceased to be the ruler of India and the British Crown assumed full sovereignty over its former dominion.

The Company's rule was brought to an end not so much from any special responsibility for the Rebellion but because 'it was felt to be an anachronism that a private corporation should, even though it were only in name, administer so vast a dominion.' Originally established 'for the purpose of extending British commerce to the East', it was able, two and a half centuries later, to transfer to the Crown 'an empire more magnificent than that of Rome.'

C. H. Philips, *The East· India Company, 1784-1834*, Indian ed., Bombay, 1961; Holden Furber, *John Company at Work*, New York, 1948; Lucy S. Sutherland, *The East India Company in 18th Century Politics*, London, 1952; Ramakrishna Mukherjee, *The Rise and Fall of the East India Company*, Berlin, 1955.

Ashley Eden (1831–87)

Ashley Eden, a nephew of Lord Auckland (q.v.), was nominated to the Indian Civil Service in 1849. After training at Haileybury College (q.v.), he arrived in Calcutta (q.v.) in 1852. Three years later he was appointed assistant to the special commissioner deputed to suppress the Santal Rebellion (q.v.); later, in recognition of his services, he was posted as the first Deputy Commissioner of that area. Subsequently, in Bengal, he took up the cause of the ryots in the course of the Indigo Riots (q.v.) in 1859 and spoke freely against the planters before the commission of inquiry. As a sop to the planters' politically powerful lobby, Eden was spirited away as Magistrate and Collector of Cuttack. During 1860-71 he acted as Secretary to the Government of Bengal and an *ex-officio* member of the Bengal Legislative Council.

Eden's experience in successfully putting down the Sikkimese incursions and concluding an advantageous commercial treaty with the Raja secured his appointment (1863) as leader of a deputation to Bhutan (q.v.) to settle the problem of the Dooars. Prevented from meeting the Deb Raja, he forced his way to the capital where he was made to sign, under duress, a treaty favourable to the Bhutanese. (This was later countermanded in Calcutta and led to war.) On return, Eden had stressed the importance of annexing the Dooars which, he maintained, contained some of the finest tea and timber lands in Bengal and were, climatically, ideally suited for European settlers.

As Chief Commissioner of British Burma in 1871-5, Eden is credited with initiating a number of administrative and educational reforms and for opening a trade route to western China. He was awarded a C.S.I. in 1874.

Eden was an additional member of the Governor-General's Executive Council between February and December 1876, when appointed Lieutenant-Governor of Bengal. Described by Lytton (q.v.) as the best administrator then under his charge, Eden supported the controversial Vernacular Press Act (q.v.). Prior to his retirement in 1882, he proposed to extend to Indian magistrates the right to try European offenders which led to the highly contentious Ilbert Bill (q.v.) that his successor Sir Augustus Rivers Thompson (1829-90) opposed vigorously.

To commemorate his long years in service, his friends in Calcutta founded the Eden Hospital for women and children, while an Eden Canal joining the Ganga with the Tista was designed to prevent floods in north Bihar. In England, from 1882 till his death 5 years later, Eden served as an active member of the Secretary of State's India Council.

DNB, VI, pp. 354-5 (Henry Morse Stephens).

Basic or Wardha Scheme of Education

Basic education, also called 'Nai Talim', is not so much a methodology of education as the expression of an idea for a new life and a new society. The premise is that only through this system of education could India build an independent, non-violent society.

The scheme was first spelt out by Mahatma Gandhi (q.v.) in 1937 in the course of a series of articles in his weekly, *Harijan*. As he himself confessed, his outpourings were that of 'a layman for the lay reader': his idea was that all education to be worthwhile must be self-supporting and his hope that in the end his scheme would pay its way except for the capital expenditure incurred. The Mahatma also stressed the need for students working at some industry during the day so that they would begin to love manual labour—and not hate or shun it. In putting forth the scheme he emphasized that the concept of free and compulsory primary education for 7 years on a nationwide scale should centre around some form of manual or productive work. All other aspects to be developed or training imparted should, as far as possible, be integrated with a central handicraft chosen with due regard to the environment of the child.

Gandhi's main thesis was that English education had created a permanent gulf between the highly educated few and the ignorant masses; that it had made its recipients ineffective, unfit for productive work; that it had harmed them physically. It was also clear that the money spent on primary education was completely wasted, for it was soon forgotten and had little or no relevance to the village or towns from which the students were chiefly drawn.

The first conference on 'National Education', as it was called, was convened at Wardha on 22-3 October 1937 to consider the new system. It apointed a committee under the presidentship of Dr Zakir Husain (q.v.) 'to prepare a detailed syllabus' in the spirit of the resolutions it had adopted. In less than two months, by December 1937, the committee had submitted its report.

In contrast to Gandhi's vague formulations, the report was 'an address of educationists to other educationists.' It outlined the principles and objectives of the scheme in terms of recognized doctrines of education and psychology, spelt out detailed syllabi for a number of crafts and made valuable suggestions regarding such important aspects of the scheme as the training of teachers, supervision and examination as well as administration. It even worked out a few possible correlations with the basic crafts of spinning and weaving.

In sum, the principal highlights of the system were: (i) introducing a basic handicraft in the syllabus; (ii) devising ways for coming into contact with the life of the community around the school through service and thereby actually building up the school community; (iii) introduction of teaching through Hindi from standard II to standard VII; (iv) removing the teaching of English from earlier years in school and beginning it only from standard VIII onwards; (v) the first 7 years of schooling to be organized as an indivisible, integral part of a free and compulsory nationwide educational system; (vi) devising a suitable technology or correlation with a view to implementing the main idea of basic education, viz., educating the child through the medium of productive activity of a suitable handicraft.

From the above it should follow that the chief characteristics of basic education are: it is child-centred; it is dynamic; it is co-operative; it is non-violent; it sets truth in the highest place. It should be added that the whole system rests upon the belief that every human being needs to *make*, needs to *love*, need to *know*.

In sum, basic education is designed to prepare the growing child for the place he or she will occupy in the future in a just and moral society, free from exploitation. It is for the shaping of the child's character and is designed to equip him for the requirements of such a society. In reality, it was the coping stone of Gandhi's socio-political edifice.

In apt phrases, a well-known educationist has defined it thus: 'Basic education lays stress on training for citizenship. Democracy in any country can function only when its citizens are enlightened...[it] aims at equipping the youngsters during the eight years of compulsory schooling with all the basic abilities, skills and attitudes which are deemed to be essential for establishing and strengthening a democratic society. The most crucial among these is the ability to work co-operatively and to discharge individual responsibilities in a corporate undertaking. [It] seeks to achieve this by providing socially useful work in the school.'

From 1937 the Indian National Congress (q.v.) which had taken office in most of the British Indian provinces was willing and indeed did implement the scheme. Towards the close of 1939, however, the party had left the reins of government which it did not assume again until 1946. During this interregnum a large measure of the earlier gains made in the shape of basic education was completely lost.

After Independence (1947), the scheme of basic education was accepted both by the Union as well as State governments as the pattern of national education at the elementary stage. It was decided to establish, gradually and in the long haul, a universal system of basic education throughout the country. The very first Five Year Plan (1951-6) indicated this new trend.

Basic National Education: Report of the Zakir Husain Committee and the Detailed Syllabus, with a Foreword by Mahatma Gandhi, Wardha, 9th reprint, 1939; J. B. Kripalani, *The Latest Fad: Basic Education*, Wardha, 2nd reprint, 1948; Salamatullah, *Thoughts on Basic Education*, Bombay, 1963; *Report of the Second National Seminar on Basic Education Held at Haunsbari* (Mysore) January 7-9, 1958, Ministry of Education, New Delhi, 1958; A. B. Solanki, *The Technique of Co-relation in Basic Education*, New Delhi, 1958; *Foundation of Living: The Principles and Practice of Basic Education*, Wardha, 1956; T. A. Avinashilingham, *Understanding of Basic Education*, Ministry of Education and Scientific Research, New Delhi, 1957.

Deccan Education Society (founded 1884)

The Deccan Education Society established by Bal Gangadhar Tilak (q.v.), Gopal Ganesh Agarkar, Mahadeo Ballal Namjoshi, Vaman Shivaram Apte, and some other dedicated educationists on 24 October 1884 grew out of the 'New English School' established four years earlier. The inspiration was that of M. G. Ranade (q.v.) and the aim 'to promote the cause of private education and to put it on a more extended basis in order to give permanence to it.' Additionally, it was to popularize education at different levels, through indigenous initiative and under Indian management. In the final list of Patrons and Fellows were Sir William Wedderburn, Principal William

Wordsworth, Professor F. G. Selby and H. G. Winter, Collector of Patna. Even Lord Ripon (q.v.) was enrolled. Wedderburn was Chairman of the Provincial Council, as also Chairman of the first regularly constituted Council of the Society.

Members were required to serve for at least 20 years on a nominal salary, starting with Rs 75 per month. So successful were the efforts of the Society that it soon secured grants-in-aid for its school as well as Fergusson College, Poona and, later, Willingdon College at Sangli. Two papers, the *Kesari* and the *Mahratta,* were started as part of the society's programme to arouse popular interest and ensure greater involvement and participation by the people.

As the years rolled by some of the Society s members began participating in political activities and, through their public organs, criticized governmental policies. On pain of losing grants, they were warned by the government to refrain from such activities. Both Ranade and Gokhale (q.v.) helped the Society steer a middle course. Thus, during the Home Rule Movement (q.v.) the Society gave its members permission to attend public and political meetings but, for itself, refrained from taking an active part.

An excerpt from the statement of the Secretary of the Society in June 1909 read: 'Many a man willingly recognizes that but for the mission of the Deccan Education Society which consists in cheapening and facilitating education, he would not have received that moral culture on Western lines which the managers of the institutions regard as an essential factor in the national progress.'

The significance of the Society's work lay in its recognition of education as the principal mode of effecting social, political and cultural advance, and its realization of the importance of the vernacular as the medium for imparting instruction. The establishment of the society is viewed as an 'outstanding' example of educational enterprise started by nationalist Indians on their own initiative.

P. M. Limaye (ed.), *The History of the Deccan Education Society (1880-1935),* Poona, 1935; A. R. Desai, *Social Background of Indian Nationalism,* 4th ed., Bombay, 1964.

The Education Despatch (1854)

Commonly known as 'Wood's Education Despatch', after Sir Charles Wood, then President of the East India Company's (q.v.) Board of Control, it has been variously described as the 'Magna Carta of English education in India' and the 'Intellectual Charter of India.' Hailed as 'one of the most statesmanlike and democratic documents in the history of educational administration', it was essentially the 'outcome of a collaborative effort' in the formulation of which the then Governor-General, Lord Dalhousie (q.v.), and his officials played an important role.

Analysing its genesis, a knowledgeable critic has suggested that the Despatch was 'a product of Baring's labours, with instructions from Wood who drew his ideas from Marshman, Bourdillon and Duff except on female education which was Duff's favourite subject.' Again, in its nature it looked 'more like codification than origination and that the laurels should be shared by Marshman, Bourdillon, Duff, Baring and Wood, if not also Dalhousie or even Lt-Governor James Thomason for his success with vernacular education except in eight districts of the North-West Provinces in the late 1840s.'

In so far as Wood seemed to take the entire credit for himself, Dalhousie was understandably sore. His diary entry for 12 October 1854 read: 'The education despatch....is a mere clap-trap put forth to the House of Commons by Sir Charles Wood whereby he seeks to filch for himself the whole credit of all that has been, or is to be, done; thus unduly detracting from the credit which fairly belongs to the Government of India and to the local administration.'

Moore spells out the various stages through which the draft passed. He identifies two plans or outlines of a draft, two manuscripts, and five printed drafts, which were annotated to show the progress of the Despatch through its successive phases. Wood wrote the outline for the guidance of Thomas G. Baring (until 1859, Secretary to Wood) who prepared and annotated the drafts. There was 'little assistance' from the papers of E. D. Bourdillon, a clerk in the Correspondence Department, and John Clark Marshman (1794-1877) but Dr Alexander Duff's (1806-78) memorandum proved to be a useful source from which to develop a 'general scheme' of 'practical education.'

The Despatch contained the first comprehensive plan for the spread of education in India and systematized the educational hierarchy from the primary through the high school and the college to the university. The medium of instruction was optional—both English and the vernacular being accepted; the latter was encouraged at the school level, the former at the university. A system of grants-in-aid was laid down so as to encourage private initiative and enterprise in the field. It was hoped that eventually state education would become education supported, where necessary, by state grants-in-aid. The secular character of the plan was highlighted by the fact that financial aid was to be given irrespective of the religious leanings of the persons or institutions concerned. In fact, it was laid down that education imparted in government institutions should be exclusively secular. Instruction in the Bible was to be given to such as volunteered for it and that too after school hours. Stress was laid on female as well as vocational education as also teacher-training. Scholarships were to be provided to meritorious students of all schools, be they government, private or indigenous. They were so planned as to connect lower schools with the higher and the latter with colleges.

To ensure the implementation of its programme, supervisory and examining bodies were to be set up. For purposes of inspection, each presidency town was to have a university, based on the pattern of the University of London, to conduct examinations and confer degrees. In pursuance, the first university in India was established in Calcutta; later that year, two more, in Bombay and Madras, were established. All teaching was to be done in colleges. To start with professorships in law, languages and civil engineering alone were to be instituted. The award of degrees was designed to bring to the notice of the government educated young men who were eligible for the public services.

The Education Despatch was by no means the brainchild of the President of the Board of Control; actually, many hands had helped give it shape and form. Among its early forebears Charles Grant (1746-1823), William Carey

(1761-1894) and Ram Mohun Roy (q.v.) may be mentioned; Dalhousie and his officials, as has been noticed, had their impact too.

Wood's 'strength', Moore suggests, 'was that he saw the problem of education as integral to the regeneration of Indian society...It was his weakness that he insisted upon the existence of "some private body or person to be added" before the government was brought into play as a financial contributor. If Indians were to "improve", they must do something to help themselves...insisting upon the applicability of the mid-Victorian doctrine of "self-help" to Indian conditions.'

The new education policy underlined the need for involvement by the community at large and stressed that no sudden or speedy result could be expected, least of all by dependence on the government alone. Needless to add, the Despatch was to form the basis for all future legislation regarding the spread of education in India.

R. J. Moore, *Sir Charles Wood's Indian Policy 1853-66*, Manchester, 1966; Prashanto K. Chatterjee, 'Authorship of the Education Despatch of 1854', *Australian Journal of Politics and History*, Vol. XIX, No. 2, August 1973, pp. 188-93.

Macaulay's Minute on Education (1835)

Written and presented by Thomas Babington Macaulay (q.v.) in his capacity as president of the committee on public instruction on 2 February 1835, the celebrated 'minute on education' was to form the basis of the John Company's (q.v.) educational policy in India. *Inter alia*, it underscored the victory of the so-called 'Anglicists' as well as 'progressive' Indians, who supported the introduction and popularization of English education over the opposing school of thought represented by the 'Orientalists' who preferred to encourage the pursuit of traditional lore.

The conflict was not a sudden flare-up in 1834, but one that had been in the making for at least a generation; its roots lay in the changing attitudes of the English towards India and its inhabitants.

The relevant provision in the Charter Act of 1813 [Charter Acts (q.v.)] stipulated that 'a sum of not less than one lac of rupees (£ 10,000) each year shall be set apart and applied to the revival and improvement of literature and the encouragement of the learned natives of India and for the introduction and promotion of a knowledge of the sciences among the inhabitants of the British territories in India.' The aim was dual: to foster oriental learning *and* western science.

The Parliamentary Select Committee, of which Macaulay was a member and which examined the affairs of the Company before the Charter Act of 1833 [Charter Acts (q.v.)], had concluded in its report (1832) that the general cultivation of English was more desirable 'both with a view to the introduction of the natives into places of trust, and as a powerful means of operating favourably on their habits and character.' By 1833, according to Charles Edward Trevelyan, Macaulay's brother-in-law, the 'oriental mania' that had begun under Wellesley (q.v.), had spent itself. Trevelyan's letters to Bentinck (q.v.) refer to the Anglicist cause as the 'popular' and 'liberal' cause, for he wished, eventually, to see the new educational policy based on English and the vernaculars as part of a comprehensive system of national education with the most proficient students duly rewarded with government jobs. He regarded the Orientalists as élitists who had little in popular education on the scale he envisaged. He also visualized, ultimately, a Christianized Asia.

In late January 1835, the two factions on the Committee—Orientalists (James Sutherland, John Shakespear, the brothers James and Henry Thoby Prinsep and Elliot Macnaghten) and Anglicists (William Wilberforce Bird, Charles Barslem Saunders, George Alexander Bushby, John Russell Colvin and Charles Edward Trevelyan)—laid their respective cases before the Supreme Council. The legal point at issue was the clause in the Charter Act of 1813 which had provided for 'the revival and improvement of literature.' The Orientalists claimed that any substantial reduction of Sanskrit and Arabic instruction would contravene that particular provision of the Act.

On 2 February 1835, Macaulay as Legal Member of the Council penned his famous minute in which he adopted and defended the views of the Anglicists on the Committee. On the basis of his minute, Bentinck ruled 'that the great object of the British Government ought to be the promotion of European literature and science among the natives of India and that all the funds appropriated for the purpose of education would be best employed on English education alone.'

What we know now is that the actual decision had been taken by the beginning of December 1834, and had been in the making for some time before that. The minute thus barely confirmed Bentinck in a decision he had already arrived at. Not unexpectedly, the Governor-General minuted (7 March) after reading it: 'I give my entire concurrence to the sentiments expressed in this minute.'

But Macaulay's minute was something more than a mere *piece d'occasion* and cleverly argued to deal with a set of special circumstances. In some ways it was 'a typical Whig document [which] reflected the Whig tendency to charge old laws with new meaning.' Bentinck's 'resolution', which eventually put the new educational policy into effect on 7 March 1835, contained the proviso that the Government had no intention of abolishing 'any college or school of native learning (the Calcutta Madrassa or the Sanskrit College) while the native population shall appear to be inclined to avail themselves of the advantages which it affords.' This stipulation, interpolated later, was not part of the original draft of the resolution drawn up for Bentinck by Macaulay.

Many factors helped the changeover: educated Indians had been seeking outlets in government employment, where knowledge of Sanskrit or Arabic did not help; the Company favoured such employment for reasons of economy in administration. In the result, a resolution based on Macaulay's 'minute' and accepted by William Bentick's government on 7 March 1835 proclaimed English as India's official language.

A brilliantly argued essay for the retention of English education, Macaulay's minute contemptuously discarded all oriental learning as devoid of utility as well as incapable of eliminating 'native' inferiority. In the light of the government's resolution referred to above, all public funds were henceforth to be divided between oriental schools teaching Arabic, Persian and Sanskrit and governmental institutions offering courses in English literature and the sciences. Through the end-products of the new system, Macaulay had argued, would emerge a class who though Indian in blood and the colour of their skins would be 'English in tastes, in opinions, in morals and in intellect.' Not only would they act as 'interpreters' between 'us and the millions whom we govern' but also further help education gradually filter down to the masses by refining 'the vernacular dialects with terms of science borrowed from the western nomenclature.'

In India, Macaulay noted, 'English is the language spoken by the ruling class of natives at the seats of Government. It is likely to become the language of commerce throughout the seas of the East.' Incidental effects of the change, Macaulay argued, would be to popularize Christianity and help train a corps of administrators who would, over the long haul, continue trade even after the British left.

Nor, Macaulay noted, were there any known constraints: 'To sum up...I think it is clear that we are not fettered by the Act of Parliament of 1813; that we are not fettered by any pledge expressed or implied; that we are free to employ our funds as we choose; that we ought to employ them in teaching what is best worth knowing; that English is better worth knowing than Sanscrit or Arabic ... that it is possible to make natives of this country good English scholars and to this end our efforts ought to be directed . . .'

Macaulay's arrogance, a critic avers, was 'not racial; he wanted to see Indians Englishmen in everything but colour. It was cultural. He could see no value in Arabic or Sanskrit literature as against English literature. Did he really prefer Restoration comedy to the Koran, Marlowe and Ben Johnson to the Bhagavad Gita, Pope and Dryden to the Upanishads?'

Macaulay's advocacy of English was helped by powerful forces then operating in the body politic. Many Indians were unmistakably in favour of western education; a number of young men had petitioned his Committee, drawing its attention to their miserable plight, job-wise, after long and elaborate courses in oriental learning; English books had claimed rapid and ready sales while those in the oriental languages had languished for want of buyers. Christian missionaries had lent the new scheme their full-throated support; 'liberally inclined' individuals, both officials as well as non-officials, favoured this course of action; the Charter Act of 1833 had, for the first time accepted, if only theoretically, the policy of admitting Indians to the administrative services.

The above notwithstanding, a number of Orientalists protested against Macaulay's proposed system and quit his Committee. Although, in retrospect, it proved to be far too literary as well as impractical and greatly discouraged elementary education in the vernaculars, English brought among the educated classes an awareness of their country's rich cultural and religious heritage which, in turn, gave birth to nationalism and the struggle for freedom.

John Clive, *Thomas Babington Macaulay*, London, 1973; G. M. Young (ed.), *Speeches of Macaulay with his Minute on Indian Education*, Indian ed., Bombay, 1935, pp. 343–61; Salauddin Ahmed, *Social Policy and Social Change in Bengal, 1818-1835*, Leiden, 1965.

The Sargent Education Report (1944)

Early in 1944, the Central Advisory Board of Education in New Delhi presented its 'scheme' on 'Post-war Educational Development in India.' More popularly, it came to be known as the Sargent Report on Education, after the name of the Board's then Chairman.

The objective which the Board set itself was 'to create in India, in a period of not less than forty years the same standard of educational attainment as had already been admitted in England.' With this end in view, the Report provided for:

a) pre-primary education for children between 3 and 6 years of age;
b) universal, compulsory and free primary or basic education for all children between the ages of 6 and 14;
c) high school education for 6 years for selected children between the ages of 11 and 17;
d) a university course of 3 years beginning after the higher secondary examination, for selected students;
e) technical, commercial and art education for full time and part-time students on an adequate scale;
f) liquidation of adult illiteracy and the development of a public libraries system in about 20 years;
g) full provision for the proper training of teachers required for the implementation and continuation of the scheme;
h) organization of compulsory physical education, medical inspection followed by after-treatment and provision of milk and mid-day meals for under-nourished children;
i) creation of employment bureaus;
j) education of the physically—and mentally—handicapped children;
k) social and recreational facilities on a fairly liberal scale.

The financial implication of the scheme was to involve a total expenditure of Rs 31,260 lakhs of which Rs 27,700 lakhs were to come from public funds.

The Sargent plan was bold in concept and went much further than any other official scheme published until then. It was comprehensive in scope and tried to meet almost every problem of Indian education. It promised higher remuneration to teachers with a view to attracting a better type of person and raising the social status of the profession.

The scheme's critics pointed out that it set before the country a very tame ideal: reaching the educational standard of England of 1939 in not less than 40 years. The result would be, assuming the report were implemented in full, 'that the India of 1984 would still be nearly 50 years behind England.' Again, the cost of implementing the scheme was reckoned to be prohibitive: Rs 313 crores per annum on the basis of population in 1940: 'If the growth of population and an upward swing of the standard of living were kept in view, its total cost would have been in the neighbourhood of Rs 1,000 crores annually.'

Additionally, it was stressed that the scheme merely pin-pointed the ideal to be reached and did not spell out a detailed programme of development. Finally, the only ideal it held before itself was the educational system of England which, in the final analysis, may not have suited Indian conditions. Actually, the experience of such countries as Russia, Denmark, even China, was deemed to be more relevant.

The author of the report, Sir John Philip Sargent, had been Education Commissioner with the Government of India since 1938 and later (1943-8) Educational Adviser to the Government.

Syed Nurullah and J. P. Naik, *A Student's History of Education in India 1800-1961*, Bombay, 1962, pp. 344-54.

Ellenborough (1790-1871)

Edward Law, later Earl of Ellenborough and Governor-General of India, had a long career as an active and vocal Tory parliamentarian with a special interest in military questions. In 1828, after a short spell as Lord Privy Seal in the administration of the Duke of Wellington (1769-1852), he was appointed President of the John Company's (q.v.) Board of Control. In this capacity he maintained direct command and supervision over the Company's Indian administration. He was energetic and popular with officials, opposed to the continuation of a permanent monopoly of the China trade, complained of the slowness of the Company's mode of transacting business and the difficulty of getting the Directors to realize that they were in reality the rulers of a large and powerful state.

After two brief tenures (December 1834-April 1835 and September 1841) in the same post, he was appointed Governor-General of India, and succeeded Auckland (q.v.) on 21 February 1842. On assumption of office, Ellenborough declared his objective to be the pursuit of a peaceful policy, particularly in regard to the Indian princes and conferring benefits on their subject peoples. Yet his tenure was to witness 'a complete reversal' of this professed intent 'to restore peace to Asia.' The fact is that his two years were witness to a series of military adventures including a war of revenge against Afghanistan, aggression against Maharaja Sindhia of Gwalior and the Amirs of Sind (q.v.).

Ellenborough brought the First Anglo-Afghan War (q.v.) to a speedy and successful conclusion, even though critics have charged him with timidity and vacillation as well as a complete disregard for the fate of English prisoners of war. The ostentatious display of retribution that followed has been ridiculed, but apologists point out that it helped to boost the morale of the army. The much-trumpeted sandalwood gates of the temple of Somnath brought all the way from Ghazni, of which so much was made, proved in reality to be those of a mosque! His protagonists however maintain that he had a thorough grasp of every detail of military administration and displayed great zeal and energy in supporting the armies engaged in combat.

Ellenborough's interest in the opening of the Indus to trade dated back to his earlier tenure in the Board of Control. In so far as the British had secured a firm base in Sind (q.v.) during the Afghan operations, he was loath to move out. He therefore found reason enough in the Amirs' allegedly disloyal actions to force on them a new treaty, which deprived them of their sovereign rights. Sir Charles Napier (q.v.), an 'impulsive...and extremely combative' general, was appointed military and political commander and given virtually a free hand. Not a soldier himself, the Governor-General achieved military glory through this intrepid commander who annexed Sind in August 1843—and this despite the objections raised by the British Cabinet and the Court of Directors.

The haste with which the Governor-General announced the Annexation of Sind (q.v.) was matched by the rapidity with which he proceeded to provide for a permanent settlement, again without awaiting instructions from England. He believed the men on the spot could create a more efficient government if unhampered by instructions from the Court of Directors for whom his respect had declined steadily.

Why did he proceed with such haste in annexing Sind? A biographer underlines: 'There were several disadvantages in such precipitate action. It not only irritated the British Cabinet and the Court of Directors...but also carried an appearance of eagerness which tended to throw more heavily upon him the burden of proving that all his measures and intentions had been just and honourable. To all these considerations he was, characteristically, blind....Moreover in the interval between 4 November (1842) when he sent his orders for the new treaties to Napier, and 5 March (1843), when he announced the annexation, he had received no intimation of disapproval from the home authorities with regard either to the principles or the details of the proposed treaties....He concluded, therefore, that the new policy, involving actual possession of certain points in Sind, met with no serious objections from them. His motive was not to achieve a *fait accompli*, but simply to exploit the occasion for effect in India without thought for English opinion.' It is important to remember that Ellenborough 'understood there would be strong objection and expressed his satisfaction that the annexation could hardly be revoked.'

The Governor-General earned further notoriety with his attack on Gwalior. It was mounted because of the alleged fear that the powerful Maratha kingdom might ally itself with the Sikhs against whom the British were then preparing for a clash of arms. Acting on the self-proclaimed doctrine that, as paramount power, the Company was justified in interfering in the internal affairs of an independent state, the Governor-General marched British troops into the state without any ostensible justification. Sindhia was badly defeated and in the subsequent treaty became virtually a British protege, although the state was spared outright annexation. Its forces, which had given an excellent account of themselves on the battlefield, were disbanded except for a contingent of 10,000 men to be officered by the English, and headed by the Resident. The state was to be administered by the British during the minority of its new ruler.

The Court of Directors, already antagonized by Ellenborough's disregard of their instructions, his pompous and impertinent letters and, most of all, by his denial of their right to patronage, could no longer stand his independent stance. In defiance of the Cabinet, they ordered his recall. Yet, to soften the harshness of the blow, he was created Earl of Ellenborough and Viscount Southam for his role in the further growth and expansion of British dominion in India!

Ellenborough's recall, it may be noted, was manoeuvred by the jealousy of the Court of Directors for their own authority over patronage and policy—a jealousy accentuated by steam navigation, by official ineptness in the Board of Control and the Cabinet, and by the Governor-General's own acid pen. It was evident none the less that the Directors lost the main issue—the question of control over Indian affairs—for Ellenborough's brother-in-law was to be appointed Governor-General and given a free hand to carry out his kinsman's policies.

Despite his brief tenure as Governor-General, the marvel is that Ellenborough accomplished as much as he did. As President of the Board of Control (1828-30), his energetic work towards effecting economy and a closer supervision and control over the Company's administration was striking. As Governor-General, his intelligent policy towards the Indian

States (q.v.), his fiscal reforms, his free trade policy and his concept of the binding moral duty of the government and of the official classes towards the subject people of India was noteworthy.

In 1846, Ellenborough was appointed First Lord of Admiralty, but resigned with the fall of government led by Sir Robert Peel (1788-1850) shortly afterwards. In 1858 he became President of the Board of Control for the fourth time. His principal task now was to muffle the cries for vengeance that had been raised in the months immediately following the suppression of the Rebellion of 1857 (q.v.) and to ensure that just and humane treatment was meted out to the 'rebels.' The Government of India Bill (1858) that he drafted was a measure of great complexity and did not elicit much public support. Earlier, his action in sending a despatch concurring in Lord Canning's (q.v.) proclamation of the annexation of the lands of all Talukdars of Oudh (q.v.) barring a few was disclaimed by Disraeli (1804-81) who questioned its propriety in Parliament. Ellenborough took the blame on himself and resigned. From now on he remained out of office albeit, as was his wont, an active and impressive orator in Parliament. He died on 2 December 1871.

The liberalism with which Ellenborough understood the struggles of constitutionalism and nationalism on the continent was conspicuously lacking in his attitude towards demands for a more extended franchise in England. To him, lower electoral qualification meant lower quality of representation in Parliament. Mediocrity and vulgarity, he argued, would replace brains and breeding. It would follow that Disraeli's adventurous scheme of building a Tory democracy by extending the franchise in 1867 distressed him deeply.

Ellenborough has been rated too stiff a Tory in his relations with the public in an age of nascent democracy. Convinced of the beneficence of aristocratic government, he conceived it to be as much his duty as ambition to rule. Proud and haughty in his public manner, with a lofty independence easily mistaken for conceit, he refused any compromise with his own convictions. His impatient utterances, rarely relieved by geniality and frequently marked by sarcasm, often needlessly offended colleagues and opponents alike. In sum, his biographer maintains, he allowed his great talents to be overmatched in contemporary eyes by his striking defects.

Ellenborough was rated an authority on military matters and was conspicuous as an orator. Vain and often theatrical, he was at the same time masterful and self-confident.

Albert H. Imlah, *Lord Ellenborough: A Biography of Edward Law, Earl of Ellenborough, Governor-General of India*, Cambridge (Mass.), 1939; Robert A. Huttenback, *British Relations with Sind*, Cambridge, 1962.

Mountstuart Elphinstone (1778–1859)

Born in 1778, Mountstuart Elphinstone was, in the early half of the 19th century, one of the great Indian administrators in a long and distinguished line that included Munro (q.v.), Metcalfe (q.v.), and Malcolm (q.v.). He came to India as a 'writer' and was among the first to be trained at the Fort William College and groomed for service during Wellesley's (q.v.) tenure as Governor-General.

Inducted into the Bengal civil service, Elphinstone reached Calcutta (1796) and was posted to Banaras. Essentially an introvert, he read extensively and, under the influence of such well-known authorities as Samuel Davis and Edward Stratchey, began a serious study of Indian literature and languages, the latter resulting before long in the compilation and publication of dictionaries in Gujarati and Marathi.

Appointed Assistant to the Governor-General's Agent in Poona (1802), Elphinstone displayed great zeal and military skill in the Second Anglo-Maratha War (q.v.) at the conclusion of which he became Resident (1804-8) at the court of the Bhonsle ruler at Nagpur. In 1808 he was selected to head a diplomatic mission to Kabul. The mission itself proved abortive, but its result was an important publication, *An Account of the Kingdom of Caubul and its Dependencies in Persia, Tartary and India* (1815).

As Resident at the Peshwa's court in Poona (1810-19), Elphinstone proved his worth as a versatile and able soldier-statesman and administrator. He maintained, as far as possible, indigenous institutions and practices (e.g., use of the vernacular in courts, the panchayat system, etc.) except where he felt these hampered good administration. He was instrumental in bringing about an understanding between the Peshwa and his jagirdars. In 1817 he was superseded temporarily by General Hislop and John Malcolm, but resumed charge when hostilities flared up in the Third Anglo-Maratha War (q.v.). After chastizing Peshwa Baji Rao II (q.v.) and forcing him to surrender, he installed the Raja of Satara as nominal head of the Maratha states.

In recognition of his services, Elphinstone was offered the governorship of Bombay in 1819, an office he continued to hold until 1827. Bishop Reginald Heber (1783-1826) was a witness to his successful rule and the peace and tranquillity that prevailed in his domain.

Far in advance of his time in the views he held on social reform and a free press, his report on education (1824) and the codification of laws (executed in 1827) are clear evidence of his liberal and humanitarian policies. His code of laws popularly known as the 'Elphinstone Code' continued to operate for well-nigh 40 years, while his system of public education gave Bombay a head-on start over other parts of the country. A college was founded in his name and endowed for teaching subjects in which he took the deepest and most abiding interest.

A firm believer in the ultimate disappearance of the British empire in India, Elphinstone's aim was to educate and train Indians so as to enable them to assume eventual control. To this end, he encouraged the teaching of European sciences and the creation of trusted posts for Indians.

Elphinstone refused a baronetcy, the Governor-Generalship of Canada, and of India, the Order of the Bath with a seat in the Privy Council. Instead he retired quietly in 1828 after 33 years service in India. On return to England (1829) after a tour of Europe, he devoted his time to study. In later years he was critical of Dalhousie's (q.v.) policy of unrestrained annexation and it would appear that his opinion influenced the altered approach to the subject adopted after 1857.

Elphinstone's attitude to life was that of an ancient philosopher—sceptical, retiring, unselfish, modest. No wonder he achieved the highest offices of state, was consulted as an oracle by the rulers of his country, who rated him as the Nestor of Indian statesmanship, and yet never derived the smallest personal advantage from his position.

Elphinstone's *History of India* was completed and published in 1841, a work for which he has been called the Tacitus of modern historians, but the *The Rise of British Power in the East* was published posthumously (1887). He died on 20 November 1859.

An Indian biographer is fulsome in his praise: 'A man of extraordinary ability, keen emotions for the good in life, great love of learning and nature, one of the finest Englishmen that came to India. A diplomat with a sense of honour and devotion to duty rarely found among any race of men....He [Elphinstone] belonged to that group of statesmen who embodied the best traditions of their race....He is a unique personality in Anglo-Indian history...a lesson in good and honourable living.'

A percipient English writer has noted that, after retiring from India—'the courtier's, soldier's, scholar's eye, tongue, sword' were now to be given to friends and books. Elphinstone was to live for another 30 years—'one of the most selfless and lovable men who ever achieved a name in the world of action.'

R. D. Choksey, *Mountstuart Elphinstone, the Indian Years, 1796-1827,* Bombay, 1971; Philip Woodruff (Mason), *The Men Who Ruled India,* 2 vols, London, 1953, I; Olaf Caroe, 'Introduction' to *An Account of the Kingdom of Caubul,* 2 vols., Oxford, reprint, 1972, pp. v-xxv; *DNB,* VI, pp. 744-6 (Henry George Keene).

Factory Act (1881)

The first Factory Act in India was passed in March 1881, and enforced four months later, in July. The need for such legislation was brought home by the growing number of workers employed; by 1880 there were 39,537 of them in cotton and 27,494 in jute mills. Initially proposed and drafted by Lytton (q.v.) who, it is said, acted under pressure from the Lancashire weaving mills, it was opposed by the various provincial governments in India and duly shelved. Ripon (q.v.), however, reopened the issue and arrived at a compromise solution with the conflicting interests involved.

As finally adopted, the Act applied to all parts of India and laid down, *inter alia,* that no child below 7 years of age was to be employed. Those between 7 and 12 were to work for only 9 hours a day; they were not to operate any dangerous machinery or be employed in two different factories on the same day. Four holidays a month and a break of an hour during working hours were provided for. There were no restrictions on the employment of adult labour, but provision was made to guard against such parts of machinery as could be dangerous if left unfenced, and for the reporting of accidents. The provincial governments were required to appoint supervisors to ensure that the law was properly implemented. The Act was not to apply to indigo, coffee or tea plantations.

Thanks to an almost complete lack of adequate inspection machinery, the Act remained a dead letter in nearly all provinces. Most factories worked from day-break to sunset, Sundays being usually working days—and if declared holidays, used for cleaning. While a small number of newspapers welcomed the Act as a humanitarian measure, a majority condemned it as an effort to strangle the infant cotton and jute industries. It was held that British industrialists, afraid of the challenge of the Indian cotton industry, were keen to impose restrictive laws that deprived the latter of its advantage of cheap labour. Additionally, it was made out that the new law was a result of the Tory anxiety to win over Lancashire, which had become alarmed at the growth of Indian industry. A feature of the Act was what its critics called an element of racial discrimination in as much as British-dominated tea, coffee and indigo plantations were exempt from its operation, without any plausible rationale. Indirectly, the Act was responsible for giving a boost to the Swadeshi Movement (q.v.).

Under the Act, the term 'factory' was defined as 'any premises (other than indigo, tea, coffee plantations) wherein work was carried on for not less than four months in any year by any process utilizing mechanical or steam power and wherein not less than 100 persons were employed.' The Act may be regarded 'a pioneering measure.' Ripon's attitude of reconciliation contrasted with the lukewarm posture of the Secretary of State, Lord Hartington, and the opposition of a majority of the members of his Council including Sir Ashley Eden (q.v.) was the more remarkable. It was the Governor-General's firm determination mingled with a conciliatory spirit that put the new law on the statute book

V. C. P. Chaudhary, *Imperial Policy of the British in India 1876-1890,* Calcutta, 1968; S. Gopal, *British Policy in India 1858–1905,* Cambridge, 1965; L. P. Mathur, *Lord Ripon's Administration in India 1880-1884*, New Delhi, 1972.

Mohammad Farrukh Siyar (r. 1713–19)

The grandson of Bahadur Shah I (q.v.), Mohammad Farrukh Siyar was the second son of Azim-us-Shan and succeeded to the throne largely with the aid of the two Sayyid Brothers (q.v.) whom he later adequately rewarded. Initially he proclaimed himself emperor at Patna (April 1712), but it was not until he had defeated his uncle, the emperor Jahandar Shah outside Agra (10 January 1713), that he enthroned himself. Soon after arriving in Delhi, he had gone through the customary blood-bath, including the murder of his predecessor, a number of likely claimants to the throne as well as some powerful nobles.

Farrukh Siyar's short-lived reign was marked by the ruthless suppression of Banda Bahadur (q.v.) and a settlement of the Mughal-Maratha conflict effected by the younger Sayyid, Husain Ali Khan. It was the emperor's refusal to accept the accord, coupled with his numerous intrigues to break the shackles imposed by the (Sayyid) brothers that led finally to his discomfiture. Another significant event of his reign was the grant of a royal *firman* to the John Company (q.v.) for free trade as well as permission to purchase 37 districts in Bengal.

Three military campaigns were undertaken during his reign to curb the incipient rebellions in the north. In Marwar, Ajit Singh had reasserted his independence and even occupied Ajmer. He was worsted in battle by Husain Ali Khan; in return, the Rajput ruler promised his daughter in marriage to the emperor, while his son Abhay Singh, was to serve at the imperial court. In the Panjab, Banda Bahadur was defeated, marched a captive to Delhi and brutally done to death. The Jat ruler, Churaman, was also brought to heel.

Farrukh Siyar's reign was witness to strong factions at the Mughal court vying with each other for power and personal aggrandizement. The Sayyid brothers wanted to lord over all, but had powerful rivals in the Alamgiri nobles, including Zulfikar Khan, Nizam-ul-Mulk (q.v.) and Mohammad Amin Khan. In so far as Husain Ali had repaired to the south (1715-18) and come to a comprehensive settlement with Raja Shahu (q.v.) which the emperor had understandably refused to ratify, the Sayyid sought Maratha help to break down imperial opposition and buttress his own position. As Husain Ali and the Peshwa Balaji Vishwanath (q.v.) marched north, the emperor found himself in dire straits.

In the 1715–18 interval, Farrukh Siyar had, through ill-advised policies, managed to annoy his friends, including Mir Jumla, Ajit Singh and Nizam-ul-Mulk. They had little confidence in his strength while Abdullah Khan, in the absence of his younger brother, had also felt increasingly frustrated. On 22 February 1719, Husain Ali had an audience with the emperor after posting his men at strategic points in the fort. The differences between the two could not be reconciled and 4 days later his brother, Abdullah Khan, had a stormy interview with Farrukh Siyar, during which the latter refused to make any further concessions, openly abused the wazir, and then retired into the harem.

Earlier, the Minister had entered the palace with Ajit Singh and his own adherents and troops, occupied the gates, office rooms and bed chambers, and placed his own guards on all sides. That afternoon, Husain Ali had marched into the city from the suburbs at the head of 30-40,000 men and a strong park of artillery. Next day, there was an unseemly brawl in the streets and the wildest 'rumours spread in the city and added to the confusion and unrest.'

All this notwithstanding, Abdullah Khan was yet in favour of keeping Farrukh Siyar on the throne and to treat him 'as Mahabat Khan had treated Jahangir' (i.e., to keep him a virtual prisoner in his hands). Thereby the brothers hoped to secure the reality of power 'without incurring the odium of raising their hands against the lawful sovereign.' Husain Ali, however, was impatient and precipitate. He demanded immediate action, failing which he threatened 'to enter the palace for settling the business.'

Farrukh Siyar was increasingly isolated and offered a tempting prey to his adversaries. The principal nobles too 'veered round in favour of deposition', even Khan-i-Dauran and Ajit Singh had concurred in this course of action. As the emperor refused to come out of the harem, a party of Afghan mercenaries was sent in. They dragged him out, blinded him and threw him into jail. A few weeks later he was murdered (29 April 1719)—the first instance of a Mughal ruler being done to death by one of his nobles. His remains were consigned in the crypt of Humayun's tomb.

A weak ruler, Farrukh Siyar was 'strong neither for evil nor for good...For seven years the state was in a condition of unstable equilibrium .... Feeble, false, cowardly, contemptible, it is impossible either to admire or regret him.' Yet his treatment by the Sayyids left a lot to be desired: 'Blinding a deposed king was the fixed usage.... But the severity of the subsequent confinement was excessive; and the taking of the captive's life was an extremity entirely uncalled for.'

Farukh Siyar had proved, it is said, to be 'the most incapable ruler of the house of Babur' that had so far occupied the throne of Delhi.

Ashirbadi Lal Srivastav, *The Mughal Empire (1526-1803* A.D.*)*, 4th rev. ed., Agra, 1964, pp. 425-9; Satish Chandra, *Parties and Politics at the Mughal Court, 1707-1740*, Aligarh, 1959, pp. 136-42, 163-5; Richard Burn (ed.), *Cambridge History of India*, IV, pp. 333-9.

Thomas Forsyth (1827–86)

Thomas Douglas Forsyth joined the East India Company's (q.v.) service in 1848, after his training at Haileybury College (q.v.). Later, at the Company's college in Calcutta, he acquired a good knowledge of Persian, Hindustani and Hindi. He served in various administrative capacities in the Panjab, while his work as special commissioner for tracking the 'mutineers' in the Rebellion of 1857 (q.v.) and looking into Nana Sahib's (q.v.) papers, was especially commended and brought him well-deserved praise. Forsyth is, however, best known for giving a boost to trade with Central Asia on the premise that an upsurge of British influence in that area would serve as a healthy check on Russian advance. He travelled extensively in this region, gathering important political and geographical information and was partly responsible for the alarming suggestion that Russia had easy access to India through Central Asia.

With a view to promoting trade, Forsyth visited Leh in 1867 and organized a fair at Palampur in Kangra to attract merchants from eastern Turkestan. Two years later, he accompanied a mission from Yakub Beg, then Amir of Yarkand and Kashgar, which had arrived in Simla. The latter had expressed a desire to establish relations with India and Forsyth was instructed to acquire information about the people and the country. This mission was not as successful as had been hoped but 4 years later (1873) Forsyth was charged afresh with concluding a commercial treaty with the Kashgar Amir. Results were gratifying and, with the removal of all hindrances to trade, it was hoped great prospects awaited this new opening. On return, he was honoured with the KCSI.

Earlier, in 1869, Forsyth had visited St Petersburg to delineate the respective British and Russian spheres of influence and to map out the territories of the Afghan Amir. It is said that he succeeded in establishing that the disputed districts belonged to the Amir and 'obtained from the Russian government an acknowledgement to that effect.'

In 1874 Forsyth was appointed an additional member of the Governor-General's Council. A year later, as envoy to Burma, he worked out a settlement about the independence of the Karen states. He resigned in 1877 to take over as director of the Indian Railway Company, visiting India six years later to check on the progress of its work. He died in 1886.

G. J. Alder, *British India's Northern Frontier 1865-95*, London, 1963; *DNB*, VII, pp. 473–74 (Edward James Rapson).

The Fourteen Points (1929)

At a meeting of the All-India Muslim League (q.v.) held in Delhi on 28 March, 1929 M. A. Jinnah (q.v.) presented a 'draft resolution' containing 'Fourteen Points' which had earlier been propounded by the Muslim

Conference held at Delhi in December 1928. (The resolution of the Conference is in fact dated 1 January, 1929.)

The resolution in question noted that the ML was 'unable' to accept the Nehru Report (q.v.) and that 'no scheme for the future Government of India will be acceptable to Mussulmans of India until and unless the following basic principles are given effect to and provisions are embodied therein to safeguard their rights and interests.' *Ad seriatim*, the 'principles' listed were:

1. The form of the future Constitution should be federal with the residuary powers vested in the Provinces.
2. All legislatures in the country and other elected bodies shall be constituted on the definite principle of adequate and effective representation of minorities in every province without reducing the majority in any province to a minority or even equality.
3. A uniform measure of autonomy shall be guaranteed to all Provinces.
4. In the Central Legislature, Mussulmans' representation shall not be less than one-third.
5. Representation of communal groups shall continue to be by means of separate electorates 'as at present'; provided it shall be open to any community, at any time, to abandon the separate electorate in favour of joint electorates.
6. Any territorial redistribution that might at any time be necessary shall not in any way affect the Muslim majority in Panjab, Bengal and the North-West Frontier Province (N. W. F. P.) (q.v.).
7. Full religious liberty, i.e. liberty of belief, worship and observance, propaganda, association and education shall be granted to all communities.
8. No bill or resolution or any part thereof shall be passed in any legislature or any other elected body if three-fourths of the members of any community in that particular body opposes such a bill, resolution or part thereof on the ground that it would be injurious to the interests of that community or, in the alternative, such other method is devised as may be found feasible and practicable to deal with such cases.
9. Sind should be separated from the Bombay Presidency.
10. Reforms should be introduced in the N.W.F.P. and Baluchistan on the same footing as in other Provinces.
11. Provision shall be made in the Constitution giving Mussulmans an adequate share, along with the other Indians, in all the Services of the State and in local self-governing bodies having due regard to the requirements of efficiency.
12. The Constitution should embody adequate safeguards for the protection of Muslim culture and for the protection and promotion of Muslim education, language, personal laws and Muslim charitable institutions and for their due share in the grants-in-aid given by self-governing bodies.
13. No Cabinet, either Central or Provincial, should be formed without there being a proportion of at least one-third Muslim Ministers.
14. No change shall be made in the Constitution by the Central Legislature except with the concurrence of the States constituting the Indian Federation.

The draft resolution mentions an alternative to the above provision in the following terms, noting *inter alia* that 'in the circumstances'

Mussulmans will not consent to joint electorates unless Sind is actually constituted into a separate Province and reforms in fact are introduced in the N.W.F.P. and Baluchistan on the same footing as in other Provinces. Further, it is provided that there shall be reservation of seats according to the Muslim population in the various Provinces, but where Muslims are in majority they shall not contest more seats than their population warrants.

The question of excess representation of Mussulmans over and above their population in Provinces where they are in minority is to be considered hereafter.

It may be useful to sum up developments preceding the Delhi meeting of the League. In the words of Choudhry Khaliquzzaman, 'Three months after the Muslim All-Parties Conference at Delhi (31 December 1928) the Muslim League Session which was postponed at Calcutta met again, in the last week of March 1929, under the presidentship of Mr Jinnah at Delhi. The Khilafatists had gone fully prepared to fight for the Nehru report and others were equally determined to see it rejected. Mr Jinnah was very late in coming to the session as he was negotiating with the Sir Shafi group their acceptance of the fourteen points.... Immediately after the election of the President (Dr Alam), discussion on the Nehru report started and was in full swing when Rafi Kidwai called me outside to inform me that there was a danger that there would be a mass raid on the hall. Hardly had he finished talking when hundreds of people from outside knocked down the doors of the hall and threw out the supporters of the Nehru report one by one, clearing the hall. Mr Jinnah came in soon after and in this meeting the fourteen points which were accepted by the Muslim League, with the modificaton that when all the other points had been accepted by the Congress, the League might agree to joint electorates. These points were later described by the Hindu press as Mr Jinnah's fourteen points.'

Another footnote may be added. At its Calcutta session in December 1928, the Muslim League had failed to come to an agreement on the recommendations of the Nehru committee. An influential section of Muslims had held a separate meeting under the presidency of the Aga Khan (q.v.). The fact is that the Muslims were deeply divided. Jinnah's draft resolution, reproduced above, 'was designed to accommodate' the various points of view. Three principal sections among the Muslims can be identified: one for the adoption of the Nehru report, another for its rejection and a third for a compromise. Attempts to reach an agreement at the Delhi session of the League where the 'fourteen points' were spelt out 'ended in failure.'

Gwyer and Appadorai, I, pp. 245-7; A. C. Banerjee, *Documents*, III, pp. 245-8; C. H. Philips (ed.), *The Evolution of India and Pakistan 1858 to 1947: Select Documents*, Oxford, 1962, pp. 235-7; Nripendra Nath Mitra (ed.), *Indian Quarterly Register*, vol. 1 (1929), pp. 365-6.

Andrew Fraser (1848–1919)

Andrew Henderson Leith Fraser who was born at Bombay had a brilliant academic career at the Edinburgh Academy and (Edinburgh) University before he passed the open examination for the Indian Civil Service in 1869. He was posted 2 years later to the Central Provinces, where he served for the next 27 years in various executive capacities. On the eve of his retirement (1898), he was appointed Secretary in the Home Department of the Government of India and later, Chief Commissioner of the Central Provinces. His interest in and knowledge of Indian administration at the district and village level warranted his appointment as President of the Police Commission (1901), which Curzon (q.v.) had set up. Credit for the resultant improvement in the police service goes to the reforms instituted on its recommendations. His biographers have rated it as his 'most substantial claim to remembrance.' So impressed was Curzon with Fraser's ability that he kept the Lieutenant-Governorship of Bengal without a permanent incumbent for over a year, until he was free to take over, in November 1903.

Fraser was among the foremost advocates of the Partition of Bengal (q.v.) and co-authored, with Herbert Hope Risley (1851–1911), an extension and enlargement of the original scheme. He had urged Curzon that there was no contact between government and people in Bengal and that only in a smaller province was more efficient and sympathetic administration possible.

Fraser reportedly did not suggest the partition of Bengal—indeed he is known to have criticized it in good measure *before* its adoption. But it is not unlikely that he hesitated to oppose a plan that Curzon had owned. By the severance of Dacca and Mymensing, both hot-beds of revolutionary activity, he hoped to segregate the unfriendly, if not seditious movements from spreading all over Bengal. He was convinced that opposition to the partition was motivated by the Calcutta bar and the 'native' press for purely selfish reasons. Contrary to his expectations, the administrative burden was increased a great deal by the partition, as the Government was caught unawares by the widespread agitation that now set in. In meeting the storm that broke out, Fraser was inhibited by his liberal dislike for all repressive measures and himself gave a fine example of great personal courage in the face of repeated attempts on his own life.

A great supporter of unhampered Christian missionary activity, Fraser was chosen (1907) moderator of the Presbyterian Church Assembly in India. He retired a year later and lived in Scotland till his death in 1919. Earlier (1911), he had published a book of reminiscences, *Among Indian Rajahs and Ryots*.

Fraser's impressions of India were affectionate and generous: 'I have found among the people of India multitudes who have elicited my kindliest feelings and who have shown the kindliest feelings towards myself and I have found not a few whom I value as the worthiest of my friends.' And again, 'I am very proud of India....I am proud of her possibilities and of the great opportunities she gives of work and influence. I am proud of her people whose patience in suffering and response to kindness have won my love.'

A. H. L. Fraser, *Among Indian Rajahs and Ryots: A Civil Servant's Recollections and Impressions of Thirty-seven Years of Work and Sport in the Central Provinces and*

Bengal, London, 3rd ed., 1912; *The Administration of Bengal under Sir Andrew Fraser 1903–1908*, Calcutta, 1909; *DNB 1912–21*, pp. 197-8 (Seymour Vesey Fitz Gerald).

John Bampfylde Fuller (1854–1935)

John (later Sir John) Bampfylde Fuller came out to India in 1875 having successfully competed and trained for the Indian Civil Service. His outstanding performance in the offices he held earned him rapid promotions, moving from the erstwhile North-Western Provinces (later the United Provinces), where he was incharge of revenue settlement and agriculture (1885-92) and continuing in the same department at Calcutta, where he moved in 1901. He officiated as Commissioner, Central Provinces (1894) and was Acting Chief Commissioner of Assam in 1900. He returned to Assam as Chief Commissioner in 1902, in which position he catered to the interests of European tea planters. He lent full support to Curzon's (q.v.) plan for the Partition of Bengal (q.v.), convinced that the Muslims of East Bengal favoured such a move.

With the partition of Bengal (1905), Fuller was appointed Lieutenant-Governor of the newly-carved province of Eastern Bengal and Assam, a post in which he was to earn a great measure of notoriety at the hands of the Indian National Congress (q.v.) in general and of the Hindus in particular. Measures which he deemed necessary to overcome lawlessness and intimidation were magnified beyond recognition by an allegedly hostile, if 'unscrupulous', press and public opinion. On the other hand, the Muslims, who constituted two-thirds of the population under his charge, rallied to his support.

In pursuance of his strong, if predetermined convictions, he left no stone unturned to suppress the growing public agitation against the partition. Thus he openly favoured the Muslims, giving them greater representation in the provincial administration and, with the help of the law courts and the police, smothered the dissenting voice of Hindus. In the process, the political atmosphere in the new province became explosive with Hindu-Muslim riots a frequent occurrence. Fuller banned the singing of 'Bande Matram', as a sequel to which came police action at a largely attended political conference at Barisal. This provoked a strong and stormy reaction in the press and he was obliged to withdraw his impugned ban. Fuller's approach in all these matters, it has been said, was 'more or less Curzonian.'He was bitter against the Bengalis—'their villainy as landlords', he declared, 'is damnable.' His remark about 'favouring the Mahometan wife' gained wide notoriety and showed him in extremely partisan colours.

Meanwhile, Fuller's policies notwithstanding, the growing popularity of the Boycott (q.v.) movement upset him tremendously. Consequently he attempted, unsuccessfully, to track down and punish all those who distributed inflammatory pamphlets. A decision taken by the teachers and students of two schools in Sirajganj to prevent the sale of foreign goods, he considered to be unforgivable. Accordingly, he asked Calcutta University to derecognise the schools. Minto (q.v.), then Governor-General, considered his action tactless and asked him to withdraw his recommendation. Impulsive and over-confident of popular backing, Fuller stuck to his decision. In a petulant letter to the Governor-General he even hinted that he might have to reconsider his position if his advice on this particular matter were not accepted. This was seized upon by the Government as a pretext for informing him, to his great chagrin, that his 'resignation' had been accepted.

Minto's decision was to mark the end of those 'ten unquiet months' during which Fuller had held charge of the new province. John Buchan, Minto's biographer, has maintained that the Governor-General had carefully concluded that Fuller 'lacked the qualities of patience and discretion which could alone, in time, abate the partition ferment'; that his resignation 'was not quite unwelcome' either to the Viceroy or the Secretary of State. Fuller, it has been held, was himself responsible for his undoing. 'People ask me', Sir Andrew Fraser (q.v.) noted, 'was it Lord Minto's doing or Mr Morley's; I say, it was Fuller's doing.'

Muslims protested loudly, albeit in vain. The Governor was given a touching send-off while newspaper reports were full of Muslim leaders and organizations throughout the country condemning the Government's action and praising Fuller. They protested, although seemingly vainly, against his removal. Morley, it is said, debated whether to appoint him to his India Council, but held back since his action might have been construed by nationalist opinion as tantamount to condoning Fuller's acts of omission and commission.

After his return to England, Fuller wrote extensively on India and, later, on philosophy. He served in World War I as a temporary officer and interested himself in local politics and philanthropic activities. His non-controversial *Studies of Indian Life and Sentiment* (1910) and *The Empire of India* (1913) were followed by some philosophical works: *Life and Human Nature* (1914) and *The Tyranny of the Mind* (1935). His reminiscences, *Some Personal Experiences*, appeared in 1930. He died 5 years later, in November 1935.

S. R. Wasti, *Lord Minto and the Indian Nationalist Movement,* London, 1964, pp. 34–52; M. N. Das, *India Under Morley and Minto,* London, 1964.

Treaty of Fyzabad (1775)

Concluded on 21 May 1775 after the accession of Nawab Asaf-ud-Daula (q.v.) in Oudh (q.v.), it was deemed necessary as the John Company (q.v.) ruled the earlier treaty (1765) to be personal to Shuja-ud-Daulah (q.v.).

The 7-article treaty laid down *inter alia* that:

i) the contracting parties with a view to maintaining reciprocal friendship 'shall not for any cause or under any pretence' encourage their ryots in committing hostilities and disturbances;

ii) the Nawab undertook 'never to entertain or receive' Kassim Ali Khan [better known as Mir Kasim (q.v.)], the ex-Subedar of Bengal and Sumro, 'the murderer of the English.' Should he lay hands on them 'he will, out of friendship make them prisoners' and deliver them to the Company;

iii) the districts of Karra and Allahabad shall remain in the Nawab's possession, 'on the same footing' as the subah of Oudh;

iv) for his defence the Nawab gave to the Company 'of his own free will and accord' sovereignty in perpetuity over all the districts dependent upon Raja Chait Singh (q.v.);

v) the Nawab shall pay for his 'aid and assistance' for a brigade of English troops, 'when stationed with him', a sum of Rs 2,60,000 per month;

vi) 'Should the Nawab need assistance from the Company' for the defence of any other of his territories, he would fix an amount 'proportional to the service.'

The treaty is referred to as a 'Translation of the proposed Articles of the treaty' with the Nawab. Appended are two 'agreements' under the Nawab's seal: one, transferring the 'possession and sovereignty' in perpetuity of Raja Chait Singh's districts to the Company, at the expiry of 'one month and a half'; two, affirming that the balance due to the Company on account of the districts of Karra and Allahabad and the salary of the troops 'according to the engagements' of the late Shuja-ud-Daulah 'shall be paid to them as it becomes due, without any dispute.'

For the new Nawab, the treaty proved to be an expensive arrangement, for while it increased his liabilities it sharply decreased his revenues. *Inter alia*, the Nawab had agreed to an increase in the payment for the Company's troops by Rs 50,000 a month (from Rs 2,10,000 to Rs 2,60,000), paying extra whenever their services were required against an outside power. Again, he had ceded them the rich districts of Banaras, Ghazipur and Jaunpur, belonging to Raja Chait Singh.

Warren Hastings (q.v.) had opposed the treaty as being at once unjust and impolitic. He further held that it was tantamount to a reversal of his earlier policy of traditional friendship with Oudh. He was, however, outvoted by a majority in his Council who ruled in its favour.

Aitchison, II, pp. 86–90; Dodwell, *CHI*, V, p. 233.

Malhar Rao, Gaekwad of Baroda (d. 1882)

Malhar Rao ascended the gaddi of Baroda in 1870. Just released from captivity for being involved in a plot to murder his predecessor, Khande Rao, he succeeded to a virtually bankrupt treasury. Before long, he embarked on a policy of punishing all those who held positions of responsibility and who, according to his line of reasoning, had thus been a party to his discomfiture. His expenses far outstripped his revenues, resulting in increased oppression of the people. The Bombay Government, on the basis of reports received from the British Resident, Colonel (later Sir) Robert Phayre (1820-97) felt compelled to intervene. A 5-member commission of inquiry was set up in 1873 to investigate complaints of maladministration. In its report, submitted in 1874, the commission held that conditions in the state bordered on the chaotic. *Inter alia*, it expressed the view that it was 'impossible to avoid the conviction from the vindictive nature of His Highness Malhar Rao's proceedings and his violent and spoliatory treatment ... that he is not a Prince who can be reasonably expected to introduce of himself the change of system absolutely necessary to reform existing abuses and to place the administration on a footing....'

In the event, Malhar Rao was warned (July 1874) that if he did not reform before 31 December 1875 he could be 'deposed from power.' His right to choose his Dewan being recognized, he appointed Dadabhai Naoroji (q.v.), an arrangement disliked by the Resident. The latter's hostile attitude led Malhar Rao to ask the Viceroy for his removal. Lord Northbrook (q.v.), then Governor-General, concurred, but before the new incumbent could arrive, Phayre discovered some dark sediment at the bottom of his glass of sherbet served at the palace and concluded that the Maharaja was privy to a plot to murder him.

Phayre was soon replaced by Sir Lewis Pelly (1825-92) who was designated 'Agent to the Governor-General.' Presently, the pace of reform in the state was interrupted by differences between Malhar Rao and Naoroji, leading to the latter's resignation. In January 1875 Malhar Rao was arrested, and the State's administration put under Pelly while a 6-member commission of inquiry under Sir Richard Couch, Chief Justice of the Calcutta High Court, was ordered. Among its 3 Indian members were the Maharajas of Jaipur and Gwalior and Sir Dinkar Rao (q.v.). The Commission could not agree on a verdict: its 3 English members found Malhar Rao guilty; one of the 3 Indian members (Jaipur) concluded he was in no way implicated in the attempted poisoning, the other two holding that the charges were not proved.

The Indian press was unfriendly towards Phayre and voiced strong support for the Gaekwad. It was even suggested that because of the Resident's enmity towards the ruler 'he himself had planned the entire poisoning affair' so as to ruin the latter. The press unanimously held the view that the charges against the Gaekwad were not proved and that he should be restored to the gaddi.

The Viceroy, dead set against restoring the Gaekwad, told his political superiors that the act would 'be a miscarriage of justice and a fatal political error [for] it would seriously weaken the British Government in India and the position of British Residents at Native Courts.'

Understandably, Northbrook and his Council recommended deposition, with which Whitehall grudgingly concurred viewing it as 'an act of political necessity, on the ground of his unfitness to govern and the bad moral effect of restoring him.'

It has been suggested that the government's attitude, inspired as it was by its earlier dispute in regard to procedure (which had gone in favour of the Gaekwad) as well as its refusal to accept Malhar Rao's legitimate son as heir, was both vindictive and tantamount to abuse of authority. The Governor-General had suggested that 'Paramountcy combined with usage had conferred on the Government of India a power halted by its own discretion.' His biographer has maintained that 'while it is true that Northbrook's action may be criticized because of its serious political effect, the alternative may have been even worse.'

A constitutional expert, while holding that the deposition was 'not inconsistent' with the John Company's (q.v.) treaties has expressed the view that the 'extreme measures'—the exclusion of Malhar Rao's 'issue from all rights, honours and privileges' appertaining 'to the sovereignty' of Baroda—indicate that 'he was punished for charges of which he had not been found guilty'; that the 'constructive interpretation' of treaties 'was indeed pushed too far'; that here the doctrine of intervention was linked with the paramount power's obligation of 'protecting the people of India from oppression.'

As a saving grace, Baroda was not annexed, while a former Gaekwad's widow, Jamuna Bai, was allowed to adopt an heir. In the result, Sayaji Rao was proclaimed the new ruler under the regency of T. Madhava Rao (q.v.). The deposed ruler was deported (April 1875) to Madras where he resided until his death in 1882.

Edward C. Moulton, *Lord Northbrook's Administration 1872-1876*, Bombay, 1968; M. P. Kamerkar, 'A Study in British Paramountcy: Baroda (1870–75)', *IHC*, Proceedings of the Twenty-fourth session, Delhi, 1961, Calcutta, 1963, pp 225–36; V. G. Khobrekar, 'How Baroda became a problem state during 1870-1874 A.D.', *IHC*, Proceedings of the Thirtieth session, Bhagalpur, 1968, Patna, 1969, pp 267-73; A. C. Banerjee, *Constitutional History of India*, 3 vols. II, pp. 490–3.

Treaty of Gandamak (1879)

The treaty of Gandamak (also spelt Guradamak, after a town about 30 km west of Jalalabad on the road from Peshawar to Kabul) between Yakub Beg, son and successor of Sher Ali, and the British marked the end of the first phase in the Second Anglo-Afghan War (q.v.). The compact signed by the Afghan Amir in the British camp on 26 May 1879 was ratified by the Governor-General four days later.

Inter alia, the treaty laid down that: (i) the districts of Kurram, Sibi and Pishin were to remain under British administration and any surplus of their revenue over expenditure to be handed over to the Amir; (ii) the Khyber and Michni passes were to be held by the British, who were additionally to retain control of all relations with the independent tribes inhabiting the territories directly connected with these passes; (iii) the Amir was to conduct his foreign relations only through the Government in India and to encourage, and protect, trade between India and Afghanistan; (iv) India was to assist the Amir with men, money and munitions in case of an external threat to his authority and pay him and his successors an annual subsidy of Rs 6 lakhs.

It has been held that the treaty deprived Afghanistan 'for the first time' of its 'traditional character of a buffer state', with its ruler virtually 'a feudatory' of the British Crown— his position 'somewhat analogous' to that of an Indian prince.

Aitchison, XIII, pp. 240–42; D. P. Singhal, *India and Afghanistan 1876-1907*, St Lucia, 1963.

Mohandas Karamchand Gandhi (1869–1948)

The fourth child of his parents, Mohandas was born at Porbandar, a coastal town in the Kathiawar peninsula of Gujarat, on 2 October 1869. His father, Karamchand Gandhi, who belonged to the Mod bania sub-caste of the Vaisya or merchant caste, was a Vaishnava and chief minister of Rajkot; earlier, Karamchand's father had held that office in Porbandar and Junagadh. Mohandas' mother was deeply religious and spent much of her time in prayer and worship.

In childhood, Mohandas is said to have been greatly impressed by the legends of Shravana's filial devotion or of Raja Harishchandra's sufferings for the cause of truth. In 1881, at the age of 12, he was married, without foreknowledge, to Kasturba, the daughter of a merchant of Porbandar. Four sons were born to the couple. At school (1881–7), a small, quiet boy, Mohandas made a barely average student and had no interest in sports. During 1888 he was briefly in college and later that year left for England to study law. It may be added that Mohandas' childhood ambition was to study medicine but, this being viewed as tantamount to defiling the community, his father prevailed upon him to study law instead.

When leaving for England, Gandhi promised his mother he would abstain from wine, women and meat. To start with, Mohandas is said to have dressed fashionably and took dancing as well as elocution lessons, trying generally to conform to English standards and ways. This he soon gave up and reverted to a life of extreme frugality, becoming, in practice, a more zealous vegetarian than ever before. It was while abroad that Gandhi's interest in religion took deep root; his approach was eclectic, it embraced all faiths. He made a close study of the *Bhagavad Gita* and was to draw inspiration from it all his life.

On return from England, Gandhi unsuccessfully attempted to practise law at Rajkot and later Bombay. Then, for a brief period, he served as a lawyer for the prince of Porbandar. To start with, it is said that he was nervous and lacked confidence as a speaker; more, the atmosphere of law courts in India was uncongenial to him. In 1893 he accepted an offer from a firm of Muslims to represent them legally in Pretoria, capital of Transvaal in South Africa. While travelling in a first-class railway compartment in Natal, Gandhi was asked by a white man to leave. He got off and spent the night at a wayside railroad station meditating on the plight of the coloured people.

The incident marks a watershed in his public career. In the result, he decided to buy a farm in Natal, return to a simpler way of life and fight racial discrimination against his people. In his own life too, there was a remarkable transformation — he began to fast and, in 1906, became celibate.

Presently, he was searching for a way of life that would satisfy his own inner needs: he ate sparingly, made continual experiments with his diet, learned to stitch his own clothes as well as those of his family and was not averse to performing the most menial household chores. A major formative influence on him was Henry David Thoreau's (1817–62) essay 'Civil Disobedience.' He was soon (1909-10) in correspondence with Leo Tolstoy (1828-1919) whose *Kingdom of God is within you* had moved him deeply, as had John Ruskin's (1819-1900) *Unto This Last* (1862).

In the second Boer war (1899-1900), Gandhi's ambulance unit was mentioned in despatches and earned him a war medal. After a while Gandhi moved to Johannesberg where he practised law and soon became a recognized leader of the Indian community in South Africa. He established his 'Phoenix Farm' near Durban. Manual labour was compulsory here, while smoking and drinking alcohol were strictly forbidden. In 1906 he raised another ambulance unit for a campaign against the Zulus, and again received a war medal.

In 1907 the Transvaal legislature enacted a law requiring all Asians to take out registration cards. The measure involved, *inter alia*, disfranchisement, physical segregation, annulment of traditional Indian marriages and imposition of a poll tax. Gandhi rated it discriminatory and launched a campaign of passive resistance, coining the phrase, '*satyagraha*'. In 1910, he established the Tolstoy Farm for all those taking part in the movement.

Gandhi's struggle against these laws, which lasted well-nigh two decades (1894-1914), was waged through public meetings, the press, as also deputations to the local and imperial governments. His principal mouthpiece was *Indian Opinion* (1903) which voiced the community's grievances in a forthright manner. There was also the peaceful march of men, women and children he led to Transvaal. Despite its initial reign of terror on a virtually defenceless people, the South African government finally yielded ground. A settlement of sorts was worked out through what is known as the June 1914 Gandhi-(Jan Christian) Smuts (1870-1950) agreement which enabled Gandhi to return to India early the next year.

In the course of the South African struggle Gandhi developed the concept of satyagraha. It is not, he explained, 'predominantly civil disobedience, but a quiet and irresistible pursuit of truth'; not an abstract absolute but a principle that had to be discovered experimentally in each given situation. It also underlined a basic concern for the means used to achieve a goal for, he was convinced, the means shaped the ends. Although less than a complete victory for the Indian cause, Gandhi felt his agreement with Smuts never the less demonstrated the efficiency of the new political weapon of satyagraha he had forged.

In 1914 while in England on his way home, Gandhi raised an Indian ambulance unit for which, on return, he received a Kaisar-i-Hind gold medal. While World War I was still on, he spoke in favour of Indians joining the British army and even conducted a recruitment drive.

Back in India, Gandhi was soon able to establish a Satyagraha Ashram on the banks of the Sabarmati river, opposite the city of Ahmedabad. During the next couple of years (1916-18) he participated in two peasant movements in the districts of Champaran, in Bihar and Kaira, in Gujarat.

In 1919 Gandhi persuaded the Indian National Congress (q.v.) to mount a campaign to redress the wrongs inflicted by the Rowlatt Act (q.v.), the Jallianwala Bagh Massacre (q.v.) and the Khilafat (q.v.), projecting it as united India's national demand. The combined assault snowballed into the Non-cooperation Movement (q.v.) which helped catapult Gandhi into the forefront of the Congress as the logical successor to Tilak (q.v.) and Gokhale (q.v.). This was more than evidenced by the fact that while at Calcutta, in September 1920, he could claim only a slender majority for his programme, at Nagpur, three months later, there was overwhelming support for him. Presently, he emerged as the party's undisputed leader and, virtually as a colossus, bestrode the political stage for the next quarter of a century.

During the Rowlatt Satyagraha of 1919–20 Gandhi used his new weapons of hartal—a downing of tools and pulling down of shutters—during which normal life ground to a halt and people organized mass demonstrations. Earlier (1920), while returning his medals to the Viceroy he declared: 'my life is dedicated to the service of India through the religion of non-violence which I believe to be the root of Hinduism.'

A campaign against the use of foreign cloth provided Gandhi with an opportunity to develop the mystique of the spinning wheel, which from now on became a cardinal tenet in his ideology, if not something of an obsession. It was to be, at the same time, a form of manual training, a spiritual exercise and the means of freeing India from the 'stranglehold of capitalist exploitation.' As the movement took a violent turn with a serious outbreak at Chauri Chaura, Gandhi suspended it to the chagrin of many of his supporters. He was arrested in March 1922 and sentenced to 6 years' imprisonment. This was the last time he was tried in a court: the British, in the long run, found such trials counter-productive. He was released less than 2 years later, in February 1924, for an emergency appendicectomy.

For the next 5 years Gandhi devoted himself to the 'constructive programme'—spinning and khadi, Hindu-Muslim unity, prohibition, village uplift. The political lull was broken with the appointment of the Simon Commission (q.v.). There was the All-Parties Conference that adopted the Nehru Report (q.v.) on a draft constitution for an Indian dominion. Later, the Congress served notice on the British that, unless Dominion Status (q.v.) was conceded by 31 December 1929, the country would opt for complete independence as its political goal.

In 1930 Gandhi launched the Civil Disobedience Movement (q.v.) which started with the famous Dandi March and the Salt Satyagraha (q.v.). It was soon to gather momentum as a mass upheaval that preached open defiance of the law. The Mahatma (as Gandhi was now called) was arrested in May 1930 and his Movement sought to be crushed with an iron hand. Less than a year later, political compulsions of a sort impelled the Viceroy, Lord Irwin (q.v.), to release Gandhi and conclude a compromise agreement called the Gandhi-Irwin Pact (q.v.). In retrospect, it proved to be a short-lived truce with a limited political objective—to persuade the Mahatma to attend the Round Table Conference (q.v.).

While in Britain in 1931 for the Round Table Conference, the Mahatma chose to stay in the modest East End of London, spun his daily quota of cotton yarn, and observed Monday as his usual day of silence. He paid brief visits to Eton, Oxford, Cambridge and Lancashire: attended, in his usual attire, a reception at Buckingham Palace, broadcast to the United States and addressed members of Parliament. He was less successful in the Conference than outside.

On returning home, Gandhi resumed the Movement and, along with a large number of front-rank leaders, was again clapped into jail. The government came down with a heavy hand: the Congress was declared an illegal organization while a veritable reign of terror was unleashed on all those who supported it. When the Communal Award (q.v.) was announced in August 1932, the Mahatma was in prison. Since, *inter alia*, it had conceded the Depressed Classes separate electorates, the Mahatma was greatly upset, the more so as he had made their cause his own. To force the government to retrace its steps he started a fast in September 1932. Five days later, the Poona Pact helped retrieve somewhat the damage Gandhi's prestige had suffered earlier. In May 1933, when he commenced another fast, the Mahatma was released from prison. He now launched the weekly, *Harijan*, which took the place of his earlier paper, *Young India* (1919-32).

Even though Gandhi severed formal links with the Congress in 1934—for not all his doctrines were acceptable to its members—he continued, until his death, to be the party 'oracle and mentor', if also perhaps its conscience-keeper. Settling down at Sevagram, near Wardha, Gandhi made it the nerve-centre of his 'constructive programme' which, as noticed earlier, focussed on the uplift and regeneration of rural India and now included an active scheme of Basic Education (q.v.) and espoused the cause of Hindi as the national language.

Although no longer a party member, Gandhi's hold over the Congress was demonstrated in 1938-9, when he frustrated Subhas Chandra Bose's (q.v.) bid to capture the organization. While, despite the Mahatma, Bose was elected president a second time, albeit by a narrow margin, the former still had the last laugh. Within weeks, Bose had not only to resign his position but was also virtually hounded out. Apart from personalities, it was a clash of ideologies too: Bose, an extremist, wanted to wrest freedom for his country without a moment's pause, singularly indifferent to the means employed. He thought it was time to strike, with Britain engaged in a life-and-death struggle. The Mahatma, scrupulous as to means, wanted to bide his time and neither wished to nor behaved that precipitately.

By 1939 Gandhi had become a convinced pacifist. Although his sympathies were with the democracies in their fight against the Axis powers, its sworn enemies, he was not prepared to countenance the use of force, even for the defence of India. In 1940, he briefly assumed leadership of the Congress but gave it up the following year when it became painfully clear that, to the party, his non-violence was an expedient, not a creed.

With World War II, the political situation in India became complicated. The British declaration of war against Nazi Germany had dragged an unwilling India into the European maelstrom. Congress protest took the form of withdrawing its ministries from the provinces where they held office, and later (1941) launching Civil Disobedience or the individual satyagraha. Many believed the Mahatma was dragging his feet and, in reality, did not wish to embarrass the British.

With the Allied reverses against Japan in south-east Asia and the failure of the Cripps Mission (q.v.), politically matters came almost to a boil. Gandhi believed it would be suicidal for India to sit by passively while the Japanese onslaught continued. Hence his last-bid call to win freedom. His slogans became catch-words: to his own people, 'Do or Die'; to the British, 'Quit India' (q.v.). No sooner did the Congress endorse his call, 8 August 1942, asking for immediate British withdrawal than he was put behind bars; so was the Congress, and most of its important functionaries. Earlier, with Japan threatening India, Gandhi expressed his strong conviction that the former would not attack a free country but if it did, the onslaught must be met with non-cooperation——even at the risk of several million lives being lost in the process.

While in detention at the Aga Khan (q.v.) Palace just outside Poona, Gandhi lost his life-long companion, Kasturba. His release came in 1944 when he engaged in the largely infructuous, if also frustrating, negotiations with Jinnah (q.v.) for a political settlement.

Gandhi's influence in the counsels of the Congress waned perceptibly after 1945. This was evident both in the events leading to as well as consequential on the Simla Conference (q.v.). The Cabinet Mission Plan (q.v.) did not enthuse the Mahatma nor did Jinnah's call for Direct Action (q.v.). Deeply distressed at the turn events now took, he travelled to Noakhali in East Bengal to heal the wounds inflicted by the shameless communal orgies of murder, rape, arson and loot. He firmly declared that he was not going to leave 'until the last embers of trouble are stamped out.' Later in Calcutta, when (1 September 1946) an angry mob broke into the house where he was staying, Gandhi began to fast: 'to end only if and when sanity returned' (to Calcutta). He now found himself virtually at the end of his tether. The June 3rd Plan (q.v.) deeply distressed him but his alternative of launching another mass civil disobedience movement had few takers—the top Congress leadership consisted, as Jawaharlal Nehru (q.v.) confessed years later, of 'tired men.' Gandhi was close to Nehru whom he had designated his political heir. Of the latter he said, 'I know this, that when I am gone, he will speak my language.'

Towards the end of his life there was grim irony in the fact that the violence he abhorred—and largely averted from the British—fell upon his own people and finally claimed him as a victim. All that he held dear seemed to fade out in the last few weeks of his life with himself a prey to brute, naked force.

Earlier, when Independence came on 15 August 1947, the Mahatma was in Calcutta trying to heal the wounds of the communal fracas. He returned to Delhi in September and spent the next few months helping restore communal peace in the capital. On 13 January 1948 he launched on another fast to press home its urgency. Seventeen days later he fell victim to the deep passions that had been aroused. Nathuram Godse, who was editor of a Hindu Mahasabha (q.v.) extremist weekly published from Poona, shot the Mahatma at point blank range while he was on his way to the evening prayer meeting. He died, with *Hai Ram* on his lips.

From 1924 onwards, Gandhi had developed a highly personalized style of dress: a white loin-cloth, white shawl and sandals. This, with his long stick and his beaming, toothless smile made him an ideal subject for caricature.

What underlay Gandhi's approach to khadi was his man-versus-machine ideology. If Indians spun their own clothing rather than buy British textile goods, he argued, the economic independence of the village would be ensured. He identified industrialism with materialism and felt it posed a dehumanizing menace to man's growth. The individual's physical and mental well-being, not economic productivity, was, he insisted, the basic desideratum, or should be. The actual form of government, to him, was of secondary interest. He had something of a distaste for organized government, whether it be foreign or indigenous. What seemed to him important was how people lived their personal—*not* their collective—lives.

Essentially, Gandhi had little understanding of the compromises and balances in which political settlements exist or are wrought. The art of statesmanship or the skilful management of human affairs was not his special *forte*. Gandhi's solution to the communal problem was simplistic. Once the British had quit, he argued, a new nation would be born to which the partition of the country would be tantamount to vivisection. Jinnah, the realist, put it the other way round: 'Divide and Quit', was what he told the British.

Gandhi's critics aver that it argued a strange lack of political understanding on the Mahatma's part that he could not, or would not, see that when a complete transfer of power at last took place, Muslim fears and pride constituted political facts of such importance that they could no longer be ignored. The harsh truth is that his pleadings with the Muslims provoked the hostility of militant Hindus who were even ready to undo Partition by force.

Gandhi's personality and methods have been a subject of considerable controversy. A British observer has summed it thus: 'What he was is perhaps less important than what people thought he was, and by the majority of Indians, even in his lifetime, he was regarded as a saint. To his opponents, and these included some sections of his own countrymen, he appeared primarily as a shrewd and even artful politician....His power lay in his influence over the masses to whom he brought a new vitality and self-respect.'

Patient in argument, he was less than receptive to other peoples' views. He confessed that his mind was narrow, that he had not read much nor travelled extensively, that he had concentrated only on a few things in life and had no interest in others. It has been suggested that he was not a profound but 'rather a muddled and wishful' thinker, that he had a tendency to ignore facts when they failed to conform to his theories. An intensely religious and pious Hindu, he disliked proselytizing and had little use for dogma or ritual. Class war to him suggested violence, which he genuinely abhorred. He disliked machinery for it undermined, he believed, the worker's individuality. His ideal was the regeneration of the Indian village, *not* its industrialization.

His compulsive fasts, and Gandhi had a strong sense of drama, were looked upon by his detractors as political blackmail. A particular merit of this weapon was that it could be brought to bear on his political adversary from behind the walls of a prison. By making the British feel morally uncomfortable, he perhaps achieved what force alone could not have accomplished so soon.

All his life Gandhi held steadfastly to a few, comparatively simple, truths. He was neither a great writer—although he wrote voluminously—nor a great orator. He gained adherents first by his example, practising what he preached, and had a genius for the mass propagation of ideas.

M. K. Gandhi, *An Autobiography, or the Story of My Experiments with Truth,* 2 vols, Ahmedabad, 1927-9; B. R. Nanda, *Mahatma Gandhi: A Biography,* London, 1965; J. B. Kripalani, *Gandhi: His Life and Thought,* New Delhi, 1970; D. G. Tendulkar, *Mahatma,* 8 vols., 2nd ed., Bombay, 1960–3; Pyarelal, *Mahatma Gandhi: The Last Phase,* 2 vols, Ahmedabad, 1956-8; Ved Mehta, *Gandhi and His Apostles,* New York, 1978; Erik H. Erikson, *Gandhi's Truth: On the Origin of Militant Non-violence,* New York, 1969; Dhananjay Keer, *Mahatama Gandhi: Political Saint and Unarmed Prophet,* Bombay, 1973.

Gandhi-Irwin Pact (1931)

An accord on the political situation reached between M. K. Gandhi (q.v.), and the Viceroy, Lord Irwin (q.v.), popularly known as the Gandhi-Irwin Pact, was signed on 5 March 1931 and published as a Government of India notification the same day.

Inter alia, it stipulated that (a) the Civil Disobedience Movement (q.v.) launched as part of the Dandi March and Salt Satyagraha (q.v.) was to be withdrawn; (b) peaceful picketing in support of the campaign in favour of purchase of Indian goods was permitted, although picketing in furtherance of the Boycott (q.v.) of foreign goods was not to be allowed outside the limits permitted by law; (c) such political prisoners as had not been found guilty of violent crime were to be released; (d) such ordinances as had been enacted recently to meet the threat of the mass movement and been strongly objected to by nationalist opinion were to be recalled; (e) the Indian National Congress (q.v.) was to take part in the second session of the Round Table Conference (q.v.); (f) the Government gave a solemn undertaking that at the Round Table talks in London it would accept as a basic principle the proposition that any reservation or safeguard in the transfer of power should be 'in the interests of India.' Accordingly, it accepted the stipulation that a federal structure and responsible government with safeguards were to be the essential bases for India's future constitutional advance; (g) Gandhi's suggestion for an inquiry into the police excesses on the satyagrahis was considered undesirable; (h) notifications declaring associations unlawful were to be withdrawn; (i) fines were to be remitted while moveable property seized in connection with the movement, if in possession of government or forfeited or attached in connection with the realization of land revenue, would be returned; (j) cases of government servants who had resigned were to be reviewed, but posts filled permanently were not to be restored to their original incumbents; (k) in the event of the Congress failing to give affect to the obligations it had accepted for itself, the government would be free to take such action as it deemed necessary.

At its session at Karachi a few weeks later the Congress ratified the 'Pact' and committed itself to participating in the Round Table Conference. Gandhi was appointed the party's sole nominee. While the Congress leaders viewed the Pact as a measure of success many bureaucrats felt unhappy that 'the highest authority of the British Government in India and the representative of the Crown had entered into an agreement with the renowned leader of the proscribed organization who, by a complex mental process, created an illusion of triumph and a concomitant spirit of defiance.'

Typical of the genre was the comment of Lord Willingdon (1866-1941), who was to succeed Irwin a few weeks later, that the layman viewed Gandhi 'as a plenipotentiary in terms of peace with the Viceroy himself and that therefore there seemed to be two kings...'

In sharp contrast, Irwin's biographer (Birkenhead) is convinced that the Viceroy drove a tough bargain. The latter, he affirms, knew that 'he was in for some fierce horse-trading and was prepared to listen for hours to Gandhi's rambling monologues...apart from the immense prestige that Gandhi won among his followers in India by bearding the Viceroy in his lair, to which Irwin was indifferent, the Viceroy drove a hard bargain and the real advantages gained were almost entirely on his side...that hard streak of Yorkshire ruthlessness and acumen, that shrewdness in a deal and that inexhaustible patience, enabled the Viceroy to prevail over an opponent as unpredictable as a snipe in flight.'

Pattabhi Sitaramayya, I, pp. 723-85; *Tara Chand*, IV, pp. 161-3; The Earl of Birkenhead, *Halifax: the Life of Lord Halifax*, London, 1965, p. 299.

Gandhi—Jinnah Talks (1944)

The All-India Muslim League (q.v.) leader, M. A. Jinnah (q.v.) having accepted M. K. Gandhi's (q.v.) proposal to meet, the talks between the two leaders began on 9 September 1944 at the former's residence at Malabar Hill in Bombay, and continued through 27 September, when the Muslim League leader announced their termination and failure to reach agreement. Later, published correspondence exchaged between the two leaders revealed *inter alia* that, while they came close to an agreement, mutual distrust and fear came in the way of a final settlement.

Regarding Partition, Gandhi had reiterated that the 'C. R. Formula' (q.v.), or a slight modification thereof that he had suggested, conceded the substance of the Muslim League demand. He did not accept the Lahore Resolution of the League because, as he pointed out, it was based on the two-nation theory. Jinnah insisted that Gandhi accept this premise and recognize that Hindus and Muslims were two independent nations. Gandhi refused, arguing that Muslims outside the north-west and the north-east regions and living in the midst of large non-Muslim majorities could not claim a nationality different from that of the people among whom their lot was cast.

Gandhi accepted the right of self-determination and even of secession of the two predominantly Muslim territories from India. This did not satisfy Jinnah who broke the negotiations, charging Gandhi with rejecting the demand for Pakistan. In essence, Jinnah wanted Pakistan first and independence later, while Gandhi insisted on independence first and secession later, *if* demanded by the majority in a mixed plebiscite. This, Jinnah argued, left Pakistan in some doubt.

A Pakistani writer has suggested that there were good reasons for Jinnah to reject Gandhi's overtures: 'In September 1944, Jinnah was not sure whether he could produce overwhelming support for his demand among the Muslims if a plebiscite were to be held....Finally, as a lawyer and as a hard-headed negotiator, Jinnah [realized that he] could not achieve Pakistan only because the [Indian National] Congress (q.v.) and the League had agreed to divide the country. The party who had the power, namely, the British Government, was not in the picture.'

Again, while the Cripps Mission (q.v.) proposals had talked of provinces opting out of the Union, both C. Rajagopalachari (q.v.) and Gandhi spoke only of Muslim majority areas doing so. This, to Jinnah, meant a truncated Pakistan, smaller than the one he had envisaged. In brief, Jinnah rejected Gandhi's proposal on three grounds: (i) he wanted the partition of India on the basis of existing British Indian provinces; (ii) he objected to the C. R. proposition that a plebiscite of the entire population take place (he held that only the Muslims had the right to vote which was tantamount to a denial of the right of the minority to express an opinion); (iii) he objected to a joint board to control matters of common concern like defence, foreign relations and communications. Jinnah felt that there could be no such common subjects between two sovereign, independent states. He also feared that a joint board might become an organization of unity, transcending the autonomy of states.

Weeks before the Gandhi-Jinnah talks, Durga Das, then *Hindustan Times* correspondent, wrote in a despatch date-lined 6 July 1944: 'Mr Jinnah will never come to an agreement during the war. While he is intransigent, he is on top; the moment he settles with the Congress, the League will get merged in the nationalist movement and will never be able to dictate terms to the Congress.'

In his entry for 30 September, Wavell recorded in his *Journal*: 'The Gandhi-Jinnah talks ended on a note of complete futility. I did not expect statesmanship or a practical solution, but I did think the two would have got down to something, if only the best way to embarrass the Government of India. Anything so barren as their exchange of letters is a deplorable exposure of Indian leadership. The two great mountains have met and not even a ridiculous mouse has emerged. This must surely blast Gandhi's reputation as a leader. Jinnah had an easy task—he merely had to keep on telling Gandhi he was talking nonsense, which was true and he did so rather rudely, without having to disclose any of the weaknesses of his own position or define Pakistan in any way. I suppose it may increase his prestige with his followers but it cannot add to his reputation with reasonable men. I wonder what the effect on HMG will be; I am afraid it will increase their dislike of any attempt at a move.'

Tara Chand, IV, pp. 430-3; Durga Das, *From Curzon to Nehru,* London, 1969, p. 211: Khalid bin Sayeed, *Pakistan: The Formative Phase, 1857-1948,* London, 1960, pp. 133–4; Penderel Moon (ed.), *Wavell: The Viceroy's Journal,* p. 91.

Ghadr Party and Movement (founded 1913)

The Ghadr party, which began as an associaton to protect and defend the rights of Indian settlers in the United States and Canada, later grew into a movement to liberate the country from alien yoke. Initially, the Panjabi immigrants had organized themselves somewhat hastily and haphazardly in their gurudwaras against increasing victimization by the whites. On 21 April 1913, Lala Har Dayal (q.v.) along with Bhai Parmanand (1874–1947) and others organized the Panjabi workers settled in the U.S.A. into an association called the 'Hindi Association of the Pacific Coast' at Astoria (Oregon).

According to Sohan Singh Bhakna (1870--1968) who was elected President—Har Dayal was General Secretary—the head office of the Association at San Francisco was to be known as Yugantar Ashram. No person was 'to get any pay for doing work in the office of the Association' though he may be given some maintenance allowance. Every worker joining the party was to contribute one month's salary towards its funds. No religious discussions were to be allowed in the party meetings and there was to be an annual election for office bearers. Kartar Singh Sarabha is said to have been the first to volunteer to join the new association, Baba Kartar Singh Latala (1896-1916) being the second. Among others, mention may be made apart from Sohan Singh Bhakna, of Pandit Kanshi Ram and Santokh Singh.

The 'Hindi Association of the Pacific Coast' was soon abbreviated into 'Hindi Pacific Association' and, before long, after its journal *Ghadr* (whose first issue was released on 1 November 1913), came to be known as the Ghadr (later, Hindustan Ghadr) party. The name was catchy and readily picked up by its members, most of whom were uneducated.

The journal which was published in several languages was circulated in almost every country of the world where Indians had settled as immigrants. Initially, it concentrated on enlightening its vast clientele about the economic expoloitation of India, avowed that the objective was to make revolution and wage an armed fight against British rule. The party established its branches in Hong Kong, Manila, Bangkok, Shanghai and Panama. It designed a tricolour national flag which was unfurled at Stockton (California) on 15 February 1914, when the Ghadrites pledged themselves to 'fight and die in the revolution under the 'National Standard'.'

Pledged to freedom of the country, the Ghadrites appealed to all patriotic Indians to take full advantage of British preoccupations in World War I to rise against them and literally throw them out. They were promised support in money and arms through Indian revolutionaries in Germany who had organized an Indian-Berlin committee. When World War I (1914-18) broke out, the party was not yet fully geared for action, but organized the return home of Indians settled abroad so as to give shape and form to its plan of action. In the result, batch after batch of immigrants sailed for India. Due to lack of proper organization and training, many were apprehended en route, or on arrival. Despite British vigilance, however, about 1,000 of the Ghadrites managed to reach the Panjab between October and December 1914; eventually, they numbered 3,125.

The Ghadrites set themselves the objective of infiltrating into the army, so as to cause disaffection in its ranks, and to incite the civil population. Any shortages in supply were to be made good by organizing guerilla raids. In the result, arms were collected, bombs manufactured, arsenals attacked and a general uprising planned. In pursuance of their plans a number of dacoities and robberies occurred in 1914 as well as early in 1915. Additionally, Rash Behari Bose, Vishnu Ganesh Pingle and Sachin Sanyal arrived in the Panjab to organize a final revolt on 21 February 1915.

According to an observer, 'India gives us the first example of what has now become the *sine qua non* of revolution—international conspiracy in the shape of the Ghadr party.' The first issue of the *Ghadr* spelt out the party ideology: 'A new era in the history of India opens today, the first November 1913, because today there begins in foreign lands, but in our country's language, a war against the English Raj....What is your name? Mutiny. Where will the Mutiny break out? In India. When? In a few years. Why? Because the people can no longer bear the oppression and tyranny practised under British rule and are ready to fight and die for freedom....time is gliding on....The whole world is waiting to see when these brave men will rise and destroy the English. Serve your country with body, mind and wealth....Pray for this rising, talk, dream, earn money, eat for it alone, make soldiers of yourselves for its sake.' There were about 8,000 Indian nationals on the Pacific coast of the U.S.A. at that time and it was not long before practically every one of them became associated with this organization, one way or another.

The Ghadr party tried to follow the methods of the Russian revolutionaries. Cypher codes were used frequently. Various members would each have a particular book and would correspond by referring to a certain page, line and word number in that book. Written signs had to be duplicated upon recognition by a confidant. Pass words were used.

The Government had been apprised of the plot by an approver and the revolutionaries apprehended in the Panjab and elsewhere in India, Burma as well as Malaya. In a series of trials held at Lahore, Mandi Shri Hargobindpur, Alawarpur, Karnna, Banaras and as far away as Mandalay and Singapore, several hundred revolutionaries were prosecuted and convicted. Of those trapped in the Panjab, trial was held under the Defence of India Act in the notorious Lahore conspiracy case; in the province, 46 were hanged, 194 sentenced to long terms of imprisonment. In the overall count, 145 were either hanged or killed in encounters with the police; 306 sentenced to transportation for life; 77 awarded lesser punishments.

The failure of the revolutionaries has been explained away by a variety of factors: their lack of experience, incompetent leadership, notorious inability to keep secrets, the mounting tension between the Germans and the Ghadrites, the efficiency of the British intelligence service which planted spies in the highest councils of the revolutionaries. No less significant were the stern measures taken by the Government of India, the brutal methods adopted by the Panjab police which compelled many of the leaders (viz., Nawab Ali, Jodh Singh, Mula Singh) to spy on their colleagues. Additionally, the climate of revolt, a necessary prerequisite to success, was conspicuous by its absence in the Panjab as well as other parts of the country. Worse, large consignments of arms smuggled from abroad miscarried or failed to arrive, while funds too either leaked or were misappropriated.

Before 6 April 1917 when it declared war on Germany, Washington had announced a policy of neutrality as between the belligerents. On 6 August 1917, the U.S. government launched its prosecution of the Ghadrites and of those who had aided them. 105 defendants were named in the indictment and the case, 'The United States of America vs. Franz Bopp *et al*', which lasted from 11 November 1917 to 23 April 1918, was launched.

Inter alia, the U.S. District Attorney told the Court: 'We will show you that the object and purpose of this conspiracy reached the entire world; that it was to engage the assistance of every Hindu and every sympathiser in every neutral country practically in the world.' In its judgement, the court pronounced everyone indicted guilty, barring one American. Sentences ranging from one to two years and fines from $2,000 to $10,000 were imposed on German officials; party members were sent to prison for terms ranging from 2 to 18 months.

It may be noted that, to begin with, the American government and people had shown sympathy for the Indian cause and the Ghadrites received their consistent encouragement and moral support. The administrations of both Presidents Theodore Roosevelt and Woodrow Wilson were not inimical to their activity. The fact is that the Ghadrites prepared their plan for revolt in India on American soil and initially at any rate that country did not bother about the diplomatic protests and pressures of the British government about their activity.

However, once the War was declared and the British and Americans became allies against Germany, the complexion changed. The Ghadrites were not only engineering a revolt for independence but had allegedly entered into a conspiracy with Germany to counteract British-American war plans. The American government, accordingly, acted swiftly; many a Ghadrite was arrested, all literature seized and their organization, the Hindustan Ghadr party, banned. It should be evident that the American government acted the way it did because of heavy pressure from the British.

Meanwhile, riddled with factions, the fortunes of the Ghadr Party in the

U.S.A. were at a low ebb. The dominant group under Bhagwan Singh accused its rivals under Ram Chander of being pro-Arya Samajist. On 7 April 1917, the latter with a number of other Ghadrites was arrested for conspiring with the Germans. Later, during the trial, he was shot by a protagonist of the rival faction.

Between 1919-25 efforts were made to revive the party, by publishing a newspaper and establishing contacts with extremist elements in India. Yet lack of proper organization and funds and the increasing impact of Gandhi's (q.v.) non-violence prevented them from making any headway. Their activities became suspect in the U.S.A. because of their increasing association with and dependence on Soviet Russia. With the subsequent arrest of its leaders (1931), the Ghadr party in the U.S.A.—it had already disappeared from the Indian political scene—made its final curtain call.

Certain salient features of the movement may be noted. The Indian migrants in the U.S.A. and Canada who formed the party backbone came mostly from Panjabi peasant stock. They were enthused by the opportunities that now came their way and made great sacrifices in giving their hard-earned money to party coffers voluntarily (German financial aid came much later). Thus, to start with, all those working on the staff of the *Ghadr* and in Yugantar Ashram met their own individual expenses.

The widely-held belief that only the uneducated took part in the movement is erroneous. It is true that some were unlettered, but not all. The comradeship they developed was remarkable, nor were they oblivious of the sacrifices called for. An insertion in the *Ghadr* of 18 August 1914 read:

Wanted:	Enthusiastic and heroic soldiers for the Ghadr in Hindustan
Pay (or remuneration):	Death
Reward:	Martyrdom
Pension:	Freedom
Field of work or battlefield:	India

The importance of the Ghadr movement lies in the fact that it was the first secular, democratic and revolutionary upsurge aiming to free India from foreign shackles. For the Sikh community, it meant the end of its long saga of unquestioned support to the Raj. No spectacular results followed. The aim was to murder and drive out the British from India. Although the vast majority of its members were Sikhs, both Hindus as well as Muslims joined. The movement was suppressed, but later it gave the Akalis their more radical aspect, for Akali terrorists, known as Babbars, were largely recruited from the ranks of the Ghadrites. Nor was that all. When they returned after serving their terms of imprisonment, the Ghadrites formed the nucleus of many a left-wing political movement in the Panjab—whether socialist, Kirti or communist.

Khushwant Singh and Satinder Singh, *Ghadr 1915: India's First Armed Revolution*, New Delhi, 1966; Gurdev Singh Deol, *The Role of the Ghadr Party in the National Movement*, Delhi, 1969; T. R. Sareen, *Indian Revolutionary Movement Abroad (1905–1920)*, New Delhi, 1979; John W. Spellman, 'The International Extensions of Political Conspiracy as illustrated by the Ghadr Party', *JIH*, 37, 1, April 1959, pp. 23–45 and 'Ghadr', unpublished Ph.D. thesis, University of London, microfilm, *NMML*; J. S. Bains, 'The Ghadr Movement: A Golden Chapter of Indian Nationalism', *Indian Journal of Political Science*, 23, 1, January-March 1962, pp. 48–59; Amarjit Singh, 'The Ghadr Party Trial and the United States of America, 1917-18', *Panjab Past and Present*, IV, 2, October 1970, pp. 401–15.

Khan Abdul Ghaffar Khan (1890–)

Abdul Ghaffar Khan (AGK, for short), the scion of a leading family of Mohamadzai Pathans, was born around 1890 in the village of Uttamanzai in the Charsadda tehsil of Peshawar district. Now in Pakistan, it then formed part of the erstwhile North-West Frontier Province (q.v.) of British India. His father, Behram Khan, had no feuds—a unique distinction for a Pathan Khan. This was, as his grandson Ghani Khan recalls, because he had forgiven all his enemies: 'He never told a lie—he did not know how to. He loved horses but was a poor rider. He was optimistic to a fault and consequently had a fine sense of humour. He was painfully honest; and therefore people loved him.'

AGK has further affirmed that both his father and grandfather 'never established any relations with the ruling power'; that the 'thought of offering them service or flattery never occurred to them.' The father was later to be arrested during an agitation led by AGK against the Rowlatt Act (q.v.). AGK's early education was on the traditional pattern, centring on the recitation of the Holy Quran. To start with, he was educated at home and also in a *maktab*. Later, he was sent to the Mission High School at Peshawar, and from there to Aligarh. The principal of his school, Wigram, and the head of the maktab, the Haji of Turangzai, had a great impact on him. It has been said that on the pleading of his mother, who was very attached to him, AGK gave up the idea of going to England to study for an engineering degree.

While still in his teens, AGK resolved to devote himself 'to the service of my country and people.' A fruitful avenue was his keen interest in the spread of education and social reform, both of which he believed to be necessary for the Pathans. In pursuance thereof, in 1921 he established the Azad High School of Uttmanzai and the Anjuman-ul-Afghania. Soon he found himself behind bars—'for inculcating the ideas of nationalism into the minds of Pathans.'

His regular nationalist career may be said to commence in 1919, when he plunged into the agitation against the Rowlatt laws referred to earlier. He was arrested and, according to Ghani Khan, 'narrowly escaped the gallows.' It was this episode which gave him the sobriquet of 'Badshah Khan.' Later (1920) he attended the Nagpur session of the Indian National Congress (q.v.) and took a leading part in the Khilafat agitation (q.v.), of which he was the principal organizer in his own province.

In 1930, AGK again plunged into the Civil Disobedience Movement (q.v.) and was arrested while the Congress itself was banned in NWFP. More specifically, he took a leading part in all the political movements launched by the Congress during 1930-47 and spent about 14 of these years in jail. In September 1929 AGK founded the Khudai Khidmatgars (literally, God's servants), a peace corps of dedicated workers who gave him his title 'Fakhar-e-Afghan' (i.e., pride of the Afghan).

The aim of the new fraternity was to inculcate among its followers the 'idea of service and the desire to serve their country and their people in the name of God', an objective that had hitherto been conspicuous by its absence. The movement was designed further to propagate the need for social change, of good behaviour and serve to check violent crimes or outbursts that were indeed not unknown to the community. Each Khudai Khidmatgar had to take a solemn vow to observe this rigid code of conduct in his personal life.

In much of this AGK was close to Gandhi (q.v.). Notwithstanding the fact that he was a blue-blooded Pathan, to AGK non-violence had been a matter of deep faith. More, he had convinced himself that his people needed to own the doctrine, if anybody else did. Much of this brought him closer to Gandhi and AGK was rated one of the Mahatama's most devoted followers and affectionately known as the 'Frontier Gandhi.'

A devout Muslim himself, the Khan did not see eye to eye with the fanatical ideology of the Muslim League (q.v.), for true faith in any religion, he argued, never warranted any ill-will or hatred towards others.

About three months after the Khudai Khidmatgars were born, the government imposed a ban on the movement. In April 1930, AGK was arrested and later sentenced to three years' imprisonment. A couple of years earlier he had started a monthly journal in Pushto, the *Pakhtoon*, which was closed in 1931 after his arrest. It was revived the following year but had to be shut down again. After a few years it reappeared as *Das Roza*, but its publication was suspended in 1941. It made an appearance in 1945 as a weekly but was closed down after two years.

In 1931, after the Gandhi-Irwin Pact (q.v.), AGK was released and, along with 100 Khudai Khidmatgars, attended for the first time the All-India Congress Committee session at Karachi.

In elections to the NWF provincial legislature held in 1936, the Khudai Khidmatgars won a majority of seats. Dr Khan Sahib (q.v.), AGK's elder brother, was invited to be the province's Chief Minister. In 1940, AGK founded a huge Khudai Khidmatgar complex on the banks of Sardaryab; it was called *Markaz-e-Alla-e-Khudai Khidmatgar*. Later (1941), he was arrested for taking part in the Civil Disobedience movement.

AGK was personally opposed to the holding of provincial elections in 1945-6. The cry of Pakistan had now been raised in all its strident fury and the political atmosphere all over the country was surcharged with communal hatred and bitterness. In the Frontier, with its preponderant Muslim majority and pronouncedly pro-nationalist leanings, the polls were viewed as extremely crucial. In the result, large numbers of students from the Aligarh Muslim University, Islamia College, Calcutta as well as important leaders of the Muslim League, with the alleged active connivance of British officials, waged an unrelenting campaign to woo Muslim voters. All this notwithstanding, Muslim League candidates were soundly defeated and the Khudai Khidmatgars emerged triumphant at the polls. This was due, in no small measure, to Badshah Khan's personal influence. Later, along with Maulana Abul Kalam Azad (q.v.) and a Muslim Leaguer, he was retuned to membership of the Constituent Assembly (q.v.) which was convened in New Delhi in December 1946.

During the hectic negotiations leading to Partition, AGK made no secret of his vehement opposition to a divided India nor the fact that the nationalist

Pathans had been let down badly by their mentors on whose side they had stood steadfast all these years. Since the elections of 1946 had clearly demonstrated the strong and powerful hold which the Khudai Khidmatgars had on the Pathans, AGK and his supporters 'refused to have anything to do' with the NWFP Referendum (q.v.) of July 1947. He viewed the whole exercise as a 'great injustice', indeed 'an insult', to the Pathans and was hyper-critical of the Congress which had delivered the province 'tied hand and foot' into the 'hands of the enemies.'

After Partition, AGK did not rest. He started an active campaign for the creation of Pakhtoonistan and was jailed a number of times by successive Pakistani regimes. He lived in exile in Afghanistan for several years and returned home at the end of 1972. Before long, he was again put behind bars but, in 1978, was allowed to go back to Afghanistan.

Pyare Lal, Mahatma Gandhi's life-long associate and later secretary, has expressed the view that the Khan 'may be broken but has never bent'; that he sought nothing for himself: neither power, nor its perquisites but only untrammelled freedom to serve his own people so that they may grow to the fullness of their stature. It is also evident that he has never known nor cared for high office and that worldly riches have never had any attraction for him. In his own inimitable words: 'The only thing my soul hungers for is, if it should please God, to deliver us from the fetters that have been put upon us to devote myself like Vinoba Bhave wholly to the service of suffering humanity.'

D. G. Tendulkar, *Abdul Ghaffar Khan, Faith Is a Battle,* Bombay, 1967; Pyare Lal, *Thrown to the Wolves: Abdul Ghaffar,* Calcutta, 1966; Mahadev Desai, *Two Servants of God,* Delhi, 1935; N. B. Narang (narrator), *My Life and My Struggle: Autobiography of Badshah Khan,* New Delhi, 1969; Ghani Khan, *The Pathans: A Sketch*, Bombay, 1947; Sen, *DNB,* II, pp. 323–6 (Meher Chand Khanna).

Lal Mohan Ghose (1849–1909)

Lal Mohan Ghose (also Lalmohan Ghosh), a lawyer and leading nationalist, came of an upper middle class Bengali family of Krishannagar. Having twice unsuccessfully attempted the Indian Civil Service examination, he turned to law, qualifying for the bar in London in 1873. He began practising in Calcutta, but despite his impressive gift as an orator, did not make any mark as a lawyer.

Ghose made his debut on the political scene when (1879) as a member of the Indian Association (q.v.), he was deputed to present a memorial to the British Parliament on the question of entry to the Indian Civil Service and the agitation connected with it. *Inter alia*, members protested against the Vernacular Press Act (q.v.), pleaded for the increasing employment of Indians in the public services and demanded raising the age for the I.C.S. examination. One result of his forceful and effective advocacy was the setting up of the Statutory Civil Service (q.v.). In 1880, he visited England again to protest against Lytton's (q.v.) highly unpopular measures. He believed that to have any impact every memorial sent to Parliament should be signed by at least half a million Indians.

Ghose was barely 30 when he made his first public appearance in Willis's room in London on 23 July 1879 under the chairmanship of the celebrated British orator, John Bright (1811-89), who remarked at the end: 'I will not spoil the effect of the magnificent oration we have heard, by any feeble words of my own.' He was known as the 'bronzed orator.' Indeed, a New Zealand Premier pinpointing 'that Black man' said, 'he speaks straight; he speaks to the point and knows when to stop.'

C. Y Chintamani, hailed the 'Pope of Indian journalism', has remarked: 'Of all the orators whom it has been my privilege to hear, I have no hesitation in according the first place (along with Mrs Besant (q.v.)) to Lal Mohan Ghose who was known as the John Bright of India.'

In India, Ghose championed the cause of unity—a unity that would 'transform the tiny brook of a feeble popular opinion into the rushing torrent of a mighty national demonstration.' The Ilbert Bill (q.v.) found in him a firm supporter, indeed the hero of the hour. He boldly defended Ripon's (q.v.) liberal measures against malicious attacks by the European community. In 1883, when in England, Ghose declared Indians were fast losing faith in British promises and their sense of fair-play. It was a shame, he argued, that a judge who could hang an Indian was not deemed competent to try or punish a European thief. He felt it was essential that Indian interests be represented in Britain's Parliament and was the first Indian to be chosen a parliamentary candidate. He stood from the Deptford constituency but, unfortunately for him, the stormy politics of the day influenced by the Irish question resulted in his defeat at the polls and his subsequent return home (1884).

In 1903 Ghose emerged from near-seclusion to preside over the Indian National Congress (q.v.) session at Madras. Introducing him, Pherozeshah Mehta (q.v.) said; 'Lal Mohan Ghose after his great exertions in England became a political yogi... We have now dragged him out of his political yogism.'

Ghose's caustic references to the Coronation Durbar held by Curzon (q.v.)—'as a pompous pageantry to a perishing people', became a by-word. He firmly believed that Indians would eventually achieve their rights by constitutional means and pleaded for compulsory primary education so as to prepare the people and to make effective use of democratic institutions. Failing health increasingly prevented his taking an active part in politics, but he lived long enough to witness the introduction of the Minto-Morley Reforms (q.v.).

The Indian Nation Builders, Madras, 1920, 3 parts, II, pp. 93-125; Asutosh Banerji, *Speeches by Lal Mohan Ghose*, Calcutta, 1884; C. Y. Chintamani, 'Mr Lal Mohan Ghose, President of the Congress', *Hindustan Review and Kayastha Samachar*, December 1903, vol 8, no. 6, pp. 569-86; Iswara K. Dutt, *Congress Cyclopaedia, The Indian National Congress; 1885-1920: the pre-Gandhian Era*, New Delhi, 1967, pp. 168-74.

Rash Behari Ghose (1845-1921)

Rash Behari Ghose (also, Rashbihari Ghosh), who rose to be an eminent lawyer, educationist, and philanthropist, was born at Torekona, a village in Burdwan district, and came of a respectable, well-to-do middle class family. In later years he was to emerge as a leading member of the Moderate group in the Indian National Congress (q.v.). After an average school career in Burdwan, he did extremely well at Presidency College in Calcutta, graduating with Honours in Law in 1871. In 1875 he was selected for the Tagore Law Lecturership and delivered 12 lectures on the 'Law of Mortgages in India.' In 1884, he was awarded the degree of Doctor of Laws. Shortly afterwards, he emerged as a front-rank lawyer of the Calcutta bar with a highly lucrative practice.

His legal preoccupations notwithstanding, Ghose retained his association with education; he was elected a Fellow of Calcutta University in 1879, a member of its Syndicate (1887-99) and President of its Faculty of Law (1893-5). He actively encouraged primary and female education, instituting later a gold medal for the best law graduate of the University. All through life he was a keen student of literature, read voraciously and acquired a good library. During the Swadeshi Movement (q.v.) he supported a scheme for national education, becoming the first President of the National Council of Education, striving hard, in particular, to encourage scientific and technical education. He donated generously to educational institutions.

A member of the Bengal Legislative Council in 1888, and of the Imperial Council (1891–6 and 1906–7), Ghose's special field of interest was legislation pertaining to legal and financial matters as well as the Civil Procedure Code Bill of 1908. His most notable contribution in the legislature was with regard to two bills, one on the partition of Hindu and Muslim families and another on the rights of debtors to buy back their properties. His most important speeches were made on the Indian financial statements for 1894-5 and 1906–7, on the Indian Tariff Bill of 1894 and the Prevention of Seditious Meetings Act (q.v.).

Without adequate reason Ghose did not indulge in criticism of the government, but at the same time did not spare it when this seemed called for. He protested openly against Curzon's (q.v.) policies and his retrogressive measures, viz., the Calcutta Municipal Act (q.v.) and the Partition of Bengal (q.v.). He supported the cult of Swadeshi hailing it as 'the cradle of New India'; it did not, he argued, even remotely imply any disloyalty to England, for it was only a means of encouraging indigenous industry and an effort to improve the economic condition of the country. He was largely responsible for setting up a match factory near Calcutta. He also criticized the Seditious Meetings Act referred to above, and dubbed it as proof of a weak administration. It was, he felt, the surest means of 'killing all political life in the country' and increasing 'secret sedition.' A moderate in politics, Ghose never the less professed his faith in the British sense of justice and their civilizing mission. They would, he had no doubt, train Indians and eventually bequeath to them 'autonomy within the empire' as they had done with their colonies.

Ghose's first active association with politics was in 1905, when he presided over a meeting in Calcutta's town hall called to protest against Curzon's extremely derogatory remarks at the University convocation.

In 1906 he was Chairman of the Reception Committee for the Indian National Congress session at Calcutta. In the following year, as president-elect of the Congress session at Surat with his candidature supported by all provincial Congress committees barring that of Berar, he lent his full-throated support to the Moderates and their policy of constitutional agitation. He was convinced that it would be unwise to ape the methods of other countries. Calling the Extremists 'pestilential demagogues' and 'irresponsible agitators', he called for a separate party of Moderates, in a bid to reduce Extremist support. He was convinced that positive governmental response to the Moderates'· demands would completely eliminate this revolutionary group.

Ghose was greatly influenced by Gokhale's (q.v.) political ideas and looked upon British rule in India as a blessing. He exhorted his people to 'have confidence in yourselves and also in the good faith of England.' At Surat (1907), he declared that the Congress ideal was 'autonomy within the Empire and not absolute independence.' More, it was 'definitely committed only to constitutional methods of agitation to which it is fast moored. If the New Party does not approve of such methods and cannot work harmoniously with the old, it has no place within the pale of the Congress. Secession, therefore, is the only course open to it.'

Following the Surat Split (q.v.) in the Congress, Ghose, along with Pherozeshah Mehta (q.v.), Dinshaw Wacha, Gokhale and Surendranath Banerjea (q.v.) announced his decision to hold an exclusive convention of the Moderates. Nine hundred delegates attended and reiterated the principal tenets of the Moderate creed. A 4-member committee including Ghose (and excluding Gokhale) was appointed to reconstitute the party. It convened at Allahabad (18–19 April 1908), was presided over by Ghose and ruled that every delegate was to express in writing his acceptance of the Congress creed.

The Madras session where Ghose presided was, in comparison with the earlier ones at Calcutta (1906) and Surat (1907), a tame affair. Proceedings began with the 'Indian National Anthem' sung to the tune of 'God Save the King' and ended with 'Cheers for the King-Emperor, Lord Morley and Lord Minto.' The first resolution tendered 'loyal homage' to His Gracious Majesty for his message to mark the 50th anniversary of the Royal proclamation of 1858! In his presidential address, Ghose maintained, 'We must be mad if we were really disloyal...Our loyalty is above all suspicion.'

As may be evident, Ghose welcomed the Minto-Morley Reforms (q.v.). Later (1917), he was a member of the Congress delegation to England. That year he presided over a joint session of the Congress and the Council of the Muslim League (q.v.).

G. A. Natesan (ed.), *Speeches and Writings of Dr Sir Rash Behari Ghose: An Exhaustive and Comprehensive Collection,* 3rd ed., Madras, n.d.; J. C. Das Gupta, *A National Biography for India,* Calcutta, 1911, pp. 222-38; Daniel Argov, *Moderates and Extremists in the Indian Nationalist Movement,* Bombay, 1967; S. P. Sen (ed.), *DNB,* II, pp. 57–9 (D. P. Sinha).

Gopal Krishna Gokhale (1866–1915)

Born on 9 May 1866 in Ratnagiri district, Gopal Krishna Gokhale came from a relatively poor Chitpavan Brahmin family of Maharashtra. A diligent student, he finished school from Kolhapur and, in 1884, graduated from Elphinstone College, Bombay. He later joined the Law College but could not complete the LL.B course. In 1886 he was appointed Assistant Master in the New English High School in Poona. Later, he enrolled himself as a life member of the Deccan Education Society (q.v.) and taught at Fergusson College, where he soon earned the title of 'Professor to Order' on account of his extraordinary ability to teach almost any subject when called upon to do so. As a student and teacher, Gokhale took infinite pains to master the English language, memorizing Burke's speeches and long stanzas from the works of important poets. During 1866-88 he contributed to the *Maharatta*, founded by Tilak (q.v.); in 1888-92 he edited the English columns of Agarkar's *Sudharak*.

Gokhale's political apprenticeship began as he came under the influence of Mahadev Govind Ranade (q.v.), whose assistant he became in 1887. A hard taskmaster, Ranade demanded nothing less than perfection and Gokhale spent years poring over books, collecting data, writing memorials and petitions as well as articles on varied problems of the day. In 1890 he became secretary of the Poona Sarvajanik Sabha (q.v.). Earlier, in 1887, he had assumed editorship of the *Quarterly*, the Sabha's journal, and continued in that position up to 1895. That year, when control of the Sabha passed into the hands of Tilak, Gokhale joined Ranade to form the new 'Deccan Sabha' and founded a journal, the *Rashtra Sabha Samachar*, of which he became editor. Deeply imbued with European liberal thought, Ranade's moderation, and belief in constitutional methods, left a permanent and almost indelible imprint on Gokhale's mind. It was to serve as a guide to his future political affiliations.

Gokhale's mode of living suggested deep spirituality. He was a front-rank reformer who deprecated the caste-system and untouchability, pleaded for the emancipation of women and championed the cause of female education as a prerequisite to national political consciousness. He advocated that primary education should be imparted free in all schools, held pronounced views on the use of the vernacular and favoured the creation of a separate vernacular university where English and Sanskrit would be taught as compulsory languages. Gokhale firmly believed that the economic results of British rule had been disastrous and spelt frightful poverty for the country. He advocated the establishment of co-operative credit societies to meet the difficulties of the farmer. These would serve a dual purpose—as banks for their savings and as credit societies to disburse loans.

Elected (1902) to the Imperial Legislative Council, Gokhale made some of his memorable speeches on the annual budgets (1902 to 1908). Sir Guy Fleetwood Wilson, then Finance Member (1908-13) of the Government, expressed the view that he frankly feared Gokhale as a virtual 'leader of the Opposition.'

Gokhale paid frequent visits to England. The first (1897) was in connection with the Welby Commission, more correctly, the Royal Commission on Indian Expenditure, of which he was a member. Later (1905) he went as a delegate of the Indian National Congress (q.v.) from Bombay to inform British public opinion of the situation in India. His next visit (1906) was for the purpose of interviewing members of Parliament and to plead with them for reform in the country's administration. The fourth (1908) was in connection with the Minto-Morley Reforms (q.v.), then on the political anvil. His fifth (1912), sixth (1913) and seventh (1914) visits were in connection with the Public Service Commission. His friendship with John Morley, then Secretary of State for India, was, to start with, of a political nature but soon matured into a genuine mutual regard for each other.

Gokhale's clear views about the baneful impact of British rule on India's economy were forcefully expressed. In his evidence before the Welby Commission, he vehemently criticized the government's financial policy with telling facts and figures. He conceded, however, that economic reconstruction was a gradual process which, in India's case, would depend among other factors on the education of the masses, the elimination of religious and sectarian differences and the spread of scientific and technical knowledge. He opposed the Swadeshi Movement (q.v.) and Boycott (q.v.) as retrogressive measures. Co-operation with the government alone, he argued, would ensure the introduction of agricultural reform and the growth of indigenous industry.

Gokhale's association with the Congress dated back to 1889 when he enrolled himself a member. From its platform he had advocated the reduction of salt duty (1890) and elaborated on the problem of Indianization of the public services (1892). In 1893 he became Secretary of the Provincial Congress Committee graduating to Joint Secretary of the all-India body 2 years later. His public apology to the British Governor of Bombay, as well as members of the Plague Committee and the soldiers engaged in relief operations, for his bitter and, as he confessed, unfounded criticism of their policy was an act of great political courage. It led to his being dubbed 'a weakling' and relegated to the backwaters in Congress politics for a few years. At one time it looked as though this traumatic experience would spell the end of his public career. In 1905, however, Gokhale was chosen to preside over the annual session of the Congress in Banaras. From then on, till 1915, he reigned virtually supreme in the party, thwarting the Extremist bid to capture control while at the same time preventing their return to or reconciliation with the parent body. It was largely due to his political moderation and the co-operation he extended to the government that made it recognize the Congress as a forum for responsible Indian public opinion.

Gokhale had great faith in the British system of government, its upkeep of law and order and the administrative unity of India that the Raj had helped to achieve. The best course open to the country, he felt, was to utilize the Raj to serve its political apprenticeship, a necessary prerequisite to the successful working of democratic institutions before graduating to the goal of self-government. Constructive criticism and co-operation, he exhorted, should guide action. Understandably, passive resistance and non cooperation did not appeal to him, for as a law-abiding citizen he disapproved of methods that by-passed or defied established authority and inculcated a sense of indiscipline among the masses. In any case, he argued, the boycott of British institutions and merchandise would do more harm than good, for Indians were not yet prepared to take so much on to their plate. Gokhale was averse to populist politics and believed that the masses had to be activated before they could achieve political reform.

Pending this, he pinned his faith on the educated elite to voice the aspirations of the masses. Not that it absolved an alien government of its responsibility. It was, in fact, the latter's duty, Gokhale argued, to help the country achieve progress in all fields—be it economic, social, political. The last could be achieved by introducing a decentralized system of administration and adopting the elective principle, thereby providing the people with added opportunities of involvement in administration, at the provincial, district and village levels. Gokhale submitted detailed memoranda on de-

centralization to the Hobhouse Commission in 1908, while the Servants of
India Society (q.v.) that he founded in 1905 reflects the importance he
attached to political apprenticeship as well as dedication to a cause.

During his tenure (1899-1901) in the Bombay Legislative Council,
Gokhale set healthy parliamentary precedents by acting as a virtual unofficial leader of the opposition. A powerful speaker, but not a demagogue, his
speeches, in particular those concerning the budget, were memorable. He
was unsparing in his criticism of policies that might in any way harm the
national interest. Thus he demanded reduction of taxation, abolition of salt
duty and a slicing of army expenditure, taxation relief for agriculturists,
Indianization of the public services, compulsory primary education, extension of scientific education and welfare schemes. Not content with his efforts
at home he made, as has been noticed above, several trips to England to
make a direct appeal to Britain's Parliament and its public. At home, he
persuaded the Congress to work the new scheme introduced by the Minto-
Morley reforms. It did not matter to him, he declared, how many
Muslims or Hindus were represented in the legislature as long as both
worked towards the same goal and in the interests of the country at large.
Earlier, Gokhale had lent support to Gandhi's (q.v.) satyagraha movement
and was largely responsible for bringing about an agreement with the South
African government.

Gandhi called Gokhale his *Rajaguru*, referred to him as 'Gokhale, the
Good' and described him as 'pure as a crystal, gentle as a lamb, brave as a
lion and chivalrous to a fault and the most perfect man in the political field.'
Conferring the CIE on Gokhale, Curzon (q.v.) wrote in a letter dated 31
December 1903: 'the honour is offered to you in recognition of abilities
which are freely bestowed upon the service of your countrymen and of which
I would ask no more than that they should continue to be so employed. I only
wish that India produce more such public men.' In 1915, Gokhale was offered
the KCIE but evidently refused to accept it.

The most urgent need of his countrymen, as Gokhale saw it, was education: in the techniques of administration, in the rudiments of public health
and sanitation, in the skills of advanced technology, in the basic principles of
communal harmony and social equality, in the methods of democratic
agitation and, as prerequisite for learning all these things, in elementary
reading and writing.

His transparent sincerity was apparent in all that he did: 'I recognize no
limits to my aspirations for our Motherland....I want our men and women
without distinction of caste or creed to grow to the full height of their
stature.'

Though he often agitated for seemingly petty reforms, Gokhale's labours,
viewed in the perspective of his lifetime, may be seen as a patient and
unremitting struggle to enshrine equality of opportunity and treatment as
the principle governing relations between England and India, and within the
empire at large.

One of his biographers has aptly summed up Gokhale's well-nigh meteoric career: 'A graduate at 18, professor and associate editor of the
Sudharak at 20....Secretary of the Sarvajanik Sabha and of the Provincial
Conference at 25, Secretary of the National Congress at 29, leading witness
before an important Royal Commission at 31, Provincial legislator at 34,

Imperial legislator at 36, President of the Indian National Congress at 39... trusted tribune of the people and a man of truth, rectitude and character in whom the rulers confided...a patriot whom Mahatma Gandhi himself regarded as his master...what a truly marvellous and brilliant career and beyond anybody's emulation.'

Gokhale and his ilk had left the Indian National Congress an instrument which, when refurbished, became a powerful weapon in the nationalist armoury. No less serviceable was the ideal they bequeathed to their successors of a humane, secular and democratic nationalism which remained a basic tenet of the Congress faith under the more vigorous and successful leadership of Gandhi and Jawaharlal Nehru (q.v.).

Gokhale handed down to Gandhi the legacy of 'spartanization of public life, unity of means and ends, secularism, a deep-rooted sense of national mission and faith in peace, justice, conciliation and progress.' Where Gokhale failed, Gandhi succeeded: he could reconcile the best of Gokhale and Tilak. Nothing perhaps can sum up the place of Gokhale in the history of modern India better than the fact that the Gandhian legacy 'in part belongs' to Gokhale.

B. R. Nanda, *Gokhale: the Indian Moderates and the British Raj*, Princeton, 1977; T. V. Parvate, *Gopal Krishan Gokhale, A Narrative and Interpretative Review of His life, Career and Contemporary Events*, Ahmedabad, 1959; D. B. Mathur, *Gokhale—a Political Biography: A Study of his Services and Political Ideas*, Bombay, 1966; Stanley Wolpert, *Tilak and Gokhale: Revolution and Reform in the Making of Modern India*, Berkeley, 1962; T.R. Deogirikar, *Gopal Krishan Gokhale*, 2nd ed., New Delhi, 1969; Dietmar Rothermund, 'Emancipation or Reintegration: the politics of Gopal Krishan Gokhale and Herbert Hope', in D.A. Low (ed.), *Soundings in Modern South Asian History*, London, 1968, pp. 131–58.

Maharaja Gulab Singh (1792–1857)

Gulab Singh, one of the four Dogra brothers in Maharaja Ranjit Singh's (q.v.) service, joined the Sikh ruler's forces as commander of a regiment after the latter had conquered Jammu. Ambitious to reunite the ancestral lands under his own leadership, Gulab Singh had in a few years not only become an important noble at the Lahore darbar who was permitted to raise his own troops but also received several jagirs as gifts. Between 1820-2 he received Jammu in farm and the hereditary title of Raja. Within the next 5 years he brought several principalities, including Reasi (1815), Rajwari and Bhimber (1820), Rehlu Rasohli (1821), Kishtwar (1822), under his control. Shrewd as well as selfish, he began consolidating his power, equipping and drilling an efficient force, confident that his brothers would safeguard his interests at Lahore. By 1841, his protege, Zorawar Singh, had conquered Ladakh and unsuccessfully attempted to subjugate central Tibet.

To realize his ambition following Ranjit Singh's death, the Dogra chief played an active role in the war of succession, making away with a lot of treasure through the connivance of aspirants to the Lahore gaddi whom he supported. Having espoused the cause of Dalip Singh's (q.v.) rival, he was imprisoned by Jawahir Singh but later released (August 1845) after payment of Rs 68 lakh. During the First Anglo-Sikh War. (q.v.), he declined the command of Sikh troops while secretly tendering his allegiance to the British on the clear understanding that he be confirmed in the possession of his territories. After the battle of Sobraon, he agreed to represent Sikh interests in the impending negotiations for peace but in the Treaty of Lahore (q.v.) accepted terms dictated by the British. This, it has been said, was due to the reward he was promised, for within a week, as a result of the treaty of Amritsar, he was to emerge as the Maharaja of Jammu & Kashmir. Gulab Singh renewed his allegiance to the British when the Second Anglo-Sikh War (q.v.) broke out, yet frustrated all their attempts to appoint a Resident at his court.

Gulab Singh's administration left a lot to be desired: his system of taxation has been dubbed 'vulturous'; he denied his Muslim subjects any significant role in the administration and neglected to improve the training and equipment of his army. On the other hand, he enforced rigorous, even stringent, measures for maintenance of law and order, outlawed Sati (q.v.) and female infanticide, imposing penal retribution on any offenders and sedulously guarded Kashmir's monopoly of the pashmina trade from British onslaughts.

Aware of the demands being made in several quarters for the annexation of Kashmir, the Maharaja adopted measures in his internal administration calculated to prevent such an eventuality. At the same time he took a variety of steps to keep the British in good humour—loaning, *inter alia*, a sum of Rs 10 lakhs to the Panjab government to pay its troops' arrears of salary and volunteering a contingent of 2,000 troops to fight (on the side of the British) against 'the mutineers' in the Rebellion of 1857 (q.v.).

A singularly controversial figure, it is hard to strike a balanced assessment of the Maharaja. On the positive side may be listed the conquest briefly noticed earlier of Ladakh, making it 'for the first time' a part of the subcontinent. A shrewd diplomat, contemporaries called him 'Ulysses of the hills' and 'Talleyrand of the East.' While his skill in the art of management of men and affairs coupled with his sharp wit and remarkable level-headedness set him apart, he was at the same time 'an unprincipled liar and a self-seeking opportunist who would stoop to any means to achieve his ends. He was a ruthless tyrant who could brook no opposition to his rule....He was faithful to no one except himself...a pragmatist who was probably the first to perceive that, in the anarchy which followed at Lahore after Dhian Singh's assassination, the extension of the Company's power across the Sutlej was inevitable...and that his future could only be insured by collaborating with the British. The Dogra ruler was a scheming, calculating and crafty strategist.'

Herbert Edwardes, a contemporary, has aptly summed up the character and role of the Dogra ruler: 'His was the cunning of the vulture. He sat apart in the clear atmosphere of passionless distance, and with sleepless eye beheld the lion and the tiger contending for the deer. And when the combatants were dead, he spread his wings, sailed down, and feasted where they fought.'

On account of ill-health, Gulab Singh handed over the administration of the state to his son in February 1856. As has been noticed, he promised assistance to the British when the Rebellion of 1857 broke out. He died shortly afterwards, in August that year.

Bawa Satinder Singh, *The Jammu Fox: A Biography of Maharaja Gulab Singh of Kashmir, 1792–1857*, Illinois, 1974 and 'Raja Gulab Singh's Role in the First Anglo-Sikh War,', *Modern Asian Studies* (Cambridge)', 5 (1971), pp. 35-59.

Treaty of Gwalior (1817)

Concluded with Daulat Rao Sindhia (q.v.), the treaty was part of the preparations made by Lord Hastings (q.v.) before launching his campaign against the Pindaris (q.v.). The Governor-General, not prepared to take chances with the most formidable of Maratha chiefs, took him by complete surprise, allowing him no time to communicate, much less work out plans, with the Peshwa, Baji Rao II (q.v.).

In sum, the 'northern' army, operating under Hastings' personal command, reached the frontiers of Sindhia's dominion on 28 October 1817. Taken unawares and with his dominion surrounded on all sides by a formidable host, Sindhia had no choice but to acquiesce in the terms of the treaty of Gwalior, negotiations for which had begun much earlier and which was concluded on 5 November 1817.

The 12-article treaty stipulated *inter alia* that (i) the contracting parties would employ their forces 'in prosecuting operations against the Pindaris and other free-booters'; (ii) Sindhia would 'never re-admit' the Pindaris to the possession of lands earlier in their occupation, nor lend them 'the smallest countenance or support'; (iii) the Maratha ruler was to place 5,000 horse in active operations against the Pindaris, plans for whose deployment were to be drawn in concert with the British. He would further ensure that these troops were maintained in a state of complete equipment and 'regularly paid'; (iv) his troops were not to change the positions designated for them 'without the express concurrence' of the British nor was he to augment his forces during the war; (v) British garrisons 'shall be admitted' into the forts of Handi and Asirgarh and charged with their care and defence; (vi) in supersession of the earlier Treaty of Surji Arjangaon (q.v.), the British were at liberty to enter into engagements with the rulers of Udaipur, Jodhpur, Kotah, Bundhi and 'other substantive states' on the left bank of the Chambal, although they would refrain from doing so in regard to the states of chiefs in Malwa or Gujarat; (vii) details of the earlier treaties of Surji Arjangaon and Mustafapur (22 November 1805) which were not affected by provisions of the new agreement were to remain in full force.

Besides underlining Sindhia's helplessness, the treaty marked him out as a mere spectator in the now impending Third Anglo-Maratha War (q.v.).

Aitchison, IV, pp. 247–53.

Amir Habibullah Khan (1869–1919)

Habibullah, the eldest son of Amir Abdur Rahman (q.v.) of Afghanistan, ascended the throne, unopposed, in 1901, and proclaimed a policy of 'national unity, resistance against foreign aggression and reform.' Sentimental, lenient and perhaps weak-kneed, he began his reign by promising to abolish the much-dreaded spy system that had been instituted by his father and granting amnesty to all political prisoners and exiles, including the tribal chiefs.

In his programme of reform also the Amir struck a middle course in an effort to win over both traditionalist as well as modernist factions in his country. Besides being a good linguist, he was well-educated and helped lay the foundations of a system of education based on the Anglo-Indian model, although it was later modified to conform to the Kemalist Turkish pattern. Two great monuments to his policy of reform were the Habibia College and the *Siraj-ul-Akhbar*, the first newspaper which he encouraged Mahmud Beg Tarzi, a public-spirited Afghan, to launch. A Royal Military College too was established in 1904. The Amir also accelerated the process of industrialization, with the result that the volume of trade with both Russia and India increased appreciably. The administrative system promulgated by his father was continued with a few minor modifications. His reign witnessed the blossoming of a nascent Afghan nationalism, influenced *inter alia* by Japan's victory over Russia (1905) and the well-orchestrated anti-British, anti-Russian propaganda in the country.

The Amir reduced taxation, relaxed the system of compulsory military recruitment, established a Council of State for tribal affairs and decreed the association of tribal chiefs with provincial governors for the adjudication of disputes among the former.

Once Tarzi and his associates had postulated an inseparable link between the monarchy, patriotism and religion, Habibullah was in a position to undertake reformist and modernist measures. These were, he argued, 'essential' to the well-being of the Afghan state and perhaps even in helping win the support of the religious establishment. He brought education under stringent government control, forcing the majority of the Mullahs to remain salaried employees of the state.

Partly with a view to allaying fears which his reforms had aroused and partly to conciliate the hereditary enemies of the ruling house, he treated with unwonted leniency the Ghilzais and Mangals of Khost, a district lying immediately to the west of the Kurram valley.

Despite his support of reform and modernization, Habibullah, like his father, was reluctant to open the country to foreign assistance—until such time as it was militarily strong. That, however, was easier said than done, for he was unable to find the wherewithal to achieve such a positon. He wavered on the question of admitting railway construction—hoping instead to obtain a corridor to the sea! His measures in the field of education, public health, industry and trade, though limited in scope, were of great significance; they assisted in the growth of an urban population and the rise of a small Afghan bourgeoisie. In fact, his reign was witness to the emergence of the first educated, and politically conscious, Afghan generation, the *Siraj-ul-Akhbar* generation, that contributed signally to the future course of Afghan development.

In his thinking Habibullah was pronouncedly anti-British. The result was that relations with the Indian government were strained during his reign and in varying degrees. The first clash came over the Afghan demand for a renewal of earlier treaties, which the Amir desired, as against Curzon's (q.v.) insistence that these had been personal to his predecessor and therefore called for fresh negotiations. Under instructions from Whitehall and during Curzon's absence on leave in 1904, Ampthill, his temporary replacement, sent a diplomatic mission to Kabul under Louis (later Sir Louis)

William Dane, then Foreign Secretary to the government. The result was a new treaty (March 1905) recognizing Habibullah as an independent ruler, albeit with the British retaining control over his country's foreign relations.

Briefly, the treaty reaffirmed the annual subsidy granted in 1893, allowing the Amir to collect £ 400,000 in undrawn subsidy payments, and re-affirmed Afghanistan's right to import arms without restriction. It implicitly guaranteed the country's territorial integrity and officially recognized the ruler as 'His Majesty, the independent King of Afghanistan and its dependencies.' It may be noted that Habibullah not only refused to grant the British trade concessions, but also declined the introduction of railways into his country. The British, who failed to establish a diplomatic mission, considered the treaty to be a renewal of the Durand Line (q.v.) agreement. If the treaty did not end Afghanistan's isolation, it was never the less an Afghan diplomatic victory and therefore important both for political and psychological reasons. It enhanced the position of the monarchy and Habibullah's personal prestige.

The Amir, who was far from happy about the British attitude towards Afghan claims in the Seistan affair, later refused to accept the Anglo-Russian Convention of 1907 in so far as it effected his country and argued that it tended to destroy his independence. In fact, the conclusion of the Convention intensified the fervour of the nationalist cum reformist cum revivalist elements in Persia as well as in Afghanistan. Afghan fears concerning the threat to their independence seemed to be particularly substantiated when the two colonial powers, disregarding Afghanistan's opposition, announced that they considered the Afghan clauses of the Convention both operative and binding. Actually, British refusal to consult the Amir before the conclusion of the Convention had, it is said, served 'to add more fuel to the smouldering fires' of Habibullah's resentment and his displeasure manifested itself, if partly, in the Afridi and Mohmand uprisings on the North-West Frontier (q.v.) in 1908.

In 1906 the Amir visited Minto (q.v.) and later repaired to England where he was much impressed by all he saw. Owing to powerful domestic compulsions, he was resentful of any attempt to push him around and had warned that if this were done, 'the Afghans would resist and in that case would look to the emperor of Russia for help.' In essence, his policy was to maintain his independence without paying court either to Great Britain or Russia. During World War I (1914-18), he maintained a friendly neutrality, which was helpful to the British cause. A Turko-German mission headed by Oscar Niedermayer and Kazim Bey visited Kabul in 1916 but failed in its immediate objective of winning Afghan support in the war. None the less it succeeded in stirring up trouble within the tribal belt where there were scattered outbreaks against the British.

Despite heavy domestic constraints, the Amir kept his turbulent people under control, strained every nerve to ensure a peaceful border, successfully countered German and Turkish intrigue among the militant groups of his own people and curbed the fanaticism of the mullahs. The October 1917 revolution in Russia, however, transformed the situation, for the Anglo-Russian alliance soon vanished. This was grist to the mills of Habibullah's enemies. The defeat of Turkey and the occupation of the holy places of Islam by a Christian power had already aroused Afghan fanaticism to fever pitch. There was the distinct feeling that the country had failed Islam in its hour of need, that the Amir had been far too dilatory in maintaining his country's independence.

Habibullah was murdered (1919) in a camp near Jalalabad while his **successor Amanullah Khan (q.v.) soon found himself thrust into an attack on British India**, leading to the Third Anglo-Afghan War (q.v.).

Vartan Gregorian, *The Emergence of Modern Afghanistan: Politics of Reform and Modernisation, 1880-1946*, Stanford, 1969, pp. 181-226; Ludwig W. Adamec, *Afghanistan, 1900-1923: A Diplomatic History*, Berkeley, 1967, pp. 28-107; Amir Habibullah, *My Life: from Brigand to King*, London, n.d.

Haidar Ali (c. 1722–1782)

Haidar Ali, known to his European contemporaries as 'Haidar Naik', was the son of Fateh Mohammad, said to be a Panjabi adventurer who traced his lineage to the family of 'the Prophet, the Quaraish of Mecca. He was a military commander and jagirdar of Budikota in Mysore. Starting as a volunteer with his brother in Chitoor, Haidar later joined service in Mysore, where he distinguished himself at the siege of Devanhalli (1749) and Arcot. He was soon given an independent command as well as the title of Khan. Though uneducated, Haidar displayed robust common sense, courage and determination, taking full advantage of every opportunity that came his way.

Haidar began by emulating the army organization and equipment of the English and the French, whom he had observed at close quarters during the Anglo-Mysore Wars (q.v.). Appointed (1755) Faujdar of Dindigul, then a Mysore stronghold, he soon subdued the surrounding Poligars and amassed a huge fortune. In 1759 he commanded the Mysore raja's army and received the title of Fateh Bahadur. By 1760, the straitened circumstances of the Mysore ruler, with his army's salary in arrears, gave Haidar Ali the opportunity he had longed for to supplant his authority; by 1761, he rose to be Dalwal or Chief Minister. Khande Rao, the Maharaja's Brahmin Minister, openly questioned Haidar Ali's newly found power; resorting to treachery, Haidar duped Khande Rao into submission.

To extend and consolidate his power, Haidar conquered Kanara and Sira, subjugated Bednur and captured all its treasure. In 1766 he defeated the Nairs of Malabar and Calicut. Control over the coastline helped him organize a small fleet and he was one of the few among his contemporaries to do so. By 1766, the Hindu ruler of Mysore became a mere titular head, while Haidar assumed unquestioned control.

Almost his entire reign was taken up with military campaigns, for the Nizam of Hyderabad, the Nawab of Carnatic and the Marathas laid their respective, and sometimes conflicting, claims to Mysore's dominion. The English too got inextricably mixed-up in their attempt to prevent any of the Indian powers from becoming too strong and thereby endangering their possessions.

The Marathas questioned Haidar Ali's credentials and overran his territories several times between 1766 and 1772 demanding *Chauth* as their legitimate share. Each time they threatened him, Haidar Ali bought peace and the evacuation of his territories. The ambitious Nawab of Carnatic was Haidar Ali's sworn enemy, seeking British aid all the time to extend his control over Mysore. He even urged the John Company (q.v.) to join the Marathas subdue the intrepid Mysore ruler, something they were most reluctant to attempt. The Nizam claimed Mysore as his territory as early as the rule of Aurangzeb's successors. He however vacillated between an alliance with the English against the Marathas, with the Marathas against Haidar—and even one with Haidar against the English!

The grant of the Northern Circars to the British by the Mughal Emperor, added to their desire to consolidate dominion, led to the First Anglo-Mysore War (q.v.). In one of the actions fought, the combined forces of the Nizam, Haidar Ali and the Marathas were defeated at Changama and Tiruvannam-alai (1767). The British, however, soon weaned away the Nizam and the Marathas, leaving Haidar Ali scrupulously alone to face their wrath. His overtures for peace were rejected. In the result, he continued to campaign alone, at one time marching his troops to within 5 miles of Madras and dictating a treaty there. *Inter alia*, it transpired that Haidar Ali had sought British help against the Marathas in 1772 but the former had failed to come to his aid. It is said that he now became a sworn enemy, resolved to avenge their (viz. British) breach of faith. This fact, among others, has invested his career with a new aura and the Mysore ruler is sometimes referred to as among the first who fought for the country's freedom.

The resumption of Anglo-French hostilities in Europe and the capture of Mahe on the Malabar coast by the British led to the Second Anglo-Mysore War (q.v.). After an initial victory at Perambahan, Haidar Ali was worsted by Eyre Coote (q.v.) at Porto Novo, while the British fleet captured Negapatam and destroyed Mysore's small navy. Haidar was hopeful of regaining his lost possessions with French assistance, but during a brief interlude in the fighting brought about by the start of the rains he died (7 December 1782) in his camp at Chitoor.

From 1760, when Haidar allied himself with the French, to 1799 when Wellesley (q.v.) destroyed Tipu (q.v.), Mysore was what has been called the 'terror of Leadenhall street.' The existence of Mysore as a strong neighbour, rich in resources, extensive in territories and formidable in power, was viewed by the John Company as a threat to the security of the Carnatic. Several factors widened the gulf between Haidar and the English. Chief among them were the latter's refusal to enter into an alliance with him against the Marathas; Haidar's irreconcilable rivalry with the Nawab of Carnatic; and his association with the French. There was also the nature of the Company's government at Madras—the unimaginative governors that succeeded to power and the want of harmony between Madras and the Company in England.

Haidar had a profound respect for the English never the less; he admired Colonel Joseph Smith and Sir Eyre Coote and regarded Pigot and Palk as able governors. He had no personal animosity against the English; it was merely that his political difficulties led to his invasion of the Carnatic, whose cause the Company owned. Bold and enterprising, and even though he never defeated the Marathas or the British in a pitched battle, Haidar 'possessed enough skill to escape a rout, enough ability to surprise a detachment and enough foresight and dash to exploit the weakness of his adversary.' A deficiency in tactical ability he remedied by discretion and prudence. As a soldier, Haidar suffered 'repeated reverses', yet 'he never despaired. He did not show any very conspicuous ability as a tactician, but he showed great ability as an organizer and his general plan of a campaign was always sound. His army compared with that of the English was inferior in leadership as also in the fighting qualities of the soldiers. In numbers, supplies and equipment, it was always superior.'

Haidar never raised a cloud of enemies against himself, as did his son who looked abroad for allies; his policy was more pragmatic, down to earth. It was a tribute to his diplomatic skill that Haidar's enemies never combined against him: he would not fight with the English unless he was on good terms with the Marathas, and he would not go to war with the Marathas unless confident that the British would not join them.

Both Haidar and Tipu were men of calibre, for whom it was difficult to submit to the paramountcy of a foreign power. The underlying principle in English relations with Mysore was the contest for power to fill the void that had been created by the disappearance of a central authority in India. The English, perhaps imperceptibly, sought a subsidiary relationship, which men like Haidar and Tipu could never agree to. Apart from being a strong-willed soldier-ruler, Haidar Ali was also a successful administrator. Tolerant of other faiths and cautious in innovation, he continued the then traditional system of administration and employed Brahmins as his advisors and administrators. Nor did he change the system of coinage with the imprint of Hindu deities on the obverse. His persecution of Christians has been attributed chiefly to his enmity with the British. He did not neglect public works and, in fact, the construction of a number of roads, gardens and fortifications in Bangalore and Seringapatam are credited to his reign.

Contemporaries rated him to be a born soldier, a first-rate horseman, heedless of danger, full of energy and resource, severe, cruel, cold. Later historians have viewed him as 'stern and gaunt, eagle-eyed and hawk-nosed, imperious, a master of men.' It has been said that with better support from the French he might have succeeded in driving the English out of southern India.

N. K. Sinha, *Haidar Ali,* 3rd ed., Calcutta, 1959; B. Sheik Ali, *British Relations with Haidar Ali 1760-1782*, Mysore, 1963; Praxy Fernandes, *Storm over Seringapatam,* Bombay, 1969, pp. 1-74.

Haileybury College (founded 1809)

To meet the pressing demand for responsible civil servants in the arts of public service, diplomacy and the administration of justice, Wellesley (q.v.) founded the College of Fort William at Calcutta (q.v.) in the opening years of the 19th century. Objecting to its location, yet conceding the necessity for its institution, an 'East India College' was established at Haileybury, close to London, in 1809. There is no gainsaying that Wellesley's 'decisive action served as the catalyst' which speeded up the Haileybury development; in fact, instruction had already begun 3 years earlier (February 1806) at Hertford castle.

During the half century of its existence (1809-57), approximately 2,000 young men appointed to Haileybury by the patronage system were posted out to India to serve in the new and varied capacities created by the reforms of Cornwallis (q.v.), John Shore (q.v.) and Wellesley.

The subjects offered for study at Haileybury were divided into two categories—'European' and 'Oriental.' The former included classical and general literature, history and political economy, general policy and the laws of England, mathematics and natural philosophy; the latter comprised a study of Hinduism, the history of Asia (this was allowed to lapse in 1837) and, among languages, Sanskrit, Persian, Arabic and the Indian vernaculars. What the students imbibed has been a subject of some contention and Professor Stokes's view that Bentham's ideas 'were disseminated among the young...civilians at Haileybury' has not found wide acceptance.

Prospective entrants to the College were nominated by the John Company's (q.v.) Board of Directors who as a matter of course and courtesy made over a proportion to the Board of Control. The incumbents came for the most part from the landed, banking and commercial classes and were between 15 and 22 years of age—the maximum, for admission, in 1853 was 21. After a 2-year course, they were sent out to India as assistants to commissioners.

Admission to the covenanted service, as it was called in those days, was conditional on a successful course through the College: its eligibility test was not severe, in so far as the aim was not to exclude, except in rare cases. The College soon became noted for its corporate life and the *camaraderie* inculcated among its trainees. Among its most distinguished products mention may be made of John Lawrence (q.v.), John Russell Colvin (1807-57), James Thomason (1804-53) and Sir Richard (later Baron) Temple (1826-1902).

In the two decades from 1793 to 1813, when the Company lost its commercial monopoly, the Directors attempted to rid the patronage system of its worst abuses. The sale of appointments, was eliminated; sponsors of young men for India as well as patrons were made to put up bonds for the individuals involved; screening processes were tightened. The entrance examinations screened out some; those not deemed qualified for civilian jobs were pushed into the military services. There were drop-outs; some were eliminated through repeated rustication and outright suspension.

There was a parallel institution, 'a military seminary' at Addiscombe (near Croydon); its objective was to prepare engineers and officers for the British Indian army. The rejects from Haileybury were often, but not always, accommodated there.

According to Bernard S. Cohn, roughly 25% of all appointments were given to relations and for a further 60% the Directors were motivated by considerations of 'friendship.' This would imply that the circle of families from which young men were drawn was 'quite restricted.' After 1830, almost all the Directors had India connections; appointments made by this coterie of men came from 50 or 60 families, inter-connected by marriage, Anglo-Indian tradition, and shipping, banking and trading interests. The Directors tended to exclude all but a few from the aristocracy.

Normally entrants attended four terms stretching over 2 years, usually departing for India in April or May. By the time they left, they were barely 18 to 20 years of age.

Suggestions to introduce competitive examinations for recruitment into the civil service had been made from time to time but were, until 1853, over-ruled. The Charter Act of 1833 [Charter Acts (q.v.)] stipulated that admission to Haileybury and to the covenanted civil service should be open to all candidates, including Indians, who could establish their claim by success in competitive examinations held in England under regulations framed by the Company's Board of Control. The latter, in turn, constituted a committee presided over by Macaulay (q.v.), which ruled in favour of candidates between 18 and 22 years of age who had received the best and most liberal education. Successful candidates were to pass through a period of probation before appointment. The first batch went to Haileybury. By now it was clear, however, that the college, excellent though it was, had outlived its utility. In the result, by an Act of 1855, it was closed down with effect from 31 January 1858.

Peter Penner, 'Haileybury: school for Anglo-Indian statesmanship', *Bengal, Past and Present*, XCIII, 1 (1974), pp. 39-58.

Abul Kasem Fazlul Haq (1873–1962)

Abul Kasem was born at Chakhar, a village in Barisal (also known as Bakerganj) district, now part of Bangladesh. His father who was a government pleader at Barisal East had good standing as a lawyer and was well known for his philanthropy. AK was brought up on traditional lore, Persian and Arabic, and joined Presidency College, Calcutta from where he graduated in 1894 with Honours in Physics, Chemistry and Mathematics. Later, he qualified in Law. He started life as a teacher, but soon shifted to journalism: was editor of the *Balak* (1901-6) and joint editor of the *Bharat Suhrid* (1900-3). For a time (1906-12), he was in government employment, which he quit to start practice at the bar. In Calcutta, he was reckoned a great favourite of Sir Asutosh Mookerjee (1864-1924).

Haq is an important figure for the political historian of the period, for he brought 'a new style' to Muslim politics in his province. Debate over the Partition of Bengal (q.v.) found him keenly supporting the measure. His first opportunity for political work, however, came in 1906, when Khwaja Salimullah, the Nawab of Dacca, 'used him as a runner' in his negotiations with Muslim leaders in other parts of northern India before the formation of the All-India Muslim League (q.v.). His reward was a place in the Provincial Executive Service where, by 1908, he rose to be Assistant Registrar of Rural Co-operative Societies. At the time of the province's reunion (1911), Haq felt aggrieved at his non-appointment as Registrar for the whole of Bengal and, in retaliation, quit the civil service. The Nawab now helped him for the Dacca Muslim seat, which returned Haq unopposed to the Bengal Legislative Council.

Although Haq had taken an active part in founding the Muslim League in Dacca (1906), his real political life began with his entry into the Bengal Legislative Council in 1913. Except for a brief interval (1934-6), when he was a member of the Central Legislative Assembly, Haq continued to serve in the provincial legislature, down to 1947. When the Nawab of Dacca died in January 1915, among his political heirs was Fazlul Haq, who, along with his friends, gained control of the Bengal Presidency Muslim League as its Secretary. Presently, he lent a hand in negotiating the Lucknow Pact (q.v.), which was hailed as a remarkable diplomatic victory for the Muslim League (except in Bengal, where it was denounced as a betrayal of the community's true interests).

During 1916-21, when Haq was President of the All-India Muslim League, he was also connected with the Indian National Congress (q.v.) and acted as its Joint Secretary. He was a member of the Panjab Inquiry Committee set up by the Congress to investigate the Jallianwala Bagh Massacre (q.v.). In 1924 Haq was a Minister under the scheme of Dyarchy in Bengal; later, he represented Muslims at the Round Table Conference (q.v.) and, in 1935, was Mayor of Calcutta.

Communal riots in Bengal in September 1918 tarnished many a Muslim image; Haq somehow came out better than others. He presided over the December 1918 session of the Muslim League, but this did him little good politically. He was dubbed a 'collaborator' who would sacrifice Muslim interests to win fame and position among the Hindus.

In December 1917 Haq, along with a group of fellow lawyers and journalists, formed the Calcutta Agricultural Association and, at the beginning of 1920, the Bengal Jotedars and Raiyats' Association. The talk of constitutional reform in general and of an extended franchise in particular had aroused the interest in politics of the Bengal peasantry, and it was in the hope of taking advantage of this awareness that these organizations had been established. They proved to be precursors of the peasant organizations formed by Muslim politicians in the mid-20s, which later provided backing for Fazlul Haq's Krishak Praja Party in the province's Legislative Council.

Under Swaraj Party (q.v.) leadership, in March 1924, the Bengal Legislative Council rejected every demand made on the 'reserved' side of the provincial administration except for the police; on the 'transferred' side, it refused grants to pay the salaries of the education department inspectorate, the medical department's establishment and the Minister himself. This last act was hailed by newspapers as a triumph for nationalism. The Governor who was determined that Dyarchy succeed, allowed Haq, and another incumbent A. K. Ghuznavi, to remain in office without drawing any salary and meantime work towards securing a majority at a fresh voting. The two, we are told, 'worked their power of patronage for all it was worth' while the vacant ministership was held out as an inducement to those with political ambitions.

During March-August 1924 Haq and Ghuznavi thus continued 'even though a majority [in the Legislative Council] had clearly shown that they would not support these two ministers.' Preceding the second vote, Haq had declared: 'As regards the point at issue I do not want to say anything except that so far as dyarchy is concerned, I wish with all my heart that it comes to an end today.' Haq's followers were solidly with the government while he was a Minister in 1924, but when forced to leave office he became embittered and his group was to side in 1925 with the Swarajists on a crucial vote.

Following elections under the Government of India Act 1935 (q.v.) that were held in January 1937, there was no single dominant party in the Bengal legislature, while a large number of members, of whatever party allegiance, claimed to represent the tenantry. One of these organized tenant groups was the Krishak Praja Samiti briefly alluded to above and founded in July 1929 with Haq as its leader. His great personal triumph lay in trouncing a former Minister and Executive Councillor, Sir Khwaja Nazimuddin (1894-1964). Haq's own road to power was opened by Congress' indecision as to whether or not its members should accept office, while his own party's electoral platform was acceptable to a sufficiently large section of the legislature as the basis for a ministerial coalition. This platform, which was to serve as a blueprint for an extended attack on Hindu *bhadralok* power, bears citation: 'In view of the fact that the land revenue system known as Permanent Settlement (q.v.) and the land laws of Bengal have arrested the economic growth and development of the province and have adversely affected the national outlook of the people, a committee of inquiry be immediately appointed to devise ways and means to get them replaced by a more equitable system and laws suitable to the needs and requirements of the people.' Other plans included amendment of the Bengal Tenancy Act to reduce rents and abolish the landlords' customary exactions, further reduction of peasant indebtedness, encouragement of co-operative societies, and provision for universal primary education.

By December 1939 Haq's ministry had honoured most of its earlier promises. It had appointed a commission to examine the land revenue system, imposed severe restrictions on the zamindars' power to enhance rents and recover arrears and ruled further limitations on money-lending. It had amended the Calcutta Municipal Act (q.v.) to provide increased Muslim representation through a system of separate electorates and given 7 general (viz., Hindu) seats to the Scheduled Castes.

In the field of education, Haq's performance was less eventful, although during his tenure Calcutta University, for the first time, had Muslim Vice-Chancellors, both in 1930-4 and 1939-42. The Secondary Education bill, which transferred control of higher schooling from the University to a Board of Secondary Education composed of elected representatives on a communal basis and government nominees, was placed on the statute book.

With its ranks sharply divided, the Congress failed to form a coalition with the Krishak party so as to keep the Muslim League out in the political wilderness. In the result, 'Fazlul Haq who was known for frequent changes of direction and a determination to stay in power, talked and wrote publicly [against the Congress] in ever harsher terms.'

In retrospect, Haq could hardly escape being branded a communalist and 'in his extramural activities' seemed to care little for his reputation. Towards the end of 1937, he accepted M. A. Jinnah's (q.v.) invitation to re-join the Muslim League.

In August 1938, when his government appeared to be threatened in the Assembly, Haq appealed to Calcutta's Muslim shopkeepers to demonstrate in its favour, tactics which his political opponents were later to emulate with a far more powerful impact. Overall, 'this aggravated the existing state of communal ill-feeling; tension mounted steadily until, in August 1940, there was a serious outbreak of Hindu-Muslim rioting, which marked the beginning of ten months of widespread violence.' Earlier, in December 1939, under his name, a pamphlet appeared on 'Muslim Sufferings under Congress rule,' which listed hundreds of acts of alleged violence perpetrated by Hindus against Muslims in provinces ruled by the Congress. Haq concluded that the 'Muslim case remains that during the Congress regime they were condemned to live in terror and to suffer these atrocities, while the law moved tardily or did not move at all.'

Haq reconstructed his government in December 1941 to include the Forward Bloc section of the Congress led by Sarat Chandra Bose, a Scheduled Caste group and the Hindu nationalists headed by Dr S. P. Mookerjee. Jinnah made a determined effort to disrupt this combination. Natural disasters, the 1942 Quit India Movement (q.v.), the growing strength of the Muslim League, and the ill-concealed disfavour of the Bengal bureaucracy to its emergence, contributed to the collapse of the coalition. Interestingly, even before the fall of his ministry in 1943, Haq had been privately speaking to Jinnah about dissolving his coalition and returning to the Muslim League fold.

During 1937-43 Bengal was witness to constant clashes between Jinnah and Haq. In September 1941, long after the League had officially adopted Pakistan as its goal, Haq in a letter tendering his resignation from the League's Working Committee and its Council protested in the strongest terms. He questioned the manner in which the interests of the Muslims of Bengal and the Panjab were being imperilled by Muslim leaders of the minority provinces and complained bitterly of the principles of democracy and autonomy being subordinated to the arbitrary wishes of a single individual. No wonder, when his coalition ministry was finally defeated in 1943, Jinnah rejoiced at the fall of this 'curse to the politics of Bengal.'

After Pakistan came into being, the Muslim League came to power in East Pakistan under Khwaja Nazimuddin (1947). A temporary alliance between two political groups headed by H. S. Suhrawardy and Haq capitalized on resentment against it, and crushed the Muslim League in the 1954 general elections held in Pakistan.

Haq was never fully reconciled to the new partition of Bengal. As late as May 1954 when Chief Minister of East Pakistan, he was reported to have said that he would take no notice of the fact that there was a political division of the province. In the result, he as well as Suhrawardy were from time to time suspected of being involved in intrigues for the re-union of Bengal and subjected to attack by their political adversaries as traitors to Pakistan. Haq was dismissed from office after 57 days, but later (1955), joined the Pakistan Cabinet as Home Minister; he rose to be Governor of East Pakistan, but once more was soon dismissed. He died in Dacca, on 27 April 1962.

It has been said that Haq was the one man who could have successfully challenged Jinnah's leadership. A skilful politician and an orator of rare quality, he was at the same time a warm hearted man whose spontaneous generosity won him friends among men of all communities. He never lost his mass following, but there were certain glaring defects in his character. He was fickle and changed sides easily. He was generous towards the poor but was not too particular about the way in which he collected funds for distribution among his proteges. In his fight against the growing intransigence of the Muslim intelligentsia, only the highest standards of 'intellectual and moral integrity' would have enabled him to win back their allegiance. While his popularity never diminished, his political support declined sharply.

Education was a passion with Haq and he considered it his duty to advance its cause, and not merely among his co-religionists. He was directly or indirectly associated with the establishment of many educational institutions viz., the Islamia (now re-named Maulana Azad) College, Lady Brabourne College, the Wajed Memorial Girls High School and Chakhar College, all in Calcutta.

Haq's generous and charitable disposition became proverbial in Bengal during his lifetime; he often ran into debt so as to provide much-needed succour to the distressed and the needy.

Haq was a new kind of Muslim leader who made his way by dint of personal ability. His education and experience in teaching, law, administration and political organization set him apart from the old leadership and made him acceptable as a *bhadralok*. While retaining his contacts with his East Bengal district, he soon established himself as an important figure in Calcutta's political life. Unlike the earlier communal leaders, he did, on occasion, make alliances with other groups in his opposition to the government. In the years that followed and under the influence of pan-Islamism and a growing distrust of British intentions, he was willing to form an alliance with the Hindus that would have horrified the older leadership.

Gifted with rare intellectual qualities and unusual vigour, Haq remained a political enigma throughout his long public career. His weakness came from a volatile temper which made him incapable of pursuing a fixed ideal, a fact that goes far to explain the sharp vicissitudes of his long public life.

Leonard Gordon, *Bengal: The Nationalist Movement 1876—1940*, New York, 1974; J. H. Broomfield, *Elite Conflict in a Plural Society*, Berkeley, 1968; Sen (ed.). *DNB*, II, pp. 135–8 (Abdus Sabhan).

Lala Har Dayal (1884–1939)

Har Dayal, son of Lala Gauri Dayal, was born in Delhi in 1884 and educated at St. Stephen's College, Delhi and, later, Government College, Lahore. He was to play a brief, albeit significant role, in the nationalist movement, being responsible for the revolutionary activities which convulsed the Panjab on the eve of World War I. With a bright scholastic career added to a flare for languages, he was awarded a government scholarship to study modern history at Oxford and it was thought he would be an aspirant for entry into the Indian Civil Service. However, his association in England with Shyamaji Krishna Varma (1857-1930), Bhai Parmanand (1874-1947) and Vinayak Damodar Savarkar (1883—1966) and his membership of 'Abhinav Bharat' dramatically altered the course of his life. He soon abandoned the idea of joining the I.C.S. and gave up the scholarship awarded to him in protest against the arrests of Ajit Singh (q.v.) and Lala Lajpat Rai in 1907.

On his return to India HD organized a training cell for political work, contributing simultaneously to the *Modern Review* (Calcutta) and the *Panjabee*. He wrote extensively for the former, especially during 1909-26, and preached a brand of 'religious nationalism' based on the revival and re-establishment of Hindu culture and society and linked to passive resistance to British authority. At the same time, he condoned communalism as pure nationalism. Convinced that the achievement of his aims was possible only through an uncompromising dedication of a band of political missionaries or ascetics, he organized such a group, setting a personal example by renouncing his hearth and home. He emphasized the three Ds—Discipline, Development, Dedication.

Har Dayal's political programme included education of the masses, criticism of all anti-national and pro-British activities and laying down broad outlines of a struggle to be waged for the attainment of Swaraj. Threatened with impending arrest following a rash of revolutionary activity in Bengal and Maharashtra, he was persuaded to leave for England (September 1908). The murder of William Wyllie (1848-1909) forced him on to Paris where, after a brief association with Madame Cama and the *Bande-Mataram* and a stay that further disillusioned him, he left for the U.S.A. in 1911. In Berkeley, he found employment as a Lecturer in Sanskrit at the University of California. Here, with the help of some affluent people, he instituted 6 scholarships to enable Indian students to study abroad and later work for the welfare of their country. But his extremist and somewhat unorthodox ideas—advocacy of a radical political change, socialism and free love—cost him his job.

In 1912-13, while secretary of the San Francisco branch of the 'Industrial Workers of the World', Har Dayal also helped to organize the Ghadr Party (q.v.). That his radical views greatly influenced the thought and activities of its members, mainly Panjabi peasants, is borne out by their determination to defy such laws as promoted racial discrimination. Sore with the victimization of Asian nationals, Har Dayal inspired the Ghadrites with national aspirations and encouraged them to return to India (while the British were preoccupied with the War) and incite people into revolting against established authority.

The Ghadrites and Har Dayal's role in the (Ghadr) party bear emphasis. It must be conceded at the outset that, except for the overseas Sikhs, those they sought to arouse were at once timid as well as tentative in their approach. The agitators for the most part stayed safely in the background and the few who tried to implement policy were tragically inept in achieving what their 'sacrifices' intended. The rhetoric of revolution was garbled, with alternative appeals to the European revolutionaries of the 19th century, the on-going Russian revolution and fanciful evocation of Indian military glory, in which heroes were idolized like gods.

The revolutionaries were often frustrated less by the British than by turncoats in their own ranks and a diffused leadership, and by repressive acts of the British who used their small but well-informed intelligence network to scotch their plans for revolution. Convinced that Har Dayal's influence had permeated the Ghadrites, the British put pressure on the U.S. authorities to have him arrested. A timely warning helped Har Dayal flee to Germany in 1914. There he tried to organize support for the struggle in India, although some scholars believe that he was not associated with the Berlin 'conspirators' till January 1915 and by that time the latter no longer wielded any influence. Har Dayal's stay in Germany proved somewhat disconcerting. Wilhelmine Germany's aim and objective of dominating the Arab lands, then ruled by the Ottoman Turks, convinced him of its false pretensions to be champion of the cause of Indian freedom. He appears to have concluded that, if imperialism had perforce to be endured, its British and French versions were more acceptable than their German or Japanese counterparts. A recent study suggests that he was also disenchanted with the Berlin 'conspirators' because they supported a Turkish-Mohammedan movement. Suspicious of his changed stance, the Germans frustrated all his attempts to leave the country, and it was only in 1918 that Har Dayal succeeded in crossing over to Sweden.

Meanwhile, converted from a radical to a pacifist, Har Dayal became a firm supporter of the Home Rule Movement (q.v.). Gradually, he was to become alienated from the freedom struggle in his own country. For 10 years Har Dayal stayed in Stockholm, lecturing at its University and studying fine arts. He also toured France and the U.S.A. In 1926, after the grant of amnesty to political agitators, he was allowed to return to Britain where he completed his doctoral thesis in 1931. Thereafter, he devoted himself exclusively to literary pursuits.

It was thus not surprising that Har Dayal and others of his ilk retired early, and disenchanted, from the nationalist scene, to expend their energies in other directions. Many retreated into religiously-oriented intellectual traditions. His three close associates—V. D. Savarkar, Bhai Parmanand and Rash Behari Ghose (q.v.)—founded the militant Hindu Mahasabha (q.v.). Most of his peers concentrated only on the importation of western political and economic ideas, but Har Dayal believed that it was more than political institutions and technology that gave the British their advantage.

The author of several books, his *Hints for Self Culture* is among the better known; another famous work is *Twelve Religions and Modern Life*. The former contains, in HD's own words, 'my philosophical and ethical propaganda (including economics and politics). It aims at preaching the ideal of free thought in a constructive fashion. The spiritual vacuum, in which most modern "advanced" peoples pass their lives must be filled in.'

HD's contribution to the national movement can be gleaned in two major, and successful, developments of the Gandhian era. Thus, his early activities may be said to have anticipated the Non-cooperation Movement (q.v.), for he had advised his followers to 'disassociate [themselves] from the British government.' Again, he stood for the active involvement of the masses in the movement; they it were, he argued, who constituted the main political force and needed to be educated to demand freedom.

It is hard to cast Har Dayal into a mould; his was an elusive personality. Over the years, there were abrupt changes in his activities and attitudes as he moved from a militant nationalist—and baiter, *par excellence*, of British pretensions—to a pacifist and internationalist who embraced not only the ideals but the homilies of the society he had once scorned and reviled.

One of his biographers has suggested that there were, in reality, three Har Dayals. As a student in India, he was overshelmingly moved by his spirit of love for humanity. In what proved to be the middle phase, he was to develop an abiding love for Hindu nationalism and finally, it took the form of love of freedom for Hindustan—a love of freedom, and, equally, a love for Hindustan.

Har Dayal died in March 1939 while on a lecture tour in the U.S.A.

C. Emily Brown, *Har Dayal: Hindu Revolutionary and Rationalist*, New Delhi, 1976; Dharma Vira, *Lala Har Dayal and the Revolutionary Movements of his Times*, New Delhi 1970 and *Letters of Lala Har Dayal*, Ambala, 1970.

Charles Hardinge (1858–1944)

Charles Hardinge, later Baron Hardinge of Penhurst, Viceroy and Governor-General (1910-16) could boast of connections with India dating back half a century; Henry Hardinge (q.v.), the first Viscount, his grandfather, had been Governor-General (1844-8) too. Educated at Harrow and Cambridge, he joined the Foreign Department in 1880 and rendered distinguished service at important diplomatic outposts: Constantinople (1881-4), Berlin (1884) and later (1885-6), Washington. He was Charge d'Affaires at Sofia (1887-9, 1890-1), with a brief stint in between at Constantinople. After being Charge d'Affaires at Bucharest (1892-3) he took over as head of the Chancery in Paris, 1893-6, followed by 2 years in Teheran and 5 as Secretary in St. Petersburg.

By now an experienced, polished diplomat, he was appointed Under-Secretary of State in the Foreign Office and accompanied Edward VII on his tours through Western Europe, following which he returned to St. Petersburg as Ambassador. In 1906, as Permanent Under-Secretary of State, he utilized his long experience in Russia to knock into shape an amicable settlement with that country, which came to be known as the Anglo-Russian Convention (1907), although a similar arrangement contemplated with Germany did not come off.

In November 1910 Hardinge arrived in India determined to pacify the vocal if disgruntled educated classes represented by the Indian National Congress (q.v.), as well as strengthen the empire by cultivating the friendship and confidence of the Indian States (q.v.) and their ruling princes.

An enlightened and liberal Viceroy, he firmly believed that Indians committed no crime in working for self-government and proclaiming it to be their 'national ideal.' At the same time, he was prepared to check any hasty realization of the goal, especially during the years of World War I, and secured a strict enforcement of repressive measures to curb all anti-government policies, alternating between political concessions and curbs.

Hardinge argued that the diminishing influence of the Moderates in the counsels of the Congress needed to be propped up and that a solution of the outstanding issues would be conducive to this end. A major area of conflict between the government and the Extremists had been the Partition of Bengal (q.v.). On a deeper analysis of the problem, the Viceroy concluded that, besides creating a psychological dilemma, a divided Bengal had failed to minimize administrative difficulties. Even though initially opposed to a reunification of the province as indicative of an obvious surrender to Extremist elements, he soon realized that a re-united Bengal was the only way of allaying discontent and curbing terrorist activities. Besides, splitting the enormous area under the Bengal Presidency into three independent units would, he argued, be an ideal solution to a complicated administrative problem.

With Whitehall's prior approval he therefore announced the annulment of the Partition as a dramatic climax to the Delhi Darbar of 1911. The measure was to take formal shape in the Government of India Act, 1912. In brief, the capital was shifted to Delhi; Bengal re-united as a province under a Governor; Bihar, Chhotanagpur and Orissa came under a Lieutenant-Governor while Assam reverted to a Chief Commissionership.

George V's visit and the holding of the Imperial Darbar (12 December 1911), briefly referred to, was a great occasion celebrated with traditional Mughal pomp and pageantry. The central idea appears to have been that the princes pay homage to the sovereign in person instead of his representative, as had been the case hitherto. The occasion was used to announce some minor concessions, viz., an enhanced grant for education, the eligibility of Indians for the Victoria Cross, all hopefully aimed at winning the loyalty of the people.

Hardinge had been labouring under the impression that the political unrest then so evident in the country was merely on the surface and posed no serious threat. A bomb attack as he made the state entry into Delhi on 23 December 1912, however, shook him out of this complacency, although he still failed to fathom the true extent of the revolutionary movement and its varied ramifications. To reassure the Moderates, he pledged that he would not deviate from his liberal policy on account of the incident.

In keeping with this declaration, he condemned the measures taken to put down passive resistance in South Africa, identifying himself with the rights of Indians and denouncing the disabilities and indignities imposed on them. As a result of his uncompromising stand, the feeling against him in South Africa and in certain Tory quarters in England was so strong that there was talk even of recalling him. Ominous war clouds over Europe and possible agitation in India against such an action, however, came in the way.

Hardinge attempted to (i) get Indians admitted as officers in the army; (ii) employ a larger number of them in the civil service; and (iii) implement the Minto-Morley Reforms (q.v.) of 1909. A Royal Commission under Lord Islington was set up to deliberate on the organization of the civil service, but made no constructive suggestions. The Governor-General also advocated better representation for India at the Imperial Conference and gave the green signal to the establishment of a Muslim University at Aligarh and a Hindu University at Banaras.

At the same time, it should be clearly understood that, as he viewed it, British policy implied (i) the principle of decentralization; (ii) an increase in the number of Indians employed in the administration; and (iii) the permanence of British rule in India. Notwithstanding this, it was evident to him that 'colonial sef-government on lines of the British Dominions is absolutely out of question' for India.

While seemingly progressive, the strenuous war years saw the Governor-General assenting to a number of repressive measures for the security of the empire. The Prevention of Seditious Meetings Act (q.v.) initiated by Minto (q.v.) was placed on the statute book by him. He tried to allay criticism of this measure by holding out a solemn pledge that it would be made applicable only to affected or proclaimed areas, and would cease to be operative as soon as conditions normalized. The Indian Criminal Law Amendment Act (q.v.) provided for the punishment of criminal conspiracies. The Delhi Conspiracy case, in which an attempt was made on the Governor-General's life, was tried under this Act and 4 conspirators sentenced to death.

Despite the measures listed above, Hardinge was unable to hold back the flood-tide of nationalist and revolutionary activity and agitation. England's preoccupations with the War had offered an ideal opportunity and, even though some moderate opinion showed a pro-British bias, the Home Rule

Movement (q.v.) born in 1916, had raised the slogan that England's difficulty was India's opportunity.

A more serious danger appeared in the Panjab, a border province and the largest recruiting ground for the army, which was flooded by Ghadr Party (q.v.) revolutionaries attempting to arouse the masses and subvert the armed forces against established authority. With the entry of Turkey into the war, and the Caliphate itself in jeopardy, political agitation took a powerful hold among the Muslims. To curb all such revolutionary activities, the Government adopted the Defence of India Act. The Ghadrites were hounded out, the Khilafat Movement (q.v.) leaders and the Congress agitators imprisoned.

In foreign affairs, Hardinge's diplomatic skill was used with success in establishing friendly relations of much value with the Amir of Afghanistan. He handled with firmness the controversy over the status of Indians in South Africa and the question of opium in China.

Hardinge steadily met the persistent demand for recruits and money to aid the British war effort. The number of men and officers sent out was the largest hitherto. The methods by which this was achieved—coercion, conscription and such other devious means—have been called into question, and held to be the principal reason for the widespread unrest that followed. The Viceroy was severely censured for grossly mismanaging the Indian expedition to Mesopotamia, which had resulted in a shameful surrender at Kut-el-Amara in 1916.

Hardinge retired from India in April 1916, to be Chairman of the Royal Commission on Ireland and presently returned to his old post in the Foreign Office. Three years later he was one of the British delegates to the Paris Peace Conference (1919). Between 1920-2, he was British Ambassador to France, after which he held no public office, returning to Oakfield, near Penhurst, where he lived till his death in August 1944.

Hardinge of Penhurst, *My Indian Years*, London, 1948; S. R. Mehrotra, *India and the Commonwealth*, London, 1965; Lala Hanumant Sahai, 'First-hand account of the bomb attack on Hardinge', *Organiser*, January 1970, pp. 37-8; *DNB 1941-50*, pp. 356-8 (Rowland Thomas Baring, Earl Cromer).

Henry Hardinge (1785-1856)

Hardinge, first Viscount Hardinge of Lahore and later Field Marshal, was Governor-General of India from 1845-8. He spent a major part of his career in the Royal Army which he had joined in 1799 and saw active service in Europe, where he earned military recognition. In 1820 he became a member of Parliament, served as Secretary of State for War (1826-30) in the Duke of Wellington's (1769-1852) Cabinet and, later (1841-44), in Sir Robert Peel's (1788-1850). He was also briefly Secretary for Ireland (July-November 1830 and December 1834-April 1835).

Hardinge's appointment as Governor-General was admirably suited to carry to fruition the expansion of British dominion begun by his predecessors. Internal conditions in the Panjab, then virtually under the uneasy rule of the Khalsa army, were near-chaotic. Hardinge, who had at first believed in maintaining a strong Sikh state as a buffer between British-ruled India and the Muslim countries beyond the Indus, soon veered round to the view that the (Sikh) community was incapable of maintaining a stable government. He thereupon embarked on a policy of deliberately weakening the Panjab by strengthening the Dogras in the hills and fortifying the Sutlej frontier with a view to annexing the state at an opportune moment. Armed preparedness therefore continued unabated. In November 1845 he had doubled the force stationed on the state's borders—having raised it to 40,000 men and 94 guns. The troops were moved up to Ferozepur, Ambala, Ludhiana and Meerut, all poised for action. Aware of the formidable Khalsa army, steps were taken to bribe its leadership and thus sabotage any chances of its victory. Fortunately for the British, some Sikh generals were amenable to such blandishments, while generous promises were made of continuing them in their positions under British rule.

The Khalsa army crossed the Sutlej on 11 December 1845. Not altogether unprepared, though a trifle surprised, Hardinge declared war. Waiving the right to the supreme command which had been exercised by Cornwallis (q.v.) and the Marquis of Hastings (q.v.), the Governor-General offered to serve under Sir Hugh Gough as his second in command, an act of great magnanimity. British victories during the First Anglo-Sikh War (q.v.) were dearly bought, and it has been held that any prolongation of hostilities might have reversed the result. With the Sikh defeat at Sobraon, where Hardinge was present, both sides were equally eager for peace and the Treaty of Lahore (q.v.) brought hostilities to a close.

Much has been made of Hardinge's 'forbearance' in not annexing the state. His appears to have been a sensible solution based on long military experience. The Khalsa army was by no means completely subdued, nor were British troops, as was common knowledge, poised for an immediate and effective take-over of the Panjab. The Governor-General therefore preferred to complete his work by stages. By the end of the year (1846), Maharani Jind Kaur (q.v.) and her faction at the court had been replaced by a regency of 8 Sardars presided over, and under the virtual control of, the local British Resident.

Hardinge's tenure of office was undisturbed by any other major event. A revolt in Kolhapur and Sawantwari was put down by Col. James Outram (q.v.) and these territories placed under a British Agent. A special agency was also set up for areas occupied by the Gonds. Internal conditions in Oudh (q.v.) were reported to be worsening, whereupon Hardinge issued a warning to its Nawab to undertake improvements.

Among other measures taken by the Governor-General were construction work on the Ganges canal, establishment of the Engineering College at Roorkee, introduction of tea-culture, especially in Assam, and the preservation of historical monuments. He increased the scale of pensions awarded to sepoys for injuries sustained in battle and originated the practice of carrying the kits of European troops at public expense. He established the first sanatorium in Darjeeling and helped Henry Lawrence (q.v.) set up an institution for soldiers' children at Kasauli.

Hardinge's son, who acted as his private secretary in India and later wrote a biography of his father, has indicated that three subjects 'strongly aroused' the Governor-General's feelings: human sacrifice, Sati (q.v.) and infanticide. It is said that as many as 16 officers were added to the staff already employed to suppress these practices among the Gonds in Orissa and, they were, in fact, 'practically' wiped out. His strong persuasion with 'native' rulers also helped to wipe out these practices in the Indian States (q.v.).

With no impending threat from the Marathas or the Sikhs, the Governor-General felt safe to go ahead with a programme of reduction in the armed forces. In this way a saving of £1,60,000 was effected in the military budget. Nor were the interests of the sepoys neglected. Additional 'batta', pensions and other perquisites were allowed. In so doing, he kept two basic principles in view. One, to maintain unimpaired the strength of the European troops in India; two, to re-deploy the entire army so that the North-West Frontier (q.v.) and the Panjab might be secured against any contingency.

His measures, it has been said, were characterized by 'moderation and vigour' and his bequest was a surplus in the budget and the possibility of a continuance of peace. In official life he has been described as plain, straightforward, just and an excellent man of business.

Hardinge retired of his own accord in 1848. After 4 years of special duty in Ireland, he served in successive military appointments as Master-General of Ordnance (1852-4) and, after the death of the Duke of Wellington (1852), General Commanding in Chief, Forces. When the Crimean war (1854-6) began, Hardinge was blamed for a manifest want of preparation by military authorities and the resultant disasters to British arms. He died in 1856, a year after his elevation to the rank of Field Marshal.

Charles, Viscount Hardinge, *Viscount Hardinge*, 2nd ed., Oxford, 1921; *DNB*, VIII, pp. 1226–9 (Henry Manners Chichester); Khushwant Singh, *Ranjit Singh*, London, 1962, pp. 40, 42n., 43n.

Hartog Committee Report (1928–9)

In May 1928 the Simon Commission (q.v.) inquiring into the working of the Montagu-Chelmsford Reforms (q.v.) appointed a 5-member Committee with Sir Philip Joseph Hartog (1846-1947), a one-time Registrar of the University of London who was at the time member of the Foreign Public Service Commission, as its Chairman. The Committee was asked to report on the growth of education in British India and indicate the potentialities of its further progress, provision having been made in the 1919 Act itself for the appointment of such a Committee before a further instalment of reforms was introduced. Apart from the chairman, the Committee's members were: Sir Amherst Selby Bigge, at one time Permanent Secretary to the Board of Education in England; Sir Sayid Sultan Ahmad (1880-1963); Sir George Anderson, then Director of Public Instruction, Panjab; Raja Narendra Nath (1864-1945), then a member of the Legislative Council of the Panjab; and Mrs. Muthulakshmi Reddi (1886-1968), then Deputy President of the Madras Legislative Council.

The Committee's report was officially called an 'Interim Report of the Indian Statutory Commission', being a 'Review of Growth of Education in British India by the Auxiliary Committee appointed by the Commission.' Usually referred to as the Education Committee Report, it was submitted in September 1928. It was actually issued on 18 October 1929 as Cd. 3407 of 1929. It was a unanimous document, except for a sharp minute of dissent by Raja Narendra Nath.

In its report, the Committee said *inter alia*; 'Responsibility for mass education through which lies formation of an educated electorate rests primarily with the state, and provision of educational facilities for all classes of the community should not be left entirely to the mercy of the local authorities.'

Among other matters, the Committee pointed out that in the 1917-27 decade, there had been a rapid growth in the education of all classes and communities and some improvements too. It was, however, far from satisfied with the progress of literacy during the years since 1882. For this it adduced two main reasons: (a) neglect of primary education; (b) far too much attention being paid to higher education. 'Primary education', the Committee had pointed out, 'is ineffective unless it at least produces literacy. On the average, no child who has not completed a primary course of at least four years will become permanently literate.'

The Committee found the general condition of secondary education satisfactory but was appalled by the large number of failures at the Matriculation examination. It felt that unitary universities alone were not adequate and that most contained a large number of undeserving students. The Committee was struck by the educational disparity between boys and girls of school-going age and went to the extent of recommending the gradual introduction of compulsion for the education of girls.

The report underlined the fact that there was considerable wastage of manpower resources and ineffectiveness, particularly in the primary system: it suggested various remedies for combating this. It concluded that the transfer of authority from the Central to provincial governments had been far too sudden and that there was need to establish a centralized education agency at Delhi. The Committee was emphatic that the transfer of control over primary education to local bodies was not desirable in so far as they were inexperienced and reluctant to consult educational experts. Larger powers thus needed to be assumed by provincial governments.

In his note of dissent Raja Narender Nath took strong exception to the Committee's proposal for reservation of seats in schools 'for the Muslims and others, if found necessary' and to its recommendation for religious education in public schools for the classes desiring it. *Inter alia*, the Raja expressed the view that 'reservations once created tend to become permanent and can be removed only by the intervention of a third party.' If the special arrangements suggested for Muslims were extended to other communities, 'much confusion will be the result.' Sir Amherst Selby Bigge in his note concurred generally but desired to make some reservations in respect of chapter V which in his view did not 'adequately represent' the serious defects of secondary education and chapter VII which seemed to him to advocate 'more rapid and extensive expansion' of female education than was wise or practicable. Dr Muthulakshami Reddi appended a note on women's education.

The Hartog report was to become the sheet-anchor of official policy in the decades before the transfer of power. A direct result of it was that such phrases as stagnation and wastage became by-words of educational terminology. With the government's increasing emphasis on 'consolidation and no expansion', as in Macaulay's filtration theory, the Hartog report frustrated the growth of primary education in the years preceding Independence.

On the other hand, it recommended improvement in the salary scales of teachers, increase in the inspectorate, improvement of curricula, emphasis on tutorial work in colleges, adult education and such cognate subjects. These were unfortunately pigeon-holed and never implemented.

Philip Hartog, *Some Aspects of Indian Education: Past & Present*, Oxford, 1939; B. D. Bhatt and J. C. Aggarwal, *Educational Document in India, 1831-1968*, New Delhi, 1969, pp. 39–41; S. N. Mukerji: *History of Education in India, Modern Period* Baroda, 1955.

Hastings (Earl of Moira) (1754–1826)

Francis Rawdon Hastings, first Marquess of Hastings and second Earl of Moira, was Governor-General in India during 1813-23. Earlier (1773-81) he had a distinguished record of military service in the American colonies; in 1788, he was promoted a Lieutenant-General and appointed commander-in-chief of the forces in Scotland. Equally active in politics, he was a member of the House of Commons (1781) and was created a peer. He opposed Charles James Fox's India Bill (1783) but later fell out with the Younger Pitt and joined the Whig opposition. He continued to be an active member of Parliament till 1812, when he was appointed to India. Here he combined his office as Governor-General with that of commander-in-chief of the army so as to prevent, in view of the unsettled conditions then prevalent in the country, divided counsels at the top.

Before assuming office, Hastings had taken strong exception to Wellesley's (q.v.) policies which had resulted in intractable wars and heavy expenditure. Yet, soon after his arrival in India there appears to have been a complete change in his views and his approach now smacked of the strong and powerful impact of Charles Metcalfe (q.v.). Later, he was to become obsessed with a 'forward' policy vis-a-vis the 'native' princes, on the premise that the British possessed the military strength for a swift campaign and, with no serious rival in the field, could easily gain control over a large part of the country. He made no secret of the fact that his true aim was 'to render the British paramount in effect, if not declaredly so.' This was to be achieved through diplomacy, if possible; by war, if necessary.

With the decline of the Mughal empire and the in-fighting among the Maratha leaders, central India had been overrun by the Pindaris (q.v.) while the Rajput states lived in terror of Pathan marauders. The so-called ring-fence policy of the British vis-a-vis the Indian States (q.v.) had resulted in the former befriending a few whom the John Company (q.v.) protected and antagonizing a host of others, who were outside its political parameters. A broad outline of the Governor-General's plan now was to suppress the predatory system and bring to heel the important states.

In order to deal effectively with the Pindaris, Hastings had first to tackle the Maratha chiefs who harboured and, indeed, lent countenance to these hordes. Above all, he feared Sindhia the most, as one capable of organizing an anti-British coalition of independent rulers. Overtures were therefore made to coerce the Marathas into some sort of an agreement to annihilate the Pindaris. Negotiations were also opened with the strategically located Rajput states, 'our natural allies and the natural enemies of the Marathas.' They had hitherto been spurned because of the Company's prior commitments and treaties with the principal Maratha chiefs, Holkar and Sindhia. While Hastings' able representatives in the states concerned were making headway with these diplomatic manoeuvres, the Governor-General on his own decided to tackle the threat posed by the rulers of Nepal.

The Gurkhas, the Company alleged, had been making insidious encroachments on British territories and refused an amicable settlement of disputes. The Anglo-Nepalese War (q.v.) broke out in 1814 and dragged on for two years with the British suffering several reverses. It was brought to a successful conclusion by David Ochterlony (q.v.) when the defeated Gurkhas signed the Treaty of Sagauli (q.v.) in 1816.

No sooner was he free of Nepal than the Governor-General drew up detailed plans and made extensive preparations for a campaign against the Pindaris, aiming simultaneously to achieve his major political objective of annihilating the Maratha confederacy. Undeterred by opposition from his Council in India and the Board of Control and the Court of Directors in London, he launched upon his campaign. The Pindari War (q.v.) began in 1817 and, as Hastings expected, the Maratha chiefs rallied to their cause. The Peshwa's sympathies were not unknown either. All this led to the short and swift campaigns of the Third and, as it proved, the last Anglo-Maratha War (q.v.). The Governor-General's ambitious plans worked out to a successful conclusion: the Pathan chief, Amir Khan, was neutralized by being made Nawab of Tonk; the Peshwa, Holkar and Bhonsle were worsted in combat while Sindhia, hedged in from all sides by British troops, remained perforce an unhappy spectator of the grim tragedy. As an aftermath, the office of the Peshwa was abolished while Raja Pratap Singh of Satara was placed at the head of the residuary Maratha state.

All the Maratha chiefs were now compelled to sign subsidiary alliances with the Company. This was followed by a series of defensive treaties with some central Indian and Rajput states. The authority of the Mughal emperor (which Hastings had refused to acknowledge, being the first Governor-General not to offer *nazar*) was now supplanted firmly and finally by that of the Company, which was in undisputed control of nearly two-thirds of the sub-continent.

The Governor-General's policy towards the Marathas came under strong censure from the Court of Directors, who denounced any further extension of territory. During the last few years of his tenure, Hastings devoted himself to the civil and financial duties of his administration. In spite of the alleged hostility of the Directors, he supported many useful measures for the education of the 'natives' and encouraged the freedom of the press. He allowed newspapers to circulate at a reduced rate of postage, and it was during his administration that 'a native journal' appeared in print.

Hastings was a tall, stately figure with an impressive demeanour. As a politician he is chiefly remembered as the friend and confidant of the Prince of Wales (the future George IV). His capacity to rule was remarkable; in addition, he was a skilful soldier and an able administrator. In his younger days he had denounced Britain's government of India as one 'founded in injustice' and 'established by force.'

Although it exterminated the political power of the Marathas, the Company maintained friendly relations with Ranjit Singh (q.v.) and the Amirs of Sind (q.v.). Hastings, though professedly against all interference in the internal affairs of the subsidiary states, wanted at the same time just enough control to 'ensure operative ascendancy.' This worked out in practice in the case of Oudh (q.v.), Mysore, Hyderabad, Baroda, Travancore and Cochin. The conduct of external policy as well as the armed forces in each case was under British supervision, apart from which their Residents enjoyed great personal discretion as to day-to-day interference in internal matters.

During Hastings' administration the salary and status of Indian judges were improved, Eurasians were employed in state service for the first time and token funds earmarked for education. His biographer has underlined the importance of Hastings' contribution by suggesting that in 1813 the Company's possessions were 'disjointed and fragmentary'; its frontiers far from 'adequately guarded and maintained'; communications both 'uncertain and difficult', while rapid access to many of the provinces was 'impossible.' Ten years later, 'All this was changed. The hostility of Nepal was overcome and the northern frontier was secured. The Maratha combination against British rule and the predatory system which threatened the Company's territories were annihilated . . .Central India was settled and pacified. In a word, the independent native states who conceived in 1813 that they could expel the English from India were defeated, and in 1823 every province in that vast region up to the Sutlej was brought into subjection to the Government of Calcutta.'

Nor were British imperial interests outside India neglected. Ceylon was subjugated and occupied in 1819; for the security of its trade, the secession of Singapore was obtained. In 1822 a mission was sent to the king of Thailand in the hope of establishing commercial contacts with that country. Several expeditions were at the same time despatched to the Persian Gulf and Arabia to put down pirate fleets. Hastings' intimate involvement in the scandals of the notorious Palmer & Co. (q.v.) and the censure of the Court of Directors for his acting contrary to the Act of Parliament (1796) led to his resignation in 1821 and his departure from India early in 1823. A year later he was appointed Commander-in-Chief of British forces in Malta. After a brief stint in the House of Lords (1825), he returned to Malta the following year. Here he died on 28 November 1826.

Major J. Ross-of-Blandensburg, *The Marquess of Hastings, KG and the Final Overthrow of the Maratha Power*, Rulers of India, Oxford, 1900; M. S. Mehta, *Lord Hastings and the Indian States*, Bombay 1930; *DNB*, IX, pp. 117-22 (George Francis Russel Barker).

Warren Hastings (1732–1818)

Warren Hastings, who rose to be the first Governor-General of the Presidency of Fort William in Bengal, came out to India in 1750 as a clerk in the employ of the East India Company (q.v.). Ambitious, industrious and endowed with unusual intelligence, he earned quick promotions and was posted (1750) at Kasimbazar where he was taken prisoner by the Nawab's men. His detention, however, was brief and after the Battle of Plassey (q.v.) he served as an assistant and later Resident at the court of the Nawab. In 1761 he was appointed a member of the Calcutta Council under Henry Vansittart (q.v.) where he assiduously supported Mir Kasim's (q.v.) rights

as a sovereign prince and objected to the malpractices of the English factors.
After a brief spell in England (1764-8), he returned as Councillor in Madras.
In April 1772 he relieved John Cartier (q.v.) as Governor of Bengal.

On appointment to this office, his political superiors in London directed
him to carry out some long overdue reforms in the administration. These
became all the more necessary as the Company was now to stand forth as
Diwan, thereby putting an end to the evils associated wth the Dual System
(q.v.). He began by strengthening the authority of the Bengal Council.
Shitab Roy and Mohammed Reza Khan, who had been acting as the Diwans
of Bihar and Bengal respectively, were charged with corruption—Maharaja
Nand Kumar (q.v.), whom Hastings disliked intensely, aiding in collecting
evidence against the two. Munni Begum, a concubine of Mir Jafar (q.v.),
was designated Regent for the minor Nawab, Mubarak-ud-Daula, with Raja
Gurdas, the son of Nand Kumar, as Diwan. The ruler's minority was taken
advantage of by the Company to effect a massive retrenchment in his long
list of pensioners, apart from scaling down the sum (from Rs 32 to 16 lakhs
annually) due to the Nawab himself. Hereditary zamindaris were abolished
and revenue collection for each pargana awarded to the highest bidder.
Zamindari chowkies were done away with and 5 main customs houses set up
in their place. In the districts, the revenue collectors were to be 'natives' but
required to function under English provincial collectors.

The Governor's 'masterful temperament' prevented him from taking
advice from people better qualified than himself in revenue matters. While it
led to a saving of Rs 50 lakhs in expenditure, this would largely explain why
the system he initiated resulted in greater corruption, if also confusion.

Hastings also brought about a reorganization of judicial institutions and
recodification of Hindu law. Courts of appeal for civil and criminal cases
were established at Calcutta, to be headed by the President of the Council
and two of its members. In criminal cases, investigation was conducted and
capital sentences passed by the Nawab's deputy, the Chief Qazi, the Mufti
and the three Maulvis.

The 'central pillar' of Hastings' foreign policy was his alliance with Oudh
(q.v.) which ensured for the British the safety of their newly-acquired
eastern territories. The Governor strengthened this bond further by sending
Robert Barker (q.v.) to witness a treaty in 1772 between the Rohillas and
Shuja-ud-Daula (q.v.). In 1774, the Treaty of Banaras (q.v.) stipulated that
the Company would assist the Nawab Wazir in conquering Rohilkhand. In
the war that followed, the Rohilla leader, Hafiz Rahmat Khan (q.v.) was
killed, his forces defeated and the Treaty of Lalding (q.v.) signed with his
successor, Faizulla Khan.

For the first 2 years (1772–4) of his tenure, the Governor's authority was
relatively unhampered, with the result that he behaved with confidence and
determination in executing policies aimed essentially at establishing British
dominion in India on a firm basis. With the Regulating Act (q.v.), Hastings
assumed his new title 'Governor-General of Fort William in Bengal' and was
charged with supervising and, to a limited extent, controlling the goverance
of the two other presidencies of Bombay and Madras. John Clavering
George Monson, Richard Barwell and Philip Francis were appointed to
assist him while a Supreme Court of judicature which would interpret the
law was set up at Calcutta with Elijah Impey (q.v.) as its first Chief Justice.

The post-1774 years proved to be a difficult phase in Hastings' career. A triumvirate in the Council (barring Barwell) led by Philip Francis, harassed the Governor-General and frustrated him in all that he attempted, subjecting him to close and embarrassing scrutiny on policy matters, as though he were *prima facie* a culprit. Ambiguity regarding the juridical limits of the Supreme Court also caused controversy and friction; it was resolved to an extent by making the Chief Justice wholly incharge of the Sadar Diwani Adalat while later legislation was to exclude the Supreme Court from interference in civil courts.

In 1775, egged on no doubt by the dissident Councillors, Maharaja Nand Kumar brought forth charges of corruption against Hastings. 'To forestall an inquiry,' and punish him for 'telling tales,' the Governor-General accused the Maharaja of forgery and later got him successfully convicted of the charge. In all this, he received the active help and support of Elijah Impey. Nand Kumar's punishment was death itself.

In the same year, in an effort to make some territorial gains the Bombay presidency concluded the Treaty of Surat (q.v.) with Raghunath Rao or Raghoba (q.v.), a claimant to the Peshwa's throne at Poona. The move was destined to involve the Company in the long drawn-out agony of a wasteful struggle, the First Anglo-Maratha War (q.v.). The Bengal government unanimously opposed it and sent Colonel Upton to negotiate afresh the terms of peace. The Treaty of Purandhar (q.v.) that followed resulted in the British withdrawing their support from Raghoba. Three years later the presence of a notorious French adventurer, St. Lu'bin, in Poona made matters worse; he declared himself an accredited agent of the French king, stayed on for over a year (1777-8) and allegedly offered the Marathas a defensive alliance with 2,500 European troops in the event of war against the British. The French menace heightened by a declaration of war persuaded the Bombay Government to pledge support afresh to Raghoba's cause. Their hasty action led to an initial rout and the conclusion of the humiliating Convention of Wadgaon (q.v.).

With the death of Colonel Monson (1776) Hastings' hitherto impossible position in the Council was substantially redeemed for, with the help of Barwell and his own casting vote he could henceforth hold his own. This enabled him to continue the war against the Marathas; reinforcements were sent to Poona and to Mysore where Haidar Ali (q.v.) was becoming increasingly active. Knowing that he could not continue for long to fight against the combined onslaught of the Marathas, the Nizam and the ruler of Mysore, Hastings used patience and skill to wean away the Nizam. He also displayed dexterity, and tact, in sowing discord in the Maratha confederacy, threw feelers for peace to Sindhia and finally persuaded him to sign the Treaty of Salbai (q.v.). It now became possible for him to fight the ruler of Mysore, who was finally defeated and made to sign the Treaty of Mangalore (q.v.) in 1784.

The prolonged state of hostilities lasting for well-nigh a decade caused enormous expenditure which the Company could ill-afford and led Hastings to resort to some questionable measures to replenish his treasury. Thus he used force to extort money from Raja Chait Singh (q.v.) of Banaras and the Begums of Oudh (q.v.); both these acts were later to earn the Governor-General considerable notoriety. It would appear, in retrospect, that Hastings was not altogether oblivious of the fact that his actions would be censured: he had accused both the parties of conspiring against the Company and collected some dubious documentary evidence to sustain his case. More, he even had this evidence verified by his friend, Elijah Impey.

Broadly, Hastings' aim was to surround the Company's territories by a chain of protectorates and buffer states. His objective regarding Oudh was to strengthen an important state upon whose security the safety of Bengal itself depended. The subsidiary system whereby an Indian state subsidized a British force for its protection was not new, the French had used it when the Northern Circars had been assigned to Bussy (q.v.) for the support of the French contingent in the service of the Nizam. As developed further by Hastings the system was a method of defence *without* incurring any expenditure, the protected state paying for its own security and the Company, instead of defending its own frontiers, undertook to guard the exposed frontiers of its ally. Hastings believed that the Company had the right to dethrone a disloyal or unsuitable ruler, the objective being to prevent any development that would impair the efficacy of the buffer state and thereby weaken the Company's defences.

The Governor-General has been blamed for the wretched condition of Oudh, but the country was no better under his successors who failed to effect any internal reforms either by remonstrance or advice. The fault lay far more with Asaf-ud-Daula (q.v.) himself than in the subsidiary system which had worked fairly smoothly under Shuja-ud-Daulah. In fact, one is forced to the conclusion that Oudh under Asaf-ud-Daula may not have been able to preserve its independence without the assistance of the Company.

It may be conceded that, to a very large extent, the policy Hastings adopted was forced upon him by his diplomatic inheritance. Hampered by the hostile majority in his Council and exposed to criticism from the Court of Directors, he was never given a free hand. His Residents were recalled, his policy condemned and even reversed. All this notwithstanding, an alliance with the strategically located buffer state of Oudh was a tragic necessity. For the Company was, after Buxar (q.v.), in no position to annex the state. A subsidiary alliance appeared to be the only viable course between annexation and complete non-intervention, for a mere alliance without any payment for the Company's troops would have been ruinous.

It has been aptly said that 'if Clive's (q.v.) sword acquired the Indian empire, it was the brain of Hastings that planted the system of civil administration and his genius that saved the empire in its darkest hour.'

A sound orientalist, Hastings had considerable knowledge of Persian and Bengali. His literary and academic pursuits, 'pandit-hunting' as his detractors were apt to call it, led to the formation of the Asiatic Society of Bengal (q.v.) and gave a great deal of encouragement to the work of William Jones (q.v.).

In 1782 Hastings resigned office in a bid to re-establish his position in England, particularly since Philip Francis had been carrying on a virulent campaign against him. But when the British Prime Minister, Lord North named Clavering his successor, Hastings had Impey invalidate the latter's appointment and stayed on. Fortunately for him, the British Government were far too occupied with the French and American wars to investigate matters. In May 1784 the House of Commons passed a vote of censure against Hastings' conduct; this did not, however, lead to the Governor-General quitting his post.

Hastings finally left India in January 1785; back in England, he was received with 'studied politeness.' Later, in April 1786, the opposition renewed its attack on him in the House of Commons. Numerous charges were brought by Edmund Burke aided by Richard Brinsley Sheridan, Charles James Fox and Gilbert Elliot (later first Earl of Minto (q.v.), 1751-1814, and Governor-General of India). In May, the House decided to impeach him for 'high crimes and misdemeanours' on 22 articles covering the entire gamut of his Indian administration. The trial itself opened in 1788, dragged on for 7 years and has been rated a 'calamitous mistake.' The final verdict acquitted Hastings on all counts.

The major attack on him was mounted by Burke who it has been said 'did not argue; he only declaimed....If it is true that violence defeats itself, since it usually implies a weak case, and the greater the violence the greater the weakness that it has to conceal, then Burke would have done better to remain silent, for every time he opened his mouth he did more harm than good to his cause.'

Burke maintained that the English language did not 'afford terms adequate to the enormity of his crimes.' More, 'I impeach him [Hastings] in the name of the English nation, whose ancient honour he has sullied. I impeach him in the name of the people of India whose rights he has trodden under foot and whose country he has turned into a desert.' Earlier, he had described the Governor-General as a 'vulture fattened upon carrion' and 'a wicked wretch.'

Michael Edwardes has maintained that at the time of his trial Hastings 'tried to conceal the truth or at least to distort it.' In extenuation, he has suggested that most Englishmen at the time were 'out for personal success and profit' and had little sympathy either for India or its people. The Directors lent no support to Hastings' reforms and their tolerance of Indian tradition was based securely on the fact that it was less expensive to tolerate than to transform. This would largely account for Hastings' failure to translate his ideas into practice: they 'remained largely in the mind.'

Nearly 20 years later when the heat and dust of earlier controversies had died down, Hastings was asked to tender evidence in support of the Company's rule. When he appeared at the bar, the Commons honoured him with a standing ovation. In 1814, he was sworn in a member of the Privy Council. He had now retired to his family home at Dalesford where he died on 22 August 1818.

The charges of personal corruption brought against Hastings lack proof and are refuted by the comparatively small savings he had on returning home after a long career. To say that he was a scrupulous politician would be to say too much. He possibly helped the ruin of Nand Kumar, instigated or connived at the spoliation of the Oudh dowagers but, in the final count, 'saved and established' the Company's empire. Said to have looked 'like a great man, and not a bad man' he was rated personally neither corrupt nor yet cruel. It has been said that he was no more than the 'scapegoat upon whose head Parliament laid the accumulated sins, real and imaginary' of the East India Company.

Warren Hastings was neither a nabob nor a *condottiere* and brought back to England a fortune a twentieth the size of Clive's. He was the first Indian civil servant and the only one to have supreme power: later Governors-General and Viceroys were all begotten of the aristocracy. An arrangement which tied India to England more effectively than any constitution: 'it is not surprising that defending Hastings's reputation became the King Charles's head of three generations of an Indian civil service dynasty like the Stracheys.'

Hastings' character remains that of a bureacratic proconsul, with an imperturbable, if steely temperament. His latest biographer criticises those who, like G. R. Gleig, painted him as a saint. His only qualification to be thus regarded is that all through life he is said to have lost his temper three or four times; that he became authoritarian only when people opposed him.

A. Mervyn Davies, *Warren Hastings: Maker of British India*, London, 1935; Penderel Moon, *Warren Hastings and British India*, London 1947; Keith Feiling, *Warren Hastings*, London, 1966; C. Colin Davies, *Warren Hastings and Oudh*, Oxford, 1939; Michael Edwardes, *Warren Hastings: King of the Nabobs*, London, 1976; P. J. Marshall, *The Impeachment of Warren Hastings*, Oxford, 1965.

All-India Hindu Mahasabha

The hazy beginnings of the Hindu Mahasabha synchronize broadly with the awakening of Muslim consciousness in the first decade of the 20th century. As a reaction to the formation of the All India Muslim League (q.v.) at Dacca in December 1906, a provincial conference of the Hindus of Bengal noted with apprehension a 'decrease in the normal growth' of the province's Hindu population and set up a committee to inquire into its causes. About the same time, a provincial Hindu Sabha was founded in the Panjab with a view to 'watching and safeguarding the interests of the entire Hindu community in all respects.' Four years later, at the time of the Minto-Morley Reforms (q.v.), the Panjab committee submitted a memorial drawing attention to the 'differential treatment in the distribution of government patronage' and the 'disadvantageous position' in which the Hindus would be placed in the matter of representation in the porposed (1909) scheme of constitutional reforms. More formally it was at Allahabad, in 1910, that the All-India Hindu Mahasabha was born; a few years later it was re-christened the Akhil Bharatiya Hindu Mahasabha.

Among the Mahasabha's first major problems was the proverbial inability of a majority to organize; there was the additional fact that the Indian National Congress (q.v.) evoked a better response because of its wider, broad-based appeal. The fact was that Hindu-Muslim riots largely provoked Hindu consciousness, as did waves of conversion from the Hindu fold. The latter was due partly to the discontent of outcastes and the proselytizing zeal of Islam and Christianity, as well as gains secured by the Muslims and other minority communities under the Minto-Morley and Montagu-Chelmsford Reforms (q.v.). There was the additional difficulty that, as numerous attempts made by the Congress to achieve Hindu-Muslim unity misfired, the minority community's intransigence grew apace. Unfortunately for its cause, even though a large number of Hindus had a sneaking sympathy with the Mahasabha, when it came to elections and representative institutions, the party's showing was singularly poor.

In its formative phase, the Mahasabha derived a great deal of strength from the Arya Samaj (q.v.). *Shuddhi* (reconversion to the Hindu faith), for instance, had wider ramifications than would be apparent on the surface, the connotation being by no means exclusively religious or theological. The fact is, it had powerful, if sinister, overtones on the national plane. For if the Muslims multiplied in numbers, it was argued, the centre of political power was bound to shift in their favour. One of the Arya Samaj objectives, it may be recalled, was to work for reclaiming all those who had been lost to the Hindu fold and faith.

The early 1920s, described as the 'dawn of Hindu renaissance', witnessed the twin movements of *Shuddhi*, referred to above, and *Sangathan*, a call for (Hindu) unity. It has been estimated that 1922-3 alone saw 450,000 Muslim Rajputs reconverted to Hinduism. In the result, the Banaras session of the Mahasabha (1923) was rated a great success. Party rules were amended, provincial and branch Sabhas organized, while conferences were convened in different parts of the country. Prominent among those who took an active part were the great Arya Samajist leader, Swami Shradhanand (1856-1926) as well as Lala Lajpat Rai and Pandit Madan Mohan Malaviya (q.v.).

Muslim reaction to the activities of the Mahasabha was manifest in the violence of the Moplah Rebellion (q.v.) and the rash of Hindu-Muslim riots that followed in its wake. There were also the *Tabligh* and *Tanzim* movements which aimed at blunting the edge of Hindu propaganda. The worst in all this was a climate of growing discord and mounting suspicion among the two communities. A book illustrating the best way of converting 'kafirs' to Islam received widespread notoriety. Swami Shradhanand, it may be recalled, was murdered (1926) in cold blood as were some other prominent advocates of the Hindu cause.

At its Delhi session (1925-6), the Mahasabha resolved that in the forthcoming elections to the provincial legislative councils candidates inimical to Hindu interests would receive short shrift and that the party would put up its own candidates to oppose them. For the rest, it was not to oppose nominees of the Congress. The accommodation with the latter inherent in the foregoing arrangement did not last for, with the advent of Bhai Parmanand (1874-1947) and Dr B. S. Moonje (1872-1948), the party acquired a more aggressive and militant character. Earlier, it had stood for a strong and united Hindu community and was viewed by many as no more than an adjunct of the Congress.

In the later 20's and the early 30's came such important political developments as the Simon Commission (q.v.), the Round Table Conference (q.v.) and the Communal Award (q.v.). The announcement of the Award and the initial Congress stance of neither accepting nor rejecting it drove a deep wedge between that party and the Mahasabha. The latter now started a vigorous campaign contending that the British dispensation was pronouncedly pro-Muslim and thus gravely unjust to the Hindus. To fight the Congress from within, Pandit Madan Mohan Malaviya and M. S. Aney (1880-1968), both of whom wielded considerable influence on the rank and file, formed the Congress Nationalist Party which was to act as a powerful pressure group.

It may be useful at this stage to sketch out the Mahasabha's political goal as it evolved over the years. In 1918 it had demanded 'responsible self-government' within the British empire. At the same time it was strongly opposed to any considerations of caste, creed or colour in the matter of representation in the legislative councils. Seven years later the party unreservedly opposed communal electorates as well as communal representation in national institutions and public services, holding these to be harmful to wider national interests.

In doing all this, the Mahasabha appealed to its 'non-Hindu brethren' to give up their 'anti-national' demands and thereby help the majority community establish national solidarity and oneness. In 1926 it reiterated that 'communal representation and separate electorates' would hinder the upsurge of national feeling as well as the smooth working of municipal, district, provincial and national representative institutions. In 1928, while opposing separate communal representation, the Mahasabha laid down broad principles that could well form the basis for any future constitution of the country.

The 1932 session of the Mahasabha had unreservedly condemned the British government's Communal Award; in the following year, it debated the feasibility of making an appeal to the League of Nations on the problem of Indian minorities. The party's 1935-6 session condemned the Government of India Act 1935 (q.v.), in so far as it sacrificed the interests of the Hindu majority at the behest of the minority communities. At the same time, the Mahasabha resolved to contest the forthcoming elections under the Act with a view to 'protecting and upholding Hindu interests.' In 1937, the party ruled that, despite its serious lacunae, Hindus should make use of the 1935 scheme of reforms for the larger interests of the country and urged the government to expedite the introduction of the federal part.

That year (1937) the Mahasabha declared its political objective to be the attainment of complete independence by all peaceful and legitimate means. At its Nagpur session (1938), the party urged its provincial branches to organize *akharas* to improve the physique of young men and to start rifle clubs to train them in the handling of arms. The following year it urged the organization of a volunteer corps to be called the Hindu Militia.

During the post-1937 period, even as the Muslim League grew into importance, so did the Mahasabha. In 1940 the party was recognized important enough to be represented in the Governor-General's Executive Council, although 5 years later, at the June 1945 Simla Conference (q.v.), it was completely ignored. The Mahasabha's importance in later years stemmed largely from the fact that it was a foil to an increasingly aggressive Muslim League. As the Congress determinedly, if uncompromisingly, set its face against any compromise with the Muslim League, the Mahasabha's fortunes slumped further. In the 1945-6 general elections to the central and provincial legislatures it was completely routed.

Earlier, on the outbreak of World War II, the Mahasabha demanded: (i) introduction of immediate responsible government at the centre; (ii) redressal of Hindu grievances stemming from the Communal Award; (iii) removal of restrictions for recruitment to the Indian army; (iv) modification of the Indian Arms Act (q.v.); (v) expansion of the Indian Territorial Force as well as the University Training Corps.

At its 1940 session the Mahasabha expressed appreciation of the fact that both the Viceroy as well as the Secretary of State had recognized that the party's co-operation was vital in solving the country's constitutional problems. During the years of World War II, the Mahasabha figured prominently in advocating more aggressive opposition to Muslim claims; at one of its sessions members renounced their titles and hinted that they would launch a mass movement for 'national liberation and the vindication of Hindu rights.' When the Congress went into the political wilderness in 1942, the Mahasabha again came into the limelight as it was now the only political body to which Hindus could turn in meeting what seemed to be the rank communalism of the Muslim League.

In the autumn of 1943 V. D. Savarkar (1883-1966) resigned from the party leadership and, though re-elected president for another year, stayed away under medical advice. The silver jubilee session of the Mahasabha held at Amritsar was presided over by Dr Shyama Prasad Mookerji (1901-53) and inaugurated by the Maharaja of Cossimbazar, whose father had been the first President of the party. In 1944-5, the Mahasabha suffered a series of reverses owing to the release of Gandhi (q.v.) from detention and the return of the Congress to active political life. It protested vigorously against the 'CR' Formula (q.v.); at its annual session at Bilaspur, in December 1944, it adopted a draft constitution embodying the principles for which it had stood. Later, the party registered its strong condemnation of the Wavell Plan (q.v.), which had sought to break the constitutional impasse by setting up an Interim Government (q.v.).

In August 1945 the Mahasabha deplored the official attitude towards the legitimate rights of the Hindus, condemned the government's 'increasingly hostile stance' and, in protest, asked its leaders to renounce their British-conferred titles.

The Mahasabha was not much in evidence either during the Cabinet Mission Plan (q.v.) negotiations with political parties in 1946 or their aftermath. It was virtually ignored at the time of the Interim Government and the June 3rd Plan (q.v.) for the country's partition.

Indra Prakasha, *Hindu Mahasabha: its contribution in India's politics*, New Delhi, 1966; V. D. Savarkar, *Hindu Rashtra Dharma: A Collection of Presidential Speeches delivered from the Hindu Mahasabha platform*, Bombay, 1949; Bruce E. Cleghorn, 'Religion and Politics: the Leadership of the All-India Hindu Mahasabha', In B. N. Pandey (ed.), *Leadership in South Asia*, New Delhi, 1977, pp. 395–425; N. C. Chatterjee, *The Message of the Mahasabha: Collection of Speeches and Addresses*, Calcutta, 1944.

Yashvantrao Holkar (1776–1811)

An illegitimate son of Tukoji Holkar, Yashvantrao (more commonly, Jaswant Rao) was born in 1776. Taking advantage of the chaotic state of affairs at Poona owing largely to the policies of Peshwa Baji Rao II (q.v.), who had the equally incompetent Daulat Rao Sindhia (q.v.) as his adviser, he rose into prominence. Initially, however, after the accession of his brother Kashi Rao who was supported by the Poona regime, Yshvantrao was a virtual fugitive. Gathering some loyal Bhil followers from the regions of the Tapti and the Narmada, Yashvantrao began raiding large areas in the Doab and Malwa and was soon powerful enough to invest the territories of Sindhia and equally challenge Kashi Rao, whom he eventually replaced in 1802.

A confrontation with Sindhia soon became inevitable. Though the sc ores were even, Yashvantrao had established a reputation as a strong leader. Imbued with the utmost confidence in his prowess, he demanded the custody of Khande Rao (the posthumous son of Malhar Rao) from the Peshwa; to pressurise him, he carried out depredations into the latter's territories. Baji Rao's refusal to comply and his confiscation of Yashvantrao's estates brought matters to a head. In the war that ensued the combined forces of the Peshwa and Sindhia were defeated at Hadaspur on 25 October 1802. The Peshwa's flight to Bassein that followed was unexpected. Yashvantrao recognized the serious implications of requesting British help and tried, albeit unsuccessfully, to persuade Baji Rao to desist. To prevent the British from entering Maratha territories to re-install the Peshwa, he put Amrit Rao (brother, by adoption, of Baji Rao) on the throne at Poona.

Simultaneously Yashvantrao sought Nizam Ali's as well as Bhonsle's help against the British. Uncertain of Sindhia's reaction, he was persuaded by the British commander, Colonel Arthur Wellesley, later Duke of Wellington, to withdraw from Poona. All further chances of a coalition among the Maratha chiefs were marred by the British through questionable means.

Later, when the John Company (q.v.) refused to conclude peace on his terms, Yashvantrao declared war. After some initial successes he was defeated by General Lake's forces at Dig and Farrukhabad (1804) as well as at Bharatpur (1805). Unable to muster help either from Sindhia, the Jodhpur raja, or even Ranjit Singh (q.v.), the Holkar chief concluded a treaty of peace with the English at Rajpurghat (q.v.) and returned to Indore.

With his heart full of mediaeval passions, Yashvantrao was singularly unfortunate both in private as well as public life and moved in an atmosphere that was both politically and socially vicious. Strange impulses and whims lent gruesome colour to all his actions. It may be recalled that he was the son of a concubine, exceptionally unlucky both in his upbringing and early associations. In private life, his utter lack of morality made John Malcolm (q.v.) talk of 'his licentious passions' which 'brooked no control.' Maharaja Ranjit Singh described him as a *pakka haramzada* (confirmed rogue), but it has been suggested that Yashvantrao 'was not a hypocrite.'

His strategy for war had a modicum of originality in so far as he made war pay for war; his tactics were 'to disperse for plunder and combine for battle.' Owing to his preoccupations in continuous wars against Sindhia and the British, besides roving campaigns in different places necessitating his living in camp outside the state, Yashvantrao had little time to devote to internal administration. His empire, it has been said, was indeed the empire of the saddle.

Yashvantrao took a keen interest in the organization of his army. Henry Thoby Prinsep has remarked that it was 'the whole machinery of his government' and was, 'at all times, kept in motion so as to enforce contributions from reluctant tributaries. His English contemporaries viewed him as 'savage', 'a demon of destruction' and a 'devil.' Yet it is worth noting that in morals, public or private, he was neither better nor much worse than his other contemporaries—Baji Rao II, Shah Alam II (q.v.), Nawab Asaf-ud-Daula (q.v.), or Daulat Rao Sindhia. In the words of Jadunath Sarkar, all were products of an age of 'rottenness at the core of Indian society.'

Qanungo has maintained, that, in spite of his great failings, the 'golden rogue' of Maratha history was perhaps 'the only man among the Marathas then living' who 'felt vaguely a national pride, an impulse to move forward and a yearning towards achievement.' Sardesai contends that, whatever his methods 'he rose to power from initial nothingness entirely by dint of his personal valour and spirit of adventure.'

After 1806, Yashvantrao found himself in a dreadful predicament with a large following on hand and no funds to maintain it, nor any aptitude for civil administration. His restless spirit would never allow him to take to a peaceful mode of living. Utter disappointment stared him in the face everywhere. He became fretful and impatient of opposition, unable to distinguish between friend and foe. Convinced of the need for a strong artillery arm against the British, he opened a gun factory at Bhanupura and exerted himself in its cause day and night. Some time in October 1808 he was seized with a fit of insanity induced by the death of his nephew, Khande Rao, whom he had poisoned along with his mother—he suspected both of intriguing with his disaffected soldiery. There was also his excessive addiction to liquor. He lingered on in that condition for 3 years—a raving lunatic—and died at Burhanpur at the youthful age of 35. His short career of 9 years full of daring incidents and hair-breadth escapes, he was both loved and feared by his men.

Though Yashvantrao had the foresight to recognize the potential danger to the country posed by the John Company, his failure lay in his inability to set aside factional differences with other Maratha chiefs and to organize effective resistance against the British.

G. S. Sardesai, *A New History of the Marathas*, 3 vols, Bombay, 1968, III; Sudhindra Nath Quanungo, *Jaswant Rao Holkar—the Golden Rogue*, Lucknow, 1965.

The Home Rule (Leagues) Movement

The two Home Rule Leagues established by B. G. Tilak (q.v.) and Annie Besant (q.v.) in April and September 1916 respectively, were the manifestation of a new trend in Indian politics, of which the two leaders were pioneers or even pace-setters.

The term 'Home Rule' was borrowed from a similar movement in Ireland and had figured often in the deliberations of the Indian National Congress (q.v.), being first employed by Shyamaji Krishnavarma (1857-1930) in 1905 in London. The credit for using it meaningfully in terms of organizing and sponsoring the movement goes however to Tilak and Annie Besant.

The birth of the two Leagues marks the advent of a period of aggressive politics aggravated by widespread disappointment with the Minto-Morley Reforms (q.v.) of 1909. Additionally, there was mounting resentment at the continuing repressive policies of the government and of British preoccupations with World War I. An effort was made from 1914 onwards both by Mrs Besant and Tilak to present a united front against the British by bringing the Moderates and the Extremists to a common platform. The former, wedded to a programme of reform in measured stages, used delaying tactics to prevent the Congress from adopting the goal of 'Home Rule.'

His path blocked in the Congress, Tilak, technically an outsider and released from detention in 1914, broke fresh ground. He appeared at the

Bombay Provincial Conference in Poona on 8 May 1915 exhorting the delegates to demand immediate Swaraj or home rule. Off his own bat, he organized a conference at Poona on 23-24 December 1915 which appointed a committee whose report was placed before another conference convened at Belgaum on 27-29 April 1916. The latter resolved *inter alia* to establish the Indian Home Rule League so as to 'attain Home Rule or Self-Government within the British empire by all constitutional means and to educate and organize public opinion in the country towards the attainment of the same.'

The Belgaum conference adopted, at Tilak's instance, a resolution exhorting the Extremists to return to the Congress fold. But his principal objective for the moment was to organize his Home Rule League. To lend him a hand, Mrs Besant came all the way to Poona to address a large meeting at which Tilak took the chair. At the Belgaum conference on 28 April the League was born. Tilak's principal political aides were present. They included Ganesh Shrikrishna Khaparde (1854-1938), Narasimha Chintaman Kelkar (1872-1947) and Balakrishna Shivaram Moonje (1872-1948). Joesph Baptista (1864-1930), his legal advisor and confidant, was elected president of the League, Kelkar its Secretary, and Tilak's personal friend and bodyguard, D. V. Gokhale (1885-1962), named Under Secretary. As for himself, Tilak held no office in the organization.

According to Mrs Besant India's salvation lay 'in Swaraj, Self-Rule, Home Rule; nothing else can preserve and renew her vitality—slowly ebbing away before our eyes.' In her paper, *New India*, dated 25 September 1915, Mrs Besant had indicated her desire 'to start a Home Rule League with "Home Rule for India" as its only objective as an auxiliary to the National Congress here and its British Committee in England.' The Bombay session of the Congress in 1915, however, ruled out her plea to nail Home Rule to its flag-mast. Her League, it is said, was formally launched in Madras towards the end of 1915 at a conclave at which Dadabhai Naoroji (q.v.) presided.

As noticed, a Home Rule (English Auxiliary) League had been formed in England in 1915, in aid of the Indian national movement. The League, Mrs. Besant noted, 'republished a little book of mine, *India—A Nation* when the English government in 1916, persuaded the publishers to withdraw it from publication.' Underlining the importance of her movement, Mrs. Besant put forth the view that 'the cry for Home Rule, Swaraj (Self-rule)…is really a cry for that which is most priceless in a Nation's life, for the life of its very soul, for its right to grow, to evolve, on its own National lines.' Organizationally, her Home Rule League had Sir S. Subramania Iyer (1842-1924) designated Honorary President, C. P. Ramaswami Iyer (1879–1966) and P. K. Telang as General Secretaries, B. P. Wadia as Treasurer and George Sydney Arundale (1878-1945) as Organizing Secretary. Mrs Besant was the powerful President of her League.

There was 'enough rivalry' between Tilak and Annie Besant to make each plough his/her own lonely furrow, but before long, with 'nice reciprocity', he joined her 'Home Rule for India League' and she his 'Indian Home Rule League.' Many others joined both, as did Jawaharlal Nehru (q.v.). While Tilak broadly restricted his League's area of operation to Maharashtra and Karnatak, Mrs Besant's extended generally over the south, although it also embraced Bihar, Bengal, the United Provinces, Gujarat and Sind.

Starting with a small membership and 6 branches, Tilak's League had some 32,000 members on its rolls by 1918. Mrs Besant began with 500 members (among whom were understandably a number of Theosophists) and 10 branches and expanded at a relatively slower pace. The objective in either case was to attain a system of self-government for India within the British empire. The protagonists were not interested in piecemeal reform of the existing system of administration which they wanted replaced by a system of responsible government related only to management of internal affairs. The agitation made rapid strides during 1916-17 and, while broadly active in many parts of the country, registered noticeable progress in the south.

Tilak had elaborated 'Home Rule' to mean 'representative government' or government over which the people would exercise a measure of control. To achieve this end both he and Mrs Besant engaged in extensive pamphleteering, endless tours and lectures, social and educational work, intended both to inform and agitate the masses and involve them in the freedom struggle, instead of letting it remain, as hitherto, an elitist effort. Their initial design to capture power in the Congress failed but, by the end of 1917, the Home Rulers were in command, with the result that Annie Besant was chosen President of the Congress session for that year. Opposition to the two Leagues came principally from Anglo-Indians, Muslims and non-Brahmins of the south who felt their existence threatened if power were transferred to Indian (and, by definition, the majority were Hindu) hands.

The Home Rulers felt that India's World War I contribution in men and money warranted political progress and nothing could accomplish this better than the grant of self-government. An added incentive at a later stage came from the Russian Revolution (1917) and the declaration by President Woodrow Wilson, early in January 1918, that the war was being waged to relieve people from unbridled autocracy. It followed that Britain's autocratic rule in India was an obvious anachronism.

Earlier, Governmental reaction to Home Rule propaganda was characteristic of its well-worn policies—a stern handling and suppression of what it viewed as 'sedition.' A case was instituted against Tilak, who was served with notice to deposit Rs 40,000 as surety for his good behaviour; on appeal, the decision was rescinded by the High Court. In the sequel, orders were served on him prohibiting his entry into the Panjab and Delhi. Presently, Mrs Besant too forfeited security on her paper, *New India*.

Notwithstanding governmental pressure, the two Leagues continued with their programme of relentless propaganda. Their zeal and devotion inspired members of the Congress and enthused them with a new spirit. Tilak's exhortation to that party as well as the Muslim League (q.v.) resulted in a co-operative effort to draw up the Lucknow Pact (q.v.). More and more Muslims, among them M. A. Jinnah (q.v.), were drawn into the movement. By 1917, a phenomenal increase in the number of adherents of the two Leagues was causing the government considerable anxiety. Annie Besant's internment in June of the same year brought a volley of protests, and the Congress showed its appreciation of her work, by electing her (as noticed earlier) President for its annual session.

To stem the tide of Home Rule popularity, both Delhi as well as Whitehall decided to placate the Moderates who, they realized, were fast losing faith in Britain's traditional sense of justice and fairplay. The objective was to be attained by putting forth a concrete scheme for reform. The decision to grant responsible government to India was made in the August (1917) Declaration (q.v.); prior to that the Home Rulers had decided to launch a movement of passive resistance on 26 August. In the light of Whitehall's gesture, the sponsors gave up their threat and sent instead an all-India deputation to meet the Viceroy.

Mrs Annie Besant's release from internment in September 1917 marked an important landmark, for paradoxically in less than twelve months to come she succeeded in isolating herself completely from the various groups and forfeited all claims to leadership in the nationalist movement. Two reasons may be adduced for this. *One*, the united front she had forged of Moderates, Extremists and young men in the Congress were basically unstable.*Two*, her change of strategy after her release from prison was singularly inept. As to the latter, she opposed passive resistance and in her presidential address to the Calcutta session affirmed: 'I cannot promise to please you always.' While saying all this she took no positive steps to restrain or control the young men whom she had enthused and who owed her allegiance. The fact is that she tried to keep their loyalty as well as that of the Moderates—which meant pursuing ambivalent policies.

Meanwhile, the Moderates, alienated by her inconsistency, refused to attend either the Special Congress or the party's annual session in December 1918. What was more, Mrs Besant did nothing to improve the organization either of the Congress or the Home Rule League. She did not strengthen the Congress at the district level, much less integrate the League with it. 'As her position waned in mid-1918, Mrs Besant at last began to realize that she had no organization for restraining those whom she had excited to agitation... In any case she had no programme of action which would give expression to the feelings of young Congressmen. By alternately fostering agitation and then cooling it off...she simply succeeded in frustrating these feelings.'

By the close of 1918 her leadership had been rejected and in so far as Tilak had virtually reliquished his authority, the Congress was leaderless while the Home Rule movement had been weakened beyond hope of revival. In sum, by early 1919, the Home Rule Movement had lost its hold for: (i) lack of organization among the Home Rulers; (ii) growth of communal tension as a result of Hindu-Muslim riots in 1917-18; and (iii) announcement of the Montford Reforms (q.v.) with its resultant schism in the Home Rulers' camp.

Its failure notwithstanding, some positive gains had been registered. For one, emphasis in the freedom movement had now shifted from the educated élite to the masses, which gave it a new dimension if also sense of urgency. Again, the Montagu-Chelmsford reforms of 1919 may be viewed as an outcome of the Home Rule agitation. On a larger plane, it may be said to have prepared the country for the Gandhian style of political action in the years ahead, and the eventual achievement of freedom.

It may be useful to highlight that at 67, Mrs Annie Besant, her eloquence and commanding personality untarnished, had helped launch what was tantamount to a new political venture. A great contemporary, Lala Lajpat Rai affirmed that 'she helped young India to feel sure of the greatness of Indian culture and religion.' Again, the deaths of Gokhale (q.v.) and Pherozeshah Mehta (q.v.) in 1915 helped facilitate Tilak's re-entry into Congress. He not only subscribed to the Home Rule ideology but raised its banner in his home province and rallied his followers to the cause.

With the adoption of the Home Rule Leagues' objective of self-government on the model of governments in the Dominions, a great stimulus was given to the national movement. This lent added strength to Mrs Besant's political standing while her hurricane campaigns in Lucknow and Allahabad captured the popular imagination.

What did the movement achieve? Measured by their initial goal of obtaining Home Rule, the two Leagues obviously failed. None the less, the British government's promise of advance towards self-government (20 August, 1917) may be traced largely to the Home rule agitation. In the long run, the importance of the two Leagues must be measured by their impact on the national movement, and here their principal contribution lay in deflecting it permanently from the course mapped out by the previous Moderate leadership. Thus in 1916-17 political agitation had been mounted on a nationwide scale for the first time, even though it was far from being active in the Panjab or Bengal. In the former, this was due to a generous use of war-time emergency legislation and no theosophy (thanks to the Arya Samaj (q.v.)); in the latter, 2,000 suspected terrorists were nabbed early in the War while Moderates such as Surendranath Banerjea (q.v.) and C. R. Das (q.v.) were still powerful.

Maharashtra and Karnatak, however, were vigorously stirred—thanks to a network of Tilak's Chitpavan Brahmin lieutenants. As for Mrs Besant's League, its strength lay in the city of Bombay, Gujarat, Saurashtra, U.P., Bihar and southern India. In these areas her Theosophical Society (q.v.) had been the strongest and there was little by way of well-established, political movements, either extremist or moderate.

The Theosophical Society had penetrated into Madras presidency and it was through its numerous 'lodges' that Mrs Besant owed her great success in setting up branches of the League and mobilizing popular support for it. In the result, the Home Rule Movement drew into its vortex many areas which had hitherto been inactive in the national upsurge.

In their separate yet combined endeavour, both the Leagues had sought to win control over the Congress by obtaining the readmission to it of Tilak and his extremist followers and inducing members of their respective Leagues to join it. Thus they were instrumental, in the end, of reviving the organization as a worthy instrument of Indian nationalism. The Home Rulers lent a sense of importance to the national movement as a whole. Their impact can be seen in 1920, when Motilal Nehru (q.v.) among others prevailed upon Gandhi (q.v.) to put forward the demand for Swaraj before he and his coterie would support the Mahatama's campaign for Non-cooperation (q.v.).

On the surface, the demand for Home Rule was simple and forceful—but impossible to satisfy in the short run. By initially demanding the maximum, Mrs Besant had limited her room for manoeuvre; any attempt to change her strategy in relation to the British exposed her to the charge of apostasy by her followers. By fostering agitation to the point where passive resistance was called for and then back-sliding, she as well as Tilak succeeded in frustrating their followers—and thereby provided much needed steam to Gandhi's satyagraha campaign in 1919-20.

H. P. Owen, 'Towards Nationwide Agitation and Organization: The Home Rule Leagues 1915-18' in D. A. Low (ed.), *Soundings in Modern South Asian History*,

London, 1968, pp. 159-95; Gopi Nath, 'The Home Rule Movement in India', unpublished Ph.D. dissertation, Agra University, 1962, referred to in *Quarterly Review
of Historical Studies*, Vol. III (1963-4), pp. 142-3; Annie Besant, 'India: Bond or
Free?', vol. 5. in *The Besant's Spirit*, Adyar, Madras, 1939, pp. 191–221; K. R.
Shirsat, *Kaka Joseph Baptista: Father of Home Rule Movement in India*, Bombay,
1974; S. R Mehrotra, 'The Home Rule Movement in India' in *Towards India's
Freedom and Partition*, New Delhi, 1979, pp. 124-34.

Allan Octavian Hume (1829–1912)

Allan Octavian Hume, known as the 'father and founder' of the Indian
National Congress (q.v.), initially came to India as a member of the Bengal
Civil Service in 1849 after having been trained at Haileybury College (q.v.)
and done a course in medicine and surgery at University College, London.

Hume had developed an abiding interest in the systematic study of birds
and his work in the field was to earn him the well-merited sobriquet, 'pope of
ornithology.' From his father Joseph Hume, who served in Parliament, he
had inherited radical reformist views and a bias in favour of the 'natives.'

In India, the courage he showed as magistrate at Etawah (1849-67) in the
North-Western Provinces during the Rebellion of 1857 (q.v.) won him recognition and an award. Later, he was to display great moderation towards
the people of India and was convinced that foreign rule could be successful
only to the extent that it conformed to the best interests of the people. At
Etawah he set a precedent for reform by establishing schools, instituting
scholarships, helping to found a vernacular paper (the *People's Friend*),
organizing an efficient police force and opposing the Ambari revenue (which,
he argued, only tended to increase drunkenness).

As Commissioner of Inland Customs (1867-70), Hume reduced the 2,500
mile barrier in Rajasthan which had hitherto safeguarded the government's
monopoly. Appointed Secretary in the Home Department, he got himself
transferred. Incharge of the Revenue and Agriculture Departments (1870–9),
he proposed to introduce greater care of the country's cattle wealth and
adopted several measures, including the establishment of an agriculture
bureau, to reduce the cultivators' indebtedness.

Mayo's (q.v.) death and budget cuts nullified Hume's efforts in the direction of
improving the agriculturists' lot while Northbrook (q.v.) was sceptical about
his reformist ideas. In the result, Hume fell from favour. Found disagreeable
and obstructive, he was transferred (1879) under a cloud to the provincial
revenue board at Allahabad.

Although the official version of Hume's 'demotion' has never been made
public, his biographer, Sir William Wedderburn, a civil servant and great
nationalist sympathizer, opines that Hume's offence lay in overboldness when
expressing opinions unpalatable to the authorities. The (Calcutta)
Statesman felt that he had been 'shamefully and cruelly' removed and the
(Lucknow) *Pioneer* characterized the act as 'the grossest jobbery ever
perpetrated.'

It was at Allahabad that Hume came under the influence of theosophy,
joining the Theosophical Society (q.v.) in 1881. Earlier, he tried unsuccessfully to secure a seat in the Viceroy's Council during Lytton's (q.v.) regime
having refused an appointment for governorship of the Panjab. In 1882 he

retired from service and this marked the beginning of his long association with nationalist leaders and the founding of the Indian National Congress.

Strongly in favour of a paternalistic form of government, Hume was convinced that India had benefited in the past and would greatly benefit in the future, from British rule. Yet the 'mutiny' (Rebellion) of 1857 (q.v.) had left him with an obsessive fear that there existed a formidable undercurrent of discontent which, unless properly harnessed, would spell the doom of the Raj. For the latter's continuation therefore, it was imperative to take account of Indian aspirations. He argued that the only solution lay in an efficient, honest and just administration based on the consent and co-operation of the ruled. A callous bureaucracy steeped in racial bias was the principal culprit in creating an unfriendly Indian middle class that would otherwise be ideally suited to bridge the gulf between the rulers and the ruled.

In short, in supporting India's political claims, Hume was motivated by (a) the desirability of self-government for the people; and (b) an anxiety that ties between India and England should not be broken by the former being pushed into violence to achieve her goal of self-government. As early as 1876, Hume had warned Lytton that 'we have now between us and destruction' nothing but the bayonets and that the 'fate of the empire is trembling in the balance.' In 1884, in order to channelize the prevalent unrest, he conferred with Dufferin (q.v.), requesting *inter alia* that Indian volunteers for the armed forces be treated on par with Europeans.

On 1 March 1883 Hume addressed a circular letter to the graduates of Calcutta University whom he termed 'the salt of the land.' *Inter alia*, he exhorted them to 'scorn personal ease and make a resolute struggle to secure greater freedom for themselves and their own affairs.' He set them a three-fold objective: 'the fusion into one national whole of all the diverse forces that peopled the country'; 'the gradual regeneration along lines spiritual, moral, social and political of the nation thus evolved'; 'the consolidation of the union between England and India by securing the modification of such of its conditions as may be unjust or injurious.' As long as Ripon (q.v.) was at the helm of affairs, these plans went unopposed, for the Viceroy had a good appreciation of the situation and a progressive outlook. In fact, Hume became, despite his somewhat superficial knowledge of Indian thinking, a trusted go-between in nationalist as well as governmental quarters by projecting himself as a spokesman for both sides. He is said to have enjoyed at this stage the confidence of Dufferin, with whose tacit approval the Congress came into being in December 1885. The Viceroy none the less ruled against governmental participation at its meetings. Hume concurred, for at no time did he contemplate promoting Indian interests at the cost of the empire's. Understandably he was totally unprepared for the shape the Congress was to assume in the years to come. Critics aver that it was the perpetuation of Britain's vested interests, and *not* India's cause for freedom, that he truly served.

Initially what Hume organized was the Indian National Union which was to convene at Poona on 25 December 1885. As the proposed conference had received widespread support, it assumed the name of 'Indian National *Congress*', while at the last moment its venue was changed from Poona to Bombay where it did eventually convene.

In a letter to a friend in May 1886, Dufferin described Hume as 'a mischievous busybody . . .a cleverish, a little cracked, vain, unscrupulous man . . .very careless of truth'; in another communication the viceroy called him 'idiot enough.' With all this, Hume was the guiding spirit behind the formative years of the Congress, its programme of constitutional agitation and the building up of a group in England that was sympathetic to Indian aspirations. He constituted a 'British committee of the Congress' in London in 1889, and raised Rs 45,000 for its maintenance. He founded a journal, *India*, in 1890 and an Indian Parliamentary party, and was the fount of a lot of pamphleteering criticizing the government and defending the aims and objectives of the new political party. In 1894, Hume left India but remained in touch with the Congress and was elected its Secretary year after year, guiding its policies and programmes until 1906 when he finally retired.

A widely accepted albeit long-exploded belief persists that Hume, under the direction of Dufferin, organized the Congress with two main objectives in view—first, to provide a 'safety-valve' to the anticipated or actual discontent of the Indian intelligentsia; and two, to form out of the latter a quasi-constitutional party analogous to the opposition in England.

In defining the Hume-Dufferin relationship, it is necessary to remember that (i) it was only after the second annual session of the Congress that Dufferin began to pay any real attention to the latter body; (ii) even then, far from being alarmed by the Congress, he looked upon it with a mixture of curiosity and disdain; (iii) there is no evidence to suggest that Hume was Dufferin's spokesman; on the other hand, Dufferin later thought Hume was a liar and a 'traducer' of his administration; (iv) Dufferin took time to form an opinion on or about the Congress. Available data would make one deduce that Dufferin was by no means Hume's adviser or even amused sympathiser, that he was 'an amused critic of the Congress, not its anxious parent.'

Hume's 'organizing ability, his immense courage and general humanitarianism were indispensable, historically speaking, for the development of the Congress *as an organization*. Even so, the Congress *as a movement* both preceded his entry into Indian politics and exceeded his expectation of what it was supposed to be even before his death.' A critic has pointed out that Hume did much to enliven loyalty to the British Crown. If Indians had some grievances, Hume attributed these to the insolence and callousness of the bureaucracy, or ignorance of the British people of Indian problems, and *not* due to any deliberate policy or exploitation. The British Crown, Hume argued, stood for the welfare of the Indian people.

Hume believed in social reform but as a slow, and gradual, process. A strong advocate of compulsory education, he opposed early marriage as the cause of physical debility. In England, after his retirement, he stayed at Upper Norwood, not far from London, and took an active interest in local politics and a botanical project.

A naturalist and a botanist, Hume established and endowed the South London Botanical Institute. While still in service, he conducted a journal called *Stray Feathers*. His transfer from Simla to the Revenue Board at Allahabad not only closed a brilliant official career but also dealt a disastrous blow to his scientific studies and explorations. He had by then spent about £ 20,000 in accumulating an ornithological museum and library of Asian birds. In collaboration with Colonel G. F. L. Marshal of the Indian army, Hume wrote a standard work, *The Game Birds of India, Burmah &*

Ceylon (Calcutta, 1879-81), and in 1885 presented a collection of his bird skins and bird eggs to the British Museum of Natural History in South Kensington.

William Wedderburn, *Allan Octavian Hume, C.B., Father of the Indian National Congress, 1829 to 1912,* London, 1913; T. V. Parvate, *Allan Octavian Hume* in Makers of Modern India, Delhi, 1964; Anthony Parel, 'Hume, Dufferin and the Origins of the Indian National Congress,' *JIH,* 42, 3, December 1964, pp. 707-25; B. L. Grover, 'Allan Octavian Hume's Political Testament: an appraisal', *Modern Review*, CXVI, October 1964, pp. 269–74; *DNB 1912–21*, pp. 277–8 (H. V. Lovett).

Indian Education (Hunter) Commission (1882–3)

During Lord Ripon's (q.v.) administration, the government appointed (3 February 1882) an Indian Education Commission headed by Sir William Wilson Hunter (1840-1900). The 22-member predominantly official Commission comprised 8 Indians, among whom Syed Ahmad Khan (q.v.), Ananda Mohan Bose (q.v.) and Kashinath Trimback Telang (1850-93) were the more prominent. The aim was not so much to overhaul the existing system as to inquire 'particularly into the manner in which effect had been given to the principles of the (Education) Depatch of 1854 (q.v.); and to suggest such measures at it may think desirable in order to the further carrying out of the policy therein laid down.'

Another principal objective was an inquiry into the 'present state of elementary education throughout the Empire and the means by which this can everywhere be extended and improved.' Still another issue was that of religious education—'should it be imparted in schools or not?' While the general operation of the universities as well as professional colleges was outside the Commission's purview, an allied field of investigation was whether the government should withdraw from direct educational enterprise in favour of missionaries.

On 16 March 1883, the Commission concluded its deliberations after examining 193 witnesses and receiving 323 memoranda; 222 resolutions were passed, 180 unanimously. Its report was submitted in September 1883; a year later (October 1884) almost all its proposals, barring one, were accepted by the government.

Broadly, the Commission concluded that the system of education prescribed by the Despatch of 1854 was sound and all that needed to be done was to support and strengthen it further. Education, it averred, 'must be national in a wider sense than is implied in mere state management, and must be managed in a great measure by the people themselves . . . .Government should not only curtail the expansion of its institutions, but should also withdraw from direct enterprise.' This was to be valid especially in the case of collegiate and secondary education.

Thirty-six of the Commission's most important recommendations related to popularization of elementary education through the medium of the vernaculars. Stressing the latter's importance and the need for further expansion, the Commission recommended encouragement of indigenous schools in every province. In particular, primary education was to be extended to the backward and tribal classes. Indigenous schools were to be encouraged and improved so as to cope with more modern needs. All elementary schools were to be subject to the inspection and supervision of the government's educational officers and were to be made over to district and municipal boards, whose educational responsibilities were to be defined by legislation.

The Commission's more important recommendations on other subjects may be briefly listed:

i) Primary education should have 'an almost exclusive claim on local funds set apart for education and a large claim on provincial revenues.' The first charge on provincial funds for primary education should be 'the cost of its direction and inspection and the provision of an adequate supply of normal schools';

ii) the work of assisting indigenous schools should be assigned to district and municipal boards who were likely to be more sympathetic than the Education Department;

iii) 'Public funds of all kinds—local, municipal and provincial—should be chargeable in an equitable proportion for the support of girls' schools as well as for boys' schools';

iv) Missionary institutions 'should be allowed to follow their own independent course under the general supervision of the state' in so far as there was room and need for every variety of agency in the field of education;

v) 'Natives of India must constitute the most important of all agencies', if educational means 'are ever to be co-extensive with educational wants';

vi) At least one model high school 'may be established in such districts where they may be required in the interests of the people.'

The Commission recommended that in the upper classes of high schools there be two divisions—one leading to the entrance examination of universities; the other, of a more practical character, intended to fit youth for commercial or non-literary pursuits.

Local governments were to be invited to consider the question of establishing special colleges or schools for the sons and relations of Indian chiefs and noblemen. where such institutions did not already exist.

The importance of physical as well as literary education was stressed. In financing it, local funds—those of municipal and district boards as well as of provincial government—were to provide the principal support. The latter was expected to supplement local budgets by means of grants-in-aid from about one-third to one-half of the total expenditure.

State aid to all higher educational institutions, the Commission recommended, should be withdrawn gradually, while grants-in-aid were to be given only when local aid was forthcoming. The Commission's priorities in this context were clearly defined in so far as 'means of primary education may be provided without regard to local co-operation, while it is ordinarily expedient to provide the means of secondary education only when adequate local co-operation is forthcoming.'

Rules for fees and scholarships were laid down for high schools and colleges and provision made for opening libraries, laboratories, the purchase and servicing of teaching apparatus and furniture, etc. The Commission proposed that special encouragement be given to female as well as Muslim education. While the former may receive grants from provincial funds, the latter was to be encouraged through scholarships and free studentships. Provinces were to be encouraged to publish their own textbooks. Additionally, the Commission suggested the reorganization of the educational service with a view to attracting better personnel to it.

Three separate Minutes were appended to the report: a long and well-reasoned one by Telang and two relatively brief ones by David Barbour and Arthur Howell.

The institution of a secular textbook on morals to guide students was perhaps the solitary recommendation made by the Commission that was rejected by the government.

Report of the Indian Education Commission, Calcutta, 1883; Sir Alfred Croft, *Review on Education in India in 1886 with Special Reference to the Report of the Education Commission*, Calcutta, 1888; M. R. Paranjpe (compiler), *A Source Book of Modern Indian Education. 1797 to 1902*, Macmillan, 1938.

Hunter Inquiry Committee Report (1920)

Officially called the 'Court of Inquiry to investigate Recent Disturbances in Bombay, Delhi and the Punjab, Their Causes and Measures Taken to Cope with Them', the Hunter Inquiry Committee was set up on 14 October 1919 by Governor-General Reading (1860–1935) with Whitehall's prior approval. The decision was taken in response to a persistent public demand that the government should urgently look into the origins of the disorders that had spread like wildfire all over the Panjab and Bombay and had necessitated the proclamation of martial law in the former province. It was an overt attempt to conciliate the nationalists whose attacks on government policies were being widely disseminated by the vernacular press, thereby spreading the contagion of discontent.

Apart from Lord Hunter who was its President, the following were members: Justice Sir George Rankin, W. F. Rice, Major-General Sir George Barrow, Pandit Jagat Narayan, Sir C. H. Setalvad and Sardar Sahibzada Sultan Ahmad Khan. H. Wilson of the Indian Police was Secretary to the Committee.

The Committee commenced its work on 29 October 1919 and held hearings for over 46 days, mostly in public; it examined a large number of witnesses, including Brigadier Dyer (q.v.) as well as the martial law officers and a number of those involved in the disturbances. The Panjab Government placed at its disposal a large plethora of records, including the proceedings and orders of the martial law courts and commissions. The Indian National Congress (q.v.) boycotted its proceedings.

On 8 March 1920 the Committee presented a 140-page report to the government. Split down the middle on racial lines, its English members produced majority findings while the 3 Indian members, disagreeing with the conclusions arrived at, detached themselves to produce a minority report.

The findings of the majority were that (i) the disturbances were of the nature of a rebellion which might have developed into revolution; (ii) the outbreaks were the work of a definite organization and all inter-connected; (iii) the proclamation of martial law in the cities was wholly justified and that firing was necessary to put down mob excesses; (iv) the Government of India were blameless; (v) Dyer's action was open to criticism for firing without warning and continuing to fire too long and excessively; (vi) Dyer's objective of producing a sufficient moral effect was a mistaken conception of duty.

The minority disagreed with the first two findings and argued that while firing was justified, flogging, salaming, etc. were intended to terrorize and humiliate Indians.

On Dyer's conduct the Indian members commented more severely than did their European counterparts. They compared his acts with the acts of brutality committed by the Germans in Belgium and France in 1914, and rated them 'a great disservice to the interest of British rule in India.'

The two reports presented a detailed narrative of events and the measures taken to suppress violence. The majority contended that a state of rebellion existed but saw no reason for the decision to relinquish civil authority to military command. It admitted that Dyer had 'committed a grave error' and condemned his action mildly, as 'a mistaken conception of duty.' The minority disagreed with these conclusions and laid the blame on the governor, Michael O'Dwyer (q.v.) for the turn events took. Both reports were agreed that the general discontent was due to a variety of causes, which were explained more elaborately by the Indian members, who viewed them as being relevant to conditions in the Panjab. Listed among them was the recruiting scheme, war subscriptions, Michael O'Dwyer's speeches and the press restrictions imposed in the province, dissapointment with the Montagu-Chelmsford Reforms (q.v.), famine and epidemic following on the heels of restraints imposed during the War years. The minority expressed disagreement with the majority's conclusion that the satyagraha movement was responsible for engendering a sense of pride among the people in disobeying regulations and endangering public safety. The minority condemned the sadistic regulations enforced during martial law, which the majority barely questioned.

The differences between the majority and minority reports necessitated 'a careful examination of the extent to which Dyer should be held blameworthy.' The government concluded: 'Giving all due weight to these considerations, the deliberate conclusion....that General Dyer (i) exceeded the reasonable requirements of the case and showed a misconception of his duty which resulted in a lamentable and unnecessary loss of life...' Montagu too ruled that Dyer had acted 'in complete violation' of the sound principle that, when military action in support of civil authority is required, 'the minimum force necessary' is to be used.

In retrospect, the report of the Hunter committee failed to serve any useful purpose. Public opinion in India was totally disillusioned by the fact that no adequate punishment had been meted out to the guilty British officers. In England, on the other hand, the Tory press condemned the Government of India for taking whatever action it did.

Disorders Inquiry Committee Report, Government of India, Calcutta, 1920; Arthur Swinson, *Six Minutes to Sunset*, London, 1964; V. N. Datta (ed.), *New Light on the Punjab Disturbances in 1919: Volumes VI and VII of Disorders Inquiry Committee Evidence*, Indian Institute of Advanced Study, Simla, 1975.

Treaty of Hyderabad (1768)

Nizam Ali Khan (q.v.), who was once an ally of Haidar Ali (q.v.), had defected to the John Company (q.v.) in the middle of the First Anglo-Mysore War (q.v.), both because he was apprehensive of a Maratha attack on his dominions as well as alarmed by the news of a British force marching towards Hyderabad. A peace treaty between the Madras Presidency and Mohammad Ali, the Nawab of Carnatic, on the one hand and the Nizam, on the other, comprising 12 articles, was therefore concluded on 23 February 1768 and ratified three days later. Under its terms:

(i) the Nizam confirmed the grant of the 5 Northern Circars to the Company for which a *firman* had earlier (1765) been made by the Mughal emperor;

(ii) the Company agreed to 'Bazalut Jung, the Nizam's brother', temporarily holding the circar of Moortizanugger provided 'he neither keeps with nor receives from Hyder Naique any vakeel or correspondence' and lives at peace with the Company, failing which the latter would be 'at liberty' to resume the circar;

(iii) the English were to retain possession of the fort of Condapillee with its jagir;

(iv) in return for the Northern Circars and the circar of Condavir, the Company agreed to pay, as from 1 January 1774, Rs 7 lakhs annually; until then (viz., 1768-74) they would pay Rs 2 lakhs (with Rs 1 lakh more for the circar of Condavir) annually;

(v) Mohammad Ali and his heirs and successors were to enjoy (in lieu of Rs 5 lakhs already paid to the Nizam in 1766), the government of the 'Carnatic Payen Gaut as an ultumgah or free gift.' For this and other parganahs, villages, forts and districts, the Nizam issued sannads;

(vi) the Nizam declared 'Hyder Naique' as 'rebel and usurper' and as such 'divests him of and revokes from him' all territories, grants and sannads and in anticipation of their reversion granted the Company their Diwani. In return, the Company agreed to pay Rs 7 lakhs annually 'in two equal payments', provided the Nizam 'assists the said Company' and the Nawab of Carnatic 'in punishing' Haidar Ali;

(vii) besides Diwani to the Nizam, the Company was to pay the Marathas 'regularly and annually without trouble for the whole chout [*chauth*],' the Nizam to use his good offices for the purpose of making a settlement:

(viii) the Company and the Nawab promised to send to the Nizam 2 battalions of sepoys and 6 guns whenever he should require them; these were to be maintained at the Nizam's expense as long as in his service.

The treaty ended the Nizam's influence on the Northern Circars, his less than glorious campaign in the Carnatic and his alliance with Haidar Ali. From the Nizam's point of view it was politically disastrous, for its terms were much less favourable to him than any earlier compact. Additionally, he had now been made to recognize Mohammad Ali as the independent ruler of the Carnatic.

Aitchison, V, pp. 21-35; *Gribble*, II, pp. 65–7.

Treaties of Masulipatam and Hyderabad (1759, 1766)

In the conflict between England and France during the Third Anglo-Mysore War (q.v.),Nizam Salabat Jung's (d. 1763) assistance was sought by his French allies. Yet before support could reach them, the French had surrendered to the British under Colonel Francis Forde (d. 1770). This fact as well as rumours of an uprising at Hyderabad made the Nizam only too eager to come to terms with the John Company (q.v.) who, in turn, dictated to him the Treaty of Masulipatam on 14 May 1759.

Under its terms, the Nizam agreed to (i) relinquish the French alliance; (ii) drive the French troops south of the river Krishna in 15 days' time; (iii) undertake never to allow them to settle in his country, nor yet employ nor assist them 'nor call them to his assistance.' He further agreed to cede to the British the circar of Masulipatam with its 8 districts while bestowing on them the circar of Nizampatam and its 2 districts as *inam*. The Raja of Vizianagram, an ally of the Company, was to continue to pay tribute to the Nizam, but no arrears of dues were to be realized from him. Both parties agreed not to assist each other's enemies. The compact took the unusual form of 'A copy of Requests made by Colonel Forde to Nawab Salabut Jung and his compliance thereto in his own hand.'

In agreeing to the 'Requests', the Nizam swore 'by God and his Prophet and upon the holy Alcoran' not to deviate from the terms 'even an hair's breadth.' The British were the principal gainers for they successfully replaced French influence, extended their territories 80 miles along the coastline north to south and 20 miles inland, besides obtaining an additional revenue of Rs 40 lakhs. The Nizam gained virtually nothing, 'not even a promise of military assistance from the British.'

On 12 August 1765 Robert Clive (q.v.) obtained a 'Firmaun' from the Mughal emperor which freed the northern circars—'Circar of Siccacole etc'—from the Nizam's nominal control. When Brigadier General John Calliaud was sent to take possession, which he did without much ado, the Nizam, enraged at being bypassed, returned from his western border where he was then engaged in an encounter with the Marathas, to oppose him; luckily, no fighting ensued, for matters were settled amicably.

A 14-article treaty of 'perpetual honour, favour, alliance and attachment' between the Nizam and the Company was signed on 12 November 1766 at Hyderabad. It stipulated *inter alia* that (i) in return for the cession by the Nizam of the 5 circars of 'Ellour, Siccacole, Rajahmundry, Moostafurnugger and Moortizanugger' as free gift, the Company would maintain a body of troops ready to settle his affairs 'in everything that is right and proper, whenever required'; (b) if the assistance of its troops was not required, the Company would pay the Nizam a sum of Rs 9 lakhs per annum, in 3 instalments; (c) the diamond mines and the villages located in the territory ceded to the Company 'shall remain' in the Nizam's possession as hitherto; (d) the fort of Condapillee would be entirely garrisoned by the troops of the Company; (e) the Nizam too would assist the Company with his troops when required but would be at liberty to withdraw 'the whole or any part thereof.'

As may be evident, the treaty was aimed, if indirectly, at Haidar Ali (q.v.), whose activities now posed a threat to the interests both of the British as well as the Nizam.

Aitchison, V, pp. 11–18; Gribble, *History of the Deccan*, II, pp. 59–64.

Ilbert Bill (1884)

The Criminal Procedure Amendment Code Bill, popularly known as the Ilbert Bill (after Sir Courtenay Peregrine Ilbert (1841–1924), then Law Member in the Governor-Generals Executive Council), was introduced in the Imperial Legislative Council on 2 February, 1883. It sought *inter alia to* invest District Magistrates and Sessions Judges with the right to try European and British offenders. The Local Governments were to be authorized to appoint Justice of the Peace from among the covenanted (and the 'native') civil sevice on the basis of training and experience regardless of colour, caste or creed. The change sought had the concurrence of the Local Governments and the Secretary of State.

The announcement of the proposed legislation however brought forth a storm of indignation and protest from European officials and non-officials alike. The latter organized themselves into a 'European and Anglo-Indian Defence Association' to protect the rights and privileges they had hitherto enjoyed. The stage was thus set for an open confrontation, with Indians applauding the measure and deprecating all attempts to repeal it. Ripon (q.v.) refused to withdraw the bill, but agreed to a climb–down. A settlement, known as 'the concordat', was drawn up by Sir Griffith Evans (1840–1902), member of Governor-General's Legislatve Council, 1877–99, on behalf of the European and Anglo-Indian Defence Association and Sir Auckland Colvin (1838-1904) representing the Government of India. The amended bill was passed into law on 25 January 1884.

The compromise measure laid down that all District Magistrates and Sessions Judges would be *ex-officio* Justices of the Peace, empowered to try European and British subjects, and pass a sentence of up to six months' imprisonment or a fine of Rs 2,000, or both. But, and herein lay the compromise, a European or British-born subject could claim the right to trial by jury, half of which was to consist of Europeans or Americans. The 'concordat' so-called was thus a virtual disavowal of the essential part of the law initially proposed.

The successful agitation mounted by the European community against the original bill had a powerful impact and hastened the development of national consciousness, resulting soon enough (1885) in the foundation of the Indian National Congress (q.v.). The solidarity displayed by the European community, their agitational approach and resultant success were to serve as object lessons for Indian nationalists; it is held that the idea of a national organization to represent and fight their cause 'became a staple for discussion' in India in 1883.

Ripon is often blamed for his 'lack of firmness' on the Ilbert Bill. It has also been suggested that he was 'not the man for the crisis.' In all this, it is necessary however to keep track of the totality of circumstances which he faced: 'the united opposition of the British and European community in India did not unnerve him. But the opposition of all the members of his Council except Ilbert and Baring—and after Baring's departure of Ilbert alone—forced him to think seriously whether he should overrule their opinions on an issue which according to him was not unimportant (as important?) as other measures like local self-government. The opposition of the governors and the officials was also a factor to reckon with.'

Nor was that all. He was conscious that Gladstone and his Cabinet were not willing to go beyond general assurances of confidence in him and had refused to take a specific decision, much less a House of Commons vote. All that he could do in the circumstances was to resign. He did not, for he attached no great importance to this issue and did not make it a question of prestige.

Edwin Alan Hirschman, *White Mutiny*, New Delhi, 1980; Nemani Sadhan Bose, *Racism, Struggle for Equality and Indian Nationalism*, Calcutta, 1981; S. Gopal, *Viceroyalty of Lord Ripon*, Oxford, 1953.

Imperial Conference (1926)

By the British Parliament's North America Act of July 1867, Canada's four chief provinces, viz., Quebec, Ontario, Nova Scotia and New Brunswick, constituted themselves into a Federation under the title 'Dominion of Canada.' The Commonwealth of Australia was not proclaimed until 1901; the Union of South Africa until 1910 and New Zealand until 1917.

At the Imperial Conference of 1911, the then British Prime Minister, H. H. Asquith, recognized the guiding principle of decentralization in Imperial affairs by proclaiming: 'We each of us are, and we each of us intend to remain, masters in our own house.' Yet even as he spoke, his definition had no absolute validity.

During World War I, the Imperial War Cabinet was brought into being as a means whereby Dominion leaders might be more effectively associated with the prosecution of the war effort. At the Versailles Peace Conference (1919), the empire was represented not by a delegation from the United Kingdom but by one from the British empire. Similarly, the treaty was signed by the delegates of different Dominions as well as India separately, each representing his own country.

In September 1922, at the time of the crisis at Chanak (Turkey), it seemed well-nigh certain that Great Britain may be involved in hostilities leading to war. Understandably, it appealed for Dominion support and even their armed assistance. The claim was contested by Mackenzie King, then Canada's Prime Minister, who insisted that a decision concerning any involvement could only be taken by his country's government and its Parliament.

Earlier, the Imperial Conference of 1921 had declared itself satisfied that no reconstruction of imperial relations was desirable. Emphasis was laid on the value of the Imperial Conference itself as a means of recognizing differences of view and thereby securing unity of policy. It was agreed to allow the Anglo-Japanese Alliance of 1902 to lapse and replace it by regional agreements on lines favoured by the U.S. government and later embodied in the four- and nine-power Washington Conference treaties of 1921–2.

The most important step in defining the position and mutual relations of Great Britain and the Dominions was taken at the Imperial Conference of 1926. In a report prepared by Lord Balfour's Inter-Imperial Relations Committee, the Dominions were defined as: 'autonomous communities within the British Empire, equal in status, in no way subordinate one to another in any aspect of their domestic or external affairs, though united by common allegiance to the Crown and freely associated as members of the British Commonwealth of Nations.'

A word on what followed may be of relevance. The Imperial Conference of 1930 adopted the report of a committee set up after the Conference of 1926 to study proposals to give legal effect to the decision to remove limitations on the freedom of the Dominions and thus paved the way for the enactment of the Statute of Westminster. The Conference of 1930 also resolved that henceforth Governors-General in the Dominions shall be appointed by the Crown on the advice of and in consultation with their respective governments.

In 1937, the Imperial Conference took note of the then rapidly deteriorating international situation and expressed the view that an overriding consideration should be to avoid war and ensure that differences between nations are settled by negotiation. It put its faith in conciliation and took a decision to adopt measures to ensure that each member fulfilled its respective international obligations.

The Indian National Congress (q.v.), which had at its Lahore session (1929) rejected the goal of Dominion Status (q.v.) and taken a pledge for complete independence, reversed its attitude at the time of the actual transfer of power in 1947. For, as a prerequisite to independence, the country was divided into the two separate Dominions of India and Pakistan. When it proclaimed itself a sovereign, independent, democratic republic 3 years later, India decided on its own to continue to be a member of the Commonwealth of Nations.

J. D. B. Miller, *The Commonwealth in the World,* London, 1958; Nicholas Mansergh, *The Commonwealth and its Nations,* London, 1948; Ernest Barker, *The Ideas & Ideals of the British Empire,* revised ed, London 1951; W. K. Hancock, *Survey of British Commonwealth Affairs,* 2 vols., London, 1937-42.

Elijah Impey (1732–1809)

The son of a merchant, Elijah Impey had a brilliant school career at Westminster where, among others, he met and befriended Warren Hastings (q.v.). Later he moved to Trinity College, Cambridge and Lincoln's Inn. He was called to the bar in 1756 and 16 years later successfully represented the East India Company (q.v.) in the House of Lords, arguing against a bill seeking to restrain it from sending supervisors to India. In 1774 he was appointed Chief Justice in the Supreme Court of Judicature established under the Regulating Act (q.v.) and landed at Calcutta on 19 October 1774.

Impey has been accused of beginning his tenure of office by being party to a judicial murder—the execution of Maharaja Nand Kumar (q.v.) on an allegedly trumped-up charge of forgery. In defence, he pleaded that the law in force in England at the time applied to India as well and since political power in Bengal had been surrendered to the Company, all delinquents there were necessarily subject to its jurisdiction. Whatever the merits of the case, there is little doubt that he had convinced himself that Nand Kumar was guilty, with the result that he relied far too heavily on evidence tendered by witnesses for the prosecution.

In extenuation, however, it has been pointed out that according to the ill-defined and badly drafted letters patent which Impey himself had helped to frame, the newly established Supreme Court at Calcutta was to have a broad jurisdiction including all cases of treason, murder, felonies and forgeries committed in the provinces of Bengal, Bihar and Orisa. In regard to Maharaja Nand Kumar's trial, while the Court's decision may not be viewed as bad, the fact was that the letters patent constituting it had not made it clear as to what law it was called upon to administer. A difference of opinion on the point was thus inevitable. Again, a reference may have been considered had the Governor-General himself not been involved as deeply as he, in fact, was. Worse, Impey tried to safeguard Hastings' position against any future accusations when he collected dubious affidavits in cases relating to Raja Chait Singh (q.v.) of Banaras and the Begums of Oudh (q.v.).

Impey is credited with introducing into India the rule of law, the law of evidence, the law of procedure and writs guaranteeing the 'fundamental rights to personal property, speech and action'. He endeavoured to maintain the independence of the Supreme Court and treat Europeans and Indians alike in the eyes of law. He refused to allow Hastings to influence his decision in the celebrated Kasipore case (1779–80) wherein the Supreme Court and the Supreme Council virtually confronted each other in a legal battle of considerable complexity.

To resolve the conflict between the Supreme Court and the civil courts, Hastings appointed Impey judge of the Sadar Diwani Adalat on a salary of Rs 5,600 per month. Here he framed a code of procedure for the Adalats which remained in force for 6 years (being modified later in 1781) and brought about a much-needed uniformity in the administration of justice.

The establishment of the rule of law was a great British contribution to modern India. When this was first introduced into Bengal by Impey and his fellow judges, there arose conflicts and a certain degree of confusion. The Mughal system of government which the Company had adopted in Bengal was dictatorial, arbitrary and coercive. Thus the conflict between the Supreme Court and the Supreme Council was in fact a conflict between the rule of law and arbitrary methods of government.

It involved the judges in a dual role. On the one hand, they had to struggle against the Supreme Council for the independence of the Supreme Court; on the other, they had to protect Indians from the arbitrary and corrupt exercise of powers by the Company's servants.

As for Nand Kumar's forgery, the judges might have given him a respite had his case not turned into an issue of independence of the Supreme Court which his trial and execution fully vindicated. From now on the conflict between the Court and the Council took other shapes and forms.

Members of the Governor-General's Council had envied the precedence Impey enjoyed. Philip Francis tried to settle scores with him in England. A committee for the administration of justice in India under the chairmanship of Edmund Burke, inspired by Francis, was set up in 1781 and reported against Impey's acceptance of the office of judge of the Sadar Diwani Adalat. In the result, the House of Commons recalled him in July (1782) to answer the charge. Impey returned in January 1784 but continued to hold office till November 1787 when Gilbert Elliot, later Lord Minto (q.v.), again brought up the case against him while 6 articles of the charge were prepared and printed. The principal accusations related to the trial and execution of Nand Kumar and the exercise of extended judicial powers under the Government of Bengal. Impey requested and was granted permission to defend himself at the bar of the House. This he did on 4 February 1788 when the question of impeachment was debated at some length. On 9 May the House divided, and the motion for impeachment was lost (by 73 votes against 55) on the first and most important count. The impeachment was thereupon dropped. Later, during 1790–6, Impey served as M. P. for Romney. He died in October 1809.

Hastings' support for the Supreme Court was weakened by his prime need for money to finance the wars with the Marathas and his short-lived alliance with Francis. He soon realized, however, the great need for reorganizing the Company's courts, of bringing them under the supervision and control of a competent authority and of bridging the wide gulf between them and the Supreme Court. Accordingly, as has been noticed, he reorganized the courts and brought them under the supervision and control of Impey by appointing the latter as judge of the Sadar Diwani Adalat. It was during Impey's brief tenure that the courts assumed, for the first time, a semblance of justice; he gave them a code of rules and procedure and a professional guidance which they needed most. The enemies of Impey and Hastings led by Burke and Francis misinterpreted these measures as a monstrous arrangement, devised to establish in India a Hastings-Impey supremacy. Hence Impey's recall.

It is held that Impey was essentially a vain man and that a certain weakness of character led him to yield at times too readily to the commanding will and intellect of Hastings. But there is not enough reason to doubt the honesty of his intentions. He did not amass a fortune (as did most of the Company's servants) during his 9 years' service in India. However, thanks to Burke (prompted by Francis) and to James Mill's *History,* followed by the writings of Edward Thornton (1799–1875) and Macaulay (q.v.), Impey was long regarded as 'one of the ogres of Indian history, a traditional monster of inequity.'

B. N. Pandey, *Introduction of English Law into India: the career of Elijah Impey in Bengal, 1774-83,* Bombay, 1969; N. Majumdar, *Justice and Police in Bengal, 1765-1793: A Study of the Nizamat in Decline,* Calcutta, 1960; *DNB,* X, pp. 418–22 (Henry George Keene).

Inam Commission (1852)

'Inams' were rent-free tenures of land, sometimes comprising entire villages, gifted to individuals or religious and charitable institutions. They were bestowed either as reward for public service or distinguished talent or as an endowment for maintenance. Usually an inam took the form of an assignment of land revenue due to the state and was thus liable to abuse by manipulation of records especially in cases where state supervision was lax. Inams might be complete or partial, made in perpetuity or for a specified period. They were freely granted for the maintenance of Brahmins or learned Muslim divines.

In the political anarchy of the 18th century this mode of intercepting state revenue had attained alarming proportions—most of the inams being spurious deals indulged in by unscrupulous land revenue officers. To plug the leak, from 1793 onwards the John Company (q.v.) authorized its collectors to resume or re-assess such lands whose holders were unable to furnish rightful title deeds. Later, in 1811, collectors were authorized to resume and assess such lands, while aggrieved parties could contest the resumption through a suit in a court of law.

Despite its harshness and the resultant discontent, the policy was vigorously pursued by the framing of more detailed regulations in 1819 and 1828. Rigorous restrictions were placed on further grants by regulations made in 1831 which curbed the practice of 'granting.' In 1845, it was ruled that tenures should not go beyond 'existing lives.'

Dalhousie (q.v.) appointed an Inam Commission in 1852 to inquire into rent-free tenures. In the result, in Bombay Presidency alone more than 20,000 estates were confiscated! A parallel inquiry by Coverly Jackson, the Chief Commissioner of Oudh (q.v.), served to exacerbate 'native' feelings further. Though begun earlier, the resumption of lands held for generations under rent-free tenures, was pursued with relentless severity during the regime of Lord Dalhousie and reduced to penury a large number of landholders who had imagined that long years of possession were more valued than title deeds. Many of them belonged to 'high families, proud of their lineage, proud of their ancestral privileges, who had won what they held by the sword and had no thought by any other means of maintaining possession.'

Repercussions of what appeared in retrospect to be a land grab policy on behalf of the government were widespread discontent among the landed gentry and may be rated one of the major causes for the Rebellion of 1857 (q.v.).

Independence Pledge

On 2 January 1930 the Working Committee of the Indian National Congress (q.v.) at the party's annual session at Lahore decided to observe Sunday, 26 January 1930 as 'Purna Swarajaya' (Complete Independence) Day all over India. The declaration to be read at all meetings held that day was:

'We believe it is the inalienable right of the Indian people to have freedom to enjoy the fruits of their toil and have necessities of life, so that they may have full opportunities of growth. The British Government of India has not only deprived the Indian people of their freedom but has based itself on the exploitation of the masses and has ruined India economically, politically, culturally and spiritually. We believe that India must sever the British connection and attain Purna Swarajaya....

We hold it to be a crime against man and God to submit any longer to a rule that has caused this four-fold disaster to our country. We recognize, however, that the most effective way of gaining our freedom is not through violence. We are convinced that if we can but withdraw our voluntary help and stop payment of taxes without doing violence even under provocation the end of this inhuman rule is assured... We therefore hereby solemnly resolve to carry out the Congress instructions issued from time to time for the purpose to establish Purna Swarajaya.'

In subsequent years, 26 January came to be observed as 'Independence Day'; after 1950, when free India's new constitution became operative the date is celebrated as Republic Day.

B. Pattabhi Sitaramayya, *History of the Indian National Congress*, 2 vols, 2nd reprint, Delhi, 1969, I, pp. 363–4.

Government of India Act, 1935

The Government of India Act, 1919, better known as the Montagu-Chelmsford Reforms (q.v.), even though well received initially, soon led to a degree of disillusionment. In brief, it failed to satisfy the country's political aspirations so that all parties soon joined hands to agitate for a further revision of the constitutional set–up. Even in the first few years of the life of reformed Provincial Councils, a resolution moved in the Central Legislative Assembly had urged the establishment of full responsible government in the provinces and a simultaneous transfer of control of all the central departments, barring the army and foreign affairs.

The pressure of public opinion in the Legislative Assembly led to the appointment of the Muddiman Committee (q.v.) under the then Home Member. Its terms of reference were narrow and, even though the majority report held that the new system had not been a given a fair trial, the minority underlined that the dyarchic experiment had failed and that no alternative, transitional system could be devised. More, there was need for a constitution which ensured 'stability in the government and willing co-operation of the people.'

Understandably, the British government refused to go beyond the majority report and, in 1927, Lord Irwin (q.v.) even warned that Parliament could not be stampeded into a decision by the Indian National Congress (q.v.) policy of coercion. Later in the year, the appointment of the Simon Commission (q.v.), two years before the time laid down in the statute, was eloquent testimony of the government's changed thinking. The Commission functioned in an atmosphere of boycott and non-cooperation; its thunder stolen by the All-Parties Conference and the Nehru Report (q.v.). The latter, it may be recalled, had recommended *inter alia* immediate establishment of full responsible government, both at the centre and in the provinces.

Meanwhile, Lord Irwin's announcement on Dominion Status (q.v.) as the goal of India's political aspirations and the decision to call a Round Table Conference (q.v.) made the Simon report look irrelevant. The Congress took on 31 December 1929 the complete Independence Pledge (q.v.) and affirmed its new political objective. After the last session of the Round Table Conference was over, the Secretary of State affirmed that (i) the new constitutional structure would be a federation if 50 per cent of Indian States (q.v.), in terms of number and population, acceded; (ii) Muslims would be assured 33⅓ per cent of British India's representation in the central legislature; (iii) Sind and Orissa would be separate provinces. Later, in 1933, the RTC proposals were embodied in a White Paper, comprising 202 paragraphs. It rested on *three* major principles as the bases for the proposed constitutional set-up: a federation, provincial autonomy and special responsibilities and safeguards vested in the executive, both at the centre and in the provinces.

The White Paper proposals formed the basis for the new legislation which, in so far as it evoked controversy, was entrusted to a Joint Select Committee of both Houses of Parliament with Lord Linlithgow (q.v.) as chairman. Twenty-one delegates from British India and the Indian States were associated as assessors. The Committee submitted its report in Novermber 1934. The Government of India Bill based on its recommendations passed through Parliament and received Royal assent on 2 August 1935.

The new Act comprised 451 clauses with 15 schedules, making it the longest and the most complicated piece of legislation ever adopted by Parliament. Its two notable features were: absence of a preamble and a proposal to prescribe the franchise, after the passage of the bill, by Orders-in-Council, subject to Parliament's approval.

In the provincial sphere, Burma was separated from India and two new provinces—Orissa and Sind—created. In view of the federal form of government at the centre, the provinces were endowed with legal personality. Dyarchy was abolished and all provincial subjects transferred to popular control. In the words of the Joint Select Committee: 'It is a scheme whereby each of the Governors' provinces will possess an executive and a legislature having precisely defined spheres, broadly free from control by the Central Governmant and Legislature.'

Governors were appointed on the advice of the Secretary of State for a period of 5 years. As a general rule, senior officers of the I.C.S. were chosen, although there was no bar to an outsider being appointed. The Governor's salary and allowances were a charge on the provincial revenues and were therefore not subject to the vote of the legislature. He acted in three distinct ways: on the advice of his ministers; in his individual judgement, where he might consult the ministers even though he was not bound to abide by their advice; in his discretion, where he would act without consulting his ministers.

The Governor chose his Council of Ministers to aid and advise him in the discharge of his duties. They were appointed in consultation with a person who, in his view, commanded a majority in the legislature so as to foster a sense of joint responsibility among them. They held office during his pleasure. The Governor's special powers and responsibilities embraced: (i) prevention of any grave menace to the peace and tranquillity of the province; (ii) safeguarding the legitimate interests of minorities; (iii) securing the legal and equitable rights and safeguarding the legitimate interests of the public services; (iv) prevention of discrimination against British subjects domiciled in the U.K. or companies incorporated in that country; (v) securing the peace and good government of the partially excluded areas; (vi) protection of rights of any Indian State and the rights and dignity of its Ruler; (vii) securing the execution of orders or directions issued by the Governor-General in his discretion.

The Governor acted in his individual judgement in the appointment and dismissal of the Attorney-General of a province. The entire executive authority of the province was vested in the Governor, who had special powers in the financial field. Thus, a finance bill could only be introduced on the recommendation of the Governor. He directed an annual financial statement to be laid before the legislature in two parts: (i) sums charged on the revenues of the province; (ii) sums required to meet other expenses proposed to be incurred from the revenues of the province.

Under (i) were included salaries and allowances of the Governor and his staff; of members of the public services, ministers, judges; public debt charges; and expenses incurred on excluded areas in the province. The Governor could, in his discretion, decide whether or not an item was a charged item which, in turn, made it non-votable. The legislature could accept, refuse to accept or accept with reduction of expenditure all items except the charged items. However, it had no power of enhancement. In case of refusal to grant the sums asked for, or their reduction, the Governor could, in his discretion, restore the demands if he felt that their denial would have an adverse effect on the proper discharge of his special responsibilities. The Governor could also lay before the legislature a supplementary budget, if necessary.

The Governor exercised important powers in the legislative field. He could summon a meeting of the legislature or a joint session of the two houses whenever necessary. He determined rules of procedure of the legislature; address a meeting thereof or send messages to it. He could give his assent to a bill passed by the legislature, withhold assent, return it for reconsideration or reserve it for consideration of the Governor-General. He could prorogue the two houses or dissolve the lower house.

The Governor's previous assent was necessary for introducing bills (i) relating to any Governor's Act or Ordinance promulgated by him in his discretion; (ii) regarding any matter relating to the police force. He could issue ordinances when the legislature was not in session; or even when the legislature was in session, in regard to certain subjects; or enact Governor's Acts which had the force of law. The Governor was not to issue such ordinances without the previous sanction of the Governor–General, but if he was not able to contact the latter he could issue the ordinance and then report (to the Governor-General).

It is accepted that the real test of a parliamentary system lies in the extent of responsibility of the executive to the legislature. Either the executive is responsible to the legislature or the latter is dissolved and a new legislature elected whose confidence the executive gains. Under the 1935 Act, however, a third alternative was provided. Under Section 93, if at any time the Governor was satisfied that a situation existed in which the government of the province could not be carried out in accordance with the provisions of the Act, he could, by proclamation, take upon himself the administration of the province. In the light of this, it has been suggested that the parliamentary system in the provinces was of a 'controlled' type, with its leading strings in the hands of the Governor.

A word on the provincial legislature. Assam, Bengal, Bihar, Bombay, Madras and the United Provinces had bicameral legislatures—a Legislative Assembly and a Legislative Council, the lower and the upper houses respectively. The other five provinces (viz., Panjab, NWFP, Sind, Orissa, CP & Berar) had a unicameral legislature—a Legislative Assembly only.

Members of the legislature were elected on the basis of constituencies demarcated on religious, racial or interest affiliations. Separate electorates were provided for Muslims, Sikhs, Anglo-Indians, Indian Christians and Europeans. Besides the 'general' constituencies, special interests recognized for representation were industry, commerce, landholders, the universities and labour. A small number of seats was reserved for women who were, however, not debarred from contesting other seats.

Election was direct. Franchise varied from province to province but generally rested on the basis of a minimum land revenue a person paid or the house rent he derived. A certain minimum educational qualification or military service were also considered adequate. Some 14% of the population, as against only 3% under the 1919 Act, had the right to vote. The term of the Assembly was 5 years. The Council however was a permanent body, with a third of its members retiring every 3 years. A great majority of members of the Council were to be elected directly, others indirectly and the rest nominated by the Governor in his discretion. Voters for the Council election had high property qualifications or paid income-tax in a high slab, or received rent or held high positions in the government or were title holders.

Except in financial matters, both Houses had equal powers. All money bills had to be initiated in the Assembly, with the Council having no voice in the matter of grants. In case a conflict between the two houses persisted for over 12 consecutive months, the Governor could summon a joint session to resolve the deadlock.

The legislature could make laws on all subjects embodied in the provincial list. There were, however, two limitations: (i) when two or more provinces, by resolutions of their legislature, authorized the federal legislature to legislate on a subject included in the provincial list; (ii) when the Governor-General, through a proclamation of emergency, authorized the federal legislature to legislate on provincial subjects.

The provincial legislature could also make laws on subjects listed in the concurrent list so long as such legislation did not conflict with any federal law. Even when such a conflict existed, it was stipulated that, should the Governor-General give his assent to the provincial law, it would prevail over the federal law.

As noticed earlier, the Act of 1935 envisaged the creation of a federal structure of government. In order to do so, it sought first to break the existing British Indian government into autonomous provinces and then unite them in a federal framework expected to include the Indian States. An Instrument of Accession was devised to rope the States in. Theoretically, it could vary from State to State and thereby create as many federal compacts as there were Indian States in the federation.

The Governor-General was appointed by the Crown usually for a period of 5 years on an annual salary of Rs 250,000. In addition, he was entitled to allowances so as to maintain the prestige and dignity inseparable from his office. His emoluments were a charge on the Consolidated Fund of India and, therefore, non-votable. The Governor-General had a dual role. He was Governor-General with regard to British India as well as Crown Representative in dealings with the Indian States. In the former capacity, he was head of the federal executive, but in his latter role he held charge of royal prerogative, being the paramount authority in relation to the States.

In matters relating to defence, foreign affairs, ecclesiastical affairs, governance of excluded and partially excluded areas, he acted in his discretion. There were three Counsellors to assist him in this work. Responsible only to him, their functions were purely advisory in character. While acting in his discretion, the Governor-General was responsible to the Secretary of State and, through him, to the British Parliament.

In so far as the executive at the Centre was of a dyarchic character, in such areas as were 'transferred' to popular control the Governor-General was aided by a Council of Ministers responsible to the federal legislature. Technically, the Governor-General acted as a constitutional head in the 'transferred' field. But the authority exercised by the ministers suffered from certain limitations. Broadly, these included (i) the erosion of authority consequent upon the creation of the Reserve Bank of India and the Federal Railway Authority with autonomous powers and statutory privileges; (ii) the special responsibilities of the Governor-General in respect of the protection of minorities; and (iii) provisions in respect of commercial discrimination.

The federal legislature was bicameral. In the Council of States, the upper house, Indian States were allocated 40 per cent of the seats while in the House of Assembly, the lower house, the proportion was 33⅓ per cent. Allocation of seats in the Council was based on the relative rank and importance of the individual State; in the Assembly, on the basis of population. Only a few States were large enough to be entitled to individual representation; the rest, divided into two groups, returned representatives either by rotation or jointly, as laid down in the Act. Procedure for the selection of members for seats earmarked for the States was left to the Ruler or Rulers concerned: it was hoped, though, that a system of popular election would be devised.

As for British India, the allocation of seats among the provinces in respect of both houses was on the basis of population. Representation of communal and special interests was on familiar lines with Muslims entitled to 33⅓ per cent of British Indian seats. It was hoped that a convention would develop, to the satisfaction of different communities, regarding the composition of representatives from the States in the legislature.

British India members of the upper house were to be returned in general by direct election through territorial constituencies, while those of the lower house were to be returned, by direct election through electoral colleges composed of members of the provincial legislatures. In other words, members of those communities—general, Muslim, Sikh—who were also members of the provincial legislative assemblies would elect them on the basis of a single transferable vote.

The lower house, called the House of Assembly, was to have a maximum of 375 members—250 from British India and 125 from the Indian States, thereby giving the latter 33⅓ per cent representation with a population that was barely 25 per cent of the total. Of the membership from British India, 3 represented commerce and industry and 1 labour. The term of the house was 5 years.

The Council of States was to consist of 260 members—156 from British India and 104 from the Indian States, thereby giving the latter over 40 per cent representation. Of the members from British India, the distribution was: 7 Europeans, 1 Anglo Indian, 2 Indian Christians and 6 nominated by the Governor-General in his discretion, with the rest distributed among the provinces. The Council was a permanent body with a third of its members retiring every 2 years.

The Governor-General was an integral part of the legislature. Acting in his discretion, he could summon either house to meet at a place and time he thought fit. He could prorogue either chamber or dissolve the Assembly at his discretion. He was to make rules for any matter concerned with his discretion or individual judgement and was to secure timely completion of financial business. He was to prohibit discussion on certain matters and had the right to address or send messages to the two houses. He could give his assent to a bill passed by the legislature, withhold it, return it for reconsideration or reserve it for His Majesty's pleasure. The Governor-General could issue ordinances when the legislature was not in session; on subjects within his purview, even when the legislature was in session. He could enact permanent laws in the form of Governor-General's Acts on subjects which were his special responsibility.

Broadly, it would appear that the federal legislature enjoyed its role only by courtesy. For both in the legislative and financial fields its hands were tied and powers restricted. Thus it had no powers of initiative in raising revenues and exercised little control over items charged on the revenues of the federation.

A large number of subjects fell within the purview of the Governor-General's individual judgement. These included (i) prevention of any grave menace to the peace and tranquillity of India or part thereof; (ii) safeguarding the financial stability and credit of federal government; (iii) safeguarding legitimate interests of minorities; (iv) securing of legal and equitable rights and safeguarding of legitimate interests of members of the public services; (v) prevention of discrimination by executive action against British subjects domiciled in the UK and companies incorporated in that country; (vi) prevention of executive action which would subject goods from U.K. or those of British origin imported into India to discriminatory or penal treatment; (vii) protection of rights of any Indian State or its ruler; (viii) securing of due discharge of functions with regard to which he was required to act in his discretion or exercise his individual judgement.

Such sweeping powers which cut across the entire gamut of administration were justified by the Joint Select Committee as being necessary 'to hold the scales evenly between conflicting interests and to protect those who have neither influence nor ability to protect themselves.'

The Act envisaged that some time was bound to elapse before negotiations for the establishment of the Federation could be completed. It therefore stipulated that provisions in respect of provincial autonomy were to come into force immediately as well as those in respect of the Federal Court, the Federal Public Service Commission and the Federal Railway Authority. As regards other matters relating to the centre, the provisions of the Act of 1919 were to continue in force until such time as the federation was established.

The Federal Court was to consist of at least 3 judges—a Chief Justice and 2 Associate Judges—and located at Delhi. Its judges were to be appointed by the Crown and to hold office until they were 65 years of age. Their salaries were fixed at the time of appointment and were not to be altered subsequently to their disadvantage. A judge could be removed only on proven misbehaviour. He was entitled to a pension on retirement on the basis of his length of service. His conduct as a judge was not to be a subject of debate in the legislature or outside.

The court had a triple jurisdiction: original, appellate and advisory. In the first, it was to hear all disputes between the units of the federation, between the units and the centre alone, or with one or more units on one side and one or more on the other, where an interpretation of the Constitution was involved. In the second, it was to hear every case decided by the High Court in which the latter affirmed that it involved interpretation of a provision of the Constitution Act. The Court's advisory opinion was given whenever sought, on a matter of law or fact, by the Governor-General. Appeals against a decision of the Federal Court could be taken to the Judicial Committee of the Privy Council.

Under the 1935 Act, the Council of the Secretary of State was abolished, its place being taken by three to six advisors. The Secretary of State continued to be responsible to Parliament for the conduct of the Governor-General and the Governors in all such matters as were not transferred to popular control.

A few special features of the federal structure, as contemplated in the Act, may be noted. While the provinces were to send elected representatives to the federal legislature, the States were to send nominees of the Rulers and, as already noticed, were given larger representation than was their due on the basis of population. The control exercised by the Centre over the provinces was so tight that the scheme appeared almost quasi–federal. Again, residuary powers were vested neither in the centre nor in the units but in the Governor-General who could, in his discretion, empower the federal legislature or the provincial legislature, as the case may be, to enact a law on the subject. Residuary powers in the case of States were vested in the Rulers thereof.

Under the Act, the centre had more administrative powers over the provinces than over the States. Federal officials could administer federal laws in the provinces; in the administration of provincial subjects, the Governor did, in fact, function under the control of the Governor-General acting in his discretion. In the case of the States, however, the Rulers alone would enforce or administer federal laws. The number of federal units—there were over 600 princely States—was disproportionately large. More, there were striking disparities in regard to their area, population, resources and systems of internal administration. Nor, as may be expected, were the units federating in respect of a common list of subjects. The provinces desired a larger number of subjects in common than did the States. In the case of the former, federal jurisdiction extended over all the 59 subjects included in the federal legislative list as well as concurrent legislative list in respect of which both the federation and the provinces had jurisdiction. The princes on the other hand were expected to federate only in regard to the first 45 items of the federal list. As certain adjustments and groupings would have to be made to suit the needs and conditions of particular States, the extent of federal jurisdiction was likely to vary from State to State. In much the same manner, there were bound to be variations between the States and the provinces in respect of the fiscal arrangements and the manner in which the administrative authority of the federation was to be exercised.

A word on the working of the Act of 1935 during the relatively normal period between its introduction in mid-1937 and the outbreak of World War II, two years later. For the first time, Indian political leaders had the opportunity to form governments based upon joint responsibility. The terms Prime Minister and Council of Ministers came to be used in India for the first time. Minority representation did not figure as a major problem necessitating either the intervention of the Governor or hampering the smooth functioning of the Cabinet. None of the Governors had an occasion to dismiss any ministry; nor did the latter, as a result of fundamental differences, submit its resignation. Distribution of work and its allocation among different ministers was done mainly on the discretion of the ministers rather than of the Governor. Parliamentary secretaries to ministers were appointed so as to train potential leadership in government. There was little opposition from the Governor to any of the new legislation enacted. Governors, for the most part, acted as constitutional heads and there was the 'substance of independence' in the provincial field. The representative character of the legislature and the executive's responsibility to it worked out smoothly, in practice.

Gurmukh Nihal Singh, *Landmarks in Indian Constitutional and National Development*, 2 vols, 6th reprint, Delhi, 1973; II; A. C. Banerjee, *Constitutional History of India* 3 vols, Delhi, 1977–8, III, pp. 126–59; M. V. Pylee, *Constitutional History of India, 1600-1950*, reprint, Bombay, 1972, pp. 69–98.

Indian Arms Act (1878)

The first Indian Arms Act came into force on 14 March 1878; its ostensible objective was to ensure the maintenance of law and order by preventing pilferage especially by 'wild tribes and other dangerous classes.' It was explained that the existing law was inadequate to prevent the smuggling of arms and fresh legislation was thus called for. Arms, it was held, found their way into the hands of organized bands of dacoits who thus managed to defeat the police's efforts to eradicate lawlessness.

Under the provisions of the Act, provincial governments were directed to impose a fixed duty on the import of all arms as well as place restrictions on their sale. A license had to be obtained for their possession and failure to do so was regarded a criminal offence. By a gazette notification of 2 January 1879 some categories of persons were declared exempt from the purview of the Act. These included all officers, Europeans, East Indian subjects, Anglo-Indians, Americans and Armenians. Later, to mollify opposition, all titled persons, those who had received a sword or certificate in the public Darbar, members of municipal committees of approved loyalty and good position and, finally, those who were exempt from personal attendance at civil courts, were declared immune too.

The measure aroused bitter criticism. What was resented most was the government's open distrust of its subjects, more especially its tinge of racial discrimination against the 'natives.'

V. C. P. Chaudhary, *Imperial Policy of the British in India (1876-1880)*, Calcutta, 1968.

Indian Association (founded 1876)

Founded in Calcutta in July 1876 through the efforts of Surendranath Banerjea (q.v.) and Ananda Mohan Bose (q.v.), the Indian Association which rose as a rival to the Indian League, founded about a month earlier, aimed 'to represent the people and promote by every legitimate means, the political, intellectual and national advancement of the people.' It emphasized that some of the existing associations hardly represented the 'oppressed cooly or the oppressed ryot,' that it alone would be 'capable of keeping up and stimulating public opinion.'

The controversy over the Ilbert Bill (q.v.) and the contempt case against Banerjea provided the requisite impetus and there was a spontaneous agitation all over India. To make the Association into a national body, Banerjea undertook countrywide tours and powerfully agitated the 'Civil Service question.' Village associations were encouraged to make it a mass movement and, to that purpose, a national conference of all parties was convened in Calcutta in December 1883.

With the establishment of the Indian National Congress (q.v.), the Association became essentially a provincial organization. Its members however attended the annual sessions of the Congress and co-operated fully in tackling that party's organizational problems in Bengal. The Association protested vigorously against the Calcutta Municipal Act (q.v.) and the Partition of Bengal (q.v.). After 1914, with the Extremists predominating the Congress, differences arose between it and the Congress. The Association welcomed the Montagu-Chelmsford Reforms (q.v.) as a step towards self-government; the Congress criticized them. Determined to give the Act of 1919 a fair trial, some members of the Association were elected to the provincial legislatures. A year later, the two bodies finally parted company over Gandhi's (q.v.) Non-cooperation Movement (q.v.) which the Association considered to be pregnant with mischief. It also protested against the Civil Disobedience Movement (q.v.) launched by the Congress and welcomed the Viceroy's promise of Dominion Status (q.v.) to India. Though it continued to voice opinion on national issues and often co-operated with other political parties, the Association had, by the early 1930's, lost its previous popular hold and was soon relegated to the limbo.

The Association's true import lies in the fact that it was the first political body to foster national awakening and organize its programmes on a national scale.

Jogesh Chandra Bagal, *History of the Indian Association, 1876–1951*, Calcutta, 1953; B. B. Majumdar, *Indian Political Associations and Reform of Legislature,* Calcutta, 1965.

Indian Councils Acts (1858, 1861, 1892)

In striking contrast to (British) Parliament's earlier enactments, the Charter Acts (1793-1853) (q.v.) did not specify for how long the John Company's (q.v.) rule was to last. The traumatic experience of the Rebellion of 1857 (q.v.), however, brought matters to a head for the Crown decided to take over direct responsibility for the governance of India.

Indian Councils Act, 1858

Officially 'An Act for the Better Government of India', the Act invested the newly-designated Secretary of State for India with the 'superintendence, direction and control of all acts, operations and concerns which in any wise relate to the government or revenues of India.' In this task, he was to be assisted by a Council of 15 members, 8 of whom were appointed by the Crown and 7 elected, in the first instance, by the Court of Directors of the now-defunct East India Company and thereafter by the Council itself. They held office during good behaviour but could be removed on an address by both Houses of Parliament. The procedure was so devised as to remove the possibility of their becoming party men, much less strain their relations with the Secretary of State, especially after a change in government.

The Council was intended to serve as a check on the Secretary of State. It was stipulated that whenever the latter acted in opposition to a majority of his Council, he was to state, and place on record, his reasons for doing so. Similarly, a Councillor whose advice was not accepted or adopted, could place on record his reasons for such advice. Again, the Secretary of State was required to convene the Council at least once a week. He was to abide by the majority view in the case of election of members to his Council and in matters of expenditure out of the revenues of India. He was also obliged to place before the Council all despatches to, and from, India. In urgent and secret matters, however, such as war and defence, he was authorized to send instructions without prior intimation of the Council.

It has been said that the change-over in 1858 was 'rather a formal than a substantial change' for all real power had long passed to the President of the Board of Commissioners, more popularly the Board of Control, constituted under Pitt's India Act (q.v.). Over the years, the Directors had been reduced to the position of an advisory council, albeit with considerable powers of initiative. It may be recalled that already, under the Charter Act of 1853, membership of the Court of Directors had been reduced from 24 to 18, of whom 6 were nominees of the Crown. The above notwithstanding, the new law did not represent a mere change of masters in so far as it brought to a close the age–old duality between the Court of Directors and the Board of Control. Clever Governors-General had often succeeded in exploiting this rivalry to their advantage; not infrequently, it had resulted in the Company's inability to pursue a strong and vigorous policy.

Lord Curzon (q.v.) was to describe the change in 1858 as the 'final decapitation' of the Company, ending its system of dual government 'with all the incongruities and misadventures': the 'two rival fictions' of the Board of Commissioners and the Court of Directors disappeared while the Home government of India was 'reconstructed' on 'its present basis' with a Secretary of State assisted by an India Council.

The Directors had protested against the transfer of authority to the Crown but conceded that a 'clamour which represented the government of India by the Company as characterized by nearly every fault of which a civil government can be accused' was succeeded by 'an almost universal acknowledgement that the rule of the Company has been honourable to themselves and beneficial to India.'

Indian Councils Act, 1861

The Act stipulated that legislative power was to be restored to the Councils of Bombay and Madras, while new Councils were allowed to be established in other provinces—in Bengal (1862), the North-Western Provinces (1886), Burma and the Panjab (1897). The Councils were to confine themselves to legislation only. Previous sanction of the Governor-General was necessary for legislation by local Councils in certain cases. Additionally, in every case a law passed by the local Council and assented to by the Governor required the assent of the Governor-General for its validity

The Executive Council of the Governor-General was enlarged by the addition of a fifth member who was to be a jurist—'a gentleman of the legal profession, a jurist rather than a technical lawyer.' Of the five, at least three were to be drawn from the Civil Service with at least 10 years' experience, while the fourth was to be a barrister of at least 5 years' standing. The Secretary of State had the power to appoint the Commander-in-Chief as an extraordinary member of the Council. Again, a Governor or a Lieutenant-Governor could be co-opted a member if a meeting of the Council was held in a provincial capital. The Governor-General was empowered to make rules for the more efficient transaction of business in the Council. This enabled Lord Canning (q.v.) to introduce the portfolio system investing individual members with specific tasks of governmental responsibility. For purposes of legislation, the Governor-General's Council was enlarged by the addition of not less than 6 and not more than 12 members. They were nominated for a period of 2 years, with at least half of them being non-officials.

A limitation on the legislative powers of the Council was that the Governor-General was vested with the authority to issue ordinances which were valid for a period of 6 months. He was empowered to promulgate them without the prior consent of his Council.

In regard to provincial legislation, the Governor of each Presidency was to nominate an Advocate–General and not less than 4 nor more than 8 as additional members of his Council, provided that not less than half of them were non-officials.

The power of local legislation under the Act was concurrent, *not* exclusive. Thus, while the provincial Council might legislate, the legislative power of the Governor-General in Council was to remain unimpaired. In so far as it deprived the Legislative Council of any independent power, the Act was a retrograde measure, for the Council exercised no control nor check upon the executive. More, even its legislative functions were circumscribed by far too many limitations.

The above notwithstanding, it was a memorable Act for two reasons. *One*, it sketched out a framework which the Government of India was to retain to the very end, all subsequent changes being made within that framework. *Two*, it ushered Indians into the higher counsels of government. Lord Canning in 1862 appointed the Maharaja of Patiala, the Raja of Banaras and Sir Dinkar Rao (q.v.) to his newly constituted Legislative Council.

The provincial Councils in Bombay and Madras operated under the same restrictions as the Governor-General's Council in the making of 'Laws and regulations.' Apart from the authority exercised by the Governor, the previous sanction of the Governor-General was necessary before any regulations could be made on such all-India subjects as currency, copyright, posts and telegraph or the penal code.

Indian Councils Act, 1892

The Act laid down that the Governor-General's Legislative Council was to have not less than 10, nor more than 16 additional members. They were to be nominated by municipalities, university Senates and various trading associations.

In the case of the Councils of Bombay and Madras, the corresponding increase was to be not less than 8 nor more than 20; not more than 9 of these were to be officials. The maximum for Bengal was fixed at 20 and for the North-Western Provinces and Oudh at 15 each. Here too, the non-official members were to be nominated by municipalities, university Senates and various trading associations.

As for the Governor-General's Council, it was decided to appoint 10 non-official members: 4 selected by the provincial Legislative Councils (one each for Bengal, Bombay, Madras and the NWP), 1 nominated by the Calcutta chamber of commerce and 5 nominated by the Governor-General. In this manner, the representative, if not the elective, principle was cautiously introduced into the Councils, though as yet both in the supreme as well as the provincial bodies an official majority was assured. The Act empowered the Governor-General to make regulations for nomination of additional members and to prescribe the manner in which such regulations should be carried into effect. This would enable him to introduce indirectly, and through the backdoor as it were, the elective principle.

The functions of the Councils were enlarged. They were allowed to hold a discussion on the annual financial statement, and members were permitted to ask questions under prescribed rules. While earlier the Governor-General's Council could discuss the budget only when fresh taxation was sought to be imposed, under the new dispensation the budget was to be laid each year before the Council while every member, rising in turn, could discuss and criticize it. The right of interpellation was also granted.

The Act marked a notable step forward in Indian participation in governmental functioning. Even though members of the Council could not outvote the official majority, they yet exercised considerable influence on policy. It was incumbent upon officials to meet criticism levelled against administrative measures.

Gurmukh Nihal Singh, *Landmarks in Indian Constitutional and National Development*, 2 vols, 6th reprint, Delhi, 1973, I, pp. 61–3, 68–70, 107–9; A. C. Banerjee, *Constitutional History of India*, 3 vols., Delhi, 1977-8, II, pp. 11–12, 41, 48, 84, 305–9.

Indian Criminal Law Amendment Act (1908)

The objective of the Act was to provide for the more speedy trial of certain offences and for the prohibition of associations rated as dangerous to public peace. Initially applicable to the provinces of Bengal and Assam, in January 1910 the Act was extended to the rest of the country.

Under its provisions, the Indian Penal Code was drastically amended so that trials of suspected law-breakers could be expedited. Changes were also made so as to refuse bail to the accused, admit the evidence of witnesses and to prohibit appeals by a special bench of 3 judges of the High Court (without the aid of a jury) whose decision was to be deemed final.

Any association considered to be anarchist in its leanings was declared illegal, its property seized and confiscated if it were found that it was being used for unlawful purposes. All those who had anything to do with such associations were to be apprehended and punished severely.

However, murders, dacoities and sabotage continued despite the above measures, culminating in an attempt on the life of Governor-General

Charles Hardinge (q.v.). In the result, in 1912 a further tightening of the law was deemed necessary. Amending the Indian Penal Code once again, the new law added chapter V to it. Act VII of 1913, it was called 'An act to further amend the Indian Penal Code and the Criminal Procedure Code of 1896' and received the assent of the Governor-General on 27 March 1913.

The Act was divided into two parts, the first dealing with 'Special Procedure' the second with 'Unlawful Associations.' The latter, in the singular, was now defined as involving 'two or more persons agreeing to commit an illegal act or an act by illegal means', the guilty were punishable by death, transportation for life or rigorous imprisonment. The same punishment applied to abettors of a crime. The famous Delhi Conspiracy Case connected with the bomb thrown at the Viceroy was, among others, tried after this amendment became operative.

The Unrepealed Central Acts, vol. V, from 1908 to 1910, both inclusive, 2nd ed., Delhi, 1949, pp. 380–6; R. C. Majumdar (ed.), *Struggle for Freedom*, Bombay, 1965, pp. 109–10, 189; *Tara Chand*, III, p. 335.

Indian Independence Act (1947)

In its final incarnation, the Indian Independence Bill consisted of 20 clauses and 3 schedules. Departing from known procedures, the draft Bill before its presentation to (British) Parliament was shown to Indian political leaders and their comments taken fully into account. In accordance with the June 3rd Plan (q.v.), the Bill provided that the Constituent Assembly (q.v.) of each of the two Dominions would also act as its respective legislature. It followed that, in New Delhi, the then Central Legislative Assembly and the Council of State stood automatically dissolved.

The Bill stipulated that until the Constituent Assemblies of the two Dominions made alternative provisions, each would be governed in accordance with the Government of India Act, 1935 (q.v.) suitably modified and adapted. Actually, the 1935 Act, with the requisite modifications and adaptations, was brought into operation by the India (Provisional Constitution) Order, 1947, made by the Governor-General on 14 August.

The pivotal clause 6 of the 1947 Act dealt with the powers of the new Dominion legislature. It established beyond doubt, or dispute, the sovereign character of the legislature with the fullest measure of independence. Sub-clauses 2, 4 and 5 removed every possible element of subordination to, or dependence on, the British Parliament. In particular, the power to amend or repeal 'this or any existing or future Act of Parliament' in so far as it affected the new Dominions, constituted a complete and unreserved transfer of sovereign power.

The Bill was rushed through Parliament in the short span of 12 days (4–16 July) and received Royal assent on 18 July. *Inter alia*, it fixed 15 August 1947 as the date for setting up the two Dominions. It indicated the territorial division of India and the constitution of two provinces each in the former Panjab and Bengal of British India. In provided a separate Governor-General for each Dominion, a legislature with full authority to make laws unhindered by the British Parliament. As a result, the British Government's responsibility in India was brought to an end while the suzerainty of the Crown over the Indian States (q.v.) lapsed (on 15 August). The Act also laid down temporary provisions for the government of the Dominions by giving to the two Constitutent Assemblies the status of parliaments with the full powers of a Dominion legislature. It authorized the Governor-General to issue temporary orders for making such provisions as appeared to him necessary or expedient to bring the Act into operation. Finally, the Act prescribed the conditions and terms of the Secretary of State's Services and the Indian armed forces, the continuance of the jurisdiction or authority of the British Government over the British Army, Navy and Air Force.

On the eve of the Bill being presented in Parliament, a question was posed at a press conference addressed by Sardar Vallabbhai Patel (q.v.) and V. P. Menon (then Secretary in the Department of States) as to whether clause 1 prevented the subsequent recognition by the British Parliament of more Dominions than the two stipulated therein. Patel's reply was that it had been made clear that the jurisdiction of the British Parliament over India ceased with the Bill.

As should be evident, legal sanction for Partition, accompanied by conferment of Dominion Status, was contained in the Bill. In respect of the functions of the constitution-making body, it laid down: 'In the case of each of the new Dominions, the powers of the legislature of the Dominion shall, for the purpose of making provision as to the Constitution of the Dominion, be exercisable in the first instance by the Constituent Assembly of that Dominion, and references in this Act to the Legislature of the Dominion shall be construed accordingly.'

V. P. Menon, *The Transfer of Power,* Calcutta, 1957, pp. 390–3, 516–32; B. Shiva Rao, *The Framing of India's Constitution: A Study,* New Delhi, 1968, p. 91.

Indian Press Act (1910)

The Newspapers (Incitement to Offences) Act of 1908 having proved ineffective, a bill was brought before the legislature to secure control over printing presses, the means of publication, publishers, importation into India and transmission by post of seditious and objectionable matter, as well as suppression of newspapers deemed to be undesirable or seditious. It provided for a deposit of security by the proprietors of presses and publishers. Offences against the Act made the person concerned liable to forfeiture of security. The law came into force on 8 February 1910.

The Act was intended essentially to eradicate all manner of terrorist activities which had erupted after 1907 and showed no signs of abatement despite several respressive measures. The government, it appears, had come to the conclusion that the 'continued recurrence of murders and outrages' necessitated fresh measures 'to deal with anarchy and sedition.'

S. P. Sinha (q.v.), then Law Member in the government, was initially opposed to this legislation but changed his stance at the news of the murder by an anarchist of a police officer in the Calcutta High Court. Gokhale (q.v.) faced much the same dilemma and yielded ground on a similar consideration.

Under the Act, the government was empowered to instruct its solicitor to go before the presidency magistrate to demand security from any newspaper publishing matter considered offensive. Punitive action was to be taken at the discretion of the executive. John Morley, then Secretary of State for India, formally approved the measure, but has left on record the view that, initially reluctant, his hands were later forced.

Apart from the nature of the legislation, the manner in which it was administered was a source of constant complaint on the part of the Press; modifications were suggested and its total repeal demanded. It was pointed out that the new measure had substituted the discretion of the executive for the rights of publicity, audience and appeal. Furthermore, it violated a fundamental principle of jurisprudence by directing the accused to prove that he was innocent; even though appeal was provided for, the High Court had no power to question the discretion of the executive authority. Journalists were asked to furnish security, at the discretion of the executive, before they could publish a newspaper. This was a humiliation to which no respectable journalist would ordinarily submit.

The Act was directed against the press, who were considered to be the prime motivators and instigators of sedition. It declared *inter alia* that all newspapers, books and documents which contained any seditious words or expressions or incited the defence forces, provoked racial or class conflict, threatened the security of officials and others, or intimidated them and disturbed the public peace would be banned. The printing presses and publishers responsible for them would forfeit their security deposits and asked to furnish these afresh. The Act empowered district magistrates to demand fresh securities ranging from Rs 500 to 5,000. The final authority in all cases vested with the Local Government, albeit an appeal lay to the High Court. The Anglo-Indian press was declared exempt from the provisions of the Act.

The Act was said to exercise a 'vague terror' upon all law-abiding citizens who had anything to do with printer's ink, for journalists were made to feel like criminals. As was feared, in its working, the Act stifled the press. Although the government gloated over Gokhale's support of the measure, it ignored his protest at the ruthless implementation of the 'sedition hunt' as he called it later. Punishments meted out were often too severe. Thus, the publisher of a so-called seditious pamphlet was punished with transportation for 7 years while another was sentenced to life imprisonment.

Within 10 years of its operation, 350 printing presses and 300 newspapers had paid penalties in cash, while several hundred were compelled to close down. As many as 500 publications were proscribed and Rs 50,000 collected as security. Aurobindo Ghosh's (q.v.) publications closed down, while Mrs Annie Besant (q.v.) forfeited security for her paper. Worse, the measure encouraged 'official terrorism', for district magistrates tended to become virtual tyrants, disallowing even a legitimate ventilation of public grievances.

In 1921 the government bowed before persistent popular protest and demands for the repeal of the Act by asking Tej Bahadur Sapru (q.v.) to constitute a committee of inquiry into its working. As a result of the latter's recommendations, the measure was repealed in 1922.

Margarita Barns, *The Indian Press: A History of the Growth of Public Opinion in India,* London, 1940, app. II, pp. 442–9; S. Natarajan, *A History of the Press in India,* Bombay, 1961, pp. 357–65; 'Press Legislation', *Modern Review,* XV, 2, February 1914, pp. 242–3.

Indian Press Ordinance (1930)

On 27 April 1930 the Indian Press Ordinance was promulgated, ostensibly to 'provide for the better control of the press', but in reality to revive the provisions of the Indian Press Act of 1910 (q.v.) with some modifications. In less than 2 months, 131 newspapers had been called upon to pay securities and 9 suspended publication, while a sum of Rs 250,000 was deposited in the state coffers.

This apart, 6 other ordinances of a similar nature were promulgated between 19 April and 7 July 1930, all directed towards controlling the Civil Disobedience Movement (q.v.). Through them, the government came down heavily on the newspapers and the young nationalist news agency, the *Free Press News*. In princely India, the Indian States (Protection against Disaffection) Act was widely used to curb the hostility of the press against the government.

Under the Press Ordinance, magistrates were empowered, in their discretion, to demand a security of not less than Rs 500 and not more than Rs 2,000 from any person keeping a printing press who was required to make a declaration under Section 4 of the Press and Registration of Books Act (1867). For publishers of newspapers it was necessary to make a declaration under Section 5, wherein too the magistrate could demand a security. Power to declare such securities forfeit was confirmed whenever it appeared to the Local Government that any published matter was likely to incite or seduce or bring into hatred or contempt lawful authority. On one security being forfeited any printer making a fresh declaration had to deposit with the magistrate a further amount of not less than Rs 1,000 and not more than Rs 10,000. From publishers, too, securities of a like amount were demanded. If this security were forfeited, the Local Government could, by notice in writing, declare forfeit the further security, the printing press as well as copies of the offending publication.

Appeals could be preferred to the High Court to set aside such orders within 2 months from the date of their execution. Such applications were to be heard by a special bench of the High Court composed of three judges, or, where the High Court consisted of less than three judges, of all the judges.

Through the Ordinance the government changed tactics by penalizing the press, instead of the editor. Newspapers were now asked to deposit securities whenever they made a fresh declaration to publish. These were later declared forfeit and new securities demanded in lieu. For more serious offences even the printing press was confiscated. Thus N. C. Kelkar of the *Kesari* was fined Rs 5,000 for contempt of court, while the *Bombay Chronicle* forfeited a security of Rs 1,500 for criticizing a magistrate.

The Press Ordinance raised a storm of protest throughout the country and led to the first largely attended, and representative, conference of Indian editors held under the presidentship of A. Rangaswami Iyengar, who was not only editor of the *Hindu* but a parliamentarian, constitutional expert and co-founder of the Swaraj Party (q.v.) in South India.

Alarmed by the prevalent conditions—with civil disobedience raging like wildfire on the one hand and the draconian ordinances on the other—a number of nationalists resigned from the Central Legislative Assembly. In May 1930, the Council of the All India National Liberal Federation (q.v.) appealed for the immediate repeal of the Press Ordinance as well as the release of all political offenders who had not been found guilty of violence.

In 1931 the state's emergency powers were invoked for only one year to meet the recrudescence of large-scale terrorist activities and of political hostility to the government in journals and elsewhere. A government publication, *India 1931–2*, justified the use of these powers which had earlier been approved by the Central Legislative Assembly.

S. Natarajan, *A History of the Press in India*, Bombay, 1962, pp. 212–14; Medig Krishna Murthy, *Indian Journalism*, Mysore, 1966, pp. 88–9; Margarita Barns, *The Indian Press: A History of the Growth of Public Opinion in India*, London, 1940, pp. 370–2.

Indian Universities Act (1904)

The deplorable state of education at all levels—primary, secondary and college or university—was discussed at length at an apparently secret if also non-official conference sponsored by Lord Curzon (q.v.). Convened at Simla in 1901 the Viceroy invited to it Directors of Public Instruction from the provinces, apart from the Reverend William Miller of Madras Christian College. No Indian educationist was called. The conference sat for 15 days (1–14 September) and embodied its conclusions in a series of 156 resolutions, each of which Curzon himself had a hand in drafting. He presided over its sessions, six hours a day, all the days and, in the result, suffered a physical collapse.

As an outcome, a 3-member Commission of Inquiry under Sir Thomas Raleigh, then law Member in the Governor-General's Executive Council, with Sir Syed Husain Bilgrami (q.v.) and Dr Gooroodass Banerjee (q.v.) was constituted. It was directed ' to inquire into the conditions and prospects of the universities established in British India, to consider the proposals for improving their condition and working, to recommend measures to elevate the standards of university teaching and to promote the advancement of learning.' The Commission recommended the need to fix minimum fees and the gradual abolition of second-grade colleges. Dr Banerjee in his note of dissent had suggested that poor students should not be denied education by the fixing of minimum fees, but Curzon was opposed to this viewpoint demanding 'quality, not quantity.'

The Commission's recommendations were incorporated in the Indian Universities Act VIII, made into law on 21 March 1904. A sequel was the Indian Universities Validation Act (February 1905) whereby the government were empowered to change or add to regulations submitted for its sanction. Under the new law, university Senates were to consist of a minimum of 50 and a maximum of 100 ordinary Fellows, one–tenth of whom were elected by graduates of five years' standing. One-fifth of the total membership was to retire every year, though there would be no retirement for the first three years. The Syndicate was to consist of the Vice–Chancellor as Chairman, the Director of Education as an *ex–officio* member and some 9–15 members elected by the Senate. They were to serve a 2–year term. The Vice-Chancellor's appointment was to be made by the government.

Stringent rules were laid down for affiliating or dis–affiliating colleges and recognizing schools, a final decision in the former case resting with the government. The framing of curricula and appointment of professors and lecturers was also subject to the approval of the government. Second grade colleges were to be gradually abolished and post-graduate studies encouraged. A minimum amount to be paid as fee was fixed and the pass marks in English were increased.

There were two principal criticisms against the new reforms. *First*, the proposed reconstruction of the Senates, it was held, would increase official control and destroy the limited autonomy that the universities enjoyed. *Secondly*, the new measure would restrict the growth of higher education. Its provisions, critics charged, recognized the government's intention of controlling education as it limited the number of senators and syndics and thereby created a preponderance of nominated members among the former. Furthermore, it lessened the importance of the educated class, then in the forefront of the nationalist movement, especially in matters relating to post-graduate teaching, the appointment of university professors, lecturers and equipment for laboratories and museums.

Gokhale (q.v.), underlining 'the undoubted hostility of the educated classes' to the new law, stressed that it would operate 'to the prejudice of indigenous enterprise in the field of higher education' and warned that, while the good its provisions 'may do is at least [best?] problematical, the injury that they will do is both certain and clear.' He called the new measure the 'narrow, bigoted and expensive rule of experts.' His critics notwithstanding, Curzon had hoped that his reforms would lay the foundation of a system 'that ought to satisfy' the country for the 'next quarter of a century.' This, however proved to be a wild boast; within 10 years a new bill was drafted while the Sadler Commission (1919) ruled that 'an effective synthesis between college and university was still undiscovered', and that 'the foundations of a sound university organization had not yet been laid.'

The idea of official control was new in Curzon's time but subsequent progress would demonstrate that it was a step in the right direction. Curzon's thinking on university education, it has been suggested, was sound but far in advance of his times. A critic has aptly called the Act of 1904 as 'the real charter of present day education in India.'

Aparna Basu, *The Growth of Education and Political Development in India, 1898–1920*, Delhi, 1974, pp. 13–31; V. C. Bhutani, 'Curzon's Educational Reforms in India,' *Journal of Indian History*, LI, 1, April 1973, pp. 65–92.

Indigo Riots (1859–60)

Until the last quarter of the 18th century, indigo was a prized dye-stuff that formed an important item in the commerce of the East India Company (q.v.). By 1780, the latter had entered directly into its cultivation and, in the process, imported European planters from the West Indies and made considerable monetary advances to them to encourage the supply of the commodity. The typical planter, ill–educated and ill–bred at best, was literally a slave driver. He did not cultivate the plant but employed local peasants under a system of cash advances. The cultivator who accepted the advance became, to all intents and purposes, a serf. Various charges were realized from him—for supply of seeds, stamps for the agreement he concluded, and the carting of produce. To cap it all, the price paid him was normally ⅓ to ½ of the market rate.

In the 1830's Macaulay (q.v.) had observed that, partly through the operation of the laws and partly through their defiance, the cultivators had been reduced to 'a state not far removed from that of predial slavery'; more, he pronounced it 'a system of bloodshed' wherein the cultivator 'was deprived of his free will.' Despite their apparent clash of interests, the fortunes of the planter as well as the cultivator were intimately tied to the fluctuating prices of indigo in the European market. In the post-1849 period, these had come tumbling down and the worst hit was the cultivator. By now virtually a slave, he not only continued growing the crop under duress, but at low rates so as to ensure an undiminished share of the planter's profit. Non–compliance with the latter's dictates meant arbitrary punishment—locking up in godowns and even physical beating. Under heavy debt to the planter who kept loaning him money, he submitted to his master's commands and lived in abject poverty.

In 1859, there were about 143 indigo concerns in Bengal employing well over 500 well-paid European planters. Under them was a hierarchy of ill–paid Indian middlemen who augmented their meagre incomes with a cess imposed on the ryot. Appeals to justice or fair play were virtually impossible since 29 Europeans and a solitary Indian planter, appointed honorary magistrates, exercised a complete judicial stranglehold. Besides, as the law then stood, Europeans were not answerable for their acts in the mofussil law courts. As the oppression on cultivators increased, voices were raised, some official, demanding an end to the system. Though John Peter Grant (1807–93), then Lieutenant-Governor at Fort William, admitted that 'indigo cannot be supported at the expense of justice', he could not ally himself openly against the planters' interests.

Some modicum of relief to the cultivator came through petty zamindars and moneylenders who helped him pay the enhanced rents on land. The cultivator's cause was also advocated and widely publicized by the 'native' Indian press in Bengal and by European missionaries. Emboldened by this overt support, the cultivators rebelled: they refused to grow indigo, attacked the planters and sued them in courts of law for maltreatment and coercion. So great was their popular appeal that the planters countered by forming a Planters' Association. There had been rumblings of the storm earlier but it broke out in full fury in 1859. Europeans were assaulted, their supplies stopped, standing indigo crops destroyed and factories plundered and burnt. As the riots spread, the Lieutenant-Governor, under considerable popular pressure, agreed reluctantly to some temporary legislation to check them. Act XI of 1860, effective for 6 months, required the cultivator to keep his part of the contract. Failure to abide by it would entail payment of a fine and a term of imprisonment.

Around this time the Bengali play, *Nil Darpan Natakam* by Dinabandhu Mitra (1830–73) about life on an indigo plantation was translated into English by Michael Madhusudan Datta (1824–73) and published and distributed by the Reverend James Long (1814–87). Its stark, down-to-earth realism shook government and popular imagination with startling revelations of the atrocities committed by the planters.

Public sympathy understandably was on the side of the underdog. Newspapers published harrowing tales of the cultivators' suffering; letters were published from the areas where indigo grew; songs were composed and plays staged. Long's trial and later conviction on a technical offence made him and *Nil Darpan* a *cause celebre*. Three men who did major work in this cause stood out: Harish Chandra Mukherji (1824–61) of the *Hindoo Patriot;* Ram Gopal Ghosh (1814–68) whose *Remarks on the Black Acts* proved a curtain-raiser; and Shishir Kumar Ghose (1840–1911), founded-editor of the *Amrit Bazar Patrika.*

The government suppressed the riots with a firm hand and set up the Indigo Inquiry Commission to report on the situation. This 5–member body under W. S. Seton-Karr, then Secretary to the Bengal Government, submitted its findings on 27 August 1860. In forwarding the report, Lieutenant-Governor Grant wrote an able albeit lengthy minute (17 December 1860). Most of the recommendations, which were unambiguously in favour of the cultivators and pronounced an end to coercion through intimidation, were accepted by the Government and embodied in Act VI of 1862. Grant incurred considerable unpopularity with the planters in his determination to do justice to the cultivators at a time when he was up against troubles from the tribes on the frontier. In both these capacities he showed great ability, in writing, in speech and in action.

The importance of the indigo riots cannot be over–emphasized. They have been viewed, not unjustly, as the 'first revolution' in Bengal after the establishment of British rule.

R. C. Majumdar (ed.), *British Paramountcy and Indian Renaissance,* Bombay, 1963, pp. 914–37.

Interim Government (1946–7)

Soon after the Cabinet Mission left India on 29 June 1946, Lord Wavell (q.v.) asked Jawaharlal Nehru (q.v.) to approach M. A. Jinnah (q.v.) and persuade him to enter the coalition interim government that had been envisaged as part of the (Cabinet) Mission's Plan (q.v.). Jinnah however refused to co-operate unless he was assured that (i) in the proposed set-up, the power of veto would vest with the Governor–General, as had been the case hitherto; (ii) the new government would not be responsible to the legislature, but to the Viceroy; (iii) a nationalist Muslim would not be included in the interim cabinet.

On 22 August, Nehru wrote to the Viceroy that he was willing to form a coalition government but would neither submit to the Muslim League (q.v.) nor subscribe to its thinking on the subject. Two days later, the personnel of the new government was announced: Jawaharlal Nehru, Vallabhbhai Patel (q.v.), Rajendra Prasad (q.v.), Asaf Ali, C. Rajagopalachari (q.v.), Sarat Chandra Bose, Dr John Matthai, Baldev Singh, Sir Shafat Ahmed Khan, Jagjivan Ram, Ali Zaheer, C. H. Bhabha. Two more Muslim members were to be appointed later. That evening (August 24), the Viceroy in a radio broadcast while announcing the formation of the new government repeated his earlier offer to take 5 Muslim Leaguers in it. Jinnah's rejoinder was to accuse him (Wavell) of making a misleading statement and to repeat his earlier charge of breach of promise.

The new government assumed office on 2 September. A few days later, Nehru, as its head, appealed for the co-operation of all concerned: 'We are perfectly prepared for and have accepted the position of sitting in sections [his reference was to the Cabinet Mission Plan] which will consider the question of formation of groups...we seek agreed and integrated solutions with the largest measure of goodwill behind them.' The Muslim League's reaction to the formation of the new government was to announce that 2 September would be observed as a day of mourning when Muslims all over the country were asked to display black flags. Gandhi's (q.v.) grim prognostication was: 'We are not in the midst of civil war but we are nearing it', for consequent on Jinnah's call violence broke out in Bombay, Panjab, Bengal and Bihar.

From the start, Wavell had been overly keen to induct the Muslim League into the new government under all circumstances. He was equally clearly persuaded that he would rather lose the co-operation of the Indian National Congress (q.v.) at the centre and in the provinces than go ahead with constitution-making on a one-party basis, which the Cabinet Mission had never intended in any case. On 13 October, Jinnah informed the Viceroy that he and the League's Council had decided to join the Interim Government and suggested the following 5 names: Liaqat Ali Khan (q.v.), I. I. Chundrigar, Abdur Rab Nishtar, Ghazanfar Ali Khan, Jogendra Nath Mandal.

It is interesting to note that before inducting it into the government, the Viceroy did not seek the League's prior commitment to the Cabinet Mission Plan of 16 May, even though Nehru had asked for a clear and categorical assurance on the subject. Nor was one readily forthcoming. All that transpired was that the Viceroy had explained to Jinnah that his party's entry into the government must be considered conditional on his acceptance of the Mission's long-term plan. The League leader replied by affirming that as soon as he was satisfied that the Mission's original Plan of 16 May would be honoured, he was prepared to call a meeting of his Council to reverse its earlier Bombay decision of a total rejection.

With the 5 League nominees sworn in on 26 October, three Congress nominees—Sarat Chandra Bose, Shafat Ahmed Khan and Ali Zaheer quit the Government. The personnel and the portfolios of the composite 14-member Government were: Jawaharlal Nehru (Vice-President of the Executive Council, External Affairs and Commonwealth Relations); Vallabhbhai Patel (Home, Information and Broadcasting); Baldev Singh (Defence); Dr John Matthai (Industries and Supplies); C. Rajagopalachari (Education); C. H. Bhabha (Works, Mines and Power); Rajendra Prasad (Food and Agriculture); Asaf Ali (Railways); Jagjivan Ram (Labour); Liaqat Ali Khan (Finance); I. I. Chundrigar (Commerce); Abdur Rab Nishtar (Communications); Ghazanfar Ali Khan (Health); Jogendra Nath Mandal (Law).

In the government that now emerged, it was evident that all the *three* parties were working at cross purposes. The Congress wanted a united government exercising joint responsibility and pursuing common goals. It deluded itself into believing that the Muslim League in government would somehow be induced to co-operate in the tasks that lay ahead. The League on its part had made it clear that its entry into the Interim Government was designed only to secure a foothold in the citadel of power so as to fight for its cherished goal of Pakistan. Echoing Jinnah, Liaqat Ali Khan had affirmed that the Government had been formed under the existing Constitution and there was thus no question of joint or collective responsibility. As if this were not clear enough, the League leader affirmed that, 'as he saw it, the Interim Government consisted of a Congress block and a Muslim block, each functioning under separate leadership.' Opposed to the views of the two political rivals, Wavell hugged the fond hope that they might come round to the realization that a British presence was necessary in India and hence accept his guidance, if not actual direction, in the administration of the three central subjects.

In his *Journal* entry for 15 October following the League's agreement to join the interim Government, the Viceroy noted: 'although I have at last succeeded in announcing a coalition Cabinet, I felt no elation over it, rather depression over the difficulties still ahead. I wonder whether I can induce them to work together.' Ten days later, on the eve of the new Government being inducted into office, Wavell confided: 'So I have at last got a coalition Government safely in office but I am in no way inclined to optimism over the future and do not feel in the least like celebrating the event; though I hope I may sleep better tonight. The new Government will be sworn in tomorrow under ominous auspices—the riots in East Bengal, restlessness in Bombay and Calcutta, the resentment of the Congress at having to take in the League without acknowledgement of Nehru's position as self–appointed premier, the deep mistrust between the party leaders . . . . The correspondence over the portfolios shows the difficulty of settling matters between two parties . . .that an agreement has been reached at all is I suppose something of an achievement.'

The life of the Interim Government was traumatic. Thus on 20 November 1946, on the morrow of the Viceroy issuing invitations for the inaugural meeting of the Constituent Assembly (q.v.), scheduled for 9 December 1946, Jinnah categorically declared that the League would keep out. Wavell had sent for Liaqat Ali Khan and 'told him that he could not agree to the representatives of the League remaining in the Interim Government unless the League accepted the long term Plan.' In reply, the League leader predicated his group's resignation once certain assurances were forthcoming from the British Government. On 5 February 1947, the Viceroy received a demand from the Congress and minority members in the Government for the resignation of the League's representatives in so far as the latter had not only not joined the Constituent Assembly but were 'committed to a policy of direct action, i.e., of active opposition to the Government of which it formed a part.' When Wavell faced him with this demand, Liaqat Ali countered by saying that the Congress 'had not in fact accepted the Cabinet Mission Plan.'

On 15 February Vallabhbhai Patel made it clear in a press interview that the Congress would withdraw from the Interim Government if representatives of the Muslim League were allowed to remain in it. Prime Minister Attlee's statement on 20 February 1947 announcing his government's firm decision to transfer power by June 1948 and the replacement of Wavell by Lord Mountbatten put a new complexion on the political scene. Attention understandably shifted to the new Viceroy and his future course of action. On 1 March the Congress Working Committee demanded that in the light of HMG's new commitment, it was necessary, pending the transfer of power, to recognize the Interim Government 'as a Dominion government with full control over the services and administration.' The demand did not find much favour with the League. Another veritable storm was created by Liaqat Ali Khan's budget for 1947–8. He proposed, *inter alia*, a 25% tax on all business profits of more than Rs 100,000. The Congress viewed this as an attempt to penalize Hindu capitalists (who largely financed it) and to sow dissension between its right wing and a small, albeit vocal, socialist group.

These and several other issues of contention gradually receded into the background in the face of the speed with which the new Viceroy proceeded to unfold his plan of action. Within less than 10 weeks of his arrival, he had made the two parties agree to 'the June 3rd Plan' (q.v.), thereby anticipating the actual transfer of power by many months. As the impending Partition with its resultant creation of Pakistan became a grim reality, the Interim Government lost its basic purpose.

On 10 July a new arrangement was given effect to. All the portfolios held hitherto by League members of the Government were withdrawn and re-allocated to the Congress wing of the Cabinet, which now took charge of affairs pertaining to the embryonic Dominion of India. Similarly, the League members took charge of the corresponding portfolios in so far as Pakistan was concerned. Matters of common concern to both Dominions were to be dealt with jointly by both wings under the chairmanship of the Governor-General. Thus, in effect, two separate provisional governments were established, one for India and another for the future Pakistan, each to deal with its own business and to consult the other on matters of common concern. Thus the Interim Government had in effect ceased to be.

Tara Chand, IV, pp. 473–5, 484–8; Penderel Moon (ed.), *Wavell: The Viceroy's Journal*, London, 1976, pp. 359-64; V. P. Menon, *The Transfer of Power*, Calcutta, 1957, pp. 280-317, 324-7, 335-7, 395-6.

Irwin (1881–1959)

Edward Fredrick Lindley Wood was born in 1881 and created first Baron Irwin in 1925; after the death of his father, in 1934, he became Viscount Halifax. He was Viceroy of India during 1926–31 and later (1938–40) Secretary of State for Foreign Affairs. In 1941 he was appointed British Ambassador in Washington D. C. and continued there until 1946. In England, he had a long political innings—Under Secretary of State for the Colonies (1921–2), Minister of Agriculture (1924–5), President of the Board of Education (1932–5), Secretary of State for War (1935) and Lord Privy Seal (1937–8).

Born with an atrophied left arm which had no hand, Irwin shrugged off his disability even as a child. He was educated at Eton and Christ Church College, Oxford, where, in 1903, he took a first class in history and became a Fellow of All Souls College. He taught history, hunted twice a week and travelled around the world. During 1910–25 Irwin was a Conservative member of the House of Commons; in 1914 he joined the army as a Yeomanry Officer (1915–17) in the Yorkshire Dragoons—he fought in France and was mentioned in despatches. His appointment as Governor-General, which was announced in November 1925, was suggested by King George V.

Immensely tall, with a fine domed head and the face of an ascetic, Irwin
bore himself majestically. His aim, he told one of his staff in June 1926, was
'to keep a contented India in the Commonwealth twenty-five years hence.'
The exclusion of an Indian from the Simon Commission (q.v.) was on his
advice. He had reasoned that a mixed body would fail to reach agreement;
that the Muslims could be persuaded to co-operate with an all-British
Commission; that the Hindus would follow suit, however reluctantly, rather
than allow their traditional opponents to be heard unchallenged. For his
part, Birkenhead, the Tory Secretary of State who had 'extreme and firmly
held' views on India, feared that an alliance in a mixed commission between
the British Labour Party and Indian members may produce dangerously
inconvenient majority conclusions. 'He [Birkenhead] must share responsibility', it has been said, 'for the gravest mistake of Irwin's Viceroyalty.'

The Viceregal announcement in October 1929 regarding a Round Table
Conference (q.v.) and the British view that the natural issue of India's
constitutional progress was Dominion Status (q.v.) evoked hostile comment
at home. Birkenhead and Churchill were predictably vehement among
Conservatives; Lord Reading condemned Irwin with the authority of a
popular ex-Viceroy; Sir John Simon was annoyed that by his announcement
Irwin had stolen his (Simon's) thunder, viz., anticipated his Commission's
report.

India again passed through the 'weary cycle of resentment, rebellion,
repression and reprieve.' Nothing was more important during his tenure of
office than the political problem. In a letter of 18 May 1926 Irwin confided: 'I
am always racking my brain as to how to get out of this futile and vicious
circle by which we say, no advance without co-operation; and they say no
co-operation without advance. I cannot help feeling that it is a question
much more psychological than political. One of the extreme Swaraj people
said to me the other day that if only they could trust us it wouldn't matter to
them whether they waited five or fifty years. How then to make them believe
that we mean what we say?'

In January 1931, combining magnanimity with political shrewdness, Irwin
ordered Gandhi's (q.v.) release. The two leaders met eight times and, after
protracted parleys, concluded the Gandhi–Irwin Pact (q.v.). It has been
said that 'few pro-consuls other than Irwin could have demonstrated a
subtlety of mind to match that of Gandhi or driven so hard a bargain clothed
in the language of friendship.' The Pact marked the climax of his Viceroyalty. On political and constitutional issues, despite his Council, 'almost
every decision was taken by Irwin.' Every Viceregal speech and statement of
policy bears the clear imprint of his personality. Herbert Emerson, then Home
Secretary, gradually won the Mahatma's confidence to an extent where the
latter 'willingly entrusted to him [Emerson], the drafting of the [Gandhi–
Irwin] settlement.'

Within a year of Irwin sailing for England in April 1931, the political
horizon in India was bleak: the second Round Table Conference ended
inconclusively; the Civil Disobedience Movement (q.v.) was widespread and
Gandhi once again in prison. Irwin's imprint of tact and patience and a
remarkable courage that recognized neither political expediency nor physical fear was deeply felt and sorely missed.

In a lifetime of public service, the Viceroyalty must be accounted Irwin's most exacting task. But for all his vision, sympathy and administrative skill, he could not secure an immediate measure of constitutional progress or a calming of racial strife.

Appointed GCSI and GCIE in 1926, Irwin was made KG in 1931, becoming Chancellor of the Order in 1943. In 1933 he was nominated unopposed as Chancellor of Oxford University in succession to Lord Grey of Fallodon. His lifelong resort to regular and unhurried worship brought him consolation at times of stress, a serenity transcending the cares of statecraft, and a detachment from the evil realities of life. As Chancellor of Oxford, Irwin gave more than formal attention to the University's problems and took every opportunity of renewing his links with All Souls, 'a second home for more than fifty years.' Two more honours came to him in 1947, when he was appointed Chancellor of Sheffield University and High Steward of Westminster. They were doubly welcome in that he was fond of pomp and pageantry.

Irwin's character was of 'baffling opaqueness.' On some contemporary minds he left the imprint of statesmanship suffused by Christian faith; others suspected that his churchmanship concealed a strain of shrewd worldliness and expediency. Even the habitual moderation of his speeches might be variously interpreted either as a humble search for truth or as a form of verbal insurance against the unexpected. Those who saw him only on official occasions thought him aloof and consciously representative of an aristocracy whose continued and effortless lien on political power seemed anachronistic, even dangerous. Gopal has summed up the man thus: 'Free of meretricious ornament, there was in it [his character] no element of the florid or the facile; it was formed not of colour and fire but of dignity, human warmth and the "plain good intent" which Burke rated above all other qualities in public life.'

Irwin died on 23 December 1959 after a short illness.

J. F. C. Watts, *Viceroyalty of Lord Irwin 1926–31: with special reference to political and constitutional development*, Oxford, 1973; S. Gopal, *The Viceroyalty of Lord Irwin 1926–31*, Oxford, 1957; Earl of Halifax, *Fullness of Days*, London, 1957; Earl of Birkenhead, *Halifax: Life of Lord Halifax*, London, 1965; Alan Campbell-Johnson, *Viscount Halifax*, London, 1941; *DNB 1951–1960*, pp. 1072–80 (Kenneth Rose).

Mir Jafar (d. 1765)

Mir Mohammad Jafar Ali Khan (better known as Mir Jafar), the uneducated son of an Arab, Sayyed Ahmed Najafi, began to be important in Bengal politics after his marriage to the half-sister of Alivardi Khan (d. 1756). The latter elevated him to the position of Deputy Governor of Orissa, Faujdar of Midnapur and Hughli as well as paymaster of the army—this after he had led successful campaigns against some recalcitrant local rulers as well as the Marathas.

In 1747 Mir Jafar's underhand conspiracy to overthrow the Nawab misfired, with the result that he was relieved of his responsibilities and dismissed from the Darbar. Later, however, when the Afghan insurrections recurred, he was reinstated. He swore allegiance to Siraj-ud-Daula (q.v.) on the latter's accession but, suspecting his loyalty, the new Nawab dismissed him from service.

Mir Jafar then turned to other disgruntled court officials, viz., Yar Lutf Khan, Rai Durlabh (q.v.) and Jagat Seth. He also established liaison with the equally frustrated if ambitious John Company (q.v.), conspiring with them to depose the Nawab on the understanding that he be placed on the throne instead. When the latter heard of the plot and attempted to seize him, Mir Jafar appealed to the British for help, accepting in turn all the conditions laid down by them. Later, he again swore fealty to the Nawab but secretly pledged help to the British. At the Battle of Plassey (q.v.) which followed, he ensured British victory by playing the traitor and remaining a mere spectator on the battlefield. The Nawab, now a fugitive, was later hounded down and murdered by his orders.

On 29 June 1757 Clive installed Mir Jafar as Nawab at Murshidabad. The latter gratefully distributed generous presents to his English benefactors, but presently realized the full implications of his earlier deal with the Company. It was evident that he would be 'allowed to govern but never to rule', for the English constantly interfered in all matters of domestic policy. The mutiny in his army, the revolt of the zamindars, the attempted conquest of Bihar by Prince Ali Gauhar, later Shah Alam II (q.v.), and the Maratha raids on Bengal prevented him from dispensing with the English contingent. All this tended further to reduce his authority, while enhancing the prestige of the Company.

Mir Jafar's attempt to neutralize British superiority by allowing commercial privileges to the Dutch was frustrated by the latter's defeat at Biderra. The royal treasury depleted, the Nawab appealed to Mir Kasim (q.v.) to help pay the arrears of salary due to the troops. Meanwhile, he also ran into difficulties in payments due to the British, with the result that the latter conspired with the all-too-willing Mir Kasim to overthrow the Nawab (20 October 1760). The British alleged he had neglected affairs of state and granted Mir Jafar an ample pension. After a brief interlude, Mir Kasim too failed to live up to British expectations and, when a clash with him seemed inevitable, the Calcutta Council unanimously resolved to restore the mild, and much more amenable, Mir Jafar to the throne (1763). In the treaty drafted to bring about this coup, the old Nawab made further promises— cession of three districts, more trade privileges, reduction of his army and a payment of Rs 30 lakhs for losses incurred by the Company. On 24 July 1763 Mir Jafar re-occupied the palace. Now old, lethargic and narcotic-addicted, internal dissensions made him completely dependent on the English till his death, early in 1765, at the age of 74.

Mean and despicable as a general, Mir Jafar was still more so as a pusillanimous ruler. A puppet of the English, he possibly did more harm to Bengal by his weakness and ineptitude than by the initial treachery that raised him to the throne. At Plassey, Mir Jafar obligingly agreed to play the role of 'Colonel Clive's jackal' and the puppet of the Nawab of Bengal. The latter's debacle was to start a long chain of developments which utterly changed the face of India; the system of her economy and government were transformed.

It was not Plassey, it has been said, but the two short periods of Mir Jafar's reign (1757–60, 1763–5) that mark the transition from Muslim to British Bengal; it was 'his inefficient reign and lack of personality' that largely account for the change. Yet it was not merely a singular lack of wisdom, honesty and sense of duty on his part or that of his entourage; the blame must be shared by the nobility and people at large. Mir Jafar's conduct was nothing out of the ordinary: these were times when 'mean intrigue and treacherous conspiracy were the very breath of the life of the nobles' and their retinue.

Atul Chandra Roy, *The Career of Mir Jafar Khan. (1757–65)*, Calcutta, 1953; Dodwell, *CHI*, V, pp. 147–52, 164–72.

Jallianwala Bagh Massacre (1919)

The Jallianwala Bagh massacre (13 April 1919) has, over the years, become an inseparable part of the Indian national movement. Part of the British government's repressive policies towards a resurgent nationalism, it marked an important watershed in Indo-British relations.

Essentially, it has been held, the fear of an impending loss of the Indian empire prompted British bureaucrats to crush a great patriotic upsurge among the people with 'one crushing blow.' Uncharitable critics aver that 'with this objective in view they planned the great massacre' at Amritsar.

The venue, Jallianwala Bagh, had been initially laid out as a garden in the middle of the 19th century by one of Maharaja Ranjit Singh's (q.v.) courtiers, Pandit Jalla and came to be known after him. Later, the garden fell into disuse. Long before 1919 houses had been built all around the 'Bagh' with their back walls abutting it. Only on one side and over a small length there was no large construction, but here too a small stretch of low boundary wall, about 5 ft high, existed. Four or five narrow lanes led into the Bagh, each barely 3-4 ft wide, and there was one small *samadhi* (tomb) in its premises. The level of its land was not even; a small strip, near the entrance from the direction of Jallianwala bazaar, was on a higher plane; for the rest, the plinth level was lower, by 4–5 feet.

With the end of World War I came the Rowlatt Act (q.v.) which had ignited as it were the smouldering discontent of the people into open defiance of law–makers and the authority they wielded. The Panjabis, groaning under the burden of a global war to which they had contributed liberally, both in men and money, reacted strongly against the politically restrictive nature of the new legislation. The Ghadr and Khilafat Movements (qq.v.) had led to an awareness of political rights as well as the government's efforts to deny these. In their wake the Indian National Congress (q.v.) gave a call for observing a hartal on 8 April (1919), which received unqualified popular support. *Inter alia*, it resulted in attacks on public as well as private property and personnel. Finding itself unequal to the situation, the civil government in the Panjab decided to hand over the administration to the military authorities under Brigadier-General Dyer (q.v.).

As a background, it is necessary to recall that on 10 April in Amritsar a mob had allegedly, and without provocation, killed 5 Englishmen, gutted several public buildings, looted an English woman and left her for dead. Dyer arrived on the scene the next day at 9 p.m. when the local civil authority abdicated power into his hands. He banned all public meetings while important political leaders were apprehended. A determined effort was mounted to stamp out subversive elements, crush nationalist activities and teach people a sound lesson for indulging in anti-government acts. On 13 April 1919 a public meeting was called at Jallianwala Bagh in open defiance of the ban. It has been maintained that the meeting was prearranged by the British to serve an ulterior purpose. Be that as it may, a motley crowd had gathered at the Bagh when Dyer, apprised of the situation, marched in and, without warning, opened fire into the crowd. The crowd converged toward the exits on either side in a frantic effort to get away—'jostling, clambering, elbowing and trampling over' each other. Seeing this movement, Captain F. C. Briggs, Dyer's confidant, drew his attention to it. Imagining that they were getting ready to rush him, Dyer directed the fire of his troops straight at them. The result was 'a horror.' Men screamed and went down, to be trampled by those coming after. An approximate 20,000 people were caught beneath the hail of bullets, all frantically trying to escape from a place that had become 'a screaming hell.' The firing, which continued for 10 to 15 minutes with 1,650 rounds being discharged (i.e., 33 rounds per rifleman), ceased only after the ammunition ran out. Dyer admitted later that if more of the latter were available that too would have been used.

Reporting to the General Staff Division on 25 August 1919, Dyer wrote: 'I fired and continued to fire till the crowd dispersed and I considered that this is the least amount of firing which would produce the necessary moral and widespread effect it was my duty to produce if I was to justify my action. If more troops had been at hand the casualties would have been greater in proportion. It was no longer a question of merely dispersing the crowd, but one of producing a sufficient moral effect, from a military point of view, not only on those who were present, but more especially throughout the Panjab. There could be no question of undue severity.'

His apologists have maintained that Dyer fired because of a 'mistaken conception of his duty' or 'an error of judgement.' It has also been suggested that he may have run amuck on the spur of the moment owing to his excitable disposition or due to a mysterious mental disease.

In his statement to the House of Commons on 3 July 1920, Dyer developed 6 main reasons for his action: '(a) I found abundant signs that a determined and organised movement was in progress to destroy all Europeans; (b) I knew of the clouds from Afghanistan which broke three weeks later; (c) I had before me in the Jallianwala Bagh not a fortuitous gathering but a mob which was there with the express intent to challenge Government and defy me; (d) I knew that if I shirked the challenge....there would infallibly follow a general mob movement which would destroy all the European population; (e) I knew that ineffective action would endanger my small force; (f) I knew that on the four occasions when firing took place on the 10th in Amritsar, its effect in restoring order had been quite ineffective.'

A word may be added on the situation on the eve of the massacre. To borrow John Lawrence's words (used in the 1860's) it may be described 'as quiet as gunpowder.' Volumes V–VI of the Hunter Inquiry Committee Report (q.v.) underline the fact that, as the government viewed it, the situation in 1919 'was critical.' Authority 'was nervous and was prone to run for the nearest shelter;' it felt, 'it was not competent enough to cope' with the situation. The British believed 'they were sitting on the edge of an abyss. They were concerned that the story of 1857 was going to be repeated.' There was information about the wreckage of railway lines, the burning of mills, stores, of a great railway strike, the shifting loyalty of Indian troops, Gandhi's (q.v.) plans to overthrow the government and the impending Afghan attack on India. Furthermore, available evidence led them to believe that the army, which held India, was in such a condition of dissatisfaction that, if Gandhi's Satyagraha movement fell into the hands of violent agitation, the country would be plunged into a revolution and would no more be amenable to control.

If the above were accepted as sound, we may see some justification for the action of men like Dyer. It would, however, appear to be a somewhat exaggerated, if unrealistic assessment. Datta holds that 'essentially the situation lacked the revolutionary profile' which was imputed to it by the Panjab officials. A British observer, Arthur Swinson, has, in retrospect, emphasized that the massacre exploded the 'coy myth' that one nation could govern another 'in a decent, civilized manner'; it showed that 'sooner or later domination led to barbarity.' Nor should Dyer alone share the blame; part of it was that of the politicians: 'Dyer had to be destroyed: how else could the politicians pride themselves that there was no blood on their own hands.'

The Jallianwala massacre was not an isolated incident; the same gruesome tale was repeated at other places. The Panjab was treated more or less as newly conquered enemy territory; its people taught not to dare challenge or criticize the government on pain of condign punishment.

Alfred Draper underlines that the view that O'Dwyer (q.v.) was equally responsible for the situation in the Panjab was, in fact, shared by Edwin Montagu and other members of the Cabinet Committee set up to consider the findings of the Hunter Committee. Unfortunately their forceful condemnation was watered down: 'What emerges is a story of deception and moral cowardice on the part of Edwin Montagu.'

In the aftermath, Edward Thompson noted an articulate Indian's reaction: 'This [the massacre] ends the British connexion with India.' The fact is it gave a tremendous impetus to the freedom struggle. From now on, political activity increased rapidly and thousands of hitherto uncommitted people were drawn into the vortex of political activism. The freedom movement had at last acquired a national character. It induced a reappraisal of Congress policies and marked the commencement of the Non-cooperation Movement (q.v.). Tagore (q.v.) said later that what happened at the Bagh was 'a monstrous progeny of a monstrous war.' Gandhi noted: 'Plassey (q.v.) laid the foundation of the British Empire; Amritsar has shaken it.'

After Independence, a Jallianwala Bagh memorial trust was established and Rs 5,65,000 collected to acquire the Bagh. A 45-feet high pylon of red stone with its basement of rare granite, symbolic of the flame of liberty, was put up as a national memorial to the 2,000 odd martyrs. The Bagh has been transformed into a memorial garden with the base of the pylon resting in a pool flanked by 4 big lanterns. As one enters, there is a pagoda or open terrace, 60 feet by 100 feet, made of Kotah stone. This was the spot where Dyer's soldiers started firing. There is also a children's bathing pool, lawns and flowers; 250 cypresses have been planted. On all four sides, in 4 languages, Hindi, Gurmukhi, Urdu, English, the following is inscribed:

In memory of Martyrs
14th April 1919

V. N. Datta, *Jallianwala Bagh*, Ludhiana, 1968; Arthur Swinson, *Six Minutes to Sunset; The Story of General Dyer & the Amritsar Affair*, London, 1964; Raja Ram, *The Jallianwala Bagh Massacre: A Premeditated Plan*, Panjab University, Chandigarh, 1969; Rupert Furneaux, *Massacre at Amritsar*, London, 1963; Alfred Draper, *Amritsar: the Massacre that ended the Raj*, London, 1981.

Jayaprakash Narayan (1902–1979)

Jayaprakash Narayan, more popularly known as 'J.P.', was born on 11 October 1902 at Sitabdiyara in Saran district on the borders of U. P. and Bihar. His family were respectable, middle class Kayasthas of long-standing. His mother was a simple, deeply religious woman. 'J.P.' was educated at the Patna Collegiate School, Bihar Vidyapith and Banaras Hindu University. In 1922 he was awarded a scholarship by an association in Calcutta and went to the U.S.A. where he stayed for 8 years, studying at Iowa, Chicago, Wisconsin, California and Ohio. Earning his way through college, he engaged in a variety of jobs including that of a farmer and factory labourer. While in the U.S.A., 'J.P.' came under powerful socialist influences and, temporarily, even joined a communist cell. He was influenced by M. N. Roy (q.v.) and developed a grave distrust of Gandhi (q.v.). His wife, Prabhavati, however, came closer to the Mahatama because she lived at his ashram while 'J.P.' was away.

On his return, 'J.P.' joined Banaras Hindu University as Professor of Sociology. Later, moved by Jawaharlal Nehru's (q.v.) speeches at the Lahore session (1929) of the Indian National Congress (q.v.), he quit his job and joined the party's labour wing. While in jail during the Civil Disobedience Movement (q.v.) he met Achyut Patwardhan (1905–), Minoo Masani and Acharya Narendra Dev (1889–1956) and, in 1934, organized the All-India Congress Socialist Party. A trenchant critic of British rule, he lent strong support to violent agitation during the Quit India Movement (q.v.). His exploits during World War II became a byword for national fervour and captured the popular imagination.

A radical, 'J.P.' advocated abolition of zamindari, nationalization of natural resources, peasant proprietorship, nationalization of heavy and basic industries and rural uplift. After Independence in 1947, support for violence and Marxism waned in 'J.P.'; in 1948, he led his socialist group out of the Congress. Later, he veered closer to Vinoba Bhave's *Bhoodan* and developed his own *Jeevandan* and *Sarvodaya*. In 1953, he declined Jawaharlal Nehru's offer to join his government, thereby turning his back on wielding or sharing in political power. In the result, at one time rated as Nehru's logical successor, he ceased to be a realistic possibility for the office of prime ministership in the 1960s. He remained, on the other hand, a leading personality and an example of that small group of nationalist leaders who operate outside the parameters of political party and government.

In the mid-70s 'J.P.' launched a veritable crusade against Indira Gandhi and her 'authoritarian' ways: he opposed with great vigour the imposition of the 'emergency' and was, along with hundreds of other political leaders, jailed. Later, he succeeded in launching an anti-Indira Gandhi combine of political groupings called the Janata party. He lived to see the latter installed in office with a convincing majority but half-way through its parliamentary lease of five years was a witness to its discomfiture with large defections leading to political instability and the holding of fresh elections.

'J. P.'s own illness brought about by a failure of his kidneys while in detention deteriorated after his release. Despite intensive care he never could, however, fully recover. Failing health added to his age and growing weakness and he died in his sleep in October 1979 mourned by a grateful nation that bade him a touching farewell.

Two different approaches to 'J. P.'s socialism are to be found in Margaret Fisher and Joan Bondurant's *Indian Approaches to a Socialist Society* (1956) and Welles Hangen, *After Nehru Who?* (1963). 'J. P.'s own writings were extensive and include *Why Socialism* (1936); *Towards Struggle* (1946); *A Plea for the Reconstruction of Indian Polity* (1959); *From Socialism to Sarvodaya* (1959); and *Swaraj for the People* (1961). A representative selection of his writings is available in *A Revolutionary's Quest* (1980) and reveals a political and social thinker of great depth and lucidity.

Maharani Jind Kaur (d. 1863)

Jind Kaur, better known as Maharani Jindan, came of lowly origins, being the daughter of a trooper who served under Maharaja Ranjit Singh (q.v.). The latter is said to have married her by proxy, sometime around 1835. Reputed to be a ravishing beauty, she grew up to be extremely ambitious.

Taking advantage of the coups and counter-coups after the death of her husband, the Maharani advanced the claims of her son Dalip Singh (q.v.) whose paternity, like most of the Maharaja's other sons, was suspect. The fact that she had been able to produce a male child, a bare 10 months before Ranjit Singh's death, pitchforked her into the limelight. Later, amid the confusion that followed the assassination (September 1843) of Maharaja Sher Singh and his only legitimate son, Partap Singh, she pressed her son's claims with the help of her brother, Jawahir Singh.

Once Dalip Singh was installed on the throne by Hira Singh Dogra, the Maharani began her subtle moves to win over the Sardars and the Khalsa army, and gained strong enough support to be declared regent. After Hira Singh was killed (21 December 1844), Jindan emerged as the virtual ruler of the state. The Khalsa army, completely blind to the Darbar's financial bankruptcy, soon made it evident that she owed her position to its support. To appease them, she made lavish promises, met some of their most unreasonable demands and distributed presents—her only concern being the retention of her power and position.

Before long Jindan had delegated authority to her drunken and debauched brother, Jawahir Singh, and her slave girl, Mangla. It seems that the former's primary concern, after being made Wazir (15 May 1845), was to keep the Khalsa occupied with military campaigns so as to prevent them from intriguing with his political rivals who might offer more liberal terms. The campaigns against Jasrota and Jammu did not take long but, in the process, Jindan found a rival in Raja Gulab Singh (q.v.), who soon emerged as a keen competitor in her game of lavishing favours on the army and thereby winning its support. At one time the Rani contemplated flight to British territory but, dissuaded by her brother, abandoned the idea. Unable to meet demands made by the troops whom the Maharani had pampered,

Jawahir Singh resorted to the stratagem of inciting them against the British. His day was soon done for, provoked by the murder of Peshawra Singh, the last of Ranjit Singh's surviving sons, the army put him to death in September 1845. In the aftermath, Gulab Singh shrewdly turned down the offer of Wazirat made by the Darbar, with the result that Missar Lal Singh, the Maharani's paramour and an Anglophile, was appointed to the post (8 November 1845). He soon convinced himself, and the Maharani, that safety lay in diverting the attention and energy of the troops from their domestic squabbles on to the British and of conniving with the latter to blunt the troops' strength.

Betrayed by its commanders, the Khalsa army fought bravely but was badly mauled in the encounters of the First Anglo-Sikh War (q.v.). After the Sikh debacle, Jindan, who regained her position as regent, soon became an obstacle to the fulfilment of British political ambitions. The Governor-General had by then concluded that 'in any agreement made for continuing the occupation of Lahore, her deprivation of power is an indispensable condition.' Consequently, by the Treaty of Bhyrowal (q.v.), she was divested of all power and authority and in lieu thereof awarded an annual pension of Rs 1½ lakhs while the regency was entrusted to a council of eight Sardars. The Rani made two unsuccessful attempts to rally the latter around her so as to challenge the British. *Inter alia*, she forbade Dalip Singh to put the tilak on Tej Singh's forehead at the latter's investiture with the title of Raja, a development that gave the British their long-sought excuse to be rid of her.

Accused of conspiring against the British, Jindan was confined (August 1847) in the fort of Sheikhupura. Spirited, strong-willed, and confident of regaining her power, she continued secret intrigue with some chiefs and sepoys. These manoeuvres, however, did not succeed and she was removed to Banaras (23 May 1848). Before long, it was discovered that she was in secret correspondence with Diwan Mul Raj (q.v.), the governor of Multan whose revolt was to mark the beginning of the Second Anglo-Sikh War (q.v.). Later, Jindan was transferred to the fort of Chunar. Undaunted by her confinement there, she managed to escape and on 29 April 1849 entered Kathmandu, having sought the prior sanction of the Rana, Jung Bahadur, to do so. The Lahore Darbar's defeat in the second war and the annexation of the Panjab that followed in its wake did not deter the ex-Maharani from attempts to arouse the Sikh chiefs against the British, especially during the Rebellion of 1857 (q.v.). In a bid to check her seditious activities, she was allowed in May 1861 to visit Dalip Singh in England and died there two years later—by then 'prematurely old, well-nigh blind, broken and subdued in spirit.' Her stay in England however was not entirely in vain, for she had, during this brief interval, imbued her son with some of her own restlessness and dissatisfaction with all that the British had done to him and his patrimony.

It has been suggested that Rani Jindan's passions over-ruled her reason, coloured her vision, and led her to embark on a course of action that was wanton, wayward, bereft of all political sagacity and statesmanship. Headstrong, though not whimsical, she lacked patience, tact, caution and the ability to manoeuvre political events and situations to her advantage. It was not in her character to patiently win over men or use them to strengthen her position; she behaved more like an autocrat than a shrewd and far-seeing statesman.

It was her personality that brought about a succession of events which weakened and disintegrated the Sikh empire beyond redemption. In the final analysis, the Rani may be held largely responsible for the downfall of the Khalsa; she never played her cards well while opportunity beckoned.

Bakshish Singh Nijjar, *Maharani Jind Kaur: the Queen Mother of Maharaja Dalip Singh*, New Delhi, 1975; M. L. Ahluwalia and Kirpal Singh, *Punjab's Pioneer Freedom Fighters*, Bombay, 1963, pp. 79–105.

Mohammad Ali Jinnah (1875–1948)

According to his school register Mohammad Ali was born at Karachi on 20 October 1875 but he always maintained that the date was 25 December 1876. His father, Jinnah Poonja (also spelt Punja) was a small hide merchant who came of a lower middle class family of Khojas. He hailed from Kathiawad and rose to be the principal proprietor of the Valji Punja Company. He had two sons, one of whom remained somewhat obscure in life, and three daughters, of whom one, Fatima, was to be Mohammad Ali's life-long companion.

A word on the Khojas. A knowledgeable source contends that the community is possessed of a 'keen, jealous spirit of competition' and enjoys a good business reputation. Said to be 'neat, clean, sober, thrifty, ambitious', they are credited with having 'great regard for their religion.'

After an elementary education in his mother tongue, Gujarati, M. A. Jinnah received his secondary education in Karachi and Bombay. He was in England during 1892-6, being called to the bar in the latter year. On returning home, he read in the chambers of the Attorney General and then acted for 6 months as a presidency magistrate in Bombay. Soon he built a lucrative practice at the bar and acquired a considerable reputation for his ability to destroy an opponent's case.

Jinnah's first wife was a Khoja girl who died young; his second, Ruttie Petit, was the great-granddaughter of Sir Dinshaw Petit, an eminent Parsi. They were married in 1918. Ruttie was half Jinnah's age: she separated from him a few years later and did not live long, dying in 1929. Jinnah's only close personal contacts after her death appear to have been his daughter (whom he however later disowned) and his sister, Fatima, who outlived him.

Jinnah came to politics quite early in life. Starting as a Moderate in the Indian National Congress (q.v.), he grew up to be a great admirer of Gokhale (q.v.). His rising reputation as a barrister and enthusiastic support of the nationalist movement led to his election, in 1909, as the Bombay Muslims' representative on the Imperial Legislative Council. He introduced, in 1913, the Waqf Validating Bill, the first private member's bill to become law. That year Jinnah joined the All India Muslim League (q.v.) although continuing to remain a loyal member of the Congress. The League under his leadership was as truly nationalist as the Congress, although it stressed special safeguards for the Muslims as a minority. In 1919 Jinnah resigned from the Imperial Legislative Council in protest against the Rowlatt Act (q.v.). Soon a widening gulf formed between him and Gandhi (q.v.), whom he later accused of being a perpetual cause of Hindu-Muslim disunity.

Jinnah came under varied influences. In his formative years it was

Dadabhai Naoroji (q.v.), whom he briefly served as private secretary at the
Calcutta session (1906) of the Congress; later, there were Surendranath
Banerjea (q.v.), Gokhale and Pherozeshah Mehta (q.v.); after the
1920's it was the impact of Sir Syed Ahmed (q.v.) and the great Urdu poet,
Sir Mohammed Iqbal (1877–1938). In 1906, at the time of the Muslim
League deputation to Lord Minto (q.v.), Jinnah had signed a memorandum
against separate electorates for his community. Three years later, as has
been noticed, he was elected to the Imperial Legislative Council from a
Muslim constituency in Bombay. Almost without a break for the next two
decades, he was a member of the Legislative Assembly at the centre. As a
parliamentarian he had few equals, for his sharp intellect, legal acumen, and
dauntless courage created a deep impact.

Jinnah had a hand in framing the 1912 League constitution which embodied the Congress ideal of self-government by constitutional means
and specifically mentioned the promotion of national unity and co-operation
with other communities. In May 1914, Jinnah went to London as member
of a Congress deputation on the reform of the legislature and the following
year was instrumental in bringing the Congress and the League together,
which resulted in the conclusion of the Lucknow Pact (q.v.). In 1917 Jinnah
joined Annie Besant's (q.v.) Home Rule Movement (q.v.) and was elected
President of its Bombay branch. In 1918, he organized a protest demonstration against the then Governor of Bombay, Lord Willingdon; a grateful
public raised funds to put up a Jinnah Hall in Bombay to commemorate the
occasion. He was a signatory to the 'Memorandum of the 19' (1916) that had
put forth concrete proposals for constitutional reform.

Disapproving strongly of Gandhi's Non-cooperation Movement (q.v.),
Jinnah resigned from the Congress as well as the Home Rule League. His
breach with the former was more or less complete, for he was never again
to return to its fold. In the words of a biographer, 'Jinnah was opposed
to the religious metaphysical politics of Gandhi as well as to the abandonment of constitutional means. In 1920 he was the only person out of more
than 14,000 delegates in the Congress pandal to speak out against the use of
civil disobedience for the Khilafat (q.v.) cause, which in any case he had never
favoured. He rejected Gandhi's invitation to join the politics of mass agitation because "If by new life you mean your methods and your programme, I
am afraid that it must lead to disaster." Jinnah had "scented danger in all
that was happening and saw in this mass awakening a symbol of Hindu
revivalism—a threat to his own community", and wrote to Gandhi in 1920
accusing him of having "already caused split and division in almost every
institution you have approached hitherto".'

Though no longer a Congressman, Jinnah's stance still continued to be
that of a nationalist. In 1929 he formulated his famous Fourteen Points
(q.v.) which summed up the Muslim credo. Like other parties, the League
had boycotted the Simon Commission (q.v.). Shortly afterwards, he was
sorely disappointed with the All-Parties National Convention in Calcutta,
which had been called to accept the Nehru Report (q.v.).

A word on what transpired at Calcutta may not be out of place. The All-
Parties Convention had convened on 22 November 1928 to consider the
Nehru Report (q.v.) and the draft constitution prepared by the All-Parties
Committee. The League was invited and, along with the Khilafat Committee,

moved amendments to the proposed draft constitution. It demanded, *inter alia*, 1/3 representation for Muslims in the Central Legislature, Muslim representation in proportion to population in Panjab and Bengal, and allocation of residuary powers to the provinces, *not* the centre. Jinnah pleaded and warned: if minorities felt insecure, the result would be 'revolution and civil war.' Tej Bahadur Sapru (q.v.) supported Jinnah; M. R. Jayakar opposed him. In the end, Jinnah's amendments were rejected and he was taunted that he spoke for no one but himself and had no right to represent the Muslims. Jamshed Nusserwanjee, a Parsi and later Mayor (and builder) of Karachi noted: 'The first time I saw [Jinnah] weep,' was after his amendments had been rejected. Leaving Calcutta next day, Jinnah said to him: 'Jamshed, this is the parting of the ways.'

Jinnah's breach with the Congress, as has been noticed, marked the advent of Gandhi whose methods he deplored as 'unconstitutional.... based on an appeal to the mob.' He was at the same time no great admirer of the League whose leaders he dubbed 'flunkeys of the British or camp followers of the Congress.' A powerful figure in the League, he presided over its Lahore session in 1924, as well as the Calcutta session four years later.

About the time he broke with Gandhi and the All-Parties Convention, there was the great personal tragedy of his life—the death of his second wife, in February 1929. In the result, a keen contemporary observer has noted, Jinnah felt not only 'rebuffed in politics' but also that 'failure' stared him in the face in his personal life. 'Something I saw had snapped in him. took her death "as a failure and personal defeat in his life." He never recovered from his loneliness, and to the bitterness of his life this bitterness, born out of his personal loss and disappointment, travelled into his political life.'

At the Round Table Conference (q.v.), Jinnah's position was ambivalent: 'The Hindus thought he was a Muslim communalist, the Muslims took him to be a pro-Hindu, the princes deemed him to be too democratic. The Britishers considered him a rabid extremist, with the result that he was everywhere but nowhere. None wanted him.' At the Conference, he is reported to have said that the Hindu attitude shocked him: 'it led me to the conclusion that there was no hope of [Hindu-Muslim] unity.'

In retrospect, it may be seen that, particularly during the twenties, in all his negotiations either with the British or the Congress, Jinnah appeared to be trying to bring about a workable compromise; later, however, there was a complete change: 'In other words, there were two Jinnahs—the Jinnah of the twenties and the Jinnah of the late thirties and of the forties. During the twenties, Jinnah's object was to reach a Hindu-Muslim settlement on the basis of an acceptable compromise. Later, in the late thirties and forties, when this approach had failed, he adopted a seemingly rigid attitude and negotiated from a position of considerable strength which was based on the political power that he had mobilized.'

In 1930, Jinnah went to live in London and started practising at the Privy Council. Towards the end of 1935, he succumbed to the temptation of returning home and assumed undisputed leadership of the Muslim League as a counter-poise not so much to a 'Hindu' Congress, as to Gandhi's Congress. Liaqat Ali (q.v.) had visited Jinnah in England while Iqbal too had appealed to him to return.

In the result, even as Jinnah returned home, the Muslim community was looking for a political leader. 'Thus, there took place a congruence between the personal need and ambition of a leader like Jinnah and the needs of the Muslim community. Jinnah had a dominating personality.... Since he could not get along with others, he needed an organization which he could dominate and through which he could put his point of view. In the dominant role that he played in the Muslim League movement after 1937, he found an outlet for the political talent and qualities of leadership that he possessed.' It may be noted that, in 1934, on the eve of Jinnah's return, the Muslim League was in a moribund condition, its organization weak, its programme nebulous, its leadership divided, half-hearted, removed from the masses. In less than a decade, his remarkable organizing ability made the League a force to be reckoned with.

The 1936–7 general elections were Jinnah's first trial of strength, and his party did not emerge poorly from these. In 1937 he is said to have suggested the formation of coalition governments with the Congress in the provinces, an offer which was, allegedly (and thoughtlessly), turned down. The Congress, having spurned a similar initiative from Fazlul Haq (q.v.) in Bengal, made the latter lean upon the League for his political survival. In fact, in 1937 when the Congress formed governments in various provinces, it insisted that minority representation to Muslims would be given only to those prepared to join the party. In October that year, Jinnah stated the Muslims could get neither justice nor fair play from Congress governments; he alleged that there was a rising crescendo of 'atrocities' on Muslims in Congress-ruled provinces. In the result, by 1939 the breach between the Congress and the League, as well as between Gandhi and Jinnah, was complete.

1937 thus proved to be a turning point for Jinnah; from now on, he completely changed his tune, and tone. Starting with protests against alleged repression of Muslims by Congress governments and a demand for adequate safeguards for minority rights, it culminated in the Lahore (1940) resolution demanding the creation of Pakistan. During the years World War II raged, while the Congress went into the political wilderness, Jinnah reaped a bumper political harvest. Spurned by the Congress, the British, for obvious reasons, now leaned heavily on Jinnah and in return gave him unqualified political support and backing. His political success after 1937 was the more striking since he possessed few of the qualities that make for a popular politician. A friend—and Jinnah had few personal friendships—described him as 'tall and stately, formal and fastidious, aloof and imperious of manner.'

In September 1944, the Gandhi-Jinnah Talks (q.v.) took place in Bombay at the former's initiative; marked by hair-splitting arguments on the two-nation theory, a complete deadlock ensued. Developments in 1945-7 played into Jinnah's hands: the Simla Conference (q.v.) was abandoned because of his intransigence; the Cabinet Mission Plan (q.v.) was first accepted by the League and then rejected; he first spurned the offer to join the Interim Government (q.v.) and then retracted. The 1945-6 elections had, however, completely vindicated his claim to be Muslim India's undisputed leader. In each of these encounters the Congress was worsted—at the hustings or across the negotiating table. Jawaharlal Nehru (q.v.) proved to be no match for a stubborn, resilient and fighting Jinnah. The Muslim leader may or may not have had any faith in the two-nation theory; he adopted it as a weapon to achieve his political objective. As a ruler of Pakistan, he certainly did not practise its tenets.

Jinnah's strategy was, broadly, to discredit the Congress claim that it represented both Hindus and Muslims. As a logical corollary to this, he wanted the Congress to recognize the League's claim to being the sole spokesman of Indian Muslims. He insisted, despite opposition from many quarters, on celebrating 'Deliverance Day' on 22 December 1939. It was deliverance, he claimed, from 'tyranny, oppression and injustice during the last two and a half years (1937–39)' of Congress rule.

The Muslim League's Lahore resolution of 23 March (1940) was vague and spoke 'of more than one sovereign state' and referred 'in a very general way' to territorial adjustments. The vagueness was deliberate for Jinnah's immediate goal was both 'to mobilize and maximize' his support among the Muslims. In July 1941, Jinnah demanded from the Muslim Premiers of Panjab, Bengal and Assam that they resign from the National Defence Council which had been set up to boost British India's war effort. This they did. Later, in 1942, during the negotiations on the Cripps Mission (q.v.) proposals he was satisfied with his modest gains in that the possibility of Pakistan was recognized by implication. But a greater triumph awaited him during the Gandhi-Jinnah talks. His two major gains from the latter were: recognition as 'the most important leader' of the Muslims; acceptance of the fact that a Congress-League settlement hinged on the Pakistan issue. His refusal at the Simla conference to a non-League Muslim being included in the Governor-General's executive council spelt the doom of Wavell's well-meant initiative. Later, in the Cabinet Mission Plan, Jinnah felt the 'basis and foundation' of Pakistan had been conceded.

Jinnah's call for 'direct action' in July 1946 was largely a result of speculation about the Congress accepting the Cabinet Mission Plan, thereby short-circuiting partition: 'But such speculations do not take into account the personality of Jinnah and the consistent strategy he had followed.' Jinnah's leadership may be explained by the aphorism that 'a society when it is faced with a desperate situation surrenders itself to the leadership of desperate and domineering men.' Yet Jinnah was so unlike his own people—for the Muslims are a 'warm-hearted' people and Jinnah 'so austere and so remote': 'One explanation is, and it is not a complete one, that this power-conscious man promised to them the political power which the Quran had promised to them and which their forbears had wielded in India.'

Jinnah, it has been said, was the most secular of all Muslim leaders. He was least interested in Islam and did not have a deep knowledge of it. As a person, Jinnah was a man of few words, and seldom relaxed in public or showed any emotion. He cared little for other people's feelings. In dress, manners, style of living, he was more English than the English. In social outlook, he was generally a progressive, but when his daughter married a Parsi, turned Christian, he disowned her immediately.

While on a visit to India in 1917-18, Edwin Montagu, then Secretary of State for India, noted: 'At the root of Jinnah's activities is ambition.' Lord Casey, a one-time Governor of Bengal, noted: 'He (Jinnah) is dogmatic and sure of himself. I would believe that it does not ever occur to him that he might be wrong.' His flashes of anger, his bitter sarcasm and righteous indignation in the law courts, have become legendary.

Lord Linlithgow's (q.v.) assessment of the League leader bears mention: 'I do not frankly feel any deep confidence in him and I suspect he is one of those political leaders who can play a personal hand but no other, and whose permanent control on the allegiance of their followers is frequently open to question.'

Lord Mountbatten is reported to have said of Jinnah: 'I have never been treated in my life like this.' Nehru, giving his own estimate of Jinnah observed that the secret of his success 'and it had been tremendous—[lay] in his capacity to take up a permanently negative attitude.'

Jinnah combined to a remarkable degree inflexible incorruptibility and an uncanny sense of tactics which stood him in good stead in his dealings with the British and the Congress. Added to his tactical ability were his complete sincerity and capacity to take a long-term view.

In later years Mountbatten had some interesting, revealing, things to say about Jinnah: 'If Jinnah had died of this illness (J. had for years suffered from tuberculosis, a fact that had been kept a closely guarded secret) about two years earlier, I think we would have kept the country unified. He was the one man who really made it impossible. I didn't realize how impossible it was going to be until I actually met Jinnah.' The Quaid-i-Azam, Mountbatten soon concluded, had a closed mind: 'I then realized that he had this faculty of closing his mind to the thing—he could see points, he was an able debater, he had a well-trained mind, he was a lawyer, but he gave me the impression of having closed his mind, closed his ears; he didn't want to be persuaded; he didn't want to hear. I mean whatever one said, it passed him absolutely by.'

The former Viceroy and Governor-General confessed to a sense of complete helplessness: 'I will at once confess that I failed with Jinnah. But let me tell you this, nobody else would have been more successful. I don't believe there was any more you could do with Jinnah. I must take the responsibility myself.' And therein lay Jinnah's strength: 'His great strength . . .he got all this by closing his mind and saying "No". And how anybody could fail to see Jinnah held the whole key to the situation, to the continent in his hand, I fail to understand. I was under no illusions.'

Unlike Syed Ahmed Khan and Iqbal, Jinnah was concerned neither with religion nor philosophy, mysticism nor poetry. He was not a social reformer, an educationist, or a pan-Islamist. Jinnah was essentially a politician—'a pure politician'—and an ardent nationalist, but he was primarily a Muslim nationalist and *not* a nationalist Muslim. Montagu called him 'a giant among politicians' (1917) and, as early as 1910, long before Gandhi or Nehru appeared on the political stage, he was a member of the Imperial Legislative Council, a dauntless figure ready to cross swords even with the Viceroy.

M. H. Saiyid, *The Sound of Fury: A Political Study of Mohammad Ali Jinnah*, New Delhi, 1981; Saleem M. M. Qureshi, *Jinnah and the Making of Nation*, Karachi, 1960; Hector Bolitho, *Jinnah, Creator of Pakistan*, London, 1954; Khalid bin Sayed, *Pakistan, the formative phase, 1857–1948*, 2nd ed., London, 1948 and 'The Personality of Jinnah and his Political Strategy,' in C. H. Philips and M. D. Wainwright (eds.), *The Partition of India: Policies and Perspectives, 1935–1947*, London, 1970, pp. 276–93; Ahmad Hasan Dhani (ed.), *World Scholars on Quaid-i-Azam Mohammad Ali Jinnah*, Islamabad, 1979; V. V. Nagarkar, *Genesis of Pakistan*, New Delhi, 1975; Jamil-ud-Din Ahmed (ed.), *Speeches and Writings of Mr. Jinnah*, 2 vols, 6th ed., 1960–64; S. S. Pirzada, *Quaid-i-Azam Jinnah's Correspondence*, 2nd ed., Karachi, 1966; Larry Collins and Dominique Lapierre, *Mountbatten and the Partition of India, March 22-August 15, 1947*, New Delhi, 1982; *DNB 1941–1950*, pp. 433–4 (P. J. Griffiths).

William Jones (1746–94)

A brilliant oriental scholar and linguist, William (later Sir William) Jones was born in London in 1746. His father, a well-known mathematician, was a Fellow of the Royal Society; his mother was a remarkable woman who had an excellent grasp of mathematics and the theory of navigation. When Jones was a child an unfortunate accident permanently impaired the vision of one of his eyes. However, even as a boy, his memory was prodigious—he once wrote out Shakespear's *The Tempest* by heart—and it was matched by a refined taste and grace of expression. Jones was educated at University College, Oxford. His knowledge of French is said to have been the envy of King Louis XVI of France!

Jones began translating and copying oriental manuscripts while working as a private tutor and, later, practising at the bar in London. He translated a life of Nadir Shah (q.v.) from Persian into French (1770) and wrote a grammar of Persian (1771) which was reprinted several times and long remained a standard work. Unsuccessful as a lawyer and unable to enter Parliament, Jones sought a lucrative appointment in India and obtained it in 1783 as a puisne judge in Calcutta's supreme court of judicature.

His ten years in India (1783–94) were the most important of his life. He performed his judicial functions with great ability, but his main pursuits were literary and juristic. He came to India with a mind imbued not only with enthusiasm for oriental studies, but one intent also on gaining a wider knowledge of classical and other literatures than most men possessed. The extraordinary range of his knowledge caused him to be regarded as a prodigy of learning. He is said to have known 13 languages thoroughly and 28 fairly well!

Founder-president of the Asiatic Society (q.v.), he was its chief contributor and largely responsible for the wide interest it evoked in India and her culture. Described variously as 'Oriental' Jones, and the 'father of Indology', he studied Sanskrit, collected rare manuscripts and befriended learned Indian scholars. He devoted much time to the translation and publication of the laws of Manu, *Shakuntala* and *Hitopadesa* and, just before his death, was engaged in compiling a digest of Hindu and Muslim laws!

The first volume of Jones's *Asiatick Researches* added to his already phenomenal reputation as an orientalist and linguist. Its first four volumes were translated into German and two into French, while 'Selections' were published in London and later Dublin. Of the 'Digest', nine large volumes were complete, with the two final ones to be collected and studied before he translated them.

According to his biographer, Jones constituted 'the West's greatest contribution to the East', a kind of 'Oriental martyr' who sacrificed his life to monumental projects designed to help the British govern India more justly. The 'truly remarkable' quality of his achievements, it has been said, was that he made these in the face of constant and severe obstacles. Additionally, 'he tried to show the West the proper relations with the Orient—a humanistic exchange of material and cultural resources that maintains a deep respect for human rights and the brotherhood of man, and a government of the people in the spirit of their institutions and culture.... perhaps the only significant

European administrator...who was non-political, honest and completely sympathetic to the native peoples.'

While his primary purpose was to extend the frontiers of human knowledge and experience by unlocking the treasures of Asiatic literature, Jones was also determined to use this new wealth of language and imagination to revitalize the literature of the West. His importance in the history of English poetry, critics maintain, cannot be gainsaid. Posterity remembers Jones chiefly as a pioneer of Sanskrit learning. Among his major contributions was the introduction of the principles of transliteration in the study of oriental languages and the identification of 'Sandrocoptus' of Greek historians with Chandragupta Mauraya. Jones died in Calcutta on 27 April 1794.

One of his biographers has summed up his career thus: 'His idealism consorted ill with the contemporary scene....To his plain speaking and honest convictions....India, with a new world of knowledge and experience to explore, his mind which recognized no frontiers of race or colour and accepted no limits of interest or capacity, was free to pasture at will the rich broad plains of wisdom, human and divine.'

Garland Cannon, *Oriental Jones*, Bombay, 1964, and 'The Indian Affairs of Sir William Jones (1726–94)', *Asian Affairs* (Journal of the Royal Central Asian Society), IX, 3, October, 1978, pp. 280–94 and X, 1, February 1979 pp. 27–41; S. N. Mukherjee, *Sir William Jones: A study in 18th century British attitudes to India*, Cambridge, 1968; A. J. Arberry, *Asiatic Jones: the life and influence of Sir William Jones (1746–94), pioneer of Indian Studies*, London, 1946; *DNB*, X, pp. 1062–5 (Henry Morse Stephens).

N. M. Joshi (1879–1955)

Narayan Malhar Joshi was born in June 1897 at Goregaon in the Colaba district of the old Bombay Presidency. He came of a lower middle-class Deshastha Brahmin family, received his early education at the New English School and later (1901) graduated from Deccan College, both in Poona. Subsequently he worked as a teacher in private schools as well as government high schools at Ahmednagar, Poona and Bombay. In 1909 he joined the Servants of India Society (q.v.) and retired in 1940. Earlier (1911), he had founded the Social Service League of which he rose to be Vice-President and then President.

Joshi's interest in labour and its problems started early. Thus, he was instrumental in establishing a number of welfare classes in labour areas as well as night schools, reading rooms, medical clinics and centres for industrial training. He was also responsible for building two big halls for the use of labour, founded (1937–8) the Bombay Civil Liberties Union and was its President ever since its inception. In 1921 Joshi became the founding father of All-India Trade Union Congress and worked as its General Secretary in 1925-9, and again, in 1940-8. In 1929 he left the AITUC to form a rival, the Trade Union Federation.

In 1919 the government nominated Joshi to attend the first International Labour Conference in Washington D. C.; from then onwards, right down to 1948, he was invariably nominated to represent Indian labour at the ILO Conferences at Geneva. During 1922–4 he was Deputy Member of the governing body of ILO and a Full Member during 1934-44 and again in

1946-8. In 1947 Joshi was nominated a member of the Central Pay Commission. He was also a government nominee at the Round Table Conference (q.v.) and served on the Joint Parliamentary Committee that gave shape and form to the Government of India Act, 1935 (q.v.). Earlier, in 1929–30, he had been a member of the Whitley Commission (q.v.) on Indian labour.

For 26 years (1921–47) Joshi was the sole nominated member of the Central Legislative Assembly to represent labour and was often referred to as 'the father' of the house. He took an active interest in several labour enactments: amendments of the Factory Act of 1881 (q.v.), the Women's Compensation Act (1924), the Indian Trade Union Act (1926), the Payment of Wages Act (1936) and the Employment of Children Act (1938). Each owed a great deal to his personal zeal, initiative and drive.

Joshi's efforts along with M. K. Bose to develop a united front in the labour movement in 1953–4 and eventually build a Labour Party, an Indian counterpart of its British namesake, were bogged down by certain ideological and practical difficulties. Essentially, Joshi belonged to the liberal school of politics and wanted not only a compromise between capital and labour but also the co-operation of the government in advancing labour interests. With the rise of militancy in the Trade Union Movement (q.v.), his influence understandably tended to decline.

V. B. Karnik, *N. M. Joshi: Servant of India*, Bombay, 1972; Sen, *DNB*, II, pp. 261–3 (G. V. Ketkar).

The June 3rd Plan (1947)

Lord Louis Mountbatten was sworn in as Governor-General on 24 March 1947. According to the instructions drawn up for him by the British government, he was (i) to aim at establishing a government in India on the basis of the Cabinet Mission Plan (q.v.) of 16 May 1946; (ii) in case (i) was not achieved by 1 October 1947, to report to the government in England on the steps considered necessary to hand over power by June 1948; (iii) not to hand over power and obligations under Paramountcy (q.v.) to any successor government earlier than the transfer of power, yet negotiations with individual Indian States (q.v.) for adjusting their relations with the Crown were to be initiated straightaway; (iv) to treat the Interim Government (q.v.) with the same consultation and consideration as a Dominion government and to give it the greatest possible freedom in the day-to-day administration of the country; (v) to maintain the closest co-operation with Indian leaders; (vi) to ensure that the transfer of power was effected with full regard to the defence requirements of India, and of avoiding any breach in the continuity and organization of the army and a collaboration in the security of the Indian ocean.

In return for the above and before being inducted into office, Mountbatten asked for a time-limit on the transfer of power. This was accepted and announced by the then Labour Prime Minister, C. R. Attlee, in the House of Commons on 20 February 1947. The new Viceroy asked for, and received, the assurance that he would have the authority to decide matters without constant reference to London or interference by the British Government.

To discharge his responsibilities effectively, Mountbatten drew up two sets of plans. The first visualized maintenance of the integrity of the existing provinces that would initially become independent successor states; their later unity under an emasculated centre was envisaged as a sequel. The second plan contemplated a partition of the provinces of Panjab, Bengal and Assam into two parts each, separating the Hindu-dominated districts from those controlled by the Muslims. Two separate independent Dominions of India and Pakistan would thus emerge, each with its own Governor-General.

By January 1947, the Indian National Congress (q.v.) had accepted the 16 May Cabinet Mission Plan in its entirety along with the interpretations put on it by HMG in December 1946. Even though it had accepted it earlier, the All India Muslim League (q.v.), however, now completely repudiated the Plan and demanded for Pakistan the five Muslim majority provinces of Panjab, Sind, the North-West Frontier Province (q.v.), Bengal and Assam along with Baluchistan and a corridor through India. It demanded a sovereign, independent Pakistan and refused to accept any provision for common links or any organization of state to discharge such functions. It visualized two defence forces and two separate heads of state.

A committee consisting of Mountbatten, Lord Ismay, his Chief of Staff, and his two principal advisers, Sir Eric Mieville and George Abell, discussed the Viceroy's first plan with Nehru, Patel, Jinnah, Liaqat Ali Khan (qq.v.) and Baldev Singh. The draft itself had been drawn up by Ismay, Mieville and Abell, ignoring the viewpoint of V. P. Menon who was then Reforms Commissioner in the Government. On 2 May the first three flew to London along with the draft of the plan. On 10 May they returned with the broad approval of HMG albeit with slight modifications on details. Mountbatten now prepared to consult Nehru and Jinnah, both of whom, however, reacted, sharply. It has been said that Nehru's reactions were so violent that Mountbatten immediately retracted, convinced that in the face of the former's opposition, he could not carry it through. He now entrusted Menon with the responsibility of working out an alternate plan.

On 17 May, Mountbatten, accompanied by Menon, flew to London with a draft of his new plan. He returned on 31 May and invited seven leaders of the Congress, the League and the Sikhs (Nehru, Patel, J. B. Kripalani, Jinnah, Liaqat Ali Khan, Abdur Rab Nishtar and Baldev Singh) to meet him on 2 June He gave each a detailed outline of the plan which, while failing to concede the demands of any party in full, represented what appeared to the Governor-General to be the largest measure of common agreement.

According to V. P. Menon, 'immediately after his meeting with the party leaders the Viceroy communicated to the Secretary of State the assurances given him by Nehru, Jinnah and Baldev Singh in regard to the acceptance of the plan. Attlee announced the plan in the House of Commons on 3 June; hence it came to be known as 'the June 3rd plan.'

In essence, the June 3rd plan, as it came to be called, envisaged that:

1. The work of the existing Constituent Assembly (q.v.) was not to be interrupted. But the constitution framed by the Assembly would not apply to all those parts of India unwilling to accept it;

2. In order to ascertain the wishes of the different parts, two methods were suggested:

a) through the existing Constituent Assembly which would be joined by the representatives of the dissident parts; or

b) through separate Constituent Assemblies of representatives of the dissident parts.

3. As for the provinces, the following arrangements were envisaged:

a) in the Panjab and Bengal the Legislative Assembly would be divided into 2 sections, one for members belonging to the Muslim-majority districts and the other for the non-Muslim districts. If they opted for partition of the provinces, each section would join the Constituent Assembly the province would join;

b) the Legislative Assembly of a province would decide which Constituent Assembly the province would join;

c) in the N.W.F.P. this choice would be exercised through a referendum of the electors (viz., voters) of the Legislative Assembly;

d) the district of Sylhet in Assam would also decide its choice by means of a referendum;

e) the Governor-General would prescribe the method and mode of ascertaining the will of the people of Baluchistan;

f) there would be elections in parts of the Panjab, Bengal and in Sylhet to chose representatives for their respective Constituent Assemblies.

4. There would be negotiations:

a) between the successor governments concerning the Central subjects in regard to the administrative consequences of partition;

b) between the successor governments and HMG for treaties in regard to matters arising out of the transfer of power;

c) between the parts of the partitioned provinces concerning the administration of provincial subjects.

5. So far as the Indian States were concerned, the policy contained in the Cabinet Mission memorandum of 12 May 1946 would apply, namely, HMG would cease to exercise the powers of Paramountcy, and the rights surrendered by the States to the Paramount power would revert to the States. It would then be open to the States to enter into political relations with the successor governments.

In its penultimate paragraph, the June 3rd plan envisaged 'the earliest transfer of power' in India. With this end in view, the British Government affirmed that 'they are willing to anticipate the date June 1948 for the handing over of power by the setting up of an independent Indian Government or Governments at an even earlier date. Accordingly ... .HMG propose to introduce legislation during the current session for the transfer of power this year on a Dominion Status (q.v.) basis to one or two successor authorities according to the decisions taken as a result of this announcement.'

Mountbatten handed over the above statement to the three leaders and asked them to communicate to him their acceptance by midnight. Nehru generally accepted, as did the Congress Working Committee. Jinnah, however, was reluctant to commit himself. When he saw the Viceroy that evening the latter handed him a message from the British Conservative leader, Winston Churchill, indicating that, if Jinnah did not accept the plan, it would spell the death-knell of his dream of Pakistan. On the night of 3rd June, Mountbatten, Nehru, Jinnah and Baldev Singh broadcast over All-India Radio their respective statements on the new plan.

Mountbatten reiterated that, as a result of his plan, 'Power can be transferred many months earlier than the most optimistic of us thought possible, and at the same time leave it to the people of British India to decide for themselves on their future, which is the declared policy of HMG.' Nehru announced his party's decision to accept the plan; Baldev Singh maintained that the plan was worthwhile; Jinnah however struck a neutral note. Gandhi (q.v.) accepted the plan and indicated that the blame for the partition envisaged was not the responsibility of the Governor–General: 'If both of us, Hindus and Muslims, cannot agree on anything else, then the Viceroy is left with no choice.'

The Council of the League convened on 9 June and passed a resolution accepting the plan. On 14 June, the All–India Congress Committee accepted its Working Committee's earlier resolution of 2 June, thereby giving its approval to the plan.

Gwyer & Appadorai, II, pp. 670-5; V. P. Menon, *The Transfer of Power in India*, Bombay, 1957, pp. 350-86; Alan Campbell-Johnson, *Mission with Mountbatten*, London, 1951, pp. 99–113; *Tara Chand*, IV, pp. 515–18.

Mir Kasim (d. 1777)

Kasim Ali Khan, more popularly known as Mir Kasim (Qasim), was the son of Bazi Khan. From contemporary accounts of his scholastic attainments it may be inferred that he had received a good education but, apparently, little or no military training. With his marriage to Fatima Begum, daughter of Mir Jafar (q.v.), he entered active court politics in Bengal. His first administrative post as Governor of Rangpur synchronized with his father-in-law's elevation to the Nawabship. Presently, the treasure he had collected from the harem of the deceased Siraj-ud-daula (q.v.) helped him equip a small personal force.

As a military commander, Mir Kasim failed to distinguish himself either in the course of the Anglo-Dutch hostilities (1759), when Mir Jafar had toyed with the idea of shifting his allegiance from the English to the Dutch, or in the war against the Marathas (1759-60). Keenly interested in a ministerial post, he failed to achieve his ambition because of his rivalry with Miran, the son of Mir Jafar. A shrewd judge of men and a clever diplomat, Mir Kasim had hoped to be nominated heir but was disappointed at being designated a mere Faujdar of the district of Purnea. Ambitious, he bought over the all-too-willing Vansittart (q.v.) and his Council who, confronted by an empty treasury and a bankrupt and resentful Nawab, were seeking for alternatives. Another coup was therefore planned and, after deposing Mir Jafar, Mir Kasim made Nawab (20 October 1760). The British, it is said, 'deceived by his elegance of manners and convinced of his skill in the finances of Bengal' had raised him to this position.

Mir Kasim soon brought order out of chaos, punished refractory vassals and zamindars, forcibly collected arrears of revenue, paid off the John Company's (q.v.) debts and gave sizeable sums as 'gifts' to the Governor and his Council. As Nawab, he took great interest in the improvement of internal trade, introducing several reforms in the revenue system, checking the power of hereditary officials, especially the zamindars, and economizing on expenditure. Once a modicum of peace had been restored, the Nawab shifted his capital to Monghyr, in Bihar. His motives in doing so were mixed.

He wanted, *inter alia*, to bring the province completely under his control, to escape continuous British interference in day-to-day affairs, check the misuse of British trade privileges and extend his control over Nepal. Before long, his efforts to improve the conduct of internal trade brought him into an open clash with the Company's factors. The Nawab had in the meantime sharply reduced the hitherto largely untrained rabble of his army and transformed it into an efficient force of 25,000 men, equipping and training them on western lines under European officers.

By 1763, however, Mir Kasim's fortunes took a turn for the worse; the expedition to Nepal proved a disaster as well as a heavy drain on the treasury. The English traders, too, were up in arms because of the stringent check by the Nawab's officers on their defiance of rules and regulations. What they sought was outright exemption from payment of duties on articles of internal and private trade; they were not prepared to compromise and thereby forego the enormous profits made by monopolizing such necessities of daily life as grain, tobacco, betel-nut etc. The Nawab had made several representations to the Calcutta Council about the high-handedness of William Ellis (d. 1763), the Company's factory chief at Patna. When the councillors instead objected to the behaviour of the Nawab and his men, he abolished, in March 1763, all inland customs throughout his domain. This was not acceptable to them either, for it would place the English on the same footing as the 'native' traders. The Governor was disposed to make a compromise but was overruled by his Council. Both Ellis and the Nawab were now on a collision course and the former took the initiative by attacking Patna. As hostilities commenced, Mir Kasim, in turn, recaptured the town and offered terms for bringing about peace. Behind the scenes, however, the English had already negotiated with and decided to reinstate Mir Jafar.

Mir Kasim was not a General and miserably lacked the physical courage to lead the army. More, he heavily depended upon Europeans—the brigades of Marker and Sumroo. The latter even though they showed some initial activity and annihilated the British forces stationed at Patna, subsequently backtracked. Thus, when it came to fighting decisive battles, their inactivity and retreats even when winning lends weight to the widely held belief that Europeans did not like to defeat Europeans 'for their Indian masters.'

Not a good commander himself and distrusting his own best officers, Mir Kasim was defeated successively in the battles of Katwa, Murshidabad, Gheria, Monghyr, Patna and Udwanala, after which he escaped to Oudh (q.v.). According to Beale, 'incensed to madness' at his reverses, he cruelly ordered the massacre of the English in his power. There were 50 gentlemen including 'Ellis, Hay, Lushington, and others, and 100 of lower rank.' On the 5th October (1763) 'they were brought out in parties and barbarously cut to pieces, or shot under the direction of a German, named Samru or Sombre.' Shuja-ud-Daula (q.v.) who had long sought Bihar for himself at first gave Mir Kasim asylum, but later had him imprisoned.

After Buxar (q.v.), when the British army advanced to overrun Oudh, its Nawab Wazir 'refused to deliver up Mir Qasim, though he had seized and plundered him.' Later MK made good his escape with a few friends and some jewels 'which he had saved from the fangs of his late ally, the wazir' and sought refuge in the Rohilla country. Presently, however, 'his intrigues' led the Rohilla chief to be rid of him. The ex-Nawab, now a helpless fugitive, took shelter with the Rana of Gohad and later repaired to Jodhpur. In 1776 (1774, according to Beale's *Dictionary*) he beseeched help from the Mughal Emperor Shah Alam II (q.v.). In this too, he was disappointed. He died at Kotwal, an obscure village near Delhi, in 1777. With him, it has been said, 'ended, virtually, the powers of the Subahdars of Bengal.'

Nandlal Chatterjee, *Mir Qasim*, Allahabad, 1935; Ram Gopal, *How the British Occupied Bengal: A corrected account of the 1756–1765 events*, Bombay, 1963; D. C. Verma, *Plassey to Buxar: A Military Study*, New Delhi, 1976; *Beale*, p. 315.

Dr Khan Sahib (1885–1958)

Khan Sahib was born in the village of Uttamanzai in the Charsadda tehsil of Peshawar district. His father, Khan Bahram Khan, was the village headman, an influential Mohamadzai landowner who was widely respected. Khan Sahib was educated at the Peshawar municipal board school and the Mission High School and, later, at the Medical College, Bombay. He proceeded to England in 1909 to study medicine, qualified for an MRCS and worked for a time at St. Thomas's Hospital. Here he married his second wife, an English woman, and sat successfully for the Indian Medical Service. Later, he served briefly in France during World War I before returning to India. In 1921, now Captain, his unit was ordered to proceed to Waziristan. Determined not to fight his own kith and kin, Khan Sahib quit and established his own private practice at Nowshera.

Khan Sahib was close to Gandhi (q.v.) and, even more so, to Jawaharlal Nehru (q.v.) with whom he had made friends while in London. Police firing in the Qissa Khani bazaar of Peshawar in April 1930 brought him into active politics. He was arrested and sentenced to 3 years' rigorous imprisonment. Later, during 1935–6, he was elected, in absentia, a member of the Central Legislative Assembly from his province. The alliance that now emerged between the Muslim Pathans and the allegedly caste Hindu-dominated Indian National Congress (q.v.) was a development of the utmost political significance which only Khan Sahib and his younger brother Abdul Ghaffar Khan (q.v.) could have brought about.

In the 1937 general elections, the Congress scored an impressive majority in the N.W.F.P. (q.v.) Legislative Assembly. Khan Sahib was chosen party leader and took over as Chief Minister. His first term of office was marked by several useful measures for the economic development of the province, but there was also some controversial legislation which alienated the sympathies of the big landowners as well as other conservative elements in the body politic. Nevertheless, his standing as an incorruptible and conscientious administrator was proved beyond question. In 1939 Khan Sahib resigned office at the bidding of the top Congress leadership, yet his influence was so powerful that the province gave little trouble during the British war effort.

Big enough to accept his mistakes, in 1954 Khan Sahib was briefly a member of Pakistan's coalition cabinet as Minister of Communications; a year later, he emerged as Chief Minister of the one-unit West Pakistan, a scheme of which he was the author. The resultant split with his brother Abdul Ghaffar Khan, who bitterly opposed the merger, was now complete.

In the years before 1958, when President Ayub Khan emerged on the political stage in Pakistan, Khan Sahib regained wide respect. When the Muslim League (q.v.) leaders defected from his coalition, he formed a new Republican party which retained a majority, albeit a shaky one, until president's rule was imposed in West Pakistan in March 1957. In December that year, Khan Sahib formed an anti-Muslim League group in the Central Assembly and a measure of the wide respect he commanded may be gauged from the fact that members of all parties in the group, which outnumbered the League, pledged their support for premiership to any person nominated by him.

On 9 May 1958, Khan Sahib was done to death in Lahore by a petty official, Atta Mohammed, who nursed a personal grudge against him. The assassination had no political motives, but proved to be a tragedy for Pakistan.

Khan Sahib's first wife was a Pathan, from whom he had three sons; his second wife was the mother of a son (who died young) and a daughter who was to marry, in the teeth of bitter opposition, a young Christian officer in the Indian Air Force.

Khan Sahib was a man of exceptional qualities. Quiet, patient and courteous in manner, incorruptible and of deep sincerity, he had the stature of a statesman. He was loved for his largeheartedness and integrity by his people and, indeed, by people of all communities with whom he came into contact. A man of all–India reputation he held a special appeal for intellectuals. His honesty and integrity, were above board, as also his straightforwardness. A man of broad and catholic views, he withstood considerable opposition (viz., to his daughter's marriage to a Christian). Handsome and stocky, he wore khadi habitually and led a simple and unostentatious life.

Mohammad Yunus, *Frontier Speaks*, Lahore, 1942; Mahadev Desai, *Two Servants of God*, Ahmedabad, 1935; Sen, *DNB*, II, pp. 329–31 (Meher Chand Khanna); *DNB 1951-60*, pp. 581-2 (F. M. Innes).

Baba Kharak Singh Ahluwalia (1867–1963)

The son of an army contractor, Kharak Singh was born at Sialkot. Little is known of his family background or early life, apart from the fact that he was one of the first graduates of Panjab University. Later he studied law and was a student at Allahabad.

Kharak Singh was chairman of the reception committee of the fifth Sikh Educational Conference held at Sialkot in 1912 and later (1920) presided over the historic session of the Central Sikh Educational Conference at Lahore in 1920. Here Mahatma Gandhi (q.v.), the Ali brothers—Maulana Shaukat Ali (q.v.) and Mohamed Ali (q.v.)—and Dr Saifuddin Kitchlew (q.v.) were present and advised the Sikh community to throw in their lot with the Indian National Congress (q.v.). In 1921, he helped found the Shiromani Gurdwara Prabandak Committee and was unanimously elected its president. He held that office subsequently on several occasions.

The Sikh Gurdwara movement in which Kharak Singh took an active part was soon to merge with the Non-cooperation Movement (q.v.) of the

Indian National Congress. He was also involved in the first Akali morcha in 1921. In the following year, when Lala Lajpat Rai was arrested, Kharak Singh was chosen to work as President of then Panjab Provincial Congress Committee. Popularly known as the 'Keys morcha', the agitation aroused a storm of protest against the government and was a resounding success for the Sikh cause. It infused a new energy and vigour into the political life of the Panjab; Gandhi called it the 'first decisive battle won for India's freedom.'

In 1928, Kharak Singh took part in a mammoth, yet peaceful, demonstration against the Simon Commission (q.v.) during its visit to Lahore. Later, he voiced a strong protest against the Communal Award (q.v.). In 1937 he rejected the offer of a ministership in the Panjab provincial cabinet for, he argued, provincial autonomy was inadequate. He was arrested again in 1940. In 1944, Kharak Singh presided over the Akhand Hindustan Conference held at Gujranwala in the Panjab. Arrested a number of times, there were thirteen convictions against him and he spent nearly 20 years of his life in jail.

Kharak Singh was founder-president of the Shiromani Akali Dal. A staunch nationalist, he broke from the Akali movement led by Master Tara Singh (q.v.) and founded the Central Akali Dal. Jawaharlal Nehru (q.v.) expressed the view that 'There are few hands which can uphold the honour and preserve the dignity of the national flag better than those of Babaji [Baba Kharak Singh].'

Kharak Singh is said to have never yielded to what he considered wrong or evil, whatever the cost. For many years, he was reckoned as the most powerful leader of the Sikhs—their *betaj baadshah* (literally, 'uncrowned king').

Khushwant Singh, *The Sikhs*, London, 1953; *The Indian Annual Registers*, 1934–7; Sen, *DNB*, II, pp. 337–38 (Prithvi Singh Azad); Fauja Singh, *Eminent Freedom Fighters of Punjab*, Patiala, 1972.

The Khilafat Movement (c. 1920–22)

The Khilafat movement was largely the end-result of resentment among Indian Muslims over the defeat in World War I of the Ottoman Turkish empire, along with its European allies, Germany and Austria-Hungary. The harsh terms of the Treaty of Sevres (1920) with Turkey further exacerbated the situation. Revolts in Arab lands engineered, at British instigation, against the Sultan's empire which was thus threatened with a complete break-up made a complicated tangle more complex and played havoc with Muslim sentiments in India. The Muslim ideology underlying the movement was based on the mediaeval Western view that identified the institution of the Caliph, the religious head of the Muslim world, with the Ottoman Sultanate of the Turkish empire. It pandered to Muslim loyalty to the faith. As will be noticed presently, some Khilafat leaders in India went to the extent of inciting their co-religionists to migrate (*hijrat*) and, in turn, ask the Amir of Afghanistan to invade India so as to liberate it from the clutches of a non-Muslim government!

In December 1918 the All India Muslim League (q.v.) had held its annual session in Delhi where M. A. Ansari (q.v.), chairman of its reception committee, denounced Husein ibn Ali of Hejaz who had raised the standard of revolt against his acknowledged sovereign, the Ottoman Turkish Sultan. *Inter alia,* Ansari demanded the maintenance of the integrity and independence of the Muslim states and the restoration of the *Jazirat-ul-Arab* (viz., Arab lands) to the Caliph.

The Delhi session was of significance for two reasons. In the first place, M. A. Jinnah (q.v.) and Mohammad Ali, the Raja of Mahmudabad (q.v.) withdrew from the Muslim League because of their opposition to its resolution on the Khilafat; secondly, a number of the ulama including Abdul Bari (1879-1926), Azad Sobhani, Ibrahim Sialkoti, Ahmad Said and Abdul Latif were present.

The Indian National Congress (q.v.) echoed Ansari's sentiments and Gandhi (q.v.) lent his strong support to the Muslim cause. In April–May 1919 the All-India Khilafat Conference was brought into being on the initiative of Abdul Bari and a large number of the ulama. At a conference in Lucknow in September 1919, with Ibrahim Haroon Jafar presiding, an All–India Khilafat Committee was formed with Seth Chhotani of Bombay as President and Maulana Shaukat Ali (q.v.) as Secretary. The next Khilafat conference was held at Delhi on 23 November 1919 under the chairmanship of Fazlul Haq (q.v.); Gandhi, Motilal Nehru and Madan Mohan Malaviya (qq.v.) attended. In his address, Gandhi stressed that the proper remedy for the wrongs done to the Muslims was non-cooperation and *not* boycott. In December 1919 during the Congress session at Amritsar, the Khilafat Committee also met. Gandhi discussed with the Khilafat leaders ways and means of achieving their objective. In the result, a deputation waited on the Viceroy in Delhi (February 1920) and another was sent to meet the British Prime Minister in London (March 1920). At its session in Delhi in January 1920, Gandhi had presented to the Congress his programme of non-cooperation which was accepted at another meeting in Meerut a few days later.

At the Khilafat conference in Calcutta (February 1920) held under the leadership of Maulana Abul Kalam Azad (q.v.), a resolution was adopted in favour of non–cooperation while a Khilafat day was to be observed. In the succeeding months a number of other meetings were held. In so far as the deputations to the Viceroy and the British Prime Minister yielded no results, it was decided to inform the Viceroy that, if the Khilafat demands were not conceded, the Non–cooperation Movement (q.v.) would start on 1 August.

According to Khan Abdul Ghaffar Khan (q.v.), at the (1920) Khilafat conference in Delhi, the *hijrat* (literally exodus/migration) of Muslims to Afghanistan had been advocated. A Hijrat Committee was constituted in Peshawar, which undertook to provide the intending migrants all kinds of facilities and comforts. The mullahs issued a *fatwa* in November 1920 lending support to the move. It has been estimated that nearly 18,000 Muslims from Sind and the North-West Frontier (q.v.) left for Afghanistan. Even though King Amanullah (q.v.) was initially well-disposed, permission to proceed was refused to the intending migrants, with the result that the exodus proved to be a veritable disaster.

Immediately after the terms of the Treaty of Sevres with Turkey were announced on 15 May 1920, the Central Khilafat Committee met at Bombay, took note of Muslim demands and announced its decision to resort to non-violent non-cooperation. Its four-fold programme was to be implemented in the following order: renunciation of titles and honorary posts; resignation from jobs held in the civil service; resignation from jobs in the police and the army; refusal to pay taxes.

In July 1920 another Khilafat conference was held in Sind which, among others, was attended by Gandhi. On 28 July the Mahatma announced that non-cooperation would be launched on 1 August with fasting and prayer and suspension of business. Later, along with Maulanas Mohamed Ali (q.v.) and Shaukat Ali, he toured extensively all over the country arousing popular enthusiasm and laying stress on Hindu-Muslim unity.

A special session of the Congress held at Calcutta in September 1920 endorsed the party's earlier decision 'to inaugurate the policy of non–cooperation.' At the Nagpur session, in December 1920, a resolution in support of the Khilafat Movement was carried overwhelmingly. Additionally, it evoked strong support from nearly 900 ulama of the Jamiatul-Ulma-i-Hind. The latter had earlier issued a *fatwa* calling upon Muslims to boycott elections, government schools, colleges and law courts and renounce their titles and ranks.

Both the Congress and the Khilafat committee had agreed upon the triple purpose of non-cooperation—redressal of the Panjab grievances, rectification of the Khilafat wrongs and the establishment of Swaraj. More specifically, the Khilafatists demanded: '(a) maintenance of the religious prestige and temporal power of the Caliph—the Sultan of Turkey. This did not necessarily imply reimposition of Turkish rule upon the Arabs; (b) guaranteeing the sovereignty of the Muslim states and, by implication, forbidding British and French mandates in Iraq and Syria or the converting of Palestine into a Jewish home.'

The Muslim case in regard to the office of the Caliph rested on the solemn assurances which two British Prime Ministers, Herbert Henry Asquith and David Lloyd George, and the Viceroy, Charles Hardinge (q.v.), had given before the War; these, the Muslims alleged, were now being shamelessly flouted. By mid-1921, the movement had thoroughly roused the country but made little impression upon the British who kept the issue hanging in mid-air, as it were. In the result, the all–India Khilafat conference at Karachi held on 8 July 1921 called upon Muslim soldiers in the Indian army to quit as their association with the latter was deemed to be religiously unlawful.

Gandhi's suspension of the Non-cooperation movement early in 1922 sharply divided the Khilafatists. A large number of them lost faith in the Mahatma and his leadership, and turned to the government for help; others continued to believe in his methods which, they argued, could alone lead India to its cherished goal.

Meanwhile, the Kemalist revolution in Turkey (1922) and the abolition of the office of the Caliph (1924) took the wind out of the agitation's sails. It was also clear that the Governor-General, Reading, had been sympathetic to the Muslim cause and had pleaded forcefully with Whitehall. A telegram he had sent on 28 February 1922 to the Secretary of State on the subject received wide publicity and was used effectively to blunt the agitation. *Inter alia*, he had urged on the British Government 'three points which...we ourselves regard as essential: (i) the evacuation of Constantinople; (ii) the Sultan's sovereignty over the Holy places; (iii) restoration of Ottoman

Thrace, including the sacred Muslim city of Adrianople and the unreserved restoration of Smyrna.'

In India, it must be conceded, a large number of Muslims did not appreciate the deeper, underlying meaning of the Movement nor yet the thinking of its leaders. They had co-operated with the Congress which, under Gandhi's leadership, had lent its whole-hearted support to their cause. Even the use of the word 'Khilafat' was interpreted to signify 'opposed to' or 'against' the foreign masters.

It has been maintained that, had it not been for the fact that the Non-cooperation movement was abruptly suspended, Muslims may have continued for a time to array themselves against the British. The agitation however lost its *elan* when, as has been noticed, the Turkish nationalists under the leadership of Kemal Ataturk (1881–1938), abolished the monarchy (1922). The new Caliph, shorn of all temporal authority, was little better than a figurehead. Nor did he last long. Cumulatively, these developments created confusion in Muslim ranks and hit the nationalist cause adversely. In the result, the Khilafat Movement ended in a miasma of communal riots and even forced religious conversions.

Reading's telegram sharply divided Muslim ranks at a time when the imprisonment of Gandhi and Maulana Mohamed Ali had left the rank and file leaderless and without a forceful guide. Thus, when the Turks put an end to the Sultanate and separated the Caliphate from the state, Muslims in India felt completely disillusioned and nonplussed. It should also perhaps be emphasized that the Khilafat committee had paid little attention to the practical aspects of their objective and showed no awareness of the currents of political thought in Turkey which had manifested themselves long before the War ended.

At the start, as has been noticed, the Ali brothers joined the movement and emerged as its foremost champions among the Muslims. None the less their known extra-territorial loyalties as well as orthodoxy hampered the cause of national liberation. It has been argued that the Khilafat shift in Indian politics was far from indicative of any fundamental change in the political attitude of the Muslims, for their anti-British posture did not imply an anti-imperial stance.

Pared to the bone, the genesis of the Movement is not difficult to spell out. The scanty regard shown by the government for Muslim sentiments over such issues as the Partition of Bengal (q.v.), the Aligarh Muslim University and the Kanpur Mosque episode had left Muslims disillusioned and deeply hurt. The Khilafat leaders therefore joined hands with the Congress against the British who, they argued, had failed to fulfil the community's aspirations. By forging a common front, they reasoned, it would be possible to settle their scores with a regime that had steadfastly refused to appreciate the value of their loyalty.

The nationalist stance implied a slight change in emphasis. The resentment felt by the Muslims during the Khilafat Movement had synchronized with the passage of the Rowlatt Act (q.v.) which led to an upsurge of resentment that was fully exploited by the Congress. Soon however this nationalist orientation in the Khilafat agitation proved to be an empty facade, for the separatist ideology of Syed Ahmad Khan (q.v.) was upheld by the Movement's ideals of universal Muslim brotherhood i.e. *Millat* or *Ummat.*

Equally, the leaders were far from ready to merge their separate Muslim identity into that of Indian nationalism.

It has been maintained that the Khilafat Movement provided some of the essential ingredients on which later the edifice of Pakistan itself was raised by the Muslim League.

M. Naeem Qureshi, 'The Indian Khilafat Movement (1918–24)', *Journal of Asian History,* 12, 2 (1978), pp. 152-68 and 'The Khilafat Movement in India', Ph.D. thesis, University of London, 1973; P. C. Bamford, *History of the Non-cooperation and Khilafat Movements,* reprint, Delhi, 1974, pp. 110-210; Sukhbir Choudhary, *Indian People's Fight for National Liberation: Non-Cooperation, Khilafat and Revivalist Movements,* New Delhi, 1972, pp. 213-386; Prabha Dixit, 'The Ideology of the Khilafat Movement: Some Observations', Unpublished research article, *NMML;* Gail Minault, *The Khilafat Movement: Religious Symbolism and Political Mobilization in India,* Delhi, 1982; Gopal Krishna, 'The Khilafat Movement in India, the first phase, September '19–August '20', *Journal of the Royal Asiatic Society of Great Britain and Ireland,* 1968, xerox copy, *NMML;* Francis Robinson, *Separatism among Indian Muslims,* New Delhi, 1975, pp. 307-8, 311-6, 334-5; *Tara Chand,* III, pp. 426-7, 487-503, 505-6.

Saifuddin Kitchlew (c. 1888–1963)

Saifuddin Kitchlew was born at Amritsar and educated both there as well as in Aligarh; later, he took his B.A. degree from Cambridge, Bar-at-law in London and Ph.D. from Germany. Kitchlew practiced law at Amritsar and presently became a municipal commissioner. In 1919 he led the anti-Rowlatt Act (q.v.) agitation in the Panjab and joined the Khilafat Movement (q.v.). Arrested in 1921, he was, on release, elected President of the All-India Khilafat Committee. In 1924 he was General Secretary of the Indian National Congress (q.v.) and five years later, chairman of the reception committee of the party's session at Lahore that adopted the Independence Pledge (q.v.) resolution which he had seconded.

Kitchlew was singularly critical of the British. Thus at the 44th (Lahore) session of the Congress he stated: 'What did we get under British domination? Poverty, unemployment, indebtedness, pestilence, disease, famine, starvation, death.... We cannot bring about the economic salvation of our country without the sovereign control of its destinies in our hands.'

In the course of the Akali agitation at the Jaito Morcha Kitchlew was arrested (21 February 1924). He was President of the Panjab Provincial Congress Committee for a term and a member of the All-India Congress Committee for a number of years. He took a prominent part in the Civil Disobedience Movement (q.v.) of 1930–3. In all, he is said to have spent 14 years in jail.

In the mid-20s Kitchlew developed a close association with the 'Tahrik-i-Tanzim' among the Muslims with the ostensible objective of countering the *Sangathan* movement of Pandit Madan Mohan Malaviya (q.v.). In furtherance of the cause, he brought out the Urdu daily *Tanzim* from Amritsar. Later, he organized the *Tabiligh* movement to fight Swami Shraddhananda's *Shuddhi* (taking back into the Hindu fold Muslims whose forefathers had been converted to Islam).

Ideologically, Kitchlew was an extremist who did not believe in the political supremacy of any particular religious community and stressed that

India's future masters were its peasants or tillers of the soil and its industrial workers. At the Lahore Congress session (1929), he had declared that the country's problem was 'not religious or merely political. It is essentially economic.'

Opposed to the country's partition and the creation of Pakistan, Kitchlew viewed the latter as a 'surrender of nationalism in favour of communalism.' In the post-Independence era he was soon disillusioned by Congress policies and joined the Communist Party of India. He was elected President of the All-India Peace Council. The Soviet Union conferred on him its much-coveted Stalin Peace Prize—he was the first Indian to receive it—just before his death in 1963.

Fauja Singh, *Eminent Freedom Fighters of the Punjab*, Patiala, 1972, pp. 220–1; Sen, *DNB*, IV, pp. 21–2 (Mushirul Haq).

Komagata Maru Incident (1914–15)

The *Komagata Maru*, a Japanese steamer, was commissioned by one Gurdit Singh, a civilian contractor operating in Singapore and the Malaya states. The objective was to transport Indian immigrants to Canada. This became necessary in the wake of the Canadian government's decision, taken in consultation with the British and Indian authorities, to invalidate the Immigration Act of 1910 as from 24 November 1913. With a view to preventing indiscriminate immigration, the new law required every aspiring immigrant to possess $200 and travel *directly* to Canada. The latter clause was aimed at disqualifying Indians and other Asiatics whose growing numbers, it was felt, posed a threat to Canada's white population.

376 passengers who travelled in the Japanese boat finally reached Vancouver in British Columbia on 23 May 1914; but they were prevented by the Canadian authorities from disembarking or obtaining any legal aid, or even collecting supplies. Despite two months of wrangling, Ottawa was unrelenting in its refusal and the government in India unwilling to help. In the result, the *Komagata Maru* was compelled to retrace its steps, starting back on its voyage in July 1914 with Calcutta as its destination.

The hapless passengers, all except 25 of whom were Sikhs, fared no better on return. The British, apprehending a conspiracy, herded them, no sooner than they arrived at Budge Budge, into waiting trains and bundled them off to the Panjab. Those among them who protested and marched towards Calcutta were rounded up, maltreated and manhandled by the police. All this sorely tried public opinion in Bengal and the Panjab. Succumbing to mounting nationalist pressure, the Viceroy, Charles Hardinge (q.v.), ordered an inquiry (1914), but the Commission, comprising 3 Englishmen and 2 loyalist Indians, inspired little confidence. It exonerated the police of all blame, putting it fair and square on the immigrants. It maintained that the *Komagata Maru* passengers had carried firearms and that the first shot was fired by them.

The government's apathetic attitude towards the immigrants was born of a conviction that a conspiracy had been hatched and that the ideas of equality and freedom which had been imbibed were dangerous and indeed, subversive of the established order. Canada's policy of racial discrimination that was openly practised, and now unashamedly demonstrated, aroused the nationalists at home and abroad. Coming as it did when the Ghadr party's (q.v.) activities had reached a climax, it took no great persuasion to make Indian immigrants return home, thirsting for revenge, and all set to drive out their alien masters.

Hugh Johnston, *The Voyage of the Komagata Maru: the Sikh challenge to Canada's colour bar,* Delhi, 1979; Khushwant Singh and Satinder Singh, *Ghadr 1915: India's First Armed Revolution,* New Delhi, 1966, App. IV, V, pp 64-5; Harinder Singh, 'Fateful Voyage of the Komagata Maru', *Modern Review,* CXXXIV, 3, March 1974, pp. 225-30.

Kunwar Singh (d. 1858)

Babu Kunwar Singh of Jagdishpur in Shahbad district (Bihar) was the central figure in the Rebellion of 1857 (q.v.) in his part of the country. A Rajput landlord, he had inherited his father's extensive landed estates along with a huge debt the rigours of which his generous and unsuspecting temperament did nothing to mitigate. His lands, the total annual rental of which amounted to Rs 3 lakhs, were so heavily mortgaged that the government in 1855 undertook their management so as to enable him to pay back his creditors. He however felt badly hurt by their refusal to stand security for the repayment of the loan he was attempting to raise to clear his revenue dues. The British were wary on account of rumours alleging that he was inciting the troops at Dinapur.

Be that as it may, in July 1857 Kunwar Singh joined as their leader the mutinying troops of the 7th, 8th and 40th Native Infantry at Arrah. The town was besieged and Kunwar Singh set up his own administration. But two months later he was driven out by a relieving British force. Thereafter, unable to match the military superiority of the British, he took to warfare, inciting rebellion everywhere on his march west to join other groups or their leaders. He extended his operations to Rewa, Banda and Kalpi and aided Nana Saheb (q.v.) in his fight against the British in Kanpur district. From the latter place he proceeded to Lucknow. Here he was warmly welcomed by the boy Wali, invested with a robe of honour and granted a *firman* for Azamgarh.

Worsted in battle by a formidable host, Kunwar Singh retraced his steps to his ruined home at Jagdishpur. Around Arrah, a British force under Captain Le Grand opposed his progress. Despite his war-worn, ill-armed men, he inflicted a crushing defeat on the British on 23 April 1858; the following day, the brave leader expired.

In 1857 Kunwar Singh was long past the prime of his life, being about 70 years old and by no means in robust health. However, he was not alone in this fight; among his principal lieutenants were his brother Amar Singh and his friend Nishan Singh, then a man of 60; the Government had announced a reward of Rs 2,000 (later raised to Rs 5,000) for the apprehension of Amar Singh who had engaged in successful guerilla fighting. A reward of Rs 1,000 had been announced for the capture of Nishan Singh. With Rajput blood in their veins they were determined to prove that its valour was not a thing of the past.

K. K. Datta, *Freedom Movement in Bihar,* 3 vols, I, pp. 15–50; Surendra Nath Sen, Eighteen Fifty-Seven, New Delhi, 1957, pp. 254–63.

Treaty of Lahore (1846)

Concluded on 9 March 1846, along with a supplementary treaty two days later, the 16-article Treaty of Lahore signalled the end of the First Anglo-Sikh War (q.v.). By no means strong enough to annex the Panjab immediately, British policy seemed to be to cripple it economically so as to ensure its complete absorption in the near future. The treaty's terms were therefore understandably harsh. These stipulated *inter alia* that Maharaja Dalip Singh (q.v.) (i) renounces for himself and his heirs all claims to the cis-Sutlej territories; (ii) cedes, in perpetuity, all lands in the Doab 'or country, hill and plain' situated between the Beas and Sutlej rivers and 'all forts, territories, rights and interests' between the Beas and the Indus, including the provinces of Kashmir and Hazara; (iii) surrenders the latter provinces, in lieu of an indemnity of Rs 1 crore; the remaining Rs 50 lakhs of a total indemnity of Rs 1½ crores to be paid in cash 'on or before' ratification of the treaty; (iv) disbands the mutinous Khalsa army and retains at the outset 12,000 cavalry—25 battalions of infantry of 800 men each; (v) surrenders to the British 'all the guns, 36 in number' which had been pointed against British troops; (vi) directs that control of the Beas and Sutlej 'with the continuation of the latter commonly called the Gurrah and the Punjab' shall, in respect of tools and ferries, vest with the British government; (vii) allows the passage of British troops through his territory as and when necessary; (viii) asks the Darbar to recognize 'the independent sovereignty' of Maharaja Gulab Singh (q.v.) in such territories and districts in the hills as may be made over to him; (ix) accepts that in cases of dispute with regard to the treaty he 'engages to abide' by the decisions of the British government; (x) agrees that the limits of Lahore territories were not to be changed 'without the concurrence' of the British government. On their part, the British undertook not to interfere in the administration of the Lahore state except in cases referred to them.

On 11 March 1846, 8 'Articles of Agreement' were concluded between the British government and the Darbar stipulating *inter alia* (i) stationing, 'till the close of year', of a British force adequate for 'protecting the person of the Maharaja and the inhabitants' of Lahore; (ii) placing a British force 'in full possession of the Fort and the city of Lahore' from whence the darbar's troops were to be removed; (iii) the darbar was to proceed vigorously with reorganization of its army but, should it fail to do so, the British 'shall be at liberty' to withdraw their men; (iv) the British undertook to respect the bona fide rights of jagirdars attached to the families of Maharajas Ranjit Singh (q.v.), Kharak Singh and Sher Singh during their lifetime within the territories ceded to them; (v) from territories ceded (to the British) the darbar was at liberty to recover arrears of revenue due as well as from the forest therein 'all treasure and state property, with the exception of guns'; (vi) commissioners were to be appointed immediately 'to settle and lay down the boundary' between the two states.

Within a week of the Treaty of Lahore, the British concluded a 10-article treaty with Maharaja Gulab Singh at Amritsar. Its terms laid down *inter alia* that (i) 'all the hilly or mountainous country with its dependencies, situated to the eastward of the river Indus and westward of the river Ravi, including Chamba and excluding Lahul' be transferred to Maharaja Gulab

Singh; (ii) in lieu thereof, the Maharaja was to pay a sum of Rs 75 lakhs '50 to be paid on ratification and 25' on or before 10 October; (iii) the eastern boundary of the Maharaja's territory was to be laid down by a commission appointed by the Maharaja and the British; (iv) the eastern limits of the Maharaja's dominion were not to be changed 'without the consent' of the British; (v) the Maharaja was to accept British arbitration in any disputes between himself and the British; (vi) the Maharaja was neither to take nor retain in his possession 'any British subject or the subject of any European or American state'; (vii) the British were to aid the Maharaja 'in protecting his territories from external enemies'; (viii) in acknowledgement of the supremacy of the British government, Gulab Singh was to present annually 'one horse, twelve perfect shawl goats of approved breed (six male and six female) and three pairs of Kashmiri shawls.'

The upshot of the two treaties and the articles of agreement needs no elaboration. The British were determined that the Sikh state be cut to size. Kashmir was the easiest limb to lop off and Gulab Singh the only man to whom it could be handed over with confidence. The British felt sure that, whatever his other failings, he would not betray their interests.

Aitchison, II, 259–66, 375–7; Khushwant Singh, *A History of the Sikhs*, 2 vols., edn., Delhi, 1977, II, pp. 56–9, 342–9.

Rani Lakshmi Bai (c. 1835–1858)

Rani Lakshmi Bai, whose role as a rebel leader constitutes one of the most colourful episodes in the Rebellion of 1857 (q.v.), was the widow of Gangadhar Rao, the ruler of Jhansi. Her maiden name was Manakarnika or Manu Bai. She was the daughter of Moropant Tambe who belonged to the retinue of Chimnaji Appa and lived at Banaras. Later, he was attached to the court of Baji Rao II (q.v.). Brought up at Bithoor, she became skilled in such manly arts as horse-riding and sword-fencing. The story of her being a playmate of Nana Saheb (q.v.) and Tatya Tope (q.v.) 'must be apocryphal' for both were considerably older. Her marriage (1851) to Gangadhar was shortlived; she was much younger than her husband and he died, issueless, two years later.

Ambitious and talented, the Rani discarded purdah and took over the reins of administration while petitioning the British that Damodar Rao, adopted heir a day before her husband's death, be recognized as the ruler. This the John Company (q.v.) was not willing to allow. In consequence, on 27 February 1854, Lord Dalhousie (q.v.) ruled that the state stood lapsed on account of the failure of a male heir, since its ruler had held power granted to him by the British government.

The annexation was in clear and flagrant violation of an earlier (1817) treaty and constituted a breach of promise. Lakshmi Bai vacillated before accepting an annual pension for life of Rs 60,000 and was permitted to live in the city palace. Conscious of her inability to challenge the Company nearer home, the Rani appealed to the Directors to right the injustice done to her and the minor child. It cost her a fortune but proved to be of no avail. Presently, she retired into the background, though not for long. On 5 June 1857 the sepoys at Jhansi rebelled and murdered their officers. The Rani did not reject any British requests for succour or protection, nor did she overtly side with the rebels. With the last soldier disappearing towards Delhi to join the great cause, she took over the state's disrupted administration and appointed ministers in charge of various departments. The local British officer, the Commissioner of Saugor, to whom she communicated her decision, concurred in that she continue ruling on behalf of the British till order had been restored.

Rumour held the Rani responsible for the murder of some Englishmen at Jokhan Bagh, in collaboration with the mutineers. The Governor-General ordered an inquiry into her conduct and marshalled evidence to 'prove' her 'guilt'. It was at this stage that the Rani decided to defend her honour by armed resistance to the British—convinced that her choice was limited to a hangman's rope on the one hand and a heroic death in the battlefield on the other. She chose the latter course to vindicate her honour, and determined to wage a war to the bitter end.

Taking over complete control of the state, the Rani formulated plans of attack, organized an army of 40,000 men, recruited women, started arsenals, collected ammunition and established contact with other rebel leaders. Tatya Tope who reached Jhansi after it had been invested by Hugh Rose, was defeated and retreated to Kalpi, about 80 km south-west of Kanpur (Cawnpore). Lakshmi Bai escaped to join him there when the fort was stormed on 3 April. Pursued by British forces, the two leaders were defeated at Kunch, not far from Kalpi. Undaunted, the Rani conceived the bold idea of marching to Gwalior to win over Sindhia's troops. Contrary to her initial plans, much time was lost and the British caught her men in a state of virtual unpreparedness. Clad in male attire, bold and fearless to the end, the Rani rallied her troops to a fight. Unfortunately, her horse stumbled and she was cut down by a hussar on the second day (17 June 1858) of the battle.

To underline the true nature of her role, it is necessary to recall that, in the words of her biographer, the Revolt of 1857 was 'an unorganized, sporadic and desultory affair with no co-ordination and effective liaison between the various centres of disaffection and personalities involved....Popular revolts in any country or age are never brought about by ready–made plans and blueprints. They deal with basic passions and prejudices.'

It has been suggested that the Rani 'joined the revolt for personal reasons and that if Lord Dalhousie had treated her more gently and justly', she might have backtracked. It may be recalled that both John Pym (1584–1643) and John Hampden (1594–1643) started their fight against the Stuart king of England because of personal grievances and wrongs.

S. N. Sen has aptly summed up her career: 'If the reverence of her own people is any compensation for vilification by her enemies, the Rani of Jhansi stands more than vindicated. Thousands of unsophisticated villagers still sing of the valours and virtues of the woman who held her own against her Bundela enemies to fall under a British bullet.'

More than anyone else in the Revolt, Rani Lakshmi Bai represented her country's urges and aspirations, hopes and fears, passions and hatreds. 'To fight against the English' she declared at the moment of crisis, 'has now become my Dharma.' More than any other leader of the time, she had some vision of the free India of the future.

D. V. Tahmankar, *The Ranee of Jhansi*, London, 1958; Surendra Nath Sen, *Eighteen Fifty-seven*, New Delhi, 1957, pp. 268–9; Shyam Narain Sinha, *Rani Lakshmi Bai of Jhansi*, Allahabad, 1980.

Treaty of Lalding (1774)

After the Rohilla War (q.v.), a treaty of peace was concluded on 7 October 1774 between Shuja-ud-Daula (q.v.), the Nawab Wazir of Oudh, and Faizulla Khan, the son of Ali Muhammad Khan. It was attested by Colonel Alexander Champion, Commander of the John Company's (q.v.) forces. The Colonel was later to level serious and, as it appeared, highly exaggerated charges against the Nawab and his troops for the cruelty inflicted on the peasantry in general and the family of Hafiz Rahmat Khan (q.v.) in particular.

The 'treaty' so–called is in the form of a declaration signed and sealed by the Nawab Wazir spelling out the terms and conditions he had granted to Faizullah Khan, the Rohilla chief (d. 1794). Alongside is another 'treaty' signed and sealed by the latter agreeing to all that the Nawab had put in in the preceding document. Both 'treaties' bear the seals of Colonel Champion and are dated 'Rajab 1188' (i.e., October 1774).

Essentially, the Nawab Wazir purloined most of the Rohilla dominion, its new chief retaining only such territory as was bequeathed to him by his father (Ali Mohammad) along with the city and district of Rampur, yielding in all an annual revenue of Rs 14,75,000. He further undertook not to keep more than 5,000 men under arms, of which 2,000–3,000 were detailed to assist the Nawab Wazir whenever the latter required their help; a part of this clause was later (1783) rescinded in return for a payment of Rs 15 lakhs. Such Rohillas as were left on this side of the Ganges were to be expelled to the other side, 20,000 being thus affected. Faizullah Khan also pledged to remain 'a firm associate' of the Oudh ruler, 'both in adversity and prosperity' and was not to correspond direct with anyone—'the English chiefs excepted.'

Aitchison, II, pp. 11–13; Dodwell, *CHI*, V, pp. 219–23.

Thomas Arthur, Comte de Lally (1700–66)

The son of an Irish exile, Lally had inherited from his father an implacable hatred for the British and was employed in the French army. He distinguished himself in the Franco–Austrian war (1734–5) as one of the more promising French officers. In 1756, he was appointed Governor-General and Commander-in-Chief of the French expedition to India charged with the task of expelling the British from the subcontinent. While invested with full civil and military power, he was yet denied any control over the navy. Among France's other misfortunes, this division of command was to prove fatal. There was, additionally, discord within the French forces.

Though possessed of great military skill, Lally was hot-headed and hasty, and failed to co-ordinate the different arms of his war machine. Due to lack of planning, he had to raise the siege of Madras and later (1759) of Tanjore. His alliance with Haidar Ali (q.v.) in 1760 proved to be of no material help, with the result that he was defeated by English forces under Eyre Coote (q.v.) at the Battle of Wandiwash (q.v.). Two months later, he was forced to surrender Pondicherry. He was captured and taken a prisoner of war to England. Earlier, the recall of Marquis de Bussy (q.v.) from the Deccan in

1758 to strengthen Lally's forces for the war in the Carnatic left the northern Circars exposed to an English attack from Bengal. The Circars were promptly lost along with the two old settlements of Masaulipatam and Yanam.

The failure of the French in India in the Seven Years War (1756–63) is generally attributed to a number of factors—the rashness and arrogance of Lally, the violent discord between him and his Company's officers at Pondicherry, the acute want of money and the timidity at sea of Vice-Admiral Comte d' Ache, which deprived Lally of much-needed naval support at every critical moment.

Lally's own dismal failure against the British was due principally to the latter's marked naval superiority. *Inter alia*, it enabled them to receive supplies of food and money from Bengal; recruits, in men, from Europe; and grain from their northern settlements. In sharp contrast, the French could receive nothing and were continuously weakened. Additionally, the British were financially much better off, while Lally was harried for lack of means to pay his troops, obtain material or engage work-people. The Deccan by itself was too poor to sustain large numbers and there was little succour that Bussy gave or could have given him. Lally's personal character too was a liability: his hastiness, his violent temper, his uncontrolled and cutting speech were serious handicaps.

On his return to France in 1763, Lally was imprisoned in the Bastille and brought to trial for lack of foresight in his Indian campaigns. Found guilty, he was executed in 1766. In 1788, however, the sentence was annulled and his estate restored to his son.

Martin, a French historian, disliked Lally's choice: 'Such a person had been given the resources which Dupleix never had at his disposal.' Yet, however critical, he absolves him of the ultimate blame: 'The real criminal on whom posterity would fasten the responsibility for the loss of India was not the Comte de Lally but the King who had ordered his death.'

S. P. Sen, *The French in India 1763–1816*, Calcutta, 1958; Dodwell, *CHI*, V, pp. 158–65.

Land Tenancy Acts (1868)

The Oudh and the Panjab Land Tenancy Acts XIX and XXVIII respectively, were adopted in 1868 during the tenure of John Lawrence (q.v.). The peasantry was traditionally rack-rented and there was a clear need to grant it a modicum of security against eviction and high rents. Lawrence's own stance was pro-peasant, but it was imperative and expedient to conciliate the landed gentry; the result was a compromise formula.

The Oudh Tenancy Act conferred the rights of occupancy on all those who possessed a hereditary title dating back 30 years before the state's annexation (1856). This benefited only a small percentage of the ryots. Originally, it was calculated, they comprised 20% of the entire body of cultivators; in actual fact, it was found, they were a bare 1%. In cases of increase in rent, a tenant may demand compensation for improvement. Rent could be raised only if equity so demanded and an application to that effect submitted to a court of law was accepted.

The consequences of the new law were disastrous. By 1873, notices of eviction were being issued at the rate of 60,000 annually—with the object not so much of clearing the land as of forcing the tenant to submit to an enhanced rent. Ten years later, inquiries revealed, rents had gone up by 25%. The new law strained relations between the landlord and the tenant, as the former was found perpetually engaged in litigation to increase the amount of rent due. While the law encouraged subletting among occupancy tenants, tenants-at-will suffered from the nagging insecurity of eviction.

The Panjab Tenancy Act, granted occupancy rights to all tenants in possession of such rights, unless the contrary was proved in a court of law through a regular suit. Furthermore, only a court was to decree a rise in rent which, in any case, must be 15% below the rack rent. The new legislation secured the landlord's interest in so far as occupancy rights could not be acquired through lapse of time alone (as under Act X) while occupancy tenants could be evicted on payment of compensation.

The two Acts came into force in 1869. Though altering but little the position of the landlords, the mere fact of their focussing attention on the cultivator made way for future legislation.

T. R. Metcalfe, *The Aftermath of Revolt,* Princeton, 1965, pp. 195–6,200.

Lansdowne (1845–1927)

Henry Charles Keith Petty-Fitzmaurice, fifth Marquess of Lansdowne, succeeded to the Viceroyalty in 1888. A wealthy landlord and member of the House of Lords at 21, he was reluctantly drawn into politics largely owing to his family's long-standing Whig traditions and connections.

Beginning as a junior lord of the treasury in 1869, he successfully rose to be Under Secretary of State for India in 1880. Broadly, his public career may be divided into four periods. To start with, as a Liberal he held (1869-83) minor posts in Gladstone's two administrations; later, as Governor-General of Canada and Viceroy of India (1883–94); still later, he was Secretary of State for War and Foreign Secretary in two consecutive Unionist administrations (1895–1906); and finally, as leader of the Conservative opposition (1906–16) in the House of Lords.

In Canada, Lansdowne's tenure (1883–8) saw the completion of the Canadian Pacific Railway (1886) and the settlement of a long-standing dispute with the United States over the Newfoundland fisheries. In between, he had declined a post in Salisbury's Tory cabinet. In 1888 he replaced Dufferin (q.v.) in India.

Largely dependent on official advice and decisions in Whitehall, Lansdowne's internal policy proceeded without any spectacular change. In so far as the existing Legislative Councils lacked local knowledge and authority, Lansdowne favoured a part of the provincial Councils being elected; he opposed a uniform system for all the provinces, urging the need for adequate representation of the aristocracy, which would not only add to the weight of the Councils but also perhaps act as a counterpoise to the influence of the elected members. The reformed Councils, he hoped, would counteract the activity of the self-constituted bodies and conciliate the more reasonable section of the educated people. Apart from a considerable increase in their membership, he favoured vesting them with rights of interpellation, calling for papers and a substantial measure of control over a portion of local finances. He also favoured an enlargement of the Governor-General's Executive Council. However, Whitehall rejected these proposals (1890), agreeing only to the nomination of some additional members. Constantly urging the necessity of appeasing educated Indian opinion, Lansdowne's tenure finally witnessed the enactment of the 1892 Indian Councils Act (q.v.).

Lansdowne felt that the system of trial by jury needed to be uniform throughout India. Accordingly, he proposed a review of the offences which were to be tried by jury and formulated his Juries Bill (1893). The latter was designed to remove criminal cases in some parts of Bengal from the purview of juries who were known to be notoriously afraid to convict. In this too Lansdowne was overruled by Whitehall. A popular, though not unexpected, agitation led to the appointment of a commission of inquiry to conduct a thorough probe into the whole system.

The Governor-General's attitude towards the Indian National Congress (q.v.) was one of sufferance. He was prepared to treat it with a measure of 'good-humoured indifference' as long as it confined its activities to drawing the government's attention to genuine problems in a constitutional manner and refrained from what its critics called seditious pamphleteering. He argued that the party could be prevented from becoming hostile by strengthening the Moderates, but in this, too, he was soon disillusioned. For, to his great resentment, the Congress, when disappointed with his scheme of reform, decided to appeal directly to the British public. Besides, he was convinced that the activities of the cow protection associations, instigated by the Congress, had resulted in communal riots in the North-Western Provinces and in Bombay (1893). The Age of Consent Bill, giving legal protection to girls up to the age of 12, was opposed by some Congressmen, including Tilak (q.v.).

Lansdowne did not resort to repressive measures to curb Congress activity, but reverted to the traditional pattern of supporting the landed gentry and evoking their sentiment of loyalty to the Raj. His short-lived honeymoon with the Congress was thus soon over.

The only formidable problem his Viceroyalty faced was the sharp decline in the value of silver and a consequent fall in the exchange value of the rupee from 2 shillings to 1. The government and its officials were most vitally affected, the former in that it had to pay more to discharge old debts and the latter in so far as their remittances and savings diminished sharply in value. Recourse was immediately had to increased taxation, while the unpopular income-tax and salt duty were enhanced. These, however, were to no avail. When the International Monetary Conference (1892) failed to provide a satisfactory solution, the Governor-General took the drastic step of ordering the closure of all Indian mints (Act VIII of 1893), thereby restricting the supply of currency. In the result, the rupee gained in price and stability and, a few years later (1899), it became possible to fix its value at 1 s. 4d. by a legal enactment.

Lansdowne's tenure also witnessed an anti-opium agitation, principally in England. A sizeable portion of the Indian revenue had for long been derived from the growth and sale of this drug and it was urged that, since it would be impossible to prevent its use, it was better that the traffic remain in government hands rather than with private individuals. After some excited debates in Parliament, the matter was finally referred to an Opium Commission which broadly supported the Indian position.

By the Convention of Peking (1886), the British conquest of Burma was recognized by China. There followed 5 years of guerilla warfare. The Shan states beyond the Irrawaddy submitted in 1890, as did the Lushais in 1892, but fighting with the Chins continued until 1896. Earlier, in 1892-3, the frontier between Thailand and the trans-Salween Shan states was finally demarcated. In the North-West Frontier (q.v.), a strategic railway line was constructed from Quetta to the Bolan Pass making the advance to Kandahar easier. The 'pocket handkerchief states' of Hunza and Nagar on the Afghan frontier, near Gilgit in Kashmir, were annexed after a brief military operation in 1892. Kalat, too, was brought under British protection (1893).

Following a moderately forward foreign policy, the Governor-General was preoccupied with establishing British control over the north-eastern and north-western frontiers. 'Spheres of influence', he argued, should be demarcated whenever the dominions of two great powers tend to meet, thereby giving each the right to act independently in areas deemed to be under its protection. Keen to settle all boundaries, Lansdowne declared Sikkim a protectorate and, in 1888, demarcated its frontier with Tibet. In much the same manner, the border between north-east Bengal and Burma was settled.

In Afghanistan, Lansdowne was influenced by military advice under Lord Roberts (1832–1914) to extend British influence up to Kabul and Kandahar by improving and extending railway and telegraph communications on the border and exercising a measure of control over the tribes. He also tried to assert his authority over Afghanistan's foreign relations while broadly refraining from interference in its internal politics. Amir Abdur Rahman (q.v.) viewed these moves with a sullen misgiving. Overruled in London, Lansdowne decided to embark on direct negotiations, but the Amir refused to meet Roberts, the much-hated author of the forward policy, who was now designated as the Indian envoy. In the result, the Amir dragged his feet until the army chief had left India and then accepted Sir Mortimer Durand's (q.v.) mission. With the drawing up of an agreement between the two sides, efforts to demarcate a boundary commenced in 1894, resulting in the establishment of the Durand Line (q.v.).

The Viceroy professed a policy of non-intervention in regard to the Indian States (q.v.), but during his tenure interceded actively in the succession dispute in Manipur where, unhappily, three English officers, including the Resident and the Chief Commissioner of Assam, had been killed. The rebel leaders were executed, a minor scion of the family enthroned and a political agent placed incharge of the administration during his apprenticeship. In Kalat, the ruler's execution of his wazir and a few other individuals gave the Viceroy an opportunity to strengthen British control. The ruler was deposed and his son acknowledged as his successor.

Lansdowne retired in 1894 and received an honorary Doctorate of Law from the University of Oxford. He figured prominently in political circles, holding the appointment of Secretary of State for War in 1895. Later, he served a five-year tenure as Secretary of State for Foreign Affairs, a period that witnessed the formation of two alliances—with Japan (1902) and France (1904). He did not enjoy the same success in settling the issue of the Venezuelan blockade and the Alaskan boundary dispute with the U.S.A. Thereafter he was leader of the Tory party in the House of Lords, but resigned in 1912. During Asquith's coalition cabinet in World War I, Lansdowne was briefly Minister Without Portfolio, but found no place in Lloyd George's government that succeeded Asquith's fall in December 1916. In favour of peace and ending hostilities, Lansdowne forcefully expressed his views in a letter to the *Daily Telegraph* (29 November 1917) strongly criticizing the party to which he owed allegiance. Broadly, he advocated an end to a war of attrition and demanded a clearer definition of the Allied war aims. However laudable his objective, his views, critics averred, were bound to arouse fears among Britain's allies and some hope amongst her enemies of a weakening of purpose. In the result, his letter was violently repudiated.

Of a modest and even retiring disposition, Lansdowne was quick at getting to the heart of a question and in expressing his conclusions clearly and concisely; his official minutes and memoranda were models of lucidity and terseness. Superficially aloof, severe and unbending, he was in reality a kind friend, a lover of nature and poetry and a good classical scholar.

Hiralal Singh, *Problems and Policies of the British in India, 1885-1898*, Bombay, 1963; *Speeches by the Marquis of Lansdowne: Viceroy and Governor-General of India, 1888-1894*, Calcutta, 1895; Lord Newton, *Lord Lansdowne: A Biography*, London, 1929; R. K. Perti, *South Asia: Frontier Policies, Administrative problems and Lord Lansdowne*, New Delhi, 1976; *DNB 1922-1930*, pp. 667–75 (Lansdowne).

Doctrine of Lapse

The Doctrine of Lapse may be said to have been first defined by John Pollard Willoughby in an elaborate minute wherein he drew upon his long and varied experience in the political department. A member of the Bombay Council, he had on the death (1848) of the Raja of Satara without a male heir asserted the prerogative of the imperial power 'to refuse to recognize heirs by adoption,' suggesting in the result the annexation of the state. As it turned out, his proposal was rejected, although Dalhousie (q.v.) gave it unprecedented support when he advanced the right of the British government 'not to neglect any rightful opportunity of annexation.'

To justify annexation the then Governor-General ruled that, while he 'would not seek to lay down any flexible rule with respect to adoption, I hold that on all occasions where natural heirs shall fail, the territory shall be made to lapse and adoption should not be permitted, excepting in those cases in which some strong political reason may render it expedient to depart from this general rule.' Dalhousie elaborated his thesis further by suggesting that sovereignty in states which were the creation of the British government would lapse to the paramount power in the absence of a natural heir. Tributary and subordinate states would lapse if the adopted heir was not recognized, the discretion lying with the sovereign authority. It may be noted that Dalhousie was careful to confine action under this policy to 'dependent states.' Thus, despite prodding by the Directors he refused to interfere in the case of Hyderabad or in Bahawalpur where there had been lawlessness. He was emphatic that he 'never advised' annexation unless a state 'lapsed naturally' for want of heirs, or 'was forfeited' for misconduct.

It was argued that an adoption entitled the heir to the private property of his adoptive father but *not* to the state, for which authority vested with the paramount power. Accordingly, Dalhousie annexed Satara (1848), Jaitpur and Sambhalpur (1849), Baghat (1850), Udaipur (1852), Jhansi (1853), Nagpur (1854) and Karauli (1855). The culminating point was the annexation of Oudh (q.v.) in 1856.

Though unlawfully annexed, Jaitpur, Sambhalpur and Baghat were small states and of no great consequence. Satara, Jhansi and Nagpur were major Maratha states which were not created by the British; they could have been annexed after the Third Anglo-Maratha War (q.v.), but the British had preferred to recognize them in the first instance.

Satara belonged to the house of Shivaji and by a treaty concluded in 1819 with Pratap Singh Narayan, the British had recognized his right and that of his heirs and successors to rule. Later, Pratap Singh was forcibly deposed (1839) and the adopted son of his third brother and successor Appa Sahib (alias Shahji) refused recognition. On the plea that no legal adoption had taken place, the British annexed the state if partly to ensure continuity of military communication in the Bombay Presidency.

Jhansi, the only state in Bundelkhand which broke the British territorial link in the area, had been confirmed in the possession of its ruler Shib Rao Bhau and his successors. Refusal in 1853 to recognize the adopted son of Gangadhar Rao and Rani Lakshmi Bai (q.v.) appeared only to be a ruse to annex the state. Nagpur was the largest of all these states—its 80,000 square miles of area was rich, fertile, cotton land. Besides increased revenues, its incorporation would mean erecting a ring fence of sorts around the Nizam's dominions. The British therefore rejected all requests of the widow of Raghuji Bhonsle III to recognize Appa Sahib, Raghuji's grand nephew, adopted after his death in 1853, as heir. Though not based strictly on the doctrine of lapse, Carnatic was annexed (1855) on the ground that the state had been allowed hereditary succession; Tanjore, because a female child could not be recognized as heir. In both cases, the rank as well as pension of the rulers was abolished.

It is only fair to suggest that Dalhousie did not originate the theory or practice of lapse which had been anticipated much earlier by Wellesley (q.v.). Again, for a correct perspective, it is necessary to recall that, in 1834, the Court of Directors had laid down that whenever it was optional for the Government of India to give or withhold its assent to adoption, 'the indulgence should be the exception and not the rule and should never be granted but as a special mark of favour and approbation.'

Its origin notwithstading, the mode and method of its practical application was, however, not always clear or even consistent. Thus, Dalhousie's predecessors did not fail to take advantage of the Directors' ruling by applying the right of lapse to states like Kolaba and Mandvi. Dalhousie could have taken over more states that were 'sovereign' and 'subordinate' if he were so minded, for the declaration of 1841 'to persevere in the one clear and direct course of abandoning no just and honourable accession of territory or revenue', was both clear and categorical.

Far from being aggressive and unrelenting, it has been suggested that

Dalhousie's attitude towards the Indian States (q.v.) was 'unnecessarily moderate.' His apologists contend that the fact that more than 500 principalities 'survived annexation' is proof of his moderation. The alleged 'independence' of states provided a basis for the policy of non-interference followed by Dalhousie; he tried to practise consistent non-interference under the pretence of respecting the states' 'independence.' In general, he interfered only where vital British interests were concerned and on such occasions, 'the political fact of paramountcy became operative, and gave an irresistible force to Government's actions.'

Paramountcy enabled the government not only to annex offending states without declaring war, but also provided a basis for the doctrine of lapse. There could be no question of a state lapsing to the Company unless the latter was its paramount authority, a fact 'which reduced to absurdity the argument of Dalhousie that the same principality was also a "sovereign", "independent" and "foreign" state.' But to admit the disastrous consequences of Dalhousie's annexations is not to deny the over-riding necessity for them. It is this virtual inevitability of all that happened which lifts his administration 'from a blind and blundering impetuosity—a statesman run amuck—to something like a Greek tragedy.'

As early as August 1848 the Governor-General had expressed the view that he could not conceive it possible for anyone 'to dispute the policy of taking advantage of every just opportunity which presents itself for consolidating the territories that already belong to us, by taking possession of states that may lapse in the midst of them, for thus getting rid of these petty intervening principalities which may be made a means of annoyance.'

Whether lapse was sanctioned by morality or expediency is a matter of opinion and historians are sharply divided on the issue. A knowledgeable authority has, however, suggested that it is difficult to maintain that the Company was within its rights, merely by an executive fiat in the absence of any legislation, to annul the adoption of an Indian ruler, to annex his state on the ground of failure of male issue.

Lapse, it has been argued, had no precedent in Indian practice, where the paramount power could not, under any circumstances, withhold recognition of the heir, even though it could demand a larger tribute (*nazrana*). It follows that here was an unjust innovation of the British aimed at eliminating petty states and consolidating British rule. There is no gainsaying that a continuous stretch of territory would ensure speedier construction of railways and road communications, facilitate traffic and increase trade. No less tempting to the British were the rich lands and the increased revenues the newly-acquired territories would bring in their train.

Extremely unpopular, these annexations left a smouldering discontent which was to flare up later into the Rebellion of 1857 (q.v.).

Sri Nandan Prasad, *Paramountcy Under Dalhousie*, Delhi, 1964.

Henry Lawrence (1806–57)

Henry (later Sir Henry) Montgomery Lawrence was born in Sri Lanka, but educated in England where he entered Addiscombe (1822) and joined the Bengal Artillery a year later. Wounded in the First Burmese War (q.v.) and sent home, he joined the Trigonometrical Survey in Ireland. Shortly after his return to India (1830), he was appointed assistant surveyor to Robert Bird and later surveyor at Moradabad (1833-8). Early in 1840 he was sent as assistant to George Clerk at Ludhiana; two years later, he accompanied General Pollock's army to Afghanistan. After brief tenures in Mussoorie and Ambala he was posted to Kaithal which had by then lapsed to the John Company's (q.v.) control. It was here that he was introduced to the Panjab. Reluctant to leave the north-west, he nevertheless served briefly as Resident in Nepal (1843-6).

Lawrence's contribution in the political and administrative field began in January 1847, when he was recalled from leave to replace Major Broadfoot as Agent to the Governor-General for foreign relations and the affairs of the Panjab. Though opposed to the annexation of the state, he speedily put an end to all possible opposition following the First Anglo-Sikh War (q.v.), personally leading a force against Imam-ud-Din, the Sikh governor in Kashmir, and bringing about its surrender to Maharaja Gulab Singh (q.v.), expelling Lal Singh and exiling Maharani Jind Kaur (q.v.) on charges of disloyalty and intrigue.

During the Second Anglo-Sikh War (q.v.), Lawrence returned from leave to resume his work as British Resident on the conclusion of hostilities. After the annexation of the Panjab (1849) he was appointed president of a newly-constituted 3-man 'board of administration', along with his brother John Lawrence (q.v.) and Charles Mansel. In addition, he was to act as Agent for the Governor-General. In this uphill task he chose a band of efficient subordinates and invested them with civil and military authority to settle the new state's borders. He disliked Dalhousie's (q.v.) militant policy towards the Sikhs while the latter no doubt disapproved of his system of administration. Meanwhile, serious differences arose between the two Lawrence brothers on questions of land revenue; the Governor-General sensibly dissolved the board and posted Henry to Rajasthan as his Agent.

Understandably Lawrence was mortified at not being selected to govern the Panjab alone for, during his 4-year tenure, he had reconstructed and pacified a hostile state and made it 'as safe as Calcutta' for an Englishman. Later (1853), he declined to be Resident at the Nizam's court in Hyderabad.

Four months before the Rebellion of 1857 (q.v.) Canning (q.v.) offered Lawrence the post of Chief Commissioner and Agent to the Governor-General in Oudh (q.v.). With the outbreak of the revolt, he was promoted to the rank of Brigadier-General and invested with military control over all the troops in Oudh. He none the less failed to hold back the 'rebels' who converged upon Lucknow after the fall of Kanpur (Cawnpore) and besieged the Residency (30 June). Hit by a bullet on 2 July, he died two days later. Lawrence wrote his own epitaph: 'Here lies Henry Lawrence who tried to do his duty.' Three weeks after his death, but before it was known in England, he was appointed to succeed Canning in case the latter had been incapacitated in an accident.

Henry Lawrence was a man of hot and tempestuous temperament. Possessed of great energy; he was indefatigable in his work, and essentially straightforward, generous and disinterested. His disregard for money or personal comfort was said to be the secret of his influence, particularly with the 'natives'. He gave a large part of his salary to the establishment of Lawrence asylums in the hill stations for the care of children of European soldiers. In manner brusque and in appearance gaunt, his shrewd, sharp understanding attracted attention. His great failings were over-sensitiveness and impatience of contradiction.

A biographer has maintained that, in so far as he had no pedestal to stand upon, asked 'no honorific phrases from his fellows', clung to 'simple duties performed with austere directness', he did not catch the eye or master the memory of the undiscerning mass— 'which is the British empire.'

In the course of a varied life, he was doing what he called, 'real' things: toiling in camp at honest survey work 'with Honoria by his side'; giving a hand to drag the guns up the Khyber pass (in 1842); talking face to face, 'careless of all proconsular safeguards to his dignity', with Sikh sardars or Maharaja Gulab Singh; desperately eager to get at the heart of the discontent among the sepoys in Oudh; speaking and acting simply in religion 'as though Jesus meant the words He spoke.'

His memorials are scattered north-west from Lucknow: the cornerstone with nothing on it but the words he asked for; the unspoiled simplicity of the Residency gardens; the Lawrence schools and, especially, that at Sanawar where he and William Hodson tried their hand at architecture.

Of a literary bent of mind, Lawrence contributed regularly to the *Calcutta Review* and the *Delhi Gazette*. Among his writings, the following may be listed: *Some passages in the life of an Adventurer in the Punjab* (1842), *Adventures of an officer in the service of Ranjeet Singh* (1845), *Essays, Military & Political* (1859), and *Essays in the Indian Army & Oudh* (1859).

J. L. Morison, *Lawrence of Lucknow, 1806–57, being the life of Sir Henry Lawrence retold from his private and public papers*, London, 1934; *DNB*, XI, pp. 699-706 (Robert Hamilton Vetch).

Sir John Lawrence (1811–1879)

John Laird Mair Lawrence, first Baron Lawrence, who rose to be Governor-General of India (1864-69) had a long and distinguished career in the Indian Civil Service. He arrived in Bengal in 1830 after 2 years of training at the John Company's (q.v.) Haileybury College (q.v.) in England. Later, after a thorough grounding in languages at Fort William College, he was posted to Delhi, as Assistant Magistrate under Sir Charles Metcalfe (q.v.). He rose to be Collector and, in 1839, became settlement officer at Etawah in the then North-Western Provinces. After a short spell as civil and sessions judge at Karnal, he was appointed (1844) Collecter and Magistrate of Panipat and Delhi. Two years later, during the First Anglo-Sikh War (q.v.), he successfully organized a convoy of military equipment to reinforce British troops then engaged in desperate battle. The convoy managed to reach the front-line just before the battle of Sobraon and was a great help in ensuring eventual British victory.

In the result, Lawrence was entrusted with the charge of the trans-Sutlej region, combining it with acting Resident at Lahore during his brother Henry Lawrence's (q.v.) leave of absence. Through alternate coaxing and cajolery, Le prevented the chiefs, and the people of the Doab, from joining the insurrection which led to the Second Anglo-Sikh War (q.v.). Like Dalhousie (q.v.), he had favoured immediate annexation of the province and, on the conclusion of the War, was appointed as member incharge of fiscal matters in the board constituted to administer the province under the presidentship of his brother, Henry. John, a hard-headed administrator, failed to see eye to eye with his brother on such vital issues as collection of land revenue, management of finances and the treatment of jagirdars.

Dalhousie took advantage of the rift between the brothers to dissolve the board in 1853, appointing John Lawrence Chief Commissioner of the new province. He now carried the administration with minor modifications— assisted by two Commissioners, one for finance and the other for judicial affairs. He got an opportunity to wield absolute power and act independently when Calcutta was cut off during the early months of the Rebellion of 1857 (q.v.). He organized the European troops in his state as efficiently as he could, disarmed mutinous Delhi, raised loans and even took the grave risk of dispatching the Panjab troops to Delhi under the intrepid British commander, John Nicholson (1821-57). After the fall of Delhi, Lawrence personally supervised the restoration of law and order in that metropolis, repeatedly exhorting his compatriots to be moderate in punishing the rebels. For services rendered he was created a baronet and a Privy Councillor and awarded the G.C.B. Additionally, the John Company granted him an annuity of £2,000 from the date of his retirement.

Lawrence returned to England in 1859 to serve in the India Office; a year later, he refused an appointment as Governor of Bombay. Having established a reputation as a cautious and sound administrator, he was appointed Elgin's (1811-63) successor in November 1863, assuming charge early in the new year. It was noted that, with a solitary exception, no Indian civilian since Warren Hastings (q.v.) had held for its full tenure the post of Governor-General.

Lawrence's term of office was noteworthy not only for his initiatives in foreign policy but also for some major measures of domestic reform. Among the latter mention may be made of his ambitious plans for a vast and comprehensive network of irrigation canals in different parts of the country. Railways too were steadily extended. The Governor-General pressed for sanitary improvements in towns, barracks and jails. Additionally, he created the Indian Forests Department and reorganized the 'native' judicial service. He was the first to move the entire government of India to Simla during the summer months.

Barring an exception here or there, Lawrence was lucky in his Council. In financial matters he had three able members in succession—Sir Charles Trevelyan, William Massey and Sir Richard Temple. With his first Commander-in-Chief, Sir Hugh Rose, his relations were somewhat strained, but his successor, Sir William Mansfield was far more cooperative. Lawrence did not work well with two military members of his Council—Sir Robert Napier and Sir Henry Durand. In all this one has to bear in mind the fact that, being a member of the ICS, the Governor-General 'never fully' attained that mastery over his colleagues which the head of government should normally possess.

The keynote of Lawrence's administration, it has been said, was 'masterly inactivity'—and not only in the field of relations with Central Asia. Thus, (i) he rejected proposals to give political officers larger powers of influence in the administration of the tribes; (ii) while approving the location of a British officer in the Naga hills, he directed that the latter confine himself to protecting the lowlands from tribal incursions (and not extending British control); (iii) he overruled the project of linking Rangoon by rail with China in so far as it would endanger peaceful relations with Burma.

However, there was the other side of the coin too. Thus the Governor-General (i) placed forest administration on an efficient basis (Act VII of 1865 laid down the rules and regulations for forest conservancy); (ii) appointed Colonel Richard Strachey as Inspector-General of Irrigation in 1867; (iii) advocated state-managed railways; (iv) appointed health officers in cities and built central and district jails.

An administrator *par excellence*, Lawrence tried, albeit unsuccessfully, to apply to the entire country the highly centralized system that he had known and worked in the Panjab. His detractors charged that he aimed at 'Panjabizing' the whole of India. Championing the cause of the ryot, and with the help of revenue experts John and Richard Strachey, Lawrence had the Panjab and Oudh Tenancy Acts (q.v.) enacted in 1868. Comprehensive regulations for relief measures were laid down following the disastrous famine in Orissa in 1866; in the result, the Rajasthan famine which came immediately thereafter was controlled better. However, government finances, which were in a bad way following the commercial crisis of 1866, worsened as a result of the heavy expenditure incurred on public works. Thus, the treasury was left with a deficit of £2½ millions at the end of Lawrence's five-year tenure.

For the peace of the frontier, Lawrence preferred to cultivate the friendship of the troublesome tribes in the region between the Panjab and the Afghan frontier. In Afghanistan, he asserted the British government's right to recognize the *de facto* ruler and to stay away from the bloody war of succession taking place in that country. Thus, the Governor-General recognized each ruler that came after 1863, till Sher Ali recaptured Kabul, and power, in 1868. Non-committal to the last, Lawrence agreed to the Amir's request for help, but only to the extent of presenting him with arms and money. Refusing to be awed by the Russian advance in Asia, he urged the home authorities to come to an understanding with St Petersburg about their respective spheres of influence. For defence, he would rather reinforce the Indian borders than deploy force outside the periphery. In its essence, his frontier policy, based on first-hand knowledge of the area and its people, was one of cautious maintenance of the status quo, making the people within the frontier prosperous and contented; and beyond it, independent. There was to be no overt interference in the latter's affairs. This succinctly summed up his reaction to a Russian advance as well as an Afghan threat. Earlier, Canning (q.v.) had noted that it was difficult 'to exaggerate' Lawrence's 'ability, vigilance and energy' and that it was 'through him' that, in the Rebellion of 1857 (q.v.), Delhi fell and the Panjab became a source of strength.

Lawrence retired in January 1869 and was immediately raised to the peerage as Baron Lawrence of the Panjab and Crately. Later (1870-3), he acted as Chairman of the London School Board. Death claimed him on 26 June 1879 and he was buried in Westminster Abbey.

Dharm Pal, *The Administration of Sir John Lawrence in India, (1864-1869)*, Simla, 1952; Sir Richard Temple, *Lord Lawrence*, London, 1903; R. Bosworth Smith, *Life of Lord Lawrence*, London, 1883; *DNB*, XI, pp. 708-14 (John Andrew Hamilton).

Lee Commission (1923)

Officially known as the 'Royal Commission on the Superior Civil Services in India' the Lee Commission was appointed on 15 June 1923 by Lord Peel, then Secretary of State for India, to inquire into the question of pay and emoluments of the Superior Civil Services and the problems attendant on their progressive Indianization. Apart from Lord Lee of Fareham who was Chairman, its members were Sir Reginald Henry Craddock, B. N. Basu, Sir Cyril Jackson, Sir M. Habibullah, H. Kaul, D. Petrie, Professor R. Coupland of Oxford and N. M. Samarth. Its report was submitted in March 1924.

The Commission's recommendations were accepted by the government except in some matters of detail and despite considerable opposition in the Central Legislative Assembly, where members were quick to point out that the progress of Indianization had been painfully slow.

The all-India services with which the Commission was primarily concerned were the Indian Civil Service, the Indian Police Service, the Indian Forest Service, the Indian Educational Service, the Indian Agricultural Service, the Indian Veterinary Service and the Indian Medical Service (Civil). Three of these (the I.C.S., I.P.S. and I.F.S.) and the Irrigation Branch of the Indian Agricultural Service operated in what was called the 'Reserved' field in the provinces, as stipulated in the Montagu-Chelmsford Reforms (q.v.) of 1919. The Commission concluded that they comprised Services upon which public security and finance mainly depended. It, therefore, recommended that the Secretary of State should continue, as hitherto, to recruit for these Services and his control, with its implied safeguards, should continue to be maintained.

The Indian Service of Engineers, Indian Educational Service, Indian Agricultural Service and the Indian Veterinary Service, as also the buildings and roads department of the Service of Engineers operated in the 'Transferred' field in every province. So did the Forest Service in Bombay and Burma where 'Forests' had been designated a 'Transferred' subject. The Commission, therefore, recommended that the control of provincial ministers over some of these should be made more complete by closing all-India recruitment to them. It was thus stipulated that no fresh recruitment was to be made to them from 1925 onwards. While the existing incumbents would remain and no change was to be made in their position (viz., they retained all the rights of officers in an All-India Service), they were to be replaced by the Provincial Services when fresh vacancies occurred on their retirement. Recruitment in future would be made by provincial governments and they would constitute Provincial Services.

One of the findings of the Commission was that, except in the case of the I.C.S. and I.P.S., and in such technical jobs as irrigation, engineering, etc., the process of Indianization had definitely taken root. It followed that the elimination of Europeans would be phased out over a period of time. The Commission rejected the charge that there had been any deliberate slowness in the policy of Indianization.

To meet the political demand for the provincialization of the Superior Services, the Lee Commission divided the main Services into three classes: All-India, Central and Provincial. The All-Indian Services were recruited by the Secretary of State for work in any part of India and, although generally assigned to one province, their members were subject to being transferred to any other while a certain number were borrowed from the provinces to assist in the discharge of the central functions of the Government of India. The Central Services dealt *inter alia* with the Indian States (q.v.) and foreign affairs, with the administration of Indian Railways (q.v.), with posts and telegraphs, customs, audit and accounts, with scientific and technical departments like the Survey of India, the Geological Survey and the Archaeological Department.

Another contribution of the Lee Commission was to accelerate the pace of Indianization. In the light of the recommendations of the Islington Commission (appointed 1912, reported 1917) the Government of India had laid down as early as 1919-20 that recruitment of Indians in the All-India Services should be 33 per cent in the Indian Police and 50 per cent in the Agricultural, Educational and Veterinary Services and the Indian Service of Engineers. A resolution of the Central Legislative Assembly adopted in 1922 had demanded further action in the same direction. The Lee Commission therefore examined the question *de novo* in the light of past developments and tried to accommodate Indian political opinion.

For the I.C.S., the Commission recommended that 20 per cent of the superior posts should be filled by the appointment of Provincial Service officers to 'listed posts' and that direct recruits in future should be Indians and Europeans in equal numbers. It calculated that on this basis half the Services would be Indian by 1939. For the Indian Police, direct recruitment was to be in the proportion of 5 Europeans to 3 Indians; allowing for promotion from the Provincial Service, to 20 per cent of all vacancies, the Commission felt that 50 percent of the Service would be Indian by 1949.

The Commission dealt not only with the question of methods of recruitment and the problems posed by Indianization but also with the grievances of the Services themselves and the special difficulties in the way of recruitment in England for the All-India Services. The Commission's proposals for the removal of Service grievances were generally accepted as adequate, while its recommendations regarding British personnel were designed to remove apprehensions amongst officers of the impact that constitutional changes might have on their careers. *Inter alia*, the Commission recommended that any British officer employed in the 'Reserved' field should be free to retire on a proportionate pension, if the department in which he served was 'transferred' to the control of ministers responsible to a legislature. The option was to remain open for one year from the date of such transfer.

Another recommendation related to the establishment of a Central Public Service Commission, which was later (1926) set up for the All-India and the higher Central Services. Its constitution and functions were laid down in statutory rules.

Reviewing the impact of the Lee Commission's recommendations, the Simon Commission (q.v.) in its report concluded that 'the improvement in the financial position of the Services and the safeguards recommended by the Lee Commission combined with an improvement in the political position in India had two results. The retirements on proportionate pension decreased rapidly and many officers who had taken leave preparatory to such retirement returned to duty. The effect on recruitment of British personnel was equally good.'

Gwyer and Appadorai, I, pp. 111-14; *Report of the Royal Commission on the Superior Civil Services in India*, Cd. 2128, London, 1924.

The Lhasa Convention (September 1904)

The Lhasa Convention signed on 7 September 1904 at the Dalai Lama's Potala marked the culmination of the Younghusband Expedition (q.v.) to Tibet in 1903-4. It was signed by the British Commissioner representing His Majesty's Government on the one hand and Lo Sang Gyal-Tsen, the Ga-den Ti Rimpoche, who deputized for the absentee Thirteenth Dalai Lama (q.v.), on the other. Also present were representatives of the Tibetan Council, the three principal monasteries (viz., Sera, Ganden and Drepung) and the National Assembly (Tsongdu) who dutifully affixed their seals to its terms.

The Convention stipulated *inter alia* that (i) Tibet would recognize the Anglo-Chinese Convention of 1890 and open two new trade marts at Gyantse and Gartok besides the one already provided for at Yatung; (ii) Tibet would levy no taxes other than those mutually agreed upon, and keep all roads to the marts in a suitable state of repair; (iii) to cover the expenses of the expedition and reparations for 'insults' to the British Commissioner, Tibet would pay Rs 75 lakhs in yearly instalments of Rs 1 lakh each; (iv) the Chumbi Valley would remain under British occupation until such time as the indemnity was paid or for a period of 3 years, whichever was later.

The Tibetan government further agreed neither to let any foreign power interfere in its affairs nor admit any foreign agents. It would neither cede nor mortgage any portion of its territory, nor yet give concessions for railways, telegraphs, etc., nor pledge any of its revenues to a foreign power. Though by no means a part of the treaty, an agreement was also arrived at permitting the British Trade Agent at Gyantse to repair to Lhasa should it be deemed necessary for settling any points of dispute between the two governments.

Later, on Younghusband's (q.v.) return from Lhasa, the British Government refused to ratify the Convention as it stood maintaining it violated their explicit instructions to the Commissioner. The latter's defiant attitude, Whitehall insisted, had put them in a false position in so far as an understanding had been given to Russia of British disinterestedness in occupying any portion of Tibetan territory. Despite India's strong protests, the indemnity was reduced by Whitehall to Rs 25 lakhs and was to be paid in three equal annual instalments. The separate agreement regarding the British agent's visit to Lhasa was also disallowed. Thus modified, the Convention was ratified by Ampthill (then acting Governor-General in place of Curzon (q.v.) who was away on leave) on 11 November 1904.

The treaty revealed, as Curzon had rightly argued, Tibet's ability to conclude international agreements independently of her suzerain and of the latter's demonstrably negligible and weakening control in Lhasa. Such gains as accrued from a modified Lhasa Convention were subsequently compromised at the Anglo-Chinese Convention signed in Peking (1906) and the

Anglo-Russian Convention (1907). The British approach vis-a-vis Tibet had now changed to a hands off policy. In the result, China emerged as the only gainer, for both Britain and Russia recognized her suzerain rights in Tibet and refrained from seeking any form of concession for themselves.

Parshotam Mehra, *The Younghusband Expedition, an Interpretation*, Bombay, 1968; Charles Bell, *Tibet, Past & Present*, Oxford, 1924; H. E. Richardson, *Tibet and Its History*, London, 1962.

Liaqat Ali Khan (1895–1951)

Born on 1 October 1895 in an aristocratic family at Karnal, now in Haryana, Liaqat Ali was the second son of Rukunuddaulah Shamsher Jang, Nawab Rustam Ali Khan, who claimed descent from King Nausherwan of Iran. He was educated at M. A. O. College, Aligarh and later Exeter College, Oxford where he took the shortened honours course in jurisprudence in 1921. Later he was called to the Bar from Inner Temple.

In 1926 Liaqat Ali became a member of the U. P. Legislative Council and in 1931 its deputy president. In 1940 he was elected a member of the Central Legislative Assembly, where he was Deputy leader of the All India Muslim League (q.v.) party. He soon made his mark, was regular in attendance and, in speech, a hard hitter.

Liaqat Ali quickly came to the top in the Muslim League and, in 1936, was elected the party General Secretary. The same year he was appointed to the League's parliamentary board, which supervised the party's legislative activities at the centre and the provinces and chose candidates for election to the legislature. All this brought him into close touch with M. A. Jinnah (q.v.) who, in 1934, had become permanent President of the Muslim League. The two gradually drew closer to each other and this bond helped Liaqat Ali reach, and retain, the near-top position in the party hierarchy.

His 'self-effacing modesty and cool temperament' made LA an ideal second-in-command. He was General Secretary of the Muslim League in 1936 and in 1940, on being elected, Liaqat Ali was chosen deputy leader of the party in the Central Legislative Assembly. In the Interim Government (q.v.) in 1946, he became Finance Member in the Governor-General's Executive Council.

The Jinnah-Liaqat Ali duumvirate made an impressive debut and, by the time of the Cripps Mission (q.v.), the League emerged as a factor of major political importance. Later, Liaqat Ali's talks with Bhulabhai Desai, leader of the Indian National Congress (q.v.) party in the Central Legislative Assembly, led to the Desai-Liaqat Formula (q.v.) which was to form the basis for determining Congress-Muslim League representation in the Interim Government. Earlier, Liaqat's role in the convincing Muslim League triumph in the elections (1945-46) to the provincial and central legislatures left little room for doubt about his place as Jinnah's right-hand man.

It has been said that Liaqat Ali was to Jinnah what Jawaharlal Nehru (q.v.) was to Gandhi (q.v.), the only difference being that Liaqat was less articulate and never opened his mouth on important issues unless Jinnah had given his prior nod. Years later Mountbatten described the Jinnah-Liaqat relationship graphically: 'When Jinnah came to see me, he always sat there (relaxes, sits back easily). Ali Khan (viz. Liaqat Ali Khan), when he came with Jinnah sat right on the edge of his chair. He'd keep saying, "Yes, Qaidi". He would not even sit back.' In public, Liaqat Ali was an enthusiastic debater, one who particularly loved to take on a hostile audience.

As Finance Member in the interim Government, Liaqat's budget proposals (in what came to be known as the 'poor man's budget') created an acute controversy. *Inter alia,* he had imposed a wealth tax, a capital gains tax, and an increase in general taxation. Congress members in the government bitterly opposed these measures, charging that they had been deliberately designed to strike at the party's political base. The resultant stalemate could be resolved only with the partition of the country.

With the birth of Pakistan on 14 August 1947, Liaqat was the obvious choice as Prime Minister. On Jinnah's death, in September 1948, he emerged as the virtual ruler of his country, for the new Governor-General, Khwaja Nazimuddin (1894-1964), was a political light-weight.

At the Karachi session of the Muslim League in December 1943, Jinnah sponsoring Liaqat Ali's re-election as Honorary Secretary of the Muslim League, had described him as 'my right-hand man'. His services to the Muslim cause, he averred, were hard to enumerate. Assuming the mantle of the dead Quaid-i-Azam in 1948, Liaqat Ali was able to provide the cohesive force that his country so badly needed and soon became widely known as *Quaid-e-Millat.* In 1949-50, when Indo-Pak relations were sorely strained, he pulled his country from the brink of another disastrous conflict with India. The Nehru-Liaqat Agreement (1950) on the protection of minorities was a measure of his statemanship. Earlier, it was his government which had accepted the cease-fire with India in Kashmir, a bold political decision.

A more difficult task was the framing of Pakistan's new constitution. Here he faced stiff opposition from the orthodox ulama who demanded a theocratic framework of state structure in sharp contrast to Liaqat's preference for a secular approach. The resistance in the Pakistan Constituent Assembly to the interim report of the Basic Principles Committee presented in September 1950 was rated a great personal setback. Unfortunately, before much headway could be made, Liaqat Ali was assassinated by a fanatic (Said Akbar) at a publc meeting in Rawalpindi on 16 October 1951.

Although a Nawabzada, apologists underline that Liaqat Ali was a thorough-going proletarian in his sympathies. His second wife, whose maiden name was Miss Rana Irene Pant, was a Christian from Uttar Pradesh. She later embraced Islam and came to be known as Rana Liaqat Ali Khan. After her husband's death, she was to serve as Pakistan's Ambassador in several western capitals.

S. M. Ikram, *Modern Muslim India and the Birth of Pakistan (1858-1951),* 2nd ed., Lahore, 1965; *DNB 1951–1960,* pp. 632–3 (P. J. Griffiths).

All-India National Liberal Federation

A definitive breach between the moderate and extremist elements in the Indian National Congress (q.v.) during its special Bombay session in August 1918, led to the birth of the National Liberal Federation. The party held its first session in Bombay on 1-2 November 1918 under the chairmanship of

Surendranath Banerjea (q.v.). Designated as the 'All-India Conference of the Moderate Party', it proved to be the nucleus of the NLF. It adopted for its creed the old Congress goal of gradual progress towards self-government, which had by then been left way behind by the parent body. In the result, the NLF became a rallying point for moderately progressive nationalist opinion which favoured peaceful and consitutional means as opposed to the 're-volutionary' creed and policy of the Congress. The 'Conference of the Moderates' was in no sense a departure from the line of action once laid down by the Congress. Rather, it was a vindication of the latter as against the new departure sought to be imposed by what may be called the radical left wing of the Congress.

The Chairman of the Reception Committee of the NLF was Sir Dinshaw Wacha and the President, as noticed, Surendranath Banerjea. In the words of its secretary, H. M. Samrath, the key note of the NLF's political philosophy was: 'Whatever I consider to be right according to my lights and according to my reason, I will say freely, frankly and fearlessly to Govern-ment and the public, whether it pleases them or not, is not my concern. What is good to them, I will administer, however unpalatable the dose may be.' Throughout the years from 1920 to 1943 the party acted upto this principle. It did not flatter the Congress, nor yet did it criticize that body simply to spite it; it did not speak in malice or for the sake of personal triumph.

During the first 5-6 years of its existence, the new party gained in strength and exercised a measure of influence. However, the death in England in 1922, of E. S. Montagu, at one time Secretary of State for India, proved to be a great set back and 'liberal' influence gradually waned. The Round Table Conference (q.v.) brought the party again into prominence but the 'reactionary provisions' of the Government of India Act, 1935 (q.v.) ad-ministered another powerful shock. General elections under the new Act further confirmed the political eclipse of the Liberals: few of the party candidates contested and of those who did hardly any was successful. All this notwithstanding, for many years the party did make a significant contribu-tion in the political field.

In his address to the NLF in 1937, V. S. Srinivasa Sastri (1869-1946) said: 'Maybe the days of our power are gone. But the days of our influence are by no means gone. Few though we are, we are not without the power of warning against danger, of advising in difficulty, of pointing out the way of safety and sanity.'

Briefly, the return of the Congress to the constitutional path in the post-1935 years ousted the Liberals from active politics. The main scope for their activity now was to act as mediators between extremist groups rather than as principals. In so far as their leaders were mostly drawn from retired administrators who owned no party affiliations or had severed their party allegiances, this was a great help.

In 1943 Sir Maharaj Singh expressed a viewpoint echoed by many: 'Liberals may diminish in numbers and our party may disappear...but liberalism represents something which is of lasting value. It is a habit of mind or outlook in life. It is progressive and constructive, not revolutionary or destructive. it is opposed to the dictatorship of wealth, of the privileged classes and vested institutions; and it advocates the widest possible diffusion of property and power, but at the same time it disapproves totalitarian tyranny.' Later, he cited a verse: 'Winds shift, tides ebb and flow, the boat swings, only let the anchor hold.'

The 1946 general elections completed the rout of the Liberals who now ceased to be an active force in the country's political life. Their place appears to have been taken by the right-wing of the Congress often referred to as the 'old guard' with which they had no pronounced differences in terms of the goals envisaged: they advocated Dominion Status (q.v.), as against complete independence to which the radical Congress was wedded. Again, in the means to be adopted for the achievement of their goal, the Liberals were opposed to direct action; instead, they swore by constitutional forms of agitation to help accelerate the pace of political progress. Another difference related to the Liberals' allegiance to, and abiding faith in, the British connection and the potentialities for good of the British empire. Hence their stake in British victory in both the World Wars.

Before Independence in 1947, the Liberals advocated a dual policy: on the one hand, they supported the war effort; on the other, their political demands were little different from those of the Congress. The years 1942-5, when the Congress was in the political wilderness, may be regarded as the moderates' era in Indian politics. Not that the party regained its lost influence or that the masses abandoned what the Liberals viewed as 'political extremism' of the masses.

The harsh truth is that 'extremism' became more extremist. None the less, it was a 'moderate' period in the sense that the 'moderates' occupied the centre of the political stage as India's British rulers made an earnest bid to listen to them. Typical of the accommodating Liberal approach to political issues was the party's annual session in 1944, when Sir Maharaj Singh as party President and Sir Cowasjee Jahangir as Chairman of the Reception Committee expressed diametrically opposite views on the political situation in the country from the same platform. Earlier, in June 1944, the party's Council had met in Poona and made a two-fold appeal: to the Government, to release all Congress leaders unconditionally; to the Congress, to withdraw its August 1942 resolution. In October 1944 the Council met at Allahabad and placed on record its stern opposition to the All India Muslim League's (q.v.) two-nation theory, declaring the latter was opposed to reality. It also reiterated its earlier view that the League's demand for a plebiscite confined to Muslims was unfair to other communities.

After the failure of the 1944 Gandhi-Jinnah Talks (q.v.), Sir Tej Bahadur Sapru (q.v.) had constituted a Conciliation Committee to examine the communal question from a political-cum-judicial viewpoint and proffer a solution. The Committee, which had Gandhi's (q.v.) blessings, was established in December 1944. While C. Rajagopalachari (q.v.) lent it his support, as did many public men in England, Jinnah (qv) refused either to recognize the Committee or give countenance to its parent, the Non-party Conference. When Sapru wrote to Wavell (q.v.), who was then in England, suggesting a way out of the political impasse, Jinnah countered by insinuating that the Liberal leader and his men were 'handmaids of the Congress' and 'playing to the tune of Gandhi.' Not surprisingly, the League leader unreservedly denounced the subsequent Liberal proposals.

1945-46 was designated the jubilee year of the NLF and witnessed the formulation by Sapru of a compromise formula on India's future constitution.

It may be noted that, while Sapru as well as other leaders of the Non-party Conference were not strictly members of the NLF, their views on many subjects were identical. The future constitution of India as spelt out by the Sapru Committee rested on *two* basic premises. *Firstly*, that Hindus minus the Scheduled Castes should enjoy parity with the Muslims in the constitution-making body, the future central legislature, as well as the executive; *secondly*, that joint electorates as well as the unity of India were tenets on which there could be no compromise. The Committee rejected Pakistan as a solution of the prevalent political impasse but accepted the proposition that any province could accede to the future Indian union or secede therefrom. Among its other recommendations were the transfer of Paramountcy (q.v.) to the union, a declaration of fundamental rights, the setting up of a minorities commission and special safeguards for minorities in the Panjab.

At the Poona session of the Council of the NLF in July 1946 an appeal was made to all major political parties in the country to enter the Constituent Assembly (q.v.), frankly acknowledging and accepting the basic principles of the Cabinet Mission Plan (q.v.). After the June 3rd Plan (q.v.) for partition had been announced, the Council of the NLF, meeting in Poona once more, expressed deep regret that the country's unity had been abandoned. It reiterated the view that the partition then envisaged would go against the country's economic and strategic interests.

Unlike the Congress or the Communists, the NLF had no political organization at the provincial, much less the district level. At best, it held an annual session at which resolutions on important subjects were adopted. The delegates to the sessions were, for all practical purposes, self-chosen. In between the sessions there was no political activity worth notice, as individual members addressed gatherings or issued statements on their own. In fact, the NLF was more a body of like-minded individuals than a political party in the accepted sense of the term. Their well-informed, sober and constructive criticism was useful; so was their role as mediators in disputes between one political group and another. Their leaders played a prominent part in the administration of the country and represented it with distinction at international forums. While the Liberals declined as a party, individual leaders found much wider scope for service. Among some of their distinguished members, the following may be listed: Alladi Krishnaswamy Iyer, M. C. Setalvad, B. N. Rao, Raja Maharaj Singh and A. Ramaswamy Mudaliar.

V. N. Naik, *Indian Liberalism*: *A Study 1918-43* (Silver Jubilee Volume), Bombay, 1945.

Linlithgow (1887–1952)

Victor Alexander John Hope, second Marquess of Linlithgow, was born in 1887 and educated at Eton. Keenly interested in agriculture, he was Chairman of the Committee on the Distribution and Prices of Agricultural Produce and, later (1928), of the Royal Commission on Agriculture in India which conducted a masterly survey of the subject. In 1933-4, he was Chairman of the Joint Select Committee of both houses of the British Parliament on Indian constitutional reforms; its report was to form the basis of the Government of India Act, 1935 (q.v.).

Linlithgow was Viceroy and Governor-General of India from 1936 to 1943; it fell to him, under the 1935 Act, to introduce provincial autonomy, prepare for a scheme of federation and superintend the separation of Burma which had hitherto been an Indian province. He was the first Crown Representative to deal with the Indian States (q.v.) in terms of integrating them with British India. Linlithgow's great effort was to bring in the federal scheme and persuade the princes as well as British India's politicians to troop in.

In the matter of all-India federation, Linlithgow was unable to mould events as he had wished; his hands were tied. Yet his tireless efforts to bring the princes around may be gauged from the fact that during 1937-9 he conducted intensive negotiations, with the rulers and, to meet their objections, revised the earlier version of the Instrument of Accession. Additionally, he had repeatedly and from the outset warned Lord Zetland, then Secretary of State for India, that time was not on his side. This would show, his apologists maintain, how ludicrous was the criticism levelled against him years later that he had dragged his feet. The fact is, that, by September 1939, two-fifth of the states were willing. They had 20 seats out of a total of 52 allocated to all the states and a population of 11 out of 39 millions. Linlithgow himself believed that he would have secured federation by July 1941 had the War not supervened.

It has been pointed out that Linlithgow's efforts in this direction were frustrated not only by the recalcitrance of the princes but also (a) the Indian National Congress (q.v.) which wanted no whittling down of responsibility at the Centre; (b) the All India Muslim League (q.v.) which was opposed to a unified centre; (c) his own Political Department, whose half-hearted efforts could not, or would not, rise to the occasion.

In 1941 there was expansion of the Governor-General's Executive Council from 7 to 15 members; of these, excluding the Governor-General and the Commander-in-Chief, 10 were Indians and 3 Europeans, only two of the latter being officials. There was also enhancement of India's international stature consequent on her representation in the British War Cabinet—at Washington D.C., in Chungking, and on the Middle-East Council, in Cairo. In 1941, a National Defence Council was constituted with British Indian representatives as well as those of the Indian states.

Earlier, all the eight provincial Congress ministries had remained in power till October 1939, when they demited office on the issue of Britain's war and peace aims in the context of India's freedom. This was followed by the Muslim League's celebration of a 'Day of Deliverance' (22 December 1939) to mark, as their spokesmen put it, the emancipation of Muslims 'from the monstrous misrule' of the Congress. The League's Lahore resolution on Pakistan followed (22-24 March 1940), an ominous declaration whose very vagueness heightened its dangerous implications. Both the resolution as well as the later 8 August (1940) Offer (q.v.) of the British Government on some minor political concessions may best be viewed in the context of New Delhi's allegedly overt and covert encouragement of the League.

After the Congress ministries resigned office in the provinces and the party's Ramgarh resolution (which was an unalloyed indictment of Whitehall's unresponsiveness), Linlithgow may be said to have turned his back completely on the party leadership. With the Congress in opposition, the Viceroy had to look to Jinnah (q.v.) and the Muslim League, whose cooperation and support he could not afford to lose. As a natural consequence, this led to the building-up of the Muslim League. By resigning office the Congress, for its part, had shown a lamentable lack of foresight and political wisdom.

By playing one party against the other, Linlithgow succeeded in retaining the initiative in his own hands. He was convinced that, but for the successful prosecution of the War, no diminution of his own authority could be allowed—a fact that would largely explain the failure of the 1942 Cripps Mission (q.v.). In this he had ample support from Prime Minister Churchill and his cabinet.

After World War II had been declared, the Viceroy's supreme concern, according to his detractors, was two-fold: (i) to maximise the war effort, no matter the cost; (ii) to try and keep the country safe for the empire by instigating the internal forces of disruption. Linlithgow's contribution to India's war effort was highlighted by a refusal to be deflected by Gandhi's (q.v.) fast (1943), and by the dispatch of Indian troops to Iran in 1941. His interest in internal administration was largely confined to rural uplift, the problems of the district officer, archaeology, improvement of the imperial capital and publicity.

As for criticism about the Bengal Famine (q.v.) and the Viceroy's failure to visit the province, his apologists maintain that 'Bengal was self-governing and the problem, grave and terrible as it was, was constitutionally a provincial problem. He was not prepared to put Wavell (q.v.) at risk by a visit which might have been seized upon by the politicians as unwonted interference and as proof of the hollowness of self-government granted by the British...He felt the whole tragedy deeply and he brooded over it but he would not change his mind even though his wife herself begged him to go. He may have been wrong. He was certainly tired out.'

Linlithgow, who had the longest tenure of any Governor-General in the twentieth century, laid down office on 20 October 1943. Some comments on his Viceroyalty may bear mention. V. P. Menon, who served under him as Reforms Commissioner, states: 'His 7½ years regime—longer than that of any other Viceroy—was conspicuous by its lack of positive achievement. When he left India, famine stalked portions of the countryside. There was economic distress due to the rising cost of living and the shortage of essential commodities.' Sir Tej Bahadur Sapru (q.v.) commented: 'Today I say after 7 years of Lord Linlithgow's administration, the country is much more divided than it was when he came here.' And Jawaharlal Nehru (q.v.) said: 'Heavy of body and slow of mind, solid as a rock and with almost a rock's lack of awareness, possessing the qualities and feelings of an old-fashioned British aristocrat, he sought with old integrity and honesty of purpose to find a way out of the tangle. But his limitations were too many.'

Linlithgow's son and biographer has stressed his father's long tenure as Viceroy and his courage through even longer years of strain 'such as few have had to bear.' Thus, at 16, he was stricken by polio. He recovered well but a physical lagacy persisted in that the muscles of his neck were permanently weakened so that he was never able to turn his head without turning his shoulders as well. In later life, this was to make him appear rather formidable to a stranger sitting next to him. Glendevon has maintained that his father acknowledged Gandhi's greatness but 'his [Gandhi's] judgement he never ceased—in interests of India—to deplore.' He 'was bound' to hold Gandhi and the Congress 'primarily responsible' for the eventual partition of India which he (Linlithgow) 'regretted so deeply.'

Linlithgow was a keen sportsman, a bird shot of unusual skill and a good golfer. A man of rocklike stability, cool judgement and firm resolution, he was unshaken by adverse fortune.

John Glendevon, *The Viceroy at Bay: Lord Linlithgow in India 1936-43*, London, 1971; V. P. Menon, *Transfer of Power*, pp. 151-2; *DNB 1951-60* pp. 498-500 (Gilbert Laithwaite); Gowher Rizwi, *Linlithgow and India*, London, 1978 and 'Lord Linlithgow and the Reviewers', *South Asia*, new series, I, 1, March 1978, pp. 114–19.

Lucknow Pact (1916)

The Lucknow Pact, which embodied the scheme of constitutional reform unanimously agreed upon by the Indian National Congress (q.v.) and the All India Muslim League (q.v.), was an historic event. It marked the coming together of the two principal political parties in the cause of national unity and a larger national interest.

Those politically active Indian Muslims who swore loyalty to the Raj had been feeling increasingly betrayed. The annulment of the Partition of Bengal (q.v.) was followed by the British empire arraying itself against Turkey in World War I (1914–18). Understandably, the arrests and detention of Muslim leaders who supported the Turkish cause followed. The advent of Gandhi (q.v.) on the Indian scene and the emergence of Jinnah (q.v.) as a leader were conducive to a rapprochement between their respective parties. In 1915 the concurrent Congress-League sessions in Bombay, in which both parties put forth a demand for self-government, marked the beginning of a joint effort to arrive at a compromise on communal questions—separate electorates and weightage for Muslims in provinces where they were a minority. In the sequel, both the Congress and the League appointed committees to work out a common scheme. Motilal Nehru (q.v.) figured prominently in guiding and literally coercing the two committees into arriving at a compromise and framing suitable proposals for reform. The proposed scheme spelt out in the following paragraphs was considered and deliberated upon at a joint meeting in Calcutta in October 1916. (Almost identical proposals were later recommended and embodied in a memorandum drawn up by 19 members of the then Imperial Legislative Council.)

At their respective annual sessions at Lucknow in December 1916 both the Congress and the League declared unreservedly for parliamentary government in India. Additionally, the League resolved to send a deputation to England immediately after the War to present India's political claims in conjunction with the Congress. Specifically, the two agreed upon the modalities of representation of the Muslim community in the provincial legislatures. In the two Muslim-majority provinces of the Panjab and Bengal, it was to be 50% and 40% respectively. Elsewhere the break-up was: 30% in the United Provinces for a population of 14% of the total; 25% in Bihar for a population of 13%; 15% in the Central Provinces as well as Madras for populations of

4% and 7% respectively; and 33 1/3% in Bombay for a population of 20%. The percentages in all cases were of the total elected for Indian members. It was clearly understood that, except electorates representing special interests, no Muslim was to contest in the general constituencies.

Additionally, no bill nor any clause of a bill much less a resolution introduced by a non-Muslim member affecting one or the other community was to be proceeded with if 3/4th of the members of that community in the provincial or Imperial Council opposed the bill, or resolution. Elections based on as broad a franchise as possible would elect members for a term of 5 years. Greater powers were to be delegated to the provinces in the spheres of internal administration viz., collection of revenues, raising loans and incurring expenditure. The executive authority was to be responsible to the legislative council even though the Governor would be allowed to exercise the power of veto. Indian members in the Executive Council were to be increased so as to constitute at least half its total strength; elected by the legislative council, the executive was to hold office for 5 years.

The same pattern was to hold good for government at the centre. The central legislature was to consist of 150 members, 80% of whom would be elected with 1/3rd of the elected members being Muslim. Reservation for the latter was to be in the same proportion in which they were represented in the provincial councils. This was tantamount to giving a weightage to the Muslims from the minority provinces both in provincial councils and the Imperial Legislative Council.

As noted earlier, power to discuss and vote upon the budget as well as other important legislation was vested in the councils. The judiciary was to be independent of the executive authority, the Government of India independent of the Secretary of State in legislative and administrative matters and the India Council in London abolished. Enrolment in the defence services was to be thrown open to all. Defence, foreign and political affairs—war, peace and treaties—were to be outside the purview of the Imperial Legislative Council.

It may be noted that the political atmosphere at Lucknow, where the annual sessions of the Congress and the League convened in December 1916 to endorse the pact, was strikingly cordial. Thus of some 433 Muslim delegates at the Congress sesssion, a bare 30 had come from outside; the rest were local. And of these, a large majority were admitted free of charge to the delegates' seats, to board as well as lodging. According to an eye-witness account, 'some Hindu delegate gets up and calls for three cheers for Muslim delegates and the response is so enthusiastic as to be beyond description.'

At the League session Jinnah was cordiality personified. 'Towards Hindus', he declared 'our attitude should be of good will and brotherly feelings. Co-operation in the cause of the motherland should be our guiding principle.'

It is widely accepted that the Pact was a result of concessions offered by both sides. Jinnah was at his best in composing constitutional differences and offering compromise solutions likely to be accepted by both sides. The Congress, for its part, had conceded separate electorates and was even agreeable to their introduction in the Panjab and the Central Provinces, where these had not existed before. In the Panjab, Muslims got 9/10th of the seats to which they were entitled on a purely numerical basis; in the result, their representation rose from 25% under the Minto-Morley Reforms (q.v.) of 1909 to 50% as a result of the Pact. In Bengal, they were given only 3/4 of the seats to which they were entitled on a population basis. Against these minor losses in the Muslim majority provinces, in the Muslim minority provinces they obtained a representation almost double of what they would have got on a purely numerical basis. Similarly, at the Centre they obtained ⅓ representation in the legislative council from separate Muslim constituencies. For the record, it may be noted that most of these principles as well as other constitutional provisions adumbrated in the Pact were incorporated later in the Montagu-Chelmsford Reforms (q.v.) of 1919.

As a backdrop to the Pact it may be recalled that, after the resignation of the Aga Khan (q.v.) in 1913, the Muslim League under the 'liberal and dynamic' leadership of Jinnah had abandoned its old creed of toadying to the British and accepted self-government for India as its ultimate goal. The change did not come easily, for at its 1915 session in Bombay the President, Mazhar-ul-Haq, 'was described as a man who cannot be called a Mohammedan.' Nor was that all. The anti-Congress Muslim elements in Bombay, led by Seth Sulaiman Kasam Mitha indulged in such hooliganism that the opening session of the League had to be adjourned and could only be convened the following day at the Taj Mahal hotel. Meanwhile, Tilak (q.v.), the responsive co-operator, and Annie Besant (q.v.), the radical politician, had joined hands to rouse the country. In 1916, at Lucknow it so happened that the old Moderates and the Extremists as well as advocates of the Home Rule Movement (q.v.) had come together. Thus, the Pact seemed to follow almost effortlessly in the prevalent political climate in the two parties.

The importance of the Lucknow Pact lies in the fact that it was 'a mutually acceptable solution of the Hindu-Muslim problem' representing a 'political agreement freely entered into between two separate political entities on a footing of equality.' In retrospect, however, it is necessary to point out that it contained within it seeds of the country's future discord and disunity. The Muslims were to become dissatisfied with the fixed and disproportionate percentage of the seats they had earlier accepted. And, by recognizing the separate political identity of the Muslims, the Hindus had, perhaps inadvertently, committed themselves to the idea of a separate state for them.

Syed S. Pirzada, *Foundations of Pakistan*, Vol. 1, 1906-1924, Dacca, 1969, pp. 324-97; Choudhry Khaliquzzaman, *Pathway to Pakistan*, Lahore, 1961, pp. 32-41; Mohammad Noman, *Muslim India*, Allahabad. 1942, pp. 138–69; Jamal-ud-din Ahmad, *Muslim Political Movement: Parliamentary Phase*, Karachi, 1963, pp. 72-80.

Lytton (1831–91)

Statesman and poet, Edward Robert Bulwer, first Earl of Lytton, was born in London in 1831. Prior to his appointment in India, he had served in various diplomatic assignments in Europe and had established a literary reputation which was much enhanced in 1860 by the publication of his poem, 'Lucile.'

In January 1876, a year after declining the governorship of Madras, Lytton received the offer of the Indian Viceroyalty which he accepted at the urgent instance of the then Prime Minister, Lord Beaconsfield (1804–81).

Unacquainted with Indian affairs, but an energetic and ambitious imperialist, he was keen to make his tenure momentous. Sharing the Tory ethos articulated by Salisbury and Disraeli, Lytton sought to perpetuate the worst facets of British rule in India, with disastrous consequences. Thus, his internal policy alienated educated Indians, while his foreign policy resulted in severe British military as well as diplomatic reverses and even his own recall.

Lytton's domestic policy was based on a series of measures intended to ensure continued British ascendancy. He had little faith in the ability of the 'Babus' as he roundly, and somewhat contemptuously, dubbed the new class of educated Indians. To meet their clamour for greater participation in the administration and appointment in the civil service, he created the Statutory Civil Service (q.v.), designed above all to open avenues for employment to the 'natives', although the top posts in the bureaucracy were to be retained by Europeans.

Lytton had great faith in regal pageantry to impress the 'natives', hoping thereby to draw to the British cause the loyalty of aristocratic classes among them. Thus he went ahead with lavish preparations for the Imperial Darbar (q.v.) in 1877, which was to mark the assumption of the title of 'Empress of India' by Queen Victoria. And this despite growing starvation and the existence of virtual famine conditions in large parts of the country, particularly in the south and the west.

Lytton proposed the constitution of an Imperial Privy Council comprising leading Indian princes as an exclusive consultative body. He worked on the premise that the princes would respond with avowed loyalty for the honour thus conferred on them, while the rest of the populace, in awe of royalty, would rally around. His proposal, however, was summarily turned down by the Secretary of State's India Council.

A popular outcry against the Imperial Darbar had put Lytton on guard. To stave off any further criticism, he enacted the Vernacular Press Act (q.v.) which put curbs on seditious writings. His Indian Arms Act (q.v.) was designed, critics averred, to disarm Indians in the interest of maintaining law and order. Another instance of his discriminatory policy was the abolition of duties on the import of coarse cotton goods and, subsequently, a reduction of imports on all cotton manufactures. Characteristically, the Governor-General failed to see a growing sense of nationalism among the people: in fact, these very measures encouraged Indian political associations, which now gained in popularity. Though at heart a liberal, Lytton came to be rated the 'most reactionary' of Governors-General.

In the realm of foreign policy, he viewed the Afghan problem as part of a larger threat from Russia and saw his role as one of establishing British political ascendancy in Afghanistan. Confident of the home government's support in whatever manner he chose to tackle the situation, he felt free to override his Executive Council in their policy of patience and moderation. A Russophobe, Lytton viewed every advance of the Tsarist regime in Central Asia as an attempt to push the frontiers of their empire which, through control over Afghanistan, would presently knock at the doors of Britain's Indian dominion. To counter these designs, he aimed at making Afghanistan subservient by insisting upon the appointment of British officers as residents on the Central Asian frontiers of the country. The Amir's refusal to fall into line he attributed to the latter's lack of enthusiasm for the British, or worse, Russian instigation. Much to the discomfiture of his political superiors in London, Lytton concluded that he was left with only two alternatives—a war with Russia, or forcible division of Afghanistan into semi-independent principalities under a vague British tutelage which would give India the scientific frontier it had long sought. The home government, alarmed by his aggressive intent, advised him to restrict his activities to diplomatic overtures to win over the Amir.

It was too late. By March 1878, acting with hasty arrogance, Lytton broke off all relations with the Amir. With the reception accorded to the Russian mission in August, all restraint placed on the Indian potentate crumbled to dust and he hastily dispatched a British mission under Neville (later Col. Sir Neville) Fitzgerald Chamberlain to Kabul. On the permission being refused, he served an ultimatum on the Amir. Despite the British cabinet's advice to use caution, Lytton was precipitate, sought and received the Secretary of State, Cranbrook's, approval to launch military operations. British troops entered Afghanistan on 21 November 1878 and the Second Afghan War (q.v.) had begun. Soon the British were in full control of the country.

The brilliance of the initial military operations during Lytton's tenure was somewhat overcast by the discovery that the expenditure was greatly in excess of estimates. Yet the Treaty of Gandamak (q.v.) briefly demonstrated the apparent success of his policy.

Peace none the less was short-lived. With the cold-blooded assassination of the British commander, Sir Pierre Louis Nepoleon Cavagnari in September 1879, the state of belligerency returned. Before Lytton could install a British protege at Kabul and negotiate the sale of Herat to Persia, he was recalled, largely because of his repudiation by the new Whig government of William Ewart Gladstone (1809-98). The 'true inner history' of Lytton's tenure in India, 'greatly criticized yet little understood', has been ably presented by his daughter, Lady Betty Balfour.

Back in England, Lytton defended his policy in Parliament. Later, he was to devote himself increasingly to literary pursuits. In 1887 he was appointed Ambassador to France, where he died four years later (November 1891).

Lytton's position among public men of his day was unique. It recalled the life of an Elizabethan noble—a scholar, a diplomatist, a magistrate, a courtier, a man of letters, all rolled into one. Few have touched life at so many points as he did, have enjoyed such variety of experience or so profoundly fascinated their intimates.

Lady Betty Balfour, *The History of Lord Lytton's Indian Administration, 1876 to 1880:* compiled from his letters and official papers, London, 1899; *DNB*, XII, pp. 387-92 (Richard Garnett).

Thomas Babington Macaulay (1800–59)

A well-known English historian, jurist, man of letters, Macaulay happily combined literary activity with politics all through his life. He gave up a career in law to be a member of the House of Commons and yet spent his leisure hours in writing articles for popular journals and magazines. As a commissioner for the John Company's (q.v.) Board of Control he developed a deep interest in acquiring an extensive knowledge of Indian affairs; later, as the Board's Secretary, he ensured renewal of its charter by the Charter Act (q.v.) of 1833. That year he also accepted an appointment as Law Member in the Governor-General's Executive Council in India.

Macaulay took up this work in June 1834. A self-imposed 'exile', as he later called this period, his main object was to put by enough money for a comfortable retirement in England. In the result, he made no effort to learn the Indian languages, much less study the Indian classics. Nevertheless, he was able to squeeze into his less than 4-year term a phenomenal amount of work.

By the time Macaulay arrived in India, the stage had been set for the enactment of an educational policy (for India) in the face of diametrically opposed views on the subject held by the so-called 'orientalists' and 'anglicists'. Charles Trevelyan's brilliant espousal of the latter school was taken up by Macaulay, now president of the committee of public instruction, and supported by a number of eminent Indians. Convinced of the superiority of European civilization, he felt it his bounden duty to make Indians imbibe European values. This would be possible, Macaulay argued, through a western-oriented system of education. Having received the approval of the then Governor-General, Bentinck (q.v.), he penned his famous Minute on Education (q.v.) in 1835, giving form and content to the foundation of English education in India. He foresaw and indeed welcomed the day when Indians, educated under the new system, would demand representative institutions; for the time being, however, he was convinced that the British must rule by the sword.

Appointed president of the Indian Law Commission to inquire into the administration of justice and the operation of all the laws, Macaulay proposed a system that would take into account the differences of religion, caste and creed and ensure a 'single standard of justice' for all parts of India. The deliberations of the Commission led to the formulation of the Indian Penal Code, the Codes of Civil and Criminal Procedure and other codes of substantive and adjectival laws. The emergence of a unified system of laws, a uniform judicial procedure and a uniform judicature, to all of which Macaulay's contribution was immense, gave a powerful stimulus to the growth of unity in the country. Macaulay had worked almost single-handed on the Codes for two years to complete his work by the end of 1837; however, these were to become law much later, in 1860. His proposal for prison reform—to go alongside the codification of laws—was rejected by the Court of Directors in England.

The home government, the European community and the press deprecated the support Macaulay gave to the so-called 'Black Act' (Act XI of 1836), by which appeals from British residents in India were transferred from the Supreme to the Sadar Court. It destroyed a privilege the Europeans had enjoyed hitherto. Macaulay also argued vigorously, and successfully, against the maintenance of the old system of press censorship. He advocated selection of candidates for the administrative service through competitive examinations and ensured the inclusion of a clause to that effect in the Charter Act (q.v.) of 1853.

After his return to England early in 1838, Macaulay was engaged in writing his five monumental volumes on the history of England; the first two appeared in 1848, the next two in 1855 and the last, posthumously, in 1861. He was also involved in active politics, although over the years he came to devote more time and attention to literary pursuits. None of these: his parliamentary career, his *History* or his literary output had any special connection with India or active politics. He refused a professorship of modern history as well as an offer to join Lord Russell's Cabinet in 1852, even though continuing intermittently to be a member of the House of Commons. Two years before his death, he was created Baron Macaulay of Rothley.

Macaulay was, in the final analysis, not a professor but a journalist of very high order, writing for an educated, but *not* a learned, audience.   He was a loyal Whig and, as a member of that party, his principal endeavour was to encourage it further accentuate the new forces released by the French and Industrial Revolutions, to contain democracy on the one hand and blind Toryism on the other; that is to say, to steer a middle course. In this light, Macaulay may appear to be a propagandist for the governing classes, one who helped supply the ideological and historical dimensions for a holding operation on their behalf.

It has often been maintained that Macaulay 'reflected' Victorian attitudes. It would be truer to say, his biographer suggests, that he helped to mould them. Not because he was an original thinker, but because the amalgam he popularized in his essays met the needs of a middle class, either educated or in need of education, which liked to see its own position glamorized. Macaulay helped to fulfil that wish.

Sir G. O. Trevelyan, *The Life and Letters of Lord Macaulay,* enlarged and complete ed., London, 1909; John Clive, *Thomas Babington Macaulay: the shaping of the Historian,* London, 1973; G. M. Young (ed.), *Speeches of Lord Macaulay with his minute on Indian Education,* Oxford, 1935; *DNB,* XII, pp. 410-18 (Leslie Stephen).

James Ramsay MacDonald (1866–1937)

James Ramsay MacDonald was a great Labour leader and statesman who, with Edwin Samuel Montagu (1879-1924), made a signal contribution to the cause of Indian independence. Born at Lossiemouth, in the Scottish highlands, MacDonald had little formal schooling and was largely self-educated. As a young man, he joined the Fabians and the Independent Labour Party. His marriage (1895) brought him not only financial independence but a companion who possessed a genius for friendship. In 1896 he was elected a member of the national administrative council of the Independent Labour Party, where he was viewed as remarkably cautious; from 1894 to 1900 he served on the executive of the Fabian Society which considered him a dangerous intransigent! With Keir Hardie (1856-1915), MacDonald drafted the resolution by which, in 1899, the British Trade Union Congress convened a special convention to devise plans for returning more Labour members to Parliament.

Arthur James Balfour (1848-1930) called him 'a born parliamentarian' and it has been suggested that, but for his influence during the seminal phase, the Labour party between the two World Wars might have preferred revolution to evolution. The party did not approve of the declaration of World War I nor of Britain joining it, but the War having been declared, it wanted England to win. It was also strongly opposed to a harsh, military peace with Germany.

Labour welcomed Kerensky's revolution (March 1917) in Russia and wanted to send a friendly mission to Petrograd. This, however, was not possible because the crew of the boat that was to carry MacDonald would not accept him on board! During the war years he was a 'most unpopular and mistrusted man' in Britain. However, after MacDonald succeeded in persuading the annual conferences of the ILP and the Labour Party to reject communism in 1920, the extremists seceded from the movement, which fact restored MacDonald's reputation with the general public.

In the 1923 general elections, Labour won 191 seats and, with Liberal support, ousted the Conservatives from power. The first Labour government in Britain was formed in 1924 with MacDonald combining the offices of Prime Minister and Foreign Secretary. This not only proved very strenuous personally but led to a great neglect of domestic affairs. His premiership enhanced his reputation and that of his government, for over such matters as parliamentary tradition, public ceremonial and relations between the Cabinet and the Crown he made no breach with established practice. In the 1924 elections, the Zinoviev letter (which was later proved a fake) undid MacDonald and his party. In 1928, however, Labour with 267 seats was again the largest single party and with the tacit support of the Liberals, MacDonald formed his second government.

The economic crisis of 1929 led to the formation of the 'National' government under his leadership. At first he viewed the coalition as no more than a temporary expedient for overcoming the great Depression and the resultant financial cirsis, but its continuance led to a good deal of controversy and even bitterness with his former colleagues and followers. Critics charged MacDonald with having plotted to bring about the fall of his own government.

In the October 1931 elections, Labour with 59 seats in Parliament, was in shambles. MacDonald as head of the 'National' government formed his fourth, a predominantly Conservative, administration. His breach with his own party was now complete. The White Paper on national defence (March 1935), which advocated re-armament, clearly bears his imprint. But his powers were impaired by continuous over-strain and the remorseless vendetta waged against him by some of his former colleagues. He resigned office in June 1935. MacDonald died on 9 November 1937, while on a holiday voyage to South America.

The Labour leader's association with India may be traced back to 1915 when he was appointed, along with Gokhale (q.v.), a member of the Royal

Commission on the Public Services. His 1924 administration lasted a bare 10 months, yet in the course of it he declared: 'Dominion Status (q.v.) for India is the idea and the ideal of the Labour government'. The 1925 resolution of the Labour Party's annual conference on India affirmed that it recognized the 'right of the Indian people to full self-determination'.

With George Lansbury (1859-1940), the veteran Labour leader piloting it, the Commonwealth of India Bill, a brain-child of Mrs Annie Besant (q.v.), got its first reading in the House of Commons in 1926. Mrs Besant had striven hard to persuade MacDonald that it become an official Labour Party measure, but he was unwilling to commit the Party to all its provisions.

At the 1928 Commonwealth Labour Conference, MacDonald had said, 'I hope that within a period of months rather than years, there would be a new Dominion added to the Commonwealth of our nations, a Dominion of another race, a Dominion that will find self-respect as an equal within the British Commonwealth. I refer to India.' When it took office, the first step of the second Labour government, was to invite the then Governor-General, Irwin (q.v.), for consultations.

MacDonald was in favour of the Round Table Conference (q.v.) and, before it was convened, had authorized the Viceroy to declare that it was implicit in the Declaration of August 1917 (q.v.) that the natural issue of India's constitutional progress as contemplated there was the attainment of Dominion Status.'

Later, the British Prime Minister told the Round Table Conference delegates: 'In such statutory safeguards as may be made for meeting the needs of the transitional period, it will be a primary concern of HMG to see that the reserve powers are so framed and exercised as not to prejudice the advance of India through the new Constitution to full responsibility for her own government.

'Finally, I hope and trust and I pray that by our labours together, India will come to possess the only thing which she now lacks to give her status of a Dominion amongst the British Commonwealth of Nations—the responsibilities and the cares, the burdens and the difficulties, but the pride and the honour of responsible government.'

The Gandhi-Irwin Pact (q.v.), which enabled the Indian National Congress (q.v.) to attend the second session of the Round Table Conference owed a lot to MacDonald. Thanks however to the political compulsions in Britain and a complete repudiation by his own party, MacDonald, who had played a prominent part in the first two sessions of the Conference, was conspicuously in the background and did not address the third session even once. It must have been humiliating to him, isolated as he was from his former colleagues, to watch the Tories translate the decisions of the Round Table Conference into legislative proposals, whittling down in the process much that he had advocated and stood for. The safeguards, 'in the mutual interests of India and Britain' (words used in the Gandhi-Irwin Pact), had finally emerged, in Arthur Neville Chamberlain's (1869-1940) apt description, as 'all that the wit of man could devise' for the purpose of safeguarding Britain's financial and economic interests. However, it is a tribute to MacDonald's great vision and courage that he chalked out a course which, with all its turns and twists, led India finally to her freedom.

Much has been written about 'this strange man and his strange career'. He has been violently attacked or strongly praised according to the point of view of the individual critic. Some regard him as a double-dyed traitor who destroyed his own child in 1931; others, as a man of high patriotic motives who consciously took a decision which he knew would blacken his reputation but which he believed to be in the national interest. His critics have maintained that MacDonald had 'a natural sympathy' for the Conservatives, especially its Tory and aristocratic elements. It was the 'aristocratic embrace' which, as Lord Passfield said, ultimately destroyed him.

Partisanship apart, MacDonald's career was remarkable. He created a great party; brought it into office for the first time in Britain's history, and repeated this feat five years later. Although by his decision in 1931 he seemed to destroy his own creation and doom the Labour movement to a long spell in the political wilderness, he acted honourably and in accordance with what he deemed to be his duty.

Harold Macmillan, *The Past Masters: Politics and Politicians, 1906-39,* Macmillan, 1975, pp. 79-95; B. Shiva Rao, *India's Freedom Movement: Some Notable Figures,* Bombay, 1972, pp. 98-106; *DNB 1931-1940,* pp. 562-70 (Godfrey Elton, Baron).

William Hay Macnaghten (1793–1841)

Macnaghten was the son of a former Supreme Court judge at Calcutta and joined the John Company's (q.v.) service at Madras 1809. A brilliant linguist, he served in the army till 1814, in which year he was posted to the Bengal civil service. Subsequent to his training at Fort William College, he was appointed assistant registrar and later (1816–22) registrar in the Sadar Adalat, where he perfected his knowledge of Hindu and Mohmmadan law.

Macnaghten's political career began towards the close of 1830, when he accompanied Bentinck (q.v.) as secretary during the latter's tour (1830–3) in the upper and western provinces. *Inter alia,* it provided him a first-hand acquaintance with Ranjit Singh (q.v.), the Sikh ruler. On returning to Calcutta, he took charge of the Secret and Political Department and held that sensitive and vital post for the next 4 years.

In October 1837 Macnaghten accompanied Auckland (q.v.) on his tour of the north-western provinces and soon became one of the Governor-General's most trusted advisers. In this capacity he was to play a pivotal role in the formulation of Afghan policy. Initially, under the Tripartite Treaty (q.v.), which he had helped to negotiate, the British role was limited to providing European officers to discipline and command the Shah's army but, before long, its scope expanded and ended in a British armed expedition to Kabul to place Shah Shuja, a virtual puppet, on the Afghan throne. Macnaghten was completely identified with this policy in all its varied ramifications. He assisted in the preparation of Auckland's manifesto of 1 October 1838, which was later to earn such notoriety.

Macnaghten had the unhappy faculty of believing what he wished to be true and failed to notice the signs of unrest and rebellion in Kabul that surrounded the British army of occupation. Created a baronet and appointed Governor of Bombay in recognition of his services, he was preparing to leave Kabul in November 1841 when the storm burst. Alexander Burnes (q.v.) was murdered and Macnaghten himself compelled to negotiate with Dost Mohammad's (q.v.) son, Akbar Khan. He agreed *inter alia* to the withdrawal of British troops from Afghanistan, the release of Dost Mohammad, and the deposition of Shah Shuja. Later, Macnaghten was tricked into another conference with the Afghan chiefs and treacherously murdered on 23 December 1841.

Macnaghten's role in the negotiations with Akbar Khan, has been criticized, as also in the formulation of policy leading to the Afghan war. All this notwithstanding, there is no gainsaying his high personal character, courage, and outstanding attainments. The historian Kaye noted that Macnaghten combined 'a profound knowledge' of oriental languages and cultures with 'an extensive acquaintance' with all the practical details of government. Thus, he made an admirable secretary, unwearying and facile, a fluent writer of dispatches and an assiduous official. At the same time, he was a little too impulsive, too optimistic and self-confident. Towards the end, while up against heavy odds, he was yet courageous and steadfast. It must also be conceded that the task which was set him, that of governing the Afghan people without direct authority over them and of preserving the seeming independence of Shah Shuja while leaving him only a power for mischief, was in itself a hopeless one. The Afghan army was unreliable; Shah Shuja showed no signs of becoming either a capable or a popular ruler, while the financial burden of the Afghan operations became increasingly unbearable. The English were the only real authority in Afghanistan but they retained their hold by force; they were saddled with conspicuously inefficient (English) commanders and, besides, distributed money among the Afghan chiefs in order to retain even their fleeting support.

DNB, XII, pp. 683–87 (John Andrew Hamilton); Dodwell, *CHI*, V, pp. 494–97, 500–9.

Arthur Henry McMahon (1862–1949)

McMahon was born in 1862, educated at Haileybury College (q.v.) and later won the sword of honour at the Royal Military College, Sandhurst. In 1887 he was posted to the Panjab Frontier Force; 3 years later, transferred to the Political Department, where he achieved great success in various diplomatic missions to which he was assigned.

McMahon was political agent in Zhob (1890-8), accompanied the successful mission of Mortimer Durand (q.v.) to Afghanistan and later helped demarcate the frontier (1894–6) between that country and Baluchistan. Subsequently, he was political agent in Dir, Swat and Chitral (1899-1901). Between 1903-5, as British Commissioner on the Seistan Mission (q.v.), McMahon accomplished the task of arbitration in Seistan on the boundary dispute between Persia and Afghanistan, begun earlier (1870–2) by Sir Frederic Goldsmid (1818–1908). During these negotiations McMahon struck a lifelong friendship with Amir Habibullah (q.v.) of Afghanistan which, extending to the Amir's two successors, helped to stabilize a difficult relationship between Delhi and Kabul.

In later years, McMahon always recalled with a certain nostalgic pride how the Bugti chief of Baluchistan provided him a personal bodyguard throughout the years (1903–5) he spent in open camp while demarcating the Persian frontier. In 1905–11 McMahon was appointed Chief Commissioner and Governor-General's Agent in Baluchistan, being transferred, in 1911, to the Foreign Department as Secretary to the Government of India. From October 1913 to July 1914 he was British plenipotentiary as well as Chairman of the Simla Conference to determine, *inter alia,* Tibet's political status and her boundaries. A firm believer in buffer states, McMahon attempted during the negotiations to establish a British representative at Lhasa who would serve as a check on Chinese attempts to suborn Tibet as well as a counterpoise to Russian intrigue. The home government, however, were strongly opposed at the time to any British presence in Lhasa and the idea had therefore to be abandoned. The Tibetan boundary line was delineated and after him called the McMahon Line. It was designed to ensure the security of the Assam Himalaya and confirm India's sovereignty over the tribal belt in this region.

McMahon was the last Foreign Secretary in India to hold the combined Foreign and Political Departments under his charge. From 1914–16 he was Britain's first High Commissioner in Egypt, where a contemporary observer described him as 'slight, fair, very young for 52, quiet, friendly, agreeable, considerate and cautious'. With courage, determination and patience he conducted negotiations with the Arabs, but at the end of 1916 was abruptly recalled. His agreement with Amir Husain Ibn Ali, later king of Hejaz, was to become the subject of considerable controversy. At the Peace Conference in Paris (1919) he served as the British Commissioner on the Middle Eastern International Commission.

A keen freemason, McMahon founded a chapter in 1908 at Quetta, and enrolled Amir Habibullah as a member when the latter visited India. In addition to founding several lodges in this country, on his return to England he rose to be grand senior warden of the Grand Lodge of England, grand commander of the Temple and sovereign great commander of the Supreme Council 33 degree. After his retirement from official life, McMahon was also active in various other societies, being President of the National Council of Y.M.C.A., a member of the Royal Society of Arts, the Society of Antiquaries and the Zoological Society. He was fellow of the Royal Geographical and Geological Societies, and Chairman of the Fellowship of the British Empire. Highly decorated, he had received the C.I.E. (1894), C.S.I. (1897), K.C.I.E. (1906), G.C.V.O. (1911) and G.C.M.G. (1919).

Sir Ronald Storrs, *Orientations,* London, 1943; E. H. Cobb, 'A Frontier Statesman', *The Piffer,* London, V, 6, May 1963; *DNB 1941-1950,* pp. 563-4 (Henry Holland).

Treaty of Madras (1769)

Having suffered several reverses at the hands of British forces, Haidar Ali (q.v.) opened negotiations for peace. When these were spurned he was driven to fight and marched towards Madras on 27 March 1769 at the head of a body of cavalry. Four days later, English troops converging on him were ordered to halt, the Mysore ruler dictating terms of peace which signalled the end of the First Anglo-Mysore War (q.v.).

The treaty signed on 3 April 1769 between the John Company (q.v.), the Raja of Tanjore, the Malabar ruler, Ram Raja and Morari Rao, 'who are friends and allies to the Carnatic Payen Ghat', on the one hand, and Haidar Ali on the other, comprised 5 articles. It provided *inter alia,* that (i) a mutual restitution of conquests take place except for Karur and its districts, which were to be retained by the Mysore ruler; (ii) in case either of the parties was attacked, the other would rally to its assistance. The salary of the troops who thus assisted was fixed; (iii) all the 'officers, Europeans and sepoys' belonging to the Presidency of Madras and the 'Sirkars and people belonging to the Carnatic Payen Ghat' were to be released; (iv) the Raja of Tanjore was to be treated as a friend and ally of Haidar Ali; (v) the trade privileges of Bombay Presidency and other English factories were to be restored.

Aitchison, V, pp. 276–7; N. K. Sinha, *Haidar Ali,* 3rd ed., Calcutta, 1959.

Mahalwari Settlement

The question of introducing a settlement of land revenue in the 'Ceded and Conquered Provinces' came to the fore in the opening years of the nineteenth century. The 'provinces' included territory *ceded* by the Nawab of Oudh (q.v.) and his tributary, the Nawab of Fyzabad, in 1801-2 and *conquered* by the British in 1803 as a result of Lord Lake's victories over the Marathas. As of 1818, they comprised the following districts: Meerut, Saharanpur, Bulandshahr, Aligarh, Bijnor, Moradabad, Budaun, Bareilly, Shahjahanpur, Farrukhabad, Etwah, Etah, Mainpuri, Allahabad, Kanpur, Lalitpur, Banda, Hamirpur, Azamgarh, Gorakhpur, Basti. To start with, they formed a part of the Government of Bengal, which in 1803 and again in 1805 proposed to introduce here the Permanent Settlement (q.v.) of Cornwallis (q.v.) with which it was so familiar. However, both the Court of Directors and the Board of Commissioners (appointed in 1807) demurred. In the result, for some time a system of periodical or short-term settlements continued. These were based 'on no very definite principles' except to suggest that the state was entitled to the entire net assessment of land. The task of revenue collection, resting on the 'excessive exactions of the displaced Indian rulers', was awarded at the highest bid made by a revenue farmer. Understandably, in the first ten years of British rule in these territories revenue receipts went up—over what the Nawab had realised—by 19 per cent! It was an oppressive settlement.

It is interesting that as late as 16 September 1820 the Governor-General, Hastings (q.v.), and members of his Council still harked back to Cornwallis in their revenue letter to the Directors: 'It is then our unanimous opinion that the system of a Permanent Settlement of the land revenue, either upon the principles of a fixed *jumma* or by assessment determinable by a fixed and invariable rate ought to be extended to the Ceded and Conquered Provinces.'

The Court in London however turned down the recommendation unceremoniously. Earlier, on the basis of a recommendation of the Board of Commissioners, Holt Mackenzie had drafted his minute of 1 July 1819 in which, *inter alia,* he revealed the existence of village communities and recommended a settlement with them wherever they existed, after a systematic survey and inquiry. While undertaking the operations, a record of the rights was to be prepared—village communities being represented by headmen called 'lambardars' (viz., persons having a 'number' in the Collector's register of persons liable to pay land revenue to the state). The objective was that the rates of assessment should be equalized rather than enhanced and that revenue payees should have their rights recorded such as they were.

With all ideas of the Bengal system finally abandoned in 1821, Mackenzie's minute became the basis for a new settlement. In essence, his plea was that revenue be fixed at a moderate rate and the settlement made with the landlords (viz., 'zamindars') or peasant proprietors where they existed and with the village communities where they held land in common tenancy. Landlords or talukdars who claimed rights in the land were generally granted compensation from the government treasury, the sum being later collected from the village zamindars. As the revenue settlement was to be made village by village and estate by estate and as an estate is called a 'mahal', it came to be known as the Mahalwari Settlement. The basis of the settlement was 'net produce', that portion of the gross produce of land which remained after deducting the expenses of cultivation, including the profits of stock and wages of labour (i.e., expenditure on labour and capital by the cultivators).

Mackenzie's minute, which formed the basis for Regulation VII of 1822 recommended a cadastral survey of land; the settlement officer was to compute the actual produce per *bigha* of land and the cost of its cultivation. The gross income of the cultivator was worked out on the basis of the average price over several preceding years and the revenue was assessed after deducting the expenses of cultivation. The state demand was fixed at 85 per cent of gross rental. Revenue officers were further empowered to grant leases to cultivators, specifying the rents payable by them. In cases where estates were held in common tenancy, it was ruled that the state demand might be raised to 95 per cent of the rental, the Collector making a fresh partition of the land of the village and determining the proportion of the state demand payable by each cultivator.

It may be noted that, in sharp contrast to British practice, indigenous Indian rights in land were complicated and lacked any precise legal definition. The primary aim of the investigation of rights, therefore, was to determine the persons—whether individuals or quasi-corporate bodies—who were entitled to the profits of landholding and who would therefore be responsible for the payment of land revenue, or with whom, in technical terms, a settlement could be made. It was by no means an easy task because of the 'vague nature of the existing rights and the obliterations which they had suffered in the recent political chaos as well as from the mischievous methods of revenue administration, inherited from Bengal which characterised the first twenty years of British rule in the United Provinces'.

In actual practice, the exercise proved to be impossible: rents paid in cash were rare, so that rental calculations depended largely upon estimates of the value of grain produce and of the cost of cultivation, a process carried out holding by holding. Romesh Chunder Dutt (q.v.), a keen student of Indian economic history, concluded that the Regulation of 1822 'prescribed no equitable standard of rents payable by cultivators except the judgement of the Revenue Collector. It prescribed no equitable margin of profits except a bare 17% of the rental . . . it swept away virtually the whole of the rental of the community leaving landlords and cultivators equally impoverished. It made any accumulation of wealth and any improvement in the material conditions of the people impossible; and it fixed no limits to the state demand in future and recurring settlements after the brief period of the first settlement was over.'

It has been maintained that, despite all the talk of 'remedying over-assessment', the 1822 settlement was never intended to reduce the total assessment. In practice, excessive assessment in certain villages was distributed over others deemed to be under-assessed. In sum, the 1822 settlement proved a failure: inquiries needed for a system of record of rights made no progress; detailed investigations relating to produce of individual fields 'proved vexatious and futile'; state demand computed at 80 per cent and above was both 'severe and impracticable'.

After his 1831 tour of northern India, Bentinck (q.v.) felt there was need for long leases to give landlords and tenants a motivation for improvement, and for a *moderate* demand that would leave with them some part of the profits from the soil. Above all, there was need for preserving village communities which, as Charles Metcalfe (q.v.) noted in his minute of 1830, were 'little Republics having nearly everything that they want within themselves and almost independent of any foreign relations. They seem to last where nothing else lasts . . . I wish therefore that the village communities may never be disturbed.'

In 1833, in consultation with his Council, members of the Board of Revenue and the Court of Directors, Bentinck convened a conference at Allahabad. The upshot was Regulation IX of 1833 which is said to constitute 'the true basis' of the land settlement of northern India. In sum, it meant the transfer of judicial cases from the court of Settlement Officers, a simplifying of the estimates of produce and rent and a system of average rents for different classes of soil. The general use of the field register and the field map was prescribed. More, government demand was reduced to two-thirds of the gross rental and the settlement which took 16 years, 1833-49, to complete, was made for a period of 30 years.

1833 also witnessed a simplified system of land assessment which was to be further elaborated by two remarkable individuals, R. M. Bird and James Thomason. The standard demand was reduced to two-third of the net rental and a less theoretical method of assessment, known as 'aggregate to detail', was devised. Land revenue was fixed with 'reference to general considerations affecting the tract under settlement, such as agricultural and economic resources, past fiscal history and the level of money rents paid by tenants, or those estimated to be fairly payable, wherever such rents had come into common use.'

The direction of this vast operation carried out for every village on the basis of a prior scientific, topographical survey executed by professional officers fell principally on Robert Merttins Bird who is rightly known as 'the father of land settlement in northern India'. Originally a judicial officer, he emerged as a great revenue administrator. In 1842, Bird noted that there was 'on the whole . . . just reason to consider that a moderate, fair and equal demand on the land such as can and ought to be collected without interfering with the accumulation of property and the march of agricultural prosperity, has, generally speaking, been fixed.'

While appearing before the Select Committee of the House of Commons ten years later Bird lucidly explained how he went about it: 'I first of all proceeded to make a survey of all the land . . . The next process was to make a map, including every field . . . Then . . . professional survey of the boundary made by an educated officer, that shows the cultivated and the uncultivated land, and the real shape of the village is taken by a regular survey . . . . We then proceeded to investigate the assessment of the Government land tax upon that tract . . . As soon as that was ascertained . . . . we fixed the amount of the Government tax we should require upon the whole of that tract, and then we proceeded to set down the amount that we should require upon each village . . . . (Complaints made by the villagers were then investigated) . . . The assessment upon the whole tract was not strictly maintained; it was not our object to do so.' Asked what was the proportion of Government revenue to the produce of the soil: 'My general impression is that it was not above a tenth of the produce.'

While by no means oblivious of the contribution made by European settlement officers, a recent writer has pointed out that the part played by the great body of Indian personnel 'has been under-rated'. Here it is necessary to underline that the British came upon a run-down, broken, administration and that their most outstanding achievement was its reconstruction. This was made possible by a large number of experts, skilled in revenue business, which the indigenous Indian administration bequeathed to its successor. The greatest name among them was that of Chhatar Mal of Agra whose work *Diwan Pasand* came to be used 'as a practical guide' in all revenue matters. Not only was its author handsomely rewarded but the work itself was translated (*c.* 1824) into English.

Bird's successor on the land revenue front was James Thomason, who was Lieutenant-Governor of the North-Western Provinces from 1843 to 1853. His *Directions for Settlement Officers* drawn up in 1844, are said to constitute the first complete code of land settlement compiled in India. Coupled with his *Directions for Revenue Officers* published five years later, they continued to be looked upon for many years as the standard reference for official purposes of all that related to revenue. The underlying principles of the land settlement of northern India, the Mahalwari, are enunciated in a preface to these *Directions*. In brief, these were:

i. All the inhabited parts of the country were to be divided into portions with fixed boundaries called 'mahals'; on each mahal was assessed a sum for a term of 20 or 30 years. It was so calculated as to leave a fair surplus over and above the net produce of the land and for the punctual payment of that sum the land was held to be perpetually hypothecated to the government.

ii. It was determined who were entitled to receive this surplus profit. The right thus determined was declared to be heritable and transferable and the persons entitled to it were considered to be proprietors of the land, from whom the engagements for the annual payment of sum assessed by the government on the mahal were taken.

iii. All the proprietors of the 'mahal' were, severally and jointly, responsible in their persons and property for the payment of the sum assessed by the government on the mahal.

As has been noticed, under Bentinck the land revenue assessment had been fixed at two thirds of the rental, but under Dalhousie (q.v.), and the famous Saharanpur Rules of 1855, it was limited to half the rental. The latter was soon to have an all-India applicability: in Madras and Bombay, by Sir Charles Wood's (q.v.) despatch of 1864; in Northern India, by the Saharanpur Rules of 1855. Interestingly enough land reforms in northern India were effected once every eleven years between 1822 and 1855.

A few broad observations on the revenue settlement in the North-Western Provinces may be in order. To start with, while 'over-assessment' has been rated a 'characteristic feature' of British administration, the term itself defies definition. There is little doubt that in the imposition of high assessment, there is the distinct influence of the Ricardian theory of rent which, while supporting the appropriation of the net produce as revenue, yet cautioned that the limit should not be overstepped. It is also worth notice that, while the Ricardian thesis may have influenced persons who framed policy, it had relatively little effect on the pitch of the demand, or on its actual value which was determined primarily by objective economic factors.

In other words, the new land revenue settlement was aimed at the abandonment of the earlier reckless and ignorant methods of assessment, in favour of a more scientific criterion for relating the demand to the cultivators' capacity to pay. None the less the 'minimum level of demand was determined by the government's financial requirements which were dictated by the Company's liabilities in England and by its expenses in India.'

It may also be noted that in the post-1833 period of economic depression and fall in prices of agricultural produce, there was large-scale export of bullion and silver. In as much as land revenue was the principal source of exported treasure, Asiya Siddiqi has pointed out that it served as the medium whereby, in these years of commercial imbalance, the Indian agricultural producer 'was made to shoulder the main burden of the (John) Company's (q.v.) payments to England'.

Wiser by its experience in Bengal, British administration in the North-Western Provinces was keen to define as well as protect the interests of tenants. In so far as a practical classification was difficult, it was decided to evolve a working rule that a tenant on proving twelve years' continuous occupation of his holding was admitted to a permanent and heritable tenure at a judicially fixed rent. The rule was later embodied as Act X of 1859—the earliest Indian legislation which defined and protected tenant right' in Bengal as well as the North-Western Provinces. The first regular settlement in the latter area was effected in 1833-42, barring the Banaras districts where the Permanent Settlement had already been introduced. Cadastral surveys were carried out here in 1877 and record of rights prepared.

Apart from the North-Western Provinces and Oudh, the mahalwari system was prevalent, with some local modifications, in Ajmer-Marwara, the Central Provinces and the Panjab.

B. H. Baden-Powell, *The Land Systems of British India,* 3 vols, II ('The System of Village or Mahal Settlements'), Oxford, 1892; Asiya Siddiqi, *Agrarian Change in a Northern Indian State: Uttar Pradesh 1819–1833,* Oxford, 1973; Romesh Chunder Dutt, *The Economic History of India,* 2 vols, 3rd reprint, New Delhi, 1976, I; Dodwell, *CHI,* VI.

Madan Mohan Malaviya (1861–1946)

A leading nationalist and patriot, Madan Mohan Malaviya belonged to an orthodox and devout Hindu family of Allahabad that originally hailed from Malwa. Under the influence of his father and grandfather, both learned Sanskrit scholars, his education in that language began early at home and at his first school, Pandit Hardev's Dharma Gyanopadesh Pathshala. He moved on to a zilla school where he acquired a good working knowledge of English. After school, he graduated from Calcutta University in 1884. Subsequently, financial limitations compelled him to abandon his plan to take a Master's Degree and he sought employment as a school teacher. Later, however, he was persuaded by A. O. Hume (q.v.) among others to take up law and successfully completed his LL.B., in 1891.

In 1893 Malaviya enrolled himself as a High Court vakil and soon developed a successful and lucrative practice. Preoccupations with public and political affairs however compelled him to withdraw from the legal profession by 1909. The only known exception was when he supported and fought a law suit for 225 persons condemned to death in the famous Chauri Chaura case during the first Civil Disobedience Movement (q.v.).

All through life, Malaviya kept up an abiding interest in journalism. His early associations were with the Hindi weekly *Hindustan* (1887–9) and the English-language *Indian Union* (1885-90). Realizing the importance of this medium of mass communication and the urgent need to publish newspapers in the vernacular so as to reach the masses, educate the public, publicize the nationalist movement and voice the people's grievances and demands, he established a Hindi weekly *Abhyudaya* in 1907, converting it into a daily in 1915. Two Hindi monthlies were also started: *Maryada* in 1910 and *Kisan* in 1921, the latter catering to rural interests. *Leader,* an English daily, made its appearance in October 1909. Most of these papers played a notable role in the nationalist movement. Later (1942–6), Malaviya was Chairman of the Board of Directors of the *Hindustan Times*.

Convinced that his true calling lay in public service, Malaviya began attending the annual sessions of the Indian National Congress (q.v.) from 1886 onwards and rarely if ever missed an opportunity to do so thereafter. Two of these sessions, in 1888 and 1892, were held at Allahabad at his invitation; four times (1909, 1918, 1932 and 1933) he was elected President. On the last two occasions, his election took place while he was under detention.

Malaviya eschewed extremism in national politics and stood for a moderate course of action, such as achievement of Dominion Status (q.v.) through constitutional and peaceful means. He was one of the signatories of the 'Memorandum of the Nineteen' presented to the government in 1916 to press demands for constitutional reform. In 1918, he welcomed the Montagu-Chelmsford report (q.v.) as being at once liberal and beneficial to the nationalist cause; he stressed, however, that it be suitably modified and broad-based, to meet the country's requirements. In 1921, he refused to toe the line of his colleagues in boycotting the visit of the then Prince of Wales, the future Edward VIII, and instead conferred on him an honorary LL.D. degree at Banaras Hindu University. Malaviya did not favour the Non-cooperation Movement (q.v.) and is said to have persuaded Gandhi (q.v.) at Bardoli of the futility of having launched it without first educating and disciplining the masses who were to be involved. In 1923, he joined the Swaraj Party (q.v.) lending his full support to its decision to contest seats in the legislature and fight British rule from within the Councils. Later, convinced that the Congress was not adequately safeguarding Hindu interests, he founded the short-lived Nationalist Party with Motilal Nehru (q.v.) and C. R. Das (q.v.).

Malaviya's active involvement with municipal politics in Allahabad led to his election to the Provincial Legislative Council (1902) and the Imperial Legislative Council (1909-1920). In both these bodies, he was known for his fearlessness in opposing government policies that were deemed inimical to national interests. His disapproval of the Non-cooperation Movement, did not in any way imply a breach with the Congress and, in keeping with the party policy, he did not seek election to the Imperial Council in 1921.

A trenchant critic of the government's repressive measures, Malaviya had warned that the Prevention of Seditious Meetings Act (q.v.) would promote, and not cure, the evil it sought to check. He protested against the Press Act of 1910 (q.v.) and opposed indentured emigration of Indians. In 1924, he opposed the recommendations of the Lee Commission (q.v.) on the Indianization of the services and 4 years later led a demonstration against the Simon Commission (q.v.). On account of the government's continuing repression and the Congress decision to counter it by Civil Disobedience Movement (q.v.), Malaviya walked out of the Central Legislative Assembly in 1930 and participated in the Salt Satyagraha (q.v.), courting arrest along with other national leaders. Later, however, it was largely due to his mediation that the Gandhi–Irwin Pact (q.v.) was concluded and the Round Table Conference (q.v.), to which he was an invitee, convened.

Himself intensely religious and a devout Hindu, Malaviya was yet extremely tolerant and of broad catholic views where the susceptibilities of others were concerned. He did much to promote the welfare of Hindus and their religious beliefs. He figured prominently in campaigns to ban cow slaughter; established a Hindu Dharma Parvardhini Sabha at Prayag and (in 1906) the Sanatan Dharma Mahasabha, travelling all over the north to help set up its branches. The Hindu Mahasabha (q.v.), of which he was a founder-member, became a powerful organization under his stewardship and he presided thrice over its annual sessions. At one of these, Malaviya proposed that Hindu converts to other religions be encouraged to return to the Hindu fold. In this he differed with Gandhi, who sought to raise the status of **untouchables** through legislation and thereby prevent them from seeking shelter in other religions.

An architect and, indeed, the principal driving force behind the establishment of Banaras Hindu University, the University soon emerged as a living monument to Malaviya's keen interest in the education of the mind and the spirit. Its foundation was laid by Lord Hardinge (q.v.) in 1916 and the University itself formally declared open in 1921. Malaviya's capacity to raise funds for the University was unsurpassed, largelv because his integrity and motives were beyond reproach; he has been aptly called tne 'prince of beggars'. His initial target for Rs 1 crore was exceeded and by 1939 over Rs 1.5 crores had been collected. He was Vice-Chancellor of the University from 1919 to 1938, when he resigned owing to ill-health; but continued to be its Rector till his death, in 1946.

Dressed invariably in immaculate white, Malaviya was called 'the spotless Pandit'. Although a man of great gentleness and humility, he did not yield where principles were concerned and dared differ violently from Gandhi on important issues. Both by precept and example, he awakened the national consciousness and served as a great source of inspiration to countless people.

Sitaram Chaturvedi, *Madan Mohan Malaviya,* New Delhi, 1972; B. J. Akkad, *Malaviyaji,* Bombay, 1948; Puran Batrai, *Malaviyaji—His Life & Work,* Agra, 1955; S. L. Gupta, *Pandit Madan Mohan Malaviya: A socio-political Study,* Allahabad, 1978. G. A. Natesan, (ed.), *Speeches and Writings of Pt. Madan Mohan Malaviya,* Madras, 1919 and *The Hon. Pt. Madan Mohan Malaviya—His Life and Speeches,* Madras, 1920; Sen, *DNB,* III, pp. 31–5 (H. N. Kunzru).

John Malcolm (1769–1833)

Malcolm came out to India as a subaltern in 1782. Ten years later he was at the siege of Seringapatam under Cornwallis (q.v.); he was present at the taking of the Cape of Good Hope; and, again, the capture of Tipu Sultan's (q.v.) capital in 1799. Though serving in different military outposts, he longed for a diplomatic assignment to improve his chances for promotion, which also explains his acquiring early on a good knowledge of Persian.

In 1799 Wellesley (q.v.) chose Malcolm as an envoy to Persia whence a French invasion, in collusion with the Afghan chief Zaman Shah, was believed to be imminent. In Teheran, the young diplomat successfully concluded a treaty of friendship with the Shah. Back in India, he was appointed a political officer under Colonel Arthur Wellesley, later Duke of Wellington, during the Second Anglo-Maratha War (q.v.) and was mainly responsible for drawing up the Treaties of Surji Arjangaon (q.v.) and Burhanpur (1804). Later, as Resident at Sindhia's court (1804), and at Mysore (1805), he strongly disagreed with the John Company's (q.v.) policy of appeasing the Maratha chiefs. He served in varied capacities and enjoyed great administrative authority.

In 1807 when the Treaty of Tilsit between Napoleon and Tsar Alexander I of Russia raised the bogey of a French overland invasion of India, the First Earl Minto (q.v.) chose Malcolm to head a mission to Persia; this was foiled by French intrigue. He was sent to Persia again in 1810 but was over-shadowed by Sir Harford Jones-Brydges (1764-1847) who had been sponsored direct by Whitehall. Malcolm now published his *Political History of India* and, in 1815, a *History of Persia*. On furlough in England from 1812 to 1817 he was awarded a K. C. B. and a doctorate at Oxford.

On his return to India, Malcolm was promoted a Brigadier, served in the Third Anglo–Maratha War (q.v.) and was chiefly responsible for subduing Holkar and persuading Baji Rao II (q.v.) to surrender. Disappointed at being superseded for the governorship of Bombay and Madras by his juniors, Malcolm left for England in 1822. Five years later, he returned as Governor of Bombay, his time there taken up largely by a quarrel with the local Supreme Court. After a brief administrative stint, he returned home in 1830.

It is to Malcolm and Elphinstone (q.v.) that most of the credit must go for settling the Maratha country, though both learnt from Munro (q.v.). Malcolm was older in service than Elphinstone by some 10 years. Certainly ambition was a part of his character in a sense it never was in Munro's or Elphinstone's. He did, in his own words, 'court every kind of service that can increase his chance of notice and distinction', as the other two did not.

Malcolm was the author of several books, among which the better known are *Sketch of the Sikhs, Central India, Government of India, Life of Clive*. A member of Parliament for Launceston, 1831-2, he died of a stroke on 30 May 1833. Malcolm was a man of stature and strength of character. He had a remarkable versatility, being a diplomat, soldier, administrator and historian. It has been said that he was 'Boy Malcolm' to the last: 'He was a great man in a different way from the others of the great quartet (viz. Elphinstone, Metcalfe, Munro, besides himself) he had the same qualities and in the same proportion, as a hundred other English officers of the empire-building days—energy, high spirits, good humour, justice, honesty, quick wits, the power to command men and be obeyed—but he had more of each. That was all'.

Philip Woodruff, *The Men Who Ruled India: The Founders*, London, 1955, pp. 204–11, 244–7; *DNB*, XII, pp. 848–56 (John Andrew Hamilton); John Malcolm (ed. K. N. Panikkar), *The Political History of India from 1784 to 1823*, 2 vols, Reprint, New Delhi, 1970.

Treaty of Mandasor (1818)

A 17-article treaty was concluded at Mandasor (40 miles due south-east of Gwalior) on 6 January 1818 after Malhar Rao Holkar II's rout at Mahidpur on 12 December 1817 by Sir Thomas Hislop in the course of the Third Anglo-Maratha War (q.v.).

Inter alia, the Maratha ruler agreed to (i) 'confirm' a British commitment to the Pindari chief, Nawab Amir Khan, and renounce all claims to territories guaranteed to him; (ii) cede in perpetuity to Raja Zalim Singh of Kotah the four parganas rented by the Raja; (iii) cede to the British claims of tribute and revenues on the Rajas of Udaipur, Jaipur, Jodhpur, Kotah,

Bundhi and Karauli; (iv) renounce all rights and titles to territories within or north of the Bundhi hills; (v) cede to the British all territories and claims south of the Satpura hills; (vi) station a British field force 'to maintain the internal tranquillity of his dominion' whose supplies and provisions were to be exempt from any duties; (vii) discharge his superfluous troops while agreeing not to keep a larger force than what his revenues could sustain; at the same time, he was to retain in service, 'ready to co-operate' with the British, a body of 'not less than' 3,000 horse; (viii) not to employ 'any European or Americans of any description' without the Company's knowledge and consent; (ix) receive an accredited British minister (and 'shall be at liberty' to send a vakil to the Governor-General).

All the cessions listed were to take effect from the date of the Treaty. In turn, the British undertook never to permit the Peshwa or his heirs and successors to claim or exercise any sovereign rights over Malhar Rao or his heirs and successors.

Aitchison, IV, pp. 294–8.

Mangal Pande (d. 1857)

To Mangal Pande belongs the unique distinction of firing the first shot in the Rebellion of 1857 (q.v.). A resident of Faizabad in what is now Uttar Pradesh, he had enrolled in the 34th Native Infantry, then stationed at Barrackpore, outside Calcutta. Intensely religious, he was perturbed by the rumour of lard-coated cartridges used in the Enfield rifle. Earlier, on 26 February 1857, the 19th Native Infantry, then stationed at Behrampur, about 200 km due west of Calcutta, had risen as one man on much the same issue. In the result, a court of inquiry, although treating it as a 'local incident', had recommended the disbandment of the regiment. As men of the 34th Native Infantry had paid a routine duty visit to the 19th earlier, they held themselves morally responsible for the punishment meted out to the latter and felt a certain sense of shame about it.

On Sunday, 29 March 1857, Mangal Pande turned out in front of the quarter-guard of the regiment and fired at Sergeant-Major Hughson (also Hewson). Later he wounded the adjutant, and even aimed at the officer commanding, Sir John Bennet Hearsey (1793-1865). Overpowered and arrested, Mangal Pande and Iswar Pande, jamadar of the recalcitrant guard, were later tried and executed on 8 April 1857. In the result, the 34th Native Infantry was disbanded. Its dishonoured sepoys returned to their homes in Oudh (q.v.) in a sullen mood to give the wildest credence to the story of the cartridges greased with the fat of the cow and the pig.

Pande was one of the first martyrs to the cause of open rebellion against the John Company (q.v.). British officers later immortalized him by referring to the sepoys of the rebellious regiments as 'Pandeys' or 'Pandies'.

Surendra Nath Sen, *Eighteen Fifty-seven*, pp. 49-50; R. C. Majumdar (ed.), *British Paramountcy and Indian Renaissance*, Part I, pp. 469-70; J. A. B. Palmer, *The Mutiny Outbreak at Meerut in 1857*, Cambridge, 1966.

Treaty of Mangalore (1784)

Signed on 11 March 1784, the 10-article treaty of Mangalore brought the Second Anglo-Mysore War (q.v.) to a close. The signatories were Tipu Sultan (q.v.) who had succeeded his father Haidar Ali (q.v.) and the Madras government under George Macartney. Both parties were eager for peace, for while Tipu had lost French support with the conclusion of the War of American Independence (1776-83), the Madras government were confronted by an empty treasury, the grim prospects of large-scale famine and instructions from the Court of Directors to bring hostilities to a close. Even though the British troops had been recalled, Tipu continued with the siege of Mangalore till its capitulation, a fact that gave him the upper-hand in the peace parleys.

The Treaty stipulated *inter alia* that (i) the signatories were not to assist each other's enemies directly or indirectly, nor make war on each other's allies; (ii) trade privileges granted to the English by Haidar Ali in 1770 were to be restored, although no additional benefits would accrue; (iii) the two parties agreed to a mutual restoration of possessions (barring the forts of Amboorgur and Satgur), to be effected within 30 days of signature; meanwhile, Tipu undertook not to make any claims on the Carnatic in future; (iv) Tipu was to release all prisoners of war 'whether European or native', and 1,680 of them were later freed; (v) Tipu was to restore the factory and privileges possessed by the English at Calicut until 1779 and 'Mount Dilly and its district belonging to the settlement of Tollicharry'.

The earlier 1782 Treaty of Salbai (q.v.), which laid down that Haidar Ali was to restore the territory he had taken from the English and the Nawab of Arcot and had succeeded in isolating the ruler of Mysore, was to be ignored—a major achievement for Tipu. While later historians have viewed its terms as 'not unreasonable', Warren Hastings (q.v.) called the compact a 'humiliating pacification' and moved for Marcartney's suspension in so far as he had disobeyed the orders of the Supreme Government.

The fact is that at Madras, Macartney had expressed the view that 'peace was necessary for us', for the financial burden of the war had become unbearable. On the other hand, Tipu's position, it has been said, was much more favourable: his armies were intact, he possessed a full treasury, his kingdom had suffered very little from the devastations of war and, because of his victories, his prestige stood high. He made peace because of his anxiety to consolidate his power and crush those refractory chiefs who had disputed his authority.

The alleged maltreatment of the British commissoners by Tipu's men and the fabrications against them embittered relations. Added to the disappointment of an early peace, which was widely viewed as a diplomatic debacle for the John Company (q.v.) and one that had failed to bring it any territorial gains, the Treaty came to be looked upon as 'merely a truce which would not last very long'. The Company's servants, indeed, expressed the 'hope' that it was 'only meant to be temporary.'

Aitchison, V, pp. 141-5; Mohibul Hasan, *History of Tipu Sultan*, 2nd ed., Calcutta, 1971; Dodwell, *CHI*, V. pp. 288–9, 333–5.

First Anglo-Maratha War (1775–82)

The War was precipitated by the British authorities in Bombay signing the Treaty of Surat (q.v.) with Raghoba (q.v.), one of the claimants to the then

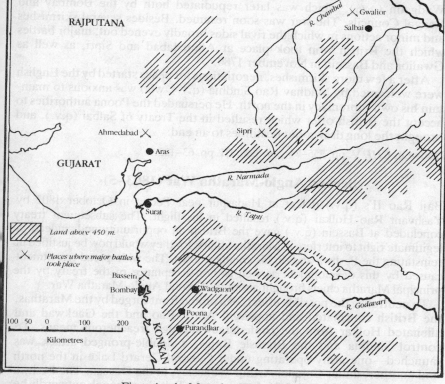

First Anglo-Maratha War (1775–82)

vacant Peshwaship at Poona. The John Company (q.v.) aimed at taking advantage of the notorious domestic squabbles of the Marathas to acquire territory on the coast near Bombay for its own trade and security.

The combined forces of Raghunath Rao (viz. Raghoba) and the British were defeated at Aras (18 May 1775) by Hari Pant, a Maratha commander. On hearing the news, the Calcutta Council condemned this action of the Bombay authorities and ordered them to recall their troops. During the lull that ensued, a Calcutta envoy, Colonel John Upton, was sent out to negotiate and successfully concluded the Treaty of Purandhar (q.v.). In defiance of its terms, the Bombay government gave asylum to Raghoba. Soon afterwards, Nana Phadnis (q.v.) welcomed a French adventurer,

Chevalier de St. Lubin, to Poona thereby renewing British fears of French involvement. Continued internal dissensions in the Maratha capital favoured a renewal of war, especially since the Court of Directors had approved the action of the Bombay authorities.

Hostilities were resumed in November 1778. The battle of Talegaon (11-12 January 1779) resulted in a British defeat and the Convention of Wadgaon (q.v.), which was later repudiated both by the Bombay and Bengal Councils. The war was soon resumed. Besides several skirmishes and minor actions in which the rival sides broadly evened out, major battles which the British won took place at Ahmedabad and Sipri, as well as Gwalior and Bassein in November 1780.

After a few more skirmishes, negotiations for peace started by the English were welcomed by Madhav Rao Sindhia (q.v.), who was anxious to maintain his own supremacy in the north. He persuaded the Poona authorities to accept the British offer which resulted in the Treaty of Salbai (q.v.), and brought the long drawn-out hostilities to an end.

Dodwell, *CHI*, V, pp. 255–71; *Sardesai*, III, pp. 63–132.

Second Anglo-Maratha War (1803–5)

Baji Rao II's (q.v.) defeat at Hadaspur near Poona in October 1802 by Yashvant Rao Holkar (q.v.) resulted in his flight. The subsequent treaty concluded at Bassein (q.v.) gave the British an opportunity and, indeed, a legitimate right to interfere in Maratha affairs, for they would now be justified in reinstating the Peshwa and do his enemies down. The widespread resentment caused by this development as well as non-acceptance of the treaty by the principal Maratha chiefs brought about the Second Anglo-Maratha War.

To neutralize the possible effects of a united front forged by the Marathas, the British conciliated and appeased Amrit Rao and the Gaekwad and alienated Holkar from the confederacy through treacherous means. To control Sindhia and the Bhonsle Rajas, a double-pronged attack was launched—one army operating under General Gerard Lake in the north and another, under Colonel Arthur Wellesley, in the Deccan. The Peshwa secretly urged the Maratha chiefs to resist the British, although outwardly he appeared to be their ally, albeit an unwilling one. On Sindhia's refusal to move out from the area bordering the Nizam's dominions in Central India, Wellesley opened hostilities on 7 August 1803. It is generally held that the Marathas numbered 250,000 men besides a force of 44,000 trained by the French; the English totalled approximately 55,000 men. In the Deccan, the Marathas suffered a series of reverses. Wellesley captured Ahmadnagar (12 August 1803), won a brilliant victory at Assaye (23 September), took Burhanpur (16 October), and achieved another success at Argaon (29 November). With the fall of the fortress of Gawilgarh, Raghuji Bhonsle sued for peace and, in December, signed the Treaty of Deogaon (q.v.). While hostilities proceeded apace in the south, in the north General Lake occupied Aligarh (5 September 1803), defeated General Perron (q.v.), Sindhia's erstwhile French commander at Delhi (11 September), took Agra

(17 October) and Laswari (1 November 1803). In Orissa, Jaggannath and Balasore and in Gujarat, Broach, Champaner and Pawagarh had surrendered by the end of September.

Such quick successes alarmed Sindhia and compelled him to sign a treaty of peace in December (1803) at Surji Arjangaon (q.v.). Officially it marked the end of the war, even though sporadic hostilities continued, for Holkar took up arms and the Raja of Bharatpur rallied to his cause. Sindhia too soon broke the peace. Yet Holkar's defeat at Delhi (7 October 1804), Farrukhabad (14 November 1804) and, finally, Deeg (13 November) and his failure to rally the Sikhs to his cause made him sign the Treaty of Rajpurghat (q.v.) in December 1805. The end result of the war was that the Marathas

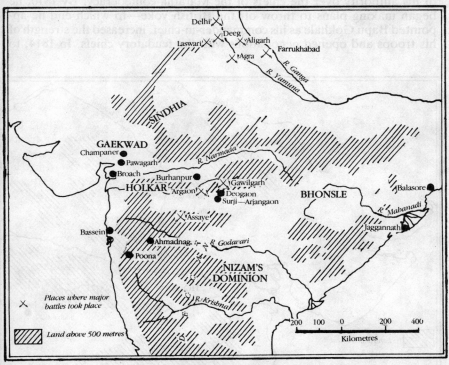

Second Anglo-Maratha War (1803–5)

were subdued, French influence well-nigh eliminated, English control over the Mughal Emperor, Shah Alam II (q.v.) firmly established, while the entire eastern sea-board passed securely under British control.

The principal British campaign in the Maratha war, brilliantly planned and executed, lasted no more than 4 months (August-December 1803) and bears witness to an almost complete rout of the Peshwa and his confederates. The Maratha debacle was partly due to the abandonment of their traditional guerilla tactics and the utter worthlessness of their French-trained hosts when pitted in battle against the British.

Roberts, pp. 256–8; *Advanced History of India*, pp. 695–6: *Sardesai*, III, pp. 379–438.

Third Anglo-Maratha War (1817–18)

The years following the Second Anglo-Maratha War (q.v.) were superficially trouble-free. Inwardly Baji Rao II (q.v.) was chafing under the excessive and irksome control imposed by the British, and the self-confessed loss of his authority over the chiefs of the Maratha confederacy. By 1810, he began making plans to throw off the British yoke—to which end he appointed Bapu Gokhale as his commander-in-chief, increased the strength of his troops and opened negotiations with the feudatory chiefs. In 1814, to

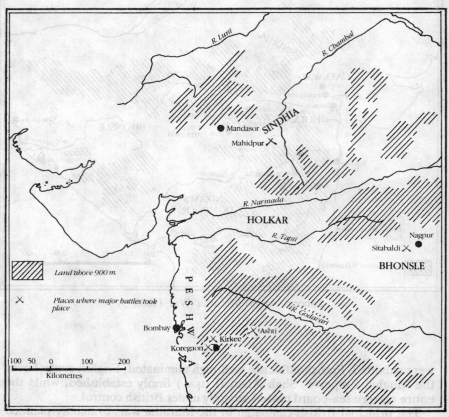

Third Anglo-Maratha War (1817–18)

settle his long-standing differences with the Gaekwad, Gangadhar Shastri came to Poona under a British assurance of safe conduct. Before any concrete results could emerge, he was murdered, presumably by the Peshwa's notorious adviser, Trimbakji, whom the British arrested and imprisoned.

Soon Trimbakji escaped from custody and, with the Peshwa's refusal to disclose his whereabouts, relations with the John Company (q.v.) became strained. Apprehensive of the Maratha leader's designs in mustering his forces, the British, under threat of withdrawing their support, made him sign the humiliating Treaty of Poona (q.v.) on 13 June 1817. Two months later, the Peshwa agreed to help the Company in its campaign to liquidate the Pindaris (q.v.). Behind the scenes, however, he was banking on the support of the principal Maratha chiefs, Sindhia, Bhonsle and Holkar. For even if their dominions were in utter confusion and their armies in worse disorder, they were not truly reconciled to the Company's yoke which with the years had become more unbearable.

Not unaware of troop movements nearby, Elphinstone (q.v.), then Resident in Poona, made defensive arrangements, at the same time asking Baji Rao to withdraw his men. The latter refused to comply and on 5 November 1817 with an army of 27,000 men attacked and burnt down the Residency. That day however the Peshwa's forces were defeated at Kirkee by a small posse of 2,800 men under Colonel Burr. Appa Sahib, whose troops were worsted at Sitabaldi (17 November), fled to the Panjab and Holkar, who was routed at Mahidpur (21 December), signed peace at Mandasor (q.v.). Baji Rao, fleeing from Kirkee, was pursued and defeated at Koregaon (1 January 1818) and Ashti (20 February). Soon deserted by his men, he decided to surrender (3 June 1818) and laid down his arms before John Malcolm (q.v.).

This final debacle led to the abolition of the Peshwa's hereditary office and an almost complete annihilation of Maratha power as a likely challenger to the Company's authority. A Maratha scholar has aptly called the period from the battle of Kirkee (Novemeber 1817) to the end of the war as the 'last phase'. He has expressed the view that only after his surrender is Baji Rao truly deserving of 'sympathy and forgiveness'.

Sardesai, III; R. D. Choksey (ed.), *The Last Phase*, Bombay, 1948, pp. 162-87; Dodwell, *CHI*, V, pp. 380-3.

Mayo (1822–72)

Richard Southwall Bourke, sixth Earl of Mayo, succeeded John Lawrence (q.v.) as Viceroy and Governor-General in 1869. Born and educated at Dublin, he took to the sports of country life and was a clever shot, an accomplished rider and a good swimmer. In 1852, he was appointed Chief Secretary for Ireland, a post he continued to hold until his arrival in India.

No Russophobe himself, Mayo's travels in that country (1845-6) had convinced him that all Anglo-Russian problems were negotiable and a settlement on the basis of the two countries' respective spheres of influence easily arrived at. To project the Indian point of view, he sent an experienced civil servant, Thomas Douglas Forsyth (q.v.) to St. Petersburg. Another way to hold back the Russians, he argued, was to encourage British commercial interests in Central Asia. For this purpose he felt it necessary to have a strong and friendly Afghanistan. Understandably, he readily endorsed the policy of his predecessor with a slight modification in terminology: instead of 'masterly' inactivity he called it 'friendly' inactivity.

Afghanistan had returned to normalcy after a decade of civil strife following the death of Dost Mohammad (q.v.). Consequently, its new Amir, Sher Ali, was invited to meet the Viceroy at Ambala. Much pomp and pageantry marked the occasion. The Amir had come prepared to demand: (i) official recognition; (ii) a treaty of mutual assistance; (iii) a subsidy; Mayo successfully avoided binding commitments on any account. The meeting ended on a note of cordiality with the Viceroy promising some arms accompanied by a letter of friendship and general support. To keep Persia from encroaching on Afghan territories, particularly in Seistan (q.v.), a boundary delimitation commission was set up. With Russia and Afghanistan thus pacified, commercial interests in Central Asia were pursued more vigorously. A mission under Douglas Forsyth was sent to Yarkand and the ruler of Kashmir persuaded to grant it transit facilities.

The 'cardinal' principle of Indian policy vis-a-vis the peripheral states (Kalat, Afghanistan, Yarkand, Nepal and Burma) as visualized by Mayo, was to foster 'intimate relations of friendship' and make them feel that although the British were 'all powerful' there was need 'to support their nationality'. The Governor-General further argued that 'when necessity arises, we might assist them with money, arms, and even perhaps, in certain eventualities, with men. We could thus create in them outworks of our empire.'

Under Mayo's predecessor, governmental expenditure had exceeded revenue. To put things aright, the Governor-General instituted measures of strict economy and sought means to enhance revenue. Salt duties were raised uniformly and income-tax increased from 1% to 2½%, though a further increase (to $3^{1/8}\%$ in 1871) was postponed. Military expenditure was reduced by nearly half a million sterling. The Viceroy's emphasis on 'decentralization' was a corollary to his fiscal policy. An elaborate scheme was drawn up to have some essentially local expenditures taken out of local funds; central control was, however, maintained in the appointment of provincial officials and in fixing their salaries.

Another reform suggested by John Lawrence and carried into effect by Mayo was that of constructing extensions of the Indian Railways (q.v.) by means of funds borrowed by the government instead of entrusting this to private companies. The decision that the Permanent Settlement (q.v.) of land revenue based on the system established by Cornwallis (q.v.) should not be extended to other provinces was mainly due to Mayo. He also advocated the development of primary education and suggested special measures for promoting the education of the Muslim community.

A hard-headed imperialist and imbued with the notion of the white man's civilizing mission, Mayo felt it his bounden duty to initiate Indians into training for government service. A number of junior judicial posts were therefore thrown open to them. This move was also aimed at effecting economy in expenditure, for Indians were paid lower salaries than their **European** counterparts.

Conditions in India were far from satisfactory, even though a superficial tranquillity prevailed. Near-famine conditions were rampant in large parts of the country. There was unrest among the Muslims and communal riots occurred from time to time. The Wahabi Movement (q.v.) had not quite died down and its Hindu/Sikh counterpart, the Kukas, were becoming increasingly militant. The latter's activities however did not unduly worry the Governor-General, for the Wahabi leaders alone were singled out for exemplary punishment. Nor was he upset by the Kuka attack on Malerkotla (Jan. 1872), strongly disagreeing with the local Deputy Commissioner's decision to summarily punish some of their leaders. Mayo was confident that the British army was capable of quelling any uprising, should such an eventuality ever arise. On 8 February 1872, while on an official visit to Port Blair, then a penal settlement in the Andaman and Nicobar group of islands. Mayo was attacked and killed by an Afghan convict, believed to be a Wahabi.

W. W. Hunter, *The Earl of Mayo*, Rulers of India, Oxford, 1891; S. Gopal, *British Policy in India*, Cambridge, 1965; *DNB*, II, pp. 929–32 (Alexander John Arbuthnot).

Mehboob Ali Khan, Nizam (1869–1911)

Mehboob Ali Khan, the only son of Afzal-ud-Daula (q.v.), was a minor barely three years old when he ascended the throne in 1869. A Regency was therefore established consisting of Sir Salar Jang (q.v.) and Shams-ul-Umra. Educated by English teachers, John and Claude Clerk, Mehboob Ali assumed full powers only in 1884. As a friend of the British, he assisted them in 1887 and offered a sum of Rs 60 lakhs for frontier defence. Hailed as 'a faithful ally', the Nizam, whose finances were now stable and well-organized, asked for the restoration of Berar, a request which the British turned down. The Hyderabad contingent which had served in the Rebellion of 1857 (q.v.) was now delocalized and incorporated in the Indian Army.

Mehboob Ali's reign was witness to a series of agreements with the British. Thus, an 1870 agreement provided for the construction of a railway line to connect Hyderabad with the Great Indian Peninsular Railway. The Nizam was to provide the capital for its construction, maintenance and working, including the provision of land, payment of compensation and cost of service, while the British were to construct and manage the railway on his behalf. Twelve years later, a postal agreement was executed making provision for the interchange, under certain conditions, of mails between the British and the Nizam's postal officers. In October 1904, the Nizam delegated to the Government of India full criminal and police jurisdiction in 11 jagirs and other villages within the Secundrabad cantonment limits.

The 1902 agreement on Berar concluded between the Nizam and Lord Curzon (q.v.) leased the Hyderabad portion of Berar to the British in perpetuity in return for a fixed annual rental of Rs 25 lakhs, the Nizam's sovereignty being acknowledged by hoisting his flag and firing a salute annually on his birthday.

A valuable ally, the Nizam was the recipient of several honours by the British, including the G. C. S. I. (1884) and the G. C. B. (1903). He died in

August 1911.

Harriet Rouken Lynton & Mohini Rajan, *The Days of the Beloved*, Berkeley, 1974; K. L. Gauba, *Hyderabad or India*, Delhi, 1948, pp. 38–43; *Chronology of Modern Hyderabad, 1720–1890*, Hyderabad, 1954; *Gribble*, II.

Nawab Mehdi Ali Hasan, Mohsin-ul-Mulk (1837–1907)

Mehdi Ali Hasan, better known as Nawab Mohsin-ul-Mulk, was born at Etawah in Uttar Pradesh on 9 December 1837. The scion of a well-known Barha Syed family which had played an important role in shaping the fortunes of the Mughal dynasty, he rose to be an active member of the Aligarh Movement (q.v.), a great promoter of Muslim welfare and education and one of the prominent initiators of a political association that fought for Muslim interests and aspirations.

Though of noble lineage, Mehdi Ali was poor, had received only a smattering of elementary education in a madrassa and was largely self-taught. Necessity drove him to seek employment early, and he began life as an *Ahalmad* (i.e. clerk) in the service of the East India Company (q.v.) in 1857. His industry and devotion to the cause of his employers earned rich dividends—by 1861 he had risen from the position of a *Paishkar* and *Sheristadar* to that of the Tehsildar of Etawah, his home town. Subsequently, he competed successfully for the provincial civil service and with the recommendation of A. O. Hume (q.v.), then Permanent Collector of Etawah, was appointed Deputy Collector of Mirzapur (1867). In addition, he acted as Superintendent of the Dudhi and Rae Bareli estates.

Impressed by his administrative ability, Sir Salar Jung (q.v.) invited Mehdi Ali to Hyderabad. Accepting the invitation (1874) he served the Nizam for nearly two decades (1874-93) in various capacities, paying special attention to agricultural problems and revenue assessment. Initially appointed Inspector General of Revenues, within 10 years Mehdi Ali rose to be Financial and Political Secretary to the Nizam. In recognition of his meritorious services he was awarded, in 1884, the title of Munir Nawaz Jung, Mohsin-ud-Daulah, Mohsin-ul-Mulk. Henceforth his own name went into the background and the world outside came to know him by his last title, Mohsin-ul-Mulk. In 1893 political intrigue—the 'factious designs of some interested persons'—compelled him to resign and he retired to Aligarh. Among his reforms in Hyderabad, mention may be made of the introduction of Urdu (in place of Persian) as the court language in the capital and the mofussil.

Mohsin-ul-Mulk's active participation in the Aligarh Movement starts only after his retirement, although he had been in touch with Sir Syed Ahmad (q.v.) for almost two decades, relieving a financial crisis in Aligarh now and then and contributing regularly to his paper *Tahzib-ul Ikhlaq*. In one of his articles in the journal, Sir Syed wrote: 'Moulvi Mehdi Ali's learning, personal merits, charming conversation, sincerity, honesty and eloquence are such that our community, had not its mind's eye been blind, would have been proud of him.'

Because of his close association with and active involvement in the Aligarh Movement, Mohsin-ul-Mulk was considered the chief lieutenant of Sir Syed, taking over as Secretary of Aligarh College after the founder's death. 'By the unanimous consent of the whole community, the mantle of Sir Syed fell' on Mohsin-ul-Mulk. In order to popularize the Movement, he tactfully achieved the hitherto denied approval of the orthodox ulema, who had earlier branded his mentor an apostate. He also managed to win over the participation of Badruddin Tyabji (q.v.). Later, he won the support of the Aga Khan (q.v.) too.

Mohsin-ul-Mulk was convinced that education was the sole means of uplifting the Muslim community so as to bring it on par with the Hindus. Until that stage was reached, he argued, Muslims must assiduously avoid all political connections, especially such as were disposed to be critical of British policies. The latter's faith in the community had to be carefully nurtured and used to further the cause of Muslim regeneration.

Mohsin-ul-Mulk organized the Muhammadan Educational Conference to convene annually. At first he was its secretary but later presided over two of its sessions. *Inter alia,* the aim was to discuss ways and means of popularizing a modern approach to education. He also initiated a move to convert the M. A. O. College at Aligarh into a Muslim university. An ardent promoter of Urdu since his Hyderabad days, he urged all Muslims to take to its study.

In 1900, Sir Antony Patrick MacDonnell, then Lieutenant-Governor of the North-Western Provinces, ruled that for administrative convenience, the government should accept petitions in Hindi and translate its orders into that language. Curzon (q.v.) promptly agreed and asked MacDonnell (1 June 1900) to ignore Muslim protests which he compared to the spleen of a minority 'from whose hands are slipping away the reins of power'. In protest and at the invitation of the Muslims of Aligarh, Mohsin-ul-Mulk convened a conference in defence of Urdu 'which was attended by many nawabs with their "quail cages" to protest' against the Governor's *diktat* recognizing Hindi. It was at this meeting that he read the verse. ('It is the coffin of Urdu, let it be taken out with great eclat').

اُردو کا جنازہ ہے، ذرا دھوم سے نکلے

An Urdu Defence Association that soon came into being unanimously adopted a resolution demanding withdrawal of the recognition accorded to Hindi. The Nawab declared that Muslims who did not wield the pen, had 'the strength to wield the sword' and expressed his amazement that the community was forsaken and ignored by the government. The entire Muslim 'nation', he maintained, felt aggrieved. His activities provoked the Governor, who promptly conveyed his displeasure; in the result, the Nawab, we are told, 'withdrew into his shell' at M. A. O. College.

It was obvious that if he persisted in the agitation in favour of Urdu. Mohsin-ul-Mulk's continuance at the helm of the College would seriously affect its welfare. The fact is that he resigned from the College but, under pressure, was later compelled to backtrack. None the less, his withdrawal from the pro-Urdu front meant an early end of that movement. One important by-product of this controversy was Viqar-ul-Mulk's (q.v.) coming out of his seclusion after retirement.

Besides his many other 'services' to the Muslim community, 'the greatest boon' that the Nawab is said to have conferred on his people was that of 'separate electorates'. The Simla deputation, of which he was a member, was *not* a command performance; 'facts', we are told, 'do not justify such a conclusion'. Nor was the demand for separate electorates made 'at the instance of Dunlop Smith', then secretary to Minto (q.v.). That 'the idea was the outcome of British agents . . . . . is at once a calumny against the British and a slander against Nawab Mohsin-ul-Mulk'. Writing in 1955, the Aga Khan has, however, maintained that the idea of separate electorates originated with the Nawab.

While the Aga Khan had advised Muslims to establish a political organization of their own, we are told that it was Mohsin-ul-Mulk, who invited the leaders from all over India to meet in Dacca in the last week of December 1906. Earlier (1901), Viqar-ul-Mulk had unsuccessfully tried to set up a similar body. At the Dacca session of Muslim leaders on 30 December 1906, where a decision was taken to organize the All-India Muslim League (q.v.), both Mohsin-ul-Mulk and Viqar-ul-Mulk were appointed Joint Secretaries to draft a constitution for the new party. Mohsin-ul-Mulk was not able to do much as he died in October 1907, before the League convened for its first formal session at Karachi.

The Nawab felt that reform in all fields, political, educational and social, could be initiated and progress made *if* it had the support of religious leaders. He therefore welcomed the formation, in 1894, of the Nadwat-ul-ulema (literally, 'synod of Muslim divines'), a body that was not averse to imbibing modern influences. Mohsin-ul-Mulk believed firmly in the distinctiveness of his community and gave it a firm root in Indian polity. The Muslim deputation to the Viceroy, had resulted in the acceptance of the demand for separate electorates in the Minto-Morley Reforms (q.v.) of 1909, and in a certain sense anticipated the creation of Pakistan.

A man of parts, the Nawab has been rated to be a brilliant and effective orator who was at the same time an able journalist, a renowned theologian, a formidable debator and classical writer. In addition, he had proved to be a capable administrator, a veteran educationist and a successful social and political reformer.

The poet Altaf Hussain Hali's tribute to him bears citation,

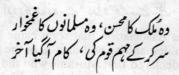

وہ مُلک کا محسن، وہ مسلمانوں کا غمخوار
سرکر کے ہم قوم کی، کام آگیا آخر

('He to whom the country was indebted and who was solicitous of Muslim interests, having fought the nation's battle, died at long last'.)

Eminent Mussalmans, Madras, 1926; Rafiq Zakaria, *Rise of Muslims in Indian Politics: an analysis of developments from 1885 to 1906*, Bombay, 1970, pp. 319–21; Aziz Ahmad, *Islamic Modernism in India and Pakistan 1857–1965*, London, 1967, pp. 64–71; S. M. Ikram, *Modern Muslim India and the Birth of Pakistan (1858–1951)*. 2nd ed., Lahore, 1965, pp. 82–95; Lal Bahadur, *The Muslim League: its history, activities and achievements*, Agra, 1954.

Pherozeshah Mehta (1845–1915)

Pherozeshah Mehta, a pioneering nationalist and popularly known as the 'uncrowned king of Bombay', belonged to a middle-class Parsi family. A brilliant student, he graduated at 20 and later took an M. A. degree—being one of the first Indians to secure higher western education and, indeed, the first Parsi to acquire a Master's degree. Mehta received the Jamsetji Jeejibhai award to pursue law studies abroad. Called to the bar in London in 1868, he returned to Bombay to practice law. However, it was his work in the mofussil, mainly in Gujarat and Kathiawar, that earned him a reputation as a criminal lawyer and, in the bargain, a lucrative practice.

Mehta's interest in public life was aroused when, as a student in England, he became a member of the East India Association. At its gatherings, he imbibed and developed his ideas of liberalism and made a lifelong friendship with such contemporaries as D. N. Wacha (1844–1936), K. T. Telang (1850–93), Badruddin Tyabji (q.v.), W. C. Bonnerjee (q.v.) and Dadabhai Naoroji (q.v.). Like many other Moderate leaders, Mehta too accepted British rule as a divine dispensation. He had concluded, that parliamentary government would be a long time taking root in India but efforts should never the less be directed towards it as the ultimate objective. He put great faith in the British sense of justice and fairplay and expressed the hope that they would guide India to a more progressive and prosperous future.

In Bombay, Mehta was to be actively involved in local municipal politics for nearly half a century. The Corporation, as it finally emerged, was substantially the result of his untiring efforts. He advocated the principle of election and it was due to him that the municipal laws of 1872 and 1888 were enacted, the latter aptly called the Magna Carta of municipal freedom in India.

Along with Badruddin Tyabji and K. T. Telang, Mehta formed the Bombay Presidency Association which, under his tutelege, served as the organizational wing of the Indian National Congress (q.v.) in the metropolis for nearly thirty years (1885–1915). He was also a founder-member of the Congress and, as Lal Mohan Ghose (q.v.) later affirmed, it was Mehta who virtually dominated the Congress behind the scenes for many years. A typical moderate and loyalist, Mehta's approach, in the words of his political detractors, was to draft memorials to the government criticizing such of its policies as seemed inimical to national interests. He strongly questioned the efficacy of Dadabhai Naoroji's scheme to fight India's battles in Britain's parliament. Mehta's control of the central Congress organization during the years 1894–1904 was almost as effective as Gandhi's (q.v.) in the 1920s and 1930s. In 1904, when the party's annual session was held at Bombay, Mehta was chairman of the reception committee and commanded the allegiance of an overwhelming majority of the delegates. At most of the party's annual sessions, his lead was invariably followed, whether or not he himself was present.

Such innovations as a constitution for the Congress appeared to be a nuisance to Mehta; apart from the risk of upsetting established procedures, they were bound to make demands on his time. It followed that he was insensitive, even hostile, to the new forces emerging in the country; he looked askance at the new men and their ideas; they threatened, he argued, to disturb the harmony of the Congress organization and, one may add, his hegemony over it! Impatient of criticism, irascible, inaccessible, forbidding, Mehta failed to discern the impact of these new forces then emerging in the Congress and the country.

Mehta had a lively distrust of Tilak (q.v.), which was partly ideological and partly temperamental. This hindered mutual understanding and even mutual comprehension between the Congress establishment in India—of which Pherozeshah Mehta was the virtual chief—and Tilak, the popular hero. At the Surat session (1907) of the Congress, Mehta is said to have brought into the pandal 40 hired men armed with sticks, a fact that would underline his strong determination to expel the Extremists. The shoe hurled at Tilak hit Mehta and Surendranath Banerjea (q.v.), the Moderate leaders seated on the dais. After it was all over, Mehta told the *Times of India* that the Surat Split (q.v.) was inevitable if the Congress were not 'to submit itself to the rule of the Extremists'. He labelled their aspirations 'unreasonable and unrealizable', and unacceptable to the 'bulk of the Congress'.

Following the dissolution of the old Congress, a 5-member committee, including Mehta, decided to hold an exclusive session of the Moderates. The latter decided to convene an 'All-India Conference' and appointed a 4-member committee, including Mehta, to reconstitute the party. The committee met at Allahabad in April 1908 and drew up a rigid constitution outlining that the party objective was the attainment of self-government within the British Empire by strictly constitutional means and gradual reform of the existing system of administration. Each delegate was to express his acceptance of this article of faith 'in writing'. Mehta declared later that there was no intention of receiving the Extremists back into the fold and that the cleavage was irreparable.

In 1915, with Gokhale (q.v.) dead, Mehta was 'always a little suspicious of the Congress. He thought, with very good reason, that Gokhale was somewhat weak and that he was negotiating with the Tilakites and arranging a sort of compromise so that the Extremists could come back to the Congress'. Of Gandhi's aims and methods both Wacha and Mehta had an instinctive dread. Mehta's condemnation of Gandhi would have been 'clear, complete and caustic', for the latter had no patience with the judicious frame of mind which weighs pros and cons with meticulous precision: 'I confess to a natural aversion from cocksure, uncompromising, final judgements in any sphere of human conduct. One can never know enough to judge aright.'

In 1886, Mehta was appointed a member of the Bombay Legislative Council and was later (1892), elected to it. During 1898-1901 he was a member of the Imperial Legislative Council; poor health however forced his resignation in 1901. He spoke eloquently and boldly on questions of the day criticizing mismanagement of the country's finances and waste of its revenues on frontier wars and expeditions mounted in alien lands. He always spoke in his characteristic, hard-hitting style and assailed government with scorn and sarcasm.

A nationalist in the true sense, Mehta claimed to be an Indian first and a Parsi afterwards. He advised his community not to isolate itself from the national mainstream, for their 'birthright was more important than a mess of pottage'. A pragmatist, he realized that India's economic progress depended on the development of indigenous industry and was, therefore, a strong supporter of Swadeshi. Among the first to invest in cotton spinning and weaving mills, he also financed a soap manufacturing concern and set up a swadeshi bank (later the Central Bank of India). He gave Bombay its first daily newspaper, the *Bombay Chronicle,* with B. G. Horniman (1873–1948) as its editor.

Mehta's early training and education in England was under the powerful influence of Dadabhai Naoroji 'who inspired him with his own burning love of the country and enthusiasm for the cause of progress and liberty.' By temperament, Mehta was 'a robust optimist' who faced the problems of the day 'with severe courage and confidence'. Like many others of his generation, he was a firm believer in the benefits of the British connection, recognizing the essential justice and humanity of England's rule in India. Allied to this was his deep-seated respect for constituted authority. The distinguishing features of Mehta's methods of controversy were fearlessness, a keen sense of fairplay and a regard for the decencies of public life. He had an abiding interest in education which he called the 'greatest gift of British rule'. Even as a student he read a paper on the 'Education system in Bombay' and, in 1869, criticized the system of grants-in-aid. Although in favour of reform in education, he was firmly of the view that such change should have the approval of the people. He criticized Lord Curzon's (q.v.) Universities Act and stoutly denied the charge that university senates were bodies that abused their power of patronage. He censured British efforts to run universities as government departments. In March 1915, he was appointed Vice-Chancellor of Bombay University; 5 months later, a D. Litt. (*honoris causa*) was conferred on him. He had also received the C. I. E. in 1894 and was knighted in 1904.

The *Times of India* obituary notice on Pherozeshah Mehta was a warm tribute: 'In his devotion to Bombay he was, we think we may say without exaggeration, the greatest citizen any city has ever produced. He gave it his best for over 40 years . . . . The dauntless patriot and the eminent citizen will never be replaced'. A biographer has maintained that nobody should grudge Mehta the 'eminent position' he acquired, 'but it is to his greater merit still as he used all these opportunities not for selfish ends at all, but exclusively and altogether for the benefit of the people . . . . His were no narrow ambitions. He did not rise to greatness on the ruins of other people's reputations'.

Mehta's great example of devotion to municipal reform drew to Bombay a wealth of talent and experience. The unsurpassed influence of Mehta and his men in the Corporation 'was never perverted to any jobbery or patronage but exerted to keep policy and principle free from all taint of unworthy ends'. A British journalist has expressed the view that Mehta had 'stood alone against the bureaucracy, had displayed a courage equal to Gokhale's, an eloquence hardly second to Surendranath Banerjea's and power of sarcasm hardly rivalled by Motilal Ghose's'. Hardinge (q.v.), then Governor-General, described him in 1915 as 'a great Parsi, a great citizen, a great patriot and a great Indian'.

In the eyes of the educated class in the last decade of the nineteenth century, Pherozeshah Mehta epitomized national self-respect. He was admired for his grasp of constitutional law, command of the English language, robust common sense, unquestioned integrity as well as freedom from religious or regional partisanship. During his long sway in the Bombay Corporation, even his worst critics did not accuse him of nepotism.

V. S. Srinavasa Sastri, *Life and Times of Sir Pherozeshah Mehta,* Madras, 1945; Sir Homi Mody, *Sir Pherozeshah Mehta: A Political Biography,* reprint, Bombay, 1963; B. R. Nanda, *Gokhale,* Oxford, 1977.

Charles Theophilus Metcalfe (1785-1846)

Charles (later Baron) Metcalfe, son of Major Thomas Metcalfe, an officer in the John Company's (q.v.) army, was born in Calcutta on 30 January 1785. Educated at Eton, he returned to India in 1800 as a 'writer' in the Company's service and was among the first to join the college for civil servants established at Fort William where he acquired a good knowledge of oriental languages. He later served in various administrative capacities—as Secretary in the Governor-General's office, Assistant Resident at Gwalior and Delhi, head of Lord Minto's (q.v.) friendly mission to Ranjit Singh's (q.v.) court in 1808-9, a brief stint in the army as Political Officer under Lord Lake in 1804 and again at Combermere's storming of Bharatpur in 1826. As Resident at Hyderabad in 1820 he earned Marquess of Hastings' (q.v.) disapproval for reporting adversely on the activities of William Palmer & Co. (q.v.) in which the then Governor-General had special interest.

Metcalfe was an outstanding public servant in the second quarter of the nineteenth century. He was a liberal to the core and, as early as 1815, expressed the view that 'all that rulers can do is to merit dominion by promoting the happiness of those under them'. The judicial and administrative systems proposed and adopted by him as Resident were largely indigenous to the soil, with some minor modifications, and have been aptly described as a new structure resting on old foundations. He visualized a free press as a safety valve that released pent-up resentment and yet left the government unmolested. In 1827 as Councillor at Calcutta, he influenced Bentinck's (q.v.) policy in regard to the press: later, as acting Governor-General (1835-6), he annulled the restrictions of 1823 by his Press Act (1835). Metcalfe also championed the extension of western learning amongst Indians and foresaw the emergence of an urban middle class, itself a product of western culture. To energize and activate the sluggish Indian economy, he encouraged Europeans to settle down in the country and induct foreign capital and skill.

In evolving his Delhi system—in contrast to the Bengal pattern—Metcalfe had followed the principle of unity of authority and completeness of control. What was more, it conformed to Indian practice. A certain contradiction was nonetheless noticeable in his thinking. While admittedly in favour of a despotic form of government wherein the executive arm tended to control the law-making as well as the justice-dispensing agencies, he also spoke of public opinion and the freedom of the press which are essentially attributes of a modern free society. The first duty of the state was to safeguard its security from 'internal and external enemies'; he rated the former more dangerous than even a Russian invasion. He believed that 'a natural antipathy' existed between the rulers and the ruled; hence the need for a strong army under European commanders as well as a strong, vigilant and swift government. Having provided for such a government, he also wanted it to be a 'good government'. The objectives of the Delhi land-revenue system were similar to those followed elsewhere—promotion of agriculture, well-being of the agricultural community and security of revenue to the state. Land was a major source of well-being for the people, for property formed the basis of human endeavour. A right to property guaranteed individual initiative and promoted social good.

The Court of Directors showed their disapproval of Metcalfe's Press Act by passing him over for appointment as Governor of Madras. To vindicate his position, Metcalfe resigned and returned to England. He was now elevated to the Privy Council and appointed Governor of Jamaica (1839–42) and later (1843–5) Governor-General of Canada; but cancer of the cheek and failing health cut short his career. In January 1845 he was raised to the peerage; in December, he returned home, seriously ill. He died on 5 September 1846.

In public life, Metcalfe showed broad vision combined with a sense of hard realism. Bentinck once wrote to Lord Melbourne about him thus: 'I think no man has shown greater rectitude of conduct or more independence of mind! We served together for nearly seven years. His behaviour for me was of the noblest kind. He never cavilled upon a trifle, and never yielded to me on a point of importance.' Lord Auckland (q.v.) ruled that he 'would rather have his [Metcalfe's] opinion and his reasons and his co-operation with me on any great measure than any other man in India'. Metcalfe has been rated an able and sagacious administrator, a man of great honesty of purpose and untiring industry. Contemporaries admired his self-reliance and good humour, as also his undeviating straight-forwardness. His epitaph, written by Macaulay, was not ill-deserved: 'A statesman tried in many high posts and difficult conjunctures and found equal to all. The three greatest dependencies of the British Crown were successively entrusted to his care . . . In India, his fortitude, his wisdom, his probity and his moderation are held in honourable remembrance . . .'

D. N. Panigrahi, *Charles Metcalfe in India, Ideas and Administration 1806–35*, Delhi, 1968; Edward Thompson, *The Life of Charles, Lord Metcalfe,* London, 1937; *DNB*, XIII, pp. 303–6 (George Fisher Russell Barker).

First Earl Minto (1751–1814)

Sir Gilbert Elliot, later the first Earl of Minto, was Governor-General of India from 1807 to 1813. He had taken an active interest in Indian affairs even as a Member of Parliament, which he became in 1776. Earlier, he had been in school with the French revolutionary leader, Comte de Mirabeau (1749-91), and was a friend of Burke (1729-97). He collaborated with the latter in preparing the impeachment proceedings against Warren Hastings (q.v.) and, in 1787, carried a motion in Parliament condemning the conduct of Elijah Impey (q.v.) basically over misconduct in the trial of Maharaja Nand Kumar (q.v.). Subsequently, Minto tried but failed to be elected Speaker of the House of Commons. He was appointed his country's diplomatic representative at Toulon (1793), Corsica (1794-6) and Vienna (1801) from where he was recalled. He became President of the Board of Control in 1806 and was soon appointed Governor-General.

Against the background of the Treaty of Tilsit (1807) between Tsar Alexander I and Napoleon, Minto on arrival in India became preoccupied with the possibility of a Franco-Russian invasion and the measures to be adopted to protect Britain's Indian possessions. The result was that important internal matters, then awaiting urgent attention, were temporarily shelved. Instead, four diplomatic missions were dispatched to the rulers of territories that might serve as buffers against an overland invasion—Sind (q.v.), Afghanistan, Persia and the Panjab.

Minto deputed John Malcolm (q.v.) to Persia, even though the Home Government had independently sent another diplomat, Sir Harford Jones. The Persians, then negotiating with the French, rejected Malcolm's advances, but Jones, whom Minto refused to recognize, was more successful and signed with the Shah what came to be known as the Preliminary Treaty (1809). The Governor-General was instructed to accept the Treaty and defray the expenses of the mission. On his second visit (1810), Malcolm was made welcome by the Persians, but both the English envoys were soon recalled and the treaty itself finalised in 1811 by Sir Gore Ouseley.

Representing the John Company (q.v.) at the Lahore court, Metcalfe (q.v.) carried on prolonged negotiations with Maharaja Ranjit Singh (q.v.) and finally persuaded him, through diplomacy, threats and a show of force, to sign the Treaty of Amritsar (q.v.). Minto rejected the defensive alliance drawn up by Captain Seeton with the Amirs of Sind (q.v.). The latter became suspicious of the British *volte face* and Smith, who replaced Seeton, could make no headway till 1809 when the Amirs finally agreed to sign the Treaty of Hyderabad. Elphinstone's (q.v.) mission to Afghanistan proved infructuous, for the treaty drawn up with Shah Shuja, and ratified in June 1809, was nullified by the Afghan Amir's deposition soon after its conclusion.

During Minto's tenure of office, the French and Dutch settlements in the East Indies were also over-powered, leaving England in an unrivalled position. His successful expeditions to the Persian Gulf, Mauritius, Bourbon (Reunion) and the eastern archipelago, more especially Java, received applause unlike those of his predecessor Wellesley's (q.v.). In the result, Amboyna (1810), the Molucca Islands, the Isle of Bourbon and Mauritius were annexed.

By the end of 1808, Minto was forced to attend to internal affairs. Travancore, whose subsidy was in arrears, was in a state of rebellion under the leadership of its Diwan, Velu Thampi; the latter was defeated by February 1809 and the state made into a British possession. English officers had been chafing against the invidious treatment meted out to the Bengal and Madras armies and the cut in their extra allowances: they mutinied under Lieutenant General Macdowall in January 1809 and despite efforts to check it, the mutiny spread. Sir George Barlow (q.v.), who had ordered the suspension and removal of some officers, refused to relent and, with the help of Indian officers and soldiers, outmanoeuvred the rebels. By the time Minto arrived in Madras, peace had been restored, the officers having signed a declaration eschewing violence.

In his relations with the Indian States (q.v.), Minto generally steered a middle course between extremes, compelling some rulers to accept defensive alliances while others were subjected to intervention through admonition and advice. But his moderate policies made him ignore the activities of the Pindaris (q.v.), the Gurkhas and the Burmese who, it is held, if checked in time, may not have posed major problems to his successors.

Minto attempted to improve the administration of justice and took a genuine interest in education. He took steps which were soon to result in the establishment of a number of Muslim colleges and the reform of the (Muslim) Madrassa in Calcutta. Additionally, he helped in broadening the curriculum of the College of Fort William. Though not averse to the spread of Christianity, he was known for his tolerance and secular outlook, which were exemplified in his admonition to the Serampore missionaries not to circulate inflammatory and prejudicial literature against Hinduism and Islam. He also forbade the use of Indian converts in proseleytisation.

Towards the end of Minto's tenure in office, the Charter Act (q.v.) of 1813 was passed. His term was marked by a substantial advance in the material prosperity of India as well as by a considerable extension and consolidation of the power of the Company. His administration was 'moderate and pacific' on the whole. The preservation of British power in the east by the elimination of European rivals was the crowning achievement of his tenure; for although there was no extension to the political map, he did much to consolidate the influence of his government.

Minto retired in February 1813 and died a year later, in June 1814.

S. R. Bakshi, *British Diplomacy and Administration in India, 1807–13*, New Delhi, 1971; *DNB*, VI, pp. 673–5 (James McCullen Rigg).

Fourth Earl Minto (1845–1914)

Gilbert John Murray Elliot, the fourth Earl of Minto, was Governor-General and Viceroy of India from 1905 to 1910. He could boast of connections with this country stretching over three generations. Thus, his great-grandfather, the First Earl of Minto (q.v.), was an able and vigorous ruler of India, while his mother's father had commanded the Deccan army in the Marquess of Hastings' (q.v.) Pindari and Maratha Wars (qq.v.).

After schooling at Eton and graduating from Trinity College, Cambridge, Minto served with the Scots Guards for 3 years. Subsequently he saw a great deal of military action—in Europe, Asia and Egypt; in the Second Afghan War (q.v.), he was attached to the staff of Sir Frederick (afterwards Earl) Roberts in the Kurram valley. During 1883-5, he was military secretary to Lord Lansdowne (q.v.), then Governor-General of Canada. Failing to get elected to Parliament in 1886, Minto directed his energies to local county politics until, in 1898, he was appointed Governor-General of Canada. The most important events of his period of office there were the sudden shifting of the Klondyke gold mines; Canada's adoption of preferential tariffs for British goods; the dispatch of Canadian forces to the Boer War (1899-1902) and the settlement of the Alaskan boundary dispute with the U.S.A. His successful tenure in Canada made Minto an eligible candidate for the Indian appointment as Lord Curzon's (q.v.) successor.

Although an appointee of the Unionist government (1895-1905), Minto's tenure of office synchronized with that of John (later Viscount) Morley (1838-

1923), the lineal descendant of philosophical radicals at the India Office. Despite their diametrically different backgrounds, they co-operated fully with each other. The political atmosphere in India was one of uneasy distrust and uncertainty, a direct result of Whitehall following extremely controversial policies in recent years. Minto had come prepared to achieve his twin objectives—of re-establishing rapport between the Government and aspiring Indian nationalists through a policy of reform, combined with stern suppression of all those elements that endangered this objective. Fortunately, with Morley as the new Secretary of State, there was little likelihood of any opposition to this policy. At the same time, Minto was exposed to a great deal of interference in the petty details of day-to-day administration from an over-enthusiastic, if also overbearing, Secretary of State.

Tory by birth and conviction, Minto was none the less fully alive to the nationalist ferment in India and recognized the presence of the Indian National Congress (q.v.) as the most important and formidable force to be reckoned with. After carefully surveying the situation, he came to the conclusion that an acceptance of the demands made by the Moderates was the only way of securing Indian support for governmental policies. This would serve the purpose of indirectly undermining the influence of militant sections among the nationalists.

The rapidly increasing influence of the Extremists haunted Minto, and he was aware that the unappeased educated middle-class membership of the Congress might accept militancy as a surer way of securing its demands. All this notwithstanding, he was not prepared to recommend 'self rule' for India. At the same time, he conceded the need for larger Indian representation in the Legislative Councils, a greater share in the administration of the country and even accepted the necessity of having more Indian members in the Executive Council of the Viceroy and the Secretary of State's India Council.

To check the increase in terrorist activity, all seditious and inflammatory literature was banned and suspected terrorists apprehended. The Viceroy affirmed that the Partition of Bengal (q.v.) was 'a settled fact' albeit conceding, in private, that there was reason enough for agitation. To prevent militant nationalists from gaining ground, he accepted the resignation of Sir Bampfylde Fuller (q.v.), then Lieutenant-Governor of the newly-created province of East Bengal and Assam. All literature pouring in from revolutionaries abroad was proscribed, while the Press Act of 1908 clamped down stringent restrictions on everything printed within the country. The convening of mass meetings where speeches subversive of established authority might be delivered was thwarted by the Prevention of Seditious Meetings Act (q.v.). This was followed by the Indian Criminal Law Amendment Act (q.v.), which declared all terrorist associations illegal.

As these draconian measures became operative, all suspects arrested between 1907-10 were prosecuted. Many more were deported, especially those connected with the Maniktala bomb conspiracy and the Muzzafarpur murders. Tilak (q.v.) too was deported for showing sympathy towards violence in political acitivity, as also Lala Lajpat Rai (1865-1928) and Ajit Singh (q.v.), presumably for mounting an agitation against the Panjab Colonization Bill. It appears that Morley did not favour deportation, but

Minto went full steam ahead, resenting the Secretary of State's interference in situations where be felt the latter's information was far from complete or even adequate.

During Minto's tenure political consciousness among the Muslims found expression in the dispatch, in 1906, of a deputation to the Viceroy outlining Muslim demands, and later in the year in the formation of the All-India Muslim League (q.v.). The Viceroy recognized in these developments an ideal opportunity to develop a counterpoise to the Congress so as to undermine its standing as an all-India body representative of all communities and sections comprising Indian society. Keen students of the contemporary political scene concede that Minto felt the same concern for Muslims as he did for the princes, the landholders, etc. Thus, it is evident that in the Minto-Morley Reforms (q.v.), then on the political anvil, he made sure that Muslims obtain separate representation. While he may not have initiated a separatist Muslim movement, Minto did undoubtedly encourage it.

M. N. Das maintains that Minto was the prime author of the Anglo-Muslim rapprochement which had become necessary on account of a number of developments both in and outside the country. The Viceroy's philosophy, in terms of his advocacy of communal electorates, was to weaken Indian nationalism and in this objective he was singularly successful for 'when communal conservatism united with an apprehensive imperialism, still at its height, insurmountable obstacles arose to national unity and revolutionary programmes. That was the beginning of the tragedy of Indian nationalism.'

To counterbalance the disaffection caused by the repressive measures and to appease the Moderates led by Gokhale (q.v.), Minto evinced great interest in the passage of the Government of India Act, 1909. Though Morley has often been credited with initiating the reforms, a careful scrutiny of records shows that the senior partner was Minto, the Conservative Viceroy, *not* Morley, the Liberal minister. Minto himself affirmed that the reforms had their genesis 'in a note of my own addressed to my colleagues in August 1906 . . . . It was based entirely on the views I had myself formed of the position of affairs in India. It was due to no suggestion from home.' *Inter alia,* the Viceroy took the initiative in the appointment of an Indian to his Executive Council and was in favour of sweeping away the official majority in the Supreme Legislative Council. This, however, was too drastic a proposal for Morley to support.

Minto's acceptance of enlarged legislative councils did not imply that he had any faith in the institution of representative government, for, while conceding the demand, he insisted on an increase in the Viceroy's authority so that the executive would be independent of legislative control. Membership of these councils, Minto had argued, should be through election and nomination while Morely showed a preference for electoral colleges.

Anticipating adverse Muslim reaction to the appointment of an Indian to his Executive Council, Minto tried to prepare his ground. In the process, he came to the conclusion that the time had come to overrule the bureaucracy, should it oppose the measure. He realized that educated Indians were no longer prepared to accept humiliating treatment. His proposed measure faced opposition in the House of Lords, yet eventually S. P. Sinha's (q.v.)

appointment to the Governor-General's Council was confirmed. Minto had carefully made his selection so as to avoid giving the Congress a sense of victory. With the princes, the Governor-General maintained friendly relations and even suggested the constitution of a Council of Princes. The proposal was rejected in Whitehall but its wisdom was evident in the loyalty of the princely states during World War I.

A feature of Minto's viceroyalty was the increasing influence of the Secretary of State upon the policy of the Indian government. This was due, *inter alia,* to Whitehall's determination to extend liberal principles in the governance of the empire, the dominant personality of Morley and the Viceroy's disinclination to quarrel with him. Constitutional pundits noted with grave misgiving the tendency of both the Viceroy and the Secretary of State to neglect their councils and permanent officials: they raised and all but settled important questions through an intimate private correspondence.

His detractors rated Minto's administration a disaster: 'K[itchner] and the secretaries run the government, Lady Minto runs the patronage and H. E. [His Excellency] runs the stables.' Minto's policy has been called one of counterpoise, conciliation and repression. He sought support for British rule in its traditional allies—the ruling princes and the landed aristocrats—so as to counteract the growing influence of the leaders coming up in the new middle class. A possible foil to the Congress was his projected council of chiefs and landlords. Additionally, he strove to conciliate the loyalists by giving them a larger share in the executive administration and the enlarged councils. At the same time, he curbed the activities of the Extremists and terrorists by using the 'strong hand', greatly strengthening the coercive apparatus with a view to eradicating 'anarchist crimes' and 'cowardly conspiracies'.

India's foreign relations during Minto's tenure were completely dominated by the home government's desire to maintain peace with China and Russia. Morley therefore rejected Minto's proposal to take up the threads of Tibetan policy more or less where Curzon had left them and consequently, in February 1908, despite protests from the Indian authorities, troops were withdrawn from the Chumbi valley inside Tibet. Earlier, the Anglo-Russian Convention (1907), on which the Indian government had strong reservations, was pushed through, Morley making it clear that the policy of *entente* with Russia was not a matter for debate, much as the Indian government might be consulted over its details. *Inter alia,* the *entente* guaranteed non-interference by the two European powers in Tibet and recognized the status quo in Afghanistan. Unhappily at the time of its conclusion, it ignored the Amir whose friendship the Indian government had been assiduously cultivating to help keep peace on the north-west frontier. Though apprised of the Convention, the Afghan Amir Habibullah (q.v.), who had earlier visited India and England, refused to abide by its terms or even accord it recognition.

Minto left India in 1910 and died suddenly 4 years later. On returning home, he was the recipient of the Order of the Garter and the freedom of the cities of London and Edinburgh, besides other honours.

Syed Razi Wasti, *Lord Minto and the Indian Nationalist Movement 1905–1910*, Oxford, 1964; M. N. Das, *India under Morley and Minto: politics behind revolution, repression and reform*, London, 1964; Pardaman Singh, *Lord Minto and Indian Nationalism, 1905–10*, Allahabad, 1976.

The Minto–Morley Reforms (1909)

Officially known as the Government of India Act, 1909, the Minto-Morley Reforms take their name after their official sponsors, Minto (q.v.), then Governor-General, and John Morley (1838–1923), Secretary of State for India.

In 1908, the British Parliament had appointed a Royal Commission on Decentralization to inquire into the relations between the Government of India and the provinces and suggest ways and means to simplify and improve them. More specifically, it was asked to suggest 'how the system of government could be better adapted both to meet the requirements and promote the welfare of the different provinces and without impairing its strength or unity to bring the executive power into closer touch with local conditions.' Later in the year, on the basis of its recommendations, a Bill was introduced in Parliament which, in May 1909, emerged as the new scheme of constitutional reform.

Its authors claimed that the chief merit of the Act lay in its provisions to further enlarge the legislative councils and at the same time make them more representative and effective. This was sought to be done under two main heads—constitutional and functional. Constitutionally, the councils were now bigger, their numbers doubled in some cases and more than doubled in others. Thus, whereas the Indian Councils Act (q.v.) of 1892 had authorized only a maximum of 16 additional members, that figure was now raised to 60. In much the same manner, the number of additional members for the Presidencies of Madras, Bombay and Bengal was raised, from 20 to 50.

The proportion of official to non-official members in the Governor-General's Council was substantially reduced, the new figures were 36 to 32. Of the latter (32), 27 were to be elected and 5 nominated. In this way, the Council continued to have an official majority. This was deliberate policy, for it was understood that 'in its legislative as well as executive character [the Council] should continue to be so constituted as to ensure its constant and uninterrupted power to fulfil the constitutional obligations that it owes and must always owe to H M's Government and to the Imperial Parliament.' In the Provinces, there was to be a non-official majority for the first time. In Bengal there was even an elected majority, outnumbering both the official as well as nominated non-official blocs—28 to 20 and 4 respectively.

The system of election was introduced in an ingenious manner. The Act enabled certain recognized bodies and associations to recommend candidates who, even though there was no obligation to accept them, were rarely rejected in practice. Provision was also made for some members to be elected in accordance with regulations made under the Act with regard to the principle of representation. A necessary corollary of this was the provision for separate electorates for Muslims, landholders, chambers of commerce and universities on the plea that 'with varying and conflicting interests, representation in the European sense was an obvious impossibility'. The separate electorates thus introduced for Muslims were later viewed by the Simon Commission (q.v.) as 'a cardinal problem and ground of controversy at every revision of the Indian electoral system'.

Apart from their constitution, the functions of the councils also underwent a change. They could now, for instance, discuss the budget before it was finally settled, propose resolutions on it and divide upon those resolutions. The budget apart, members could discuss matters of public importance through resolutions and divisions. Additionally, the right to ask questions was enlarged and supplementaries allowed. It may be noted that the resolutions were in the nature of recommendations and were not binding on the government. In fact, any of these might be disallowed at his discretion by the head of the government acting as President of the council. No resolutions could be moved in matters concerning the army, conduct of foreign relations, the Indian States (q.v.) and sundry other subjects. Of 168 resolutions moved in the Imperial Legislative Council to the end of 1917, only 24 were accepted by the government; 68 were withdrawn; 76 rejected.

A word on the voters and constituencies. The latter, composed of non-official members of the provincial councils, returned 9 members; on an average they had only 22 voters, and in one case a bare 9. The total number of votes by which all the elected members were returned was around 4,000, less than 150 for an average member! Constituencies were small—the largest had only 650 electors. Of 27 elected members, 7 were to be chosen by landowners, 5 by Muslims, 2 by chambers of commerce and the rest through provincial legislatures. The total membership of the Councils was now 370 as against 139 in 1892, and the number of elected members was 135 as against 39 (in 1892).

A much-trumpeted change was the appointment of an Indian to the Executive Council of the Governor-General; Indians were also appointed to the councils in Madras and Bombay. Satyendra Prasanna Sinha (q.v.), later Lord Sinha, was the first Law Member. Two Indians were appointed to the Council of the Secretary of State in London. In Madras and Bombay, the Executive Councils were enlarged from 2 to 4. Such councils were also to be formed in provinces ruled by Lieutenant-Governors. An executive council was thus constituted in Bengal (1909) and Bihar and Orissa (1912). The United Provinces however gained such a council in 1915.

The 1909 Reforms did not envisage responsible government. The executive could not be driven out of office by an adverse vote of the legislature and the Governor-General in Council remained responsible to the British Parliament through the Secretary of State for India. It was this bottleneck which made the authors of the Montagu-Chelmsford (q.v.) Report confess that the 1909 reforms 'afforded no answer and could afford no answer, to Indian political problems . . . . Responsibility is the savour of popular government, and that savour the present councils wholly lack'.

Morley however was quite clear as to what his objective was: 'If I were attempting to set up a parliamentary system in India, or if it could be said that this chapter of reforms led directly or indirectly to the establishment of a parliamentary system in India, I for one would have nothing to do with it. . . If my existence, either officially or corporeally, were to be prolonged 20 times longer than either is likely to be, a parliamentary system in India is not at all the goal to which I for one moment aspire.' The idea of India emerging as a self-governing colony was, Morley noted, 'for many a day to come—long after the short span of time that may be left to us—this was a mere dream'.

Curzon (q.v.) who none the less saw the 'inevitable result' of the new scheme as the emergence of parliamentary government in India was 'under the strong opinion' that, in the process, the government would tend to become 'less paternal and less beneficient to the poorer classes of the population'.

Anil Chandra Banerjee, *Constitutional History of India*, 3 vols, New Delhi, 1977–1978, II, 1858–1919; M. V. Pylee, *Constitutional History of India, 1600–1950*, reprint, Bombay, 1972; S. R. Mehrotra, 'The Morley-Minto Reforms' in *Towards India's Freedom and Partition*, New Delhi, 1979, pp. 115–23.

Maulana Mohamed Ali Jauhar (1878–1931)

Mohamed Ali Jauhar of Khilafat fame belonged to a family of Najibabad in the district of Bijnor. After 1857 the family had moved to a town near Moradabad. A student of Aligarh, he graduated with honours and was sent to Oxford with the intention of competing for the Indian Civil Service examination. Unable to qualify for the I. C. S., he remained in Oxford, where he read history.

On return home, Mohamed Ali did a brief stint as Education Officer in the state of Rampur in U. P. Dissatisfied, he resigned and tried unsuccessfully to take a law degree from the University of Allahabad. Subsequently, he served in Baroda for 7 years. During this period he became increasingly interested in the contemporary political scene and began giving expression to his views in newspapers. He eventually concluded that his true calling lay in journalism and active politics. He left Baroda for Calcutta, where he started a weekly, *Comrade*, in January 1911. Mohamed Ali affirmed that his objective was 'to serve his community and to bring about better relations' between the rulers and the ruled. The following year he shifted to Delhi, the country's new capital. Here, in addition to the English weekly, he started an Urdu daily called *Hamdard* through which he hoped to reach and involve the Muslim masses against government policies deemed inimical to their interests. The paper's popularity is said to have earned the displeasure of the government and it was suppressed in 1915.

In the Balkan wars (1912–13), where Turkey faced the combined onslaught of Serbia, Bulgaria, Greece and Rumania and was completely routed, the sufferings of its soldiers moved Indian Muslims to sympathy and action. In the result, a Red Crescent mission to Turkey was organized (1912) under the leadership of Mohamed Ali and Dr M. A. Ansari (q.v.).

Mohamed Ali's own interest in Muslim welfare can be traced to his education at Aligarh and the inspiration he derived from the movement that bore its name. He maintained his contacts and was among the co-founders of the All India Muslim League (q.v.) in 1906, giving full-throated support to the idea of a Muslim university and helped to raise funds for it. He assisted in setting up the Jamia Millia Islamia which was later transferred to Delhi.

In the field of politics, Mohamed Ali was responsible for some major developments—active involvement of the masses, political extremism among the Muslims and the cult of pan-Islamism which manifested itself in the Khilafat Movement (q.v.). He used religion effectively as the motivating force—activating Muslims to emerge from their apathy and forging a mass movement against a foreign-dominated government. He declared that the Muslims had no need to remain loyal to the British; the latter had betrayed them in India by rescinding the Partition of Bengal (q.v.) and, overseas, by the treatment meted out to Turkey. And in so far as Islam knew no geographical, caste or colour barriers, he exhorted Muslims from all over the world to unite and oust the foreigner. To Mohamed Ali, politics and religion were inseparable, which made him demand an independent, religion-oriented India. His fiery speeches, newspaper appeals and attacks on government policies landed him and his brother Shaukat Ali (q.v.) in jail in May 1915.

Mohamed Ali's detention lasted until December 1919. The Khilafat Movement, of which he was the principal author, was directed towards arriving at a 'compromise between pan-Islamism and Indian nationalism'. Essentially, the Maulana demanded that the Jazirat-ul-Arab, including Mesopotamia, Arabia, Syria and Palestine with all the Muslim holy places situated therein, must remain under the direct suzerainty of the Caliph. Unfortunately, the peace treaties (1919-20) did severe violence to such demands and thereby generated powerful tensions among the Muslims. After his release from jail, the Maulana became painfully aware that Muslims by themselves may not be able to achieve their objective. Only a united attempt by all Indians, Hindus and Muslims alike, would shake the Raj's foundations. Fortunately for him, Gandhi (q.v.), who had emerged as leader of the Indian National Congress (q.v.), was a firm believer in Hindu-Muslim unity. Gandhi placed great faith in the Ali brothers and raised no objection to their preoccupation with Islam.

Mohamed Ali raised the 'Caliphate in danger' slogan and mobilized the Muslims for what some term an anti-imperialist, anti-British movement while others prefer to describe it as pure and simple pan-Islamism. Apart from the need to win over Hindus to the Khilafat cause, Mohamed Ali had no compunction about the means to be employed to ensure the safety of the Caliph. He wholeheartedly joined the Non-cooperation Movement (q.v.) organized by Gandhi. In August 1921 he and his brother were sentenced to two years' rigorous imprisonment.

Meanwhile, with the emergence of Kemal Ataturk in Turkey, the Khilafat agitation died down for the Caliphate itself was abolished and Mohamed Ali's efforts to revive it came to nought.

The failure of Non-cooperation brought the Congress nearer the Swaraj Party (q.v.) with its plea for Council entry. The Maulana was called upon to guide the special Congress session at Delhi, which ratified the new demand. Later that year he was to preside over the annual session of the Congress at Kakinada. This, however, proved to be a short-lived honeymoon. With the all-parties conference and the Nehru Report (q.v.), the political situation underwent a sea-change and the Maulana now hitched his wagon to the prevailing winds. A one-time votary of Hindu-Muslim unity, he changed his tune and declared that, once in power, Hindus would 'make the 70 million Muslims dependent on the Hindu Sabha'.

Though a loyal Indian, Mohamed Ali was also an intensely fervent Muslim, which accounts for his remark that 'the worst Muslim sinner and criminal was better than Mahatmaji (viz. Gandhi).' Some historians contend that, while this and similar remarks show his over-protectiveness towards Islam, they do not necessarily mean his intolerance of other faiths. To Mohamed Ali, nationalism meant the ability of each community to flower according to its genius, without fear of subjection in an independent country.

Convinced that the case of Indian Muslims would not be effectively argued at the Round Table Conference (q.v.), Mohamed Ali went to London despite ill-health. Soon after the first session was over, he collapsed (4 January 1931). His body was taken to Jerusalem where he was buried.

The Maulana's priorities were badly mixed up. Thus, while pan-Islamism was 'the concomitant of his rigid orthodoxy; the Khilafat Movement was a means to achieve the object of pan-Islamism. He also stood for the independence of the country. His thought abounds in contradictions and inconsistencies. He attempted to reconcile the realities of Indian nationalsim with pan-Islamism, but could hardly succeed. He was at once the advocate of the supremacy of Islam and the "Federation of Faiths". His ideas about democracy are vague, immature, irrelevant, and betray a lack of realistic understanding'. His ideology, it has been said, was the 'extreme type of Mullaism, which included prejudice, superstition, orthodoxy, hatred and intolerance because to the discussion of every problem he used to bring in God and His Prophet', an approach that is repugnant to rationalism.

The Khilafat Movement, as anyone could see, had meant the chaotic collection and maladministration of huge public subscriptions: 'The funds were legion, the accounts few and in financial matters, the politicians, the Ali Brothers in particular, came to be trusted by no one. They lived well. It is a fair presumption that they lived well on the proceeds of pan-Islamic politics.' From the end of the Khilafat to his death, the Maulana tried to remain in touch with the masses and guide them, a task in which, a critic contends, 'he sank to the level of the cheapest, fanatical and most ill-informed of Muslim mullahs'.

Mohamed Ali showed no clear road; yet 'no one— and certainly not Mr Jinnah (q.v.)—could challenge' him before the Muslim masses. 'It is a sad reality' that those who followed his technique and strategy 'fought the battle of Pakistan and won it.'

Mushirul Hasan, *Mohamed Ali: Ideology and Politics,* New Delhi, 1980, also (ed.), *Mohamed Ali in Indian Politics: Selected Writings,* Delhi, 1982; Allah Baksh Yusufi, *Life of Maulana Mohamed Ali Jauhar,* Karachi, 1970; Afzal Iqbal, *Life and Times of Mohamed Ali: an analysis of the hopes, fears and aspirations of Muslim India from 1878 to 1931,* Delhi, 1978, also (ed.) *Select Writings and Speeches of Maulana Mohamed Ali,* 2 vols, reprint, Lahore, 1969; G. A. Natesan (ed.), *Eminent Mussalmans,* Madras, 1926, pp. 508–44.

Mohammad Ali Muhammad of Mahmudabad (1879–1931)

A Shia from the small town of Mahmudabad in the Sitapur district of U.P., Mohammad Ali claimed descent from a thirteenth century Siddiqui Shaikh. His grandfather, Nawab Ali Khan, who greatly augmented the family estates in the last decades of Oudh's (q.v.) independent existence, played a prominent role in the Rebellion of 1857 (q.v.) and surrendered shortly before his death in the following year. His father, Raja Sher Mohammad Amir Hasan Khan, was one of the leading men of the province in the later part of the nineteenth century, the Mahmudabad estate being the second largest in U.P. (the largest was that of Balrampur). He was Vice President of the British Indian Association in 1871 and its President during 1882-92. He was also a member of the Viceroy's Council and was the recipient of many titles from the government.

Mohammad Ali received no formal education and was, in fact, taught by a private tutor. He became a Fellow of Allahabad University in 1906 and was elected a trustee of Aligarh College the same year. He was a member of the U.P. Legislative Council (1904-9) and the Governor-General's Council (1907-20) where he represented the landlords of Oudh. It is said that for fear of offending the Hindu talukdars, he did not attend the meeting of Muslim leaders in September 1906 at Lucknow to approve the memorandum presented to the fourth Earl Minto (q.v.).

A close friend of Syed Wazir Hasan (1872-1947) and a vigorous supporter of the 'Young Party' among Muslims, Mohammad Ali was an activist in politics during 1913-16 and took a leading part in an agitation over the Kanpur mosque (1913). This taste of early success in a populist cause propelled him to stake a strong claim for the leadership of the community.

The lawyers and sycophants whom U.P.'s Lieutenant Governor James Scorgie Meston (1865-1943) later characterized as the Raja's 'vile entourage', were the nucleus of the 'Young Party' in Lucknow and the source of his influence in the All India Muslim League (q.v.). It is said they 'gorged his vanity and he fed them from his purse—they gained a living and he acquired a voice in Muslim politics'. For as long as the Raja could combine his reactionary talukdari position with his progressive political allegiances, Mahmudabad made it possible for several young men to have time for politics.

At the annual session of the Muslim League in Bombay in December 1915, the 'Young Party' was shaken by the non-sectarian and nationalist presidential address of the youthful Mazharul Haq (1866-1929). The following day, Kasim Mitha, a Sunni leader of the Bombay Presidency Muslim League's opposition faction, infiltrated a body of Pathans, *julahas* and local toughs into the session and at a crucial moment broke it up with cries of 'This is the (Indian National) Congress (q.v.)' and 'they want to join the Congress'. The League leaders retired to the Taj Mahal Hotel where in a session to which attendance was by invitation they passed a resolution appointing a committee to frame a reform scheme and, where necessary, to confer with other communities and organizations. Then—'to cap Lucknow's triumph over Bombay'—the Raja of Mahmudabad was elected president of the League in place of the Aga Khan (q.v.).

Even though heavily in debt during his 'Young Party' days, the Raja had acted as paymaster and employer of many a Muslim leader, including Maulanas Mohamed Ali (q.v.) and Shaukat Ali (q.v.), Raja Ghulam Hussain and Choudhry Khaliquzzaman. He was president of the Muslim League session at Calcutta in 1917 as well as of the party's special sessions at Bombay in 1917 and 1918. It was the arrival of Spencer Harcourt Butler (1869–1938) as Lieutenant-Governor of U.P. in 1918 that pulled the Raja out of 'Young Party' politics. Butler's predecessor, James Meston, is also said to have administered a stern warning to the Raja by threatening to revoke his talukdari sanad unless he functioned more moderately. In the result, the Raja did pull himself back. But a contributory factor to the Raja's *volte face* was the drubbing he and Wazir Hasan received at the Delhi Muslim League session in December 1918—treatment ill-befitting a talukdar and nobleman—which made them leave Delhi 'in disgust'. Both now resigned from the League, for it was no longer easy for them to reconcile the growing hostility towards the government as well as themselves by many members of that body. In the circumstances, an active association with the League would, they argued, belie their hope of receiving the rewards of collaboration from the British and come in the way of what they deemed best for the Muslims. In the following two years, the Lucknow clique, like many of the Congress leaders with whom they had formed the joint reforms scheme, left the front line of nationalist politics.

It is said that Harcourt Butler made the Raja's support of the Montagu-Chelmsford Reforms (q.v.) certain by promising him the post of Home Member in the first administration formed under the new constitutional dispensation. Whether the story be true or not, Mahmudabad was more moderate at the special session of the League over which he presided in September 1918 for the League now refused to join the Congress in condemning the Montford scheme of reforms.

Thereafter the Raja received much official patronage. He was Home Member in the U.P. government between 1920-5, President of the British Indian Association between 1917-21 and again in 1930-1 and Vice-Chancellor of Aligarh Muslim University, 1920-3. In 1925, the personal title of Maharaja was conferred on him. Mahmudabad was president of the Calcutta session of the Muslim League in 1928.

Francis Robinson, *Separatism among Indian Muslims, the Politics of the United Provinces' Muslims, 1860–1923*, Delhi, 1975; Sen, *DNB,* pp. 40–1 (M. S. Jain).

Montagu–Chelmsford Reforms (1919)

Officially, the Government of India Act, 1919, the Montagu-Chelmsford Reforms, named after their principal co-sponsors, E. S. Montagu (1879-1924), then Secretary of State for India and Lord Chelmsford (q.v.), then Governor General, were a logical sequel to the historic Declaration of 20 August 1917 (q.v.). Prior to it, the accepted principle of government had been that both authority as well as responsibility for the governance of India was vested in the King-in-Parliament who exercised it through the agency of the Secretary of State in London, the Governor-General in Council in India and the governors-in-council in the different provinces. The association of Indians in the legislative sphere was designed only to acquaint the rulers with the thoughts and aspirations of the governed.

Since, in terms of the August Declaration, there was to be a gradual transfer of authority to Indian hands, the mode and measure of such transfer required to be worked out. Again, to the extent that transfer of responsibility in the provincial sphere as a whole was considered premature, a system of dyarchy was established. A signal contribution in working out the details was made by Lionel George Curtis (q.v.) and his Round Table group and finds its fullest elaboration in his work entitled *Dyarchy* (1920). Under it ministers responsible to the legislature held charge of such subjects as were 'transferred' to popular control, while the governor and his councillors were to be incharge of 'reserved' subjects for which they were responsible to Parliament.

Broadly, 'transferred' subjects included: local self-government, medical administration, education other than European and Anglo-Indian, agriculture, fisheries, co-operative societies, excise, the development of industries and religious endowments. 'Reserved' subjects comprised land-revenue administration, famine relief, the administration of justice, police and prisons.

The broad criteria for 'transferred' subjects were: those which afforded most opportunity for local knowledge and service; in which Indians had shown themselves to be keenly interested; in which mistakes, even though serious, would not be irremediable; which stood most in need of development; which concerned the interests of classes that would be adequately represented in the legislature (and not those which could not be so represented).

While the functions of the 'reserved' and 'transferred' areas were clearly defined, their sources of revenue were combined. The allocation of expenditure by the two was a matter of agreement; the governor acting as an arbiter in case of differences. A taxation measure or proposal was to be discussed by the entire government, but a decision on it was to be taken only by the part that initiated it. The governor was to regulate business in such a manner as to make sure that responsibility of the two halves in respect of matters under their respective control was kept 'clear and distinct'. He was to encourage the habit of joint deliberation between his ministers and councillors.

Even though power had been transferred in certain areas, the governor could yet refuse his ministers' advice 'if [he had] sufficient cause to dissent from their opinion'. He could over-rule them, and act on his own, if by accepting the advice in question—the safety and tranquillity of the province was likely to be threatened; the interests of the minority communities—communal or racial—or of the members of the public services were affected; or when unfair discrimination was made in matters affecting commercial or industrial interests. In all this the governor was to keep the major objective of the reforms constantly in view, viz., that people were trained to 'acquire such habits of political action and respect such conventions as will best, and soonest, fit them for self-government'. As with provincial administration, there was also to be complete popular control 'so far as possible' in the field of local government; it was, largely independent of the Government of India and responsible, if partly, to popular representatives.

On the legislative side, the councils were considerably enlarged. The proportion of elected members was not less than 70%, and of officials not less than 20%. In 1926 the composition of the legislatures of all the provinces taken together was: 14.5% officials; 8.6% non-officials nominated to represent aborigines, backward tracts, depressed classes, Anglo-Indians, labour; 9.9% elected members representing special interests—landholders, universities, commerce and industry and 67% elected members, returned through territorial constituencies.

The last category, members elected through territorial constituencies, comprised 'general', Muslims, Sikhs (in the Panjab), Indian Christians (in Madras), Anglo-Indians (in Madras and Bengal) and Europeans (in all the provinces except the Panjab, the Central Provinces and Berar and Assam). The 'general' constituency included such voters as did not find a place in any of the communal or special constituencies. In the distribution of seats, the minority communities were given weightage—viz., representation in excess of their population ratio. As for franchise, property qualifications were considerably lowered and women given the right to vote in all the provinces. In 1926, the proportion of those enfranchised to the total population stood at 2.8%.

Normally, all legislative measures and annual budgets were to be passed by the provincial councils. However in so far as the 'reserved' half was outside the purview of a council, the governor was empowered to certify such bills and restore such grants as had been rejected by the legislature if he considered such action necessary for the proper fulfilment of his responsibility to Parliament.

While the 1909 Act had laid down the maximum number of seats in the councils, the act of 1919 specified the minimum. Thus, as against a maximum of 50 in the provinces, the new chambers had a minimum of over 100. Madras had 118, Bombay, 111 and Bengal, 125. The term of a council was three years. After its dissolution, a new council was to be elected within a period of 6 months.

Since uniform territorial constituencies were deemed unsuited to Indian conditions, constituencies were designed to represent particular communities (e.g., Muslims) or special interests (e.g. landholders or chambers of commerce). Franchise was restricted. It revolved around i) residence in the constituency for a minimum period of time; ii) ownership or occupation of a house which had a minimum rental value; iii) payment of a minimum municipal tax or income tax or some other tax or receipt of a military pension.

Members could ask questions as well as supplementaries. They could discuss resolutions to ventilate public grievances and move for adjournment to take note of matters of urgent public interest. Not only did they have a general discussion on the budget but they also voted on grants. Their major limitation lay in the special powers with which the governor was vested both in law-making as well as voting on the budget.

In regard to central administration, the two cardinal principles of the Act were: (i) the Government of India was to remain responsible to Parliament, although the Imperial Legislative Council was to be enlarged and popular representation and influence in it enhanced; (ii) the control of Parliament and the Secretary of State over the Government of India (and the provinces) was to be relaxed in proportion to the changes contemplated in (i).

The 'devolution rules' which were part of the Act distinguished carefully between the spheres of the central and provincial governments, even though the demarcation was not as rigid as it usually is in a federal set up. In the sphere of financial devolution, the provinces now framed their own budgets whereas previously provincial budgets were part of the central budget. Additionally, they made their own taxation proposals; previously prior sanction of the Governor-General was necessary to do so. In legislative devolution a measure of central control was exercised. Thus an authentic copy of every Act to which the governor had given his assent had to be sent to the Governor-General who may or may not accord his assent to it. If the Governor-General gave his assent, a copy of the Act had to be sent to the Secretary of State who, again, may or may not give his assent.

As there was no transfer of power at the Centre, the Governor-General-in-Council continued to be responsible to Parliament through the Secretary of State in Council in respect of all matters. Before the 1919 Act, the strength of the Governor-General's Executive Council was 6 ordinary and 1 extraordinary member. Under the new Act, there was greater elasticity in the size of the Council, while the number of Indians on it was raised from 2 to 3.

The legislature at the Centre was bicameral, consisting of the Legislative Assembly, the lower house, and the Council of State, the upper house. Elections to the lower house were direct, the principle of communal or separate representation was recognized while industry, commerce and landholders were given special representation. The Legislative Assembly was to have 145 members, although its strength could be increased, if necessary. At least five-sevenths of its total membership was elected while one-third of the remainder were to be non-officials. The representation of communities and special interest was broadly on lines similar to those followed for the provincial legislatures. Except in special constituencies, elected members of both houses were returned through territorial constituencies on the basis of a high property franchise—qualifications in respect of the upper house being set much higher than those for the lower house.

As in the provincial legislatures, normal procedure laid down that all legislative measures as well as the annual budget relating to the Centre should be passed by the central legislature. But in so far as the Governor-General's ultimate responsibility was to Parliament—and not to the central legislature—he was, in his individual capacity, empowered to certify bills and restore grants that had not been approved. He was also empowered to issue ordinances.

In the legislative field, the powers of the Council of State were coordinate with those of the Assembly. Since the government could always depend upon a majority of the Council to support its measures, the popular majority in the Assembly could not enforce its will against it in any legislative matter. In the budget, a number of items were non-votable, with the result that the legislature was not even allowed to discuss them.

The Governor-General's powers in the legislative field were extensive. He could refuse permission to introduce certain bills where such advance permission was necessary. If the legislature rejected a bill recommended by him, he could certify its being essential 'for the safety, tranquillity and interests' of British India. The only check on him was that such Acts were required to be laid before Parliament for at least 8 days prior to their receiving Royal assent. The Governor-General could refuse assent to bills passed by the legislature whenever he deemed it necessary. In financial matters, he could restore, if necessary, any grant rejected or cut by the Assembly.

As regards the Home Government, it was clearly understood that, to the extent power had been constitutionally transferred to Indian hands, intervention by Parliament and its agents should cease. Thus the Speaker of the House of Commons ruled in 1921 that parliamentary criticism should not extend to 'transferred' subjects in the provinces. As for the central government and the 'reserved' subjects in the provinces, since legal responsibility for them vested in Parliament, there could be no abrogation of control. Even here the Joint Select Committee on the India Bill (1919) ruled that 'in the exercise of his responsibility to Parliament which he cannot delegate to anyone else, the Secretary of State may reasonably consider that only in exceptional circumstances should he be called upon to intervene in matters of purely Indian interest where the government and legislature of India are in agreement'. This was to be particularly so in matters of fiscal policy. The Committee had expressed the view that the relations of the Secretary of State and the Governor-General-in-Council should be regulated by similar principles so far as 'reserved' subjects were concerned.

The fiscal convention in respect of tariff policy was accepted, although Indian opinion was less than happy. The Governor-General and a majority of his Council, the latter argued, consisted of Englishmen whose first loyalty naturally lay elsewhere. The proposed convention in respect of 'reserved' subjects in the provinces found appropriate reference in the Instrument of Instructions issued to the Governor-General.

Peter Robb has suggested that the 'lynch-pin' of the Act of 1919 'in so far as techniques of political control were concerned was the attempt to create a "free-market" polity for India'; that, despite criticism, the scheme of dyarchy served India for 15 years and was adapted to a further stage of advance with dyarchy, in effect, at the Centre under the Government of India Act 1935 (q.v.). Algernon Rumbold who as civil servant in the India Office had first-hand experience of the formulation of the Montford reforms has put forth a powerful, and well-argued, thesis that the reforms were 'unnecessary, badly conceived and went too far'. In the result, he avers, they tended to divert Indian political development to the wrong path.'

Anil Chandra Banerjee, *Constitutional History of India*, 3 vols, New Delhi, 1978, II, 1858–1919; M. V. Pylee, *Constitutional History of India, 1600–1950*, reprint, Bombay, 1972; P. G. Robb, *The Government of India and Reforms Policies towards Politics and the Constitution*, Oxford, 1976; Algernon Rumbold, *Watershed in India, 1914–1922*, London, 1979.

The Moplah Rebellion (1921)

The 1921 Mappilla, more popularly Moplah, Rebellion broke out at a time when the Non-cooperation and Khilafat Movements (qq.v.) and some sundry peasant upheavals were gaining ground in Malabar. In all these, religious, economic and political factors were inextricably mixed. Thus, the then Governor of Madras, Lord Willingdon, informed the home government that the Khilafat Movement 'fomented and worked by Mohammadan and Hindu Non-cooperators was essentially responsible for the disastrous occurrence'. Nationalist opinion viewed the Rebellion as a reaction to the oppression and folly of the district authorities. More specifically, they alleged, it was the rash and unwise behaviour of the local officials that brought matters to a head, and grievously injured the religious susceptibilities of the Moplahs. Others maintain that it was the rage and fanaticism of an ignorant and illiterate community (viz. the Moplahs) that was responsible for much of the destruction of life and property.

Essentially, the Moplahs include Malayali converts to Islam as well as descendants of the Arabs and Malayalis settled in the Malabar region for over a thousand years. They were mostly small agriculturists or petty traders. Poor and ignorant, they were under the influence of their Qazis and Maulvis known as Thangals. Rebellions among the Moplahs have been endemic. There were several in the nineteenth century; between 1836–54 there were as many as 22. In 1849, 64 Moplah rebels were killed; three years later there were hideous murders in which Hindu women as well as children were not spared. These were ascribed to religious fanaticism and, as a preventive measure, Moplahs were deprived of their war-knives. This did not help, for there were serious outbreaks in 1873, 1880 and another 5 during 1883–5! A major uprising disfigured the land in 1894, followed by another 2 years later. A common feature was the 'pillaging, maltreatment and murdering of Hindus'.

It should be evident that violent if small-scale Moplah disturbances were a recurring feature of the south Malabar interior between 1836–1919. These 'outbreaks' may be viewed as attempts by rural Moplahs in the south Malabar taluks of Ernad and Walluvarad to curb the British fortified power of the high-caste, mainly Brahmin and Nair, Hindu *jenmis* or landlords by means of what were, in effect, ritual challenges to British rule. What is little realized is that the defiance of British power by the Moplahs against the population of the interior in south Malabar dates from the earliest period of the rule of the East India Company (q.v.), the decade after the Muslim ruler of Mysore, Tipu Sultan (q.v.), ceded the province in 1792.

In 1921 the trouble started in the village of Pukottur, part of a thickly populated area about 5 miles north-west of Merjeri in Ernad taluk. Most of the land here was held by the Nilambut Raja, one of the richest landlords in these parts, with a large majority of the Moplahs being the Raja's tenants, sub-tenants or wage-earners. The starting point was an unseemly dispute at the Raja's palace between Mammad, a Moplah leader in the Khilafat agitation of the area, and the Raja's local agent, Thirumalphad. The police and district authorities exaggerated the situation beyond measure, and a request was relayed to the Madras government for police assistance against an anticipated communal riot. The Moplahs were outraged by the arrival of further police forces and broke out in open defiance of the law, starting virtual guerilla warfare with swords and spears, pitted in an unequal fight against guns and rifles. They committed terrible atrocities against the administration as well as their Hindu neighbours. The government called in troops to suppress the rising and measures of extreme severity were resorted to. In the middle of October, martial law was proclaimed; by the year-end, peace of a sort was restored. It appears in retrospect that the District Magistrate, E. R. Thomas, was worried not so much by the communal situation as the progress of the Khilafat and Non-cooperation Movements and the slight regard with which the public and political leaders treated him. Hence his reign of terror, in which he is said to have 'out-Dyered Dyer'.

The rebellion claimed many forcible conversions, large-scale looting and plunder of the property and belongings of non-Muslims. It has been estimated that nearly 2,500 forced conversions were made; that about 600 citizens lost their lives; that the rebels completely controlled the entire area for well-nigh six months. It may also be conceded that measures for the suppression of the rising were savage in the extreme. The troops deployed—Gurkhas, Garhwalis, Kachins—were carefully chosen so as to be devoid of any sympathy for the rebel cause and were concentrated to enforce the rigours of martial law. Of the rebels, 2,226 are said to have been killed in action; 1,615 wounded; 5,688 were captured while 38,256 surrendered. The worst-known incident was the packing of 150 Moplahs in the wagon of a goods train that slowly wended its way from Calicut to Madras in the scorching heat of summer; when opened at a wayside station it was discovered that 66 had died of suffocation while the rest were seriously unwell.

It has been held that the Rebellion, which was initially directed against landlords and their British patrons, later took on a communal character. Observers have viewed it against the background of the poor economic conditions of the Moplah peasantry, the pattern of rebel activity and the class to which the participants belonged. In some respects, the Rebellion appears to have been a continuation of the agrarian conflicts of the nineteenth century. British officials have ascribed it not to such economic factors as the land-tenure system but political incitement, fruit of the seed 'which Annie Besant (q.v.) sowed and Gandhi (q.v.) watered'. It has been suggested that by July 1921 the Moplahs had become extremely suspect about the effectiveness of the Non-cooperation Movement and the resultant disillusionment burst into open defiance of authority. Unlike the earlier rebellions of the nineteenth century, which were localized in extent and limited in scope, that of 1921 was far more intense and widespread. It embraced in its entirety the Moplah peasant populations of Ernad and Walluvarad taluks. An important after-effect of the Rebellion was large-scale famine in these areas and, to remedy it, the adoption of comprehensive tenancy legislation in the 1930's.

Asked by the government of Madras, William Logan, at one time Collector of Malabar, probed the causes of the rebellion and produced a monumental report. It demonstrated how the British owing to their faulty understanding of the land revenue system in Malabar, and their deliberate policy of bolstering up a group, ended by creating a class of 'jenmis' who came to be

looked upon as absolute proprietors of land. They were by and large caste
Hindus i.e. either Nairs or Namboodris while the preponderant majority of
the cultivating tenants in Ernad and Walluvarad taluks, the scene of the
rebellion, were Moplahs. They were subjected to arbitrary eviction, rack-
renting and numerous other exactions. Logan concluded that the class
antagonism thus generated was at the root of the Moplah revolt. By under-
playing this factor and over-emphasising the religious aspect, Dale has given
an alibi to the diabolical role of the British government. He depicts the
revolt as an attempt by Moplah Muslims to create a theocratic state based on
the tenets of Islam in Kerala. The motives of individual leaders notwithstanding, this may not hold true for the vast majority of the rebels. In
essence, there were three disparate factors merging into a single stream in
the Moplah rebellion: the Non-cooperation movement for Swaraj; the
Khilafat Movement for undoing the wrongs done to the Muslims by the
abolition of the Caliphate; the movement for tenancy reform. It was the
exigent combination of these three currents that made the movement so
powerful, so explosive.

Outside Malabar, the 1921 disturbances struck a severe blow to the
euphoria of Hindu-Muslim unity and co-operation. The stories of atrocities
that filtered out brought a rude and indeed harsh awakening to the
signatories of the Lucknow Pact (q.v.). Hindu leaders raised the cry of
Hinduism in danger and the Arya Samaj's (q.v.) *shuddhi* and *sangathan*
movements gained in momentum. This, in turn, stoked the fires of Muslim
separatism. To start with, Muslim leaders either denied the atrocities or
underplayed their import; worse, the Moplahs were praised for their zeal
and bravery. In the result, a vicious circle of accusation and counter-
accusation started leading to a grave set-back to all efforts at national unity.

Stephen F. Dale, *The Mappilas of Malabar 1498-1922: Islamic Society on the South
Asian Frontier*, Oxford, 1980; also 'The Mappilla Outbreaks: Ideology and Social
Conflict in 19th Century Kerala', *Journal of Asian Studies*(Ann Arbor, Michigan),
XXXV, 1, Nov. 1975, pp. 85–97; Conrad Wood, 'The First Moplah Rebellion
Against British Rule in Malabar', *Journal of Modern Asian Studies*, X, 4 (1976), pp.
543–76; J. Hitchcock, *History of the Malabar Rebellion*, Madras, 1921, pp. 81-6;
Richard D. Lambert, 'Hindu-Muslim Riots', unpublished thesis of the University of
Pennsylvania, 1951, microfilm, *NMML;* T. Prakasam and T. V. Venkatarama Iyer,
Non-official Report on Malabar Disturbances, Madras Provincial Congress Commit-
tee, 1921; K. N. Panikkar, 'Malabar Rebellion of 1921', unpublished article, pp.
1–35, *NMML;*

Motilal Nehru (1861–1931)

Born posthumously at Agra in May 1861, Motilal's father, Gangadhar, was
the kotwal of Delhi at the time of the Rebellion of 1857 (q.v.); his grandfather, Lakshmi Narayan, had been the first vakil of the John Company
(q.v.) at the Mughal court. Motilal's childhood was spent at Khetri in
Rajasthan where his brother Nandlal was employed. Later, his brother
practised law at Agra and when the High Court moved to Allahabad, he
settled there. The Nehrus initially hailed from Kashmir but had moved to

Delhi at the start of the eighteenth century.

As a boy Motilal was fond of outdoor sport, especially wrestling; he was a great enthusiast and full of zest for life. His early schooling was in Persian and Arabic. He attended a high school in Kanpur and matriculated from Central College in Allahabad. Although he did not complete courses for the B. A. degree, he passed the vakils' examination in 1883 with distinction. Deeply influenced by western culture and institutions, his English teachers implanted in him an intelligent, rational and sceptical outlook towards life. After completing his law studies, Motilal started practising at Kanpur and later moved to Allahabad. Here he purchased a house, rebuilt it and called it 'Anand Bhavan'. His lucrative practice meant progressive westernization, a steep rise in his standard of living and frequent visits to Europe.

Motilal's early incursions into politics were reluctant, brief and sporadic. The list of 1,400 delegates to the Allahabad session (1888) of the Indian National Congress (q.v.) included the following entry: 'Pandit Motilal, Hindu, Brahman, Vakil High Court, N.W.P. [North-Western Provinces]'. In the epic struggle between the Moderates and the Extremists after the 1907 Surat Split (q.v.), Motilal was on the side of the former. His sympathies were with the 'constitutional agitators' for, he argued, 'the reforms we wish to bring about must come through the medium of constituted authority'. In 1917, he was elected President of the Allahbad branch of Annie Besant's (q.v.) Home Rule League (q.v.). In the following year however he parted company with the Moderates and attended the Bombay Congress session which demanded *inter alia* radical changes in the Montagu-Chelmsford Reforms (q.v.). In February 1919 he launched a newspaper, the *Independent*, a counter-blast to the Anglo-Indian diehard, *Leader*.

A host of factors brought Motilal into deeper political activity. Among these, Gandhi's (q.v.) entry into politics, his son Jawaharlal's (q.v.) return from England, the Rowlatt Act (q.v.) Satyagraha and Jallianwala Bagh Massacre (q.v.) may be listed as the most important. 'Amritsar', C. F. Andrews noted, 'shook the very foundations of the faith on which Motilal had built up his life'. Motilal served on the unofficial committee set up to inquire into the Panjab disturbances. Later, he was elected to preside over the Amritsar session of the Congress in December 1919.

At the Calcutta session in September 1920, Motilal lent active support to Gandhi's Non-cooperation Movement (q.v.), being the only front-rank Congress leader to do so. Immediately thereafter he quit his legal practice, resigned from the U. P. Legislative Council and radically changed his style of living. In December 1921, both Motilal and Jawaharlal were arrested and sentenced to 6 months' imprisonment. Three years later, with C. R. Das (q.v.) and others of the same persuasion, he formed the Swaraj Party (q.v.) which had an impressive membership in the Central Legislative Assembly and in some of the provincial councils.

From 1923 to 1929 Motilal dominated the Assembly as leader of the opposition. His commanding personality, incisive wit, powerful intellect, knowledge of law, brilliant advocacy and combative spirit made him an impressive parliamentarian and a formidable opposition leader. At first he was able to command sufficient support from the moderate elements and the Muslim legislators to out-vote the government; after 1926, his party was increasingly riven by factions and divided by personal squabbles.

To start with, government measures were resisted and much delayed, but soon enough mere wrecking tactics were abandoned and the party took its full share in the work of select committees. The Simon Commission (q.v.) and the All-Parties Conference that followed pitchforked Motilal into further importance. The latter body chose him to be chairman of the committee which was to determine the principles of India's future constitution, later embodied in the Nehru Report (q.v.). Based on the concept of Dominion Status (q.v.) for India, it was anathema to the radical wing of the Congress which, led by Jawaharlal and Subhas Chandra Bose (q.v.) formed the 'Independence for India League'. The Calcutta session of the Congress resulted in a compromise to the effect that if Dominion Status were *not* granted by the end of 1929, the Congress would opt out for complete independence.

On the proscription, in 1930, of the Congress Working Committee, of which he was Chairman, Motilal was sentenced to 6 months' imprisonment, but after a few weeks' detention was released on grounds of ill-health. Later, he was imprisoned in the Salt Satyagraha (q.v.), when his health gave way. He died at Lucknow on 6 February 1931.

Motilal's outlook on life was at once rational, robust and secular. A brilliant lawyer, he was at the same time an eloquent speaker, a great parliamentarian, and a good organizer. Before entering politics he was a fearless, strong-willed, imperious man who lived the life of an English country gentleman, and imported one of India's first automobiles. A moderate realist early in his political career, he became, paradoxically, increasingly revolutionary with age. To a group of several thousand people he proclaimed: 'The government has openly declared a crusade against our national aims . . . Are we going to succumb to these official frowns?'

Ravinder Kumar in a biographical assessment has aptly summed up Motilal's place in the saga of India's freedom struggle: 'That an individual who grew up as an admirer of British values and institutions should have become an adversary of the Raj, speaks volumes of its exploitative character in India. It speaks equally forcefully of Motilal's love for his country; of his ability to outgrow the milieu in which he had achieved intellectual maturity and professional success; that he plunged into the struggle . . with a rare sense of commitment and sacrificed everything . . When men like Motilal, who were so deeply influenced by the liberal political culture of Great Britain, turned against the British Raj . . For this reason, and also because of the distinguished leadership he provided to the nationalist cause, Motilal occupies a position of lonely eminence in the history of the struggle for freedom in India.'

B. R. Nanda, *The Nehrus: Motilal & Jawaharlal Nehru*, London, 1962; S. P. Chablani (ed.), *Motilal Nehru: Essays & Reflections on his Life and Times*, New Delhi, 1961; Ravinder Kumar and D. N. Panigrahi (eds.), *Selected Works of Motilal Nehru*, I, New Delhi, 1982; *DNB 1931-1940*, pp. 648–9 (F. H. Brown).

Muddiman Committee Report (1925)

On 16 May 1924, a 9-member 'Reforms Enquiry Committee' under the

Chairmanship of Sir Alexander Muddiman, then Home Member, Government of India, was set up to examine broadly the working of Dyarchy as laid down in the Montagu-Chelmsford Reforms (q.v.). This was the aftermath of an almost complete breakdown of constitutional machinery when the Central Legislative Assembly, under the leadership of the Swaraj Party (q.v.) and its allies, either refused or drastically cut down demands contained in the budget estimates for 1924-5. On 17 March 1924, the Finance Bill itself was thrown out. The Committee's appointment shortly afterwards was designed to mollify public criticism of the working of the Reforms.

The Muddiman Committee consisted of 9 members, 3 officials and 6 non-officials. Apart from the Chairman, there were Sir Muhammad Shafi, then Law Member in the Governor-General's Executive Council, Bijay Chand Mahtab, the Maharaja of Burdwan, two European members—Arthur Froom and Henry Moncrieff Smith. Together, they were to constitute the majority, reporting separately from the minority who comprised M. A. Jinnah (q.v.), Sir R. P. Paranjpye (1876-1966), Tej Bahadur Sapru (q.v.) and Sir P. S. Sivaswami Iyer (1864-1946).

The Committee's brief, as noticed earlier, was 'to inquire into the difficulties arising from or defects inherent in the working of the Government of India Act (1919) and the Rules thereunder . . . and to investigate the feasibility and desirability of securing remedies for such difficulties or defects, consistent with the structure, policy and purpose of the Act'. More specifically, the working of the central government and the status of the Governors' Provinces was to be examined in terms of 'the structure, policy and purpose of the Act'.

The Committee held its meetings from August to December 1924 and took oral as well as written evidence from all those 'past and present' Indian ministers and Executive Councillors from the provinces who had first-hand, practical knowledge of the working of the Councils. Its report, submitted in March 1925, fell broadly into two parts. The majority suggested that the system had not been given a fair trial and, therefore, called for a review with minor changes. They argued that it was too early to undertake a revision and that the working of the Act was capable of improvement without any radical alteration in the structure. 'The partial dyarchy which was introduced is clearly a complex, confused system . . . The existing constitution is working in most provinces . . . While the period during which the present constitution has been in force has been too short to enable a well-founded opinion as to its success to be formed, the evidence before us is far from convincing that it has failed.'

The minority, on the other hand, felt that dyarchy had clearly failed and that, as the Government of the United Provinces put it, the Act was 'a complex, confused system, having no logical basis, rooted in compromise, and defensible only as transitional expedient'. Furthermore, 'the system has been severely tested during the course of this year and its practical breakdown in two provinces, viz., Bengal and the Central Provinces, as a result of the opinions of the majority of the members of the councils of those two provinces who refuse to believe in the efficacy of Dyarchy and the tension prevailing in the other Legislatures for similar reasons, point to the conclusion that the constitution requires being overhauled . . . We think that the Bihar Government has correctly summed up the position by saying that Dyarchy is working "creakily" and "minor remedies may cure a creak or two".'

The minority suggested that what was needed was a constitution framed on a permanent basis with a provision for automatic progress in the future so as to secure a certain stability in the government and the willing co-operation of the people. With this end in view, it recommended the appointment of a Royal Commission or any other agency with freer terms of reference and a larger scope of inquiry.

The Muddiman Report was the subject of a debate in the Central Legislative Assembly in September 1925. An official motion accepting the underlying principle of the majority report and its detailed recommendations was defeated. Instead, an amendment by the Swaraj Party leader Motilal Nehru (q.v.) suggesting that Parliament recognize the right of India to responsible government and convene forthwith a round table conference to frame a constitution on that basis was carried by 45 to 14 votes.

Earlier, on 7 July 1925, Lord Birkenhead, then Secretary of State for India, had announced that it was only on the basis of the majority report that immediate action could be taken and that the recommendations made by the minority could not be accepted.

Report of Reforms Enquiry Committee, Cd. 2360, HMSO, London, 1925; Maurice Gwyer and A. Appadorai, *Documents,* I, Oxford, pp. xxxvi-vii, 80-9; A. C. Banerjee, *Indian Constitutional Documents,* 3 vols, 3rd ed., Calcutta, 1961, III, pp. 118–27.

Diwan Mulraj (d. 1851)

Diwan Mulraj whose revolt became the forerunner of the Second Anglo-Sikh War (q.v.) succeeded his father Diwan Sawan Mal as the governor of Multan in 1844. Unable to meet the demands of Hira Singh Dogra and Lal Singh, ministers of the Lahore darbar, for a *nazrana* of Rs 30 lakhs, which was to be reckoned as a succession fee, and opposed to their innovations in revenue and judicial matters, Mulraj was at the end of his tether.

An expedition sent in 1846 to coerce him to pay was defeated. While confirming Mulraj in his post, the British Resident assessed the Diwan for Rs 20 lakhs, but at the same time took away the district of Jhang, nearly a third of his estate, and abolished the excise duty on goods transported by river which had hitherto constituted a substantial part of his income. In December 1847, Mulraj submitted his resignation but was persuaded not to press it. In March 1848, a new Resident, Frederick Currie (1799-1875), replaced Henry Lawrence (q.v.) and acted with undue haste. Mulraj's resignation was accepted and Kahan Singh Man, his replacement, accompanied by two British officers, P. A. Vans Agnew and Lieutenant W. A. Anderson with an escort of the troops of the Darbar, repaired to Multan.

The take-over was smooth but feelings had been badly ruffled. Multan's disbanded soldiery forced Mulraj to be their leader and fraternized with the Darbar troops. In the result, the British camp was robbed and its two officers killed.

Reluctantly, Mulraj took up arms but it was Dalhousie's (q.v.) deliberately delayed action that made him into a public hero. Herbert Edwardes at Dera Fateh Khan and General Van Cortland at Dera Ismail Khan converged on Multan from the south. Dera Gazi Khan fell in May 1848 and Mulraj, badly beaten at Kineri on 18 June, retreated to Multan. Bhai Maharaj Singh rallied to his cause, as did Sher Singh Attariwala. It was the latter's call to arms that precipitated the Second Anglo-Sikh War.

British forces soon besieged his fortress and on 22 January 1849, Mulraj was compelled to surrender. Tried as a rebel for the murder of two British officers, he was found guilty and sentenced to death. The court however held that the Diwan had been a 'victim of circumstances' and Dalhousie in confirming the sentence commuted it to 'imprisonment for life with banishment from India'.

Taken to Calcutta, *en route* to the 'black water', Mulraj fell seriously ill and died on 11 August 1851 near Buxar. He was then 30 years old.

Sitaram Kohli, *Trial of Diwan Mulraj,* Monograph no. 14, Punjab Government Record Office, Lahore, 1932; Ganda Singh, *Private Correspondence Relating to Anglo-Sikh Wars,* Amritsar, 1955; Khushwant Singh, *History of the Sikhs,* 2 vols, Princeton, 1965, II.

Muhammad Shah (1719–48)

Surnamed Roshan Akhtar, and son of Prince Khujista Adktar Jahan Shah, the youngest son of Bahadur Shah I (q.v.), Muhammad Shah was raised to the throne by the Sayyid Brothers (q.v.) after the short-lived reigns of Farrukh Siyar's (q.v.) two immediate successors.

Muhammad Shah's 29-year long rule falls into two unequal halves marked by the invasion (1739) of the Persian scourge, Nadir Shah (q.v.). Besides petty court intrigue which knew no end, its main interest in the political sphere centred around the steady expansion of Maratha power and influence and their mounting pressure on the imperial domain. Under the redoubtable Balaji Baji Rao I (q.v.), the Marathas were now a power to reckon with all the way from Gujarat to Bengal and from the Narmada to the Yamuna.

For more than a year after his accession, Muhammad Shah remained a virtual prisoner of the Sayyid brothers. That stranglehold was, however, soon broken; Husain Ali was done to death (March 1720) and Abdullah taken prisoner. No sooner were the brothers disposed of than the Emperor fell into the hands of another clique. His new wazir, Muhammad Amin Khan Chin, a cousin of the Nizam-ul-Mulk (q.v.) proved, if anything, more domineering than the Sayyids. Muhammad Shah's share in government, it has been said, 'was only to sit on the throne and to wear the crown'. The other nobles could see for themselves that the Emperor was powerless, and, in turn, they too were afraid of the wazir. The Chin group was supplanted in 1732; seven years later the new clique replacing it gave way to yet another faction that ruled the roost to the last day of the Emperor's reign.

After 1736, the threat from Persia and Nadir Shah began to loom large. Envoys had been sent to the Mughal court informing it that Persia's new ruler, who had already captured Herat and Balkh, proposed to punish the

Afghans of Kandahar, beseeching that the Mughal Governor at Kabul close the frontiers of his province to the fugitives. Muhammad Shah, negligent of affairs of state and his nobles hell-bent on petty factional squabbles, offered little if any sense of direction: 'Each envoy returned with a favourable answer but nothing was done'.

Nadir Shah's progress was unchecked and inexorable. Kandahar fell in March 1738, Ghazni and Kabul the following June. In November, Nadir Shah defeated at Jamrud the Mughal Governor of Kabul and marched relentlessly towards the goal he had set himself: 'On 27 December he crossed the Indus at Attock and in January 1739 . . . [took] Wazirabad. The Governor of Lahore met the invader at a distance of 12 miles . . . made his obeisance and presented a peace offering.' Muhammad Shah, unprepared to face the challenge of the Persian invader, tactfully decided to stave off disaster by a diplomatic offensive mounted through the Nizam-ul-Mulk. It might have succeeded but for the petty jealousies and rivalry between the Nizam and Saadat Khan which the invader exploited to the full. In the result, Nadir Shah ravaged the populace and pillaged the imperial capital in a manner that had few parallels. Nor did the Emperor display any strength of will or qualities of leadership. Both by birth and upbringing, he was far too weak to handle the situation.

In the aftermath of the Persian holocaust, the imperial court presented a tragic picture of confusion and discord: Saadat Khan was dead, the Nizam-ul-Mulk called to the Deccan to meet the growing Maratha threat; Jai Singh retired to Rajasthan. The new band that filled the void included royal favourites like Kuki Jiun and Shah Abdul Ghafur and had only personal enrichment as its primary objective. They were self-seekers and ill-equipped to discharge their responsibilities in conditions of constant strife and struggle. The harsh truth is that the Empire had been rudely shaken and was now almost beyond repair. The central government wielded little authority while the army was a rabble. The imperial domain had shrunk beyond recognition: the six subahs of the Deccan and the viceroyalties of Oudh (q.v.), Bengal, Bihar and Orissa were well-nigh independent; Malwa, Bundelkhand and Gujarat were Maratha possessions; the Rajput states accepted no control; European traders in the south dreamt of territorial dominion.

In sum, Muhammad Shah's reign was witness to a period of base intrigue, underhand dealings, treachery and blood-letting on a scale rarely encountered hitherto. The Emperor's name remained a mere symbol of titular sovereignty, bereft of any real authority or prestige. There was a proliferation of cliques or groups resting neither on religious affinity nor political loyalty. Their allegiance to the Emperor's person was dubious at best.

Another characteristic feature was a precipitate decline in public morality. The Emperor no less than the nobles led a life of lechery and licentiousness; no wonder the court itself became a forum for jest and frivolity, much to the annoyance and disgust of a large section that had known better days. At its best, here was an assembly presided over by a sovereign 'sunk in indolence and debauchery' who wasted away his years in 'secluded palaces, chewing bhang; fondling concubines, and listening to buffoons'. Nor were Muhammad Shah's favourites identified with any particular policy or group of nobles at the court; their influence was 'erratic and fitful', their political importance meagre. They hindered the pursuance of any coherent state policy and sometimes caused great resentment and annoyance to the ministers.

It has been suggested that the Emperor 'demands our pity if he may not command our respect. Placed in a position which called for a genius, he was a very ordinary person... the tragedy of his situation was that the most absolute devotion to business by a man of his mental calibre would in no way have altered the course of events... he appears to have realized both the hopelessness of the situation and his own powerlessness to amend it. The seeds of decay had been sown by Aurangzeb and the process was now nearly complete'.

Zahir Uddin Malik has expressed the view that 'to emphasise the political failings of the Emperor as the principal cause of decline is to ignore the basic defects in the working of the existing institutions'; that Muhammad Shah's one great personal disadvantage was that 'he was destitute of military valour and incapable of leading armies and conducting campaigns'. The Emperor was nonetheless a distinguished patron of the arts: 'a polished gentleman, a poet and himself well-versed in music.'

Zahir Uddin Malik, *The Reign of Muhammad Shah 1719–1748*, Bombay 1978; Satish Chandra, *Parties & Politics at the Mughal Court, 1707–1740*, Aligarh, 1959; A. L. Srivastav, *Mughal Empire, 1526–1603*, 3rd ed., Agra, 1959; Sir Richard Burn (ed.), *Cambridge History of India*, Vol. IV.

Hector Munro (1726–1805)

Popularly known as the hero of Buxar, Major (later Sir) Hector Munro joined the army in 1747, and came out to India in 1761 in charge of a new corps of Highlanders. In 1764 he replaced Major John Carnac in Patna where he successfully, albeit brutally, quelled a sepoy mutiny. Aware of a build-up of the combined forces of the deposed Nawab of Bengal, Mir Kasim (q.v.), Shuja-ud-Daula (q.v.), the Nawab Wazir of Oudh (q.v.), and Shah Alam II (q.v.), the Mughal Emperor, Munro opened secret correspondence with the officers of the Oudh army with a view to subverting their loyalty; in this, however, he was unsuccessful. He then led an attack against the combined forces and defeated them decisively at the Battle of Buxar (q.v.) on 22 October 1764. Shortly afterwards, he resigned his command and left for England.

Munro came back to India in 1777 as a Councillor at Madras, taking over command of the army in the following year. A successful soldier, he captured Pondicherry in 1778, commanded the right division in Eyre Coote's (q.v.) army that worsted Haidar Ali (q.v.) at Porto Novo and captured Nagapatam from the Dutch in 1781.

Munro returned to England and rose to be a general in 1798. He died at his estate in Novar on 27 December 1805. Contemporaries rated him a firm but humane disciplinarian and, although not a great tactician, a brave. enterprising and successful soldier.

Dodwell, *CHI*, V, pp. 283–4, 286; *DNB*, XIII, pp. 1202–4 (Henry Manners Chichester).

Nawab Mushtaq Hussain, Viqar-ul-Mulk (1841–1917)

Mushtaq Hussain, better known as Nawab Viqar-ul-Mulk, hailed from a village in the Moradabad district of western U.P. Starting life as an assistant teacher, his dedicated work and concern for Muslim welfare brought him to the notice of Sir Syed Ahmad (q.v.). While employed on famine relief work, Viqar-ul-Mulk rose further in Sir Syed's estimation and was appointed a personal reader to him. Simultaneously, he participated in the activities of the Aligarh Movement (q.v.), promoting the educational plan of his mentor and taking special interest in the management of the printing press and the scientific society. In 1875 he found employment at Hyderabad in the Nizam's government, which he was to serve for 17 years. It was here that the title by which he is commonly known (viz., Viqar-ul-Mulk) was conferred upon him. He resigned under pressure, on account of local intrigue and because the then Nizam had lost faith in him.

Although in touch with the Aligarh Movement all along, Viqar-ul-Mulk took no active interest in Muslim politics after he retired and settled down in Amroha. However the Urdu-Hindi controversy in the North-Western Provinces in 1900 brought him out of his political isolation and, along with Mohsin-ul-Mulk (q.v.), he agitated for the retention of Urdu as an official language. He also urged the revival of the Anglo-Oriental Defence Association which, earlier in 1893, had seen brief activity.

In the wake of the language controversy referred to, Viqar-ul-Mulk made common cause with such Muslim leaders as Mian Mohammed Shah Din, Fazl-i-Hussain and Mohammad Shafi to put forth the view that Muslim political rights could not be protected without an adequate organization. In the result, at a meeting at Lucknow on 20-1 October 1901, it was resolved that Muslims in India should (i) form an organization to safeguard their social and political needs and interests; and (ii) keep away from the Indian National Congress (q.v.) because its objectives were 'manifestly inimical' to Muslim interests. The February 1903 issue of the *Aligarh Institute Gazette* emphasized the need to organize and consolidate the scattered Muslim forces and added that the 'Mussulmans of India, on account of their religious unity, were the first to become a nation'.

From 1901 onward, Viqar-ul-Mulk undertook extensive tours to propagate his ideas, but did not make much headway. In 1903, however, a Mohammadan Political Association was formed at Saharanpur at a public meeting convened by him. It had the objective of co-operating with the government and opposing the Congress demand for representative institutions. Viqar-ul-Mulk underlined the distinctness. In a letter of 16 August 1903 to the *Pioneer* he wrote: 'The two movements are essentially different; not only in their most important objects, but also in their *modus operandi*'. Among the Association's other aims the following may be listed: to impress upon the Muslims that 'their well-being and prosperity' depended entirely on the stability and permanence of British rule in India; to lay 'in a moderate and respectful manner' Muslim grievances before government; to refrain from assuming hostile attitudes towards other countries; to oppose Congress demands regarding representative government and competitive examinations. However, in retrospect, the Association did not do much work and little was later heard of it.

Viqar-ul-Mulk presided, in December 1906, at the Dacca meeting of Muslim leaders where he declared that 'so much was their cause bound up with that of the British raj that they must be prepared to fight and die for the Government if necessary'. Their motto, he averred, was 'defence, not defiance'. He was the first General Secretary of the All-India Muslim League (q.v.).

Earlier in the year, at an educational conference at Dacca, the Nawab listed three issues on which Muslims had serious differences with the Congress: (i) some of the demands put forth by the latter body would imperil the very existence of British rule; (ii) many of its leaders at their annual sessions used aggressive and violent language against the government; (iii) some of its demands were prejudicial to Muslim rights. In case British rule was withdrawn, he argued, Hindus would rule the country; in such a contingency, 'our property, our honour, our religion—all will be in jeopardy'.

On the death of Mohsin-ul-Mulk, the Nawab was unanimously elected Secretary of Aligarh College; he encouraged the study and practice of the tenets of Islam and regular attendance at prayer. His tenure, however, gave rise to sharp Sunni-Shia differences and undermined the unity of Muslims. Differences between him and W. A. J. Archbold, then principal of Aligarh College, led to the latter's resignation.

At the League council meeting held in December 1912, a resolution amending the aims and objectives of the party was passed by a large majority. Apart from fostering loyalty to the Crown and advancement of the political and other interests of Muslims, the League sought to promote friendship and union with other communities. More, in co-operation with them, it was to work through constitutional means for the 'attainment of a system of self-government suitable to India by bringing about a steady reform of the administrative system'. The adoption of this resolution marked the loss of exclusive control over the League by the Ashraf aristocracy.

Viqar-ul-Mulk stoutly opposed this change and argued that the time for self-government had not yet come. But the founding father of the League was overruled by M. A. Jinnah (q.v.) and others.

Viqar-ul-Mulk's reaction to the annulment of the Partition of Bengal (q.v.) was sharp. The government's policy, he averred, was 'like a cannon which passed over the dead bodies of Muslims without any feeling whether amongst them there was anyone alive and whether he would receive any painful sensation from the action of theirs'. His friends called him an 'incurable loyalist', yet he was once constrained to admit: 'It is now manifest like the midday sun that, after seeing what has happened lately, it is futile to ask the Muslims to place their reliance on Government.'

He wrote in the *Aligarh Institute Gazette* of 20 December, 1911: 'Now the days of such reliances [Muslim reliance on the British] are over. What we should rely on, after the grace of God, is the strength of our arm, for which we have, before us, the example of our worthy countrymen.' Since the promotion of Muslim welfare was dependent on British co-operation, he yet took pains to demonstrate his own and his community's loyalty towards the government. Understandably, therefore, the annulment of the partition was a great shock to him.

Although disillusioned with British policy and acutely conscious of Congress gains as a result of the annulment of the Partition of Bengal, Viqar-ul-Mulk continued to oppose Muslim association with the nationalist movement. In his last two years as secretary of the M.A.O. College, he made a clear departure from his earlier stance and sometimes criticized government policies that he deemed to be inimical to Muslim interests. His call for Hindu-Muslim unity was hedged in by the clear proviso that Muslim interests were not to be sacrificed; as a matter of fact, he pleaded that each community have an independent platform from which to project its own separate demands. His disenchantment with the British notwithstanding, he retained a vested interest in the continuation of the Raj for its end, he argued, would be calamitous for Muslims.

Even though no longer actively engaged in the activities of the M.A.O. College after 1913, Viqar-ul-Mulk felt deeply concerned about Turkey's predicament in joining World War I against the Allied powers. Until his death in 1917, he was the patron of an institute. Nazaratul Maarif, which imparted religious instruction to the young. Apart from changes in the control and administration of the College, and the twist Viqar-ul-Mulk gave to Muslim political policy, his tenure is known for a deepening of the religious life of Aligarh College, and its popularity even with the most orthodox sections of the community. Mohsin-ul-Mulk had tried to win the ulama with his suavity and tact, but Viqar-ul-Mulk attracted them because he was really one of them.

S. M. Ikram, *Modern Muslim India and the Birth of Pakistan (1858-1851)*, 2nd ed., Lahore, 1965, pp. 110–23; Rafiq Zakaria, *Rise of Muslims in Indian Politics: an analysis of developments from 1885 to 1906*, Bombay, 1970, pp. 99–100, 108; Lal Bahadur, *The Muslim League: its history, activities and achievements*, Agra, 1954.

All-India Muslim League

The All-India Muslim League was born at Dacca in December 1906. Its founder, NawabViqar-ul-Mulk (q.v.) had tried as early as 1901 to start a political organization of the Muslims. The League's first session was held under his presidentship, thereby completing the life-work of one who has been called 'a great benefactor' of Muslim India. Actually, after the Muslim deputation had waited on the fourth Earl Minto (q.v.) in October 1906, the Aga Khan (q.v.) had put in a strong plea that Muslims establish a separate political organization of their own if the policy initiated by his Simla deputation was to make any headway.

The next decade in the history of the League was uneventful, although by 1916 it was rated important enough to enter into an agreement, the Lucknow Pact (q.v.), with the Indian National Congress (q.v.). Over the years, the League had largely remained confined to indoor political shows, its annual sessions being held eitner in well-decorated *pandals* or in big halls where a few distinguished visitors were allowed by special invitation. Mass public meetings were unknown to the League. From 1906 to 1910 the party's central office remained at Aligarh, functioning more as an adjunct of its educational institution than as a separate political entity. It was only after the League's headquarters had moved to Lucknow that it increasingly attended to political affairs, albeit within safe bounds. The income from its membership and annual subscriptions was not deemed adequate for it to maintain a decent office, much less to work among the masses. The party subsisted largely on an annual grant of Rs 3,000 from the Raja of Mahmudabad (q.v.), this being its main fixed income.

In 1910, the Muslim League was a debating society many of whose members seemed to have more important things to do than take part in politics. Led by Maulanas Mohamed Ali and Shaukat Ali (qq.v.), Fazlul Haq (q.v.), Mazharul Haque (1866–1930) and Fazl-i-Hussain (1877–1936), by 1912 not only young Muslims of the professional classes but many Muslim members of the Congress also joined the League, albeit not to the exclusion of their membership of the former body. The 'objectives' resolution of December 1912, with its demand for self government in a form 'suitable' for India, its proclamation of loyalty *not,* as hitherto, to the British government but to the Crown, and its call to promote national unity by fostering public spirit among the people of India and by co-operating with other communities, spoke a very different language from that of the Simla deputation which had begged 'most respectfully' to approach Lord Minto with an address for his 'favourable consideration'.

During the years of the Khilafat Movement (q.v.), the party lived largely on paper, holding its sessions wherever the Khilafat Conference or the Congress held theirs. After the breakup of the Khilafat Movement, the League's guardianship came to vest for all practical purposes in a small coterie of landed aristocrats. Their measure of 'sacrifice' was the fact of travelling in state to attend its annual sessions, to win some applause and relax together.

The proceedings of the sessions were duly sent to the press while knowledgeable British officials were aware of every word spoken or heard during party deliberations. The end of a session was the end of the organization for the year and 'no one took notice' of what had been said or done except for the official record of the Government of India. It has been maintained that it was the leadership, not the masses, who were to blame for this moribund condition of the party; the Khilafat agitation (1920-4), had clearly demonstrated the keen interest Muslims took in political activity. After it died down, the League reverted to its earlier state of near-complete inertia.

The party's 1931 session was held in a private house in Delhi for fear the Ahmadiyah agitation, then rampant in the metropolis, might disturb the proceedings. Of the 1932 session there is no known record. In 1933, Mian Abdul Aziz, a barrister of Peshawar, managed to become president of the League. He was a staunch supporter of the recently-announced Communal Award (q.v.) of the British government. Since his views were not particularly popular, the Calcutta branch of the party was worried lest a session presided over by Aziz should provoke a riot. In the result, Aziz held a meeting (21–22 October) with the help of the police in which the Communal Award was supported. There was another meeting (25-26 November) presided over by Khan Bahadur Hafiz Hidavat Hussain Khan in New Delhi, of which Nawab Mohammed Yusuf, U. P.'s then Minister for Local Government, was the principal organizer. It followed that the party had two presidents—Mian Abdul Aziz and Hafiz Hidayat Hussain Khan. At its general meeting on 4 March 1934, Mian Abdul Aziz resigned and M. A. Jinnah (q.v.) took his place as President, while Hafiz Hidayat Khan became the party secretary.

When Jinnah took over, the League's fortunes had been at a low ebb. In 1927, the party's total membership was 1,330; in 1930, at the Allahabad session, when Dr Muhammad Iqbal (1877–1938) presented his historic address demanding the establishment of a north-western Muslim state in India, the annual general meeting did not have even its quorum of 75! Hafeez Jallundri, the well-known Urdu poet, had to read his 'Shamma-i-Islam' to keep those present entertained while the organizers were busy enrolling new members in the town! The 1931 annual session was described by an eye-witness as a 'languid and attenuated house of scarcely 120 people in all'. To gain a larger popular base, the party subscription was reduced from Rs 6 to Rs 1 a year, while the admission fee of Rs 5 was abolished. The party's declining fortunes may be gauged from the fact that the quorum for party meetings was now reduced from 75 to 50. No annual session was held in 1935 and the Khilafat Conference too had long been dormant.

A word about the party's attitude to the Lucknow Pact (1916) briefly referred to earlier. The 1915 session of the League had been held in Bombay under the presidentship of Mazharul Haque, a staunch nationalist, who was sternly opposed to the demand for separate electorates. The anti-Congress Muslim elements in Bombay allegedly encouraged by government officials and led by Sardar Suleiman Haji Kasim Mitha had indulged in hooliganism, with the result that the inaugural session had to be adjourned. It was convened again the next day at the Taj Mahal Hotel where a committee was formed to discuss the settlement of communal matters with the Congress. The latter too was then holding its session in Bombay and had directed its Committee to negotiate with the League and frame a joint scheme for constitutional reform. Later, the committees of the two parties met and unanimously decided to prepare a draft for approval by their parent bodies. In this task Motilal Nehru (q.v.) played an important role, for meetings of the two committees were held at his house, Anand Bhavan, at Allahabad. It was obvious that the Montagu-Chelmsford Reforms (q.v.) as well as prospects of further constitutional advance meant opportunities for more political power in the legislatures and outside. This was reflected later (1928) in the setting up of the All-Parties Muslim Conference. Again, the publication (1933) of the Communal Award as well as the White Paper on reforms made the position even more explicit.

The Muslim League Parliamentary Board was nominated by Jinnah in 1936 to contest elections to the provincial assembly as well as the Central Legislative Assembly. A meeting of the Board, in December 1936, to raise party funds has been described as a 'very poor show'. A sum of Rs 21,000 was announced as donations, of which Rs 9,000 were shared equally by three patrons—the Rajas of Mahmudabad and Salampur as well as Mahomed Wasim, a brother-in-law of Choudhry Khaliquzzaman. In the Panjab, Jinnah drew a blank, for Fazl-i-Hussain held back, maintaining he was far too occupied with the Communal Award which gave the Panjab Muslims a bare 86 out of a total of 175 seats in the provincial legislature. The fact was that, having retired from the Governor-General's Executive Council, Fazl-i-Hussain had returned to his home state to revive and resuscitate the Unionist Party. He not only advised Jinnah to keep 'his fingers out of the Panjab pie' but ruled against setting up a Central Parliamentary Board for the League, arguing that provinces such as the Panjab may have to work in harmony with non-communal organizations. Sir Fazl-i-Hussain apart, Jinnah's electoral prospects were rated so bleak that even the Aga Khan lent financial support to the Unionist Part and *not* the League. The Majlis-i-Ahrar which supported the League in the Panjab had only a weak political base in urban areas and none whatsoever in its rural parts.

Within a short time, however, the League was to succeed in galvanizing Indian Muslims into a political force second only to the Congress. Henceforth, both the government and the Congress were compelled to consider the Muslim viewpoint before embarking on any measure affecting the country in general. Even at this early stage the two-nation theory was largely influenced by the League's concept of a homogeneous Muslim nationality. Despite the initial limitations, Jinnah and the League did not fare too badly in the elections. The party contested altogether a little more than half the seats reserved for Muslims in separate constituencies and won around 60% of these. Except for Bengal, it drew almost a blank in the Muslim-majority provinces. In the Panjab, it won a solitary place out of 86 Muslim seats; in Sind, 3 out of 33; none in the N.W.F.P. In Bengal, the League got 39 out of 117; in Bombay, 20 out of 29; in U.P., 27 out of 64; in Madras, 10 out of 28 and in Assam, 9 out of 34. An impressive gain none the less was that, for once, the League's branches came to be established in all parts of the country.

At Lucknow, in 1937, the League's creed was up-dated; at Lahore, in 1940, it was to demand a partition of the country. The Lahore resolution affirmed *inter alia* 'that . . . no constitutional plan would be workable in this country or acceptable to the Muslims unless it is designed on the following basic principles, viz., that geographically contiguous units are demarcated into regions which should be so constituted, with such territorial readjustments as may be necessary, that the areas in which the Muslims are numerically in a majority as in the eastern or western zones of India should be grouped to constitute "independent states" in which the constituent units shall be autonomous and sovereign'. The Indian nationalist press hailed this as the 'Pakistan resolution', although the word itself was not mentioned in the speeches made or in the text of the resolution.

The League grew in strength during World War II (1939-45) largely because the Congress had gone into the political wilderness and, anxious to lean back on some political prop, the government gave covert aid to the League. Jinnah claimed that by 1938 hundreds of thousands of Muslims had joined the League. Six years later, the League had a membership of some 3 million, its organization had penetrated the countryside and those who remained openly hostile to it were not considered Muslims by their co-religionists. By the end of 1944, the Bengal Muslim League claimed a membership of 5,00,000; the Sind and Panjab Leagues had 2,00,000 each.

Lord Wavell's (q.v.) attempt in 1945 at the Simla Conference (q.v.) to form a Congress-League coalition without prejudice to either party's claims, or counter-claims, failed owing to Jinnah's intransigence. In the general elections to the legislatures that followed, the League did remarkably well and captured almost all the Muslim seats both at the centre and in the provinces. The League polled about 4.5 million or 75% of the Muslim vote in the elections, winning 460 out of 533 seats in the central and provincial legislatures.

What did account for the League's phenomenal rise after 1939? The answer, it has been said, lay partly in the short-sightedness of the Congress in excluding Muslim League representatives from its provincial governments; its abdication of governmental authority in the provinces it ruled; and additionally, in the alleged persecution of the Muslims by the latter.

The British Cabinet Mission (q.v.) in 1946, after its marathon sessions, with almost all political groups in the country, ruled that Pakistan was impracticable and inadvisable and decided in favour of a Constituent Assembly (q.v.) to frame a three-tier constitution. It was to consist of a limited union centre, 3 groups of contiguous provinces (one in the north-west, a second in the centre and a third in the east) and 11 provincial constitutions. It also ruled in favour of setting up an Interim Government (q.v.) pending the framing and introduction of a future constitution. The League at first accepted the Mission's proposals but later went back on its word and resolved upon launching Direct Action (q.v.). In the late autumn of 1946 it again decided upon co-operating and sent its representatives to the Interim Government. After the arrival of Lord Mountbatten and the June 3rd Plan (q.v.), Pakistan, the League's long-sought goal, came to be accepted as a harsh reality and was born, as a political entity, on 14 August 1947.

According to political analysts there is little doubt that the British government contributed to the League's growing strength. This helped the party, but the real momentum came only after the Pakistan resolution had been accepted. Thus, neither Jinnah's organizing ability nor the alleged Congress mis-rule by themselves transformed the League into a mighty popular movement. The collective Muslim desire for political power and seeming reluctance to live under those whom they had once governed perhaps partly explain the demand for Pakistan. Like the Congress, the Muslim League was not a political party in the accepted sense of that term; it was a national movement whose sole aim came to be the establishment of a separate sovereign state of Pakistan.

It has been suggested that by reason of its origin, character and objective, the League under Jinnah, borrowed the Nazi techniques wholesale. The emphasis was on relentless propaganda—based on false premises and on projecting an image of the leader that was larger than life. In this case the watchword was pan-Islamism and a policy that was calculated to appeal to all provinces of India. A catchy phrase to start with, Pakistan acquired strong religious overtones. Its propaganda was made through such slogans as the Urdu couplet

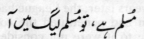

('if you are a Muslim, come join the Muslim League').

The organs of the Muslim League were a President, a Working Committee, and a Council. Reading through the party constitutions of 1940, '41 and '44, one is struck by the fact that there was a steady centralization of power in the hands of the President and his Working Committee. Jinnah may or may not have exercised his 'rod of iron' but there is no denying that most members more or less came round to his point of view; the Qaid-i-Azam's power, experience and personality were such that they accepted his leadership without qualification. He cleverly kept the League scrupulously out of all controversial issues. Himself a Shia and a Khoja, he said his public prayers with the Sunni Muslims. Since a state was yet to be born, he kept out of all contention and polemics as to the form of Islam which Pakistan was to establish or practise. The League's own brand of Islam was at once simple and straight-forward, free of theological and doctrinal subtleties. This intellectual naivete of the party leadership was a great asset in keeping the organization closely knit together.

Mutiur Rahman, *From Consultation to Confrontation: A Study of the Muslim League in British Indian Politics, 1906-1912,* London, 1970; Lal Bahadur, *The Muslim League:its History, Activities & Achievements* (A Ph.D. thesis of Agra Univ.), Agra, 1954; A. B. Rajput, *Muslim League: Yesterday and Today,* Lahore, 1948; Mohammad Noman, *Muslim India: Rise & Growth of the All-India Muslim League,* Allahabad, 1942; Deepak Pandey, 'Congress-Muslim League Relations 1932-39: 'the parting of the ways', *Modern Asian Studies,* 12, 4 (1978), pp. 629-54.

First Anglo-Mysore War (1767–9)

The years of peace, 1761–6, between Haidar Ali (q.v.) and the East India Company (q.v.) at Madras were rudely shattered by the latter in 1767. Afraid of antagonizing the Nizam over the Northern Sarkars, threatened by the Marathas in Bengal and fearful of the prospect of a Maratha-Nizam-Haidar Ali coalition against the Nawab of Carnatic who was their protege, the English made Haidar Ali, the Mysore ruler, a scapegoat and succeeded in turning all the other powers against him. It is true that Haidar Ali managed to break up this confederacy, but not before the misguided British had brought about a war.

To start with, Haidar Ali swooped down from the passes leading into British-held Madras and took the offensive, although the initial encounters at Changama and Tiruvannamalai proved indecisive. From then on, his policy was to avoid pitched battles, spring a surprise or ambush the English detachments while ravaging their territories. By January 1768, he had been driven out of the Carnatic, but the recapture of Mangalore (May 1768), where he produced much-needed gun-powder and artillery, was to prove a powerful shot in the arm. Haidar Ali once again took the offensive and defeated the English at Malbagal (4 October 1768). Frequent changes in (English) command gave him virtually a free hand. Later, successfully avoiding British armies, he reached the gates of Madras on 27 March 1769 and dictated a Treaty (of Madras, q.v.) there a week later.

Dodwell, *CHI,* V, 276–7; B. Sheik Ali, *British Relations with Haidar Ali 1760–82,* Mysore, 1963.

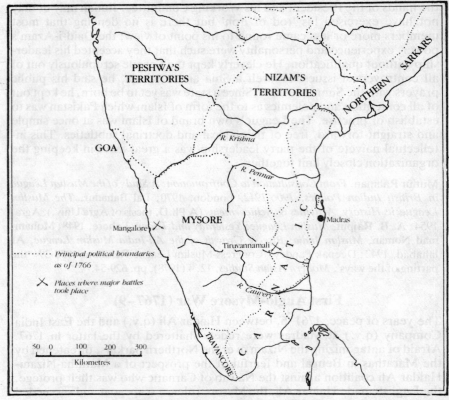

First Anglo-Mysore War (1767–9)

Second Anglo-Mysore War (1780–4)

In 1770, when the Marathas invested Mysore, Haidar Ali (q.v.) according to the terms of the Treaty of Madras (q.v.) sought British aid. In this, however, he drew a blank. What made matters worse for the Mysore ruler was the fact that the Marathas continued to ravage his dominions until 1772. To add to his discomfiture, the East India Company (q.v.) captured Mahe (later a French possession), which then formed a part of his territory, and stationed a force at Guntur. In retaliation, Haidar Ali threatened to capture Adoni, a small town now in Andhra Pradesh. This made the British dispatch a force, marching through Haidar's dominion to aid the Nizam, Basalat Jang. The Nizam was visibly upset on the British take-over of Guntur without his prior knowledge or permission while the Marathas too were alienated by the support which Bombay Presidency gave to Raghoba (q.v.). By 1780, the Marathas, Mysore and the Nizam had composed their differences and were allied against the British.

With an army of 80,000 men and 100 pieces of artillery, Haidar Ali invaded the Carnatic in July 1780. In the first two engagements at Parambakam and Pollibur, British forces under William Baillie (d.1782) suffered serious reverses. This forced them to retreat and gave Haidar Ali unrestrained freedom to overrun the country. With the arrival of a Bengal force under Eyre Coote (q.v.), Haidar Ali suffered defeat at Porto Novo on 1 July, and

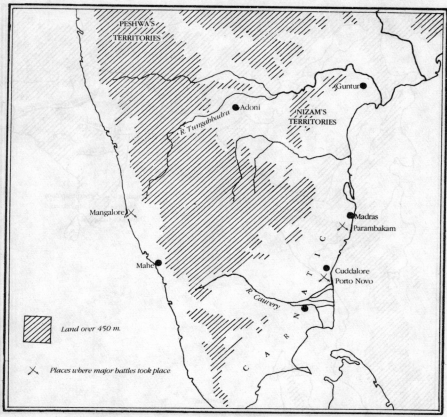

Second Anglo-Mysore War (1780–4)

Sholingur on 28 September 1781. The war dragged on with many an indecisive engagement. On 17-18 February 1782 the Company's troops were defeated by Tipu Sultan (q.v.) at Annagudi. By September 1783, the Dutch had been worsted too. French assistance arrived only after Haidar Ali's death, and played a part in the successful defence of Cuddalore on 13 May 1783. Meanwhile in Europe the conclusion of the Treaty of Versailles had brought the War of American Independence (1776-83) to an end and opened the way for peace negotiations. Tipu was amenable to overtures for peace and after the capture of Mangalore signed a treaty (q.v.) there on 11 March 1784.

Dodwell, *CHI*, V, 276–7; B. Sheik Ali, *British Relations with Haidar Ali 1760-82*, Mysore, 1963.

Third Anglo-Mysore War (1790–2)

The peace following the Treaty of Mangalore (q.v.) proved to be a 'hollow truce', for both the English and Tipu Sultan (q.v.) were aspiring to be

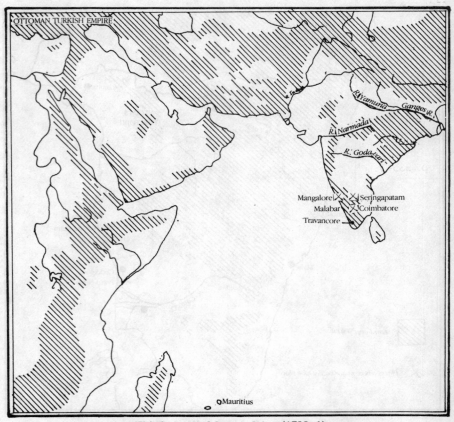

Third Anglo-Mysore War (1790–1)

dominant powers in the Deccan. Aware of British leanings towards the
Marathas and the Nizam, Tipu, the Mysore ruler, made futile attempts to
seek an alliance with the French revolutionaries in Mauritius and the Ottoman Turkish Sultan who, as Caliph, was the acknowledged head of the
Islamic world. Aware that he could not rely on Tipu's assistance in the event
of an Anglo-French war, Lord Cornwallis (q.v.) provoked him further by
co-operating with other Indian powers not friendly to the Mysore ruler.
Additionally, the English sent help to Raja Rama Verma of Travancore,
with whom Tipu was at war. The English also successfully concluded an
alliance with the Marathas and the Nizam against Tipu, and even promised
the restoration of Hindu dynasty to the deposed Rani of Mysore. Tipu's
efforts to avert hostilities were ignored, for the English, afraid of his growing
strength, were understandably determined to chastise him.

   The war was fought in two phases. To start with, English troops numbering approximately 30,000 men commanded by General Sir William Medows
(1738-1813) achieved some successes in Malabar, although Tipu by forced
marches, elusive movements and surprise attacks had the upper hand. In
January 1791, Cornwallis himself assumed command. Meanwhile, the
Marathas as well as the Nizam's forces kept the Mysore ruler busy on his

northern frontier. The first major loss for Tipu was the capture of Mangalore (21 March 1791). During the rains that followed, Cornwallis decided to retreat there. Tipu in the mean time re-captured Coimbatore (3 November 1791). Having received some reinforcements early in 1792, Cornwallis marched towards Seringapatam. The fort was invested on 6 February; two days later, Tipu opened negotiations after acknowledging he had been the aggressor and promising reparations to all of the John Company's (q.v.) allies. On 21 February, the fort was stormed and taken and two days later preliminaries for peace initiated. The Treaty of Seringapatam (q.v.) which brought hostilities to an end was signed in March 1792.

Mohibul Hasan, *History of Tipu Sultan*, 2nd ed., Calcutta, 1971; Dodwell, *CHI*, V, pp. 335–7.

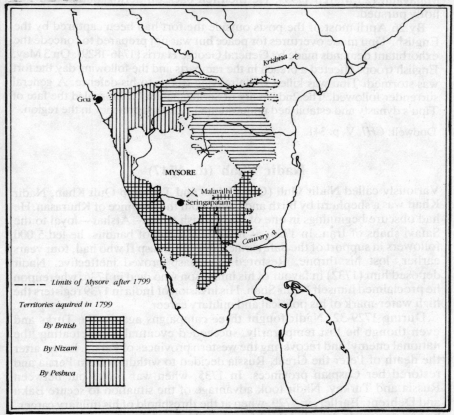

Fourth Anglo-Mysore War (1799)

Fourth Anglo-Mysore War (1799)

The amazing rapidity with which Tipu Sultan (q.v.) recovered from the ravages and reverses of the Third Mysore War (q.v.) alarmed the British. They were conscious that he would not accept for long the humiliating terms of the Treaty of Seringapatam (q.v.). His appeal for help to the French in Mauritius and his ill-concealed flirtations with them disturbed the English even more. Rumours about a Tipu-Zaman Shah (the Afghan ruler) alliance were rife too.

Wellesley (q.v.), a Francophobe and hypersensitive to revolutionary designs, found this reason enough to cripple permanently Tipu's power and capacity for intrigue with the John Company's (q.v.) sworn enemies. While professing friendship outwardly, Wellesley made preparations for war, concluding a subsidiary alliance with the Nizam and offering an equal share in the fruits of conquest to the ever-evasive Peshwa.

On 14 February 1799, British troops numbering roughly 42,000 men marched towards Mysore. Tipu's three principal generals—Purnaiya, Qamaruddin and Mir Sadiq—turned traitors to his cause and remained inactive, thereby causing his defeat at Siddeswara (5 March 1799) and later Malavalhi (25 March 1799). He then fell back on Seringapatam and was hotly pursued.

By 26 April most of the posts outside the fort had been captured by the English. Tipu made overtures for peace but was not prepared to concede the exhorbitant demands made by General George Harris (1746-1829). On 3 May, English troops effected a breach in the ramparts and the following day the fort was stormed. Tipu was killed while rallying troops to his defence. A general surrender followed. The 2nd Treaty of Seringapatam (1799) sealed the fate of Tipu's dynasty and established unquestioned British supremacy in the region.

Dodwell, *CHI*, V, p. 341.

Nadir Shah (d. 1747)

Variously called Nadir Quli (Qoli) Khan and Tahmasp Quli Khan, Nadir Khan was a shepherd by birth and came from the province of Khurasan. He had obscure beginnings in one of the Turkish tribes—Afshar—loyal to the Safavi shahs of Iran. In 1726, as head of a group of bandits, he led 5,000 followers in support of the Safavi ruler Shah Tahmasp II who had, four years earlier, lost his throne. Restored, Tahmasp proved ineffective. Nadir deposed him (1732) in favour of his infant son who died in 1736, whereupon he proclaimed himself Nadir Shah. His invasion of India in 1739 registers the high water-mark of his political and military career.

During 1729-32, Nadir fought three campaigns against the Turks and even though he lost temporarily, succeeded eventually in defeating 'the national enemy' and recovering the western provinces of Persia. Later, after the death of Peter the Great, Russia decided to withdraw from Persia and restored her Caspian provinces. In 1735, when war broke out between Russia and Turkey, Nadir took advantage of the situation to secure Baku and Dehrent. Earlier, in 1729, when at the threshhold of his military career, he had decisively defeated the Afghans and hunted them across to their own land.

Having settled accounts with Turkey and Russia, Nadir turned his attention one more to Afghanistan. In March 1738, he scored a convincing victory at Kandahar and stormed his way into the town. His progress from now on was unchecked; such resistance as he encountered 'was swept away as a flood sweeps away a handful to chaff'. Ghazni and Kabul fell in June; in

November he defeated the runaway Mughal governor of Kabul, at Jamrud. Relentlessly, he now marched to the goal he had set himself; on 27 December 1738 he crossed the Indus at Attock and in January 1739 captured Wazirabad. The Governor of Lahore soon surrendered without a fight.

Nadir Shah's real motive for marching into India was greed for gold, apart from a vaulting political ambition to walk in the foot-steps of the great Alexander'. His immediate pretext was the Mughal Emperor Muhammad Shah's (q.v.) alleged disregard of his repeated requests to deny asylum to the Afghan rebels.

After Zakariyah Khan, the Lahore governor, had purchased his life and limb by offering the invader Rs 20 lakhs, the Persian troops hovered around Karnal where the Mughal emperor in a last vain bid to stem the tide, mounted a half-hearted offensive. Out-manoeuvred and out-generalled, the Emperor decided to buy off Nadir Shah; the latter was offered Rs 50 lakhs, to be paid in instalments. The Emperor prayed that in lieu he and his capital be spared the Persian holocaust. Nadir Shah's calculations, however, were different and, thanks to the mutual jealousies of the highest in the land, viz, Burhan-ul-Mulk Saadat Khan and Nizam-ul-Mulk Qulich Khan (q.v.), he made up his mind to invade Delhi. On the former's advice, he had earlier at Karnal taken the Mughal ruler, his nobles and his harem captive. Nadir was now doubly determined to march on the imperial capital and march there he did with the Mughal Emperor, a prisoner, in tow.

On arrival in Delhi, the Persian ruler occupied the Diwan-i-Khas, the then imperial residence and, demonstrative of his unchallenged sovereignty, had the *khutba* read and the *sikka* struck in his name. Presently, the news of Saadat Khan's suicide, allegedly on account of his inability to collect the large sum promised the invader, spread consternation in the Mughal camp. Later that evening, as wild rumour circulated in the town that Nadir Shah had met an untimely death, some 3,000 Persian troops fell prey to wanton attacks of mob fury. The following day, a bullet barely missed the Shah as he rode to the city mosque for prayer. Enraged, he ordered a general massacre of Delhi's inhabitants.

The troops who began their dreadful carnage at nine in the morning 'forced their way into shops and houses killing the occupants and laying violent hands on anything of value . . . No distinction was made between the innocent and the guilty, male and female, old and young.' The bloodbath continued for six hours and is said to have claimed a toll of anything from 8,000 to 40,000 lives. The Shah's lust for human life was matched by his unsatiated greed for worldly treasure. In the result, the Mughal emperor and his nobles disgorged Rs 70 lakhs in treasure, besides the jewel-studded peacock throne and the celebrated Koh-i-Noor diamond. The Shah confiscated many a noble's property and sent a strong contingent of his men to Oudh (q.v.) to bring back the treasures of Burhan-ul-Mulk.

After two months' strenuous exercise of collecting a huge indemnity, on 16 May 1739, Nadir Shah marched out of Delhi on his way home; his progress was punctuated by occasional raids on the flanks and rear of his army. The Khyber, in particular, proved extremely difficult and its Afridi tribesmen almost succeeded in robbing the Shah of his life and treasure. In the aftermath of Nadir Shah, the Mughal empire was badly shaken, the royal court presenting a tragic picture of confusion and discord. The invasion itself had been a bloody holocaust, a shameless record of wholesale destruction, blood-curdling massacre, plunder and rapine.

In 1740, the Shah led a successful campaign against Bokhara; later that year, he invested Khiva. His major military reverse was the campaign (1741-2) against the fierce tribesmen of Daghestan, the Lesghians.

An Afghan contingent, of which the Afridis formed the largest support (though the Ghaljis too were well-represented) constituted the *corps d'elite* of Nadir Shah's army. This body had accompanied him to India; it was the murder of some of them that led to the notorious massacre in the imperial capital. More, they played a signal role in extricating him from the Afridi tribesmen who beset his men in the Khyber on his way home from India. The preference Nadir Shah showed his Afghan mercenaries led to great jealousies among his own Turkmen, the better known Qizilbash, and became the main cause of his assassination by Muhammad Khan Qajar, the founder of the dynasty that succeeded Nadir Shah on the throne.

Always harsh and ruthless, in later years the Shah is said to have become ever more 'capricious, proud and tyrannical'. He even ordered the blinding of his own son, whom he suspected of plotting against him. More, he sought to convert his subjects from their Shia sect to a form of the Sunni faith that he supported. The measure met with stout resistance at home and a Turkish onslaught from without. His suspicions continued to grow and, wherever he went, he had people tortured and executed. In the end, Nadir Shah was assassinated by some of his own troops in 1747. At the time, the Abdali contingent of the Afghan corps was commanded by Ahmad Khan, the future Ahmad Shah Abdali (q.v.).

L. Lockhart, *Nadir Shah: A Critical Study based mainly upon contemporary sources*, London, 1938; Jadunath Sarkar, *Nadir Shah in India*, reprint, Calcutta, 1973; Satish Chandra, *Parties & Politics at the Mughal Court, 1707–1740*, Aligarh, 1959, pp. 242–57.

Nana Phadnis (1742–1800)

The son of Janardhan Bhanu and Rukmabai, Balaji Janardhan, better known as Nana Phadnis, was born on 12 February 1742. On his father's death (1756) while barely 15 he was appointed *karkun* or *fardnavis* (literally, 'record writer'), a hereditary post. From contemporary accounts it would appear that the hereditary appointment held by Nana was different from the post of Phadnis in Poona to which he was appointed by Peshwa Madhav Rao I (1761-72). A keen and conscientious worker, Nana took great interest in day-to-day administration and, as a young man, was present at the Third Battle of Panipat (q.v.), of which he kept a detailed account.

The office of *phadnis* meant control over accounts or the public purse and was concerned with the earnings and expenditure of the state. In this task Nana was perfectly adept and, indeed, had few equals. He had acquired this efficiency under his rigorous task-master, Madhav Rao I, whom he had served for many years. After the latter's death, he conducted the whole administration practically on his own responsibility, improving the system of accounts and never letting the state remain in want. The charge usually levelled against him—that he accumulated a private fortune of several crores at the expense of the state—is debatable.

After the death of Peshwa Balaji Baji Rao (q.v.) in 1761, Nana was dismissed by Raghunath Rao or Raghoba (q.v.) but later (1768) reinstated by Madhav Rao. He combined in his person the duties of administrator and police officer. In little less than a decade he was to become in fact, if not in name, the chief minister of the Peshwa. On Raghoba's brief usurpation after the murder of Narayan Rao (1773), Nana and Sakharam Bapu (a known partisan of Raghoba and Nana's principal adversary) organized the 'Barbhai', successfully challenged Raghoba's succession, proved his guilt in the murder of the young Peshwa and hounded him out of Poona. Narayan Rao's infant son, Madhav Rao Narayan (d. 1795), was recognized the new Peshwa and a council of regency consisting, among others, of Nana and Narayan Rao's widow (Gunga Bhai), ruled the state, until a few years later when Nana was to emerge as supreme.

Encouraged by internal dissensions at the Maratha court and keen to enhance their own power and influence, the John Company (q.v.) at Bombay espoused Raghoba's candidature. A past-master in diplomacy, Nana's vigorous appeals against the Bombay government's action forced Warren Hastings (q.v.) to take action and conclude the Treaty of Purandhar (q.v.) whereby the Company retracted on its pledge of protection to Raghoba. Nana had in the meantime arranged for Haidar Ali's (q.v.) neutrality through several treaties and compromises. Having thus neutralized the power and influence of Raghoba, Nana came to wield almost sovereign authority in the state on behalf of the infant Peshwa.

Confronted by the English and Tipu Sultan (q.v.), Nana tried to ensure the neutrality of the one, while he crushed the other. When Tipu attacked the English, Nana joined the latter, leading to the discomfiture of the Mysore ruler and thereby restoring Maratha territories which he (Tipu) had purloined earlier. To chastise the Nizam, he defeated him at Karda in 1795.

Fiercely anti-British, Nana opened negotiations with the French which led to a renewal of hostilities with the English Company and the outbreak of the First Anglo-Maratha War (q.v.). In this long drawn-out struggle (1772-82), credit for forging a united front of all Maratha chiefs should go entirely to Nana who recognized in Madhav Rao Sindhia (q.v.) an efficient military leader and appointed him commander of the Peshwa's forces. In 1782, he ratified the Treaty of Salbai (q.v.) bringing the war to an end.

Sindhia's initiative at Delhi in putting Emperor Shah Alam II (q.v.) on the *masnad* boomeranged. Documentary evidence suggests that Nana was deeply interested in Sindhia's bold enterprise and extremely anxious to support his cause at all costs, whatever the results. It has been suggested that in so doing, the Maratha state deferred the downfall of the Mughal empire by about 30 years.

Since, contrary to their treaty commitments, the British had failed to aid the Marathas in their confrontations with the Nizam and Tipu, Nana refused them help during the Third Anglo-Mysore War (q.v.). Had he been a military commander, Nana may well have founded an independent dynasty, for Madhav Rao Sindhia on whose military prowess he relied, was his political rival too. After the latter's death in 1794, Nana was, for a short while, at the height of his power and prestige.

When Peshwa Madhav Rao Narayan allegedly committed suicide, Raghoba's son, Baji Rao II (q.v.), came to the fore. Amrit Rao (d. 1824), his brother, appeared to be the consensus candidate and Baji Rao, it is said, could have been kept out. But Nana's methods gave rise to 'low intrigue and selfish venality' thereby damaging the prospects of a smooth administration. This showed his 'lack of magnanimity' and failure to sink his own individuality 'for the public good'. In so far as Baji Rao succeeded, Nana fled from the court to escape retribution, but was seized and imprisoned. He was, however, soon reinstated in recognition of his great administrative ability. Despite their known differences, Nana prevented Peshwa Baji Rao II from falling into the snare of Wellesley's (q.v.) system of subsidiary alliances as long as he was alive. He breathed his last on 10 March 1800.

For a man of his times, Nana's great drawback was his ignorance of warfare—this compelled him to depend upon others and launched him into all sorts of trouble and suffering. His great credit was the success he achieved in co-operation with Madhav Rao Sindhia over the Company in the First Maratha war. Similarly, Nana's most glaring failure was his deplorable handling of the situation after the death of Peshwa Madhav Rao Narayan. So long as Haripant Phadke, his loyal co-operator, lived, Nana's administration was successful. But thereafter Nana appeared to have no fixed policy and allowed vacillation and temporary shifts to have their course. During his last five years, it has been suggested, his mind was quite confused.

Contemporary British estimates uniformly commend his services. Haidar Ali in a letter noted: 'Nana is far-sighted, and iron-willed; his respect and rectitude for his word are indeed great, he is well-versed with the intrigues and machinations of the English'. Nana's great predecessor and political rival, Sakharam Bapu observed: 'so long as Nana is there, there is no cause for fear'.

His administration rested on a network of reporters and personal envoys who were indeed the pillars of his politics. Nana was against modernizing the Maratha army, for he was convinced that the new-fangled techniques compelled the army to fight when flight was more judicious. This was to have a marked effect on the future of the Maratha state. The fact is that Nana did not cultivate the goodwill of the army.

The number of known letters dealt with by Nana between 1762 and 1800 total 14,122, out of which those in English number 2,185. In administrative etiquette he was a polished man, but among his glaring failures was the 'galling tutelage' devised by him for Narayan Rao which, it has been held, was partly responsible for the untimely death of that Peshwa, a development that brought in its wake 'most deplorable consequences'.

Grant Duff has maintained that Nana's principal defects 'originated in the want of personal courage and in an ambition not always restrained by principles'. His life was entirely public; in private, he was 'a man of strict veracity, humane, frugal and charitable' and shines out as 'the last genius produced by the Maratha nation' of the time. After Nana's death there was a strange contrast and, indeed, irony in the Maratha and British personnel. **Madhav Rao Sindhia, Haripant Phadke, Ahalyabai, Madhav Rao**

Narayan, Tukoji Holkar and Nana all died within a short period, leaving two incompetent youths—Baji Rao and Daulat Rao Sindhia (q.v.) to handle affairs. In sharp contrast, on the British side there were the Wellesley brothers, Metcalfe (q.v.), William Kirkpatrick (1754-1812), Barry Close (1756-1813), Elphinstone (q.v.), Malcolm (q.v.), Richard Jenkins (1785-1853) and Munro (q.v.).

The significance of Nana's political strategy is revealed by 'the stupendous endeavours' that he, along with Madhav Rao Sindhia, made in the teeth of such a disruptive climate as prevailed at Poona. Called the Indian Machiavelli, Nana was at once capable and crafty. He combined a keenly analytical intellect—as evidenced in his autobiographical fragment—with a flair for practical politics. It has been said that he was the 'last of a group with whose passing away the tottering structure of the Maratha empire collapsed like a pack of cards'.

Y. N. Deodhar, *Nana Phadnis and the External Affairs of the Maratha Empire*, Bombay, 1962; *G. S. Sardesai*, III.

Nana Saheb (died c. 1859)

Govind Dhondu Pant, popularly known as Nana Saheb, and one of the principal leaders of the Rebellion of 1857 (q.v.), was adopted heir and successor by Peshwa Baji Rao II (q.v.) in 1827. He succeeded to the Peshwaship in 1851, but a pension of Rs 8 lakhs enjoyed by the previous incumbent was discontinued. His numerous representations to the Governor-General and the John Company's (q.v.) Court of Directors against this decision, culminating in the dispatch of Azimullah Khan to England to plead on his behalf, were of no avail. Notwithstanding his disappointment with their behaviour, Nana Saheb continued to maintain good relations with the English at Kanpur. When the first news of the Rebellion spread, the local magistrate Hillersden sought the Nana's help to protect the treasury; the latter also proffered shelter to English families.

There is no broad agreement as to how and when Nana joined the 'rebels'. Some historians hold that his action was premeditated, that he had been touring the country accompanied by Azimullah Khan and had, in fact, visited Delhi and Lucknow, inciting rebellion. Others hold that by nature weak and vainglorious, he was either compelled or tempted by the 'rebels' to join them.

At Kanpur, when the outbreak took place on 4 June, Nana was chosen leader and, with Azimullah, headed for Delhi; at Kalyanpur, a few miles out of town, the march was however countermanded and a return ordered. Nana's *Ishtaharnama* said *inter alia*, 'I have committed no murder. By means of entreaties I have restrained my soldiers, and saved the lives of 200 English women and children.'

Nana warned General Hugh Wheeler (1789-1857) to expect an attack and his men later besieged the Residency. The British resisted for nearly three weeks, until their resources ran out, laying down arms after Nana promised safe passage to Allahabad. His subsequent notoriety rests on two alleged instances of the massacre of his English captives at Sati Chaura Ghat and

Bibighar. At the former place, the captured men were fired upon immediately after their boats moved away, opinion being sharply divided as to who fired the first shot—the English or the Indians. Nana, it may be recalled, had deputed Tatya Tope (q.v.) to supervise the affair and may not therefore have been personally responsible.

The survivors, along with some captives from Fatehgarh, were kept in custody at Bibigarh. On 16 July, a fortnight after Nana was proclaimed Peshwa in the midst of great public rejoicing, British reinforcements under General Henry Havelock (1795-1857) arrived at Kanpur and took the town without much ado. All the prisoners at Bibighar were massacred before Nana himself marched out to challenge the British; in the engagement that followed, his forces were routed and he himself compelled to flee. Later, Tatya Tope made several unsuccessful attempts to recapture Kanpur, even securing the help of the Gwalior contingent for the purpose. He was, however, finally defeated in December 1857.

On the question of Nana's alleged involvement in the massacres, it is fair to assert that his main objective, as of other Indian leaders, was the 'overthrow of foreign domination'. It thus seems unjustified to conclude that he planned or ordered the massacres.

Nana, who had once contemplated escaping to Chandernagore (q.v.) and seeking French help, now joined the revolting forces of Oudh (q.v.) under Begum Hazrat Mahal (d. 1879), a wife of Wajid Ali Shah (dethroned 1856), the last Nawab of Oudh. Together they fought several unsuccessful engagements in Rohilkhand and Shahjahanpur, Colin Campbell (1792-1863) pursuing them relentlessly from place to place. Earlier, a reward of Rs 1 lakh and free pardon for Nana's captor had been announced. At the end of 1858, it was reported that Nana had escaped to Nepal. The Nepalese Prime Minister, Jang Bahadur (1816-77), unwilling to displease the British, granted asylum only to the women in the fugitives' party. From Nepal in April 1859, Nana is said to have written letters to the Queen, the British Parliament and the Viceroy, containing some seemingly paradoxical statements. *Inter alia*, he proclaimed his innocence and prayed for pardon. He is also said to have declared: 'There will be war between you and me as long as I have life, whether I be killed or imprisoned or hanged. And whatever I do will be done with the sword only.'.

Major Richardson, the British Resident in Kathmandu, asked Nana to surrender unconditionally, which he refused, not unmindful of the fate that might await him. In October 1859, Jang Bahadur informed Richardson that Nana was dead. Efforts to round up Nana continued, however, and several people resembling him were apprehended and later released after interrogation. To put an end to the undue excitement that ensued every time such news spread and the resultant loss of money and effort involved, the government finally issued an order to the effect that even if Nana were found, he should be let go scot free and then ignored.

Anand Swarup Misra, *Nana Saheb Peshwa and the Fight for Freedom*, Lucknow, 1961; P. C. Gupta, *Nana Sahib and the Rising at Cawnpore*, Oxford, 1963; Surendra Nath Sen, *Eighteen Fifty-seven*, New Delhi, 1957.

Maharaja Nand Kumar (1705–75)

Nand Kumar was the son of Padmanav Roy, an *amil* of two or three parganas in West Bengal. Born in the district of Birbhum in 1740 he had served as *amil* of the parganas of Murshidabad and Hooghly and, after changing several jobs, emerged as the Diwan of Hooghly in 1752. Temporarily removed, he was confirmed in this post by the new Nawab, Siraj-ud-Daula (q.v.), who later elevated him to the post of *faujdar* as well. Later still, Nand Kumar acted as Dewan of the Nawab of Bengal at Murshidabad and combined this with collection of the John Company's (q.v.) 'tuncaw' in Burdwan, Nadia and Hooghly. It is said that as early as 1761 the Company's authorities in Calcutta (q.v.) had begun to suspect that Nand Kumar was not well disposed towards the English, whose growing influence over the Nawab's administration he deeply resented.

As Diwan, Nand Kumar enjoyed the supreme confidence of Nawab Mir Jafar (q.v.) and received the title of Maharaja from the Mughal emperor. Soon after the Nawab's death, he was removed by the Company to Calcutta on a false allegation that could not be sustained. Here he spent his time as a virtual prisoner.

Rattled and disgruntled by such treatment, Nand Kumar's hopes were raised by the arrival of the three new Councillors (John Clavering, George Monson and Philip Francis) under the Regulating Act (q.v.) in October 1774. In a long letter presented to the Council by Philip Francis on 11 March 1775, Nand Kumar accused the Governor-General, Warren Hastings (q.v.), of accepting bribes from highly placed officials of the Nawab, such as Muhammad Reza Khan, Raja Shitab Rai, Munni Begum and even himself. Refusing to be tried by the Council, the Governor-General in turn accused Nand Kumar (11 April 1775) of conspiring with Joseph Fawke and others against himself and Richard Barwell, a member of the Council who was pronouncedly pro-Hastings in his leanings. A few days later one Mohan Prasad accused Nand Kumar of forgery, on which charge the latter was imprisoned and brought to trial. The proceedings during 8–11 June were before an all-English jury which declared him guilty; Elijah Impey (q.v.), then Chief Justice of Calcutta's Supreme Court, pronounced the sentence of death.

The importance of Nand Kumar's trial lies in the fact that it was considered by many contemporary observers as tantamount to 'judicial murder' committed with the connivance of Warren Hastings in a bid to save himself from disgrace. Some later writers, however, tried to justify the action taken while others admit that ulterior motives were involved. It is held that while forgery was punishable under Hindu law, it certainly did not invite capital punishment. The sentence meant therefore that the newly-constituted Supreme Court had applied English law, then itself barbarous, to Indian conditions. It has been maintained that the Supreme Court's jurisdiction in this case was dubious and that the particular section of the English law applied was not applicable to the citizens of Calcutta.

In extenuation, however, it may be pointed out that English laws had been applied in Calcutta for quite some time, even though no records exist of punishment by death for forgery except in a solitary case where the offender was pardoned. It is, therefore, held that, if Nand Kumar had not dared attack the Governor-General, he too may have been acquitted. On the other hand, it is contended that the Supreme Court in taking this decision averted a more violent settlement of differences in the Council itself and may even have prevented civil strife.

A scholar has underlined 'certain facts' about Nand Kumar's case that deserve to be noted: 'From 16 June to 4 August, from the day of his conviction to that of his execution, petitions presented to the Court were grounded on the petitioner's ignorance of law. None of these were grounded on the prisoner having preferred a charge against the Governor-General;

'The majority members of the Council who had publicly supported Nand Kumar before and during his trial and had interfered with the processes of the Court on his behalf, abandoned him altogether after he was found guilty. If they believed that the prosecution was malicious or the punishment severe, they had more than one opportunity to move the court for a suspension of the sentence;

'As for the alleged conspiracy between Warren Hastings and Impey, it may well be argued that Nand Kumar's accusations did not expose Hastings to any unforeseen danger. By destroying Nand Kumar, "he would have aroused suspicions about, rather than saved his honour and reputation." Further it has been suggested that if Hastings and Impey had conspired in 1775 to ruin Nand Kumar, they would not have wrangled as they did in 1780. Their relationship in the years after 1775 did not smack of an element of conspiracy.'

It is interesting that the House of Commons did not include Nand Kumar's case as a charge against Warren Hastings during his impeachment. Impey too was later exonerated on this count.

After his execution, Nand Kumar's treasure and effects were passed on to his son, Raja Gurdas. It is said that a sum of Rs 52 lakhs in cash and about the same in jewels and precious goods were found. The *Siyar-ul-mutakharin* mentions that in his house forged counterfeit seals of several eminent persons were discovered.

According to some authorities, Hastings has been improperly charged with Nand Kumar's murder, and James Stephens exonerates him completely. A recent biographer maintains that Nand Kumar, an efficient and intelligent officer, 'showed in full measure' the vices of his age, that he was a typical civil servant who was ready to lend his services to anyone who paid for them. He was also an intriguer and played into the hands of members of the Council who for their own reasons were hostile to Hastings. There is little doubt that Nand Kumar was inordinately ambitious and that his aspirations for status, wealth and fame knew no bounds.

Strictly, the laws of the Supreme Court did not apply to him for Nand Kumar was not a resident of Calcutta but had been kept there under detention. It would, however, be an exaggeration to view him as a great patriot or a martyr. The fact is that he was a victim of the intrigues in which he was himself so deeply enmeshed. A recent biographer has concluded that Nand Kumar fell victim to a well-planned scheme hatched by his political opponents 'who were not prepared to tolerate his opposition to their ambition'.

B. N. Pandey, who has closely studied the career of Elijah Impey, concludes that 'there existed no conspiracy' between the Governor-General and the Chief Justice of the Supreme Court to ruin Nand Kumar, and that at the same time one has to accept the fact that Nand Kumar, in fact, did forge the Persian bond. Further, 'By snubbing the Court, censuring the conduct of the judges and publicly sympathizing with the prisoner to the extent of making him expect everything from power and nothing from justice, the majority members of the Council in fact compelled the judges to vindicate their powers and independence by rigidily adhering to the strict letter of the law. Nand Kumar, till the last moment of his life, expected that the Council would force the judges to deliver him. By fabricating the evidence during the trial and ignoring the judges after the trial, he had made them merciless. Had these special circumstances not attended his case, his original guilt would not have brought about his destruction.'

Benoy Krishna Roy, *The Career and Achievements of Maharaja Nand Kumar, Dewan of Bengal (1705–75),* Calcutta, 1969; B. N. Pandey, *The Introduction of English Law into India: the career of Elijah Impey in Bengal 1774–83,* Bombay, 1969.

Dadabhai Naoroji (1825–1917)

Dadabhai Naoroji came of a priestly Parsi family and rose to be 'the grand old man' of India. He had lost his father while still young and thus came under the powerful impact of his mother Manekbhai who, he said later in life, 'made me what I am'. Dadabhai graduated from Elphinstone College in Bombay where later, in 1845, he was to start life as a 'native' Head Assistant. Earlier, Jamesetji Jeejeebhoi, a well-known Parsi philanthropist, had declined to share the expenses of his law studies abroad, for fear Dadabhai be lost to the community. Promoted Assistant Professor of Mathematics and Physics in 1850, Dadabhai became Professor four years later, being the first 'native' to reach that position. Acutely conscious of the deplorable condition of his people, he involved himself increasingly in political and social reform movements for their uplift. Initially using the short-lived Bombay Association as his forum, he petitioned the government for the redress of genuine grievances of the people. He had already started a weekly, the *Rast Goftar,* giving expression *inter alia* to his ideas on social and religious reform. To improve the lamentable state of women in Indian society he founded a girls school and a widow remarriage association.

Dadabhai's life spanned three-quarters of the nineteenth century and seventeen years of the twentieth. It falls into five distinct periods: the first, his years of childhood and youth, from 1825–55; the second, from 1855 when he first went to England and up to 1881, when he left there with the intention of never returning again; the third, from 1881 to 1886, when he did in fact return to England with the intention of trying to enter Parliament; the fourth, from 1886 to 1907, when he finally returned to India; and the fifth, the ten years of retirement from 1907 up to his death in 1917.

In 1855, as agent and partner of Messrs Cama & Company in England, he took charge of their London branch; but he set up his own business in 1862. In England, Dadabhai played an active role in the deliberations of the council of Liverpool, the 'Athaneum' and the National Indian Association. In effect, he was looked upon as India's unofficial ambassador, fighting for the cause of his country and its people. From now onwards until his retirement, Dadabhai commuted regularly between India and England. In 1865 he established the London India Society in collaboration with W. C. Bonnerjee (q.v.) and was to be its President till 1907. Its objective was to publicize Indian grievances and seek British support in remedying them. Soon afterwards (December 1866) Dadabhai started the East India Association, which threw open its membership to non-Indians. At the same time (1856–66) he had been teaching Gujarati at University College, London.

After his return to India and while on a lecture tour of western India, Dadabhai met the Gaekwad of Baroda who, in 1874, offered him his state's Diwanship, which he accepted. Opposed by the courtiers in his efforts to reform the state administration and by the British Resident, Robert Phayre (1820-97), who disliked being superseded in importance, he resigned a year later when the Gaekwad too failed to support him. Between 1869 and 1874 Dadabhai had occupied himself with municipal reform, besides writing a book on the poverty of India, explaining how, despite the best intentions of the British, their rule had proved to be disastrous for the country. The appointment of a Parliamentary Committee in 1873 to inquire into Indian finances was due to his untiring efforts. At the end of his one-year (1875–6) tenure as municipal commissioner, Dadabhai left for England; later, on returning from England, he occupied (1881–5) the same position. At the same time, he was working for the formation of an all-India political association and was, in fact, a founder-member of the Indian National Congress (q.v.). Away briefly once more in England to contest the election to Parliament (1886)— he was unsuccessful— Dadabhai returned home just in time to preside over the second annual session of the Congress. Six years later (1892) he was returned to the House of Commons from Central Finsbury on a Liberal (Party) ticket.

In 1885 Dadabhai joined the Bombay Legislative Council. In that year he was also elected Vice President of the Bombay Presidency Association and, as has been noticed, took a leading part in founding the Congress; thrice, in 1886, 1893 and 1906, he was to be its President. During his tenure (1892–5) as a member of the British Parliament, he drew pointed attention to the cause of Indian poverty. In the result, he was instrumental in the appointment (1895) of a Royal Commission on Indian Expenditures under Lord Welby (of which he himself was a member).

Politically a moderate, Dadabhai believed that English interests were identical with India's own and that both countries could work to their mutual benefit. He was further of the view that Indian grievances should be ventilated through constitutional agitation which, however, had to be intensified and made continuous. The Bengal anti-partition movement had shown, he argued, how to organize and appeal to the masses.

Dadabhai was convinced that nothing much could be achieved without removing British apathy and ignorance. While enlightening the English public about Indian affairs, he did not fail to warn it about an upsurge of nationalism and the possibility that his country's loyalty may fail. The British, he counselled, must not rely too much on the policy of divide and rule for Indians were bound to unite in a common national cause. For his part, he decried militancy and avoided commenting on such movements as the Boycott (q.v.), for he still set great store by the British sense of justice and fair play. His loyalty had an empirical base for he appreciated the benefits of the British link by way of education, communications, justice, law and order.

Dadabhai popularized the nationalist cause in England and was actively involved in giving it shape and form. In 1899 he helped set up a committee for the Congress in London with Sir William Wedderburn (1838-1918) as Chairman, a body that was dissolved only in 1921. He espoused India's cause, supported the demand for constitutional reform and called for admissible changes in the scheme of things. As President of the Indian National Congress he laid down moderate guidelines; in 1903 he averted a split in Congress ranks by declaring 'Swaraj' (or self-government) to be the national goal even though, to him, it meant 'colonial self-government'. Later, he was to accept the Presidentship of the Home Rule League (q.v.) although Wedderburn had counselled him not to join hands with the extremists. Dadabhai had a large number of English friends, including, apart from Hume (q.v.) and William Wedderburn, Henry Mayers Hyndmann, a British socialist, Sir George Birdwood (1832-1917), Sheriff of Bombay, and the radical parliamentarian, Charles Bradlaugh. Among his Indian friends, mention may be made of Sorabjee Bengali, the author and social reformer; K. R. Cama (1831–1909), the orientalist; Jamsetji Tata (1839–1904), the industrialist; Pherozeshah Mehta (q.v.), Gokhale (q.v.), Dinshaw Wacha (1844–1936), the business magnate, and Gandhi (q.v.).

Coming under the impact of scientific socialism during his sojourn in England, Dadabhai began to appreciate more vividly the economic implications of imperial rule in India and became a high priest of the 'drain' theory. There was in India, he argued, an export surplus while India's imports were made for unproductive purposes. Besides, there was the drain through pensions payable to personnel who had retired to live in England. All this led to financial exhaustion and the impoverishment of a people whose per capita income was barely Rs 20. Equally depressing was the moral drain caused by English officials monopolizing the higher posts while qualified and experienced 'natives' had no opportunities to fill these positions. The 'drain' was a kind of built-in mechanism which extorted resources out of a low-level colonial economy and the surplus thus generated, was drained out of the economy through a complicated mechanism. The processes were those of external trade, the dynamics of which was supplied by the unilateral transfer of funds in an equally complicated kind of way. The functioning of this mechanism of transfer of resources was uniquely determined, according to Dadabhai, by a number of objective political factors, such as: India being a colonial economy governed by remote control; unlike the other white colonies in the world's temperate zone, the country did not attract labour or capital for economic development; India was saddled with an expensive civil administration and an equally expensive army of occupation; it had to bear the burden of empire-building within as well as outside the country; colonial exploitation by the British meant, among other things, creating highly paid jobs for foreign personnel; her colonial rulers did not spend their money or resources inside the country.

In a resolution adopted on 28 December 1897 at a meeting under the auspices of the India Society, the principal cause of India's ills was identified as the 'unrighteous and un-British system of government which produces an unceasing and ever-increasing bleeding of the country, and which is maintained by a political hypocrisy and continuous subterfuges, unworthy of the British honour and name and entirely in opposition to the British nation and sovereign.' In 1905, he roundly computed the annual drain at Rs. 51.5 crores. In sum, 'owing to this one unnatural policy of the British rule of ignoring India's interest and making it the drudge for the benefit of England the whole rule moves in a wrong, unnatural suicidal groove.'

Having become a moderate socialist, Dadabhai espoused the cause of labour in England; at home, he exhorted the government to use its taxation money for the welfare of the country and its people. In economics, he believed in self-sufficiency and the importance of cottage industries. A champion of Swadeshi (q.v.), he viewed it as 'a forced necessity for India in its unnatural economic muddle.' This did not, however, prevent him from supporting heavy industry such as Tata's iron and steel plants.

Dadabhai demanded that in the 'faithful and conscientious fulfilment' of solemn pledges, India expects and demands that the British sovereign, people, parliament and government should make honest efforts towards 'self-government under British paramountcy' or true British citizenship. He came back to India (1907) in poor health and lived in complete retirement at Versova. In 1915, he donated his library to the Bombay Presidency Association. A year before his death (in June 1917), Bombay University conferred on him an honorary degree of Doctor of Laws.

R. P. Masani, *Dadabhai Naoroji: the Grand Old Man of India*, London, 1939; *Dadabhai Naoroji*, Builders of India, New Delhi, 1960; Dadabhai Naoroji, *Poverty and Un-British Rule in India*, first Indian ed. in the Classics of Indian History and Economics, New Delhi, 1962; B. N. Ganguli, 'Dadabhai Naoroji and the mechanism of external drain', *Indian Economic and Social History Review*, II, 2, April 1965, pp. 85–102; R. P. Patwardan (ed.), *Dadabhai Naoroji Correspondence*, II, parts 1 and 2, Bombay, 1977; vol. 1 has yet to appear.

Charles Napier (1782–1853)

Charles Napier entered the army in 1794 at the age of twelve; he served in Ireland till 1803, and later (1808) in Spain and the USA (1813), besides being a veteran of the Peninsular War (1809–14) in which he achieved some distinction. After two years' (1815–17) study at the Military College, Farnham, he became Resident at Caphalonia (1822–30), an island off the west coast of Greece. Later, he lived in England in obscurity and on half pay, till he was posted to command the Poona division in 1838. Napier's stay in Poona was uneventful, except for his drilling of the troops, which attracted notice. In 1839 he was transferred as commander of Sind (q.v.) having achieved that position through the influence of his brother, William. He was convinced that this was the call to glory he had awaited so long and that it would be the most eventful period of his life.

Napier went to Sind with preconceived ideas: 'we have no right to seize

Sind, yet we shall do so and a very advantageous piece of rascality it will be'. The Governor-General's dependence on and, indeed, implicit faith and trust helped Napier to manoeuvre the course of events in a manner that resulted in the outbreak of open hostilities, despite Outram's (q.v.) efforts to the contrary. The successful Annexation of Sind (q.v) made his name a household word in England. He received £70,000 as his share of the spoils.

As governor of Sind, Napier made sure that the administration was carried on by military personnel rather than by the 'civil villains', as he called the civilians. A benevolent despot, with a capacity for leadership, his military rule was inexpensive and at the same time effective. Harsh to the Amirs, he tried to be just to the people, making short shrift of bribery and corruption, encouraging public works, setting up schools and introducing social reform. Despite these measures, his administration witnessed a decline in cultivation and large-scale unemployment, the province's economy being sustained through the illegal smuggling of opium.

Early in 1845 a three-month, rigorous campaign was undertaken by Napier against the troublesome tribes of the Cutchee hills. During the First Anglo-Sikh War (q.v.), Napier volunteered to seize Multan and by early February 1845 had reached Rohri with his troops but was disappointed to learn that his help was no longer required. Two years later, his wife's ill-health persuaded him to resign.

Napier's relations with the Court of Directors had in the meantime deteriorated due to his unrestrained criticism of that body as one interested exclusively in profit and therefore unable to recognise the services of troops who had won them an empire. By making all appointments in the army himself, he also deprived the Directors of their much-coveted patronage.

During the Second Anglo-Sikh War (q.v.), British reverses made the Duke of Wellington (1769-1852) suggest that Napier act as a replacement for Hugh Gough. Understandably, the Court of Directors initially opposed the move vigorously. Later, however, under pressure, they acquiesced. But Napier was frustrated to find on his arrival in May 1849 that the war had already been successfully concluded. During his later tenure as Commander-in-Chief (1849–50) he clashed with Dalhousie (q.v.) on the measures adopted to suppress a mutiny of Indian troops and on the subject of compensatory allowance to be paid to the 'native' army. Reprimanded by the Governor-General, he resigned office and left India on 16 November 1850.

A prolific writer, Napier had almost completed a book, 'Defects, Civil and Military of the Indian Government' when he died on 27 August 1853. He described his career 'a wayward life of adventure'. His biographer calls it 'A life that glowed with love and war, and endless disputes, and furious rows with his superiors over the rights of private soldiers whose champion he became: a life pulsating with embers when blown upon by bellows, till they blazed into flame! There was a kind of bravura about this old warrior who was given his first commission at twelve! He inspired wherever he went either admiration or fury.' Thomas Carlyle called him 'A fiery, lynx-eyed man with the spirit of an old knight in him more than in any modern I have ever met,' and Napier's statue at Trafalgar Square in the heart of London bears witness to the affection he inspired: 'Erected by public subscription, the most numerous contributions being Private soldiers.'

Lambrick, after 'a thorough examination' of Napier's career, views it as 'a remarkable example of the power of personality and propaganda'. Its force 'and strange charm' backed by his own sharp and skilful pen was projected by his brother's literary fame, while the support of the Duke of Wellington 'secured for him the implicit trust of thousands'. A legendary figure in his own lifetime, his apologists dismissed the calumnies pressed against him as 'an additional proof of his eminence'. For the Sindhis and Baluchis he possessed the greatest virtues 'of strength and success'; although he treated the Amirs harshly 'he tried hard to do justice to their people.' Lambrick concludes that he may have made mistakes as a ruler 'but at least he ruled'. Contemporary accounts noted that Napier looked and behaved a hero with his keen, hawk-like eye, aquiline nose and impressive features. His disregard of luxury, simplicity of manner, careful attention to the wants of soldiers under his command and enthusiasm for duty and right were proverbial. His journals testify to his deep religious convictions, while his life was a prolonged protest against oppression, injustice and wrong-doing. Generous to a fault, a radical in politics yet an autocrat in government, hot-tempered and impetuous, Napier inspired strong affection or inveterate hatred. On his statue in St Paul's Cathedral in London are inscribed the words, 'A prescient general, a beneficient governor, a just man'.

Rosamond Lawrence, *Charles Napier: Friend and Fighter, 1782-1853*, London, 1952; H. T. Lambrick, *Sir Charles Napier and Sind*, Oxford, 1952; *DNB*, XIV, pp. 45–54 (Robert Hamilton Vetch).

Nasir-ud-Daula, Nizam (1792–1857)

Mir Farkundah Ali Khan, the eldest son of Sikandar Jah (q.v.), succeeded the latter in 1829 and assumed the title of Nasir-ud-Daula. He asked the John Company (q.v.) to discontinue all interference in the internal administraton of his state, to which the then Governor-General, William Bentinck (q.v.), agreed. Nasir-ud-Daula was illiterate, but knew the art of governing his court. Kind and just, he had to be literally forced into passing a sentence of death.

However, the old minister Chandu Lal (d.1863), who was a British protege, had assumed control of the administration and presently, the condition of the people and the economy deteriorated beyond repair. The British Resident refused, on grounds of policy, all requests for help as conditions worsened, though interfering whenever anything seemed to upset British domination at the court. The main cause of oppression and corruption was the heavy cost (Rs 42 lakhs annually) of maintaining the British subsidiary\forces. In 1835 the Court of Directors warned the Nizam that misrule and disorder would not be allowed to continue; eight years later, Chandu Lal, who paid heavily for the subsidiary troops so as to buy the support of the British, was unable to carry on the administration and resigned. It has been suggested that the resignation was instigated by the British Resident, General James Fraser.

The Nizam took a long time appointing a successor while the state's financial bankruptcy worsened. He is said to have spent Rs 2 crores from his own treasury to clear part of the state debt. Ellenborough (q.v.) was willing to advance a loan if the entire administration of the state were taken over by the British after making an allowance for the Nizam—an offer which the latter refused to accept. By December 1850, the Nizam owed Rs 70 lakhs to the Company, which now set him a time-limit (viz., January 1851) to clear the arrears.

When the Nizam was unable to pay the entire amount, Dalhousie (q.v.) coerced him by threatening the use of force into signing a treaty (1853) whereby he agreed to cede the province of Berar and the Raichur Doab in perpetuity to the English for the maintenance of the subsidiary troops. Additionally, the latter were to maintain the Hyderabad contingent while the surplus revenue (from Berar), after defraying the cost of troops, was promised to the Nizam.

Nasir-ud-Daula died on 11 March 1857 and was succeeded by his son Afzal-ud-Daulah (q.v.).

M. Rama Rao, *Glimpses of Dakkan History*, Bombay, 1951, pp. 149–50; *Gribble*, II, pp. 171–222.

Nationalist Muslim Party (founded 1929)

The rise of the Nationalist Muslims as an organized group is said to have been the 'most significant' development of 1929. The beginnings may be traced to the formation of the Congress Muslim Party at a meeting in Bombay on 29 July where Yusuf Meherally (1903-50) and S. A. Brelvi (1891-1945), both well known for their socialist leanings, were present. In the same month, at another meeting at Allahabad, Maulana Abul Kalam Azad (q.v.) presided over the first All-India Nationalist Muslim Conference, pledged to develop among Muslims a spirit of nationalism and anti-communalism.

According to Khaliquzzaman at the All India Muslim League (q.v.) session held at Delhi in March 1929, under the presidentship of M. A. Jinnah (q.v.), leaders of the Khilafat Conference (q.v.) had come out to support the Nehru Report (q.v.) while there were others equally determined to oppose it. The hall was stormed by a mob from outside and supporters of the Report were eliminated one by one. Some of those thrown out of the hall decided to form a nationalist Muslim party.

There was another initiative. The Indian National Congress (q.v.) was naturally anxious that nationalist Muslims should have an independent organization to support its programme and the Nehru Report. The beginnings were made at the All-India Congress Committee meeting at Allahabad on 5 July 1929. According to Khaliquzzaman he, along with some representatives from the Panjab and Bengal, as well as Dr Sheikh Muhammad Alam, formed the new Muslim Nationalist Party. The Party chose Dr M. A. Ansari (q.v.) to be its President and Khaliquzzaman as its Secretary. Two prominent Muslims in the Congress, Maulana Abul Kalam Azad and Rafi Ahmad Kidwai (1894-1954) did not oppose the formation of the new party but, at the same time, kept aloof from it.

On 2 July 1930 Dr Ansari and Maulana Azad issued a public statement appealing to Muslims to respond in their thousands to the Congress call for the freedom struggle. Soon Afzal Haq presided over another conference of nationalist Muslims at Lahore, where a similar call was given. Earlier, on 21 April 1930, at the Bengal Provincial Muslim Political Conference held in Chittagong, speakers asked Muslims to join the Congress in large numbers and make equal sacrifices with other communities in the cause of the country's freedom.

About the same time, the emergence in the North-West Frontier Province (q.v.) of the Khudai Khidmatgars or Red Shirts under the leadership of Khan Abdul Ghaffar Khan (q.v.) and Dr Khan Sahib (q.v.), had given a great boost to the nationalist Muslim cause. But according to Khaliquzzaman, the party's prospects were somewhat dim: 'By its very nature it could have no roots in Muslim society and it did not make much headway either. Under its name no doubt several conferences were held ... but it had no rules or regulations, no separate membership and no separate office. Being backed by the Hindu Sabha press it lived in the newspapers all right but beyond that it had no positive existence. My idea that it might serve to bring about some discipline in nationalist Muslim ranks did not materialize because the remedy was not potent enough to eradicate the evil.'

A significant concession to the nationalist Muslims was Lord Irwin's (q.v.) undertaking to nominate one of them in the person of Dr Ansari to the second Round Table Conference (q.v.) in London. However, when Lord Willingdon succeeded Irwin in March 1931, the government eventually chose Ali Imam (1869-1932) to attend the Conference. Ali Imam was both old and infirm, but what was worse, he is said to have been 'effectively gagged' at the Conference in September 1931. A 'willing victim', he made 'little or no contribution' to its deliberations and even 'failed' in his primary duty to represent the nationalist Muslim cause.

Choudhry Khaliquzzaman, *Pathway to Pakistan*, Karachi, 1961, pp. 101–2; V. V. Nagarkar, *Genesis of Pakistan*, New Delhi, 1975, pp. 214–33.

Jawaharlal Nehru (1889–1964)

Jawaharlal Nehru was born at Allahabad to a proud, learned, prosperous Kashmiri Brahmin father, Motilal Nehru (q.v.) and an uneducated, and tradition-bound mother, Swarup Rani. Brought up in a luxurious home—with two swimming pools and a stable—coached by English, Irish and Scottish tutors, Jawaharlal grew up in an atmosphere that was more English than Indian. He lacked nothing—in wealth, status, comfort. Until 11, he was the only child, whereafter came two sisters. As there was no company at home—and few children visited Motilal's home—Jawaharlal grew up with a strong sense of loneliness.

Early on, his Irish teacher, Ferdinand T. Brooks introduced him to Mrs Annie Besant's (q.v.) theosophy. That apart, Jawaharlal was deeply moved by her silver-tongued oratory. He developed a love for poetry and the mysteries of science. His taste for writers such as Walter Scott, Charles Dickens, Thackeray, H. G. Wells and Mark Twain as also for the political ethos of John Stuart Mill, Gladstone and John Morley was pronounced. Both Bernard Shaw and Bertrand Russell moved him powerfully.

At 13, Jawaharlal joined the Theosophical Society (q.v.); at 15, he sailed with his parents for England to join Harrow, the celebrated public school. Here he was quiet and reserved and did not make an impression on his contemporaries. Later, to university at Cambridge where, he confessed many years later: 'In my likes and dislikes, I was perhaps more an English-man than an Indian'. In London he was attracted by the then fashionable Fabian ideas on nationalism and socialism. At Trinity College, Cambridge, where Jawaharlal was enrolled, he obtained his Tripos in Natural Sciences—Chemistry, Geology, Botany. He was an average student.

Jawaharlal joined the Inner Temple in 1910—initially his father wanted him to enter the I.C.S.—and was called to the Bar two years later. On returning home, the legal profession did not hold him for long. He was stirred by the arrest of Annie Besant, then an ardent advocate of Indian Home Rule (q.v.), in 1917. After the Jallianwala Bagh Massacre (q.v.), he came under the powerful impact of Mahatma Gandhi (q.v.). Meantime, in 1916, he was married to Kamala Kaul who, ten years younger to him, came of an orthodox Kashmiri Brahmin family; it was an arranged affair. Nor were the two entirely compatible in temperament: Jawaharlal was domineering; Kamala, quiet, unobtrusive. She had little impact on her petulant husband. In the second year of their marriage, Indira was born. Never in robust health, Kamala was to die prematurely, in 1936.

In the course of the Non-cooperation Movement (q.v.), Jawaharlal came in contact with the *kisans* in U.P. He was, he confessed, 'filled with shame and sorrow . . . at the degradation and overpowering poverty of India'. It aroused his deep sympathy for the underdog which was to characterize many of his later political mores. Non-cooperation helped him to become a popular leader: 'I took to the crowd and the crowd took to me, and yet I never lost myself in it.' This was characteristic: his intimate involvement with the masses went side by side with his studied aloofness and lonely detachment.

From 1921 may be said to begin Jawaharlal's long saga of imprisonments. With jail-going a badge of political respectability, Nehru earned the latter in goodly measure: between 1920 and 1945, he had one leg in jail and the other outside; years later he was to describe prison as 'the best of universities.' In 1930, he was arrested in connection with the Salt Satyagraha (q.v.) as was his wife, Kamala. Between end-1931 and September 1935, he was free for only six months! This apart, his political rise, which was well-nigh meteoric, was helped by the self-abnegation of Gandhi and Vallabhbhai Patel (q.v.). He was chosen thrice President of Indian National Congress (q.v.), a rare distinction.

During 1926-7 Jawaharlal visited Europe for the sake of his ailing wife and attended the anti-imperialist Oppressed Nationalities' Conference at Brussels. Here he met the German dramatist, Ernest Toller who later shared his aversion for Nazi Germany. On returning home, Jawaharlal was in the thick of the Trade Union Movement (q.v.) and emerged as a doughty champion both of independence and socialism. At the Congress session at Calcutta in December 1928, he joined Subhas Chandra Bose (q.v.) and others to press the claim for complete independence as the Congress objective, in place of Dominion Status (q.v.). When the party convened at Lahore, in 1929, under his presidentship it committed itself to the new political goal. In the 1936-37 election campaign for the provincial legislatures under the Government of India Act 1935 (q.v.), Jawaharlal was the principal vote-getter for the Congress and a powerful influence in the higher echelons of the party counsels. In 1938, Jawaharlal paid brief visits to Europe and, later, China where he was to develop a great personal rapport with Generalissimo Chiang Kai-shek and his wife. In the 1930s, his undiluted sympathies lay with Fascist-ravaged Abyssinnia and Republican Spain. Independent India's foreign policy was as much his gift as a backwash of Indian tradition. International disputes, Nehru insisted, should always be worked out by negotiation as well as arbitration.

Jawaharlal was to play a major role in negotiations with Sir Stafford Cripps (q.v.) in March 1942 as well as developments leading to the Quit India Movement (q.v.). Later, after his release from prison, he was the pivotal negotiator on behalf of his party at the time of the Simla Conference (q.v.) as well as all that followed: the Cabinet Mission (q.v.) and the June 3rd Plan (q.v.).

Even though he differed with Gandhi on fundamentals—in many ways they were worlds apart—Jawaharlal developed great respect and admiration for the Mahatma. Gandhi's verdict on him could scarce be bettered: 'Jawaharlal is pure as a crystal, he is truthful beyond suspicion. He is a knight *sans peur, sans reproche*. The nation is safe in his hands.' No wonder the Mahatma designated him his political heir, thereby eliminating Patel from the contest which, but for the latter's vow of obedience, could have been bitter.

In September 1946, Nehru was the head of the Interim Government (q.v.) and Vice-President of the Governor-General's Executive Council. It has been suggested that he was partly responsible for Wavell's (q.v.) recall. The close rapport that Jawaharlal developed with Lord Louis Mountbatten helped smoothen a lot of difficulties in the eventual transfer of power.

With Independence on 15 August 1947, Jawaharlal emerged as the undisputed choice for Prime Ministership of the Indian dominion. He was to occupy that office until his death, on 27 May 1964. Under his stewardship, the country launched a major planning offensive with three Five Year Plans, large-scale industrialization, especially in the key sector of heavy industry, and increased food production. In foreign policy, Jawaharlal advocated non-alignment and a stern refusal to be a camp follower of any of the two powerful blocs in which the world was then sharply split. Friendly towards China to start with, an increasing bitterness developed in his relationship with that country as the border conflict came to the fore. The Chinese armed offensive in October-November 1962 proved a veritable death blow to Jawaharlal—to his policies and to him personally.

Jawaharlal's death in May 1964 left a void. His countrymen, echoing his own words, might well have said: 'The light has gone out of our lives and there is darkness everywhere.' A democrat to the core, he helped consolidate democratic foundations in India. His agnosticism and opposition to all forms of organized religion paved the way for secularism. Under his stewardship, the customary Hindu law was codified, giving women equal rights of inheritance and divorce. Jawaharlal hated narrow nationalism and stood for freedom of intercourse with the rest of the world. Unlike Gandhi, non-violence with him was not an article of faith, yet he forswore violence for the attainment of social transformation. Again, even though he rejected Gandhi's theory of economic trusteeship, he refused to promote class war. As head of the government, Jawaharlal fostered national unity but the States' Reorganization Scheme—to restructure the states on the basis of linguistic affinities—led to a host of problems which proved intractable. He wanted to give India her own national language—Hindi, yet his policies succeeded only in giving a longer lease of life to English.

His emphasis on planning, science and technology, led to a chain of national scientific laboratories, the decimal system of coinage and a drastic reform of weights and measures. A great advocate of the freedom of the press, Jawaharlal avowed: 'I would rather have a completely free press with all the dangers involved in the wrong use of that freedom than a suppressed or regulated press.'

His critics charge that Jawaharlal left a host of unsolved problems—communalism, poverty, Indo-Pakistan estrangements, the backlog of a bitter, armed conflict with China, vacillation and lack of decision on Kashmir. These apart, a great deal in his Five Year Plans by which he set much store, they aver, went awry. Critics also charge him with backsliding. Thus in the 1930s he backed out of the Congress Socialist Party when Gandhi frowned on the leftists, thereby parting company with socialists like Jayaprakash Narayan (q.v.) and Ram Manohar Lohia. Essentially, it has been said, Nehru behaved less as a radical or socialist and more as 'Bapu's (Gandhi's) obedient boy'

Jawaharlal's alleged refusal to compromise with the Muslim League (q.v.) after the 1937 elections has been rated as a great political blunder which helped communal forces and encouraged M.A. Jinnah's (q.v.) intransigence over the partition of the country. Another grave error attributed to him was his refusal to allow Fazlul Haq (q.v.) permission to form a coalition with the Congress in Bengal. The repercussions were to prove disastrous. Jawaharlal's injudicious speech on the Cabinet Mission Plan stating that once the Congress entered the Constituent Assembly (q.v.) it would be free to decide what part of the original plan it would accept and what it would not, led to grievous consequences. Abul Kalam Azad (q.v.) called it 'one of those unfortunate events which change the course of history'. Jawaharlal's acceptance of the June 3rd Plan, when he had vehemently opposed partition of the country all along, has been explained by the party's unwillingness to go again into the political wilderness. 'The truth is', he confessed years later, 'we were tired men'. The partition 'offered a way out and we took it'.

Added up and even multiplied, all these criticisms show some of Jawaharlal Nehru's failings and his occasionally poor judgement; but they do not detract from his greatness. It would not be straying far from the truth to say that Nehru was to Gandhi what Lenin was to Marx.

On the plus side, it was Jawaharlal alone who saw to it that India did not become a Hindu state and thus an anti-thesis of Pakistan. The long if harsh struggle that he waged to reform the Hindu laws of marriage and property in favour of women and the self-imposed task of transforming a mediaeval society by substituting technology for tradition and science for superstition need no emphasis. If Gandhi was India's liberator, Nehru was its modernizer.

In every single field, the essence of his failure was his inability to match his aspirations with achievements. He devoted too much attention and energy to building an ambience and perhaps too little to getting things done. The fate of the land reforms by which he swore is a telling example.

Jawaharlal's detractors emphasize his capacity to tolerate corruption almost under his nose and his woefully poor judgement of men whereby he was taken in easily by seemingly dynamic crooks and frauds. There was also his total refusal to stray away from the democratic path which, combined with an almost obsessive concern for national unity and a punctilious regard for proprieties, made him absolutely unwilling to force the pace on any issue.

Whatever his failings, Jawaharlal's love for his land and people remained undimmed. In his own words, he was one 'who, with all his mind and heart, loved India and the Indian people. And they, in turn, were indulgent to him and gave him of their love most abundantly and extravagantly.' 'Great men', said Stalin, 'need not be good men'. Nehru was no doubt an exception to the rule—a rare blend of greatness and goodness.

A keen English observer has underlined some seeming inconsistencies in Nehru's character: 'an unusually complicated man, a leader harbouring powerful contradictory impulses: agitator and mediator, a politician often bored with politics, and wanting power not for himself but for a cause. A Brahmin not without vanity who loathed caste, an aloof intellectual preferring his own company who had a unique relationship with the Indian masses..' At the same time Jawaharlal was 'blessed with extraordinary gifts of intellect, of energy and physical resilience, and of a captivating presence . . (his) loyalty, courage, self-discipline, and a dedication to a free and democratic India . .'

Galbraith records that faced with challenges, Nehru could hardly think of a root-and-branch solution; his problem, as he told Malraux, was the creation of a just state by just means. Walter Crocker, a percipient observer who as New Zealand High Commissioner in New Delhi came to know Jawaharlal intimately, noted that 'Nehru had less of the common and less of the mean than all but a few men. And he is to be numbered among the small band of rulers in history whose power has been matched with pity and mercy . . . Nehru's public face differed scarcely at all from his private face.'

Introspective and lonely, Jawaharlal was often animated by women's company. Among Indian women Padmaja Naidu was very close to him. Lady Edwina Mountbatten's wit and beauty charmed him as did Madame Chiang Kai-shek's and Jacqueline Kennedy's.

Nehru wrote prolifically, with feeling and an engaging felicity. His books, for the most part, were composed during his interminable jail detentions. His *Glimpses of World History* (1934-35) is in the form of letters to his daughter Indira; his *Autobiography* (1936), largely a saga of the nationalist struggle for independence; his *Discovery of India* (1946), a foray into India's historical, predominantly cultural past. Jawaharlal's *Selected Works* running into several volumes and far from complete (15 have been published) as of date, add up to a vast store-house of human endeavour in varied fields.

Sarvepalli Gopal, *Nehru: A Biography,* New Delhi, vol. i, 1977, vol. ii, 1979 and (ed.), *Jawaharlal Nehru: An Anthology,* Delhi, 1980; Michael Brecher, *Nehru: A Political Biography*, New York, 1960; B. N. Pandey, *Nehru,* London, 1976; Walter Crocker, *Nehru: A Contemporary's View,* London, 1966; *DNB 1961–1970,* pp. 783–88 (T. H. Beaglehole); Sen (ed.), *DNB,* III, pp. 253–62 (Ajit Prasad Jain).

Nehru Report (1928)

Officially called 'Report of the Committee by the All-Parties Conference to determine the principles of the constitution of India', it is more popularly known as the Nehru Report, after its Chairman, Pandit Motilal Nehru (q.v.). The president of the Conference was Dr M. A. Ansari (q.v.) and the Committee's members were Tej Bahadur Sapru (q.v.) of the Liberal Federation (q.v.), Ali Imam (1869-1932), M. S. Aney (q.v.), M. R. Jayakar (1873-1959), N. M. Joshi (q.v.), the labour leader, Mangal Singh who represented the Sikh League, Shuaib Qureshi, General Secretary of the Indian National Congress (q.v.), Subhas Chandra Bose (q.v.) and G. R. Pradhan to represent the non-Brahmin view-point. Joshi was unable to attend any sitting of the Committee; Ali Imam attended only one and Pradhan attended meetings only up to 12 June 1928.

The Report comprised seven chapters, two schedules and three appendices. Chapter 7, comprising 24 pages in print and entitled 'Recommendations', contains the broad outlines of the constitutional framework.

A word on the background. Towards the end of 1927, with the almost unanimous opposition to the appointment of the Simon Commission (q.v.), most Indian political parties drew closer to each other. In pursuance of a resolution of the Madras session of the Congress in December 1927, an all-parties conference was convened at Delhi on 12 February 1928. Representatives of 29 organisations including the Central Khilafat Committee, the Central Sikh League, the South Indian Liberal Federation, the Central Council of All-Burmese Associations, the Indian States' Subjects Association, the Indian States' Subjects Conference, the Parsi Panchayat, the Bombay Non-Brahmin Party, the Communist Party of Bombay and the Bombay Workers' and Peasants' Party attended.

After acute differences of opinion about the objective of the proposed constitution had been sorted out by adopting a compromise formula of full responsible government, the conference appointed a Committee with instructions to report on such subjects as a bi-cameral or uni-cameral legislatures; franchise; a declaration of rights; the rights of labour and the peasantry and the future of the Indian States (q.v.).

The committee's labours came up against serious obstacles and at a meeting held in Bombay on 19 May 1928, the parent All-Parties Conference adopted a resolution appointing another committee with Motilal Nehru as its Chairman to consider and determine the principles of the constitution of India after giving the fullest consideration to the Congress resolution on communal unity as well as resolutions of other parties and organizations.

The Committee was asked to report before 1 July and the Conference was to convene early in August to consider its report.

After seeking advice from a number of eminent people and representatives of communal parties and holding 25 sittings in June and July, the Nehru Committee presented its report to the fourth session of the All-Parties Conference which meeting at Lucknow in August 1928 adopted in principle the constitution outlined and recommended by it in the report.

The report was signed by all members, barring Shuaib Qureshi who was not present at the final meeting of the Committee. The draft was sent to him and he intimated that chapter III should specify that one-third of seats in the central legislature be reserved for Muslims. Further, he added: 'I agree with the resolution adopted at the informal conference of 7 July but do not subscribe to all the figures and arguments produced in its support.' Ali Imam, Bose and G. R. Pradhan were also unable to be present, but signified their concurrence with the report after seeing the draft.

The highest common denominator in the Committee's recommendations was the assumption that the country's new constitution would rest on the solid base of Dominion Status (q.v.). In retrospect, this was viewed as a great climb-down by the radical wing of the Congress led by Subhas Chandra Bose and Jawaharlal Nehru (q.v.) who, in opposition, founded the 'Independence for India League'.

Among the other principal recommendations of the Report were: (a) that provision be made for freedom of conscience, profession and practice of one's religion; (b) that lower houses in the central legislature and the provincial councils consist of members elected by joint mixed electorates with reservation of seats for Muslims at the centre and such provinces where they constituted a minority, and, similarly, reservation of seats for Hindus in the North-West Frontier Province (q.v.); (c) that there should be no reservation of seats for Muslims in the Panjab and Bengal; (d) that the reservation of seats should be on the basis of population and for a fixed period of 10 years; communities whose seats were reserved were to have the right to contest additional seats; (e) that adult universal suffrage was to be provided; (f) that Sind (q.v.) and Karnataka were to be separate provinces; (g) that lists of subjects on which the central and provincial governments were to exercise authority were to be provided in the schedules.

The Nehru Report was not an attempt to draft a constitution as such. The Committee had made it clear that its recommendations were similar to the clauses of a draft bill but were not intended to be treated as such. It had also made explicit the fact that the Report was nothing more than an indication of the principles involved and that, in compiling it, members had drawn freely on the constitutions of other dominions of the British Empire. Since it was visualised that India would enjoy that status too, it would have, like other dominions, a parliament with power to make laws for the peace, order and good government of the country and an executive responsible to that parliament. The country was to be styled and known as the 'Commonwealth of India'.

It may be recalled that the Lucknow meeting of the All-Parties Conference in August 1928 had adopted a resolution which accepted the constitutional framework of the Nehru Report in its main principles. It now further re-appointed the earlier Committee with powers to co-opt, and authorized it to select and appoint a parliamentary draftsman. His task was to give the constitutional outline a concrete shape and recommend it in the form of a bill that may be placed before the convention of representatives of all political, commercial, labour and other organizations.

The Committee met at Lucknow and decided to co-opt Annie Besant (q.v.), Dr M. A. Ansari, Pandit Madan Mohan Malaviya (q.v.), Lala Lajpat Rai, Maulana Abul Kalam Azad (q.v.), M. A. Jinnah (q.v.), C. Vijairaghavachariar and Maulana Abdul Qadir Kasuri. The resolution was circulated to members not present at Lucknow and their approval sought; with the exception of Jinnah, who was not in the country, all agreed. On his return from Europe, Jinnah declined to act.

The earlier idea of a bill was however dropped and publication of the Committee's Report on points referred to it by the Conference considered adequate. The supplementary report of the Committee was thus published towards the end of 1928 and has an appendix containing its earlier recommendations with some consequential amendments. This Report was considered by the All-India Congress Committee at its meeting in Delhi on 4-5 November 1928 and accepted with some amendments. It was next placed before the All-Parties Convention at Calcutta which witnessed a violent clash between Jinnah representing the All India Muslim League (q.v.) and M.R. Jayakar, who put forth the All India Hindu Mahasabha (q.v.) viewpoint. The former demanded, *inter alia*, that one-third of the total seats in the proposed central legislature be reserved for Muslims; that in the Muslim majority provinces of Panjab and Bengal, too, there should be reservation of seats for Muslims on a population basis and that residuary powers of the federation be vested in the provinces. Jayakar, on the other hand, questioned Jinnah's *locus standi* as a representative of the Muslims and warned the Convention against going back on the Report. Jinnah's proposed amendments were overwhelmingly out-voted.

Later at the Convention, Gandhi (q.v.) expressed his satisfaction at the acceptance of the main recommendations of the Nehru Report which, according to him, reflected the will of the nation on the principles of a constitution. He voiced much the same views at the January 1929 session of the Congress at Calcutta which witnessed a lively debate on the political goal of India, viz., Dominion Status versus complete independence. The Convention adopted a resolution welcoming the report 'as a great contribution towards the solution of India's political and communal problems.' Furthermore, it viewed the constitution recommended by the Committee 'as a great step in political advance' and undertook to adopt it 'if it is accepted by the British Parliament on or before the 31 December 1929'.

Few, if any, references to the Muslim demand were articulated at the Congress session. The net result was a parting of the ways and a near-alienation of two well-known Muslim leaders, Jinnah and Maulana Mohamed Ali (q.v.), from the mainstream of the national movement. This was grist to the imperial mill and led inevitably to the Report proving, in retrospect, to be a non-starter and an historical museum piece.

All-Parties Conference 1928: *Report of the Committee appointed by the Conference to determine the principles for the constitution of India*, General Secretary, AICC, Allahabad, August 1928; All Parties Conference: *Supplementary Report of the Committee*, General Secretary, AICC, Allahabad, 1928; The Committee Appointed by

508   *Anglo-Nepalese War*

the All-Parties Conference 1928, *The Nehru Report: an anti-separatist manifesto*, reprint, New Delhi, 1975; Mushirul Hasan, 'Communalism in Indian Politics: a study of the Nehru Report', *Indian Historical Review*, 4, 2, January 1978, pp. 379–404; 'All Parties Committee Report' and 'The Nehru Supplementary Report', *Indian Review*, xxx, 9, September 1928, pp. 625–7 and Ibid., xxx, 12, December 1928, p. 873; *Tara Chand*, IV, pp. 111–15; A. C. Banerjee, *Indian Constitutional Documents*, III, pp. 201–7; S. Srinivas Iyengar, *Swaraj Constitution*, Madras, 1927.

Anglo-Nepalese War (1814–1816)

The Gurkhas who had occupied Nepal in 1767 were, by the end of the eighteenth century, in possession of the whole country between the rivers Teesta in the east and the Sutlej in the west, their ill-defined southern frontier bordering, for most part, on British-governed districts. Earlier, efforts to check frequent Gurkha inroads into these territories had been, from the British point of view, singularly unavailing. In December 1813, the Marquis of Hastings (q.v.), failing to settle matters amicably, demanded a complete evacuation of areas ruled by the John Company (q.v.). Under the pretext of compliance, the Nepalese commissioners who negotiated moved out, but in a surprise attack on Bhutwal (14 May 1814) killed a number of British personnel. This made the British decide to go on the offensive, but they waited till after the rains to declare war (November 1814).

A large army comprising approximately 20,000 men and 55 guns was assembled by the British for a double-pronged campaign. Colonel Ochterlony (q.v.) and Major-General Robert Gillespie were to operate from the west, near the Sutlej, and Major-Generals Bennet Marley and George Wood from Patna and Gorakhpur in the east, while over them all was Hastings directing operations from Lucknow. The Gurkhas under Amar Singh Thapa numbered 12,000 regular and some irregular troops, most of them poorly armed.

The first year of the campaign proved disastrous for the British, for they were complete strangers to the hilly terrain and the guerilla tactics adopted by the Gurkhas. Though Ochterlony achieved some success in pushing on to Bilaspur, Gillespie was killed at fort Kalanga, near Dehra Dun; his successor, Major General Gabriel Martindell, was defeated at Jaitak, while the two eastern commanders proved absolutely ineffective. The initial successes of the Gurkhas and the ineptitute of the British served as an eye-opener to the Company's rulers. Metcalfe (q.v.) wrote with evident mortification that there were 'numbers on our side and skill and bravery on the side of our enemy'.

These successes emboldened the Gurkhas who now concentrated on the western frontier. But on 14 April 1815 the redoubtable Amar Singh Thapa was defeated by Ochterlony, who invested Malaun. Another defeat was inflicted on the Gurkhas at Almora and when, on 15 May, a breach was made at Malaun itself, the Nepalese commander offered to negotiate. Even as the terms and conditions of the treaty were being worked out, Hastings continued with preparations for a possible renewal of hostilities. The Nepalese failed to ratify the draft agreement to which they had consented earlier. Ochterlony thereupon took the offensive, decisively defeating the Gurkha cammander at Makwanpur on 27 February 1816. A direct result was

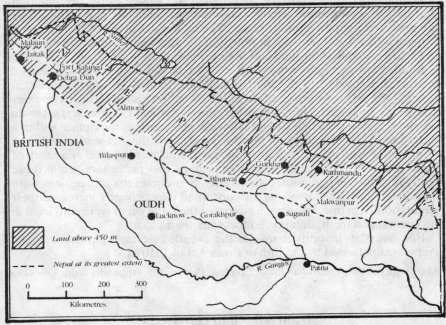

Anglo-Nepalese War (1814–16)

that the official seal was now affixed to the Treaty of Sagauli (q.v.) bringing
the Anglo-Nepalese War to an end.

John Pemble, *The Invasion of Nepal: John Company at War*, Oxford, 1971; Dodwell,
CHI, V, pp. 378–9.

Newspapers (Incitement to Offences) Act (1908)

Like the Explosive Substances Act, this measure followed a spate of terrorist activities, and in particular the Muzaffarpur bomb incident, in the
opening years of the twentieth century. The Act was intended to stop
seditious writings in newspapers, pamphlets and books and incitement
against British rule. Applicable to the whole of British India, the aim of the
Act was 'to make better provision for the prevention of incitements to
murder and to other offences in newspapers'. It empowered the authorities
to take judicial action against the editor of any paper which published matter
which, in their view, was an incitement to rebellion.

The Act authorized the government to ban the publication of newspapers
and to seize printing presses if they were found guilty of publishing news
which could incite to murder or any other violent act, or violate the Explosive Substances Act. A district magistrate was the ultimate authority, but
appeals lay to the High Court, after fifteen days.

In enacting this measure the government was guided by the presumption that Indians, being unprepared for constitutional agitation, may be misled by the press to disrupt the public peace. The moderates in the Indian National Congress (q.v.) and outside, hoping that the Act was a temporary measure to ensure law and order, had lent their support to it.

In all, 9 prosecutions were instituted: 7 resulted in the confiscation of 4 presses in Bengal, 2 in the Panjab and 1 in Bombay. In one instance, in Bengal, the presses were restored to the owner on his tendering an apology and giving an undertaking; in another, the government's order was set aside on an appeal to the High Court. All these prosecutions took place within a year, but in the eleven years that followed, until the Act was repealed, it remained a dead letter. Moreover, its provisions were evaded as a result of mere nominees declaring themselves printers and publishers, while those really responsible maintained anonymity. Sometimes the proceedings were protracted and in the process, the concerned papers 'vastly increased their circulation'. On one occasion, 5 editors of the same paper were convicted in succession and fresh, dummy, editors took their place.

Because of its inability to muzzle the so-called seditious publications, the Act was superseded by the Indian Press Act of 1910 (q.v.).

Margarita Barnes, *The Indian Press*. London, 1940, p. 325, Appendix 1, pp. 439–41.

Nizam Ali Khan (1761–1803)

Nizam Ali, the fourth son of Nizam-ul-Mulk Asaf Jah (q.v.), succeeded to the Nizamat in 1761 after dethroning and imprisoning his brother Salabat Jung. Anxious to extend his dominion, he devastated the Carnatic in 1765, but was driven back by the Nawab of Carnatic and his English allies. Later, menaced by the Marathas and Haidar Ali (q.v.), he concluded a treaty of alliance with the John Company (q.v.) at Madras (q.v.), agreeing *inter alia* to keep some subsidiary troops. Vacillating in his foreign policy, Nizam Ali soon joined the Mysore ruler and the Marathas against the English, but was weaned away by the latter through the Treaty of Masulipatam. The loss of Guntur in 1780 once again alienated him from an alliance with Haidar Ali. The British demand for it was ignored after the death of Basalat Jang till Cornwallis's (q.v.) military preparations forced Nizam Ali to surrender it. In 1790, the latter concluded a defensive and offensive alliance with the Company, and aided the British in the Third Anglo-Mysore War (q.v.).

In 1794, when the Marathas renewed claims upon the Nizam for arrears of *chauth* and *sardeshmukhi* he appealed to the then Governor-General, John Shore (q.v.), for the assistance he had been led to expect; Calcutta, however, fearing a war with the Marathas, proclaimed neutrality. In the sequel, the Nizam's army was routed by the Marathas at Kharda, near Ahmadnagar. The result was a humiliating treaty which imposed heavy pecuniary damages, loss of considerable territory, including the districts of Daulatabad, Ahmadnagar and Sholapur, and the surrender of his principal minister to Poona as a hostage.

Nizam Ali now retaliated against the Company by dismissing his English troops, increasing his French contingent and opening negotiations with Tipu Sultan (q.v.) for an alliance against the Marathas. Wellesley (q.v.), the Governor-General, at first sought to conciliate by helping Nizam Ali during the rebellion of his son, Ali Jah, in 1797. He next encouraged Mir Alam, Nizam Ali's Anglophile minister, to persuade his master to see reason. Overwhelmed, Nizam Ali decided to conclude a subsidiary alliance with the British in September 1798. Under its terms, he agreed *inter alia* to maintain a British force, subject all external relations to British control and supervision and expel all foreigners, principally the French adventurer Michel Raymond (1755–98), from his dominions. In the result, Nizam Ali's troops fought alongside the British against Tipu in the Fourth Anglo-Mysore War (q.v.). He was soon asked to maintain a subsidiary force and, in payment, surrender all the territorial gains made in the earlier wars of 1792 and 1798, as well as those acquired after Tipu's final discomfiture at Seringapatam. Henceforth Nizam Ali was a ruler in name only. He died in 1803.

As for his relations with the Mughal Emperor, the Nizam is said to have gone in procession to receive the Mughal Emperor's *firman* from Delhi in 1772, the Emperor graciously acknowledging the *nazr* which the Nizam had sent. In December 1773, a turban and a special imperial upper-robe with half sleeves was sent together with a *firman* by the Emperor and received by the Nizam with due ceremony at Humnabad.

Nizam Ali made Hyderabad the seat of his government and was succeeded by his son Nawab Sikandar Jah (q.v.).

Gribble, II, pp. 90–3; Dodwell, *CHI*, V, p. 370; *The Chronology of Modern Hyderabad (1720–1890)*, Hyderabad Government, Hyderabad, 1954.

Nizam-ul-Mulk, Asaf Jah (1671–1748)

Qamar-ud-din, Chin Qulich Khan, later given the title Nizam-ul-Mulk, Asaf Jah, was the son of Ghazi-ud-din Khan Jang, a favourite Turkman officer of the Emperor Aurangzeb (r. 1658-1757) under whom he had distinguished himself. Born at Agra in 1671, Chin Qulich participated in the early campaigns of his father, including that of Adoni. He played an active role in the Mughal capture of Wakhinkhera (1705) and, as a result, is said to have acquired great influence with the old Emperor. From now on, his keen rivalry for mounting political ambition with a contemporary, Zulfikar Khan, was to constitute almost 'a fixed point' in Mughal court politics for more than a quarter century.

Under Bahadur Shah I (q.v.), Chin Qulich was raised to the highest rank, accorded the title of Khan-i-Dauran, and made the Governor of Oudh (q.v.) and the *faujdar* of Gorakhpur. In that brief reign however he and his group do not appear to have played any significant role in state affairs. It is not unlikely that they felt themselves out of step with the spirit and policy of Bahadur Shah's administration. Thereafter, during the 9–month reign of Jahandar Shah that followed Chin Qulich kept his counsel and did not play a partisan role in the civil war leading to the victory of Farrukh Siyar (q.v.) who became Emperor.

When the Sayyid Brothers (q.v.) became anxious to conciliate powerful nobles at the Mughal court, they invested Chin Qulich Khan at an early stage with the rank of 7,000/7,000, the title of Nizam-ul-Mulk, and appointed him Viceroy of the Deccan. He was given wide ranging powers to select the lands to be held in *jagir* and to suggest the *mansabs* to be granted to the chief zamindars there. Later, as a counterpoise and at Mir Jumla's instance, Farrukh Siyar made Haidar Quli, Diwan of the Deccan with equally wide powers. In as much as Nizam-ul-Mulk did not see eye to eye with his Diwan, he ordered him to go back to Delhi, thereby gaining supreme control of the executive as well as revenue affairs of the Deccan. This did not last; for his first tenure (1713–14), soon drew to a close.

In September 1714, Husain Ali, the younger Sayyid, demanded and obtained for himself the viceroyalty of the Deccan in place of Nizam-ul-Mulk. His initial intent was to revive an earlier practice of discharging the duties of his office through a deputy and himself remain at the capital. This was, however, overruled by the Emperor. In the result, Husain Ali had to take over his new charge in person. Nizam-ul-Mulk showed great resentment at his peremptory supersession by neglecting to call on the Sayyid while the two passed each other in transit, the one on his way to, and the other from, the imperial capital.

Appointed *faujdar* of Moradabad, Nizam-ul-Mulk was summoned (August–September 1718) by the Emperor to the court along with a number of other friendly nobles in an ostensible demonstration of strength against the Sayyids. That stratagem did not work for, in his 'usual heedless way', Farrukh Siyar soon succeeded in alienating his friends: he took away the *faujdari* of Moradabad from Nizam-ul-Mulk, converted it into a province and conferred it upon his new favourite, Muhammad Murad. To no one's surprise, therefore, in the last round of the battle between the Emperor and the Sayyids, Nizam-ul-Mulk stayed more or less neutral.

Soon appointed Governor of Bihar, Nizam-ul-Mulk was later moved to Malwa (March 1719). He accepted the appointment on the clear understanding that the new charge would not be taken away from him—'at any rate, not for a long time'. However, a change did occur and Nizam-ul-Mulk was asked to give up Malwa and choose between Agra, Allahabad, Burhanpur and Multan. As a preliminary to taking up his new post, he was asked to repair to the court. Fearing for the worst, he decided to disregard the imperial fiat, left Ujjain, ostensibly to return to Delhi, but turned south instead and crossed the Narmada into the Deccan.

Presently he emerged as the hub of an anti-Sayyid front which charged that the brothers were out to subvert the Timurid dynasty, 'ruin and disgrace' all Irani and Turani nobles and, allying themselves with the Hindus, pursue 'anti-Islamic policies detrimental to the empire'. The Sayyids hit back: Dilawar Khan was ordered to proceed against Nizam-ul-Mulk from the north, while Alam Ali, Husain Ali's deputy in the Deccan, marched from the south. The strategy was to crush Nizam-ul-Mulk between their combined forces. Nor was that all. For letters were dispatched to the Marathas, Raja Shahu (q.v.) and Balaji Vishwanath (q.v.), requesting them to assist Alam Ali in his anti-Nizam assault.

The Nizam, however, was to prove too quick and clever for the Sayyids.

He fell upon Dilawar Khan and completely routed him (June 1720) in the battle of Husainpur, near Khandwa, about 32 miles north of Burhanpur. Soon after, Alam Ali was worsted too. In one of their quick somersaults, the Sayyids granted the victorious Nizam the viceroyalty of the Deccan afresh. This, his second tenure, was to last a bare two years, 1720–22.

After the defeat and downfall of the Sayyids, Emperor Muhammad Shah (q.v.) invited Nizam-ul-Mulk to assume the Wizarat; he took over in February 1722. While a life-long ambition was thus fulfilled, it proved to be an impossible charge. The interference of royal favourites in day-to-day administration and the 'sleepless jealousy' of the Chief Bakshi created great difficulties for the new Wazir. More, the latter was witness to a state of affairs that bordered on the chaotic: 'the established rules of business had been thrown to the winds, the old nobility was neglected, income was declining and the Empire was fast sinking into its grave.'

No wonder, on the pretext of putting down Haidar Quli, Governor of Malwa, the new Wazir set out for Gujarat (December 1722). Here he met the young Peshwa, Baji Rao, in February 1723 and reached a mutually satisfactory accord with him. After appointing his cousin to be his deputy in Gujarat, the Wazir turned back towards Delhi. With a view to restoring the efficiency of administration and putting the finances of the Empire in trim, he drew up a detailed plan and presented it to the Emperor. The latter gave it his formal assent but, in reality, shelved it, thereby placing his Wazir in a difficult position.

The Wazir's options were limited: for one, he could reduce the Emperor to the position of a mere puppet; for another, he could depose him and set up a new dynasty. Neither course appealed to the Nizam. Nor yet did he relish the prospect of staying at the capital as a helpless onlooker and, in the bargain, weakening his position in the Deccan. Equally, there was no dearth of critics who pointed out that in his person there had been an unusual concentration of authority. Thus, it was argued, that apart from the office of Wazir, his retention of the viceroyalty of Deccan in addition to the absentee Governorships of Gujarat and Malwa, posed a serious threat to the monarchy!

In December 1723, Nizam-ul-Mulk marched to his jagir in Moradabad, ostensibly for 'a change of air'. From Agra he hastened towards Malwa and Gujarat to repulse the Maratha onslaught. Mean while, news reached him that he had been superseded in the viceroyalty of the Deccan by his deputy and that a mighty coalition was now afoot against him. He was not slow to react. In October 1724, with the aid of Baji Rao, he defeated his replacement, Mubariz Khan at Shakarhelda not far from Aurangabad.

Rated one of 'the decisive battles of India', Shakarhelda is said to mark the establishment of the 'independent' principality of Hyderabad. 'The break-up of the Mughal Empire', a percipient observer has noted, 'had begun'. In the aftermath, according to Sir Jadunath Sarkar, 'a new scene opens' in the history of the Mughal Deccan: 'The constant succession of short-term viceroys, the discord due to the six different officers, and the civil strife between rivals for the viceroyalty henceforth ceased. There was now one ruler for the whole tract, he made it his home and planted his dynasty there

.His strong hand brought peace to that unhappy land harried by war for forty years since the invasion of Aurangzeb.'

During his second sojourn, the Nizam-ul-Mulk had stayed in the imperial capital for a little less than six months, July–December 1723. His departure marks the end of an epoch in the history of the Mughal Empire. Before that, a long line of ambitious nobles had attempted to save the Empire from dissolution by concentrating supreme power in their own hands and carrying out reforms in the administrative system. Henceforth, ambitious nobles would devote their energies to the carving out of separate principalities for themselves.

The Nizam's defeat of Mubariz Khan soon led to his acquiring complete control over 'the entire Mughal Deccan', where revenue now began to be collected 'regularly': 'The Emperor recognized the accomplished fact by pardoning the Nizam [for waging war against his appointee, Mubariz Khan] and confirming him in the viceroyalty of the Deccan, with the title of Asaf Jah (June, 1725). This [to mark] the foundation of the present state of Hyderabad'.

In 1728, affairs between Nizam-ul-Mulk and Baji Rao moved towards an outbreak of hostilities. After 'a brief but brilliant' campaign, the Peshwa worsted the Nizam in Battle. In the result, by the Treaty of Mungi Shivagaon (6 March 1728), the Nizam reaffirmed Raja Shahu's claim for *chauth* and *sardeshmukhi* and agreed not to offer protection to Tara Bai's (q.v.) son, Shambhuji II of Kolhapur.

The Nizam who had ostensibly been pursuing an anti-Baji Rao policy of late 'changed sides' and concluded a secret pact with the Peshwa in 1732, leaving the latter free to pursue his own schemes of conquest in the north. This evoked such suspicion in the minds of the Emperor and his ministers that they sought a separate agreement with the Maratha leader stipulating *inter alia* that Nizam-ul-Mulk must be 'taken care of'.

The harsh truth is that Nizam-ul-Mulk's policies were viewed with a deep distrust in Delhi. For the record, he had befriended the Marathas in 1725 and 1728, and yet betrayed them on both occasions. In 1731, he had proposed a joint (Delhi-Hyderabad) campaign against the Peshwa and then (1732) concluded peace with Baji Rao. In 1735, he moved up to Burhanpur to support the Wazir's campaign in Malwa—and yet no one in the imperial court had any confidence in his word.

The Nizam-Baji Rao armed encounter at Bhopal (1737) bears a mention. The former's 'heavily armed and slow moving' troops were hemmed in by the numerically superior, swift and lightly armed Maratha cavalry; his plight was worsened by his suspicion of his Rajput allies. In the result, the Nizam could neither move away nor yet come out and fight, while his provisions were fast running out. After much hard bargaining, the convention of Duraha Sarai (7 January 1737) was concluded. It stipulated *inter alia* the grant to the Peshwa of the *subah* of Malwa; the levy of tribute from the rajas in the region between the Narmada and the Chambal; and a promise of Rs 50 lakhs as war indemnity.

Despite his critics, the fact is that the Nizam's policy towards the Marathas had been pragmatic and seemingly far from consistent. At best, it represented a clever admixture of checks and balances. For up against 'the implacable hostility of the Delhi court, (he) was not loth to acquiesce in Baji Rao's schemes of expansion towards the north. At the same time he could not afford to let the Marathas grow so powerful as to bring Malwa and Gujarat completely under their sway. This would isolate him from Delhi and jeopardise his position in the Deccan.'

Not long after, the Nizam was summoned to Delhi to meet the Persian threat in the person of Nadir Shah (q.v.). His negotiations with the latter had turned essentially on the amount of indemnity to be paid by the imperial court. The Nizam stipulated a sum of Rs 50 lakhs, of which 20 were to be paid immediately and the rest in instalments. But Nadir Shah changed his mind and, playing upon the rivalry between Nizam-ul-Mulk and Saadat Khan, had his way. In retrospect, the Nizam forfeited the confidence of the Emperor for his sorry role in the battle of Karnal and, soon after the Persian ruler had left, decided to repair to the Deccan, leaving the Mughal ruler much to his own devices.

Nizam-ul-Mulk became the founder of the dynasty from which the later Nizams of Hyderabad were descended. He died on 22 May 1748—37 days after the death of Emperor Muhammad Shah.

A man of letters, he composed poetry in Persian under the pseudonym 'Shakir'. His 'Diwan Asaf Nizam-ul-Mulk' was later found in the library of Tipu Sultan (q.v.).

According to Yusuf Husain, Nizam-ul-Mulk's early experience in the Deccan 'accustomed him to danger and hardship.' A man of parts 'work was his greatest pleasure. His genius shone forth in action . . . No dangers were too threatening for him to face, no obstacles too formidable, no tasks too laborious . . . He possessed to a supreme degree, a deep and lively sense of reality in politics . . . He is the only statesman in the early eighteenth century in India whose political aims have been completely fulfilled.'

In summing up his career, Sir Jadunath Sarkar calls Asaf Jah 'the most outstanding personality' in the Mughal Empire for a quarter century: 'He was universally regarded as the sole representative of the spacious times of Aurangzeb and of the policy and traditions of that strenuous monarch . . . [he was] undoubtedly the foremost general of his time in India. In statecraft and diplomacy he was no less eminent. He had the true statesman's length (*sic.*) of vision and spirit of moderation, his conduct . . . throughout marked by prudence, the avoidance of waste or unnecessary expenditure, and simplicity of living, worthy of a pupil of Aurangzeb.'

Yusuf Husain, *The first Nizam: the life and times of Nizam-ul-Mulk Asaf Jah I*, 2nd ed., Bombay, 1963; Satish Chandra, *Parties & Politics at the Mughal Court, 1707–1740*, Aligarh, 1959; Sir Richard Burn (ed.), *Cambridge History of India*, IV, pp. 371–85; Beale (ed.), *An Oriental Biographical Dictionary*, Indian reprint, 1971.

Non-cooperation Movement (1920–1922)

The Non-cooperation Movement was launched on 1 August 1920 with fasting and prayer and a suspension of business. Gandhi (q.v.) had earlier served an 'ultimatum' on the Viceroy accompanied by 'a heart-felt prayer to the tyrant to desist from evil'. Besides, he condemned the government's 'unscrupulous, immoral and unjust' attitude and, in high dudgeon, returned all the medals which had been conferred on him by the British.

At its special session at Calcutta in September 1920, the Indian National Congress (q.v.) approved and ratified the decision to launch the Movement. It put forth the view that 'there is no course left open for the people of India but to approve . . . . the policy of progressive non-violent, non-cooperation' until 'swaraj is established'. The Calcutta decision was later ratified unanimously at the Nagpur session in December 1920. Gandhi described his Movement as 'a state of peaceful rebellion' and called for defiance of 'every single state-made law'.

The objective was two-fold: first, to raise a fund of Rs 1 crore in the name of Tilak (q.v.) to finance the country's non-cooperation activities; secondly, to enrol a volunteer corps of one crore members to help promote various boycotts—social, educational, legal and economic. There was to be a boycott of law courts by lawyers; of schools and colleges owned, aided or recognized by the government; of elections to the Central Legislative Assembly and the provincial councils; of honours, titles and official functions; of British goods. Swadeshi (q.v.) was to be encouraged as also the use of khaddar; there was to be prohibition on drinking all liquor.

The Tilak Fund was soon over-subscribed. This apart, the Movement evoked an enthusiastic public response. Lawyers of the eminence of C. R. Das, Motilal Nehru, Rajendra Prasad, C. Rajagopalachari (qq.v.) gave up their lucrative legal careers; thousands of students came out of college while many new national institutions were founded (e.g., the Kashi Vidyapeeth, the Jamia Millia Islamia). Subhas Chandra Bose (q.v.) quit his career in the I.C.S. and Jawaharlal Nehru (q.v.) his practice at the bar in Allahabad. The number of students in colleges and secondary schools fell, as did excise revenues. As for the boycott of elections, moderate politicians and sundry others did contest, but Congressmen and their sympathizers abstained from voting, thereby exposing the unrepresentative character of those elected. The boycott of foreign cloth adversely affected the import of British piece-goods.

By July 1921, the Non-cooperation Movement had thoroughly roused the country, although it appears to have made little immediate impression on British policy. Thus, when the Prince of Wales (the future King Edward VIII) visited India in November 1921, there were large-scale popular demonstrations against him and, during December 1921–January 1922, nearly 30,000 people were imprisoned.

Meanwhile, the Moplah Rebellion (q.v.) in Kerala had raised the ugly spectre of Hindu-Muslim antagonisms while the Chauri Chaura holocaust demonstrated how the seeds of violence were imbedded deep in the national psyche. On 6 February 1922, the day following Chauri Chaura, Gandhi decided to suspend the Movement and at the same time abandon the proposed Civil Disobedience (q.v.) campaign at Bardoli in Gujarat. On 16 February, he published 'My Confession': 'The drastic reversal of the whole of the aggressive programme may be politically unsound and unwise, but there is no doubt, it is religiously sound . . . . Civil Disobedience is a preparation for mute suffering . . . Let the opponent glory in our so-called defeat. It is better to be charged with cowardice than to sin against God.'

Some of the highlights of this 20-month Movement may be briefly noted. In November 1920 a *muttafiqa fatwa* (literally, 'joint pronouncement') was issued by Muslim theologians declaring India to be Dar-al-Harb, thereby leaving Muslims with two alternatives: of waging *jihad* (holy war) against the infidels or *hijrat* (migration). In so far as the latter course alone was deemed feasible, 18,000 Muslims, mostly from Sind and the North-West Frontier (q.v.), left for Afghanistan. The Kabul Amir, however, refused to admit them, adding further to their misery and privation.

At its Nagpur session, in December 1920, the Congress adopted a new constitution which declared that its objective was 'the attainment of swara-jaya . . . by all legitimate and peaceful means'. Additionally, the new goal was sought to be attained 'within one year' through 'non-violent, non-cooperation'. The Karachi meeting (July 1921) of the Khilafat Movement (q.v.) had called upon Muslim soldiers to quit the army. This decision was endorsed by the Congress Working Committee on 5 October. The visit to India, in November 1921, of the Prince of Wales as noticed was the occasion for hartals, demonstrations and political meetings, marred by scenes of mob violence and police reprisals in Bombay.

In December 1921, some Indian leaders, including Pandit Madan Mohan Malaviya (q.v.) and M. A. Jinnah (q.v.), interceded with the Viceroy to find some solution to an already deteriorating situation. The latter was agreeable to a round table conference to discuss the issue. However, as a precondition to convening of such a conference, Gandhi demanded that all prisoners including those connected with the Khilafat agitation, be released. On the Viceroy refusing this, the proposed parleys fell through. At the Congress session at Ahmedabad, in December 1921, it was decided to launch both individual and mass civil disobedience movements. An appeal was made to all men over the age of 18 to join the volunteer corps. Gandhi was to be the 'sole dictator' of the movement.

Later, during the All-Parties Conference in January 1922 where, among others, Gandhi, Jinnah and M.R. Jayakar (1873–1959) were present, a request was made to the Congress Working Committee to postpone its proposed civil disobedience campaign and this was agreed to. Unfortunately, behind-the-scene parleys with the government, then in progress, proved of no avail. In the result, on 1 February 1922 Gandhi wrote to the Viceroy announcing his intention of launching the Movement at Bardoli in Gujarat in case the government failed to settle the Khilafat question and undo the Panjab wrongs.

But Chauri Chaura intervened and finally persuaded Gandhi to countermand the agitation and retrace his steps. Additionally, there had been mounting pressure in the same direction by such liberals as Pandit Madan Mohan Malaviya and Jayakar from inside the Congress and of the veteran social reformer Kamakshi Natarajan and Jinnah from outside.

It may also be recalled that serious differences had developed among Congressmen on the correctness of Gandhi's stand in withdrawing the Movement because of the strains to which the party had been exposed. In serious doubt about his precipitate step, the Congress Working Committee set up a Civil Disobedience Inquiry Committee entrusted with the task of touring the country and reporting on the feasibility of restarting the Movement. After an extensive survey, the Committee submitted a report (August 1922) underlining that conditions were far from ripe for doing so.

The sudden if abrupt countermanding of the Movement which had raised popular enthusiasm to a high pitch created strong resentment and even political confusion. The Congress was sharply split, as were the Khilafatists. Seizing the opportunity, the government, which had hesitated hitherto, arrested Gandhi on 10 March and sentenced him to six years in jail.

The Non-cooperation movement brought Gandhi into the limelight of all-India politics. He now emerged as the logical heir of Tilak. Another significant impact was that the imprisonment of thousands of people from all walks of life removed from the popular mind the sense of terror and ignominy associated hitherto with jail entry; it became respectable and presently a badge of honour. Again, the fear complex inspired by alien authority, thus far a dominant feature of public life, dissolved. People were no longer afraid.

Judith M. Brown, *Gandhi's Rise to power: Indian Politics 1915-1922*, Cambridge, 1972; *Tara Chand*, III, pp. 493-6; Sukhbir Choudhary, *Indian People Fight for National Liberation (Non Cooperation, Khilafat And Revivalist Movements) 1920-22*, New Delhi, 1972; B. M. Taunk, *Non-cooperation Movement in Indian Politics 1919–1924: A Historical Study*, Delhi, 1978.

Lord Northbrook (1826–1904)

Born in 1826, Thomas George Baring was the eldest son of Sir Francis Baring, first Baron Northbrook. Educated privately and later at Christ Church College, Oxford, he entered Parliament in 1857 as a Whig and joined Palmerston's administration as Civil Lord of the admiralty; in 1867 he succeeded his father as second Lord Northbrook and moved to the House of Lords. Between 1859-64, with a brief interval, he served under Sir Charles Wood as Under-Secretary of State at the India Office. In 1872, on the assassination of Mayo (q.v.), he was appointed Governor-General.

A quiet and undemonstrative man, his aim, as no doubt of Gladstone's Whig administration, was to continue John Lawrence's (q.v.) policy of 'masterly inactivity', so far as Afghanistan was concerned, and at the same time safeguard the integrity of the empire. Consequently, Northbrook tried to avoid any major upheavals so as to 'give the land rest'. His critics aver that he nearly slipped into a 'state of inertia'. Northbrook's main purpose, as he saw it, was 'steady government', in respect both of foreign and domestic policy. In the teeth of much expert opinion, he decided on the non-renewal of income-tax, but retained the salt duty, and this despite strong pressure to the contrary from England. An ardent free trader, he refused to be convinced that the impost in question amounted to protective tariff.

Northbrook disallowed the Bengal Muncipalities Bill and ordered a modification of certain local imposts. He took financial matters under his special care, exercising rigid and effective control over expenditure on public works, both civil and military. The result was that during his tenure there was a surplus of not less than a million pounds.

In regard to the militant Kukas and Wahabis (q.v.), Northbrook countinued with the earlier policy of their trial and conviction, leading to deportation of the principal ring leaders.

Aware of an undercurrent of distrust and discontent in the country occasioned, if partly, by educated unemployment, Northbrook solicited the Home Government's advice. After a great deal of debate, it was resolved to employ Indians in junior posts, at lower scales of salary, in the hope of promoting them later to the covenanted service. However, during his tenure of office no appointments were made in this cadre. The Home Government was also opposed to Northbrook's proposal to revise the maximum age for the civil service examination to 22. He did, however, manage to allay widespread resentment by appointing Ramnath Tagore and, later, Narendra Krishna Deb to the Imperial Legislative Council. The Governor-General also ruled that drafts of proposed bills and amendments be published in the vernacular languages; refusing to gag the vernacular press on the plea that it helped to supplement the government's inadequate knowledge of the feelings and sentiments of the people. Nor were Muslim interests ignored; Northbrook lent support to Syed Ahmad Khan's (q.v.) efforts to diffuse education among his community.

To deal with the famine of 1873-4, said to be the worst in a century, Northbrook went out of his way to adopt measures to feed the hungry and save life. This, he argued, would serve a dual purpose—prevent loss of land revenue following loss of life, as well as win over the masses in dire distress by giving them timely aid. Understandably the expenditure incurred was enormous, but the rigours of the famine had been averted. His policy in this case was vindicated when the Indian Famine Commission (1880) accepted his organization of relief measures as the basis for future famine administration in the country.

While deprecating undue interference in the affairs of Indian States (q.v.), Northbrook asserted the unquestioned right of the paramount power to check alleged maladministration in Baroda. The Resident, Sir Robert Phayre, had reported misrule and a complaint of poisoning. A commission of inquiry against Malhar Rao Gaekwad (q.v.) was divided in its opinion, rating the evidence to convict him as unsatisfactory. The Governor-General decided none the less to depose the ruler. While Indian opinion condemned his action as both unfair and unjust, his own compatriots rated his policy to be far too lenient. To prevent the Nizam of Hyderabad from becoming unduly powerful, he tactfully postponed the restitution of the Berars to their ruler.

Not easily ruffled, Northbrook preferred to be at peace with Afghanistan. Russia, he felt, posed no problem militarily; more, he argued, all disputes in Asia could be settled amicably between Britain and that country. After the Russian occupation of Khiva, he conferred with the Amir's envoy and suggested greater control over his external relations by promising help in men and money, whenever need for it arose. Gladstone, then Prime Minister, opposed any such binding commitments. Later, with the change of government in England, the Tories bent over backwards to reverse gears. Northbrook was particularly averse to the aggressive overtones of Salisbury's policy of insisting on stationing a British resident at Kabul on the flimsiest of pretexts. While conceding the necessity for an agent at Meshed (Persia) and even Herat, the Governor-General was however unwilling to push the Amir around and thereby risk another war. Aware that his differences with the Home Government were widening (the cotton tariff had also added to difficulties), he requested to be relieved of his post on personal grounds.

In contrast to the rather unenthusiastic attitude of the British press and the strong hostility of Anglo-Indian newspapers, the Indian educated classes had, according to his biographer, much praise for Northbrook. Most vernacular newspapers no doubt considered his Baroda policy a blot on his career, yet Northbrook had paid close attention to Indian public opinion as evidenced by his enthusiastic promotion of education, his attempt to raise the age-limit for the civil service examination and his refusal to restrict freedom of the press. In an editorial (17 November 1904) at the time of his death, the *Bengalee* referred to Northbrook as a 'pro-Indian Viceroy'.

Back in England, Northbrook took an active interest in the controversy over Lytton's (q.v.) disastrous Afghan policy. In 1880, he joined Gladstone's cabinet as First Lord of the Admiralty and continued to be that government's principal advisor on Indian affairs. After 1885 his relations with Gladstone became somewhat strained and he refrained from active politics. He none the less retained strong liberal sympathies and as late as 1903 withdrew his support from the Unionist Party at the commencement of its agitation in favour of tariff reform.

After 1890, Northbrook confined his attention to local government, serving in various capacities in the county council till his death in November 1904.

Edward C. Moulton, *Lord Northbrook's Indian Administration 1872—1876*, Bombay, 1968; *DNB 1901–11*, pp. 93-6 (Bernard Mallet).

North-West Frontier & (N W F) Province

In 1858 the districts west of the Yamuna ceded in 1803 and known as the Delhi territory were transferred from the North-Western Provinces to the Panjab. In the result, the chief commissioner of Panjab became a lieutenant-governor. In 1901 the frontier districts of the Panjab beyond the Indus were put into a separate charge under a chief commissioner and called the North-West Frontier Province.

Because the Panjab frontier was too long and mountainous to be defended by the army alone, a great deal depended upon what was called the political management of the tribes. At first there was no special agency for dealing with tribal tracts and relations with the tribes were conducted by deputy commissioners of the six districts of Hazara, Peshawar, Kohat, Bannu, Dera Ismail Khan and Dera Ghazi Khan. In 1876, the three northern districts were formed into the commissionership of Peshawar and the three southern into that of Derajat. The system of political agencies was not adopted until two years later, when a special officer was appointed for the Khyber agency during the Second Afghan War (q.v.). Kurram became an agency in 1892 while three others, Malakand, Tochi and Wana, were created in 1895-96. Malakand was placed under the direct control of the Government of India from the outset, the other three remaining under the Panjab government. This was the arrangement until the creation of the NWFP in 1901.

A word on the tribes before discussing the constitution of the new province. They initially came into contact with the British with the latter's occupation of the Panjab (1849). Sporadic clashes with one tribe or another over control of communication routes and alleged prestige issues arose from 1857 onwards. Tribal uprisings were encouraged by Syed Ahmed of Rae Bareli, the Wahabi (q.v.) leader with his headquarters at Sithana. To meet this threat, a regular campaign was undertaken in 1868, which resulted in the establishment of an uneasy truce.

A reversion to the so-called 'forward policy' from 1878 onwards, accelerated during the 1890's by the building of roads, bridges and railways to strengthen control over the frontier and in particular the passes leading into Afghanistan, brought about a recurrence of tribal uprisings. In the Durand Line (q.v.), the tribes read a British plan to occupy their country: the Mahsud uprising in 1894 was followed by a rash of others until, by 1897, the whole tribal area was simmering with discontent that often erupted into open rebellion. The regular Malakand and Khyber Field Forces were organized and campaigns launched by the government to control the most inflamed areas. In all, 75,000 troops were engaged for three years in checking uprisings and pacifying the area. During 1905-8 the Afridis were in open revolt and in 1919 the Wana Wazirs and Mahsuds. The Third Afghan War (q.v.), in which the tribes co-operated with the ruler of Kabul and his levies, was followed by the 'relatively quiet' twenties.

The creation of NWFP in 1901 was the consummation of Curzon's (q.v.) frontier policy. For at least a quarter century preceding it, however, Viceroys and frontier administrators had put forth varied proposals for a new administrative arrangement. Lytton (q.v.) for instance had suggested the formation of an enormous trans-Indus province comprising the six frontier districts of the Panjab and the trans-Indus district of Sind (q.v.), with the exception of Karachi. Besides, Lytton's scheme of 1877 proposed giving the central government a more direct control over frontier administration and policy so as to help improve the relations of districts with their trans-border neighbours. He envisaged an immense frontier province stretching all the way from Peshawar to the sea.

Curzon's minute of 27 August 1900 justifying the creation of the new province underlined the anomaly of the existing situation. He pointed out that, as then constituted, between the frontier areas and the authority of the Viceroy there was placed a subordinate government (the Panjab) through whose hands all frontier questions had to pass: 'between itself (viz., Government of India) and the Frontier (there was) the Panjab government which often knows less and which for 20 years has been an instrument of procrastination and obstruction and weakness.' Curzon argued that this militated against rapidity of action and swiftness of decision, both essential on an exposed frontier.

Politically, the new province was divided into two: the settled districts of Hazara, Peshawar, Kohat, Bannu and Dera Ismail Khan and the trans-border tracts which lay between its administrative and Durand boundaries. The trans-border area, in addition to the five political agencies of Malakand, Khyber, Kurram, Tochi and Wana, embraced the tribal tracts under the political control of deputy commissioners of the adjoining settled districts. The cis-Indus tract of Hazara was not included in the scheme as originally drafted by Curzon. Between Dera Ismail Khan and Hazara, one trans-Indus tract was not taken away from the Panjab, the *tahsil* of Isa Khel.

The head of the new unit was to be a chief commissioner and agent to the Governor-General, to be appointed by the latter and responsible to him. In addition, there was to be a revenue and a judicial commissioner. The civil and judicial administration of the settled districts approximated to that obtaining elsewhere in British India—each of the five districts being placed under a deputy commissioner assisted by *tahsildars, naib-tahsildars, kanungos* and *patwaris.*

The purpose of Curzon's scheme was a recognition of the Pathan conception of oneness. It provided, in the words of a knowledgeable student of frontier affairs, 'first an administrative and later a political soil in which this idea could take root and, carefully nurtured, grow into active life. It laid out this area at a time when the allegiance of the frontier people was uncertain and groping . . . . At the same time, by arranging for a greater concentration of effort and expertise at the decisive point, it did something to draw together the districts and the tribal territory . . . . Not entirely consciously, Curzon had provided a focus for Pathan self-esteem, and so done much to consolidate a firm frontier.' The new province's greatest justification, it has been suggested, lay in that it provided a 'focal point' for Pathan identity and not in terms of the country's defence and foreign policy.

With the exception of the Ambela campaign of 1863, no very serious tribal risings had taken place before 1890. Later, gun-running in the Persian Gulf and other factors, such as the generosity of the Amir of Kabul and thieving in British cantonments, had flooded the tribal areas with arms and ammunition. There was an enormous growth of the arms traffic in the Persian Gulf which, both at Bushire and Muscat, was initially in the hands of British traders. It was not until 1910 when Britain established a rigorous blockade of the Gulf that this pernicious traffic was in any way checked.

Apart from the arms traffic and historic geographical and economic factors other developments such as Bolshevik propaganda across the border added to the turbulence of the region. Essentially, political propaganda after 1890 has been the most potent factor for unrest, which is not to under-rate the impact of Afghan intrigues. The revolts were either instigated directly from Kabul with full cognizance of the Amir, or carried out by his local officials. Considerable unrest resulted too from the British practice of dealing with the tribes through Arabs or Pathan middlemen.

The 'frontier' under the British attracted a number of outstanding soldiers and administrators. Names such as Edwardes, Hodson and Nicholson are still household words; others such as Abbot, Battye, Cavagnari, Chamberlain, Handyside, Roos-Keppel and Warburton are only slightly less well-known. People were attracted to the area because of the challenge of 'a real, live man to deal with'; or the 'difficult, dangerous and responsible' job it posed; it was a challenge in an area of sharp contrasts. Finally, it was 'perhaps the biggest political backwater' and the British kept it that way as long as they could.

In the quarter century after its creation, there was in the new province a growing awareness for administrative reform. An inquiry committee recommended the establishment of a legislative council in the province. Khan Abdul Ghaffar Khan (q.v.) and his elder brother, Dr Khan Sahib (q.v.) began to figure prominently in provincial politics in the later twenties. They had been in close touch with Gandhi (q.v.) even though formal affiliation with the Indian National Congress (q.v.) came about only in 1931.

In regard to frontier affairs and their management, by the end of 1932 one thing was clear. Any extravagant claims for the 'modified forward policy' had proved just as illusory as similar claims in the preceding years for a 'non-involvement policy', a forward policy', or one of 'masterly inactivity'. Many soldiers and administrators realized by now that so long as the British remained on the frontier, they would have to fight. The fact is that the British never had and never could have had a uniform policy for the whole frontier zone. They never had or could have a settled policy either. There were two distinct problems they were up against: tribal control and imperial strategy. Depending upon the situation, British administration on the frontier was marked by sudden advances interspersed with ill-timed retreats.

In the long haul, neither 'masterly inactivity' nor yet 'meddling interference' had proved successful. The one had been tantamount to a shirking of imperial responsibilities, the other had led to incursions which bred suspicion in the minds both of the tribesmen and the Amir of Afghanistan.

On the constitutional front, it may be noted that in 1932 the frontier was given the status of a Governor's province. This was followed by the induction of complete provincial autonomy on the implementation of the Government of India Act 1935 (q.v.). With the provincial elections over, a popular ministry under Dr Khan Sahib was installed (1937). Resigning office in 1939, he was returned to power only in 1946—the All India Muslim League (q.v.) holding virtual sway in the interim period. Communal disturbances rocked the province from February to July 1947, when it was decided to hold a (NWFP) Referendum (q.v.). The latter took place on 20 July 1947 and was organized by a commissioner and a team of 40 British officers, all experienced in 'frontier' affairs. The Congress officially boycotted the poll in so far as the Khan brothers advocated independence for the province, a free Pakhtoonistan. The vote for Pakistan was overwhelming, and in its wake it was decided to demit the province to Pakistan.

The formal accession to the central government of Pakistan by the tribes up to the Durand Line and the chiefs of the four frontier states of Dir, Swat, Chitral and Amb was completed by 1948. The former had signified their loyalty in open *jirga* and the latter, by means of Instruments of Accession. In 1955, the North-West Frontier Province was amalgamated into a one-unit West Pakistan. To the passionate Pathan individualist, the slogan 'one-unit' seemed far from attractive. The union was undone 16 years later (1971) when the province regained its earlier separate identity.

A footnote on defence may be relevant. In 1944, the Commander-in-Chief in New Delhi appointed a committee to review defence policy over the

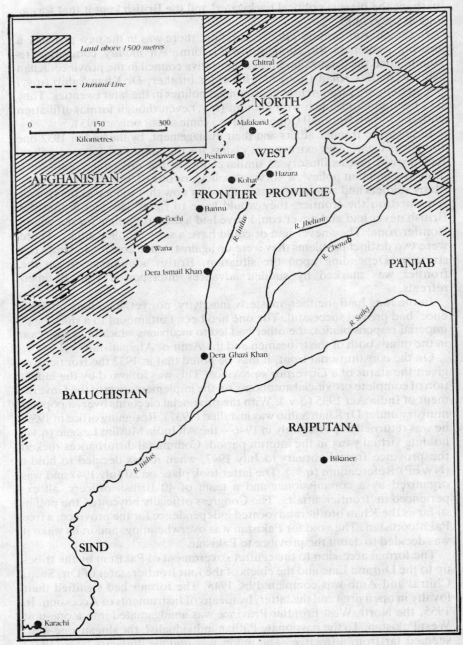

North-West Frontier and the NWF Province

whole of the frontier. Under Lt. Gen. Francis Tuker, the committee broadly recommended the withdrawal of the army from tribal territory to cantonments along the administrative border. From here troops were to be available to reinforce the Scouts whose equipment at the same time was to be stepped up to enable them to deal with more serious opposition without having to call on the army for help. Air support was to be forthcoming independent of what the army did or did not do. In September 1947, the Pakistan government put this policy into effect and ordered the evacuation of all regular military forces from Waziristan. The operation was called 'Curzon', signifying a return to the earlier Viceroy's policy of 1899–1903.

The North-West Frontier is not represented by any particular boundary line: it is a zone or belt of mountainous country of varying width, stretching over a distance of about 1,200 miles from the Pamirs to the shores of the Arabian Sea. The vulnerable part of the frontier lies between Peshawar and Quetta. To protect it, it is necessary to hold both the eastern and the western extremities of the five principal mountain passes. British predominance in the Gulf was essential for the safety of the Indian empire. Were it not for Afghanistan and other political intrigues, the local problem of tribal control would have been solved a long time ago.

C. Collin Davies, *The Problem of the North-West Frontier 1890-1908, with a survey of policy since 1849*, 2nd ed., London, 1975; Major-General J. G. Elliott, *The Frontier 1839-1947: a study of the North-West Frontier of India*, London, 1968; Arthur Swinson, *North-West Frontier: People and Events, 1839–1947*, London, 1967; Olaf Caroe, *The Pathans, 550 B.C.–A.D. 1957*, London, 1965; Parshotam Mehra, 'A Frontier Governor and his conflict with Authority', paper presented at *30th International Congress of Human Sciences in Asia and North Africa*, Mexico, 3-8 August, 1976.

NWFP Referendum (July 1947)

Much against the wishes of the Indian National Congress (q.v.) members of the Interim Government (q.v.) and the provincial Congress ministry in Peshawar, it had been decided to hold a referendum in the NWFP to decide its future political affiliation as between India and Pakistan. The June 3rd Plan (q.v.) therefore offered to the voters of the legislative assembly in the province the choice of either joining a *new* Constituent Assembly (q.v.) or of continuing in the existing one.

Khan Abdul Ghaffar Khan (q.v.) objected to a referendum on what appeared to him to be a purely communal question and urged that the voters should also have the additional choice of asking for an independent Pakhtoonistan, When the question was put to Lord Mountbatten, his reply was that he could not change the procedure laid down without the consent of the two major political parties. While the Congress was willing to abide by the wishes of Ghaffar Khan, the All India Muslim League (q.v.) and M. A. Jinnah (q.v.) were firmly opposed. They characterized the Khan's demand as 'insidious and spurious', declaring that in the new Pakistan envisaged, the NWFP would enjoy full autonomy.

With its demand rejected out of hand, the Congress appealed to its followers to boycott the referendum in the province and pledged itself to a new struggle for the establishment of an independent Pakhtoonistan. This, it has been argued, was tantamount to conceding defeat 'even before the contest'.

The fact is that, having accepted Pakistan, the Congress could not have logically opposed the referendum 'without appearing to be unreasonable'. It therefore accepted the referendum 'to the utter discomfiture' of the NWFP Congress. To the latter, the referendum meant not only a complete disregard of its elected majority in the provincial Legislative Assembly, but also its subjection to a fresh battle for votes in a severely adverse communal climate. Not unexpectedly, the meeting of the Provincial Congress Committee at Bannu on 21 June 1947 accepted the lead given by the parent body: it decided to boycott the referendum and pledged itself to a new struggle for the establishment of a free Pakhtoonistan. Towards the end of June, Sir Olaf Caroe, then provincial Governor, had proceeded on two months' leave of absence and been replaced by General Sir Rob Lockhart. In the meanwhile, the Afghan government had begun taking an interest in the matter, claiming that all the territory west of the Indus was peopled by Afghans; it followed, they argued, that the latter should have a right to decide their future. The Afghan stance was firmly countered by the British Government.

The referendum in the NWFP was held between 6–17 July. It was entrusted to British officers of the Indian Army with experience of frontier affairs under a Referendum Commissioner, Brigadier J. B. Booth. Of the total 572,798 registered voters slightly over 50 per cent took part in the referendum; of these 289, 244 voted for and 2,874 against joining a new constituent assembly. Those who exercised the right to vote constituted a bare 9.52 per cent of the total population of NWFP.

For the record, it may be stated that Jawaharlal Nehru's (q.v.) estimate was that in a referendum, the Congress chances of winning were '50:50'. Whatever the basis for this forecast, it should not be dismissed as illusory. Thus, in the 1946 elections, 41.45 per cent of the Muslim voters had voted for the Congress as had nearly all Hindus and Sikhs. In June 1947 two additional factors operated in favour of the Congress: Abdul Ghaffar Khan and the promise of a Congress campaign for the inclusion of the NWFP in India 'with the largest measure of independence and freedom for the frontier'.

A keen student of frontier affairs has expressed the view that 'even the operation of these factors might not have brought victory to the Congress, but they could at least reduce the margin of defeat. Whether a fortunate, slender Congress victory would have put Pakistan in jeopardy or not, a marginal defeat could have embarrassed Jinnah to the extreme and facilitated the cause of a future Pakhtoonistan.'

As a result of the referendum, on 14 August 1947 Pakistan came into being with the NWFP as an integral part of its territory. Dr Khan Sahib's (q.v.) incumbent ministry which had refused to resign and awaited a general election in vain was dismissed from office barely a week later, on 22 August 1947 to be precise.

Amit Kumar Gupta, *NWFP Legislature & Freedom Struggle 1932–47*, New Delhi, 1976; V. P. Menon, *The Transfer of Power*, New Delhi, 1957.

David Ochterlony (1758–1825)

Famed as the 'Conqueror of Nepal', David Ochterlony came out to India in 1777 as a cadet in the Bengal army of the East India Company(q.v.). He participated in the Second Anglo-Mysore War (q.v.) and later served under General Lake in the northern campaigns of the Second Anglo-Maratha War (q.v.). In 1803 he was appointed Resident at the Mughal Emperor's court in Delhi, a city he defended (1804) successfully against Yashvantrao Holkar (q.v.). Subsequently he held various military appointments and, by 1814, had been promoted to the rank of Major-General.

Hastings (q.v.) appointed him one of his commanders in the Anglo–Nepalese War (q.v.). Undaunted by heavy odds, Ochterlony's forces achieved victory (1815); he was, in fact, the lone British commander who was successful. This brought him the much-coveted K. C. B., a baronetcy and a pension from the Company; he added a G. C. B. to these decorations by the ultimate rout of the Gurkhas within 20 miles of Kathmandu. 1816 saw him actively engaged in the Pindari War (q.v.), wherein he commanded a column and made a treaty and an amicable settlement in 1818 with Amir Khan. In that year he was appointed Resident in Rajputana and commander of troops that concluded treaties with several Rajput states. Later, he was made Resident at Delhi.

In 1821 Ochterlony assumed charge of the newly created agency of Malwa and Rajputana states. This proved to be a stormy period in his career, when he came into open conflict with his subordinates as well as his superiors. In 1822, his jealousy and constant criticism of James Tod's policy in Udaipur and Jodhpur led to the latter's resignation. Ochterlony's resentment against Tod was not unknown to the Governor-General or his Council, nor were they unaware of his eagerness to humiliate Tod. In the result, the latter's technical lapses were magnified and his weakness—an emotional involvement with the Rajput past—misinterpreted.

Ochterlony's detractors charged that he constantly interfered in the internal affairs of Indian States (q.v.), adding to the existing confusion. His action involving British forces and incurring extra expenditure in the war of succession at Bharatpur (1825), which was deemed hasty initially, but later vindicated, was severely criticized by Amherst (q.v.) who was already beset with difficulties arising from reverses suffered in the First Anglo-Burmese War (q.v.). Ochterlony, hyper-sensitive to criticism, chose to resign rather than suffer a 'repudiation of his policy'. The 'Ochterlony papers' help us to view his humiliation, after years of distinguished service, 'in its proper setting'.

Ochterlony had been deeply hurt and maintained that, after 48 years' experience, the supreme government should have exhibited a certain confidence in his discretion. The feeling that he had been injured and disgraced however preyed upon his mind and is said to have caused his death (15 July 1825) at Meerut, where he had gone for a change of air.

The diplomatic achievements of Ochterlony were no less conspicuous than his soldiership; with a vigorous intellect and consummate address, he possessed an intimate knowledge of Indian character, language and manners. Popularly known as 'Akhtar Loony' among Indian rulers, he lived in style like a nawab with an impressive retinue of wives and attendants. A column was erected in Calcutta on the western extremity of the Maidan, facing Chowringhee, which is known as the Ochterlony monument. Put up in 1841 to commemorate his long association with this country, it is said to be one of the tallest (165 feet high) and, architecturally, oddest memorial pillars in India.

N. K. Sinha & A. K. Das Gupta (eds.), *Selections from the Ochterlony Papers 1818–25 in the National Archives of India*, Calcutta, 1964; Sukumar Bhattacharyya, *The Rajput States and the East India Company from the close of the 18th century to 1820*, New Delhi, 1972; *DNB*, XIV, pp. 798-802 (Robert Louis Vetch); Eardley Latimer, *Handbook to Calcutta and Environs*, 2nd ed., Calcutta, 1966, pp. 23-4.

Omi Chand (d. 1758)

Omi Chand, variously spelt as Amin or Amir Chand, was a leading Panjabi merchant of Bengal. English historians have emphasized that he was *not* a Bengali and K. K. Datta maintains that he was, in fact, a Sikh adventurer who at one stage even expressed a desire to go on a pilgrimage to Amritsar. It has been suggested that he was a Hindu bania, either a Khatri or an Arora. The Calcutta (q.v.) Council believed that he had played a treacherous role in the capture 'of the town of Siraj-ud-Daulah (q.v.) and in instigating' the alleged Black Hole tragedy. He is said to have encouraged the English to attack the French settlement of Chandernagore (q.v.); hatched a plot to install Yar Lutuf Khan as Nawab, a contingency Clive (q.v.) opposed by his intrigues with Rai Durlabh (q.v.); and caused delay in securing Mir Jafar's (q.v.) agreement to the terms which the English offered.

Initially, Omi Chand had got along well with the John Company (q.v.) and is known to have interceded on their behalf when Maratha troops stopped a British fleet between Kasimbazar (Cossimbazar) and Calcutta and plundered their goods. Earlier, he made an immense fortune as the Company's principal contractor; it is said that many of the best houses in Calcutta were owned by him. He became a camp follower of Siraj-ud-Daula after the latter's conquest of Calcutta, when he is said to have lost goods worth Rs 4 lakhs. At the same time, Omi Chand continued to maintain his English connections and was their principal agent in negotiating the Treaty of Alinagar (q.v.). He then became the British resident's advisor and agent at Murshidabad, taking a keen interest in all the intrigues that were rife to replace Siraj-ud-Daula. He is said to have proposed that the Nawab be replaced by Yar Lutuf Khan who was 'a man of good character and had the support of the Seths.' When the English decided to support Mir Jafar, Omi Chand threatened to disclose their plans unless given 5 per cent of all the money that accrued from the Nawab's treasury, a part of his jewels as well as other sundry concessions adding up to a sizeable sum. It was only after the Battle of Plassey (q.v.) that Omi Chand discovered to his dismay that the treaty awarding him his share of the booty was a forged document. He is then believed to have become insane and later to have gone to Malda on a pilgrimage.

A recent scholar has suggested that it was at Clive's instance that the

Malda pilgrimage was planned and that it is certain Omi Chand did not become insane. In any case, he died shortly afterwards, on 5 December 1758.

Clive is not known to have felt any qualms about his forging the treaty to out-smart Omi Chand, convinced that such a treatment was fully warranted.

K. K. Datta, *Alivardi and his Times*, Calcutta, 1963, n. 1, p. 1; Michael Edwardes, *The Founding of an Empire*, London, 1959; Ram Gopal, *How the British Occupied Bengal*, Bombay, 1963; Nirad Chaudhri, *Clive of India*, London, 1975.

Mir Osman Ali Khan, Nizam (1884–1967)

Mir Osman Ali Khan, the seventh and last of the line of Hyderabad's Nizams, succeeded to the gaddi on 29 August 1911, having earlier been groomed for his role by English tutors. Over the years, the government of India had continued its interference in the administration of the state and warned him (1911 and 1919) that he was on trial, that the British would take over the administration in the event of continued misrule in the state. Before long, the Nizam raised the question of the retrocession of Berar, additionally underlining the fact that the British had no right to interfere in the domestic affairs of his state. In a famous reply (1925), Reading, the then Viceroy, asserted categorically that the sovereignty of the British crown was supreme in India, that it had the right to intervene in the internal affairs of Indian States (q.v.), that the Nizam did not stand on a footing of equality vis-á-vis the British government and, in fact, was on much the same pedestal as the rulers of other Indian states. As for Berar, by an agreement concluded in 1936 the sovereignty of the Nizam over this territory was re-affirmed; the specified rent was to continue to be paid as before, but administratively the area was to be treated as a part of the Central Provinces of British India.

In July 1947, on the eve of transfer of power from British to Indian hands, the question of Berar, of the possible grant of Dominion Status (q.v.) to Hyderabad and of its accession to the Indian Union came up when a delegation from Hyderabad met Lord Louis Mountbatten. In August, the Nizam declared that he wished to retain an independent status and to remain neutral as between the two newly constituted dominions of India and Pakistan. He maintained he had inalienable religious ties with Pakistan but since India was a neighbour he was prepared to enter into a treaty with her. In the mean while, the Government of India had assured the Nizam that nothing would be settled by force. Unfortunately the political and administrative chaos caused by the Razakars, a politically militant paramilitary group led by one Kasim Razvi, who enjoyed the tacit support of the Nizam, made armed intervention imperative. On 13 September 1948, the Indian army converged on Hyderabad; four days later the Nizam acceded to the Indian Union. He was then called upon to become the Rajpramukh; on 23 November 1949 he extended the Indian constitution to Hyderabad by a public proclamation.

The Nizam died on 25 February 1967.

D. F. Karaka, *Fabulous Mogul: Nizam VII of Hyderabad*, London, 1955; V. P. Menon, *The Story of the Integration of Indian States*, Reprint, Bombay, 1969.

Oudh or Awadh

Oudh (or Awadh)

In the second half of the eighteenth century the province which takes its
name from the ancient city of Ayodhya or Awadh had an area of roughly
24,000 sq. miles and was securely under Mughal control until and during
Aurangzeb's reign (1658–1707). Subsequently (1732) it became independent under its then governor, Saadat Khan. He was succeeded in 1743 by his
son-in-law, Safdar Jang (1743); under both, Oudh was a fertile province,
enjoying a measure of prosperity. Shuja-ud-Daula (q.v.), who succeeded to
the Wazirship in 1753, tried to take advantage of the struggle between Mir
Kasim (q.v.) and the East India Company (q.v.) to extend his dominion so
as to include Bihar. Unable to do so, he allied himself with Mir Kasim and
Shah Alam II (q.v.) against the British. With his defeat at Buxar (q.v.), and
the treaty with the English that followed, Oudh was reduced to the status of
a semi-independent state.

From now onwards, while the British continued to grow stronger, the
ruling house weakened perceptibly with each succeeding incumbent to the
throne. The English, who controlled the foreign policy of the state, began to
interfere actively in its internal affairs, with results that were far from happy.
While little effort was made by the English to improve local conditions,
larger and larger sums of money were extorted by the Company on one
pretext or another. Later, under Nasir-ud-Din Haidar (r.1827–37), Muham-

mad Ali Shah (r.1837-42) and Amjad Ali Shah (r.1841–47), conditions deteriorated precipitately. Each successive Governor-General pointed to the alleged maladministration, and threatened to assume the government of the state.

In 1851, Colonel 'Thuggee' Sleeman (q.v.) was asked to submit a report on conditions in the province, on the basis of which Dalhousie (q.v.) took over its government (1856) from Wajid Ali Shah, its last independent ruler. In the Rebellion of 1857 (q.v.), the whole of Oudh was affected, the 'rebels' occupying it for a time. None the less, by 1858 the English had recaptured most of the state. In 1877 a part of Oudh was amalgamated with the North-Western Provinces. Later the two together constitued the new 'United Provinces of Agra and Oudh'. Lucknow, its capital, became the administrative headquarters of the new province.

Imperial Gazetteer, New Ed., Calcutta, 1907-9, 26 vols., XIX, pp. 278-85.

Begums of Oudh

The expression 'Begums of Oudh' refers principally to Bahu Begum, the widow of Shuja-ud-Daula (q.v.) and to his mother Sadrur Nisa Begum. Shuja had bequeathed to his wife the estates of Gonda and Faizabad as well as a treasure estimated at Rs 2 crores. The Begums maintained an armed force of some 4,000 men, which was commanded by their eunuchs Jowar and Bahar Ali Khan, who governed the *jagirs* independently of the Nawab, with the assistance of Mirza Shafi Khan.

When Asaf-ud-Daula ascended the throne of Oudh (q.v.) in 1775, the subsidy due from Oudh to the John Company (q.v.) was in arrears. He professed his inability to pay on the plea that all the property was in the hands of the Begums. On the intervention of Nathaniel Middleton. the British Resident in Oudh, Bahu Begum agreed to part with £550,000 (approximately Rs 50 lakhs only) if the Company in return guaranteed that there would be no interference in her possession and administration of the *jagirs* held by her and made no further demands. This being agreed to, the money was transferred.

As a backdrop it should be noted that, broadly, the period up to 1798 may be divided into two parts in terms of the financial relations between Oudh and the Company—(i) upto 1786; (ii) 1786-98. During the first period very large sums had been realized from Oudh and the province was used as a financial resource of the Bengal Government when the latter was in monetary distress. Such indeed was the case during the whole period of Warren Hastings (q.v.) administration.

During Sir John Macpherson's Governor-Generalship (1785-6) patronage added considerably to the Company's receipts from Oudh. Under Cornwallis (q.v.) an honest effort was made not to levy any extra burdens on the province but, from 1793 onwards, the Company's finances in India began again to be unfavourably disturbed.

In 1781 the Nawab Wazir of Oudh owed the Company Rs 1.5 crores in arrears while his resources had been completely depleted. Haidar Beg, his wily minister, suggested that the money be raised from the Begums. Warren

Hastings, then desperately in need of funds for the First Maratha War (q.v.), concluded a treaty with the Nawab in which the latter agreed *inter alia* to the resumption of all *jagirs*, including those of the Begums.

On the pretext that the Begums were aiding and abetting an insurrection in Banaras led by Raja Chait Singh (q.v.) and otherwise acting against the interests of the Company's government, Hastings ruled that they were not entitled to any protection. He further deemed it politic to deprive the Begums of *jagirs* which provided them, he argued, with the means for inciting revolts. The result was that the Company's troops aided an increasingly reluctant Nawab driven to desperation by Middleton and his successor John Bristlow, both acting under remorseless pressure from their masters in Calcutta (q.v.). In February 1782, Middleton confessed that 'no further rigour than that which I exerted could have been used against females in this country'; four months later, Bristlow expressed the view that 'all that force could do has been done'. This aspect apart, it was evident that the Company had gone back on its plighted word, that it interfered in what was essentially a domestic and intimate situation in the Nawab's household and that Hastings was the moving spirit egging on an unwilling Nawab on the one hand and reluctant British residents and officers on the other.

The paltry forces of the Begums were soon overcome and their commanders arrested, tortured and humiliated. The palace was invested and no provisions allowed to enter. After suffering numerous indignities, the Begums surrendered. The Nawab ransacked the palace, taking Rs 50 lakhs in cash and an equal amount in gold and silver. The loot purloined by the Company was sold at a public auction in Calcutta.

Recent research reveals that 'in the light of the facts' the view that the Begums of Oudh 'were opposed to and acting against the welfare of the people and the rulers' is erroneous: 'they were remarkable women of courage, determination and far-sightedness whose concern was the preservation of the dynasty and the welfare of their subjects' which they had to accomplish against two powerful forces—'intriguing ministers of the court and the covetous officials of the East India Company.'

When facing impeachment, Warren Hastings was severely censured for this act of robbing and pillaging the Begums.

K. S. Santha, *Begums of Awadh*, Varanasi, 1980; Purnendu Basu, *Oudh and the East India Company 1785-1801*, Lucknow, 1943; Richard B. Barnett, *North India Between Empires: Awadh, the Mughals and the British 1720-1801*, Berkeley, 1980.

James Outram (1803–1863)

James Outram entered the John Company's (q.v.) army at the age of 16. He served in a combined military-cum-political capacity from 1833 onwards, successfully subduing and winning over the Bhils in Khandesh and putting down refractory chiefs in Gujarat (1835–8). Though opposed to Auckland's (q.v.) policy of advancing into Afghanistan in preference to the British maintaining defensive positions on the Indus—he nevertheless served with distinction in the Afghan operations. He was attached to the Bombay army under John Keane in its progress through Kandahar and Ghazni to Kabul.

From the latter place he led the pursuit of Amir Dost Mohammad (q.v.) across the Hindu Kush.

In January 1840 Outram was posted as Resident in Lower Sind (q.v.) and a year later of the combined agency for the entire province. Devoted to the welfare of the people, he at the same time carefully cultivated the trust and friendship of the Amirs. In 1843 he was superseded by Charles Napier (q.v.), but was shortly recalled from Bombay to help in formulating new treaties with the Amirs (q.v.). Despite his best efforts, no understanding could be reached with the latter as Napier's actions had aroused the Amirs' suspicions about British *bona fides* and the honesty of their intentions. Grievously hurt, Outram warned Napier that he would consider every life lost as tantamount to murder. In the war that followed, he heroically defended the Residency against 8,000 Baluchis and managed to escape just in time.

After the Annexation of Sind (q.v.), when Napier took over the administration, Outram proceeded to England on leave after requesting a friend 'to pay every regard to their [the amirs'] comfort and dignity'. While in England, he pleaded the cause of the despoiled Amirs, achieving a just condemnation of the Company's policy towards Sind but earning, in goodly measure, the chagrin of both Napier and Ellenborough (q.v.).

Returning to India towards the close of 1843, Outram served for a few years in relatively unimportant posts. His request to serve under Hugh Gough in the First Sikh War (q.v.) was rejected by Ellenborough. As Resident in Baroda (1847), he became deeply involved in a campaign against *khutput*, or corruption, allegedly involving some Bombay government officials. Thoughts of supersession and rejection now began to prey on his mind and to recoup both mental and physical health, Outram was granted permission to proceed to Egypt where he stayed for 15 months. His report on alleged widespread corruption in the administration after his return to Baroda led to his temporary removal in 1852; later, in 1853, he returned to the same post. After a brief interlude (June–November 1854) in Aden as Commander and Political Agent, he was posted as Resident in Oudh (q.v.).

Reversing his previous role as the champion of 'native' states, Outram now prepared, on Dalhousie's (q.v.) request, an exhaustive report on conditions in Oudh. Herein he represented conditions as deplorable and reluctantly recommended the state's annexation as the only available remedy. The annexation was achieved in February 1856.

In November 1856 Outram served as Commander of the East India Company's troops in Persia. Back in Calcutta (July 1857) in the midst of the Rebellion of 1857 (q.v.), he was given command of two Divisions of the Bengal army for the relief of Lucknow. Characteristically magnanimous, he allowed Havelock to continue in command and took over only after the relief of the city had been secured. On the second relief in November, Outram retired to the Alambagh and held it against 120,000 'rebels' until the final capture of Lucknow in March 1858.

Later that year he was appointed Military Member of the Governor General's Council and continued in that capacity until 1860, when he retired. Many important matters, such as the reorganization of the Indian army were subjects on which he wrote mature and carefully argued minutes. Possessed of great courage, a strong individuality, a warm temper, untiring energy and good physique, Outram was at the same time kind-hearted and considerate. A Bombay saying had it that 'A fox is a fool and a lion a coward compared with James Outram'. In all that he did, he had a strong feeling of personal responsibility. His exploits and his character—brave, humble, modest, chivalrous, high-minded—have made him conspicuous among the British heroes of Indian history.

In an address presented at a public meeting in Calcutta on the eve of his departure (July 1860) for England, he was referred to 'as our noble, disinterested fellow countryman who has preserved all his chivalry of feeling unchilled through the wear and tear of a laborious life and who will ever be remembered as emphatically as "the soldier's friend", that we would wish to testify our admiration and affectionate respect, and to preserve the memory of your career as an example to ourselves and to those who come after us.'

Lionel J. Trotter, *The Bayard of India: A Life of General Sir James Outram*, Everyman ed., London, 1909; *DNB*, XIV, pp. 1260–8 (Robert Hamilton Vetch).

Bipin Chandra Pal (1858–1932)

Bipin Chandra Pal, popularly known as the 'father of revolutionary thought in India', hailed from a well-to-do Kayastha family of Sylhet, now part of Bangladesh. A voracious reader while still in school and Presidency College, Calcutta, he published some essays and poems but did not take the university examination. At an early age Pal showed signs of rebellion against accepted beliefs and traditions. Thus, while at college, his conversion (1877) to the Brahmo Samaj (q.v.) resulted in a temporary estrangement from his father. Undaunted, he abandoned his studies to work in Cuttack, Bangalore and other places, yet never stuck to any job for long. Continuing his journalistic career simultaneously, he started (1880) *Paridarsak*, a weekly, and later took over as assistant editor of *Bengal Public Opinion* and the *Tribune*.

After a brief stint as a librarian in the Calcutta Public Library, Pal took up mission work in the Sadharan Brahmo Samaj in right earnest; the latter sponsored his visit to Oxford (1898), where he studied comparative theology for a year. This was followed by a lecture tour of England, France and the United States. In the States he encountered a strong unwillingness among people to accept anything from a subservient nation. Understandably, he returned home an avowed nationalist, determined to raise his country and its people to their rightful place. Another journalistic venture, *New India*, was started in 1901 to propagate his brand of nationalism.

Pal's interest in active politics, which dated back to his student days, was summed up in strong protests against the unjust policies of an autocratic government. Nevertheless, when he joined the Indian National Congress (q.v.) in 1886, he accepted Surendranath Banerjea (q.v.) as his political guru, but at the same time refused to question the *bona fides* of the government. He set out to democratize the Congress organization and at his suggestion younger members were given a voice in party deliberations by the election of their representatives to its subjects committee. The latter was to discuss and draft resolutions to be placed before the party's plenary session.

Pal also advised the setting up of local committees, which would be active in between sessions, to reach out to people in villages and thereby gradually involve the nation in Congress programmes. Unless it preached and practised 'equal rights and privileges', a 'common destiny of all men' and the dawn of 'a new era' in the country, he argued, the Congress would come to a premature end. Additionally, he laid stress on cultural rather than political unity and exhorted his people to appreciate their own culture and derive strength and unity from it.

Gradually, however, Pal began drifting away from the Moderates as the impending failure of their constitutional methods became apparent. The Partition of Bengal (q.v.) clinched the issue and Pal switched over to radical protest resting on independence and self-reliance. Along with Lala Lajpat Rai and Balgangadhar Tilak (q.v.) they became the 'Lal, Bal, Pal' trio that was associated in popular imagination with revolutionary activity. The fact is that Aurobindo Ghosh (q.v.) and Pal were recognized as the chief exponents of a new national movement revolving around the ideals of Purna Swaraj, Swadeshi (q.v.), Boycott (q.v.), and national education. The passive resistance that Pal preached implied active but not agressive opposition, and he was responsible for the boycott resolution of 7 August 1905.

Pal felt that the *feringhis* had destroyed all faith in political training under them; it followed that the people had to unite, fight for their rights and prepare themselves for an independent India. *Bande Mataram*, started in 1906 and edited by Aurobindo Ghosh as well as Pal, became a powerful organ propagating the extremist ideology. The latter now vowed to break up what he called the 'old lawyers rings' of the Congress and plant the seeds of democracy from which a new leadership was to emerge.

A brilliant and indeed fiery orator, Pal undertook extensive tours of Bengal to propagate his ideals. So great was the impact he made that the government soon labelled him an 'arch seditionist' and chief among the itinerant demagogues. His lecture tour of Madras was viewed as a major cause of unrest in the south. Though opposed to the Surat Split (q.v.), he preferred to side with Tilak, when it did occur. The same year (1907) he was sentenced to six months' imprisonment on account of his refusal to tender evidence against Aurobindo during the latter's trial in the 'Bande Mataram' sedition case. The 'New Party', as the extremists came to call themselves, had plans for a democratic and representative organization all the way from the province down to the district and village levels. However, such an organization existed only on paper, although some groups called 'national volunteers' put in an appearance.

Pal's imprisonment (March-August 1908) marks a major change in his thinking which took on a more concrete shape and form during his self-imposed exile (1908-11) in England. It has been suggested that he returned home 'more moderate and idiosyncratic' in his ways and thus 'unable to work effectively' with any organized party during the remaining 20 years of his life. Whereas during 1906-8 Pal had been a powerful exponent of Indian swaraj outside the British Empire, the major trend of his speeches in England during 1908-11 was an attempted reconciliation of national aspirations with the imperial system of Great Britain. The swaraj ideal of the Nationalist school, of which he was one of the earliest and most articulate advocates, now seemed to him to be too idealistic; consequently, he prescribed a practical substitute for it in the form of Indian freedom under a British Imperial Federation.

By 1911 Pal began to view the national movement as a manifestation of the divine will and was repelled by terrorism and violence. Additionally, he emerged as an advocate of internationalism, stressed the unity of independent nations and the salvation of mankind and founded an English monthly, the *Hindu Review*. He was not only opposed to modern man's selfish pursuit of individual goals but was also apprehensive of the dangers lurking in modern nationalism. Independence, he averred, must be coupled with interdependence. Competition, it followed, was a slogan of the past; it had to be replaced by co-operation. He now advocated Dominion Status (q.v.) for India in an emerging federation of states, an equal partnership with Britain and other self-governing colonies in the Empire geared to a co-operative endeavour. Pal felt that this would provide a real solution to the country's problems. His faith in a federal structure was further strengthened by the growing separatist tendencies among the Muslims.

Writing in the *Hindu Review* in April 1914, Pal put forth the view that expansion of the legislative councils was not what had been wanted, that 'a little more freedom of self-expression and self-reliant civic activities' was in fact sought, that the Minto-Morley Reforms of 1909 (q.v.) had only strengthened the conviction that any 'reasonable reconciliation between popular rights and the British connection with this country' was impossible. He now joined the Home Rule Movement (q.v.) of Annie Besant (q.v.) and Tilak and came back to the Congress fold in 1916. Three years later he went to England as a member of the Home Rule League and Congress delegation. On return home, he acted as editor (1919-22) of the *Independent,* founded by Motilal Nehru (q.v.).

In 1920 Pal, like C. R. Das (q.v.), aspired to national stature. 'Blind reverence for Gandhi's (q.v.) leadership', he wrote, 'would kill people's freedom of thought and would paralyse by the dead weight of unreasoning reverence their individual conscience'. In a letter of 10 September 1920 to Motilal Nehru, he decried 'the inspiration of mediaeval religion' which alone explained Gandhi's hold on the populace and feared this would encourage a slave mentality 'which is the root of all our degradations and miseries'. Pal thought Gandhi's priorities were lop-sided and took strong exception to the latter's statement that 'he [Pal] did not care for swaraj'. More, 'the Khilafat [q.v.] has precedence in his [Gandhi's] thought and endeavour over the Panjab tragedies. It is just here that I sense a great danger to let ourselves be led by him.' When Gandhi sought to launch the Non-cooperation Movement (q.v.), in September 1920, Pal moved an amendment seeking to accept the principle but delay its implementation. His concern, he explained, was to avoid failure on a national scale. His amendment to the official resolution was, however, overwhelmingly defeated. In the result, he bowed to the majority decision but resolved to work for its reversal at the end of the year.

At the provincial conference at Barisal over which he was asked to preside (1921), Pal voiced his opposition to Gandhi's non-violent non-cooperation.

He ridiculed the Mahatma's ideal of swaraj in one year; unfortunately for him, his political idealism fell flat on the audience. For 'Barisal saw the end of his public and political life. In Pal's thought the Gandhian upsurge was too circumscribed and too conceited in its leadership at the top to admit of fresh thinking from any source outside it.' In a series of lectures, later reprinted as *Non-cooperation*, Pal gave the movement only grudging support. He maintained that Bengal had been the first to adopt non-cooperation during the Swadeshi Movement, argued for 'constitutional non-cooperation', and felt strongly against bringing in anarchy or disorder.

Pal attacked the Montagu-Chelmsford Reforms (q.v.) as a sham but argued that the council chambers should not be given up to the Moderates. After 1921, his importance as a public figure declined precipitately and he retired from active politics even though continuing to express his views on national questions through books and articles. In fact, from now on, until his death in 1932, he lived in a virtual political wilderness and died in dire poverty. It has been well said that if Pal rose by conquering the Moderates, he 'naturally fell a victim to his own moderation'.

In social reform, Pal set himself a stringent code of personal conduct, twice marrying widows belonging to castes higher than his own. Educating women, he believed, was the surest and most effective way of elevating their position in society and of bringing about moral and social regeneration. He lent all his support to the Age of Consent Bill (1891), opposed the caste system and other rigid rules concerning inter-dining and inter-mixing. After his Brahmo youth, Pal's religious views drifted to the Vedantic philosophy of Shankaracharya and, finally, under the influence of Bijoykrishna Goswami, he was drawn to the Vaishnavism of Shri Chaitanya.

A firm supporter of the national education programme, Pal particularly stressed the need for a study of science and technology. He was also deeply involved in the labour movement. As early as 1901 he had drawn pointed attention to the condition of workers as 'a matter of profound significance to the present economic problems of the country'. He had also urged the repeal of the Emigration Act of 1882 which had reduced the coolies on estates to a condition of semi-slavery. Powerfully moved by the 1917 Bolshevik Revolution in Russia, he suggested that the only way to prevent economic exploitation in the country was to organize labour.

The British viewed Pal as 'their great enemy'. The *Historians' History of the World* described him as a preacher of sedition; no wonder Minto (q.v.) had wanted to deport him.

Pal was a noted writer of serious essays in Bengali. In the words of Srinivasa Shastri, he could speak 'words hot with emotion and subtly logical'; of his 1907 lecture in Madras, Shastri said 'oratory had never dreamed of such triumphs in India; the power of the spoken word had never been demonstrated on such a scale'. But that which distinguished Pal most and was the source of his power as a writer and speaker was his capacity for thinking. Power, position, money and even the applause of his countrymen had no lure for him when it was a question of conscience or conviction.

B.C. Pal, *Memories of My Life and Times*, 2 vols. (Vol. I, *In the Days of My Youth, 1857-84*, Vol. II, *Memories of My Life and Times, 1886-1900)* 2nd ed., Calcutta, 1973;

Haridas and Uma Mukherjee, *Bipin Chandra Pal and India's Struggle for Swaraj*, Calcuttá, 1958; Alexander Lipski, 'Bipin Chandra Pal's Synthesis of Modernity and Tradition', *JIH*, 50, 2, August 1972, pp. 431-40; Jnananjan Pal, 'Bipinchandra Pal' in Atulchandra Gupta (ed.), *Studies in the Bengal Renaissance: in commemoration of the first centenary of Bipinchandra Pal*, Calcutta, 1958, pp. 556-80; *Writings and Speeches of Bipinchandra Pal*, Calcutta, 1958.

William Palmer & Co (f. 1814)

Ostensibly a banking and commercial concern, William Palmer & Co. was started in 1814 by a superannuated army officer, William Palmer (1780-1867). On retirement from the Nizam's army, he founded the banking house named after him at Hyderabad. Henry Russell, then British Resident in Hyderabad, lent him firm support. To those who invested their savings, and they included several servants of the John Company (q.v.), an interest of 12% was paid while business was transacted at double that figure. Owing to its British parentage and patronage Palmer & Company was identified with the government in the popular mind and its cause further strengthened by the fact that Sir William Rumbold, husband of one of the Marquess of Hastings' (q.v.) wards, was a principal shareholder. In violation of a long standing law which barred any European from entering into financial transactions with an Indian ruler, the Company was granted permission by the Bengal government in 1816 to loan a huge sum to the Nizam's efficient, but notoriously extravagant and corrupt minister, Chandu Lal.

It was known that Palmer & Company was prepared to lend money at a lower rate of interest than Indian bankers; hence Hastings' sanction referred to, on the understanding that his government would not be responsible for the repayment of any sums thus loaned. Meanwhile, information regarding a loan of Rs 60 lakhs transacted in 1820, and repayable in 6 years at the rate of Rs 16 lakhs a year, reached the Directors who censured the government in India for such scandalous deals and forbade all further transactions.

Charles Metcalfe (q.v.), who took over as resident in Hyderabad in December 1820, investigated the matter further and expressed the view that the loans had been misapplied. He revealed that nearly a million pounds sterling had been lent and then wasted in highly irregular expenditure, including the grant of pensions to members of the firm, while as much as 24% was charged as rate of interest. Metcalfe's efforts to check the oppression of the people who raised these sums to pay off the debts of the Company were condemned by Hastings as tantamount to unnecessary interference in Hyderabad's internal affairs. On specific orders from the Directors, however, the Nizam was advanced a loan of Rs 80 lakhs and the Company liquidated. The latter's appeal for redress and the heated exchanges that followed revealed Hastings' partisan attitude, although his actions were later condoned as having resulted from an erroneous judgement. His implied censure by the Directors however made him resign from the Governor-Generalship.

Dodwell, *CHI*, V, p. 576; *Buckland*, p. 328; Karen Leonard, 'Banking Firms in 19th century Hyderabad Politics', *Modern Asian Studies*, 15, 2, April 1981, pp. 177-201.

Third Battle of Panipat (1761)

Panipat, the site of three important battles (in 1526, 1556 and 1761) lies some 20 miles to the south of Karnal and a bare 55 miles north of Delhi. Once a large town, its importance was due *inter alia* to its strategic location on the high road from Sirhind to Delhi.

The third battle of Panipat was fought on 21 January 1761 between the Maratha armies under Sadashiva Rao Bhau and a large Afghan host under Ahmad Shah Abdali (q.v.). It lasted from 9 in the morning to 3.30 in the afternoon. Conflicting accounts of the troops engaged in the fighting have been given by two eyewitnesses—Kashiraj and Muhammed Jafar Shamlu, the former's estimate being rated more accurate. According to Kashiraj, Abdali had 41,800 horse, 38,000 foot soldiers, 200 camel swivels and 40 pieces of artillery. His erstwhile Indian allies, Najib-ud-Daula (d.1770) and the Rohillas, Shuja-ud-Daula (q.v.) of Oudh (q.v.) and other assorted friends accounted for 1,14,000 foot soldiers with 185 guns. In numbers, firing power, body armour and the quality of their mounts, the Afghan forces had a decisive edge over the Marathas who were not easily amenable to discipline and team-work. In the final count, the superiority of the Afghan general and his captains over the Marathas, added to their higher morale and discipline, won the day.

Initially, as the fighting commenced, the advantage lay with the Marathas, but with the arrival of reinforcements for Abdali's troops, the position was reversed. The battle ended in a complete Maratha rout in which Vishwas Rao, the young son of Peshwa Balaji Baji Rao (q.v.), as well as his uncle and mentor, Sadashiva Rao Bahu, perished on the battlefield.

The Afghan losses have been estimated at 20,000 men killed, of which roughly three-quarters were Rohillas. The Marathas lost over 50,000 men, besides most of their 45,000 horses, 2,000 bullocks and 500 elephants.

A close scrutiny of events preceding and following the battle does not support the view that it was a contest between the united Hindus of India and a confederacy of Muhammadan chiefs like Najib and Shuja-ud-Daulah. It is true that the latter rallied to the side of the Afghans, but, on the other hand, the Rajputs, Jats and a number of Hindu chiefs were conspicuously absent from the side of the Marathas, and some among them even shed their blood for the Timurid empire. The Marathas fought for no apparent cause and lost, but the victorious Abdali gained no lasting benefits either.

Although the Marathas lost the Panjab, in the long run it was gained not by Abdali, but by the Sikhs. The treacherous Najib-ud Daula, the arch-villain of the piece, outwardly succeeded in warding off the Marathas, but eventually found himself thrown between two millstones—the Sikhs from the north and the Jats from the south. The Marathas too came back to rule in Delhi and uprooted Najib's family together with his buried bones. The trans-Ganges Rohillas under Hafiz Rahmat Khan (q.v.) also experienced the wrath of the Marathas after Najib's death and Shuja-ud Daulah with the help of the British became their annihilator. In fact, the ultimate result of Panipat was to pave the way, smooth and clear, for the English.

The defeat of Panipat was a disaster of the first magnitude but was not conclusive. For Abdali, it was an empty victory. The Marathas too had received a severe blow but within a decade they were back in the north, acting as guardians of the Mughal Emperor, Shah Alam II (q.v.), whom they escorted from Allahabad to Delhi in 1771. It is equally doubtful if a Maratha victory at Panipat would have made much difference to the subsequent history of India. Spear has expressed the view that 'what Panipat really did was to reveal, as in a lightning flash, the political bankruptcy of the Afghan chiefs and the material poverty of the Marathas.' The fact that it took them ten years 'to recover from the blow is evidence not so much of the severity of the defeat, as of their lack of reserves.'

Hari Ram Gupta (ed.), *Marathas and Panipat*, Chandigarh, 1961; T. S. Shejwalkar, *Panipat: 1761*, Deccan College Monograph Series, Poona, 1946: T. G. P. Spear, *Twilight of the Mughals*, Cambridge, 1951, pp. 3–4.

Paramountcy and the Indian States (1946–7)

At the 1930-2 Round Table Conference (q.v.), the Indian princes had accepted the idea of a federal union for the whole of India embracing both the British-ruled provinces and the Indian States (q.v.) ruled by their Maharajas and Nawabs. The Government of India Act 1935 (q.v.) which envisaged a federal form of government at the centre, was never implemented, for while the provincial part of the Act was introduced in 1937, the federal was kept in abeyance for a variety of reasons. However, the Cabinet Mission Plan (q.v.) of 16 May 1946 promised self-government to India on the model of the British Dominions under a constitution prepared by the Indians themselves.

There were in all 562 Indian states covering 40 per cent of the total area and 25 per cent of the country's entire population, their territories intermixed with those of the British-ruled Indian provinces. In area and importance they differed widely: Kashmir, with an area of 82,000 square miles, was as large as England; Hyderabad had a population of 16 million; Mysore 7 million; Travancore 6 million; Kashmir and Gwalior 4 million each. The total area covered by the states was 720,000 square miles and their population 93 million.

In status, authority and honours accorded, the states differed widely. Yet their relationship to the paramount power was defined by the term 'paramountcy', which implied both a system of rights as well as duties. Broadly, the duties of the Crown were to protect the ruler and his territory from internal and external danger, to conduct the external relations of the state, provide for its defence, regulate disputed successions, administer it during the possible minority of a ruler and intervene in cases of gross misrule.

The function of paramountcy, at best nebulously defined, was exercised by the Crown through the Viceroy in his personal capacity. On 29 January 1947 a conference of rulers was held to consider the terms on which they should approve the Cabinet Mission Plan. *Inter alia* this meeting resolved that (i) the final decision about entering the Union would be made through negotiation and would be imposed by the Union government; (ii) the federal union would exercise only such powers as were delegated by the states; (iii) the status of an Indian state would be that of a sovereign power; there would be no interference with its constitution, territorial integrity, succession and dynastic rights; (iv) the states would continue to enjoy internal autonomy and there was to be no interference in their exercise of it.

On 8-9 February 1947 the States Committee of the Indian Constituent Assembly (q.v.) under the chairmanship of Jawaharlal Nehru (q.v.) met the Negotiating Committee of the Chamber of Princes (q.v.) for talks. After discussion, they resolved that the states would be represented by 93 seats in the Constituent Assembly in such a manner that 50 per cent of the representatives would be nominees of the rulers and the remaining 50 per cent elected through different types of electoral bodies.

There were acute differences among the rulers of various groups of states. These were articulated by the Nawab of Bhopal, then Chancellor of the Chamber of Princes, on the one hand and the Maharajas of Patiala, Baroda and Bikaner, on the other. The former held that the states should join the Constituent Assembly only at the last stage, when the constitution of the Union itself was under consideration. His group was also determined to defer a decision regarding entry into the proposed federation till the constitution had been finally adopted. The latter group felt that the states' representatives should be present at the earlier deliberations of the Assembly and not stay out of the union. The first ruler to toe this line was Baroda, followed by eight others on 28 April. In July, 37 more princes joined, including Gwalior and Mysore. In opposition to them, Bhopal unsuccessfully attempted to form an independent state in Madhya Pradesh.

The June 3rd Plan (q.v.) had reiterated the Cabinet Mission's policy of 16 May regarding the states. Later, the Governor-General made it clear that the states as such would not be allowed to become members of the British Commonwealth. Under the influence of the politically powerful Ittihad-ul-Muslimin, Hyderabad declared its intention of setting up an independent monarchy. Travancore, with C. P. Ramaswamy Aiyer as its Diwan, took the same line. Bhopal resigned his Chancellorship of the Chamber of Princes and established contacts with M. A. Jinnah (q.v.). Lord Mountbatten, British India's last Viceroy and Governor-General, invited the princes to meet him in New Delhi on 25 July. The meeting appointed a committee of rulers and their ministers to discuss the Instrument of Accession and the Standstill Agreement which had been drafted by the new States Department headed by Sardar Vallabhbhai Patel (q.v.) with V. P. Menon as its Secretary and moving spirit.

Before signing the two documents, some princes tried to open negotiations with Jinnah and the Muslim League (q.v.) to obtain what they hoped would be better terms that would enable them to stay out of the Indian Union. Among them was the ruler of Jodhpur who appears to have been promised ownership of a port on the Rann of Cutch, a railway line from Jodhpur to Karachi and sundry other concessions. Jaisalmer was also persuaded by Jodhpur to join this plan. The rulers of Indore and Dholpur, however, proved recalcitrant, while Travancore was maturing its plans, in collusion with Jinnah, for a wholly independent status. Despite those who were not very willing, a large majority of the rulers gradually decided to join the Union. By 15 August 1947 the only states that remained obdurate were Junagadh in Saurashtra, Kashmir and Hyderabad and two small states under

Muslim rulers in Kathiawar.

On 1 August 1947 the Government of India had announced that standstill agreements would be entered into only with those rulers who had executed the Instrument of Accession with New Delhi. Jinnah objected to the policy of accession and told Mountbatten that he considered it utterly wrong. He also made it clear that he would guarantee the independence of the states in Pakistan.

In the Indian Independence Act (q.v.), clause 7 was mainly concerned with the future of the states. Understandably, the general tendency among the rulers was that they should make as good a bargain as possible, given the situation created by the lapse of paramountcy. The fact that in the course of World War II many of them had strengthened their armed forces had not gone unnoticed.

V. P. Menon, *The Story of the Integration of the Indian States*, Reprint, New Delhi, 1969, pp. 68-118; *Tara Chand*, IV, pp. 333-40.

Partition Council (1947)

After the acceptance by Indian political leaders of the June 3rd Plan (q.v.), Lord Louis Mountbatten presented them a paper entitled 'The Administrative Consequences of Partition'. After 'many meetings and much argument', the Governor-General persuaded the politicians to set up a Partition Committee consisting of Vallabhbhai Patel (q.v.) and Rajendra Prasad (q.v.) belonging to the Indian National Congress (q.v.), as well as Liaqat Ali Khan (q.v.) and Abdur Rab Nishtar of the All India Muslim League (q.v.), with himself acting as Chairman. Later, when the provinces decided on Partition, the Committee came to be known as the Partition Council. The Congress continued to be represented by Patel and Rajendra Prasad, with C. Rajagopalachari (q.v.) as an alternate member; while M. A. Jinnah (q.v.) and Liaqat Ali Khan, with Nishtar as an alternate member, represented the Muslim League.

By an order of the Governor-General under the Indian Independence Act (q.v.), the Partition Council continued to function even after 15 August 1947. Its composition was then altered to include two members drawn from each Dominion cabinet. India continued to be represented by its original members and Pakistan by such ministers as were able to attend meetings in New Delhi.

The Council functioned through a steering committee of two senior officials—H. M. Patel for India and Chaudhri Mohamad Ali for Pakistan. The steering committee was assisted by ten expert committees of officials representing both countries. They covered the entire gamut of administration: organization, records and personnel; assets and liabilities; central revenues, contracts, currency and coinage; economic relations (trade and controls); domicile; foreign relations and the armed forces. The steering committee was meant to ensure that concrete proposals were evolved and put up within a specified time to the Partition Council for decision, and thereafter take steps to implement them.

The expert committees which began their investigations in the third week of June were able to put up agreed recommendations on a large number of subjects, while the steering committee was saddled with a few unsettled issues. Only a few points remained to be sorted out by the Arbitral Tribunal (q.v.) after 15 August. Even these matters Mountbatten was determined to resolve by a mutual give and take. With this end in view, the Pakistani representatives, Ghulam Mohammad and Sir Archibald Rowlands, met Sardar Patel, Rajendra Prasad and Rajagopalachari who, after discussion, remitted the outstanding issues to the steering committee. The latter was able to resolve differences and evolve mutually acceptable compromises. The result was that all references to the Arbitral Tribunal were withdrawn.

V. P. Menon, *The Transfer of Power in India*, Bombay, 1957.

Vallabhbhai Patel (1875–1950)

There is no record of Vallabhbhai's exact date of birth, but he was born at Nadiad, a small town not far from Surat and his generally accepted date of birth is 31 October 1875. He came of an agricultural family of the Lewa Patidar community; his background was lower middle-class and the family did not have a tradition of education. As a Patidar, or peasant proprietor, Vallabhbhai's father, who held a share in the village land, is said to have fought in the Rebellion of 1857 (q.v.) under Rani Lakshmi Bai of Jhansi (q.v.). Vallabhbhai was educated at Karamsad and later Nadiad, where he matriculated at the age of 22.

Initially Vallabhbhai practised law at Borsad, a town in Kheda district. During 1910-13 he was in England and called to the bar from Middle Temple. On his return to India, he established himself at Ahmedabad and attained a prominent position in public life. Even though he met Gandhi (q.v.) in 1916, he kept himself 'cynically and sarcastically aloof', for the Mahatma's Franciscan idealism had no appeal for a hard-headed realist who 'dressed in tip-top English style'.

In 1917 Vallabhbhai was elected a municipal councillor of Ahmedabad; during 1924-8 he was Chairman of the Municipal Committee and paid particular attention to the city's civic amenities. His devotion to the public weal is revealed by his dedicated work during the plague (1917) and famine (1918) epidemics that betook the town. His entry into politics came through the Gujarat Sabha, a political body which was later of great assistance to Gandhi in his political campaigns. In 1918 Patel was associated with the Kheda satyagraha which was launched to secure the cultivators' exemption from payment of land tax for the crops that year had failed. Gandhi later expressed the view that but for Patel the campaign would not have been carried 'so successfully'. In the final count, despite government repression and brutality, the peasants stood their ground and won.

By 1922 Patel had renounced his legal practice and devoted himself wholly to political and constructive work, touring villages and addressing meetings. In 1928 he was engaged in a mass peasant upheaval against the provincial government's decision to increase land revenue from the Bardoli taluka by 22 per cent and, in some villages, by as much as 50-60 per cent. Other means of redress having failed, the agriculturists decided, under Patel's leadership, to withhold payment of land revenue. The government unleashed a **verit-able** reign of terror: mass arrests, police barbarities and hired Pathan ruffians were let loose. Organized resistance however was so strong that the government ultimately yielded. An inquiry was instituted to determine if the proposed increase was justified, and realization of enhanced revenue was postponed. 80,000 peasants had been involved in the satyagraha, a triumph of powerful leadership; in recognition of Patel's great work, Gandhi now called him 'Sardar', an honorific that stuck.

Later, Patel was to join the Salt Satyagraha of 1930. After the failure of the Round Table Conference (q.v.) and Gandhi's arrest, he was with the Mahatma in the Yervada jail; for 16 months (January 1932-May 1933), they were thrown together. After the Congress decided to accept office in the provinces under the Government of India Act 1935 (q.v.), Patel was chairman of the Congress parliamentary board, which supervised the working of the party's ministries in the Congress-ruled provinces. He was soon to play an active role in the individual Civil Disobedience (1940-1) and Quit India Movements (qq.v.). On both occasions, he was sentenced to long terms of imprisonment.

Patel was Home Member of the Governor-General's Executive Council in the Interim Government (q.v.) formed in September 1946. In the events leading to the transfer of power by the British, he was, with Jawaharlal Nehru (q.v.), the principal negotiator on behalf of the Indian National Congress (q.v.). With Independence (August 1947), Patel became Deputy Prime Minister, his portfolios including Home, the Indian States (q.v.) and Information and Broadcasting. His tact, power of persuasion and statesmanship brought about the integration of some 562 states and princely domains into 26 administrative units, bringing into the Union 80 million people, a little over a quarter of the country's population. This has aptly been rated the crowning achievement of his political career. In this task Patel acted swiftly, yet quite ruthlessly. The smaller states were merged into the contiguous provinces, and larger conglomerations were formed into unitary systems. On the issue of Junagadh, armed intervention was deemed necessary; in Hyderabad, there was 'police action' by the military followed by armed occupation. Within two years, the old princely India had been well-nigh completely integrated into the rest of the body politic.

As Minister for Home Affairs after 1947 Patel helped control communal strife and tackled the myriad problems arising out of Partition, principally the rehabilitation of millions of refugees. He accomplished this herculean task with the skill and efficiency of a great administrator. He reorganized the public services which had been badly depleted with the departure of the British. The new Indian Administrative Service was born to take the place of the old I.C.S. and provide a stable administrative base.

Throughout his political career, Patel was the party boss who organized and controlled the Congress party machine effectively and efficiently. No one prior to him had given so much time or thought to the need for an adequate party organization which could be geared to fight political campaigns.

Kewal Panjabi has referred to Maulana Azad's (q.v.) *India Wins Freedom* wherein 'by copious inaccuracy in his statements, coloured with **excessive** self-esteem', the Sardar's image has been tarnished. He has underlined Patel's skill 'in manoeuvring' the course of events: 'He understood as few others did, the anatomy and mechanics of power in a democratic state. And he organised and planned so well that he retained control over the limbs of the body politic.' The Sardar, he avers, was 'shy of emotional demonstrations'; was 'too blunt and honest' and therefore lacked mass appeal: his singular objective in life was 'to build a strong and united India. It was not merely an intellectual craving or a political aspiration with him. It had become his mission in life . . . It was a living faith.'

The inscription on his bust in the Indian Merchants' Chamber in Bombay aptly describes him—Apostle of Reality: Statesman-Patriot.

The Sardar has been compared to the nineteenth century Prussian statesman, Prince Otto von Bismarck (1815-98), yet the parallel does not really hold. True, like the Iron Chancellor, he was courageous and realistic; but, unlike him, he was at once honest and far from cynical. Patel was an idealist and, though his natural temper was authoritarian, he never imposed his will on others. He accepted the discipline he enjoined; was loyal to the ideal of a secular state and, even on Kashmir was veering round to a peaceful settlement towards the end of his life. He was a man of courage, discipline, sturdy individualism, tough stability and a sense of the practical. Lord Mountbatten has remarked that 'at heart he was a gentle and kind man'. For despite the unhappy legacy of the freedom struggle against the British, Patel had no bitterness against the latter, either on the individual plane or collectively as a people.

Patel was broadly identified with the business community and as one generally opposed to Nehru's socialism. By background a staunch Hindu, he tended to be conservative in politics.

After a brief illness, the Sardar died on 15 December 1950, leaving behind a son, Dahyabhai, and a daughter, Maniben.

Narhari D. Parikh, *Sardar Vallabbhai Patel*, 2 vols, Bombay, 1953-56; P. D. Saggi, *Life and Work of Sardar Vallabbhai Patel*, Bombay, 1953; V. P. Menon, *The Transfer of Power in India*, Bombay, 1957; Kewal K. Panjabi, *The Indomitable Sardar*, 2nd ed., Bombay, 1964; D. V. Tahmankar, *Sardar Patel*, London, 1970; Durga Das (ed.), *Sardar Patel's Correspondence 1945-50*, 10 vols., Ahmedabad, 1971-3; V. Shankar (ed.), *Sardar Patel (Select Correspondence 1945-50)*, 2 vols, Ahmedabad, 1978.

The Permanent Settlement (1793)

One of Lord Cornwallis's (q.v.) major achievements was the Permanent Settlement of land revenue in Bengal. For a quarter century after the grant (1765) of Diwani Rights (q.v.) to the John Company (q.v.), the revenue settlement had been on an annual basis, though a permanent system, later christened 'assessment forever' had been 'vaguely anticipated'. On 10 February 1790, however, the Governor-General announced a decennial settlement; a perpetual settlement was to follow 'provided such continuance should meet with the approbation of the Court of Directors. . .And not otherwise'. Three years later it was approved by the Directors and made permanent as of 22 March 1793. It constituted Regulation I in the series of regulations passed by the Calcutta Supreme Council on 1 May and collectively known as the Cornwallis Code (q.v.).

Under the new dispensation, the zamindars were recognized as proprietors of land, which was to be leased to the highest bidder for 10 years. Land revenue was to be fixed, there being no enhancement of dues to the government, nor could the zamindar in return expect any remissions or postponement of dues.

Cornwallis argued that these measures would encourage landlords to obtain the maximum produce as well as reclaim waste land, ensure a permanent income to the government, and save time and effort hitherto wasted on annual settlements. By accepting the hereditary status of zamindars, however, the settlement completely ignored the interests of cultivators and ryots who were thus thrown to the tender mercies of big landlords. It was clear that the latter would rack-rent the peasantry and thereby add to their own profits. The Governor-General's views were opposed by most of his advisors, including John Shore (q.v.) and Charles Grant. Shore wanted a proper survey to be carried out *before* a perpetual assessment was made; Grant was doubtful about the zamindars' proprietary rights to the land without an exhaustive study of the records. Ironically, Shore who succeeded Cornwallis, was to bear witness to the first results of the Permanent Settlement he had so steadfastly opposed.

Sirajul Islam concludes that the Permanent Settlement 'laid the foundations of the British administrative system in Bengal . . .(albeit) at the expense of social order.' The changes it brought about 'proved to be mere social disorders. The loss of rights of ryots, growth of sub-infeudation, conflicts between old and new houses, absenteeism, pressure of the sale laws, inadequate law courts and police system, exclusion of the natives from the important offices, decline of trade and commerce and industries—all contributed to an extremely tense and unstable social environment. Within that atmosphere, the zamindars failed to stand for improvement. Instead of becoming improving landlords they turned out to be tyrannical and unproductive.'

Ranajit Guha has expressed the view that the Settlement was not the logical culmination of a mere process of experimentation through trials and errors. There were communication gaps between London and Calcutta as well as between and within different levels of the administration. Besides, the two highest organs of the Company's government in Bengal were at war with each other. As a result broad and far-sighted decisions did not emerge. In actual fact the Settlement was the result of a complex causation in which ideas too played a role to the extent that these were relevant to mundane interests and provided a decent appearance to them. Guha concludes that Cornwallis not only legitimized a heavy tribute in the form of rent; he also made its collection rigid and harsh. His ideas represented British ruling classes' immediate interests as well as their false view of Bengal's social reality.

Viewed in its purely commercial and financial aspects, the Settlement resulted in considerable loss of future revenues. As an administrative measure, its completion required a stronger statutory base and more vigorous executive management than were forthcoming. But looking at the measure solely from a political point of view, it was the means of allaying apprehensions and removing doubts amongst a class of Indians.

Sirajul Islam, *The Permanent Settlement in Bengal: A Study of its Operation, 1790-1819*, Bangla Academy, Dacca, 1979; Ratnalekha Ray, *Change in Bengal Agrarian Society c. 1760-1850*, New Delhi, 1979; Ranajit Guha, *A Rule of Property for Bengal: An Essay on the idea of Permanent Settlement*, 2nd ed., New Delhi, 1982; W. S. Seton-Karr. *The Marquess of Cornwallis*, Rulers of India, Oxford, 1893; Dodwell, *CHI*, V, pp. 449-51, 456.

General Perron (c. 1755–1836)

Pierre Cuillier, better known as 'General Perron', was born in 1755 at Chateau du Loire, in Sarthe (France). He inched his way from the position of a petty peddler, a handkerchief hawker in his native land, to be appointed a governor in India and the chief commander of Mahadji Sindhia's (q.v.) forces.

In 1780, Perron arrived off the Malabar coast. Around 1781, he had discarded his old name and assumed the *nom de guerre* of Perron. Beginning as a petty officer in small Indian state armies, he finally managed to get employment under Benoit de Boigne (q.v.) in Sindhia's army. He saw action at the battle of Kharda (1789), where Maratha forces decisively worsted the Nizam.

In 1790 de Boigne, who had formed a favourable impression of Perron's capacity as a soldier and an artisan skilled in the work of cannon-foundry appointed him captain-lieutenant in a new brigade which was being raised. Perron was given command of the Burhanpur battalion. During 1792-3 Perron was associated with Ambaji Inglia, a general of Gwalior who served under Mahadji Sindhia, and Rana Khan in the subjugation of Mewar and assisted in establishing the former as *subahdar* of that district. Mahadji himself accompanied the army in this task and, when it was successfully accomplished, marched to Poona while Perron and his brigade returned to their headquarters. In 1794, Perron returned to the Deccan to strengthen the position of his master there. From 1797 to 1800 Perron was in command of the army of Hindustan. The battalions he commanded were veterans, undefeated in combat, their spirit and organization unexcelled.

Early in 1800 Lakwa Dada, the champion of the Bhais, advanced into Rajasthan to collect the tribute due to his master and was supported by Perron's second brigade under Major Pohlman. The result was the successful rout of the rulers of Jaipur and Jodhpur. By 1801 Perron was at the zenith of his career. He had brought nearly the whole of the north under his control and was supreme within the boundaries of Sindhia's northern possessions. The following year however saw a major reverse at Ujjain through the victory of Yashvantrao Holkar (q.v.). This was partially retrieved for Sindhia by the defeat inflicted at the battle of Indore when Holkar's general, George Thomas, was taken prisoner.

Upon the declaration of war by Wellesley (q.v.) in 1803, Sindhia's regular brigades numbered 39,000 men with 5,000 Hindustani horse and 464 guns. It was then that General Lake continuously pressurized Perron into surrendering his position by Sindhia's side. The French adventurer was shaken in his hour of decision; he abandoned his master's cause, resigned his command and sought British protection: 'Never surely did a master of so many legions fall so swiftly and so ignominiously. Not a single blow had he struck to uphold that sovereign power which he had wielded for 7 years...With a lie on his lips, and his trembling hands squandering gold to bribe the soldiery he dared not trust, Perron fled from his kingdom, followed by the execrations of his troops and the exultant denunciation of his fellow countrymen.'

A number of factors had unnerved Perron—Lake's campaign undertaken at the height of the monsoon; the fall of Aligarh in a single day (4 September 1803); his own supersession by Sindhia's close confidant, Ambaji Inglia; the defection of some of his brigades, and the fact that he had been deposed from his command by Louis Bourguien and his life threatened.

In retirement, de Boigne kept up a steady correspondence with Perron, inscribing his letters with 'your ever devoted and affectionate friend'. De Boigne was pronouncedly Anglophile; Perron, though remarkably well treated by Wellesley and General Lake, could never forgive the British for their refusal to help him collect and remove the last of his fortune. Reaching Europe in 1805, Perron lived in retirement in France until his death in 1834.

Shelford Bidwell, *Swords for Hire: European mercenaries in eighteenth century India*, London, 1971; Herbert Compton, *A Particular Account of the European Military Adventurers of Hindustan from 1784 to 1803*, Reprint, Oxford, 1976; A. Martineau, *Le General Perron*, Paris, 1931; P. K. Tatineni, 'European Mercenaries in Moghul India', *Imprint* (Bombay), June 1982, pp. 51-4; *Buckland*, p. 334.

Pindaris

The Pindaris were armed predatory hordes, forming the rear-guard of a conquering army, engaged not so much in fighting as in plundering and laying waste the country they passed through, besides perpetrating cruelties on local inhabitants. Their headquarters were in central India, but they laid claim to no particular area, much less professed a common religion. New recruits were initiated into the fold on Vijay Dashami or Dussehra.

The exact derivation of the term 'Pindari' is unknown; some take it to be a corrupted form of 'Bidari'—the armed and privileged robbers earlier known to Mughal rulers; others attribute the name to their consumption of the intoxicating drink called *pendha*. It has also been suggested that the term is composed of two Marathi words, *pendha* (a bundle of grass) and *hara* (one who takes), the 'pindaris' having originally been collectors of forage. Sardesai is uncertain about the etymology of the word but refers to the Pindaris as 'a body of stragglers equivalent to Burga or Bazar Bunga of the regular armies'. Hordes similar to the Pindaris existed under the Pathan chiefs Mohammed Shah and Amir Khan, ancestors of the Nawabs of Tonk. They exploited the fears of powerful princes to extort large money payments.

Irvine *(Indian Antiquary,* May 1900) puts forth the view that the Pindaris had initially settled down in the region of Pandhar—a place somewhere between Burhanpur and Hindia on the Narmada—and took their name from it. Sardesai calls them 'a bandit cavalry' that reinforced all Indian armies and maintains that British accounts referring to them as 'enemies of society' and 'loathsome pests' are biased; that at one time the Pindaris were called 'a convenient ingredient' of the system of warfare developed by the Marathas. Essentially, he contends, they were 'a class of unpaid auxiliaries' attached to each chief's fighting quota whose duty it was to step in the moment a battle ended and thereafter finish the enemy by seizing his property and camp equipage, thus destroying his power of recovery. The Pindaris received no regular pay and lived on plunder and devastation of the enemy country. Hardy horse-riders, the characteristics of the Pindaris were an amazing mobility and rapidity of movement; their chief arms were the lance and the sword.

The Pindaris do not find any mention in the Maratha army during the time of Shivaji (1627-80). Later, however, under Peshwa Balaji Baji Rao (q.v.) they emerge as a common, albeit restricted, feature of the Maratha forces. In Holkar's army the Pindaris are said to have preponderated over the paid mercenaries. In so far as they cost their employers little or nothing, they eased their way into the service of every chief.

As long as the Maratha state was a viable political entity, these 'predatory bands', unmatched in their long and swift marches, were considered quite helpful and *not* obnoxious. But with the decline of the Maratha power, their cavalry, no longer gainfully employed, went to swell the ranks of these freebooters. The major portion of the Pindari bands was in the service of Maratha chiefs, Sindhia and Holkar, and had even received the distinctive titles of Sindeshahi and Holkarshahi. Mahadji Sindhia (q.v.) was served by two Pindari chiefs, Hira and Burhan. To the British, the Pindaris were the best organized 'anti-social element' encountered; yet in this respect the Pindaris were essentially a by-product of British rule. It was Wellesley's (q.v.) system of subsidiary alliances which had resulted in the disbandment of state armies and these unemployed soldiers invariably swelled the Pindari ranks.

The majority among the Pindaris were Muslims, although there were Hindus of the lower castes too, and as a group they are known to have had 'neither caste nor conscience'. Their main branch is said to have been descended from Nusru, a Muslim of the Talaye tribe who had served under Shahji Bhonsle, the father of Shivaji.

The last decade of the eighteenth century and the first two of the nineteenth may be said to embrace the Pindari phase; their story falls broadly into two nearly equal halves. In the first, they were a constituent part of the armies of the various Maratha chiefs as well as of the Nawab of Bhopal and Amir Khan, the Pathan leader. Until about 1803, they remained subordinate to the Maratha chiefs but, after that date, made rapid strides towards near-independence. In 1794 Sindhia granted them lands in the valley of the Narmada. For the Marathas, the Pindaris constituted a source of income, paying a tax called *palpatti* to the general whose forces they accompanied in return for the protection they received from him.

The Maratha debacle in their long drawn-out struggle against the John Company (q.v.) helped the rise of the Pindaris; it not only made the latter virtually independent but swelled their ranks. After the Second Anglo-Maratha War (q.v.), they constituted a menace in a vast area stretching from Mirzapur in the north to Guntur in the south, from Surat in the west to Cuttack in the east. Even though lacking a separate political identity, in the opening decades of the nineteenth century the Pindaris had come to be an important political force, given the general lawlessness in the heart of India. In 1804 their number stood around 10,000; it shot up to 26,000 in 1811 and, six years later, to 60,000. By then they were a powerful and hostile confedera-tion under such leaders as Karim Khan, Chitu, Dost Muhammad, Namdhar Khan and others. The contemporary Indian powers had neither the will nor the strength to stop their depredations.

By 1812 powerful Pindari leaders had carried fire and sword far and wide into British territory, the Nizam's dominions and as far as the Northern Sarkars. To put an end to their recurrent depredations the Marquess of Hastings (q.v.), with the approval of the Court of Directors, mounted a regular war against them. The well-organised Pindari War (q.v.) had nearly succeeded, by the end of 1817, in expelling the Pindaris from Malwa and across the Chambal; by January 1818, they were practically annihilated. As the Pindaris had an intimate association with the Holkar family, formed an integral part of Sindhia's army and were ready auxiliaries of Amir Khan, the Pathan leader, Hastings made sure that as the Company launched its opera-tions against them, the Pindaris received no help from these quarters.

B. K. Sinha, *The Pindaris (1798-1817)*, Calcutta, 1971; M. P. Roy, *Origin, Growth & Suppression of the Pindaris*, New Delhi, 1973; Bishwanath Ghosh, *British Policy Towards the Pathans & the Pindaris in Central India 1805-1818*, Calcutta, 1966; S. N. Sen, *The Military System of the Marathas*, New Delhi, 1958, pp. 62-3, 75-6.

Pindari War (1817–18)

The depredations of the Pindaris (q.v.) and their erstwhile allies, the Pathans, had gradually spread to areas directly held, or indirectly ruled, by the John Company (q.v.). Thus the districts of Shahbad and Mirzapur were ravaged in 1812, the Nizam's dominion in 1815 and the Northern Sarkars a year later. This finally clinched the issue in so far as the Company was concerned. With the approval of the Court of Directors, the Marquess of Hastings (q.v.), assembled a large force, 113,000 men and 300 guns, to round up and exterminate the seemingly lawless Pindari hordes. A pincer-like operation was planned to surround them from all sides: in the north and east, from Bengal; in the west, from Gujarat; in the south, from the Deccan. The northern force of four divisions was to be commanded by the Governor-General himself; the southern by General Thomas Hislop (1764-1843), who was assisted by John Malcolm (q.v.). Each of the Pindari chiefs, Karim

Khan, Wasil Muhammad and Chitu, commanded some seven to eight thousand men.

Even as the armed conflict raged, Hastings in a swift diplomatic move neutralized the formidable Pathan leader, Amir Khan, by installing him as the Nawab of Tonk. Negotiations were also opened with the Rajput rulers and the Maratha chiefs. Surrounded in Malwa, the Pindaris fled to Mewar

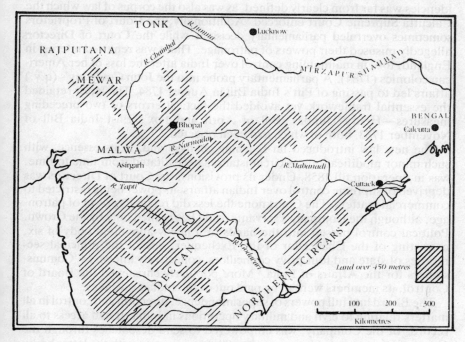

Pindari War

but were forced to retrace their steps, suffering a severe reverse on their return to Malwa. Karim Khan surrendered and was offered an estate at Gawashpur; Wasil Muhammad sought asylum with Sindhia but was made to lay down arms and died in captivity; Chitu was defeated and lost in the Asirgarh forests. In the operations lasting over a year, the Pindaris were virtually annihilated.

B. K. Sinha, *The Pindaris (1798–1817),* Calcutta, 1971; Mohan Sinha Mehta, *Lord Hastings and the Indian States: Being a Study of the Relations of the British Government in India with the Indian States 1813-23,* Bombay, 1930.

Pitt's India Act (1784)

Some glaring defects that had come to light in the working of the Regulating Act (q.v.) made new parliamentary legislation imperative. To list some of the lacunae, the Governor-General's control over the subordinate presidencies was far from clearly defined, as was also the corpus of law which the Calcutta Supreme Court enforced. Additionally, the Court of Proprietors sometimes overruled parliamentary decisions while the Court of Directors allegedly misused their powers of patronage. There was renewed interest in England, too, in maintaining control over India after the loss of her American colonies (1784). A parliamentary probe into the John Company's (q.v.) affairs led to passing of Pitt's India Bill in August 1784. The latter retained the essential framework yet avoided the tactical errors of two preceding measures—Henry Dundas' Bill of April and Fox's East India Bill of November 1783, both of which had been rejected.

The new law introduced far-reaching changes and, in its essence, with such minor modifications as circumstances necessitated from time to time, was in operation till 1858. Under its provisions, the Court of Directors was deprived of supreme control over Indian affairs, its power being restricted to commercial matters. The Court none the less did retain its power of patronage, although the Company's servants could be recalled only by the Crown. Political control passed into the hands of a newly-appointed body of six, consisting of the Chancellor of the Exchequer, one of the principal secretaries of state and four privy councillors, collectively known as 'Commissioners for the Affairs of India.' More popularly christened the Board of Control, its members were to be paid out of the Indian revenues.

The Board had full powers of superintendence, direction and control in all matters relating to civil and military operations in India. It had access to all records of the Company, was empowered to send despatches through the Court of Directors, to change or alter those originating with the latter body, if deemed necessary, and, in cases of emergency, bypass the general body of Directors by acting through a secret committee of three members of the Court.

The changes introduced by the Act in Indian affairs were relatively less important. The Governor-General's Council was to consist of three members (instead of four) who were to be recruited only from the covenanted service. The same applied to Council appointments in other Presidencies. The Governor-General's superiority over the Presidency Governors was underlined by the fact that disobedience to his orders could lead to the suspension of the offending official.

The Act mentioned for the first time the Company's territories as 'British possessions', but stipulated that 'all schemes of conquest and extension of dominion' would not necessarily receive official countenance. The Company's servants were to refrain from fiscal transactions with Indian princes. All British offenders were to be tried by a special court of three judges, four peers and six members of the House of Commons.

Critics aver that under the new dispensation members of the Board were affiliated to and, in fact, were political appointees, their tenure dependent upon the party in power. Furthermore, the Directors, afraid of endangering their power of patronage, would ordinarily hesitate to challenge the authority of the President of the Board. Again, the Governor-General would now be responsible to two masters—the Directors as well as the Board—which made the performance of his duties difficult if not onerous. Despatches to and from India, because of this dual control, were subject to interminable delays, thereby making efficient administration impossible. Finally, parliamentary control over the Company's affairs still remained illusory, for the ministry in power kept Indian affairs farther and farther removed from the scrutiny of Parliament.

A. C. Banerjee, *Constitutional History of India,* I, pp. 123-61; M. V. Pylee, *A Short Constitutional History of India,* Bombay, 1967; Sri Ram Sharma, *A Constitutional History of India,* 2nd ed., Bombay, 1954.

Battle of Plassey (1757)

Plassey, more correctly 'Palasi' (from the Palas trees that abound in the area), is the name of a village and pargana in Kasimbazar, a bare 20 miles from Murshidabad. It is a tract of country approximating to 240 square miles in area. In June 1757 it was the scene of a battle which had historic, and far-reaching, consequences, for it helped transform a British company of merchants into territorial conquerors and set them on the road to the establishment of an empire in India. The field of Plassey no longer exists, for the site of the mango-grove and the hunting lodge have been lost in the depths of the river. By the new village of Plassey the river no longer flows, having changed its course a long way off.

The battle was fought between the British forces and those of Nawab Siraj-ud-Daulah (q.v.). The former, under Robert Clive (q.v.), numbered 613 European infantry, 100 Eurasian soldiers, 171 pieces of artillery and 2,100 Indian infantry; the latter was estimated at 35,000 infantry, 15,000 cavalry, 53 pieces of artillery under the command of forty or fifty Frenchmen. The battle itself began at 9 a.m. on 23 June 1757 and lasted until 4 p.m. when the Nawab's troops were put to flight. Considering the numbers involved, the losses on both sides were insignificant, the English casualties being 52 sepoys and 20 Europeans killed or wounded, while the Nawab's numbered about 500.

In essence, it was an unequal fight. On the one hand there was an unsteady youth like Siraj-ud-Daulah, scatter-brained and addicted to all manner of vice; on the other, an astute person like Clive, cool and calculating, whom nothing could daunt or deter. The agility and far-sightedness of the English, coupled with their unscrupulous employment of treason, intrigue and conspiracy in the enemy's camp, crippled the strength of the Nawab's army. The French contingent commanded by St. Frais and four guns occupied a position 200 yards from the British. Nearer to the river, there were 2 heavy guns

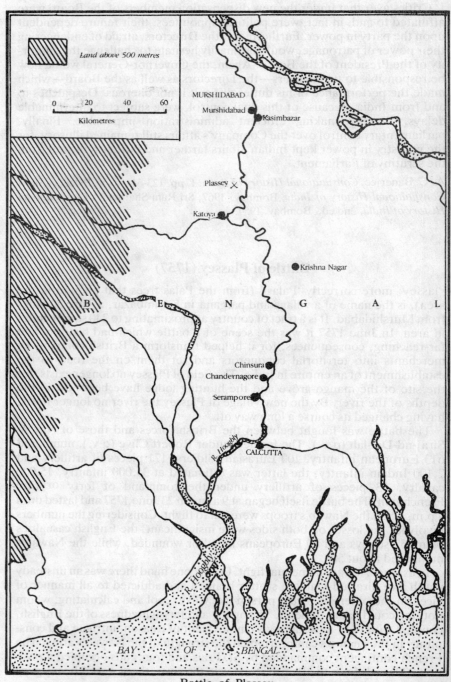

Battle of Plassey

under a 'native' officer. Only two generals, Mir Madan and Mohan Lal fought, while the other three Mir Jafar (q.v.), Yar Lutuf Khan and Rai Durlabh (q.v.), secretly in league with the John Company's (q.v.) agents, stood aside as mere spectators. Comparatively little fighting took place at Plassey and it has been described as less a 'battle' than an 'armed demonstration', an 'imposing red-coat drill of a few hours'. Clive's report on the battle was apt: 'Mir Jafar, Rai Durlabh and Yar Lutuf Khan gave us no other assistance than standing neutral....' It was, for the John Company and its intrepid commander, no mean feat. The English never rated it a great conquest; some called it a revolution, others a revolt.

Tapanmohan Chatterji, *The Road to Plassey,* Bombay, 1960, pp. 126–45; Michael Edwardes, *The Founding of an Empire,* London, 1969; Ram Gopal, *How the British Occupied Bengal,* Bombay, 1963; D. C. Verma, *Plassey to Buxar: A Military Study,* New Delhi, 1976.

Poona Sarvojanik Sabha (founded 1870)

The 'Poona Association', started in 1867, was reorganized to form the Poona Sarvojanik Sabha on 2 April 1870. Between the government and the people, it was to be something 'of a mediating body which may afford to the latter facilities for knowing the real intention and objects of government as well as adequate means for securing their rights, by making a true representation of the circumstances in which they are placed.' Its distinguishing feature was to be the representative character of its membership. A prospective member was required to produce a *mukhtiarnama* (an affidavit) signed by at least fifty adults of the place he hailed from, authorizing him to speak or act on their behalf. This requirement could be waived only under certain conditions. Provision was made for territorial and vocational representation and, to make it thoroughly democratic, the Sabha provided for the election of office-bearers for one year only at a time.

Within four months of its establishment, the Sabha claimed a membership of about 100 (who had acquired *mukhtiarnamas* from nearly 7,000 people); in a little over a year, there were 140 members representing nearly 17,000 constituents. Each member solemnly pledged that he would impartially, and according to his best judgement and ability, perform such duties as may be assigned to him.

Its constitution enjoined the Sabha to take up broadly all matters connected with the public weal—more specifically, all bills, regulations and Acts published in the government gazette; all bills of regulations, Acts, circulars and rules which were in force or which might come into force; the operation of municipalities and the management of *devasthans* (religious endowments). Any religious subject, dispute or case that affected particular individuals only did not come within its prescribed beat, nor did its rules specify any uniform annual membership fees.

The Sabha had a managing committee of not more than twenty members, elected for a one-year term. It was to convene a general body meeting every three months where 25 members were to constitute a quorum. The first president and vice-president were first-class Sardars; the former being

Shriniwas Rao Parshuram Pandit (alias Rao Saheb Pant Pratinidi), the chief of Aundh, who continued to hold that office until 1897. The annual subscription was one day's income of an individual member. A meeting of all the constituents of the Sabha, 'the electors of the *mukhtiars'*, was to be convened annually. Branches affiliated to the Sabha were established at Satara, Sholapur, Wai and Nasik.

A stronghold of the Chitpavan Brahmins during its first ten years, the Sabha soon came to represent the affluent, educated urban section of the community. It was composed of Sardars, landholders, businessmen, retired government officials, lawyers and teachers. It was also patronized by the southern Maharashtra princes. Most of its members were Hindus who, in any case, formed the bulk of the population, but there was also a fair number of Parsis, Muslims and Christians. Of the Hindus, a large majority were Brahmins, the traditional elite in Poona and the Deccan. The president and vice-president were invariably drawn from the princely chiefs, such as those of Aundh, Jamkhindi, Jat, Karandwad and Sangli. The Sabha's managing committee was dominated by superannuated government officials and lawyers; in its formative years, among the most active were G. V. Joshi (1851-1911), the eminent statesman and thinker; S. H. Sathe, a Poona lawyer; and S. H. Chiplonkar, a lawyer and journalist of Bombay and a close friend of M. G. Ranade (q.v.).

During its first few years, the Sabha made representations to various authorities on such diverse matters as procedure for recovery of costs in revenue cases, reduction of liquor shops in the city of Poona, management of the Parvati Temple endowment, the desirability of opening a vernacular school in Poona cantonment against enhancement of taxation, desirability of appointing an Indian judge to the Bombay High Court, the necessity of publishing the text of official bills and debates in the legislative councils in the vernaculars; clashes between European soldiers and Indians; and the necessity of some rules for regulating relations between Indian chiefs, their subjects and the British. In 1872, the arrival in Poona of Ranade infused new life and vigour into the Sabha; barely 30 at the time, he soon emerged as its real mentor. The life and soul of the Sabha, however, was G V. Joshi. A pleader in a local court, he was not highly educated but was a born agitator and leader. His zeal and devotion earned him the title of the 'Sabha Kaka' (literally, 'uncle of the Sabha'). Between Ranade and Joshi, the Sabha was soon to emerge as the leading association of the progressive party in western India.

In 1872 and again in 1876-8, the Sabha organized famine relief in the Deccan and won the approbation of both the people and the government. In the former year, it appointed a sub-committee of its members to conduct an elaborate inquiry into the condition of the agricultural classes in the Deccan. Later, in 1874, it raised funds for the famine-stricken population of Bengal, and in 1875 submitted a petition to the House of Commons demanding direct representation of Indians in the British Parliament. The memorial shows how educated Marathas were trying to press their demand for self-government 11 years before the birth of the Indian National Congress (q.v.). The memorial was signed by several thousand people.

The Sabha invariably espoused the cause of the Indian princes, for its members argued that the states offered scope for Indian statesmen such as Dinkar Rao (q.v.), T. Madhav Rao (q.v.) and Salar Jang (q.v.) to display their constructive ability while in British India such avenues were barred.

As from 1876, the Sabha took an active interest in organizing arbitration courts (*nyaya sabhas*) for private settlement of civil disputes without recourse to the ordinary courts of justice. The objective was two-fold: to revive the ancient institution of the panchayat and to curb the growing evil of expensive and often ruinous litigation. The arbitration courts thus established were not, however, a great success.

The Sabha was suspected by British officials, especially in the wake of its leading role in the 1875 agitation against the deposition of Malhar Rao, Gaekwad of Baroda (q.v.) and the threatened annexation of his state. Its 'representative' character and claim to speak on behalf of the people of the Deccan irked the bureaucrats. Not unexpectedly, in 1878, two prominent members of the Bombay government described the Sabha as 'a seditious association'. Convinced that Ranade was the mastermind behind it, he was transferred (early in 1878) to Nasik and from there to Dhulia, where his allegedly 'pernicious influence upon his fellow country-men' was expected to have less impact. Two years later, his promotion to the High Court bench was successfully blocked on the specious plea of his connection with the Sabha and his 'strong patriotic, national feelings'.

The leaders of the Sabha were actively involved in the confabulations which took place after A. O. Hume's (q.v.) arrival in Bombay in mid-December 1884. It is not improbable that, before he moved on to Madras early in March 1885, Hume had already persuaded the Sabha to play host to the first session of the Congress scheduled to be held in December that year. The Sabha had completed all the arrangements for this when an outbreak of cholera in the town forced the organizers, in the third week of December 1885, to shift the venue to Bombay.

How relevant the Sabha had become may be gauged from the fact that as early as 1873 it appointed a sub-committee of 12 persons to conduct an elaborate statistical survey regarding the condition of the agricultural classes, the pressure of land revenue, the increase of local and central taxation and the working of forests. Again, in 1876, it suggested the constitution of a chamber of princes, a permanent settlement of land revenue throughout British India, against increase of local and central taxation and better working of forests. The second issue of its *Journal* contained an article on a subject that is relevant even today: 'Over-population and marriage customs'.

In 1895, the Balgangadhar Tilak (q.v.) group captured almost all the key positions in the Sabha, including membership of its executive committee. Under the new management, the Sabha followed a distinctly anti-government policy; its propaganda, confined hitherto to the educated classes, was now carried to the masses. Two years later, the government declared that the Sabha 'must cease to be recognized' as a body that had 'any claim to address' it 'on questions of the public policy'. This by itself may not have mattered much had the Sabha been able to carry its propaganda work to the masses. Unfortunately, it failed to do this and its *Journal* was defunct from April 1897 to April 1916. The Sabha was so distrusted by the government that the Gaekwad of Baroda incurred official displeasure for visiting its offices in 1909!

The Sabha however continued to enjoy representation in Congress ses-sions; in 1896 Tilak attended the Party's annual session as a representative of the Sabha. After the Surat Split (q.v.), the Moderates ruled that only such political associations as were recognized by the Provincial Congress Com-mittees would be entitled to elect representatives to the party's annual sessions. In the result, the Sabha could not secure recognition till 1916. According to the Bombay police records, in July 1919 the Sabha played host to Gandhi (q.v.), when Tilak was present.

The Sabha made common cause with the British Indian Association (q.v.) and the Indian Association (q.v.) on many occasions. Along with the latter, the Sabha took the unprecedented step of issuing appeals to the free electors of Great Britain and Ireland on behalf of the unrepresented millions of India beseeching them to return candidates belonging to the Liberal party to the new Parliament.

In 1887, the Sabha's *Journal* published a vigorous plea for reforming the jury system in India. In 1888, it sent a memorandum regarding certain affairs in the Poona Government High School. Another victory for the Sabha was to secure representation for Central Division (Poona) in the Bombay Legislative Council.

In its issue of 1916, the Sabha's *Journal* computed that during the 25 years of its existence it had addressed 108 letters, petitions and memoranda to the government; 'of these 64 failed to elicit any kind of reply, 28 were answered by something like a formal acknowledgement and only 16 were honoured by any sort of official notice'. The Sabha's views were however accepted with alacrity by a large proportion of the educated classes. It acted as a sounding-board for public opinion, while the standard of articles published in its *Journal* was quite high.

Biman Behari Majumdar, *Indian Political Associations and Reform of Legislature, (1818-1917),* Calcutta, 1965, pp. 106-30; S. R. Mehrotra, *The Emergence of the Indian National Congress,* New Delhi, 1973.

Treaty of Poona (1817)

The British were apprehensive lest Peshwa Baji Rao II (q.v.), in collusion with his favourite minister Trimbakji Danglia who had escaped from their custody, stir up anti-British sentiments as well as strengthen his army for hostile action. Determined to render him incapable of creating further trouble, the John Company (q.v.) threatened that the Peshwa would be seized and his country occupied if he did not comply with their fresh demands. With little or no alternative open to him, the Maratha leader gave way. A new compact was accordingly drawn up and signed on 13 June 1817; it was ratified on 7 July (1817). In essence, it was a supplement to the earlier Treaty of Bassein (q.v.).

According to the terms of this 18-article compact, the Peshwa (i) declared Trimbakji responsible for the murder of Gangadhar Shastri, the Gaekwad's plenipotentiary (who had earlier repaired to Poona under a British safe conduct to negotiate with the Maratha chief) and promised to arrest and deliver him to the Company; (ii) engaged not to admit into his territory any subject of a European or an American power without the previous consent of the British; (iii) recognized the dissolution 'in form and substance of the Maratha confederacy' and renounced all connections with its chiefs; (iv) surrendered all past claims on the Gaekwad in return for an annual payment of Rs. 4 lakhs; (v) agreed to rent the Ahmadnagar farm to the Gaekwad for Rs 4½ lakhs annually; (vi) gave up in perpetuity the fort of **Ahmadnagar** to the East India Company and renounced his rights and interests over Bundelkhand, in Malwa and all his possessions north of the Narmada; (vii) engaged 'never more' to interfere in the affairs of Hindustan; (viii) agreed to pay to the British for the upkeep of a force of 5,000 cavalry, 3,000 infantry and a due proportion of ordnance and military stores.

Attached to the Treaty was a schedule of the 'lands and revenues' ceded in perpetuity in terms of its seventh article. It was also stipulated that all the articles in the Treaty of Bassein, not contrary to the new compact, stood confirmed.

For the Peshwa, the Treaty of Poona was a heavy cross to carry. Indeed, so harsh were the terms he now accepted that the Peshwa considered this an enormous price for the Company's dubious alliance. He found himself hemmed in far too tightly under a yoke that was extremely galling to bear. Elphinstone (q.v.) has expressed the view that the terms 'could not have been harsh' if made at the end of a successful campaign and that 'no independent prince' could have submitted to them 'unless compelled by force of arms'. It may be noted that many of the Peshwa's adherents had urged him to take recourse to arms instead of submitting, that 'sullenly' he ratified the Treaty, protesting he had accepted it for want of power to resist. In the final count, the Treaty achieved merely a postponement of hostilities which culminated in the Third Anglo-Maratha War (q.v.) that was to break out a few months later.

Aitchison, III, pp. 79–88; P. C. Gupta, *Baji Rao & the East India Company, 1796-1818*, rev. ed., New Delhi, 1964, pp. 165-7; Dodwell, *CHI*, V, p. 379.

Dr Rajendra Prasad (1884–1963)

Rajendra Prasad was born on 3 December 1884 in an obscure village in the Saran district of north Bihar. His great uncle, Chandhur Lal, had built the family fortunes in terms of a great zamindari. His father, Mahadev Sahay, was a country gentleman, a scholar of Persian and Arabic and interested in wrestling and horticulture. His devout mother, Kamleshwari Devi, fed the young boy on stories from the Ramayana. Later in life the great epic became Prasad's constant companion, though he also browsed through the Upanishads and other scriptures as well. His father shunned ostentation, lived simply and mixed freely with people in the village.

At the age of 5, Rajendra Prasad was put under a Maulvi to learn Persian; later he moved on to Hindi and arithmetic. At 18, he passed the entrance examination of Calcutta University, securing the first position in the first division. At Presidency College, Calcutta, he took a first in the M. A. and a first in the LL.M. He impressed the University's Vice-Chancellor, Sir

Asutosh Mookerjee (1864-1924) so deeply that the latter offered him a lecturership in Presidency Law College. In 1911, Prasad started his law practice at Calcutta; he shifted to Patna in 1916 when the High Court for Bihar and Orissa moved there. His transparent honesty and sincerity above all soon made him attain a marked ascendancy in the profession.

Long before he met Gandhi (q.v.), the Swadeshi Movement (q.v.) and the Dawn Society (founded by S. C. Mukherjee to help students) had deeply influenced Prasad. He helped Gandhi in the Champaran satyagraha in 1917 and participated in the Non-cooperation Movement (q.v.) campaigns of 1919 and 1921-2. Forsaking his legal practice, he became Principal of National College in Bihar, edited nationalist newspapers and mobilized peasant support for the movement. In the 1920's he was a spokesman for the 'No Change' group, which wholeheartedly supported Gandhi's constructive programme, particularly the production of hand-spun khadi.

Prasad was in jail when, on 15 January 1934, a devastating earthquake overtook Bihar. He was released two days later; though still ailing, he set himself immediately the task of raising funds and organizing relief. His fund swelled to Rs. 38 lakhs and was administered with model efficiency.

In 1937, along with Maulana Azad (q.v.) and Vallabhbhai Patel (q.v.), Prasad was a member of the Congress parliamentary board entrusted with the task of supervising the work of Congress ministries in the eight Governor's Provinces ruled by the party. In the Interim Government (q.v.) inducted into office in September 1946, he held the Food and Agriculture portfolio. He gave the country the now well-known slogan 'Grow More Food', even though he was in office for just about a year. Had he continued longer, he may well have zealously pursued his plans for the development of the country's cattle wealth on scientific lines and mobilized the resources of the government as well as support of the people for such programmes.

As President of the Constituent Assembly (q.v.), Prasad guided, regulated and controlled with infinite patience, skill, grace and firmness the full, free and frank discussions in the House on the future constitutional set-up of the country. On his election as President of the Constituent Assembly, Dr. S. Radhakrishnan had said of Prasad: 'He is the soul of goodness, he has great patience and courage, he has suffered . . . Rajendra Prasad is the suffering servant of India.'

On 26 January 1950, Prasad was chosen interim President of India; in May 1952, he was formally elected to the office. Five years later, in May 1957, he was re-elected for a second term. As President, Prasad exercised his moderating influence, moulding policies and actions silently yet unobtrusively. He was, to all outward appearances, so self-effacing that many thought that during his tenure he neither reigned nor yet ruled. In all his work, Prasad often drew upon the words and achievements of his mentor, Gandhi and gave importance to the need for more extensive educational programmes, particularly the implementation of the Mahatma's Basic Education Scheme (q.v.).

Prasad retired in September 1962. An illness in 1961 had completely shattered his health. The death of his wife, Rajbansi Devi, early in September 1962, was a great shock. Frail and an invalid for a long time, she had been the very embodiment of the spirit of renunciation, selflessness, self-effacement and devotion. His own health had been indifferent and shocks, both personal as well as national, shook him completely. He died on 28 February 1963.

Prasad's innate integrity and purity of character were phenomenal and his admirers a legion. Sarojini Naidu (1879-1949) said that he was to Gandhi what John was to Christ. Jawaharlal Nehru (q.v.) called him 'the symbol of Bharat' and found 'truth looking at you through those eyes'. Gandhi said of him, 'there is at least one man who would not hesitate to take the cup of poison from my hands'. Prasad shared the Mahatma's great vision, the making of a new man in a new society. In Rajendra Prasad, it has been said, Gandhi saw a great deal of himself: his living faith in god, his humility of spirit, his habit of disinterested action and his devotion to dharma.

Rajendra Prasad made a success of whatever he took up. As a student, he was brilliant and won many scholarships despite his ill health. In the legal profession, he had risen to the front rank without influence or patronage. In social service, he had proved himself to be earnest, sincere and indefatigable.

Prasad's outstanding book in Hindi is his *Atmakatha,* once adjudged the best autobiography in that language. The talks he gave in jail were later published as *Gandhiji ki den.* His other works include *Champaran Satyagraha*; *Bapu ke kadmon men*; *Sahitya, shikshan aur sanskriti* and *Bharatiya shikshan.* Written in lucid Hindi, they also reveal his scholarship in the Persian, Sanskrit and Bengali languages and bear the impress of a warm personality. Among his works in English, his *Autobiography* (1957), *At the Feet of Mahatama Gandhi,* and *India Divided* (1946) bear mention.

Of his colleagues in politics, Prasad was closest to Sardar Patel. They had much in common; both had sprung from the soil and spent their childhood in the village; both achieved distinction at the bar. Simple and unassuming in manner, Prasad looked like a peasant—a typical son of the soil. His benevolent appearance reflected his goodwill towards all. Although his mind was capable of broad sweeps, it rarely omitted even the smallest of details.

Kewal Panjabi, *Rajendra Prasad, First President of India,* London, 1960; Rajendra Prasad, *Autobiography* (translated), Bombay, 1957.

The Indian Press

Before 1835 the printing of books and newspapers in India was subject to the issue of a licence by the Governor-General in Council; licences were issued or relaxed at the government's discretion. Act XI of 1835 merely required registration of the printer and stipulated a few other minor requirements. This was replaced in 1867 by the Press and Registration of Books Act. During Ripon's (q.v.) administration, Lytton's (q.v.) controversial Vernacular Press Act (q.v.) was repealed. From 1882 to 1907 there was no direct press legislation *per se,* sedition being dealt with by the adoption, in 1898, of Section 124A of the Penal Code. Additionally, Section 153A was introduced in the Penal Code and Section 108 into the Civil Procedure Code. In 1908 the Newspapers (Incitement to Offences) Act (q.v.), dealing with news reports and comment inciting people to murder or acts of violence, was passed. The

Indian Press Act of 1910 (q.v.) was wider in scope; its aim was to keep the press generally within the limits of legitimate discussion. Together, however, both the 1908 and 1910 Acts led to the closure of several presses and newspapers.

Broadly, the press in India was an English institution. The first newspaper appeared in Calcutta in January 1780—the Regulating Act (q.v.) itself having been passed only seven years earlier. In 1789 Bombay's first newspaper was published, the *Bombay Herald;* it was soon followed by the *Bombay Courier.* Later, in 1861, the *Courier* was to be amalgamated with the *Times of India.* The first Calcutta newspaper was the weekly *Bengal Gazette,* also called the *Calcutta General Advertiser,* though best known as 'Hickey's Gazette' or 'Journal', after the name of its founder, J. A. Hickey. It turned out to be essentially a medium for publishing gross scandal and soon disappeared. Another, the *Indian Gazette,* lasted nearly 50 years; in 1833, it merged with the *Bengal Harkaru.* The *Calcutta Gazette,* which commenced publication in 1784, later became the official gazette of the Bengal government. In 1821 a syndicate of European officials and merchants began publication of *John Bull in the East,* a daily which provided a faithful mirror of Tory opinion in Britain. In 1836, its name was changed to the *Englishman.*

Understandably, the Company's administration was extremely sensitive to all public criticism. During 1791-9, several editors were deported without trial to Europe and some were censured and had to apologise. In 1801, the government promulgated stringent rules for the press and instituted an official censor. This continued until 1818 when the Governor-General, Marquess of Hastings (q.v.), abolished censorship and made the rules milder. After Hastings, both Amherst (q.v.) and Bentinck (q.v.) were liberal and mild. Metcalfe (q.v.), who briefly succeeded Bentinck, brought about what has been called the emancipation of the press and removed all restrictions imposed on it.

The first vernacular newspaper appeared in 1818, the *Samachar Darpan* in Bengali. Its promoters were the well-known Serampore missionaries—William Ward, William Carey and Joshua Marshman. In 1830, a Gujarati newspaper, the *Bombay Samachar,* was brought out; it still exists. From 1835 to 1857 the press sprouted in other metropolitan towns—Delhi, Agra, Gwalior and Lahore. Canning's (q.v.) infamous (Gagging) Act No. XII of 1857, which restored the system of licenses in addition to the existing registration procedure, and whose aim was to control vernacular journalism remained in force only for a year. Nevertheless, the Act's victims included the *Bengal Harkaru,* owned by Dwarkanath Tagore; the Indian printers and publishers of *Doorbeen,* the *Sultan ul Akhbar* and the *Samachar Sudhaburshan,* who were prosecuted in the Calcutta Supreme Court for publishing allegedly seditious matter. Of the 33 popular publications extant in 1853, only six survived the Rebellion of 1857 (q.v.). At the time there were 30 newspapers in the North-Western Provinces of Agra and Oudh alone. For most part, they were published in Urdu and edited by Muslims; only three are known to have survived the Rebellion.

In 1858 Canning established an 'Editors Room' which journalists could visit to examine official papers relating to the public interest. Some official papers were printed and pasted on notice boards while others were attached to the official gazette for public information. Metcalfe's Press Act No. XI of 1835, a great liberator of the press, was repealed by Act No. XXV of 1867 which was designed ostensibly for the regulation of printing units and newspapers. With slight alterations, it is still in force.

In 1864, John Lawrence (q.v.) revived the idea of a government newspaper; his successor, Mayo (q.v.), discussed it with Whitehall. In the result, not a newspaper but Act XXVII of 1870 became law. *Inter alia*, it ruled that 'Whoever by words either spoken or intended to be read or by signs or by visible representation or otherwise, excites or attempts to excite feelings of dissatisfaction to the government established by law in British India shall be punished by transportation for life for any term, to which fine may be added; or with imprisonment for a term which may extend to three years, to which fine may be added, or with fine.' All the provisions of this section were later incorporated in the Indian Penal Code, as Section 124A.

With Lytton's Vernacular Press Act IX of 1878 becoming law, the language press all over India, was muzzled. Ostensibly designed for the better control of publications in different languages, it was a great blow to the freedom of the press and more specifically the language newspapers, which suffered heavily. The Viceroy's Council was divided on the issue and some members wrote strong minutes of dissent. Gladstone opposed it vehemently in the British Parliament.

In order to 'keep the press fully posted which accurate and current information', Lytton instituted the office of Press Counsellor for India, Sir Robert Lethbridge being its first incumbent. His function was to supply correct, early and accurate information with regard to public measures, to act as a liaison between the government and the Indian language press.

The immediate effect of the Vernacular Press Act was felt by the *Amrit Bazar Patrika,* a bilingual daily published in English and Bengali; to evade the rigours of the law, it became a full-fledged English daily. The *Hindu* was born on 20 September 1876 largely to protest against Lytton's Act in the south; in 1883, it was converted from a weekly to a tri-weekly.

The birth of the Indian National Congress (q.v.) heralded a new era in the history of journalism. The *Illustrated Weekly* (1878) was born in Bombay and *Capital* founded in Calcutta as a commercial and financial weekly (in 1888). Special interests were served by *Indian Engineering, Eastern Engineer* and the *Asian and Indian Planters' Gazette.* Sachidananda Sinha founded in 1899, and edited the *Hindustan Review,* a monthly devoted to a review of matters of political, historical and literary interest.

The public postal service established in 1870 provided for a uniform rate of payment irrespective of distance. Invention of the electric telegraph, of paper-making machinery and the laying of cables between India and Great Britain followed; the Suez Canal was opened in 1869. Soon came the invention of a printing press operated by steam power. All these developments did not overly benefit Indian newspapers because of their limited resources and circulation, but the *Statesman* was the first to import a rotary printing machine. *Reuter's* office in India was established in 1866, but the formation of *Associated Press of India* was a deathblow to the system of special correspondents who soon disappeared. *API* reports were viewed as biased and the agency dubbed a purveyor of official news, the activities of commercial magnates, big landlords and other vested interests.

The twentieth century witnessed a new era in the growth of the press. G. A. Natesan (1873-1949) of Madras started a monthly, the *Indian Review,* in 1900. He specialized in editing and publishing numerous political biographies of outstanding Indians. C. Y. Chintamani (1880-1941) and N. C. Kelkar (1872-1947) were among the budding journalists; the latter edited B. G. Tilak's (q.v.) *Kesari* and the *Mahratta.* The *Bombay Chronicle,* inspired by Pherozeshah Mehta (q.v.), was launched on 3 March 1913. An Englishman, Benjamin Guy Horniman, who had worked with the *Manchester Guardian* and the *Statesman,* became its editor and identified himself with most of the Indian nationalist causes. Of the *Leader* (Allahabad), Pandit Madan Mohan Malaviya (q.v.) was the chief organizer. It was essentially a mouthpiece of the Liberals, including Pherozeshah Mehta, Gokhale (qq.v.), and Dinshaw Wacha.

With a view to popularizing her Home Rule League (q.v.), Annie Besant (q.v.) bought the *Madras Standard* and re-christened it *New India.* It was widely accepted that she was 'an enthusiastic, devoted, idealistic and supremely earnest journalist' despite her political preoccupations. She pioneered a course in journalism at her 'National University' at Adyar in Madras. However, three days after World War I, Ordinance I was promulgated to secure 'the control of the press during the war' and 'to control the publication of naval and military news and information'.

The *Servant of India* made its appearance on 18 February 1918 with V. S. Srinivasa Sastri as its first editor. Its appearance marked the third death anniversary of Gokhale. In 1919, Motilal Nehru (q.v.) started the *Independent* which lasted a bare four years; another newspaper to come into being as a result of the 1919 Montford Reforms (q.v.) was the *Hindustan Times.* The *Servant of India* continued till 1939, its last editor being S. G. Vaze. Gandhi (q.v.) was another eminent nationalist to nourish the world of journalism: in South Africa the Mahatma had founded *Indian Opinion.* Back in India, he established *Young India,* an English weekly with its Gujarati counterpart, *Navajivan. Young India,* which accepted no advertisements, soon touched a circulation of 45,000.

Meantime, a Hindi daily, the *Aj,* supporting the Congress programme and patterned on the London *Times,* was established on 5 September 1920. It 'set the standard for Hindi journalism' while consciousness of Hindi gave a fresh impetus' to Hindi journalists. To support the Swarajists and their objective of entering the legislatures, the *Hindustan Times* had Sardar K. M. Panikkar (1895-1963) as its first editor. The original owners were Sikhs— actually, Akali funds had been used, for the need was felt to advocate Sikh reform and strengthen the revolutionary movement. The Akalis did not keep the paper long and sold it to a group of Swarajist leaders who, in turn, constituted a company to run it as the official organ of the Swaraj Party (q.v.).

The first national news agency, the *Free Press of India,* was established in 1927. Among its sponsors were Annie Besant, M. R. Jayakar, Purshotamdas Thakurdas (1879–1962), G. D. Birla (1894–1983) and Walchand Hirachand, with S. Sadanand as the managing editor.

To 'provide for the better control of the Press', the Indian Press Ordinance was promulgated in 1930. The Ordinance spread its net wide in curbing the freedom of the press, for the definition of an offence was made more comprehensive. Press reaction took the form of a meeting of editors under the chairmanship of A. Rangaswamy Iyengar (1877-1934), editor of the *Hindu*. The government did not budge. N. C. Kelkar of *Kesari* was fined Rs 5,000 for contempt of court while the *Bombay Chronicle* forfeited a security of Rs 15,000 for criticising a magistrate. In princely India, the Indian States (Protection Against Disaffection) Act was mercilessly used to curb the hostility of the press. Lord Willingdon, then Viceroy, promulgated six notorious ordinances to control the Civil Disobedience Movement (q.v.). One such was the Indian Press (Emergency Powers) Act of 1931, 'an Act to provide against the publication of matter inciting to or encouraging murder or violence'. The powers conferred on the executive were very wide and the curbs imposed included prohibition of the publication of any kind of Congress propaganda, including messages from persons arrested or jailed. Securities were demanded from almost all papers which had pledged support to the Congress—the *Bombay Chronicle, Ananda Bazar Patrika, Amrita Bazar Patrika* and *Free Press Journal* were among the principal targets.

1932 saw two more Acts: the Criminal Law Amendment Act No. XXIII which amended the 1931 Act by (a) embodying all those phrases incorporated in the 1930 ordinance which the Act had originally omitted and (b) making the Act permanent. The Government controls were more or less the same as in 1910. The second was the Foreign Relations Act to provide 'against the publication of statements likely to prejudice party relations between H M G and the Goverments of certain foreign states'.

During the Civil Disobedience Movement of 1930, unauthorized, undeclared and unregistered mimeographed news-sheets were common; these contained news about satyagraha and details of all such activities as had been banned. Among nationalist papers, the *Indian Express* appeared in 1933, and *Dinamani* (in Tamil); both were established in Madras. *Harijan*, a weekly in English, appeared on 11 February 1933. The paper was soon self-supporting and Hindi and Gujarati editions were planned. The *Hindustan Standard* and *Jugantar* were founded in 1937 in Calcutta, the *Star of India* was also started there to support the All-India Muslim League (q.v.). *Dawn*, founded by M. A. Jinnah (q.v.), had Pothan Joseph (1894-1972) as its editor. The *Hindustan*, a Hindi counterpart of the *Hindustan Times*, was established about this time, while *Blitz*, a weekly, appeared in Bombay, in 1941.

In 1939, the Indian and Eastern Newspaper Society was founded. Among its principal aims the following may be listed: to act as a central organ of the press of India, Burma and Ceylon; to promote and safeguard the business interests of its members as affected by the legislatures, governments, law courts, municipal and local bodies; to collect information on any topic of practical interest for members and communicate it to them; to promote co-operation in all matters affecting their common interests; to make rules to govern the conduct of members and ensure that no infringement takes place; to maintain a permanent secretariat; and to help the interchange of views.

Rule 41 of the Defence of India Rules (1939) applied to the press. It required that, 'for the defence of British India and the efficient prosecution' of the War, 'any matter shall before being published be submitted for scrutiny to an authority specified'; it also 'prohibited or regulated the printing or publishing or the use of any printing press.'

In 1930 the Press Ordinance had netted securities worth a total of Rs. 2,40,000 and struck at 131 newspapers. Over 450 papers ceased to exist in 1935 as they could not afford to deposit the securities demanded. In the same year, about 72 newspapers were awarded penalties and a sum exceeding Rs. 1 lakh was asked to be paid as securities. Only 15 newspapers chose to deposit the sum demanded to keep their publications alive. In August 1942, the government suspended 96 newspapers and journals and demanded heavy securities within a period of three weeks following the start of the Quit India Movement (q.v.).

In 1940, a conference of editors was called at Delhi by K. Srinivasan (1887-1959) of the *Hindu* with a view to discussing the restrictions imposed by the government under the Defence of India Rules. At a subsequent meeting, the All-India Newspapers Editors' Conference (AINEC) was born; its aim was to meet the extraordinary situation created by the government's panicky order of 26 October 1940 imposing severe restrictions on the press. The AINEC adopted a constitution with the following objectives: to preserve high traditions and standards; to serve and safeguard the interests of the press in regard to the publication of news and comment; to secure facilities and privileges for the discharge of its responsibilities; to represent the press in its relations with public and private institutions; to establish contact with associations with similar objectives in other countries.

In August 1942 the government placed further restrictions on the press. *Inter alia*, it ordered (a) the registration of correspondents; (b) limitation on the number of messages regarding civil disturbances; (c) prohibition of news regarding acts of sabotage; (d) limitations on the headlines and space given to news on disturbances; (e) compulsory press advice; and (f) arbitrary censorship. Several newspapers protested and stopped publication, among them the *Harijan, National Herald* and *Indian Express*. In the result, the standing committee of the AINEC negotiated with the government to have the restrictions withdrawn. The latter's failure to do so led to an all-India newspaper strike, as a result of which no newspaper or magazine was published on 6 January 1943. The press also resolved not to give publicity to (a) all circulars from Government Houses; (b) New Year Honours list; (c) speeches of members of the British government, the Government of India and provincial governments. Thanks to this demonstration of solidarity, the government's prohibitory orders were withdrawn six days later and, in response, the press ban on government news ceased to be operative.

The 1945-6 outbreak of communal violence compelled many provincial governments to promulgate ordinances arming themselves with special powers. These were later enacted into law by special legislation. To this there was no serious objection from the press in India.

The principal objective of the standing committee of the AINEC, which was broadly representative of editors of English as well as Indian-language newspapers and news agencies, was to keep itself in touch with the Government of India. Its meetings were generally attended by an official spokesman or representative. Provincial press advisory committees functioned in most provinces and a senior official or minister in the Home Department kept himself informed of developments. From time to time a procedure was laid down by these committees regarding the constraints to be observed in the publication and dissemination of matter affecting the country's peace and security.

On 15 March 1947 the government appointed a committee of official and non-official members to review press laws and suggest reform. While provincial governments were in favour of the retention of existing laws and even of tightening them, journalist opinion on the whole seemed unfavourable. The committee submitted its report on 19 August 1948 and recommended *inter alia* the repeal of the Indian Press (Emergency Powers) Act, 1931, even though some of its provisions were to be incorporated into the ordinary law of the land. Among its other recommendations the following may be listed: exemption of the press from Section 144 of the criminal law and the adoption of a separate law, if deemed necessary, for dealing with the press in urgent cases of apprehended danger; annulment of Section124A, of the Indian Penal Code, so that only incitement to violence against government established by law be treated as sedition.

Nadig Krishna Murthy, *Indian Journalism: Origin, Growth & Development of Indian Journalism from Asoka to Nehru,* Mysore, 1966, pp. 49-111; Margarita Barns, *The Indian Press: A History of the Growth of Public Opinion in India,* London, 1940; S. Natarajan, *A History of the Press in India,* Bombay, 1962.

Chamber of Princes (1921–47)

In the years following the Rebellion of 1857 (q.v.), the need had been felt for a joint consultative machinery that would bring the Indian government and the Indian princes together to discuss matters of common interest. Lytton (q.v.) had proposed the establishment of an 'Imperial Privy Council', Curzon (q.v.) a 'Council of Ruling Princes' and Minto (q.v.) an 'Advisory Council' of rulers and big landholders: none of these suggestions, however, found favour in Whitehall for one reason or another.

However, World War I and the mobilization of resources in the Indian States (q.v.) brought a sea change in the situation. The result was that both under Hardinge (q.v.) as well as Chelmsford (q.v.), conferences of rulers became a regular feature. The need was now increasingly felt for a permanent institution to give the rulers an 'opportunity of informing the government as to their sentiments and wishes, of broadening their outlook and of conferring with one another and with the government'.

In so far as constitutional reforms were being contemplated in terms of the August (1917) Declaration (q.v.), the Montford Report had recommended the institution of a 'Council of Princes' whose opinion could be 'of the utmost value'. In its wake, 'a permanent cousultative body', the Chamber of Princes, became an integral part of the 1919 Montagu-Chelmsford Reforms (q.v.).

Brought into being by a Royal Proclamation which promised, *inter alia,* that the 'privileges, rights and dignities' of the princes would remain unimpaired', the Chamber was inaugurated on 8 February 1921 by the King's brother, the Duke of Connaught, at the Diwan-i-Am of the Red Fort in Delhi. The royal message read on the occasion assured the Chamber that, 'My Viceroy will take its counsel freely in matters relating to the territories of Indian States generally and in matters that affect these territories jointly with British India or with the rest of my Empire. It will have no concern with the internal affairs of individual States or their Rulers or with the relation of individual States with my Government, while the existing rights of these States and their freedom of action will in no way be prejudiced or impaired.'

The Viceroy was to be President of the Chamber and its members were to elect annually a Chancellor and a Pro-Chancellor from among their own ranks. There was to be a Standing Committee consisting of 7 members, including the Chancellor and the Pro-Chancellor. The Chamber was to comprise, in the first place, 108 rulers who were to be members in their own right. Status-wise, all of them were entitled to 11 or more gun salutes. There were to be 12 additional members elected by the rulers of 127 non-salute states. There was also a third category of such members as 'qualified' in the Viceroy's opinion.

Earlier, when the problem of codification of political practice became a live issue in the wake of World War I and the August Declaration, a committee comprising 6 Rulers, the Law Member of the Governor-General's Council and Secretary of the Political Department, was constituted to look into it. In 1921, with the Chamber coming into being, this work was entrusted to its Standing Committee.

Even though provision had been made for joint deliberations of the Chamber with the Council of State, the upper house of legislature at the centre, no such meeting between the two in fact ever took place. The result was that the gradual bringing together of the states and British India remained a pious hope.

The promulgation of the Government of India Act, 1935 (q.v.) was followed by protracted negotiations with the princes to accede to the federation contemplated under it. During these parleys, the draft of the proposed Instrument of Accession underwent several changes for the worse. The princes' approach to the problem was governed by the view that, while their accession to the federation involved a process of levelling down so far as their internal sovereignty was concerned, it was a process of levelling up for the provinces as semi-autonomous units. They argued that the provinces and the states could not thus be treated alike. While the stalemate persisted, World War II broke out (3 Sept 1939) and Lord Linlithgow (q.v.) announced abandonment of the federal scheme until after it was over.

The Nawab of Bhopal as Chancellor of the Chamber of Princes in 1944 made a major, but unsuccesful, effort to forge that body into an effective instrument for developing the rulers into a 'third force' between political parties in British India on the one hand and the government on the other.

As outlined above, the Chamber was 'a deliberative, a consultative and advisory but *not* an executive body.' Its establishment did not affect the individual relations between any state and the representative of the Crown. It could not discuss 'treaties and internal affairs of individual States, rights and interests, dignities and powers, privileges and prerogatives of individual Princes and Chiefs, their States and the members of their families, and the actions of individual Rulers'. Its real import lay in the fact that it marked the end of the paramount power's policy of treating each state as an isolated unit apart from its neighbours, but its political relevance diminished because some important states—such as Mysore and Hyderabad—held aloof.

With the lapse of Paramountcy (q.v.) following the transfer of power to the dominions of India and Pakistan on 15 August 1947, the Chamber of Princes was wound up.

White Paper on Indian States, New Delhi, 1950, pp. 20-1; *A. C. Banerjee,* III, pp. 88-9.

Public Service Commission (1886)

To mollify and conciliate educated Indian public opinion and pacify the persistent demand for greater employment opportunities in the administration, a 15-member commission headed by Sir Charles Aitchison (q.v.), then Lieutenant-Governor of the Panjab, was appointed in 1886. Its other members included a trained English lawyer; six incumbents of the covenanted service; a representative each of the non-official European and Eurasian communities; a member of the uncovenanted civil service, and six Indians selected from various provinces as 'sufficiently representative of the different classes and modes of thought'.

Initially, the government's resolution of 4 November 1886 had called for an inquiry into employment of Indians in the posts ordinarily reserved for the covenanted service and in the executive and judicial branches of the uncovenanted service. At a later stage, it held an inquiry into questions relating to such special departments as Accounts, Archaeological Survey, Customs, Education, Forests, Geological Survey, Jails, Meteorological Survey, Mint, Opium, Pilot Service, Post Office and Telegraph, Police, Public Works, Registration, Salt and Survey. The second part of its inquiry, held under a resolution of 8 March 1887, also embraced the question of admission of Indians and Europeans to these services. The objective was to devise 'a scheme which may reasonably be hoped to possess the necessary elements of finality and to do full justice to the claims of Natives of India to higher and more extensive employment in the public service'. Questions relating to the induction of English candidates into the I.C.S. were outside its purview.

After examining witnesses at length, the Aitchison Commission submitted its report on 23 December 1887 and recommended, *inter alia,* that no major departure be made from the policy enunciated in the Queen's Proclamation of 1858 eschewing all racial disqualifications. The existing covenanted civil service, which the Commission had proposed to designate as the Imperial Civil Service and later, in deference to the views of the Secretary of State, called the Indian Civil Service, was to stay. Recruitment was to be made by competition in England, the service being open, without distinction of race, to all natural-born subjects of Her Majesty. The lower and upper age limits for entry were to be 19 and 23 years respectively.

The uncovenanted service was to be called the Provincial Civil Service—later distinguished by the name of the province viz., the 'Panjab Civil Service', the 'Bombay Civil Service', etc. Recruitment was to be made separately in each province by a competitive examination, promotion from the subordinate services, or a combination of the two. The P.C.S was to hold the higher appointments of the existing uncovenanted service, together with a certain number of appointments then ordinarily reserved by law, or practice, for the covenanted civil service which were now to be transferred.

The Commission recommended the abolition of direct recruitment for the specially transferred I. C. S. posts and directed that these be filled from senior personnel of the P.C.S. 108 covenanted posts were to be thus transferred. This figure, which was arrived at on the basis of one-sixth of the appointments made under the statutory rules, was to be excluded from the Schedule to the Act of 1861. With a view to meeting the requirements of changing conditions, the Commission recommended an amendment of the Act of 1861 in such a way as to give power to the Secretary of State, subject to the control of Parliament, to make from time to time such alterations in the Schedule as might be deemed necessary.

The continuance of the London test was strongly defended; the Commission's stand against the proposal for simultaneous examinations was unequivocal. The paramount consideration appeared to be to maintain a strong, permanent official English element in India for which, it felt, the competition in England provided the surest guarantee. It rejected the suggestion for a separate examination in London for Indian candidates, as distinct from European candidates.

The Commission ruled that the Statutory Civil Service (q.v.), introduced under the rules formulated in 1879, be abolished. It further recommended that its incumbents be absorbed into the P.C.S.

The recommendations of the Aitchison Commission, which the government accepted, imparted a finality to the structure of the public service that emerged in the 1890s and at the turn of the century. The Commission may be said to have fulfilled its purpose by devising a scheme for the division of the general administrative staff into three branches, the Indian Civil Service, the Provincial Civil Service and the Subordinate Civil Service, which has been sustained almost to the present day. The objective of filling by promotion from the P.C.S. one-sixth of the posts, so far set apart for the I.C.S., was not, however, fully attained. By 1923 there were only 88 listed posts out of a total of 700 superior posts, and not the full quota of 116, which the P.C.S. would have held had the proportion been worked out fully. On 1 January 1930, the number, now increased, was 153.

The effect of the new scheme was nevertheless to admit to higher appointments selected officers of the P.C.S. The channel of entrance into the I.C.S. was open, as noted above, to Indian candidates of a younger age, whose admission to it was facilitated by raising upper age limit for the examination from 19 years to 23.

The Commission's findings were not popular with educated Indians whose status, it was argued, remained essentially unchanged. The provincial and subordinate services occupied an inferior position while the reservation of higher posts exclusively for Europeans created a *corps d' elite*. The Commission envisaged a 'delay of at least a generation' before its proposals would be fully implemented, but the fact is that as noticed, until 1923, only 88 covenanted posts had been transferred to the provinces!

It may be recalled that political activity in India began largely as part of an agitation to secure increasing employment opportunities for Indians in the 'superior services' of the government. To start with, such activity related to Indians versus Europeans and Anglo-Indians, but soon it extended to Hindus versus Muhammadans with repercussions filtering down as political democracy expanded in scope and content.

B. B. Misra, *The Administrative History of India, 1834-1947: General Administration.* Oxford, 1970; Hira Lal Singh, *Problems and Policies of the British in India 1885-98,* Bombay, 1963, pp, 44–9; L. S. S. O'Malley, *The Indian Civil Service, 1601–1930,* 2nd ed., London, 1965, pp. 216-19.

Treaty of Purandhar (1776)

In return for some territorial gains, the Bombay Presidency decided to lend its support in 1773 to Raghunath Rao's (q.v.) claims to the Peshwaship, promising *inter alia* to assist him with troops against the army of the ruling Maratha faction at Poona. This was done without informing or taking the prior approval of the Bengal government which, under the Regulating Act (q.v.), had nominally become the supreme executive authority in regard to the two other Presidencies. The Calcutta Council unanimously disapproved of Bombay's decision calling it 'unjust, impolitic and unauthorized'; it asked Bombay to reopen negotiations with the ruling group in the Peshwa's court and despatched Lieutenant-Colonel John Upton as its envoy to oversee arrangements.

On 1 January 1776, Upton met the Peshwa's representatives, Sakharam Bapu and Nana Phadnis (q.v.), at Purandhar, a hill fort 20 miles to the south-east of Poona. Protracted negotiations ensued, the Marathas refusing to let the British retain the territories they had occupied. On 1 March, when a resumption of hostilities appeared to be certain, the Maratha ministers gave way and signed a treaty. It was ratified by the Calcutta Council in May 1776.

The principal terms of the Treaty were: (i) The John Company (q.v.) was to restore Salsette (q.v.) and its surrounding islands subject to the approval of the Governor-General in Council; in case the latter agreed, the Peshwa was to give, 'in exchange', territory near Broach worth Rs 3 lakhs as *chauth*. Broach and its revenues were ceded to the Company in perpetuity; (ii) Poona agreed to pay Rs 12 lakhs as war indemnity within two years; (iii) the British were to restore 'any part of the Gujarat country ceded to them' by Raghunath Rao or the Gaekwad. They were also to withdraw their forces and Raghunath Rao to disband his troops 'within one month'. He was to be paid Rs 25,000 per month to maintain a retinue of 1,000 horse and some domestic attendants on condition that he retired to Kopergaon; (iv) all treaties made with Raghoba and the Gaekwad stood annulled, while those of 1739 and 1756 concluded with the Peshwa's court were re-affirmed.

Orginally comprising 20 articles, article 13 (relating to Bhonsle's claim for the *chauth* of Bengal) and article 17 (regarding the Peshwa's jewels allegedly lodged by him with the Company) were omitted altogether at the time of ratification, while the concluding words of article 7 (regarding Raghoba's treaties with the Company 'to be destroyed in the presence of the Peshwa's ministers') were deleted. An 'additional clause' made it clear that the British did not intend relinquishing the islands of Salsette, Caranjia, Elephanta and Hog.

It has been said that the Treaty represented 'a patch-work of compromises' and neither party accepted it either sincerely or wholeheartedly. The Bombay Council in particular felt extremely unhappy and rated it as 'highly injurious' to the Company's interests and reputation. The vagueness of some of its terms made the later resumption of Anglo-Maratha hostilities inevitable.

Aitchison,\III, pp. 33–9; Dodwell, *CHI*, V, pp. 260–3; G. S. Sardesai, *New History of the Marathas*, 3 vols, III (1772–1848), Bombay, 1968, pp. 56–60.

Quit India Movement (1942)

The Quit India Movement followed in the wake of the failure of the Cripps Mission (q.v.). When Sir Stafford Cripps (q.v.) arrived in India in March 1942 the political situation both within and beyond the country's borders was anything but reassuring. For one, from the day Japan declared war, 7 December 1941, its onslaught had been unrelenting—Singapore had falen on 15 February 1942; Rangoon, on 7 March; the Andamans, on 12 March. It was clear that the seas around India were now dominated by the Japanese. It might be worth noting that while Cripps was engaged in intensive negotiations with Indian leaders, bombs had fallen in Trincomalee, Cocanada and Vizagapatam; that the government of Madras had moved its offices from the coast far into the interior and that panic had spread along the eastern sea-board, all the way from Trincomalee in Sri Lanka to Calcutta. The All-India Committee of the Indian National Congress (q.v.), which convened at Allahabad on 29 April, resolved *inter alia* that the Indian people should offer complete non-violent non-cooperation to the invading forces and refuse to render them any assistance. It conceded none the less that in places where the British and the invading forces were engaged in active combat, Indian non-cooperation would necessarily be fruitless and even unnecessary.

Cripps' failure to resolve the political impasse created what appeared to Gandhi (q.v.) a moral crisis; the latter was determined, as he put it, to free Britain from the taint of hypocrisy and, at the same time, restore the dignity, self-reliance and integrity of the Indian people and convert their ill-will into good-will. It has been suggested that the term 'Quit India' was coined by an American journalist during an interview with Gandhi. Writing in the *Harijan* on 26 April, the Mahatama had instead used the expression 'orderly and timely British withdrawal from India'. Again, 'under my proposal they have to leave India in God's hands but in the modern parlance, to anarchy and that anarchy may lead to internecine warfare for a time or to unrestrained dacoities. From these a true India, will rise in the place of the fake one we see.'

On 14 July the Congress Working Committee appealed to Britain to withdraw from India with goodwill so that a provisional government might be established which would co-operate with the United Nations in resisting aggression. The Committee however affirmed that 'should this appeal fail, the Congress cannot view without the greatest apprehension the continuation of the present state of affairs . . . . . The Congress will then be reluctantly compelled to utilize all the non-violent strength it might have gathered since 1920. Such a widespread struggle would inevitably be under the leadership of Gandhiji.' The Committee also decided that a meeting of the AICC be held in Bombay on 7 August 1942.

The government had made up its mind to take drastic action, for the resolutions of the AICC (April-May 1942) and the Congress Working Committee (14 July) were, in its view, fraught with the utmost danger. There was growing discontent among the people and serious doubt in Britain's capacity to defend India, while British propaganda had not been particularly successful in gaining public support in the United States and China.

As scheduled, the AICC convened in Bombay on 7 August and adopted a resolution which justified the demand for the British to 'quit India' and explained its implications. *Inter alia,* it formulated the broad outlines of the constitution of a provisional government including its composition and aims, outlined a solution to the communal problem and declared India's aspirations for world peace and amity. The operative part of the resolution read: 'The Committee resolves, therefore, to sanction for the vindication of India's inalienable right to freedom and independence, the starting of mass struggle on non-violent lines on the widest possible scale so that the country might utilize all the non-violent strength it has gathered during the last 22 years of peaceful struggle.' Gandhi was to be incharge of the new mass movement. Anticipating a stage when the Congress may be unable to issue instructions because of government reprisals, the resolution noted that in such a contingency 'every man and woman who is participating in this movement must function for himself or herself within the four corners of the general instructions issued'.

On 8 August the Government of India adopted a resolution charging that the Congress was preparing for 'unlawful, dangerous and violent activities' directed towards the disruption of communications and public utility services; the organisation of strikes; tampering with the loyalty of government servants; and interference with defence measures, including recruitment. Government measures to crush the Movement were launched on the morning of Sunday, 9 August with the police descending on Birla House where Gandhi and his companions were staying in Bombay. He was arrested along with his wife Kasturba, his secretary, Mahadeo Desai, and Sarojini Naidu, all of whom were taken to the Aga Khan Palace at Poona. Simultaneously, all members of the Congress Working Committee were taken to the Old Fort at Ahmadnagar. Arrests were made throughout India and a large number of Congress leaders of the movement at all levels—all-India, provincial, district, *taluqa* and town were summarily rounded up and put behind bars.

What followed was not a Movement but an outburst of blind anger—

unorganized, unrehearsed and undirected—by a harassed and distracted people. The leaderless masses were deeply moved, swayed by a multiplicity of influences and knew not what to do. They were a mixed lot: the terrorists; the revolutionaries; the Forward Bloc of Subhas Chandra Bose (q.v.); the socialist followers of Jayaprakash Narayan (q.v.) who were part of the Congress, albeit opposed to its policy of non-violence; and a vast number of non-descript, anti-social elements always on the look-out for opportunities for mischief.

The British viewed the situation as a challenge. The Viceroy confided in the British Prime Minister that it was 'by far the most serious rebellion since that of 1857, the gravity and extent of which we have so far concealed from the world for reasons of military security.' Cruel and indeed atrocious reprisals followed on the one hand while there was a mass upsurge on the other. Bihar, with the exception of its southern districts, and eastern U. P., were the main nerve-centres of lawless activities. The district of Ballia excelled all others in U.P. The people here opened the jail gates when one of the prisoners took the lead, cut off communications and, for a few days, maintained what they called panchayat raj. In Bengal, the district of Midnapore defied British *fiat*. In Tamluk, a national government was installed with all the paraphernalia of administration. The district was subjected to violent activities relating to police, railways and roads.

In the Central Provinces and Berar, two places were especially affected— Ashti and Chimur; in Madras Presidency, the railway track between Renugunta and Bezwada, a distance of 130 miles, was uprooted. In Bombay there were large strikes in mills and factories. Railway dislocation was especially pronounced in the North-West Bengal, East India, Madras and Southern Maratha Railways. Furious mobs not only attacked government buildings, offices and stores but assaulted officers, injured many officials and even killed some.

The government's retaliatory measures were extremely cruel. Every canon of morality, of human decency was violated in the name of preserving law and order. Mobs were dispersed by lathi charge, by rifle, pistol and occasionally machine-gun fire from the air. Men were mercilessly flogged, beaten and subjected to inhuman torture. They were cross-examined throughout the day and not allowed to sleep at night, kept hungry, thirsty and humiliated. Women were stripped, assaulted, raped; even children were not spared. In a village numerous houses were razed to the ground; many were burnt down. People were undressed, tied to trees and beaten. Large numbers were thrown into prison without trial and long terms of imprisonment were awarded. Imposition of collective fines was the order of the day; what was worse, these were ruthlessly realized. The objective was to terrorize the people, teach them a lesson and efface from their minds all thought of defiance. Students were foremost in this national upsurge. Many abandoned their studies; schools and colleges were closed and Authority made frequent use of bullets in quelling disturbances.

According to official records, the total civilian casualties from August to November, were 1,028 killed and 3,125 seriously injured. This would appear to be a gross under-estimate in the light of the fact that 8 British brigades and 57 Indian battalions were used to crush the revolt. According to unofficial figures, those killed alone might vary from 4,000 to 10,000.

In Bombay, 'Congress Radio' broadcasts were made by Usha Mehta and her friends for a few months in 1942; a parrallel government was set up at Satara by Nana Patil and his companions. Some technical skill and perception was no doubt evident in destroying railway property and installations and intensive foresight in disrupting transport and communications so as to isolate places and establish a 'people's government'. These stray cases apart, the disturbances lacked both coherence as well as sound planning. The result was that in a few weeks the peak of their fury had been reached, to be followed by a rapid decline in overt action while the movement was driven underground. The government did not relax its whip-hand until satisfied that there was little chance of the movement reviving. Thereupon it ordered the release of Gandhi on 4 May 1944, 21 months after his arrest.

A post-script may be added. From August 1942 onwards, intelligence organizations of the Central and Provincial governments were engaged in collecting evidence, from every possible source, of Congress responsibility for the disturbances. A year later the evidence had become so voluminous as to be difficult to handle. Accordingly, New Delhi decided to ask one T. Wickenden, an ICS official and then a judge in the Central Provinces and Berar, to prepare a report. The Wickenden Report, officially called 'Report on the Disturbances of 1942-3', was submitted to the government on 29 November 1943.

In Wickenden's own words, 'The short effect of the conclusions from the material as a whole is that there was a concerted course of action by Gandhi and the Working Committee to which the All-India Congress Committee made themselves a party, for the overthrow of the Government of this country . . .where its incidents were not deliberately conceived, they were inherent in the circumstances and responsibility for them would be none the less'. Wickenden conceded, however, a major lacuna, namely; 'Most of the material would be utterly inadmissible if legal proceedings were in contemplation and it would appear out of place therefore to attempt any legal appreciation of the evidence—whether it is sufficient to establish the existence of a conspiracy to overthrow the existing Government. For that purpose the evidence would reduce to little more than Gandhi's writings, speeches which could be proved, a few letters, and possibly statements of persons who might conceivably stand as approvers.'

In assesing Gandhi's motive for launching the Movement, Wickenden listed the latter's desperation at the failure of the individual satyagraha movement; rejection on Cripps' proposals; the general demoralization in Congress ranks; the growing danger of the British acceding to the Muslim League (q.v.) demand for Pakistan and the presence of a large number of American troops in India. 'Above all, however, and in part proceeding from these factors, was Gandhi's conviction of Britain's defeat in the war, without which conviction, I am satisfied, this movement would never [have] come into being.'

The 'prime responsibility' for all that happened, Wickenden concluded, must rest with Gandhi. Yet, the Congress apart, the intervention of the Congress Socialist party, the Forward Bloc and other revolutionary groups intensified the movement further.

A great deal of interest has been evinced in the US reactions to the Quit India movement. A competent study makes the point that the response of the Roosevelt administration 'had been largely negative': that the President 'was disinclined' to engage in a controversy with Winston Churchill, 'his valued ally'; that American elite groups remained 'unresponsive' albeit 'a relatively small' number 'refused to remain silent.'

P. N. Chopra (ed.), *Quit India Movement, British Secret Report,* Faridabad, 1976; *Congress Responsibility for the Disturbances,* New Delhi, 1943; *Tara Chand,* IV, pp. 362-81; D. G. Tendulkar, *The Mahatma,* 8 vols., 2nd ed., New Delhi, 1960-63 pp. 1481-86; M. S. Venkataramani & B. K. Shrivastav, *Quit India: The American response to the 1942 struggle,* Delhi, 1979.

Raghunath Rao (Raghoba) (d. 1783)

The younger son of Peshwa Baji Rao I and father of the last Peshwa, Baji Rao II (q.v.), Raghunath Rao, better known as Raghoba, is held to be solely responsible for legalizing British interference in the internal affairs of the Maratha state with the disastrous consequences that ensued from it.

During his brother Balaji Baji Rao's (q.v.) reign, Raghoba had served as an army commander, leading two military expeditions (1753-5 and 1757) to the north. Weak and incompetent, he had incurred a disproportionately heavy expenditure in men and money, apart from arousing the hostility of the Rajputs and Jats against his compatriots. Gullible, he was easily persuaded by Malhar Rao Holkar to release Najib-ud-Daula, a Rohilla chief and sworn enemy of the Maratha cause. Among his other omissions and commissions, Najib had been responsible for inviting Ahmad Shah Abdali (q.v.) to invade India with the object of pushing the Marathas back to the Deccan where, he argued, they legitimately belonged. Present at the Third Battle of Panipat (q.v.), Raghoba was among its few principal survivors and fled after that defeat had turned into a variegated disaster.

An aspirant to the Peshwaship, Raghoba opposed Narayan Rao's nomination after the death, in 1772, of Madhav Rao I. Unable to seize power, Raghoba conspired to bring about, in August 1773, the murder of his nephew and was proclaimed Peshwa by his supporters. Veteran Maratha statesmen, the Barbhais, however, sought to protect Ganga Bai, the widow of Narayan Rao, and after the birth of her son took vigorous steps to oust Raghoba, whose guilt and direct involvement in the murder of the Peshwa had been established. With the birth of Madhav Rao (April 1774), Raghoba's claims to the Peshwaship stood 'finally extinguished', for the child was formally invested Peshwa and a council of regency proclaimed.

From then on the 'pretender' becomes, in fact, 'a mere pawn' in the web of complicated intrigue that now beset the Maratha state. Thomas Mostyn, the John Company's (q.v.) agent in Poona, recognizing this to be an ideal situation for his masters to step in, encouraged Raghoba to seek the Bombay government's support and, after his defeat, arranged to whisk him away. By the Treaty of Surat (q.v.), Raghoba gave the British the right to restore him to the *masnad.*

The result was the First Anglo-Maratha War (q.v.), in which the British initially suffered reverses. Later, the Calcutta government forsook Raghoba's cause, though the Bombay authorities continued to give him asylum. In 1778, when Nana Phadnis (q.v.) seized power and recalled Raghoba, the British did not lend the latter any support and his plans fell through.

A renewal of Anglo-Maratha hostilities revived Raghoba's hopes, but the disaster to British arms at Telegaon and the Convention of Wadgaon (q.v.) forced him to surrender. He managed to escape while being escorted to Jhansi and joined the British commander, Thomas Goddard's troops. The English finally renounced Raghoba's cause by the Treaty of Salbai (q.v.). Despite this, Raghoba continued to stay at Surat and for a time was the recipient of an allowance from the Company. Deeply disgruntled with the latter, he even sent a deputation to George III of England to seek help in retrieving his fortunes. The one-year sojourn (1781-2) of his two-man 'embassy' was singularly barren of results. In 1783, Raghoba wrote another cringing letter to the British ruler—but to no avail.

Raghoba surrendered to Mahadji Sindhia (q.v.) when the Company stopped his allowances in 1783. It is said that Mahadji treated him 'generously', that for his part Raghoba adopted an extremely soft and humble tone and not only acknowledged Madhav Rao's position as the new Peshwa but was cordial and respectful towards Nana Phadnis too. Raghoba died in December 1783 at Kopargaum, on the Godavari near Nasik, the place fixed for his residence. He was barely 48.

G. S. Sardesai, *New History of the Marathas*, 3 vols, III; *Beale*, pp. 324–5.

Hafiz Rahmat Khan Rohilla (c. 1710–1774)

In the eighteenth century, Rohilkhand with an approximate area of 11,805 square miles, extended all the way from Hardwar along the foot of the Kumaon and Garhwal Himalaya to the frontiers of Oudh (q.v.). The original name of the tract was Katehar. The Rohillas were Afghans who had settled in the Terai region, along the foot of the Himalaya. The derivation of the term is disputed. Some ascribe it to the Pushtu word *rohelah* — from *rohu* (mountain), signifying a mountain dweller of Afghanistan; others to *roh*, a name by which a large part of eastern Afghanistan is said to be known.

The Rohillas were mostly Sunni Muslims of the Yusufzai tribe. They were free-booters and soldiers of fortune who settled down in Rohilkhand after overpowering and subjugating its Hindu population. Not long after the death (1707), of the Mughal emperor, Aurangzeb they rose to political power, revolted under their chief, Ali Muhammad Khan in 1744 and made themselves independent of Mughal control.

Rahmat Khan who traced his descent to the Kutah Khail, known also as the Badalzoi tribe of Kandahar, was born in Afghanistan about the year 1710. His people later settled among the Yusufzais near Peshawar, whence his father Shah Alam had moved down to Katehar in the Doab, towards the close of the seventeenth century. Rahmat Khan had served under Ali Muhammad Khan, his nephew, who, before his death (1749), appointed him Hafiz or chief guardian of his four minor sons. For a while Rahmat Khan remained busy in quarrels with rival chiefs and neighbouring powers, but by

1754, in disregard of his word, assumed control over a large part of Rohilkhand—assigning some small districts to the two older sons of his late master.

Unable to face continuous raids from the Marathas, Rahmat Khan sought, in 1759, Shuja-ud-Daula's (q.v.) help, and in 1772-3 promised to pay the latter a sum of Rs 40 lakhs for his services. Earlier, in 1761, he had joined Ahmad Shah Abdali (q.v.) against the Marathas at Panipat and thereby gained from the latter the districts of Etawah and the country between Agra and Kalpi.

As ill-luck would have it, after the Maratha raid in 1773 conditions in Rohilkhand deteriorated further, thanks to mutual rivalries among the Rohilla chiefs who devastated each other's lands. The administration of justice, revenue collection and commerce ground virtually to a halt. Unable to secure the co-operation of other chiefs to pay Shuja-ud-Daula his due and failing in his efforts either to get the amount scaled down or its payment staggered, Rahmat Khan decided to die fighting. In the Rohilla War (q.v.) that followed, he fell in the battle of Miranpur Katra.

Besides being a successful ruler, Rahmat Khan was a poet and a man of literary tastes. John Strachey mentions four of his Persian poems as well as his 'very great' collection of books which, after his death, was purloined by the Nawab of Oudh. He was the author of *Khulasat-ul-Ansab*. Rahmat Khan made studied efforts to please his Hindu subjects; contemporary accounts testify that under his rule they were fairly treated and prosperous.

With Rahmat Khan's complete military rout in 1774, most of Rohilkhand was annexed to Oudh, with the Nawab retaining control only of Rampur and the immediately neighbouring area. In 1801, the Nawab of Oudh ceded the recently acquired area to the East India Company (q.v.). Under the British, it comprised the districts of Bijnor, Moradabad, Badaun, Shahjahanpur and the Terai, with headquarters at Bareilly. At present, Rohilkhand may be equated broadly to the Bareilly division of Uttar Pradesh.

John Strachey, *Hastings and the Rohilla War,* Oxford, 1892; *Imperial Gazetteer,* vol. 8; *Hobson-Jobson,* pp. 766-7; *Beale,* p. 148.

Rai Durlabh or Durlabh Rai (d. 1770)

The eldest son of Raja Janki Ram, Raja Durlabhram Rai, more popularly known as Rai Durlabh, began his career as commander of the army and deputy governor of Orissa when Siraj-ud-Daula (q.v.) was Nawab. Unsuccessful in this post, he was later made the Nizamat diwan. Far from happy with Siraj-ud-Daula's conduct of affairs, he conspired with Robert Clive (q.v.) to bring about his downfall, turning a traitor to the Nawab at the Battle of Plassey (q.v.). Later, working in close liaison with the British, he clashed with Mir Jafar (q.v.) who wanted to be independent of British control. This made Rai Durlabh unpopular and, in fear for his life, he was moved to Calcutta (q.v.) under British escort.

With the coming of Warren Hastings (q.v.), the Rai fell from grace in 1761, but was reinstated in 1765 as Diwan of the Khalsa Cutchery, mainly as a check on Maharaja Nand Kumar (q.v.) who was deemed a greater menace. After the accession of Najm-ud-Daula as Nawab of Bengal, the Rai became more or less a minister for the John Company (q.v.) till his death in 1770.

K. K. Datta, 'Durlabh Ram, a prominent Bengal officer of the eighteenth century', *Indian Historical Quarterly* (Calcutta), XVI, 1940, pp. 20-39; Abdul Majeed Khan, *The Transition in Bengal 1757-75*, Cambridge, 1969.

Indian Railways

Only after they had proved successful in England was the extension of railways to India seriously contemplated. To start with, three experimental lines were sanctioned in 1845: the East Indian Railway, from Calcutta to Raniganj (120 miles); the Great Indian Peninsular Railway, from Bombay to Kalyan (32 miles); and the Madras Railway, from Madras to Arkonam (30 miles).

Broadly, the development of Indian railways may be divided into five distinct phases reflecting, in large measure, the varying emphasis and impact of growing public opinion on the government of the day. These were: (a) the 'old guarantee system', 1849–69; (b) state construction and ownership, 1869–82; (c) the 'modified guarantee system', 1882-1924; (d) nationalization, 1924-44; and (e) integration and regrouping, 1948-52.

Indian railroad building began in earnest after Lord Dalhousie's (q.v.) 1853 Minute on the subject. Herein the Governor-General stressed the great social, political and commercial advantages accruing from railway construction, suggested an ambitious programme of trunk lines linking the presidencies with each other and the hinterland with the principal port towns. The Rebellion of 1857 (q.v.) hastened this process for, in its aftermath, it was widely recognized that speedier communications would have been a great help in quelling the uprising.

In the light of later developments, an excerpt from Dalhousie's Minute of 4 July 1856 makes interesting reading: 'I trust they [East India Company (q.v.) and the Government of India] will ever avoid the error of viewing railways as private undertakings and will regard these as national work over which the Government may justly exercise, and is called upon to exercise, a stringent and salutary control. This control should not be an arbitrary right of interference, but a regulated authority, defined and declared by law, which is not to be needlessly or vexatiously exacted, but which, in my humble judgement, is necessary at once for the interests of the state and for the protection of the public.'

As no large-scale private capital for these huge undertakings was forthcoming, the Company ruled that English companies, interest on whose capital investment would be guaranteed by the state, be constituted to take up this work. By the end of 1859 contracts with eight such companies for the construction of 5,000 miles of railroad, involving a guaranteed capital of £52 million, were signed. These were the East Indian; the Great Indian Peninsular; the Madras; the Bombay Baroda and Central Indian; the East Bengal; the Indian Branch (later the Oudh and Rohilkhand State Railway and, still later, the East Indian Railway); the Sind, Punjab and Delhi (later the

North-Western) Railway.

In all these cases the government under-wrote the capital and guaranteed a 5 per cent return on it, coupled with a free grant of all land required for construction. In return, the companies were called upon to share the surplus profits with the government—after the guaranteed interest had been met, the interest charge being calculated at 22 pence to the rupee. The railroads were to be sold to the government on stipulated terms at the close of 25 years, while during this period the government was to exercise control both over their expenditure as well as working.

The average profit on the turnover worked out to 3 per cent leaving the remaining 2 per cent to be borne by the public exchequer. The latter did not get efficient service, for with the companies non-resident and the guarantee absolute, there was no impetus to render good, effective service. In essence, the shareholders were not only relieved of all risks to their capital investment but also assured of a margin of profit over and above the guaranteed interest. The state, in turn, obtained powers of supervision and the ultimate right of purchase. Some attributed the losses to the unnecessarily high standard and consequent high cost of construction, as well as to the construction engineers' ignorance of local conditions. By 1869, the deficit on the railway budget had added up to a total of Rs 166 lakhs.

It should be obvious that the two most controversial features of the arrangement were the ownership of railways by private companies and the guarantee by the government of a minimum return on their capital, especially the latter. During 1858-1900, the Government of India paid a sum of £51,527,307 out of general revenues to make up the dividend to the guaranteed figure; of this £44,700,000 came to be recovered during the next 19 years.

In the second phase of railway construction from 1869 to 1892—a powerful fillip had been the Panjdeh incident (1885) under Dufferin (q.v.)—both India as well as Whitehall now accepted the policy of state construction. Progress in this field however was by no means rapid. Thus between 1869-91 the mileage added through government agency totalled 3,297. The state proved as good an agent as the companies in construction and administration, sometimes even better. It could have been far more successful but for lack of unity of management, absence of amalgamation and pooling of resources, lack of an equitable distribution of railway lines and prevention of monopoly abuse. There was the additional fact that Whitehall put a stern face on all state construction and management.

In his Minute dated 9 January 1869, John Lawrence (q.v.), then Governor-General, strongly recommended state construction and ownership of railways. Under the prevalent guarantee system, he averred, the 'whole profit would go to the company, and the whole loss to the government. It is an abuse of language to describe as an interference with private enterprises what is only a refusal to support private speculators and to guarantee them from all possible loss by the credit of the state. [The company administration was] as bad and extravagant as anything which the worst opponent of government agency could suggest as likely to result from that system'. In July 1869, the Duke of Argyll, then Secretary of State, while accepting the policy of state construction and ownership ruled that 'both in

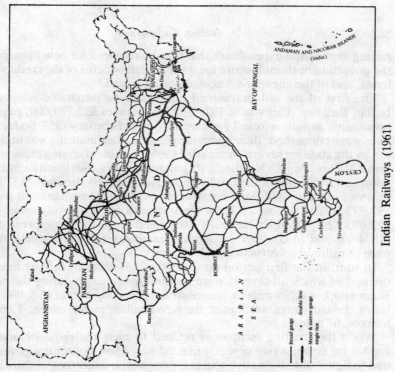

Indian Railways (1961)

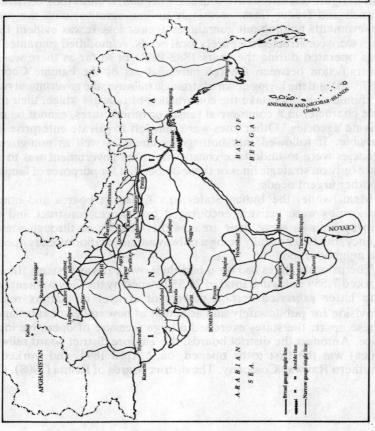

Indian Railways (1901)

raising capital and expenditure that may be required for new lines in India, the government should secure for itself the full benefits of the credit which it lends, and of the cheaper agencies at its command.'

The first of the old guaranteed railways to be purchased was the East Indian Railway. This was in 1879 and for a sum of £32,750,000, payable in terminable annuities from 1 January 1880 to 14 February 1953. So far as new lines were concerned, their commitment as well as financing was underwritten by the state for several years after 1869; prominent among these were the Indus Valley, Punjab Northern, Rajputana, Malwa, Northern Bengal, Rangoon and Irrawaddy Valley and Tirhoot Railways. By the end of 1879, 6,128 miles of railways had been constructed by various companies at a cost of £97,872,000 as against 2,175 by the state at a comparatively lower cost of £23,695,726. Through the 1870's the need to tackle widespread famine (1874-9), and to conduct the Afghan campaign (1878-9), accelerated the pace of railroad construction in the country.

In sum, in the first period up to 1870, 4,255 miles of railway lines were opened of which all save 45 were on the broad gauge; during the next ten years another 4,239 miles were constructed making a total of 8,494. Of the latter, broad gauge accounted for 6,562 miles; meter gauge, 1,865; and narrow, 67 miles.

When the existing companies refused to raise the requisite additional capital for constructing urgently needed new lines, the central government had to figure out alternative sources. *Inter alia*, it undertook construction of branch and feeder lines, seemingly unremunerative, with the provincial governments holding out guarantees against loss. It was evident that such lines were constructed for purely local needs. A 'modified guarantee' system thus operated during the years 1882-1924. In so far as there was a clear contradiction between the recommendations of the Famine Commission (1878-80) and the laying down of strategic railways, the government ruled that it 'should only undertake the construction of railways which, their unprofitable character in a commercial sense, or other causes, cannot be made by private agencies.' Other lines were thus left to private enterprise as far as possible. It followed that both government as well as non-government agencies were to undertake construction; the government was to concentrate only on strategic lines or those demanded for purposes of famine relief or other urgent needs.

Mean while, the Indian States (q.v.), district boards and other local authorities were actively encouraged to finance, construct and operate railway lines to serve their areas, either directly or through some other agency, the latter usually being a railway administration already operating in the neighbourhood.

The princely states too soon had their own railway systems. In all, they worked 7,559 miles in a total of 25,550 owned by the Government of India. The latter exercised certain powers of control in matters relating to provision for public safety and adoption of new routes or rates and fares. These apart, the states exercised a large measure of operative independence. Amongst the district boards, the Tanjore district board railway (112 miles) was the first to be opened, on 2 April 1894, and worked by the Southern Railway Company. The district boards of Kistna (1908), Coimbatore (1915), Guntur (1916) and Salem (1917) soon followed suit.

In accordance with the government's policy, three companies were formed with a guarantee—the Bengal Central in 1881, the Bengal and North-Western, and the Rohilkhand and Kumaon, the latter two in 1882. Three with a 'modified guarantee' were the Southern Mahratta, in 1882; the Indian Midland, in 1885; and the Bengal-Nagpur, in 1887. In all these six instances, the government had the right to acquire the lines at the end of 25 years or at subsequent intervals of 10 years, on repaying the company's capital at par. A large number of other railways, mostly narrow gauge, branch and feeder lines were built by companies under various contracts between 1896 and 1923 and were worked either directly by the owning company, by managing agents or by adjoining railways. While entitled to exercise its right to purchase the lines of the 'old guarantee companies' as and when they fell due, the government allowed company managements to continue in most cases.

On 31 March 1923 the total mileage of railways in India stood at 37,618 of which more than 66 per cent was owned by the government, its subordinate agencies and the Indian states, although most of the railways were managed by private companies. Only three principal railways, North-Western, Eastern Bengal, and Oudh and Rohilkhand and two small lines, Jorhat (Provincial) and the Aden railways, were under the direct management and control of the government, the remaining being worked by companies.

In 1900 the railways showed a small profit for the first time. In succeeding years the net receipts grew rapidly; in the 4 years ending 1907-8, they averaged close upon £2 million a year; in 1918-19 railway earnings totalled £10 million. This bright phase ended with 1920-1, for in the following year there was a loss of over £6 million. Following a breakthrough in railway finances immediately after World War I, the Acworth Committee (see below), far from approving the contracts already entered into, ruled in 1921 that their number be reduced by amalgamating some of the existing companies. Besides, it held that private enterprise should be encouraged only when adequate government funds were not available.

In 1924-5 railway finances were separated from the general budget. 1933-4 was the first year to show some signs of recovery after the great economic depression (1929-31), with the earnings of state-owned railways increasing from Rs 84 crores (1932-3) to Rs 95.48 crores (1936-7). As the old contracts guaranteeing a 5 per cent dividend at 22 pence per rupee lapsed, the government began revising them. The process helped to swell the revenues and assets of the state and improve the financial position of the railways.

In railroad construction up to 1900, emphasis had been laid on the provision of trunk lines. However, with the construction of the Nagda-Mathura line, which provided an alternate route from Bombay to Delhi through eastern Rajasthan, the trunk system was virtually complete. The sudden spurt in trade activity meant growing emphasis on improving equipment, providing new and better yards, terminal facilities as well as increase in rolling stock. The Inchape Committee had suggested an annual allotment of £12 million on railway improvement. In actual fact, however, even this paltry sum could not always be provided in the budget.

In 1901, Thomas Robertson was appointed special commissioner to examine the entire system of the organization and working of the Indian railways. *Inter alia*, he proposed (1903) drastic changes, criticized both centralization as well as departmentalism, and recommended the constitution of a Railway Board with a chairman, two members and a secretary. The Board was formally set up in March 1905 and made subordinate to the government, wherein it was represented by the Department of Commerce and Industry. Its administrative duties included construction of new lines, improvement of railway management with regard both to economy and public convenience, arrangements for through traffic, settlement of disputes between competing lines and a general supervision over the working and expenditure of lines managed or run by private companies.

In 1907, the Secretary of State, John Morley, appointed a committee under Sir James Mackay to examine the financial and administrative structure of the railways. The committee found that the objective of the Railway Board, namely, an expeditious and speedy disposal of business, was only imperfectly realized; that there was friction between the Board and the government; that defects existed in the constitution of the Board itself, with attention being given to matters which could normally have been left to individual railways.

As constituted in 1905 and modified in 1909, and again in 1914, the Board did not work satisfactorily. Initially, its chairman and members were men with considerable knowledge and railway experience. This was modified in 1914, when a member with financial and commercial qualifications was appointed. The position was reversed in 1920, when it was decided that all the three members should possess experience of work in the railways. The Board was hampered, too, by the Secretary of State who gave detailed instructions on important matters as well as the Government of India who did no better. As if that were not bad enough, the Member for Commerce and Industry in the Governor-General's Executive Council treated the Board as a step-child, his interest in its functioning being peripheral. The Board's duties were of a routine character and its functions multifarious. In 1909, when the Imperial Legislative Council came into being, it expressed itself strongly against the Board and the powers with which it was vested. The Council, however, had only advisory functions, for the Secretary of State was still all-powerful.

After 1921, when the government assumed direct responsibility for the state railways, it delegated all its powers to the Railway Board. The latter, however, was not rated sufficiently important to be entrusted to the care of a single Member of the Executive Council, although the Member for Public Works, and later that for Commerce, were supposed to look after it. The Acworth Committee was later to rule that a Member of the Governor-General's Council should be in constant touch with railway business. Accordingly, a Member for Communications was appointed in 1937 who, in the course of World War II, became transformed into the Member for War Transport and Railways. After 1947 there was a Minister for Transport and Railways in the Union Cabinet; in 1957, Transport was taken away from his charge and transferred to a Minister for Communications, so that there was now a separate, full-fledged Minister for Railways.

Before 1947, the Members incharge of railways in the Governor-General's Executive Council were mostly drawn from experienced officers of the I. C. S. All those who held the charge were above 47 years of age at the time of their appointment, possessed wide administrative experience and had the ability to deal with legislative work. There were two exceptions: one was a politician, Mr Asaf Ali, a member of the Interim Government (q.v.) and another, a business man, Sir Edward Benthall; they held the portfolio briefly before 1947.

Before its reorganization according to the Acworth Committee's recommendations the Railway Board was 'semi-independent' both in theory as well as practice. It became collectively the Railway Department, distinct from and independent of the Department of Commerce and Industry, with its President (or Chairman) having direct access to the Viceroy. There was criticism and apprehension regarding the Board's powers and hence a persistent demand in the legislature for its abolition. The fact is that the Board's powers were related largely to day-to-day administrative supervision and control of certain staff matters and technical questions. It enjoyed autonomy only in the sense that, within its defined sphere, it could pass orders. This however did not prevent the Minister or the Member concerned from giving instructions regarding any or every matter of railway administration. All questions involving policy and major administrative arrangements were submitted to him for orders. Cases with financial implications were examined by the Financial Commissioner. In this way decisions of the Board were normally viewed as government decisions.

While public opinion strongly demanded state management of the railways, the provincial governments were sharply divided on the issue. On 1 November 1920 the Secretary of State announced the appointment of the East India Railways Committee under the chairmanship of Sir William Acworth to go into the whole question of railway policy, finances and administration and to 'recommend suitable methods of management, to examine the functions, status and constitution of the Railway Board and the system of government control over the Railway administration, to consider arrangements for the financing of railways in India and to make such other recommendations that may seem germane to the inquiry.'

The Acworth Committee consisted of 10 members, experts in railway matters or finance and administration or commerce and industry. Among them, 3 were Indians — V. S. Srinivas Sastri, a member of the Council of State, Sir Rajendranath Mookerjee, an eminent Calcutta industrialist and Sir Purshotamdass Thakurdas, a Bombay industrial magnate. *Inter alia* the Committee was asked to weigh the relative advantages of (i) direct state management; (ii) management through a company domiciled in England with its board of directors in London; (iii) management through a company domiciled in India with a board sitting in India; and (iv) management through a combination of (ii) and (iii). The Committee unanimously rejected (ii) and (iii) and, by a majority decision, ruled in favour of state management.

The Acworth Committee's recommendations were to form the basis of much of the later development of the Indian railways. It was to spell out the basic form and structure of a centralized railway administration, the shape of its finances and the manner of its development on sound economic and commercial lines.

The Committee unanimously recommended that the 'English companies shall be brought to an end on the broad ground that they represent a system essentially unworkable'. Supporting state management, it ruled that company management 'does not encourage' the development of indigenous industries, 'gives preference' to the import and export of goods and 'to large profits' to private British interests while higher appointments to Indians remained few and training facilities for them nil. Further, the Committee ruled: 'There is also, in addition, a positive feeling caused by an awkward national self-consciousness that Indians should have more control in the management of the railways in their own country. We therefore do not hesitate to recommend that in India the state should manage directly the railways which it already owns.'

The Acworth Committee also recommended the appointment of a Chief Commissioner of Railways. He took the place of President of the Railway Board and was solely responsible, under the Government of India, for decisions on technical matters and on matters of railway policy. Unlike the President of the Board, he was not to be out-voted or overruled by his colleagues. The first incumbent, C. D. M. Hindley, was appointed on 1 April 1923.

The Railway Board thus came to consist of a Chief Commissioner, a Financial Commissioner and two Members. Its work was divided into various fields, Members concerning themselves largely with questions of broad policy. For technical subjects there were the Directors of Civil and Mechanical Engineering, Traffic, Establishment and Finance. In addition, there were 11 Deputy Directors and 2 Assistant Directors. There was also the Central Publicity Bureau under a Chief Publicity Officer, first appointed in 1927. Two years later a third Member of the Board was appointed whose main duties related to resolving labour problems and effecting improvements in the service conditions of railway staff, especially of lower-paid employees. As a result of the report of the Indian Railway Inquiry Committee (1936-7) presided over by Sir Ralph Wedgewood (see below), the Central Accounts Organization of the railways was taken over by the Railway Board. In 1930, a Central Standardization Office was established to provide the necessary machinery for standardizing all railway equipment.

The question of separating general finances from railway finances was debated by the Acworth Committee which recommended that it be examined in the first instance by the railway finance committee and the Central Legislative Assembly. The latter ruled on 20 September 1924 that the yearly contribution by the railways be placed at 10 per cent of the capital charge, instead of 5-6 per cent; that if the surplus remaining after this payment to general revenues should exceed 3 crores, only two-thirds of the excess over this amount be transferred to railway revenues, with the remaining third accruing to general revenues. Nearly 20 years later (1943), an amendment by the legislature stipulated that a decision on the allocation of the surplus on commercial lines between the railway reserves and the general revenues be taken each year.

In 1932-3 a committee under the chairmanship of P. A. Pope was set up to inquire into all aspects of railway operations. It perfected a system of detailed investigation into individual items of railway working known as 'Job Analysis'. A second report, in 1933-4, on the progress of work and possibilities of further economy was submitted. Some of the important recommendations of the second report included an intensive use of locomotives, of rolling stock, of machinery and plant; disposal of uneconomic wagons; combining resources between different railways; handling and transport of small traffic; ticketless travel; methods of increasing earnings.

On the recommendations of the Public Accounts Committee of the Central Legislative Assembly, the Indian Railway Inquiry Committee was appointed in October 1936 under Sir Ralph Wedgewood to secure an improvement in net earnings and devise means to place railway finances on a sound and remunerative basis. Its report, submitted in June 1937, was duly considered by the Railway Board who decided upon early action to implement some of its recommendations.

As a result of the recommendations of the Standing Finance Committee on Railways, the government appointed a Railway Inquiry Committee in 1947 with K. C. Neogy, then a member of the Central Legislative Assembly, as Chairman. *Inter alia* the Committee was to (i) suggest ways and means of securing improvements in net earnings; (ii) effect economies in all branches of railway administration; (iii) ascertain the extent of staff surplus to requirements; and (iv) suggest practical methods of absorbing them in railway service. Owing to the then disturbed and uncertain conditions in the country, the Committee soon dispersed, hoping it would be able to convene again, which it never did.

A few other facets of the growth of railways in India may be taken note of. Thus it may be of interest to recall that in the four decades that followed the first phase of railroad construction (1882-1924), an effort was made to encourage private enterprise, unaided by the state. Four companies—the Bengal Central (1881), Rohilkhand-Kumaon (1890), Bengal and North-Western Railway (1882), and Southern Maratha Railway (1882)—were launched. The experiment well-nigh flopped with the result that these ventures had either to be purchased by the state or aided by joining them to other lines that were economically viable. The Southern Maratha Railway, however, continued and two other companies were set up on terms and conditions that bore a close parallel to it.

Unlike the old guarantee companies, the new ones functioned merely as agents to manage and work property belonging to the government. Additionally, they undertook to raise money and construct new lines. As for terminating the original contracts with the older companies, the government did not adopt a uniform policy and left each case to be decided on its own merits. Interestingly enough, both Thomas Robertson, who was appointed to inquire into the administration and working of the railways, and the Mackay Committee recommended the transfer of some state-managed lines to private management.

After a great deal of vacillation but with mounting public pressure, the government accepted in principle the policy of taking over the East Indian and Great Indian Peninsular Railways; this it actually did in January and July 1925 respectively. Solid support was lent to this decision when a resolution on the separation of railway finance from general finance was discussed and later adopted by the Central Legislative Assembly. Prior to 1924, the government had worked only those railway lines from which, because of their unremunerative character, private companies had shied away; under the new policy, it agreed to accept responsibility for operating such lines as had yielded profits.

In sum, after 1924 the central government was broadly committed to a policy of state management, yet no definite official line as such was formulated and, as has been noticed, every case was left to be judged on its merits. The Wedgewood Committee and the European community, on the whole, desired company management but Indian public opinion, expressed through resolutions in the legislature, the tabling of questions, budget debates, as well as discussions in the Railways' Central Advisory Council, was sternly opposed to what was deemed to be the official line.

The total route mileage of Indian railways in 1924 was 38,039. Between 1924–32, a total of 5,360 route miles were added at a cost of Rs 44.90 crores. During the Great Depression of the thirties and the crippling effects of World War II railroad construction was virtually halted. Meanwhile, by 1944, the nationalization of practically the entire railway mileage network in India had been completed. In 1946 the total railway mileage was: broad gauge 20,686.60; meter gauge 16,004.23; and narrow gauge 3,827.08.

Broadly, prior to 1944 railways in India fell into the following categories: (i) state-owned lines managed by the state; (ii) state-owned lines managed by private companies; (iii) company-owned lines managed by the companies; (iv) lines belonging to the Indian government; (v) miscellaneous lines, company lines or District Board lines. By 1944, (ii) and (iii) had been completely nationalized; almost all, barring some 533 miles, were either directly with the government or with its agencies.

Railway administration and control was mostly conducted from England by boards of directors dominated by ex-officials of the Government of India. Thanks to their rich knowledge of India, many among them exercised a thorough, detailed supervision; because of their overall usefulness, a few continued to function even beyond the age of 90 years or so.

With growing national consciousness in India, the control of the Secretary of State and his exercise of near-absolute power and authority on railroad building was understandably very unpopular with Indian public opinion. Only as late as 1925 were his powers in this regard considerably curtailed; most of these now devolved on the Government of India. In the result, the latter could now sanction an expenditure up to Rs 50 lakhs—instead of Rs 20 lakhs, as hitherto—on open lines.

Since there were no state-managed railways before 1869, various legislative enactments had been made from time to time to exercise regulatory control. A law enacted in 1879 replaced those of 1854, 1867, 1870 and 1871 on the subject. *Inter alia*, the new measure invested the government with authority to determine the route, the number, the speed and the times of trains. State construction, which was undertaken after 1884, involved collection and organization of a large railway staff and determination of a suitable machinery for management and control. From 1882 to 1905 a two-fold tendency was noticeable: that of greater centralization as well as bureaucratic and departmental administration.

Broadly, about two-thirds of the Indian railway revenue came from freight traffic, although the figure in individual railways might have varied. The pattern of traffic changed slowly over the decades, parallel with changes in the economy. Foodgrains and coal were the two largest items of freight from 1870 to 1947 and even later; foodgrain traffic, on an average, was the biggest by weight and revenue; then came coal and coke, followed by oilseeds, salt, jute and sugar.

With the partition of the country in 1947 sections of the North-Western Railway in the west and the Bengal and Assam Railway in the east went to Pakistan; along with the Sind section of the Jodhpur railway, the total route mileage handed over to Pakistan was 6,958. The section of the North-Western Railway left in India was now called the Eastern Punjab Railway; the broad gauge of the Bengal-Assam Railway was added to the East Indian Railway, while its meter gauge formed a separate Assam Railway.

Report by Thomas Robertson on Railway Administration, Calcutta 1903; *Committee on Indian Finance and Administration (Mackay Committee) Report,* Calcutta, 1908; *East India Railway Committee (Acworth Committee) Report & Volumes of Evidence,* Delhi, 1920; *Report of the Indian Railway Inquiry Committee,* New Delhi, 1937; Amba Prasad, *Indian Railways: A Study in Public Utility Administration,* Bombay, 1960; M. A. Rao, *Indian Railways,* New Delhi, 1974; J. N. Westwood, *Railways of India,* London, 1974.

Chakravarti Rajagopalachari (1879–1972)

Chakravarti Rajagopalachari belonged to a Vaishnavite Brahmin family, his father being a village *munsif* (judicial officer) in Salem district in the then Madras Presidency. Some of his family members were pandits in the royal court of Mysore. 'C. R.' was the youngest of three sons.

Educated at Bangalore and Madras, he had read the works of such authors as Shakespeare, Walter Scott, Tolstoy and Thoreau when a boy. As a young man he was powerfully influenced by Dadabhai Naoroji (q.v.) as well as the terrorist activities in Bengal, Maharashtra and South India itself. In the wake of the Rowlatt Act (q.v.) and the Jallianwala Bagh Massacre (q.v.), he joined the national movement.

'C. R.' had been Chairman of the Salem municipality, secretary of the Prohibition League of India and member incharge of the Indian National Congress' (q.v.) anti-drink campaign. Later, as Chief Minister of Madras, he was to introduce prohibition in his state. His period of political apprenticeship, however, was prolonged. Thus, for over a decade after World War I, while C. R. Das (q.v.) and Motilal Nehru (q.v.) were busy building the Swaraj Party (q.v.) and challenging British might on the legislative front, 'C. R.' was 'content to devote his energies to Gandhi's (q.v.) constructive programme', espousing in addition the cult of the spinning wheel and the removal of untouchability.

'C. R.' led the famous Salt Satyagraha (q.v.) march which galvanized

political activity in South India. Earlier (1921-2), he was General Secretary of
the A.I.C.C., a member of the Congress Working Committee and President
of its provincial committee for many years. During 1937-9 he was the Chief
Minister of Madras Presidency. Behind Gandhi's success at the Round
Table Conference (q.v.) and, earlier, in the Gandhi-Irwin Pact (q.v.), there
is strong evidence of 'C. R.'s quiet work and dogged persistence. In 1937 he
was responsible for evolving the formula that led the Congress to accept
office in the provinces in which it had won a majority.

'C. R.' pleaded strongly for the social and economic reform of Indian
society, especially the removal of untouchability. As Chief Minister of
Madras he was responsible for the Madras Temple Entry Act (1939). A
contemporary observer has noted that 'there was acknowledgement' on all
sides that during the Congress' tenure in office in the provinces, 'for efficiency of administration and good relations between ministers and the civil
service', Madras, under 'C. R.'s stewardship, 'was well ahead of all other
provinces'. 'C. R.' was opposed to the Congress abdicating responsibility in
the provinces on the outbreak of World War II. It was, to him, a blunder of
the first magnitude, for the abandonment of a position of strength was to
prove fatal to effective negotiations 'whether with the British or with the
Muslim League (q.v.)'. Like a number of other people, he was caught in a
vortex of conflicting forces: 'Congress left-wing demands being matched by
British short-sightedness'.

At the Allahabad meeting of the Congress Working Committee (July
1942), 'C. R.' came out with the bold suggestion that the party accept the
principle of partition as the basis for an understanding with the Muslim
League. He held the 'Quit India' policy to be misguided and detrimental to
India's long-term interests. The 'C. R. Formula' (q.v.) which formed the basis
of the 1944 Gandhi-Jinnah Talks (q.v.), relied on the premise, implicit
in the formula itself, of a treaty of separation which would provide 'for the
efficient and satisfactory administration of foreign affairs, defence, customs,
commerce and the like which must necessarily continue to be matters of
common interest between the concluding parties'. It is important to remember that neither Gandhi nor 'C. R.' contemplated an abrupt separation.
In the establishment of Pakistan as a sovereign, independent state, an
essential feature, from his point of view, was the treaty of separation to
provide for a difficult period of transition.

In March-April 1942, 'C. R.' was among a small minority of Congress
leaders who favoured acceptance of proposals by the Cripps Mission (q.v.)
with a view to breaking the existing political deadlock. Four years later, he
advised acceptance of the Muslim League's demand for Pakistan as the price
which had to be paid for independence. Having criticized the Congress for
rejecting the Cripps Mission proposals, he refused to join the Quit India
Movement (q.v.) that came in its wake. With the Japanese poised for a
frontal assault, the Movement seemed to him to reflect an attitude of
neutrality towards the Axis powers. Not for the first time, was he thus to
strike a discordant note that, he knew, would almost completely isolate him
from the mainstream of the nationalist movement.

'C. R.' believed a compromise with the Muslims was essential and the 'C.
R. Formula' was intended to provide the Muslims a choice either to join a

federated India, a confederation of free units or carve out a separate sovereign state. When the Congress endorsed the Quit India call, he resigned from its Working Committee and expressed the hope that Britain would win the war and establish a democratic government in India.

After the War, 'C. R.' was a member of the Governor-General's Executive Council (1946-7); Governor of West Bengal (August-November 1947); Governor-General of India (1948-50); Minister Without Portfolio (May-December, 1950) and Minister for Home Affairs in the Central Cabinet; he was once more Chief Minister of Madras during 1952-4. Thereafter, 'C. R.' gradually drifted away from the Congress mainstream and was instrumental in the formation of the pronouncedly rightist and anti-Congress Swatantra Party.

'C. R.' played a prominent role in the international movement against the nuclear bomb and was a strong advocate of religious instruction in public schools. He published a highly regarded, abridged edition of the Mahabharata. In later years he repeatedly, and without qualification, denounced the Government of India for its alleged corruption, bureaucratic obscurantism, inefficiency and lack of impartiality.

Known for his mordant wit, 'C. R.' pleaded for the retention of English as the *lingua franca* of India. He wrote a small tract, *Mudiyuma*, to establish that even Tamil could be used as a medium for scientific ideas and underlined that Hindi should not be imposed on the South. 'C. R.' told one of his biographers: 'I don't want any [office]. I have held and finished with the highest offices open to anyone. I have received honours and tokens of utmost regard and affection, for all of which I am grateful. I have kept my record clean and have led life honestly throughout. I say what I feel and what appears to be just and right.' General Chatterjee, his principal staff officer during his tenure as the first Indian Governor of Bengal and later as the last Governor-General, has noted that 'C. R.' was a 'multi-faceted genius of sparkling intellect, deep erudition, transparent honesty, bubbling humour, intense humanism, bold conventions and an unceasing zest for living a full life . . . This rare combination of age and ardour, catholicity and conservatism, volubility and taciturnity, serenity and pugnacity, his detachment in the midst of power, his religiosity mingled with a latitudinarian outlook . . . A pious soul of staggering moral heights, he was still practising all that he preached.'

Raj Mohan Gandhi, *A Warrior from the South*, Bombay, 1978; Monica Felton, *I Meet Rajaji*, London, 1962; A. R. H. Copley: *The Political Career of Chakravarti Rajagopalachari: A Moralist in Politics*, London, 1978; B. Shiva Rao, *India's Freedom Movement*, Delhi, 1972; Sen, *DNB*, III, pp. 439-44 (T. P. Meenakshisundaran); Masti Venkatesa Iyengar, *Rajaji: A Study of His Personality*, 2 vols, Bangalore, 1975; Bimanesh Chatterjee, *A Thousand Days with Raja Ji*, New Delhi, 1973.

'C. R. Formula' (10 July 1944)

The 'C. R. Formula' was an honest if ingenious attempt to break the political impasse following the virtual failure of the Quit India Movement (q.v.) and the growing strength of the Muslim League (q.v.) demand for the creation of

Pakistan.

Gandhi (q.v.) had been released from jail on 9 May 1944 and soon repaired to Panchgani to recuperate his shattered health. His interview with Stuart Gelder of the (London) *News Chronicle* appeared on 4 July and aroused much public interest. Six days later C. Rajagopalachari (q.v.) published his formula designed to break the Congress-League political deadlock.

Its principal provisions were: (i) The Muslim League was to endorse the demand for independence of the country and co-operate with the Indian National Congress (q.v.) in the formation of a provisional Interim Government; (ii) At the end of the War, a commission would demarcate those contiguous areas in the North-west and North-east in which Muslims were in an absolute majority and in these areas a plebiscite of *all* the inhabitants would decide whether or not they should be separated from India. If the majority decided in favour of forming a sovereign state such a decision would be given effect to, without prejudice to the right of districts on the border to choose either state; (iii) It would be open to all the parties to advocate their respective points of view before the plebiscite was held; (iv) Any transfer of population would only be on an absolutely voluntary basis; (v) In the event of separation, mutual agreements would be entered into for safeguarding defence, commerce and communications and for other essential purposes; (vi) These terms should be binding only in the event of transfer by Britain of full power and responsibility for the governance of India.

It has been said that Gandhi approved the formula in March 1943 at the time of his 21-day fast in the Aga Khan palace at Poona. It was communicated to M. A. Jinnah (q.v.) on 8 April 1944 by 'C. R.', who also indicated it had Gandhi's 'full approval', and was made public for the first time on 10 July 1944. Raja Maheshwar Dayal, a prominent member of the Hindu Mahasabha (q.v.), has maintained that, in essence, Jinnah had agreed to these terms as early as September 1942 having proposed them himself. The League leader, however, later denied that he had made any such proposal or commitment.

The Formula was to form the basis for the September–October 1944 Gandhi-Jinnah Talks (q.v.) which ended in failure. Jinnah placed the Formula before his party's Working Committee on 30 July, but made no secret of the fact that personally he considered it unsatisfactory. *Inter alia*, he told his committee: 'Mr Gandhi is offering a shadow and a husk, a maimed, mutilated and moth-eaten Pakistan'.

Later the League leader was to charge that both Gandhi and Rajagopalachari 'are putting the cart before the horse when they say that all these clauses can have any value or can become effective only if Britain transfers power to India'. His meaning was unambiguously clear; he wanted Pakistan first and independence afterwards, as against Gandhi's reversal of the priorities.

In his *Journal*, Wavell noted in the entry for 11 July 1944: 'Jinnah is a mass of vanity and no statesman but he is much too wary to accept the rather vague proposals put forward by Rajagopalachari without more definition ... We are undoubtedly in for a period of political manoeuvring which may lead to trouble. I wonder if we shall ever have any chance of a solution till the three intransigent, obstinate, uncompromising principals are out of the way: Gandhi (just on 75), Jinnah (68), Winston (nearing 70).' There is no doubt, however, that the 'C. R. Formula' was a subtle attempt to reduce the League's hitherto vague demand for Pakistan to a concrete and intelligible strait-jacket.

Sandhya Chaudhri, 'Gandhi and the Rajagopalachari Formula', *Gandhi Marg* (New Delhi), IV, 2, February 1983, pp. 934-8; D. G. Tendulkar, *Mahatama*, 8 vols., 2nd ed., Bombay, VI, p. 267; *Tara Chand*, IV, pp. 428–30; Gwyer & Appadorai, *Speeches & Documents on the Indian Constitution 1921–47*, II, pp. 548–9; Penderel Moon (ed.), *Wavell, the Viceroy's Journal*, Oxford, 1973, pp. 78-9.

Treaty of Rajpurghat (1805)

When the British commander, General Gerard Lake (1744-1808) refused to accept the terms of peace demanded by Yashvantrao Holkar (q.v.), the Maratha chief re-opened hostilities along with his ally, the Raja of Bharatpur. The latter gave in after his fort had been invested for many months. Holkar, however, fled to Panjab where he vainly sought the help of Ranjit Singh (q.v.), while at the same time sending desperate messages to Sindhia. Unluckily for him, with no aid forthcoming, he agreed to sign a treaty of peace at Rajpurghat on 24 December 1805.

Inter alia, the 9-article Treaty stipulated that Holkar (i) renounce 'all right and title' to the districts of 'Tonk, Rampoora, Boondee, Lekherree, Samey-dee, Bhamungann, Dass' and other places north of the Bundi hills (Article II); and to the district of Kunch in Bundelkhand; (ii) engage never to entertain in his service 'Europeans of any description'. On their part, the British undertook (i) not to disturb Holkar's possessions in Mewar, Malwa and 'Harrowtee' or interfere with the rulers south of the Chambal; (ii) to 'deliver immediately' such of his possessions as were situated south of the river Tapti.

While ratifying the Treaty on 2 February 1806, the Governor-General added 'Declaratory articles' whereby the British renounced all claims to territory listed in Article II. The Treaty marks the end of the Second Anglo-Maratha War (q.v.).

Aitchison, IV, pp. 289–93; Dodwell, *CHI*, V, p. 375.

Ramakrishna Mission (founded 1897)

The Ramakrishna monastic order and Mission, formally registered in 1909, had been officially established in 1887, and more systematically founded ten years later in 1897 by Swami Vivekananda (q.v.), the chief disciple of Swami Ramakrishna Parmahansa (1836-86) of Dakshineswar. A year after his death, about a dozen young men, including Vivekananda, had taken monastic vows at Baranagore and dedicated themselves to propagating the gospel of the master. The latter had preached the equality of all religions which point the way to achieve God. A practical Vedantist, Ramakrishna realised 'divinity in humanity', viz, in the service of man, and thereby found communion with a loving and vibrating humanity.

The means for spiritual life and salvation were spelt out, Ramakrishna said, in the ancient scriptures. He also sanctified the worship of images which, he had argued, were only different forms of one God. It has been suggested that Ramakrishna has in large part contributed to the growth of national (or Hindu) self-consciousness. His influence on social reform after his death in 1886 was a curious mixture of traditional and modern ideas.

The principal objective of the Mission was to ward off the materialist influences of western civilization. It idealized Hinduism, including its practice of idol worship and polytheism. For a revived Hindu faith, it visualized the spiritual conquest of the world. A monastery was established at Mayavati near Almora and in 1899 the headquarters of the Math were moved to Belur on the banks of the Ganges, near Calcutta. The Math is a registered religious trust and the Mission a charitable society under the Societies Registration Act of 1860. Though legally distinct from each other and endowed with separate funds, the Mission and the Math are virtually a single body, the members of the Math constituting the principal workers of the Mission while its trustees form the governing body. The Belur Math is the headquarters of both.

At Mayavati, young men who joined the Mission were trained as *sanyasis* for religious as well as social welfare work. They lived dedicated yet ascetic lives actively engaged in alleviating human suffering and devoted to study, meditation and prayer. Two papers, *Prabhuda Bharat* (in English) and *Udbodhna* (in Bengali), were published to propagate the message of the master.

To the Math, which was the centre for spiritual culture, Vivekananda added the Mission—devoted to social service inspired by Ramakrishna's ideal of 'service of man, for man was God'. The mission also aimed at training missionaries and preachers to work in India and abroad—spreading the Vedantic teachings as propounded by the master and in bringing about an equality among different sections of people through mass education and appropriate training. Though deeply religious and steeped in Hinduism, the Mission feels one with the followers of other religions too. It is not a proselytising body, nor is it sectarian in its outlook. Its chief aim is to project and propagate the principles of Vedanta, convinced that with that background, a Hindu (or a person of any faith) would be a better representative of his or her faith.

The Math was to perform different roles in different countries, for in some only spirituality is needed; in others, some amount of material comfort is extremely necessary. In India, the first and foremost task was the propagation of education and spirituality among the masses: 'it is impossible for hungry men to become spiritual unless food is provided for them'. The Math was not to pay much attention to social reform, for 'social evils are a sort of disease in a social body and if that body be nourished by education and food, the evils will die out of themselves. Hence, instead of using its energy in the trumpeting of social evils, it should be the aim of the Math to nourish the social body.' The Mission's role was to bring about on a new basis of equality, respect and understanding, a closer link between East and West. The movement has always preserved its dual character—a contemplative Math and a socially active Mission. The latter, with all its hospitals, schools, and relief projects, is necessarily involved in the affairs of the world. It has had to learn how to accept help and co-operation in these projects while refusing to be governed by the worldy policies of its helpers.

The Mission officially shied away from political involvement; nevertheless, a number of young Bengali revolutionaries like B. C. Pal (q.v.) and Sister Nivedita (Margaret Elizabeth Noble, who took the name of SN; 1867-1911) did indulge in anarchist activities, inspired by Vivekananda's call to patriotism and dedication to the cause of the country above all else.

Over the years, the Mission has grown. By 1966, it had 113 branch centres and attached to these 22 sub-centres with roughly 700 monks and *brahamcharins*. India apart, the Mission operates in Argentina, Bangla Desh, Burma, England, Fiji, France, Mauritius, Singapore, Sri Lanka, Switzerland and the United States. The Math and the Mission have brought out a large number of publications on Vedanta in the English language. For its finances, it depends mainly on voluntary contributions from the public, supplemented by state grants in India and some countries abroad. The Mission operates a number of centres in Europe and the United States, where its members engage themselves actively in relief work of all kinds and in providing medical aid to the needy, besides holding devotional meetings and religious discourses.

In the West, the work is mainly concerned with preaching the universal principles of religion while in the East the Mission's activities include running cultural centres, schools, colleges, libraries, orphanages, hospitals and dispensaries and the organization of various types of social service and emergency relief work.

Swami Gambhirananda, *History of the Ramakrishna Math & Mission*, Calcutta, 1957.

Raja Ram Mohun Roy (1772–1833)

A pioneer religious, social and political reformer, Ram Mohun Roy is best described as the father of modern India. He was born in an orthodox and well-to-do family at Radhanagar, in the Hooghly district of West Bengal. The family surname was Banerjee 'but the title of Roy-Rayan', conferred by the Nawab of Bengal, had become hereditary. As he grew up, Ram Mohun acquired a good knowledge of languages. Bengali was his mother-tongue; Persian and Arabic he acquired at Patna; Sanskrit at Banaras. English came early on and, later in life, he was to gain a working knowledge of Latin, Greek and Hebrew. He had a smattering of French too. Ram Mohun was a prolific writer and the author of two books in Persian, three in Hindi, thirty-two in Bengali and forty-seven tracts, letters and books in English.

As was then customary, Ram Mohun was sent to Patna to study Persian and Arabic and the extensive reading he did there was responsible for the great influence of Islam on his religious thinking. Driven away from home as a result of a treatise against idolatry, he is said to have visited Tibet during his wanderings. He also stayed at Banaras where he studied the Hindu scriptures and found a 'Brahmanical equivalent' of certain features of Islamic faith that he so admired. He moved back to Murshidabad after his father's death and, taking advantage of a local press, published his *Tuhfat-ul-Muwahhiddin* (literally, 'A gift to the Unitarians') which derives inspiration from Islamic thought and is a protest against idolatry and superstition. His other work in Persian was *Munazarat-ul-Adyan* (literally 'Discussions/ Debates on Religion'). In 1822-3 he published a weekly journal, *Mirat-ul-Akhbar*.

Between 1791-4, Ram Mohun set up a modest money-lending business in Calcutta (q.v.) and bought some property. Presently he began a study of the English language and, in 1797, joined the John Company's (q.v.) service in the revenue department. For a short spell in 1803 he worked for Thomas Woodforde, then Collector of Dacca, and, during 1805–11, for John Digby at Ramgarh, Jessore, Bhagalpur and Rangpur, continuing to work for him privately after the latter's retirement. It was due to Digby's encouragement that Ram Mohun became deeply involved in English language and literature. Subsequently, unable to secure any permanent employment, he left for Calcutta where he settled down.

During his years of employment with the Company, Ram Mohun had undertaken a serious study of Tantric and Jain literature as also Christian theology and Muslim sufi and *mutazillite* thought. He had, as a result, come to the conclusion that there was a basic unity underlying the Hindu, Muslim and Christian religions. His contribution, it is said, lay in separating the 'essentials of religion from non-essentials' and in presenting a 'positive and rationally sound system of ethico-religious thought'. To him religion was an all-embracing principle operating in every sphere of individual, social and national life.

After moving to Calcutta, Ram Mohun formed the short-lived Atmiya Sabha (1815-19) to propagate the monotheistic doctrine of Hindu scriptures. He believed in God as being omnipresent, omnipotent, formless and unseen. First and foremost a religious reformer, he accepted the truth of all religious texts and their teachings. A pioneer in the comparative study of religions, he undertook a serious study of the Bible with the help of one William Adam and drew upon the originals in Hebrew and Greek. As a result, his *The Precepts of Jesus* (1820) proved highly polemical and caused unending controversy with the Serampore missionaries. Later, with the backing of Adam, Ram Mohun started a Calcutta Unitarian Committee, which was short-lived. In 1828 he established the Brahmo Sabha, later the Brahmo Samaj (q.v.).

Initially using the platform of the Atmiya Sabha, Ram Mohun launched a programme of social reform and expressed himself boldly against Sati (q.v.), child marriage, polygamy and the caste system. Though he preferred reform from within rather than through legislation, he deserves credit for creating a strong public opinion against these social evils, thereby making the task of British administrators (who were to implement reform) relatively easier. Slanderous propaganda against him did not dampen his determination to effect the emancipation of women; he suggested, *inter alia*, a change in the law of property in their favour. He was also a relentless crusader against the rigidity of the caste system and held that a democratic society was possible only if the system were completely eliminated.

Ram Mohun had implicit faith in mass education as the sole means of eradicating pernicious social and religious practices and elevating individual character. He pressed for the substitution of English for Persian as the official language of the country and for the introduction of a westernized system of education. Simultaneously, he advocated a more scientific approach to the study of the eastern classics, establishing the Vedanta College (1825) to teach the Hindu monotheistic doctrines and foster a proper study of Sanskrit. Nor did he ignore the vernaculars which he rated an ideal vehicle for disseminating modern knowledge. He wrote textbooks in Bengali on grammar, geography, astronomy and geometry for use in the Anglo-Hindu school that he had established. For the impetus thus given to the language he is considered the 'maker' of modern Bengali prose; it was on foundations he laid that Bankim Chandra (1838-94) and Vidyasagar (1820-91) later built the edifice of Bengali literature.

Ram Mohun viewed British rule as beneficial. More, he supported European colonization which would, he argued, improve the social, educational and political condition of India. He felt it would prepare the people for a constitutional and democratic form of government and expedite the process of modernizing the social and economic life of the country. He was among the first to launch a spirited protest against the Jury Act (1827) and the Press Act (1828). In his weekly journal *Sambad Kaumadi* he suggested improvements in the British system of administration and an increasing association of Indians in policy-making. As a realist, Ram Mohun was conscious that the country was not immediately ready for freedom and therefore argued strongly in favour of organizing the Company's rule on more rational principles. He urged respect for a free press, the rule of law, civil liberties, individual rights and the sanctity of ownership of private property.

Ram Mohun was keen to visit England, and it was arranged for him to do so as an envoy of the then Mughal ruler, Akbar Shah II (q.v.), to the court of St James's, to which end the title of Raja was bestowed on him. He was expected to represent to the British sovereign the inadequacy of the stipend granted to the Mughal emperor. The Company's government did not recognize Ram Mohun's title, but it allowed him to proceed to England in his individual capacity.

The Raja was no narrow bigot and the world to him was one. He grieved over the loss of freedom to Naples, rejoiced over the establishment of a constitutional règime in Spain, warmly greeted the news of the July 1830 revolution in France and vowed unstinted support to Lord John Russell's Reform Bill (1832) in England. Welcomed by English scholars, historians and philosophers and introduced in the House of Lords, the Raja was befriended by many among the royalty. Unsuccessful in his original mission, Ram Mohun died at Bristol in September 1833 a few months after a visit to France.

It is necessary to remind ourselves that many generalizations about Raja Ram Mohun Roy have no objective relevance to events during the age in which he lived but were formulated after his death for various reasons. Recent assessments have brought out the realization that a sharp tradition-modernization dichotomy is not conducive to an appreciation of the complex processes of change in the colonial situation of which the Raja was merely a part. The three main influences in the Raja's thought—Persian, Vedantic and Occidental—were imbibed by him successively, strictly in that chronological order, a fact which cannot be emphasized too often. His career exhibited a complex and inconclusive process of modernization in which three strands may be detected: a consolidation of the position of the traditional high-caste rural gentry on the land; the transition of a medieval literati into a modern intelligentsia and the transition from Company monopoly to free-trade imperialism. Ram Mohun's achievements as a modernizer were invariably both limited and extremely ambivalent—for society was undergoing a change from pre-capitalist moorings towards its weak and distorted caricature, all that colonial subjection permitted. However, his personal greatness was never in doubt: the sweeping clarity of his thought, the striking modernity of his philosophical premises and social vision, and the concrete achievements of his fruitful career in Calcutta that led to the emergence of a modern urban culture containing the seeds of future Indian nationalism.

Saumyendranath Tagore has cited with approval R. Venkata Ratnam's fulsome tribute: the Raja 'was distinctly different from the other great men of India before his day. In range of vision, in reach of sympathy, in versatility of power, in variety of activities, in coordination of interests and in coalescence of ideas . . . (he) is a unique figure in the history of India, if not in the annals of the race.'

Upendra Nath Ball, *Rammohun Roy: A Study of his Life, Works and Thoughts*, Calcutta, 1933; Iqbal Singh, *Ram Mohun Roy: A Biographical Inquiry into the Making of Modern India*, vol. I, Bombay, 1958; Saumyendranath Tagore, *Raja Rammohun Roy*, New Delhi, 1973; V. C. Joshi (ed.), *Rammohun Roy and the Process of Modernization in India*, New Delhi, 1975.

Mahadev (Mahadeo) Govind Ranade (1842–1901)

An eminent social reformer who rose to be a judge of the Bombay High Court, Mahadev Govind Ranade is widely accepted as the 'father of the renaissance' in western India. After a brilliant academic career in India he was sent on a scholarship to Edinburgh to complete his education. On returning home, he joined the civil service and was appointed a sub-judge in Poona. He stagnated in minor posts all through Lytton's (q.v.) règime, but subsequently obtained higher positions through successive promotions and retired as a puisne judge of the Bombay High Court.

A man of varied interests, an economist, politician, historian and social reformer, Ranade did not let his official work interfere with his duty to the country and its people. He sketched out a policy that would make India progress economically; a keen historian, he took a special interest in reinterpreting Maratha history. He was also an active member of the Poona Sarvojanik Sabha (q.v.), the Deccan Education Society (q.v.), and the Prarthana Samaj.

Ranade's principal *forte* was social and religious reform. He relied upon legislation to do away with social ills and worked unceasingly for the eradication of child marriage, the purdah system and the prohibition of widow remarriage. To encourage consideration of social problems on a national scale, he inaugurated the Indian National Social Conference, which for many years met for its annual sessions alongside the Indian National Congress (q.v.).

Ranade presented to friends and visitors a stern and severe aspect, and being devoid of light or amusing talk, was not a convivial companion. A voracious reader, he lost one of his eyes largely through excessive reading in insufficient light. He never forgot that reform was for all—and not merely for a few. At bottom, Ranade's heart was gentle and peace-loving. Cast in a big mould, both in body and mind, he was a veritable giant; his scholarship had amplitude and depth far beyond the common. History, politics, economics, blue books, German and Marathi literature—these made up his gargantuan fare. Like a true rishi, he had toleration and mercy for all and planned and laboured for all alike. *Inter alia*, he rehabilitated the character of Shivaji and the empire that he founded, laid the groundwork for Indian economics, enumerated the elements that go into the making of a great man—'earnestness of purpose, sincerity in action, originality, imagination and, above all, the power of magnetism'. All these qualities he possessed, and in rich measure.

On questions relating to religious superstition and orthodoxy, Ranade believed in reformation from within as against the revivalism that was then popular in many parts of the country. While official duty prevented his engaging in political activity, he exercised a tremendous impact on the Congress in general and its policy-making in particular. A moderate, he decried militancy and advocated peaceful progress through constitutional means. He believed, with some reservations, in the benevolent nature of British rule and tried to convince his compatriots that they had much to learn from their alien masters. Though never a spectacular figure on the Indian political stage, Ranade is credited with arousing national consciousness among the people and guiding them into responsible political roles.

Tilak (q.v.) has talked of Ranade's 'unique greatness,' in breathing life into that 'cold lump of flesh and bones' that was Maharashtra before him and he did it 'by all possible remedies in all possible ways.' Gokhale (q.v.) recalled his 'great, massive intellect . . . . an earnest and dauntless spirit, an infinite capacity for work . . . and an humble faith in the purpose of Providence that nothing shook.'

Called 'the modern rishi', Ranade achieved elevation as well as detachment—his life one long and unbroken sacrifice, his soul 'like a star that dwelt apart.' Circumstances did not permit him heroic actions; essentially, his was the role of a constructive nation-builder. Subjecting himself to severe discipline, he cultivated marvellous self-control, forbearance and equanimity. No man judged himself more severely than he did. He was scarcely known to lose his temper and chose the path of conciliatory co-operation. Gokhale said of him that if he had been born two centuries earlier 'Ranade would have found his place by the side of saints like Tukaram or Eknath'. Ranade's biographer maintains that he stood 'for the liberation of conscience from external authority; of the country from political and economic dominion and of the intelligentsia from prejudices and prepossessions, beliefs and superstitions'.

P. J. Jagirdar, *Mahadeo Govind Ranade*, New Delhi, 1971; T. V. Parvate, *Mahadev Govind Ranade: A Biography*, Bombay, 1963; V. S. Srinivasa Sastri, *Centenary of the*

Birthday of M. G. Ranade, 18 January 1942, Madras, 1942; B. R. Ambedkar, *Ranade, Gandhi and Jinnah* (address delivered on the 101st birth anniversary of Ranade, held on the 18 January 1943, Poona) Jullundur, 1964; Mahadeo Govind Ranade, *Rise of the Maratha Power*, Reprint, New Delhi, 1961.

Ranjit Singh (1780–1839)

Ranjit Singh was born (1780) at Gujranwala and succeeded his father Maha Singh as head of the Sukarchakia *misal* in 1793. Illiterate and unlettered, he displayed remarkable intelligence, political sagacity and dynamic leadership in creating a powerful Sikh state in the Panjab. The administration of his possessions was taken over by his mother Raj Kaur, ably assisted by Diwan Lakhpat Rai. In 1797, taking advantage of the Diwan's murder, Ranjit Singh took the administration into his own hands, appointing Dal Singh, his maternal uncle, as his chief minister. He also undertook to fulfil his self-appointed task of uniting all Sikhs under his banner and forming a large and unified state of Panjab. His rival *misaldars* were, happily for him, in a state of decline, although Zaman Shah of Afghanistan, Sansar Chand of Kangra and the Gurkhas under Amar Singh Thapa constituted a formidable trio, each hoping to gain control over the Panjab.

Zaman Shah, the grandson of Ahmad Shah Abdali (q.v.), led his fourth expedition into the Panjab in 1798, hoping this time to extirpate the Sikhs. Ranjit Singh faced the invader gallantly and so impressed him with his prowess that, in return for the recovery of his guns, the Afghan ruler appointed him governor of the Panjab. The Sikh chief thus occupied Lahore without much resistance from the Bhangi *misaldars* after defeating a confederacy of the neighbouring Sikh and Muslim chiefs at Bhasin; on 12 April 1801, Sahib Singh Bedi proclaimed him Maharaja of the Panjab.

To pursue his plan of systematic aggression, Ranjit Singh first won over the loyalty of such powerful *misals* as the Kanhayas, Ahluwalias and Ramgarhias, through tactful diplomacy. With their active support he now chastised, annexed and demanded tribute from weaker principalities—Kasur, Jhaurian, Kangra, Akalgarh, Gujrat, Jhang, Sahiwal, Chiniot, etc. Unscrupulous and self-assertive, he did not always resort to military means to achieve his ends.

Ranjit Singh next turned his attention to the cis-Sutlej states which, after the fall of George Thomas (1756?-1802), had come under the influence of the Amirs of Sind (q.v.). In 1802 Perron (q.v.) and in 1805 Yashvantrao Holkar (q.v.) sought his help against the British. Shrewdly, the Maharaja refrained from entering into a political grouping with a stronger Indian power, preferring instead to sign the Treaty of Lahore (1806) with the British. In the result, the Marathas were soon driven out and the cis-Sutlej states left to the mercy of Ranjit Singh. Aware of British disinterestedness, the Sikh chief undertook two invasions, conquering and exacting *nazarana*, or tribute, from all these states. With the British rejecting their plea for help, the states reconciled themselves to Ranjit Singh's supremacy and, by 1808, had formed subordinate alliances with him.

The Treaty of Tilsit (1807) between Napoleon Bonaparte and Tsar Alexander I led to a British diplomatic offensive in India; as part of this,

Charles Metcalfe (q.v.) repaired to the court of Lahore to elicit Ranjit Singh's help in case of French aggression. The wily Sikh chief deputed Fakir Imamuddin to meet Metcalfe at Patiala, implying thereby an indirect extension of his sovereignty over the area. Again, before the talks had got underway, he launched upon a series of conquests—annexing Faridkot, Ambala, Malerkotla, Thanesar, Kasur, Pathankot and Sialkot, while at the same time exacting tribute from Basoli and Chamba. The Maharaja hoped that the British would recognize his fresh conquests in return for friendship and support against the French.

By January 1809, however, a favourable turn of events in Europe had brought about a sea change in British policy which now made a firm demand that Ranjit Singh sign a treaty on terms dictated by them. The Maharaja hesitated to fight and expose his infant state to strains it might have been unable to bear even though some of his confidants advised him to seek the co-operation of the Marathas, the Rohillas, and Begum Samru. His subsequent acceptance of the Treaty of Amritsar (q.v.) was ostensibly a diplomatic defeat and a fatal blow to his dreams of a united Sikh empire. In so doing he clearly renounced his claims to the cis-Sutlej areas conquered after Metcalfe's arrival at his court.

Spurred on by the freedom of action which his compact with the British allowed him in the trans-Sutlej areas, Ranjit Singh turned his attention to annexation and consolidation of his power there. By the end of 1809, he had taken Kangra, Kasur, Sialkot, Sheikhupura and the Gheba states; a year later he had subjugated all the independent principalities including the Makkar and Kanbaja *misals*. In 1815 he abolished the Gurumata, the central body that exercised some vague, if ill-defined, control over the affairs of the Sikh community, thereby taking over as undisputed leader of the state.

Earlier, in 1812, Ranjit Singh had allied himself with Fateh Khan of Kabul to crush Atta Muhammad Khan of Kashmir. In the course of the campaign Mohkam Chand managed to rescue the former Afghan Amir, Shah Shuja, a prisoner of Atta Muhammad, and brought him to Lahore where the Sikh chief is said to have forced him to disgorge the famous Kohinoor diamond. Deprived of his share of the spoils of Kashmir, Ranjit Singh retaliated by taking Attock, then deservedly regarded as the 'sentinel' of India. Fateh Khan rallied other Muslim chiefs and attacked, but in the pitched battle at Chach that followed the Sikhs were victorious. A more confident Ranjit Singh now attacked Kashmir but was unsuccessful. In June 1818 Multan was occupied and the fort capitulated in the seventh expedition sent against it. A year later he successfully occupied Kashmir, conquered Dera Ghazi Khan (1820), Derajat, and Dera Ismail Khan (1821).

The most important Sikh conquest was that of Peshawar. Although he had occupied Peshawar in 1818, Ranjit Singh had then left it in the hands of a Muslim governor. Four years later Muhammad Azim of Kabul seized it, leading to a *jehad* against the Sikhs; Azim was, however, defeated in the battle of Nowshera. Peshawar, none the less remained a source of trouble till 1834 when, taking advantage of the civil war in Kabul, Ranjit Singh annexed it to his dominion and appointed Hari Singh Nalwa as its governor. Amir Dost Mohammad's (q.v.) attempt to reconquer Peshawar (1835) ended in dismal failure. Two years later the Afghans were again forced to retreat after their victory at Jamrud where the Sikh governor fell fighting. Between 1831-6, Dera Ismail Khan, Bannu, Tonk and Dera Ghazi Khan, which had hitherto been occupied by local chiefs, were brought under the direct rule of the Sikh state. In 1834 Ladakh was conquered by the Dogra general, Zorawar Singh.

Ranjit Singh's interest in expanding his dominion towards Sind (q.v.) and occupying Shikarpur came into direct clash with British plans to establish a vague protectorate over Afghanistan, thanks to the conclusion of the Treaty of Turkomanchai (1828) between Russia and Persia. Alexander Burnes (q.v.) was deputed to explore the possibility of navigating the Indus under cover of sending some horses as a gift to Ranjit Singh. Bentinck (q.v.) later met the Maharaja at Rupar (1831) and persuaded him to recognize the commercial treaty which the John Company (q.v.) had concluded with the Amirs of Sind. In 1838, in pursuance of British plans to reinstate Shah Shuja, Ranjit Singh was persuaded to sign the Tripartite Treaty (q.v.), thereby putting an end for all time to his dream of conquering Shikarpur.

The Maharaja's ambition of a unified Panjab had been achieved within the territorial limits set for him by the British. A well-trained army led by able Indian generals as well as capable European mercenaries, the Sikh chief's unshaken determination and generous treatment of the defeated chiefs—all helped him accomplish the goal he had set himself. A distinct feature of his rule was its secular character, for among those he appointed to trusted posts were Muslims, Hindus and Sikhs.

After his meeting with Auckland (q.v.) in December 1838 at Ferozepur, Ranjit Singh's health, already failing, became worse. His condition kept deteriorating and he died in June 1839 after appointing his eldest son, Kharak Singh, as his successor. Ranjit Singh's deathbed decision—taken on the advice of Fakir Azizuddin—that Kharak Singh should succeed him with Dhian Singh as his chief minister 'was the best course practicable'. The former was the rightful heir and needed the Dogra leader's guidance and support. In the event, this strange compromise did not work. The simple-minded Kharak Singh succumbed to court intrigue, allowed himself to be deposed and imprisoned within four months of his accession and was slowly poisoned to death in another year's time.

Among Ranjit Singh's principal achievements, his very successful defence of his kingdom against the Afghans may be rated the most important. Yet, his is a 'supreme example of an intellect without a conscience. He forgot that force, stratagem and policy alone can create a very rude organization. He so completely centralized everything pertaining to his government in himself that his disappearance caused not a vacancy but a void in which the entire structure of government was submerged. He left the jagirdars weak and the army too powerful for his weak successors to control.' It was an unhappy coincidence that nearly all his able generals—Mohkam Chand, Diwan Chand, Hari Singh Nalwa, Ram Dyal—died during his lifetime. Those left were 'crafty, designing men, either weaklings or traitors'.

A major 'external cause' of Ranjit Singh's failure lay in his relations with the British, who limited his power on the east, on the south and would have done so on the west too, if that were possible. A clash of arms between his military monarchy and British imperialism was imminent, but it occurred after his death, 'under far less able men, chaos and disorder had already supervened and whatever hope there had been when he was living, there was no more when he was dead . . . . In his relations with the British government, Ranjit Singh is seen at his worst. He never grandly dared. He was all hesitancy and indecision.'

The image that persists of Ranjit Singh is of a popular ruler, well-known to his people through frequent appearances in their midst, ready to listen to them and to redress their grievances at all times, and looking upon all his subjects, irrespective of caste and creed, with one eye. One of his recent biographers has compared the Sikh ruler to his two famous contemporaries: Napoleon Bonaparte of France and Mohammed (Mehemet) Ali of Egypt. He has expressed the view that the Maharaja was neither a selfless patriot nor an avaricious freebooter, neither a model of virtue nor a lascivious sensualist; that his political success was due largely to the fact that he aroused among his people a sense of nascent nationalism.

N. K. Sinha, *Ranjit Singh*, 3rd ed., Calcutta, 1951; Khushwant Singh, *Ranjit Singh, Maharaja of the Panjab 1780–1839,* London, 1962; Fakir Syed Waheeduddin, *The Real Ranjit Singh*, Indian reprint, New Delhi, 1976; Lepel Griffin, *Ranjit Singh*, Indian reprint, Delhi, 1967.

Dinkar Rao (1819–96)

Born in 1819 in the district of Ratnagiri, Dinkar Rao was a Maratha Brahmin and educated both in Sanskrit and Persian. He began life as an accountant in Gwalior where he later succeeded his father as *subahdar* of a division.

Dinkar Rao made his mark as an administrator and statesman in his capacity as Diwan (1851-9) of Gwalior state. His difficulties were immense. The Maharaja, Jayaji Rao, was a minor, the sardars powerfully entrenched and opposed to all reform. The officials were permeated with self-seeking tendencies and there were no well-founded laws and no administration worth the name. Dinkar Rao's revenue, judicial and police reforms were of a far-reaching character.

Loyal to the British, it was mainly his efforts which kept the powerful Gwalior regiments from joining the 'mutineers' in the Rebellion of 1857 (q.v.). In recognition of his services, the Viceroy and the Maharaja conferred on him sizeable *jagirs* in Banaras district. However, when accused of attempting to assume all power in the state and on losing the Maharaja's confidence, Dinkar Rao resigned in 1859. Three years later, he was appointed a member of the Governor-General's Supreme Council, its other Indian members being the Maharajas of Patiala and of Banaras. Earlier, he had served in Dholpur, Rewa and Devas. Dinkar Rao considered British rule benevolent, but that did not make him a silent spectator in the Council. He held that a contented populace alone could indicate the success of government, and thus directed attention to measures for improvement in the lives of the people. Appointed to the Baroda tribunal (1875) to try Malhar Rao (q.v.) Dinkar Rao, along with its other Indian members, found him not guilty and thereby helped to avert a tragedy. Two years later, he was honoured with the title of Munshi-i-Khas Bahadur and, later still, his title of Rao Raja was made hereditary.

Dinkar Rao's public conduct is said to have been 'spotless' and his private life 'saintly'. By nature reticent, his public speech was 'always charming, animated, full of meaning and gravity'.

He died in Allahabad on 2 January 1896.

G. A. Natesan (ed.), *Indian Statesmen: Dewans and Prime Ministers of Native States*, Madras, n.d.; *Buckland*, p. 350.

T. Madhava Rao (Row) (1829–91)

One of the most eminent and progressive Indian statesmen and administrators of the nineteenth century, Madhava Rao came to be known as 'the Turgot of India'. He was a Maratha Brahmin who served successfully as Diwan in three princely states.

After a brief spell as a teacher of mathematics and natural philosophy in Presidency College and a stint in the Accountant-General's office, both in Madras, Madhava Rao was appointed tutor to the princes of Travancore (1851), who were destined to be its future rulers. Seven years later, he took over as Diwan in that state, and for the next fifteen years devoted himself to straightening out its affairs. He adopted methods of government that were a synthesis of the old and the new, and followed a wide-ranging policy of judicial, revenue and social reform. With important fiscal changes, he not only cleared all the debts of the state, but undertook public works on a large scale. Given the disadvantage of being regarded 'with suspicion and fear' as the representative of the British, his success was all the more remarkable. In his own words, his objective was 'to provide for every subject, within a couple of hours' journey, the advantages of a doctor, a school-master, a judge, a magistrate, a registering officer and a post-master'. It has been said that he found Travancore a den of misrule and left it 'a model native state'.

Madhava Rao's work soon brought him recognition, for he was knighted and nominated to the Viceroy's Council in 1873. He declined the latter offer to become Diwan of Indore. During his two-year tenure there, he brought the long simmering Holkar-Sindhia feud to an end. In 1875, at the instance of the Government of India, he assumed office as Diwan of Baroda after the deposition of Malhar Rao (q.v.). For five years he guided the policy of that state and groomed its youthful ruler, Sayaji Rao III, for the duties of kingship.

A moderate reformer, Madhava Rao preferred change brought about by social compulsion rather than through legislation. In politics he is said to have been 'more practical than theoretic, more accurate than wordy, more moderate than enthusiastic, more cautious than precipitate'. Loyal to the British, he was not unaware of the defects of their rule. He did however prefer constitutional means to achieve national goals and deprecated any attempt at popular agitation. Accordingly, he condemned the Rebellion of 1857 (q.v.) and, as Chairman of the Reception Committee at the 1887 session of the Indian National Congress (q.v.), advised its delegates against disloyalty to the paramount power.

Towards the close of his life, Madhava Rao suffered in the estimation of some of his countrymen and was attacked by his detractors as an enemy of reform. Others set him down as a mediocre thinker. The reason was largely his contributions under the *nom de plume* of 'A Native Thinker'. Besides, his reputation suffered with his withdrawal from the Congress because of what he regarded as its radical election scheme for the reform of the Legislative Councils in India, proposed by the party's Madras committee and adopted by the parent body at Bombay in 1889. As may be evident, in matters of social and political reform, Madhava Rao was a conservative. Thus he was a staunch advocate of the caste system; he opposed the craze for the English language and supported the nomination of the propertied classes to the legislative councils. He regarded the system of 'election' to the legislature as 'premature', 'wild and mischievous' and 'disturbing' to the country's peace and tranquillity.

Madhava Rao lived in Mylapore in Madras after his retirement (1882) and until his death in 1891.

G. A. Natesan (ed.), *Indian Statesmen: Dewans and Prime Ministers of Native States*, Madras, n.d.; Sen, *DNB*, III, pp. 528–9 (K. N. V. Shastri).

Rebellion of 1857

The great upsurge of 1857, invariably referred to as the 'Mutiny' in most contemporary accounts, took on the dimensions of a rebellion as the princes and people of India, following the lead given by the sepoys, challenged their British masters. The question of the greased cartridge which proved to be its immediate cause was but the culminating point in that cauldron of seething discontent and unrest then coming to the boil in many parts of the country.

The discontent of the sepoys who suffered from numerous disabilities, apart from the lack of prospects for further promotion, had manifested itself in periodic mutinies from 1806 onwards, and in all parts of the country. Additionally, the administrative and judicial innovations made by the British in the country were half-understood, much less appreciated, by the masses, and no doubt resented by the privileged classes. Mention may be made in this context of the Inam Commission (q.v.) which meant large-scale deprivations, or of the Doctrine of Lapse (q.v.) that unnerved most rulers of princely states. The British reluctance to recruit educated Indians into the covenanted services was taken as an insult to the capacity and competence of this new and relatively vocal class of people. Their (British) refusal to treat Indians as social equals, the proselytizing activities of missionaries and the rapid pace at which social reform, such as the abolition of Sati (q.v.), was introduced aggravated the situation further. Such innovations as the introduction of Railways (q.v.) or the postal services under Dalhousie (q.v.) also upset a traditional society. Added to this was the ruthless economic exploitation of the country which the colonialists had turned into a source of supply of raw materials to feed the rapidly growing industrialization of England. This meant the steady but sure strangulation of indigenous cottage industries which had been the traditional backbone of the country's economy. The vast mass of cultivators felt equally oppressed by revenue assessments which were deemed to be unrealistic and on the high side.

As briefly mentioned, the immediate cause for the 1857 upheaval was the sepoys' refusal to bite the lard-coated cartridges that went into the Enfield rifle. It was widely held that the lard was made from the fat of the cow and the pig. Mangal Pandey (q.v.), who openly defied the authorities in his regiment, was tried and executed. But the contagion had caught on and incidents of a similar nature were repeated at Lucknow on 2 May 1857 and Meerut (10 May). With the news of the successful capture of Delhi by the sepoys from Meerut and the proclamation of an unwilling Bahadur Shah II (q.v.) as Emperor of Hindustan, the whole of north India was convulsed with military uprisings supported and, in many cases, preceded by civil rebellion. Although widespread, the centres of intensive activity were, however, confined to the North-Western Provinces, Rohilkhand, central India and Bihar.

From the outset, the British understood the extreme urgency, if only for purposes of prestige, of recapturing the imperial capital of Delhi which fell into their hands on 19 September 1857. The feat was accomplished by the concerted efforts of Sir Colin Campbell (1792-1863), the newly appointed commander-in-chief of the British forces, aided by a contingent of the Panjab moveable column under John Nicholson, later mortally wounded. At Lucknow, the 1,700-strong English force in the Residency struggled hard against 100,000 mutinying soldiers led by Begum Hazarat Mahal of Oudh (q.v.) and Maulvi Ahmadullah Shah of Faizabad. They were relieved early in March 1858 by James Outram (q.v.) and Campbell. The two Indian leaders who inspired the sepoys were also said to have 'incited' the Oudh zamindars and the populace to give the uprising a mass base.

Canning's (q.v.) proclamation of March 1858 taking away the proprietary rights of the zamindars steeled the latter into continuing resistance to British arms till December that year. Their back was finally broken in a relentless campaign organized by Campbell. At Kanpur, intermittent fighting continued between Nana Saheb (q.v.) and Tatya Tope (q.v.) on the one hand and the British on the other until the former, driven out by Henry Havelock, an intrepid British commander, joined Rani Lakshmi Bai (q.v.) of Jhansi. The latter led the revolt in central India, but was defeated and killed in June 1858. In Bihar, Babu Kunwar Singh (q.v.) challenged British might; when driven out from his stronghold he continued to harass the British forces in south Bihar, the North-Western Provinces and central India till his death on 5 May 1858.

In the Panjab, Rajasthan, Assam and areas south of the Narmada, the British successfully put down all sporadic cases of rebellion by apprehending local leaders and, in some instances, disarming them in good time. In Bengal and Madras there was widespread unrest but no organized movement *per se*. By the end of 1858 most of the 'rebel' leaders had been killed, captured or driven across the border into Nepal. By the beginning of 1859, all resistance had been crushed. In the final analysis, the revolt collapsed as it had failed to grow into a coherent movement. Additionally, there was the complete absence of a common goal and a singular lack of effective leadership coupled with a woefully inadequate military command.

Divergent opinions have been expressed as to the nature of the outbreak and later historians have waxed eloquent in support of their respective formulations. Contemporary observers too have expressed diverse opinions. Thus Benjamin Disraeli, then leader of the Tory opposition, called it a 'national revolt' and *not* a 'military mutiny'; Ellenborough (q.v.) thought hostilities in Oudh had more the 'character of a legitimate war than that of rebellion'. Justin McCarthy, writing long after the event, refused to call it 'a merely military mutiny', for it was 'a combination of military grievances, national hatred and religious fanaticism against the English occupation of India'; Charles Bell called it the 'rebellion of a whole people'.

The uprising has also been called a Muslim conspiracy; a sepoy revolt; a plot initiated by Rani Baiza Bai of Gwalior which was supported and popularized by Nana Saheb. Fancifully, its origins have been attributed to an underhand deal between the moribund Mughal Emperor, Bahadur Shah II, and the Persian ruler aided by Russia, mysteriously linked up with the circulation of *chapatis* all over the country. In the result, some have called it a mutiny; others, a popular revolt; still others India's first national war of independence.

To the extent that the alien rulers had given mortal offence to the dignity and self-respect of the ruling class and had antagonized the masses by their oppressive land revenue policy and economic measures (which ruined their arts and crafts), the Rebellion may be called a war for the liberation of India from the yoke of the foreigner. According to R. C. Majumdar, 'the so-called popular upsurge' to start with, 'was really a scramble for power and plunder', and even the popular cry of 'drive away the English' (he underlines), 'lost its force and fervour after the first orgy of riots' was over. In the first place, the 'popular upsurge' had nothing to do with the achievement of independence or freedom from British control, for that task was already done for the people by the mutinous sepoys. If there was any war, 'it was for maintaining and *not* gaining independence'. Again, one 'looks in vain' for any evidence to show that the civil population appreciated the importance of recovering lost independence, or made an organized, and determined effort, to maintain it by evolving a suitable plan of defence. Thus the idea of a common national endeavour to free the country from the yoke of the British is conspicuously absent in the proclamations issued by various leaders.

The rebellion of the chiefs and their people in Oudh constitutes the chief claim of the outbreak of 1857 to be regarded as a war of independence. There were, however, numerous earlier instances of civil resistance to British authority. If, however, the revolt of several *talukadars* and chiefs of Oudh who took advantage of a general mutiny of 'native' sepoys to rise against the British, is to be viewed as a war of independence, Majumdar argues, 'we must regard such war to be in continuous operation in more extensive regions in India almost throughout the first century of British rule'. 'It is difficult', Majumdar continues, to accept that the Mutiny 'was regarded at the time or for many years afterwards, as a war of independence'. All the elements 'of disaffection and discontent which combined to produce the great conflagration' were not only present, but 'made themselves felt in sporadic outbursts' throughout the previous century. 'Only their unique combination and the vast scale of operations' distinguished the outbreak of 1857.

According to Tara Chand, the outbreak of 1857 may be viewed at best 'as the first great and direct challenge to the British rule in India, on an extensive scale. The memory of 1857-8 substantiated the later movement, infused courage into the hearts of its fighters, furnished a historical basis for the grim struggle, and gave it a moral stimulus . . . [its] memory distorted but hallowed with sanctity, perhaps did more damage to the cause of British rule in India than the revolt itself. . . . Whatever might have been its original character, it soon became a symbol of challenge to the mighty British power in India. It remained a shining example before nascent nationalism in India in its struggle for freedom from the British yoke.'

Majumdar's comment, 'On the whole it is difficult to avoid the conclusion that the so-called First National War of Independence of 1857 is neither First, nor National, nor a War of Independence' — appears to be 'neither appropriate nor just' to S. B. Chaudhuri. His own conclusion is: 'It was both a Mutiny and a Rebellion, perhaps more of a rebellion than an undoubted mutiny, which either followed or preceded the sweeping participation of the people.' He argues that the upsurge of independence could be felt 'in the passion with which Savarkar invoked the spears of the Marathas, the swords of the Rajputs, the kirpans of the Sikhs, the crescent of the Islamites as elements in the common endeavour'. Unfortunately, Savarkar's 'undoubted emotional involvement' detracted from the 'historical worthiness' of his account. According to Chaudhuri, the year 1857 was a turning point in British history 'at which India failed to turn'.

Some sort of crude nationalistic feeling was concealed 'in the individual and collective loyalties of the people to their landed chiefs fighting against an alien power' and indeed 'in the profound desire of the rebels to end foreign domination for all' and 'in the general popular support' extended to the movement. Nationalism is after all a tendency, an impulse, a developing attitude of mind rather than an objective, fixed, determinate thing. The rising of 1857 was national because it represented 'the evolutionary, though variable and undoubtedly developing nature' of the manifestations of nationalism.

According to Maulana Abul Kalam Azad (q.v.) two facts stand out clearly in the midst of the tangled story of the rising: 'the remarkable sense of unity among the Hindus and the Muslims' of India and 'the deep loyalty which the people felt for the Mughal crown'.

There is however the 'sad conclusion' that the leaders of the revolt 'could never agree'. They were 'mutually jealous and continually intrigued against one another', personal jealousies and intrigues that were largely responsible for the Indian defeat. Most of those who took part — barring Maulvi Ahmadullah Shah of Faizabad and Tatya Tope — 'did so for personal reasons'. They did not rise against the British till their personal interests had been damaged. Again, the uprising was 'not the result of careful planning nor were there any master minds behind it'.

Nor were they forward-looking. 'The Mutiny leaders', S. N. Sen contends, 'would have set the clock back, they would have done away with the new reforms, with the new order, and gone back to the good, old days . . .'

Majumdar stresses the role of the sepoys whose risings destroyed British authority in certain areas thus creating power vacuums into which a motley array of aggrieved landlords, dacoits, predatory tribals, princely chiefs, rushed, each for his own advantage. His conclusion: 'The miseries and bloodshed of 1857-8 were not the birth-pangs of a freedom movement in India, but the dying groans of an obsolete aristocracy and centrifugal feudalism of the mediaeval age.'

Whatever way one may look at it, the outbreak began as a revolt of the sepoys and gradually took on the dimensions of a rebellion as people in most parts of the country, more particularly in the north, demonstrated their utter distrust of and dissatisfaction with the John Company's (q.v.) government. At the same time there is no denying the fact that it lacked the patriotic zeal and organized effort which go into waging a war of independence. In Tara Chand's considered judgement the rising 'was an attempt— the last attempt of the medieval order— to halt the process of dissolution and to recover its lost status . . . [it was] a general movement of the traditional elite of the Muslims and the Hindus— princes, landholders, soldiers, scholars and theologians . . . . The class composition of the insurgents reflects the geographical disposition of the movement, and sheds light upon the motives of the participants. There is little doubt that practically all those who belonged to this order were disaffected although some of them abstained from active participation because of their peculiar circumstances'.

The rebellion was foredoomed to failure, for it was not inspired by any positive or creative ideas. It was 'an almost spontaneous, episodic outburst' lacking a 'stable, well-ordered organization' to sustain the movement. There was neither a plan, nor yet a programme, nor any funds. There was little discipline among the rebels and their loyalties were fragile. Additionally, they were pitted against a foe whose military technique was based upon modern science and whose processes of reasoning were more in accord with logical and rational principles. Both in strategy and tactics, the British forces were far superior to their Indian counterparts, while their commanders were well-trained and possessed extensive experience.

Among a host of others, one of the chief results of the rebellion was the firmer establishment of British power in India as the administration of the Indian empire passed from the hands of the John Company into those of the British Crown.

S. N. Sen, *Eighteen Fifty-seven,* New Delhi, 1957; R. C. Majumdar, *The Sepoy Mutiny and the Revolt of 1857,* Calcutta, 1957; S. B. Chaudhuri, *Theories of the Indian Mutiny (1857–59): A study of the views of eminent historians on the subject,* Calcutta, 1965; Michael Adas, 'Twentieth Century Approaches to the Indian Mutiny of 1857-58', *Journal of Asian History* (Wiesbaden), V, 1, 1971, pp. 1-19; J. A. B. Palmer, *The Mutiny Outbreak at Meerut in 1857,* Cambridge, 1966; Valeire Fitzgerald, *Zemindar,* London, 1981; Christopher Hibbert, *The Great Mutiny: India, 1857,* London, 1980; H. Chattopadhyaya, *The Sepoy Mutiny, 1857: A social study and analysis,* Calcutta, 1957; P. C. Joshi (ed.), *Rebellion: 1857, A symposium,* New Delhi, 1957; A. T. Embree, *1857 in India,* Boston, 1963; V. D. Savarkar, *The Indian War of Independence (National Rising of 1857),* Bombay, 1960.

The Regulating Act (1773)

The affairs of the East India Company (q.v.) began to attract a great deal of critical attention in England following its acquisition, in 1765, of the Diwani

Rights (q.v.) over the provinces of Bengal, Bihar and Orissa. The anomaly of a commercial combine exercising political control, the resultant administrative anarchy, the ill-gotten wealth of the Company's 'Nabobs' and its unsatisfactory administrative control in England were sharply questioned in Parliament.

The Company, which had announced an enhanced dividend of 12½ per cent and a payment to the exchequer of £400,000, was soon face to face with financial bankruptcy. It emanated from wars necessitated by the need to defend its newly-acquired territories. In 1772, its application for a loan was utilized by Lord North's government in England to set up a Select and a Secret Committee to probe into its affairs. The reports of the two Committees paved the way for an Act of Parliament called the Regulating Act to enforce governmental control and regulate the affairs of the Company. It was tantamount 'in reality to a delegation of the whole power and sovereignty of this kingdom, set into the East.'

The Act, passed in May 1773, remodelled the Company's constitution at home and changed the structure of its government in India. To make the Court of Directors more responsible, and responsive, to public opinion a system of renewal was established whereby elections to the Court were to be held every four years, with ¼ of the members replaced annually. The voting power of the Court of Proprietors was restricted to a minimum of one-year holders of £1,000 stock. Parliamentary control was ensured by having the Directors submit copies of all dispatches and communications from India to the Treasury in case of revenues and a Secretary of State over civil and military affairs.

In India, the governor of Bengal was henceforth designated Governor-General of the Presidency of Fort William in Bengal, with a Council of four appointed by the British government for five years. Bengal Presidency was to exercise control over the other two Presidencies in all matters of war and peace. The latter could, however, act independently in emergencies, itself undefined, or on direct orders from the Court of Directors. Rules and Regulations made by the Governor-General in Council and adopted by a majority vote were to be submitted to the Supreme Court before they became valid.

The emoluments of the Company's servants were increased and such malpractices as acceptance of bribes and presents, private trading and lending money were rigorously barred. An independent Supreme Court of judicature consisting of a Chief Justice and three puisne judges was set up at Calcutta. Appeals from its decisions could only be made to the King in Council in England.

The Regulating Act proved, in retrospect, a half-way house, vague and defective in some important respects, such as the powers of the Governor-General in relation to his Council or of the supreme government in Calcutta over the two other presidencies. Its true import lies in the fact that British parliamentary control was established, making possible for future legislation to guide and direct the Company in its new political role. Its major defects were sought to be remedied by subsequent legislation, such as the Act of 1786 which vested the Governor-General with authority to overrule the majority in his Council on his own responsibility. In much the same manner, Pitt's India Act (q.v.), established the unquestioned superiority of Bengal Presidency over the other two, while the Amending Act (1781) defined the powers of Calcutta's Supreme Court and other courts under the jurisdiction of the Governor-General in Council.

M. V. Pylee, *A Short Constitutional History of India*, Bombay, 1967; S. R. Sharma, *A Constitutional History of India*, Bombay, 1949; A. C. Banerjee, *Constitutional History of India*, 3 vols., Delhi, 1977–1978, I (1600–1858), pp. 47–122.

Lord Ripon (1827–1909)

George Frederick Samuel Ripon, first Marquis of Ripon, began his public career in 1849 and his parliamentary career three years later. He served in various ministerial posts in the British government and was the first among India's Governors-General to have served both as Under Secretary (January-July 1861) and later (1866-73) Secretary of State at the India Office. He resigned following his conversion to Roman Catholicism, but re-entered public life after Gladstone's victory at the polls (1880) and was, soon after, designated Governor-General of India.

A thorough-going liberal, many believed Ripon would be a 'friend of India' and help smother controversies aroused by the domestic and foreign policies of his predecessor, Lytton (q.v.). *Inter alia*, he was 'charged' by his political superiors with putting governmental finances on a sound footing, reversing the policy of imperial expansion and establishing a certain rapport with public opinion in India.

The Governor-General set off on a partial reversal of the forward policy in Afghanistan by recalling British troops and, against the better judgement of some of his colleagues, leaving that country to its own devices to choose its new ruler. In the final analysis, the British agreed to help the Afghan chief Abdur Rahman (q.v.) with arms and money when the need arose, withdraw from his country and refrain from negotiating the issue of Herat bilaterally with Persia. In turn, the Amir accepted the stationing of a non-European British agent and the retention by India of the districts of Sibi and Pishin. Before a withdrawal could be effected, Ayub Khan of Herat defeated a British force under General Burrows, inflicting heavy losses. The British commander, General Frederick Roberts, who was dispatched to relieve Burrows, initially defeated Abdur Rahman but later helped him take Herat. Ripon also persuaded Wali Sher Ali, the erstwhile ruler of Kandahar, to abdicate, thereby leaving a friendly Abdur Rahman reasonably well-entrenched in his own country.

The Governor-General believed in direct negotiations with Russia and in refusing to make Afghanistan a pawn between two imperialist giants. Even though Russia had accepted a measure of British interest in Afghanistan on the conclusion of the Second Afghan War (q.v.), its own movement towards that country's frontiers caused anxiety and remained unchecked. For its part, Britain felt no need for a formal treaty, trusting to the sincerity of Russian declarations of a 'hands off' policy; but while it looked on complacently, the Czar's government occupied Merv (1884). Since verbal protests had been of no avail, the British began negotiating with Russia at the diplomatic level; in the result, the latter agreed to a joint demarcation of the boundary between their empire and Afghanistan.

The nub of the Governor-General's domestic policy was to bind the 'educated Indian class to British rule, trust their leaders . . .and find legitimate outlets for their aspirations'. His initial efforts aimed at conciliating Indian opinion constituted only 'an undoing process'. The Vernacular Press Act (q.v.), the hated legacy of his predecessor, was repealed, and the Factory Act (q.v.) finalized and passed. Ripon's liberal approach was manifest in the reforms he introduced subsequently, resting on the firm conviction that British rule in India constituted a 'trusteeship' and devolved a heavy responsibility on Britain not only to govern beneficiently, but also to train Indians for self-government.

To encourage a greater participation of non-official Indians in the work of local government and to train the educated among them in the art of administration and political responsibility, Ripon preferred to begin at the municipal and district level. An elaborate scheme of 'de-provincialization' was drawn up with such subjects as health, education and public works transferred to local bodies. Legislation was to be introduced under the supervision of provincial governments, who would be allowed access to new sources of revenue and a share in other imposts and thus no longer depend wholly on a fixed grant. The system held no appeal for the bureaucracy, without whose co-operation it was bound to be ineffective. In the result, it worked only partially in the North-Western Provinces, the Panjab and Madras, but was ineffective in Bengal, Bombay and the Central Provinces.

Subsequent legislation that Ripon introduced fared no better. His Land Tenancy Bill was vigorously opposed and criticized by the zamindars, the one class whose sympathies the government could least afford to alienate. Subjected to a review, the decision as to its final shape and form was left to his successor. The Famine Commission's (1878-80) recommendations, formulated into a 'Famine Code', were shelved on account of financial constraints, aided by an apathetic bureaucracy. Ripon's proposals to encourage the iron and steel industry were rejected by the Secretary of State. The Governor-General tried, albeit unsuccessfuly, to reframe rules in the provincial civil service to provide for competitive examinations instead of nominations.

However, it was the Ilbert Bill (q.v.), introduced in February 1883, that brought on Ripon the wrath and fury of the bureaucracy as well as non-official Europeans. The measure, which sought to give Indian judges jurisdiction over Europeans in criminal cases, was not exclusively Ripon's brain child. It had been in the making for a long while as more Indian civil servants received additional administrative and judicial powers. Nor was it framed overnight; in fact, official opinion had been sought, provincial governments consulted and, except for Madras, there had been no voice of dissent. The proposed measure had also received the green signal from the home government. Besides being unexpected, the storm that broke over it was out of all proportion to the import of the measure introduced and, understandably, caught Ripon unawares. His request to Gladstone to get a House of Commons vote on the Bill was rejected. Though admitting to an 'error in tactics', the Governor-General was not prepared to withdraw the Bill.

As the agitation against the Bill became more militant and better or-ganized and a so-called 'white mutiny' appeared imminent, Ripon au-thorized Sir Auckland Colvin to conduct negotiations for a compromise. Indian opinion, which had initially hailed Ripon as a 'deliverer' and ap-plauded the measure, was sorely disappointed at his apparent retreat. To protect their rights, arouse public opinion and mount an agitation, the first National Conference was called at Calcutta, a development Ripon had all along hoped to avoid!

In financial matters, the Governor-General strictly rejected innovation, adhering to the taxation policy outlined by Sir Richard Strachey. Major Evelyn Baring (later Earl Cromer) in 1882 removed tariffs on all imports, but Ripon rejected his recommendations for direct taxation. His sustained protest against saddling India with the expenses of imperial campaigns resulted in a partial payment by Britain of the costs of the Afghan war and of an Indian contingent dispatched to Egypt.

After his initial success in enacting the Factory Act of 1881 and the repeal of the Vernacular Press Act, Ripon failed to carry out the policy of his party in other matters. As noticed, his proposals for tenancy reform and the implementation of the Famine Commission's recommendations were delayed or altered so drastically either by the home government or the local governments that their purpose was to a large extent defeated.

Of the major local governments Ripon could only count on the support of Sir Charles Aitchison (q.v.), then Lieutenant-Governor of the Panjab. Besides the delaying tactics or opposition of these governments, the vast majority of senior officials in Calcutta and the provinces were not at all reconciled to Ripon's policies. They were apathetic, if not hostile.

Ripon had tried hard to ensure a continuation of liberal imperial policies but has been criticized as a 'reckless innovator' who followed a 'policy of sentiment'. A major problem appears to have been the pace of reform, Ripon's inability to foresee European reactions and his misfortune in having an executive council opposed to his policies, an indifferent home govern-ment, and a conservative India council baulking at change. His Indian administration, it has been maintained, 'did not rise above mediocrity', but his impact on the Indian people was tremendous judging from the rousing farewell he received before sailing back to Britain at the end of his tenure in India. Paradoxically Ripon was detested by the vast majority of Englishmen in India. 'The starched society of Anglo-India' ever viewed his activities with bewilderment and pain and found it difficult to forgive him. On the other hand, the 'tenacious affections' of the Indian people 'have clung to him' with the result that his name has become almost a symbol and a legend in India.

Ripon's disadvantages, in fact, were 'not acquired but innate'. His person-ality, a biographer maintains, had no sparkle, his intellect was not of first-rate quality and his oratory was turgid. 'His style is that of a sermon', remarked an admirer. Steady-going but something of a mediocrity, Gran-ville summed him up as 'a very persistent man with wealth.' Most of the graces of life had been denied to him. He was cautious but not tactful; he could never conciliate or win over an opponent and kept too much to himself. The genuine simplicity of his character made him a faulty judge of men. He had not the capacity, so essential in the head of a government, to seize quality in others. He had the creed of a first-rate man and the prowess of a second-rate man. All this notwithstanding, Ripon's moral tone and compassion, his 'sincerity and sympathy and vision impart to his work something better and higher' than is to be found in the guiding principles of most viceroyalties.

Local seif government as visualized by the Viceroy would have led to a representative system and this in turn could have expanded into a fully democratic state. Ripon's efforts, however, were frustrated by his countrymen, 'by the frenzy of those in India and the inertia of those in England'. None the less his 'sad failures' bore within them the seeds of eventual success: 'he whom the English condemned as Indophile beçame the most English of all Viceroys in that he was the prophet and champion of their freedom'. It has been suggested, that the four years of Ripon's viceroyalty form 'one of the successful failures of history'. 'What is now my dream', he wrote to a friend in England in January 1883, 'may become a reality when I have long finished my task on earth, and . . . perhaps it may be given me if I am not too unworthy, to look down hereafter on the completion of the task which I have now begun'.

Back in England, Ripon vigorously defended his administration. He also served as First Lord of the Admiralty (1886), in the Colonial Office (1892-1894), and finally, as Lord Privy Seal and leader of the Whigs in the House of Lords (1905-8). He retired barely a year before his death in 1909.

S. Gopal, *The Viceroyalty of Lord Ripon 1880–1884*, Oxford, 1953; L. P. Mathur, *Lord Ripon's Administration in India (1880—84)*, New Delhi, 1972; Mark Bence-Jones, *The Viceroys of India*, London, 1982; E. A. Hirschmann, 'Ilbert Bill Controversy as a Crisis in Imperial Relationships', unpublished Ph. D. thesis, University of Wisconsin, 1972, microfilm, *NMML; DNB 1901–1911* Supplement, 3 vols., III, pp. 216–21 (William Lee-Warner).

Rohilla War (1774)

Among the principal causes of the Rohilla War, itself a sequel to repeated Maratha invasions of Rohilla country, was the excessive fear entertained by the English of Maratha designs. From Rohilkhand, the Marathas were uncomfortably close to the John Company's (q.v.) newly-acquired dominion. Additionally, there was the desire of the Rohillas for protection, not to gainsay the ambitions of the Nawab of Oudh (q.v.), Shuja-ud-Daula (q.v.): while the latter had continuously extended his sway, the Rohillas had been weakened by repeated Maratha depredations.

In 1773 the combined forces of the Nawab and the British, who had helped drive the Marathas away from Rohilkhand, demanded compensation in terms of the Treaty of Shahbad (q.v.). Hafiz Rahmat Khan (q.v.) made desperate efforts to keep the treaties with a view to averting war, but failed. Shuja was unrelenting, raising his demand to Rs 2 crores. The English were conveniently non-committal, bound as they were by the secret clauses of the Treaty of Banaras (q.v.) to help Oudh. As a result of confabulations between the Nawab and the British in August-September 1773 the latter were to loan a brigade to punish the Rohillas, in return for a subsidy bearing the expenses of the campaign and payment of a sum of Rs 40 lakhs.

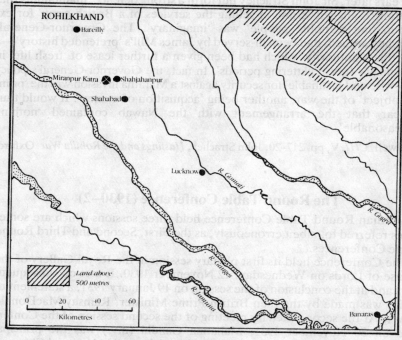

Rohilla War (1774)

It was against this background that the appeals made by the Rohillas through Colonel Alexander Champion, later C. in C. of the Bengal Army, evoked no response. On 13 April 1774 Shuja issued a last warning, and four days later troops entered Rohilkhand. In less than a week, at Miranpur Katra, 20 miles west of Shahjahanpur, a solitary battle took place which was to prove decisive. Rohilla troops numbering 40,000 were defeated, with Hafiz Rahmat Khan and 2,000 of his men dead; losses sustained by the English and the Oudh army were nominal. Faizullah Khan, who was chosen new Rohilla leader, fled to Garhwal but, hotly pursued by the British, surrendered on 2 October and signed the Treaty of Lalding (q.v.).

A few facts may be noticed about the war. First, all the three Indian parties involved—the Nawab, the Rohillas as well as the Marathas, were 'utterly unscrupulous' and disinterested in each other. Secondly, the letter of the Treaty of Shahbad was against Hafiz Rahmat Khan and his compatriots in so far as they were honour-bound to pay the Nawab Rs 40 lakhs on his obliging the Marathas to retire from their country, 'either by peace or war'. Thirdly, in the campaigns of 1773 both the Nawab Wazir and the British brigade had, by the mere fact of their presence on the spot, quelled the threatened Maratha invasion.

The Rohilla War constituted one of the major indictments against Warren Hastings (q.v.) in his impeachment. It was held that the Governor-General had deliberately sold away the lives and liberties of a free people and condoned the horrible atrocities perpetrated by the Nawab and his minions.

Years later, Sir John Strachey put forth a strong defence, maintaining that Hastings's alleged 'crime in selling the services of a British army' for exterminating a 'noble people' was 'imaginary'. The Governor-General, Strachey argued, had been ill-served by James Mill's 'pretended history'—a 'worthless authority' which had been given a further lease of 'fresh life' in Macaulay's (q.v.) 'glittering periods'. In fact, the Governor-General's policy was 'wise and justifiable' for security against a Maratha invasion was the 'primary object' of the war, another being 'acquisition of money'. It would thus appear that the arrangement with the Nawab contained 'nothing unreasonable'.

Dodwell, *CHI*, V, pp. 217–20; John Strachey, *Hastings and the Rohilla War*, Oxford, 1892.

The Round Table Conference (1930–2)

The Indian Round Table Conference held three sessions which are sometimes referred to, albeit erroneously, as the First, Second and Third Round Table Conferences.

The Conference held its first plenary session in the Royal Gallery of the House of Lords on Wednesday, 12 November 1930. It met on subsequent days and at the conclusion of the session on 19 January 1931, a statement of policy was made by the then British Prime Minister, Ramsay MacDonald (q.v.). At the second plenary meeting of the second session of the Conference on 30 November 1931, Mahatma Gandhi (q.v.) was the principal speaker. He was the solitary representative of the Indian National Congress (q.v.) which had boycotted the first session. A day later, a statement of policy on India's future political set up was made to the Conference by the British Prime Minister. The third session of the Conference convened during November-December 1932. It was poorly attended; neither the representatives of British political parties nor yet a number of Indian political leaders, including Gandhi, were present.

In the first session of the Conference, the three principal political parties in Britain (Labour, Conservative and Liberal) were represented by 16 members; British India by 57, all nominees of its Governor-General; and the Indian States (q.v.) by 16; the total membership of the Conference being 89. As has been noticed, the Congress was not represented in the first session. Prominent among the Indian Liberals who attended were Tej Bahadur Sapru (q.v.), V. S. Srinivasa Sastri, M. R. Jayakar and the well-known journalist, C. Y. Chintamani; among the Muslims, the Aga Khan (q.v.), Muhammad Shafi, Maulana Mohamed Ali (q.v.), A. K. Fazl-ul-Haq (q.v.) and M. A. Jinnah (q.v.) attended; among the Sikhs, Sampuran Singh. The Hindu Mahasabha (q.v.) was represented by Dr B. S. Moonje; the Depressed Classes by Dr B. R. Ambedkar (q.v.); Indian Christians by K. T. Paul; the British business community by Sir Hubert Winch Carr; and Anglo-Indians by H. A. J. Gidney. Among Indian princes, there were the rulers of Alwar, Baroda, Bhopal, Bikaner, Kashmir, Patiala and a few other smaller states. Hyderabad was represented by Sir Akbar Hydari, then a member of the Nizam's executive council; Mysore by Sir Mirza Muhammad Ismail, then its

Prime Minister; and Gwalior by Colonel K. N. Haksar, a member of the state's council of regency.

The first session did result in the British government accepting the principle that in India's future constitutional set-up, the executive authority of government should be responsible to the legislature both at the centre and the provinces. This was conditional on the acceptance of the principle of federation between British India and Indian India. In his address on 19 January 1931, at the conclusion of the session, the British Prime Minister declared: 'The view of HMG is that responsibility for the government of India should be placed upon legislatures, central and provincial, with such provisions as may be necessary to guarantee, during the period of transition, the observance of certain obligations and to meet other special circumstances, and also with such guarantees as are required by minorities to protect their political liberties and rights.'

The work of the first session of the Conference was taken up in its numerous sub-committees—the federal structure sub-committee, the provincial constitution sub-committee, the franchise sub-committee, the Sind sub-committee, the NWFP sub-committee, the defence sub-committee, the Services sub-committee, and the minorities sub-committee.

The second session of the Conference opened on 7 September 1931. Among the new comers were Gandhi, Sir Muhammad Iqbal, the celebrated Urdu poet, Dr S. K. Datta, a leading Indian Christian, G. D. Birla, the business magnate, Pandit Madan Mohan Malaviya (q.v.), Mrs Sarojini Naidu and Ali Imam. The session grappled with the problem of communal representation in general and of Muslim representation in particular. It closed on 1 December 1931. Despite its failure to solve the communal problem, the structure of the federal judiciary had taken shape; the intricate question of the distribution of resources between the centre and the provinces had been examined, if not settled. The main points, besides the communal issue, on which agreement was still to be worked out were the composition of the federal legislature and the manner in which the states were to be fitted into the federation.

The main work of the second session was done by two large sub-committees—on federal structure and the minorities—which re-examined and amplified the reports presented by the corresponding sub-committees of the first session. As the contentious debate on communal representation could not be settled by mutual agreement, the British Prime Minister made this the reason for announcing, 4 August 1932, what was called the 'Communal Award' (q.v.). It provided for separate representation not only to the recognized minorities but also to the Depressed Classes. Gandhi fasted on the latter issue, with the result that the Poona Pact modified the original award substantially in regard to the representation of the Depressed Classes.

The third session of the conference agreed upon certain broad principles for the future constitutional set up. These were published later as a White Paper (March 1933), which was referred to a Joint Select Committee of both Houses of Parliament for examination and scrutiny. Eventually, the Committee's report was to form the basis of the Government of India Act, 1935 (q.v.).

In his speech to the third session on 24 December 1932, Sir Samuel Hoare, then Secretary of State for India, made two points: 'the great achievement of the First Round Table Conference was to establish...that the new bond must be the bond of an all-India Federation with the rights of each of the three parties effectively safeguarded... The second conference...was to start on foot the whole series of inquiries that led to the government's communal award...this [third] conference....has clearly delimited the field upon which the future constitution is going to be built...we have delimited the sphere of activity of the various parts of the constitution...we have created an *espiri de corps* amongst all of us (that is) determined to see the building...both complete in itself and completed at the earliest possible date.....'

Some extraneous events had an important impact on the third session of the Conference. The Labour government in England had been replaced by a 'National' government under Ramsay MacDonald shortly before the session convened, while Sir Samuel Hoare had succeeded. William Wedgwood Benn as Secretary of State for India. In June (1932) the government had informed Parliament that India's financial resources had been considerably strained and it might be obliged to ask Parliament to assist in 'maintaining the credit of the country pending the settlement of the constitutional problem'. The Statute of Westminister, which was progressing through its later stages in Parliament when the Conference first opened, received its final assent ten days after it closed.

The background to the convening of the Conference may be briefly summed up. On 31 January 1929 the Governor-General, Irwin (q.v.), announced the British government's decision to convene a Round Table Conference to settle the question of India's future political set-up. Additionally, he had affirmed that the attainment of Dominion Status (q.v.) was the natural goal of British policy in India. Earlier, on 21 July 1923, at the British Commonwealth Labour Conference, Prime Minister Ramsay MacDonald had expressed the hope that 'in a few months' a new Dominion, would join the Commonwealth as an equal member. Understandably, many Indian leaders assumed that the Conference announced by Irwin was intended to settle the basis of a constitution of the Dominion-type resting on the principle of equality among constituent members as laid down by the Imperial Conference of 1926. However, neither the British Liberals nor the Conservatives accepted such radical ideas. In the result, when Gandhi met Irwin on 23 December 1929 the latter denied that the projected conference would draw up a scheme for full Dominion Status. A little later the Congress at its Lahore session (December 1929) retaliated by defining complete Independence as India's political goal.

In the earlier stages of the Conference, politicians in British India had welcomed the idea of forging along with the princes a common front against British control and had opted for a federal set-up. Yet the princes had kept their own interests in view and, in any case, a majority of them were Hindus. The British commercial community also favoured a federation. It may be noted that in the initial stages of the Conference, the then Labour government was in political control and powerfully influenced by the conviction that a democratic set-up could not be long withheld from the Indian people.

Understandably, the result of the first session was the acceptance of the proposition of ministerial control on such questions as external relations and defence. It was further stipulated that the Governor-General as well as the Governors in the provinces must protect the interests of the minorities and ensure the independence of the public services.

The proceedings of the second session were made difficult for the British government by Gandhi's categorical assertion that he spoke for the people of India as a whole, thereby completely denying, by implication, the representative character of spokesmen for the minority communities. At the second plenary meeting of this session, on 30 November 1931, the Mahatma affirmed that 'the Congress claimed to represent over 85 per cent of the population of India, that is to say the dumb, toiling, semi-starved millions . . . the Congress claimed also by right of service to represent even the Princes . . .and the landed gentry, the educated class . . . . All the other parties at this meeting represent sectional interests. Congress alone claims to represent the whole of India, all interests. It is no communal organization; it is a determined enemy of communalism in any shape or form. Congress knows no distinction of race, colour, or creed; its platform is universal . . . . And yet here I see that the Congress is treated as one of the parties. I don't mind it; I do not regard it as a calamity for the Congress; but I do regard it as a calamity for the purpose of doing the work for which we have gathered together here.'

There were, additionally, the problems precipitated by the international financial crisis of 1931 and the fact that Ramsay MacDonald now continued as Prime Minister without support from his party which had, indeed, repudiated him. By the time of the third session, the Labour party had completely withdrawn from the Conference, as it had from the government, thereby introducing a clear-cut political, if also partisan element into its proceedings. The absence of the Congress from the third session made things even more difficult.

Reginald Coupland, *The Constitutional Problem in India*, 3 parts, Oxford, 1944, I, pp. 113–31; A. C. Banerjee, *Constitutional History of India*, 3 vols, Delhi, 1977–1978, III, pp. 98–112; A. C. Banerjee, *Indian Constitutional Documents*, 3 vols., 3rd ed., Calcutta 1961, III, pp. 226–43; A. B. Keith, *A Constitutional History of India*, Oxford, 1936, pp. 294–318; Gwyer and Appadorai, *Speeches & Documents on the Indian Constitution 1921_47*, 2 vols, Oxford, 1957, I, pp. 225–41.

Rowlatt Act (1919)

The Anarchical and Revolutionary Crimes Act (1919) is popularly known as the Rowlatt Act after its author, Sir Sydney A. T. Rowlatt. The latter was president of a committee appointed by the government on 10 December 1917 to look into the nature and extent of subversive activities then widely prevalent. Among the other members were two High Court judges, Sir Basil Scott from Bombay and Diwan Bahadur C. V. Kumaraswami Sastri from Madras and two non-officials, Sir Verney Lovett, then member of the UP Board of Revenue and Provash Chandra Mitter, a well-known lawyer.

The committee met as from January 1918 and submitted its report four months later on 30 April 1919. It was based exclusively upon the evidence submitted by the central and provincial governments. Broadly, it concluded that 'in Bombay the revolutionary movement was confined mostly to Chitpavan Brahmins, in Bengal the conspirators were young men belonging to the educated middle class who committed the outrages. Elsewhere, the movement had not taken any roots.' More specifically, the committee gave a detailed history of the revolutionary and anarchical activities in the various regions of India, particularly Bengal. It made recommendations principally to arm the government with powers to subdue all unlawful and dangerous activities in the future. It was imperative to do so, it had argued, in view of the fact that the Defence of India Act would cease to be operative with the termination of the War.

On the basis of this report, the government drew up and published, on 18 January 1919, two Bills—one seeking to alter the Penal Code and providing for greater and stricter control over the press; the other empowering the government to short-circuit the due process of law so as to check terrorist activities. The objective was to dispense with as much of the ordinary procedure as possible for the trial of a person accused of crime and to secure his speedy conviction. A special court from whose judgement there could be no appeal, trial *in camera* and consideration of evidence not admissible by the law of evidence were provided. Extraordinary powers of search, arrest, demand of security, etc. were conferred on provincial governments.

The two measures were presented to the Imperial Legislative Council on 6 February 1919. The better known of the two was the Anarchical and Revolutionary Crimes Bill referred to above which was enacted into law, despite vehement protests by a number of public men and the press. In the Imperial Legislative Council all elected Indian members, irrespective of their political alignments, opposed the measure. V. S. Srinavasa Sastri warned that it would 'hurt the good as well as the bad' and cautioned that if it was adopted, despite opposition, everyone would deem it his duty to 'join the agitation.' M. A. Jinnah (q.v.) was convinced it would lead to 'discontent and agitation, the like of which you have not witnessed.' Put to the vote, 22 Indian members voted against, and 35 official members in favour, the only Indian among them being Sankaran Nair, then a member of the Viceroy's Executive Council (from which he resigned a few months later in protest against the Panjab atrocities). The press was highly critical, calling the measure 'monstrous' (*New India*, Madras), a 'gigantic blunder' (*Amrita Bazar Patrika*, Calcutta), and 'repression in *excelsus*' (*Bombay Chronicle*, Bombay); the *Hindu* (Madras) thought its provisions would be read with 'shame, indignation and disgust.'

The Act, which was applicable to all parts of India and to be operative for three years, was divided into five parts. It stipulated that, should anarchical conditions exist, the Governor-General had the authority, to make the Act applicable to any area and to order a speedy trial of offences. In the interests of public safety, suspected persons could be arrested and confined, while any place or premises were liable to be searched. It provided that persons interned under the Defence of India Act may not be released; that even if an affected area was declared safe, the trials and investigations ordered when the Act was operative would continue unaffected and uninterrupted. Juries in such cases were to be dispensed with.

Opposition to the Black Act, as it came to be known, was widespread. Criticism was directed to the composition of the Rowlatt committee and the powers given to the executive uncontrolled by the judiciary. The term 'crime' was not defined while all activities included in the schedule could be labelled anarchical. More than anything else, it displayed the British distrust of Indians and nullified all hope of political reform and advance to which the government had pledged its honour.

No sooner had the bills been introduced in the legislature than Gandhi (q.v.) had a pledge drafted which committed its signatories 'to refuse civilly to obey those laws . . . and until they were withdrawn.' As soon as the bills became law, an all-India *hartal* was announced for 24 February 1919 (postponed to 30 March and later 6 April). It was to mark the beginnings of a satyagraha campaign which, Gandhi told the Viceroy, constitutes 'an attempt to revolutionize politics and restore moral force to its original position'. Meetings were held all over the country to signify popular disapproval of the Act and the press gave full support to the mass agitation.

The response to the Mahatma's call was unprecedented. Almost all parts of the country joined. To the British two important portents of danger were the fraternization of Hindus and Muslims and the general excitement among the masses. An unfortunate aspect of the satyagraha was the rash of violence it provoked—in the Panjab (Amritsar, Lahore, Kasur, Gujranwala), Gujarat (Ahmedabad, Viramgam, Nadiad) and Bengal (Calcutta). Gandhi, deeply upset, admitted that in launching his movement without prior preparation he had committed a 'mistake of Himalayan magnitude' and announced his decision to suspend passive resistance.

Briefly, the Rowlatt satyagraha set into motion a chain reaction culminating in the Jallianwala Bagh Massacre (q.v.) and widespread disorders in many parts of the country, which had significant repercussions. It led to the emergence of Gandhi on the political stage and a change in (Indian National) Congress (q.v.) policies. It alienated moderate opinion from the government and gave a unity of purpose to all shades of public opinion. No less significant was the change it effected in British policy which, for a time at any rate, refrained from the use of the repressive measure.

(Rowlatt) Sedition Committee Report, reprint, Calcutta, 1973; R. Kumar (ed.), *Essays on Gandhian Politics: The Rowlatt Satyagraha of 1919,* Oxford, 1971; Arthur Swinson, *Six Minutes to Sunset,* London, 1964, pp. 9-12.

M. N. Roy (1887–1954)

Narendra Nath Bhattacharya, better known by his later assumed name of Manabendra Nath Roy, was born on 21 March 1887 in the small village of Arbelia in the district of 24 Parganas in West Bengal. His father was a Sanskrit teacher in a junior high school in Arbelia and later moved to Kodalia. Apart from school, Narendra Nath did not receive any formal instruction and was thus essentially a self-educated man.

As a boy, Roy is said to have been very religious. Arrested in connection with the Partition of Bengal (q.v.) agitation, he turned to politics and revolutionary literature. From his early childhood he had a thirst for knowledge and maintained that knowledge is freedom; that the latter is, in fact, inherent in every man and must be achieved through knowledge.

In 1905, when his father died, Roy and his brothers came to Calcutta to fend for themselves. During the next ten years he lived with one or another of his non-political brothers or with one of his several revolutionary comrades. During his Calcutta years from 1905 to 1915, Roy moved from job to job, house to house, managing all the while to live on the periphery of respectable society.

Roy was attracted to politics early in life, his first 'action' being a political dacoity. Later, he was involved in the Howrah Conspiracy Case (1910-11) and a host of other similar events. He now came into close touch with Jatindranath Mukherjee (1879-1915), the celebrated leader of the Yugantar group who was known to his many admirers as 'Bagha-Jatin' or 'Jatin-Bagh' (i.e. Jatin the Tiger). Years later Roy referred to him as 'a good man . . . I have still to find a better one.' Between 1905 and 1930 Roy was arrested on a number of occasions. Each time he either escaped while on bail or was released.

Yugantar, the weekly that had been suppressed, served as a rallying point for the Aurobindo (q.v.)-Barindra group of Calcutta; the title was also used by others belonging to different groups. The Yugantar party does not appear to have been formed until late in 1914 or early 1915. It meant an alliance between different groups for the largest revolutionary 'action' yet planned. One aspect of revolutionary activity was its network of overseas connections. In the two decades preceding 1915 a number of revolutionaries had travelled to England and Europe trying to gain support and assistance. In the years following the failure of the German conspiracy to assist Indian revolutionaries fight the British, Roy was to become one of the most famous overseas revolutionaries, propagandists and organizers. Disguised as a Father Martin he hoodwinked the British and travelled through South-east Asia, first to Japan and then the United States. He met some of the Indian nationalist and revolutionary leaders living in exile during his tour and attended meetings and studied in New York. While in California, he took the name Manabendra Nath Roy and it stuck. He was arrested in New York as a member of a revolutionary conspiracy and fled, while on bail, to Mexico.

Much later in life Roy wrote his *Memoirs* covering the years 1915-23 and beginning with his journey, across the Pacific, to the United States. These observations, made at the end of his revolutionary years and just before his communist phase was to begin, are of extreme interest. Although he liked to think of himself as a heretic, Roy held fervently to each new faith that he adopted until disillusionment set in. The older Roy saw the young Narendra Nath Bhattacharya as a romantic idealist, ignorant of social theory and the world of letters, a rather stiff and silly puritan and teetotaller. He viewed his earlier faith in India's mission to be constricting and immature as he passed first into his communist and then into his humanist phase.

Roy's writings in 1916-17, mostly in Spanish and probably done with the assistance of an anonymous Spanish writer, present a black and white view of India and her past. This was largely political propaganda to counteract ideas which he thought were completely incorrect. He considered the projected Montagu-Chelmsford Reforms (q.v.) a sham and the men elected to the legislatures as toadies. His writings present a simplistic view of politics, society and history with their rationalization of nationalist revolution and anarchism. India, Roy averred, had a mission, a global historical role.

After the success of the Bolshevik Revolution in Russia, followed by its failure in western and eastern Europe, attention focussed increasingly on the nationalist struggles and revolutionary possibilities in Asia. Among the Indian emigre, the third communist international chose Roy as their 'premier theoretician and organizer' for India. He now founded the Communist Party of Mexico, the first such party to be established outside Russia. On an invitation from Lenin he visited Moscow just before the Second World Congress of the Communist International in 1920. Presently he developed acute differences with Lenin on such issues as revolution in the colonies, the role of the national bourgeoisie and the relation of communists to the bourgeoisie in national and democratic movements. This was part of his 'revolution from below' thesis in contrast to Lenin's 'revolution from above.' The 'International' adopted a compromise resolution between the two extremes.

Before long, Roy rose high in the communist hierarchy: in 1922 he was a candidate-member of the executive committee of the 'International' and in 1924 a full member. Later, he became a member of the Presidium and of the secretariat of the movement in Asia and placed incharge of the training and education of communists in Asian countries. Roy visited China in 1927 where his acute differences with Mikhail Borodin, the Soviet advisor to Sun Yat-sen's Kuomintang movement since 1923, soon surfaced.

The Sixth World Congress of the Communist International under Stalin's influence adopted an ultra-leftist line of communist purism and criticized Roy who, for all practical purposes, now severed his connections with the 'International'. Much later, in 1934, Roy's position was vindicated when the Seventh World Congress of the 'International' adopted a 'Popular Front' approach towards the non-communist left.

In 1922 appeared Roy's *India in Transition*, a Marxist view of Indian nationalism. His objective herein was to show the relationship of class structure to nationalism. Through the 1920's he called for the formation of a workers' and peasants' party within the Indian National Congress (q.v.), dispatched a stream of political pamphlets and propaganda, a number of agents and some funds home to organize the Communist Party of India. But the C.P.I. had just about begun in the 1920's; the government of India, nevertheless, held two 'show' trials at Kanpur in 1924 and at Meerut in 1929 to curb the communist threat, such as it was. After some underground activity in 1930-1, Roy was finally captured by the police, prosecuted under an old conviction in the Kanpur case and sentenced to imprisonment. He was released after 6 years.

During the years of his association with the 'International', Roy tried to develop a revolutionary movement in India and published two papers, *Vanguard* and *Masses*. Some copies were smuggled into India where Roy was widely believed to be the founder of the communist movement. Through almost a decade of effort to organize the C. P. I. from Europe, and even with numerous agents and friends to help, Roy was constantly hampered. There were few whom he could trust, his letters were invariably being intercepted by the government's intelligence branch while he was trying to convince his people from a distance that a foreign-based ideology was relevant to the Indian struggle for freedom and the conditions prevalent there. Meantime he had also developed an intense hatred of Gandhi (q.v.).

While the Comintern and the C. P. I. were veering round to the left (1928-34) and viewing the Congress as an enemy rather than a potential ally, Roy was moving from his former left, sectarian position towards a much more positive view of the Congress. He argued that the leftists should work within the Congress and the trade unions, but was opposed to forming an autonomous party until 1940. when he split with the Congress on the War issue.

In 1937 Roy had joined the Congress and was elected a member of the A. I. C. C.; his professed aim now was to democratize the national movement. With Soviet Russia joining the War (1941) against the Axis powers, he unreservedly upheld the Allied cause and avowed the defeat of fascism. In support of the War effort, he organized the Radical Democratic Party and other sympathetic labour organizations. Presently, Roy's thinking evolved from that of a radical democrat to a radical humanist; he was to acclaim humanism as the ideology of the future.

Roy had supported Subhas Chandra Bose's (q.v.) candidature for the presidentship of the Congress in 1939. After Bose's election, Roy wanted a homogeneous leftist Working Committee and the position of General Secretary of the party for himself. This proved to be a pipe dream, for Roy's isolation in Indian politics was well-nigh complete by the time World War II ended in 1945. During the War, Roy took the position that it was a struggle against fascism and for democracy and pleaded that a fascist victory would sound the death-knell of democracy. He also argued that, by the time the War drew to a close, the British government would be weakened if not completely exhausted. For this attitude, Roy was not only misunderstood and opposed but maligned. He was called an enemy of India and a lackey of British imperialism. Critics recalled that he had started his political career as a communist and, for many years, was an admirer of Stalin and the Soviet Union without realising that democracy could not be equated with Marxism. On the other hand, the so-called Marxists called Roy a revisionist. His reply was that, if there was to be no possibility of revision, Marxism ceased to be Marxist.

The development of Roy's thought towards what he termed scientific humanism brought him quite close to the essence of Gandhi's teachings. Though he and the Mahatma started from entirely different premises, their thinking seemed to converge in underlining the pre-eminence of man on the basis of love and justice. Roy maintained that structural changes in society from above were not possible and that a philosophical revolution was a necessary precursor as also a precondition of social revolution. To further this cause, he founded the Indian Renaissance Institute. The basic tenet of the radical humanism he now propounded was that man is the archetype of society, that co-operative social relationships contribute towards developing individual potentialities which, in turn, are a measure of social progress.

It would thus appear that, starting as a nationalist revolutionary and spending nearly 20 years in the vanguard of the Marxian revolution, Roy ultimately crowned his career as a philosopher of the modern renaissance. He was unique in embodying in his person a love of freedom, unimpeachable integrity, a sense of loyalty, courage of conviction, a passionate interest in ideas and their human implications and an unqualified involvement in the struggle for freedom combined with a scrupulous detachment from the game of power politics. It has been suggested that there was something of the universal man in Roy, whose company made even the most mediocre of his comrades feel that life, with all its ugly patches, was exciting and beautiful. In essence, Roy declared: 'New Humanism is cosmopolitanism. A co-operative commonwealth of spiritually free men will not be limited by the boundaries of national states—capitalist, fascist, socialist, communist or of any other kind which will gradually disappear under the impact of the twentieth-century Renaissance of Man.'

A fall in 1952 during a trekking expedition developed into cerebral thrombosis. Roy was taken ill in August 1953 while the fatal attack came six months later. His wife Ellen (*nee* Gottschalk) survived him but was done to death (December 1960) in a gruesome, murderous assault.

Roy was a prolific writer. His well-known books, *Fascism* and *Historical Role of Islam* were written in jail. A pamphlet on developments in China was published as *China in Revolt*. His controversy with Sir Shah Suliman, Chief Justice of the Allahabad High Court, was published later as *Heresies of the Twentieth Century*. His last great work, *Reason, Romanticism and Revolution* has been published in two volumes, even though his *magnum opus,* 'The Philosophical Consequences of Modern Science' is still awaiting publication.

M. N. Roy, *Memoirs,* Dehra Dun, 1964; V. B. Karnik, *M. N. Roy: A Political Biography,* Bombay, 1978; Leonard A. Gordon, *Bengal: the Nationalist Movement 1876-1940,* Delhi, 1974.

The Royal Titles Act (1876)

Since the assumption of direct power by the Crown after the Rebellion of 1857 (q.v.), need had been felt for an appropriate title for the British sovereign.The Tory leader, Benjamin Disraeli, later Lord Beaconsfield (1804-81), had been very keen about this as far back as 1858; so was Lytton (q.v.), albeit much later. Salisbury, the Secretary of State for India (1874-8), was far from enthusiastic however, and when the proposed change came in for severe criticism from the Liberals, regretted the move even more. A British critic considered it 'one of the most gratuitous of blunders', but the Viceroy 'who had a stronger sense of theatre' than his political bosses lent it powerful support.

The Queen herself was persuaded to view the matter 'as a formal and emphatic expression of the favourable sentiments which she had always entertained towards the princes and people' of India. Accordingly, by the Royal Titles Act (1876), the British sovereign was authorized to make, through a royal proclamation, any 'such addition to the style and titles appertaining to the Imperial Crown of the United Kingdom and its dependencies as to Her Majesty might seem meet.' Invoking its provisions on

28 April 1876, Queen Victoria added to her titles the words '*Indiae Im-peratrix*' (Empress of India), which was rendered into the vernacular as 'Kaiser-i-Hind.'

Disraeli, then Britain's Prime Minister, viewed the title as 'providing his concept of imperialism' with a 'symbol.' Lytton carried matters to a magnificent *finale* at the grand Imperial Darbar (q.v.) held in Delhi on 1 January 1877, where the Queen was formally proclaimed Empress of India. Arranged with great pomp and show despite widespread famine in the country, the Darbar was later dubbed as 'pompous pageantry to a perishing people.'

S. Gopal, *British Policy in India (1858-1905),* Cambridge, 1965.

Ryotwari Settlement

Not long after Cornwallis (q.v.) introduced the Permanent Settlement (q.v.) in Bengal, the question of extending it to other territories acquired by the John Company (q.v.) from time to time presented itself. The capture in 1792 of Baramahal and Dindigul from Tipu Sultan (q.v.) in the Second Mysore War (q.v.), and the cession, two years later, of the Northern Sarkars as a jagir brought issues to the fore. In 1799, Tanjore and Coimbatore and, in 1801, Malabar and the territory of the Nawab of Arcot had been annexed to Madras presidency. Among the first officials to be associated with land-revenue settlement in these areas were Alexander Read and Lionel Place. Thomas Munro (q.v.) was one of Read's assistants; in 1800, he had been transferred from Kanara to the Deccan districts ceded by the Nizam of Hyderabad.

While these officials were busy sorting out the tangled skein of revenue affairs under their charge, Lord Wellesley (q.v.), then Governor-General, issued a peremptory order to the Madras government to introduce the Bengal system of Permanent Settlement in its newly acquired dominion. The directive was not well received, for, as Munro and his assistants gained in experience, they became extremely critical of the Bengal system; more, they were able to sell their seemingly new-fangled ideas to the local administration. In particular, William Bentinck (q.v.), then Governor of Madras (1803-7), was attracted by what they were doing and ruled that further progress with zamindari settlement be stayed. Later (1808), permission was accorded to experiment with village panchayats, apart from the ryotwari system.

The ryotwari system had its staunch champion in Munro. As a result of earlier experience in Tanjore, Hodgson, then powerful in the Madras Board of Revenue, was keen on village panchayats. In 1808-9, the ryotwari experiment was being tried in most of the districts while, much to Hodgson's discomfiture, reports regarding village leases were uniformly unfavourable. The Fifth Report of the Select Committee of the House of Commons bore the clear imprint of Munro's thinking. In the result, from now on he had the ear of the Court of Directors, which he later used to full advantage to remodel the Madras administrative system.

It needs to be heavily underlined that, unlike their Mughal or Maratha predecessors, who adopted the existing practices, the British were keen to build an administration and land taxation system in consonance with their own ideas on the subject. Their acquisition of new territories led, under-standably, to a great deal of initial dislocation and even anarchical condi-tions. Additionally, the relative ignorance of early administrators, coupled with their zeal and the commercial character of the Company, led initially to excessive demands of revenue which proved, for the most part, ruinous to the peasantry. And all this while the ravages of war and anarchy persisted over large areas of their newly-acquired dominion.

In Madras, by 1818, the subjugation of the landed aristocrats, the *poligars,* the establishment of judicial courts and the improvement of the revenue system had been ensured, although in the bargain, they had claimed a heavy toll. As soon as Munro became Governor in May 1820, the system was declared generally operative in all parts of Madras Presidency, barring areas already under the Permanent Settlement. As to the latter, every opportunity was taken of getting back, on account of lapses or by means of purchase, the zamindari *mootahs* and such other tenures as existed with a view to introducing the new system therein. It followed that those village leases as had survived were rapidly got rid of.

The special feature of Munro's system was that the government demand on land was now permanently fixed and each cultivator could take or reject the field he was offered if he thought its rent to be excessive. Munro reduced the assessment from roughly half (45 or 50 or 55 per cent) to one-third of the estimated produce; even so, the latter represented in many cases the entire economic rent and was thus, by definition, oppressive. Two other factors impinged on the situation: first, the cultivator had to pay a fixed sum of money irrespective of the actual yield or the prevalent price; secondly, the rent was not calculated through local bodies, as in the North-Western Pro-vinces, but by low-paid agents who made unjust extortions and used oppres-sive methods. It is to Munro's credit that he strove all through his seven-year administration to lower the assessments and keep the evils of the system under constant check. After him Madras was to become 'a scene of oppres-sion and of agricultural distress unparalleled in India in that age'.

In 1838 the Sadr Board of Revenue made a strong protest to Calcutta against the attendant evils of the ryotwari system: the fraud and oppression of the low-paid revenue officials as well as the harassment and inquisitorial searches made into the cultivators' means. Nor were the evils accidental; they were inherent in the system itself. In 1852, George Campbell (1824-92), who was later to become Lieutenant Governor of Bengal and an M.P., noted: 'Only imagine one Collector dealing with 150,000 tenants, not one of whom has a lease, but each pays according as he cultivates and gets a crop and with reference to the number of his cattle, sheep and children . . . . [In so far as the Commissioner was a foreigner and liable to frequent transfers] the native subordinates could . . . do as they liked . . . the abuses of the whole system, and especially that of remissions, is something frightful; chicanery and abuse of all kinds . . .' James Bourdillon (1811-83), one of the better-known Madras officials, said in 1853 that, barring 'a very small proportion . . . the large majority of the cultivators . . . were always in poverty and generally in debt.'

In the course of a parliamentary inquiry during 1850-3 the abuses of the system were fully exposed and remedial steps taken. The latter were based on 'an accurate survey and careful settlement of the land revenue'. It was conceded that the then existing burden on the cultivator meant 'a vast extent of unoccupied land with a peaceful and industrious population scantily fed and scantily employed'. Earlier, a Government of India Commission of Inquiry had noted that 'the practice of torture for the realization of the Government revenue existed . . . and that injured parties could not obtain any redress'.

In essence, the ryotwari system stipulated that the registered occupant (i) was free to alienate, encumber and devise his land at his discretion so far as government was concerned; (ii) may at any time relinquish any portion of his holding, yet may never be ousted unless he failed to pay regularly the assessment fixed on the land or any other charge by law recoverable as land revenue, in which case his land could be attached and sold to the extent necessary to discharge the debt; (iii) would not pay any additional charge as a result of improvement effected at the ryots' expense, but a separate charge could be made for minerals extracted. The rate of assessment was liable to alteration only on the expiry of the specified period for which it had been fixed.

The various changes in the ryotwari system up to the mid-1850s had left untouched its principal defect—an excessive, unequal and unsystematic assessment. It was not until 1855 that the government forced a long overdue reform and proposed to carry out a professional field survey of Madras Presidency accompanied by a detailed classification of soils and their evaluation for assessment. In fact, it was only in 1864 that a decision was taken that the state's share be limited to half the net value of the crop and that the period of each settlement be fixed for 30 years.

In Madras, the ryotwari system evolved in three stages: early, middle and late, the only description common to all being that it was a mode of settlement with small farmers. These characteristics represented a gradual growth, none of which applied to *early ryotwari* which, as has been noticed, was introduced by Read, approved by the Directors as an experiment, widely extended by Munro and others, and abruptly brought to an end in some districts by the zamindari settlement and in others by village leases. The re-introduction of the ryotwari system between 1813 and 1822 marks the beginning of *middle ryotwari,* a decade plagued by widespread administrative chaos. To begin with, there was no proper basis of survey: no boundary marks, no maps and very few survey records of any sort, and little was done to remedy these shortfalls. With the middle phase ending in each district and the introduction of settlements under the scheme of 1855, the final stage for *late ryotwari* was reached.

Two aspects of the ryotwari system deserve more than passing notice: the state's share in the yield and the ryot's inalienable right to the land. By age-old custom, the ryot and the state shared the crop or its cash equivalent. In theory, the ryot was meant to get about half, but in practice he got one-fifth or less. Alexander Read assigned to the state one-third of the gross value of the crop on dry land and two-fifths on irrigated land. In the ceded districts, Munro was forced to give the state nearly half but regarded one-third as the correct figure. Under the Company, assessment was always fixed in money and the rates attached to different soils had no corresponding relationship to output even where efforts were made to establish such a relationship.

On an average, the earliest assessments under the Company were too high. The imposition upon early ryotwari of a zamindari settlement here and village leases there made matters worse. The innumerable rates of middle ryotwari were supposed to represent 50 per cent on wet land and 33 per cent on dry; these traditional imposts were, in general, excessive, variable and based on no principle. As for the ryot, in a thoughtful minute recorded on 31 December 1824, Munro noted: 'The ryot is the real proprietor, for whatever land does not belong to the Sovereign belongs to him ....It is the ever-varying assessment which has prevented, and so long as it continues will prevent, land from becoming a valuable property. When it is fixed, all uncertainty is removed and all land ... soon acquires a value which is every day increased by improvements, made in consequence of the certainty'.

Munro had laboured all his life to obtain for the Madras cultivator a fixity of rental so that all improvements made by him led to his own profit. An official report of 1855-6 noted that the Madras ryot, 'cannot be ejected by Government so long as he pays the fixed assessment.... The ryot under the system is virtually a proprietor on a simple and perfect title, and has all the benefits of a perpetual lease.' The Board of Revenue observed in 1857 that a Madras ryot 'is able to retain the land perpetually without any increase of assessment'. The Madras government said in a communication to the Supreme government in Calcutta in 1862: 'There can be no question that one fundamental principle of the ryotwari system is that the Government demand on the land is fixed for ever'.

Lest a fixed state demand appear as a panacea for all the ills of the cultivator, a Marxist historian's interpretation should help to serve as a necessary corrective: 'A system which establishes fixed revenue assessments in cash at a uniform figure for thirty-year periods at a time irrespective of harvest or economic changes, may appear convenient to the revenue collector or to the government statesmen computing their budget; but to the countryman, who has to pay the uniform figure from a wildly fluctuating income it spells ruin in bad years, and inevitably drives him into the hands of the money lender. Tardy suspensions or remissions in extreme conditions may strive to mitigate, but cannot prevent this process.'

In 1880, Lord Ripon (q.v.) laid down that, as a rule, the land tax 'would not be raised except on the equitable ground of a rise in prices' in districts which had once been surveyed and settled. It was the best compromise after the right of an absolutely fixed rental had been ignored and gave some modicum of security to the original cultivators. Ripon's rule was, however, cancelled by the Secretary of State in January 1885.

The ryotwari system of the Malabar coast also demands some notice. There was no village system among the settled farmers of its sequestered valleys, for the ruler took his dues in military service alone. Thus, the ryotwari system was applied right from the outset. In 1805, it was notified that settlements would be with the principal landholders or *jammis*. Yet many of the latter had fled, with the result that the government often settled with the principal occupants or *kanomdars*, who alone were held responsible for the revenue. In 1889, the Madras High Court ruled this practice to be illegal. The result was Act III of 1896 enabling the Collector to determine in whom the ownership vested and permitting, in certain cases, a joint registration of both the landholder and the occupant. The fact was that in the distribution of the produce in Malabar three persons—the state, the landholder and the occupant—were taken into account, and *not* two.

The ryotwari settlement of South Canara bore a close resemblance to that of Malabar. In the Bombay area the Maratha system of farming out the land revenue was adopted to start with: the districts were farmed out to *desais* and later to *patels* of villages. The Collector or his agent, the *mamlatdar* or *kamavisdar,* had to make the best possible deal with the *desai* for the annual revenue and, provided the amount was duly paid, kept out of the way as far as the *desai*'s methods were concerned. After 1816, the ryotwari system was introduced and the *talti,* or village accountant, appointed directly by the Bombay government, superseded the *desai* or *patel.*

Initially, the position of the *mamlatdar* or *kamavisdar* in the Gujarat area was not satisfactory for he was both poorly paid and, by reason of being a police official, required to attend to numerous additional chores entailing long absences from the district. These difficulties were gradually removed with the re-introduction of the ryotwari system which brought the villages and the cultivators in direct contact with government officials and at the same time increased revenue, which was now more equitably distributed. Additionally, there was 'better management and fuller assertion of the public rights'. The system itself was introduced first by a Commissioner charged with inquiring rather than innovating and, secondly, by Collectors trained in the delicate business of acquainting themselves with the actual state of affairs.

Apart from the Madras and Bombay (including Sind) presidencies, the ryotwari system, with such modifications as local conditions demanded, was also prevalent in Berar, Assam, Burma and Coorg.

B. H. Baden-Powell, *The Land Systems of British India: being a manual of the land-tenures and of the systems of land-revenue administration prevalent in several provinces,* 3 vols, Oxford, 1892, III; Romesh Chunder Dutt, *The Economic History of India,* 2 vols, 3rd impression, New Delhi, 1976, I; Dodwell, *CHI,* VI; A. R. Desai, *Social Background of Indian Nationalism,* 5th ed, Bombay, 1976; Nilmani Mukherjee, *The Ryotwari System in Madras, 1791–1827,* Calcutta, 1962; Thomas R. Metcalf, *Land, Landlords and the British Raj: North India in the Nineteenth Century,* Oxford, 1980.

Treaty of Sagauli (1816)

The draft treaty signed at Sagauli on 2 December 1815 was ratified by the Nepalese government only on 4 March 1816, after the Gurkha rout at Makwanpur on 27 February 1816. Under the terms of this 9-article compact, Nepal and the John Company (q.v.) pledged to maintain perpetual peace and friendship. Additionally, it stipulated that Nepal (i) would renounce 'all claim' to the lands which were disputed between it and the Company before the war and accept the latter's sovereignty over them; (ii) cede 'all the low-lands between the Rapti and the Ganduk, between the Ganduk and the Coosah, between the rivers Mitchee and Teesta, within the hills eastward of the river Mitchee'; (iii) renounce 'all claim to or connection with' the countries lying to the west of the river Kali; (iv) engage 'never to molest or disturb' the Raja of Sikkim in the possession of his territories; (v) undertake 'never to take or retain in service' any British subject nor the subject of any European or American state.

To indemnify the chiefs and Barahdars whose interests would suffer as a result of the alienation of lands ceded, the British agreed to settle on them pensions worth Rs 2 lakhs per annum. The chiefs were to be selected by the Nepal ruler who would also determine the proportions in which the amounts were to be disbursed. It was also laid down that 'accredited Ministers from each [viz., the Nepal Darbar and Company] shall reside at the court of the other.'

In sum, the Gurkhas ceded what came to be known as the Garhwal and Kumaon divisions and withdrew from Sikkim. The Treaty, besides removing all danger that had hitherto threatened them from their northern neighbour, gave the British sites for some of their best hill stations. They also discovered an excellent recruiting ground for first-rate human material, the Gurkhas, for their armies.

John Pemble, *The Invasion of Nepal: John Company at War*, Oxford, 1971; *Aitchison*, II, pp. 205–7.

Salar Jang (1829–83)

Salar Jang, whose real name was Mir Turab Ali Khan, is best known as the maker of modern Hyderabad. His forebears had been in the service of the Nizam as ministers of state; he himself served as prime minister under two successive rulers, Nasir-ud-Daula (q.v.) and Afzal-ud-Daula (q.v.), and as co-regent during the minority of a third, Mehboob Ali Khan (q.v.).

With no formal education, Salar Jang had studied Persian, Arabic and, later, English on his own. His interest in business and administration was initially aroused while looking after the family estates. Subsequently, as *taluqdar* of Telingana, he so impressed the British that they installed him as prime minister of Hyderabad in 1853, much against the Nizam's wishes. Salar Jang was least favoured by the Nizam among the candidates—he was barely 24 and was the nephew of the minister who had negotiated and concluded the treaty by which Berar was transferred to British control! Faithful and indebted to his benefactors, Salar Jang firmly suppressed all attempts at revolt in the Rebellion of 1857 (q.v.). The danger was the more acute in so far as the Nizam, Nasir-ud-Daula, had just died while Salar Jang himself had been in office for less than 4 years.

A good administrator, Salar Jang restored law and order in the state, disbanded a large retinue of Arab troops, started public works, improved finances, reduced military expenditure and paid back a large part of the debts owed by the state to the British government. He opened a number of

schools and colleges in a bid to spread education in the state. Despite
herculean efforts, including a visit to England, he was unable to have the
Berar territory restored to Hyderabad.

Salar Jang's fate was typical of that of a loyal servant—he was an object of
suspicion to his jealous master, and even the British suspected him of
intriguing with Persia behind their back. After 1866 he had to face a
'permanent opposition' offered by 'his jealous and powerful enemies' and a
degree of the 'most vexatious and senseless interference' on the part of the
Nizam. It is said that Salar Jang was seldom admitted to the Nizam's
presence and 'when he was, he used to be almost pale from agitation.' As he
was considered a British protege and therefore unpopular, more than one
attempt was made to assassinate him. However, the Nizam's efforts to
replace him were foiled by the supreme government in Calcutta.

To the British, Salar Jang repeatedly stressed that under his stewardship,
Hyderabad did not join the general revolt of 1857 and thereby stopped the
disaffection from spreading farther down to the south. The British appreciated
his services and the Governor-General in Council informed him that the
'ability, courage and firmness' with which he discharged his duty entitled
him to Government's 'most cordial thanks.' In 1877, the Government of
India bestowed the G.C.S.I. on him and at the Imperial Darbar (q.v.) at
Delhi on 1 January, 1877, a salute of 17 guns was fired as a mark of special
favour to him.

With the death of the co-regent, Nawab Shams-ul-umrah, Salar Jang
became the virtual ruler of Hyderabad. But he did not live to enjoy this
position long, he died on 8 February 1883.

G. Natesan (ed.), *Eminent Mussalmans*, Madras, 1926; *Chronology of Modern
Hyderabad (1720–1890)*, Central Records Office, Hyderabad, 1954.

Treaty of Salbai (1782)

Salbai is a small town some 32 kms to the south of Gwalior. The Treaty that
bears its name was signed between Mahadji Sindhia (q.v.), acting as
plenipotentiary for the Peshwa Madhav Rao, and the British, represented
by David Anderson, on 17 May 1782. It signalled the end of the First
Anglo-Maratha War (q.v.); Warren Hastings (q.v.) ratified it at Fort William on 6 June 1782 and Nana Phadnis (q.v.) at Poona; instruments of
ratification were formally exchanged on 24 February 1783.

The 17-article 'treaty of perpetual friendship and alliance' stipulated *inter
alia* that (1) the John Company (q.v.) would restore all 'countries, places,
cities and forts' captured by them (including Bassein) to the Peshwa, and
return to him and the Gaekwad territories taken in Gujarat. The latter ruler
undertook further to accept the suzerainty of the Poona court; (ii) Salsette
(q.v.) and its three neighbouring islands of 'Elephanta, Carranja and Hog'
as well as the city of Broach, were to remain British possessions; (iii)
territories granted earlier to the Company by Raghunath Rao (q.v.) were to
be restored to the Marathas; (iv) 'within a period of four months',
Raghunath Rao was to fix his place of future residence, after which the
British were not to afford him 'any support, protection or assistance'; (v) the
Peshwa would make Haidar Ali (q.v.) relinquish his claims to British territ-

ory (a commitment his successor Tipu Sultan (q.v.) later blatantly ignored); (vi) both parties would not molest each other's allies, while the Peshwa would neither support any other European power nor allow it to settle in his dominions without previously informing the English; (vi) the Company's trade privileges would be restored; (viii) Mahadji Sindhia would guarantee that both parties to the Treaty would abide by its terms.

The importance of the Treaty cannot be over-emphasized. For the Company, it was a turning point in its career, securing peace with the Marathas for nearly 20 years to come and establishing beyond dispute its predominance as an important controlling factor in Indian politics. It added a new feather to Hastings' cap for having successfully terminated seven years of a continuous, if wasteful struggle.

In the career of Mahadji Sindhia, too, Salbai was to mark a watershed. For hitherto, even though he had disregarded the authority of the Peshwa, he had still rated himself a vassal; from now on, ignoring Poona's *fiat*. he pursued with the utmost tenacity, but within limits, his policy of personal aggrandisement in the confident belief that the British would leave him a free hand. It is worth noting that the Treaty itself was concluded at Salbai 'in the camp of Maharaja Soubahdar (Mahadji Sindhia).'

Aitchison, III, pp. 49–55; Dodwell, *CHI,* V, pp. 270–2.

Khawaja Salimullah Khan, Nawab Bahadur of Dacca (d. 1915)

A leading Bengali Muslim and founder-member of the All-India Muslim League (q.v.), Nawab Salimulla Khan was the son of Nawab Ahsanulla Khan of Dacca, who had been a great friend of the British.

Many Bengali Muslims consider the Dacca Nawab's family as outsiders. His forebears, who came from Kashmir, were influential at the Mughal court, and moved to Sylhet in the eighteenth century; they later shifted to Dacca and held property there and in Barisal, Patna and Mymensingh. During the Rebellion of 1857 (q.v.) they supported the Raj and were thereafter generally loyalists.

Salimullah began to figure prominently in politics, especially Muslim politics, when the Partition of Bengal (q.v.) became imminent. Initially opposed to the scheme, he was persuaded to lend his support to it during Lord Curzon's (q.v.) tour, in 1905, of East Bengal. Some attribute his *volte face* to the fact of a loan of £100,000 given him at a nominal rate of interest; it helped rescue him from financial bankruptcy. Thereafter, the Nawab was not only a vocal supporter of the Raj (to which he was now attached by interest as much as sentiment) but also an active organizer of a strong Muslim opposition to the Swadeshi Movement (q.v.) and the reunification of Bengal.

Salimullah could not join the Simla deputation (1st October 1906) because of an eye operation, but took the first concrete step towards establishing a separate Muslim organization. In November 1906 he circulated a scheme for the formation of a 'Muslim All-India Confederacy', the embryo from which the Muslim League emerged.   In December 1906 his scheme became the basis of discussion among Muslim leaders who had assembled from all parts of India to attend the All–India Mohammadan Educational Conference at Dacca. It is true that his 'scheme was not adopted in its entirety as the phraseology of parts of the document did not seem quite happy to the majority of the delegates and the term *confederacy* grated on the years of not a few. The spirit of the Nawab's scheme was however adopted and the essence approved. Therefore the object, the establishment of a central political organization for Muslims, was achieved.'

Salimullah presided over and played host to the first session of the All-India Muslim League at Dacca in December 1907, the League having come into being exactly a year earlier, on 31 December 1906.

To revert to the Partition. In 1906, Salimullah allegedly wrote a communal pamphlet in Bengali and instigated the mullahs to spread his separatist message through the East Bengal countryside; his visit to Comilla in March 1907 sparked off serious clashes between the communities. The tone of his campaigns was, understandably, at once anti-zamindar and anti-mahajan. Writing in the same tone, Salimullah voiced Muslim optimism about the new province of Eastern Bengal and Assam. He was convinced that Muslims would have 'the largest share' of the 'many good things in store' for them and hailed it as their 'golden opportunity.' In fact, he was soon to emerge as Sir Bampfylde Fuller's (q.v.) 'chief unofficial advisor' and 'main agent' in the distribution of patronage in the new political entity of Eastern Bengal and Assam. In the result, East Bengal's Muslims were recipients of many concessions in the decade upto 1911. Salimullah's advice in countering nationalist influence in his community was highly valued and the government of Eastern Bengal and Assam gave him every encouragement to advance Muslim interests. Unhappy with Fuller's resignation, Salimullah advocated the formation of a united Muslim front. Earlier, he had been heartened by Lord Minto's (q.v.) favourable response to the Muslim deputation (1906), of which he was chosen a member (even though he did not finally go). Two years later, he welcomed the Minto-Morley Reforms (q.v.) in so far as the latter conceded the Muslim demand for separate electorates.

After the Partition was countermanded in 1911, Salimullah became doubly determined to gain all he could for his community. Unhappy with the government, he yet 'could see no viable alternative to a policy of dependence on the British', and was convinced that his compatriots had to maintain the 'right balance between their demands and their expression of loyalty.' In so far as Muslims could not hold their own against the Hindu *bhadralok* 'in the rough and tumble of electoral or agitational politics' while the British were worried by the growing strength and 'increasingly aggressive tone' of Hindu nationalism, he urged that Muslim leadership should 'serve as a counter-poise.' It should proclaim its loyalty to the Raj and, in return, Muslims would be able to advise and at the same time receive advice from the highest quarters in the land and hope for a favourable treatment in any constitutional or political settlement.

Salimullah's resentment of the government decision is well brought out in his presidential address to the Muslim League session at Calcutta in March 1912: 'The annulment of the Partition had all appearance of ready concessions to the clamours of an utterly seditious agitation. It has appeared to put a premium on sedition and disloyalty, and created an impression in the minds of the irresponsible masses that even the Government can be brought down on its knees by a reckless and persistent defiance of constituted authority.'

The government conferred on Salimullah the KCSI and, two years later, the GCIE. These rewards, it is said, were designed to silence his opposition to the annulment of the Partition.

Failing health prevented Salimullah's active association with the League after 1912; thereafter, he continued to be its Vice-President in Bengal until his death in January 1915.

J. H. Broomfield, *Elite conflict in a plural society: twentieth century Bengal*, Berkeley, 1968; Leonard A. Gordon, *Bengal: the Nationalist Movement 1876–1940*, Delhi, 1974; Syed Sharifuddin Pirzada, *Foundations of Pakistan: All-India Muslim League Documents: 1906–47*, 2 vols., Karachi, 1969, vol. 1, 1906–24.

Salsette

'Salsette' is a corruption of the Marathi word, 'Shatshasthi', literally eighty-six, which was the number of villages in the territory as it was originally composed. It is 150 square miles in area and much the largest of the many islands near Bombay, with those of Dravee and Versova just off its shores. It is connected with Bombay by a causeway and bridge at Sion, 2 miles east of Mahim. It is beautifully diversified and well-peopled with many ancient rock temples.

Salsette, along with some neighbouring islands, was in the possession of the Portuguese, but was not part of the group handed over to the English King Charles II (r.1660-85) as dowry when he married Catherine of Braganza. In 1738, Salsette was captured by the Marathas. The English had for long desired to control it owing to its strategic location for the proper defence of Bombay. Through it, they wanted to command the passes too by which goods travelled inland. The Bombay Presidency, taking advantage of the confused state of affairs at Poona, took sides in supporting a rival faction at the Peshwa's court, thereby involving themselves in the First Anglo-Maratha War (q.v.). Along with Bassein, the island was taken by the British on 28 December 1774; a little later, Raghoba (q.v.), whose candidature the Bombay Presidency had supported, ceded to them the two islands as well as the revenues of the district of Broach.

Edward Balfour, *Encyclopaedia of India*, 3 vols., 3rd ed., Graz, 1967, III, pp. 503–4.

Santal Rebellion (1855–7)

Essentially a primitive community, the Santals were harassed and ruthlessly exploited by 'civilized people' from Bengal and Bihar, not to speak of the railway construction companies. They were often unable to seek, much less obtain, justice in far away courts whose law and procedure they did not understand. The heavy demands made compelled them to depend upon moneylenders, the 'mahajans', to whose sharp practices they fell an easy prey. The John Company's (q.v.) revenue officials were far from understanding and the railway companies paid their wages fitfully, if at all. The primary cause of the Santal revolt was thus economic, *not* political; they turned against the government only when they realized that, instead of helping them against their oppressors, it shielded the latter. Driven to desperation, they took the law into their own hands and under the leadership of two brothers, Sidhu and Kanhu, with such others as Chand and Bhairah, who claimed divine authority, they broke out in open revolt.

Beginning with stray cases of looting, arson and murder, in June 1855, the revolt soon assumed the proportions of a formidable rebellion; by August, 30,000 men were up in arms. The Santals assembled in large groups in different areas, proclaimed the end of the Company's rule and their own independent state. Before many weeks had passed, the countryside was completely ravaged and everyone they could lay hands upon—English planters, railway officials, police personnel, tradesmen, peasants, men, women and children—were done to death.

The British were taken completely by surprise, but their reprisals were awesome. A regular military campaign was mounted and the Santals hunted down like wild beasts. By February 1856, the situation was well in hand; by August, the rebellion had been firmly suppressed.

After the worst was over, by Act 37 of 1855, the Santal parganas were constituted into a separate Non-Regulation district, placed under the control of the Commissioner of Bhagalpur, to be administered by a Deputy Commissioner at Dumka and four Assistant Commissioners. The aim was to create closer personal contact between the rulers and the ruled.

The insurrection was 'not a mere spasmodic outburst of the crude instincts' of the Santals; it was the product of a 'long course of oppression silently and patiently submitted to' by an unsophisticated people unaccustomed to fight for their own rights. Nor would it be correct to dismiss the revolt as 'a mere local rising of no importance.' For more than six months it remained a dreadful menace to the Government, the zamindars and the people of the affected areas. Its suppression heavily taxed the energies of the troops. At the same time, the movement was not anti-British in the beginning but directed chiefly against the mahajans and the traders.

Kalikinkar Datta, *The Santal Insurrection of 1855-57*, University of Calcutta, Calcutta, 1940.

Tej Bahadur Sapru (1875–1949)

Tej Bahadur Sapru was born at Aligarh in an aristocratic Brahmin family once based in Delhi. He attended high school in Aligarh and matriculated from Agra where he also took his law degrees. After apprenticeship at Moradabad, he moved to the Allahabad High Court. In 1907, Sapru entered active politics and joined the moderate wing of the Indian National Congress (q.v.). Later (1917) he was one of the first to enroll in Annie Besant's (q.v.) Home Rule League (q.v.). As a member of the Imperial Legislative Council, he was a signatory (1916) to 'the Memorandum of the 19' (members) embodying proposals for constitutional reform.

During the visit of the Prince of Wales to India (1921), which the Congress had decided to boycott, the Governor-General, Reading, used Sapru's good offices to bring about a rapprochement, promising substantial concessions on the political plane. Unfortunately Gandhi's (q.v.) insistence on the release of the Ali brothers, Mohamed Ali and Shaukat Ali (qq.v.), as a precondition to any political parleys led to a deadlock.

In 1921 at the age of 46, Sapru was appointed Law Member in the Governor-General's Executive Council. Here he was instrumental in removing restrictions on the press. As a result of his efforts, the Indian Press Act of 1910 (q.v.) and the Indian Criminal Law Amendment Act of 1908 (q.v.) were withdrawn from the statute book. He resigned in 1923 after being in office for a little over two years and returned to law and political life. He was awarded the KCSI on his resignation from the Executive Council and chosen president of a national convention which had the support of many political parties, though not of the Congress. Sapru was of the firm view that HMG's control over the Government of India was a major hindrance to the country's constitutional progress. He considered Whitehall to be a citadel of reaction and felt that until New Delhi was freed from the stranglehold of its control, progress in constitutional reform would be without substance.

Sapru was the principal architect of the Commonwealth of India Bill which Annie Besant had sponsored and which was introduced in the British Parliament in 1926 by George Lansbury, a Labour Party front ranker. In 1924, he was the author, along with P. S. Sivaswamy Aiyer, M. A. Jinnah (q.v.) and R. P. Paranjpye, of the minority report of the Muddiman Committee (q.v.). Later, he was an active member of the committee appointed by the All-Parties Conference, of which M. A. Ansari (q.v.) was chairman. The Nehru Report (q.v.), in the making of which Sapru played a pivotal role, was a further step in the direction already taken by the Commonwealth of India Bill. *Inter alia*, the Report had urged that the next stage of constitutional advance must be the establishment of an all-India federal union, including both British Indian provinces as well as the Indian States (q.v.).

As a liberal favouring moderate change within the existing constitutional and legal framework, Sapru worked untiringly in the role of mediator between the British authorities and Indian nationalists and between Hindu and Muslim leaders. He sought, for instance, albeit to no avail, to mediate between Whitehall and Indian nationalists and between the two principal communities at the Round Table Conference (q.v.). Here, thanks to his close contacts with many of the Indian princes and their faith in his integrity and soundness of judgment, he came to be regarded as 'easily the most outstanding delegate.' Successful in his efforts with the Gandhi-Irwin Pact (q.v.), Sapru reacted strongly not only to the Congress tactics of Civil Disobedience Movement (q.v.) as being prejudicial to compromise, but also to the imprisonment of Congress leaders by the government.

Sapru held that despite its many limitations, the Government of India Act, 1935 (q.v.) could be implemented in a spirit that might lead, in the long haul, to full responsible government. In 1942, he along with C. Rajagopalachari (q.v.) and B.N. Rau helped Sir Stafford Cripps (q.v.) evolve a formula on defence. Cripps thought well of it. The subsequent failure of the Cripps Mission (q.v.) he viewed as a disaster both for India as well as Britain. Similarly, Sapru regarded the Quit India Movement (q.v.) of the Congress as a tactical blunder. During the politically dark days of 1940-4, Sapru made numerous efforts to break the constitutional deadlock, particularly through the Non-Parties' Congress held at Allahabad in December 1942.

Sapru told Gandhi, after the latter's release from prison in 1944, that the 'C. R.' Formula (q.v.) would pave the way for partition and Pakistan, a course to which he was unalterably opposed. In the wake of the failure of the Gandhi-Jinnah Talks (q.v.), in September 1944, the Non-Party conference elected him chairman of its 29-member committee charged with examining the whole communal question in a judicial framework. The committee, after a detailed analysis, made a strong plea against the partition of the country. Sapru was also a member of the defence committee in the 1945 Azad Hind Fauj (q.v.) trials. In 1946 Sapru was offered membership of the Constituent Assembly (q.v.) but ill-health prevented his accepting it. His advice was however sought frequently, especially on matters relating to the judiciary and its functioning.

Sapru represented India at the Imperial Conference in London in 1923; 20 years later he was the first President of the Indian Council of World Affairs, which he helped to found and which honoured him by naming its headquarters, in New Delhi, as Sapru House. He supported Hindu law reform and was a good scholar of Urdu and Persian. In regard to tenancy legislation, Sapru was strongly in favour of a fair deal to the tenants in the zamindari districts of Bihar and U.P. Essentially a constitutional pandit and a constructive statesman, his standards of honesty and personal integrity were above reproach.

'In many ways', B. Shiva Rao rates him as 'the most remarkable Indian personality' he had known in public life: 'Few men in India of this century had his breadth of vision; and certainly no one was endowed with his warm-hearted generosity, his absolute integrity and the complete freedom from pettiness and malice which characterized his public and personal life.' He had 'the vision to see the solutions' of many of the country's political problems and the courage to stand by them.

S. K. Bose, *Tej Bahadur Sapru 1875–1949*, New Delhi, 1978; D. A. Low, 'Sir Tej Bahadur Sapru and the First Round Table Conference', in D. A. Low (ed.), *Soundings in Modern South Asian History*, London, 1968, pp. 294–329; C. H. Philips and M. D. Wainwright (eds.), *The Partition of India: Policies and Perspectives, 1935–1947*, London, 1970; B. Shiva Rao, *India's Freedom Movement: Some Notable Figures*, New Delhi, 1972, pp. 89–97; Sen, *DNB*, IV, pp. 48–51 (B. Shiva Rao).

Sati

Broadly, *sati* (or 'suttee') means a chaste and virtuous woman; however with the passage of time, the term has come to connote a woman devoted to her husband in life who, on his death, immolates herself on his funeral pyre (*Sahagamana* or *Sahamaran*). Voluntary in some instances, the practice was no doubt forced in most cases and was sometimes brought about even by the administering of drugs to the widow. Said to date as far back as 400 B. C. and at its worst in periods of political uncertainty, it came to acquire, as time passed, the approval of most devout Hindus. By the first quarter of the nineteenth century in Bengal alone about 800 satis took their lives every year.

Officials and missionaries during early British days enjoined on the government to stop this baneful custom but effective action was hampered by the then widely accepted policy of *laissez faire* in matters of religion. Some organized efforts however were soon evident to minimize its incidence. Thus regulations were made in 1812, and later supplemented in 1815 and 1817, to ascertain whether a sati was voluntary or not. There was also a ban on girls under 16 years of age committing sati, as also for those who were pregnant or had infant children.

By 1817 enlightened Indian opinion, spearheaded by social reformers like Dwarka Nath Tagore (1794-1846) and Raja Rammohun Roy (q.v.) asserted itself powerfully in favour of abolishing the practice of sati in a quiet yet gradual phasing out so as not to hurt seriously the religious sentiments of orthodox Hindus. A section among the latter actually mounted a counter-agitation under Raja Radha Kanta Deb (1783-1867). William Bentinck (q.v.), encouraged and sustained by liberal Indian opinion, undertook an extensive inquiry into the possible reaction of Indians to the abolition of this rite; a broad conclusion reached was that it would not provoke any violent opposition.

With the approval of the Governor-General's Council, a measure was enacted on 4 December 1829 and published, as Regulation XVII, in the official gazette five days later. Under its provisions, sati was declared illegal, an act of culpable homicide punishable by fine, imprisonment or both. Even those associated with or conniving at it were to be treated as offenders under the law. When enforced, the Regulation referred specifically to Bengal but was later (1830) extended to Madras and even Bombay. There was a loud clamour of protest and an appeal against it was preferred to the Privy Council which, in 1832, summarily dismissed the petition. Thus it was that this measure received legal sanction.

B. H. Hjejle, 'The Social policy of the East India Company with regard to Sati, Slavery, Thagi and Infanticide', unpublished D. Phil thesis, Oxford, 1958; G. Seed, 'The Abolition of Suttee in Bengal', *History*, XL, 1955; Kalipada Mitra, 'Suppression of Suttee in the province of Cuttack', *Bengal Past and Present*, XLVI, Nos. 91-92, July-December 1933, pp. 125-31.

Dr Satya Pal (1885–1954)

An eminent physician-cum-politician of Amritsar, Dr Satya Pal had received his medical education at Lahore. He was commissioned into the Royal Medical Service during World War I (1914-18) at the termination of which he evinced a keen interest in current Indian politics. Soon he was completely absorbed in the anti-Rowlatt Act (q.v.) agitation in the Panjab and, along with Dr Saifuddin Kitchlew (q.v.) toured the province, rousing its people into political action. His other compatriots were Mahashe Rattan Chand and Chaudhari Bagga Mal. The historic Indian National Congress (q.v.) session at Amritsar in December 1919 owed much of its success to Dr Satya Pal's untiring efforts.

Stamped dangerous, Satya Pal had been arrested on 10 April 1919, and interned at Dharamsala to await transportation for life. He was released with the declaration of an amnesty on 26 December 1919 but continued his political work with the Panjab Provincial Congress Committee under the guidance of Gandhi (q.v.). He took an active part in the Non-cooperation and Civil Disobedience Movements (qq.v.). A staunch believer in Hindu-Muslim unity and toleration towards all religions, Satya Pal took an active interest in promoting social reform. He contributed articles on political subjects and co-authored a book, *Sixty Years of Congress*. For some time he published an Urdu newspaper, called the *Congress*, from Lahore.

Satya Pal rejoined the Indian Medical Service during World War II (1939-45), but this did not diminish his interest in active politics. Initially he had favoured Dominion Status (q.v.) because it spelt a peaceful transfer of power; later he was converted to the ideal of complete independence. Soon after Partition (1947), he shifted to Simla and, in 1952, was elected Speaker of the East Panjab Legislative Assembly, in which office he died two years later.

Sen, *DNB*, IV, pp. 89–90 (V. S. Suri); Fauja Singh, *Eminent Freedom Fighters of Punjab*, Patiala, 1972, pp. 205–7.

Sayyid Brothers

The brothers Hasan Ali (afterwards Abdullah Khan) and Husain Ali Khan belonged to a numerous and respected family descended from Sayyid Abul-Farah of Wasalt (in Iraq) who settled in India in 1217. The Sayyids of Barha (from *bara,* or twelve, villages held in Muzaffarnagar district) were as distinguished for personal bravery as were their kinsmen of Bilgram, in Oudh (q.v.), for their learning.

The Sayyids first attracted attention during the reign of Akbar (r.1556-1605) when they won the hereditary right to lead the Mughal vanguard in battle. Though reckoned to be brave, doughty fighters, they had, over the years, also acquired a reputation for 'unreliability and ambitiousness'.

Hasan Ali and Husain Ali Khan were the eldest sons of Abdullah Khan Sayyid Mian. In the service of the Chief Bakshi of Aurangzeb (r.1658-1707), the latter rose to be Subahdar of Bijapur and later of Ajmer. In the last decade of Aurangzeb's rule, his two sons had attached themselves to the cause of Prince Azim-ush-Shan, the second son of Emperor Bahadur Shah I (q.v.). Under his patronage, Abdullah Khan rose to be Deputy Governor of Allahabad, while Husain Ali occupied a corresponding position at Patna.

As Farrukh Siyar (q.v.) succeeded in his struggle (1711-13) for the throne, the two brothers, more especially Abdullah Khan (who had helped smoothen the future Emperor's relations with Husain Ali too), espoused his cause as their own. Farrukh Siyar's success brought them generous rewards: Abdullah Khan was made Wazir with the title of Qutb-ul-Mulk, Zafar Jang Sepah Salar, and Husain Ali promoted Mir Bakshi, Amir-ul-umra Firuz Jang; the rank of 7,000 *zat* and 7,000 *sowar* was also conferred on both.

An early measure to which they attended was the formal abolition by the Emperor of the *jaziah,* while the pilgrim tax too was not to be realized from a number of centres. The Marwar campaign (1713-14), which Husain Ali led against Raja Ajit Singh, resulted in a settlement that was satisfactory both for the Rajputs as well as the two brothers. In the bargain, Ajit Singh became Subahdar of Gujarat and Jai Singh of Malwa.

Meanwhile, as the brothers endeavoured to exercise the substance of power in terms of the offices they held, the Emperor and his favourites sabotaged their efforts. The principle of personal rule by the monarch was invoked against the Wazir as well as the Mir Bakhshi's right to run the administration according to their lights. This was to emerge as the central issue in party politics during Farrukh Siyar's reign.

In March 1714, Husain Ali demanded and secured for himself the viceroyalty of the Deccan in place of Nizam-ul-Mulk (q.v.). His intention was to discharge the functions of his new office through a deputy while himself remaining at the court. The Emperor, however, refused to concede this and ordered Husain Ali to proceed to the Deccan. Abdullah Khan was thus left alone to face a treacherous master and a hostile court until such time as the brothers gained enough strength to settle the issue finally in the manner they desired.

During 1715-18 both Farrukh Siyar as well as the Sayyid brothers engaged in a life-and-death struggle to recruit fresh allies for their respective, if rival, causes. The Emperor turned to the old Alamgiri nobles—Muhammad Amin Khan, Nizam-ul-Mulk, Zulfikar Khan—apart from trying to enlist the support of Ajit Singh and Jai Singh; while refusing to alienate the old nobility, the Sayyid brothers tried to gain fresh allies among the Jats and the Marathas.

Husain Ali's stewardship of the Deccan (1715-18) was remarkable in giving shape and form to his earlier conviction that a political settlement with Raja Shahu (q.v.) and his Peshwa was a *sine qua non* for the return of sanity to a war-ravaged land. For more than a quarter of a century since Aurangzeb marched thither in 1681, the Deccan had known no peace. Bahadur Shah I was already before his death feeling his way towards a political settlement with the Marathas and even the Nizam-ul-Mulk had been forced to recognize the new-gained strength of the Peshwa and his sardars.

Nizam-ul-Mulk had initially refused to accept his predecessor Daud Khan Panni's agreement for the payment of *chauth* and *sardeshmukhi* to Raja Shahu and had ousted Maratha revenue collectors from Aurangabad and several other districts; Husain Ali too had followed suit. However, his position was rendered more difficult by Farrukh Siyar secretly encouraging the Maratha ruler as well the zamindars and Diwans to oppose his own Viceroy! That apart, the Emperor began to interfere actively in the matter of official appointments in the Deccan. It was against this background that, in mid-1717, Husain Ali opened negotiations with the Marathas, culminating in the agreement of February 1718. It conceded the principal Maratha demand for the right of collecting *chauth* and *sardeshmukhi* from six subahs of the Deccan as well as recognizing their recent conquests in Berar, Gondwana and Karnatak. Asked to confirm the agreement, the Emperor dragged his feet. It was clear to Farrukh Siyar as to anyone else that, in essence, the agreement was aimed against him.

Early in 1718, Abdullah Khan had written to Husain Ali to return to the north at once; his relations with the Emperor had worsened to a degree where he feared for his life. In October 1718, the Sayyid left Aurangabad; at Burhanpur, he was joined by a Maratha army of 10,000 horse under Peshwa

Balaji Vishwanath (q.v.). The ostensible pretext for his coming to the court, without permission, was that an alleged son of Prince Akbar handed over by Raja Shahu had to be escorted to Delhi!

Haughty as well as hot-headed, Husain Ali had already made up his mind to depose Farrukh Siyar. He entered Delhi with drums beating, 'like an independent sovereign'. In spite of a clear breach between the brothers and the Emperor, Abdullah Khan was in favour of keeping Farrukh Siyar on the throne and maintaining the *khutbah* and the *sikkah* in his name. Husain Ali however was impatient and precipitate. In the result, the Emperor was deposed. This proved to be a fatal move, for 'in destroying Farrukh Siyar, the Saiyids had thus destroyed their most effective shield against the old nobles'.

The deposition has been rated as the brothers' biggest political error. The question has been argued on a moral plane, and yet the Emperor's execution, although marked by 'unnecessary cruelty', appeared to be 'a logically unavoidable' corollary to his deposition. After it occurred, the Sayyids began to be considered as traitors and tyrants and their action condemned as 'an act of infamy and disgrace'.

Considering the weakness of their position, the brothers blundered politically as their rivals could now pose as the champions of the Timurid monarchy. Again, in deposing Farrukh Siyar, the Sayyids had 'overestimated their strength and resources, disagreed among themselves about the policy to be pursued towards the powerful Chin group and ultimately precipitated a premature show-down with it'.

The deposition and execution of Farrukh Siyar were more than a personal tragedy and nullified the brothers' efforts to evolve a composite ruling class consisting of all sections of the Mughal nobility as well as the Rajputs and the Marathas. The emergence of such a ruling class might have enabled them to consolidate and develop the political structure evolved earlier by the Mughals. As Satish Chandra emphasizes, the real significance of the Sayyids' 'new' wizarat lay precisely in that it 'made a definite break with narrow, exclusionist policies and moved in the direction of establishing a state essentially secular in approach and national in character'.

The brothers' downfall did not automatically imply a negation of the process which they had stimulated and strengthened, 'it continued to work apace and influenced the political and cultural developments of the succeeding period'. But the instability which followed was not conducive for the development of new institutions.

In any proper assessment of their work it is imperative to remember that the brothers did not enjoy political power long enough to make any impact on policy. After Farrukh Siyar's deposition, two emperors followed in quick succession; both were proteges of the Sayyids. The first, Rafi-ud-Darajat, already a sick man, lasted a little over three months and was a complete puppet in the Sayyids' hands. Nor did his elder brother Rafi-ud-Doulah, who succeeded him, fare any better. Even before he ascended the throne, he fell prey to an advanced stage of consumption.

While the number of their enemies multiplied, there were not many to befriend the Sayyids. Emperor Muhammad Shah (q.v.), now elevated to the masnad, was weak and inexperienced, while the open rebellion of Nizam-ul-

Mulk posed a serious threat. To counter it, Husain Ali accompanied the Emperor on his way to the Deccan. Not far from Agra, at a place called Toda Bhim, he was done to death on 9 October 1720 by a trooper, Mir Haidar Beg Dughlat. Presently, Abdullah was decisively defeated at the battle of Hasanpur, near Agra. Taken prisoner, he was poisoned and killed in 1723.

The mortal remains of Husain Ali were transferred to Ajmer for burial while Abdullah was buried at Delhi.

Satish Chandra, *Parties & Politics at the Mughal Court 1707-1740*, Aligarh, 1959, pp. 86-167.

Prevention of Seditious Meetings Act (1907–11)

Promulgated as an Ordinance on 11 May 1907 and called the 'Regulation of Meetings Ordinance 1907', the aim of the Prevention of Seditious Meetings Act was to control meetings in connection with, or the curbing of, political agitation in Bengal and the Panjab. It stipulated that no public meeting could be held in any proclaimed area for the discussion of any question unless notice had been served at least 7 days earlier to the appropriate authorities to that effect. The latter were authorized to prohibit the holding of such meetings. A meeting held in contravention of the law rendered the holders of the meeting liable to imprisonment or fine. A prohibited meeting was deemed to be an unlawful assembly.

Passed on 1 November 1907, the Act sought to prevent the spread of sedition and the mushrooming of secret anarchist organizations. Additionally, its aim was to preserve law and order by cordoning off certain territories as 'proclaimed areas' where all public meetings would be banned. Under its provisions, permission to hold meetings of more than twenty persons would have to be obtained from the local authorities who had the right to forbid them or authorize the local police to attend and report on what transpired. In every case a notice of three days was required to be served. Rash Behari Ghose (q.v.) and G. K. Gokhale (q.v.) had opposed its passage—as had the Secretary of State, John Morley, initially. They feared it would encourage 'secret sedition', for local authorities invested with so much power would be apt to misuse it.

Understandably, the new legislation failed in achieving its purpose, with the result that terrorist organizations and their activities multiplied and the need was felt to continue the measure after its expiry in August 1910. Extended up to March 1911, the Act was then made, with some modifications, into the permanent 'Prevention of Seditious Meetings Act 1911, Act No. X.' The objective was 'to consolidate and amend the law relating to the prevention of public meetings likely to promote sedition or to cause a disturbance of public tranquillity.' 'A public meeting' was defined as one 'open to the public' notwithstanding the fact that 'it is held in a private place . . . and admission thereto may have been restricted by ticket or otherwise.'

Penalties for a person 'concerned in the promotion or conduct' of a public meeting, contrary to provisions of the Act, 'may extend to six months or with fine, or with both.' A person delivering a lecture at such a meeting 'may be arrested without warrant and shall be punished with imprisonment' for six months with fine. Though applicable to the whole country, the Act was to be operative in the disturbed or proclaimed areas for a period of six months, unless extended for a longer period with the permission of the Governor-General in Council. Meetings covened by government officers or under legal authority were immune from its operation. While the conveners of all unlawful assemblies were liable to punishment, authority to try breaches of this Act was conferred only on Presidency Magistrates or First Class Magistrates or Sub-Divisional Magistrates.

Ostensibly designed to preserve law and order, the measure was, in reality, aimed at paralysing the Indian national movement.

The Unrepealed Central Acts, 10 vols, Delhi, 1938–42, vol. VI, from 1911–1916, pp. 106–8; Tara Chand, IV, p. 355.

Seistan Missions (1870–2, 1903–5)

Seistan is a border district between Persia and Afghanistan, for the most part a sandy dune interspersed with lakes, streams and marshes. Originally a part of Persia, it was captured by Ahmad Shah Abdali (q.v.), so that at the time of his death (1773) the entire disputed area of Seistan right up to the banks of the Helmund was in Afghan occupation. The Persians, who coveted it no less than did the Afghans, invoked the terms of the Treaty of Paris (1857) to seek British mediation in settling the dispute. However, under the impact of its policy of non-intervention in Afghan affairs, Britain let matters drift. The civil war (1863-9) in Afghanistan following the death of Amir Dost Mohammad (q.v.) however provided an ideal opportunity for the Persians to establish their control in a large part of Seistan; later (1870), they sought British mediation in the hope that it would legalize their occupation.

British interest in settling the dispute arose from a desire to forestall Russian influence in Persia and Afghanistan, both of whom she was anxious to retain as allies. Besides, Seistan occupied a strategic position, affording easy access across the Helmund to Kandahar and India. In response to a Persian request, Maj Gen Sir Frederick Goldsmid of the Indian army was dispatched to demarcate the boundary and was to be assisted by Persian and Afghan commissioners. After a thorough study and investigation, he handed down what is known as the 'Seistan Award' in 1872.

Under its terms, Seistan proper was assigned to Persia while the Afghans were given possession of the right bank as well as part of the left bank of the Helmund. This was designed to prevent Persia from falling prey to a Russian advance, while establishing Afghan control over the river. Neither country was satisfied, for while Persia reluctantly evacuated occupied territory, Afghanistan was loath to lose the fertile plains Persia still held. In the result, the Award aggravated problems of British India's defence.

It has been suggested that the Seistan Award was very much in favour of Persia because it was important for the British to ensure that Persia did not go over to the Russians. To pacify Sher Ali of Afghanistan it was decided to give him monetary assistance. Though neither side was wholly satisfied with Goldsmid's decision, they adhered to it in practice.

Disputes arose afresh on the question of the distribution of river waters and alleged Persian encroachments on Afghan territory, as the Helmund changed its course. Asked to mediate in the dispute, the Government of India deputed A. H. McMahon (q.v.) to head the Seistan Arbitration Mission, which commenced work in February 1903. There was now a greater urgency in the situation for both the Germans as well as the Russians were rapidly receiving important economic and political concessions in Persia.

The task regarding the distribution of the river waters was two-fold—to delineate a more precise riparian boundary and to distribute the waters more equitably. After an extensive survey of the area, an interim award was handed down on 11 November 1903, wherein the major portion of the boundary still followed the course of the Helmund. A subsequent award handed down on 10 April 1905 gave Persia the right to one-third of the river's water supply, a right she could not alienate without Afghanistan's prior permission. No new irrigation works which interfered with an equitable distribution of the river's waters were to be allowed. Both countries accepted the boundary, although Persia declined to accept the award on the waterway. The British however had achieved their primary objective of retaining their influence in the region and preventing any Russian penetration along this frontier.

G. P. Tripathi, *Indo-Afghan Relations 1882-1906,* New Delhi, 1973; Mridula Abrol, *British Relations with Frontier States (1863-1875),* Delhi, 1974; Louis Dupree, *Afghanistan,* Princeton, 1973.

Treaty of Seringapatam (1792)

The Treaty of Seringapatam, negotiations for which had begun on 8 February 1792 and whose preliminary terms were signed fourteen days later, brought the Third Anglo-Mysore War (q.v.) to an end. Tipu Sultan (q.v.) initially keen to wriggle out, for the terms were somewhat harsh, soon realized his inability to face his combined enemies and signed on 18 March 1792.

Comprising eight articles, the 'Definitive Treaty of Perpetual Friendship' was concluded between the John Company (q.v.) and its two allies, the Nizam and the Peshwa on the one hand and Tipu on the other. *Inter alia* (i) it confirmed the earlier treaties between the British and the rulers of Mysore, with Haidar Ali (q.v.) on 8 August 1770 and with Tipu on 11 March 1784; (ii) by article 4 of the Preliminary Treaty, Tipu was to cede half his dominion. He was to make immediate payment of half the indemnity agreed upon while the remainder was to be given in specie only—in three instalments, not exceeding four months; additionally, he was to order the release of prisoners of war. Pending fulfilment of these terms, two of his sons were to be detained as (British) hostages; (iii) it specified that the territory to be ceded to the allies (viz, the Nizam and the Marathas) was to be 'adjacent to their respective boundaries and subject to their selection accordingly.' A general abstract of 'countries' to be thus ceded was attached; (iv) villages and talukas to the north and east of the river Cauvery were to be part of the Company's dominion and those to the south and west of the river Tipu's; such adjustments as this necessitated between the two were to be effected; (v) districts and forts to be ceded by Tipu were to be delivered 'without any cavil or demand', as also those to be handed over to him.

In terms of territory, the Nizam obtained the lion's share, his dominion now extending all the way from the Krishna to beyond the Pennar river, with the forts of Ganjikotah and Cuddapah thrown in. With their newly-acquired territory, the Maratha boundary now extended to the Tungabhadra and the Krishna. The English secured large chunks on the Malabar coast from the north of Cannanore to the south of the Ponnani river, with Coorg as its defensive hinterland. In addition, they obtained the Baramahal district as well as Dindigul. The Raja of Travancore, on whose behalf ostensibly the war had been fought, got virtually nothing.

Apart from territory, Tipu was required to pay an indemnity of Rs 3.6 crores, of which Rs 1.6 crore was to be paid immediately and the rest in three instalments at intervals not exceeding four months each. All prisoners held by the combatants since the time of Haidar Ali were were to be released.

The harsh terms of the Treaty sapped the economic, financial and military resources of Mysore; more, it took away all the natural barriers protecting the state. In fact, Tipu's dominion was now surrounded by British territory except on the north-west and the north-east where the Marathas and the Nizam had made sizeable gains. The cession of Malabar and Coorg cut Mysore from the western seaboard, the surrender of Baramahal deprived Tipu of access to the passes through which his father had descended on the Carnatic. In sum, for all practical purposes, the Mysore ruler was confined and shut in and Cornwallis (q.v.) who fought the war, and concluded the peace, felt that the British had now 'effectively crippled our enemy without making our friends too formidable.'

Aitchison, V, pp. 147-57; Dodwell, *CHI*, V, pp. 336-7; *Roberts*, p. 235.

Servants of India Society (f. 1905)

The Servants of India Society was founded on 12 June 1905 by Gopal Krishna Gokhale (q.v.) and continues to function today with its head-quarters at Shivaji Nagar, Poona and branches in Madras, Bombay, Delhi, Nagpur and Allahabad. In addition, it has working centres at Cuttack and Kozhikode. Pandit H. N. Kunzru continued to be the society's president from 1936 until his death some 40 years later.

A non-communal, non-sectarian body, the Society recognizes no caste distinctions; it was registered in 1928 with 13 individual members; in 1948, the membership was 24. It operates throughout India and, in 1963, had a budget of Rs 400,000. Its principal organ is the *Hitvada*, an English daily published from Nagpur and Bhopal. Another Maratha daily, the *Dnyan Prakash*, has also served as a mouth-piece.

Gokhale's aim in setting up this body—'to spiritualize public life and fill the heart with love for the country'—was shared by its first members: N. A. Dravid, A. V. Patwardhan and G. K. Devadhar. The objective was to be achieved by bringing together and training a band of selfless and dedicated young men. 'National missionaries' as Gokhale called them, they were to devote themselves to the cause of the country and its uplift with a religious fervour and zeal. *Inter alia*, the Society's constitution accepted 'the British government as ordained . . .for India's good.' Each member was to undergo training for five years. As a probationer, he was neither allowed to write nor speak in public without the prior permission of the founder members. In the result, it has been compared to the monastic order of the Society of Jesus, except for the latter's vow of celibacy. None the less, as V. S. Srinivas Sastri explained, 'it was a politico-social organization of life-workers, without a religious bond.'

Having been accepted into the fraternity, each member was to take seven vows, viz., (i) that the country will always be first in his thoughts; (ii) that in serving the country he will seek no personal advantage for himself; (iii) that he will regard Indians as brothers and will work for the advancement of all; (iv) that he will be content with such provision for himself and his family . . .as the Society will be able to make; (v) that he will lead a pure personal life; (vi) that he will not engage in personal quarrels with anyone; (vii) that he will always keep in view the aims of the Society and watch over its interests.

The Society paid its members, while the latter's earnings went to fill its coffers. In addition, an applicant for membership was required to pass through a period of probation during which he might be removed any time. As may be evident, becoming a member was not easy. By December 1916, when the Society's first report was presented, there were 10 ordinary members, with another 8 under training. Ten were released from their vows for a variety of reasons. Gokhale's mantle fell on V. S. Srinivas Sastri, who succeeded him as Senior Member.

From its very inception, the Society's work was put under six broad categories: (i) creating among the people—by example and precept—a deep and passionate love of India and seeking its highest fulfilment in service and sacrifice; (ii) organising the work of political education and agitation, basing it on a careful study of public questions; (iii) promoting goodwill and co-operation among the different communities; (iv) assisting educational movements, especially for workers, the Backward Classes as well as industrial and scientific education; (v) helping the industrial development of the country; (vi) improving the lot of the Backward Classes.

Politically, the Society and its members gradually drifted away from the Indian National Congress (q.v.) towards the National Liberal Federation (q.v.). Thus, V. S. Srinivas Sastri wrote (December 1916) his *Self Government for India under the British Flag* and was closely associated with the 'Memorandum of Nineteen.' Gokhale and Sastri devoted themselves mainly to political work; N.M. Joshi (q.v.), another member, founded the Social Service League (1911) and, in the 1920s, the Trade Union Movement (q.v.). Pandit Kunzru founded the Seva Samiti (1914) while Sri Ram Bajpai, the Seva Samiti Boy Scouts Association. Other institutions, such as the Poona Seva Samiti and the Bhil Seva Mandal, speak volumes for the society's work. It has also been conducting a model Depressed Classes mission in Mangalore while its work during the Moplah Rebellion (q.v.) made it a household-name in Malabar.

As of date, the Society's activities embrace, *inter alia,* welfare work for the Adivasis, Harijans, Backward Classes and tribals. It administers distress relief, maintains primary and junior high schools for children, runs hostels, leprosy clinics—and the Gokhale Institute of Politics and Economics in Poona. Its modest budget for the year ending 31 March 1979 was of the order of Rs 26.25 lakhs. As of 1 October 1979, the Society claimed an overall membership of 15 including the President (S. R. Venkataraman), the Vice President (R. S. Misra) and 4 'Senior', 3 'Ordinary', 5 'Members under Training' and a solitary 'Attache'.

Though Gandhi (q.v.) did not enrol himself a member, he continued to take a keen interest in the Society's activities. An official organ of the Society, *The Servant of India*, continued to be published from 1918 to 1939.

Servants of India Society, Report for 1978–79, Poona, 1979; Bimanbehari Majumdar, *Indian Political Associations and Reform of Legislature (1818-1917)*, Calcutta, 1965, pp. 133-8; B. R. Nanda, *Gokhale*, New Delhi, 1977; Planning Commission (India): *Encyclopaedia of Social Work in India*, 3 vols., New Delhi, 1968, III, p. 90.

Reorganization of Civil Services (1947)

On the eve of Indian independence, the government of India announced that it would undertake to give those members of the Secretary of State's services who continued to serve at the centre or in the provinces their existing scales of salary, leave and pensionary benefits. The compensation provided for European officers who would continue to serve after 15 August 1947 was assessed differently from their Indian counterparts. In the latter category an exception was made in regard to such Indian officers who (i) had not been invited to serve after the transfer of power; (ii) could satisfy the Governor-General that their actions in the course of their service prior to the transfer of power had damaged their prospects; (iii) could demonstrate that the appointments offered to them were such that may not be viewed as satisfactory in their altered circumstances; (iv) could prove to the satisfaction of the Governor-General that they had legitimate cause for anxiety about their future in the province in which they were placed. The same principles of compensation applied to European officers and other ranks of the defence services and the Indian Medical Service.

While the Government of India accepted responsibility for the payment of retiring benefits or proportionate pensions, the British government undertook to compensate European officers as well as Indian officers in the special categories listed above, for loss of their careers and prospects. In the case of European officers who would no longer be serving under the ultimate control of the British Parliament, compensation was deemed necessary, for they would hold their appointments under changed conditions.

The result of these rules was that most European officers on the civil side opted for compensation and retired. But in the defence services a large number of officers elected to remain in the service of the Government of India.

V. P. Menon, *Transfer of Power*, pp. 400-1; *Tara Chand*, IV, p. 533.

Statutory Civil Service

The Statutory Civil Service instituted in 1879 during Lord Lytton's (q.v.) viceroyalty was a device to appease educated Indians who were agitating for employment in the Covenanted Civil Service. The Government of India Act, 1870 had laid down *inter alia* that no law then in force 'should restrain the authorities . . . from appointing a native of India to any such place, office or employment' to which he may not have been admitted in the manner 'prescribed by law.' In other words, even those who had not been selected through competition could be admitted.

The rules framed in 1875 to give effect to this intent of Parliament were found inadequate; in an attempt to remedy this, Lytton's government decided to institute a new 'native branch' of the civil service. Appointments were to be generally confined to young men of 'good family' and social position 'possessed of fair abilities and education.' Their proportion was not to exceed one-sixth of the total number of Covenanted Civil servants appointed in any one year by the Secretary of State. Recruitment was to be from among 'natives' selected in India by the local governments, subject to the approval of the Governor-General in Council. Save in exceptional circumstances, selected candidates were to be on probation for two years. Their salary scales were to be lower (being two-thirds of the salary given to English civil servants) and they were debarred from certain posts such as that of Secretary to the government, chief magistrate of a district and commissioner of a division or of customs. They were generally to be appointed in the province from where they were selected.

A word here on the Covenanted Civil Service and the positions held by them may be useful. In all the Provinces including the Presidencies of Madras and Bombay, the chief administrators were aided by secretaries of various departments who also belonged to the covenanted service. There were five of these secretaries in the Government of India and 48 who served local governments in various capacities. In the whole of British India there were 235 administrative units called districts. Traditionally considered as the core of British administration, the covenanted administrator in each was called a Magistrate or Collector in 'Regulation' provinces and a Deputy Commissioner in 'Non-Regulation' provinces. Commissioners of Divisions, 41 in all, had a supervisory role, over 3 or more districts. On the judicial side, covenanted servants held most of the District and Sessions judgeships, 111 in all, and a proportion of seats in all the provincial High Courts. Below these major administrative positions were approximately 277 inferior posts of Assistant or Joint Magistracies of three grades where young civilians gained training and experience. All these positions with a few miscellaneous appointments constituted the cadre reserved for covenanted civil servants.

In instituting the Statutory Service, the British had none the less made sure that the educated middle class in the country was largely kept out, while top posts were retained by their own compatriots to ensure proper implementation of policies. The numbers taken were meagre: by 1886, a bare 69 including 27 Hindus, 15 Muslims, 2 Parsis and 2 Sikhs had been appointed. In essence, the scheme sought to confine Indians to minor posts. Its worst aspect was the introduction of a system of nomination in place of competition and the neglect of merit at the altar of birth. This drove a wedge between the middle class and the 'native' aristocracy. The fact that the new incumbents were discriminated against in terms of the posts they filled as well as their salary and status was further underlined by the appearance of a separate civil list; they were not to be part of the list showing Covenanted Civil Servants.

'Native' opinion apart, Authority was none too happy either. It held that, 'generally speaking', the incumbents did not possess adequate educational qualifications and were 'often found unequal' to their responsibilities. Consequently, the experiment was pronounced a failure as a means of admitting Indians to the higher services. The Public Service Commission (appointed by Lord Dufferin's (q.v.) government) in 1886 ruled that the Statutory Civil Service stood 'condemned for sufficiently good reasons not only by particular sections of the native community but also by the very large majority of officials, both Europeans and natives, who had enjoyed practical experience of its working.' In the result, the Commission recommended the abolition of the Service and the absorption of its members into the provincial covenanted services.

V. C. P. Chaudhary, *Imperial Policy of the British in India 1876-80*, Calcutta, 1968; S. Gopal, *British Policy in India 1858-1905*, Cambridge, 1965; Bradford Spangenberg, *British Bureaucracy in India: Status, Policy & the I.C.S. in the late 19th century*, Delhi, 1976.

Mian Muhammad Shafi

Muhammad (later Sir Muhammad) Shafi was born at Baghbanpura near Lahore; his father, Mian Din Muhammad belonged to an aristocratic family. Shafi was educated at Government College as well as Foreman Christian College, Lahore. Later, he qualified for the Bar. He practised at Lahore and, in 1917, was elected President of the Panjab Chief Bar Association.

Shafi promoted the cause of Indian Muslims through educational progress and political organization when a trustee of M. A. O. College, Aligarh as well as a member of its governing body; and later, as vice-president of the All-India Muslim university association. As Education Member of the Government of India, he was responsible for the Muslim University (Aligarh) Bill, which he later piloted successfully through the Imperial Legislative Council.

Presiding over the Lucknow session of the All-India Muslim League (q.v.) in 1913, Shafi opposed joint electorates. Later, he felt extremely unhappy when the March 1927 session of the Muslim League accepted joint electorates with reservation of seats on a population basis in the provinces and with one-third of the total number of seats in the central legislature (subject to the condition that reforms be introduced in the N.W.F.P. and Baluchistan and that Sind (q.v.) be formed into a separate province). To counter these moves which claimed M. A. Jinnah's (q.v.) backing, he floated his own Shafi League in the Panjab. The Calcutta session of Muslim League presided over by Sir Mahomed Yaqub, then Deputy Speaker of the Central Legislative Assembly, however endorsed the party's Delhi decisions (20

March, 1927). Here the Shafi League came in for severe criticism and Maulana Zafar Ali Khan, founder of the Ahrar party, went so far as to demand its sponsor's elimination from the parent body.

Twice, in 1909 and again in 1912, Shafi was nominated to the provincial legislative council. In 1911, 1914 and 1917, he was a member of the Imperial Legislative Council too. After World War I (1914-18), Shafi was nominated a member of the Governor-General's Executive Council, acting as its Vice-President from 1922 to 1925. He was Member for Education and Health and later also for Law. He owed his position, it was said, principally to his pro-British leanings in general and for spearheading Panjab's revolt against the Lucknow Pact (q.v.) in particular.

Shafi was a major leader of the Muslim community, but never rose above communal politics and loyal co-operation with the British.

G. A. Natesan (ed.), *Eminent Mussalmans*, Madras, 1926; Chaudhari Khaliquzzaman, *Pathway to Pakistan*, Lahore, 1961; Durga Das, *From Curzon to Nehru*, London, 1969, p. 90; Sen, *DNB*, IV, pp. 138-40 (M. M. Ahluwalia).

Shah Alam II (1728–1806)

Son of the Mughal Emperor Alamgir II, Shahzada Ali Gauhar, later Shah Alam II, was born on 15 June 1728. He was intelligent, well-educated and wrote good Urdu and Persian verse (under the pseudonym 'Aftab'). However, as a ruler he turned out to be an administrator and leader of mediocre ability. Essentially, he felt insecure and unsure of himself and was easily swayed by the counsels of his ministers in whom he placed unreserved confidence.

To start with, in August 1758, the Wazir, Najib-ud-Daula's hostility compelled him, when a prince, to flee from Delhi to Miranpur. This enabled the Wazir to declare the prince a rebel and to appoint Hidayat Baksh as the Subehdar of Bihar. Meanwhile, as the British were engaged in consolidating their authority over Bengal and Bihar after Plassey (q.v.), Ali Gauhar made three attempts to assert his sovereignty, by then a mere figment, over the eastern subahs of the Mughal empire. This was an uphill task in which he was singularly unsuccessful. When, in May 1759, he heard the news that his father Alamgir II had been murdered, he proclaimed himself Emperor and assumed the title of Shah Alam II.

In January 1761, on the day following the Third Battle of Panipat (q.v.), the Emperor suffered a reverse at the hands of Major John Carnac whereupon his troops gradually deserted him. He now solicited the help of the English who, in turn, sought the Nawab of Bengal, Mir Kasim's (q.v.), concurrence 'in providing the Emperor with a daily allowance from the revenues of Bihar.'

Ahmad Shah Abdali (q.v.), the Afghan victor of the battle of Panipat, proclaimed Shah Alam Emperor while leaving Delhi in March 1761. In June, the fugitive ruler crossed the Karamnasa on his way to Delhi, but Shuja-ud-Daula (q.v.) of Oudh (q.v.) stopped him *en route* and dragged him half-heartedly into another fight with the British. After Shuja's defeat, in 1764, at the Battle of Buxar (q.v.), the Emperor threw himself once again, and unreservedly, at the mercy of the English. When Shuja finally surrendered, he was forced to give up the districts of Kora and Allahabad which the John Company (q.v.) handed to the Emperor; in return, Shah Alam granted them the Diwani Rights (q.v.) for the provinces of Bengal, Bihar and Orissa.

For obvious reasons, the Company was reluctant to let the Emperor leave Allahabad, making excuses whenever he asked for an escort. Meanwhile, Najib-ud-Daula, the Rohilla leader, could no longer safeguard his interests in Delhi, so that when the Marathas advanced to the north and established their control over the Doab, Shah Alam sought their assistance in the hope of regaining the throne. Najib-ud-Daula died in 1770 and Ahmad Khan Bangash and, later, Zabita Khan who assumed power were defeated by powerful Maratha forces. The latter now made Jawan Bakht, the Emperor's son, regent, a development that forced Shah Alam to agree to their terms for escorting him to Delhi. Mahadji Sindhia (q.v.) welcomed the Emperor at Anupshahr and together they entered Delhi on 6 January 1772. On hearing the news, the English disavowed Maratha sovereignty and Warren Hastings (q.v.), on the plea of the Emperor's shifting loyalties, took back Kora and Allahabad and stopped the remittance of revenues that had been granted to him. Mirza Najaf Khan now took over as Wazir, but the Emperor was in such sore financial straits that he could not even pay the Marathas the Rs 50 lakhs promised as their reward.

Najaf Khan's attempt, aided and abetted by Shah Alam, to defeat the Marathas failed, with the result that he was replaced by Zabita Khan, a Rohilla chief and son of Najib-ud-Daula. The change was short-lived, for soon the Maratha armies were recalled to Poona in the wrangles for succession following the death of Peshwa Madhav Rao and the disputed claim of his uncle Raghunath Rao (q.v.). This enabled Najaf Khan to resume power, which he continued to exercise with skill and some success till his death in 1782. His successors, however, wasted themselves in a bloody civil war, leaving the field open for the return of the Marathas. The Emperor now appealed to Mahadji Sindhia to take over the administration.

Without counting the cost in terms of claims which the Emperor would make on available resources, the Maratha leader repaired north. The Emperor conferred on Mahadji the title of regent (*vakil-i-mutlaq*), an amalgam of the offices of Wazir and Mir Bakshi. He was the Emperor's deputy and, next to him, the highest dignitary in the state. Mahadji Sindhia worked assiduously to resist attempts made by the Company to regain ascendancy at the Mughal court. As it was, the Emperor never followed a steady policy and was easily swayed by rival factions competing for his favours.

Unfortunately, while the Maratha leader was at Mathura, busy with the Rajputs and the Jats, Ghulam Qadir, Zabita Khan's son, assumed control of Shah Alam's palace (July 1788). On 10 August the Emperor was defeated, tortured and then blinded. Mahadji, however, soon rallied support, reoccupied Delhi, drove out Ghulam Qadir and reinstated the blind Shah Alam. The Emperor now solicited the help of the ambitious, albeit weak Afghan ruler, Zaman Shah, the grandson of Ahmad Shah Abdali to help re-establish his authority for, in reality, he resented Maratha control. In 1792, when Mahadji returned to the south, Shah Alam and his court again fell into decay.

The British victory over the Marathas in the Second Anglo-Maratha War (q.v.) gave them control over Delhi, and Shah Alam. In September 1803, General Lake, pursuing Holkar found the Emperor, 'blind and aged, stripped of all authority and reduced to poverty.' Wellesley (q.v.) described the British victory as 'the happy instrument of Your Majesty's restoration to a state of dignity and tranquillity *under the power of the British crown.*' Shah Alam hoped in vain to cover the *de facto* supremacy of the English 'with the Mughal ceremonial mantle as far as he could.' In 1805, however, he passed under the absolute control of the English Company. The preceding year, David Ochterlony (q.v.) had been appointed Resident on behalf of the British and armed with a definite 20-point detailed set of instructions. Shah Alam thereafter spent the last days of a miserable career as a British pensioner in his own capital till his death on 19 November 1806, but the fiction of Mughal rule was to be virtually extinguished in the time of Lord Hastings (q.v.).

Shah Alam's career has been viewed as a commentary on the history of India during the eighteenth century which, for various reasons, was a period of turmoil and tragedy. His personality naturally combined good and bad qualities, but the latter, under various adverse circumstances, cruelly overshadowed the former. Thus, after his installation in Delhi, he became a prey to superstition, sloth, indolence and excesses of the harem which heightened the tragedy of his life. Shah Alam's career excites pity but no praise or admiration. He and his courtiers were, in the final analysis, typical representatives of the decadent old order of the eighteenth century which collapsed due to its own internal weaknesses.

K. K. Datta, *Shah Alam II and the East India Company*, Calcutta, 1965; T. G. P. Spear, *Twilight of the Mughals*, Cambridge, 1951; A. L. H. Polier (ed. P. C. Gupta), *Shah Alam II and His Court: A Narrative of the Transactions at the Court of Delhy from the year 1771 to the present times*, Calcutta, 1947.

Treaty of Shahabad (1772)

Concluded on 13 June 1772 between Shuja-ud-Daula (q.v.), Nawab Wazir of Oudh (q.v.), Hafiz Rahmat Khan (q.v.), Zabita Khan and 'all the other Rohilla sirdars', the Treaty was *witnessed* by General Robert Barker (q.v.), Commander-in-Chief of the John Company's (q.v.) forces whose initiative and intervention alone had brought it about. Essentially, it was part of British efforts to prevent an alliance between the Marathas, Oudh and the Rohillas and was the inevitable sequel to the Maratha invasion of Rohilkhand (1772).

The Treaty comprises two 'agreements'. The first laid down that 'if any enemy should make an attempt against us, and the Vizier', the two 'shall use our joint endeavours to join and unite' in any measures determined by the Nawab for the benefit of Zabita Khan. The second 'agreement given by Hafiz Rahmat Khan to the vizier' laid down that it was for Shuja-ud-Daula to put the Rohilla leaders 'in full possession of their country . . . either by peace or war.' If the Marathas entered Rohilkhand, retreated owing to the monsoon 'and after that is elapsed, commit disturbances', it was for the Nawab to quell them. The Rohilla leaders 'after the aforesaid business do agree to pay the sum of 40 lakhs of Rupees.' Ten lakhs were to be paid 'in ready money' after the Rohillas came from their hide-outs and the rest 'discharged in three years.'

Aitchison, II, pp. 9-11; John Strachey, *Hastings and the Rohilla War*, London, 1892; Dodwell, *CHI*, V, pp. 217-18.

Raja Shahu (r. 1707–49)

Shahu (also Sahji, Sahuji or Sau Bhosla II) was the son of Sambhaji and grandson of the great Shivaji (1627-80). After Sambhaji's death (1689), Shahu was acknowledged as Raja, while his uncle, Raja Ram, was nominated regent during his minority. Subsequently, Shahu fell into the hands of the Mughal Emperor Aurangzeb (r. 1658-1707) and, as a boy, was brought up in the imperial harem. The common belief that Shahu had led a life of ease and comfort does not take account of the fact that he had never been to Delhi, much less tasted its palace life. The truth is that he had constantly to experience the same privations and hardships as the fighting members of the Emperor's camp. That apart, he was a closely watched prisoner, a pawn in the imperial game, to be used as and when necessary.

During the captivity of his nephew, Raja Ram proclaimed himself ruler and, on his death (1700), his widow, Tara Bai (q.v.), became regent for her 2-year old son, Shiva. Seven years later, on the death of Aurangzeb, Shahu was released from confinement by Prince Azam, whereupon he repaired home. One of Shahu's major political rivals was Tara Bai who, understandably, refused to accept his claims. Initially, she maintained that Shahu was an impostor, parading falsely as the genuine claimant. Later, she put forth the view that the Maratha state founded by the great Shivaji had been lost by Sambhaji, Shahu's father. On its ashes, her husband Raja Ram raised the edifice anew, defended it against the Mughal onslaught and was therefore, she argued, the founding father of the new Maratha state. It followed that the latter, by right, belonged to her son and Shahu's claim to Shivaji's patrimony was at once false and unjustified.

What weighed the scales heavily in Shahu's favour, however, was that the common people and the soldiers rallied to his cause. So did Balaji Vishwanath (q.v.) and Khando Ballal, Shivaji's hereditary secretary. In the result, Shahu worsted the combined forces of his adversaries at Khed (12 October 1707). The victory opened to Shahu the heart of Maratha country, the hilly territory of Poona and Satara, where Shivaji had started his political career. Presently, the hill-forts of Rajgarh, Torna, Rohida and Vichitragarh fell into his hands. In January 1708, he entered Satara in triumph; in March, he was crowned king.

The fratricidal conflict with Tara Bai proved to be at once wasteful and protracted. Bahadur Shah I (q.v.) who had repaired to the south to put down the revolt of his youngest brother, Kam Bakhsh, exploited the situation to the utmost. He refused to negotiate a settlement, to Shahu's great chagrin, with either of the two contending parties. Nor was that all. Presently,

Shahu's *senapati*, Chandrasen Jadhav, launched a major revolt against constituted authority; worse, it proved a signal for a general rising all around. The man who helped Shahu most in stemming the tide was Balaji Vishwanath who, by his 'activity, watchfulness and tact' foiled Chandrasen's conspiracy and defeated his master's rivals. Before long, Balaji was appointed Peshwa (November 1713) and granted a fresh jagir of six *mahals* and two forts. His later conciliation of Kanhoji Angria, the most powerful chieftain of Tara Bai's party, was a master-stroke and a bloodless victory for Shahu's cause.

Meanwhile, Peshwa Balaji Vishwanath's settlement with Husain Ali, one of the Sayyid Brothers (q.v.) who was anxious to end the prolonged Mughal-Maratha conflict, was enshrined in the Treaty of Delhi (March 1718). It helped further to boost the prestige of his new master at Satara.

Shahu died on 15 December 1749. There had been hectic activity at Satara in the years immediately preceding that event. Peshwa Balaji Rao (r. 1720-40) was desirous of uniting the rival houses of Kolhapur and Satara, thereby ending the seemingly unending fratricidal conflict. Behind the back of his master he had thus agreed secretly to support the succession (to Satara) of Sambhaji II, then ruler of Kolhapur. Shahu, however, had a bitter personal hatred for his cousin. The latter had at one stage joined hands with the Mughals to oust him, and on another occasion sent assassins to murder him. Shahu thus refused to fall in line with his Peshwa and chose instead Tara Bai's grandson, Ram Raja, to be his successor. The latter proved to be weak and incompetent and a puppet in the hands of the Peshwa. More, Tara Bai revealed him to be an impostor! To no one's surprise, therefore, the power of the Maratha state gravitated inevitably into the hands of the Peshwa.

Invariably called 'the good', Shahu was an amiable and religious man, known for his intense conservatism. Able and unambitious, he could be magnanimous to a fallen foe and happy to pass his time hunting, fishing and hawking. However, according to H. G. Rawlinson, Shahu was not 'a mere puppet', a view forcefully endorsed by Mahadev Govind Ranade (q.v.): 'He was not the titular head of the Maratha government. He directed all the operations, ordered and recalled commanders and ... exercised a great controlling power on the chiefs, though he had no armies in the field'.

Refuting the widely-held belief that Shahu was 'no judge of men', that he was 'too soft to wield power' and 'rule men', that he was 'ignorant of Indian politics' and devoid of 'sternness required in managing the intricate concerns of a large growing state', Sardesai maintains that 'the very fact of his recognizing the great qualities of Bajirao and giving a free scope for their play, gives a lie to that narrow view. He ensured the expansion of Maratha power by conciliating the Emperor. He effected a lasting friendly understanding with Swai Jaysingh and other Rajput princes in the interests of a general Hindu regeneration.' Nadkarni underlines that Shahu who had inherited 'the gentleness and prudence' of his good mother Yeshubai rather than the 'savage rashness of his father' had an innate common sense and sympathetic heart. At the same time his 'vacillation and mismanagement' were notorious and his administration far from progressive.

All in all, Shahu's legacy was not a happy one: 'There was no conception of a centralized and integrated state .... [What he bequeathed to his successors] was merely a loose collection of feudal entities. It was only in the Swaraj territory that there was some centralized and unified administration. The outlying parts ... were administered by the military sardars to whom they were assigned as military grants.'

R. C. Majumdar (ed.), *The Maratha Supremacy (1707–1818)*, Bombay, 1977; Richard Burn (ed.), *The Cambridge History of India*, vol. IV, Delhi, 1957; G. S. Sardesai, *New History of the Marathas*, 2nd ed., Bombay 1958, vol. II; Brij Kishore, *Tara Bai and her Times*, Bombay 1963; R. V. Nadkarni, *The Rise and Fall of the Maratha Empire*, Bombay, 1966.

Maulana Shaukat Ali (1873–1938)

Shaukat Ali, who was to play a prominent role in the Khilafat Movement (q.v.), belonged to a respectable Muslim family of Najibabad in the district of Bijnor (U.P.) The family had moved to a town near Moradabad after 1857. He received what has been called a 'modern liberal education', first in the Collegiate school at Bareilly and later at the M.A.O. College, Aligarh. Known in college as 'Bare Dada' ['the elder brother' of Maulana Mohamed Ali (q.v)], he was a good sportsman, being particularly fond of cricket. After graduating in 1885 he obtained employment as Assistant Opium Agent, but continued to have an abiding interest in his *alma mater* and, for a time, was editor of the Alumni Association's magazine, the *Old Boy*. Later, he gave his services to the Aga Khan (q.v.) to raise funds for making the Aligarh College into a university.

Shaukat Ali's involvement with the promotion of Muslim interests led him to establish the 'Anjuman-i-Khuddam-i-Kabah' (literally, Association of the Servants of Kabah), which aimed at facilitating the Haj pilgrimage to Mecca and protecting the Kabah itself from the Saudis, then on the warpath with their political masters, the Ottoman Turks. Maulana Abdul Bari was closely associated with him in this venture. Along with his brother Mohamed Ali, Shaukat raised a loud protest against the British government's anti-Turkish policies. Black-listed as a rabble-rouser who was agitating the Muslim masses, he was arrested on 30 May 1915.

Shaukat Ali's most significant contribution to the freedom struggle began with his release from detention in December 1919. From now on starts his active association with the Indian National Congress (q.v.) and Gandhi (q.v.), under whose influence he organized and encouraged Muslims to join the national mainstream. At the same time, Muslim welfare being the focus of his attention, he joined the Khilafat movement, of which his brother Mohamed Ali was one of the principal protagonists. In 1923, Shaukat Ali presided over the annual session of a committee at Kakinada, where a resolution to improve social conditions in the country was adopted. Accordingly, the Hindustani Sevak Dal was founded with Shaukat Ali presiding over its first session at Belgaum in 1924. He was tireless in his efforts to popularize the Non-cooperation Movement (q.v.) among the Muslims, since the Congress had identified itself with and supported the Khilafat demands. In this context, he strongly deprecated the Arya Samaj (q.v.) which, he argued, was causing deep cleavages and endangering this new-found communal harmony through its *Shuddhi* and *Sangathan* movements. For the time being, however, he advised his fellow Muslims to ignore the Samaj for the higher goal of achieving freedom and swaraj.

By nature quick-tempered and uncompromising, Shaukat Ali broke with the Congress on the issue of the future of Muslims in independent India, fearing that his community's rights and interests would be smothered by the vast Hindu majority. The Nehru Report's (q.v.) allegedly discriminatory treatment of Muslims further alienated the two Ali brothers from the national mainstream. Shaukat charged that Congress support for the Muslim cause was merely a facade put up until such time as independence was attained. After severing his connection with the Congress, albeit never becoming its vicious opponent, he reverted to being a full-time worker in the Muslim cause.

In 1929, Shaukat Ali was nominated a member of the Round Table Conference (q.v.) and took the opportunity to travel widely in Muslim countries to organize a world Muslim conference. In 1933 he was invited to the U.S.A. to deliver lectures on India and Islam. A member of the Central Legislative Assembly from 1935 onward, Shaukat Ali died on 26 November 1938.

G. A. Natesan, *Eminent Mussalmans*, Madras, 1926; P. C. Bamford, *Histories of the Non-cooperation and Kilafat Movements*, reprint, New Delhi, 1974; Sen, *DNB*, IV, pp. 176-8 (Mushirul Haq).

John Shore (1751–1834)

John Shore, First Baron Teignmouth, came to India as a 'writer' in the service of the John Company (q.v.) in 1768. After working in various capacities in the Political and Revenue Departments and as a Persian translator at Murshidabad, he was appointed a member of the Revenue Council at Calcutta (1775-1780) and later Revenue Commissioner for Dacca and Bihar. On leave in England from 1785 to 1787, he returned as a member of the Supreme Council in Bengal. Well-informed on fiscal and judicial matters, he completed the decennial revenue settlements of Bengal, Bihar and Orissa by 1789, preferring a settlement for 10-30 years in the hope that it would conduce to the welfare of the people.

It was his knowledge of judicial and fiscal affairs that helped in the reforms instituted by Cornwallis (q.v.). Shore's minute of 18 June 1789, which spans 562 paragraphs, still remains the classic text on the subject of the Bengal zamindari system. Though Shore recommended caution and further inquiry and expressed himself strongly against fixation, his decision in favour of the proprietary rights of the zamindars was hastily ratified by Cornwallis and formed the basis of his much-discussed, and controversial, Permanent Settlement (q.v.).

In 1792 Shore was appointed Governor-General. He assumed the role in October 1793 and continued in that office until March 1798. A quiet, honest, conscientious and religious man, he was not a 'policy-maker' and preferred to avoid the burden and responsibility of a decision. In regard to the Indian

States (q.v.), he favoured maintenance of the *status quo*, avoiding interference in their internal affairs as well as the formation of new political alliances. He helped settle the succession problem in Oudh (q.v.) and held strong views over the treatment of the Nawab of Arcot and the Raja of Tanjore, believing in the adage that 'what is wrong morally cannot be politically right.'

Shore followed the inglorious if also unambitious policy of non-intervention laid down by the Home Government and is often criticized for his timidity. It was during his tenure that the Sikhs asserted themselves, while the Marathas invaded the Nizam's dominion and defeated him; the Company adopting a neutral stance in either case. Presently Tipu Sultan (q.v.) was on the offensive and many apprehended an alliance between him and Zaman Shah, the Afghan ruler, who had threatened to invade India. Characteristically, Shore refused to believe in such wild rumours, though he took appropriate measures when the need arose. He also checked the mutiny of army officers in Bengal, though discontent simmered. He was more interested in extending trade than in adding to territorial dominion and made strong efforts to open up commerce with Nepal and Burma.

The period of Shore's rule as Governor-General was comparatively uneventful. He implicitly obeyed the pacific injunctions of the British Parliament and the Company and pursued a thoroughly unpretentious and equitable policy. Being more anxious to extend trade than territorial domain, jingoists attacked his policy as 'temporizing and timid.' Shore's Indian administration is generally overlooked, falling as it does between those of Cornwallis and Wellesley (q.v.), both powerful proconsuls. According to Furber, Shore was that 'comparatively rare political phenomenon in British Indian history at this period, an honest man'; it was he who 'oversaw and worked out' the details of many of Cornwallis's salutary internal reforms. In London, his 'talents, integrity and candour' had won the respect of the Crown's ministers.

Three major problems of Shore's administration may be briefly listed: (i) hostilities between the Nizam and the Marathas, 1793–5; (ii) the 'all but open mutiny' in the British army in Bengal, 1795-6; (iii) the 'revolution' in Oudh, 1797.

There was nothing in the existing treaties which bound the Governor-General to support the Nizam in a case of this sort. What the treaties had contemplated was the joint co-operation of the Nizam, the Marathas and the British against Tipu. Additionally, British support to the Nizam would have meant the hostility of the Marathas—an enmity far more formidable than that of the Muslim ruler. It is also worth noting that the French officers with the Marathas, the corps of De Boigne (q.v.), were by no means violent partisans of the French revolution while Michel Raymond (1766-98), commander of the French officers with the Nizam, was. Besides, Shore's long Indian experience had led him to believe that the victors in a war would inevitably quarrel over the spoils.

Shore's 'tactful conciliation' in handling the Bengal army has been commended. The vagaries of the Dual Government (q.v.) meant at the least a year's time to consult the 'whims and prejudices' of the Directors. To have maintained an empire under such conditions was a truly remarkable achievement.

Shore was 'an honest and conscientious civil servant' whose alleged faults were: neutrality in war, refusal to assert British prestige, a policy of concilia-tion and a degree of vacillation in reaching decisions. These, it is held, 'are not the marks of great statecraft.' Yet, all this notwithstanding, he 'kept the ship of state on an even keel until he could hand it over to an abler pilot.' Thus, even though he could not 'forge ahead, he could hold the rudder true amidst many dangers.'

Philip Mason (who writes under the pseudonym of Woodruff) makes the point that when Shore left after 30 years in India, a settlement of the land revenue had been made; the district officer was firmly established as the basis of administration; the civil service of the Company had become a true service: its functions reasonably clear, its branches established, the salaries and prospects of its members settled. Shore's tenure, he maintains, consists of that period of settling down; he was the last Governor-General till John Lawrence (q.v.), to be a member of the Covenanted Service. Mason con-tends that Shore did not arouse warmth of feeling— 'there is no strong love or hate, there is no passion in his life.' He was fair, thorough, painstaking, temperate, honest; his conscience driving him unremittingly to duties that he sometimes found mildly distasteful.

It is a temptation to belittle Shore, but one that ought not to be indulged. 'Solemn, conscientious, a little heavy on the bridle-hand, Shore plods through his thirty years at the dogged stone-breaking trot of a battery-wheeler..He was the first of a new age, born a Victorian long before Victoria.' In March 1798 he left India and later in the year was created Baron Teignmouth. From 1807 to 1828 he served as a member of the Board of Control and twice tendered evidence on Indian affairs before the House of Commons. He died on 13 July 1834.

Holden Furber (ed.), *The Private Record of an Indian Governor-Generalship: the correspondence of Sir John Shore, Governor-General with Henry Dundas, President of the Board of Control, 1793-1798*, Harvard, 1933; Philip Woodruff, *The Men who Ruled India: the Founders*, 6th impression, London, 1955, pp. 133–50; *DNB*, XVIII, pp. 149–51 (George Fisher Russel Barker).

Shuja-ud-Daula (c. 1731–75)

Mirza Jalaluddin Haidar, better known as Shuja-ud-Daula, was born at Delhi in January 1731 to Sadr-ul-Nisa, the daughter of Saadat Khan (Gover-nor of Oudh (q.v.) and Mansur Ali Khan Safdarjang, Nawab Wazir of Oudh. Taught by renowned teachers, he soon acquired mastery over Per-sian, Arabic, Turki and Hindustani. In 1748, after the accession of Emperor Ahmad Shah (r.1748-54), he was given the title of Shuja-ud-Daula and appointed head of the imperial artillery. He officiated as Wazir during his father's absence in 1750 and three years later moved, along with him, to Lucknow as Deputy ('Naib') Governor of the provinces of Allahabad and Oudh. On his father's death in 1754, he succeeded to the governorship and was nominated Wazir by the Emperor, Shah Alam II (q.v.), in 1759.

The first few years were taken up in consolidating his power. Thus the

Nawab subjugated Raja Balwant Singh of Banaras and worsted in battle the chiefs dispatched against him by Ahmad Shah Abdali (q.v.) on the intercession of one his close underlings, Ahmad Khan Bangash, the Nawab of Farrukhabad. Even though he had sought Maratha help in 1756, Shuja became wary of their growing strength and, in 1761, at the Third Battle of Panipat (q.v.), lined up with Ahmad Shah Abdali against them.

Shuja vacillated between recognizing Mir Jafar (q.v.) and aiding Mir Kasim (q.v.) and gave asylum to the latter when he was fleeing from Bengal after his defeat. The same year (1764), along with a reluctant Shah Alam he fought the English and was defeated at Buxar (q.v.). Shuja was reduced to the position of a virtual fugitive, but the Marathas as well as the Pathans refused to come to his help. The English, who had by now secured Shah Alam's neutrality, pursued Shuja until he finally surrendered unconditionally to John Carnac at Jajman. Thereafter he proceeded to meet Robert Clive (q.v.) at Banaras and, on 12 August 1765, signed with him the Treaty of Allahabad (q.v.).

This virtual surrender made Shuja painfully aware of British military superiority, even though Clive had restored him in Oudh and made him an ally. Presently, the Nawab directed his efforts to large-scale military reform, employing British officers and equipment to raise an efficient infantry force and subjugate the neighbouring rajas and chiefs. By a show of strength, the English compelled him to drastically reduce his troops. A sagacious politician, aware that any territorial expansion would necessitate British help, Shuja now began sedulously cultivating their friendship and trust. Through their intervention he secured the powers and jagirs of the Wazirship conferred on him earlier by Emperor Shah Alam. He tried to maintain friendly relations with the Marathas too, without at the same time alienating the British who wanted him to give shape and form to a north Indian coalition against the former. A clash with the Marathas, however, became inevitable after the Emperor solicited their help to restore him to Delhi (1770); two years later, the Marathas planned to invade Rohilkhand, an ambition Shuja had also harboured for years.

Shuja now started negotiations with the Rohillas but, before anything could materialize, the Marathas overran Rohilkhand. Frustrated, Shuja sought British assistance against them by promising John Company (q.v.) a sizeable sum of money as reward. To pursue his designs on Rohilkhand, he bought a Maratha retreat for Rs 40 lakhs and British aid for Rs 50 lakhs. When Hafiz Rahmat Khan (q.v.), the Rohilla chief, was unable to pay the Rs 40 lakhs promised to Shuja (the latter having weaned away the Marathas), the former was routed at Miranpur Katra. An English brigade had engaged in these operations—a transaction for which Warren Hastings (q.v.) was later severely censured. Shuja acquired Pilibhit, Bareilly, Aonla and Basauli as well as Rs 15 lakhs from Faizullah Khan (who had succeeded Hafiz Rahmat Khan) after the latter surrendered.

Soon after his victory, Shuja, who had been keeping indifferent health fell ill and died, at Faizabad, in January 1775.

Srivastav has maintained that Shuja could not escape the odium of 'having actively helped the forces of reaction against those of nationalism' at Panipat in 1761. More, he had placed his personal interests above those of the country; in retrospect, his immediate ends were served, but in the long run the battle proved a disaster. However, his intrigues against Imad-ul-Mulk (the Mughal Emperor's Wazir), with whom he had a hereditary feud, and his desire to strike a balance between Najib-ud-Daula and the Marathas were 'unexceptionable according to the standards of the age.'

Prior to the Treaty of Allahabad, Shuja was virtually an independent ruler, but soon thereafter sank into a secondary position. He fell an easy prey to the subtleties of English diplomacy and began to show them undue deference, accepting, in the bargain, a somewhat inferior position. A singular result was the treaty of 1768 which slashed his military strength; seven years later, the treaty of 1775 was to reduce his successor to the position of a subordinate ally. It may be worth recalling that contrary to the terms of the 1768 Treaty, British garrisons had continued to be stationed at Chunar and Allahabad, the two most important strategic forts in the Wazir's dominions. The result was to force English superiority upon the Nawab Wazir, besides securing for them important military and political results.

Shuja's own political ambitions too contributed to his gradual eclipse. Thus, he sought out the Bengal Governor, Harry Verelst (q.v.), as a virtual arbiter and judge in his unedifying quarrels with Shah Alam over whose affairs Shuja wanted to exercise virtual control. In the result, his position was no better than that of a mere petitioner begging English aid for the settlement of a domestic dispute! His aggressive designs against the Rohillas, too, necessitated help from the Company. This meant the latter's continued presence at his seat of authority, which had a demoralizing effect on his power both from the military as well as political points of view. Eventually, it was to lead to the appointment of an English political resident at Faizabad. Again, the non-payment of the salaries of English troops and the debts into which Shuja ran worsened an already difficult situation.

A. L. Srivastava, *Shuja-ud-Daula*, 2 vols., Lahore, 1945, I, 1754–65; II, 1765–75; H. R. Gupta (ed.), *Marathas and Panipat*, Chandigarh, 1961.

Sikandar Jah, Nizam (1771–1829)

Akbar Ali, who had received the title of Sikandar Jah from his father, was the second and only surviving son of Nizam Ali Khan (q.v.) and succeeded to the Nizamat in 1803. As soon as the Mughal Emperor assented to his accession, Wellesley (q.v.), then Governor-General, and the new Nizam agreed to maintain all the treaties concluded hitherto between the two parties.

The Nizam fought alongside the English during the Second Anglo-Maratha War (q.v.). In the settlement with the Marathas that followed, Sikandar Jah made sizeable territorial gains. At the same time, cessions of territory by the Nizam resulted in Hyderabad state being surrounded on all sides by territory ruled directly by the East India Company (q.v.). This apart, the presence of a British Resident at Hyderabad acted as a further check on the Nizam.

During Sikandar Jah's stewardship, British interference in the day-to-day adminstration of the state increased. Thus in 1804 the Company raised its own protege, Mir Alam, to ministership, in preference to Raja Mahipat Ram who had been chosen by the Nizam. The latter's assent, contemporary British observers noted, was extorted from his timidity. Four years later, the British installed another of their cronies, Chandu Lal. The fact was that the Company had taken advantage of the Nizam's heavy indebtedness to control the affairs of his government through their own nominees. No wonder the Nizam was progressively barred from interfering in matters of administration, the latter deteriorating as the burden of heavy payments to be made for the subsidiary troops continued to mount.

Corruption was rife. The Nizam, it is alleged, troubled himself little about public affairs and 'was content as long as he was left to his own amusements, and provided with sufficient funds to indulge in them.' Sikandar Jah was not interested in affairs of government which broke down completely, preceded by utter financial ruination.

The British Resident, Henry Russell, who found the army of the Nizam in a worthless condition, set about reorganizing it. Chandu Lal tried to find funds for this work and the scandal concerning the notorious Palmer and Company (q.v.) involved a number of people, including Chandu Lal, Russell and the Nizam himself. The supreme government advanced a sum of Rs 60 lakhs to the Resident to clear the Nizam's debts; in return, the Nizam remitted permanently to the Company the *peshkush* of the Northern Sarkars.

In 1820, Charles Metcalfe (q.v.), who succeeded Russell, took over the revenue administration, overhauled the affairs of Palmer & Company, to whom the Nizam was heavily in debt, and punished refractories including the Nizam's son on charges of gross misconduct. The Nizam, it was widely believed, harboured strong anti-British sentiments in private; he was rarely seen out of the palace, allegedly because of the disgust he felt at being controlled by a minister (Chandu Lal) who was in the pay of the British.

Sikandar Jah died on 21 May 1829.

M. Rama Rao, *Glimpses of Dekkan History*, Madras 1951, pp. 148-9; *Gribble*, II; *Beale*, p. 384.

First Anglo-Sikh War (1845–46)

Internal strife in the Panjab, exacerbated and indeed fully exploited by the functionaries of the John Company (q.v.), precipitated developments culminating in the First Anglo-Sikh War. The years 1839-45, following the death of Maharaja Ranjit Singh (q.v.), had been a traumatic experience marked by a succession of violent deaths among a number of rival claimants to the throne and the wazirship. The result was the elimination of what might have been capable rulers and the consequent rise to ascendancy of the Khalsa army. The latter, taking advantage of chaotic political conditions, became the arbiter of Sikh furtunes—by selling the army's services to the highest bidder. Maharani Jind Kaur (q.v.), the mother of Maharaja Ranjit Singh's minor son Dalip Singh (q.v.), was playing into the hands of Lal Singh and Tej Singh, both of whom, being unscrupulous, and extremely ambitious, had gradually worked their way into the Maharani's favour and

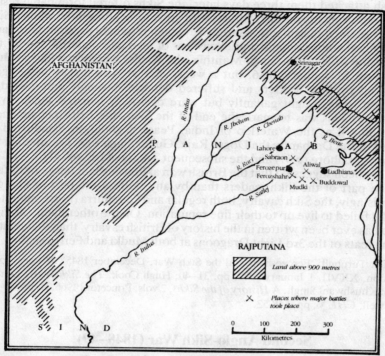

First Anglo-Sikh War (1845–6)

assumed unbridled power in the state. The two-some succeeded in diverting people's attention from the true state of affairs and fanned anti-British sentiments in the disgruntled army by raising the bogey of an impending British invasion.

An outer facade of devotion to Sikh interests notwithstanding, behind the scenes both the Maharani and her paramours had secretly sought the Company's help so as to be confirmed in power as well as cut the army to size. The military build-up and preparations of the British at Ferozepur, their Annexation of Sind (q.v.), combined with aggressive pronouncements and acts of responsible officers like Charles Napier (q.v.) and the notorious Major George Broadfoot, the British agent at Ludhiana, confirmed the worst apprehensions of the Sikh army. Ellenborough (q.v.), and his successor Henry Hardinge (q.v.), who considered hostilitites with the Sikhs a foregone conclusion, did nothing to mitigate mounting suspicions. Goaded by the Maharani, the Sikh army, on 11 December 1845, crossed the Sutlej unopposed.

Two days later, the British declared war. Their army, commanded by Hugh Gough, confronted the Khalsa in a series of bloody battles. In the first of these, at Mudki on 18 December 1845, the English won a narrow victory through the treachery of Lal Singh who, *inter alia*, prevented the Khalsa from investing a tired enemy force at Ferozeshahr. Subsequently, when the

British attacked them three days later, the Sikhs offered formidable resistance, repulsing the infantry thrusts with great force. Presently, when a Sikh
victory seemed reasonably assured, Tej Singh retreated precipitately, causing general confusion and a grievous loss of men and material. Under the
leadership of Ranjosh Singh Majithia, the Khalsa were victorious at Bud-
dowal on 21 January 1846, but a week later at Aliwal they were again
betrayed by their leaders and suffered debacle. Strongly entrenched at
Sabraon, they fought gallantly but were decisively worsted there on 10
February. This was to mark the end of the War, the British commander
describing it as the Waterloo of India. Peace negotiations conducted on
behalf of the Darbar by the Dogra Raja, Gulab Singh (q.v.) resulted in the
Treaty of Lahore (q.v.) and the subsequent Treaty of Bhyrowal (q.v.).

It has been suggested that the British won at Ferozeshahr 'more by default
on the part of the Sikh leaders than by any skill on the part of Gough.'
Surprisingly, the Sikh cavalry, both regular and Gurchurra (horse-mounted)
totally failed to live up to their fine reputation. On the other hand, 'no finer
page has ever been written in the history of British cavalry' than that relating
to the feats of the 3rd Light Dragoons at both Mudki and Ferozeshahr.

Patrick Turnbull, 'Ferozeshahr and the Sikh War, December 1845', *History Today*,
London, XXVII, 1 January 1977, pp. 31–40; Hugh Cook, *The Sikh Wars*, London,
1975; Khushwant Singh, A *History of the Sikhs*, 2 vols, Princeton, 1966, II, pp. 40–54;
Dodwell, *CHI*, V, pp. 548-52.

Second Anglo-Sikh War (1848–49)

In the Panjab a superficial peace had reigned following the stormy events of
1845-6 which had brought the First Anglo-Sikh War (q.v.) to a conclusion.
The large-scale retrenchment and disarming of Sikh soldiery, the constant
interference of the British Resident in the minutest details of administration
and the reforms initiated by him had resulted in a great deal of discontent,
both overt and covert. Fuel was added to the fire by the banishment of
Maharani Jind Kaur (q.v.), the widowed mother of the minor Maharaja
Dalip Singh (q.v.), to Sheikhupura on account of her alleged involvement in
anti-British activities. The rebellion of Diwan Mulraj (q.v.) following the
murder of two English agents sparked off a smouldering discontent. Except
for some independent action taken by Herbert Edwardes, Assistant Political
Agent at Bannu, the Governor-General followed a policy of 'deliberate
inactivity', letting the revolt develop into a full-scale rebellion so as to justify
his more ambitious plans to annex the whole of the Panjab. Chattar Singh
Attariwala of Hazara and his son Sher Singh, sceptical about British intentions of restoring Panjab to Dalip Singh and incensed at the brutish behaviour of Captain Saunders Abbot (with Chattar Singh), the British Resident's representative, joined the rebels at Multan. They negotiated with and
received promises of help from the Afghan Amir Dost Mohammad (q.v.)
and several frontier tribes. The stage was thus set for the sequence of events
leading to the Second Anglo-Sikh War.

Having made elaborate preparations for action, the British army, commanded by General Hugh Gough, moved across the Sutlej and, towards the

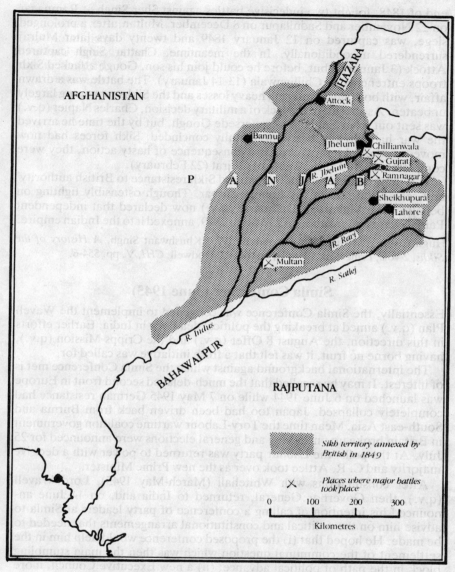

AFGHANISTAN

HAZARA

Attock

Bannu

Jhelum

R. Jhelum

Chillianwala

Gujrat

Ramnagar

Sheikhupura

Lahore

P A N J A B

Multan

R. Ravi

R. Satlej

R. Indus

BAHAWALPUR

RAJPUTANA

Sikh territory annexed by
British in 1849

× Places where major battles
took place

0   100   200   300

Kilometres

Second Anglo-Sikh War (1848–9)

end of 1848, fought two indecisive battles against Sher Singh at Ramnagar on 22 November and Sadullapur on 8 December. Multan, after a prolonged siege, was captured on 12 January 1849 and twenty days later Mulraj surrendered unconditionally. In the meantime, Chattar Singh captured Attock (3 January), but, before he could join his son, Gough attacked Sikh troops entrenched at Chillianwala (13-14 January). The battle was a drawn affair, with both sides suffering heavy losses and the Sikhs remaining largely unbeaten. As a result of the lack of a military decision, Charles Napier (q.v.) was sent out from England to supersede Gough, but by the time he arrived the war had already been successfully concluded. Sikh forces had now moved to the Jehlum where, as a consequence of hasty action, they were completely routed at the battle of Gujrat (22 February).

This marked the end of all 'organised Sikh resistance to British authority' and sealed the fate of the Lahore darbar. Though ostensibly fighting on behalf of the Maharaja, Dalhousie (q.v.) now declared that independent Panjab was no more and, on 29 March 1849, annexed it to the Indian empire.

Hugh Cook, *The Sikh Wars*, London, 1975; Khushwant Singh, *A History of the Sikhs*, 2 vols, Princeton, 1966, II, pp. 66–82; Dodwell, *CHI*, V, pp. 554-6.

Simla Conference (June 1945)

Essentially, the Simla Conference was convened to implement the Wavell Plan (q.v.) aimed at breaking the political deadlock in India. Earlier efforts in this direction, the August 8 Offer (q.v.) and the Cripps Mission (q.v.), having borne no fruit, it was felt that a fresh initiative was called for.

The international background against which the Simla Conference met is of interest. It may be recalled that the much-delayed second front in Europe was launched on 6 June 1944 while on 7 May 1945 German resistance had completely collapsed. Japan too had been driven back from Burma and South-east Asia. Mean time the Tory-Labour wartime coalition government in Britain broke up on 25 May and general elections were announced for 25 July. At the polls, the Labour party was returned to power with a decisive majority and C. R. Attlee took over as the new Prime Minister.

After consultations with Whitehall (March-May 1945), Lord Wavell (q.v.), then Governor General, returned to India and, on 14 June announced his intention of calling a conference of party leaders at Simla to advise him on the political and constitutional arrangements that needed to be made. He hoped that (i) the proposed conference would help him in the settlement of the communal question which was then the main stumbling block in the path of political advance; (ii) a new Executive Council, more representative of organized political parties, would be brought into being. This was to consist of an equal number of caste Hindus and Muslims, working under the existing constitution and almost entirely Indian in complexion except for the Viceroy and the Commander-in-Chief (the latter was to retain his position as War Member).

The main functions of the Council would be: (a) to prosecute the War; (b) to carry on the government of India; (c) to consider ways and means whereby a new permanent constitution may be agreed upon and a long-term solution facilitated. It was understood that the portfolio of External Affairs, hitherto held by the Viceroy, would be transferred to an Indian member.

The Viceroy also announced the immediate release of all members of the (Indian National) Congress (q.v.) Working Committee. The latter convened on 21-22 June, deliberated upon the proposals and accepted the Viceroy's invitation to attend the Conference at Simla scheduled for 25 June. For its part, the All-India Muslim League (q.v.) entered two caveats: that (i) the list of members of the Executive Council to be submitted by it would be deemed final and the Viceroy's demand for a panel of names out of which he would make a selection was unjustified; (ii) Muslims nominated to the Council should all be members of the Muslim League.

Invitees to the Conference included the Premiers of British Indian provinces, where popular ministries were functioning; ex-Premiers of provinces ruled by the Governor under Section 93 of the Government of India Act 1935 (q.v.); the Presidents of the Congress and the Muslim League; the deputy leaders of the Congress and Muslim League parties in the Central Legislative Assembly and their respective leaders in the Council of State; leaders of the Nationalist party and of the European group in the Assembly; one representative each of the Scheduled Castes and of the Sikhs. Gandhi (q.v.) was present at Simla while the Conference was in session but did not attend it.

In his address to the plenary session, Wavell declared: 'it is not a constitutional settlement, it is not a final solution of India's complex problems that is proposed. Nor does the plan in any way prejudice or prejudge its final issue.' On 26 June, the Viceroy posed two sets of questions to the Conference: Part A related to the scheme of the new Executive Council as explained in his declaration of 14 June; Part B related to the strength and composition of the Council, the method of submitting panels of names for it to the Viceroy so as to enable him to make his choice for appointment. In 'A', the main divergence of opinion concerned the question of parity between Muslims and caste Hindus, but on the whole parity was not denounced. As for 'B', it was decided to adjourn the Conference to give the Congress and the League time to come to a settlement through informal talks.

The parleys unfortunately failed. Wavell suggested that the parties submit to him lists of their nominees: 8-12 each from the Congress and the League, 4 from the Scheduled Castes and 3 from each of the remaining delegations. The Congress submitted a list on 6 July; Jinnah (q.v.) hedged, insisting on an assurance that Muslim members would be nominated exclusively by the League. This was turned down by the Viceroy, with the result that Jinnah refused to submit a list. Wavell made his own list of 4 members from the Muslim League and one from the Unionist Party in the Panjab. Jinnah demurred; he would not accept any Muslim from outside the League, and would not join the Council unless special safeguards for Muslims were provided. On 14 July, Wavell announced the failure of the Conference. He confessed to making every possible effort but had made no headway.

Maulana Azad (q.v.) has expressed the view that it was not advisable to have rejected Wavell's offer. However, as a percipient observer has pointed out, the Viceroy's offer was less generous than that of Cripps (1942): there was no provision in it for a long-term solution; no promise of complete independence; no transfer of the War (viz. Defence) portfolio; no surrender of the Viceroy's veto or other powers and, unlike the Cripps offer, it treated the Congress and the League on terms of equality.

It has been argued that in accepting Wavell's offer, Congress leaders had demonstrated that they were tired of the political struggle and were anxious to arrive at a settlement on the terms proposed. Jinnah, on the other hand, was confident and aggressive. Even before the Conference convened, it is suggested, he was sure of Muslim electoral support and was eagerly looking forward to a fresh poll.

On 11 July, Wavell noted in his *Journal:* 'I fear I have to record the definite failure of the Conference and so of this fresh effort to make progress in Indian self-government....He [Jinnah] refused even to discuss unless he could be given absolute right to select all Muslims and some guarantee that any decision which the Muslim League opposed in Council could only be passed by a two-third majority; in fact, a kind of communal veto. I said that these conditions were entirely unacceptable and the interview ended . . . .So ends my attempt to introduce a fresh impetus and a fresh spirit into Indian politics. . . .I am afraid that the result may be an increase in communal bitterness and agitation in India . . .'

Tara Chand, IV, pp. 442–54; Penderel Moon (ed.), *Wavell, The Viceroy's Journal*, Oxford, 1973, pp. 144–56.

Simon Commission (1927–1930)

On 8 November 1927 the Secretary of State for India, Lord Birkenhead, in London and the Viceroy, Lord Irwin (q.v.), in New Delhi, announced the setting up of the Indian Statutory Commission under Sir John Simon. It consisted, in addition to the Chairman, of six members. Party-wise, there were four Conservatives, two Labourites and one Liberal; it was an all-white Commission with no Indian representation.

Apart from the Chairman, the Commission's members were Viscount Burnham, Baron Strathcone, both members of the House of Lords, George Fox, Edward Cadogan and Clement Attlee, all three members of the House of Commons. The sixth, Vernon Hertshorn, was a Welsh socialist and a miners' leader who replaced Stephen Walsh. Two Indian civil servants, J. H. Bhore and S. F. Steward were appointed secretaries of the Commission.

A word on the Commission's genesis. Owing to the 'inevitable and ever-rising claims' of Indian nationalism and the signal success of the Indian National Congress (q.v.) in the provincial Council elections of 1926, the government had been increasingly sceptical about the smooth working of the Montagu-Chelmsford Reforms (q.v.). This is said to have been 'a compelling consideration' for an early start of the work of the Commission. Section 84A of the Reforms of 1919, had stipulated that 'at the expiration of ten years after the passing of that Act' a Royal Commission would inquire into the working of the Indian constitution. In its early (December 1927) induction, the stipulated date of appointment of the Statutory Commission (December 1929) was thus anticipated by two years.

The Commission was 'to inquire into the working of the system of government, the growth of education and the development of representative institutions, in British India, and matters connected therewith and should report as to whether and to what extent it is desirable to establish the principle of responsible government or to extend, modify or restrict the degree of responsible government then existing therein including the question whether the establishment of second chambers of the local legislatures is or is not desirable.' It was stipulated that the proposals made by the Commission would be referred to a joint select committee of the two Houses of Parliament. The latter was to invite 'the views of the Indian Central Legislature by delegations' as also of any other bodies whom the parliamentary committee 'may desire to consult.'

Technically, the composition of the Commission, which was presently to become a subject of acute controversy, was one for decision by the British Parliament and government. The then Governor-General (viz., Irwin) was 'decidedly opposed' to the inclusion of an Indian among its members, a view-point in which HMG concurred. Again, its procedure was to be settled by the Commission itself and was not a subject of correspondence or consultation between New Delhi and Whitehall.

Throughout 1928 there was intense excitement all over India on account of the impending visit of the Commission which evoked a popular political and even social boycott. Apart from their manifestos, statements and resolutions, all the major political parties—the Indian National Congress (q.v.), the All-India Liberal Federation (q.v.), the All-India Muslim League (q.v.), the Hindu Mahasabha (q.v.)—as well as the Federation of Indian Chambers of Commerce and the Millowners' Association were signatories to a statement declaring that India could not 'conscientiously take any part or share in the work of the Commission as at present constituted.' The Central Legislative Assembly too expressed its vehement opposition. It would thus be obvious that those who undertook to welcome the Commission were either splinter groups, such as a section of the Muslim League led by Mian Muhammad Shafi (q.v.), or representatives of special or sectarian interests, i.e. Europeans, Anglo-Indians, the Depressed Classes, etc.

The Commission thus worked in an atmosphere of boycott and non-cooperation. Nor did its report mend matters. When submitted on 27 May 1930, it confirmed in fact the worst fears of the nationalists. *Inter alia,* it omitted any mention of Dominion Status (q.v.) even as a distant goal for the country's political progress and rejected all ideas of transfer of power at the centre which was to remain, as hitherto, politically irresponsible. The introduction of indirect elections for the central legislature was another retrograde step. So were provisions such as removal of the entire subject of defence from the legislature's purview, failure to provide for Indianization of the army, retention of the Secretary of State's India Council and the maintenance of Whitehall's undiluted control over the Government of India.

Autonomy in the provinces, which was to replace the Montford version of dyarchy, was rated as nothing but a camouflage. Thus, the centre was to have special powers in financial matters; there were to be non-votable items and the Governor was to have the power of restoring grants and certifying bills rejected by the legislature. Provincial cabinets were to have one or two officials from the civil service. Communal representation, against which the Commision had expressed itself in no uncertain terms, was none the less endorsed and indeed sought to be perpetuated.

The proposals were understandably found to be completely unacceptable to the major political parties in the country, including the Muslim League. Motilal Nehru (q.v.) declared that, while the Commission was a farce, its Report was 'an even greater farce'. Lord Irwin, viewed its findings as 'lacking in imagination' and sought to soften the shock by side-tracking its importance and stressing the independent role of the forthcoming Round Table Conference (q.v.). In fact, the Commission's findings were outpaced by events. The Nehru Report (q.v.) as well as the Viceroy's declaration of 31 October 1929 that the 'natural issue of India's constitu- tional progress' was the 'attainment of Dominion Status' had stolen the Commission's political thunder. For while Indian nationalist opinion de- manded the immediate establishment of full responsible government, both at the centre and in the provinces, the Commission's proposals were practi- cally limited to the transfer of responsibility in the provincial sphere and that too hedged in by several qualifications. Thus, in sharp contrast to the attention it received in Whitehall, Indian political opinion virtually ignored the Commission as well as its report as somewhat irrelevant.

It may be of interest to note that the total cost of the Statutory Commis- sion was estimated at £146,000, exclusive of the cost of the Auxiliary (viz. Hartog) Committee (q.v.) on Education and of the Indian Central Commit- tee and Provincial Committees.

Report of the Indian Statutory Commission, 1930, 2 vols, I-Survey; II- Recommendations; I, London; II, Publication Branch, Government of India, Calcutta; S. R. Bakshi, *Simon Commission and Indian Nationalism*, New Delhi, 1977 also, 'Simon commission—a case study of its appointment', *JIH*, 50, 2, 1972, pp. 561-72; C. F. Andrews, *India and the Simon Report*, London, 1930.

Sind

'Sin' is an Indo-Scythic or Tartar term, the river Indus being the 'Abe-Sin' or 'father-stream.' The province which takes its name from the river is bounded on the west by Baluchistan; on the north, by Baluchistan, the Panjab and Bahawalpur; on the east, by the Rajasthan region of Jaisalmer and Jodhpur; on the south, by the Arabian Sea and the Rann of Kutch. Its sea-coast is that of the delta of the Indus.

To the western Arabs, all land eastward of the Persian Gulf was known as 'Hind', but they distinguished the two regions on and beyond the Indus river by the expression, *Hind-wa-Sind*. The term Sind is mentioned both by Pliny and Arrian.

Geographically the term applies only to lower Sind (the Indus river's delta), although its political boundaries embrace Kohistan and parts of the Thar desert. By the latter part of the eighteenth century, the province was populated by the Baluchis, Sindhis, Panjabi Hindus and Afghans.

In the early eighteenth century the Kalhotra, a Sind tribe, took possession

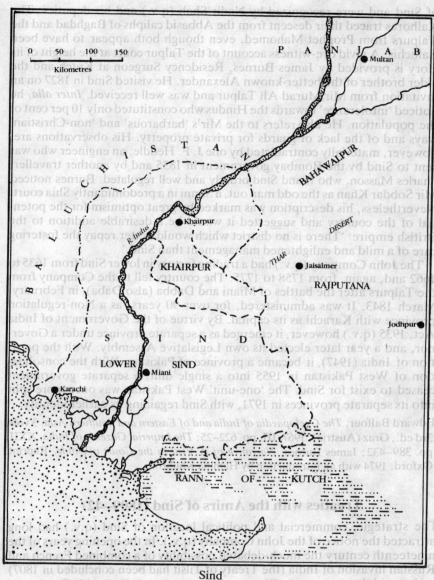

Sind

of Sind and were recognized by Nadir Shah (q.v.) and his deputies. The Kalhoras traced their descent from the Abbasid caliphs of Baghdad and the Talpurs from Prophet Mahomed, even though both appear to have been Baluchis. A vivid eye-witness account of the Talpur court at the height of its glory is provided by James Burnes, Residency Surgeon at Kutch and the elder brother of the better-known Alexander. He visited Sind in 1827 on an invitation from Mir Murad Ali Talpur and was well received. *Inter alia,* he noticed 'intolerance' towards the Hindus who constituted only 10 per cent of the population. He also refers to the Mir's 'barbarous' and 'non-Christian' ways and of the lack of guards for private property. His observations are, however, materially contradicted by one J. F. Heddle, an engineer who was sent to Sind by the Bombay government in 1835 and by another traveller, Charles Masson, who found Sind orderly and well regulated. Burnes noticed Mir Sobdar Khan as the odd man out, a Sunni in a predominantly Shia court. Nevertheless, his description was marked by great optimism for the potential of the country and suggested it would be a desirable addition to the British empire: 'There is no district which would better repay the fostering care of a mild and enlightened management than Sind.'

The John Company (q.v.) had a trading factory in lower Sind from 1635 to 1662 and, again, from 1758 to 1775. The country fell to the Company from the Talpurs after the battles of Miani and Dabba (also Daba), in February-March 1843. It was administered, for over 90 years, as a Non-regulation province with Karachi as its capital. By virtue of the Government of India Act, 1935 (q.v.) however, it emerged as a separate province under a Governor, and a year later elected its own Legislative Assembly. With the partition of India (1947), it became a province of Pakistan. With the consolidation of West Pakistan in 1955 into a single unit, a separate government ceased to exist for Sind. The 'one-unit' West Pakistan was once more split into its separate provinces in 1971, with Sind regaining its earlier identity.

Edward Balfour, *The Cyclopaedia of India and of Eastern and Southern Asia,* 3 vols, 3rd ed., Graz (Austria), 1967, III, pp. 622–25; *The Imperial Gazetter of India,* XXII, pp. 389–432; James Burnes, *Narrative of A Visit to the Court of Sinde,* Reprint, Oxford, 1974 with an introduction by Hamida Khuhro.

Treaties with the Amirs of Sind (1809–42)

The strategic, commercial and political location of Sind (q.v.) had long attracted the notice of the John Company (q.v.). In the opening years of the nineteenth century the much-debated possibility of a combined French and Russian invasion of India (the Treaty of Tilsit had been concluded in 1807) and a widely rumoured alliance of the Amirs of Sind with Persia and France expedited the dispatch of a British diplomatic mission to Sind. The initial Treaty of Hyderabad, negotiated in July 1808 by Captain David Seton, was rejected by the Company as it committed the British to some mutual defence clauses which they found to be politically inconvenient. Subsequently, Hankey Smith concluded the first 4-article Treaty on 22 August 1809. According to its terms, the Amirs agreed *inter alia* to a mutual exchange of agents and to exclude ' the tribe of the French' from their country. The Treaty, initially concluded with Hyderabad in Sind, was deemed to be binding on the Amirs of Khairpur and Mirpur as well. Eleven years later, on 9 November 1820, the 1809 Treaty was renewed. According to the new 4-clause agreement, the Amirs engaged to restrain the depredations of border tribes and keep them from making inroads into British territory. Additionally, they undertook not to permit 'any European or American' to settle in their dominion.

A 4-article Treaty with Mir Rustam of Khairpur, concluded on 4 April 1832, stipulated that the Mir would grant the use of the river and roads of Sind to the merchants of Hindustan 'on whatever terms may be settled' with the government of Hyderabad. Additionally, he was to furnish a written statement 'of just and reasonable duties to be levied on all goods' under the Treaty. Sixteen days later, on 20 April 1832, a 7-article treaty was concluded with Mir Murad Ali Khan Talpur of Hyderabad. It laid down that 'the merchants and traders' of Hindustan would be allowed use of the river and roads of Sind on three conditions: 'no person shall bring any description of military stores; no armed vessels or boats shall come by the said river and no English merchants shall be allowed to settle [in Sind].' Additionally, the Hyderabad ruler was to fix 'certain proper and moderate duties' to be levied and undertook that there would be no arbitrary departure from the schedule.

Two days later, a 3-article 'Supplemental Treaty' to the above laid down that the Hyderabad ruler would furnish the British with a statement of duties, etc. These would be scrutinized to ensure that they were 'fair and equitable' but, should they appear 'too high', the British would inform him to that effect and he 'will reduce the said duties.' It was also laid down that in so far as the Khairpur ruler was to abide by the terms arrived at, copies of the Treaty would be sent to the Amir 'for his satisfaction and guidance.'

On 2 July 1834, a 5-article 'Commercial Treaty' was concluded between the Company and the government of Hyderabad. It was in pursuance of Article I of the 'Supplemental Treaty' in regard to the fixation of fair and equitable duties on trade which were now laid down. Procedures were also worked out to settle any disputes that might arise. Two years later, on 28 November, 1836, 11 'Commercial Articles' were entered into between Colonel Henry Pottinger and the government of Hyderabad. They sought to clarify certain difficulties that had arisen in actual practice.

A 2-article Treaty between the Company and the Amirs of Sind signed on 20 April 1838 laid down that (i) the Governor-General in Council would 'use his good offices to adjust the present differences' between the Amirs and Maharaja Ranjit Singh (q.v.); (ii) 'to secure and improve' the relations between the signatories, 'an accredited' British minister 'shall reside' at Hyderabad; the latter would change 'his ordinary place of residence' from time to time whenever 'expedient' and be attended by such escort 'as may be deemed suitable' by his government. The Amirs too would be at liberty to depute a vakil to reside at the court of the British government.

A 10-article Treaty between Mir Rustam of Khairpur and Alexander Burnes (q.v.) on behalf of the Company was concluded on 24 December 1838. It laid down that the British would protect the Amir's state which would act in 'subordinate co-operation' with them. The Amir was not to enter into negotiations with any 'other state or ruler without their (the Company's) prior knowledge and sanction'; and would accept 'arbitration and award' in matters of dispute. An accredited British representative would reside at Khairpur. A 'separate article' laid down that if the Governor-General 'in time of war should seek to occupy the fortress of Bukkar as a depot for treasure and munitions', the Amir would not object.

On 7 February 1839, a 2-article 'agreement' for the surrender of Karachi was signed.

A 14-article Treaty between the British and the Amirs of Hyderabad was signed on 11 March 1839. It stipulated *inter alia:* (i) the stationing of a British force of 5,000 men at Thatta 'or such place westward of the river' as the Governor-General may determine; (ii) the payment of Rs 1 lakh by Mirs Noor Mahomed, Nuseer Mahomed and Meer Mahomed every year as 'part payment' for the maintenance of the force; (iii) that no negotiations with foreign chiefs or states were to be permitted; (iv) that the Amirs were to act 'in subordinate co-operation' with the British.

A 14-article Treaty between the British and Amir Sher Mahomed Khan of Mirpur was concluded on 18 June 1841 more or less on the pattern of the 1839 Treaty with Hyderabad. Additionally, it laid down that the territories disputed between the Mir and the Amirs of Hyderabad would be submitted to arbitrators appointed by the contending parties 'and an umpire' appointed by the British Political Agent.

Two 'draft treaties' of 12 articles with the Amirs of Hyderabad and of 10 articles with the Amirs of Khairpur, both dated Simla, 4 November 1842 are to be found in *Aitchison*. It would appear that their actual conclusion was overtaken by events.

Aitchison, VII, pp. 34–69; Kala Thairani, *British Missions to Sind*, New Delhi, 1973; R. A. Huttenback, *British Relations with Sind*, Berkeley, 1962; P. N. Khera, *British Policy towards Sind upto Its Annexation–1843*, 2nd ed., Delhi, 1963.

Annexation of Sind (1843)

British relations with Sind (q.v.) in the early part of the nineteenth century had been, to start with, purely commercial in nature. The potential wealth of the province and of the Indus which served as a highway for the commerce of its rich hinterland, apart from considerations of defence and security, made the John Company (q.v.) steadily but surely encroach upon the authority of the Amirs. By alternately using intimidation, coaxing and cajolery, they were made to accept treaties (Treaties with the Amirs of Sind (q.v.)) which eventually subordinated them to British power and control. In pursuance of the Afghan policy of Auckland (q.v.), the Amirs who were not a party to the Tripartite Treaty (q.v.) were none the less forced to finance Shah Shuja's military campaign as well as allow Sind to be used as a base for British military operations. To retrieve the Company's badly shaken prestige following the disasters of the First Afghan War (q.v.), Ellenborough (q.v.) decided to annex Sind. Charles Napier (q.v.) who was in complete accord with this plan was appointed military commander, replacing James Outram (q.v.), who was known to sympathize with local aspirations.

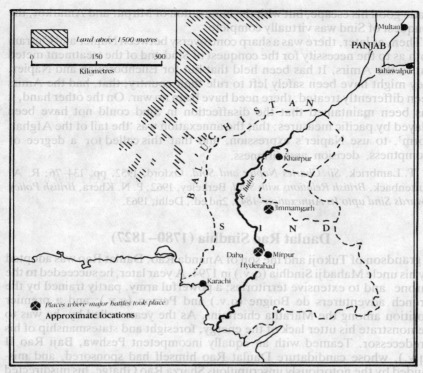

Annexation of Sind (1843)

Napier's subsequent actions were directed towards one goal, bringing about the annexation of Sind by means fair or foul. To this end, he produced incriminating evidence of dubious validity, accused the Amirs of disloyalty to the British cause, took sides in a succession squabble in Khairpur and tried to force the cession of lands to Bahawalpur, which provoked the Baluchis into action.

The hesitation shown by the Amirs in signing fresh treaties drawn up at Simla in November 1842 which threatened their very existence was dubbed as insubordination on their part. While Outram was negotiating, Napier blew up the fortress of Imamgarh (January 1843) without even declaring war on the Amirs. It was patent that this action was designed to precipitate matters. The Amirs, driven to sore straits and fearing further military action, sent out a call for their levies. The infuriated Baluchis attacked the Residency at Hyderabad, from which Outram just about managed to escape.

The war, now formally declared, was 'short and sanguinary.' A Baluchi army of 22,000 men was defeated at Miani on 17 February 1843 by Napier who commanded a force of 2,800 men and 12 guns. Sher Muhammad of Mirpur and 24,000 Baluchis who had held out were defeated at Dabba (also Daba) on 24 March by a reinforced British army of 6,000 men. The Amir made good his escape, but with the annexation of Mirpur and Amarkot, the conquest of Sind was virtually complete.

Then, as later, there was a sharp controversy between Napier and Outram both as to the necessity for the conquest of Sind and of the treatment meted out to the Amirs. It has been held that but for Ellenborough and Napier, they might have been safely left to rule their country; that, had the Amirs been differently treated, there need have been no war. On the other hand, it has been maintained that the disaffection in Sind could not have been allayed by pacific measures; that the annexation was 'the tail of the Afghan storm', to use Napier's expression, and that this called for a degree of promptness, decision and firmness.

H. T. Lambrick, *Sir Charles Napier and Sind,* Oxford, 1952, pp. 134–76; R. A. Huttenback, *British Relations with Sind,* Berkeley, 1962; P. N. Khera, *British Policy towards Sind upto Its Annexation–1843,* 2nd ed., Delhi, 1963.

Daulat Rao Sindhia (1780–1827)

A grandson of Tukoji and the son of Ananda Rao, Daulat Rao was adopted by his uncle Mahadji Sindhia (q.v.) in 1794. A year later, he succeeded to the throne and to extensive territories; a powerful army, partly trained by the French adventurers de Boigne (q.v.) and Perron (q.v.); and a premier position among the Maratha chieftains. As the years rolled by, he was to demonstrate his utter lack of the energy, foresight and statesmanship of his predecessor. Teamed with an equally incompetent Peshwa, Baji Rao II (q.v.), whose candidature Daulat Rao himself had sponsored, and misguided by the notoriously unscrupulous Sharza Rao Ghatge, his misdirected actions were destined soon to result in a near-eclipse of Maratha power in the Deccan.

Not unlike Mahadji, Daulat Rao's great amibition was to rule the roost at Poona. In this he came into an open conflict with Nana Phadnis (q.v.) whom, through a clever stratagem, he briefly (1797-8) arrested. The two had clashed over the question of succession to the Peshwaship after the death of Madhav Narayan Rao, with Nana supporting the candidature of Chimnaji Appa and staunchly opposing that of Baji Rao, the son of his sworn enemy, Raghoba (q.v.). Yashvant Rao Holkar (q.v.) too joined the fray, as did Chhatrapati Shivaji, Raja of Kolhapur, albeit indirectly. The campaigns of the two contending armies devastated the countryside; villages were ravaged, towns plundered. Neither the rich nor the poor were spared and, in the bargain, anarchy reigned supreme in the Maratha heartland.

With his superior military strength, Daulat Rao finally succeeded in putting Baji Rao II on the *masnad* at Poona, thereby retaining his pre-eminence at the citadel of Maratha authority. This, however, was to prove a pyrrhic victory. For no sooner had he retired to the north than Yashvant Rao defeated the Peshwa (1802) and drove him out of Poona. The latter was thus compelled to seek refuge within the enemy's gates—under the John Company (q.v.) at Bassein.

Earlier, with Nana's death (1800), all semblance of the Peshwa's authority save in the Maratha council had vanished and Sindhia emerged all-powerful.

Ghatge who had been initially employed by Nana to spy on Daulat Rao switched loyalties and, after the latter's marriage to Ghatge's daughter (1798), emerged as Daulat Rao's principal advisor. The latter's extravagant personal expenditure and the maintenance of an enormous army resulted in an almost perpetual financial deficit, relieved from time to time by forcible extortions from every possible source—bankers, merchants, city-dwellers and the rack-rented peasantry. In the result, depredations and plunder by the army reduced the countryside to near-starvation.

Daulat Rao soon provoked a fierce family quarrel with Mahadji's wives by failing to keep a settlement he had arrived at with them earlier. What was worse, he embroiled himself without reason in the disputed Holkar succession, thereby aggravating the traditional rivalry between the two chiefs. In the result, Yashvant Rao and Vithoji took up cudgels against Daulat Rao (1801) and raided his territories. 1801-2 witnessed several engagements between the contenders, with varying fortunes. Provoked further by Vithoji's murder, the Peshwa's confiscation of his estates and Daulat Rao's refusal to surrender Khande Rao (the son of Malhar Rao), Yashvant Rao marched upon Poona. Daulat Rao's failure at this juncture to send timely aid resulted in the Peshwa's defeat at Hadaspur. On hearing this, Daulat Rao promptly left Ujjain for Poona, yet despite his pressing advice to the contrary, Baji Rao fell into the British trap and signed the Treaty of Bassein (q.v.).

Unlike Yashvant Rao, Daulat Rao failed to grasp the crucial significance of this new development and ignored opportunities for a friendly understanding among the Maratha chiefs. Holkar and Amrit Rao tried in vain to sell him the idea of a new government at Poona and the need for combined resistance to the Peshwa's return there as a British protege. Unfortunately for him, Daulat Rao continued to entertain illusions of his ascendancy in Maratha affairs even after the Peshwa's restoration under the Company's auspices.

Only too eager to prevent a common front by the Maratha chiefs, the British sent a representative to Daulat Rao's court to ascertain his approval of their earlier Treaty with the Peshwa. Daulat Rao's reply was non-committal, as was his response to Raghuji Bhonsle's attempt to narrow down his differences with Holkar. Once Holkar moved out and Baji Rao was re-installed at Poona (April 1803), Sindhia engaged in frantic negotiations with Bhonsle and other Maratha chiefs so as to evade a declaration of loyalty to the restored Peshwa. His refusal to comply with the British directive to move his forces away from the Nizam's borders brought about the Second Anglo-Maratha War (q.v.).

The War proved crucial in the fortunes of Daulat Rao. The British launched a combined asault on his dominions, north and south. General Lake marched to Aligarh and routed Sindhia's forces under Perron, and later took Delhi (September 1803). In the Deccan, Arthur Wellesley worsted his forces at Assaye and captured the fortress of Gawilgarh. The Treaty of Surji Arjangaon (q.v.) followed, whereby Sindhia virtually signed away his independence.

In the years that followed, till his death in 1827, Daulat Rao was to play no significant role in Maratha politics. Revenue was collected, as was usual, by force, and the neighbouring petty chiefs ruthlessly subdued. In 1810, he shifted his headquarters to Gwalior. Seven years later, and now virtually surrounded on all sides by British troops, Daulat Rao hesitated to give a positive response to the Peshwa's entreaties for help, while reluctantly promising the British aid against the Pindaris (q.v.). With the establishment of an unchallenged British paramountcy on the conclusion of the Third Anglo-Maratha War (q.v.), Daulat Rao faded into insignificance.

J. N. Sarkar, *et al*, *Daulat Rao Sindhia and North Indian Affairs (1794–99)*, Poona Residency Correspondence, vols. VIII-XII, Bombay, 1951.

Madhav Rao (Mahadji) Sindhia (1727–94)

The son of Ranoji, Madhav Rao Sindhia, popularly known as Mahadji Sindhia and among contemporary writers as Maharaja Patel, was born in 1727. Wounded at the Third Battle of Panipat (q.v.) and rescued by a water-carrier, he repaired to the Deccan from Malwa in 1762, to take charge of the family estates. Unable to pay the stipulated *nazrana*, Raghu Nath Rao (q.v.) in supersession appointed his brother Kedarji as head of the family. Two years later, however, Mahadji forcibly took charge of his patrimony, devoting time and effort to consolidating his dominion and strengthening his military prowess. In 1766, he accompanied Raghu Nath Rao in a campaign against the Jat ruler of Gohad. The expedition, not altogether successful, had entailed heavy expenditure, compelling the Marathas to retreat. Two years later (1770), however, Mahadji dealt successfully with the Rohillas and their leader Ahmad Khan Bangash of Farrukhabad.

Meanwhile, Shah Alam II (q.v.) approached Mahadji for help to return to Delhi, but kept vacillating about the terms. To force the issue, Mahadji placed his son Jawan Bakhat on the throne *ad interim*. Shah Alam relented and, in January 1772, was escorted by the Maratha chief to Delhi. At the end of the year, Mahadji repulsed the imperial troops who, secretly encouraged by Shah Alam, had attacked the Marathas. The death of Peshwa Madhav Rao and the issue of succession that now cropped up called for an early withdrawal of Maratha forces from Delhi. Mahadji, a brave soldier and shrewd diplomat, remained a seemingly disinterested observer in the civil war then raging in Poona until lack of military strength compelled Nana Phadnis (q.v.) to appoint him commander of the Maratha forces. Later, in 1780, he was to lead his people to near-victory in the First Anglo-Maratha War (q.v.). When hostilities were renewed, the British concentrated their major attacks against his territories. Conscious that the war-worn, impoverished English were keen to conclude peace, he made equally certain that this would be on terms favourable to him. On condition therefore, that all his possessions, including Gwalior and Ujjain, would be restored, he concluded with the English the Treaty of Salbai (q.v.) and pledged himself to make the other chiefs in the Maratha confederacy accept its terms.

Not a man to take hasty or precipitate action, Mahadji did not rush to Delhi when, in 1782, after the death of Najaf Khan, the Emperor Shah Alam invited him to take over control of affairs. Before proceeding to the north, Mahadji was keen to establish a strong base in Bundelkhand for, he argued, in case of need he may not get any help either from Poona or even Delhi.

Hamdani, the keeper of the fort at Agra, who resented Maratha penetration, had Muhammad Shafi and Afrasial Khan, both pro-Maratha in their sympathies, murdered. Mahadji now paid his first visit to the Emperor, who conferred on him the title of Wakil-i-Mutlaq.

Cool, moderate and calculating, Mahadji made great efforts to secure a regular territory and income for the Emperor. With this end in view, he conciliated the Sikhs while the Rajputs and Hamdani came into an open confrontation in an indecisive battle at Lalsot where Hamdani was killed. The reverse thus suffered was a serious blow to Maratha prestige, for Mahadji's enemies now rose against him on all sides. Ghulam Qadir Rohilla, after defeating the Maratha garrison at Delhi, took the Emperor captive in August 1787; he was deposed, tortured and even blinded.

Mahadji, frustrated by the petty jealousies of the Maratha chiefs and the lack of timely help from Poona, retired south of the Chambal to make preparations to retrieve his position. Later, in a clever move with the help of troops from Nana Phadnis and de Boigne (q.v.), he defeated Ghulam Qadir in April (1788) and by June was firmly in the saddle at Delhi again. By the end of 1791, all northern India, from the Sutlej to the Narmada, came under Mahadji's nominal control. His independence of Poona completely washed out the Peshwa's influence in the affairs of the north and Mahadji acknowledged the Peshwa's authority only in so far as it helped him in his objectives.

Having consolidated his hold, Mahadji now used his French-trained troops successfully against the Rajputs. In 1790 he had refused to help Cornwallis (q.v.) in the south, but on learning that Nana Phadnis had agreed to loan him 10,000 men and that Tukoji Holkar was attempting to undermine his influence at the Peshwa's court, Mahadji returned to the Deccan for a time. Additionally, his aim was to organize all the Indian powers in a combined bid against the British who were fast establishing their sway in different parts of the country. On this count alone, he is rightly considered one of the more far-sighted statesmen of his time.

Leaving his French commander incharge of affairs in the north, Mahadji reached Poona in June 1792 and resumed his position at the Peshwa's court, where he soon regained his master's earlier confidence. He now powerfully influenced the Peshwa's policy, while de Boigne successfully defended Mahadji's interests in Delhi. This was too good a position to last. On 12 February 1794, Mahadji died suddenly at his camp at Wanavadi, his death depriving the Marathas of their last great soldier-statesman.

Mahadji, impressed by the superiority of European-trained troops in battle, had resolved early to raise an army on their model. To this end, he employed a number of French officers, including de Boigne, to recruit and train his men. This proved to be an extremely expensive proposition and could only be sustained by keeping his other troops starving. Nor was that all, for the loyalty of the foreign soldiers was never certain and, in the final analysis, they were to prove traitors.

According to Sardesai, Madhav Rao's career falls into four clear parts. The first comprised the pre-Panipat (1761) days when, entirely obscure, he was over-shadowed by his brilliant brothers. The second, from 1761 to the restoration of the Mughal Emperor (viz., 1772) was one of apprenticeship in which Mahadji acquired the supreme fitness which enabled him to cooperate with Nana Phadnis and the Poona ministers in fighting the British. In the third period (1772-82), Mahadji gained experience of war and diplomacy on his own initiative which he put to actual test. The fourth period commenced with the Treaty of Salbai and ended with the crowning successes he gained in north India. Sardesai concludes that, if 'one man' could be credited 'with the authorship of fulfilling the Maratha dream of Hindu-pad Padshahi', that man admittedly was Mahadji Sindhia.

Keene noted that Mahadji was 'an Indian ruler of successful capacity in times of exceptional difficulty.' Jadu Nath Sarkar has remarked that Mahadji 'towers over Maratha history in military grandeur, a ruler of India without an ally, without a party.' He laments that Nana Phadnis did not back Mahadji from the outset or else 'the unchallengeable position' which Mahadji gained in January 1778 would have been achieved 'fully four years earlier.' He triumphed in the end. but that triumph was dearly purchased at the expense of years of frustration, of swaying fortunes and of immense personal sufferings. Sarkar calls him 'a heroic personality [that] dominates the northern Indian history of his time like a colossus.' Sardesai notes that Mahadji shines 'far above' his contemporaries in every respect. Hindus and Muslims alike respected him. A man of devout temperament, he led a life 'entirely unsullied and scrupulously chaste.'

Henry George Keene, *Madhava Rao Sindhia*, Rulers of India, Oxford, 1891; G. S. Sardesai, *A New History of the Marathas*, 3 vols, II, pp. 263–72; Dodwell, *CHI*, V, pp. 261–3, 265–8, 270–2.

S. P. Sinha (1864–1928)

Satyendra Prasanno Sinha, later first Baron Sinha of Raipur, was born in June 1864 in the village of Raipur in Birbhum district of Bengal. His father was a petty Kayastha landowner. At the age of 14, S. P. entered Presidency College (Calcutta) but left for England without taking a degree. An outstanding student, S. P. distinguished himself in his studies, annexing several coveted awards and scholarships. He was called to the Bar (1886) from Lincoln's Inn. On returning home he enrolled in the High Court at Calcutta, working with great devotion and dedication. He soon built up a lucrative practice, earning the reputation of the 'greatest verdict-winner and the best cross-examiner' in the Presidency town.

Sinha's talent and ability were soon recognized and he was appointed Standing Counsel to the Bengal government in 1903. Five years later he became Advocate-General, which was followed in 1909 by his appointment as Law Member in the Governor-General's Executive Council. Differences over the Indian Press Act of 1910 (q.v.) caused him to resign, but later its promised reconsideration and modification persuaded him to stay on.

Honours poured in, thick and fast. In 1914, Sinha was knighted; three years later he gave up his appointment in the Bengal Executive Council to become one of the first Indians to participate in the deliberations of the British Cabinet. *Inter alia*, he attended meetings of the Imperial War

Cabinet and the Imperial Conference and later represented India at the peace conference in Paris. In 1919, he was appointed Parliamentary Under Secretary for India and was raised to the peerage as Baron Sinha of Raipur. It fell to him to pilot the Government of India Bill (1919), better-known as the Montagu-Chelmsford Reforms (q.v.), through the House of Lords. The following year saw Sinha installed as the Governor of Bihar and Orissa, an office he held for just about a year. Nominated a member of the Privy Council in 1925, he was appointed to its Judicial Committee in 1926.

Though not an active politician, Sinha was well-informed about current events and closely observed political trends in India. He never figured prominently in the annual sessions of the Indian National Congress (q.v.), except in 1896 and later, in 1915, when he presided over them. On the latter occasion, in a closely reasoned address which was hailed as a 'triumph of careful advocacy as well as a statement of deep convictions', he pleaded for an authoritative definition of the ultimate goal of British policy for India. His faith in British fair-mindedness and benevolence remained unshaken and he preached and practised cautious moderation in his relations with them. He was convinced that conditions as they prevailed in India did not warrant a revolutionary change to an autonomous form of government; that political change, to be meaningful, should be evolutionary, not revolutionary. This did not however make him a henchman of the British, for he openly advocated industrial growth in India to ensure prosperity and the imposition of tariffs to protect the country's nascent industry from unfair foreign competition. He also insisted on the right of Indians to join the defence services. Sinha's primary interest lay in his own profession of the law, he was never so happy as at the Bar and his brief tenure on the judicial committee of the Privy Council gave ample proof of his high judicial capacity.

A great advocate of the need for compulsory primary education, Sinha also supported technical education as a desideratum for progress in the country. On social questions, he held progressive views and decried untouchability and the caste system. Converted to the Sadharna Brahmo Samaj (c. 1886), he put great faith in the education of women as a cure for many social ills.

Apart from other honours, Sinha received the freedom of the City of London in 1917. In 1926 he was made a bencher of Lincoln's Inn. Indeed, he came to be the accepted type of educated Indian whom British politicians could summon to a share in the government of India and the counsels of the empire. Hence the numerous honours and official positions, some of which he was the first Indian to hold. In turn, what endeared him to the British was his abiding article of faith, a firm belief in British character, their sense of fair play and justice.

Sinha's failing health twice compelled him to winter in his own country towards the end of his life, and during the second of these trips he died—on 4 March 1928.

G. A. Natesan (ed.) *Speeches and writings of Lord Sinha, with a portrait and a sketch*, Madras, 1919; *DNB 1922–1930*, pp. 776–8 (S. V. Fitz Gerald).

Nawab Siraj-ud-Daula (1733–57)

Born Mirza Mohammad, Siraj was the son of Amina Begum, the daughter of Alivardi Khan, and Zin-ed-Din Ahmed Khan, the son of Haji Ahmad, Alivardi's brother. His birth (1733) had synchronized with Alivardi's own elevation to the post of Deputy Governor of Bihar. The latter fact goes a long way to explain the grandfather's excessive attachment to the young boy who was educated in the arts of government and administration, but soon developed some of the common vices of his age due to parental indulgence. From 1741 onwards, Siraj accompanied his grandfather on his military campaigns. Married to Mirza Iraj Khan's daughter in 1746, Siraj was appointed Deputy Governor of Bihar two years later. In 1752-3 he was formally adopted as the son and successor of Alivardi Khan (who gave him the title of Siraj-ud-Daula, literally, 'lamp of the state'), and became the Nawab on his grandfather's death in 1756.

Siraj's short, barely 2-year reign, was an interlude of growing tension with the East India Company (q.v.) in Bengal. He objected to the British fortifying Calcutta (q.v.) without consulting him; of misusing their trade privileges which deprived him of well-deserved revenue; of refusing to give him the custody of one Krishan Dass who had been asked to clear his accounts, and of even offering him asylum. His notes of protest against the Company's high-handedness were answered in offensive language and sometimes even ignored. He then marched against the English, having warned them of his intention to annihilate them. On 24 May (1756), Siraj captured Kasimbazar and on 19 June Calcutta, failing none the less to follow up his victory by evicting the English from Falta, where they had taken refuge.

The so-called Black Hole tragedy was a sequel to this victory over the English and is still a subject of live controversy. It is alleged that on the morrow of his success (i.e. on 20 June) the Nawab confined 146 English prisoners during the night in a small room (18 × 14 sq. ft.); on the following morning, 123 are said to have died of suffocation while a bare 23 survived to tell the ghastly tale. Many question the authenticity of Holwell's lurid account and maintain that it was a complete fabrication. Those who accept it at face-value exonerate the Nawab of the charge of cruelty, for he was probably ignorant of the treatment accorded to the prisoners, whose number is doubtful in any case. It is further held that the dead were possibly those who had been actually wounded or grievously hurt in the preceding battle.

Siraj-ud-Daula had placated both the French and the Dutch before his assault on the English but failed to receive the help he had sought from them. After his success, he demanded and received a huge war indemnity from both. In the meantime, the British openly intrigued with the disgruntled nobles in Siraj's court and, at the same time, sought the help of such Indian merchants as thrived on their business or trade interests with the Company. Once reinforcements arrived from Madras under Robert Clive (q.v.) and Charles Watson, the English recaptured Hooghly and Calcutta without much ado from its then compliant Governor, Raja Manik Chand. Nor was Siraj-ud-Daula averse to the British returning so long as they obeyed his laws. Negotiations were therefore resumed while the Nawab marched with his troops to Calcutta (3 February). Clive's agents, John Walsh and Luke Scrafton, carried proposals for peace on 3 February 1757 and at the same time spied the land for details of the Nawab's men and the deployment of his forces. The next day, 5 February, Clive led a surprise attack on the Nawab's camp, killing 1,300 of his men and retreating to the fort as soon as the 'native' troops began to rally. Instead of pursuing the British, Siraj-ud-Daula, who had in the meantime received news of the victorious Ahmad Shah Abdali's (q.v.) intention to march east, preferred to accept the British proposals for peace, and signed the Treaty of Alinagar (q.v.)

The British now captured Chandernagore (q.v.) from the French and demanded that the Nawab hand over such other French factories as he had assaulted; Maharaja Nand Kumar (q.v.), who had been deputed by Siraj-ud-Daula to aid the French in offering resistance, had in the meantime been bribed by Clive and chose to stay away. Hostilities were therefore resumed, the English determined to remove the intractable Nawab and replace him by the more pliable Mir Jafar (q.v.). While preparations were being made for war, intrigue and treachery were let loose in and around the Nawab's camp. At the Battle of Plassey (q.v.) which followed, nearly three-fourths of the Nawab's men remained mere spectators of their ruler's ill-deserved debacle, the English winning an easy victory over what remained of the rest.

A few basic facts about the background to the Nawab's struggle with the English need to be underscored. The opulent nature of the Company's Bengal trade in a period when both the central and the local authorities throughout India were undergoing a graded process of disintegration, carried the seeds of conflict between the Nawab and the Company. It would be difficult to accept the view that the Nawab's campaign against the English (1756-7) was motivated by avarice and a desire for plunder. The fact is that not only did he try to resolve the dispute without use of force, but also took good care of such English property that fell into his hands. There was no attempt on his part of any act of deliberate brutality towards the English. The return of the English to Bengal was designed to engineer a *coup d'etat* against Siraj-ud-Daula and to dispossess the French of their establishments in Bengal.

In the spring of 1757, the Nawab had foolishly engaged in negotiations with the French, underestimating English opposition to any such move. With the presence of a large body of English troops in Bengal and with the threat of an impending invasion by Ahmad Shah Abdali from the north, the balance of power had shifted in favour of the English. In June 1757, the Nawab had two choices before him—to fight for his interests either in concert with the French or alone. He chose the latter course, for the former would have meant the establishment of a French protectorate over him. He had to win alone. At Plassey, where he lost, there was on one side a prosperous Company aligned with the English government and with growing economic and political power; on the other, a Nawab beset with internal dissensions and devoid of any support from the Mughal authority.

Whether Siraj-ud-Daula could have achieved a *modus vivendi* with the English to avoid a violent show-down remains a moot point. He made an attempt but his attack on Calcutta brought an expeditionary force under Clive to safeguard British interests. Could the Nawab have saved himself from his debacle at Plassey after Clive's arrival in Bengal? Two factors militated against it. The first was the commencement of the Seven Years' War in Europe (1756-63); the second was Abdali's threatened, if perhaps problematical, invasion of the Nawab's dominions. In the circumstances, the Company felt constrained to wage a war against the French and then establish in Bengal a Nawab who would be loyal to them. If only Siraj-ud-Daula had been able to eliminate dissensions at his court, he might well have held the English back. But the fact that these existed made the latter hatch a conspiracy with dissident nobles and Hindu compradors.

After the battle, the defeated Nawab fled towards Murshidabad but was captured at Raj Mahal on 30 June. On 2 July he was murdered by Mohammed Beg, on orders given by Miran, a son of Mir Jafar.

Brought up as a spoilt child, Siraj had grown to be both wilful and vain. He had offended the high and the low by his rapacious, arbitrary and cruel dealings. There was a hostile faction in the army and a disaffected subject population. However, whatever his other failings, Siraj was entirely in the right in his demands on the English. They had failed even to acknowledge his accession to the throne, given unlawful shelter to a fugitive from his justice and expelled one of his officials from Calcutta, still a part of his dominion. Worse, they had raised fortifications and increased their garrisons without so much as informing him, much less seeking his permission.

Brijen K. Gupta, *Siraj-ud-daulah and the East India Company, 1756-57: Background to the Foundation of British Power in India*, Leiden, 1966; K. K. Datta, 'Siraj-ud-daula and the English before 1756', *Indian Historical Quarterly*, XXII, 1 March 1946, pp. 155–6; Dodwell, *CHI*, V, pp. 141–9; Ram Gopal, *How the British Conquered Bengal*, Bombay, 1963; Irish Macfarlane, *The Black Hole or the Making of a Legend*, London, 1975.

William Henry Sleeman (1788–1856)

William (later Sir William) Henry (popularly known as 'Thuggee') Sleeman came out to India and was gazetted an ensign in the Bengal army in September 1810. At Allahabad, on his way back from the Anglo-Nepalese War (q.v.), he came across a document on 'Thuggee' and developed an abiding interest in the subject. He also acquired during this period a good mastery over Hindi, Arabic, Persian and Gurkhali and opted for the civil service.

Sleeman served in the Nepal war (1814-16) and four years later was appointed assistant to the agent to the Governor-General for the Saugor and Narmada territories. During 1825-35 he served as magistrate and district officer in various parts of what is now Madhya Pradesh and was most intrigued by the government's hesitation in crushing the Thugs (q.v.) for fear of injuring the religious susceptibilities of the Hindus. He also made the chance discovery that the Thugs conversed in a secret language called Ramasi; he mastered it with the help of an approver.

In 1826 Sleeman was given the responsibility of tracking down the Thugs over a wide region; three years later, in addition to his district work, he acted as assistant to the official charged with dealing with their crimes. Initially,

Sleeman could not achieve much success—the Thugs were patronized by rich landlords; officials in charge of different districts resented his interference; district courts refused to deal with cases outside their jurisdiction; people associated with the Thugs went about unpunished. By 1832, however, he had surmounted most of these hurdles and organized a firm plan of action. Every officer under him was provided with detailed information about the gangs and their genealogical tables, while detailed sketches of their areas of operation were drawn up. By means of approvers, the relentless pursuit of individuals and groups, and the capture and punishment of their leaders, many a gang was tracked down and eliminated. Under Bentinck (q.v.), a department for the suppression of Thuggee was set up and Sleeman appointed first its general superintendent and later, in 1839, as commissioner for Thuggee and dacoity. The area under his control extended all the way from Lahore to the Carnatic; three years later, he was appointed Agent to the Governor-General in Bundelkhand. Here he undertook measures to suppress dacoity.

Sleeman was opposed to the absorption of 'native' Indian States (q.v.) by the John Company (q.v.) and both as Resident at Gwalior (1843-9) and later (1849-56) Oudh (q.v.) he opposed undue interference in their internal affairs. Dalhousie (q.v.) based his decision for the annexation of Oudh on James Outram's (q.v.) report who, in turn, had drawn heavily on Sleeman's detailed account of the prevalent conditions there and, more specifically, its maladministration. He had, however, opposed the Governor-General's proposal to annex Oudh and suggested the setting up of a regency council instead.

The author of *Rambles and Reflections of an Indian Official* (1844), his second work, *A Journey Through the Kingdom of Oudh in 1849-50*, was published, posthumously, in 1858.

Broken down in health, Sleeman, in 1854, repaired to Mussorie to recoup. In January 1856, he left for England on board the *Monarch* but died on 10 February *en route*.

Francis Tinker, *Yellow Scarf: the story of the Life of Thuggee Sleeman*, London, 1977; *DNB*, XVIII, pp. 373–4 (Stephen Wheeler).

Explosive Substances Act (1908)

The Explosive Substances Act was designed to curb terrorist activity and prevent sedition, which had increased rapidly since 1905, and had remained unaffected by the preventive legislation passed hitherto. The immediate cause and the resultant urgency with which it was passed in one day (8 June 1908) lay in a bomb outrage at Muzzafarpur on 30 April 1908. There was also the discovery of the Maniktola group of explosive manufacturers, followed by the murder of the Deputy Superintendent of Police and the Public Prosecutor conducting the Alipur Conspiracy Case. The Act was to extend to the entire country, including the Indian States (q.v.). Any person who used an explosive substance (which was elaborately defined), was liable to transportation for life or imprisonment up to ten years. And one who possessed explosives could be transported for twenty years or imprisoned for seven years along with a fine. Again, a person who 'by the supply of or solicitation for money, the providing of premises, the supply of materials, or in any manner whatever, procures, counsels, aids, abets, or is accessory to (explosives) . . .' was liable to draconian punishments. No court was to try a person for offences against this measure except with the consent of the Governor-General in Council.

The Unrepealed Central Acts, 10 vols, Delhi, 1938–42, vol. II, from 1908 to 1910, pp. 342–3.

The Surat Split (1907)

The Indian National Congress (q.v.) had from its very inception followed a loyalist and constitutional policy towards the government, confident that the latter would gradually effect changes beneficial to the people. By 1905, however, the British attitude towards reform, and particularly Curzon's (q.v.) retrogressive measures, had made it evident that this approach had been singularly barren of results. A more radical group which had in the meantime emerged was impatient to implement the programme of passive resistance on a large scale to shake off British complacency.

Essentially, both the moderate as well as the radical wings were disillusioned by government policy, but while the former were content with sending memorials and petitions, the latter advocated a more vigorous approach based on 'self-reliance and *not* mendicancy.' They made a concerted but unsuccessful effort at Banaras (1905) to make the Congress declare 'Boycott' (q.v.) constitutional and prevent the dispatch of a telegram of welcome to the then Prince of Wales (the future King George V) on his visit to India. The Moderates, however, held the fort, content with passing what their detractors viewed as mild or weak resolutions.

Ominous clouds appeared as the Extremists (or Nationalists, the name by which the New Party came to be called), began to gather momentum and work tirelessly to make themselves heard. The alternatives became clear enough: either the Extremists would capture control or there would be a parting of ways. To prevent the latter contingency from occurring, the 80-year old Dadabhai Naoroji (q.v.) who was universally respected and whose election to the party presidentship went unchallenged, was asked to preside over the Calcutta session in 1906. Here, as a result of a protest walk-out by the Extremists, compromise resolutions were adopted legitimizing the boycott movement in Bengal, accepting the cult of the Swadeshi (q.v.) and recognizing Swaraj as the country's ultimate political goal.

Both sides none the less remained deeply dissatisfied. 1906-7 saw each group launch large-scale campaigns to collect funds and muster support. At the district conference at Midnapore, in December 1906, the Extremists fared badly, while police aid had to be sought to enable the organizers conduct the proceedings. Meanwhile, the Moderates had engendered a widespread feeling that the compromise resolutions adopted at Calcutta would be flouted.

Gokhale's (q.v.) talks in London with John Morley, then Secretary of

State for India, had boosted Moderate confidence in the Liberal government's *bona fides*. In the result, they disliked presenting a stance that smacked of any lack of loyalty to the Raj or would delay an early implementation of the proposed scheme of reform. Determined to retain control and browbeat the Extremists, they accordingly changed the venue of the Congress session from Nagpur, admittedly an extremist stronghold, to Surat, rated pronouncedly moderate in its leanings.

A certain uneasiness pervaded the atmosphere as the delegates gathered in full force at Surat. The Extremist position was clear—no going back on the resolutions of 1906; more, a clear-cut declaration favouring an all-India boycott. At a conference of the 'New Party' before the plenary session, it was resolved not to secede from the main body if the status quo were maintained. The Moderates were equally determined not to give in. Behind the scenes, and without consulting the Extremists, they are said to have changed the wording of the resolutions, giving them a milder complexion, and withholding the text from the scrutiny of their political antagonists.

Neither self-government nor national education, subjects on which the Extremists had set their heart, figured in the subjects committee list. Thus, the only way left to the Extremists was to oppose the election of Rash Behari Ghose (q.v.), and propose instead the candidature of Lala Lajpat Rai. The latter, however, disappointed his supporters by agreeing, at Gokhale's personal intercession, not to offer himself for election. In the past, presidential candidates had invariably been selected by a coterie but, at Surat, the Extremists challenged this method as arbitrary. Besides, they demanded a role in the preparation of resolutions scheduled for discussion in the subjects committee. Desperate, if also seemingly helpless against a large and articulate majority, the Extremists, led by Tilak (q.v.) and Aurobindo Ghosh (q.v.), and supported principally by delegates from Bengal, Maharashtra, the Panjab and the Central Provinces, now prepared to obstruct the proceedings. On 26 December they prevented Surendranath Banerjea (q.v.) from seconding the motion for the election of the president; in the open session, Tilak opposed it.

So great was the confusion and the noise this occasioned that T. N. Malvi, chairman of the meeting. suspended the session for the day. When it reconvened on the morrow, Tilak's request to speak was ignored. The rebuff notwithstanding, the latter forced his way on to the rostrum, and even as he did so, the Moderates made a loud demonstration. Tilak's protagonists, not to be out-manoeuvred, joined in the clamour. A Maratha shoe aimed at Tilak flew into the air, hitting Pherozeshah Mehta (q.v.) and Banerjea instead: 'It flew, it fell, and, as at a given signal, white waves of turbaned men surged up the escarpment of the platform. Leaping, climbing, hissing the breath of fury, brandishing long sticks, they came, striking at any head that looked to them Moderate . . . . .'

It was to become the 'legendary symbol of the break-up of the Congress.' Utter confusion prevailed while the police, at the request of Pherozeshah Mehta, cleared the *pandal*. The Congress had split. A graphic eye-witness account of the great encounter notes: 'Restraining the rage of Moderates, ingeminating peace if ever peace ingeminated, Mr Gokhale, sweet-natured even in extremes, stood behind his old opponent, flinging out both arms to protect him from the threatened onset. But Mr Tilak asked for no protection. He stood there with folded arms, defiant: calling on violence to do its worst, calling on violence to move him, for he would move for nothing else in hell or heaven. In front, the white-clad audience roared like a tumultous sea.'

The Moderates retained control. They met immediately afterwards in a convention and drafted the party's new creed stipulating that only those who accepted it would be eligible for membership. The Extremists were thus automatically excluded. Politically isolated, they had, in addition, now to face the full and determined repression that the government unleashed against them. In retrospect, it is evident that the tragedy at Surat was the outcome of a clash of principles as well as of personalities, of mistrust as well as miscalculation. It has been held that while Pherozeshah Mehta had the decisive voice in the counsels of Moderates, Gokhale had to bear the brunt of the schism that followed.

In his account of the Surat session, Aurobindo has given 'himself a considerably larger role' than any other contemporary observer ascribes to him. In his own words, committed to writing many years later, he observed: 'very few people know that it was I (without consulting Tilak) who gave the order that led to the breaking of the Congress and was responsible for the refusal to join the new-fangled moderate convention which were the two decisive happenings at Surat.' According to Bimal Prasad, it 'will not be proper to give the entire credit—if at all it was a credit—for the breaking up of the Surat Congress to Aurobindo.' In whatever light the split may be viewed, a large measure of responsibility for it would appear to belong to the Moderates who were unwilling to compromise and were determined to have their political rivals quit the party ranks if they failed to modify their demands.

At Allahabad, in April 1908, the Moderates adopted a new constitution declaring their political goal to be the 'attainment by India of self-government similar to that enjoyed by other members of the British empire.' Every party member was to pledge himself to political action by constitutional means only. In the aftermath, the Moderates met with declining attendance and enthusiasm in what one of them called a 'rump Congress.'

The Moderates reorganized the Congress without the Extremists. In this they easily succeeded and maintained their exclusive control over the party from 1908 to 1915. But the Extremists had the last laugh, they re-entered the Congress in 1916 and soon established such a dominant position in that body that, in 1918, the Moderates voluntarily seceded from it. The latter were to emerge as the National Liberal Federation (q.v.) to play a small, if marginal role. The secret behind this sequel to the Surat split was that 'while the Moderates controlled the organization in 1907, the Extremists had historical forces on their side, they represented the wave of the future.'

H. W. Nevinson, *The New Spirit in India,* London, 1908, pp. 257-8; Bimal Prasad, 'The Congress Split at Surat' in B. R. Nanda and V. C. Joshi (eds.), *Studies in Modern Indian History,* No. 1, New Delhi, 1972, pp. 144-76; Pardaman Singh, 'The Indian National Congress—Surat Split', *Bengal Past and Present,* LXXXIV, 2, July-December 1965, pp. 121–39; N. L. Chatterjee, 'The Congress session of 1907', *JIH,* 38, 2, April 1960, pp. 131-7; Daniel Argov, *Moderates and Extremists in the Indian Nationalist Movement—1883-1920,* New Delhi. 1967.

Indian States

The Government of India Act, 1935 (q.v.) defined an Indian state as 'any territory, whether described as State, an Estate, a Jagir or otherwise, belonging to or under the suzerainty of a Ruler who is under the suzerainty of His Majesty and not being a part of British India.' Politically, it was a community 'occupying a territory in India of defined boundaries and subject to a common Ruler who enjoyed or exercised, as belonging to him, any of the functions and attributes, of internal sovereignty duly recognized by the Paramount Power.' The latter expression may, broadly, be equated to the British government in India.

Using the above yardstick, the Butler Committee Report (q.v.) and the Simon Commission (q.v.) identified 562 such units; the Joint Parliamentary Committee on constitutional reforms leading to the 1935 Act however referred to 600 such units as states.

Out of a total area of 1,581,410 square miles of pre-Partition India, the Indian states covered 715,964 square miles, approximately 45 per cent of the whole. There were 15 states which had territories of more than 10,000 square miles and 67 ranging between 1,000 to 10,000 square miles; 202 had an area of less than 10 square miles. Of a total pre-Partition population (1941 *Census*) of 389 million, the states claimed 93.2 million or about 24 per cent. Overall, about 25 per cent Hindus, 16 per cent Muslims, 46 per cent Indian Christians and 27 per cent Sikhs lived there. 16 states had a population of over a million; 4 ranged between 750,000 to a million. All these 20 were assigned individual representation (11 of them to 2 or more) in the Indian Constituent Assembly (q.v.), claiming 60 seats, as against 33 allocated to the rest. Of the latter, 13 ranged in population between 500,000 and 750,000; 140, between 25,000 and 500,000. The revenue receipts of 19 states totalled Rs 10 million or more; of 7, between 5-10 million. Some states claimed ancient lineage, as in Rajasthan; others claimed Muslim rulers or viceroys as their forebears. There were still others which the British recognized in the final stages of their consolidation of power in the subcontinent.

Prominent as yellow patches and jostling inextricably with the pink of the British Indian provinces on the map, the states were spread all over the country— from Baluchistan, through Kashmir and Sikkim, down to the deep south. In the north-east there were Cooch Behar, within Bengal, and Manipur, surrounded by Assam. There were several around Chattisgarh and Orissa and, farther south, the large entities of Hyderabad and Mysore. Facing the Indian Ocean were Travancore and Cochin. On the western coast there were Baroda and Kutch, Nawanagar, Bhavnagar and Junagadh. There were also the central Indian states, including Gwalior, Indore, Rewa, in addition to the Rajasthan states of Bikaner, Jaipur, Jodhpur and Udaipur. In U.P., there were the isolated pockets of Tehri-Garwal, Rampur, and Banaras. In the Panjab, there were Patiala, Jind, Nabha. Kapurthala and, further west, Bhawalpur and Khairpur.

The Butler Committee classified them thus: states whose rulers were members of the Chamber of Princes (q.v.) in their own right—108; states whose rulers were represented in that Chamber by 12 members of their order, elected by themselves—127; estates, jagirs and others—327 in all.

Forty states had treaties with the Paramount Power and a much larger number some form of engagement or *sanad* (viz., acknowledgement of concession, authority or privilege generally coupled with conditions proceeding from the Paramount Power); the remainder enjoyed in one form or another recognition of their status by the Crown. The scope of the treaties, engagements or *sanads* covered a wide field. The more important related to mutual amity and defensive alliances providing for territorial integrity, internal sovereignty or protection, prohibition of external intercourse and mutual aggression. There was also the right of the British government to advise in certain circumstances and, in some cases, the payment of tribute. A number of treaties dealt with such matters as exchange, the cession and gift of territory, the cession of jurisdiction for railroad and other purposes, cantonments and Imperial Service troops. There were treaties dealing with important financial and economic matters including postal communications, currency and coinage arrangements, engagements for opium, salt agreements and arrangements for the exchange of postal correspondence, telegraph and telephone lines. There were agreements concerning trade arrangements, construction of canals, leasing of forests and construction of waterways. The rights and obligations arising from these agreements varied, as may be evident, from state to state.

The paramountcy of the British Crown in practice was not co-extensive with the rights of the Crown flowing from the treaties. It was based on treaties, engagements, and *sanads* as supplemented by usage and sufferance and by decisions of the Government of India and the Secretary of State embodied in political practice. The right claimed by the Paramount Power in exercise of the functions of the Crown covered both external as well as internal matters.

The state as a unit had no international existence and thus no power of negotiation or legation. It was the Paramount Power that had exclusive authority of making war or peace or negotiating or communicating with foreign states. The Paramount Power assumed rights and duties and was responsible for implementing its international commitments; the princes were required to give effect to them. The right of the Paramount Power for intervention in internal matters could be exercised for the benefit of the ruler of a state, of India as a whole or to give effect to international commitments. Other reasons for intervention were the prevention of dismemberment of a state; suppression of a rebellion against the lawful ruler; economic growth of India as a whole and offences against natural law or public morality.

In so far as it was responsible for the defence of British India as well as the Indian states, the Paramount Power exercised full control over all matters such as the establishment of cantonments, regulation of the strength of the armed forces of the states, procurement of supplies, free passage of troops, supplies of arms and ammunition.

The Paramount Power had the exclusive right to settle precedence and grant honours as well as regulate ceremonies. It recognized succession and disputes thereof; imposed or remitted *nazrana* or succession duties; took charge of the states where the rulers were minors and provided for their education. Above all, it imposed a duty of loyalty to the Crown.

In the evolution of treaty relationship between the Indian states and the British government extending all the way from the Battle of Plassey (q.v.) to the Partition of the country in 1947, four distinct phases may be easily ear-marked. The first two pertain to the period of the John Company (q.v.); the last two, that of the Crown which succeeded (1858) it. The period witnessed the birth and growth into a mighty instrument of what became the major British instrument for intervention—Paramountcy—and its ultimate demise.

The first phase of the Company's treaty-making activity extends broadly from the morrow of Plassey in 1757 to the close of the first Earl Minto's (q.v.) tenure in 1813. Starting with a desire to confine British interests to trading in and around the territories in which they possessed settlements, it saw the Company emerge as an important political force with ambitious territorial designs. To begin with, the Company, then struggling for a foothold in India, recoiled from the expense and danger of extending its commitments beyond the ring fence of its own territorial acquisitions.

To this general policy of non-intervention, if also non-involvement, Wellesley's (q.v.) tenure (1798-1805) was a notable exception. Strictly enjoined by his political masters at home to keep the peace and not meddle with Indian rulers while at the same time husbanding the depleted resources of the Company, he openly defied the Directors, paying them scant attention. The Governor-General soon persuaded himself that in the then prevalent conditions, the British must become the paramount power in the country. To achieve this objective, he evolved the notorious subsidiary system. Briefly, a state accepting an alliance under this system was not to make war or carry on negotiations with another state without the Company's prior knowledge and consent. In addition, the bigger states were to maintain armies commanded by British officers for 'the preservation of public peace' and their rulers to cede certain territories for the upkeep of these forces. The smaller states, however, were to pay a tribute, in lieu of territory. In return, the Company was to afford protection to one and all against external aggression as well as internal rebellion. In every state that accepted the system, a British Resident was to be installed.

The system was tantamount to what has been aptly described as 'Trojan-horse tactics' in empire-building. It gave the Company a stabilizing authority vis-a-vis the states in as much as the 'Governor-General was present by proxy in every State that accepted it.' More, well-trained bodies of troops were posted in key, strategic positions without any cost to the Company in territories the fidelity of whose rulers was assured.

Wellesley, who had to his credit great successes in Hyderabad, Travancore, Mysore, Baroda and Gwalior, could claim two big assets. One was his brother, Arthur Wellesley, the future Duke of Wellington—a

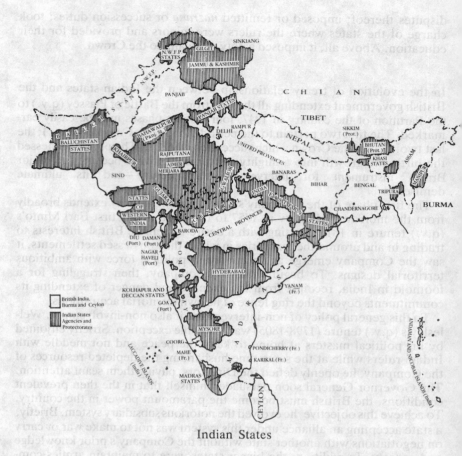

Indian States

master strategist and a most successful commander in battle. Two, there was
a team of gifted men who were ready to hand, men like Malcolm (q.v.),
Metcalfe (q.v.) and Elphinstone (q.v.). The Governor-General's own contribution was no less significant. 'Inspired with imperial projects', he laid
down, as his 'guiding principle', that the British must act and be accepted as
the Paramount Power in India. Nor was that all. Native princes, it followed,
'could only retain the personal insignia of sovereignty by surrendering their
political independence.'

Wellesley's subsidiary system contained within it the essentials of the
framework for princely India as it was developed and maintained under the
John Company. It had two distinct advantages: one, it ensured the states'
fidelity by the presence of the subsidiary force within their territory; two, it

enabled the Company 'to throw forward their military considerably in advance of their political frontier.'

British policy in the second phase, 1813–57, has been called one of 'subordinate isolation.' Even a casual glance at the treaties concluded in the course of these forty odd years would show that such phrases as 'mutual amity', 'friendly co-operation' and the reciprocal obligations of the first phase now give place to compacts exhorting 'co-operation', 'allegiance' and 'loyalty'. There is also the stark fact of the emergence of the British as the dominant power, a development made all the easier by the defeat and discomfiture (1818) of the so-called Maratha confederacy.

Metcalfe, one of the principal architects of the new policy, spelt it out in a lettter written in 1816: 'They [rulers of Rajput states] said that some power in India had always existed to which the peaceable states submitted and in return obtained protection against the invasions of upstart chiefs and the armies of landless banditti, that the British government now occupied the place of that protecting power and was the natural guardian of weak states.' Ten years earlier, he had expressed this idea even more succinctly 'Sovereigns you [the John Company]are, and, as such, must act.'

The first clear, and categorical, expression of the doctrine is in a letter written by David Ochterlony (q.v.) to Metcalfe on 21 March 1820: 'I hope His Lordship [the Governor-General] will in virtue of his Power and Paramountcy forbid all future invasions of Surhoi and fix himself a sum which the Rajah must take.' The Marquess of Hastings (q.v.) had frequently used the term Paramountcy, which he had picked up from his officers. The fact is that his predecessor, Wellesley, had always felt and, what is more, acted as the Paramount Power; and his immediate subordinates adopted much the same attitude. Hastings' own successive campaigns against Nepal, the Pindaris (q.v.) and finally the Marathas carried British dominion over north and central India; in their wake, he extended the Company's supremacy and protection over almost all the Indian states. By the time he left, in 1823, the British empire in India had been formed and its map drawn in all its essentials; every state in India outside the Panjab and Sind (q.v.) had passed under the Company's control.

In the wake of Hastings' treaty settlement, the influence of the Company over the states' internal administration increased. Soon its Residents became transformed 'from diplomatic agents representing a foreign power into executive and controlling officers of a superior government.' Evocative of the authority they now wielded is a letter written by a certain Colonel Macaulay to the Raja of Cochin: 'The Resident will be glad to learn that on his arrival, near Cochin, the Rajah will find it convenient to wait on him.' Even as the British Resident grew in power and importance, the ruler sank into impotence. A percipient observer of the scene in the middle of the nineteenth century noted: 'The sovereigns of what are called independent states live in a state of abject dependence upon the will of the British agency at their various courts. The whole functions of government are in most cases exercised by the Residents, in fact if not in appearance . . .To know the character of his rule and the seeming tendencies of his disposition, it is sufficient to have a knowledge of the capacity and likings of the British Representative.'

This concentration of power *without* responsibility bred corruption and favouritism. In so far as the rulers were guaranteed their position, not only against external aggression but also against internal revolution, there was no incentive for good government and, in fact, a certain premium on indolence. No wonder that 'in most of the States, the revenues were dissipated between the mercenaries of the Residency and the minions of the Court.' Despite the stink they emitted and the pallid story of bad internal administration, the Company viewed the princes as useful adjuncts 'not only as buffers but as cess-pits into which the accumulating miseries of the rest of India would seep and like warring germs prey upon each other . .[as a sink] to receive all the corrupt matter including that which they [the British] discharged.'

The Charter Act of 1833 [Charter Acts 1793–1853 (q.v.)], which put an end to the Company's trading monopoly, marked a radical change in its policy towards the states. Partly with a view to eliminating irritants, especially any future threat to its domain, and partly to augmenting its revenues, the Company desired additional territories. In 1841, the Court of Directors ruled that the Governor-General was 'to persevere in the one clear and direct course of abandoning no just and honourable accession of territory or revenue.' Earlier, Coorg was annexed in 1834 on the plea of maladministration by the ruler. Nine years later Sind was conquered without any justifiable reason. The culminating point was reached by Dalhousie (q.v.), who acquired vast dominions. Through his Doctrine of Lapse (q.v.), he annexed Satara, Nagpur, Jhansi, Sambhalpur and Bhagat. He conquered the Panjab and thereby pushed the country's frontiers to 'the natural limits of India, the base of the mountains of Afghanistan.' Oudh (q.v.) 'whose wretched princes were so absolutely loyal that no excuse could ever be imagined for depriving them of their power' was annexed because, in Dalhousie's words, 'the British government would be guilty in the sight of God and man if it were any longer to aid in sustaining by its countenance an administration fraught with suffering to millions.' The fact is that left to himself, the Governor-General would have been content with taking over the Nawab's administration but the Directors willed otherwise.

Territory apart, Dalhousie swept away the titles and pensions of the deposed rulers or those who died without leaving behind any natural heirs. Nor was his policy an aberration. Annexation, according to William Lee-Warner, an administrator who wrote perceptively on the subject, 'was not a mere incident arising from the peculiar views of a single Governor-General or from a temporary reaction against the king-making policy of the previous administration.' It was a distinct policy, clearly understood by the Court of Directors in England and the Company's Agent in India; Dalhousie was its principal exponent; its clear objective was extension of dominion by absorbing 'the mischievous anomalies' represented by yellow patches on the map.

In 1858 a new policy was born and adumbrated in the Queen's Proclamation of that year: 'We desire no extension of our present territorial possessions and while we will permit no territorial aggression upon our dominions or our rights to be attempted with impunity, we shall sanction no encroachment on those of others. We shall respect the rights, dignity and honour of Native Princes as our own; and we desire that they as well as our own subjects should enjoy that prosperity and that social advancement which can only be secured by internal peace and good government.' The final clause in 'An Act for the Better Government of India' in 1858 [Indian Councils Acts (q.v.)], provided that 'all treaties made by the Company shall be binding upon Her Majesty.' Thus, Dalhousie's policy of vigorous annexation gave place to one of perpetuation of the states as separate entities.

On Canning's (q.v.) recommendation in 1860, *sanads* were granted to rulers under which, in the event of the failure of natural heirs, they were authorized to adopt their successors according to their laws and customs. This was designed to remove mistrust and suspicion and 'to reassure and knit' them closer to the Paramount Power. Annexation was no longer heard of, for the new policy was to punish the ruler for extreme misgovernment and, if necessary, to depose him but *not* to annex his state. This worked towards closer identity—'the territories under the sovereignty of the Crown became at once as important and as integral a part of India' as those under its direct control. Canning's new policy towards the states, it has been suggested, was in the long-term interests of British capital that demanded such change. It was a cautious policy of denuding the native states of their real power and reducing them to no more than satellites of the British imperial government.

Over the next fifty years a machinery was evolved to control the states through the medium of the Political Department which functioned under the direct charge of the Governor-General. It was manned by the Indian Political Service, to whom personnel from the I.C.S. and the army were seconded. It had at its disposal a police force financed jointly by the central government and the states. The Political Department maintained Residents and Political Agents in all the important states or groups of states. The Secretary of State kept a close watch principally over matters affecting the rights and privileges of the rulers. The Crown's relationship with the states was conducted by the Governor-General in Council. In so far as he held charge of the Political Department, the Council left the states' affairs to the Governor-General so that, in fact, the Political Department came 'to assume the position of a government within a government.'

The Political Department and its functionaries exercised compulsive, albeit unwritten, authority. In the smaller states their attitude was one of superiors towards inferiors; even in the bigger states they went much their own way. While inter-state dissensions and jealousies were sedulously fostered, the princes remained, and indeed were made to remain, isolated from British India. Over the years, the Department built up a series of rights not always sustained by treaties. One of these was recognizing succession in the case of natural heirs. In 1884, it had ruled that 'the succession of a native State is invalid until it receives in some form the sanction of British authority'; in 1891, that it was the right and duty of the government 'to settle succession in the protected States of India.' It followed that the Government of India would assume the guardianship of minor princes and arrange for the administration of the state during a minority. More, the ruler did not appear so much to inherit his throne as that he received it as a gift from the Paramount Power. In the result, the rulers found themselves drawn closer to the Crown.

Further encroachments by the Paramount Power were necessitated by the country's overall political and economic consolidation. Subjects such as railroad and telegraph construction, limitation of armaments, coinage and currency, opium policy, administration of cantonments, required an approach that swept away an individual ruler's whims and caprices. The result was that a body of usage influencing the government's relations with the states grew up which 'however benevolent in intention', was 'none the less arbitrary.'

This exercise of authority by the Crown regarding the states, loosely called Paramountcy, became the coping stone of the imperial edifice in India—at once a link as well as a barrier. While on the one hand it provided a nexus between British India and the Indian states and thereby integrated the economic and administrative life of the country, on the other it helped to drive a wedge between the two parts of India. The concept, it has been noted, was ingenious, 'ambiguous to the point of being delightfully vague and flexible.' More, it worked remarkably well—'though only from the British point of view.' Here, if in anticipation, it may be useful to mention the Butler Committee's legitimate boast that paramountcy served the 'shifting necessities' of time.

The impact of World War I on the states was profound. Growing economic and administrative compulsions underlined the need for common action and a common approach to problems. The War demanded the mobilization of resources of the entire country and thus a closer co-ordination between British India and what was called Indian India. There was also increasing emphasis on the unity of the British empire as a whole. All this occurred while constitutional changes in British India went apace and raised important issues. Until 1909 these were largely administrative in nature. The Minto-Morley Reforms (q.v.) led to what was essentially a 'constitutional autocracy' and did not materially alter the shape of things. As John Morley, then Secretary of State for India, confessed: 'Not one whit more than you [viz., Minto, then Governor-General], do I think it desirable or possible or even conceivable to adapt English political institutions to the nations who inhabit India.' With the Motagu-Chelmsford Reforms (q.v.) a decade later, things however were different. Indian India was now more apprehensive about the possible repercussions of the constitutional liberalization in the provinces and its 'fall- out' on neighbouring territories. The British too, for their part, were a little less than sure whether, as a result of the growing administrative unity between the two Indias, the states' role as breakwaters would not be seriously compromised. In the result, a major effort was mounted to convert the states 'into an Indian Ulster by pressing constitutional theories into service.'

The battle was joined on two fronts. One related to bringing the states together on a common platform; it found its ultimate consummation in the birth of the Chamber of Princes. The second was to attempt a codification of political practice to make sure that the rights of the states were not eroded; it led to the appointment of the Butler Committee. Briefly, the Chamber was designed to give counsel to the Viceroy on matters relating to the territories of the states and in areas affecting their relations with British India and the rest of the empire. As for the Butler Committee, it ruled in sum that there could be no transfer of paramountcy to British India without the states' own agreement.

As the political tempo in British India mounted in the two decades between the Simon Commission (q.v.) and the transfer of power (1947), the princes were drawn more and more into the political maelstrom. Although the Simon Commission Report proved stillborn, it may be useful to recapitulate what it had to say in relation to the states. Broadly, it endorsed the recommendations of the Butler Committee that the exercise of paramountcy should be in the hands of the Viceroy, that a serious effort should be made to define 'matters of common concern' between British India and the Indian states, that a standing consultative body comprising representatives from the two sides should deliberate on areas of common ground. 'What we are proposing', the Commission concluded, 'is merely a throwing across the gap of the first strands which may in time mark the line of a solid and enduring bridge.'

At the Round Table Conference (q.v.), the rulers of states avowed their faith in a federation with British India which they would join, even though a small minority among them plumped for a confederation of their own before any association with British India was worked out. Their enthusiasm for the federal scheme however was short-lived. By the time the Government of India Act, 1935 came into operation, nearly all the states began dragging their feet over the Instrument of Accession which each was to execute. All the safeguards provided were not deemed adequate to persuade a sizeable number among them to come forward. This despite the fact that the authority of the federation to perform such functions was to be exercised 'only in respect of those matters accepted by the ruler as federal in his instrument of accession' and subject to such limitations as might be specified in the 'instrument.' Similarly, the rulers' relationship with the Paramount Power was safeguarded by creating the post of a Crown Representative in addition to as well as distinct from that of the Governor-General. It was clearly stipulated that in the conduct of their affairs as members of the federation, the states were to deal with the Governor-General as head of the federal government; in their relationship with the Paramount Power, they were to deal with the Crown Representative.

Lord Linlithgow (q.v.) did his utmost to rope the princes in. His special envoys toured the states in the winter of 1936-7; the latter were reluctant, holding out to win more concessions. By August 1939, on the eve of World War II, the federation, as far as the princes were concerned, seemed as distant as ever. The major political parties in British India, each for diametrically different reasons, were opposed to it too. On 11 September 1939, the Viceroy confessed as much in his address to the Central Legislative Assembly: 'the compulsions of the present international situation and the fact that, given the necessity for concentrating on the emergency that confronts us, we have no choice but to hold in suspense the work in connection with preparations for federation.' This marked a watershed and a useful halt to take stock of the situation. Thus it has been argued that the Princes were doomed even before the Government of India Act, 1935 opened the way for the transfer of substantial powers to elected politicians in India; that by not forcing political reform on the states in the 1920s and later, the Political Department virtually condemned the princely order to extinction. Most writers agree that the fate of the princely states was probably settled much earlier and the halt to constitutional reform in the 1930s only confirmed this.

From now on, the pace of political developments was swift and it may be useful to see where the states stood at each turn of the wheel. The princes were associated with the National Defence Council set up in pursuance of the August 8, 1940 Offer (q.v.). The Council comprised 22 members from British India and 9 from the states. During the Cripps Mission (q.v.), negotiations with the states were at a low key. Sir Stafford Cripps' (q.v.) principal objective, it would appear, was to set up a wartime government at the centre consisting of representatives of British India's political parties. His abortive Mission did however bring home to the states the somewhat uncomfortable realization that if the interests of British India and the states ever came into conflict, the British would almost certainly let the states down.

Taking maximum advantage of the Indian National Congress (q.v.)— Muslim League (q.v.) impasse in British India, the Nawab of Bhopal, as Chancellor of the Chamber of Princes (1944–6), tried hard to forge that body into an effective instrument for developing the rulers into a *third* force. In their negotiations with the Cabinet Mission (q.v.), the states' representatives broadly took the position that Paramountcy could neither be retained by the Crown nor yet transferred to a successor government, and that it should lapse. Additionally, the states could not be forced to join any Union or Unions; that there should be *prima facie* no objection to the formation of a confederation of states if the rulers so desired; and that there should be no interference in their internal affairs by British India. Under the Mission's proposed plan, the states were to retain all subjects and powers other than those ceded to the Union, namely, defence, foreign affairs and communications. In the preliminary stage, they were to be represented in the proposed Constituent Assembly by a negotiating committee; later, by their own representatives, not exceeding 93 members. The mode of the latter's selection was to be determined after consultation between the parties concerned. After the provincial and group constitutions had been drawn up by the three sections of the Assembly, the representatives of the sections and of the Indian states would re-assemble for the purpose of settling the Union constitution.

On 22 May (1946), the Cabinet Mission published a 'Memorandum on States' Treaties and Paramountcy', better known as the 'Memorandum of 12 May.' Three days later the Mission affirmed that the question of how the states' representatives should be appointed to the Constituent Assembly was not a matter for decision by itself but must clearly be discussed with the states. By a resolution of 21 December 1946, the Constituent Assembly appointed a committee to confer with the negotiating committee set up by the Chamber of Princes to (a) fix the distribution of seats in the Assembly not exceeding 93 in number reserved for the Indian states; (b) determine the method by which the representatives of the states should be returned to the Assembly.

Representatives of Baroda, Cochin, Jaipur, Bikaner, Patiala and Rewa took their seats in the Assembly on 28 April 1947. Subsequently, with the exception of Hyderabad, all the remaining states, entitled to individual representation, also sent their representatives. They were returned, in due course, by groups consisting of states which did not have individual representation.

In so far as the states were concerned, the June 3rd Plan (q.v.) stipulated: 'H. M. G. wish to make it clear that the decisions announced above [about the partition of the country] related only to British India and that their policy towards Indian States contained in the Cabinet Mission Memorandum of 12 May 1946 remains unchanged.' The Indian Independence Act 1947 (q.v.) released the states from all their obligations to the Crown. As for the Dominion government in India (as in Pakistan), all it inherited from the Paramount Power was the caveat to Section 7 of the Act which provided for the continuance, until denounced by either of the parties, of agreements between the states and the provincial governments in regard to specified matters such as customs, posts and telegraphs.

On 27 June 1947, the Government of India announced the establishment of a new States Department with Sardar Vallabhbhai Patel (q.v.) as Member in charge and V. P. Menon as Secretary. The existing Political Department and Political Advisor were to give all possible assistance and advice in its formation. It was the States Department that invited all the rulers to accede to the Dominion on the three subjects of defence, foreign affairs and communications, negotiations in this regard being entrusted to the new department and *not* the older Political Department.

Barring Hyderabad, Kashmir and Junagadh, all the states within the geographical limits of India acceded to the Dominion government by 15 August 1947. It may as well be noted here that by 1947 the princely states were, except for perhaps a handful, such an anachronism as could not have survived the British withdrawal. Standstill agreements, the acceptance of which was conditional on the accession of the states concerned, were entered into between the Dominion government and the acceding states. These provided for continuance, for the time being, of all subsisting agreements and administrative assignments, in matters of common concern, between the states and the Dominion of India.

William Lee-Warner, *The Protected Princes of India,* London, 1894 and *The Native States of India,* London, 1910; V. P. Menon, *The Story of the Integration of the Indian States,* Bombay, 1956; S. R. Ashton, *British Policy Towards the Indian States, 1905–39,* London, 1982; S. R. Mehrotra, 'The Problem of the Indian States in historical perspective', in *Towards India's Freedom and Partition,* New Delhi, 1979, pp. 233–50; Conrad Corfield, *The Princely India I Knew: from Reading to Mountbatten,* Madras, 1975; Mihir Kumar Ray, *Princely States and the Paramount Power,* New

Delhi, 1981; Robin Jeffrey (ed.), *People, Princes and the Paramount Power: Society and Politics in the Indian Princely States,* Oxford, 1979; Ian Copland, *British Raj and the Indian Princes: Paramountcy in Western in India, 1857–1930,* London, 1982; *White Paper on Indian States,* Delhi, 1950.

Treaty of Surat (March 1775)

The East India Company's (q.v.) directors in England had over a period of time been asking the Bombay Presidency to acquire among others the strategically located islands of Salsette (q.v.) and Bassein by peaceful means, if possible, or by force, if necessary. Bombay dispatched Thomas Mostyn as its envoy to Poona to gain first-hand intelligence of the intrigues at the Peshwa's court with a view to taking advantage of any opportunity that might come his way. Mostyn who remained at Poona for about three months (November 1767–February 1768) was keen to secure the Peshwa's neutrality as well as prevent his joining either Haidar Ali (q.v.) or Nizam Ali (q.v.). On 17 January (1768) he heard that the Nizam had concluded peace with the Nawab of Arcot and advised that forming a junction with the Marathas 'thus appeared the less necessary.' In February, the Bombay government sent an expedition against Haidar Ali's fleet and possessions on the western coast and instructed Mostyn to secure the Peshwa's neutrality.

The death of Peshwa Madhav Rao (1772) proved to be a godsend for the British, as both Raghoba (q.v.) and Narayan Rao were rival claimants to the now-vacant throne. Raghoba had Narayan Rao murdered in 1773. Knowledge of his involvement in this heinous crime turned the Maratha sardars under Nana Phadnis (q.v.) squarely against him. Raghoba, who had been secretly negotiating with the British, now fled to Surat and sought the Company's help and protection. The Bombay government, only too eager to fish in troubled waters, signed with him a treaty on 6 March 1775 which was ratified ten days latter.

Among its principal terms were the following: (i) the earlier Treaties of 1739 and 1756 between the Company and the Peshwa were confirmed; (ii) a contingent of 2,500 men, including 700 Europeans, was to be placed at the disposal of Raghoba whose candidature for the Peshwaship the English agreed to support in the hope that he would soon establish himself at Poona; (iii) Raghoba agreed to deposit jewellery worth Rs 6 lakhs as security in British custody, as well as pay Rs 1½ lakhs every month for the upkeep of the army; (iv) he undertook to cede to the British, in perpetuity, Bassein, Salsette, 'Jambooseer and Orpad' and the four islands of Karanja, Kanheri, Elephanta and Hog, adjacent to Bombay; (v) Raghoba was to defray such expense as may be incurred in occupying the islands, promising at the same time to secure for the British the Gaekwad's share of revenues for the districts of Broach and Surat; (vi) Maratha raids into Bengal and the Carnatic were to cease; (vii) any peace made by Raghoba with the authorities in Poona was not to exclude the English.

In fulfilment of its terms, Raghoba issued 16 *sanads* transferring the territories and revenues mentioned in the Treaty to the Bombay government. Additionally, he mortgaged his jewellery worth Rs 6 lakhs to the Company; after many vicissitudes, the jewellery was eventually returned to his son Baji Rao II (q.v.) in June 1798.

In pursuance of the Treaty, a British force left Bombay under the command of Colonel Thomas Keating and reached Surat on 28 February, five days after Raghunath Rao had arrived there. Later (15 March), the force accompanied by the Maratha leader left Surat for Cambay by sea (to put down the ministerial armies then camping in Gujarat) and was eventually to reach Poona.

The Treaty settlement was later to involve the Company actively in the prolonged hostilities of the First Anglo-Maratha War (q.v.).

Aitchison, III, pp. 24-32; Dodwell, *CHI,* V, pp. 257-8; G. S. Sardesai, *A New History of the Marathas,* 3 vols, III, pp. 49–51.

Treaty of Surji Arjangaon (1803)

Having detached the Bhonsle raja from the Maratha confederacy, Major-General Arthur Wellesley (later Duke of Wellington) turned all his attention to Daulat Rao Sindhia (q.v.) who, conscious of his inability to face a determined British assault on his dominions, agreed to come to terms.

By the 16-article Treaty of Surji Arjangaon concluded on 30 December 1803, Sindhia agreed to (i) cede all territory between the Ganga and the Yamuna; (ii) give up his control over the imperial cities of Delhi and Agra as well as the Rajput states; (iii) accept an 'accredited minister' at his court—John Malcolm (q.v.) was designated as the first British envoy (Sindhia could also station a vakil at Calcutta); (iv) surrender parts of Bundelkhand, Ahmadnagar, Broach and territories west of the Ajanta hills; (v) recognize the Treaty of Bassein (q.v.) and the validity of such other treaties as the British had concluded with his feudatories; (vi) renounce all claims on the Peshwa, the Mughal Emperor, the Nizam, the Gaekwad and the John Company's (q.v.) administration and agree to accept the latter as a sovereign authority; (vii) promise not to employ in his service 'any Frenchman, or the subject of any other European or American power whether European or native of India, indeed any national', without the consent of the British.

In addition to the above, the Company undertook to (i) provide the Maratha ruler within 2 months a force of six battalions of infantry 'with their complement of ordnance and artillery', its expenses being defrayed from the revenues of lands ceded by Sindhia; (ii) restore to Bhonsle the fort of Asirgarh, the city of Burhanpur, the forts of Powanghur and Dohud and territories in Khandesh and Gujarat depending on these forts.

While there is no schedule as part of the original Treaty, a 'memorandum' is attached to its copy in the archival records. This lists the 'forts, territories and rights in the Doab or the country situated between the Jamna and the Ganges, and all his forts, territories, rights, and interests in the countries which are to the north' of those of the rulers of Jaipur, Jodhpur and Gohad, which Sindhia was to cede to the Company in terms of Article 2 of the Treaty.

It has been held that by concluding the Treaty, Daulat Rao 'from a pinnacle of glory and power plummeted to the lowest depths of misery.' As a matter of fact, D. R.'s singular lack of men and resources led to the supplementary Treaty of Burhanpur (27 February 1804), whereby the British agreed to his request to support him with a subsidiary force. Later, when Holkar took up arms, Sindhia also renewed hostilities to make good his losses. This phase, however, was short-lived for by the Treaty of Mustafapur (22 November 1805), the terms of the earlier Treaty of Surji Arjangaon were confirmed and, in the process, somewhat modified. The earlier defensive alliance was not renewed; Gwalior and Gohad were given back and the Chambal became the new boundary— British dominion lying to its north, Sindhia's to its south. The British also gave up their alliance with the Rajput states, leaving them, as hitherto, at the mercy of the Marathas. This has been viewed by historians as a discreditable deal— for the Rajput chieftains had all along lent the Company unquestioned support. The latter also agreed not to interfere in the territories Sindhia had acquired from Holkar.

In November 1817, on the eve of the Third Anglo-Maratha War (q.v.), the Treaty of Surji Arjangaon was amended a third time. Under the new compact known as the Treaty of Gwalior (q.v.), while Sindhia bound himself to give assistance against the Pindaris (q.v.), the British abrogated a clause of the earlier Treaty which debarred them from concluding alliances with the Rajput chieftains. As may be evident, the latter welcomed the new dispensation.

Aitchison, IV, pp. 221-32; *Roberts*, pp. 258, 265, 285.

Swadeshi Movement in Bengal

A vow was taken at the Town Hall in Calcutta, on 7 August 1905 by those opposed to the Partition of Bengal (q.v.) to 'abstain from the purchase of British manufactures' so long as the Partition resolution was 'not withdrawn'. This was to mark the formal revival of the Swadeshi Movement in Bengal which soon spilled over provincial boundaries and embraced U.P., the Panjab, Maharashtra and other parts of India. Calcutta, however, continued to remain the nerve-centre of activity and gave a lead in the formulation of programmes and the prescription of methods for agitation.

On the occasion of the Mahalaya festival on 28 September a ceremony was held at the Kalighat temple in Calcutta where the worshippers took the following pledge: 'I will not use foreign-made goods as far as practicable, I will not buy at foreign merchants' shops articles that are available at the shops of the people of the country and I will not get anything done by a foreigner which can be done by a countryman of mine.' This may be said to sum up the essence of the Movement— eschewing the use of foreign goods and encouraging indigenous manufactures.

The Movement passed through three phases. In the first, which commenced sometime in the middle of the nineteenth century, the idea of Swadeshi had begun to emerge. In Maharashtra, the columns of the *Prabhakar* proved invaluable to the cause; in Bengal, the Hindu fair provided a platform. Among its principal protagonists, the following may be listed: Dadabhai Naoroji (q.v.) V. N. Mandlik, Ranade (q.v.), G. V. Joshi and Tilak (q.v.) in western India; Bolanath Chunder, Surendranath Banerjea (q.v.) and Krishna Kumar Mitra in Bengal; Madan Mohan Malaviya (q.v.), Murlidhar and the Arya Samaj (q.v.) leaders like Sain Das in northern India. Organizations such as the Sarvojanik Sabha (q.v.) in Poona gave the Movement a big boost. The Movement received a powerful impetus in 1896 from the imposition of countervailing excise duties on Indian cotton goods under pressure from powerful British interests in Manchester. In 1902, Surendranath Banerjea in his presidential address at the Indian National Congress (q.v.) session put forth the view that, in so far as the government 'refused to protect Indian industries by tariff, Indians should resolve to use indigenous goods to stimulate the growth of Indian industry.' In Panjab, one of the planks of Arya Samaj propaganda was Swadeshi.

As may be evident, Bengal's Partition vastly extended the scope and area of the Movement. Industrialists like J. N. Tata (1839-1904) associated themselves with the cause of Swadeshi and the professional classes invested their capital in indigenous enterprises. The Movement was not merely economic but had developed into a political weapon; more, it soon became the expression of India's yearning for political independence and the manifestation of the country's determination to realize its national identity. Swadeshi was the positive aspect of a programme of which Boycott (q.v.) was the defiant and dynamic aspect. The most zealous workers for the Movement were students from schools and colleges.

The Movement had a powerful impact on the import of British goods, especially in textiles. In reverse, a large crop of cloth mills were started with Indian capital. The latter took the fullest advantage of the political upsurge in favour of indigenous goods to make rapid strides. Before long, they wholly displaced Manchester's products in the Indian market.

Swadeshi as well as Swaraj and boycott were interpreted in different ways by the Moderates and the Extremists in the Congress; in the result, the events of 1906-7 culminating in the Surat Split (q.v.) increased the gulf between the two. The Moderates laid stress on the economic aspects of Swadeshi and viewed boycott as a transitory measure to be used cautiously and only for the revocation of the Partition. The Extremists, on the other hand, viewed it as a weapon of political warfare against an imperialist regime. Inevitably, they judged the Movement from the point of view of its effectiveness in rousing national pride and self-reliance. It was noticed that one of the results of the Movement was to make 'the general attitude of the Bengali . . . [both] insolent and aggressive.'

Swadeshi was not a new idea, its philosophy having earlier been accepted in the Panjab (1881) and Maharashtra (1897). Its later importance, however, lay in the fact that it synchronized with an overall national awakening and assumed considerable dimensions. Some historians even maintain that the call it gave was the first historic announcement of India's will to independence and freedom. The nerve-centre of the movement remained in Bengal but its emotional overtones affected the whole country, especially in Maharashtra and the north.

All classes of people— the zamindars, professional groups such as lawyers, teachers and journalists, doctors, students and even the illiterate masses—unhesitatingly answered the call, thereby involving themselves in the Movement. The religious overtones of its appeal did, to an extent, restrict Muslim participation. Politically, Swadeshi became synonymous with opposition to the Partition; Swaraj (self-government) was declared to be its goal and passive resistance the means of achieving it. It was the first bold, organized challenge offered not only to British rule, but also to the then existing nationalist leadership in the country.

The economic aspect of the Movement underlined the need for the establishment of indigenous— Indian-owned and Indian-managed— industry, its adoption of modern techniques and stress on the purchase of its finished products. It took on a new form in the guise of handicraft and cottage industry products and organized attempts to sell these through exhibitions and special shops. The major aim appeared to be to increase opportunities for employment. The boycott of foreign goods was a necessary concomitant of Swadeshi. The foreign items especially earmarked were goods such as Manchester cotton, Liverpool salt, sugar, liquor, enamelled goods, leather-ware, glassware and other articles of luxury.

The positive side of the Movement was reflected in the establishment of 'national education' institutions, a council to work out its programme of implementing Bengali as the medium of instruction, and of guiding education along scientific and technical lines. As the Movement spread all over Bengal, mass meetings were organized and the creed of Swadeshi preached. Huge bonfires of foreign goods were a common sight and students boycotted university examinations. There was an upsurge of patriotic writing in songs, plays, articles and treatises. *Bande Matram* was the new watch-word. The British, who had initially ignored this propaganda, came down heavily as the Movement caught the popular imagination. Student agitators were indicted and their scholarships declared forefeit, while the affiliation of colleges was withdrawn by an official circular. Mass meetings were banned and leaders of the Movement arrested.

With the annulment of the Partition (1911), the Swadeshi Movement in Bengal petered out, albeit not without a sense of national achievement. Industry had received a powerful stimulus and the same applied to (Swadeshi) banking, insurance and inland trade. The national education movement did not long survive except for institutions such as Rabindra Nath Tagore's (q.v.) Shantiniketan. It did none the less leave behind among its enduring memorials the first efforts at promoting a national language through the Eka Lipi Vistera Parishad. Its cultural impact was so impressive that the period has been called 'the golden age that dawned in Bengal.' More than anything else, Swadeshi (and boycott) had come to stay as part of a programme to achieve independence and was made use of by the Congress more than once to pressurize the government.

Sumit Sarkar, *The Swadeshi Movement in Bengal (1903-1908)*, Calcutta, 1973; Leonard A. Gordon, *Bengal: the Nationalist Movement 1876–1940,* Delhi, 1974, pp. 77–100.

Swaraj Party

The foundations of 'the Congress-Khilafat-Swarajya party', later known as the Swaraj (Swarajya) Party, were laid on 1 January 1923. Its ideological birth may be traced to the Gaya session of the Indian National Congress (q.v.) in December 1922, when some leading members (of the Congress) including C. R. Das (q.v.), Motilal Nehru (q.v.), Hakim Ajmal Khan (1863-1927), Vallabhbhai Patel (q.v.) and others, declared that the Non-cooperation Movement (q.v.), as reported by the Inquiry Committee set up by the Congress itself, had been a failure and, with the detention of Gandhi (q.v.), had lost its momentum. They proposed an alternative programme of diverting the Movement from a widespread mass civil disobedience programme to a restricted one which would encourage Congress members to enter the legislative councils established under the Montford Reforms (q.v.) of 1919 and to use moral pressure to compel Authority concede the popular demand for self-government. A large and powerful section under C. Rajagopalachari (q.v.), however, opposed any diversion from Gandhi's known objectives and programmes.

Presently, C. R. Das issued a manifesto announcing the formation of the new party *within* the Congress. While the new party accepted the parent organization as well as its programme, it was prepared to seek entry into the legislative councils and take an oath of allegiance to an alien government. The aims were identical, namely, the achievement of self-government; yet the methods employed would be different. *Inter alia*, an effort was to be made to prevent in the councils all regressive legislation as well as that which was inimical to national interests and retarded the country's progress towards the attainment of its goal of Dominion Status (q.v.). The Swarajists also planned to ensure that the constitution finally adopted would be suited to the 'conditions of the country and the genius of the people.' If the government was uncooperative, they would obstruct normal functioning through the councils. No member was permitted to hold any office under the crown. These objectives were accepted at the special Delhi session of the Congress, which Maulana Mohamed Ali (q.v.) was called upon to guide.

Apart from council entry, the 'New Party' did not regard civil disobedience as the exclusive monopoly of the most ardent non-cooperators—it would favour spontaneous and local civil disobedience without any elaborate preparations. The Swarajists believed that the government could be compelled to yield to public opinion simply by the moral pressure they would exert on it. In retrospect, they were able to destroy the charm that had been woven around the 1919 Reforms by the bureaucracy. In actual fact, their success in the legislatures fell far short of what Gandhi had achieved outside, although they succeeded in pushing some of the (legislative) Liberals out of the fold of the government.

Responsibility for the temporary secession of the Swarajists lay mainly on those who were not prepared to take up civil disobedience when the country wanted it and who allowed the programme to remain cold and soul less without trying to modify it. In the Central Legislative Assembly, they scored a victory over the government now and then, but they could not overcome the disillusionment at the frustrating task they had to perform in that body. Before the Congress passed its boycott resolution at Lahore (1929), many had resigned from the legislatures or advocated that course of action.

It may be recalled that in February 1923, efforts were made by Maulana Abul Kalam Azad (q.v.) to narrow down the differences between the two

Congress factions, and in response thereto the Swarajists agreed to suspend all their activities until April that year. In May, the Congress Working Committee endorsed the Swaraj Party demand to contest elections on its own resources and without using Congress influence. By September, the Congress further agreed not to hinder the Swarajists' efforts in any way. Gandhi continued to oppose council entry after his release in 1924, but relented by 1925 and tried to close the rift in Congress ranks by accepting the Swaraj Party as its political wing. Completely in control of the parent body by 1927, the Swarajists declared their goal to be *Purna Swaraj* or complete independence.

Earlier, in its election manifesto, in October 1923, the party had affirmed its support for agricultural reform and the transfer of power from the bureaucracy to the people. In the following month, it successfully fought elections and routed both the Moderates as well as the Liberals. In the Central Provinces, it gained an absolute majority of seats while in Bengal, the United Provinces, Bombay and Assam its gains were sizeable. Forty-eight members of the party were returned to the Central Legislative Assembly. Here they combined with the Independents, under M. A. Jinnah (q.v.), to form what was called the Nationalist Party.

The Swarajists voiced grievances, demanded the release of political prisoners, an increase in the number of Indians recruited into the Indian Civil Service as well as the defence services. They also attacked government policies, demanding a repeal of repressive laws and exposing its various acts of omission and commission. In the Central Provinces, they were able to throw out the entire budget, compelling the government to use its emergency powers which, in turn, they criticized as undemocratic. Similar moves were initiated in other provinces; in Bengal, a number of resolutions proposed by the Swarajists were carried. In the Central Legislative Assembly the party, led by Motilal Nehru, assured the government of its co-operation provided the latter acceded to the demand for Dominion Status. The government's hesitation in entrusting Indians with democratic responsibilities resulted in Motilal Nehru's famous amendment, adopted by a majority of 76 to 48, which demanded a representative round table conference. The latter was to draw up a constitution protecting the rights of the minorities and a dissolution of the Central legislature, while the scheme itself was to be presented to the British parliament. The ding-dong duel continued till the government was really perturbed when the finance bill was rejected and thrown out in 1925. To pacify the Nationalists and Independents, it set up the Muddiman Committee (q.v.), whose purpose was to inquire into the working of the Reforms of 1919. Some of the Swarajists took the cue and argued that it was unwise to paralyse the entire functioning of the government.

In the ranks of the Swaraj Party now appeared a number of dissenters who wanted to accept office under the government and work with it in 'responsive co-operation.' There were others who wanted to get out of the legislatures; communal tensions had weakened their electoral position. In the elections of 1926 the party lost much ground— faring especially badly in the Panjab and the United Provinces and not much better in Madras, Bengal and Assam. With the Congress adopting the resolution on Civil Disobedience

Movement (q.v.) in 1929. the Swarajists boycotted the legislatures and returned to the parental Congress fold. In 1934 the party was revived again as the political wing of the Congress to contest the elections.

The Swarajist triumph had been short-lived. Though the party did not have any spectacular victories to boast of, it would not be correct to dismiss it as a study in failure. It had re-awakened political consciousness when the Non-cooperation Movement was in the doldrums. Its effective opposition to government measures and a persistent demand for political reform resulted in a positive response from the latter in the form of various inquiry committees. It also provided a good training ground for Indian parliamentarians.

Lal Bahadur, 'The Swaraj Party', unpublished D. Litt. thesis, Agra University, 1958, microfilm, *NMML;* B. B. Misra, *The Indian Political Parties, an historical analysis of political behaviour up to 1947*, Oxtord, 1976, pp. 213–31; Goverdhanbhai J. Patel, *Vithalbhai Patel: life and times*, 2 vols, Bombay, n.d., II, pp. 537–1096; Manoranjan Jha, *Role of the Central Legislature in the Freedom Struggle*, New Delhi, 1972, pp. 80–160; N. C. Kelkar, *The Passing Phase of Politics*, Poona, 1925, pp. 187–204.

Syed Ahmad Khan (1817–98)

Syed (also Sayyid) Ahmad was born in Delhi in April 1817, the scion of a well-established family that had migrated to India in the seventeenth century and held high positions at the Mughal court. He received no formal education but developed an early acquaintance with the world of letters by contributing regularly to an Urdu journal, founded and edited by his elder brother.

Convinced that British rule in India had come to stay, Syed Ahmad preferred service under the John Company (q.v.) rather than the decaying Mughals, as had been the age-old family tradition. To start with, in 1838 he joined the Company's judicial department as a *Sheristadar* at Delhi. A year later he became *Naib Mir Munshi* to Robert Hamilton, then Commissioner of Agra. He passed the *Munsif's* examination with credit and was posted to Mainpuri in 1841. The Mughal court bestowed on him the family title 'Nawab Jawad-ud-Daula'. From 1846 to 1854 he remained at Delhi as *Sadr Amin*. Here he resumed his duties and wrote his famous work *Ansar-e-Sanadid*, mainly dealing with the ruins, architecture and mausoleums of Delhi.

In 1855, Syed Ahmad was transferred to Bijnor as *Sadr Amin* and found time to edit Abul Fazl's *Ain-i-Akbari*, for which Henry Blochman, the famous linguist, later paid him a handsome tribute. At the time of the Rebellion of 1857 (q.v.), Syed Ahmad was at Bijnor and earned the government's gratitude for his work in saving the lives of many Englishmen during those days. In 1858 he wrote his famous pamphlet on the *Causes of the Indian Mutiny*, published in 1863, and later translated into English by Auckland Colvin, a former Governor of U.P.

The alleged repression suffered by Muslims in the post-1857 period resulted in Syed Ahmad's dedication to the cause of uplift and rejuvenation of his community. His plans were designed to serve a dual purpose—to reconcile and promote understanding between the English and the Muslims on the

one hand and to disseminate education among his community, so as to
release it from the clutches of obscurantism, on the other. He also initiated a
programme of liberalization—reinterpreting Muslim religious beliefs and
practices and advocating a more progressive, westernized, approach to
education. His ideal was a Muslim community that could 'maintain steadfast
loyalty to Islam, without sacrificing the rewards of worldly progress.'

Syed Ahmad began by establishing an English-medium school at
Moradabad (*c.* 1861) and later Ghazipur (1864), and the following year
founded a Translation Society for rendering useful English books into Urdu;
it was later moved to Aligarh and rechristened the Scientific Society. To
propagate his ideas, he started the bilingual (English-Urdu) *Aligarh Institute
Gazette*. His programme of educational reform took concrete shape with the
establishment of the Muhammadan Anglo-Oriental College at Aligarh in
January 1877. It rested broadly on the Oxbridge pattern and was the result
partly of an earlier visit (1869-70) to England where Syed Ahmad had
studied the functioning of English educational institutions. The Muhammadan Educational Congress was founded in 1886; after 1890, it came to be
known as the Muhammadan Educational *Conference*. While propagating his
ideas of liberal education among Muslims, Syed Ahmad favoured both
technical education for the community as well as higher education for
women. These measures, for the most part unpopular, swelled the ranks of his
detractors among the orthodox, culminating in a dastardly attempt on his
life.

Convinced like many of his Muslim and Hindu contemporaries of the
usefulness and necessity of British rule in India, Syed Ahmad along with
Raja Jaikishan Das took the lead in establishing (1866) at Aligarh 'the
'British Indian Association, North-Western Provinces.' Though superficially
it would appear to be a branch of the British Indian Association (q.v.), in
fact, it was not. The 'leading aim' was 'to improve the efficiency' of the
British Indian government and 'to promote its best interests by every legitimate means.' The Association was short-lived—surviving a bare four
years— and proved to be a far from active body.

Syed Ahmad's opposition to the Indian National Congress (q.v.) and his
formation, in 1888, of the Indian Patriotic Association stemmed largely from
his conviction that the activities of the former smacked of sedition. The
latter body presently split—a development that led eventually to the formation of the United Indian Patriotic Association.

Initially, Syed Ahmad was convinced that the 'Indian Nation'—'an
amalgam of different religious and cultural communities'—was not mature
for self-rule. He regarded the Muslims in many ways as 'different and
distinct' from the Hindus. His sense of loyalty to his community, the experience of British distrust of that loyalty and his desire to remove that distrust
led him to rule that Muslims should not be associated with the Congress,
even in their individual capacity. In the result, he skirted the idea that
Hindus and Muslims were members of one 'Indian Nation.' It may be added
that he was convinced that the Congress ideology of open competition for
jobs and elected legislative councils would be detrimental to Muslim interests. Orthodox Muslims distrusted Syed Ahmad's advocacy of social
intercourse with Christians, his comparatively liberal interpretation of the

Quran so as to give it a scientific bias, as well as his ideas on socio-religious problems.

Prem Narain has suggested that Sir Syed's political views considerably influenced Muslim attitude to the Congress, that figures about Muslim delegates to Congress sessions speak for themselves. In 1898, the year Sir Syed died, only 10 Muslim delegates attended the Madras session of the Congress and none of them came from outside the Presidency. After his death there was a perceptible tilt among the Muslims towards the Congress. This none the less was short-lived. Nizami has maintained that Sir Syed's 'opposition to the Congress was based not on communal but on practical grounds. He believed that if the Congress demands were accepted, at a time when there was great disparity in the level of education among various sections and communities in India, there would be great imbalance in the life of the country.'

Syed Ahmad applied himself to the more fundamental questions on a priority basis without undermining the ultimate objective of arousing political consciousness. Thus, maintenance of law and order and avoiding risks of the recurrence of 1857 so that backward Muslims might make up for deficiencies of education and material prosperity were the bases of his political views and were synonymous with loyalty to the ruling power.

Divergent views are held as to whether Syed Ahmad was responsible for encouraging communal tendencies in the body politic. His loyalty to the British, whose help he reckoned was indispensable for Muslim uplift, was proverbial. At the same time, his antipathy to the Congress and its functioning was axiomatic; he had argued that Muslim participation in its activities would retard his reform movement. It was this which no doubt earned him the opprobrium of being a communalist. Even though Syed Ahmad did not join hands with the majority community politically, he maintained that differences in political outlook were not incompatible with patriotism and that brotherly relations with Hindus had nothing to do with his political views. Jawaharlal Nehru (q.v.) in his *Discovery of India* has put forth the view that Syed Ahmad opposed the Congress because 'he thought it was politically too aggressive and he wanted British help and co-operation . . . . He was in no way anti-Hindu and communally separatist.' It would be wrong to say that Syed Ahmad even thought of the partition of the country. All that he wanted was 'an Indian freedom in which all minorities— Muslims, Sikhs, Christians and others– would have their legitimate share.'

Syed Ahmad's activities brought warm appreciation from the government; in 1869 he was awarded the CSI and, later, KCSI. He was nominated to the Viceroy's Executive Council for two successive terms (1878-80 and 1881-6). Besides, he was a member of the (Hunter) Education Commission of 1882 (q.v.) as also of the Public Service Commission of 1886. Graham's biography, typical of the British stance, was written while Syed Ahmad was still alive. To use Graham's own words, it was designed to demonstrate 'how a native gentleman of high and distinguished family, but poor, had raised himself to the highest rung' of the 'offical ladder' and emerged as 'the foremost Mohammedan' of his day.

Syed Ahmad gradually handed over charge of his activities to his chosen heir, Mohsin-ul-Mulk (q.v.). The Aligarh Movement (q.v.) continued uninterrupted long after his death in 1898. The impact of Syed Ahmad's personality on his community was profound. The College and the Educational Conference deeply influenced Muslim intellectuals, while his political posture of complete dissociation from the Congress remained a basic tenet of Muslims for many years. Referring to Syed Ahmad, Maulana Mahomed Ali (q.v.) said:

سکھایا ہے تجھیس نے قوم کو یہ شور و شر سارا
جو اِس کی انتہا ہم ہیں، تو اِس کی ابتدا تم ہو

(You alone taught the community [nation] all this agitational approach; if we are the ultimate [in this], then you were the beginning)

Shan Muhammad, *Sir Ahmad Khan: A political biography,* Meerut, 1969 and *Writings and Speeches of Sir Syed Ahmad Khan*, Bombay, 1972; K. A. Nizami, *Sayyid Ahmad Khan*, reprint, New Delhi, 1974; Prem Narain, 'Political Views of Syed Ahmad Khan: Evolution and Impact', *JIH*, LIII, 1, April 1975, pp. 105–53; G. F. I. Graham, *The Life and Work of Sir Sayyid Ahmad Khan*, 5th ed., reprint, Delhi, 1974; Aziz Ahmad, *Islamic Modernism in India and Pakistan 1857-1964*, London, 1967; S. K. Bhatnagar, *History of the MAO College, Aligarh*, Bombay, 1971.

Rabindranath Tagore (1861–1941)

Rabindranath was born at Jorasanko in Calcutta (q.v.) on 7 May 1861, the youngest of the seven sons of Maharishi Debendranath Tagore (1817-1905). Owing to his father's frequent absences from home, Rabindranath's childhood care was in the hands of servants, tutors and school masters. But the vast mansion teemed with creative activity and in the poet's own words, 'we wrote, we sang, we acted, we poured ourselves out on every side.'

Rabindranath belonged to the affluent and cultured Tagore family of Jessore (now in Bangladesh), which had long been settled in Calcutta. Being the youngest child, he was exposed to powerful cultural influences from his early years in the abundant artistic, literary and dramatic activities of the family. Later, he was to imbibe a love for folk song and fable from his numerous students. A truant at school, most of his education was undertaken at home. It was, however, a tour with his father (when Rabindranath was barely 11) to the Himalayas, via Bolpur, that left a lasting impression on his young mind. For Debendranath now instructed him in Sanskrit, English and astronomy and taught him the ancient Hindu religious texts.

Rabindranath revealed his literary talent early, publishing his first poem in the *Tattvabodhini Patrika* in 1874. Four years later, he accompanied his brother Satyendranath, the first Indian to be admitted to the Indian Civil Service, to England where he studied English at University College for a little over a year. Encouraged by other members of the family, he continued to write poems, essays and make translations, most of which were published in the family publications, *Bharati* and *Balak;* he became editor of the latter in 1885.

Rabindranath came to painting much later in life, but his musical talent developed early—soon his songs became very popular; he had started writing verse from the age of 8! His writing was based on a good knowledge of the Sanskrit classics, the English Romantics, notably Shelley, and the poets of Bengal. His early work is said to have been imitative, but with his book *Evening Songs* he broke with tradition and is said to have 'found his genius.'

Entrusted with the management of the family estates, Tagore moved to Shieleida on the banks of the Ganges. The ten years he spent there proved to be the most creative period of his life: a second edition of his collected poems, published in 1903, ran into 13 volumes. The period witnessed, *inter alia*, the emergence of the Bengali short story; most of his writings were published in the *Hitavadi* and, later, *Sadhana*, founded by the poet himself in 1891. Of his novels, several of which were written between 1901 and 1907, the best known is *Gora*. Its theme revolves around educated young Bengalis who had become westernized and broken with their own traditions.

Rabindranath's innate love for the country soon convinced him that the village was the most important unit of political life and that the solution to India's problems lay not so much in a blind imitation of the West as in constructive social work, beginninng with the rural masses. His ideas on education were given shape and form, and practised, on his own children first. Later, in 1901, he opened a school at Shantiniketan (near Bolpur) and presently moved there.

Rabindranath's genius as a writer was recognized in Bengal as well as outside it. In 1912 the Bangiya Sahitya Parishad felicitated him on his fiftieth birthday. The same year he left for England with a prose translation of his *Gitanjali* (literally, 'song offerings'). *Gitanjali* consists tor the most part ot lyrical and devotional poems akin to the songs of the Vaishnavas. Introduced to literary circles by the English painter William Rothenstein, Tagore's work impressed W. B. Yeats, Ezra Pound, A. C. Bradley and other eminent literary personalities of the time, who drew pointed attention to its merit and helped popularize it. A year later (1913) Tagore shot into the limelight as the recipient of the Nobel Prize for Literature. There followed a lecture tour of the United States (1912-13) and England in the summer of 1913. Two years later, a knighthood was conferred on him.

A prodigious writer, Tagore kept experimenting with new forms and has to his credit over 1,000 poems, 2,000 songs and many short stories, plays, dance dramas, essays, works of criticism, novels and translations. He composed music for his songs, popularly known as Rabindra Sangeet, which did not conform to the straitjacket of the ragas. He also emerged as an important painter despite the fact that he took to the art late in life.

Infrequently and unsystematically, Tagore wrote on economic problems, for poverty and the low standard of living of the peasants bothered and depressed him. Education alone, he felt, could change their attitude and outlook. The country's economic and social progress, he further argued, depended entirely on rural rehabilitation. Beginning with co-operative farming and encouragement of cottage industry with only local and indigenous resources, Tagore later felt the need for the import of scientific knowledge and agricultural training. Besides agriculture, village children, he averred, need to be instructed in local arts and crafts so as to occupy them during the idle seasons on the farm. At Sriniketan, a few miles from Shantiniketan, he tried to give shape and form to his ideas of social and economic reconstruction.

Shantiniketan, Sriniketan and Visva Bharati emerged as concrete manifestations of Tagore's educational ideas. Like Rousseau, Tagore advocated
living close to and learning from nature, with the freedom and time to
analyse and synthesize one's own experiences. He also emphasized the use
of the mother tongue as the medium of instruction in creative and practical
activities and the need for a close rapport between the teacher and the
taught. Visva Bharati, established in 1918, saw the fulfilment of his dream
of international brotherhood and understanding, for here students from all
parts of the world were welcome to live and learn together.

Tagore made no claim to originality as a philosopher. He set out not so
much to analyse or speculate about the Indian tradition of the Upanishads
and the Bhagvad Gita as, by expressing it in his own vivid phrases and
homely analogies, to show their relevance to life in the contemporary world.

While still in his teens, Tagore had become a member of the short-lived
albeit radical Sanjivani Sabha, participated fitfully in the activities of the
Indian National Congress (q.v.) but was committed neither to Moderate nor
Extremist ideology. During the 1905 anti-Partition of Bengal (q.v.) agitation his song 'Amar Sonar Bangla' was immensely popular and, at his
suggestion, the mass Rakshabandan ceremony was revived. He abhorred all
violence and withdrew from active politics in 1908. Three years later, 'Janaa
Gana Mana' was composed though not, as is sometimes believed, in honour
of King George V's visit to Calcutta. Through the good offices of his friend
and admirer the English missionary, C. F. Andrews, he met Gandhi (q.v.) in
1915. Though Tagore admired the latter's dedicated patriotism, he became
apprenhensive lest Gandhi's charismatic personality make his followers stop
thinking independently and obey the Mahatma blindly. He disagreed with
Gandhi's attitude towards the Khilafat Movement (q.v.) and the launching
of the Non-cooperation Movement (q.v.).

Though not unaware that it was the mischievous intent of the British
policy of divide and rule that lay at the root of the communal problem,
Tagore firmly held that the Khilafat slogan only provided a transitory unity.
The communal problem, he stressed, could only be solved by improving the
social status of Muslims. Non-cooperation he considered suicidal, and the
charkha and home-spun ineffective, for a poor country. He believed that
non-violence was for those who sought spiritual perfection and that it was
not safe to impose it upon all sorts and conditions of men. Again, the
machine could clothe many more, at lesser cost. Tagore stayed scrupulously
clear of Congress activities after the Jallianwala Bagh Massacre (q.v.),
although as a personal protest he renounced his knighthood in 1919. In
doing so, he expressed the hope that the British would realize their folly and
recant.

In his later years, Tagore was much occupied by his university and with
travel abroad to propagate his ideal of universal human brotherhood and
world unity. It met with diminishing response as the international situation
deteriorated and the horizon grew visibly darker. In 1940, he delivered the
Hibbert Lectures at Oxford, which were published later as the *The Religion
of Man*. At a special convocation, Oxford University conferred upon him an
honorary D. Litt. degree. His *Religion of Man* and *Sadhana* (originally a
series of lectures at Harvard) are at once thoughtful and provocative, while

his essays, *Towards Universal Man* (1961), show him as a social and political theorist.

Gradually, Tagore turned away from nationalism as it had evolved in the West. He viewed it as parochial and divisive and favoured internationalism, world unity and understanding among nations. Asia, he felt, had a special role to play as a leader in fostering the spiritual unity of the world. He elaborated this idea during his tour of Asian countries but failed to find receptive audiences in China and Japan and was only partially accepted by the political leadership in India. Despite his obsession with internationalism in later years, he expressed the hope, a few months before his death (August 1941), that India would soon win back its 'lost heritage.'

In the midst of mounting gloom on the international horizon, Tagore's last message on his eightieth birthday (7 May 1941) breathes his unswerving faith in man: 'As I look around, I see the crumbling ruins of a proud civilization strewn like a vast heap of futility. And yet I shall not commit the grievous sin of losing faith in man. I would rather look forward to the opening of a new chapter in his history after the cataclysm is over and the atmosphere rendered clean with the spirit of service and sacrifice.' He did not long survive his birthday. Towards the end of July he was taken seriously ill and on 7 August life ebbed away, slowly. It was, in the words of a biographer, 'an eventful and glorious life . . . as fascinating as his poetry.'

The basic and most robust characteristic of Tagore's philosophy of life, according to Krishna Kripalani, was 'his emphasis on the development of the human personality and his deep-set conviction that there is no inherent contradiction' between the claims of the so-called opposites—the flesh and the spirit, the human and the divine, love of life and love of God, joy in beauty and the pursuit of truth, social obligation and individual rights, respect for tradition and the freedom to experiment, love of one's people and faith in the unity of mankind. These seeming opposites, the poet argued, could and must be reconciled. 'My mission', Tagore said, 'is to urge for a world-wide commerce of heart and mind, sympathy and understanding and never to allow this sublime opportunity to be sold in the slave market for the cheap price of individual profits to be shattered away by the unholy competition in mutual destructiveness.'

Stephen Hay argues that no man in his own lifetime had tried harder than Tagore to establish this 'world-wide commerce of heart and mind' and historians reviewing his life need to judge him more fairly by what he tried to do than by what he failed to achieve. As with every pioneer, Tagore's vision of the better world to come was so clear and strong that it blinded him to some of the specific realities of the world around him.

'True modernism', Tagore said in his lectures on *Nationalism,* 'is freedom of mind, not slavery of taste. It is independence of thought and action, not tutelage under European school-masters. It is science, but not its wrong application in life.' What Tagore did accomplish, according to Hay, was a first step towards a distant goal. His ultimate hope was that 'gradually world ideals will grow in strength until at last they have fulfilled their highest mission—the unification of mankind.' His unique contribution to this aim was 'to articulate and strive to exemplify in a modern setting the ancient Hindu ideal of man as identical with that eternal and universal Self that dwells in all men.'

Tagore who 'represented the quintessence of Indian culture' and functioned as his country's 'living force' was a man of great sincerity and nobility of character; an aristocrat of gentleness and courage; of grace and wit; a thinker, a dreamer and, above all, a lyrical poet inspired for over sixty years by the wonder of the created world. Three elements come out powerully throughout his life: a profound desire for freedom, both personal and national; an idea of the greatness of Asia and especially India's contribution to the world of the spirit and poetry expressing both of these. The (London) *Times,* in an obituary notice, rated him 'the most notable Indian writer . . . of the whole period of British administration in India.'

Rabindranath Tagore, *My Reminiscences,* London, 1917; Stephen N. Hay, *Asian Ideas of East and West: Tagore and his Critics in Japan, China and India,* Harvard, 1970; Krishna Kripalani, *Rabindranath Tagore: a biography,* Oxford, 1962; Hiranmay Banerjee, *Rabindranath Tagore*, New Delhi, 1971; Marjorie Sykes, *Rabindranath Tagore,* London, 1943; G. D. Khandolkar, *The Lute and the Plough: A Life of Rabindranath Tagore,* Bombay, 1963.

Tara Bai (1675–1761)

The daughter of Hansaji Mohite, better known by his title, Hambir Rao, Tara Bai was born in 1675 and given the name Sita Bai. It was changed to Tarau Saheb or Tara Bai when she was married to Raja Ram, the younger son of Shivaji (1627–80) who had been made captive by his half-brother, Chhatrapati Sambhaji. Earlier, barely a month before his death, Shivaji had married Raja Ram to Janki Bai, a daughter of his *senapati*; he later married Rajas Bai and Ambika Bai.

Tara Bai's conjugal life was not particularly happy for, despite her beauty, she is said to have been 'less lovable and less feminine' than Raja Ram's other consorts. She was feared and respected, but *not* loved, for her 'domineering personality and political sagacity'; in comparison, both Raja Ram and his other wives were 'indifferent mediocrities'.

After the capture and execution of Sambhaji (1689), and the captivity of his son Raja Shahu (q.v.) in the Mughal harem, Raja Ram escaped to Jinji, where Tara Bai soon joined him. It was in that beleaguered fortress that she gave birth, in June 1696, to her one and only child, Shivaji.

Tara Bai's political career may be said to begin with Raja Ram investing her, in a 'nominal capacity', with the work of administration through the *Hakumat-Panah* issued to Ramchandra Nilkanth on the eve of his own departure, in disguise, for Jinji. Even during her husband's lifetime, Tara Bai is said to have acquired a reputation for mastery of 'civil and military' affairs that was the envy of many. This was accentuated by her vaulting political ambition for her son.

On the eve of the fall of Jinji (February 1698), Raja Ram barely escaped, but Tara Bai became a prisoner in Mughal hands. It appears that she was later escorted, unmolested, to Maratha country. Mean while, her husband, hotly pursued by the Mughal army, started on his hazardous northern expedition. He was virtually hunted down and, ill in body, died in March

1700 at Singhgarh, at the youthful age of 30. Tara Bai, by now an experienced hand in the game of political chicanery, outwitted the Amatiya, Ramchandra Nilkanth and, with the help of some powerful sardars, performed the sacred thread ceremony as well as coronation of her son at Vishalgarh. A mere 4-year old, he was designated Shivaji III, while the supreme direction of affairs vested with Tara Bai, the dowager queen.

Pitted in an unequal battle of war and diplomacy with the mighty Aurangzeb (r. 1658-1707), Tara Bai proved to be more than his equal. According to Khafi Khan, by no means a friendly witness, she showed 'great powers of command and government' and in a bitter, 7-year life-and-death struggle with the Mughals displayed remarkable skill: 'Her strategy consisted in widening the area of operations. She had decided to carry war to the settled provinces of the Mughal Empire in the north to relieve pressure on the Deccan. Her field armies and freelance captains were overrunning Khandesh, Berar and Malwa.'

It was a difficult task. Not only had Tara Bai to enlist allies in her crusade against the Mughals, but she also had to keep her own mutually jealous and warring sardars pacified. Impelled by political compulsions inherent in the situation, she continued an indiscriminate award of jagirs even though, in principle, she was opposed to the practice.

The Marathas took the maximum advantage of the difficulties of their adversaries and spread throughout the length and breadth of the Deccan. Even at Ahmadnagar, the Emperor had little peace, for the Marathas hovered around the imperial camp, a bare four miles away. Their forts had yielded not so much to Mughal bravery, as to 'bribing the qiladars'. In the result, the Maratha garrisons held out as long as they could and then surrendered on payment of huge sums of money. Tara Bai's greatness rests largely on her resounding success in this war of wits with the ageing Emperor.

With Aurangzeb's death (1707), and the release of Shahu from Mughal captivity, a new phase opens in Tara Bai's life. To start with, she seemed to have held her own. She declared Shahu an impostor and charged that, by accepting Mughal vassalage, he had bartered away national independence for personal gain. More, she felt that her husband, Raja Ram, had created an altogether new kingdom by his own exertions. Unfortunately for her, the battle of Khed (1707) was won by the generous-hearted and genial Shahu.

Tara Bai's political ambitions knew no bounds. She raised a veritable storm for Shahu by openly challenging his position when Bahadur Shah I (q.v.) came to the south in hot pursuit of his youngest brother, Kam Baksh. She also consolidated her position at Panhala and proclaimed her son a rival Chhatrapati. The internecine struggle was to last another twenty years and, even though Shahu's gains were impressive, Tara Bai fought back and carved out the Kolhapur region as her stronghold. Later, even Shahu is said to have connived at her usurpations beyond the Warna river.

After a diligent scrutiny of all the charges Tara Bai levelled against Shahu, Brij Kishore concludes on a sombre note: 'Her own conduct was inconsistent with her professions . . . her claims and professions were not based on any sound logic or moral principle; she was an adventurer and an opportunist and wanted to cling to power irrespective of the fact whether her cause was just or unjust and whether the means employed to gain her ends were fair or unfair.'

The Maratha civil war itself was complicated by the emergence of the Peshwa, the first incumbent of that office being Balaji Vishwanath (q.v.) who sedulously, even though unwittingly, did mortal damage to the office of Chhatrapati. Nor was that all. For the rise of the Nizam-ul-Mulk (q.v.) as the powerful viceroy of the Deccan and Sambhaji II's alliance with him to spite Shahu, may not have been possible if only Tara Bai had held her hand.

In 1714, in a palace revolution, Tara Bai and her son were captured and taken prisoner. Sixteen years later, in March 1730, she was captured again by Shahu's forces. Later, she was instrumental in bringing about the treaty of Warna (April 1731), when the civil war between the rival houses of Satara and Kolhapur drew to a temporary close. Not that it marked the end of Tara Bai's political ambitions. Her grandson, Ram Raja, whom the childless Shahu had adopted heir on his deathbed, was revealed by her to be a pretender. To be sure, she was keen that he free himself from dependence on the Peshwa and rule by her, and her partisans', advice. In so far as Ram Raja failed to oblige, she denounced him unreservedly. As matters stood, he had proved to be a broken reed: unsteady in matters of state and singularly unsure of himself. By a clever ruse, Tara Bai clamped him into the fort of Satara (November 1750) where, a virtual prisoner, he was to pine away until her own death. It was not until 1763 that Peshwa Madhav Rao restored him to the throne.

Earlier, in October 1751, Peshwa Balaji Baji Rao (q.v.) brought about a compromise with Tara Bai which was solemnly affirmed a year later (September 1752). It stipulated, in essence, that she was to be left to her own devices at Satara, while the Peshwa would not insist on the release of the captive Ram Raja. The compact is said to mark the end of Tara Bai's active political life, although Balaji, aware of her capacity for mischief, paid her all outward deference and occasionally consulted her on important affairs of state. Tara Bai died on 9 December 1761, a few months after installing Balaji Bajirao's second son, Madhav Rao, as the new Peshwa.

Tara Bai was at her best in the struggle against the great Mughal Emperor, Aurangzeb. In waging the fight her 'wonderful powers of organization' as well as 'administrative genius and strength of character' have been uniformly commended. But the half century and more separating that event from her death greatly detracts from her signal achievements; after 1707, she became an 'arch conspirator and the prime intriguer' in much of the mischief, and misfortune, that dogged the steps of Shahu and the first three Peshwas. Truly, there 'must have been something very remarkable about Tara Bai who successfully kept at bay Aurangzeb and three generations of Peshwas. [She turned] her prison in the Satara fort into a citadel of defence against the Peshwa and essayed to rule in her own right by throwing the accredited Chhatrapati into prison .... She died as the only legitimate authority who did her last great service to the nation by investing young Madhavrao as the successor of Balaji as Peshwa'.

Brij Kishore, *Tara Bai and her Times,* Bombay, 1963; G. S. Sardesai, *New History of the Marathas*, 3 vols., Bombay, second impression, 1958, II; R. V. Nadkarni, *The Rise and Fall of the Maratha Empire,* Bombay, 1966.

Tara Singh (Master) (1885–1967)

Nanak Chand later named Tara Singh was born on 24 June 1885 at Haryal, a village in Rawalpindi district where his father, Bakshi Gopi Chand was a village *patwari*. He was educated at Rawalpindi; Khalsa College, Amritsar; Training College, Lahore. In 1902, he embraced Sikhism and was renamed Tara Singh. He soon helped set up the Khalsa High School at Lyalpur, of which he was appointed, in 1908, Headmaster at a nominal salary of Rs 15 per month; hence the sobriquet of 'Master' that stuck.

Tara Singh was actively involved in the Gurdwara Rikabganj agitation; in the subsequent Gurdwara reform movement he emerged as one of his community's outstanding leaders. The Akali movement proved to be a great force in the political awakening of the country. With the passage of the Gurdwara Act 1925, the movement split, Master Tara Singh finding himself in a camp opposed to one led by two other prominent leaders, Giani Sher Singh and S. Mehtab Singh. Later, he opposed the visit of the all-white Simon Commission (q.v.) and voiced strong protest against the Nehru Report (q.v.); it had failed, he argued, to solve the problem of minorities, particularly that of the Sikhs. In the gurdwara elections of 1930, his party emerged as the strongest, a fact which brought him a message of encouragement from Gandhi (q.v.), among others.

Tara Singh was now president of the Shiromani Gurdawara Prabhandak Committee, a strong and well-knit organization that helped him build up his supremacy among the Sikhs. Along with other nationalist leaders, Tara Singh opposed the Communal Award (q.v.) and was pitted against the Khalsa Nationalist Party, led by Sir Sunder Singh Majithia and Giani Sher Singh who had entered into a political alliance with the Unionist Party of Sir Sikandar Hayat Khan. In the result, Tara Singh's position was completely vindicated. In 1941, Sardar Baldev Singh, Master Tara Singh's nominee, was included in the Panjab cabinet.

Tara Singh opposed the Cripps Mission (q.v.) proposals as well as the Cabinet Mission Plan (q.v.) for they failed, he argued, to do justice to the legitimate demands of his community. In 1946, on the eve of Partition (1947), Tara Singh raised his demand for 'Azad Panjab' bounded by the river Chenab on the north-west and the Yamuna to the south-east. His objective was to counter the All-India Muslim League's (q.v.) claim for including the whole of the Panjab in Pakistan. It has been maintained that it was mainly due to his uncompromising attitude that East Panjab was saved for India at the time of Partition.

After Independence, Tara Singh demanded a Panjabi speaking state and fasted unto death to get his demand conceded. He survived the ordeal but was charged with breach of a solemn pledge. All this hastened the end of his political career, for his own protege, Sant Fateh Singh, now supplanted him in the political affections of the Akali party and the Sikh masses. Forlorn and frustrated, Tara Singh died on 22 November 1967.

Politics apart, the Akali leader played a significant role in establishing Khalsa College at Bombay and Guru Nanak Engineering College at Ludhiana. For many years he was editor of the *Akali te Pardesi* and was the author of some booklets, among which three, *Baba Taga Singh*, *Prem Lagan* and *Meri Yad* (mostly autobiographical), may be listed.

Tara Singh, *Meri Yad* (in Panjabi), Amritsar, 1950; Khushwant Singh, *History of the Sikhs*, 2 vols., Princeton, 1966, II ; Sen, *DNB*, IV, pp. 223–25 (Ganda Singh); Fauja Singh, *Eminent Freedom Fighters of Panjab*, Patiala, 1972, pp. 251–3.

Tatya Tope (*c.* 1814–59)

Tatya Tope (popularly, Tantia Topi), whose real name was Ramchandra (also Ram Chandra) Pandurang, rose to prominence during the fateful days of the Rebellion of 1857 (q.v.). The son of Pandurang Rao Tope, a De-shastha Brahmin, he was a retainer of Peshwa Baji Rao II (q.v.) at Bithoor. The story of his martial leanings and service for a short spell in the East India Company's (q.v.) artillery regiment ('Tope' or 'Topi' is an artillery soldier, a gunner) may be accepted with some reservation. It would appear more likely that he had no special military experience and that such training as he received was what an average young man of his standing would have had. The fact is that Tatya's knowledge of fencing and shooting hardly qualified him for the role he was eventually to play; albeit, there is no denying the natural instinct of the Maratha guerilla tactician in him.

Tatya's involvement in the Rebellion began after Nana Saheb (q.v.) was chosen leader of the 'rebel' troops. He took part in the siege of Kanpur and is held responsible by some for the massacre of the British at Sati Chaura Ghat. After Nana's defeat at Kanpur on 11 July by a relieving force under Maj Gen Henry Havelock, Tatya Tope proceeded to Oudh (q.v.). Having reorganized his troops, he attempted, but failed, to recapture Kanpur. Undaunted, he won over the Gwalior contingent to his cause and, in November 1857, defeated Lt Gen Charles Windham and reoccupied Kanpur. A relief force under Colin Campbell ended this short-lived victory. A sense of dedication to the larger cause having been aroused, Tatya Tope decided to relieve Rani Lakshmi Bai (q.v.) who had been besieged at Jhansi. Defeated and repulsed by Maj Gen Hugh Rose, he retreated to Kalpi where Lakshmi Bai joined him. Suffering reverses in two subsequent engagements with a Gwalior contingent, he yet successfully worsted the troops who had held out in defence and took the Gwalior fort.

Tatya's broad plan of action was to rally the Marathas from all over the Deccan; the British, in hot pursuit, did not let this work. In the ensuing battle, Lakshmi Bai was killed and Gwalior fort recaptured. Tatya escaped and, unable henceforth to fight pitched battles, continued attacking enemy strongholds and disrupting communications. Above all, he eluded capture for nearly a year, collecting his own supplies and ammunition by levies whenever he passed through a princely state. Relentlessly pursued by the British, he fought his last battle at Sikar, in Jaipur territory, in January 1859. While in hiding in the Paron jungles near Sipri in the Gwalior state, he was betrayed by his own companion Raja Man Singh of Marwar. Tried by a court martial (15 April 1859), Tatya was found guilty of rebellion and of waging war, and hanged three days later. Its last great surviving leader, with his death came the end of the Rebellion.

Tatya Tope's skill and courage to defy odds needs no emphasis. From central India, he had rushed to Rajasthan in July 1858, from Rajasthan he dashed to Bundelkhand, from Bundelkhand to Madhya Pradesh and from there to Baroda, only to be pushed back to Rajasthan. Rivers such as the Chambal, the Betwa and the Narmada may have hampered the progress of his enemies, but they offered him no serious difficulty. He moved to wherever he chose.

According to a British historian, Tatya Tope was 'by far the biggest brain produced on the native side by the Mutiny of 1857-8. A few more like him and India had inevitably been wrested from the English.' His plans, somewhat Napoleonic in conception, though not in execution, reveal his strategic insight. Two of these—to capture the great rock fortress of Gwalior and to make a dash to the Deccan—were admirably conceived and testify to his great ability as a strategist. Tatya's whole thinking was governed by one important consideration—to destroy the enemy base and to disrupt its line of communications. His tactics were to preserve his army intact and not risk it in a single decisive encounter. At the battles of Kanpur (6 December 1857) and Betwa (1 April 1858) he showed masterly skill in extricating his forces—his aim, in both cases, was to carry out successful rearguard action to cover the retreat of his troops.

Essentially, Tatya Tope lacked the physical courage to lead his men in open combat; his achievement was more as a guerilla leader than as a great commander. His tactics of 'out-manoeuvring and routing his opponents, avoiding pitched battles, escaping after defeat and eluding his adversaries' meant that large British forces remained committed in chasing him across central India into Rajasthan, back and forth. It may be noted that in the end he put the noose around his neck with his own hands and walked fearlessly to the gallows.

Dharam Pal, *Tatya Tope: the hero of India's first war of independence, 1857-59*, New Delhi, 1959; Surendra Nath Sen. *Eighteen Fifty–seven,* New Delhi, 1957, pp. 231–2, 374; Indumati Sheorey, *Tatya Tope*, 2nd ed., New Delhi, 1980.

Theosophical Society (founded 1875)

The Theosophical Society was founded by Madame Helena Petrovna Blavatsky (1831-91) and Colonel Henry Steel Olcott (1832-1907) at New York in 1875. Later, in correspondence with Swami Dayanand (q.v.) who founded the Arya Samaj (q.v.) that very year, a union of the two movements was planned, but this proved very short-lived.

The two theosophist leaders reached India in January 1882 and set up their headquarters at Bombay before moving to Adyar, in Madras. By 1884 the Society had 100 branches in India, apart from several in Europe and America. Four years later, it started an esoteric school to initiate young theosophists into the practice of occultism.

In matters of religion, theosophy essentially believes in the unity of god; his three-fold emanations, viz., a hierarchy of angels; human spirits and sub-human intelligences; and universal brotherhood. Philosophically, it supports the school of idealism, asserts the primacy of consciousness and maintains that the human soul is akin to the divine. Theosophists aim at achieving a universal brotherhood of man by restoring faith in ancient religions and philosophies. Understandably, in India they asserted belief in and defended the entire gamut of Hindu practices. This included the worship of various gods and goddesses, thereby rescuing Hinduism from the derogatory criticism of Western missionaries. Educated Indians who had come to believe that socio-religious customs and polytheism were incompatible with modernization flocked to its meetings. Madame Blavatsky relayed messages she claimed to have received from savants residing in Tibet and frequently demonstrated miraculous powers to convince her followers.

Theosophy purports to be the final truth of the universe, taught in different lands and at different times by various founders of religion and teachers of philosophy, but revealed anew to Madame Blavatsky by certain masters or mahatmas said to live in Tibet and elsewhere. The system and the Society are both of great interest because of the large literature which has sprung up from the movement. Sadly, theosophic accounts both of Madame Blavatsky's life and history of the society are extremely unreliable. Colonel Olcott and other leaders of the movement themselves tell us with the utmost frankness that she was a liar, a habit from which issued the two extraordinary myths of the pretended mahatmas in Tibet and their communication with her, and the legend of her own virginity. Propagated in 1879 and 1885 respectively, these myths have very seriously contaminated theosophic literature.

Madame Blavatsky's approach was criticized by many as mere jugglery and, in the absence of a strong defence, the theosophical movement suffered a temporary setback. It was revived and revitalized by Annie Besant (q.v.) who came out to India in 1893, after the death of Madame Blavatsky. She succeeded Olcott as president of the Society in 1907 and endeared herself to large numbers of people by preaching the wisdom of Krishna and the Gita, thus turning theosophy 'into something specifically Hindu.' In fact, that would largely explain the uniqueness of this movement—it was inaugurated by a non-Indian who was a great admirer of Hinduism.

Theosophy's contribution lay in restoring among Indians a faith in Hinduism, a pride in its ancient cultural heritage and a desire to revive its glorious past. It also popularized oriental books and study in foreign countries. The movement won great popularity for its work in the education of the youth. Its most successful venture was the establishment of the Central Hindu College at Banaras in 1898, which proved to be the nucleus for Banaras Hindu University two decades later. The college apart, the Society opened schools for boys, for women, for the Depressed Classes and took part in the Boy Scouts movement. All in all, it proved to be a powerful force in awakening pride and self-respect among Indians.

Thanks to theosophy, Mrs Besant, later an acknowledged leader in the national movement, commanded a respectable following before she embarked on her political career. For under the aegis of the Society, a social and religious reform movement had taken root all over India, especially in the south.

J. N. Farquhar, *Modern Religious Movements in India*, reprint, Delhi, 1967.

Thugs

In common parlance, a thug is synonymous with a cheat, a cut-throat, a ruffian. In nineteenth-century India, Thugs were a class of professional thieves and assassins who used clever disguise and cunning to rob and kill people. Their gangs operated virtually all over the country, even as far south as Travancore, but were much more dominant in central and northern India.

Claiming a legendary origin, the Thugs were drawn both from Hindu and Muslim ranks. They carried their 'trade' invoking the goddess Kali, Durga or Bhabani, who allegedly consecrated their operative weapons—a scarf, yellow or white in colour, which was used to strangle the victim and a pick-axe for digging his grave. While they carried their depredations over a wide area, there is no evidence to suggest that the Thugs had any central or even regional organization that was hierarchical, nor did they constitute a religious fraternity, much less a social order. The widespread incidence of Thuggee in the nineteenth century may be explained as a natural consequence of the anarchy and confusion prevailing in the preceding decades, the loss of occupation by people with military instincts as a result of the annexation of 'native' states by the British as well as the latter's failure to establish an efficient system of administration. Poverty and destitution were its real and proximate causes.

The *modus operandi* of the Thugs was to disguise themselves as travellers, befriend co-travellers, their prospective victims, and strangle them when off-guard. An operation would extend over a number of days, the victims being hacked to pieces and buried. Their gangs operated during certain seasons, while masquerading as cultivators for the rest of the year. They were usually patronized by rich landlords and chiefs with whom they shared their booty. It has been estimated that in the course of his career a Thug, on an average, murdered 256 people.

Other groups who employed different methods such as the Daturias, Megpannais and the Bengali river Thugs were grouped under the same broad category. Meadows Taylor in his *Confessions of a Thug* gives a lucid account of these criminal bands and of the practices in which they indulged.

William Henry (Thuggee) Sleeman (q.v.) was given charge of eradicating this social menace. In 1835, a separate 'Thuggee and Dacoity Department' was created. A real problem faced by it was the difficulty of securing convictions; to meet this lacuna, the law was amended in 1836 and again in 1843 and 1851.

Thuggee took a long time dying down. By 1840, 3,689 of the clan had been tried; eight years later another 651 had been apprehended. By 1853 there were reports of stray cases only in the Panjab, for by then the evil had been virtually suppressed.

W. H. Sleeman, *The Thugs or Phausigars of India*, Philadelphia, 1839; Philip Meadows Taylor, *Confessions of a Thug: a Novel*, 3 vols, London, 1839; Hiralal Gupta, 'A critical study of the Thugs and their activities', *JIH*, 37, 2, August 1959, pp. 167-77.

Bal Gangadhar Tilak (1856–1920)

Bal Gangadhar Tilak, who was later to emerge as a great patriot and a pioneering radical nationalist, came of an orthodox Chitpavan Brahmin family of moderate means. He was born at Ratnagiri on 23 July 1856. Though an intelligent student and a voracious reader, his obsession with body-building during his school and early college career largely accounted for his failure to take the B.A. examination in the first instance. Later (1876), he took a first class degree in Mathematics and, after two unsuccessful attempts to pass M.A., studied law. As a student, he has been described as 'intelligent...but no book-worm...more in his element in the gymnasium and in the swimming pool than in the class-room...rather taciturn and had a caustic wit...His friends nicknamed him Mr Blunt.'

When a young man, Tilak was 'a high-spirited, wilful lad, not easily amenable to discipline and not readily agreeable' to routine. He had developed 'an independent, precise and analytical intellect: sharp, keen, perspicacious and decisive.' His endurance and imperturbability were equally remarkable. A realist, he was practical in his views and willing to compromise. Tilak's active life of about forty years (1880-1920) falls into two almost equal halves: the first spans the last two decades of the nineteenth century; the second, the first two of the twentieth.

The years 1876-80 constitute a formative period in Tilak's life, when he was keenly observing, registering and formulating some of his political and social ideas and ideals. He had by then tentatively reached the conclusion that British motives were far from altruistic and that political and national awareness could be inculcated among the masses only through popular education resting on private initiative and enterprise. He rejected outright all thought of government service and personal gain and was determined to dedicate himself to the national cause. Fortunately for him, Tilak found other like-minded friends in Vishnu Krishna Chiplunkar (1850-82), Gopal Ganesh Agarkar (1856-95) and Madhavrao Namjoshi (1853-96). Sharing some common ideals, they gave them shape and form in the establishment, on 1 January 1880, of the New English School at Poona with the objective of rejuvenating education. Four years later, an expansion of the school's activities led to the foundation of the Deccan Education Society (q.v.). The aim, *inter alia*, was to administer the school already established and set up more schools and colleges on similar lines.

Tilak's ideals found expression in two popular journals. These were the *Kesari* in Marathi, started in 1881 so as to fight the evils of 'flunkeyism and flattery', which were deemed harmful to the true interests of the country; its English counterpart was the *Mahratta*. The objective, in either case, was to educate public opinion on current political questions. In so far as their viewpoints did not always find favour with the British, the latter considered the two papers not only unfriendly but also unreliable. In fact, Tilak and Agarkar, editors of the two newspapers, were sentenced to a four-month imprisonment each in a defamation suit by Rao Bahadur Madhavarao Wasudeva Barve, Diwan of Kolhapur state. Later, in 1887, the two parted company when Agarkar started a new paper, *Sudharak* (1888). In an 'open letter' published therein (1892), Agarkar charged Tilak with lack of conviction in the social orthodoxies to which he paid lip-service, and with trimming his sails to catch the winds of popularity. It has been held that there was an element of 'personal antagonism' between the two men, which made it impossible for them to co-exist in the Deccan Education Society.

Tilak's education movement was designed to attract self-sacrificing young men with a spirit of dedication and a missionary zeal. However, he soon found himself outnumbered by those who desired no more than an increase in their emoluments and other charges. Divergent views on social reform hastened the impending crisis. Gokhale's (q.v.) interest in and appointment (1890) as Secretary of the Poona Sarvojanik Sabha (q.v.) brought matters to a head. Tilak handed in his resignation (1890) from the Deccan Education Society rather than compromise on principles.

It has been said that his resignation proved to be a gain in the long run; it enabled Tilak to devote his undivided energies to the more congenial spheres of journalism and politics. Later, giving practical shape and form to his ideas, he acquired the sole proprietorship of *Kesari* and *Mahratta* and started private coaching classes in law as an avocation.

The years that followed witnessed Tilak's increasing involvement in political questions. Here he went all the way to attract and involve the masses, convinced that the work of the Indian National Congress (q.v.), confined as it was to elitist groups, would never make much headway. Acutely conscious of the government's policy of openly favouring the Muslims and inciting Hindu–Muslim clashes, as evidenced in the Bombay riots of 1893-4, he tried to arouse national pride and Hindu unity by revitalizing well-known religious festivals, and resurrecting forgotten national heroes. Thus in 1894 he revived the Ganapati festival and two years later the Shivaji festival.

The first Shivaji festival was organized on 5 April 1896 at Raigad, consecrated by the great Shivaji's coronation and death. In the following year the festival was celebrated in June to mark the anniversary of the Maratha leader's coronation. Festivities extending over a week marked these occasions and provided a forum for discourses on Indian culture, religion and nationalism. *Inter alia*, Tilak decried the activities of Christian missionaries and reacted as an orthodox, conservative Hindu would to all social reform legislation. The stance enabled him to identify himself with the illiterate, superstition-ridden masses till such time as they were educated and prepared to accept reform of their own volition. Additionally, his approach was based on an implicit faith that political agitation must take precedence over social reform.

Ranade (q.v.) and his friends feared that the Ganapati festival by arousing the communal consciousness of Hindus was bound to provoke a reaction from the Muslim community. Tilak refused, however, to be impressed by this line of reasoning and maintained that the government was not holding the scales even between the two communities on such contentious issues as processions in public places, music before mosques and cow slaughter. To those who criticized him for playing on the emotions of the masses, his retort was that there was 'no greater folly than the educated people thinking themselves to be a different class from the rest of the society. The educated people can achieve through these national festivals results which would be impossible for the Congress to achieve.'

Tilak was a vehement critic of Behramji Merwanji Malabari (1853-1912). A Parsi social reformer of Bombay, Malabari through his journal, the *Indian Spectator*, was working for child widows; his Age of Consent Bill (1891) had sought to raise the comsummation age of marriage from 10 years (as fixed by the Act of 1860) to 12. It was, at best, a conservative and, as it turned out, ineffective measure, but raised a virtual storm of protest. While its author was no doubt inspired by humane and philanthropic considerations, his crusade came to be exploited by Anglo-Indian apologists anxious to divert public opinion from political questions. Agarkar in *Sudharak* alleged that Tilak was deliberately pampering the ignorant masses to win cheap popularity and leading a crusade in which he did not believe. In reply, Tilak denounced in *Kesari* the superior, almost supercilious attitude of his political adversary and his fellow reformers towards the man in the street.

Tilak's anti-reform stance has made his critics label him a reactionary, a revivalist and a communalist. His recent biographers however absolve him of this charge by reiterating that his prime motivation above all was to unite all Indians, that he was a progressive who desired political and social reform, but differed only in his manner of approach, that he advocated social reform through peaceful evolution rather than through a surfeit of legislation. Social reform, Tilak argued, would automatically follow, once the country was free.

The 1895 Congress session in Poona helped to widen the growing breach between Tilak and Ranade. In the result, the Pherozeshah Mehta (q.v.)— Dinshaw Wacha group in the Bombay Provincial Congress which virtually controlled the all–India organization was further alienated from Tilak. It turned on him by appointing additional secretaries to the reception committee of the Poona Congress—Gokhale being one of them. Tilak did not take the affront lying down—he resigned from the reception committee.

Deeply hurt, Tilak did not take long to strike back. On 14 July 1895 at the annual general meeting of the Poona Sarvojanik Sabha he and his friends who had enrolled new members outvoted Ranade and his cohorts. The new 34–member managing committee, a majority of whom were opposed to social reform, included a bare ten of the outgoing incumbents although Gokhale was elected one of the secretaries. To counter Tilak's obvious triumph, Ranade founded the Deccan Sabha. Presently, thanks to the Bombay government's hostile attitude, the Sarvojanik Sabha lost its effectiveness. Dadabhai Naoroji (q.v.) later remonstrated with Tilak for destroying an institution built up with such infinite patience and dedicated labour over several decades. Nor did Ranade's new Deccan Sabha prove to be a reasonable substitute or alternative; its politics were much too tame!

In the mean while, Tilak had emerged as an unsparing critic of the moderate loyalists and the elitist social reformers. Using the platform of the Sarvojanik Sabha, he waged a relentless war against British economic policies which, he declared, were the primary cause of India's poverty and of the recurrence of famine and epidemics in the country. The plague epidemic of 1896-7 found him violently criticizing the government's anti-plague measures. One unfortunate result was the murder of three concerned British officials, blame for which was put squarely on Tilak's shoulders. He was arrested (27 July 1897) on a charge of sedition, tried and convicted by the majority of a predominantly European jury and sentenced to eighteen months of hard labour.

Tilak emerged stronger from his term in jail. In the Congress, a small but articulate section which did not agree with the prevalent policy of political mendicancy now accepted him as its leader. By no means averse to the use of violent propaganda to oust the British, he lent his full-throated support to the Boycott (qq.v.) and Swadeshi Movements (qq.v.) in Bengal, encouraging similar activities in Maharashtra. 'Action' became his watchword as the Nationalists or Extremists, as they now came to be called, rejected the allegedly weak-kneed policies of inaction pursued by their political adversaries. Soon the Maharashtra-Bengal linkage in terms of the Tilak-Bipin Chandra Pal (q.v.) alliance caused deep concern not only to the government but also to the Congress leadership. Among the latter, Tilak's position had always been that of a dissident, if not a disguised rebel. Pherozeshah Mehta, Wacha and, indeed, the entire group of Bombay Moderates had a lively distrust of him that dated back to the Poona controversies of the 1890's. Its deep-rooted origins lay in ideological as well as temperamental differences.

The image of Tilak as an uncompromising champion of Swaraj, a reckless patriot hurling defiance at the mighty British Raj while the craven Moderates lay low, does less than justice to the subtlety, stamina and suppleness of a consummate politician who managed to survive the bitter hostility of the government for nearly forty years. In the eyes of British officials, Tilak was the archetype of the crafty, seditious Poona Brahmin. They persecuted him with a rare shame-facedness. Thus in 1882, as has been noticed, he had been convicted for publishing a defamatory article against Barve; in 1897, he received a sentence of 12 months for 'seditious writings' in *Kesari*; three years later he was implicated in a suit that dragged its weary course for several years. His worst ordeal, referred to in detail later, came in 1908 when he was deported to Burma and lodged in the Mandalay fort for 6 years. Nor was that the end; after his release in 1914, the Bombay authorities directed all their officers to view him as 'an enemy of the British government' and to consider people associated with him to be 'unfriendly.'

While he occasionally criticized specific policies of the Congress, Tilak posed no challenge either to its broad strategy or its leadership until the turn of the century. 1906, however, marks a turning point. On 7 June (1906) he told a Calcutta audience: 'If you forget your grievances by hearing words of sympathy, then the cause is gone. You must make a permanent cause of grievance. Store up the grievances till they are removed. Partition (of Bengal) (q.v.) grievance will be the edifice for the regeneration of India . . .'

Tilak now wanted the Congress not only to win the support of the English-educated minority which numbered scarcely a million but also to penetrate among many more versed in the vernaculars and even some layers of the country's unlettered 250 millions. He was not prepared to wait until all of them had been educated—a task for which the government had, in any case, neither the funds nor perhaps the political will.

Earlier, in December 1905 at the Banaras session of the Congress, Tilak had forged an alliance with the radicals of Bengal. A year later, with the deepening political crisis, he felt bold enough to openly challenge the Congress establishment. On the eve of the Calcutta session, Gokhale wrote (20 October 1906) of his political adversary that he 'has a matchless capacity for intrigue and he is not burdened with an exacting conscience. His great talents, his simple habits, his sturdy and dauntless spirit and above all the cruel persecution which he has had to bear at the hand of the Government have won for him the hearts of the millions.'

'You could not and would not have treated me so in Bombay', Pherozeshah Mehta told Tilak at the (1906) Calcutta Congress. 'If provoked to it', pat came Tilak's retort, 'we would show you a sample even in Bombay.' A compromise was hurriedly hammered out, the resolutions on the Partition of Bengal, Swadeshi and boycott were rephrased and secured a smooth passage in the open session. The battle was now joined. In the eyes of the Moderates, Tilak was the villain of the peace, his detractors charging him with a deliberate plot to wreck the Congress by the (1907) Surat Split (q.v.). The fact is that no one was more unhappy than Tilak at the turn events eventually took. On 28 December 1907, at the instance of Motilal Ghose (1847-1922) of *Amrita Bazar Patrika*, Tilak tried to appease his political opponents by writing what amounted to a letter of regret and waiving his political opposition to the election of Rash Behari Ghose (q.v.). He invoked the spirit of 'forget and forgive' and offered his co-operation to preserve the unity of the party. However, Motilal Ghose, Tilak's emissary, was 'bowled out' by the Moderate camp. Aurobindo (q.v.), who was in the thick of the fray at Surat, wrote years later that 'to no one was the catastrophe so great a blow as to Mr Tilak. He did not love the do-nothingness of that assembly (the Congress) but he valued it both as a great national fact and for its unrealized possibilities.'

Tilak's detractors, however, are not easily persuaded, Thus it has been suggested that, at Surat, he 'signally failed to discipline his lieutenants, whose hatred of Pherozeshah Mehta, suspicion of Gokhale and contempt for the Moderates as a group were obvious to all.' Lala Lajpat Rai (1865-1928), committed to neither group, wrote 18 months after the Surat fiasco that 'instead of leading his party, Tilak had allowed himself to be led by some of its wild spirits.' On his own testimony, Aurobindo however emerges as the hero: 'Very few people know that it was I without consulting Tilak who gave the order that led to breaking of the Congress.'

The Extremists whom Tilak allegedly led out of the Congress were far from being a homogenous or united group. Thus, there was all the difference in the world between the robust realism of Tilak, the volatile flamboyance of B. C. Pal and the messianic romanticism of Aurobindo Ghosh. And there were Extremists who were ideologically not far from the Moderates, being 'extreme in moderation.' And Moderates who were 'moderate in extremism.' This may be said to be particularly true of Tilak and Gokhale.

In 1908, as in 1897, the British bureaucracy in India was alarmed and traced a direct connection between political terrorism and incendiary writings in the press. Once again, the victim of the panic was Tilak. For articles published in *Kesari* in Poona he was ordered to be tried in Bombay. The news spread and soon the city was in turmoil. Among the charges for the prosecution was that he had attempted 'to terrorize the government by threats open or concealed to the effect that bombs will be thrown . . . .'

The trial itself began on 13 July before Justice Dunbar of the Bombay High Court. On M. A. Jinnah (q.v.) refusing to be his counsel, Tilak defended himself with great courage, skill and dignity. He spoke for 22½ hours, but a packed jury (7 Europeans and 2 Parsis), sentenced him on 22 July 1908 to six years' deportation. An appeal to the Privy Council was rejected in 1909. Contrary to the prevailing impression, the initiative for prosecution had not come from the Secretary of State John Morley, not even from Minto (q.v.), the Governor-General, but from George Clarke, the then Governor of Bombay

His solitary detention in Mandalay left a deep imprint on Tilak's personality. His outlook on life appears to have undergone a metamorphosis and he emerged a more cautious, if milder, politician. Realizing the futility of revolutionary violence, he was now prepared to accept self-government within the British empire as the country's ultimate political goal. Yet, despite his changed outlook, the Moderates continued to distrust him, for he professed his inability to petition for small crumbs. Later, Mrs Annie Besant's (q.v.) efforts to effect a reconciliation between Tilak and Gokhale came to naught, although the latter's death (1915) somewhat simplified the situation.

A pragmatist and practical politician, Tilak soon realized his ineffectiveness outside the larger Congress mainstream. To build a strong political base for that body, he put forth four desiderata: national education, swadeshi, boycott and swaraj. After his release from Mandalay, Tilak was widely acclaimed at the Bombay provincial conference (May 1915), where he advocated the Extremists' re-entry into the Congress fold. He electrified politics in Maharashtra by his Home Rule League (q.v.) and thus, in a rare comradeship with Annie Besant, helped to broaden the hitherto narrow, elitist, political base. Another of his triumphs was the Lucknow session (1916) which he attended accompanied by 300 delegates who travelled with him by special train from Poona. Here he exercised his tremendous influence in persuading the national organization to accept the terms of the agreement between the Congress and the League embodied in the Lucknow Pact (q.v.). It was his 'powerful advocacy and undisputed leadership', we are told, that made the Congress swallow the unpopular demand for separate representation for the Muslims adumbrated in the Pact. It may also be noted that Tilak lent his full support to the Khilafat Movement (q.v.). Thus the charge that he was a communalist need not be taken at its face value.

On social reform, Tilak has been much maligned by interested parties: 'He was not a social reformer. Indeed he was a conservative follower of the Sanatan Dharma. But he strongly objected to an alien government whose powers he wanted to limit and in fact scale down through attrition imposing reforms in matters which affected society so intimately. Such reforms antagonised the orthodox people and because they were opposed by a considerable section of the Hindus remained ineffective make-believe. It was not worthwhile to incur displeasure for such dubious progress.' The fact is that Tilak favoured improvement in the status of women—their participation in public affairs, education and the minimum age of marriage. His ideas about caste distinctions and untouchability were equally clear-cut.

In 1919, Tilak's views as expressed in (Narhar Shivaram) Paranjpe's words were: 'I do not hold that a social reconstruction must be undertaken prior to political emancipation...without the power to shape our own destiny, our national regeneration, in a larger sense cannot in my opinion be effected.' Again, inaugurating (1920) the Congress Democratic Party in 1920, he called for 'the removal of all civic, secular or social disabilities based on caste or custom.'

On the broad problem of cultural modernization, Tilak was a conservative. He had a profound respect for Hindu tradition—religion, philosophy and ethics. Not that he accepted it wholesale: he employed the modern critical and comparative methods of interpretation. Agarkar, as has been noticed, had alleged that Tilak's conservatism was the result of calculation rather than conviction, that he trimmed his sails to catch the winds of popularity. Tilak refuted the charge that his propagation of the Shivaji festival or the congregational twist that he had given to the Ganapati celebrations had any anti-Muslim inspiration.

Tilak's death 'at midnight preceding the dawn' of 1 August 1920 when Gandhi's (q.v.) Non-cooperation Movement (q.v.) was to be launched, was significant.

Tilak's was a multi-faceted, yet extremely controversial, personality. He had admirers who gave him the title of 'Lokmanya' and critics who claimed he was a sedition monger and the 'father of Indian unrest.' He was a scholar with many a learned work to his credit. The *Gita Rahasaya*, which he wrote while in jail, was an adept reinterpretation in which he stressed *Karmayoga* as against the earlier emphasis on Bhakti and renunciation. To broadcast its message, Tilak emphasized that *Karmayoga* is not restricted to the Kshatriyas but extended to all citizens whose bounden duty it was to resist oppression. He directed all his strength and ability into arousing the masses to seek freedom: 'Swarajya is my birthright and I shall have it', he had declared. It was his life's ambition to see India free, even though he did not live to see his ambition fulfilled. He died a bare few months after setting up the Congress Democratic Party to campaign actively for Swaraj.

A perceptive biographer underlines Tilak's monumental contribution to Indian politics: he did 'much more than germinate unrest in the minds of his countrymen. He made it vocal; he gave it shape; he directed it into constructive channels.' Nor was that all. For he was a scholar and thinker to boot: 'the *Gita-Rahasaya* will for ever remain a monument to his scholarship. But he did not merely comment on the Gita; he lived it.'

Tilak's detractors underline the fact that even if he had not died when he did it is doubtful whether he would have taken any new initiatives or suggested any new methods. It has been argued that the extremists had by 1920 run out of steam and even out of ideas and methods. However, Gandhi's obituary notice on Tilak bears a mention: 'A giant among men has fallen. The roar of the lion is hushed. For us he will go down to the generations yet unborn as a member of modern India . . . . .his bravery, his simplicity, his wonderful industry and his love of his country.'

D . V. Tahmankar, *Lokmanya Tilak,* London, 1956; T. V. Parvate, *Bal Gangadhar Tilak,* Ahmedabad, 1958; S. A. Wolpert, *Tilak and Gokhale,* Philadelphia, 1959; I. M. Reisner and N. M. Goldberg, *Tilak and the Struggle for Indian Freedom,* Bombay, 1966; N. G. Jog, *Lokmanya Bal Gangadhar Tilak,* Reprint, New Delhi, 1974; Richard I. Cashman, *The Myth of the Lokmanya: Tilak and Mass Politics in Maharashtra,* Berkeley, 1975; St Nihal Singh, 'Mr Tilak's Work in England', *Modern Review,* XXVI, 4, October 1919, pp. 367-73; D. Mackenzie Brown, 'The Philosphy of Bal Gangadhar Tilak', *JAS,* XVIII, 2, February 1958, pp. 197-206; Sen, *DNB,* IV, pp. 352-6 (Y. B. Chavan).

Tipu Sultan (1750–94)

Tipu, the eldest son of Haidar Ali (q.v.) was born on 10 December 1750 at Devanhalli. Early in life he was initiated into the arts of warfare; in addition, he took to learning languages, mathematics and science. By 1765 he began accompanying his father on his campaigns. During the First Anglo-Mysore War (q.v.), he conducted successfully a diplomatic mission to the Nizam. Later, Tipu was entrusted with the task of recovering territories captured by the Marathas. Between 1774-8 he assisted his father in strengthening and even extending the territorial domain of Mysore. He played a major military role in the Second Anglo-Mysore War (q.v.) and by his victory at Pollur acquired a great deal of self-confidence. In 1782, halfway through the War, his father died and Tipu assumed control. After several engagements with the British—in some of which he was victorious—Tipu finally forced their garrison to surrender (1784). The Treaty of Mangalore (q.v.) which followed was a great victory for the young Sultan.

Not unlike his father, the major part of Tipu's reign was devoted to wars—mainly with a view to keeping the Poligars and his newly-conquered territories under control. After 1784, relatively free from provocation by his powerful neighbours, the Nizam and the Marathas, Tipu weeded out treacherous officers, refractory nobles and the Malabar Christians who had earlier intrigued against him. He had also to quell rebellions in Coorg twice over in the years 1785-6 and punished its inhabitants with allegedly forced conversions and deportations. Meanwhile the Sultan despatched diplomatic missions to the Marathas in the hope of forging an alliance with them. His efforts to prevent a Maratha-Nizam-English coalition were singularly unsuccessful. In the event, in May 1786, the Marathas and the Nizam attacked Mysore. Tipu successfully countered the combined assault, but at the same time realized the impermanence of these victories against continuous Maratha inroads. By April 1787, apprised of Cornwallis's (q.v.) military preparations, he made overtures for peace.

Conscious of his diplomatic isolation nearer home, the Mysore ruler in the years 1784-7 endeavoured to forge a defensive alliance with the French in Mauritius as well as the Sultan of Turkey. In both cases however he drew a blank, for no active support was forthcoming from either; the French sent some artisans and the Caliph (of Turkey) recognized him as an independent ruler! Subsequently, Tipu assumed the title of 'Padshah'. The Sultan had no doubt approached the French to end his isolation at home. They held aloof partly because of their domestic troubles but also in as much as their policy in India lacked any modicum of boldness and foresight. His missions none the less succeeded in promoting commercial relations with the states of the Persian Gulf.

The chiefs of Malabar and the Raja of Coorg had been a perennial source of trouble for the Mysore Sultan, the former incited by the Raja of Travancore, a British protege. When Raja Ram Verma refused to settle some bilateral disputes amicably, Tipu attacked and defeated him (December 1789). Nor was that the end, for by May 1790 Mysore learnt that the British had mobilized their forces. Tipu made desperate efforts to negotiate a settlement and prevent the outbreak of a full-scale war, but the John

Company (q.v.), assured of support by the Marathas and the Nizam, were determined to check his rising power. In the Third Anglo-Mysore War (q.v.), Tipu offered stubborn resistance but failed to follow up his successes, and, in the face of large and superior force, was compelled to seek peace and sign the Treaty of Seringapatam (q.v.) in 1792.

His recovery however was phenomenal. In a little over two years Tipu had paid off his debts, repaired the damage inflicted by the war and was striving hard to improve his civil administration. Though his relations with the Peshwa's court improved with the emergence of Mahadji Sindhia (q.v.), disputed territories (viz. Kurnool) still embittered his dealings with the Nizam. Briefly, his relations with the English were amicable, because of Sir John Shore's (q.v.) policy of non-interference in 'native' Indian States (q.v.).

With Wellesley's (q.v.) induction into office (1798) however, things changed. Pledged to an aggressive and therefore necessarily expansionist policy, the Governor-General found a *casus belli* in Tipu's dealings with the French and his reported alliance with the Afghan ruler, Zaman Shah (r. 1793-99). After making sure that he would get no help either from the Marathas or the Nizam, Wellesley accused Tipu of being in league with the Company's enemies. The Sultan made an unsuccessful appeal to his illusory French allies but, before long, troops under General George Harris poured into Mysore, a two-pronged attack being launched from Madras and Bombay. The Fourth, and as it turned out the last, Anglo-Mysore War (q.v.) was short and decisive. Seringapatam was attacked and captured on 4 May; Tipu fell fighting, defending his fort to the last.

It may be useful to assess the causes for this debacle. After the Third Mysore War, Tipu had reduced his infantry as well as cavalry. The latter was a blunder, for according to Arthur Wellesley, later Duke of Wellington (1769-1852), it was 'the best of its kind in the world'. What was worse, Tipu placed too much reliance on the fortress of Seringapatam. Unlike his father, Tipu's handling of affairs was extremely inept. It may be recalled that in the First War, Haidar Ali had the support of the Nizam; in the Second, he was allied with the French while the Nizam was neutral and the Marathas preoccupied with hostilities with the English. In sharp contrast, in the Third War, Tipu was up against an Anglo-Maratha-Nizam coalition; while in the Fourth there was an Anglo-Nizam hook-up. Additionally, by the time of the Fourth War, the British had developed their own cavalry—in the Third, the Nizam and the Marathas had supported them with their cavalry arm while Tipu had, unadvisedly, reduced his own.

In so far as Pitt's India Act (q.v.) had enhanced the powers of the Governor-General—at the cost of the Council—both Cornwallis as well as Wellesley were able to prosecute the war against Tipu much more vigorously than Warren Hastings (q.v.) had against Haidar Ali. While the latter had fought against the Company alone, Tipu was pitted against the Company as well as the Government of England. Tipu could no doubt have saved himself and his kingdom if he had become a vassal of the Company: 'But he was too independent, too proud, able and energetic to accept such a position. The result was that he lost his life and his throne.'

Although an autocrat, the Sultan was an enlightened and cultured ruler.

He undertook reform with great fervour, applying Western methods where-ever he could, e.g., in the administrative divisions of his kingdom and the creation of a civil service of sorts. In his age there was no sense of nationalism or awareness among Indians as a subject people. In fact, it would be too much to say that he waged war against the English for the sake of India's freedom. The truth is that he fought in order to preserve his own power and independence, that he had warned the Marathas and the Nizam too of British designs. More, he even tried to form a confederacy of Indian rulers to prevent the establishment and later consolidation of British rule.

Tipu's more recent biographers no longer condemn him as a religious bigot. His treatment of the Christians of Coorg has been interpreted as a policy of providing 'political insurance' against further disturbances. While Muslims dominated the army, Hindus were in majority in the revenue and financial departments. Tipu took great interest in commerce and industry, establishing relations with foreign countries and sending trade mission to Iran, Muscat and Kutch, etc. To maintain his power, he organized a mod-ern, well-equipped and well-trained army. His political vision was prophetic, **for he alone recognized the British as a potential danger, nor did he accept** any subsidy or alliance that would compromise the independence of his state. Growing into manhood while his father was engaged in a long-drawn struggle with the British, Tipu alone of all contemporary Indian rulers fought them relentlessly till the very end.

For long the stereotype of Tipu as 'a monster pure and simple', was deliberately so painted as to justify the Company's aggression against him. Proud, vain and imperious—that is what contemporary opinion said of him. Another trait was his great ambition, but this did not consist so much of making new conquests as in retaining the kingdom he had inherited from his father; in making it powerful and prosperous. It has been held that the defeat he sustained in the Third Mysore War 'weakened his government and ruined his country.' In reality, as has been noticed, he recovered remarkably well, making his rule strong and efficient and his state prosperous.

Tipu had a spirit of innovation and curiosity, strongly reminiscent of Akbar (r. 1556-1605). Thus, he instituted a new calendar, a new scale of weights and measures, a new coinage. A Sunni Muslim, religious considera-tions did not influence his state policy, although these did not deter him either from exploiting this factor when necessary. Tipu has been criticized for his anti-English policy, his failure to win the Marathas and the Nizam to his side and his special penchant for cultivating the friendship of the French. The basic cause of English hostility to him was that he was not prepared to become a tributary of the Company. In the result, they no doubt viewed him as an obstacle to their ambitions.

B. Sheik Ali has referred to the Sultan's 'reform of coinage and currency, weights and measures, banking and finance, revenue and judiciary, army and navy' and underlines his evolving an 'efficient system' of administration by 'seeking to apply western methods.' He refutes the charge that Tipu was a fanatic: 'If he crushed the Hindus in Coorg and the Nayars in Malabar, it was because of political reasons; they were in league with the English . . . He was more hostile towards the Nizam than towards the Marathas.' In his fight against the English, Tipu was 'a solitary and lone figure' even though displaying 'the fierceness of a tiger and the tenacity of a bull-dog.' The Sultan made no compromises, 'never deviated from his goal and never ceased to exert his utmost.'

A recent biographer emphasizes that Tipu was 'the last ray of India's hope', being the solitary ruler who from beginning to end saw where British expansion was leading. Another underlines his rare quality of single-mindedness: 'As in the style of his letters, so in the shape of his life—Tipu was always recognizably himself. That is why the English feared him, even beyond reason. And he was a brave man. He may have fallen short in wisdom and foresight, but never in courage, never in aspiration, never in his dream of a united, an independent, a prosperous Mysore.'

Denys Forrest, *Tiger of Mysore*, Bombay, 1970; Mohibul Hasan, *History of Tipu Sultan*, 2nd ed., Calcutta, 1971; B. Sheik Ali, *Tipu Sultan*, New Delhi, 1972; Praxy Fernandes, *Storm over Seringapatam*, Bombay, 1969; Fazal Ahmad, *Sultan Tipu*, Lahore, 1958.

Trade Union Movement

The trade union movement in India began in a small way in 1918. The growth of industry in the country owing to the constraints of foreign rule and lack of encouragement had been haphazard to say the least; in the result, trade unionism grew unevenly. Its political leanings were neither new nor exceptional. Understandably, therefore, the biggest opposition to the movement came from the hostility and oppression of the employers. In the early days, it took many vile forms. To the employers, workers indulging in union activities appeared to be no better than communists or syndicalists; only in the late 1930's was this attitude to undergo a change.

During the years of World War II (1939-45), trade unions were recognized by the government as an important part of the national effort, a fact that made the employers also change their stance. Earlier, the Trade Disputes Act (1929) had provided a machinery to avoid strikes in the first instance and to secure an early settlement of disputes after a strike had been declared.

Modern industry in India, which started way back in the 1850's with cotton textile mills being established in Bombay, Ahmedabad, Sholapur, Nagpur and Kanpur, helped provide employment to a number of people. Similarly, the jute industry had grown in the course of about half a century or so. By 1860 there were more than 60 mills employing a sizeable labour force. A modern steel plant had started production in April that year.

Despite steps towards early industrialization, trade unionism took time to take root. Thus the first Factory Commission of 1875 found workers indifferent to the whole question of conditions of employment and, at the end of the decade (1881-90) when the government conducted an extensive inquiry into trade union and other labour activity, nothing in the nature of unionism was to be found. The opening decades of the twentieth century, however, saw some spurt in labour activity mainly because of active politicization thanks to the Partition of Bengal (q.v.), the Swadeshi Movement (q.v.) and the long, if cruel sentence (1908) on B. G. Tilak (q.v.). In consonance with the times, the methods used by the workers were 'characterized by a tendency to petition, memorialize and seek redress of grievances by mild pressure.'

Industries that had developed by the early part of the twentieth century complained of labour scarcity. There was a fluctuating labour population that consisted largely of semi-agriculturists who migrated hundreds of miles in search of jobs. There were seasonal variations in the supply of labour whch depended upon the condition of the harvest, a fact that introduced an element of uncertainty in labour supply. The Royal (Whitley) Commission on Labour (q.v.) had made the point that workers were pushed, not pulled, to the cities.

The history of labour associations in India goes a fairly long way back. Thus, a Textile Labour Association was formed as early as 1920 in Ahmedabad. Two years earlier, unions had been organized in Bombay. One had been established in Calcutta and another four in Madras—unions of motor car drivers, and oil gas workers. Unfortunately all proved to be short-lived; the moment their grievances were redressed, they ceased to exist. The majority of them had no constitution, no binding rules, no membership proforma and were thus little better than strike committees consisting of a few office-bearers and some paying members.

The first organization on the lines of a modern trade union in India was the Madras Labour Union, organized in 1918. It was an association of textile workers employed in the Buckingham and Carnatic Mills; its organizer was B. P. Wadia, later one of the better-known leaders of the national movement and an associate of Annie Besant (q.v.). In 1921, N. M. Joshi (q.v.) moved a resolution in the Central Legislative Assembly that legislation be enacted for the registration and protection of trade unions. Five years later, the Indian Trade Union Act was passed. It came into operation as from 1 June 1927 and was slightly amended in 1928. Apart from the provisions necessary for administration and penalties, the Act laid down: (1) conditions governing the registration of trade unions; (ii) obligations to which a trade union was subject after registration; and (iii) rights and privileges accorded to registered unions. The term 'trade union' was so defined as to cover combinations both of workers and of employers but not of workers and employees. Persons under the age of 15 were debarred from membership of any registered union.

The administration of the Act was entirely the responsibility of provinces and each provincial government was required to appoint a registrar of trade unions. It was stipulated that any seven or more members of a union may apply for registration but no union could be registered unless at least 50 per cent of its executive body consisted of members actually engaged in the unit or group of units which the union proposed to cover. The general funds of registered trade unions could not be spent on objectives other than those specified in section 15 of the Act, and not on political activity. However, this ban was not total, for provision existed for the creation of a separate political fund. All registered trade unions were required to submit annually to the registrar duly audited statements of accounts on a prescribed proforma. A registered trade union was to be immune from prosecution for criminal conspiracy.

The leadership of the movement was drawn from eminent public men, political leaders and social workers. Some were guided by humane considerations; others, especially the politicians, had the objective of gaining a mass base for their political organization, while the trade unionists' main interest lay in the welfare of workers. Trade unions were also involved in social work and social service, while the communists were to make use of them as training grounds for their cadres and as agencies for promoting party interest.

As noticed earlier, World War II had a powerful impact on the trade union movement. It brought about a radical change in the outlook of industrial workers owing to the 'realization' of what the Whitley Commission later called 'the potentialities of the strike.' The impact of the Western world need not be gainsaid either. Thus the early twenties saw in Europe a growing demand for 'direct action' independent of political parties, to secure workers' control in leading industries. In India, as we will notice, industrial conflict, in the immediate post-World War I period, began in Bombay and was helped by 'political turmoil which added to the prevailing feeling of unrest' that helped to provide 'willing leaders' for the movement.

In October 1920, the All-India Trade Union Congress (AITUC) held its first session in Bombay; Lala Lajpat Rai presided. Its stated objective was 'to co-ordinate the activities of all labour organizations in all trades and in all the provinces in India and generally further the interests of Indian labour in matters economic, social and political.' The number of unions affiliated to it or sympathetic towards its objective was 107. The AITUC continued to grow in importance until it split in December 1929. The first direct result of the establishment in 1919 of the International Labour Organization, an adjunct of the League of Nations, was India's representation at its Conference in Washington, where the tripartite character of the ILO was underlined. Thus there were representatives of governments, of employers and of employees.

The resolution adopted by the Indian National Congress (q.v.) at its Gaya session in 1922 enabled party workers to participate in trade union activities. From 1923 to 1927 there was not much life in the movement; after 1925 however a strong communist influence became noticeable. Two leading members, Dhundiraj Thengdi and S. V. Ghate, both strongly oriented towards Moscow, had emerged, while older leaders such as N. M. Joshi, Diwan Chaman Lall and V. V. Giri had developed close affiliations with the (British) Trade Union Congress, the (British) Labour Party and other social democratic parties in Europe. In 1928 the communists made a powerful bid to capture the AITUC. Their candidate for presidentship, B. D. Kulkarni, was however defeated by Jawaharlal Nehru (q.v.) by a narrow margin. This reverse notwithstanding, the Bombay textile strike, April-October 1928, registered a great victory for the communists and their Mumbai Girni Kargar Union.

The world-wide economic crisis in the late twenties and early thirties had a powerful impact on India. In March 1929 the government arrested as many as 31 prominent trade union leaders who were involved in the Meerut Conspiracy Case. They included communists, Congressmen and members of a youth league. All the accused were charged under section 121 of the Penal Code, with conspiracy 'to deprive the King Emperor of his sovereignty over British India.' Proceedings dragged on for four years and cost Rs 20 lakhs to the exchequer. While the removal of trade union leadership led to a temporary improvement in the industrial climate, 'far from damning communism', the latter movement spread.

A word on how the labour movement was affected by constitutional changes may not be out of place here. It was under the Montford Reforms (q.v.) of 1919 that labour was first given representation in the legislature although industrial labour, by comparison with the employees, was under-represented. The Government of India Act, 1935 (q.v.) however was an improvement. 38 seats were allotted to labour in the Federal Assembly, contrasted with 93 to employers (in the commercial, industrial, mining, planting and land-holding groups) in the various provincial assemblies and 18 in the Federal Assembly.

In 1930, under communist influence, the AITUC decided to boycott the Whitley Commission which had among its members two prominent Indian trade unionists, N. M. Joshi and Diwan Chaman Lall. It further resolved to affiliate itself to the 'League Against Imperialism', the 'Pan-Pacific Trade Union Secretariat' and to appoint the Workers' Welfare League as its agent in Britain. These resolutions were adopted in the teeth of strong opposition by the moderate elements. The latter actually walked out of the AITUC and took away with them 30 unions with a total membership of 95,039. The rump AITUC that met after the secession elected Subhas Chandra Bose (q.v.) as its president and S. V. Deshpande its general secretary. Meantime, the moderates among the trade unionists formed the Indian National Trade Union Federation (INTUF). In July 1931 the communists forced another split and deserted the AITUC to form their own separate TUC. This was accomplished through the intervention of the M. N. Roy (q.v.) group.

The splits notwithstanding, efforts were soon afoot to forge unity in the movement. An active role in this respect was played by the All-India Railwaymen's Federation. Meantime, in 1934, with their TUC fast withering away, the communists returned to the fold of the parent AITUC. In 1936, the INTUF expressed its willingness to affiliate itself as one single organization to the AITUC for a period of one year. In April 1938, at the Nagpur session of AITUC, a further step was taken in this direction. This unity was finally consummated in September 1940 when the INTUF dissolved itself, while the unions formerly affiliated to it now affiliated themselves as separate organizations to the AITUC. N. M. Joshi who had been general secretary of the AITUC in 1929 was elected to the same post in the reunited organization in 1940. Meantime, another experiment in labour relations was launched by the Textiles Labour Association of Ahmedabad under Gandhi's (q.v.) leadership.

A word on the policy of the Indian National Congress towards the trade union movement may be of relevance. The party's 1936 election manifesto pledged itself 'to secure to industrial workers a decent standard of living, hours of work and conditions of labour in conformity, as far as the new economic conditions in the country permitted, with international standards.

suitable machinery for settlement of disputes between the employees and workmen.' In so far as it was known to be sympathetic to the workers' interests, the two years (1937-8) when the Congress was in office in a large number of British Indian provinces witnessed a new upsurge of industrial unrest culminating in a rash of big strikes. Two may be mentioned—the Bengal general strike of the jute workers and the Kanpur textile strike which, beginning in 1937, developed into a general strike in 1939.

During the years of World War II, the communist strangle-hold over the AITUC increased because of the arrest and detention of a large number of Congress leaders. The first Indian Labour Conference was convened in New Delhi in August 1942. There were 22 representatives of the Central and Provincial governments, 11 representing employees and 11 employers. In May 1940, the Rashtriya Mill Mazdur Sangh was established in Bombay with the objective of organizing trade unions on constructive, positive lines; and in May 1947 the INTUC, with the active co-operation and support of all prominent leaders of the Congress and Gandhi's blessings came into being.

From the above it should be evident that, broadly, the history of the trade union movement up to 1945 falls into four parts: (i) Pre-organized trade unionism from its early beginnings to 1918; (ii) organized trade unionism from 1918 to 1926; (iii) militant trade unionism, 1926-39; (iv) moderate trade unionism, 1939-45. It may also be relevant to mention that there are three well-known schools of thought in the trade union movement: the Marxist; the British, represented by Sidney and Beatrice Webb, G. D. H. Cole and Harold J. Laski; and the American, led by John R. Commons. In India, two distinct protagonists of the movement have been Gandhi and Ashok Mehta.

An extremely important facet of the Indian trade union movement has been the fact that nerve-centres of trade union policy-making and action have remained under the control of outside leaders, the majority of whom have been—as indeed they still are—political functionaries subject to various degrees of party discipline. In other words, the backbone of the trade union movement has been constituted by its politically motivated, party-directed, non-labour leadership. In essence, it has been a political labour movement created, weaned and nourished, helped as well as exploited, by external political forces for the purpose chiefly of achieving ulterior political goals.

V. B. Karnik, *Indian Trade Unions: A survey*, 2nd ed., Bombay, 1966; Chamanlal Revri, *Indian Trade Union Movements: An Outline History, 1880-1947*, New Delhi, 1972; S. D. Punekar, *Trade Unionism in India*, Bombay, 1943; Sanat Bose, 'Parties and Politics in Indian Trade Union Movement,' *Social Scientist*, 7, 12, July 1979, pp. 3-12.

Tripartite Treaty (1838)

The Tripartite Treaty was concluded on 26 June 1838 at Lahore between Maharaja Ranjit Singh (q.v.), Shah Shuja, the Afghan Amir living in exile in India since 1809, and the John Company (q.v.), expressly with a view to reinstating the Amir to his throne at Kabul. It was necessitated by (a) the growing Russian influence in Persia, consequent upon the conclusion of the Treaty of Turkomanchai (1828) between the two countries; (b) an obsessive British fear of a Russian advance into India, through Afghanistan, precipitated by the siege of Herat; and (c) the failure of the British envoy, Alexander Burnes (q.v.), to bring about an understanding with Amir Dost Mohammad (q.v.). Its conclusion signalled the final stage of British efforts to forestall Ranjit Singh's aggressive designs on Sind (q.v.) and Shikarpur.

The 18-article Treaty stipulated *inter alia* that (i) Shah Shuja disclaim 'all titles' to territories lying on either bank of the Indus that may be possessed by Ranjit Singh, viz., Kashmir, Attock, Chuch, Hazara, Amb etc.; (ii) tribals 'on the other side of the Khyber' would not be suffered to commit robberies or aggressions; (iii) regarding Shikarpur and Sind, the Shah would abide by 'whatever may be settled as right and proper' between the British and Ranjit Singh; (iv) Shah Shuja was to relinquish 'all claims of supremacy and arrears of tribute' over Sind on condition of payment of a sum by the Amirs which was to be determined by the British. Of this, Rs 1,500,000 was to be paid by him to Ranjit Singh, whereupon article 4 of the earlier Treaty of March 1833 was to be deemed cancelled and intercourse between Ranjit Singh and the Amirs resumed; (v) Ranjit Singh was to furnish the Shah, 'when required', with an auxiliary force composed of Muslims and commanded by one of his principal officers 'in furtherance of the objects contemplated' by the Treaty; (vi) the Shah, 'after the attainment of his object', was to pay Ranjit Singh a sum of Rs 2 lakhs in consideration of the latter stationing a force 'of not less than 5,000 men' within the limits of Peshawar 'for the support of the Shah and to be sent to the aid of His Majesty, whenever the British government, in concert and counsel with the Maharaja shall deem their aid necessary.' Concluded on 26 June, the treaty was ratified on 25 July.

It is said that Ranjit Singh had often used Shah Shuja 'as a scare-crow' to frighten the Barakzais. He had supported the exiled Amir's attempt in 1833-4 to regain his throne. Seven days before the conclusion of the Tripartite Treaty, W. G. Osborne, who had been at the Sikh ruler's court, noted that Ranjit Singh 'refuses to sign the treaty, wishing to stipulate for all sorts of concessions which cannot be granted.' But finally, he did yield.

The Tripartite Treaty was based on the Treaty concluded earlier in 1833 between the Sikh ruler and the exiled Afghan Amir, with the difference that certain modifications were made and four new articles added to the 14 in the original. There was no mention of British troops being employed, while a clause relating to Sind was now deleted. Later, Ranjit Singh was to refuse the British permission to march their troops through his territory.

It has been suggested that the Sikh ruler was more or less coerced into signing the Treaty under veiled British threats. Equally, it is well-known that most of the Maharaja's close confidants were strongly opposed to its conclusion; only two, Faqir Azizuddin and Bhai Ram Singh, are said to have favoured it. The harsh truth is that it was not Ranjit Singh's venture, for Shah Shuja could not be expected to raise a force that would fight with success. It was thus not unnatural for Auckland (q.v.) to conclude that another power's troops would be needed to put Shah Shuja on the throne. Since there was no love lost between Ranjit Singh and Dost Mohammad, the

British aim was to get the Sikh chief to help Shah Shuja with troops to get back his throne while, on their own, they made no commitments. To placate Ranjit Singh, Auckland met him at Ferozepore in November 'seemingly on equal terms.' Ranjit Singh made sure his territory would not be used, that he remained in control of every pass into Afghanistan north of the Bolan. 'From a military point of view he was perhaps master of the situation', yet he could easily see that Shah Shuja would have a dependent throne. 'But if we judge it from the point of the Lahore chief's relations with the British government, the Tripartite Treaty and the subsequent developments in British foreign policy formed the most conclusive evidence of Ranjit Singh's helplessness and his own consciousness of it.' It was the conclusion of the Treaty and developments subsequent thereto that led to a full-scale British invasion of Afghanistan.

Later, the First Anglo-Afghan War (q.v.) resulted in passage through the Panjab of British forces. Nor did the Darbar have an alternative: the War actually 'weakened the independence of the Khalsa by the constant passage of British troops and British convoys through the Panjab.'

As part of overall mechanics, the Amirs of Sind (q.v.) were required to pay Shah Shuja arrears of tribute for over thirty years of his exile (since 1809), out of which, as has been noticed, Rs 1,500,000 were to be paid to Ranjit Singh for his anticipated help to the Shah.

N. K. Sinha, *Ranjit Singh*, 3rd ed., Calcutta, 1951; *Aitchison*, II, pp. 251-6.

Badruddin Tyabji (1844–1906)

A prominent Bombay barrister who rose to be a great nationalist and educationist, Badruddin Tyabji belonged to an affluent, broad-minded family of Muslims. Initially educated in a *madrassa,* and Elphinstone Institution (which later grew into Elphinstone College) in Bombay, he finished his schooling in London. Subsequently, he was to return to London to pursue his law studies and was called to the Bar in 1867. Back in India, he became the first (Indian) barrister to enrol at the Bombay High Court, where he presently made a mark.

Tyabji's interest in and entry into politics may be dated from 1879 when he made his first speech against the abolition of duties on Manchester cotton goods. Subsequently, he took a keen interest in all public questions. In 1882, he was appointed an additional member of the Bombay Legislative Council. Along with Pherozeshah Mehta (q.v.) and Kashinath Telang, he founded the Bombay Association (1885); the three of them were popularly known as 'the triumvirate', and 'the three stars' of Bombay's public life.

Tyabji was a founder member of the Indian National Congress (q.v.). Though unable to attend its first two sessions, he was unanimously elected President for the third session held at Madras in 1887. In his presidential address he reiterated his faith in the Congress ideology and exhorted the Muslims to endeavour to work with other Indians engaged in achieving political reform. Social change, he felt, could best be dealt with by each community independently. Basically, he did not differ from Syed Ahmad Khan's (q.v.) thesis that India was not a nation but 'numerous communities or nations.' Yet, Tyabji argued, the Congress was an organization that attempted to represent every community and its interests. In the result, he took upon himself the task of breaking down Muslim resistance to the Congress. He argued that by co-operating with the latter body, the Muslim community as a whole could guide its policies and activities along national lines.

At the fourth annual session of Congress it was decided, on Tyabji's suggestion, that any subject to which either Hindus or Muslims objected should be dropped for discussion, provided that the objection was sustained by a unanimous vote. He also requested A. O. Hume (q.v.) to prorogue the Congress for five years as he disliked the growing schism among the Muslims themselves, even though they were arrayed in the opposing camp. The Congress could be revived, he averred, as and when dissensions among the Muslims were eliminated. Tyabji made a determined effort to achieve Hindu–Muslim unity, refusing an invitation in 1887 by Syed Ameer Ali (q.v.) to the Mohammadan Political Conference, since it posed itself as a rival to the Congress. He wanted Muslims to consider themselves Indians first and deprecated all attempts to divide the two communities and thereby disrupt peace and amity. He was convinced that in regard to general political questions 'it is the duty of all educated, public-spirited citizens to work together, irrespective of their caste, colour or creed.'

Tyabji had great faith in education as the panacea for all the ills from which the Muslim community suffered. Along with his brother, Camruddin, he formed the Anjuman-i-Islam, a body dedicated to the uplift of the Muslims. He did not however let this come into conflict with his association with the Congress. He took an interest in the actitivites of the M.A.O. College at Aligarh and was President of the Mohammadan Educational Conference in 1903. He advocated the encouragement of female education and the discarding of Purdah—three of his own daughters giving a lead in the matter. A Fellow of Bombay University, he took an active interest in its affairs. As has been noticed, he was also a founder of the most progressive Moslem institution of western India, the Anjuman-i-Islam established 'for the betterment and uplift of Mussalmans in every direction.' He served first as its honorary secretary and from 1890 until his death as its president. He lent full support to the Age of Consent Bill (1891).

On accepting the post of a puisne judge in the Bombay High Court in 1895, Tyabji retired from active politics; in 1903, he officiated as its Chief Justice. It is said that on the eve of his death he had the prospect of being promoted as the first Indian Chief Justice of a High Court. In later years he expressed his disillusionment with the Congress which, he felt, was not maintaining a fair balance between political, social and educational reform, concentrating far too heavily on the political issues. Nor, he argued, was the representative form of government a fit solution for the political ills of an illiterate people. Tyabji died in August 1906 in England, where he had gone for treatment of an eye ailment. Compared to a number of his contemporaries, he died early—at 62: Dadabhai lived to be 92 years; Syed Ahmad, 81; Pherozeshah Mehta, 72.

A biographer has underlined the fact that 'eminent as he was as a lawyer', Badruddin 'will for ever rank among the great judges. The Bar valued his presence . . . for his forensic acumen and his independence . . able, fearless and utterly blind to differences of race or religion . .' His 'greatest service' lay 'in articulating his broad, tolerant outlook' and showing his co-religionists a path 'which would conduce both to national integration and to the preservation of Muslim culture and values.'

Gandhi (q.v.) expressed the view that 'for years [Tyabji] was a decisive factor in the deliberations of the Congress' and, in fact, one of its forefathers. Among Muslims, he was the first to create a secular political consciousness; on the national plane, he was a pioneer in making secularism the Indian ideal.

A. G. Noorani, *Badruddin Tyabji,* New Delhi, 1969; Hussain B. Tyabji, *Badruddin Tyabji: A Biography,* Bombay, 1952; *DNB 1901-11,* pp. 540-1 (Frank Herbert Brown).

Henry Vansittart (1732–1770)

Henry Vansittart, originally appointed a 'writer' in the East India Company (q.v.), came out to Madras in 1746 at the age of 13. A close friend of Robert Clive (q.v.), he also participated in the defence of Fort St. David (1746-7). By 1756 he had been promoted to the rank of a senior merchant. He was assiduous in his work and soon acquired a mastery over Persian, acting as Secretary and Persian translator to the Secret Committee. A year later, he was appointed to the Council at Madras. On Clive's recommendation, Vansittart was made president of the Council, and Governor of Fort William, taking office in July 1760. Between Clive's resignation and Vansittart's assumption of office, the English had become increasingly suspicious of Mir Jafar's (q.v.) incompetence and his attempts to become independent of British control.

An empty treasury further accentuated the difficulties of the British. Emulating the example set by Clive, Vansittart and his select committee connived at and staged another coup, replacing Mir Jafar by his son-in-law, Mir Kasim (q.v.). The latter not only paid Mir Jafar's dues, then in arrears, but assigned to the Company the revenues of the districts of Midnapore, Burdwan and Chittagong, apart from generously lining the pockets of the Governor and his Council. Vansittart tried to sort out amicably subsequent misunderstandings with Mir Kasim about revenue and trade privileges. *Inter alia,* he suggested the payment of 9 per cent duty on private trade by the Company's servants—a rate far below that levied on Indian traders—but even this move was opposed and rejected by a majority in the Council. He tried in vain to reason with them about the just rights and claims of the Nawab and the introduction of some measure of control over English traders and their agents. Complaints poured in from Patna and Dacca whenever and wherever the Nawab's officials insisted on enforcing the law. Finally, Vansittart was compelled to write to the Nawab that the traders would pay 2½ per cent duty on salt only and that the Nawab's officers should not check nor oppress any of them. This provoked Mir Kasim into abolishing the whole system of duties on internal trade.

This abolition was anathema to the Company. Vansittart deputed some

Englishmen to negotiate with the Nawab, but William Ellis, the Company s chief at Patna, spread rumours to the effect that the Nawab was preparing for war. As if in anticipation, Ellis and his men attacked. In the encounters that followed, Mir Kasim was defeated and fled to Oudh (q.v.). Though Vansittart admitted that the English were at fault, it was decided to reinstate Mir Jafar and make fresh demands on him. The Governor himself was said to have been opposed to this course of action; in lieu, he received handsome gifts and payments from the Nawab. But chagrined at the manner in which his policy had been thwarted, he resigned office in November 1764 and left Calcutta (q.v) a month later.

In 1768 Vansittart was elected a Member of Parliament and a year later a Director of the Company. The same year brought his appointment as one of the three supervisors (with Luke Scrafton and Francis Forde) to look into the Company's administration in India, and together they left for India in September 1769. They reached the Cape of Good Hope in December but were subsequently reported lost at sea.

Owing chiefly to his later quarrel with Clive, Vansittart has been treated unjustly by some British writers on Indian history. It is implied that though he was honest and capable he was rather ineffective; 'local greed', it is said, pushed him along the path of aggression and 'local jealousies' neutralized his instincts of integrity. It has also been suggested that his appointment was 'singularly unfortunate' in that he lacked the insight and vigour which his position demanded. Apologists, however, contend that Vansittart's conduct was far-sighted and his dealings with the Nawab distinguished by statesman-like moderation. Had he been vested with sufficient authority, his administration may well have been brilliant, but he found himself, as Warren Hastings (q.v.) did later, at the mercy of a hostile majority in the Council and was able only to indicate the right policy, not to carry it out.

In 1766 he published his 3-volume *A Narrative of the Transactions in Bengal from 1760 to 1764*, a standard work of reference for this period.

DNB, XX, pp. 137-140 (Edward Irving Carlyle); *Buckland*, pp. 434-5; Dodwell, *CHI*, V, pp. 168-73.

Ventura (*c.* 1792–1858)

Born at Modena in Italy, Jean Baptiste Ventura joined the army early, serving under Joseph Bonaparte in a number of campaigns. For four years (1816-20), he is said to have served with Turkish and Egyptian armies. Subsequently, in Teheran he met Allard (q.v.) and, in 1822, the two travelled together to Lahore. Employed by Maharaja Ranjit Singh (q.v.), Ventura was among the first to train Indian troops on the European model. He was continuously engaged in military campaigns, defeated the Afghans (1823), helped annex Kangra (1828) and worsted Syed Ahmed Ghazi (1832) at Peshawar. In the latter year, he was appointed Governor of Derajat and in return agreed to remit Rs 11½ lakhs in revenue annually to Lahore.

Ventura became a General and virtually commander-in-chief of the Darbar's army. During 1837-9 he had been away to Europe and returned just before Ranjit Singh's death. Later, he was posted to Peshawar and entrusted with the task of helping British forces engaged in the First Afghan War (q.v.). In Lahore during the brief reign of Kharak Singh and Nau Nihal Singh he led expeditions to subjugate Mandi and Kulu districts (1841), as a result of which he came to be known as Count de Mandi and, in France, was generally called by that title. Not a mere spectator of court intrigue, he was in active touch with Lord Ellenborough (q.v.) and kept the latter informed about developments at Lahore. He also manoeuvred and manipulated men and affairs so as to suit British designs.

Of all the European military adventurers at the Sikh ruler's court only one attained great wealth. This was Avitabile (q.v.), who held charge of an important district and, in addition, drew a high military salary. Ventura who held charge of a civil district, does not appear to have accumulated much. Allard (q.v.) died poor and Court (q.v.), who was a thrifty man of retiring disposition, also departed with only enough to keep himself in reasonable comfort for the rest of his life.

In 1843 Ventura asked for retirement, leaving Lahore in November 1844 after Sher Singh's assassination. He came back briefly but could find no employment and returned to France where he lived till his death in April 1858.

Buckland, pp. 435–6; Khushwant Singh, *A History of the Sikhs*, vol. I, pp. 258–9.

Henry Verelst (d. 1785)

Henry Verelst entered the service of the East India Company (q.v.) and arrived in Bengal in 1750, aged roughly 16-17 years. His first important assignment was to be placed incharge of the Lakhipur factory in 1757, immediately after the British re-occupied Calcutta (q.v.). He was later taken prisoner by Siraj-ud-Daula (q.v.) and released only after the Battle of Plassey (q.v.). Robert Clive (q.v.) appointed him a member of the Bengal Council; later, in 1764, he became a member of the select committee, an independent body. He strongly disapproved of the behaviour of the Council towards Vansittart (q.v.). His own tenure at Chittagong (1761-5), Burdwan (1765), and Midnapore (1766) witnessed several useful reforms, which brought about an increase in the Company's revenues. Re-appointed to the select committee in 1766, he was confirmed as Governor of Bengal on Clive's departure (1767) and continued to hold that office till the end of 1769.

To the whole of Bengal and Bihar, Verelst extended the supervision of revenue collection by English officers. This fact, according to some observers, led to the hazy beginnings of what was to emerge later as the Indian Civil Service; his detailed instructions to the supervisors, if followed, would have created a dedicated, selfless group of officers. On a complaint received from Shuja-ud-Daula (q.v.), he stopped the Company's servants from trading beyond the three provinces of Bengal, Bihar and Orissa.

Verelst was responsible for financial and military aid to Madras during the First Anglo-Mysore War (q.v.). He apprehended trouble from Shuja-ud-Daula after the latter had augmented his armed forces and, by a new Treaty concluded at Banaras (q.v.), forced the Nawab to cut down his armed strength. He tried to conciliate Janoji Bhosle who was demanding arrears of *chauth* (which had been paid earlier with a view to conciliating him) and endeavoured to obtain Cuttack from him so as to link British possessions on the Coromandel coast. He also tried to pander to the vanity of the Emperor, Shah Alam II (q.v.), who was attempting to go back to Delhi, because he felt it vital to British interests to keep him (Emperor) dependent.

In 1770, Verelst returned to England where prolonged litigation resulting from measures taken during his tenure as Governor took away most of his time, and fortune. Subsequently, he retired to the continent, where he died on 24 October 1785.

Nandlal Chatterjee, *Verelst's Rule in Bengal*, Allahabad, 1939; *DNB*, XX, pp. 248-9 (Gerald Le Grys Norgate); *Buckland*, p. 436.

Vernacular Press Act (1878)

Officially described as 'an Act for the better control of publication in oriental languages', the measure is popularly known as the Vernacular Press Act and became law on 14 March 1878, in all British Indian provinces, except Madras. The problem of seditious writing had existed for a long time, but had been generally ignored. Lytton (q.v.), however, felt no compunction in placing restrictions on the press, since he considered its liberty a gift of the civilized west, misused by 'semi-literate orientals'; in the Indian context, he regarded it 'a great political anomaly.' Unabashed criticism of his Imperial Darbar (q.v.) had fortified Lytton's determination and the Act itself was adopted in a single sitting.

The law was modelled on the Irish Coercion Act of 1870 and stipulated *inter alia* that the printer or publisher of any paper in an *Indian* language was to execute a bond with the government accompanied by a security deposit. Herein the printer or publisher undertook not to publish anything likely to excite ill-feeling among communities or disaffection against duly constituted authority that may lead to a breach of the peace or cause disturbance. In case of non-compliance, the local government was empowered to warn and, on repetition of an offence, confiscate the printing press and deposit. No printer or publisher against whom such action had been taken could have recourse to a court of law. Redress lay only in an appeal to the Governor-General in Council. All this could be avoided if the publisher was willing to submit proofs well in advance of publication. A system of censorship was framed by the government, and one of its officers appointed Press Commissioner to scrutinize all matter before publication.

The Act aroused whidespread and, indeed, bitter reactions throughout the country. Its worst feature was that it smacked of discrimination in favour of English newspapers. The press and political associations alike protested against denial of the right to voice grievances. So successful were these protests that on 7 December 1881, Ripon (q.v.) felt compelled to repeal the Act. He now affirmed that conditions no longer existed to justify its continuance.

Margarita Barns, *The Indian Press*, London, 1940, pp. 281–95; J. Natarajan, *History of Indian Journalism*, Part II of the Report of the Press Commission, New Delhi, 1955, pp. 81-92.

Swami Vivekananda (1863–1902)

Narendra Nath Dutta, better known as Swami Vivekananda, was born in a well-to-do middle class Kayastha family of Calcutta (q.v.) in January 1863. Educated in a mission school and college, he distinguished himself in philosophy. For a time he was a member of the Brahmo Samaj (q.v.) but after 1882 came under the influence of Ramakrishna Parmahansa (1836-86). The latter instinctively saw in the youth the one man destined to propagate his message far and wide. Ramakrishna said: 'Narendra is a boy of very high order. He excels in everything—vocal and instrumental music and studies. Again, he has control over his sense organs. He is truthful and has discrimination and dispassion. So many virtues in one person! Isn't he unusually good?'

Gradually, Narendra Nath came to accept Ramakrishna's teachings, to become his spiritual successor on the master's death in 1886. In accordance with the latter's wishes, he founded a monastic order in a rented house later known as Baranagore Math, the humble beginnings of what later came to be known as the Ramakrishna Math and Mission (q.v.).

On a pilgrimage that took him all over India, Vivekananda was a pained witness to the decadent state of Hindu society caused by the apathy and ignorance of the people. Ruthlessly exploited by the Brahmins, they invariably succumbed to the proselytizing activities of Christians and Muslims. At the same time, he became conscious of the potentialities of the Hindu religion as a binding force to unite the whole of India. To be able to perform that role, Vivekananda felt Hinduism would need a re-interpretation and reinvigoration. In the result, he set out to demonstrate that a belief in Vedanta was not incompatible with the study and practice of scientific knowledge. More, he restated in simple language India's ancient metaphysical thought 'in terms of modern science and philosophy'. As a representative of Hinduism to the Parliament of Religions convened at Chicago in 1893, he made a powerful impact by his personality and exposition of the faith. He introduced Vedanta and its spirituality to the west in a series of brilliant lectures in the United States and, later, in England (1893-5). Vivekananda returned home in January 1897 with three disciples (viz., Madame Louise, Mr Sandsberg and Margaret Noble), and was accorded a rousing welcome wherever he went through the length and breadth of the land.

In due course, Vivekananda planned a programme for the regeneration of his people. They must be taught to rebel, he argued, against malpractices, social and religious customs which weakened individuals as well as society, and establish a new social order based on freedom and equality. The eduation of the masses, with special stress on that of women, as well as borrowing western technical know-how, would, he felt, speedily usher in the modernizing proccess. He had no faith in a social reform programme that catered to an elitist group. He argued that education, with all that it implied, would automatically rid society of its ailments, thereby dispensing with the necessity of a formal movement. Reform, he believed, could be brought about only by uplifting the masses in whom lay imbedded the vitality of a nation. He projected the image of a classless society in which the Brahmins would help elevate the Shudras. In a certain sense, he may be said to have predicted the rise of communism when he declared that the Shudras would rule the fourth epoch of the world.

Vivekananda declared that he would talk of religion only when he succeeded in removing poverty and misery from the country, for religion could
not appease hunger. People must first be properly fed and made physically
strong. The poor should be considered equal to God and service to them
should rate as the best form of worship.

A keen sense of patriotism is evident in all the Swami's writings. His
dream was to restore to India the glory of its bygone days; to achieve this, he
exhorted the youth to dedicate themselves selflessly to the service of their
country, to do away with dissensions and come together on the basis of a
common spiritual heritage for a great cause—the freedom of India from
alien yoke. The young revolutionaries of Bengal were inspired by his teachings and one of his disciples, Sister Nivedita (originally, Margaret Noble),
later served on the executive committee of the Revolutionary Society.

In 1899 Vivekananda visited the United States a second time and while
there opened Vedanta centres in Los Angeles and San Francisco. On his way
home he highlighted the role of Hinduism as a great spiritual force at the
Congress of the History of Religions in Paris (1900). Despite the poor state
of his health, he continued organizing and guiding the activities of the
Mission until his death, in July 1902.

Vivekananda was a religious devotee *par excellence*—a saint of the highest category gifted with extraordinary spiritual powers. Of his erudition
and knowledge, his books and speeches bear eloquent testimony. His literary gifts are best judged by his writings in Bengali, which are not voluminous, for he generally wrote in English; his prose writings are elegant and
powerful; his historical knowledge was both profound and comprehensive;
he was a connoisseur of the arts.

Vivekananda's personality was completely submerged in his high degree
of spiritual fervour and saintliness. His Vedanta is to be distinguished from
Shankaracharya's Vedantism. The latter is *Advaita,* non-dualist; Vivekananda's is a synthetic Vedanta which reconciles *dvaita* (dualism) and
advaita (non-dualism), and also other theories of reality. He applied his
philosophic principles to the affairs of everyday life. Salvation, he insisted,
comes not through the life of a recluse but by serving God in man. Though
essentially a savant, Vivekananda also unwittingly made a signal contribution to the nascent nationalism of India which he 'largely created' and whose
'highest and noblest elements' he embodied in his own life. His ideal of
nationalism rested on four solid rocks: the awakening of the masses who
form the bases of the nation; development of physical and moral strength;
unity based on common spiritual ideas; and a consciousness and pride in the
ancient glory and greatness of India. His ideal of reform was based on
improving the condition of women; overhauling the educational system;
abolishing caste distinctions. He offered a synthesis between the old and the
new.

Religion, Vivekananda averred, consists of a personal encounter with the
Supreme and cannot be defined in any precise terms. This view leads to an
appreciation of every form, description and approach to the Divine. He
called himself a socialist, not because that system was perfect but 'because
half a loaf is better than no bread.' His idea of religion was one that 'will give

us faith in ourselves, a national self-respect, and the power to feed and educate the poor and relieve the misery around.'

R. C. Majumdar, *Swami Vivekananda: a historical review*, Calcutta, 1965; Bhupendranath Dutta, *Swami Vivekananda*, Calcutta, 1954; V. K. R. V. Rao, *Swami Vivekananda*, New Delhi, 1979; Sen, *DNB*, IV, pp. 436–40 (Swami Vishwasharayananda).

Treaty (Convention) of Wadgaon
(January 1779)

A sequel to the rout on 12 January 1779 of the John Company's (q.v.) retreating troops at Wadgaon, some 30 miles to the north-west of Poona, the Treaty of Wadgaon itself was concluded four days later. Mahadji Sindhia (q.v.), on behalf of the Marathas, and Colonel John Carnac, representing the committee of the Bombay army, settled its terms. *Inter alia*, it stipulated that (i) the Bombay government would no longer protect Raghunath Rao or Raghoba (q.v.) and would surrender all acquisitions made by it since 1773; (ii) the troops advancing from Bengal were to be stopped and a sum of Rs 41,000 and two hostages (William Farmer and Charles Stewart) surrendered as security for fulfilling this condition. It was noted that the Company had 'not adhered to' the earlier agreement embodied in the Treaty of Purandhar (q.v.). Under a separate clause, it was agreed that Broach would be handed over to Sindhia.

The agreement was concluded through the mediation of the Maratha chiefs Mahadji Sindhia and Tukoji Holkar. Both the Bombay and Bengal governments later disapproved of and repudiated the agreement, maintaining that Colonel Carnac had exceeded instructions and lacked authority to conclude it. British writers choose to call the Treaty a Convention. G.R. Gleig, Warren Hastings' (q.v.) biographer, has expressed the view that 'never had so disgraceful an affair' occurred since the advent of the British in India. Warren Hastings 'warmly repudiated' it and 'strained every nerve to wipe out the disgrace' by at once opening a new war against the Marathas. The Treaty has been called a 'disgraceful act', an 'ill-started venture' of the Bombay army that was to prove 'fatal' to the interests and alleged good name of the Company.

Aitchison, III, pp. 46-8; Dodwell, *CHI*, V, pp. 264-5; *Sardesai*, III, pp. 81-4.

Wahabis

The term 'wahabi' was applied by the British to the followers of Syed Ahmad of Rae Bareli. Better known as Ahmad Shah Barelwi, he was a follower of the notorious Amir Khan, one of the Pindari (q.v.) leaders, who lost his employment when his force was defeated at the end of the Pindari War (q.v.) which recognized Amir Khan as Chief of Tonk in Rajasthan. In actual fact, the movement Syed Ahmad initiated was designed to revive the ways of the Prophet (*Tariqa-i-Muhamadiya*), with its appeal chiefly among the lower middle and peasant classes. In Arabia, the Wahabi movement had reached its climax in the first two decades of the nineteenth century; in 1803-6, its followers had occupied Mecca and Medina; in 1808, they threatened Damascus. By 1818, however, Mehmet Ali (1769-1849), Pasha of Egypt, had beaten the Wahabis decisively. Active in India between 1820 and 1870, the Wahabis were by no means confined to Bengal, Bihar, the Panjab and the North-West Frontier Province (q.v.); they claimed followers in Madras as well as other parts of the Deccan.

It has been suggested that the movement was 'one of the earliest, most consistent, and protracted' and the 'most remorselessly anti-British in the political history of India' in the second half of the eighteenth and the early nineteenth centuries. Starting originally under a socio-religious impulse, it fast gained a political orientation. Later, its religious aspect was deliberately exaggerated, one of the generally prevalent misconceptions being that it was purely religious in nature and was directed solely against the Sikhs. This is not only an over-simplification but also a deliberate distortion. The fact is that the Wahabi struggle continued long after the Sikhs had ceased to exist as a political entity. The series of wars against the English from 1845 onwards, culminating in the Ambeyla campaign, had hardly any religious overtones.

Though there were striking similarities between Syed Ahmad's tenets and those of Abdul Wahab of Nejd, the impact of Shah Waliullah of Delhi (1703-63) was far more profound. Syed Ahmad preached the doctrine of restoration of Islam to its pristine purity by eradicating all un-Islamic innovations. He advocated a 3-fold programme—the exaltation of the word of God; the revival of the spirit of faith in word and deed and the practice of the holy war. As a man of action, he laid the greatest stress upon practice and rated pilgrimage to be the most meritorious form of worship. He placed special emphasis on two points—the avoidance of *Shirk* (i.e. association of another with the one God), and abjuring all innovations (i.e. *Bidat*).

Syed Ahmad's pilgrimage to Mecca (1822-4) had a profound impact on his career. There he learnt of the creed of Abdul Wahab, with emphasis added about the humiliation of Muslims at the hands of the Western powers in the lands they had conquered and suborned. In its militancy, his movement was akin to the Wahabis, but not in its theological content. But the latter transformed him into a fiery crusader with a clear intellectual resolve to fight Islam's enemies and recover the lands Muslims had once ruled.

On returning home, Syed Ahmad engaged himself in preparing for a *Jihad* and raising a corps of several hundred Muslims who elected him their *Imam*. Many of the educated followed him while among the humbler folk, the story runs, his exhortations were so efficacious that even the Delhi tailors were moved scrupulously to return remnants of cloth to their employers!The base of his operations was to be the north-west frontier region; its fanatical tribes and their mullahs provided, it was argued, fertile soil for the message of Abdul Wahab. After an agonizingly long march (January-November 1826), the faithful had reached Peshawar under Syed Ahmad, who was now designated *Imam Mahdi*. The assault on the Sikh kingdom followed, but was vigorously repulsed. His first effort, in 1828, against a strong Sikh force is said to have been successful. Later (1829) he attacked Peshawar and killed its Barakzai governor, Yar Muhammad; in 1830, Peshawar was actually held by his men for 2 months. In the battle of Balakote (6 May 1831), however, the host was badly routed and Syed Ahmad as well as his principal lieutenant, Shah Muhammad Ismail, lost their lives.

Syed Ahmad had commanded a vast following, with a hierarchy of officials, both to conduct the administration and co-ordinate its activities. A camp for training militant Wahabis was set up at Sithana, north of Peshawar, and supplied generously with volunteers and provisions from all parts of India through a massive secret organization. After his death, it was this elaborate and efficient hierarchy which kept the movement alive.

The death of Maharaja Ranjit Singh (q.v.) and the British conquest of the Panjab (1849) that came in its wake transformed the situation. The *Jihad* had a new target now—British rule, which, in turn, geared up for action. A special police department was organized to destroy the centres from where men and money had poured into the frontier. At the same time, armed expeditions were sent to annihilate those who had waged this relentless struggle; 20 such expeditions, involving 60,000 men, were dispatched between 1850 and 1863. The Wahabis had to move out of their headquarters (Sithana) in 1858 to Malka; the latter was burnt down by the British, in 1863.

Apart from these encounters which broke the back of the movement, prominent leaders (viz., Yahya Ali, Mohammad Jafar and Mohammad Shafi) were brought to trial and sentenced to long terms of imprisonment, some to transportation for life. Another weapon employed was propaganda. Religious decrees were obtained, among others from the Mufti of Mecca and a host of Ulama in all parts of the country, including Maulvis Karamat Ali of Jaunpur and Abdul Latif of Calcutta. The combined assault had expected results; by 1871, the movement was in shambles; after 1884, little was heard of it.

Qeyamuddin Ahmad, a careful student of the movement, has suggested that the followers of Syed Ahmad should more correctly have been designated *Ahl-i-Hadis* (puritans/reformists); that the insistence of the English as also some Indian writers in using the Wahabi appellation 'seems to be deliberate and actuated by ulterior motives.' The British viewed the term as synonymous with 'traitor' or 'rebel': 'Thus by describing the followers of Syed Ahmad as Wahabis the contemporary Government officers...brand them as "rebels" in the higher circles of Government and as "extremists" and "desecrators' of shrines" in the eyes of the general Muslims. The epithet became a term of religio-political abuse.'

Syed Ahmad's detractors contend that the doctrine that commanded his allegiance is in doubt, that in Arabia he had become a strict Wahabi of the Hanbali school of the *Sunnah*. His apologists however claim that, as a Hanafi, he remained loyal to what is orthodoxy among the Pathans, that the novelty of his message lay only in the reinterpretaton expressed of a true *mujaddid*. He had a host of Yasufzai and Khattak followers and his memory among the Pathans is kept green by the family of Pir Baba Sayyids who were his leading disciples along the border.

The Wahabi movement demonstrated the possibility of organizing and sustaining for years a rebellion of the have-nots under the leadership of theologians. Its eventual failure proved that, whatever its temporary successes, such a movement could not overthrow a well-organized empire. Despite their zeal, Syed Ahmad and his followers were out of step with the times;

their efforts to revive the seventh century Arab milieu foredoomed the movement to failure.

The movement left in its wake a trail of separatist or isolationist tendencies, and accounted for the Muslim community's later exclusion from the national mainstream. At the same time, it kept alive the desire for freedom among Muslims. As a purely religious movement, it may have collapsed sooner than it did; its political moorings alone would appear to account for its sustained survival.

In a side result, the movement gave a great impetus to the growth of the Urdu language, particularly Urdu prose. It left behind an inspiring tradition of a heroic and sustained struggle against the British and also a model for the formation of a well-knit all-India political organization to conduct the struggle. But it also set off a reaction symbolized by Syed Ahmad Khan (q.v.) which advocated the adoption of western education and technology by the Muslims.

The weakness of the Wahabis lay in the distance which separated their administrative headquarters from their operational centres; nor could *Jihad,* understandably, have the sympathy of Hindus, although some of them were indirectly connected with it. While on the one hand it encouraged, as has been noticed, the growth of Urdu, on the other it left the community 'susceptible to later communalistic propaganda.'

For its failure, the following factors may be listed: *firstly*, the frequent defection and intermittent hostility of the frontier tribesmen who failed to realize the true spirit of the movement and to give it their real and continuous support; *secondly*, the Wahabis' virtually complete dependence on their centres in India for all sorts of material help. The latter being completely at the mercy of the English authorities the movement was foredoomed to failure; *thirdly*, its inability to develop resources even remotely matching those of the adversary.

Syed Ahmad's teachings were later consolidated into a book, *Sirat-ul-mustaqim,* by two of his distinguished disciples, Shah Muhammad Ismail and Maulana Abdul Haily, both of whom belonged to the house of Waliullah.

Qeyamuddin Ahmad, *The Wahabi Movement in India*, Calcutta, 1966; *Tara Chand*, II, pp. 23-30; W. W. Hunter, *The Indian Musalmans*, 3rd ed., Calcutta, 1876, pp. 61-2.

Battle of Wandiwash (22 January 1760)

The town of Wandiwash lies some 60 miles to the south-west of Madras. The battle fought here was in more ways than one a continuation of the Anglo-French armed struggle and rivalry in Europe and other parts of the world. English troops, estimated at 1,900 Europeans, 3,300 Indian sepoys and 21 pieces of field artillery were commanded by the veteran English soldier, Eyre Coote (q.v.). On the other side, there were 2,250 Europeans, 1,300 Indian sepoys and a Maratha cavalry of 3,000 under Morari Rao Ghorpade (who eventually did not participate) under France's well-known commander in the east, the Comte de Lally (q.v.).

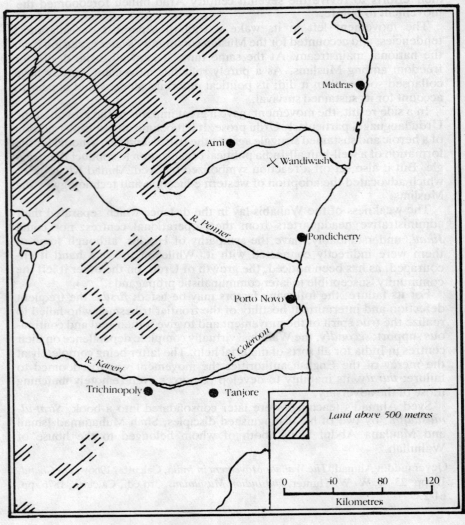

Battle of Wandiwash (22 January 1760)

The fort captured by the British in November 1759 was invested by Lally's troops on 11 January 1760. Coote advanced swiftly on Lally and in a pitched battle that followed (22 January), the French were completely routed. French losses were estimated at 230 dead and 130 wounded, besides a large stockpile of arms, ammunition and other stores. English casualties were estimated at 80 Europeans and 60 Indian sepoys killed and 124 wounded.

The battle sealed the fate of the French empire in India, for the French were now no longer in a position to challenge British superiority.

Dodwell, *CHI*, V, p. 163.

Wavell (1883–1950)

Educated at Winchester, Archibald Percival Wavell went to Sandhurst at the age of 17 and was commissioned into the famous 'Black Watch' regiment at 18. In 1901 he served as a subaltern in the later stages of the Boer War (1899-1902) in South Africa. In 1914-16 he saw service in France and was wounded at Ypres, where he lost his left eye. His dictum: 'My ideal infantry-man has the qualities of a successful poacher, a cat burglar and a gunman.' On the eve of World War II, Wavell was G. O. C.-in-C, Middle East. When, on 12 September 1940, Italy invaded Egypt, he not only defended his position but pushed the enemy back. The latter were badly routed, Tobruck and Benghazi were captured and Mussolini's empire in Ethiopia liquidated. Later, in 1941, when the Germans were successful in Greece and Crete, Wavell's counter-offensive in North Africa failed. He was now replaced by Field Marshal Sir Claude Auchinleck (1884-1981) and assumed the latter's position as Commander-in-Chief, India.

Earlier, after the Japanese entered the War (December 1941), Wavell became Allied Commander, South-West Pacific and, fighting against heavy odds, lost both Malaya and Burma. During 1943-47 he was India's last but one Viceroy. In 1943 he had been promoted Field Marshal and created Viscount Wavell of Cyrenaica and Winchester; in 1947, after retirement from India, he was made Earl. His last public service was the Viceroyalty. He accepted it with his usual willingness to shoulder an unpopular task although, as he wrote to a friend, 'I fear I have no talent for persuasion.'

Wavell's first act was administrative, and characteristic. The Bengal Famine (q.v.) was at its worst and he relieved a critical situation by an immediate personal reconnaissance followed by extensive aid administered by the army. He then set to work 'with limitless patience'. To disarm critics, he issued a statement in July 1945 taking the blame for governmental failures on himself.

One of the most controversial episodes of his Viceroyalty was the June 1945 Simla Conference (q.v.) which, in the words of V. P. Menon, then his Reforms Commissioner, 'had been convened as a gathering of politically eminent persons who would sit together and collectively advise the Viceroy about the formation of a new central government. Very soon however it became transformed into the familiar pattern of futile discussions between the (Indian National) Congress (q.v.) and the (All-India) Muslim League (q.v.), and between party leaders and the Viceroy. The formal sessions of the Conference served as a forum for party leaders to set out their points of view whilst other members functioned as the audience or chorus...C. Rajagopalachari (q.v.) expressed the view that if it had been known that the sole purpose of the Conference was to get (M. A.) Jinnah (q.v.) to agree, failing which it would have to disperse, the Congress would have told Lord Wavell at the very start that it would be a waste of energy.' The fact was that the abandonment of the Viceroy's plan 'strengthened the position of Jinnah and the League at a time when their fortunes were none too good'. Again, the Conference has been viewed as 'a last opportunity' for the forces of nationalism to fight a rearguard action to preserve the integrity of the country. When that battle was lost, the 'waves of communalism' quickly engulfed it, for 'only the Hobson's choice of partition was left.'

Nor was the political climate any the better at the time of Waveil's departure in March 1947: 'the general situation was so bleak that it looked as though the country was heading for certain disaster. With the Muslim League conducting a civil disobedience campaign against two provincial ministries and its representatives in the central government openly preaching "direct action", Hindu-Muslim differences were further accentuated. Even some members of the Services...[were] openly taking sides in the political controversy. The precarious food position, the steadily deteriorating economic situation and widespread labour unrest added to the threatening symptoms of a general collapse.'

Other eventful developments during Wavell's four years were the Cabinet Mission (q.v.) negotiations (1946) to break the political deadlock, and the swearing-in of the Interim Government (q.v.).

Wavell's tenure was 'probably the most difficult and momentous period that any Viceroy has had to face.' A shadow has been cast over it by what was tantamount to his summary dismissal from his post and Lord Louis Mountbatten's then much-appreciated performance in winding up the Raj with the full agreement of all the parties concerned. In contrast to Mountbatten, Wavell's 'unavailing effort to bring about agreement between the Congress and the Muslim League can all too easily appear in retrospect to have been fumbling and maladroit and his removal from the scene a necessary preliminary to a final ringing down of the curtain....In some recently published books references to his viceroyalty have been disparaging, even contemptuous. It has been said that he was quite unfitted for delicate negotiations, that he was defeatist in outlook...that he was often at a loss what to do and by the time of his dismissal, at the end of his resources.' In fact, Penderel Moon maintains, the 'main significance' of his viceroyalty lay in the 'two fateful political decisions' reached while he was still in office. The *first*, Labour Prime Minister C. R. Attlee's 20 February 1947 pronouncement that the British would quit India in a little over a year; the *second*, that the country should be divided. Both had, in effect, been reached by the Congress and the Muslim League before the Viceroy handed over charge to his successor.

Wavell's 'failure', such as it was, was not his fault: 'The task that he was set was a well-nigh impossible one...and he was hampered throughout by the indecision and weakness of his masters. . . . Nevertheless he came very near to success.'

According to Penderel Moon, Wavell's *Journal* reveals that, amid all his difficulties and disappointments, he never accepted defeat and was never for long at a loss what to do, that he was always looking ahead and devising ways of meeting contingencies that others had not begun to think of. The policy of scuttle that has been attributed to him was one that he strongly advised against. In the end, the British government agreed to fix a date and took the credit for this 'bold and courageous move' that Wavell had for months been vainly advocating.

As a soldier, for all his misfortunes in the War of 1939-45, Wavell's reputation ultimately stood as high as those of any of his contemporaries. In none of the eleven campaigns in which he fought did he have a preponderance in men or in weaponry. He left the Middle East; he was relieved of the command in Asia before the arrival of the material and reinforcements with which his successors were to win their country's battles and their own renown. Yet at no time, in public or in private, in print or by spoken word, did he ever complain.

A biographer underscores the point that while Wavell liked to picture himself as a cavalier, it was his fate to be remembered as the dour and indomitable slave of duty, condemned to defend one indefensible position after another and always relieved of command when victory was in sight. And yet his sturdy courage never deserted him: 'At the heart of it was a moral certainty, a distaste for humbug and the shopwindow, a devotion to truth.' He was a great man for solutions: 'reasonable, civilized, elegant, unhurried.'

In appearance, Wavell was broad and thick-set, sturdy and physically tough. His silences were proverbial, but among intimates he was the most congenial and jovial of company. He delighted in horses and horsemanship, in golf and shooting. His *Palestine Campaign* (1928) and a biography of his former chief, Viscount Edmund Allenby, produced during years of high pressure, are masterly surveys and easy to read. He had delivered the Lee Knowles Lectures at Cambridge on 'Generals and Generalship' in 1939; these were later (1941) published in book-form.

Likeable and respected by his men, as a soldier Wavell was uncomplaining and professional. A general of exceptional quality, he was, besides, a scholar and talented writer. His publications include, apart from *The Palestine Campaign*, (1928); *Allenby, a Study in Greatness* (1940); *Other Men's Flowers: an anthology of poetry* (1944). In 1947, Wavell returned to London where he died, on 24 May 1950.

John H. Robertson (John Connell, pseudonym), *Wavell, Scholar and Soldier*, London, 1964; Ronald Lewin, *Chief: Field Marshal Lord Wavell, Commander-in-Chief and Viceroy, 1939–47*, London, 1980; Penderel Moon (ed.), *Wavell: the Viceroy's Journal*, Oxford, 1973; V. P. Menon, *The Transfer of Power*, Bombay, 1957, pp. 214-5, 348-9; *DNB 1941-50*, pp. 932-5 (Bernard Ferguson).

Wavell Plan (1945)

In August 1944, the Governor-General, Lord Wavell (q.v.) had expressed the view that what the government 'had entangled, government must alone disentangle'; to break the political deadlock, he called a Conference of Governors of all the 11 British-Indian provinces. The Conference endorsed his view that the Central government should take all possible steps to break the constitutional impasse in which the country was then sadly enmeshed. The tentative plan was to assemble a conference of the principal leaders of all political parties besides Gandhi (q.v.) and Jinnah (q.v.) and discuss with them the composition of an Interim Government (q.v.).

Following the Desai–Liaqat Formula (q.v.), Wavell had in mind a Council with an equal number of Hindus and Muslims, one representative each of the Sikhs and the Depressed Classes, besides the Commander-in-Chief and the Viceroy. The Council was to function under the Government of India Act, 1935 (q.v.). Apart from its immediate duties concerning prosecution of the War and conclusion of peace, the Council would also consider the composition of the proposed constitution-making body. The proposed conference would also indicate the means of reviving responsible governments in the provinces which had been placed under the Governors' untrammelled authority under Section 93 of the 1935 Act.

It was stipulated that if the parties at the conference agreed upon the composition and personnel of the Executive Council, members would take office after the approval of the British Government. The formation of responsible provincial governments in place of those run by the Governors would follow immediately thereafter. The Executive Council would make proposals for the framing of the new constitution and negotiate with the Indian States (q.v.) for their place in it.

The scheme was submitted to Whitehall, which made counter-proposals in which the League and the Congress were shown scant consideration. Wavell did not agree with what was suggested and appealed directly to the British Prime Minister, who invited him to London for consultations. He remained there from March through May 1945. Winston Churchill was extremely sceptical about Wavell's proposed course of action but the Secretary of State, L. S. Amery, protested, and finally the Prime Minister agreed to the idea of the Conference. As he argued, 'after all we aren't giving anything away.'

Essentially, as has been indicated, Wavell's proposal was for the formation of a provisional government at the centre representing the main political parties and, with this object in view, the calling of a small conference of political leaders. His reasons for making such a move well before the end of the War, were spelt out in a letter to the British Prime Minister as early as 24 October 1944. Briefly, 'What I have in mind is provisional political government of the type suggested in the Cripps Mission (q.v.) declaration, within the present constitution, coupled with an earnest but not necessarily simultaneous attempt to devise means to reach a constitutional settlement. Amery knows my views and I drafted a paper for the Cabinet, which I have asked him to withhold for the present. I think the failure of the Gandhi–Jinnah Talks (q.v.) has created a favourable moment for a move by HMG.'

In sharp contrast to Wavell, the Secretary of State had countered with the view that the then Government of India should be given the status of a Dominion and the authority of Parliament to legislate for India abrogated, thereby virtually conceding India's demand for independence at once. The

Viceroy did not consider Whitehall's plan to be practical and had thus addressed his letter direct to the Prime Minister.

Earlier, in November 1944, Wavell had noted after meeting Bhulabhai Desai, leader of the Congress Party in the Central Legislative Assembly: 'In fact his ideas seems to bear a distinct resemblance to the recommendations I have made to HMG. He wanted a National Government under the present constitution formed of members drawn from the existing legislature and of course the release of the (Congress) Working Committee and replacement of Section 93 governments.' While in London, where he had been summoned for consultations, Wavell felt frustrated. On 24 May 1945 he noted in his *Journal:* 'A long day but some movement at least or hope of movement. I began the day by writing to Prime Minister to point out that I had been 8 weeks at home, that I had had nothing from the India Committee for 4 weeks or from himself for 7 weeks and asking for a decision.' A week later he recorded: 'The climax of my visit was an extraordinary one. At meeting of the Cabinet at 10.30 p.m., the Prime Minister made just as forcible an address in favour of my proposals as he had made in their damnation this morning . . . . He will change again but I suppose I can claim in the meantime some sort of personal triumph . . . and so at 11.30 p.m. I got my decision just 12 hours before my train was scheduled to leave Victoria. It all ended in an atmosphere of good-will and congratulation—only temporary, I fear.'

The Plan was announced in Parliament by the Secretary of State on 14 June 1945. Essentially, it was proposed that (i) the Governor-General's Executive Council be reconstituted 'from amongst leaders of Indian political life at the centre and in the Provinces with an equal number of Muslims and caste Hindus'; (ii) a conference of political leaders was to be called and a list of names invited but 'the responsibility for the recommendations must of course continue to rest with him [the Governor-General] and his freedom of choice therefore remains unrestricted'; (iii) apart from the Viceroy and the Commander-in-Chief (who would retain his position as War member) all other members of the Executive Council would be Indians; (iv) the relations of the Crown with the Indian States through the Viceroy as Crown Representative were to remain unaffected; (v) if the Central government, as envisaged, came into effect, responsible governments would be restored in such provinces where these had been earlier abrogated; (vi) external affairs (other than tribal and frontier matters) would come within the purview of an Indian member of the proposed Executive Council, while 'fully accredited representatives shall be appointed for the representation of India abroad'.

In a brief broadcast from All-India Radio the same evening, Wavell gave a matter of fact summary of what had been said in London apart from two small details. One, that it was proposed to appoint a British High Commissioner in India 'as in the Dominions, to represent Great Britain's commercial and other such interests in India.' Two, that in so far as the new Council would operate within the framework of the existing constitution, 'there can be no question of the Govenor-General agreeing not to exercise his constitutional power of control; but it will of course not be exercised unreasonably.'

A concrete outcome of the Wavell Plan was the summoning of the Simla Conference (q.v.).

Penderel Moon (ed.), *Wavell: The Viceroy's Journal*, pp. 90. 94-9, 101, 13ᴸ-6; *Gwyer & Appadorai,* II, pp. 557-60; A. C. Banerji, *Documents*, IV (1936-9), pp. 200-1; *Tara Chand,* IV, pp. 41-2.

Wellesley (1760–1842)

Richard Colley Wellesley, Earl of Mornington and later Marquess of Wellesley, was born on 20 June 1760; he studied at Harrow, Eton and, finally, Christ Church College, Oxford. After a brief spell in the House of Commons (1784) and as Lord of the Treasury (1786), he became a Commissioner of John Company's (q.v.) Board of Control (1793) under Henry Dundas (q.v.) and, three years later, was appointed Governor-General, setting forth on his appointment in November 1797.

From the outset, Wellesley was pledged to fighting renewed French interest in India, a commitment which led inevitably to an expansionist if also overtly interventionist policy. He had the active encouragement and support both of William Pitt the younger, (1759-1806), then Prime Minister, and Dundas, whose confidence he enjoyed to the fullest, in the initial stages at any rate. Soon after his arrival in India, Wellesley was persuaded that the time was ripe to undertake plans of territorial aggrandisement, for the earlier policy of non-interference and neutrality had paid poor dividends. Fully briefed on the existing state of affairs, he had drawn up his list of priorities in dealing with the 'native' Indian States (q.v.).

Tipu Sultan (q.v.), then rated the Company's most formidable opponent, was allegedly in intimate correspondence with the French revolutionaries in Mauritius (Napolean was in Egypt) as well as Zaman Shah, the ambitious Afghan ruler, grandson of Ahmad Shah Abdali (q.v.). No wonder Wellesley fully exploited the French and Afghan bogeys, re-animated the triple alliance with the Nizam and the Marathas and, through his astute diplomacy, lured Tipu into a sense of false security. Presently, in a lightning campaign he eliminated the powerful Mysore ruler and, in the bargain, made extensive gains of territory. The Sultan died fighting while a truncated Mysore was restored to the minor Wadeyar raja. The spectacular successes of the campaign and the detailed descriptions sent home of his great victories earned Wellesley an Irish peerage. He was, however, far from happy and described it as 'a double-gilt potato'—too slight a recognition for such considerable services!

Not long after he arrived in India, Wellesley concluded that the Company's earlier policy of maintaining a balance of power among the Indian states would no longer benefit the English. He therefore devised a system of subsidiary alliances whereby the 'allied' power would maintain in its dominion for its 'protection', and at its own expense, English troops who would be under the control and discipline of the Company. Abundant self-confidence and powerful support from the Directors at home made Wellesley follow his new policy boldly, making such modifications as a particular local situation might demand. The first to be inducted, in 1798, was the hapless Nizam of Hyderabad. In Tanjore, Wellesley started by giving an annuity to the Nawab and took over the state's administration, albeit later in the same year, taking advantage of a change in succession, he assumed full control and pensioned off the heir.

In 1801 Wellesley took over the Carnatic and in the process modified and re-interpreted his 'system'. Instead of monetary payments for the maintenance of troops as hitherto, he now demanded cession of territory in lieu. The change did not meet with the approval of the Home Government who questioned his policy of annexation and viewed some of its consequential responsibilities as far too onerous to bear. But Wellesley was now like one obsessed; not to talk of piecemeal gains, he even advocated the assumption of government for the whole country by the British crown! In the case of Nawab Saadat Ali of Oudh (q.v.) as well as the Nizam, he used force to compel cession of dominion. Through clever and calculated manipulation, was allegedly in intimate correspondence with the French revolutionaries in territory. In his campaigns in south India, Wellesley was greatly assisted by his brother Arthur, who later, as the Duke of Wellington, achieved even greater eminence in Europe and Britain.

By 1802 tensions between Calcutta (q.v.) and the controlling authorities in London had mounted. The Court of Directors had stoutly opposed the Governor-General's wholesale annexations; his free trade policy; his creating a college for civil service trainees and the appointment of his brothers to important posts. In the result, Wellesley asked to be relieved, but in view of the then uncertain state of affairs in the Maratha kingdom, agreed to stay on for another year. All attempts made hitherto to persuade the Peshwa enter into a subsidiary alliance had misfired. After the death of Nana Phadnis (1800), both Daulat Rao Sindhia and Yashvant Rao Holkar (qq.v.), the most powerful Maratha chiefs, wanted to dominate at Poona. Baji Rao II's (q.v.) intrigues resulted in a war between the two, in which Holkar had the upper hand. In the result, the Peshwa fled to Bassein and sought British protection—a long-awaited opportunity eagerly seized by Wellesley. On 31 December 1802, he signed the Treaty of Bassein (q.v.), accepting a subsidiary alliance and yielding territories worth Rs 26 lakhs. Wellesley's dream was now a reality, for British paramountcy was no longer a matter of dispute.

As feared by his detractors, before long the Maratha chiefs arrayed themselves into a united front against the Company and, in August 1803, commenced the Second Anglo-Maratha War (q.v.). The facade of Maratha unity however was paper-thin, for their numerous jealousies and lack of co-ordinated effort brought about many a reverse; by the end of the year, Sindhia had signed the Treaty of Surji Arjangaon (q.v.) and Bhonsle that of Deogaon (q.v.). A hurricane campaign followed, which brought unexpectedly handsome gains for the British and Wellesley's ambitious plans had nearly been fulfilled.

With the Comapany's new territorial gains, the Presidencies of Bengal and Madras were linked through British-ruled areas. However, before long, Holkar resumed hostilities and the other Maratha chiefs rallied to his side. Even though he had earlier suffered reverses, General Lake's defeat at Bharatpur decided Wellesley's fate. For the Home authorities, already at the end of their tether, then ordered his recall: his seemingly victorious campaigns had brought them grave and even unmanageable responsibilities.

In his dealings with his political masters, Wellesley had been somewhat overbearing and imperious, disregarding their directives whenever they ran counter to his own grand design. While he succeeded militarily, his successes left a smouldering resentment that was bound to endanger peace. Outwardly, his principal aim—to consolidate British dominion by absorbing the weak and dependent rulers and, through them, controlling others—was achieved to an eminent degree. Wellesley saw things in a wider perspective, too, and sent a mission to Persia under John Malcolm (q.v.) and another, under General Baird, to Egypt to help exorcise the French demon. He even wanted to capture Ceylon (Sri Lanka). By the time he left, the Company had become an imperial power of first-rate magnitude though, in the process, piling up a huge foreign debt.

On his return to England (1805), some attempts were made to impeach Wellesley, but these were finally voted down in 1808. He refused, however, to accept any assignment till his name had been cleared. In 1809, he served as ambassador in Spain before becoming Foreign Secretary. He left that office in February 1812 and was later (1821-8 and 1833-4) Lord Lieutenant of Ireland. He died in September 1842.

One of Wellesley's biographers (Torrens) refers to the poor reception given him on his return home and talks of its 'chilling nature'. A Member of Parliament tried to put him on trial as a culprit. This 'long and sordid episode' lasted nearly two years when Wellesley was subjected to a 'species of persecution perhaps unparalleled in the modern history of England'. All the proceedings used in the case of Warren Hastings (q.v.) 'were copied and parodied'. Thomas Creevey, in 1807, said the Marquess 'is a great calamity inflicted upon England' and Croker referred to his 'brilliant incapacity.'

Only in 1836, when his despatches were at long last published was Wellesley fully vindicated 'and the long injustice of their [his critics'] blindness and ignorance' recognized. Few of the great controversies of history had 'so right and gracious' an ending. His desptaches, apologists point out, are 'massively impressive in their power, their logical force and their tone of resolute decision.'

It has been suggested that Wellesley did not despise Indians nor seek to change them because they were Indians or had brown skins. He was an eighteenth century man and free of the moral vanity of the next century. His arrogance was universal; it was essential for him to feel that he knew best and, if everyone (British and Indian) did what they were told, all could be sweetness and light. He really believed this ideal situation would be achieved; hence the fury and frantic indignation, whenever his will was crossed. His private and public lives were conducted on the same lines. It was an extraordinary human achievement that in both (lives) he came so near to success.

Wellesley's biographers, it has been suggested, do not give enough credit to his younger brother; but the Duke of Wellington's biographers give too much.

The most outstanding part of Wellesley's long and distinguished career was his governance of India, for he may be regarded as one of the three men who consolidated the empire. In many respects he resembled Dalhousie (q.v.) more than he did Warren Hastings; but the difficulties which he was called upon to encounter were greater than those which confronted either the former or the latter.

P. E. Roberts, *India under Wellesley*, reprint, Gorakhpur, 1961; Iris Butler, *The Eldest Brother: the Marquess Wellesley, the Duke of Wellington's Eldest Brother*, London, 1973; Ainslie T. Embree, *Charles Grant and British Rule in India*, London, 1962; *DNB*, XX, pp. 122-34 (Alexander John Arbuthnot).

Whitley Commission (1929–1931)

The Whitley Commission on Labour, or more accurately the Royal Commission on Labour, under the chairmanship of John Henry Whitley, formerly Speaker of the House of Commons, was set up in October 1929 and its report released on 1 July 1931. The Commission consisted of 11 members; excluding the Chairman, they were: Srinivas S. Sastri, Sir Victor Sasson, Sir Ibrahim Rahimtoola, Sir Alexander Murray, A. G. Clow, Kabeer-ud-Din Ahmed, G. D. Birla, John Cliff, N. M. Joshi (q.v.), D. Chaman Lall and Miss B. M. Le Poer Power.

The Commission was asked *inter alia* to inquire into and report on existing conditions of labour in industrial undertakings and plantations in British India; on the health, efficiency and standard of living of the workers; on the relations between employers and employed. Additionally, it was to make recommendations to rectify such deficiencies in these fields that it might discover. The Commission, which cost the exchequer an approximate Rs 10.5 lakhs, examined 837 witnesses, held 128 public sittings and 71 private sessions, apart from undertaking a wide survey of industrial conditions in India, including Burma. The report of the Commission was unanimous except for a separate minute appended by Sasson and another by K. Ahmed. The Commission attempted to reply to the former, but felt that the latter required no answer. Sir Ibrahim Rahimtoola could not sign the report, having been unable to work with the Commission after his appointment as President of the Central Legislative Assembly.

Among other subjects, the Commission's recommendations related to the question of transport services; public works contracts; standard wages, fines and deductions; compensation; trade unions; joint machinery for settling disputes; recruitment of labour for tea gardens in Assam, in mines as well as the railways; labour legislation; employment of factory workers; working conditions in factories and unregistered factories.

On the all important question of standard wages, the Commission recommended that every effort should be made to put into operation a policy of standardized wages in the Bombay cotton mills, and that in the jute industry early steps should also be taken in that direction both for time and piece workers. It however conceded that the data it had been able to collect on wages was appalling. As for Assam, the Commission felt that conditions there were different from those in the rest of the country.

The Commission noted that the 'attempts to deal with unrest begin rather with the creation of an atmosphere unfavourable to disputes than with machinery for their settlement.' To establish close contacts and cordial relations between managements and employees, the Commission suggested three possible lines: the development of stable trade unions; appointment of labour officers; formation of works committees. It also recommended the appointment of conciliation officers to bring about settlements between parties in the earlier stages of disputes. Except for the appointment of conciliation officers, for which provision was made in the Trade Disputes (Amendment) Act, 1938, nothing was done for a long time to implement the recommendations of the Commission.

V. V. Giri, a prominent trade unionist who later rose to be President of India (1969-74), has noted: 'The report remains to this day the most valuable document on the conditions of workers from the early days of industrial development until the end of 1930.'

A word about the background to the appointment of the Commission. The Bombay Industrial Disputes Commission of 1922 and the Labour Commission had recommended the formation of works or shop committees on the lines of the 'Whitley committees' in England. The workers were to be represented on these committees and, along with the employers, would be responsible for the fixing and observance of conditions under which work was to be carried on. These committees were later established by the Tata group of industries and by the government in their capacity as employers.

Initially, in 1916, the British government had appointed a commission to consider ways and means of improving relations between employers and employees. Whitley, who was then Speaker of the House of Commons was its chairman. Its recommendations, popularly known as the Whitley scheme, were accepted by HMG and the Ministry of Labour was asked to implement them. The scheme's most important aspect related to the organization of joint industrial councils in most industries. These were representative both of employers and work-people and their objective was the regular consideration of matters affecting the progress and well-being of the trade. This was to be judged from the point of view of all those engaged in it, in so far as it was consistent with the general interests of the community. In partially organized industries, it recommended the appointment of works committees while regulation of wages was recommended in unorganized industries. Additionally, it proposed the voluntary establishment of a National Joint Standing Industrial Council in several industries and different councils for different areas.

The Whitley Commission in England had pointed out that it was wrong to try to establish the joint committee as a substitute for trade unions and that these committees could work successfully only in such industries where the workers were organized in unions. The constitution of a Whitley Commission for India was an aftermath of the experiment's earlier success in streamlining industrial relations in England.

Report of the Royal Commission on Labour, Government of India, Calcutta, 1931; N.N. Mitra, *The Indian Annual Register,* July-Dec. 1931, Vol. II, Calcutta, pp. 341–9; V. V. Giri, *Labour Problems in Indian Industry,* 3rd ed., Bombay, 1972; Radhakamal Mukerjee, *The Indian Working Class,* Bombay, 1945; T. N. Bhagoliwal, *Economics of Labour and Social Welfare*, Agra, 1966, pp. 194–5.

Treaty of Yandaboo (1826)

Signed on 24 February 1826, the 11–article Treaty of Yandaboo, with an 'Additional' article, brought to an end the First Anglo-Burmese War (q.v.). Both the contracting parties professed 'perpetual peace and friendship' and agreed to maintain accredited ministers at each other's courts. *Inter alia*, Burma renounced 'all claims upon and will abstain from all future interference with' Assam, Cachar and Jaintia. Additionally, it agreed to recognize Gambhir Singh, 'should he desire to return', as the ruler of the state of Manipur. It was also to pay an indemnity of Rs 1 crore in fixed instalments. The British were to retain Arakan, including the four divisions of 'Arracan, Ramree, Cheduba and Sandoway.' The Arakan mountains were to form the boundary between the two empires. Burma also ceded the provinces of Yeh, Tavoy, Megrui and Tenasserim 'with the islands and the dependencies thereunto pertaining, taking the Salween river as the title of demarcation of that frontier.' It was stipulated that 'accredited ministers' retaining 'an escort or safeguard of fifty men' shall reside at the Darbar of the other. The 'Additional' article spelt out the modalities of the payment by the Burmese of the indemnity of Rs 1 crore.

The territorial acquisitions listed above proved to be of great strategic import for the British, as they gave them a 'bridge-head on either side of Burma'; they were of great commercial value, too, in so far as the areas were centres of flourishing trade and commerce. In as much as these were all one-sided gains, it was evident that the settlement arrived at would be short-lived.

A 'Commercial Treaty' based upon the principles of 'reciprocal advantage' was to be concluded between the two countries. Burma was to abolish 'all exactions' upon British ships or vessels in Burmese ports and the King of Siam, Britain's 'good and faithful ally', was to be included in the Treaty. A 4-article 'Commercial Treaty with Ava' was signed and sealed at Ratnapura on 23 November 1826.

A. C. Banerjee, *The Eastern Frontier of British India*, Calcutta, 1946; D. G. E. Hall, *Europe and Burma*, Oxford, 1945; *Aitchison*, 5th ed., Calcutta, 1931, XII, pp. 230-3.

Francis Edward Younghusband (1863–1942)

Born at Muree, now in Pakistan, educated at Clifton Hall and trained at the Royal Military College, Sandhurst, Francis Edward Younghusband was commissioned in 1882 and posted to Meerut. Of an adventurous disposition, fond of out-door life and a keen geographer, he spent his early years in India joining numerous teams exploring the Himalayan and Central Asian regions. Accounts of these then unusual journeys and experiences were faithfully recorded, maintained and later published. In 1886, he accompanied an expedition to Manchuria and a year later travelled overland from Peking to India, reaching Rawalpindi after seven months. While exploring the passes in the Pamirs into Hunza, Younghusband encountered a Russian officer, Captain Grombtchevsky, who boasted of an impending Russian invasion of India.

Posted to the Foreign Department in Calcutta a year later,

Younghusband travelled via Yarkand to the Pamirs where he had another similar dramatic experience. Arrested by Colonel Yanoff (also spelt Ianoff) for trespassing into Russian territory, he was released only after the British Prime Minister, Lord Salisbury, had interceded on his behalf, protesting to Nikolai Giers, the Russian Foreign Minister. The information Younghusband gathered and the observations he made during these explorations besides being useful for military strategy, left him a confirmed Russophobe. At the same time, he was convinced that China was utterly incapable of blocking a Russian advance and argued that Chinese Turkestan should be used as a buffer between Russia and India. Awarded the Royal Geographical Society's Gold Medal in recognition of his explorations, he received the C.I.E. a year later.

Subsequently, Younghusband served as Poltical Officer in Hunza and later (1892-3) as Political Agent at Chitral. It was here that he renewed his acquaitance with Curzon (q.v.), whom he had met in 1892, in England. The two not only shared a common love for travel and exploration, but an almost obsessive Russophobia and the desire to protect the Indian empire from the dangers that the Tsarist regime allegedly posed. In 1903, Curzon, then Viceroy and Governor-General, singled out Younghusband as the man to lead the expedition to Lhasa. Younghusband appreciated the urgency of the need to forestall Russia, but the British government was not easily amenable to Curzon's pleas for a green signal in regard to Tibet. No less an imperialist than his political mentor, Younghusband's impatience to march to Gyantse and his conviction that Russian intrigue had deep roots matched, and sometimes exceeded, that of Curzon's. *Inter alia,* Younghusband had warned that the Tibetan countryside was swarming with hostiles building up a strong resistance and that nothing could be achieved short of a march on Lhasa.

Finally, given permission to occupy the Chumbi valley and move up to Gyantse, Younghusband, with rare optimism, over-rode all military objections to a winter campaign and, what was more, successfully achieved his objective despite the foul weather and a most difficult terrain. Obsessed with the importance of his mission, he could barely wait to move on from Gyantse to Lhasa when the Lamas refused to fall in line, much less negotiate. At the Tibetan capital, he exceeded the explicit instructions given him by Whitehall in drawing up the Lhasa Convention (q.v.). The rich valleys of Tibet, it would appear in retrospect, excited his cupidity and he set his heart on the Chumbi valley, 'the key' to the land. Thus in drawing up the terms, Younghusband adapted instructions according to his own reasoning, both in regard to the 75-year lease over the valley and the provision for the British Trade Agent to move from Gyantse to Lhasa in case of need. In the result, he was charged with open disobedience, if not defiance, and was clearly under a cloud in regard to the conferment of honours on his return. In ratification, the Convention too was modified on some vital counts.

After serving as Resident in Kashmir (1906-9), Younghusband retired. Back in Britain, he remained an active member of the Royal Geographical Society and was its President in 1919. Apart from his interest in Himalayan exploration, in later years he turned increasingly towards mysticism. He wrote a great deal and studied different religious philosophies. In 1924,

Younghusband was responsible for organizing a conference of religions of the British empire and twelve years later (1936) founded the World Fellowship of Faiths.

George Seaver, *Francis Younghusband,* London, 1952; Viscount Samuel, *Man of Action, Man of Spirit: Sir Francis Youghusband,* London, 1952; Parshotam Mehra, *The Younghusband Expedition, An Interpretation,* Bombay, 1968.

The Younghusband Expedition (1903–4)

The Younghusband Expedition (1903–4)

Tibet, India's large albeit empty neighbour to the north lying athwart the Himalayas, began to loom large in British India's foreign relations towards the close of the nineteenth century and for a variety of reasons. Attempts to open it to trade, which began as early as the last quarter of the eighteenth century, had continued intermittently thereafter but proved, for most part, to be abortive and short-lived. Negotiations in 1890 and 1893 between the Government of India and China, who claimed to be Lhasa's political sovereign, had resulted in two treaties demarcating the Sikkim-Tibet boundary and regulating trade relations between the two countries. The Tibetans, with some justification, opposed and later ignored these agreements which had lacked their overt, much less tacit, consent. During Curzon's (q.v.) viceroyalty (1899-1905), the growing menace of a possible Russian advance towards India gave Tibet a strategic importance as a buffer state, for Russia was increasingly suspected of casting covetous glances on this vast, barren and treeless waste in the heart of Asia.

Using the Sikkim-Tibet boundary dispute as an excuse, Curzon initiated a bolder policy, emphasizing the necessity of having direct relations with Lhasa. He tried to convince the Home Government that the myth of Chinese control was no more than a ruse to keep India at bay. After three unsuccessful attempts to establish a direct link with the Thirteenth Dalai Lama (q.v.), Curzon concluded that a show of force was needed to make Lhasa come to terms. On his insistence, Whitehall grudgingly allowed a mission under its Political Officer in Sikkim, John Claude White, to set up boundary pillars and clear Giagong, on the Sikkim border, of all Tibetan intruders. None the less, it refused the second part of Curzon's proposal that, should the Tibetans remain hostile, the Chumbi valley be occupied until the latter agreed to negotiate at Lhasa.

Reports mean while were pouring in of a growing intimacy between Russia and Tibet which was grist to the Dalai Lama's mill, the latter hoping to use the former as a counterpoise against China as well as the British in India. The drama was heightened by the fact that the Lama's adviser and close confidant was a Russian subject—a Mongolian Buriat monk named Aguan Dorjieff, who had, at his master's behest, undertaken several ostensibly diplomatic missions to St Petersburg. Rumours were also rife of a Russo-Chinese accord dealing with Tibet's cession to the former. The Russian government's clear disavowal of any designs on Tibet and its affirmation that Dorjieff's visits were of a purely religious character did nothing to allay Curzon's fears. He argued convincingly enough that a 'Russian protectorate' would pose a 'great menace to India' and pressurized the Secretary of State to permit the immediate dispatch of a military mission.

For a time the Home Government stalled. HMG began by making inquiries both in Peking as well as St Petersburg. While denying the existence of an agreement with Russia over Tibet, the Chinese agreed through their Amban at Lhasa to meet British representatives at a conference where Whitehall too would send its delegates. Curzon, however, was emphatic that this should be subject to two conditions. One, that besides dealing with the Sikkim border, the parleys would include the question of future relations with Tibet and two, result in a 'permanent consular representative' being stationed in Gyantse, if not at Lhasa itself. The British representative Colonel (later Sir) Francis Edward Younghusband (q.v.) was chosen leader of the mission and was to be accompanied by an armed escort, while a reserve force was to remain in Sikkim. The venue of the conference was to be Khamba Jong, some 20-30 miles within Tibetan territory. On the failure of the Chinese or Tibetan representatives to put up an appearance, the party was to push forward to Gyantse, albeit, as the Home Government reiterated, not without its prior approval.

Younghusband reached Khamba Jong on 19 July 1903. Chinese representatives of a sort arrived too. Their Tibetan counterparts however put in a belated appearance, and when they did, questioned the need of an armed escort, stipulating that they would negotiate only when the British withdrew to their own side of the frontier in Sikkim. A deadlock ensued, while Younghusband wrote to his superiors about a Tibetan military build-up around Khamba Jong and the necessity to use force in order to achieve a breakthrough. Curzon enthusiastically supported his envoy's reports, hinting at the possibility of large-scale albeit covert Russian support to the Tibetans. He sought permission therefore to march to Gyantse, which was granted after much delay, in November 1903. It was also laid down that the Chumbi valley would be occupied first.

Instructed not to annex, much less permanently occupy, any territory, Younghusband, accompanied by a sizeable armed escort, crossed the Jelap La in December 1903. A severe winter and high altitude passes did not deter the British advance and, since the Tibetans were still unwilling to negotiate, the march to Gyantse itself began on 4 March 1904. At Guru, *en route*, the British expedition met (31 March) with the first 'organized' Tibetan resistance. The fight however turned into a cruel massacre of an ill-armed, ill-disciplined Tibetan 'force', 600 of whom were slaughtered in cold blood. British casualties were, 'two wounded'. Yet, despite their enormous losses, Tibetan resistance remained alive, though in numbers they were never quite as formidable again. Gyantse was reached on 11 April. On 6 May and again on 18 July small battles were fought at Karo La where Younghusband feared strong resistance was building up; on 5-7 July, the Gyantse dzong itself was attacked and captured. With no signs of Tibetan willingness to negotiate meaningfully, Younghusband got the permission he had long sought to push forward.

The march to Lhasa itself began on 14 July; on 3 August the expedition was knocking at the gates of the Potala. The 13th Dalai Lama, disillusioned with empty promises of Russian aid, fled. After a few days of confusion and hesitation as to who was in control, the Ganden Ti Rimpoche 'was recognized' and authorized to deputize for the absentee Dalai Lama. Three weeks later the Lhasa Convention (q.v.) was signed and sealed. It has been held that the Younghusband expedition marked a solitary note of discord in an otherwise long tale of amity that had characterized relations between India and Tibet long before the British arrived and even during their rule.

Parshotam Mehra, *The Younghusband Expedition: An interpretation*, Bombay, 1968; Peter Fleming, *Bayonets to Lhasa*, London, 1961; Alastair Lamb, *The Road to Lhasa: Britain and Chinese Central Asia*, London, 1960; Premen Addy, 'Imperial Prophet or Scaremonger? Curzon's Tibetan Policy Re-considered,' *Asian Affairs* (London), 14, 1, February 1983, pp. 54-67.

Zakir Husain (1897–1969)

Zakir Husain was born in February 1897 at Hyderabad in an upper middle-class Pathan family based at Qaimganj, in Farrukhabad (U.P.). His father, Fida Husain Khan, had gone to Hyderabad to study law and had a most successful career. Zakir Husain was educated at Etawah and M.A.O. College, Aligarh; during 1923–6 he worked for his Ph.D. in economics at the University of Berlin. The subject of Zakir Husain's thesis was the agrarian policy of the British in India. German scholarship impressed him deeply; in addition, he was a keen student of Western ideas and institutions.

The three years he spent in Germany seem to have been the happiest in Zakir Husain's life. At the time of the Non-cooperation and Khilafat Movements (qq.v.), he persuaded Hakim Ajmal Khan and a number of other prominent leaders to establish a national educational institution at Aligarh. Thus was born, on 29 October 1920, the Jamia Milia Islamia. After returning from Germany, Zakir Husain rejoined the Jamia as its Shaikhu Jamia (Vice Chancellor). His rich experience in the educational field was gained here, an experience he later put to excellent use in evolving the Basic or the Wardha Scheme of Education (q.v.) launched in 1938. For the next ten years, he was President of the Hindustani Talimi Sangh located at Sevagram.

In November 1948, Zakir Husain became Vice-Chancellor of Aligarh Muslim University and was nominated a member of the Indian Universities Commission under Dr Sarvepalli Radhakrishnan. Later, he was chosen to be a member of the Rajya Sabha.

During 1956-8, Zakir Husain was India's representative on the Executive Board of UNESCO and, until 1957, Chairman of the Central Board of Higher Education and a member of the University Grants Commission. In 1957, he became Governor of Bihar; in 1962, Vice-President of India, and, five years later, President. He died in harness, on 3 May 1969, having held the highest office in the country with exemplary grace and dignity.

Zakir Husain was awarded the Padma Vibhushan in 1954 and the Bharat Ratna in 1963. All this notwithstanding, he had the sufi's indifference towards the externals of religion and, even though a deeply religious man, did not wear his faith on his sleeve. He was an inspiration for secularism and endeared himself to men of different religious communities.

In almost every respect, Zakir Husain epitomized India's composite culture, deeply steeped in the ethical, moral and spiritual principles of its saints and sufis. His nationalism, a reflection of his allegiance to the highest moral value, rested on a democratic approach, self-discipline, and an identification with the good of society that gives substance and meaning to the individual.

Zakir Husain translated Plato's *Republic* and Canon's *Elementary Political Economy* into Urdu (1920); he published a biography of Gandhi (q.v.) in German and wrote short stories, mostly for children. His convocation addresses at various universities were later published under the title *The Dynamic University*.

Tall and well-built, Dr Zakir Husain had a broad forehead, a well-kept beard and was, invariably, neatly, and tastefully dressed. An imposing embodiment of culture and refinement, he was sensitive to beauty in all its forms and had an intense passion for excellence. His varied tastes and hobbies—for roses, collections of cacti, fossils, paintings and specimens of calligraphy, objects of art and curios, and books—speak of a remarkable breadth of vision and versatility.

M. Mujeeb, *Dr Zakir Husain, A Biography,* New Delhi, 1972; Sen, *DNB,* IV, pp. 463-5 (M. Mujeeb).

Glossary

amil	revenue collector; revenue contractor
bhadralok	literally, wise, mature people; the elite
charkha	spinning wheel
chauth/chauthai	one-fourth of the total revenue
crore	one hundred lakhs (lacs); ten millions
darbar (durbar)	court; ceremonial assembly
desai	principal revenue officer of a district under 'native' rulers
deshmukh	district revenue officer
feringhi (firangi)	literally, a Frank; a European in general
firman (farman)	mandate; command; order
hartal	closure (stoppage) of work or activity
Ittihad ul Muselimin	literally, unity of Muslims; name given to a political organization in the erstwhile Hyderabad state
Jamiat ul Ulema	literally, an association of learned men
jaziah	a tribute; capitation tax levied by Muslims on their subjects of another faith; poll tax
jenmi (janimi, jammi)	An owner of land; a proprietor; the original owner or proprietor by hereditary right; hereditary owner of land in Kerala
jihad (jehad)	holy war; especially that waged by Muslims against infidels or idolaters
jirga	a council of elders in the NWFP
khutbah	in Islam: a service or oration delivered after the service every Friday in which a preacher blesses the prophet, his successors and the *reigning* monarch
kamavisdar	a functionary directly under the Peshwa who was responsible for overall charge of district administration including fixation and realization of land revenue and other imposts (see also *mamlatdar*)
kanungo	literally, expounder of the laws; village or district revenue officer
khassadar	members of a loose irregular body of troops' who appeared in the tribal areas of the NWFP, choosing their own officers and finding their own rifles
kulkarni	village accountant
lakh (lac)	one hundred thousand
misl (misal)	from Arabic, meaning similitude; clan or confederation
madrassa	a religious school for children intended for the teaching of the Quran, Arabic and Islam

mahal	estate; a group of lands regarded as a unit for land revenue purposes
mamlatdar	Indian revenue official incharge of a taluk, division or a district
mansab	military rank conferred by the Mughal government
masnad	throne; a large cushion; a prop; a chair
mujahid	literally, 'one who strives'; a warrior, especially in the defence of the true faith
nazr/nazrana	gift; forced contribution
naib tahsildar	deputy or assistant officer of tahsil
naib mir munshi	deputy or assistant chief secretary
paishkar	a deputy; agent; assistant; a minister; a manager
patel	village headman
patwari	village accountant
sadar amin	In British Bengal, a judicial functionary empowered to try causes to the extent of Rs. 1,000/-
sanad	grant; charter; certificate; deed of grant of an office; by a sovereign privilege or right
sardeshmukhi	one-tenth part of the land revenue
senapati	commander-in-chief (of the army, forces)
sheristadar	the head ministerial office of a court charged with receiving plaints and, generally, to attend to routine business
shirk	worshipping something else besides Allah; polytheism, idolatory
sikkah	stamped coin; the silver currency of the Mughals adopted by the East India Company
subahdar	provincial governor
sunnah	literally, 'path'; the normative pattern of the Prophet as recorded in the Tradition (Hadith); the orthodox standard or practice of Islam
tahsil/tahsildar	a revenue sub-division of a district or estate; administrator of a tahsil
talti	village accountant
taluka	under British administration, sub-division of a district
wazir	prime minister

Select Chronology, 1707–1947

1707	The 89-year old Mughal Emperor, Aurangzeb, dies at Ahmadnagar; Prince Muhammad Muazzam eventually succeeds him as Bahadur Shah I.
	Fort William in Bengal is becoming well-established with a number of guns and 125 soldiers, half European; Calcutta, hitherto subordinate to Madras now constituted a separate presidency.
	Union of England and Scotland under the name of Great Britain.
1708	Shivaji's grandson, Shahu, formally ascends the Maratha throne at Satara.
	Guru Gobind Singh, the last Sikh Guru, assassinated at Nanded.
	The Godolphin Award concerning the two rival English companies announced; the English Coy. and the London Coy. are henceforth to be known as the 'United Company of the Merchants of England trading to the East Indies.'
1709	The battle of Poltava, marking the emergence of Russia as a dominant power in the Baltic.
1712	Death of Bahadur Shah I.
1713	Farrukh Siyar proclaims himself Emperor.
	Shahu formally appoints Balaji Vishwanath his Peshwa or Prime Minister.
1715	A British mission led by Surman and Stephenson and accompanied by William Hamilton arrives in Delhi to secure the Emperor's protection from the oppression of Mughal functionaries in Bengal.
1716	Sikh insurrection crushed by Abdus Samad Khan; Banda Bahadur is tortured to death.
1717	The Mughal Emperor grants the Company a patent conferring the right of passing commerce duty free. Additionally, it is allowed to purchase 37 villages contiguous to Calcutta and to possess lands around its factories.
1718	Murshid Quli Khan made Governor of Bihar in addition to Bengal and Orissa.
	Act of Parliament passed to punish British merchants trading with India under foreign commissions.
1719	The Sayyid brothers depose, blind and imprison Emperor Farrukh Siyar (later in the year, he is done to death). Roshan Akhtar elevated to the throne with the title of Muhammad Shah.
	The Emperor grants sanads to Shahu agreeing to his demands of *chauth* and *sardeshmukhi* for the six subahs of the Deccan and complete restoration of *swaraj* for the old conquests of Shivaji.

1720   Asaf Jah, Nizam-ul-Mulk, marches to the Deccan.

Peshwa Balaji Vishwanath dies; his son, Baji Rao, succeeds him.

Sayyid Husain Ali, one of the Sayyid brothers, assassinated in October; Sayyid Abdullah is captured and imprisoned.

1721   The Portuguese invite co-operation from the English to meet the challenge of Kanhoji Angria, who is helped by the new Peshwa.

1722   Nizam-ul-Mulk appointed the Mughal Emperor's Wazir.

Charles VI of Austria charters the 'Ostend East India Company'.

1723   The Peshwa invades Malwa.

1724   Agreement between Nizam-ul-Mulk and the Peshwa; Mubariz Khan killed.

1725   Nizam-ul-Mulk recovers Hyderabad, thereby marking the independence and founding of the state.

During 1720–5 the English had exported to India £ 578,155 worth of goods and £ 2,770,238 in bullion.

1726   Baji Rao invades Karnataka; levies a contribution from Seringapatam; is opposed by the Nizam; gains no permanent advantage.

East India House erected in Leadenhall Street, London.

1727   Murshid Quli Jafar Khan, Nawab of Bengal, dies; succeeded by his son-in-law, Shuja-ud-Din.

The Maratha army under the Peshwa invades Khandesh and Gujarat.

The charter of the Ostend Company suspended for 7 years, thanks to stiff opposition from other European powers.

1728   The Nizam defeated by Maratha armies, agrees to the Treaty of Mungi Shivagaon.

1729   Kanhoji Angria dies; succeeded by his son Sekhoji Angria.

The Ostend Company is finally dissolved, although its factors continue to stay in Bankipur until 1733.

1730   The United East India Company's charter renewed again, till 1769.

During the year English ships from China bring 1,707,000 lbs of tea to India and 371,000 pieces of calico; between 1725–30 the Company had exported to the East £ 551,234 worth of goods and £ 2,551,872 in bullion.

1731   Dupleix assumes office at Chandernagore and restores the town's commercial prosperity.

The Swedish East India Company established in Gottenborg, by King Frederick.

Treaty of Warna concluded between Raja Shahu and his cousin, Raja Sambhaji II.

1732   Meeting and agreement between the Peshwa and Nizam; the latter is given a free hand for expansion in the south and the Peshwa in the north.

Between 1732–44, the John Company's dividend is reduced from 8% to 7%; the Dutch, on the other hand, realize 20% to 25% on their capital stock 'and never less than $12^{1}/_{2}$'.

1733	Marathas advance into Gujarat.
	Sekhoji Angria dies.
1735	Benoit Dumas, Governor of Isles de France and Bourbon, takes office as Governor-General at Pondicherry.
	Malhar Rao Holkar overruns Malwa and, with other Maratha chiefs, agrees to accept Rs 22 lakhs as *chauth*.
	Peshwa Baji Rao leaves Poona on his north Indian campaign.
	Between 1730–5, the E.I.Coy. exports to the East £ 717, 854 worth of goods and £ 2,406,078 of bullion.
1736	The Court of Directors issues a proclamation prohibiting British subjects from trading in the East Indies in a manner contrary to the liberties and privileges granted to the Company.
	Alivardi Khan acquires the title of Nawab of Bihar, independent of Bengal.
1736–95	Emperor Ch'ien Lung's reign, one of China's greatest periods.
1737	Baji Rao marches to Delhi while his commander routs the Mughal army; in panic, Muhammad Shah summons Nizam-ul-Mulk and appoints him Governor of Agra.
	Gujarat finally lost to the Mughal Empire.
1738	Baji Rao defeats Nizam-ul-Mulk at the battle of Bhopal and dictates humiliating terms.
	The Portuguese fail to take Thana, occupied earlier by the Marathas. The latter sack Daman, capture several forts and besiege Mahim.
	Chanda Sahib (real name Husain Dost Khan), now in possession of Madurai, obtains aid from the French.
	Invention of the 'Flying Shuttle' by John Kaye.
1739	Nadir Shah defeats the Mughal Emperor and takes him prisoner (February); enters and sacks Delhi (March), ordering a general massacre; later (May), he begins his homeward journey, laden with booty.
	Mir Muhammad Amin, also known as Saadat Khan, founder of the kingdom of Oudh, commits suicide.
	Shuja-ud-Din, Governor of Bengal, dies; succeeded by his son, Sarfaraz Khan.
	The Marathas wrest Bassein from the Portuguese.
	Sambhaji Angria's fleet appears off Bombay; he hoists his flag over Elephanta.
1740	Alivardi Khan, Governor of Bihar, rebels against the new Nawab of Bengal; he kills the latter and proclaims himself Subahdar of Bengal.
	Baji Rao dies at Khargon; is succeeded by his son, Balaji (also known as Balaji Baji) Rao.
	A Maratha army defeats Dost Ali, Nawab of Arcot.
	Between 1735–40, the E.I.Coy. exports £ 938,970 worth of goods and £ 2,459,470 of bullion.
	Birth of the Urdu poet Muhammad Nazir.
	Accession of Frederick the Great of Prussia and Maria Theresa of Austria.

1740–48	The War of Austrian Succession, ending with the Treaty of Aix-la-Chapelle.
1741	Raghuji Bhonsle wrests Trichinopoly (also Trichchirappalli) and captures Chanda Sahib, who is carried to Satara.
	Dumas diverts Maratha attention from Pondicherry and receives a *mansab* from the Emperor; later, de la Bourdonnais arrives with seven ships; Dumas leaves for Europe, to be succeeded by Dupleix.
	As Mughal viceroy, Jai Singh of Amber cedes Malwa to the Marathas and appoints Balaji Rao Deputy Governor with the right of collecting *chauth* and *sardeshmukhi*.
1742	Dupleix formally enters Pondicherry and receives a flag and kettle-drum from the Emperor.
	Alivardi Khan permits the English to construct a moat or ditch around their Calcutta settlement.
	A Maratha army under Raghuji Bhonsle's minister invades Bengal; Alivardi Khan's surprise attack makes it flee in confusion.
1743	Some Marathas under Raghuji Bhonsle again invade Bengal. Alivardi Khan, with the help of the Peshwa's army, drives them back.
	Raja Shahu mediates between the Peshwa and Raghuji Bhonsle and marks out their respective spheres.
1744	The Company agrees to lend the British government a million pounds sterling at 3% in return for prolongation of its charter to 1783.
	As a state of war prevails between France and England, a French fleet is dispatched to attack Madras, while an English fleet under Commodore Barnett seizes French ships in the Straits of Gibraltar.
1745	Nawab Anwar-ud-Din Khan makes a state entry into Pondicherry and is warmly received by Dupleix.
	The English fleet appears off the Coromandel coast and takes three French ships. In answer to Dupleix's appeal, the Nawab insists on no hostilities occurring in his domain.
	Raghuji Bhonsle raids Murshidabad but is repulsed.
	Zakarya Khan, the Governor of Lahore, dies; in the ensuing war of succession one of his sons invites the help of Ahmad Shah Abdali.
	Between 1740–5, the Company exports £ 1,105,750 worth of goods to the East and £ 2,529,108 of bullion.
1746	Commodore Peyton engages the French fleet under de la Bourdonnais near Negapatam; sustaining heavy losses, the French retire to Pondicherry.
	The French (under de la Bourdonnais) invest Madras and bombard Fort St George, where the English garrison surrenders.
	Orissa passes into the hands of Raghuji Bhonsle.
1747	Nadir Shah assassinated by his Persian guard. His Afghan mercenaries retreat, their leader Ahmad Khan (later Shah) marches to Kandahar and assumes sovereignty under the dynastic title of 'Durrani' (also Abdali).
	Peshwa Balaji Rao proceeds on his north Indian campaign.
	Dupleix fails in an attack upon Fort St David.

1748   Major Stringer Lawrence arrives at Fort St David to command all the Company's forces in India and to be Major of the garrison at Fort St George.

Ahmad Shah Abdali launches his first attack on India but is repulsed; between 1748–67 he raids the country 7 times.

The Emperor, Muhammad Shah, dies, preceded by the death of his Wazir, Qamar-ud-Din.

Nizam-ul-Mulk dies; is succeeded by his second son, Nasir Jang.

Pondicherry withstands siege from land and sea by Lawrence and Boscawen.

Siraj-ud-Daulah is appointed nominal Deputy Governor of Bihar.

1749   The French promise help to Chanda Sahib, who is proclaimed Nawab of Carnatic while the British-backed Anwar-du-Din is killed in the battle of Ambur.

Under the Treaty of Aix-la-Chapelle, Madras is restored to the English.

As Boscawen's fleet leaves Fort St David, the French and Chanda Sahib attack Trichinopoly.

Shahu dies.

Ahmad Shah Abdali raids India a second time and conquers the Panjab.

1750   Nasir Jang is treacherously shot, whereupon his nephew, Muzaffar Chanda Sahib and Muzaffar Jang with their French auxiliaries; Muhammad Ali joins Nasir Jang, who confirms him in government; presently Muhammad Ali is defeated by the French and Chanda Sahib; the former, under Bussy, takes Jinji.

Nasir Jang is treacherously shot, whereupon his nephew Muzaffar Jang, escapes from imprisonment and with the aid of the French assumes the viceroyalty of the Deccan.

1751   Muzaffar Jang killed; is succeeded by Salabat Jang; Bussy is appointed a nobleman of the Mughal Empire and receives the Northern Sarkars as jagir.

Safdar Jang, Nawab of Oudh, forges an alliance with the Marathas; their combined armies worst the Rohillas.

Nawab Alivardi Khan buys off Raghuji Bhonsle; cedes Orissa and agrees to pay *chauth*.

Ahmad Shah Abdali raids India for the third time, defeats the Panjab Governor, Mir Mannu, and conquers Kashmir.

Two English factories are established in the Godavari district.

1752   The Mughal Emperor enters into a defensive subsidiary alliance with the Marathas.

Chanda Sahib is killed.

A fresh treaty concluded between the Nizam and the Peshwa, to which Bussy and Raghuji Bhonsle are parties.

1754   The Treaty of Pondicherry between the English and French is signed. Earlier, Clive had returned to England on sick leave (1752) and Dupleix recalled.

Shuja-ud-Daulah takes over as the new Subahdar of Oudh.

1755	Raghuji Bhonsle dies at Nagpur, is succeeded by his son Janoji.
	Balaji Rao concludes treaty with the Company to wipe out the power of Tulaji Angria on the west coast.
	Clive, appointed Lt. Col. in England, arrives at Bombay with a force of artillery.
	Serampore is taken possession of by the Danes.
1755–63	The Seven Years' War concluded by the Treaty of Paris.
1756	Tulaji Angria surrenders to the Maratha commander after a combined British-Maratha assault.
	Alivardi Khan dies; succeeded by Siraj-ud-Daulah as Nawab of Bengal; the Nawab's soldiers storm the English factory at Kasimbazar (also Cossimbazar) and capture Calcutta.
	A squadron under Admiral Watson and Clive, with 900 Europeans and 1,500 sepoys, leaves Madras for Calcutta and, towards end-December, arrives at Falta on the Hooghly.
1757	Ahmad Shah Abdali in his fourth invasion reaches Delhi, which he plunders and pillages, the Mughal Emperor formally ceding to him the provinces of Panjab, Kashmir, Thatta and Sarhind.
	Siraj-ud-Daulah and the English conclude the Treaty of Alinagar.
	Battle of Plassey between the English and Siraj-ud-Daulah; with the latter killed shortly afterwards, Mir Jafar is proclaimed Nawab of Bengal, Bihar and Orissa.
	Clive's first governorship of Bengal commences.
	Admiral Watson dies, succeeded by Sir George Pococke.
	Raghunath Rao, the Maratha general, attacks and captures Delhi.
	Clive quells rebellion in Bengal; the district of 24-parganas is ceded to the English Company by Mir Jafar.
1758	First Maratha invasion of Panjab under Raghunath Rao, assisted by Malhar Rao Holkar, results in defeat of Abdali's governor and installation of Adina Beg Khan as the Maratha nominee; the latter does not last beyond 6 months.
	A French fleet under the Comte d' Ache, with the Count de Lally as Commander-in-Chief, appears off Fort St David; its fortifications are razed to the ground and presently the French commander returns to Pondicherry in triumph.
	The Marathas under Tukoji Holkar march beyond Attock and reach Peshawar.
1759	Dattaji Sindhia meets Wazir Imad-ul-Mulk and compels him to accept an agreement.
	Ahmad Shah Abdali, invited by the Rohilla leader, Najib-ud-Daulah, invades India and re-establishes his government at Lahore.
	Clive humbles the Dutch, captures their fleet and worsts their troops at Chinsura in Bengal.
	With Emperor Alamgir II murdered, his son Mirza Abdullah Ali Gauhar, then in Bihar, eventually succeeds him with the title of Shah Alam (II).
1759–60	Capture of Quebec by the British under General Wolfe, leading to Britain's conquest of Canada.

1760	Dattaji Sindhia killed in battle against Ahmad Shah Abdali.

1760   Dattaji Sindhia killed in battle against Ahmad Shah Abdali.

Clive leaves for England.

The Marathas under Malhar Rao Holkar defeated by Ahmad Shah Abdali. Later, Sadashiv Rao Bhau captures Delhi, advances to Kunjpura and retraces his steps to Panipat.

Abdali reaches Panipat along with his allies.

Mir Kasim made Subahdar of Bengal in place of Mir Jafar.

In Delhi, Sadashiv Rao Bhau removes Emperor Shah Jahan II and installs Shah Alam II; Shuja-ud-Daulah nominated Wazir.

1761   Lally surrenders to English troops at Pondicherry.

Ahmad Shah Abdali defeats the Marathas at Panipat (January) and later (April) leaves for Afghanistan.

An English force defeats the Emperor's troops in Bihar.

Peshwa Balaji Rao dies in Poona.

Haidar Ali takes over the government of Mysore.

1762   The Nizam invades Maratha territory but suffers a reverse.

Wazir Shuja-ud-Daulah conducts an expedition against the Bundhelkhand ruler.

The Bengal Council negotiates with Mir Kasim regarding private trade carried on illegally by the Company's servants.

1763   The Peshwa and Nizam on the warpath; Madhav Rao plunders the suburbs of Hyderabad, and the Nizam attacks Poona; later, peace is concluded between the two.

The Bengal Council breaks with Mir Kasim; the Nawab is deposed and Mir Jafar installed in his place; Mir Kasim routed at Katwa and Murshidabad, flees towards Monghyr and Patna.

Peace between England and France concluded by the Treaty of Paris.

Surajmal, the Jat ruler of Bharatpur, dies in an encounter with Najib-ud-Daulah.

1764   Clive arrives as head of the Bengal government.

Raja Nand Kumar is honoured by the Emperor Shah Alam and appointed Collector of Burdwan, Nadiya and Hooghly.

The combined forces of Emperor Shah Alam, Nawab Shuja-ud-Daulah and Mir Kasim are routed at Buxar by Major Hector Munro; Shuja-ud-Daulah is re-appointed Wazir allegedly under pressure from Clive; Mir Kasim escapes into Rohilla country.

1765   Mir Jafar dies; succeeded by his son Mir Phulwari with the title of Najm-ud-Daulah; the English Company conclude a fresh treaty with the new Nawab.

Clive arrives in Calcutta; obtains from Emperor Shah Alam the Diwani of Bengal, Bihar and Orissa; concludes Treaty of Allahabad with the Nawab of Oudh.

Postal service established between Calcutta and Murshidabad.

1766   Bengal Select Committee stops 'double full batta' for its officers; faces mutinous situation.

Najm-ud-Daulah dies; succeeded by his brother, Saif-ud-Daulah, with whom the Company concludes a new treaty.

Raghunath Rao leads expedition into Hindustan; is joined by Malhar Rao Holkar and Madhoji Sindhia's forces.

The English, the Marathas and the Nizam form an alliance against Haidar Ali.

The Court of Directors 'absolutely forbid' inland trade by private individuals.

1767 Clive leaves India; is succeeded by Henry Verelst.

Ahmad Shah Abdali invades the Panjab.

First Anglo-Mysore War breaks out; English troops defeat combined forces of Haidar Ali and the Nizam.

Thomas Mostyn sent to Poona to persuade the Peshwa join the English against Haidar Ali.

1768 Battle between the Peshwa, Madhav Rao, and his uncle, Raghunath Rao (supported by Holkar, Janoji Bhonsle and Damaji Gaekwad) in which the latter is worsted.

The English conclude a treaty with Shuja-ud-Daulah limiting his armed strength.

1768–74 Russo-Turkish War concluded by the Treaty of Kuchuk Kainarji.

1769 Peace established between Janoji Bhonsle and the Peshwa.

Treaty concluded between Haidar Ali and the Madras government, bringing the First Anglo-Mysore War to a conclusion.

Act of Parliament allows the Company to hold territorial revenues for five years and, in return, pay £ 400,000 into the British exchequer every year.

For revenue purposes, Bengal is divided into 6 divisions.

Verelst resigns, is succeeded by John Cartier.

Bengal afflicted by plague and famine.

1770 Saif-ud-Daulah dies; is succeeded by his minor brother, Mubarik-ud-Daulah, as Nawab of Bengal whose stipend is reduced from Rs 31 to 16 lakhs.

The Company sends an expedition under Capt. Kinlock to establish trade relations with Nepal.

The Rohilla leader, Najib-ud-Daula, dies.

The Mughal Emperor Shah Alam conducts secret negotiations with the Maratha leader, Mahadji Sindhia.

Invention of the 'Spinning Jenny' by Hargreave; Australia claimed for England by James Cooke.

1771 Shah Alam marches from Allahabad to Delhi.

Prithvi Narayan Shah is succeeded by his son, Partap Narayan, as ruler of Nepal.

1772 Shah Alam enters Delhi, is supported by Mahadji Sindhia.

Warren Hastings appointed Governor of Bengal.

Muhammad Reza Khan deposed from the office of Naib Diwan and Naib Subah at Murshidabad; so also Raja Shaitab (also Shitab) Rai, who held a corresponding post at Patna. Revenue business, the treasury and the law courts are transferred from Murshidabad to Calcutta.

A treaty is concluded between the Rohillas and the Nawab of Oudh.

The Company resolves to abolish the system of dual government and 'to stand forth as Diwan'.

Peshwa Madhav Rao I dies; is succeeded by his brother, Narayan Rao.

1773   The Company's application to the British government for a loan leads to the appointment of a Select Committee which brings in the Regulating Act.

The combined forces of the Nawab Wazir and the British repulse a Maratha attack on Rohilkhand.

Peshwa Narayan Rao is murdered in his palace; Raghunath Rao proclaimed Peshwa.

The Company and Shuja-ud-Daulah conclude the Treaty of Banaras.

In 1773–4 the Bengal revenues were £ 2,481,404; civil and military charges, £ 1,488,435. The army consisted of 5 companies of artillery, 1 troop of cavalry, 3 regiments of European infantry, 23 battalions of native infantry and 28 companies of invalids—a total of 27,000 men.

1774   English troops and Shuja-ud-Daulah's forces enter Rohilkhand; the Rohillas are defeated at Miranpur Katra, and Hafiz Rahmat Khan dies of wounds.

A treaty of peace with Bhutan signed at Fort William. George Bogle is to lead a mission to the Tashi (Panchen) Lama.

Philip Francis, Clavering and Monson arrive in India; first meeting of the new Council under the Regulating Act held.

Robert Clive commits suicide.

The First Anglo-Martha War breaks out.

Birth of Ram Mohun Roy.

Accession of Louis XVI in France

1775   Shuja-ud-Daulah dies and is succeeded by his son, Asaf-ud-Daulah, with whom the British conclude a new treaty. The Nawab robs the Begums (his mother and grandmother) of their property.

Raghunath Rao flees Poona, seeks shelter with the British and concludes the Treaty of Surat.

Maharaja Nand Kumar brings charges against Warren Hastings; in turn, is accused of forgery, is arrested, tried, convicted and sentenced to be hanged.

1776   The Treaty of Purandhar, concluded by Col. Upton, envoy from Calcutta, supersedes the Treaty of Surat.

Formal adoption in America of the Declaration of Independence by the Continental Congress (4 July).

1777   Upton is recalled from Poona and his place taken by Thomas Mostyn.

Mir Kasim dies.

The French adventurer, St Lubin, is received at the Peshwa's court.

1778   The Bengal Council consider complaints of the Begums of Oudh against the Nawab.

The Company renews its war against the Marathas and, in Bengal, seizes French settlements at Chandernagore, Masulipatam and Karikal.

1779   Convention of Wadgaon concluded between the Company and Marathas.

Mahe is captured by the English.

Sir Eyre Coote is appointed Commander-in-Chief of the Bengal army.

The Nizam takes an interest in the formation of an anti-British confederacy.

1780   Haidar Ali concludes a treaty with the Marathas; the latter plan a quadruple alliance with Mudhoji (Appa Sahib) Bhonsle, the Nizam and Haidar Ali.

The fort of Gwalior is surprised and captured from Sindhia's officers by Captain Popham.

The Bengal Council passes regulations for the administration of justice and Sir Elijah Impey becomes Judge of the Sadr Diwani Adalat.

Philip Francis challenges Hastings to a duel; badly wounded, the former leaves for England.

James Augustus Hickey's weekly paper, *Bengal Gazette* or *Calcutta General Advertiser*, starts publication.

The *India Gazette* is published.

Pierre Cuillier, later General Perron, arrives in India.

1781   A Board of Revenue is established in Bengal; Diwani courts are increased and the office of faujdar abolished.

A Parliamentary measure restricts the jurisdiction of the Supreme Court in India.

Sir Eyre Coote defeats Haidar Ali at Porto Novo, Pollilore (Polilur) and Solingar (Sholinghur).

Warren Hastings leaves Calcutta to chastize Raja Chait Singh; the latter is deposed, and his place taken by Mohip Narian.

Hastings founds the Muhammadan Madrassa at Calcutta.

The adventurer George Thomas lands in India.

1782   The French fleet arrives off the Coromandel coast and engages in action against the British.

Mirza Najaf Khan, Emperor Shah Alam's regent, dies.

The Treaty of Salbai between the Company and the Marathas is concluded.

Haidar Ali dies; Tipu Sultan succeeds him.

Hickey is convicted of libel and his paper closed. The *Calcutta Gazette* is published.

England recognizes American independence.

1783   With peace concluded between France and England, Pondicherry is restored to the French and Trincomalee to the Dutch.

Charles James Fox introduces in Parliament his Bill for the better governance of India.

Sir Elijah Impey is recalled to answer charges of illegality.

Warren Hastings sends Samuel Turner to Tashilhunpo.

Mir Fateh Ali Khan establishes himself as Amir of Sind.

1783–1801	Premiership of the younger Pitt.
1784	Treaty of Mangalore between the British and Tipu Sultan brings hostilities to a close.

Treaty of Yadgir between the Nizam and the Marathas restores peace between the two.

Pitt's second India Bill is passed.

Mahadji Sindhia is supreme master in Delhi.

The *Madras Courier* is published.

1785   Bussy dies at Pondicherry.

Warren Hastings resigns and embarks for England; is succeeded by Sir John Macpherson.

Mahadji Sindhia concludes a treaty of friendship with the Sikh chiefs.

1786   Charges against Warren Hastings are preferred in Parliament.

Earl Cornwallis becomes Governor-General of British India and also Commander-in-Chief.

An Act of Parliament gives the Governor-General the power of over-riding decisions of his Council; another empowers the King to recall him.

1787   After prolonged negotiations, the Marathas conclude peace with Tipu Sultan.

The rulers of Jaipur and Jodhpur combine against Mahadji Sindhia and defeat his army at Lalsot after 3 days' hard fighting.

George Thomas joins the service of Begum Samru of Sardhana, for whom he fights against the Sikhs.

Overland communication between England and India is established 'with some regularity'.

Formation of an anti-slavery league under William Wilberforce.

1788   Trial of Warren Hastings begins in London.

Ghulam Qadir takes possession of Delhi, pillages the city, deposes Shah Alam and blinds him; later in the year, Mahadji Sindhia occupies the town and reinstates the Emperor; Ghulam Qadir is captured.

1789   Lord Cornwallis's revenue reforms and decennial settlements come into force.

Death of Fateh Singh, Gaekwad of Baroda.

The *Bombay Herald* starts publication.

Storming of the Bastille and royal recognition of the National Assembly (14–17 July); adoption of the Declaration of the Rights of Man and the Citizen by the National Assembly (27 August); inauguration of the new federal government in the US with George Washington as first President.

1790   The Company declares war against Tipu Sultan who successfully attacks Travancore.

Treaty of Poona concluded between the Peshwa and the Company; a separate treaty concluded by the Company with the Nizam to secure his alliance against the Mysore ruler.

Battle of Paten between Mahadji Sindhia's troops and the Rajputs; the latter are worsted.

The British overrun the Malabar coast; Cornwallis arrives at Madras and takes over command of the army.

Ram Mohun Roy's treatise assailing Hindu idolatry lays the foundations of prose literature in the Bengali language.

1791   In the war against Tipu Sultan, Cornwallis invests Bangalore; Coimbatore surrenders to Tipu and his troops rout a Maratha detachment; the Company receives extensive reinforcements from England.

Varanasi Rajakiya Sanskrit Mahavidyalaya—later the Sanskrit Vishwa Vidyalaya—founded at Banaras by Jonathan Duncan.

Incorporation of the 'Bill of Rights' into the American constitution.

1792   Tipu Sultan concludes peace with the Company by the Treaty of Seringapatam.

Nepal opens negotiations and concludes a commercial treaty with the Company; initially the Regent had asked for military aid against the Chinese which was refused.

The '(2–7) September Massacres' in Paris; the unsuccessful Macartney Mission to China.

1793   Cornwallis institutes Zila and City courts and Provincial Courts of Appeal; at the same time, the Sadr Diwani and Sadr Nizamat Adalats are established at Calcutta.

The Company's charter is renewed for 20 years.

Taimur Shah of Afghanistan dies; his fifth son, Zaman Shah, is elected Amir at Kabul (Humayun Shah assumes authority at Kandahar and Mahmud Shah at Herat).

Holkar's army is defeated by Sindhia's at Lakheri in a hotly contested battle.

Against the advice of Sir John Shore, Cornwallis introduces his Permanent Settlement of land revenue.

With war breaking out between France and Britain, Pondicherry is besieged by the English.

Cornwallis leaves for England; is succeeded by Sir John Shore.

George Thomas fails to rescue Begum Samru.

Dr William Carey, the first Baptist missionary, arrives in Calcutta.

Execution of Louis XVI (21 January).

1794   Mahadji Sindhia dies suddenly; is succeeded by his grand-nephew and adopted son, Daulat Rao; this leaves Nana Phadnis unchallenged at Poona.

Faizullah Khan, the Rohilla chief, dies.

1795   The Peshwa's forces defeat the Nizam at the battle of Kharda.

Ahalya Bai, the window of Khande Rao Holkar, dies, leaving Rukoji Holkar the sole ruler.

Warren Hastings acquitted on all charges—the proceedings had lasted 7 years, the trial occupied 145 days and cost him £ 70,000.

Accidental death of Peshwa Sawai Madhav Rao.

The Bengal officers form a Board to enforce restoration of privileges revoked by Cornwallis.

Jonathan Duncan assumes office as Governor of Bombay.

1796 New regulations for army administration further aggravate (army) discontent; the Governor-General is compelled to modify these regulations and practically concede the original demands.

Nana Phadnis enters into a secret treaty with the Nizam; he secures a declaration of friendship from Baji Rao and returns to Poona, where the new Peshwa is invested with authority.

1797 Zaman Shah occupies Lahore, conciliates the Sikhs and threatens Delhi.

Death of Tukoji Holkar, followed by civil war in Indore with Yashvant Rao emerging victorious.

Nana Phadnis, arrested by Sindhia in a stratagem, is confined at Ahmadnagar.

60 Frenchmen form a Jacobin Club at Seringapatam and plant a 'tree of liberty' outside Tipu's palace; the Sultan's envoys leave for Mauritius.

1798 George Thomas defeats the Sikhs and carves out an 'independent' kingdom comprising Hissar, Hansi, Sirsa and Rohtak.

The Earl of Mornington (later Marquess Wellesley) takes over as Governor-General.

Nana Phadnis is released from confinement.

Wellesley concludes a subsidiary alliance with the Nizam.

Zaman Shah marches from Kabul, but is checked by the Sikhs near Amritsar; he makes over Lahore to Ranjit Singh as a chief and returns to Kandahar.

Wellesley writes to Tipu Sultan protesting against his French connections; the latter's replies are deemed unsatisfactory.

Napoleon's expedition to Egypt.

1799 War between the Company and Tipu Sultan; allied with the Nizam, British forces lay siege to Seringapatam; Tipu is wounded and finally shot by a grenadier. Mysore is then partitioned between the British and the Nizam, with the residuary state restored to Krishna Raja Wadiyar.

Earl Mornington is created Marquess Wellesley; passes a regulation to control the press.

Sir John Malcolm leaves Bombay as envoy to Persia to negotiate a treaty.

Madras imposes pre-censorship on newspapers.

The Directory overthrown in the *coup d'état* of Brumaire (9 November), leaving Napoleon Bonaparte virtual ruler of France.

1800 Death of Nana Phadnis.

Marquess Wellesley made Captain-General and Commander-in-Chief of forces in India.

Fort William College, Calcutta is established (wound up in 1854).

Govind Rao, Gaekwad of Baroda, dies.

The Barakzais revolt in Kabul and declare for Mahmud, brother of Zaman Shah.

Christian missionaries establish a printing press at Serampore.

1801 Union of England with Ireland.

Yashvant Rao Holkar defeats Sindhia's detachment under Capt. McIntyre at Newri; another Sindhia officer, Capt. Brownrigg defeats Holkar in a battle near Satwas; Holkar captures Ujjain.

Lord Lake appointed Commander-in-Chief in India.

Pondicherry restored to the French under the Treaty of Amiens.

Supreme Court is established at Madras.

Daulat Rao Sindhia attacks Indore.

The Nawab-Wazir of Oudh enters into a new subsidiary treaty with the English.

William Carey publishes a Bengali grammar.

1802 Convention of Cambay between the Gaekwad and the Company; Anand Rao enters into a subsidiary alliance with the English.

Yashvant Rao Holkar defeats the combined forces of the Peshwa and Daulat Rao Sindhia at Hadaspur; Peshwa Baji Rao II who flees to Bassein and Bombay, proposes a subsidiary alliance with the English which is formalized by the Treaty of Bassein.

Treaty of Amiens between England and France.

1803 The Peshwa returns to Poona, under British escort.

Shuja Mirza, son of Taimur Shah, proclaimed Amir at Kabul.

The English capture Broach.

The English army under General Lake defeats Sindhia's forces at Koil, near Aligarh, and at Delhi.

The Company declares war on Bhonsle and Sindhia.

Emperor Shah Alam seeks British protection; Lake enters Delhi.

Arthur Wellesley defeats combined Sindhia-Bhonsle forces at Assaye.

The English capture Burhanpur, Agra and Amirgarh and become masters of the province of Cuttack.

The English defeat Sindhia's army at Laswari, Bhonsle's at Argaon, and seize the fort of Gawilgarh.

The Company conclude the Treaty of Deogaon with Bhonsle, of Nagpur and Surji Arjangaon with Daulat Rao Sindhia.

Pondicherry and other French settlements in India are seized by the English.

Ram Mohun Roy's *Tuhfat-ul-Muwahhiddin* published.

1804 Despite Yashvant Rao Holkar's efforts, Daulat Rao Sindhia concludes a defensive alliance with the English.

The Company declare war on Holkar, who is repulsed from Mathura and Delhi and defeated in battles at Farrukhabad and Deeg.

1804–10	Promulgation of a series of legal codes in France, including the 'Code Napoleon'.
1805	Lake lays siege to Bharatpur, where Holkar had taken refuge.
	Amir Shah Shuja of Afghanistan marches to Peshawar intending to conquer Kashmir, but retires due to Barakzai rebellions.
	Lord Cornwallis assumes office for a second term as Governor-General (July); is taken ill and dies at Ghazipur (October).
	Yashvant Rao Holkar enters into a treaty with the English at Rajpurghat on the Beas.
1806	Sepoy rebellion at Vellore where Tipu's flag is hoisted.
	Ranjit Singh crosses the Sutlej to assist the ruler of Nabha against Patiala.
	Emperor Shah Alam dies.
	Birth of the Urdu poet, Mirza Ghalib.
	The Berlin Decree formally inaugurating the Continental System issued.
1807	Ranjit Singh makes further gains in Cis-Sutlej territory.
	Yashvant Rao Holkar, now virtually insane, makes extravagant military preparations.
	The Earl of Minto takes over as Governor-General in succession to Sir George Barlow.
	Lord William Bentinck recalled by the Directors for being partly responsible for the Vellore mutiny.
	Slave trade abolished in the British empire.
	Peace of Tilsit, leading to Franco-Russian alliance.
1808	Sir Harford Jones arrives in Bombay to proceed with the Company's agent, Sir John Malcolm, on a mission to Persia.
	Captain David Seton concludes an offensive and defensive alliance with Ghulam Ali of Sind, which the Bengal Council repudiates.
	A mission to Lahore, conducted by Charles Metcalfe, faces difficulties on the issue of Cis-Sutlej territory.
	Mountstuart Elphinstone leaves Delhi on a mission to Kabul.
1808–14	The Peninsular War.
1809	A Parliamentary Committee is appointed to inquire into corrupt practices in the distribution of patronage by the Company's Court of Directors.
	Treaty of Amritsar between Ranjit Singh and Metcalfe.
	Elphinstone reaches Peshawar, but an alliance with Shah Shuja is not achieved.
	Treaty between the Company and the Raja of Cochin; also, one between the Company and the Amirs of Sind.
1810	A small expedition from Madras captures Amboyna in the East Indies from its Dutch Governor.
	Malcolm reaches Teheran on his second mission, but simultaneously Sir Gore Ouseley arrives from London as the King's envoy.
	Shah Shuja, driven from Afghanistan, becomes a British pensioner at Ludhiana.
1811	Yashvant Rao Holkar dies at Bhanpura.

Thomas Manning reaches Lhasa in disguise, the first Englishman to visit the city.

Importation of slaves into India forbidden.

1812   Treaty of Pandharpur between the Peshwa and his feudatories, and another with the Raja of Kolhapur through Elphinstone, the British envoy at Poona.

William Carey writes the *Itihasmala*, in Bengali.

Napoleon's invasion of Russia.

1813   By an Act of Parliament, the Company's charter is renewed for 20 years, £ 10,000 per year out of its Indian revenues being allocated for education.

The Earl of Moira succeeds Minto as Governor-General.

Christian missionaries permitted to preach in British India.

1814   Gangadhar Shastri is sent to Poona to adjust conflicting claims of the Peshwa and the Gaekwad.

The Company declares war against the Gurkhas of Nepal.

English school established at Chinsura.

The Dutch cede their rights in Cochin to the British.

1814–15   The Congress of Vienna.

1815   General Martindale bombards and blockades Jaitak in Nepal.

General Ochterlony invests Malaun, where most of the garrison surrenders.

The Gurkha chief, Amar Singh Thapa, engages in protracted negotiations for peace.

Gangadhar Shastri is treacherously murdered at Poona by Trimbakji Danglia's hired assassins; the latter is arrested, but escapes (September 1816).

Ram Mohun Roy founds the Atmiya Sabha.

The Battle of Waterloo.

1816   Treaty of Sagauli between the Company and the Gurkhas.

Death of Raghuji II Bhonsle; his cousin, Parsoji, concludes a subsidiary alliance with the English.

David Hare, in conjunction with Ram Mohun Roy, founds Hindu College, Calcutta (formally opened January 1817).

1817   The Raja of Sikkim signs a defensive treaty with the Company.

The Peshwa signs the Treaty of Poona, allegedly under duress.

The Marquis of Hastings opens a campaign against the Pindaris.

The Peshwa's men set fire to the Residency at Poona; are later worsted at the battles of Kirkee and Yervada.

Battle of Sitabaldi between the English and Appa Saheb Bhonsle; the latter is defeated.

Battle of Mahidpur between Holkar and the English; the former is defeated.

Amir Khan of Tonk, confirmed in his possessions, agrees to disband his army.

Birth of Syed Ahmad Khan.

1818	Jodhpur is taken under British protection.
	Treaty of Mandasor, between Holkar and the English.
	Baji Rao surrenders to the British at Mhow.
	Banswara, in Rajasthan, taken under British protection.
	Publication by Carey & Marshman of Bengali weekly, *Samachara Darshana* (sometimes attributed to 1821); James Silk Buckingham publishes *Calcutta Journal*. Serampore College established.
	The Convention of 1818, permanently establishing the Canadian-American boundary.
1819	The English wrest Asirgarh.
	Ranjit Singh conquers Kashmir, thereby ending Afghan rule there.
	Elphinstone assumes office as Governor of Bombay.
1820	Fresh treaty concluded between the Company and the Amirs of Sind.
	Metcalfe appointed Resident at Hyderabad; inquires into the dealings of Palmer and Company.
	Birth of Isvar Chandra Vidyasagar.
1821	Poona Sanskrit College, later Deccan College, opened.
1822	The Native Education Society founded at Bombay.
	The *Bombay Samachar*, in Gujarati, published.
1823	The Marquis of Hastings resigns; John Adam succeeds *ad interim*.
	The Press Ordinance is passed.
	The license of Buckingham, editor of *Calcutta Journal*, is withdrawn.
	First steamship built in India, the *Diana*, launched at Kidderpur.
	Lord Amherst assumes office as Governor-General; the Wahabi leader, Syed Ahmad, leaves Bombay for upper India.
	Agra College established; Sanskrit College, Calcutta founded by Lord Amherst.
	Declaration of the Monroe Doctrine.
1824	War with Burma formally declared.
	The 47th Native Infantry, having refused to march to Arakan, are broken at Barrackpur and their name erased from the army list.
	First Indian girls school opened in Bombay.
	Birth of Swami Dayanand Saraswati.
	The Dutch surrender Malacca to the British; publication of Ranke's *Latin and Teutonic Nations 1494–1519*.
1825	Owing to differences with the Governor-General, Ochterlony resigns (May); dies (July).
	Oriental College established in Delhi.
1826	Bharatpur is stormed by the Bengal Army and taken after heavy losses on both sides.
	The Treaty of Yandaboo is signed and brings war with Burma to an end.
	Syed Ahmad, the Wahabi leader, proclaims *jihad* against the Sikhs.
	Derozio appointed a teacher in Hindu College, Calcutta.

1827   Daulat Rao Sindhia dies in Gwalior.

Lord Amherst effects important administrative reforms, including establishment of the Sadr Diwani Adalat.

The Company's troops are henceforth not to be employed in preserving order in the territories of Indian rulers.

The Jury Act passed.

1828   Lord William Bentinck assumes office as Governor-General.

The allowance of *batta* is reduced to one-half; leads to great discontent amongst officers.

Ram Mohun Roy founds the Brahmo Samaj.

English introduced in Delhi College.

1829   Regulation XVII abolishes Sati; its practice or abetment punishable as culpable homicide.

Settlement of status of Serbia and Greece by the Treaty of Adrianople; completion of the first steam-locomotive railroads in the USA.

1830   William Palmer and Co. fail; many leading business houses become insolvent.

The Great Bhor Ghat, establishing communications between the Deccan and the Konkan, is opened.

Ram Mohun Roy visits England to plead the cause of the Mughal emperor.

Isvar Chandra Gupta starts a Bengali monthly, *Sambad Prabhakar*.

Britain begins sending Indian labour to Mauritius.

French invasion of Algeria.

1831   Lt. Alexander Burnes visits Ranjit Singh, presents a letter and gift of horses from King William IV.

The Mysore Raja is divested of political power and the state administration taken over by a commissioner and 4 superintendents.

Bentinck meets Ranjit Singh at Rupar; presents are exchanged and reviews held.

Syed Ahmad the Wahabi leader, killed at the battle of Balakot.

1832   A treaty is concluded with the Amirs of Sind at Hyderabad.

The Raja of Cachar dies and the state administration is taken over by the Company.

Great Reform Bill passed.

1833   Bentinck appointed Commander-in-Chief in India, in addition to being Governor-General.

The Charter Act (1833) introduces far-reaching administrative changes.

The Company declares open its trade to India and tea trade etc. to China.

Death of Ram Mohun Roy.

Slavery abolished in Britain.

1834   Lord Macaulay arrives as Law Member of the Governor-General's Council.

Bentinck announces constitution of the new Presidency of Agra; Metcalfe is its first President.

1835   The Raja of Sikkim presents Darjeeling to the Company and receives a pension of Rs 3,000 per annum in lieu.

Corporal punishment is abolished in the 'native' army.

Bentinck's resolution on education presented.

Charles Metcalfe appointed acting Governor-General.

Calcutta Medical College opened.

Press Law passed.

De Tocqueville's *Democracy in America* published.

1836   Lord Auckland takes over as Governor-General.

Metcalfe, passed over for appointment as Governor of Madras, retires from the Company's service.

Birth of Ramakrishna Parmahansa.

1837   Alexander Burnes sent on a mission, nominally commercial, to the Afghan Amir, Dost Mohammad.

Muhammad Ali, the Shah of Persia, sets out to besiege Herat; accompanied by a Russian envoy with officers and troops.

Muhammad Bahadur Shah II ascends the Mughal throne; he is to be the last Mughal ruler of the dynasty.

By legislative order, Persian ceases to be court language in India.

Two Acts passed regulating the recruitment of Indian labour for Mauritius.

Birth of Mirza Ghulam Ahmad, founder of the Ahmadiya sect.

Queen Victoria ascends the British throne.

1838   Burnes leaves Kabul, later in the year Auckland pledges support to the restoration at Kabul of the ex-Amir, Shah Shuja, and declares war on Afghanistan.

Macnaghten leaves for Shikarpur, followed by Willoughby Cotton.

Birth of Bankim Chandra Chatterji.

Bombay Times, later the *Times of India*, published.

Zamindari Association, later Landholders' Society (Bengal), inaugurated.

1839   Burnes negotiates a treaty with the Khan of Kalat.

Maharaja Ranjit Singh dies.

A British force under General John Keane reaches Kandahar; Shah Shuja enthroned, Ghazni stormed and Kabul seized. Dost Mohammad takes flight and Shah Shuja is escorted to his palace.

General Keane leaves Kabul.

1839–42   Britain victorious in the First (Anglo-Chinese) Opium War.

1840   After a series of debacles, Dost Mohammd gives himself up; he is sent to Calcutta with an escort.

Maharaja Kharak Singh dies. His son, Nau Nihal Singh succeeds him but, on returning from his father's last rites, sustains a fatal accident. His mother, Rani Chand Kaur, becomes *de facto* ruler.

Appa Saheb Bhonsle, who had taken shelter with the Raja of Jodhpur, dies.

England formally annexes New Zealand; introduction of penny post (in England).

1841   Maharaja Sher Singh takes over the administration at Lahore.

Renewed risings of the Khyberees and the Ghilzais; Akbar Khan revolts at Girishk.

Burnes mobbed and murdered in his house at Kabul; the British treasury is plundered.

Macnaghten confers with Akbar Khan, who then murders him.

All the Bhutan Duars are annexed and a sum of Rs 10,000 paid to the chiefs as compensation; the formal annexation of the Duars is made in 1865.

1842   General Elphinstone signs a capitulation to retire from Afghanistan; the 4,500 strong British force with 12,000 camp followers besides women and children leaves Kabul; only Dr Brydon reaches Jalalabad; General Pollock relieves Jalalabad; Shah Shuja is murdered near Kabul.

Lord Ellenborough takes over as Governor-General.

Rani Chand Kaur is killed by her slave-girls.

Birth of Mahadev Govind Ranade.

Under pressure from Britain, India passes a law permitting emigration of Indian labour.

Charles Napier arrives in Sind.

Generals Pollock and Nott relieve hostages in Kabul and, after causing death and destruction, leave for Peshawar. Dost Mohammad, set at liberty, reaches Kabul and resumes as Amir.

1843   Napier defeats the Amirs' army at Miani; Sind is annexed; appointed Governor, he is directed to abolish the slave trade.

Maharaja Sher Singh and his son Pratap Singh are foully murdered; Dalip Singh installed as Maharaja.

Slavery declared illegal and abolished throughout British India.

Military expedition against Maharaja Sindhia of Gwalior.

1843–44   The USA and France sign treaties with China, leading to the 'open door' principle.

1844   Rebellion in Kolhapur; the government is put under direct British control.

The 34th Native Infantry disbanded.

Lord Ellenborough is recalled; Sir Henry Hardinge succeeds him as Governor-General.

The Governor-General issues a resolution that, in making appointment to jobs, candidates educated at government or private schools should have preference; English is thus made an essential qualification for public service.

Four Indians proceed to England for training in medicine.

A class for training engineers opened in Elphinstone Institution, Bombay.

1845   Danish possessions in India, Tranquebar, Serampore and Balasore are sold to the Company.

The Khalsa army cross the Sutlej and are worsted at Mudki and Ferozeshahr.

Grant Medical College opened at Bombay.

1846   Sikh forces defeated at Aliwal and Sabraon.

Treaty of peace signed between the Sikhs and the English; Kashmir and Jammu pass to Maharaja Gulab Singh as part payment of indemnity.

Treaty of Bhyrowal; the British Resident and force are to stay at Lahore.

1847   Raja Lal Singh banished for treachery; Maharani Jind Kaur, removed to Sheikhupura, is kept under surveillance.

Engineering College (later University) founded at Roorkee.

1848   Lord Dalhousie takes over as Governor-General.

Satara is annexed.

Vans Agnew and Lt. Anderson are murdered at Multan; revolt of Diwan Mulraj.

Maharani Jind Kaur deported to Banaras.

Second Anglo-Sikh War commences.

1848–49   Revolts and revolutions in western and central Europe.

1849   Capture of Multan and battles of Chilianwala and Gujrat.

Maharaja Dalip Singh renounces all claims; Panjab is annexed.

Michael Madhusudan Datta publishes his first work, *The Captive Ladie* (in English).

Dr Hooker and Dr Campbell are detained by the Raja of Sikkim, whose pension is stopped.

Annexation of Sambalpur.

1850   Charles Napier, censured by Lord Dalhousie, resigns as Commander-in-Chief.

Construction of Hindustan—Tibet road begun at Kalka.

Bareilly College founded.

1850–64   Taiping Rebellion in China.

1851   Col. Sleeman reports on abuses of Oudh administration and advises its take-over.

The Nizam is obliged to give up territory yielding Rs 36 lakhs in liquidation of his debt to the Company.

British Indian Association founded in Calcutta.

Dadabhai Naoroji publishes *Rast Goftar* in Gujarati.

The Great Exhibition; Julius Reuter founds the first extensive news-handling agency.

1852   Second Anglo-Burmese War; the province of Pegu annexed.

Peshwa Baji Rao dies at Bithur; his adopted son, Nana Saheb, is denied pension.

1853   Sir John Lawrence appointed Chief Commissioner of Panjab.

The first Indian railway from Bombay to Thana opened; construction is started on a telegraph line from Calcutta to Agra (completed March 1855).

For want of heirs, the states of Jhansi and Nagpur lapse to the British government; with Nagpur they are to constitute the Central Provinces.

Cheap postage is introduced.

By a treaty revision, the Nizam cedes Berar and other districts to the Company.

Haris Chandra Mukherji publishes *Hindu Patriot*.

A college department is added to Central High School (later developed into Presidency College, Madras).

1854   A Bill introduced for abolition of patronage by the Company; its charter is renewed.

1854–56   The Crimean War.

Sir Charles Wood's Education Despatch is drafted.

1855   A Santhal rising erupts in Bengal.

Titles of Nawab of Karnataka and Raja of Tanjore become extinct.

1856   Amir Dost Mohammad regains Kandahar.

Oudh is annexed and Wajid Ali Shah banished to Calcutta.

Lord Canning takes over as Governor-General.

The Company declares war against Persia for breach of 1853 treaty forbidding capture of Herat; island of Kharag is occupied.

Ramakrishna Parmahansa becomes priest of Dakshinesvara temple.

The (Hindu) Widow Remarriage Act passed.

Calcutta College of Engineering founded.

1857   Treaty with Dost Mohammad to assist him against a Persian onslaught.

The 19th Bengal Native Infantry mutiny at Berampur (Berhampore); it is later disbanded at Barrackpur.

Rebellion breaks out at Meerut, with sepoys marching to Delhi; revolts at Jhansi and Allahabad.

British forces storm and enter Delhi; Captain Hodson captures Bahadur Shah II.

Universities incorporated at Calcutta (January), Bombay (July) & Madras (September).

Keshab Chandra Sen joins the Brahmo Samaj.

1858   Trial of Bahadur Shah II; later (October) he is sent to Calcutta and transported (December) to Rangoon.

Queen Victoria's proclamation at Allahabad Darbar transfers authority from the Company to the Crown.

Lord Canning takes over as first Viceroy *and* Governor-General.

1859   Dalhousie's Doctrine of Lapse is countermanded.

Nana Saheb, with his family, seeks asylum in Nepal.

The Company's English troops, protesting against their summary transfer to the Crown, mutiny.

Death of Mountstuart Elphinstone.

James Wilson, first Finance Member of the Supreme Council, imposes income tax and issues government paper currency.

Indigo disputes and riots in Bengal.

Karl Marx's *On the Criticism of Political Economy* (later revised as *Das Kapital*) is published as also John Stuart Mill's *On Liberty*.

1860	Indian Penal Code enacted.
	Treaty concluded with the Nizam; his debt to the British government is cancelled.
	Dinabandhu Mitra's *Nil Darpan Natakam* published.
	Lahore Medical School founded.
1860 (and 1864)	Abraham Lincoln elected President in the USA.
1861	Treaty with Sikkim Raja signed.
	Acute famine conditions in the North-Western Provinces.
	Indian Councils Act becomes law.
	Code of Criminal Procedure enacted.
	Indian High Courts Act (amalgamating the Supreme and Sadr courts into High Courts) becomes operative.
	Birth of Rabindranath Tagore.
	The *Bombay Times* becomes the *Times of India*.
1861–65	The American Civil War.
1862	The Indian Penal Code comes into force from 1 January.
	Lord Elgin takes over as Viceroy and Governor-General.
	The High Court of Judicature in Bengal inaugurated.
	Its first M.A. degree is conferred by Calcutta University.
	Publication of the Marathi journal, *Induprakasha*.
1862–71	Bismarck unifies Germany.
1863	The Indian Navy is transferred to the Admiralty.
	Amir Dost Mohammad takes Herat from the Persians; he dies shortly afterwards.
	The Ambela campaign in the North-West Frontier; the pass is captured and destroyed.
	Lord Elgin dies at Dharamasala.
	Birth of Vivekananda.
	Patna College established.
1864	Sir John Lawrence becomes Viceroy and Governor-General.
	Sir Ashley Eden's disastrous diplomatic mission to Bhutan; his treaty, signed under duress, is repudiated; the Western or Bengal Duars are annexed and war declared.
	Durgesh Nandini, an historical novel by Bankim Chandra Chatterji, is published.
	Government Colleges established at Lahore, Delhi.
	Canning College founded at Lucknow.
	Indian Whipping Act passed.
	International Red Cross founded.
1865	Bhutias sue for peace; Treaty of Punakha.
	Indo-European Telegraph from Karachi, through Persia and Turkey, is opened.
	The *Pioneer* starts publication.
	The short-lived 'London Indian Society' is formed
1866	Severe famine conditions in Orissa.

Keshab Chandra Sen organizes the break-away 'Brahmo Samaj of India'.

Dar-ul-Ulum founded at Deoband.

The 'East India Association' founded and the 'London Indian Society' amalgamated with it.

1867	Amir Sher Ali, defeated by his brother Azim Khan, flees to Herat; left with Balkh in his hands. In the civil war in Afghanistan, the British maintain strict neutrality.

Prarthana Samaj inaugurated in Bombay.

Poona Sarvojanik Sabha founded.

US purchase of Alaska from the Russian Government; end of the Shogunate in Japan.

1868	Civil war in Afghanistan rages unabated.

Panjab Tenancy Bill, passed by the Viceroy's Council, is sent to the Secretary of State for his consent.

The Viceroy formally opens the railway line joining Delhi to Ambala.

Severe famine conditions in Orissa and northern Madras Presidency.

Sisikar Kumar Ghosh publishes the *Amrita Bazar Patrika*.

Indian's first evening paper, the *Madras Mail*, is published.

1869	Sher Ali defeats Azim Khan and Abdur Rahman Khan to become sole ruler of Afghanistan; the latter seeks refuge in Russian Turkistan.

Lord Mayo takes over as Viceroy and Governor-General.

At Ambala, Mayo meets Amir Sher Ali, and establishes cordial relations.

Act of Parliament for better government of India and defining the Governor-General's powers.

Surendranath Banerjea is disqualified for the ICS.

Death of the Urdu poet, Mirza Ghalib.

Syed Ahmad Khan visits England.

Opening of the Suez Canal.

1870	The railway line from Bombay to Allahabad is completed.

The Viceroy receives an embassy from Yakub Beg who has seized power in Kashgar.

Under Lord Mayo's financial settlement, provincial governments are to receive fixed annual allotments for police, education, printing, roads and public works.

M. G. Ranade joins the Prarthana Sabha.

Lahore Medical School raised to the status of a College.

1871	The 19th Madras Native Infantry mutiny.

With Henry Fawcett as Chairman, a parliamentary committee is set up to inquire into the financial administration of India.

Rise and fall of the Paris Commune.

1872	The King of Siam visits Calcutta.

Kuka rebellion in the Panjab.

Lord Mayo assassinated at Port Blair in the Andamans.

The first Earl of Northbrook takes over as Viceroy and Governor-General.

Col. Goldsmid submits his report on the Afghan-Persian boundary.

Ananda Mohan Bose organizes the (London) Indian Society.

Birth of the Marathi writer, N. C. Kelkar.

1873   T. D. Forsyth's mission to Yakub Beg of Kashgar.

Russians capture Khiva; earlier, the Khan's appeal to India for help was refused.

Sayyid Nur Muhammad, Amir Sher Ali's envoy, meets the Governor-General at Simla.

Sher Ali nominates his younger son, Abdullah Jan, to be his successor.

In England, Ananda Mohan Bose pleads for the establishment of representative government in India.

1874   Treaty of trade and transit with Yakub Beg of Kashgar.

The Marquis of Salisbury takes over as Secretary of State for India in Disraeli's Tory administration.

Yakub Khan imprisoned by his father, Amir Sher Ali.

Publication of *Nibandhamala* of Vishnusastri Chippulankar.

1874–80   Disraeli Prime Minister in Britain.

1875   British mission to Yunnan (China) through Bhamo; A. R. Margary murdered by Chinese at Nanwain; attacked, the party retreats.

The Viceroy, by proclamation, deposes Malhar Rao, Gaekwad of Baroda who is deported to Madras (dies 1882).

The Theosophical Society is founded by Madame Blavatsky,

Mayo College opened at Ajmer.

Robert Knight publishes the *Statesman* from Calcutta.

Dayanand Saraswati founds the Arya Samaj at Bombay.

International Postal Union formed.

1876   Owing to differences with it, Lord Northbrook asks the Home Government to relieve him.

Royal Titles Act passed.

Queen Victoria proclaimed 'Indiae Imperatrix' (Empress of India) in London.

Lord Lytton assumes office as Viceroy and Governor-General.

1854 treaty between British India and the Khan of Kalat renewed, with some additions.

The age-limit of competitors for the ICS examinations is lowered.

1877   Proclamation of the Queen's new title made at a Darbar held in Delhi.

Sir Lewis Pelly meets (30 January) Nur Muhammad, the Afghan envoy, at Peshawar; the latter dies (26 March) and negotiations cease.

Yakub Beg of Kashgar defeated by the Chinese and later assassinated; Kashgar taken and eastern Turkistan regained by the latter.

Severe drought followed by famine in the Central Provinces, the Panjab and Upper Provinces.

Syed Ameer Ali founds the 'National Mohammedan Association'.

Dwijendranath Tagore publishes the journal *Bharati*.

1878   Vernacular Press Act passed.

General Stolietoff's 3-man mission to Afghanistan; Abdullah Jan, the Amir's favourite son, dies.

Sir Neville Chamberlain's mission to Sher Ali refused admittance at Ali Masjid; Lytton's 3-week ultimatum is followed by a declaration of war; Sher Ali flees to Turkistan, leaving Yakub Khan to defend Kabul. Russian mission is withdrawn from Kabul.

Sadharan Brahmo Samaj founded.

A weekly, the *Hindu*, is published from Madras.

The Congress, and Treaty, of Berlin.

1879   The Burmese king, Thibaw, orders the assassination of 86 princes of royal blood and their relatives.

Amir Sher Ali dies.

Import duties on cotton goods from England are abolished.

Treaty of Gandamak concluded between the British and Amir Yakub Khan. Afghan soldiery and mobs besiege the Kabul Residency (3 September) and massacre all the inmates, including Sir Louis Cavagnari; General Roberts enters Kabul (12 October); Yakub Khan abdicates.

1880   The Marquis of Ripon takes over as Viceroy and Governor-General.

British victory at Maiwand, General Roberts marches to Kandahar; Abdur Rahman, son of Afzal Khan, who had lived in exile (1870–80) in Russian Turkistan nominated Amir of Afghanistan at Kabul.

1881   Rendition of Mysore under Maharaja Chama Rajendra Wodeyar; representative assembly is established in the state.

The first Factory Act becomes operative.

Vivekananda meets Ramakrishna Paramahansa.

The *Tribune* is published from Lahore, the *Kesari* and the *Maharatta* from Poona.

1882   A contingent of troops from India is ordered to Egypt for the war with Arabi Pasha.

The 500-mile long Sarhind Irrigation Canal is formally opened.

Ripon repeals Vernacular Press Act, 1878.

Panjab University (Lahore) incorporated.

The British occupy Egypt.

1883   C. P. Ilbert's Criminal Procedure Amendment Bill introduced amidst acute controversy.

Surendranath Banerjea sentenced to imprisonment for gross libel.

Death of Swami Dayanand Saraswati.

A. O. Hume addresses an open letter to graduates of Calcutta University.

First session of the National Conference held at Calcutta.

1884 Ilbert Bill amended and finally passed.

Amir Abdur Rahman agrees to join the Anglo-Russian Frontier Commission.

The Earl of Dufferin takes over as Viceroy and Governor-General.

Death of Keshab Chandra Sen.

The 'Mahajan Sabha' of Madras founded.

The government approves the recommendations of the Hunter Education Commission.

1885 Inauguration of Bombay Presidency Association.

Bengal Tenancy Act passed.

Amir Abdur Rahman arrives in India, meets Viceroy.

Panjdeh crisis.

The Kashmir Maharaja, Ranbir Singh, dies; Pratap Singh succeeds him.

Russian and British Afghan Delimitation Commissioners meet at Zulfikar Pass and commence work.

Third Anglo-Burmese War. King Thibaw surrenders and is interned at Ratnagiri in Maharashtra.

First session of the Indian National Congress convenes at Bombay.

1886 Burma is proclaimed part of British India.

Income Tax Bill passed.

Delimitation of Afghanistan's northern frontier completed.

1887 Queen Victoria's Golden Jubilee celebrated.

The Quetta, Pishin, Thal-Chotiali and Sibi districts of Baluchistan annexed by the British.

Allahabad University incorporated.

'Dev Samaj' founded by Sivanarayan Agnihotri.

1888 Tibetans expelled from Lingtu and Giagong across the Sikkim frontier.

Punitive expedition against Hazara tribesmen.

The Marquis of Lansdowne takes over as Viceroy and Governor-General.

Col. Beck forms the 'United Indian Patriotic Association'.

Agarkar publishes the *Sudharak*.

D. A. V. School at Lahore raised to the status of a college.

1889 Sukkur bridge over the Indus opened.

The Kashmir Maharaja, Pratap Singh, abdicates and a council of state is appointed.

Charles Bradlaugh introduces a Bill for setting up democratic government in India.

The *Hindu* becomes a daily.

1890 Anglo-Chinese Convention on Sikkim concluded; the Raja flees to Tibet, is arrested in Nepal and lives in retirement.

1891 Factory Bill for the protection of women and children passed; 'Age of Consent to Marriage Bill' adopted.

Death of Isvar Chandra Vidyasagar.

Mirza Ghulam Ahmad proclaims himself the Mahdi.

Military expedition against Manipur.

Revised totals of 1891 census of India show a population of 287,289,873 and an area of 1,553,925 square miles; of the total, 72.28 per cent are Hindus and 19.97 per cent Muslims; of the remainder, Christians, Sikhs, Jains, Parsis and Jews constitute about 2 per cent of the total.

1892	The Russian government declares the action of Captain Yanoff in interfering with Capt. Younghusband illegal, and apologizes.
	Petroleum discovered in Assam in large quantities.
	Indian Councils Act comes into force.
	Diesel engine patented.
1893	The Khan of Kalat is deposed.
	British mission to Kabul under Sir Mortimer Durand; Durand Boundary agreement is signed.
	Swami Vivekananda attends Parliament of Religions at Chicago.
	Tilak organizes the Ganapati festival.
1894	The Earl of Elgin takes office as Viceroy and Governor-General.
	Convention delimiting the frontier between China and Burma ratified.
1894–95	The Sino-Japanese War, with China badly mauled.
1895	Military expedition against Chitral.
	Settlement of Russo-Afghan frontier.
	Tilak organizes the Shivaji festival.
	Italo-Ethiopian War: an African nation defeats a European power.
1896	Severe famine all over India.
	Spanish-American War ends the Spanish empire in America and the Philippines.
1897	Widespread tribal risings on the North-west Frontier.
	Outbreak of plague in Bombay presidency; British officers Rand and Ayerst murdered in Poona.
	Vivekananda establishes the Ramakrishna Mission on a systematic basis (first beginnings in 1887).
1898	Prarthana Samaj, Bombay, starts a Depressed Classes mission.
	'Nadwat-ul-'Ulama' founded at Lucknow.
	Death of Syed Ahmad Khan.
1899	Lord Curzon takes over as Viceroy and Governor-General.
	Swami Vivekananda establishes a Math at Belur.
	First International Peace Congress at the Hague.
1899–1902	The Boer War.
1900	Famine commission report submitted.
	North-West Frontier Province formed under a Chief Commissioner.
1901	Death of Queen Victoria.
	Habibullah takes over as Amir of Afghanistan.
1902	Madame Rustam K. R. Cama leaves India to settle down in Paris.
	Anglo-Japanese Alliance.

1903	A British mission crosses into Tibet.
1904	The Younghusband expedition reaches Lhasa; concludes a convention.
	Act passed empowering universities to make appointments to teaching faculties.
	Anglo-French Entente.
1904–5	Russo-Japanese War: a major European power worsted by an Asian nation.
1905	Partition of Bengal effected, leading to widespread public agitation in and outside the province.
	Lord Minto takes over as Viceroy and Governor-General.
1906	Arundel Committee submits its report on political reforms; Minto receives Muslim deputation headed by the Aga Khan.
	The All-India Muslim League founded at Dacca.
	British Labour Party formed; the first Duma convenes in Russia.
1907	Hindu-Muslim riots at Comilla.
	Lala Lajpat Rai and S. Ajit Singh deported; Ordinance restricting the right of holding public meetings promulgated.
	The Council of India Act becomes law.
1908	Khudiram Bose is executed.
	Newspapers (Incitement to Offences) Act and Explosive Substances Act passed into law.
	Tilak sentenced to 6 years' transportation.
	Criminal Law (Amendment) Act passed.
	Young Turk Revolution in Turkey.
1909	The Depressed Classes Mission Society of Madras founded.
	Indian Councils Act passed.
	Madan Lal Dhingra shoots Curzon Wyllie dead.
1910	Imperial Legislative Council inaugurated.
	Hindu-Muslim riots at Peshawar.
	Department of Education established under a separate Member of the Viceroy's Executive Council.
	Aurobindo Ghosh retires to Pondicherry.
	Seditious Meetings Act renewed.
	Korea becomes a Japanese dependency.
1912	Delhi is proclaimed a province.
	Islington Commission appointed to consider organization of the civil service in India.
	Abul Kalam Azad brings out the Urdu paper *Al-Hilal*.
	Legislative Assembly created for Assam.
1913	Indian Criminal Law Amendment Act passed.
	The *Bombay Chronicle* started by Pherozeshah Mehta.
	Associated Press of India amalgamates with Reuters.
	The Ghadr Party founded at San Francisco.
	Legislative assembly created for the Central Provinces.

1914   Forest Research Institute and College opens at Dehra Dun.

Foundation laid of Government Commercial Institute, Calcutta and Sydenham College of Commerce and Economics, Bombay.

Tilak released from internment in Mandalay; Gandhi concludes agreement with General Smuts regarding Indians in South Africa; Annie Besant brings out *New India*.

The *Komagata Maru* arrives at Budge Budge, outside Calcutta.

Panama Canal opened.

1914–18   World War I.

1915   Gandhi arrives in India.

Muslim students from Lahore, Peshawar and Kohat join the *Mujahiddin* on their way to Afghanistan.

Gokhale dies; Rashbehari Bose escapes to Japan; Annie Besant announces the formation of her Home Rule League.

Death of Pherozeshah Mehta.

A Provisional Government of India established at Kabul.

The Mesopotamia expedition; British-Indian reverses.

1916   Maulanas Mohamed Ali and Shaukat Ali interned.

Sadler Commission on higher education appointed; Banaras Hindu University is established at Varanasi and SNDT Women's University at Bombay.

Tilak establishes his Indian Home Rule League; 19 Indian members of the Imperial Legislative Council submit a joint memorandum for constitutional reform.

1917   Gandhi tried for his role in the Champaran satyagraha.

Annie Besant interned by the Madras government.

Bhandarkar Oriental Research Institute established at Poona.

E. S. Montagu announces far-reaching political concessions.

Bose Research Institute established at Calcutta.

Rowlatt (Sedition) Committee appointed.

The October Revolution in Russia.

1917–24   Lenin as head of the Council of Peoples' Commissars in the USSR.

1918   Indians in the armed forces are now made eligible to hold King's commission.

Searchlight started at Patna under the sponsorship of Sachchidananda Sinha and the Maharaja of Darbangha.

The first All-India Depressed Classes Conference convenes.

Rowlatt (Sedition) Committee report submitted; Montagu-Chelmsford report on constitutional reform published.

President Wilson's Fourteen Points.

1919   Gandhi takes over *Young India* and *Navajivan*; government introduction of the Rowlatt Bills is marked by an all-India hartal.

Dr Satyapal and Dr Kitchlew deported; trouble breaks out at Amritsar; Dyer imposes curfew, followed by the Jallianwala Bagh massacre at Amritsar.

Third Anglo-Afghan War followed by a treaty of peace at Rawalpindi.

The Hunter Committee of Inquiry into the Panjab massacres begins work.

Government of India Act, 1919 (also Montagu-Chelmsford Reforms) becomes law.

Treaty of Versailles; League of Nations formed; founding of the Third (Communist) International.

1920   First meeting held of the All-India Trade Union Congress.

Aligarh Muslim University is established and the Central Advisory Board of Education constituted.

Hunter Committee report published.

Death of Tilak.

Shiromani Gurdwara Prabhandak Committee formed.

1921   Death of Subramania Bharati.

Scheme of reforms under the Government of India Act, 1919 comes into operation.

Moplah Rebellion in Malabar; police terror results in asphyxiation of 70 Moplah prisoners.

1921–5 Sun Yat-sen heads Kuomintang Government in China.

1922   The Chauri Chaura incident, leading to Gandhi's suspension of the Non-cooperation Movement.

Rabindranath Tagore establishes Visvabharati University at Shantiniketan.

Permanent Court of International Justice opens at the Hague.

Benito Mussolini is dictator of Italy.

1923   Surendranath Banerjea amends the Calcutta Municipal Act.

With K. M. Panikkar as editor, the *Hindustan Times* commences publication.

Banaras session of the Hindu Mahasabha attracts a large number of delegates.

Hari Singh Gaur's Civil Marriage Bill passed.

Kemal Ataturk is President of Turkey.

1924   Communist Party of India commences its activities.

The Royal (Lee) Commission on Superior Services submits its report.

Central Legislative Assembly carries Motilal Nehru's resolution on constitutional advance, rejects demand for grants under Customs and refuses leave to introduce the Finance Bill.

Bengal Criminal Law Amendment Act promulgated.

1925   The Gurdwara Law vests the management of all important gurdwaras in the Panjab in the Shiromani Gurdwara Prabhandak Committee.

Indian Sandhurst (better known as the Skeen) Committee, constituted.

Death of C. R. Das.

Vithalbhai Patel elected first Indian presiding officer of the Central Legislative Assembly.

The All-India Congress Committee permits the Swaraj Party to work in the legislatures.

1925–9	Stalin's rise to power in the USSR.
1926	Trade Union Act becomes operative.
	Inter-University Board holds its first meeting.
	Swami Shradhanand, the Arya Samaj leader, murdered.
	Imperial Conference redefines Dominion Status.
1927	The *Free Press of India* news agency started.
	Whitehall announces establishment of the all-white Simon Commission.
	Lindbergh's non-stop solo flight from New York to Paris.
1928	Royal Commission on agriculture appointed.
	Simon Commission's arrival in Bombay marked by an all-India hartal.
	All-Parties Conference considers the Nehru Report.
1929	All-Parties Conference adjourned *sine die*.
	31 members of the Communist Party arrested in connection with the Meerut conspiracy case.
	Under Jinnah's leadership, the All-Parties Muslim Conference formulates its 'fourteen points'.
	Bhagat Singh drops bombs into the Legislative Assembly.
	Imperial Council of Agricultural Research established.
	Jatin Das dies in jail after 64-day fast.
	Lord Irwin announces Dominion Status as the political goal of British policy in India.
1929–33	The Great Depression.
1930	The Congress passes Civil Disobedience resolution.
	Gandhi begins his Salt Satyagraha with the Dandi march.
	Chittagong armoury raid.
	Simon Commission report published.
	First Round Table Conference inaugurated in London.
1931	Press Emergency Powers Act becomes law.
	Gandhi – Irwin Pact concluded (March); Gandhi sails for England (August) to attend the Second Round Table Conference (September-November); returns to Bombay (December).
	Britain announces decision to constitute NWFP and Sind into separate Governors' provinces.
	Statute of Westminster confirms British Commonwealth of Nations.
1932	Whitehall announces the Communal Award; Poona Pact regarding scheduled caste representation is signed; All-India Untouchability League (later Harijan Sevak Sangh) formed.
	Third Round Table Conference (November – December) held.
1933	British government's White Paper on constitutional reforms published.
	Gandhi starts the weekly *Harijan*; he is arrested and later (8 May) released.
	Civil disobedience temporarily suspended (May); is re-started (August); Gandhi arrested (1 August) and released (23 August).
	Hitler comes to power in Germany.

1933–37	Four years of Franklin Delano Roosevelt's 'New Deal' in the U.S.A.
1934	Bihar earthquake causes havoc.
	Congress policy on the Communal Award leads to the birth of the Nationalist Party.
	Jinnah returns from London to head the Muslim League.
1935	Indo-British trade agreement signed.
	Rahmat Ali publishes a leaflet on the formation of Pakistan.
	After passage through Parliament, the Government of India Bill, 1935 receives royal assent.
1936	Death of Munshi Premchand (b. 1880).
	The Congress, Muslim League and other political parties engage in vigorous campaigning for elections to the provincial legislatures and the Central Legislative Assembly under the Act of 1935.
1937	A. Abbott and S. H. Wood submit a report on technical education.
	The Congress permits its members to accept office under the Act of 1935.
	The All-India National Education Conference under Gandhi's leadership formulates a new education policy.
	Start of the undeclared Sino-Japanese War.
1938	V. D. Savarkar elected president of the All-India Hindu Maha-sabha.
	Deaths of Sarat Chandra Chatterjee and Dr Sir Muhammad Iqbal.
	Pirpur Committee submits report.
1939	Gandhi comments adversely on election of Subhas Chandra Bose as Congress President; the latter resigns.
	India inducted into World War II by the British; Linlithgow declares Dominion Status as the ultimate goal of British policy.
	Congress ministries resign office in the provinces; Jinnah declares 22 December as a Day of Deliverance for Muslims.
1939–45	World War II.
1940	Lahore Session of Muslim League adopts the Pakistan resolution.
	Subhas Chandra Bose arrested.
	Linlithgow announces new constitutional (August) offer which the Congress rejects but the Muslim League welcomes.
	The Congress starts (17 October) and later suspends (17 December) individual Civil Disobedience.
1941	Death of Rabindranath Tagore.
	Subhas Chandra Bose disappears (January) from Calcutta and arrives (March) in Berlin.
	The Congress absolves Gandhi of responsibility to lead a Satyagraha movement.
	Germany invades Russia; the proclamation of the Atlantic Charter (British Prime Minister Churchill affirms it did *not* apply to India); Japan attacks the USA.
1942	The Japanese bomb Rangoon (January), which falls (March) as does Singapore (February).

Cripps, as the British War Cabinet nominee, fails to break the political deadlock; the Congress and League reject his proposals.

The Tokyo conference (March) of Indians in South-east Asia elects Rash Behari Bose as its leader; establishment (September) of the Indian National Army.

First Japanese aerial bombing (April) of India, followed by bombing (December) of Calcutta.

The Congress passes (9 August) the Quit India resolution; its leaders are arrested and the movement tapers off (September).

1943　　Subhas Chandra Bose leaves (February) Germany, arrives in Singapore (July), proclaims (October) the Provisional Government of Free India.

The Karachi session of the Muslim League adopts the slogan, 'Divide and Quit'.

Axis troops surrender at Stalingrad.

1944　　INA forces engage the British in Burma (March), hoist the national flag on Indian soil, capture (May) a British post which soon (September) changes hands.

Allied invasion of France (D-Day: 6 June).

1945　　Landslide victory of the Labour Party in the British general elections (June).

Wavell's Simla conference fails to break the political deadlock.

Subhas Chandra Bose arrives at Taipeh.

Elections held to the Central Legislative Assembly.

Atom bombs dropped on Hiroshima and Nagasaki to end World War II; Labour Government comes to power in Britain; UNO formed.

1945–51　Labour Party in power in Britain.

1946　　British parliamentary delegation in India; Wavell announces Whitehall's intention of setting up a politically representative Executive Council at the centre.

Large-scale mutiny of Indian naval ratings in Bombay.

Three-member British Cabinet Mission arrives (March) and , after consultations, issues its proposals (May).

India recalls its High Commissioner from South Africa and repudiates the Indo-South African trade agreement of 1927.

Elections to Constituent Assembly completed.

The Council of the Muslim League repudiates (29 July) the Cabinet Mission Plan and after Nehru is invited to form an interim government (6 August) proclaims 'Direct Action Day' (16 August) which is followed by the 'Great Calcutta killing'.

The Interim Government is sworn in (2 September); it is joined by the Muslim League (13 October).

Nehru, Baldev Singh, Jinnah, Liaqat Ali Khan and Wavell visit (3–6 December) London to break the political impasse.

The Constituent Assembly convenes (9 December).

Independent Philippines Republic created (4 July).

1947   The Muslim League declares that the Cabinet Mission Plan has failed and the Constituent Assembly is illegal.

Attlee announces the end (June 1948)) of British rule; Lord Mountbatten is sworn in (March) as the last Viceroy and Governor-General; he presents (3 June) his plan for Partition and announces (9 June) the transfer of power (14–15 August) to the separate Dominions of India and Pakistan.

Referendum held (6–17 July) in NWFP.

Indian Independence Bill introduced (4 July) in Parliament; it is passed (15–16 July) and receives (18 July) royal assent.

Pakistan's Constituent Assembly meets (11 August) and elects Jinnah as President; he is sworn in as Governor-General; Pakistan is born (14 August); with Mountbatten sworn Governor-General, India attains independence (15 August).

Cominform formed.

Governors-General and Viceroys of India: 1774–1947

Governors-General of Presidency of Fort William in Bengal (under Regulating Act, 1773)

Warren Hastings	October 1774–February 1785
Sir John Macpherson (Acting Governor-General)	February 1785–September 1786
Charles Cornwallis, 2nd Earl and first Marquess Cornwallis	September 1786–October 1793
Sir John Shore, Baron Teignmouth	October 1793–March 1798
Richard Colley Wellesley, Earl of Mornington, Marquess Wellesley	May 1798–July 1805
Sir George Barlow (Acting Governor-General)	October 1805–July 1807
Gilbert Elliot, Ist Earl of Minto	July 1807–October 1813
Francis Rawdon, Earl of Moira, Marquess of Hastings	October 1813–January 1823
John Adam (Acting Governor-General)	January-July 1823
William Pitt Amherst, Earl Amherst	August 1823–February 1828
William Butterworth Bayley (Acting Governor-General)	March–July 1828
William Cavendish Bentinck, Lord	July 1828–August 1833

Governors-General of India (under Charter Act, 1833)

William Cavendish Bentinck Lord	August 1833–March 1835
Sir Charles Metcalfe (Acting Governor-General)	March 1835–March 1836
George Eden, Earl of Auckland	March 1836–February 1842
Edward Law, Earl of Ellenborough	February 1842–July 1844
Henry Hardinge, Viscount Hardinge	July 1844–January 1848
James Andrew Broun-Ramsay, Earl and Marquess of Dalhousie	January 1848–February 1856
Charles John Canning, Viscount and Earl Canning	February 1856–October 1858

Governors-General and Viceroys of India
(under Indian Councils Act, 1858)

Charles John Canning	November 1858–March 1862
James Bruce, 8th Earl of Elgin and Kincardine (died in office)	March 1862–November 1863
Laird Mair John Lawrence, 1st Earl Lawrence	January 1864–January 1869
Richard Southwell Bourke, 6th Earl of Mayo (died in office)	January 1869–February 1872
Thomas George Baring, Earl of Northbrook	May 1872–April 1876
Edward Robert Bulwer Lytton, Earl of Lytton	April 1876–June 1880
George Frederick Samuel Robinson, Earl and Marquess of Ripon	June 1880–December 1884
Frederick Hamilton-Temple-Blackwood, Earl of Dufferin and Marquess of Dufferin and Ava	December 1884–December 1888
Victor Alexander Bruce, Earl of Elgin and Kincardine	January 1894–January 1899
George Nathaniel Curzon, Earl and Marquess Curzon of Kedleston	January 1899–April 1904 and December 1904–November 1905
Oliver Arthur Villiers Russell, Baron Ampthill (Acting Governor-General and Viceroy)	April-December 1904
Gilbert John Elliot-Murray-Kynynmond, Earl of Minto	November 1905-November 1910
Charles Hardinge, Baron Hardinge of Penhurst	November 1910–April 1916
Frederick John Napier Thesiger, 1st Viscount Chelmsford	April 1916–April 1921
Rufus Daniel Isaacs, Marquess of Reading	April 1921–April 1926
Edward Frederick Lindley Wood, Lord Irwin, Earl of Halifax	April 1926–April 1931
Freeman Freeman-Thomas, Earl and Marquess of Willingdon	April 1931–April 1936
Victor Alexander John Hope, 2nd Marquess of Linlithgow	April 1936–March 1937

Governors-General and Crown Representatives
(under Government of India Act, 1935)

Victor Alexander John Hope, 2nd Marquess of Linlithgow	March 1937–October 1943
Archibald Percival Wavell, Viscount and Earl Wavell	October 1943–March 1947
Louis Mountbatten, Earl Mountbatten of Burma	March–August 1947

Index

Entries in bold type indicate headings of articles in the main text.